SECOND EDITION

The Garden Primer

Barbara Damrosch

*Illustrations by Linda Heppes Funk,
Ray Maher, and Carol Bolt*

A REGINA RYAN BOOK

WORKMAN PUBLISHING, NEW YORK

Library of Congress Cataloguing-in-Publication Data is available.

ISBN-13: 978-0-7611-2275-3 (pb); ISBN-13: 978-0-7611-4856-2 (hc)

Recycled stock; 15% post-consumer waste, acid-free, and manufactured-elemental-chlorine–free.

Cover photograph by Matthew Benson
Book design by Barbara Balch

Illustrations by Linda Heppes Funk: pages iii, vii left, viii, 3, 15, 33, 39, 46 lower left, 48 upper left and upper right, 50 lower right, 51 upper right, 64 ant lion, assassin bug, bumblebee, orchard mason bee, ground beetle, braconid wasp, dragonfly, syrphid fly, 81, 82, 89, 95 right-angled trowel, 96, 99 collinear hoe, 109, 119, 131, 138, 140, 147 top right, 151 right, 154 right, 158 left, 160 left, 161 left, 162 left, 165, 180–181, 197, 204 left, 212 right, 215, 216 left, 217, 218, 223 left, 216 left, 244, 246, 266, 334–336, 388, 394, 399–401, 444, 485, 502, 519, 522, 528, 539, 557, 566 left, 568 left, 572 left, 574, 586, 589 left, 590, 592, 597, 600, 602, 622, 626, 628 left, 633 right, 636 left, 639, 647, 649, 651 right, 675 left, 682 left, 684, 685 left, 702 left, 709, 710 right.
Ray Maher: inside front cover, page i, vii right, 41, 53, 73, 94, 95 except right-angled trowel, 97, 99 except collinear hoe, 102–103, 105–106, 108, 111, 114, 116–117, 229, 269, 271, 272, 273, 274, 277, 279, 281, 285, 287, 290, 294, 297–298, 300, 304, 309, 312, 315, 316, 320, 322, 328, 331, 337, 340, 344, 346, 350, 352, 354, 357, 360, 363, 368–370, 373, 375, 377, 380, 383, 411, 414, 429, 432, 436, 440, 449, 457, 462, 466, 469, 472, 480, 575, 653, 689, 715, 716, 755.
All other illustrations by Carol Bolt.

Books are available at special discounts when purchased in bulk for premiums and sales promotions as well as for fund-raising or educational use. Special editions or book excerpts can also be created to specification. For details, contact the Special Sales Director at the address below.

Workman Publishing Company, Inc.
225 Varick Street
New York, NY 10014-4381
www.workman.com

Printed in the United States of America
First printing February 2008
10 9 8 7 6 5 4 3 2 1

To Eliot

Acknowledgments

A number of people made the writing of this book an easier, more pleasant task than it would otherwise have been. Regina Ryan helped to launch the original project, the late Sally Kovalchick saw it through, and the late Paul Frese lent his deep knowledge of plants and gardening. I thank Peter and Carolan Workman for their energy and encouragement, and the fine staff that kept the new book on track: my editor Suzanne Rafer, Barbara Balch, Barbara Peragine, Helen Rosner, Carol White, Ron Longe, Anne Kerman, Wayne Kirn, Robert Vargas, and most especially Mary Wilkinson for her superb and heroic efforts on the book's behalf.

Linda Heppes Funk drew all the exquisite new illustrations for this edition.

My sisters Anne Damrosch and Eloise Damrosch buoyed my spirits throughout the long process, as did many friends: Sherry Streeter, all the Akiwabas, the wonderful crew at Four Season Farm, Kathleen Beal and the dream team, and the staff of Blue Hill Books in Blue Hill, Maine. I also thank Chris Kerrigan, Melissa Coleman, Clara Coleman, and Ian Coleman, for their wit and forbearance. Joel Walther made the computer behave at crucial times. Lisa Chase helped me to clear much space on my desk. Eliot Coleman's knowledge, patience, and good cheer have been the greatest gift of all.

A Note on the Second Edition

TWENTY-TWO YEARS AGO I SAT down to write a simple little book that would introduce people to gardening. If I'd known how large it would grow, I might never have begun. Now it's 2008 and THE GARDEN PRIMER has grown again. Much of the original needed updating—new varieties, new sources, more efficient techniques, innovative tools. After a few more decades in my garden and the gardens of others, I'd learned much that I wanted to share, and I've packed as many additional plants into these pages as practicality would allow. Many are North American natives, and a number are suitable for drier conditions, a consideration for any place where water is, or could be, a scarce resource—that is, everywhere.

The march of gardening commerce is always advancing, as Katherine White so hilariously noted in her essays in *The New Yorker* (anthologized after her death in the 1977 book *Onward and Upward in the Garden*). For better or worse, flowers are commanded to produce more petals, and leaves must evolve in shades beyond green. Some trends, such as the breeding of smaller varieties for smaller yards, are quite practical. Others, such as the genetic engineering of food plants for pest or herbicide resistance, are poor substitutes for good growing practices. But if the pros sometimes disappoint, home gardeners have made great strides. Most of the ones I meet would like to use more sustainable, nontoxic methods, eat from the garden all year, enjoy more wildlife, mow less lawn, avoid invasive species, grow plants better suited to their climates and, in general, make peace with nature rather than fighting her all the way.

On balance, gardeners make the world a better place. So when they show me battered, sun-bleached, mud-spattered copies of my book and tell me it has coaxed them into the garden, I feel that I have done the job I set out to do.

Contents

Green Side Up

I FIRMLY BELIEVE THAT IN ORDER TO learn anything you have to be willing to ask dumb questions. People often say to me, "I don't know *anything* about gardening," and some of them just let it go at that. Intimidated by the sheer volume of gardening lore that exists, much of it very scientific and arcane, they leave gardening to those who presumably have lots of time to read and better yet, have a "green thumb." But others, unable to resist a pastime they suspect may be a lot of fun, wade right in. I love people who ask things like "Why should I prune my plants?" or "What is mulch?"

The aim of this book is to answer as many fundamental questions about gardening as possible. I may not be able to anticipate everything you want to know, but I will explain how pruning can make your plants bushier, more compact, or more fruitful. I will tell you that mulch is a layer of material, such as shredded bark, that you lay down on the ground chiefly to keep weeds from growing and to keep the soil moist. And I will try to come to your aid when you're standing there alone in the garden, holding a plant that looks like an amorphous tangle, and you have no idea what to do with it. If I could go out there with you, I would tell you what my nurseryman friends Mary Ann and Frederick McGourty used to tell their fledgling workers: "Plant it with the green side up." Everyone has to start somewhere.

I'm the first to admit that I have my own idiosyncratic approach when it comes to gardening. Someone once called me an "old-fashioned dirt gardener," and I guess the description fits. I use almost no commercial fertilizers and no pesticides at all, except the occasional soap spray. I prefer hand tools to power ones. I take my cues from the way nature gardens, and also from the gardens of the past. I read as much as time allows about scientific advances in horticulture, and I'm usually willing to try something new, but most of what I do has come from just plain experience. There's no substitute for spending time in your garden and using all your senses to judge the results. Are your plants' leaves a healthy green? Does your soil feel porous and fluffy when you stick your fingers into it? Does your sick plant have bugs on it, or is there evidence of disease? Far more gardens fail because the gardener is absent or not paying attention than because he or she lacks erudition. Yes, you need to know your ABCs, but the more you garden, the more you'll learn what works and what doesn't.

One of the hazards of writing a gardening book is that the author is addressing gardeners in many different localities with many different climates, soil types, and selections of plants to choose from. The more exact the information I give you, the less it may apply to the specific conditions of your very own yard. I'd have to tell you what to add to your soil, for example, without knowing what is already in it. I've tried, therefore, to steer away from formulas, though there are times when saying "Add some fertilizer" is not enough. ("Should I add a spoonful or a bucketful?" I hear you asking.) So use my recommendations as a starting point, and try to learn as much as you can about your own garden's needs. Local resources such as nurseries, universities, and the Cooperative Extension Service can be very helpful.

You'll find most of the general information about gardening in the first four chapters of this book; the rest deals with specific kinds of plants. Use the book by going back to the early chapters if you need to have one of those basic questions answered. The index will help you if a cross-reference does not steer you to the answer at the point where you need it.

Gardening, for all its down-to-earthness, has always had some mystery about it, a mystery that each culture had its own ways of expressing. In olden days you might have had a village maiden dance around the fire to woo the corn god, or made a burnt offering of the harvest to thank the deity that made it possible. Now we do soil tests, make tissue cultures, and even try to become gods ourselves in our quest to create new genetic plant material. But I don't think we'll ever shed so much light on the subject that we dampen the awe a gardener feels when the first vegetable seedlings poke up in spring. We may never explain why we're drawn to flowers just as butterflies and bees are, even though normally we have no role in their pollination. Perhaps their form and fragrance are luring us to some fateful role in their survival. We'll never know all there is to know about gardening, and I'm glad there will always be some magic about it.

So just go out there and start doing it. It's often said that a green thumb is a dirty thumb. Choose good spots for your gardens, prepare the soil well, keep a close eye on things. And remember: the green side is always up.

CHAPTER 1

What Plants Need

GOOD GARDENING IS VERY SIMPLE, really. You just have to learn to think like a plant. You can memorize sets of instructions if you want to, collect charts and tables, and follow precise recipes for soil mixes and compost. But you'll accomplish even more by learning a bit about how plants are constructed, how they grow, and what they want out of life. Once you understand what makes plants tick, you'll know what to do to help them grow well. You'll also learn how to read the sign language by which plants tell you what they need. Some plants have fussy preferences (many of these are dealt with in later chapters of this book) but most have the same universal needs.

How Plants Function

PLANTS, LIKE PEOPLE, NEED FOOD FOR survival, growth, and reproduction. They manufacture their food by means of a process called photosynthesis, from elements they find in the air, water, and soil. Sunlight provides the energy for this activity, which is in reality a chain of chemical reactions.

To get what it needs from the air, a plant "breathes," inhaling carbon dioxide and exhaling oxygen—just the opposite of animal respiration. To get what it needs from the soil, a plant absorbs water, oxygen, and certain nutrients, the most important of which are compounds of nitrogen, phosphorus, and potassium, followed closely by sulfur, calcium, and magnesium. Other chemicals, known as trace elements or micronutrients, must be in the soil in smaller quantities.

Plants also make their own vitamins and digestive enzymes, and the hormones that govern their desires, which are called tropisms. One of these (phototropism) makes a plant want to lean or grow toward a source of light and to face its flowers toward the sun. Another (hydrotropism) makes it turn its roots in the direction of water.

Working with plants gives you a great respect for them. Though silent and slow, they are resilient, relentless. We may feel quite powerful dispatching a row of garden weeds with a hoe in an instant. But turn our backs for a week or two, and there they all are again. I once went on a camping trip in the South American jungle and saw that the paths we had made with machetes on our way to the campsite had started to seal us in when we hacked our way out again a mere week later. To this day I always see a little bit of the jungle in plants, even the ones in my civilized northern garden.

PLANT STRUCTURE

To see how plants work, let's look more closely at the parts of a typical one, from the bottom up (Figure 1). A plant's roots are, in a sense, its feet, since they anchor it to the ground, but they're also responsible for absorbing all those vital elements from the soil. It is thus very important to keep in mind what a plant's roots are up to—all the more so because you can't see them. The roots' absorption of nutrients takes place through microscopic projections called root hairs; these hairs also take in oxygen from the soil, release carbon dioxide, and absorb water. The roots store water and nutrients (sometimes for long periods, in enlarged portions such as bulbs or tubers), then send them up to the leaves via fine channels (like our veins) in the stems.

The Parts of a Plant

FIG. 1

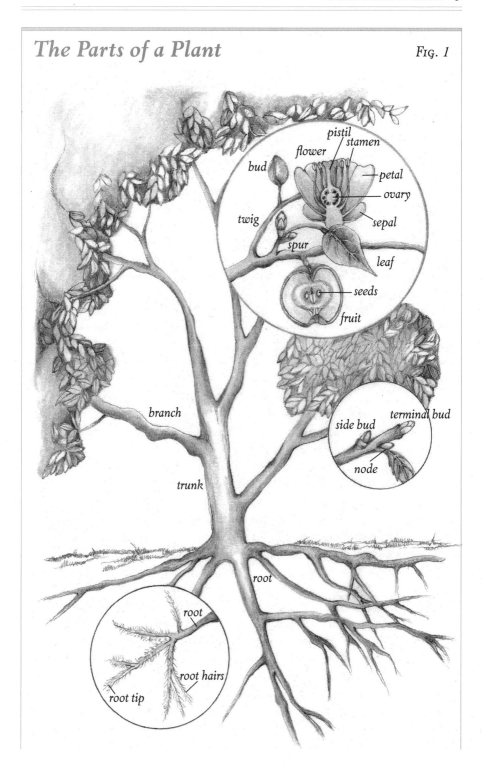

One of the plant stem's main functions is support. Unless a plant is a creeper by nature, it is always thinking "up"—trying to get its leaves up into a place where there is light and good circulation of air, and competing with other plants that have the same goal. Stems (and trunks and branches in the case of woody plants) are also the plant's most important conductors of materials—its circulatory system, so to speak. Stems bring the leaves raw materials gathered by the roots and take away food that the leaves manufacture, using some of it for their own growth and returning the rest to the roots so that they too can grow.

Although stems make some food, it is primarily in the leaves that food production takes place, from the water and nutrients brought up by the stems from the roots. (Plants can absorb nutrients through their leaves as well.) On the leaves' undersides are tiny pores, called stomata, through which carbon dioxide enters. This gas is combined with the water and nutrients, in the presence of the green chlorophyll in the leaves. The process produces the carbohydrates that nourish the plant. The by-products of these chemical reactions—water vapor and oxygen—pass out through the stomata into the air (in a process called transpiration). The more leaves a plant has, the more food it can make, and the more it can grow.

PLANT GROWTH

A plant is always growing—all over. The most dramatic growth points are the tips of the roots and the buds at the tips of the stems (terminal buds). But growth also occurs at side buds, where new stems form. Some plants, known as annuals, grow to maturity in one season, reproduce, and then die. Others, which are called perennials, produce new plants but also continue to grow themselves, persisting from season to season. From the gardener's viewpoint, it's important—with both annuals and perennials—to keep a plant's growth vigorous during the full course of its normal life.

PLANT REPRODUCTION

Plants reproduce in different ways, one of them by means of seeds. Some of a plant's terminal buds turn into leaves but others turn into flowers, which (as far as the plant is concerned) exist solely for the purpose of reproduction. A flower performs its show of color and fragrance to attract the creatures that pollinate it. When we think of pollinators, bees and butterflies come chiefly to mind, but there are a host of other pollinators that are essential to the plants they visit to feed on nectar. These include other insects such as moths, flies, bugs, beetles, thrips, and wasps. Numerous birds around the world are pollinators—hummingbirds, treecreepers, lorikeets, orioles, and parrots, to name a few. Even mammals such as bats, possums, and lemurs are known to pollinate flowers.

While these various creatures are burrowing around in the blossom to get nectar, they transfer pollen from a male part of the flower, called a stamen, onto a female part, called a pistil (a biology teacher taught me how to remember which is which by thinking "pistil-packing mama"), and the flower is thereby fertilized. (Occasionally, the male and female parts are on separate plants.) After fertilization, the flower can produce fruits or seed heads containing the seeds. These are then transported by gravity, by the wind, by water, by traveling animals who carry the seeds on their fur, or by birds that eat the fruits. The seeds land or are dropped at another spot, where the life of a new plant begins.

Plants can also reproduce by vegetative means, such as by sending up new shoots from their roots or underground stems (stolons), or by forming small bulblets at the sides of a food-storing bulb. Your plants may decide that they want to put most of their energy into one or another form of reproduction, but it is often desirable for you to change their minds. If you're trying to encourage a large harvest of fruits or a showy display of flowers, you may want to chop off suckers, the new plants that come up from the roots. Or you may want to cut the seed heads off plants that have flowered, so the plants will concentrate on forming good, productive root systems instead of maturing their seeds. (Decisions such as these are discussed in more detail in the chapters on specific types of plants.)

Plants Need Good Soil

B ECAUSE SO MUCH OF WHAT PLANTS need if they are to do well comes from the soil, establishing a good soil is the most important thing you can do for them. But gardeners often don't understand just what a good soil is or how they can achieve it. They may think it means simply improving soil fertility, and that this entails going out to buy a bag of evergreen food, bulb food, or rose food (just as they'd buy dog food), and sprinkling it on their gardens. But good soil has good structure as well as good fertility, and structure is something

you must work to build. Improving soil structure isn't difficult to do, but it does require that you understand some basic things about your soil.

SOIL LAYERS

What is soil? Most soils are composed of inorganic mineral particles, air, water, and organic matter (matter that was once living plant or animal tissue) in varying amounts. If you go out into the garden right now and dig a straight-sided hole to the depth of your spade, you'll see something like the cross-section drawing of soil on page 1. Most likely, the upper layer (the topsoil) will be considerably darker in color, lighter in texture, and easier to dig than the lower layer (the subsoil), because the topsoil contains more organic matter. In the upper layer you'll find more plant roots and more soil organisms than in the denser subsoil, although some deeper-rooted plants and some earthworms will probably have entered the subsoil as well. The subsoil is important: plant roots bring important minerals up from it, and it can be improved just as the topsoil can. When we speak of the soil structure in a garden, however, we are usually talking about the topsoil layer.

Soils vary enormously from one part of the country to another. Your topsoil may be dark brown, light brown, or brick red, depending on the kinds of minerals it contains and the amount of moisture and organic matter in it. It may be only a few inches deep, or it may be a foot deep. It may be full of rocks, or it may be fairly rock-free.

SOIL TEXTURE

Soils are classified according to the size of the particles of which they are composed. At one extreme is coarse gravel, with particles larger than 5 millimeters in diameter; at the other is clay, with particles smaller than .005 millimeter. In between is a gradation of soils with particles of decreasing size: fine gravel, coarse sand, fine sand, sandy loam, loam, silt loam, and silt. The soils with larger particles are generally characterized as light or sandy soils; those with small ones are heavy or clay soils. Loam, the happy medium, is usually considered the ideal type of soil.

Each type of soil texture has its virtues. In light soils, both water and air can move freely among the large particles, so these soils tend to be well drained and rich in oxygen. Light soils warm up fast in spring, thus stimulating early plant growth. They are also easy for plant roots to penetrate as they grow. On the negative side, water may drain out of light soils too quickly, taking nutrients with it and leaving the soil both dry and infertile.

In clay soils there is little space among the particles for air and water to circulate, so these soils are often waterlogged and poorly drained. This can rob plant roots of the oxygen the plant needs for growth, and cause the roots to rot. Because clay soils are dense, they are harder for roots to penetrate. (Imagine poking your fingers through sand, then through clay, and you'll sense what the same process feels like for plant roots.) Clay soils also warm up more slowly in spring. On the other hand, because they hold water and nutrients well, they are often fertile (this is also because clay particles have negatively charged ions that attract positively charged particles of elements important for plants, such as calcium, potassium, sodium, and magnesium). And they retain moisture better than sandy soils do in hot, dry weather.

Different plants like different soils. Some plants that need particularly good drainage are most at home in sandy soils and have evolved with roots deep enough to withstand their dryness. Others that need the extra fertility and moisture of clay soils have strong roots that don't mind the extra push it takes to penetrate them. But the ideal soil for most plants is loam, and if we are trying to grow a wide range of plants, loam is what most of us would like to have.

What kind of soil do you have in your garden? On a day when the soil is neither unusually dry nor unusually wet, squeeze a handful of it. Does it form a tight ball that doesn't come apart when you tap it? Is it sticky when wet but hard and lumpy when dry? If so, you have a clay soil. If it runs through your fingers and doesn't form a ball, it's sandy. If it holds together, but breaks when you tap it, it's loam. (The results of this informal test can vary somewhat according to the amount of organic matter in the soil, as explained below.)

The size of the particles in your soil is not the only important factor in soil structure. How the particles are organized also matters. Ideally, soil particles are clustered together in groups and are not distinct as, for example, sand particles usually are. Nor are the particles so close together that they form a tight mass, as with clay. Rather, the particles of the best soils are like crumbs of homemade bread. In fact, when we describe good soil structure we often say the soil has a "crumb," or "tilth." And usually a soil has a good crumb because it is rich in organic matter. What you want is a "friable" soil, one that feels light, almost fluffy, and is easy to stick your fingers into. It is inviting to plants, inviting to earthworms (which will always populate your garden if you have good soil), and also inviting to you! You'll find it a joy to work in because it's easy to dig and because weeds pull out of it more readily.

Now let's get back to your own soil. What if you've squeezed your handful and found it is dry and sandy, or heavy and sticky—and on top of that it has no crumb. Don't despair. Only in the direst of situations would you need to replace your soil by bringing in good (and expensive) loam, or adjust your soil by adding large amounts of soil of the opposite texture. Fortunately, there's one easy way to improve your soil no matter what is wrong with its structure: add organic matter.

THE ROLE OF ORGANIC MATTER

Organic matter is simply dead plant or animal tissue. Unless all your topsoil has been removed, there's some of it in your soil. Aboveground, animals have left their carcasses and excrement, plants have died, and leaves have fallen. Belowground, organisms such as worms and moles have also left carcasses and excrement, and plant roots have died and rotted. The actions of burrowing creatures, growing plant roots, and the freezing and thawing of the soil have mixed all these into the soil, even bringing some of the surface matter, such as fallen leaves, down to the layers below.

This varied collection of organic materials does a number of things for the soil that are greatly appreciated by plants. In the soil, plant and animal matter, with the aid of bacteria and fungi, decomposes into a substance called humus. Humus contains sticky gums that bind soil particles together into those all-important clusters, or crumbs—not densely, as with tightly packed clay, but with spaces through which water and air can pass. Thus organic matter, in the form of humus, helps to aerate the soil. It also makes it more able to absorb and conduct water, retaining some for plants to use, but enabling the excess to drain away. This is how adding organic matter can improve both clay and sandy soils. It gives them a better "structure," a term that refers to the type of aggregates in the soil—not the size of the mineral particles, but the way they stick together. In a good garden soil, they should stick together just enough so the soil resembles loose cookie crumbs—not like sugar, which you can pour from a spoon, and not like dense fudge, which must be cut with a knife. Organic matter even moderates the soil's temperature, protecting the plants and animals that live in it from extremes and rapid fluctuations of heat and cold.

Organic matter also contains important nutritional elements that plants need. In the process of decay, living things return to the soil the substances from which they were built so that other living things can use them. This happens through the action of soil microorganisms, which break down organic matter into its basic elements, in forms that can be readily absorbed by plant roots. Thus organic matter in the soil gives it a good structure and makes it fertile at the same time.

THE SOIL IS ALIVE

I cannot emphasize enough the fact that the soil is a very busy place. It is populated by numerous large creatures, from groundhogs to snakes, smaller ones like moles, and even smaller yet still visible creatures like worms, centipedes, ants, slugs, bees, beetles, and springtails. The vast majority of soil-dwelling species however are microscopic—including bacteria, fungi, nematodes, mites, slime molds, algae, rotifers, and single-celled protozoa such as amoebas. A single teaspoon of soil contains millions of bacteria alone. Entire civilizations of small organisms are interacting down there, sometimes battling, sometimes cooperating with one another, but all existing in a state of mutual inter-dependence. Without them, nothing that died on earth would ever decompose and no new life would be born, because plants would not have nutrients in forms they could use for growth. In fact, the smaller the organism, the more essential it seems to be for life on earth.

It is vitally important for the gardener to regard the soil with respect. Compacting it, tilling it excessively, and above all applying harsh or toxic substances to it can disrupt the vital web of life that makes the garden grow. The following section introduces some of the important elements that plants need, but don't think of them as a shopping list, or the ingredients in a recipe. Plant nutrition is greater than the sum of its parts. By adding organic soil amendments, you're not so much feeding your plants as you are feeding the soil itself—and the creatures within it, so that they in turn can nurture the plants' roots.

The result of this approach is a thriving community of soil populations that do much of the work for you, that compensate for your lapses in effort and judgment, that buffer the whims of climate and weather. The opposite approach, which relies on factory-produced inputs, essentially keeps your soil and your plants on artificial life support so they'll require your constant attention, expense, and effort.

SOIL FERTILITY

For the most part, plant life is more healthy and abundant in soils that are fertile—that is, rich in nutrients. But what, really, does this mean? Let's go back to the major elements that plants need from the soil to manufacture their food, and consider how nature—or the gardener—supplies them.

Nitrogen. Soil nitrogen is converted to nitrates by "nitrogen-fixing" bacteria, which take the nitrogen and change it (or "fix" it) into a form that plants can use. Nitrogen maintains plants' green color and is largely responsible for good leaf and stem growth. The effect of feeding nitrogen to plants is fast and dramatic—you can see the stems shoot up and new leaves unfurl, suffused with a healthy green color. To the plant, a dose of nitrogen probably feels the way a candy bar feels to us: like a shot of quick energy.

Important as nitrogen is to plants, they can sometimes suffer from an excess of it, especially if other important elements are lacking. You'll notice that rapidly grown tissue produced by nitrogen is often rather soft and vulnerable, easily succumbing to cold and disease and making the plant attractive to sucking insects. The stems may be weak and need staking. Nitrogen may also produce too much leaf and stem growth instead of a good root system, or instead of producing desirable fruits and flowers. So you have to learn when your plants need extra nitrogen: when you want to green up your lawn, for example, or make an ornamental foliage plant like a fern more showy, or produce a quick, abundant row of a leafy garden crop such as spinach. And you learn when plants don't need nitrogen: before the onset of cold weather, which would kill soft new growth, and when you want your plants to bloom heavily or get their roots well established instead of growing tall or leafy.

Although I use nitrogen with some caution, I am always on the lookout for a nitrogen deficiency. Nitrogen is an element that's used up by plants very quickly. It's also highly soluble in water and thus leaches out of the soil. If your plants run out of it you'll see slow, spindly growth, and foliage that is pale green, since nitrogen is a component of chlorophyll, which gives plants their healthy green color. If older parts of the plant are pale, it indicates that the plant is directing what nitrogen stores it has into new growth.

Spring is the best time to feed nitrogen to outdoor plants, for several reasons: because that's when you want lots of new growth, because the nitrogen is more available to the plants in warm weather when nitrogen-fixing soil bacteria are most active, and finally because nitrogen added in fall may leach away by springtime.

Phosphorus. Phosphorus is essential for the general growth and health of a plant, especially its root development, the production of fruit and seeds, and the ability to resist disease. It is one of those pluses a gardener can give to plants to make sure they do better than average.

When I dig a permanent bed for perennials where good root growth must continue for years, or if I am transplanting a plant and want it to put out fresh new roots right away, I try to make sure there is enough phosphorus available in the soil. Root-vegetable crops and flower bulbs, in particular, need plenty of phosphorus. Symptoms of phosphorus deficiency vary (in corn, for example, it results in purplish leaves), and a soil test is the best way to alert yourself to any lack of it. Unlike nitrogen, it is not highly soluble and thus can be applied in fall. However, like nitrogen, phosphorus can be too much of a good thing. Excess phosphorus can lead to deficiencies of zinc and iron. Also, runoff from fields where excess manure or high-phosphate fertilizers have been added are a common source of water pollution.

Potassium. Potassium is essential for a plant's growth, general well-being, and resistance to disease. Deficiency first shows up in older tissues. Excess potassium can cause magnesium deficiency.

Trace elements. In addition to calcium, magnesium, and sulfur (which are often included among the "major" elements, or macronutrients), the significant trace elements, or micronutrients, are iron, boron, zinc, copper, manganese, cobalt, and molybdenum. A deficiency in any of these will show up on a thorough soil test.

Most mineral deficiencies in the soil are hard for the average gardener to spot because they sometimes produce symptoms that could also indicate drought, excess shade, pollution, disease, and other problems. If your plants are growing poorly despite your best efforts, it's a very good idea to have your soil tested (page 10). In certain parts of the country, local soils are commonly deficient in a specific element. A soil test will pick this up.

SOIL PH

Another thing that determines whether you have good soil is the soil's level of acidity or alkalinity, as measured by the pH factor—expressed as a number on a scale of 1.0 to 14.0, with 7.0 representing a neutral pH. As the numbers decrease from 7.0, they indicate greater acidity. As they increase from 7.0, they indicate greater alkalinity. The pH of most soils is between 4.5 and 8.0.

The main reason to be concerned with soil pH is not the direct effect of excessively acid or alkaline soil substances on the plants themselves, but the effect the pH has on important soil minerals. These minerals are much more available to plants in soil that is close to neutral than they are in soil that is either very acid (sour) or very alkaline (sweet). The action of most soil bacteria is also thought to be more vigorous when soil pH is between 6.0 and 7.0.

Most plants have specific preferences as to soil pH. There are some that like really acid soil: heathers, rhododendrons, and blueberries are notorious examples. Others prefer alkaline soil: these include baby's breath, delphiniums, and beets. But most garden plants will tolerate a wide pH range. Furthermore, if you have a healthy soil that is well supplied with nutrients and organic matter, and that is also well aerated and full of earthworms and microorganisms, its pH matters less. The overall good condition of the soil will act as a buffer against any deviations from the ideal pH for any given plant.

Usually, it is only when your soil is quite acid or quite alkaline that you have to do anything about it. A soil test is probably the easiest way for you to check the pH of your soil. (For ways to alter soil pH see page 21.)

Having your soil tested. If you're new to gardening or are simply unsure about the nature of the soil in your garden, have a soil test done. You'll learn a lot about your soil. Most tests will tell you how much of the important elements your soil has (excluding nitrogen, which is hard to measure), how acid or alkaline it is, and what you need to add, in what amounts, to bring your soil to optimum condition (depending on what you're planning to grow). Often you can request organic recommendations when you fill out the form. Some test results will also include the clay and humus content of your soil and even

the levels of lead or other toxic elements. If you notice flecks of paint in your soil from nearby buildings or fences, be sure to have the soil tested for lead. Don't grow edible crops in places where the lead level is indicated as high.

You can buy fairly inexpensive soil test kits that will test for pH and many nutrients, but I think it's easier to have your soil tested professionally, and you'll also get more complete information that way. For a small fee, the local Cooperative Extension Service will provide you with a mailer and full instructions for digging up and sending soil samples in for testing, and they'll send you back a computer printout with the results. Private labs cost more but may provide more information. The best time to test the soil is before you start your garden or add nutrients to it. If you want to test an established garden, do it in fall.

Feeding the Soil

ONCE YOU UNDERSTAND WHAT YOUR plants want from your soil—good structure, available nutrients, and the proper pH—and have determined how well equipped that soil is to provide these things, you need to decide how to make up for any deficiencies the soil has, and keep it "in good heart" as the English farmers say. The relationship between plants and the soil is incredibly complex, and it often seems that the more we learn about it, the more we realize how much is still unknown. On the face of it, this would make problem-solving difficult. Here's an example: a disease of celery called black heart is caused by a boron deficiency. But it's also known that the deficiency is more common in soils with a sandy texture or a high pH or both. Which problem do you then address—the deficiency itself, the soil texture, or the pH? To me the answer is surprisingly simple. Because adding organic matter such as manure or compost improves the stucture of sandy soil, buffers the effect of high pH, and tends to be high in trace elements such as boron, I'd start by just adding more of it and seeing if the situation resolves itself. It's remarkable how many problems are solved just by doing this simple thing.

There is nothing mystical about it. Nature has been improving the soil this way for millions of years. A living organism contains a complete nutritional package that is passed along to future organisms when it decomposes in the soil. As I'll explain, adding organic matter does not always give my plants everything they want, but it does give them so much that it is the point at which I always begin.

ADDING ORGANIC MATTER

If nature has already put organic matter in your soil, why add more? Because few soils have a perfect structure to begin with, and because, after all, when you garden you want to give your plants an even more luxurious environment than nature might provide. Furthermore, organic matter is not an addition you make just once and then forget about. It is always decomposing and being used up, and therefore it must be replenished. Even the most permanent plantings such as trees, shrubs, and deep-rooted perennials benefit from a surface mulch of organic matter that will, as it breaks down, be worked into the soil by earthworms and other helpers.

Although there are many kinds of organic soil additions to choose from, here are some of the most commonly used:

Animal manures: Thousands of years ago farmers observed that plants grew better in fields manured by animals who were pastured there. Droppings collected from stabled animals and then spread on cropland produced even better results. Farm animals have been linked with agriculture ever since, above and beyond their use for meat, milk, labor, or hides. Manures of farm animals are still popular soil amendments, providing good tilth and a rich supply of nutrients as well. But there are a few things you need to know in order to use animal manures profitably.

Manures are not always balanced in a way that will benefit your particular soil or the type of plants you intend to grow. Most contain a high percentage of nitrogen, relative to phosphorus, although poultry manures can also be quite high in phosphorus—a danger in soils where phosphate fertilizers have been overused. Having your soil tested will help steer you toward an informed decision.

Manure can also be harmful to plants if it has not sufficiently decomposed. If you look at a pile of fresh horse manure on a cold morning, you'll see billows of steam rising from it because of the heat it is giving off during decomposition, and you'll be able to smell the ammonia in it as well. Both heat and caustic ammonia can burn plants' roots, just as they can burn your own hands.

I use animal manure in my garden, but I never use any that is fresh. Well-rotted manure is odorless and looks like dark soil. Often people who raise animals have piles of it that have been sitting around for years, and they're glad to have it carted away. Or they'll sell it to you for much less than it would cost to buy it in bags. I have occasionally purchased bagged, composted cow manure when I did not have a handy farm source, because it seems to benefit my garden. But I always consider it second best, especially since I don't often know what other ingredients have been added to that bag, and much of the store-bought has been of dubious quality.

There are other considerations in judging a particular manure source: one is the percentage of animal excrement versus animal bedding, such as straw, sawdust, or shavings. The bedding is organic matter too, but it is lower in nutrients and its benefits vary. Manure from horses bedded on straw is excellent because the straw decomposes readily. Sawdust or shavings, on the other hand, take a long time to break down and can tie up soil nutrients while doing so. Another drawback is that manure and bedding can contain viable seeds from hay or other animal feeds, and these can sprout in your garden, so you have to weigh the risk of introducing weeds against the benefits to your soil. (This is less a problem with cow manure.) Adding the manure to a compost pile first (page 15) is a good way to minimize this problem.

Finally, I would avoid using manures from dogs, cats, or humans, because all of these can transmit diseases to your soil and then to you.

Plant humus: The most common form of decomposed plant matter that is sold commercially is peat moss. This is made up of plants—usually sphagnum or other mosses—that have decomposed very slowly in boggy places. (Sphagnum peat is not to be confused with the undecomposed sphagnum moss that is used to keep plants moist when packed for shipping or to line hanging plant baskets.)

Peat moss comes in compressed, plastic-wrapped bales of various sizes, usually 2, 4, or 6 cubic feet. It is very, very dry. If you add peat moss to your soil directly it will draw the moisture out of the soil just as a blotter would, so be sure to moisten it. One way is to split the bale in two by cutting the plastic with a knife and letting water from a hose trickle slowly into the peat for a few hours. Another is to spread it on top of the garden and turn a sprinkler on it until the whole layer is wet before you dig it into the soil.

You can also buy "peat humus." This is more decomposed than peat moss, and much more moist. It comes in smaller bags and is darker, heavier, and more expensive.

I find that no commercial product can lighten the soil in a large area as efficiently as peat moss can, if properly moistened, because it is relatively inexpensive and light to handle. I often use it in combination with compost or rotted manure, however, because peat moss is relatively low in nutrients.

Grass clippings are a convenient source of plant humus, but don't dig them into a planted garden if they've just been cut, because they decompose rapidly in a way that can inhibit plant roots. I avoid them if they are full of especially bothersome weed seeds (such as those of dandelions), and I never use clippings from lawns where someone has applied broadleaf weed killers such as 2,4-D, which will harm garden plants. Pass up offers of free grass clippings from neighbors or municipalities unless you're sure they're herbicide- and insecticide-free.

Other sources include plant debris such as weeds (preferably those that have not yet gone to seed), annual crops that have finished producing, and thinnings from the vegetable garden, all of which will eventually turn into humus in the soil. These can be tilled directly into the soil, and you can till under annual crops in fall after they've finished producing.

Cover crops: Sometimes gardeners plant crops just to provide organic matter for their soil, especially in vegetable gardens. These are called cover crops or green manures, and are tilled under after a while unless they are being grown solely as a cover to protect the soil. They are especially good if you have a large garden, because they spare you from having to bring in a lot of organic material from somewhere else.

Planting cover crops benefits your garden in a number of ways. The growing roots help to keep the soil loose, moist, and aerated on land that is lying fallow. Deep-rooted cover crops bring valuable minerals up to the topsoil from the subsoil, something that shallower-rooted garden crops can't do. Cover crops also keep rainfall from eroding the soil, and in many cases will shade out weeds. After the cover crops are turned under, they not only add organic matter for good tilth, but often return more nutrients to the soil than they have consumed. Since some of the nutrients already in the soil would leach away if the ground were fallow, this is a double bonus.

What you decide to grow as a cover crop depends partly on your climate and partly on what you're trying to achieve. You might want a cover crop that will grow for an entire year, from one spring to another, to take care of a plot you are not going to use and/or want to revitalize thoroughly as part of your garden-rotation scheme (page 247). If so, plant a deep-rooted perennial crop such as alfalfa, perennial rye, or one of the clovers (see below for more on the benefits of these). On the other hand, use an annual cover crop if you want a quick-growing green manure to follow early vegetables, a spring cover crop to precede later-planted ones, or a crop for the fallow summer period in a hot-climate garden. Some of these are annual rye (called ryegrass), buckwheat, hairy vetch, crimson clover, and winter barley. I find annual cover crops easier to deal with because I don't have to worry about perennial roots remaining in the soil and resprouting. But with any cover crop it's essential to mow or till before the plants drop their seeds and become weeds themselves (buckwheat is a good case in point).

Cover crops that are especially good at smothering out weeds are buckwheat (an annual) and winter rye, a biennial that will survive the winter even in the north but will stop growing and die if you mow it in spring. Cover crops that are best at enriching the soil are members of the pea family (legumes) such as the clovers, the vetches, and alfalfa. Legumes enrich the soil through the process of nitrogen fixation, discussed on page 275. They have bacteria called rhizobia living in nodules that grow on their roots. The legumes will use some of the nitrogen up, but a certain amount will be available for other plants that grow in the same soil after the legumes have been removed or tilled under. You can help the process of nitrogen fixation along by dusting the seeds of the legume crop with a powder called an inoculant, although it is usually not a necessity. There are different inoculants for various legume crops, so check to make sure you've got the right one for your crop.

The most popular way to till under a cover crop is with a rear-mounted rotary tiller, but this machine cannot handle crops after they've gotten tall and thick-stalked. Either till your cover crop under when the plants are soft, green, and about a foot tall or, if they've gotten tall and tough, mow them first and leave them lying there to wilt and break down for a while before tilling. You can also put the cuttings on the compost pile or use them elsewhere as mulch, and just till in what remains. It's possible to spade under a cover crop such as buckwheat or clover by hand if you're dealing with a small area. A vigorous root producer such as winter rye will usually require mechanical tilling and may even have to be tilled twice.

As a rule, it is not advisable to plant a new crop right after a green cover crop has been tilled under, because it will not have decomposed sufficiently to provide nutrients, and because the process of decomposition will inhibit seed germination. Wait at least three weeks. A good plan is to sow an annual cover crop in late summer or fall, but not so early that it will go to seed before winter. The plants will die over the winter and start decomposing, but their roots will still hold the soil. By spring, it will be time to till them in.

There are many different cover crops you can grow, and some will be better for your own climate than others. Your best bet is to talk to local farmers, farm-supply stores, nurseries, or the Cooperative Extension Service to find out what works best in your area.

MAKING COMPOST

Another good way to add organic matter—and nutrients—to the soil is through compost. Compost is simply a big casse-role of organic matter that you assemble yourself, usually enclosed in some sort of bin, and then leave to "cook" awhile. The cooking—or decomposing—takes place fastest when there is adequate moisture, warmth, and air. It must take place in the presence of the soil microorganisms that make decomposition happen.

Making compost enables you to recycle the debris from your garden, and many of the scraps from your kitchen, and put them back into growing things so that nothing is wasted. This is nature's way. It's a handy way to deal with garden refuse and obtain a great soil amendment at the same time— one that's not only free of charge, but right next to your garden where you need it.

Compost is made by piling layers of organic material (usually interspersed with very thin layers of soil) in a pile or stack, keeping it moistened with a hose (if rain doesn't do this for you), and letting the pile decompose. This happens very quickly at the inside of the pile—the temperature there can get as high as 160 degrees Fahrenheit— though the whole pile will eventually break down successfully if it sits long enough. Patient (or lazy) composters do just that— let it sit. Those who want their compost faster turn their piles, bringing the material on the outside to the inside with a garden fork and/or shovel so that it too will have its chance at the "hot spot." This also fluffs up the pile, adding air that further stimulates the action. A handy way to do this is to turn the pile into another bin right next to it, and within a few weeks it should heat up again. Industrious composters turn their piles frequently, but even doing it only once, after a few months of warm weather, will bring you more quickly to the finished product—a dark, moist substance that has broken down enough so that you cannot easily recognize the original ingredients.

It may take longer than you think to fill a bin. The materials shrink as they settle and decompose. But when you have added as much as you can, it is time to let the pile rest and do its final cooking. I add a layer of straw on top, hose it down if the materials seem dry, and cover it with a tarp to protect the pile from dryness and excessive rain, which can leach out the nutrients.

Every composter has his or her own recipe—usually, as with most good casseroles, a blend of whatever good things come to hand (see page 16 for some suggestions). But basically what you need are some dry brown, carbonaceous materials like twigs, bark, straw, and other dead plant stems that provide bulk but break down slowly; and some moist, softer materials that break down faster and hasten the decomposition of the bulky ones—high-nitrogen substances such as green plant debris, kitchen wastes, and manure. The

Styles of Compost Bins FIG. 2

A compost bin is left open at the top so you can dump materials into it. It may also be helpful to have one side removable, for turning the contents and removing finished compost.

stacked straw bales

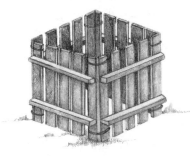

wooden boards, spaced to let air enter

stacked sapling logs

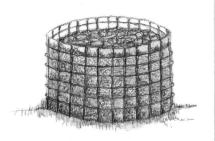

circle of wire mesh

THE MAKINGS OF COMPOST

Materials to use:

Weeds from the yard and garden

Farm animal manure

Farm animal bedding, especially straw (see page 12)

Spent crops, such as pea vines, bolted lettuce, any plant no longer producing

Grass clippings

Nonanimal kitchen scraps, such as fruit and vegetable peelings, corn husks, carrot tops, eggshells

Straw

Used mulch, such as hay or finely shredded bark

Seaweed

Alfalfa meal, or unused cat litter made from alfalfa meal

By-products from locally grown crops, such as spent hops or tobacco stems

Sod that has been removed

Coffee grounds

Bulbs that have been discarded after forcing

The tops of perennials cut back in fall, if not too woody

Dead annuals, removed after frost

Silt removed from the bottom of garden pools and ponds

Fallen fruit

Materials to use with caution:

Fish and shellfish scraps, which are a good nitrogen source but may attract animals unless well buried in the pile

Annual weeds with seeds of long viability, such as feverfew

Autumn leaves and twigs (shred with mower, or compost separately)

Wood chips, if finely chipped and in small amounts

Wood ashes, in very small amounts

Materials to avoid:

Animal kitchen scraps, which attract dogs or rats

Manure from dogs, cats, and humans; used cat litter

Colored newspapers, books, and magazines, which may contain toxic inks

Plastic materials, which will not decompose

Grass clippings containing residual weed killers, which will kill garden plants

Any refuse from black walnut, eucalyptus, and cedar trees, which will inhibit the growth of garden plants

Any plant parts from poison ivy, poison oak, and poison sumac

Coal and charcoal ashes, which contain toxic residues

key is to maintain just the right balance of carbon and nitrogen. Think of your casserole as a lasagna in which the dry brown ingredients are the noodle layers and the moist green ones the filling. High-nitrogen additions such as seaweed, dried blood, fish emulsion, or grass clippings can be added to heat things up if the heap has too much "noodle." Sprinkling in some soil now and again is a good way of introducing worker microorganisms into the pile, although during the growing season you'll find this happens anyway as you toss on weeds with soil attached to their roots.

Some gardeners sprinkle on special compost activators but these are unnecessary. The garden, yard, and kitchen usually provide most of what I need. I also avoid the use of gasoline- or electric-powered shredders to break up compost materials and thereby speed decomposition, because I dislike the noise, smell, and energy use. But I'd make one exception: if you use a power mower to mow your lawn you can use it to shred up autumn leaves and add them to the pile in small amounts as a carbon source. It's tempting to rely heavily on autumn leaves because they are so plentiful, but this is unadvisable. Tree leaves, especially flat ones like maple leaves, tend to mat and thereby exclude air. Also, their decomposition is largely fungal, whereas the desired action in a compost pile is largely bacteria-driven. The best solution is to have a separate heap for leaves, one that can break down over the course of three years to yield leaf mold—a time-honored soil improver and mulch, inspired by the decomposition of leaves on the forest floor.

You'll find that some ingredients break down faster than others. This is not really a problem. If I find undecomposed plant stalks or corncobs in my "finished" pile, I just toss them onto the pile that's still cooking, to give them another go-around. Another trick is to smash things like big, tough broccoli stems with an axe, mallet, or hatchet to break up the fibers before composting. Large woody stems from the perennial garden are best composted in a separate pile along with small and medium-size shrub and tree brush.

I try very hard to make my compost recipe as diverse as possible. The more different materials I use, the more likely I am to cover the bases in terms of plant nutrition. Each ingredient makes its own contribution of basic elements, including trace minerals. I figure that by putting together a complete enough package, I'm offering a good smorgasbord to my plants. If I've done my job, they'll in turn serve me up a whole nutritional package as well.

You can "cook" your compost in a number of different containers. It's easier to stack your pile if you enclose it, and it will also look tidier. See Figure 2 for a choice of styles. A wooden box frame with wire mesh stretched across it works fine, with one side removable, for turning. The mesh lets air into the pile to help activate it. Bins can be constructed of wooden boards (some people use the wooden pallets used in shipping). Sapling logs stacked log-cabin style can be had for free if you have a woodlot. Cement blocks stacked with air spaces between them are tidy and sturdy, though not glamorous. My dad preferred a circle of snow fence, supported by metal stakes. I like a system of straw bales, used like building blocks, because they keep the heap moist and cooking all the way out to the edges. The straw eventually decomposes and is added to next year's pile. There are also many prefabricated composting devices on the market, but most of them seem too small, too expensive, or both, and I like the do-it-yourself approach best. You may come up with your own ingenious compost receptacle.

It is possible to get by with just one compost bin. You can turn the materials by simply forking them onto the ground next to the bin, then forking them back in again. When the compost is mature you can just fork or shovel it into a tidy pile to free the bin up for new material. But I find it is helpful to have two bins, one that I am gradually filling and one that is resting.

Some gardeners, especially in town or suburban settings, worry about the smell of a compost heap and its potential for attracting dogs, raccoons, noisy birds, rodents, and other scavengers. I find that odors are rarely a problem, and if critters appear, a well-fortified enclosure with a tight-fitting cover will keep them out. A more casual approach is to site the heap in an inconspicuous spot where the occasional raid won't upset anyone's idea of tidiness. Covering the remains of a lobster feast with straw will usually keep seagulls and crows from scattering the shells.

Compost is "done" when it has broken down into pieces small enough to use easily, depending on what job you are doing. For jobs like planting shrubs and trees, or for use as a mulch, it can be fairly coarse textured. For enriching a seedbed or a potting mixture, you want compost that has broken down so much that it looks like very rich soil and nothing that went into it is still visible. When I worked at my friend Lee Bristol's nursery in Sherman, Connecticut, he kept numerous compost piles going at once, none of which were ever turned.

Most of them were large, tidy stacks in varying stages of decay. (Helen and Scott Nearing, authors of *Living the Good Life*, kept an equally impressive array in the log-sapling style at their Maine farm.) Bristol also kept a four-sided wooden bin with a removable board at the bottom of one side, from which he extracted very fine compost that had been sitting for about five years. We used this for jobs like starting seeds. If you want very fine compost without the long wait, take some coarse compost and sift it through ½-inch hardware cloth nailed taut to a frame. A small window frame, set on top of your wheelbarrow, would be fine—or better yet, build one just the right size from 2-by-4s. Then put the coarse material you sifted out back onto the heap.

If you let compost sit without being turned, it will probably take between a year and a half to two years to mature—less in warmer climates, since cold weather slows down microbial action. It can be ready in six months if you turn it often. Can you let a compost pile sit indefinitely? No. Eventually the organic matter will break down completely, your pile will dwindle, and the microorganisms in it will no longer be active.

ADDING MORE NUTRIENTS TO THE SOIL

As I've explained, much of the organic matter that you add to your soil to improve its structure also makes it more fertile. If you incorporate manure, plant residues, cover crops, or compost into your soil, it may be that you won't have to add anything else.

On the other hand, maybe you will. Some kinds of organic matter—peat moss, for example—are less nutritious than others, or are lacking in some important elements that your plants need. So you need to find materials to add to your soil solely for the purpose of increasing its fertility.

You may also need to fertilize a specific plant by giving it an extra dose of nutrients at some point in its growth. You can dig some fertilizer into the bottom of a planting hole and mix some into the soil with which you fill the hole. You can dig fertilizer into the soil around certain plants as they grow, and "side-dress" or "top-dress" plants by spreading fertilizer on the surface of the soil around them. You can also apply fertilizer in liquid form, either by watering the plant with a fertilizer solution or by foliar feeding—spraying the solution directly on the plant's leaves.

The fertilizer you use might consist of some of the organic materials mentioned in the preceding sections, but here you would be applying them chiefly for their nutritional value, not to change the structure of the soil. Before feeding a plant, always ask yourself, What kind of food does this plant really want? Keep in mind the three basic elements that plants need to get from the soil—nitrogen, phosphorus, and potassium—what kind of growth they produce in plants, and when that growth should occur.

Organic versus inorganic fertilizers. Nitrogen, phosphorus, and potassium can be obtained from organic sources (animal and vegetable matter) or from inorganic fertilizers produced by the petrochemical industry. Some gardeners are passionately committed to one or the other approach, some don't care and use whatever they have around, and others use different fertilizers in different situations.

People who favor inorganic, or "chemical," fertilizers maintain that plants don't know the difference between elements from organic and inorganic sources. All plant nutrients are chemical compounds, after all, and are absorbed and used in the same way. Organic gardeners, on the other hand, avoid the use of any petrochemical products (as well as most man-made pesticides and weed killers) because they're concerned about their effect on the soil and other parts of the environment (not to mention the environmental impact of the factories that produce them).

Chemical fertilizers are harmful to beneficial soil organisms—with the result that soon nutrients are no longer made in the soil, and the only way plants can obtain readily available nourishment is from still more chemical fertilizers. These products can also lead to the buildup of residues in the soil, which can be bad for plant growth. Some are highly soluble and lead to the contamination of groundwater. In addition, it's very easy to go overboard with any bagged fertilizers as you scatter them about, especially as a beginning gardener. With the long, steady action of well-made compost, however, it's hard to go far wrong. I also find there's more inherent satisfaction in soil-building than there is in just dosing a plant with something that comes out of a bag, a bottle, or a box. And with compost you are applying an all-purpose amendment that is somehow greater that the sum of its parts, complete with whatever x-factors nature puts in there during the transformative process of decay-and-rebirth.

When you buy fertilizers commercially, most are labeled with a formula that states the percentage of nitrogen, phosphorus, and potassium that the preparations contain, in that order. The chemical symbols for these three elements are N, P, and K, respectively, and the elements are referred to by their symbols in many discussions of them and on fertilizer bags, so it is worth memorizing them. (If, like most people, you forget which element is P and which is K, use a memory device such as "Phosphorus is P because the word has *two* Ps in it.") If a bag of fertilizer is marked "5-10-5," for example, that means that it contains 5 percent N, 10 percent P, and 5 percent K. You can then figure out, if you want to, how many pounds of each element you're adding to your soil. For example, a 100-pound bag of 5-10-5 would supply 5 pounds of nitrogen to your garden, 10 pounds of phosphorus, and 5 pounds of potassium. The rest is inert filler. Both organic and inorganic commercial fertilizers are labeled using these initial letters.

Organic sources. If I want a good, steady nitrogen source that will break down over a period of time and simultaneously improve soil structure, I add well-rotted manure. Manure is also good to use if you have lightened the soil with a material that is relatively poor in nutrients, like vermiculite or peat moss; but since in this case the soil structure would already be good, you might apply a less bulky nitrogen source such as an organic seed meal. A number of types can be found at feed or farm supply stores; cottonseed meal is a popular choice. Alfalfa meal (also available in pelleted form) is also excellent. For a fast-acting nitrogen supply, use a liquid source that will go straight to the plant roots, such as liquid fish emulsion diluted according to the directions on the bottle, or "manure tea," made by soaking manure in a bucket or tub of warm water for several hours or overnight. Although "dried activated" sewage sludge is a nitrogenous fertilizer, I don't use it. It's supposed to be free of disease-causing bacteria if it has been heat-treated, but I'm concerned that sludge might contain PCBs, heavy metals, and other toxic wastes.

Sources of organic phosphorus include bonemeal (a slaughterhouse by-product) and rock phosphate, a naturally occurring mineral deposit that has been mined and ground up. If you use manure as a fertilizer, it's sometimes necessary to add one of these because manure is relatively low in phosphorus—but only if a soil test indicates the phosphorus level in your soil is low.

Wood ashes from your stove or fireplace yield a natural form of potassium. It's also found in leaves and in compost made from them. (Hardwood trees yield a higher percentage than softwood.) Mineral sources include crushed granite and greensand (glauconite), a mineral deposit.

You can also buy commercial organic preparations that are "complete" fertilizers—mixtures of the three essential nutrients (nitrogen, phosphorus, and potassium) in pelleted form. Sometimes you'll see organic and inorganic nitrogen combined together in one product, and the label will say something like "40 percent of the N is organic." The reason for combining the two is that the inorganic nitrogen will act quickly to start the plant's growth, and the slower-acting organic nitrogen will provide for future growth. In general, using complete, prepackaged organic fertilizers is much more expensive than putting together a soil fertility program based on compost, manure, rock powders, and other individual ingredients.

Inorganic fertilizers. Most inorganic fertilizers sold are complete ones, with all the essential nutrients. Their contents are indicated by the N-P-K formula, and many different formulations are available. You can also buy bags of these nutrients singly. Superphosphate—a highly activated form of rock phosphate—provides a rapidly available supply of phosphorus, but using too much of it can cause mineral imbalances in your soil. I have not found the use of it to be necessary. Muriate of potash is a synthetic product that raises the potassium level of the soil.

There are also commercial products designed to treat deficiencies of specific trace minerals (such as boron, sulfur, or magnesium), either singly or in combination, if a soil test indicates they are needed. But dealing with such deficiencies is a rather specialized art that the home gardener rarely needs to address. The simplest path is to use a product such as greensand or a dried seaweed product such as kelp meal, which is harvested in a regulated manner from kelp beds in northern waters. Both of these supply a wide range of micronutrients. They are safe additions to the soil that act as a good insurance policy. Crab meal is also a good soil amendment, rich in calcium. Not all of these products are available at standard garden centers, and you may have to order them from suppliers of organic amendments if there's not a local source.

ADJUSTING YOUR SOIL'S PH

As explained on page 10, you may not need to do anything about your soil's pH. But if a soil test indicates you need to correct it, this can easily be done.

To raise the pH of soil that is too acidic, lime (short for "limestone") is usually added. "Lime" is the common name for pulverized rock containing calcium carbonate, a compound that also helps compensate for the calcium deficiencies to which acid soils are sometimes prone. Dolomite limestone is one that contains magnesium carbonate in a balanced proportion with calcium carbonate, and compensates for magnesium deficiencies. Bonemeal and wood ashes also raise soil pH.

A general rule of thumb for adding lime is that 5 to 10 pounds of it per 100 square feet of soil will raise the pH one scale interval. But this amount depends on what your soil is like. For example, you'll need more lime to raise the pH if your soil is clay. It's best to follow the recommendation that comes with your soil-test results. The mineral composition of soils also varies widely from one locale to another. Your soil test—and the advice from your local Extension Service—will take the specific needs of your particular area into account.

The lime you buy is a fine white powder that comes in large or small bags. Quicklime is a product that neutralizes acid soil much faster than other preparations, but it is too caustic for garden use. Hydrated lime is safer, but it too can harm plants and should be applied only to soil that you will not be planting for several months; it also will revert to ordinary lime if the bag sits around for a while.

Where I live the soil is very acid, with a pH as low as 4.3, and even lower than that when mulches such as shredded bark are used. As a result, I add quite a bit of lime when I create a new garden from scratch, unless it is a bed of acid-loving plants such as blueberries or azaleas. In subsequent years I add more lime periodically as soil-test results indicate the need. But even in gardens where I haven't used any lime at all, I am amazed at how well everything seems to grow, even in such acid soil, because of all the compost I've used.

In many parts of the country, especially in the Great Plains and in dry western areas, the soil is often very alkaline. You also might have a portion of your property that is alkaline because of the lime present in some building materials—the ground next to a mortared wall or concrete foundation, for example. To lower soil pH, pelleted sulfur can be added—but carefully, since too much can be harmful. (Again, follow the recommendations included with the soil-test results.) But the best solution is to dig in a lot of organic matter that is very acid, such as peat moss, sawdust, leaves, or bark. Organic fertilizers designed for "acid-loving plants" can benefit a soil that is too alkaline, but applying quantities of these products year after year can cause your soil to become much too acid. In a case where the calcium level must be increased to remedy a deficiency, the usual solution of adding lime would not apply in an alkaline soil. Gypsum, which provides calcium without elevating the pH, should be used instead.

TILLING YOUR SOIL

How you dig in organic matter, fertilizers, lime, and other soil amendments is just as important as what you add. You want to work these materials into the soil thoroughly, and as deeply as necessary for the plants you want to grow—usually to a depth of about 6 inches. This procedure—which also loosens the soil and breaks up large clumps—is called tilling. For growing crops on a large scale, tilling is done with heavy power equipment, and it is still the custom in some areas to have a local farmer come in and plow up the fam-

ily vegetable plot with his tractor. But now, typically, people have smaller gardens and often till their own plots.

Tilling a new bed. If you're making a new garden bed, whether it is for vegetables or flowers, you'll want to get rid of any existing sod and then till in soil amendments to get the plants off to a good start. For a large area you can rent a sod-cutting machine; for a small one you can till by hand. The sod can be used on your compost heap, or even placed in areas where new sod is needed. You would then dig in soil amendments such as compost, rock phosphate, lime, or whatever else the soil might need to make it garden-worthy. This can be accomplished with a spade or digging fork, depending on how big the garden is and on your own strength and determination. I prefer not to use power equipment when I can avoid it, but there are times when I'll use a rototiller to create a new garden, tilling under the sod and incorporating amendments into the soil at the same time. Though easier on the back, there are a few drawbacks to this approach. Both sod and the roots of perennial weeds that you till under can subsequently regrow, and you may have to till the area repeatedly, at intervals, to make sure all the vegetative matter has been smothered. Also, rototillers don't remove rocks, and you'll still have to go through the plot with hand tools and remove both small rocks and boulders, as well as whatever grass and weeds persist in resprouting. With hand-tilling all these are removed as you first encounter them.

When you till a deep bed you try to improve on nature by loosening, lightening, and enriching the topsoil layer, and if your soil is naturally very shallow you may want to do this to some of the subsoil layer as well. Increasing the depth of your topsoil layer can also be achieved just by adding more soil and humus on top, but for a deep, luxurious bed for a special group of deep-rooted plants—a garden of prize roses, perhaps—you might consider double-digging. This is an old and laborious technique that is good to know when you need to give certain plants the royal treatment. As shown in Figure 3, the soil is removed from successive sections of the bed to the depth of a spade, and set aside so that the soil beneath can be further loosened and amended as well. A simpler way to loosen the soil to a depth greater than 6 inches is to use a digging fork, as described on page 93, or a broadfork, as described on page 96.

After a bed has been tilled by any method, it's loose and fluffy—and higher than the untilled area around it. It's best to till in the fall and then let the soil settle over the winter, so at planting time there won't be any air pockets, which could dry out the plants' roots. This also gives the soil time to mellow out, the amendments time to become well incorporated, and the soil organisms time to begin their work of rebuilding. Nature is equipped to deal with disturbed soil, but it does take a while.

Double-Digging a Bed FIG. 3

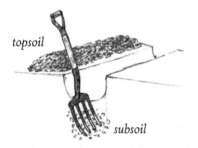

Dig a trench the width of the bed at one end, removing the topsoil. Add organic matter and other soil enrichments to the trench, and fork them into the subsoil at the bottom.

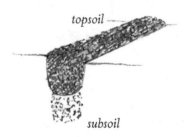

Shovel the topsoil back into the trench, enriching it with organic matter and nutrients as you go.

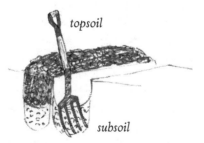

Make a second trench parallel to the first and repeat the procedure, piling the topsoil from the second trench on top of the first, then replacing it after the subsoil has been enriched. Continue, trench by trench, until the whole bed has been dug.

Tilling an established bed. Once a bed has been put in, you may never need to till it again, especially if it's a perennial garden. If you have a garden of annual vegetables or flowers, you may want to till it each year (gardeners have their own preferences about this); it's best to retill in the fall when the soil is not wet and easily compacted. Annual tilling is much less of a chore than creating a new bed. It can easily be accomplished with hand tools or with a deep-tined rototiller. But use the rototiller with care: overtilling can pulverize soil to the point that it loses its crumb. Over a period of time, rototilling can also leave a hardpan—a layer of packed soil created by the downward pressure of the tines at the bottom of their spin.

Often all an established garden needs is a light forking over in the fall, exposing clumps of soil to winter freezing and thawing, which will break them up and leave you with an excellent crumbly structure come spring. This is called frost tillage. It's even more effective if you have spread amendments (such as manure) and lightly raked them into the top several inches of soil, where frost and soil creatures can go to work on them in the quiet season.

Plants Need Light

A S EVERYONE KNOWS, MUSHROOMS grow well in the dark, and many seeds germinate in the darkness of the soil and will even send up pale shoots without light. In most cases, however, plants need light to carry on food production. Although the requirement for light is almost universal, different plants need different degrees of light. Some must have bright sunlight to do well, others tolerate or prefer part shade, and a few even grow in full shade. Plants that are small enough to be kept indoors will also do well grown in artificial light (see the houseplants chapter for more on this subject).

Before I plant something outdoors, I try to have a good idea of what its light requirements are, so that I can choose an appropriate site for it. But even so, I also watch the plant as it grows, to make sure I've made the right choice. If the plant has too little light it might let me know that by putting out fewer leaves than normal, and by remaining short and stunted. Conversely, it may send out long, leggy shoots or lean in an attempt to reach a light source. If the sun is too strong for a plant it will wilt, and the leaves may look pale and scorched.

Sometimes the decision to plant in light or shade is purely aesthetic. For example, daylilies, azaleas, and mountain laurel may grow perfectly well in shade but have few flowers. A golden-leaved hosta will thrive in shade but the color will be less intense. Coleus may do well in sun, but its leaf variegations will be less striking than they would be in shade. Lilies and roses will thrive in sun, but if it is too strong their flower colors may fade.

DEGREES OF LIGHT

To give a plant the right amount of light, it's important to understand all the different degrees of light and shade. Light requirements are often affected by other site factors and by the climate.

Full sun. Usually a plant that is said to prefer full sun needs at least six hours of sun a day, during the "prime time" for sun—10:00 A.M. to 6:00 P.M. Daylight Saving Time. This includes most fruits and vegetables and most flowers. When I grow plants that are particularly sun-loving, such as tomatoes and sunflowers, I try to give them even more sun than that. If you have a choice between a site with morning sun and a site with afternoon sun, keep in mind that afternoon sun is stronger, and that midday sun is the strongest of all.

If you live in a cool climate you'll find yourself trying to make the most of your sun, but if you live in a warm one you'll be trying to temper it, especially for plants like Oriental poppy and bellflower, which are basically sun-loving but can't take too much heat. For these, morning sun or part shade at midday may be preferable to full sun. In dry climates you may also have to guard some plants against full sun, or supply more water. Not only will soil moisture be lost through evaporation in a sunny site, but the air will be drier, and plants will lose moisture through their leaves.

Light shade or part shade. Plants that prefer neither full sun nor full shade should be given shade during the hours when the sun is strongest or else grown in a spot where the sunlight is broken in some way. This condition is variously described as filtered light and dappled shade. The most common way to provide it is by planting in the shade of a tree such as a crab apple, birch, honeylocust, or mountain ash, which does not cast full shade but lets spots of light come through its branches. A broad-leaved evergreen such as boxwood or mountain laurel, which must be protected against winter sun (see page 610), might get enough shade from a very dense stand of leafless trees in the same manner. You might also find sites that are more shaded at one time of the year than another, as the sun changes its course. These can be used

advantageously to suit the needs of particular plants. A site with winter shade would suit boxwood, and one with winter sun would be perfect for a February daphne, to encourage early bloom. Dappled shade can also be provided artificially by the use of a trellis or lath structure—thin, narrow pieces of wood nailed in rows or crisscrossed so that some part of the plant is always shaded as the sun moves across the sky.

Bright shade. Even a spot that gets no sun at all can be filled with light. The area under a tree whose branches start at a considerable height on the trunk will often be filled with ambient light from the areas around it. A sunless spot next to the white wall of a house might receive reflected light from the house, especially if sun shines on the wall. Often, plants described as liking part shade will do all right in bright shade.

Full shade and deep shade. A site in full shade that gets neither direct sun nor reflected light will only sustain truly shade-loving plants. In very deep shade almost nothing will grow. Full shade on the north side of a house may be bright enough to grow plants like hostas and rhododendrons, however, and full shade underneath a broad-leaved deciduous tree such as a linden might be appropriate for ferns and shade-loving ground covers like sweet woodruff if the tree limbs are high enough off the ground. But under the overhanging branches of large evergreen trees you may find that a mulch is your only alternative to bare soil. (Happily, many evergreens, such as pines, provide a fine mulch of their own in the form of dropped needles.)

Naturally, in the case of deciduous trees, the time of year makes a big difference in the shade they cast. There are some plants that don't mind being shaded in summer and fall as long as they get sun shining through leaf-less branches in spring—spring-blooming woodland wildflowers are the prime example. By the time the trees above them have leafed out, they have completed all or most of their growth cycles. Some even become dormant and disappear from view until the following spring. Although I always try to include some summer-blooming shade plants (such as astilbes) in my shade garden, it is always in its fullest glory in springtime. For information on growing edibles in part shade see page 235.

Finding the perfect balance of sun and shade for the plants you grow may take some juggling—giving a plant just enough sun to bloom well without burning its foliage, for example. You might have to try a plant in one spot, then move it if it doesn't perform as well as it should. If there is too little sun on your property you may have to cut down some trees, or "limb" some (cut off selected branches), to let in bright-ness. On the other hand, if there's too little shade you might need to plant some trees, choosing those that will admit just the amount of light you need, or you might build a lath screen or arbor to partially shade your garden. The portable frame shown on page 259 will provide temporary shade for smaller plants.

Plants Need Water

A LL THE CHEMICAL REACTIONS THAT take place in plants require the pres-ence of water. All movement of nutrients through plants and through the soil requires water. Water is also needed to give plant parts turgor, or firmness. You can see what happens to a plant when it dries out. The leaves shrivel, the stems flop, and the roots (if exposed) look like a handful of limp spaghetti. On the other hand, the changes wrought by too much water are just as dramatic. Below ground, roots growing in waterlogged soil, robbed of the oxygen they need, soon die and turn into a rotting mess, as does the rest of the plant. Above ground, plant stems and crowns, sitting in puddles or soggy ground, can also rot. Leaves that stay too wet are more suscep-tible to diseases. And some plant diseases travel through the medium of water.

ACHIEVING THE RIGHT BALANCE

Obviously you need to make sure that your plants have the right amount of water, nei-ther too much nor too little. This means you have to get to know your plants and their individual needs. Just as with light, the moisture requirements of plants vary greatly from species to species. For example, plants native to dry climates (like cacti and succu-lents) have evolved in such a way that they can store water in their stems and leaves, while plants native to bogs and other wet places have roots that can "breathe" in water, like fish. Even among species native to one climate, needs can vary according to plant structure. Shallow-rooted plants need water more often than deep-rooted ones. Young plants, and plants that have been root-pruned or transplanted, usually need extra water to help build new root systems. Many need more water at the time they set their flowers (otherwise the flowers may drop), or when fruits or vegetables are maturing, especially juicy ones like tomatoes.

The amount of water available to a plant depends on more than just how much falls from the sky or from your hose. The amount and strength of the sun, the degree of heat, and the force and prevalence of wind influence how much water is retained by the soil and by plant tissues, and how quickly it will evaporate before it can be used. If your site has strong sun or a lot of wind, or if the weather is hot, you'll have to work harder at keeping the soil moist. Shady sites where air circulates poorly may stay too moist and lead to plant diseases. Another fact not always accounted for is the effect of frozen soil on a plant's water supply. If woody plants, especially evergreens, go into the winter with their roots in dry soil they may suffer, because rain and melting snow will not reach their roots through frozen soil. "Winter burn" of broad-leaved evergreens can be caused by the harsh, scorching effect of sun on snow, but often the situation is made worse by the roots' having had insufficient moisture before the ground was frozen.

The type of soil in which the plant is growing also makes a big difference, as explained on pages 5 to 10. Sandy soils hold water poorly. Clay soils hold it well and may in fact drain poorly. Soils of either type that are rich in organic matter hold moisture well, and also release the excess.

CORRECTING SITE PROBLEMS

Anything you can do to improve the site of your garden before you plant will save you work later on, and solving water problems is no exception. First consider whether you need to do any grading. Go out and look at the site sometime when it has been raining all day, and see what the water is doing.

Steep slopes. If the site is on a slope, chances are the water is running downhill at a great rate and not staying where it might be doing the plants some good. It may even be taking the soil with it, leaving gullies. In this case, one solution is to terrace the land by cutting into the hill to make flat beds, and retaining the soil above them with low stone walls or timbers. If you can achieve your goal with retaining walls a foot high or less, terracing is a fairly simple matter, but if your slope is quite steep and requires higher walls, you'll need to build masonry footings to support them and install subsoil drains in the bank to prevent excess water from pushing the wall outward. If you use timbers, you'll have to anchor them into the bank. I would immediately hire, or at least consult, a professional who specializes in this type of work, and I suggest you do too. Another option is to look for a flatter area for your garden.

You can also consider plantings that will help to retain the soil on a steep bank, such as bearberry (*Arctostaphylos uva-ursi*) or shore juniper (*Juniperus conferta*)—both of them seaside plants used to keep sand dunes from eroding. Daylilies (*Hemerocallis*), whose fingerlike roots grip the soil, make a beautiful planting for a steep bank. You can also create miniature retaining walls for each plant by making a flat, round planting area shored up by a saucer like the one pictured on page 43, with the saucer only on the downhill side.

Poor drainage. If you look at your rained-on site and it's a sea of puddles, you'll need to find a way to make them drain off. If the problem is not severe, you can probably devise your own commonsense solution. If you're like most people, you enjoyed fooling around with water as a child, making it stay, making it go—whether it was in the sandbox, in a stream that you dammed up, or on a sandy beach. Just do what you did then. Make a berm of earth to channel water the way you want it to go, or dig a gulley to take it away, then fill the gulley with crushed stone—a material that helps water to drain away because of the large air spaces between the stones. Or you can lay lengths of perforated plastic pipe—just make sure your gulley slopes downhill and has somewhere appropriate to go (not your lawn or driveway, or your neighbor's). Simply placing a layer of crushed stone under the soil in your bed may help drainage, but if the problem is severe or if the soil around the bed is very compacted, the layer will act as a sump into which water will flow and where it will stay, rotting your plants' roots. If your drainage problem is very severe, you may need a more elaborate drainage system that goes below frost level. In this case I would reach for the Yellow Pages. It's a job for a landscape contractor or excavator.

Drainage problems may not always be visible, even when it rains. Water may be collecting below the soil surface when it meets a layer of hardpan (compacted soil). This situation will harm any deep-rooted plants you try to grow there. Usually you encounter the problem with your first attempt to plant a tree. You find you need a pickaxe to make the planting hole. Then, in due course, the tree dies. You can avoid such disappointments by first digging a test hole and filling it with water. If the soil is hard to dig and the water sits there for more than an hour without draining into the soil around it, you may need to choose a new site or consult a landscaping contractor.

In some cases, the simplest way for a beginning gardener to deal with poor drainage is to build a raised bed, especially if you're growing relatively small plants such as vegetables, flowers, herbs, bulbs, roses, and small shrubs. Follow the directions for the simple wooden bed on page 239, or build one out of railroad ties, landscaping timbers, or stones. More elaborate ones can be built with mortared stone or bricks.

In preparing your site, also remember that tilling the soil (page 22) and adding plenty of organic matter will improve a site that drains either too slowly or too fast. If the problem is not too severe, you may find that adding organic matter is all you need to do.

WATERING

Watering is a basic part of planting, as discussed on page 42 and in other sections dealing with specific plants. And it is very important to keep the soil around new plants moist, whether they're tiny vegetable, flower, or grass seedlings or a recently planted shrub or tree.

While garden plants are growing, their need for water varies with the type of plant, the climate, and the weather. Established trees and shrubs, in an average climate, don't need irrigation except during very dry summers or (especially if they are evergreens) during a dry fall. According to the usual rule of thumb, vegetable and flower gardens don't need to be watered unless the rainfall is less than 1 inch a week. But moisture-loving plants will need more water and drought-tolerant plants less. Mulched gardens, closely planted gardens, and gardens with clay soil or soil rich in organic matter will often get by with no watering even if less than an inch of rain falls. For raised-bed gardens, gardens in warm climates, or gardens with sandy soil an inch may be too little.

With newly planted shrubs and trees you must be especially attentive to watering. This is also true of newly seeded vegetables or flowers, and also with new perennial plantings especially if the weather is warm and dry. Certain vegetables such as tomatoes and peppers need extra water when they are forming their fruits. Others, like celery, need plentiful water for growth. I also water plants like dahlias that bloom poorly when their roots are dry, and I check my flower gardens in dry weather to see if anything is drooping.

I always try to keep a close eye on both the plants and the soil to see whether either needs more water. Plants are tricky, especially young ones with small root systems. These may wilt during the hot part of the day but revive later on. (Some mature plants, such as *Ligularia* and *Pulmonaria*, will wilt and revive, too.) But no plant should be ignored if it stays wilted for more than a few hours; if a plant passes a certain point it will not recover.

Checking the soil for moisture is easy—just dig down and see if it's moist under the surface. It doesn't much matter whether the soil surface is moist because you just watered it, or dry because the sun is out. It's the soil underneath, where the roots are, that counts.

There are a number of ways to give your garden extra water, as discussed in the chapter on garden gear (page 107). But here are some points to remember:

Try to water deeply or not at all. Everyone runs out of patience standing there with a hose and is apt to skimp at the end, but it's better to water only part of the garden and really soak it, or use a sprinkler, soaker hose, or drip-irrigation system. The goal is to "make the moisture meet." This means applying enough water to the soil surface so that it joins up with the water that lies deeper down, with no dry layer in between. One time-saving trick is to put buckets with holes punched in the bottom next to the plants, and fill the containers with water that can then soak down into the ground. Planting in furrows (page 38) or with saucers (page 43) will also help more water to soak in.

In some cases it's best to water the soil, not the leaves. Misting houseplants indoors is often beneficial, but wetting the leaves of outdoor plants may burn them if the sun is out, as the droplets act like lenses that concentrate the sun's rays. (This might happen anyway when the sun comes out after a rain, but you can at least avoid contributing to the problem.) Water can also promote disease organisms if leaves are wet at night. If diseases are a particular risk in your garden, water in the morning, at ground level, and don't work around the plants when they are wet because this might spread disease. Or use a soaker hose or drip-irrigation system, and avoid hoses and sprinklers that wet the leaves.

Don't waste water. It's a valuable resource that is getting scarcer every day. The best way to handle any water shortage is to choose plants for your gardens and landscape that rarely require extra water. When in doubt, take your inspiration from the native plants that grow in your area without coddling even during dry spells. Conserve whenever possible. Don't let your lawn sprinkler run any longer than is absolutely necessary, and don't let water run down slopes. Give the soil only what it can absorb.

The Importance of Climate

SOMETIMES WE GROW PLANTS THAT adapt very easily to our climate, and other times we choose ones that are less well suited but are so beautiful or useful that they're worth the extra trouble to make them grow, or are worth growing even if they cannot carry out their entire growth cycle. Dahlias, for example, do not survive the winter in my flower garden as they would in warm Mexico, but I'm willing to dig them up and store them over the winter so I can have their glorious late-summer bloom. Tomato plants only live one summer in my vegetable garden, whereas they live much longer than that in Peru—but never mind. I simply sow new seeds each year. I try to give dahlias and tomatoes the warmest, sunniest growing conditions I can, to make them feel at home and produce better.

If I lived in a hot climate my situation would be reversed. Plants such as delphiniums would resent the hot summer, and others, like daffodils, would mind the absence of a cold winter to send them into a dormant, resting state. I might be able to grow delphiniums as early-summer annuals, buying new ones each year. And I could give my daffodils an artificial winter by putting them into cold storage before planting them in late fall or early winter. But by and large, if I lived in a warm region I would choose among the many warm-climate plants that northern gardeners wish they could grow.

WINTER HARDINESS ZONES

It's not always possible to predict whether a plant will flourish in your garden. One general indicator that is widely used is the United States Department of Agriculture table and accompanying map of winter hardiness zones, shown on pages 756 and 757. In this system the United States and most of Canada are divided into numbered zones based on average minimum winter temperature. Plants are assigned a hardiness zone based on how low a temperature they are able to survive. For example a plant that is rated hardy to zone 5, where I live, is expected to survive temperatures as low as minus 20 degrees Fahrenheit. But a plant rated hardy to zone 9 will probably not survive temperatures lower than 20 degrees above zero. If you do not know how low the temperatures go in your area, get the figure for the annual average minimum from your local Extension Service office.

I take hardiness ratings of plants with a grain of salt, however. For one thing, a good many of them are only estimates that will continue to be reassessed and refined as more data on each plant becomes available. For another, hardiness zones are applied with a broad brush: they may refer to your geographical area but not to your particular yard. Your windy hill might be zone 6, while your neighbor's protected valley next door might be zone 7. On an even smaller scale, your lawn might be zone 7 but the garden next to the south wall of your house, zone 8. Try to identify these "microclimates" on your property so that you can choose the right site for your plants. South- or west-facing exposures are warmest, northern ones are coldest. The area around a swimming pool is often hotter and drier in summer than the rest of your yard because of the reflected glare off the water and the proximity of paving materials that hold and reflect heat. Usually the plants themselves will tell you which spots are warm and which are cold: the same plant may bloom or leaf out earlier in one spot than another.

Also bear in mind that the lowest temperature indicated for your zone is not reached every year. For example in my zone 5, there may be some zone 6 plants I can grow—most of the time. It's a gamble, to be sure, but I don't mind if the plants are, say, some asters I bought at $5 a pot. On the other hand, if they're $50 azaleas I would certainly think twice about growing one that wasn't rated zone 5, and that might be killed by a rare minus-20-degree winter's night.

Another problem is that hardiness ratings take into account only one climatic factor: minimum winter temperature. Some of the important factors they omit are the *maximum* temperature a plant can stand, the degree of dryness or moisture, the light requirements, and the type of soil plants prefer. Therefore a plant that is hardy in your zone may still do poorly for any of these other reasons.

You should also be aware that there are several different zone maps, with different systems of zone numbering; the USDA one is simply the most commonly used. So when you're told a plant's zone, check to see which map your source is using, and use the temperature chart to see which zone is yours on that particular map.

The American Horticultural Society has prepared a Plant Heat Zone Map that assigns a zone number to a plant based on the amount of heat the plant can withstand, rather than the amount of cold. Zones are delineated based on the average number of days in a given year in which the temperature exceeds 86 degrees Fahrenheit. The AHS map is of most interest to gardeners seeking plants that will thrive in their climate's heat, although it was useful to me to learn that my region's cool summers placed it in a frigid zone 2, even though our winters are hardly the coldest in the nation. (It explained why I have repeatedly failed at growing okra.) As with the Winter Hardiness Zone Map, other factors such as rainfall and soil type must also be taken into account. I have not assigned heat zone numbers to the plants described in this book, but urge you to consult Dr. H. Marc Cathey's book *Heat-Zone Gardening.*

Whether you live in a windy area is also important for your choice of plants, as is whether there are particularly windy spots on your property. A windy site calls for relatively short or strong-stemmed plants that won't be pushed over by the wind; and because wind is drying, plants in windy locations should be able to withstand dryness well. Plants native to the seashore are resistant to wind. Their leaves often have tiny hairs on them that help to prevent evaporation of water.

Plants Need a Good Start

IF YOU'RE A FREUDIAN, YOU BELIEVE that birth traumas and subsequent experiences in people's early lives can mark them for life. If you're a non-Freudian you might consider this hogwash, holding that everyone is born with a certain personality, but beyond that your life is what you make of it.

I'm not entirely sure which theory is true where humans are concerned, but with plants I'm a Freudian all the way. Yes, a rhododendron is born a rhododendron and will always curl up its leaves self-protectively on cold winter days, only to become an extroverted mound of bright-flowered joy when it gets sufficiently warm in spring. But how large that mound is, and how glorious its display, depends on *you*, its parent. You can either start it off by cramming its little roots into a stingy hole filled with meager soil, or you can give it a wonderful environment rich in love, care, and compost. Whether you're planting a tiny seed, or transplanting a large tree, the same principle applies.

GROWING PLANTS FROM SEED

The seeds that gardeners most often sow are annual vegetables and herbs, such as lettuce and dill, or annual plants grown for their ornamental flowers and leaves, such as marigolds and coleus. But in fact many kinds of plants can be started from seed: perennials, bulbs, even shrubs and trees. The main reason we don't usually grow these plants from seed is that they take

Starting Seeds Indoors FIG. 4

cell pack

pricking out seedlings in a plastic flat

peat pots

transplanting a seedling into a peat pot

longer to reach a mature size and may take up too much of our space and time while we're waiting for them to perform (a separate nursery bed and often a cold frame or propagation greenhouse might be necessary). So we buy them in a more mature state and then transplant them to our gardens. Nevertheless there is something very satisfying about growing any plant from a single seed, whether you start the seed indoors or out.

Starting seeds indoors. The main reason we start seeds indoors is to get a jump on the growing season with plants that will not withstand frost, but it's also a way of starting a plant's life in a controlled environment and making the most of every seed sown. Whether you start seeds indoors, and how many, depends on how much space you have. There are a number of systems for starting seeds, and you'll probably develop one that best suits your household.

You can start seeds in a commercially prepared soilless mix that is primarily composed of peat moss, but you can also make your own mix from various combinations of peat, perlite, vermiculite, compost, and even soil from outdoors.

Using Soil Blockers

Fig. 5

2-inch blocker with inserts creates space for mini-cubes

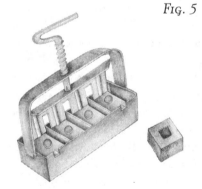

2-inch blocker with soil cube

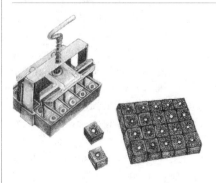

mini-blocker with soil cubes

mini-cube transplanted into 2-inch cube

Garden soil dug for seed starting is often sterilized in the oven for a few hours at 180 degrees in order to kill disease organisms in the soil (such as the fungus that causes damping off), and also to kill weed seeds that might lurk there. In the garden you wouldn't want sterility—you'd want your soil crawling with beneficial microbes—but for the few weeks your seedlings spend in your starting medium, sterile soil has its advantages. With a soilless mix, either purchased or homemade, this step is not necessary. A plastic dishpan is useful for blending small amounts of seed-starting mix; for larger amounts use a large plastic tub or a wheelbarrow.

You can start seeds in just about any container that is at least 2 inches deep and has holes for drainage. One good system is to sow seeds in small plastic flats, spacing the seeds about a half-inch apart. Large seeds such as those of winter squash are sown directly into peat pots (small pots made out of compressed peat) or cell packs (flats divided into individual compartments). Some people sow all seeds directly into individual units, then thin them to one seedling after they've sprouted. It's very hard to space tiny seeds far enough apart, but worth the effort, because this gives each one a better chance to form a root system. I find that creasing the packet to make a little V-shaped trough allows you drop them one by one into the soil, gently tapping the packet with your finger to slowly move the seeds along the crease. Proper spacing also avoids wasting seeds. Most packets give you more seeds than you need for one sowing, and since the majority of seeds will stay viable for at least several years, you won't be planting the whole packet at

once. Fold over the top edge of the packet and secure it with a paper clip. Then store any unused seed packets, whether opened or not, in a cool dry place.

The planting mix should be moistened before sowing, especially if it is peat-based (so it doesn't draw moisture away from the seeds), then pressed lightly into the flat so there are no air pockets. After dropping the seeds onto the surface, cover them very thinly with a fine layer of dry mix and moisten the surface with a spray bottle but do not cover the seeds if the packet tells you that particular seed needs light for germination. If that's the case, just press them very lightly into the soil so they'll make good contact with the mix. Label the seeds in the flat by sticking a little wooden marker in the corner, marked with a black waterproof marker pen (colored inks can fade in the sunlight). Set the small flats inside a larger one that they can drain into when watered. It's absolutely crucial to keep germinating seeds from drying out.

Every plant has an optimum temperature for germination, and either the seed packet or the catalog will probably tell you what it is. (The book *Park's Success with Seeds*, by Ann Reilly, is also a good resource.) Most do best with a warm temperature—sometimes followed by a slightly cooler one for growing. A table above a heat vent and the top of a high kitchen cupboard near the ceiling are both good sites, but if you choose the latter be careful to check at least once a day, and bring the flat down as soon as you see the color green appear. Another trick is to cover the flat with plastic cling wrap, held well off the surface by little sticks, pencils, or plant labels. This will help keep in the moisture that is so crucial for germination and create a warm little greenhouse for the emerging seedlings. Just don't seal it tightly or the seedlings will bake. Leave a loose spot where heat can escape and watch carefully so you can remove the wrap when the seeds have sprouted. You should also remove the wrap if you see any sign of mold.

As soon as seeds germinate they need an excellent light source, otherwise they'll become spindly as they grow, elongating their stems to reach for light instead of producing robust clusters of leaves. If you have a surface next to a window that gets sun for a good part of the day, this is fine. But fluorescent light is even better, especially in a spring with lots of rainy days. If your kitchen has under-cabinet lighting, you might set your flats just under the lights on a stack of bricks or books, removing these as needed when your seedlings grow taller. But if your seed-starting operation is extensive, you might want to invest in a series of fluorescent fixtures dedicated to this. Entire setups are sold for

this purpose, but I've built homemade versions by just suspending a few 4-foot-long standard shop light fixtures over a couple of old card tables. These can be hung on metal chains, either from hooks attached to the basement ceiling or a simple wooden frame. Use broad-spectrum lights, which plants prefer, available from hardware or home-supply stores. By using chains you can easily adjust the height of the lights, as shown in Figure 6, as the seedlings grow, so they're always just several inches above the plants. You can even put newly sown flats under the lights. The slight heat emanating from the bulbs will help them to germinate faster.

If something is growing so fast that I expect it will be planting size before planting time, I take it away and put it on a sunny but cooler windowsill. On the other hand, if I'm trying to hurry up warm-season crops like eggplant and peppers, I give them the choice seats, under the center of the bulb, where the light is the strongest.

Trays of Seedlings Under Fluorescent Lights

FIG. 6

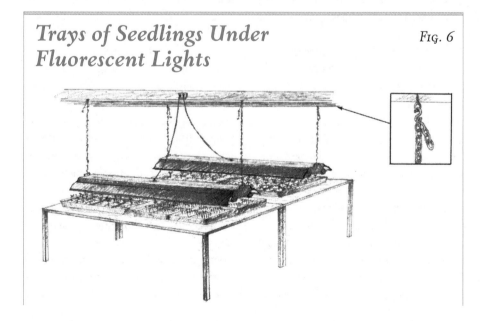

There are also rubber seed-starting mats you can buy that have heat cables inside them. These provide excellent bottom heat for seedlings.

The standard advice is to turn out the lights at night to simulate a normal growing day. This seems logical. I check the flats at least once a day to make sure the planting mix is not drying out, and I pour water not on the delicate seedlings but into the trays underneath them, where it's absorbed from the bottom up. (In a greenhouse you can use a special hose attachment with a very fine, soft spray.) But I'm careful to give them only what the soil can absorb and don't let them sit in water.

By the time seedlings have developed their second set of leaves, they need to be transplanted into containers that will give their roots more room to grow. This operation is called pricking out. These containers might be individual peat pots—especially good for plants that must be set directly into the soil with a minumum of root disturbance. Seedlings can also go into larger flats, spaced a few inches apart, or into plastic cell packs.

How you move tiny seedlings is important. They look too fragile to deal with, but they'll be fine if you grasp them by the leaves, not the stems. You can use a kitchen fork or plant label to help dislodge them, but I've found they will lift out easily by the leaves if the planting mix is a light one. Select the strongest seedlings and discard any that have little or no root system attached.

To plant the seedlings you can either dangle the roots and sprinkle dry soil mix around them or else make a hole with your finger, insert the roots, and then sprinkle. Plant them a bit deeper than they were in the germinating flat, to give the stems more

support. The mix can be the same kind you sowed the seed in, or it can be one with more soil. Commercial seed-starting mixes already contain enough nutrients for seedlings. If weak growth or pale color suggests yours need extra fertility, use a weak solution of an organic liquid fertilizer, being careful to not get any on the delicate leaves, which burn easily. Eventually you'll want to move up some seedlings (tomatoes for example) to large plastic pots, and at this stage additional feeding will be necessary.

While the program I've just described, in which seeds are started in flats and then pricked out, is the most common one and the one I used for many years, I now use soil blocks to start my seeds instead (see Figure 5). For this excellent system you need to purchase a set of soil-block makers, which are not always easy to find (Johnny's Selected Seeds currently sells them). But they are sturdy lifetime tools that well repay your effort. Start with a 2-inch soil blocker that makes four cubes of soil, each one measuring 2 inches on every side. This is done by plunging the blocker into a flat-bottomed tray of well-moistened peat-based mix. You rotate the blocker a bit on the bottom of the tray, tip it up to break the suction, then lift it and eject the cubes onto a flat surface by means of the spring-loaded handle. It's easy when you get the hang of it, and the soil cubes are surprisingly sturdy. Seeds sown in them develop superb root systems, and transplant shock is almost nonexistent.

The cleverest aspect of the blocker is its companion, a tiny mini-blocker that makes 20 baby cubes, less than an inch on each side, with a slight indentation on top to receive the seed. By attaching little plastic cubes that same size inside the larger blocker, the 2-inch cubes can be made to receive the baby cubes as soon as the seeds in them have germinated. Instead of pricking out seedlings, you're just putting a small soil cube into a hole in a big one—much easier on the plant. It's also easier on the budget. You'll still need some trays to hold your soil blocks, but you'll never have to buy cell packs or peat pots again. I've never been wholly satisfied with peat pots anyway. They don't break down as quickly as I'd like, and roots often seem to struggle to penetrate them.

It's important to label seedlings meticulously. It's helpful to write the sowing date on the label, and have that label follow the seedling as it is moved from a small flat to a larger one or into an individual pot. Sometimes this means making more labels, but often you can just keep a number of small pots grouped together with the label in one of them. Mixups may occur, but often you can tell by the foliage which plant is which, as long as at least one plant in the group is identified. Most people develop their own little systems.

Luckily you won't be planting all the different seeds at once, so they'll all be at different stages, and in different places, at any given time. It's sort of like a grade school. Some are started early either because they need a longer time to germinate and reach transplanting size, or because they can go out into the garden earlier in the spring. Just when the tables under the lights start to get very crowded, the more advanced classes might move up to the sunny windowsill, making room for the lower grades. As the weather warms you can even start moving some outdoors to harden off (that is, get used to cold, wind, and strong sun to toughen up the leaves and stems) in a spot where it's easy to keep a close eye on them. (A cold frame, described on page 39, is a great place to harden off seedlings.) I bring the little plants in at night for the first few days—or longer if the weather is cold or windy. Eventually some graduate to the garden, and others can be promoted from the fluorescent lights to the window. This way the whole house isn't filled with seedlings—it just seems that way.

Planting seedlings outdoors. When it's the right time to set plants in the ground (see the appropriate chapters for specific kinds of plants, especially annuals and vegetables), I make sure the ground in the garden is ready, then carry out a tray or two, filled with as many plants as I know I can plant that day. (They should not be left unplanted in the garden overnight to dry out or tip over.) Water these seedlings thoroughly to give them a good start. If they're in containers, watering will also help them to come out easily, with soil clinging to their roots. If they're in peat pots, tear off the top edge so that it won't draw moisture out of the soil like a wick, and carefully slit the pot on two sides and remove the bottom. In other words, leave just enough of the pot so the soil around the roots stays put when you set the plant in the ground.

To plant each seedling I make a hole with a broad trowel, fill the hole with water from a watering can, let the water sink in, set the plant in the hole a little deeper than it was in the pot (even deeper for leggy annual vegetables or flowers), and firm the soil around it. For a plant that likes abundant water, I'll make a small saucer around it to catch rain. If it needs something extra, such as rotted manure (for tomatoes) or extra lime (for larkspur), I'll dig that in before I plant. Then I'll stake the plant or label it or mulch it, depending on the type of garden and the needs of that particular plant. If I've bought seedlings of vegetables, herbs, or annual flowers from a nursery, I set those into the garden just the way I do the ones I've grown myself. But I'll often need to pull apart their matted root systems. Most nursery-grown seedlings are grown in cells that are far too small and have spent too much time in them before they reach the garden.

Starting seeds outdoors. Fun as it is to start seeds indoors in early spring, I'm grateful for those that can go straight into the garden, either because (like peas or alyssum) they can take some frost, or because (like zinnias and summer squash) they grow so fast that they make up the difference.

First I draw an iron rake through the garden, smoothing the surface and removing from the top inch or two of the soil stones and debris that might impede small seedlings' growth. If I'm planting in rows, I stretch out a string tied to a stake as a guide in making the row straight, then I make a furrow several inches deep with the blade of a hoe held at an angle. I soak the furrow very thoroughly with water several times, then place my seeds in the bottom, trying to space them as evenly as I can (the correct distance will vary from plant to plant). Then I pick up some dry earth and rub it between my hands, letting a light, powdery covering fall over the seeds, unless it is a species that must remain uncovered for germination. Then I water the surface gently with a fine spray from the hose. For large seeds that I plant more deeply, I poke a hole for each one with my finger and drop it in. Some large seeds, such as corn and beans, can be planted either in long furrows or in what are called hills—not mounds, but circles or

groups of seeds—which are later thinned to the strongest few or the strongest one. However I plant them, I always press the soil down with my hands to make sure the seeds are in contact with the soil.

I leave my seed furrows concave because this helps to keep the seeds and seedlings moist and also marks the rows so that I know where the seeds are. (A wooden or plastic marker at one end of the row also identifies it.) For wide vegetable rows or blocks, or for patches I'm seeding in a flower garden, I just plant in well-moistened broader areas, covered with soil sifted through my hands and then with a fine spray as described above. For seeds that germinate slowly, especially in warm weather, it's helpful to spread moist burlap or hay over the seedbed until the seedlings emerge, or to sow them along with a "nurse crop" such as radishes, which will shade the ground and help keep it moist. With all seeds it is very important to keep the seedbed moist and with some, such as carrots, it is especially crucial. If you're going to be away for a few days, you'll need someone to sprinkle them for you.

When the seedlings are several inches high they can be thinned to the appropriate distance apart, either by pulling up some of them or by snipping them with scissors to avoid disturbing the roots of those left. With leafy crops such as spinach, you have the wonderful opportunity of eating the small thinnings in a fresh spring salad.

If you have a nursery-bed section of your garden, you can raise seedlings there and then transplant them into the place where they will eventually grow. A part of the vegetable garden, for example, might provide a nursery for seedlings of annual flowers that will eventually be used as bedding plants elsewhere, or as fill-ins for the perennial border. Perennials that take several years to flower, or biennials that flower the second season, can also be started in a nursery bed until they're ready for prime time. A cold frame (Figure 7) also makes a good nursery bed.

PLANTING HERBACEOUS PERENNIALS

Herbaceous perennials are plants whose stems are generally soft and green, rather than hard and woody like those of shrubs.

"Perennial" means that, unlike annual vegetables and flowers, they last more than one year in your garden. Most of them go dormant during the winter, meaning that they have no green growth to be seen above the ground. How to design and prepare beds for perennials, and when to plant them, are discussed in detail in the perennials chapter, and to some extent in the herbs and ground covers chapters, since some herbs and ground covers are perennials of this type.

Planting bare-root. Certain perennials can be grown successfully from seed,

Using a Cold Frame

FIG. 7

A cold frame is a bottomless box with a glass or transparent plastic top to let in sunlight. Old storm windows work fine, attached at the top with hinges so they can be propped open. Build the sides with rot-resistant wood (not pressure-treated), bracing the corner with 2-by-2s. The windows should face south and tilt toward it for the best solar efficiency. This is done by making the back of the frame higher than the front with the back no higher than 12 inches tall. Too much space inside reduces the effect of the earth's warmth, captured by the frame and released at night.

Enrich the soil inside so you can sow early and late salad crops, or winter over tender perennials. Set flats of seedlings inside to harden them off before planting. In winter, you can bank the sides with bales of hay or straw, and cover the top with blankets on frigid nights. But heat is more of a risk to most plants. When there is any chance of overheating, prop open the frame with a stick.

either sown directly in the garden or sown indoors and transplanted outdoors as seedlings, in the manner described above. But most perennials are older plants that are set out when they're dormant or just starting to sprout, and often bare-root, with no soil around the roots.

Planting perennials bare-root is easy, but you have to be aware of one very important thing: those roots absolutely mustn't dry out. If they do they will never recover. This means you have to keep the roots moist, but also protect them from the sun and wind. If you order perennials by mail, they will usually come carefully wrapped in damp sphagnum moss or some such packing material (though some nurseries ship perennials in a soil mix, in small peat or plastic containers). If you can't plant them right away, either pot them up (page 185) or heel them into the ground. "Heeling in" means digging a trench in a cool, shady spot and laying the plants in it, in a row with their crowns (the place where stem and roots join) at soil level, then watering them and covering the roots with soil. Plants can be held that way for quite a while, but if growth starts they will eventually resent being crowded together, so don't let a heeling-in trench become a permanent residence. When you get ready to plant your bare-root perennials, never leave them lying on the ground unprotected while you're digging their holes. Cover them with moist burlap or some mulch material such as hay.

I make my planting holes with a broad trowel, spade, or shovel, depending on the size of the plants. If I feel the soil needs improvement, I might mix in some compost or bonemeal, but I avoid chemical fertilizers because they might burn the roots. I set the plant in the hole so that the crown is just at the soil surface, because burying it any deeper may cause the plant to rot. Then I spread the roots out in the hole and fill it partway with soil and the rest of the way with water. When the water has sunk in, I fill up the hole with soil and firm it well so there are no air pockets. Some perennials have special planting requirements; for these see page 184.

Plants in containers. Perennials that you've bought potted up (or that you've potted yourself) are planted in much the same way. If you must keep them for a while before planting, set them in a level, semishaded spot where they can be watered conveniently. Soak the soil in the pot just before planting time, then knock the plant out of the pot as shown in Figure 8. If the plant has been growing in the pot for a long time it may be potbound or rootbound—the roots will be thick, matted, and even growing round and round in the pot. To encourage roots to start growing outward, pull them gently apart. You might even have to slit the mass of roots vertically every few inches with a knife or hand pruners. This may sound like a brutal thing to do when I've just told you to pamper a plant's roots, but it's the kind of tough love that potbound roots need. Left alone, they'll have trouble growing out beyond the root mass—and they may even rot or starve. If the plants are in peat pots you can plant them in the pots, but tear off the rims and slit the sides vertically in several places to help the roots to escape. (For staking newly planted perennials, see page 188.)

PLANTING SHRUBS AND TREES

Woody plants are usually planted singly, in individually prepared holes, rather than together in prepared beds. (One exception is hedge plants, which may be planted in a long trench.) How you make the planting hole is important. Woody plants have two kinds of roots, each for a different purpose. One kind goes down very deep into the soil (more deeply with some species than with others) and is there primarily to support the plant; the other kind spreads out for a great distance through the topsoil and upper subsoil layers. These are called feeder roots, because through them the plant absorbs nutrients. Feeder roots need particular encouragement, so it is more important to dig a wide hole for the plant than a deep one.

Buying and planting large trees and shrubs will give you more of an instant effect, but they don't establish themselves as well as younger specimens. Obviously, they are more expensive and more laborious to transport and plant as well.

Providing a shrub or tree with a luxurious planting hole filled with compost and other soil amendments is a practice that has fallen out of favor because it encourages the plant's roots to stay with the amended spot. You may well need to improve the soil's fertility, structure, and general good health (see the earlier sections of this chapter on fertile soil), but it's best to dig or till amendments into the top 3 to 6 inches of the soil, in the entire planting area where the far-ranging roots will soon encounter them.

Planting bare-root. Many shrubs and trees that establish themselves easily are sold bare-root. Planting is almost always done when the plant is dormant, usually in early spring but sometimes in autumn after the leaves have fallen, and it's usually done when the plant is quite young. When you buy bare-root trees in a nursery, or order them by mail, they won't look like much. Often they've been, quite properly, pruned back hard. Don't let that discourage you.

The plant's roots want to be good and moist when you plant them. Soaking them for a few hours (but no longer than overnight) will help; so will "puddling in." This means mixing up soil and water in a tub or bucket so that it's the consistency of gravy, and then sloshing the roots around in it. This mud gravy will keep the root hairs moist and help them start to grow.

Dig a hole a few inches deeper than the roots and quite a bit wider. Set aside any subsoil and rocks you dig up, and put any sod clumps in a pile. It's a good idea to break up the soil along the bottom and sides of the hole with a digging fork, so that roots will be encouraged to venture out laterally. Then loosen the soil surface near

Knocking a Plant Out of a Pot   FIG. 8

the hole, and dig in some organic matter to encourage feeder roots to spread outward.

Set the tree or shrub in the hole (Figure 9) so that the beginning of the trunk is just above the soil surface (you'll see a line where the trunk bark changes color and the roots begin). It's important not to plant the trunk belowground, because the roots can be deprived of food, water, and air if they're too far down. Better to err on the side of planting too high, in case the plant settles in the hole. If the plant is a grafted one such as a dwarf fruit tree (there will be a bump where the top part has been joined onto the rootstock), the graft union should be aboveground. (There are a few exceptions to this rule, such as the practice of burying the graft of tender rose plants in cold climates.)

Spread the roots out in the hole and start filling the hole with the topsoil you dug out. As you work, make sure you don't leave air pockets, which can dry the roots. Firm the soil with your feet, but take care that the roots aren't damaged. When the hole is about two-thirds full, add water from a hose or bucket till it reaches the top, and let the water sink in. The water not only keeps the roots moist but also helps to settle the soil in the hole.

Then fill the hole the rest of the way with topsoil. Use the subsoil and rocks to build a small saucer, or circular dike, around the plant to hold water. Sod clumps can also be used for the dike, or they can be placed in the bottom of the hole, grassy side down. Your last steps are to pour water into the saucer, then apply several inches of mulch (such as shredded bark) to keep the soil around the trunk moist and free of weeds. Keep the mulch at least 6 inches away from the plant, however, to keep the

trunk from getting too damp. Trees whose trunks are susceptible to sun scald, particularly young fruit trees, can be protected by painting them with a white tree paint designed for this purpose, or by wrapping a plastic tree guard around them. See page 422 for advice on protecting newly planted trees from borers, and page 70 for nibbling creatures such as rabbits, voles, and deer.

Balled-and-burlapped plants. Many trees and shrubs that you buy will be "B-and-B"—balled and burlapped—either because they do poorly when transplanted bare-root, or so that you can plant them even when they're not dormant. A nursery will dig the plant in the field with a ball of soil around it and wrap up the root ball, usually with burlap and twine. The plant can be transported, held for a while, and planted in this state. I would not advise trying to dig a root ball yourself unless you're dealing with an easy-to-move plant or one whose life you don't mind putting at risk. Digging a ball without the soil falling apart is, as a friend of mine once put it, "like carving a ball of melting butter," and wrapping and tying it can be tricky too, especially if the root ball is large.

Plants you buy B-and-B should be planted as soon as possible after bringing them home. If you must keep them out of the ground for a while, set them close together in a group, in the shade and covered with piles of mulch, and moisten them regularly, with a sprinkler if possible. Water from a hose tends to just run down the sides of the ball, and it's not easy to duplicate the kind of care that B-and-B plants receive in a nursery. Treat the root ball very carefully, sliding it rather than rolling it, and never dropping it on the ground. Lower it into the planting hole *gently*. If you're taking a heavy ball off a truck, slide it down a stout

Planting Shrubs and Trees Fig. 9

Dig the planting hole, setting aside topsoil, subsoil, sod clumps, and rocks.

Balled-and-burlapped plant, set on inverted clumps of sod.

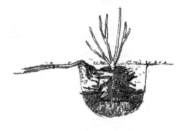

Container-grown plant, with roots loosened.

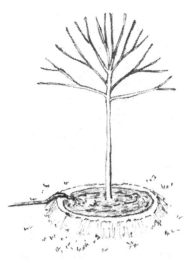

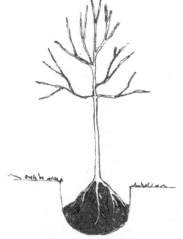

Bare-root plant, with roots spread over a mound of soil.

With all of these, add topsoil until the hole is two-thirds full, tamping with your feet. Fill the hole with water and let it sink in. Then fill the rest of the hole with more topsoil. Make a saucer around the plant, using the subsoil, soil clumps, and rocks as needed. Water again, then mulch.

wooden plank. You might even want to borrow or rent a handcart designed for moving plants. These look like the dollies you move furniture with, but the upright part is curved to hold the root ball in place.

B-and-B shrubs and trees are planted much the same way as bare-root stock, except that the size of the hole has to be calculated more carefully. It's very frustrating to dig a large hole, lower a large root ball into it, then find that the hole is too deep and the ball too heavy to lift out again. The best way to avoid this is to measure the height of the ball, then lay a tool handle flat across the top of the hole and measure from the handle to the center of the bottom of the hole, adjusting the depth accordingly. Another trick is to put upside-down sod clumps in the bottom of the hole, lower the ball, then add or remove sod clumps as needed until the bottom of the trunk is just above the soil surface.

Once the ball is in the hole you can remove the burlap, but only if the ball is a very firm one. It's safest not to remove it at all. Burlap is easily penetrated by most roots, and both the burlap and the twine will rot quickly. But if the burlap is left sticking out so it's exposed to air, it can draw moisture out of the soil, so it's a good idea to loosen the burlap near the trunk, roll it back a little, and cut that part away. If the wrapping and twine are made of plastic you *must* remove them. I usually remove the metal baskets that sometimes encase root balls, cutting them away with wire cutters so the metal doesn't harm the plant's roots when they grow larger. If a ball seems loose and removing the basket will threaten its integrity, leave it in place but remove the upper third and peel it back a bit so that it's spread out on the bottom of the hole. Fill the hole just as for a bare-root

plant, firming the soil around the ball with your feet, watering, making a saucer, and mulching in the same way.

Container-grown plants. Woody plants that have been grown in containers can be planted even when they're not dormant. They are planted like B-and-B plants, but first you must remove them from their containers, which are usually plastic, metal, or compressed peat. Trees and shrubs in plastic pots can be knocked out by the method shown on page 41, but plants in metal cans are a different story. I've never once succeeded in extricating a plant from a metal can without slitting the can down the sides with wire cutters or tinsnips. Pots made of compressed peat are easily cut away.

Aftercare. The most important thing about taking care of a newly planted shrub or tree is to give it plenty of water. Apply four or five gallons of water every day for several weeks (unless it's raining heavily), and even more than that for a large tree. This is especially important for plants set out during or at the onset of hot, dry weather. After this establishing period, make sure the plant gets weekly waterings—more if it is hot and dry.

For advice on when to plant shrubs and trees and how to stake them, and for special procedures to use with specific plants, see the chapters on shrubs and trees.

Dealing with Weeds

"A WEED," MY MOTHER USED TO SAY, "is just the right plant in the wrong place." To me this is much more accurate than defining weeds as "wild" plants as opposed to "garden" ones. Many wild plants are appropriate in gardens. In fact, a large number of the plants we regard as wildflowers are actually plants imported from other countries as garden flowers, which have escaped into the wild, liked the environment, and naturalized themselves. And many a garden plant, fine in one spot, can be an unwelcome guest in another. Even the right plant in the right spot can be weedy if there's too much of it; in that case you must weed it out along with the crabgrass, fat hen, and mile-a-minute. (Why do weeds always have the best names?)

It sometimes seems that weeds will put up with anything, but this is not so. While it's true that many weedy plants are colonizers, able to cover disturbed ground quickly or thrive in places where less finicky plants will not grow, all plants have some preferences as to climate, soil type, degree of sun, and moisture. In fact, if you're looking at a new piece of ground with an eye to gardening on it, you can tell a lot about the conditions on the spot by noting which weeds are there by choice. A field of goldenrod (depending on the species) is likely to have rather dry, poor soil; one with burdock, on the other hand, will be moister and richer in organic matter.

Every now and then a particularly attractive weed, like Cinderella, will be lifted from the ranks of weedhood because of some desirable trait. Nurseries will start selling it, hybridizers will start looking for ways to improve it. Butterfly weed, with its showy red-orange flowers and popularity with butterflies, is a fairly recent example, but your garden may have its own Cinderellas that are simply your own pet weeds. When something crops up in my flower garden that might have potential, I'll sometimes let it bloom and see if I like the way it looks there. You'd never know that the clumps of blue-eyed grass at the front of my perennial border weren't put there deliberately.

But let's face it: weeds are often just plain weeds, and you need a good way to keep them under control. It does no good to give your plants first-class soil if they must share it with weeds. These invaders will compete with your prized specimens for everything they need in life—nutrients, water, light, air, and space—both above the ground and below.

ANNUAL WEEDS

How you deal with weeds depends partly on whether they're annuals or perennials. You can never quite eradicate annual weeds because they make so many seeds—seeds that are dropped, blown, or carried into your garden or are simply lying there dormant in your soil, waiting for your hoe or trowel to bring them close enough to the surface for them to sprout. Unfortunately, in the very act of weeding you make it possible for new weeds to grow. This is one reason why mulching is helpful. It won't keep every annual weed from germinating, but it will greatly cut down on their number. Some mulches, however, such as hay and other grass crops, may introduce seeds of their own or seeds of the weeds that invaded the fields where they grew. Applied thickly they will keep the seeds from sprouting, but the seeds may come up later with a vengeance whenever the mulch is removed. Straw tends to have fewer weeds than hay, and salt hay, pine needles, or shredded bark are relatively weed-free. (For more information about mulches, see page 55.) On soil that is not (continued on page 51)

SOME COMMON WEEDS

I F THESE PLANTS WERE HUMAN THEY would probably have their pictures hanging in the post office. You no doubt have some of them where you live, but plant life varies so much from one locale to another that it may take some time to identify your own local criminal element. And please note that some of these weeds are the "right" plant if they're growing in the right place.

Bindweed. *Convolvulus arvensis.* A deep-rooted perennial with pink-white flowers shaped like those of the morning glory, to which it is related, this vine should be eradicated before it can twine around your garden plants and smother them.

Broadleaf plantain. *Plantago major.* This low-growing broad-leaved weed

has a short taproot and is not especially hard to remove with a trowel. Its strength, however, is in numbers, and it's important not to let it form thick patches in the lawn. Keeping a healthy stand of grass is the best defense, but you may have to resort to hand-pulling. It also proliferates in gardens and paths.

Burdock. *Arctium minus* (common burdock) and *A. lappa* (great burdock). You can recognize burdock by its fuzzy purple-pink flowers and the round burrs that stick to your hair, your clothes, your dog, and anything else with a textured surface. It is a biennial that forms a rosette of broad, hairy leaves the first year, then usually goes to seed the next. Don't let burdock do this. When you spot its foliage, yank or dig up its deep taproot, which is edible and quite tasty when cooked slowly in butter until tender.

Canada thistle. *Cirsium arvense.* If you can look at this weed objectively, it's a handsome plant, with fuzzy purple flowers from midsummer to fall. But the very prickly leaves are not something

you want to step on in bare feet. An extremely hardy perennial, it spreads both by suckers from the roots and by seed. Put on leather gloves and try to dig out as much of the taproot as you can.

driveway, but is equally happy filling any bare spot in your lawn, garden, or shrub border. The best prevention is to have no bare spots—by keeping the lawn healthy and by mulching your gardens. If crabgrass appears, dig it out with a trowel (it's hard to grasp with your fingers) before it can go to seed.

Chickweed. *Stellaria media.* Chickweed loves the fertile soil of gardens but will make do with a less luxurious habitat. An annual with dainty foliage and little starlike white flowers, it looks harmless but makes seeds like crazy from spring to fall and also roots along the stem. It withstands fairly cold winter temperatures. In its defense, it's easy to pull out, and is tasty in salads.

Crabgrass. *Digitaria sanguinalis.* This annual grass spreads out from the center in a stiff, flat rosette. It tolerates even the inhospitable packed soil of a gravelly

Dandelion. *Taraxacum officinale.* Dandelions need no introduction. I think the yellow flowers and fluffy round seed heads are pretty in the lawn, but they're a nuisance in the garden because they are perennials and their deep taproots are very hard to eradicate. The best way to keep them out of the lawn is by mowing them before the seeds start to blow around, and by hand-digging, but all the root must be removed.

Dock. Both broad-leaved dock (*Rumex obtusifolius*) and curly dock (*R. crispus*)

broad-leaved dock   curly dock

are widespread in lawns, gardens, and fields. The leaves of the former are wider, with smoother margins. Like dandelions, docks have deep taproots, all or most of which must be dug out or they'll resprout. It's best to remove them before they go to seed, as the seeds persist in the soil for many decades.

Galinsoga. Hairy galinsoga (*Galinsoga ciliata*) is the most prevalent species of this annoying pest. Learn to recognize the bushy plants, no taller than 2 feet, with triangular, toothed, slightly fuzzy leaves and little yellow-centered white blossoms. Almost overnight it can invade your property, showering the soil with fast-germinating seeds. Pull it out as soon as you spot it, and do this repeatedly until it's under control.

Dodder. *Cuscuta gronovii* and other *Cuscuta* species. This slender, leafless annual vine, gold in color, is the ill-famed "tares" referred to in the Bible (as in "wheat and tares"). Like bindweed, it twines around plants and kills them, but unlike bindweed it is actually parasitic on the host plant, rooting in it to suck its juices while its own roots atrophy and die. It spreads by seed. Pull it off its host as soon as you spot it.

Ground ivy. *Glechoma hederacea.* Also called gill-over-the-ground, this is a pretty weed with small round leaves and small blue flowers in spring. Usually it sneaks from the lawn into your gardens by means of thin, almost invisible runners. In the right spot it makes a nice deciduous perennial ground cover, but I try to keep it pulled out if it starts to approach any shrubs, particularly low-growing evergreens. If it gets into their branches the needles don't grow, and the plant's shape is distorted.

Johnson grass. *Sorghum halepense.* This warm-climate pest is a tall perennial grass with wide blades and vigorous creeping rootstocks. You can make a lifelong career of pulling it out, especially if you let it go to seed. Repeated close mowing will set it back in large areas but it still may have to be smothered with black plastic. Dig it out thoroughly by hand in smaller gardens.

Lamb's quarters. *Chenopodium album.* How this weed got to be associated with so many animals I'll never know, but it also goes by the names pigweed, fat hen, and white goosefoot. An annual that likes any garden soil, it has ragged-edged leaves and grows as tall as 6 feet. On the plus side, it's easy to pull out and is delicious cooked like creamed spinach. But it grows very fast, and unless you consume an awful lot of creamed greens there is always too much of it.

Poison ivy. *Toxicodendron radicans.* I spent my whole childhood learning how to recognize this plant in all its guises: the three shiny reddish green leaves as they first unfold; the three medium green leaves when half grown; the three large dark green leaves at maturity; the three red-orange leaves in fall; the ropelike vines; the fuzzy underground roots. This vigorous perennial native clinging vine gives most people a blistering rash if *any* part of the plant is touched, at *any* time of the year. Those few lucky individuals who are not susceptible can dig it out, but even they are advised to wear protective clothes and launder them immediately. If it invades your garden, an organic herbicide might be tried.

Purslane. *Portulaca oleracea.* Here's another one that looks innocent—but watch out. It resembles the bright-

flowered portulaca of the annual garden, but its water-storing leaves are rounder and fatter, and its small yellow blooms are not showy. Like garden portulaca it spreads easily by seed, especially in tilled ground. It also has a habit of rooting into the ground wherever you throw it, so drought-proof are its roots—don't leave pulled plants lying in the garden or in paths. It's best controlled while tiny, before it can make spreading mats.

Quack grass. *Agropyron repens.* Other names include witch grass and couch grass. This weed is high on my own personal enemies list. It spreads both by seed and by long white stolons that are very hard to eradicate; I recommend black plastic and/or long sessions with the digging fork. For large areas, repeated tilling may be necessary.

Ragweed. *Ambrosia artemisiifolia.* I don't know which is worse—what ragweed does to the garden or what it does to my nose. It grows at least

3 feet tall and sometimes taller than I am. Its flower spikes make vast amounts of hay-fever-producing pollen in late summer and fall. Ragweed blooms at the same time as goldenrod, which is often unjustly blamed for people's sneezes and itchy eyes. A deep-rooted annual, ragweed chooses soil that has been tilled, whether it's your garden or a cornfield, and should be pulled out before it has a chance to flower and form all that pollen.

Redroot pigweed. *Amaranthus retroflexus.* This common annual weed resembles lamb's quarters when young, but soon becomes a coarser plant with fuzzy rather than smooth leaves. It can grow to 5 feet tall, with a striking red taproot. Easily pulled while small, it should be eradicated before the dense, pointed seed clusters are formed. It is toxic to livestock.

Shepherd's purse. *Capsella bursa-pastoris.* This common annual or biennial weed grows to 3 feet, with arrow-shaped leaves on top and a rosette of leaves on the bottom. Flowers are small and white. Dig out the thin taproot promptly before seed can set.

Sheep sorrel. *Rumex acetosella.* Closely related to garden sorrel, and to the docks described above, this plant has a pleasantly sour taste when you nibble on it. Less endearing is its rapidly spreading habit, cruising along just beneath the soil surface and erupting here and there in small clusters. It can be fun to pull out the long threadlike roots and their attached plantlets—if you have nothing pressing to do with your day. Unfortunately, it loves mulch.

(continued from page 45)

being gardened, cover crops (page 13) will also keep most weeds from growing.

If you're not using a mulch, the best way to deal with annual weeds is simply to get them while they're very tiny and keep after them. It's so easy to put off weeding when weeds are small, inconspicuous, and not staring you in the face, but believe me, this is the time to attack them. Small weeds are thwarted just by slicing them with a collinear hoe or scuffle hoe, which either severs the plant from the roots or brings the roots to the soil surface, where they dry out and die. With this technique you don't even need to cart piles of weeds away—just leave them where they fall. Shallow cultivating like this also prevents disturbing lower soil layers and bringing more weed seeds to the surface.

Experienced gardeners know they must strike when weeds are small, but even the best let weeds get ahead of them from time to time. When this happens there is no alternative but to get out there and pull the weeds. With some weeds the job is just that—pulling. The ones with soft, water-filled stems come out easily when you yank them, and in fact many weeds can be pulled if you grasp them just at soil level. But if you break them off and leave the root in the ground, you're often just pruning the weed and encouraging it to branch and regrow more bushy and glorious than ever. When pulling mature weeds I always have a trowel handy for the ones that resist a tug. I stick the point of the trowel under the roots to loosen them from the soil, and *then* I yank the weed.

Sometimes, if I'm rushed, I'll just spread the weeds I've pulled between the rows of my vegetable garden as a temporary mulch, until I can get around to composting them. A blanket of dead weeds is not very attractive, but it keeps new ones from growing. I don't do this, however, if the weeds are at the point of going to seed. That would be like sowing a brand-new crop of problems. In fact, catching weeds before they go to seed is the golden rule of weeding. If you diligently keep after your garden's weeds for seven years or so, you'll have permanently reduced their numbers. But one year of neglect can put you back to square one.

Another tactic with annual weeds is to use a preemergent weed killer. The only kinds I'd be comfortable with are nontoxic ones such as those made with corn gluten, which is said to inhibit germination. This is fine for a setting such as a shrub bed, but not a garden where you're sowing seeds or encouraging plants to self-sow.

PERENNIAL WEEDS

Some perennial weeds go to seed the way annuals do, but usually their roots are their real weapons. Most perennials reproduce themselves from their root systems, and even from parts of roots that may remain in the ground after you pull or dig them up. Therefore it's important, when you go after perennial weeds, to try

and get the whole plant. Weeding them with a hoe when they're small will often work, just as it does for annual weeds, but once perennials get large you need to be more careful, especially if the weeds spread by runners, or stolons—underground stems that run through the soil and send up new plants at intervals. A digging fork is the best tool for removing these, because it's less likely to break the roots than a spade is. Almost as pernicious as weeds that produce stolons are the weeds with long, skinny taproots, like dandelions and the various species of dock. If you leave even a small amount of the root when you pull it, a new plant can sprout. Sometimes these pull out easily if they're growing in loose soil, but if you hit a stubborn one, the dandelion weeder shown on page 99 can help you get the whole weed. There are certain situations when even this tool doesn't help—especially when dandelions and other deep-rooted weeds are growing between the cracks in paving stones. For this you need ordinary household white vinegar. It's inexpensive and surefire. Pour a little over the weed and it will turn brown and die.

Mulch will control perennial weeds to some degree, but it won't help much if a number of the weeds' roots are present in the soil before you put down the mulch—many will come right up through it. Black plastic will smother them if left on long enough, but it could take a year. And if there are holes in the plastic to let water in or to let a cultivated plant grow, weeds with stolons will search around under the plastic till they find those holes and come up there.

I can hear you saying, "How am I supposed to know whether a weed is annual or perennial? I can't even tell whether something *is* a weed!" Unfortunately, the only way to learn these things is by experience, and this means spending time in the garden weeding and really looking at the plants that are there—both weed and nonweed. If you recognize the foliage and growth habits of the plants that are supposed to be there, then you know the rest are weeds by process of elimination. It's also useful to have an illustrated guide to native and non-native weeds so that you can identify ones that appear. The list of common weeds on pages 46 to 51 may help you pinpoint some, but there are many more that I don't have the space to list. In general, perennial weeds have deeper, more vigorous, and

more pronounced root systems than annuals, and are harder to get out of the ground. Just be on the lookout for ones like these, and try to get *all* the roots.

PREPARING A NEW BED

Keeping an established garden free of weeds is challenge enough, but the big task is removing them from a spot that is not yet a garden. Removing all the weeds first, especially perennial ones, will obviously save you much work and aggravation later on. There are several ways to go about this. One is to dig out any woody plants and then cut all the herbaceous ones close to the ground with a mower, brush cutter, string trimmer, or hand tool such as a sickle or scythe. Then spread sheets of heavy black plastic on the area for a year. Afterward, till under the dead weeds. If you can't wait a year to start the garden, you can dig all the weeds out by hand with a digging fork, or whatever it takes to get rid of them all.

If the site has lawn sod, you can use the black plastic technique if you have time to wait. Otherwise you'll need to strip it off or till it under, bearing in mind that grass tilled in may eventually regrow. To remove sod by hand, first mark the shape of the bed with a string tied to a stake, using it just as you would a ruler or compass. If you're making a curved bed, a garden hose (preferably one made soft and flexible by the sun's heat) is a handy way to delineate it. You can then mark the area you have laid out using small stakes or a sprinkling of lime.

Then edge the bed along its outline with a sharp spade. If you can't slice through the sod easily, lift the spade above your head with both hands as shown in Figure 10, and bring it down hard. (Don't worry—your aim

Edging a Bed with a Spade *Fig. 10*

will improve with practice.) Either roll back the sod in strips, or slice under it just below the surface, trying to remove as little of the topsoil along with the sod as possible. I sometimes cut stubborn sod into blocks and shake the excess soil out of the roots, block by block. I lift the sod with a digging fork and shake it, then stab or prod it with a pointed trowel if needed. It's a laborious process, but it leaves most of the topsoil in the ground where it belongs. What's left goes onto the compost pile. You can also rent a gasoline-powered sod stripper. Remove any large weed roots left behind in the soil.

GARDEN EDGINGS

Another way to minimize weeds in the garden is to edge it with a barrier to deter weeds and grass that come in from surrounding areas, including the lawn. Such invasions can be a real problem, and edgings do help. Edgings also give the garden a tidy, well-defined look. They can be as

---

Garden Edgings

FIG. 11

Flagstone edging. Lay flagstones in a sand-filled trench with the smooth side up. Stand on opposite corners of each stone to see if it rocks; add and remove sand as needed until the stone is level.

Brick edging. Lay bricks vertically in a sand-filled trench; tamp the top of the bricks with a rubber mallet until the tops are flush with the soil surface.

Plastic or metal edging. Dig a narrow trench deep enough to accommodate the edging strip; lay the strip so that the rim on top is just above the soil level, then fill in the trench.

Railroad tie edging. Lay railroad ties in a sand-filled trench so that the tops are just slightly above the soil level. Join them at right-angle corners with metal spikes for added stability.

simple as a prefabricated metal or plastic strip or as elaborate as a row of flagstones or brick set in sand or stone dust. They are all fairly easy to install. Some types of edgings are shown in Figure 11.

Mulch

I DON'T KNOW WHO INVENTED MULCH, but I'm sure I know where the idea came from. If you go out into the woods and examine the ground, you'll see a perfectly mulched garden. On the surface of the ground are leaves that have fallen recently. Below them are layers of leaves from seasons past, in increasingly advanced stages of decomposition. Just under the litter of leaves and twigs near the top is a crumbly substance called leaf mold; below that are duff layers that eventually crumble almost to a powder; and below them is soil— beautiful, dark, rich, light, moist, humusy soil. Forest soil is so good because of the leaf covering, which is both a natural fertilizer and a natural mulch. And achieving that kind of soil is one of the reasons why people mulch their gardens.

THE BENEFITS OF MULCH

Mulch is simply a surface covering that we apply to our garden soil. There are various materials we can mulch with, but before I advise you about which ones are best to use, let's look at some of the things mulch does.

It keeps weeds down. As I've explained, mulch won't keep every weed from coming up, especially if the roots of perennial weeds are in the soil. It will, however, keep down enough of them so that your weeding labor will be reduced. At the same time, the moister, looser condition of mulched soil will also make weeds easier to pull. Get out as many weeds as you can before you mulch, and if some do come up, try to pull them without bringing soil up on top of the mulch where more weeds might grow. This may mean pushing aside the mulch to get at a weed, especially if a trowel, fork, or spade is required to dig it up.

It conserves soil moisture. A mulch will keep moisture from evaporating from the soil surface. This is especially useful during hot, dry weather. Depending on your climate, you may have to do little or no watering if you mulch. By absorbing rainfall, a mulch can make the most of a good rain, holding water that would otherwise run off and letting it trickle down to the soil. And by holding moisture in the soil in fall, mulch helps keep the foliage of evergreen plants from drying out in wintertime (page 610).

It keeps soil cooler in summer, warmer in winter. The temperature of mulched soil is more constant than that of unmulched soil. Mulch allows you to temper both extreme heat and extreme cold by several degrees. A mulch that keeps the soil cooler in summer not only prevents moisture from evaporating, but also helps to protect plants that are intolerant of high temperatures. A number of plants such as lilies and clematis don't mind warmth on their stems and leaves but like to have their roots kept cool.

In the winter a mulch may also prevent the death of certain plants that are not quite winter-hardy in your climate, just by keeping the soil a few degrees warmer than unmulched soil. More important, mulched soil experiences less of the alternate freezing and thawing that can damage the roots of plants and even heave them out of the ground.

(continued on page 59)

MULCHING MATERIALS

HERE ARE SOME OF THE MULCHES you can try. I've left out a few that are widely used, such as peat moss (it forms a crust that sheds rain) and newspaper (it looks ugly). In applying all these mulches, try not to bury the plants you're mulching, and smooth the surface of the mulch so it doesn't look lumpy. Most of these will need to be replenished from time to time, for mulch, like compost, is not so much a product as a process. For one thing it's always decomposing, and for another it is often disturbed in the course of weeding and planting, during which mulch is worked into the soil. This is fine if you've chosen a mulch material that returns organic matter to the beds—you're mulching and composting at the same time.

Autumn leaves. Raking leaves into shrub beds at the edge of the lawn is a good way to make use of them. They tend to mat heavily, though, and can smother some ground covers and the herbaceous plants in a perennial garden. This is especially true of flat leaves such as maple. Curly ones, such as oak, make a more aerated mulch. Shredded leaves, or those chopped up by a lawn mower, are even more lightweight and make a finer mulch.

Black plastic. For the use of black plastic in the vegetable garden see page 241; for killing weeds, see page 52. Many people use it to mulch beds or paths, then cover it with a more attractive substance like bark or chips or gravel. Employed this way, plastic will keep weeds from coming up, but I find it always works its way up to the surface eventually. If you use it in a bed, make a few holes in it so rainwater can flow through, unless you're using one of the new plastic sheeting materials that are perforated with small holes to let moisture seep through to the soil.

Buckwheat hulls. This tidy, elegant mulch looks especially good in flower gardens and rose beds, spread about 2 inches deep. The hulls are tiny, dark gray papery disks that are easy to sprinkle on the garden from large bags. Since this mulch is very light, some weeds will push right up through it, but it does prevent many annual weed seeds from germinating and will help keep the soil moist. Its major drawback is that it blows around, wanders into the lawn, slides down hills, and is totally dispersed by any leaf-blowing machine that comes near it. I use it whenever I want to give a fairly flat bed a formal look, and simply replace it each year in early summer.

Cocoa shells. These are sold in bags and make a good light mulch. Don't worry if your garden smells of chocolate at first—the odor soon disappears.

Evergreen branches. The branches of evergreen trees make an excellent winter mulch for gardens such as perennial beds, where you don't want moist materials matting around the plants. They hold the snow and keep it from blowing away or being melted by the sun. Apply them after the ground has frozen. About this same time, abandoned Christmas trees can provide a handy supply. The goal is not to prevent freezing but rather to avoid alternate freezing and thawing, which can be hard on roots, especially if newly planted.

Grass clippings. These are convenient, though perhaps they look a bit messy in an ornamental planting. They decompose very rapidly and can burn herbaceous plants, so don't allow them to touch the stems of vegetables or flowers. Never use clippings from a lawn that has been treated with broadleaf weed killers.

Hay. Hay is the most traditional mulch because it's so handy. What else can you do with hay that has been spoiled by an untimely rain or by green weeds that have rotted in the bales? Farmers often sell it for mulch, sometimes at a higher price than the good hay used for horses. Try to get a second or, better yet, a third cutting that will contain fewer seeds. A hay bale breaks apart in "flakes" or "books." Simply lay these side by side between the rows of your vegetable garden.

Locally available by-products. In your quest for the perfect mulch,

check to see if any local farms or plants have organic waste materials that might be suitable. Some by-products that people use for mulches are spent hops from breweries, tobacco stems, ground corncobs, shredded cornstalks, sugarcane residue, cottonseed hulls, peanut hulls, and nutshells. Make sure that anything you use *doesn't* contain toxic substances.

Manufactured cloth mulches. There are some fabrics on the market that are less obtrusive than plastic and might be worth investigating, though I, myself, haven't tried them. There are also biodegradable plasticlike films designed for use as mulch.

Pine needles. Pine trees generally shed their old needles after they've been on the trees for two to five years, so you can find the needles lying on the ground in abundance. Pine needles make a beautiful mulch for ornamental gardens, especially shrub plantings. They are rather acidic.

Root mulch. This marvelous mulch can be hard to find, especially in bulk, and is expensive to buy in bags. It consists of chopped-up plant roots that have a dark color and are moist and easy to apply. This mulch stays put better than any I've ever used, even on a steep slope.

Salt hay. This is a better—although much more expensive—alternative to ordinary hay. It is a wild seaside grass that is harvested when it floats into shore on the water. Seeds in it will germinate only under salty conditions, not in your garden. Salt hay decays more slowly than regular hay, so you can use it a second year. However, it's quite scarce now and there are ecological concerns about its harvesting.

Seaweed. Various seaweeds make good mulch for shrub and tree plantings if you live by the ocean and find some that has washed up on shore. It's very coarse, heavy, and stringy, and not easy to handle. It makes a good winter mulch for a vegetable garden, and should be tilled in before the spring planting.

Shavings and sawdust. These can be used as mulch, but look rather unnatural until they weather to a gray color. They also can deplete the soil of nitrogen.

Shredded bark. This is an excellent mulch, particularly for shrubs and trees, and one that is readily available. You can buy it in bags at a garden center, but try to get it in bulk if you want to mulch large areas. Sawmills that strip the logs they cut into lumber will often sell the bark—a bucket loader simply dumps it into the back of your pickup truck, or you can get truckloads delivered by a local hauler. I lay it down about 3 to 4 inches thick, less for herbaceous plantings. The bark weathers to a natural grayish brown color; I think

it's a lot more attractive than the "bark nuggets" that are also sold in bags, because it looks more natural. I try to get it as fine as possible—even ground bark is sometimes available.

Stones. If you put down a mulch of small stones or pebbles several inches thick, you can suppress most weeds and provide a nice dry surface for plants whose foliage can rot if it lies on moist ground. I think organic materials are more attractive as mulches than stones are, but a stone mulch sometimes looks just right in a contemporary or Japanese-style setting.

Straw. Straw comprises the dry stalks of a grain crop from which the nutritious seed head has been removed. Harvested after it has dried, it is relatively free of viable seeds. Use it like hay (see above).

Wood chips. The best wood chips are the ones whose branches, twigs, and bark have all been put through a chipper, because they look much like the litter on the forest floor and contain more nutrients. A tree surgeon may be able to sell you some, or you may find a place where land is being cleared and there are piles of wood chips that you can beg or buy. Chips are also available at sawmills and in bags at garden centers, but these are very light colored, and they take a while to weather to a more subtle color.

(continued from page 55)

It attracts earthworms. Earthworms work hard to cultivate your garden soil, but they don't like soil that is too hot and will stay in the subsoil to get cool. A soil cooled by mulch will bring them closer to the surface.

It prevents soil erosion. Rainfall will not wash soil away if the surface has been mulched, even on a fairly steep slope.

It improves soil structure. Mulches consisting of organic matter decompose and are gradually worked into the soil, thereby improving its structure (page 7). This is what happens in the forest, and it can happen in your garden.

It improves soil fertility. These same organic mulches break down and provide the soil with nutrients that the plants need.

It keeps plants and their fruits clean. Plants growing in mulch are not spattered by rain or water from your hose. Crops such as tomatoes, melons, and strawberries, which may rest on the ground, will stay cleaner and be less prone to rot and freer from disease. Mulch also keeps flowers that flop over, such as peonies and daffodils, from getting spattered with soil.

It provides a place to walk. A mulched path in a garden, whether it's down the middle of a vegetable garden or winding its way through a wildflower garden in the woods, won't get muddy and won't need to be weeded.

It makes plantings more attractive. A mulched garden tends to have a tidy look. Although it is best to avoid walking on garden beds, mulch allows you to do so when necessary without leaving footprints. Mulch can also be an important design feature: using the same mulch throughout a bed with a variety of different plants ties the composition together. A number of separate plantings can be visually linked to one another by using the same mulching material for all of them.

WHEN NOT TO MULCH

Mulch does have certain drawbacks, and there are times when even a confirmed mulcher may forgo it, use it with caution, or use it only during a specific part of the season.

It can keep the soil too cool or moist. In the cool climate where I live, early spring is called mud season. It's the time when everything, including the soil, needs to make the most of the sun's warmth and drying power so that planting can begin. Mulch is often withheld or moved aside until the soil is warmer and drier.

It can cause plants to rot. Plants that are particularly sensitive to winter moisture, such as coral bells and blanketflower, may rot and die if water collects around their crowns (the place where the roots and stems join). Either don't grow these plants in mulched beds, or draw the mulch away in fall. Another solution is to apply the mulch thickly between the plants but leave the soil right around them bare.

Seeded areas and young seedlings can't be mulched. Don't mulch a newly planted area until the plants are tall enough so the mulch won't smother them. An exception would be a very light mulch, such as strands of hay, which will partly shade the soil, keep it moist, prevent erosion, and aid seed germination. This technique is especially useful for lawns that are seeded in hot weather. A heavier mulch, such as wet burlap, might be placed on the seeded area to help germination, but unlike straw it must be removed as soon as the seeds are up.

Mulch can impoverish the soil. Some woody mulches such as chips or sawdust have been found to deplete the soil of nitrogen while they're decomposing. If plants growing in mulch lose their green color, this might be the cause. It is best to use mulches that break down more quickly and are more nutritious. Bark, for example, contains more nitrogen and other nutrients than the wood of the tree.

Mulches attract certain pests. Voles and other rodents often burrow in mulch either to nest, hide, or look for seeds, and they can nibble on garden plants while they're there. Mulch can also harbor slugs and snails, which can do serious damage. If you have problems with these or other pests, don't use mulch on susceptible plantings.

How you use mulch is a combination of trial and error and common sense. Some gardeners use mulches so religiously that they claim they never even have to till their gardens. They insist their mulch just sits there and solves all their problems. In many cases this may be true. My advice is to experiment with several mulching materials that are readily available, using the list on page 56 for suggestions.

What to Do About Bugs

EVERY GARDEN HAS SOME INSECTS THAT the gardener would just as soon do without. I must admit I don't pay a great deal of attention to bugs because they rarely do serious damage. I tolerate a few chewed leaves or flowers in my ornamental plantings, and with my food crops I follow the old wisdom that holds, "one for the bugs, one for me," planting enough so that my yields are good despite occasional nibblers. I also find that if I choose varieties suited to my climate and give them the proper amount of sun, water, and nutrients, they are vigorous enough to resist many pests—just as people resist germs when they eat right and get plenty of exercise and sleep.

A serious infestation does need a gardener's attention, however, especially since some insects can spread plant diseases. It is important to know some safe ways to deal with them. Fortunately gardeners are becoming more aware that using toxic sprays and dusts are dangerous to themselves and their families, to their pets, to wildlife, and even to their plants. So today there's considerable interest in safe means of insect control.

A large network of insect and plant life exists in every garden. This network fits together in such complex ways that I doubt we'll ever fully understand it. And because insect and plant populations are always in flux, the balance changes from season to season. Certain insects eat some of my plants, but there are in turn other insects that attack those. If I destroyed all the insects in my garden, I'd not only be destroying the bug eaters but also insects that perform other useful functions, such as the bees, flies, wasps, and other insects that pollinate my plants, and the butterflies, spiders, and other fascinating insects I simply enjoy watching. And even if I find a means of controlling only the "bad" plant eaters, I run the risk of removing the food supply of the insects, birds, frogs, and others that feast on them. If these essential predators leave my garden, the plant eaters will become all the more

Some Common Insect Predators FIG. *12*

aphid
⅛"

Japanese beetle
½"

scale
1⁄16"

cutworm
1"–2"

leafhopper
⅛"

imported cabbage worm
1"

spotted cucumber beetle
¼"

striped cucumber beetle
⅕"

European corn borer
1"

plum curculio
¼"

squash vine borer
1"

apple maggot fly
⅜"

corn earworm
1¾"

Colorado potato beetle
⅜"

Colorado potato beetle larva
½"

numerous. This is why I balk at calling any insect good or bad. They're all part of a working system that stays more or less in balance. Sometimes I'll try to get rid of unwelcome visitors that are threatening something I've worked hard to grow, but even then I don't worry about rounding up the whole gang, just diminishing their numbers.

Each plant that gardeners grow has particular insects that consider it their favorite food, and each part of the country has its own notorious insects to deal with. Vegetables tend to be "buggier" in the south than they are in the northeast, where I live. But our fruit crops in the northeast are buggier than those of some growers I've talked to on the west coast. You will probably need more specific information than I can give you about all the creatures that might eat your plants and what you can do about them (it's a huge topic), and you'll need to consult local experts or some of the sources listed beginning on page 777. But the decision about what forms of pest control you're comfortable with is finally yours. I, for one, would no sooner use an "all-purpose" spray that killed all the bugs in my garden than I would a spray that killed all the gray hairs on my head—and all the brown ones, too.

Insects vary in the ways in which they damage plants. Some suck out the plant juices; some chew on leaves or other plant parts; others bore into the stems, leaves, or roots. Some carry specific diseases to plants or create wounds that leave them open to infection, or simply weaken plants so they resist disease less easily than healthy plants would. Insects may do damage while they're in their growing stages (as larvae) or after they've changed into the adult form in which they reproduce—or both. If you're up against a specific insect, you should check an insect field guide so you can recognize it in its different stages. Sometimes gardeners unwittingly kill an insect that they'd like to protect, such as a butterfly, because they only recognize its adult form and not the suspicious-looking caterpillar that takes a few bites of something they prize. Often when there is insect damage you can't even see the culprit because it's too tiny, or because it has hidden itself somewhere in the plant, or because it does its work in the soil. Sometimes an insect is not even at fault—a disease is, or a mineral deficiency in the soil, or some other cause of physical stress. When in doubt on any of these counts, *don't spray*. Get a positive identification. If you put the affected plant parts in a plastic bag and take or mail it to your Extension Service, they can usually identify the problem for you.

ORGANIC PEST MANAGEMENT

You may not need to spray at all. People have found, over the years, that insects often develop a resistance to the chemicals used to control them, so that not only is spraying risky, it's often futile. The people who sell you poison sprays are eager to play on your sense that nature is out to destroy your garden and that you must do battle to protect it. But experienced growers are starting to rely more and more on deterrents that work *with* nature rather than against her. Some of these tactics include crop rotation (page 247), picking off pests by hand, encouraging natural predators, sterilizing and releasing male insects that will mate but produce no young, using traps—and most important of all, identifying the specific pests, pinpointing the time and place of the damage they cause, and then making an educated decision about which control to use. Even among growers who are not strictly organic in their methods, poisons are starting to be viewed as a last resort, and the indiscriminate use of wide-spectrum ones is regarded as an uneducated choice that carries great risks.

Home gardeners have an even greater advantage because pests are often easier to deal with on a small scale. Try using some of the strategies listed below. If you grow food crops in a communal garden, where each person has a plot and many crops are being grown, it may seem as if every bug in the world has found its way there, and control may be a tricky matter. You're at the mercy not only of your neighbors' bugs, but also of any sprays they use that might drift over onto your plants. By meeting together and planning a safe, coordinated program, you may be able to help one another identify problem insects before they spread. And if the methods listed below pay off in beautiful crops, you'll be sure to win your neighbors over.

FORMS OF INSECT CONTROL

Keep plants healthy. I've noticed so many times that insect pests favor plants that are stressed. Give your plants whatever growing conditions will make them strong.

Plant extra for bugs. If something cuts back on your harvest one year, figure how many more plants you'll need next year if the visitor comes back.

Time your plantings. If the planting date for a food crop is flexible, you can often time it to avoid a pest—for example, by growing radishes after root maggots are no longer active (in late summer and fall), or

by sowing arugula after flea beetle season has passed.

Pick off the bugs. This is probably the most useful insect control there is. Picking bugs off your plants and dropping them into jars filled with soapy water may not be your favorite way to spend time, nor will you get them all. But you don't need to: even getting half the offending bugs may solve your problem. If you have children you might give them a chance to earn spending money by paying them a per-bug or per-cupful fee. Not all insects can be picked easily, of course. Some are too small, some won't sit still, and some are high above your head, eating your trees. But many are easy. Japanese beetles and potato beetles drop to the ground when disturbed, so you can just knock them or shake them into a container, or onto a cloth spread on the ground. Prowl for slugs with a flashlight at night, and check their hiding places (under rocks and boards, for instance) by day. If cutworms nibble young plants at night, probe the soil within a few inches of each plant during the day and nab them while they sleep.

Grow a trap crop. You might plant a "sacrifice" radish crop so the maggots will eat that and not your broccoli. I grow a plot of the annual butterfly weed (*Asclepias curassavica*) to give monarch butterfly caterpillars a free meal. As a result, they go easy on the perennial butterfly weed (*A. tuberosa*) in my permanent garden.

Avoid high-risk plants. Sometimes a plant is not worth repeating if you grow it and find it's a magnet for a specific pest that's hard to control. Grow those that are less susceptible.

Wait for a pest to move on. Many insects migrate or come in cycles. You might get a severe infestation of gypsy moths or tent

Some Helpful Insects

FIG. 13

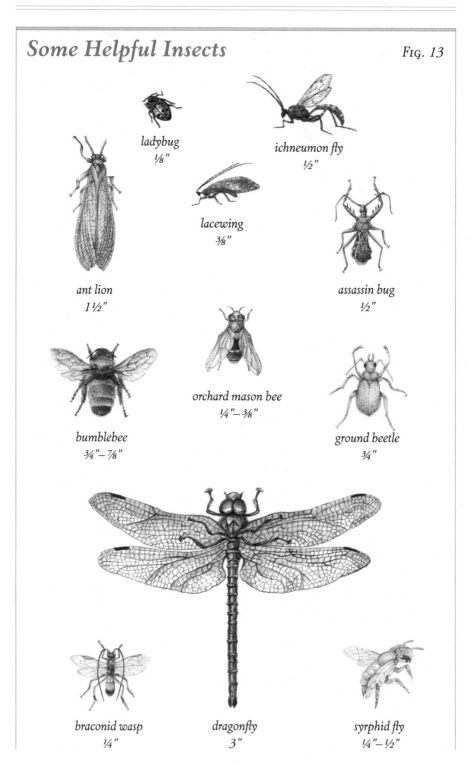

ladybug
⅛"

ichneumon fly
½"

lacewing
⅜"

ant lion
1½"

assassin bug
½"

bumblebee
¾"–⅞"

orchard mason bee
¼"–⅜"

ground beetle
¾"

braconid wasp
¼"

dragonfly
3"

syrphid fly
¼"–½"

caterpillars for a few years, for instance, then find that they cease to be a problem.

Rotate your crops. If you grow an annual food crop in the same place each year, the insects will often overwinter in the soil and come back stronger than ever. Foil them so that they hatch out *without* their favorite food handy; sometimes they never even find where you've moved it (see page 247).

Encourage beneficial predators. Many creatures that prey on insect pests will appear in your garden of their own accord, but there are things you can do to encourage them. Birds eat a lot of insects; give them trees and shrubs near the garden in which to nest. Toads do their part as well; give them flowerpots to hide in, propped open with a rock. Spiders, of course, trap and eat insects (they are not, strictly speaking, insects themselves). Some of the insects that eat insect pests are ladybugs, lacewings, ant lions, damsel bugs, pirate bugs, syrphid flies, ichneumon flies, assassin bugs, and fireflies (see Figure 13). Some of these can be bought in bulk and released into your garden, but that's often a waste of money. Ladybugs eat a few aphids and then move on. Lacewings are a notable exception and will stick around to prey on mealybugs, aphids, mites, thrips, scale insects, and whiteflies. But the best way to encourage all useful predators in your garden is to avoid using poisons.

Cover the plants. If insects attack your young plants while they are most vulnerable, try protecting them during this stage with the floating row covers described on page 260. One commercial seed producer I talked to told me these fabrics had virtually solved his pest-control problems. They're particularly helpful for insects such as leafhoppers that don't sit still long enough for you to pick them off. You'll have to remove the fabric in order to weed, however, and also when the plants are being pollinated by insects and are setting flowers.

Place physical barriers on the ground. Cutworms, which sever the stems of young plants just beneath the soil surface, can be deterred by setting collars made of paper cups or some such thing around susceptible seedlings such as tomatoes and peppers. The collars should extend several inches above the soil and an inch below it. Copper strips, which slugs hate to crawl over, are also effective. Tar paper mats spread on the ground are said to deter root maggots (lay the tar paper on the ground and plant through holes you make in it).

Control the weeds. A lot of weeds growing in the garden and just outside it can harbor insect pests. They can harbor beneficial insects too, but if your garden is particularly "buggy," try to keep the weeds down and mow weedy areas around its perimeter.

Use repellents. Some insects that eat food crops or ornamental plants are said to be deterred by sprays made of garlic or ground-up hot peppers. It's always worth a try, but be sure to reapply if rain washes them off.

Use bug juice. Many gardeners claim that if you collect pest insects in a jar, puree the bugs in water in an old blender, strain the concoction, and spray it back on the plants, it will discourage others from returning.

Turn loose the chickens. They may eat good bugs as well as bad, and they may nibble away at some plants, but if left in the garden for short stretches chickens may help to cut down on some serious pests, such as potato beetles. Introducing chickens or ducks in fall after most vulnerable crops are spent will help clean up overwintering pests.

Spray with a hose. Many pests such as aphids and spider mites can easily be knocked off with the force of a garden hose. Aphids are tiny sucking insects (usually green) that appear in throngs on plant leaves; the leaves are often crinkled or distorted. Spider mites are too small to really see, but they give the leaves a dotted, stippled look and you can sometimes spot the tiny webs they make on the undersides of the leaves. Be sure, when you're hosing off these pests, that you hit the undersides of the leaves, too.

Vacuum them. You can use a shop vacuum cleaner to suck pests off plants. The slot attachment works best and does the least harm to the leaves. This is a great way to get rid of striped cucumber beetles. Go after them at daybreak while they're still sluggish.

Trap them. You can outfox many pests with clever traps. Slugs and earwigs can be lured into saucers sunk in the ground up to their rims and filled with beer, or half-filled bottles laid on their sides (these are harder for them to crawl out of). Whiteflies can be lured, while in flight, to a piece of wood or metal painted bright yellow and smeared with a sticky substance like molasses, which works like old-fashioned flypaper. Probably the most ingenious insect trap around is a sticky red ball on which apple maggots will lay their eggs, thinking it's a ripe apple. You can buy them from mail-order catalogs. These and other sticky traps are also used to monitor insect infestations so the right pests can be dealt with at the right time.

Destroy their nests. Tent caterpillars, which build webs in the forks of trees in spring (particularly cherry trees), and fall webworms, which build webs at the ends of tree branches in fall, can be curbed if you break apart their nests and scrape the caterpillars into buckets of diluted alcohol or soapsuds.

Use oil sprays. Dormant oil sprays are applied only when the temperature is between 45 and 85 degrees Fahrenheit, to deciduous woody plants while they are in a dormant state, usually just before their buds begin to swell. There are similar formulations that can be applied later in the season and will not burn leaves the way dormant oils can. These are important controls for scale insects, which look like small bumps (usually brown) on the twigs and branches of woody plants but which are actually sucking insects.

Like many other sucking pests (including whiteflies and aphids), scale insects secrete a sticky substance called honeydew, which in turn attracts a black fungus disease called sooty mold. Oil sprays also help to control such pests as spider mites, psyllids (such as pear psylla), and leaf rollers. Your Extension Service can advise you on this.

Use soap sprays. Spraying infested plants with soapsuds is an old-fashioned remedy for such insects as aphids, earwigs, psyllids, sawflies, leaf miners (which make tunnels in leaves), spider mites, thrips, and scale. But household soaps and detergents can burn plant leaves, and it's less risky to buy a commercially prepared insect soap spray and use the concentration recommended on the label. Adding 10 percent alcohol to the spray will help it adhere.

Diatomaceous earth. This material consists of the fossilized remains of diatoms, tiny sea creatures. It damages the soft bodies of crawlers such as slugs and cabbage worms. It is harmful to breathe, however, and because I worry about hurting harmless caterpillars too, I'd use this only as a last resort.

Bt. "Bt" stands for the bacterium *Bacillus thuringiensis*. Sold under names such as Dipel and Thuricide, Bt is a disease you can intentionally give to your bagworms, gypsy moths, tent caterpillars, webworms, tomato hornworms, European corn borers, and cabbage worms. Milky spore disease, another bacterium, will eliminate many of your Japanese beetles. These remedies are rather expensive to apply and again, I'm concerned about upsetting the balance of nature and wiping out bugs I want, so they're also in the "last resort" category.

Natural organic poisons. Certain plant extracts can kill insects with less risk to humans and other warm-blooded animals than most chemical sprays present, but they all carry some risks. All can harm insects indiscriminately, besides the one you are targeting, and none should ever be applied to plants in bloom, especially at times when bees are active.

Pyrethrum, made from ground-up flowers of the chrysanthemum family, kills a number of insects, and the residue it leaves on edible crops breaks down very quickly; but it can kill some beneficial insects and fish, too, if it drifts or drains into streams or ponds. Rotenone, made from ground-up derris root, is more powerful; its residue lasts up to a week. While it supposedly won't hurt humans or pets, it kills fish and beneficial insects. Ryania has a fairly low toxicity and helps cope with worms such as European corn borer. Sabadilla dust kills many insects—including bees; nicotine is quite toxic, and I do not advise using it.

In general, be wary of *any* poison, even those that (dubiously) claim to kill "pest" insects but spare the "beneficial" ones.

As you can see, I've put even the "natural" poison sprays low on my list, because they're either something to use if all else fails, or not to use at all, depending on your philosophy. If you do use products such as these in the garden, follow the following safety rules:

Read the labels carefully, use only as directed, and heed all warnings.

Keep poisons in original containers, away from children and pets.

Don't breathe sprays and dusts.

Try not to spill poisons or splash them on humans or pets.

Don't smoke while using them.

Cover any food or water in the area that might be consumed by people or animals.

Always deal with pesticides in a well-ventilated area.

Don't mix them together.

Don't use them on windy days.

Be careful not to contaminate streams, ponds, and other water sources.

Wash yourself with soap and water after handling them; wash and flush out any equipment used to apply them.

Keep empty poison containers out of harm's way, then take them to a toxic-materials recovery site; *don't* send them to the town dump.

Coping with Diseases

PLANT DISEASES ARE NOT EASY FOR the home gardener to diagnose or treat. There are so many of them—ranging from those that make ornamental plants unsightly to those that kill or weaken food plants or make their fruits inedible or unappetizing—and it's hard to match the disease with the cure without being an expert. Even if you can get your disease identified, the cures available to you may be ineffective. Fortunately, there is quite a bit you can do to prevent plant diseases or at least keep them under control.

DISEASE PREVENTION

Here are some steps you can take to keep your gardens healthy. As with pest control, there are commercial products that can be applied if prevention fails, but you may find that you can get by without using them.

Grow disease-resistant varieties. Commercial producers of plants and seeds are always coming up with new varieties that resist the most common diseases of those plants. And in fact, gardeners have been doing the same thing for centuries simply by selecting the healthiest, most vigorous specimens from which to save seed or take cuttings. If certain diseases haunt your garden, be on the lookout for varieties that are said to resist them. Certain species of plants may also be more prone to disease in your garden because your particular climate is too different from their native one. You might simply choose to grow plants that do well in your area instead. Sometimes diseases are aggravated by growing a susceptible plant in large numbers. For example, the more lilies you grow, the more apt your flowers are to get lily virus. In this case, being content with a few healthy specimens may be more gratifying.

Buy disease-free plants. Sometimes a plant disease will permeate a given locality so that none of the seed or stock raised there commercially can be totally free of it. You might check with your local Extension Service, state university, or nursery expert to find out if there are specific diseases associated with certain plants or seeds you wish to grow. They can also advise you about where disease-free material is grown and sold. Always try to buy seeds and plants from reputable sources, and examine plants you buy for signs of disease before you bring them home.

Practice crop rotation. This practice, described on page 247, applies mostly to food gardens, but if ornamental plants do succumb to disease, you might try them again in a new location since disease organisms can persist in the soil.

Don't work in wet gardens, if possible. As you move among wet plants you can sometimes spread diseases. Usually this is not a big worry, but it's something to keep in mind in a year when you're having especially bad disease problems.

Keep plants dry. Obviously your plants are going to get wet when it rains, but keeping foliage unnecessarily moist can promote disease. If diseases are a problem, water plants at ground level.

Control disease-spreading insects. Cucumber wilt, for example, is spread by the striped cucumber beetle, so to thwart the disease you thwart the bug.

Keep your plants vigorous. We know that we get fewer colds if we exercise, keep our feet dry, eat fruits and vegetables, get plenty of sleep, and all those other things our mothers taught us. It's the same with plants. If they have great soil, no weeds, and ample water, chances are they'll have few diseases or only mild cases.

Don't crowd plants. Good air circulation among plants helps prevent many diseases.

Don't reuse potting soil. This is especially important if the previous tenant of the pot was sick.

Disinfect contaminated tools. If you're pruning out diseased portions of a plant, dipping your pruners between cuts in chlorine bleach diluted to 10 percent strength can help stop the infection's spread.

Destroy diseased plants. Tilling under diseased plants can perpetuate the problem. Even composting them may be ineffective if your pile does not heat up enough to kill pathogens. If you're in doubt, burn them, or bury them in a spot other than the garden.

Keep a tidy garden. Clean up plant debris after you harvest a food crop, and cut back herbaceous perennials after their foliage dies down in fall if they're covered with leaf spot or mildew. Disease organisms will then be less likely to winter over.

Replace the soil. As a last resort, if a disease keeps recurring each year, you can remove the top 2 or 3 inches of soil, and with it the disease organism. Replace with new, disease-free soil. Or move the garden to another spot and try again.

COMMON PLANT DISEASES

Here are some major categories of diseases that may befall your plants. They can be caused by fungi, bacteria, or viruses.

Leaf-spot diseases. These are fungus diseases that afflict both woody and herbaceous plants. There are many different ones, but in general they appear as round spots that are often a series of concentric circles in shades of brown, purple, yellow, or black (if the circles are numerous they merge to form blotches). Often they affect a plant's looks only, and can be ignored, but I have sometimes seen bad cases kill plants. The fungi overwinter in

fallen leaves, so it's best to rake up the leaves of affected plants and destroy them, and to destroy the whole plant if it dies.

Fusarium wilt. This fungus lives in the soil and attacks plants' roots. Scar tissue forms, which blocks the circulation of fluids, and the plant wilts. There's no treatment the home gardener can apply, but you can fight the wilt by growing resistant varieties, rotating crops, pulling up and destroying afflicted plants, and not letting the soil get too acid.

Mildews. Mildews afflict such diverse plants as phlox, beans, lilacs, and roses. Downy mildew produces white patches on the leaves in wet weather; powdery mildew turns the leaves a grayish white and occurs when it's hot and humid. Sulfur dust can be effective on many ornamental and food plants. Baking soda is an even simpler remedy. And many plants, such as roses and bee balm, have mildew-resistant varieties. Usually, I simply try not to look at the mildew on my phlox and lilacs.

Botrytis. This fungus disease produces brown or gray areas on leaves and stems in humid weather. Prune out and destroy all affected parts.

Rust. Yet another fungus, rust produces pustules on the undersides of leaves; these are sometimes rust colored but can also be red, yellow, brown, or black. Rust is commonly treated with fungicides, but it is better to find resistant varieties. My hollyhocks always get rust on their lower leaves. I just prune those out.

Anthracnose. A lot of things get anthracnose, from maple trees and dogwoods to cucumbers and beans. It's not always easy to identify, but it produces spots on leaves, or on pods in the case of beans. Western-grown seeds and plants are less likely to carry it.

Canker. Cankers can be either fungal or bacterial. They produce sunken areas on the twigs, stems, and trunks of woody plants. Prune them out, and if too much of the plant is affected for this to help, destroy it.

Crown galls. This bacterial disease of woody plants produces knobby growths that block the circulation of fluids. Usually the plant must be destroyed.

Other bacterial diseases. Plants afflicted with bacteria can show slime and rot, wilt, spots, and any number of other symptoms. Bacteria tend to spread quickly so it's wise to get any plant in very bad shape out of your garden fast. Plants growing in moist, nitrogen-rich soil in hot, humid weather are the most susceptible.

Four-Legged Marauders

PEOPLE WHO MOVE FROM THE CITY TO the country often ask what they can plant to attract wildlife to their yards. "That's easy," I tell them. "Plant lettuce, corn, broccoli, beans, berries, daylilies, yews. . . ." The list is very long.

I'm only partly kidding. I can empathize with someone who's tired of looking at concrete and wants to look at deer, rabbits, and raccoons instead. I'm the same way. But sometimes those of us who garden in the country wind up regarding these creatures much the way city folk regard muggers and car thieves. The trick is to find ways to enjoy the presence of wildlife and still have a garden.

I won't waste your time listing the dozens of repellents that gardeners claim work on this or that pest. No doubt some are effective. Yes, you can try dabbing your ornamentals with Tabasco sauce, cayenne pepper, and every Cajun, Creole, or Szechuan seasoning in the gourmet aisle. You can round up human hair from all the local beauticians and barbers to hang in bags around your property, and you can haunt zoos that are willing to part with their lion dung. But the best remedies are either to plant things that your local wildlife doesn't care for, or to erect physical barriers.

KNOW THE CREATURES' HABITS

You may not know what is eating your plants. Finding out about your local wildlife by consulting field guides may help you to identify the culprit. And talk to local gardeners and farmers. Each area has its own special varmints. Here are some of the most common ones.

Rabbits. Rabbits will eat a wide variety of plants. They love salad crops like lettuce but will also gnaw the bark of fruit trees or any young trees, often girdling and killing them. Rabbits reproduce prolifically, as we all know, and the little ones are the hungriest of all. Protect young fruit trees as soon as they're planted by wrapping the trunks in cylinders of hardware cloth that are buried 1 to 2 inches in the ground, and extend at least 18 inches up the tree. The cylinder should not constrict the growth of the trunk or prevent the tree from forming feeder roots below the surface.

In the vegetable garden make sure the first 2 feet of your fence is rabbit fencing made of 1- by 2-inch mesh (baby bunnies can squeeze through anything less closely woven than that). Bury it 6 inches deep or bend it outward to rest on 6 inches of soil to discourage burrowing.

For unfenced flowers and other herbaceous plants, you can use the portable frames shown on page 259 with rabbit mesh or 1-inch chicken wire stretched over them, until the plants are large enough to withstand a little nibbling.

Woodchucks. Some people call them groundhogs. They are fat, lumbering, and rather lovable except when they're eating your peas. Woodchucks are not supposed to climb fences, but I once saw a huge one hauling its heavy self over a 4-foot fence that I had built, and I've heard of them climbing much higher. They're not supposed to burrow under the fence if you bury the wire a foot down, but one did, and came up right in the middle of my garden, so you might want to go deeper than that.

Deer. It's funny, but as an area gets more built up and suburban it often has more deer. Although they are woodland creatures, deer prefer the outskirts of woodlands, or clearings in them, where they can find fresh new growth on shrubs and other understory plants. When they see former farmland growing up in scrub, or homeowners planting daylilies and phlox or rows of yews and arborvitae on one-acre lots, "Ah," say the deer, "progress!"

Deer can leap very high fences, but you generally need one only 6 to 8 feet tall to deter them effectively. Some people have had good luck with fencing that is lower but extends upward at a 45-degree angle. Others swear by two fences that are lower and spaced 4 feet apart, on the theory that deer don't like to broad jump. Commercial orchards and tree farms often use electrified strands of wire. Hardware and farm-supply stores supply apparatus for electric

fencing, as do mail-order outfits, but I still feel a very tall fence, or a double one, is the best solution if deer are a problem. In areas where the fence is conspicuous, make it from an attractive lattice and plant it with flowering or food-bearing vines. Ornamental shrubs that deer like can be wrapped in wintertime with plastic deer netting, or with chicken wire supported by metal stakes. These are removed in spring, when everything has leafed out and the deer have a wider choice of forage. Emerging tulips and other herbaceous plants can be protected by the movable frames shown on page 259, or some other cage of your own devising. There are also a number of deer repellents. I use dried blood on my tulips and other temporarily vulnerable crops. It's available in bags at garden centers and agriculture-supply stores. The rain washes it off but it's easy to reapply either by sprinkling it on or dusting the plants with an old-fashioned flit gun. It adds nitrogen to the soil as well.

Raccoons. Raccoons will raid your garbage can if the lid isn't tight, but usually the only plant they seriously threaten is corn. See page 307 for some tactical suggestions.

Rodents. Mice and voles can do the same thing to young fruit trees that rabbits can, and they're foiled by the same methods. But voles often gnaw on the roots as well, and are fond of leafy greens. You can destroy them by putting mousetraps, baited with something tasty like apple or peanut butter, in their little pathways. Better yet, set bottomless wooden boxes about a foot square in their accustomed routes. Cut out small vole-size holes in two opposite sides of the box, and place a wooden lid on top for easy removal. Then set unbaited mousetraps inside. The voles will eagerly run into the hole for cover, land on a trap, and meet their doom.

Also avoid using mulch within a foot of tree trunks because it can be a haven for rodents. For problems with flower bulbs see page 495. Moles can make a lawn very lumpy, but they are blamed unjustly for a lot of damage actually done by voles, which use mole tunnels as runs. As far as I'm concerned, moles earn their keep in the lawn by eating Japanese beetle grubs that hatch there, so I leave them alone.

Birds. Protect newly planted seeds from birds with mulch or mesh-covered frames. Plastic netting is effective on fruit crops such as raspberries and blueberries. Floating row covers can be spread over strawberries until the foliage is tall and lush enough to hide the fruits from the robins. Or just grow enough to share, and pick regularly.

The Larger Community

GARDENING IS ESSENTIALLY THE creation, for certain plants, of a more luxurious, consistent, and protected environment than those plants would find in the wild. By giving them this environment we control nature, just as plant growers have for thousands of years.

Sometimes, in our desire to achieve a predictable outcome from all our hard work, we lose sight of how much we and the other living things in nature all depend on one another. Plant and animal life is a chain of interdependence: plants feeding animals, animals feeding plants, plants feeding plants, and animals feeding animals. The death and decay of organisms is part of the process. When we eradicate living things that are part of the chain, we run some risk of disrupting it, and destroying their habitats can amount to the same thing. Good gardening is sometimes a matter of leaving nature alone, of not draining a swamp that harbors wildlife, of not clearing your woods of the underbrush and logs where creatures hide, of realizing that your soil is alive—with insects, reptiles, mammals, and microbes—and so is not the place for toxic substances. We garden in a world that is in constant motion—motion that our clumsy efforts to control the environment can bring to a halt.

My own philosophy is that most of the time I can't predict what the outcome of my manipulation of the natural world will be, because that world is so complex. So although I might regulate this or that aspect of it, I try to do the very minimum and avoid any measures I fear might be harmful. I don't try to be a perfect gardener; I don't always judge my success by the number of flowers on a plant or the size of a fruit. I happen to think that safe gardening practices give even better results than those that tamper clumsily with the balance of nature. But even if they did not, I'd probably use them anyway. If I've enjoyed growing my garden, and the countryside around it is still humming with life, that's a large part of the harvest.

CHAPTER 2

Planning Your Landscape

THE GARDENING BUG CAN BITE AT any moment. Sometimes it's on a warm day in March when the earth is just starting to smell like earth. Itching to get out there and dig, an eager gardener rushes to buy some seeds, tills up some soil, and scans the instructions on the packets to see which seeds can be planted "as soon as the ground can be worked." The peas can, so in they go.

Sometimes the bug bites on a Saturday in late June. A couple out for a drive passes a nursery where everything is 25 percent off. They pick out two dozen shrubs, 40 perennials, and a magnificent copper beach tree. When the plants are delivered the next day they triumphantly "find a place for everything."

There's no doubt that these gardeners are having a good time. But acting on impulse does not always produce satisfying results. The pea planter later decides that the front yard was not the best spot for the vegetable garden—once the tomato stakes have reared their 6-foot heads and the squash vines have taken off across the lawn and into the street. The hasty shoppers find that in five years their weekend purchases (and the many that have followed) are an unrelated collection of this and that, and their landscaping has a spotty look with no unifying theme. In 15 years the precious copper beech has to be moved at great expense because it's right where the new addition to the house has to go. So much for bargains.

You Need a Plan

LANDSCAPES—AND LIVES—ARE ALWAYS evolving, and some unforeseen changes are inevitable. Nonetheless, many missteps can be avoided by advance planning, and without taking any of the fun out of gardening. In fact for some people the planning is the best part. I like to do it in the lull after the winter holidays, when the first color-filled plant catalogs start to arrive and gardening is a grand fantasy—weedless, bugless, and crowned with success. It's a time when I'm not being rushed into planting jobs that must be done on time and can stand back and take an honest look at my surroundings as a whole.

Other chapters in this book will give you help in planning the individual segments of your landscape. The tree chapter will help you choose and place trees for shade, ornament, and other purposes. The shrub chapter will show you ways to use various shrubs in the landscape—shrub borders and plantings near the house, for example. The chapters on lawns, ground covers, perennials, annuals, herbs, bulbs, roses, vines, vegetables, fruits, and wildflowers will help you design gardens with these particular plants and place them in the landscape. As you read, however, keep thinking about how all these plantings will look together.

It's especially important to consider the overall look of the house and grounds when you build a new home, because you're starting from scratch. But an overview is also useful when you move into a home that previous owners have landscaped in a way that may or may not suit your taste and lifestyle. Even if you've lived there awhile, it's good to rethink the plan from time to time and make sure the whole thing works. A new structure or addition to existing buildings might need to be incorporated into your scheme. A shift in your way of life—new children coming along, or older ones moving away, for example—might prompt some changes. Perhaps the landscape needs to require less maintenance. Or you might just decide the place needs a fresh look.

One purpose of landscape planning is to reconcile the needs of different members of the household. Sometimes when I've been asked to advise people about their property, I've felt like a family counselor. The husband is thinking "lawn" for a spot where the wife is thinking "flowers." A couple's concept of their yard as an elegant setting for their jewel of a home conflicts with their children's use of it as a playground. Often one member of a team is a gardener and the other is not. The gardener may anticipate the other's help in the form of interest, ideas, and hard labor, but rarely will he or she get it. One may love to spend money on plants, tools, and power equipment, while the other balks. And who asks the family dog? No one, because it wouldn't do any good. Chances are the dog will run where it wants, dig where it wants, and take its own chosen path from point A to point B whether you make the walkways flagstone or brick.

It's important that the area around your home have a style or atmosphere that suits you. Some people think of their yard as very connected to the natural or social worlds around them, whether that be a street with other houses, a road where people pass by, or a secluded woodland. Other people experience their yard as very private, a little kingdom insulated from the rest of the world. Some like wide-open spaces, while others like to nestle in leafy corners. One person might want to live surrounded by an old-fashioned garden, full of nostalgic scents and associations, bursting with greenery. Another might feel more comfortable in a setting that is clean-lined and severe—more architectural than horticultural. It may not always be possible to reconcile everyone's needs within a household, but you can at least try to arrange the property in such a way that everyone will coexist, enjoy themselves, and take pride in their surroundings.

These are aesthetic and emotional issues that may take some time to think through, but first, begin on a practical note. I recommend that you take a survey of your property, map it out on graph paper, sketch in your ideas, and gradually come up with a simple master plan that you can follow in years to come. Here is how you do it.

Getting to Know Your Property

THE FIRST THING TO DO, BEFORE YOU ever put pencil to paper, is to take a long, careful look around you. If your place is newly acquired, or if you have never gardened much before, there are probably some basic things you don't yet know. Some of these you can find out right away; others you will learn only after you've lived there for a while. I sometimes advise people not to take any major steps until they have been in their house for a full year.

CHECK YOUR PROPERTY LINES AND UTILITIES

First of all, make sure you have a surveyor's map of the property, and walk the boundaries. Don't rely on someone else's vague indication of them—find all the little markers. Anything you build or plant on your neighbor's land you might have to unbuild or unplant in the future. Next find out where all your underground service lines are buried: electrical cables, water pipes, sewer lines or septic tanks and leach fields, underground oil tanks, etc. You need to know what you'll encounter if someone digs in any given spot, either by hand or with machinery. Driving over a septic field with a heavy truck can cause it to cave in; driving over water lines can damage them, too. Also look above you and be aware of any power lines or telephone wires that may interfere with trees or shrubs when they reach their full height.

CHECK THE ORIENTATION

Get a clear idea of where north, south, east, and west are, either from the surveyor's or architect's plan, or a compass. Watch the sun and see where it rises and sets at various times of the year and how high it is in the sky in different seasons. Many plants prefer a specific exposure. And as the position of the sun changes, a spot that is shady in summer may be sunny in winter and vice versa. Make a note of how much sun each part of the yard receives and at what times of the day. Whether a site is shaded, and in particular what kind of shade it gets, will strongly affect what you choose to plant there (see page 24). You may need to cut down trees, or plant trees, to alter the degree of light.

UNDERSTAND THE CLIMATE

You should be aware of your climate's vital statistics. What is the coldest winter temperature you're likely to experience? This will affect what plants you choose to grow and how you grow them (page 30). If you live in a climate where temperatures

fall below freezing, what are the dates of the average first frost in fall and the average last frost in spring? These dates will affect how you plan your vegetable garden as well as the way you grow any tender plants that can't take frost. If the weather is very dry or very wet where you live, you probably know that already, but it's useful to get statistics on annual rainfall, too. All these facts can be obtained from your local Cooperative Extension Service, and gardening neighbors can be helpful, too.

The direction of the prevailing winds at various times of the year is also something to be aware of. Winds, especially strong ones, can dry your plants in summer, chill them in winter, slow their growth, knock down tall vegetables and flowers, and even ruin the shapes of some shrubs and trees. They may also affect your own comfort. If you have strong winds you'll have to plant in sheltered areas or erect a windbreak of some sort, such as a tall wooden fence, or plant a living windbreak in the form of a hedge.

TOPOGRAPHICAL FEATURES

Look closely at the way the land is formed, and think about how this will affect the way you use it. Any major changes that require grading of the site (moving soil to change the level or degree of slope) should be done first, so you don't have to disrupt areas after they've been planted. Very often these are changes for which you'll need both expert advice and heavy equipment. For instance, if the land is so hilly that you cannot walk around it comfortably, chances are you will not be able to garden comfortably there either. Your planting areas will be easier to tend, more attractive to look at, and less prone to water runoff if you terrace them, using retaining walls of stone or timbers, and building steps of stone or wood to lead you comfortably and attractively from one level to another. It's important that all these features be installed correctly, allowing for water drainage, so they'll be permanent. Unless you're particularly good at this kind of engineering, hire a contractor to do it.

Grading may also have to be done if the property is very rocky. You may want to have a bulldozer remove rocks and add topsoil. Or if the rocks are very large, use them in your plantings by creating a rock garden. Determine which rocks are the visible outcroppings of ledge under the soil, and don't plan to put deep-rooted trees and shrubs in these areas. If it's important to you to have a flat play area, or a flat site for a formal garden, do the grading now, even if you won't be planting for a few years.

WATER

How does water behave on the property? Does it gush down slopes, eroding soil as it goes? Does it collect in puddles that don't drain, making the soil soggy? You may need to have a drainage system installed, but it might be possible to plant slopes with vegetation to slow erosion instead. If water collects and doesn't drain in a certain spot, you could make a virtue of your "problem" by landscaping with wetland plantings. If the ground is too dry, choose plants that thrive with little water, so that irrigation can be kept to a minimum.

SOIL

What is the soil like? Refer to the discussion of soil beginning on page 5, and see if you need to make changes in your soil

that might require heavy equipment. This is particularly important if there has been recent construction on the property. Rocks, rubble, and building debris may have been buried in certain areas, and would need to be removed if deep-rooted plants are to go there. It's likely that the soil has been compacted by trucks and bulldozers driving over it, and it may need to be power-tilled. The topsoil layer may have been stripped off and not adequately replaced, or not replaced at all. If so, you'll have to have topsoil brought in and spread over the area.

At this point you may be shouting, "Stop! We just wanted to put in some early peas and a few shrubs, and now you have us calling in the Army Corps of Engineers." No, my point is that if major, earth-moving changes are going to be needed, it's best to do them first, if possible, so you'll only have to create a disruption once. If major work isn't affordable at the moment, you can at least plan around future projects. It's easy to move a pea patch, but not a large vegetable garden or a 30-foot tree.

EXISTING PLANTS

What is already growing on your land? It may take you a while to find and identify all the trees, shrubs, and herbaceous plants growing on your property, and to decide which ones to keep and which ones to take out. Some people get rid of too little because they're afraid they'll kill something valuable and not easily replaced. Others get rid of too much in their eagerness to let in light and air, open up a view, or make room for new plantings. Identify and evaluate what is there before you take drastic measures; or get in a landscaper or tree surgeon to advise you.

VIEWS

Look at your house in relation to everything that's around it. Are there eyesores you'd prefer not to see? Some can be removed, such as your tumbledown shed and rusted pickup. Others must be screened from view, such as your neighbor's rusted pickup. There may, on the other hand, be attractive vistas that should be highlighted, either by cutting trees to open the view or by planting some that will frame it. Think of all the lines of sight there are on your property: the view of the house from the street, the view as you walk up the path, the views from all the windows. A view across a lawn might be enhanced by an attractive planting at the far side, or a view into a woodland area might be more dramatic if a path were cut into the woods to let you see still farther.

PRIVACY

Think about how much privacy you need. Should there be tall fences for instant screening, or have you the patience to wait for a hedge to grow? (The sooner you plant it, the better.) What creatures are likely to roam across the yard: dogs? children? cows? "Good fences make good neighbors," Robert Frost once wrote. (See also the section on using your imagination on page 85.)

Mapping the Property

AFTER YOU'VE TAKEN A GOOD HARD look around and answered these basic questions, make a map of what is on your place. You don't have to be an experienced draftsman to do this—it's very easy. And you'll learn even more about your surroundings while you're doing it. All you need is some graph paper, a piece of wood or a bulletin board to thumbtack it to, and a 100-foot measuring tape. An architectural scale ruler is useful for translating feet into inches. Unless the area to be mapped is very extensive, I use a scale of ¼ inch = 1 foot for the general scheme, and ½ inch = 1 foot for smaller, more detailed plantings such as flower gardens. But you can also just let each side of a square on the graph paper represent a foot, or half a foot, and count squares as you draw your lines.

I figure out how large a sheet of paper I will need to measure the whole area; sometimes I have to use several sheets and map various areas separately. Then I start with the buildings. I position the house, garage, and other structures in such a way that I'll have room to map the areas around them that need landscaping. If there are architect's drawings of the buildings, I can save some time by tracing those outlines onto my plan, as long as I'm using the same scale. Otherwise I simply measure with my long tape. If I don't have a partner to hold one end, I just stick a screwdriver through the metal loop at the end of the tape, and then into the ground to anchor it.

After the buildings, I measure the size and position of all the other important features such as trees, shrubs, boundaries, driveway, stone walls, paths, and large rocks. I draw them on the plan and label them "existing maple," "existing stone wall," and so forth. For trees and shrubs, I indicate both the location of the trunk and the spread of its branches by a circle with a dot in the middle (with young plants I draw in the spread they'll have when full grown). I note details such as the position of the well cover or the pipe where the oil tank is filled, and the height from the ground of windows I'll be planting things under—anything I think might be relevant to my planning. As I go, I always use the buildings as reference points, sighting along the walls to extend their straight lines and measuring the distances of other objects from those lines. It isn't as accurate as using a surveyor's transit, but for most home landscaping purposes it works fine.

When I've mapped everything, my plan is ready to be filled in with all the new features I want to add—new trees, gardens, paths, decks, or whatever. That's the fun part. But if you've never done it before you might ask, "Where do I start?" I suggest you stop for a while and do some hard thinking.

How to Begin

W HEN YOU LANDSCAPE YOUR HOME you're really doing two things: creating an environment that will be a pleasure to look at and also creating one that will be used. After you have a good sense of what's there on your property, you need to think very carefully about what will happen on it. I always feel that the best way to understand this is to compare the inside of the house with what is around it. Homes are divided into rooms for reasons—chiefly to give the people who use them private space and to separate different activities from one another. This is just as true outdoors. The grounds surrounding the great English estates were often divided into distinct "garden rooms," separated by walls or hedges.

This is rarely done today, but it is helpful to think of outdoor spaces as rooms that must serve different purposes and must have different looks to them. Some features will be purely ornamental, such as a shrub planting that frames an important entrance. Some, such as lawns or swimming pools, will be used for recreation. Others, such as storage or work areas, will be strictly utilitarian.

These areas must all be tied together in a way that looks attractive and is also easy to live with. You must plan the best way to get from one outdoor space to another, just as the traffic between indoor rooms is determined by the placement of halls and doorways. Even an informal landscape plan should define the different areas within it, and lead you subtly but deliberately from one to the next. Visitors should not be confused about which door of the house to enter—the landscaping should guide them. They shouldn't wonder about how to approach the backyard (unless of course you want to discourage people from going there!). And even the most fun-loving households function best if different outdoor spaces are well defined, both those that specific people use and those that are used in common. Transitional elements such as gates and walkways are an opportunity for creativity. They can be beautiful in themselves, and enhance the feeling of surprise when you enter a new part of the landscape.

Getting Ideas

I T IS VERY HELPFUL TO DRIVE AROUND your community, and other communities, and see what people have done to enhance their homes. You don't want to merely copy someone else's landscaping, but you may get some ideas you hadn't thought of. And when looking at places in your area, you'll get a sense of what plants do best there.

You should also take note of the style of your home and consider what style of landscaping will best complement it. For example, a large Victorian house would be well set off by a sweeping lawn, stately trees, large-specimen shrubs set at a distance from the house and perhaps some plots of bedding annuals or a perennial border. A colonial house could be enhanced by a cottage garden of herbs and flowers inside a picket fence. A contemporary wooden house stained in a natural color might look good with a Japanese-style planting, or with the abstract masses provided by interesting foliage plants such as cacti, ornamental grasses, or dwarf evergreens. Suppose you live in a low ranch house in a dry climate, but you've fallen in love with the English garden style, with its perennial borders and formal hedges. Rather than reproducing this look, plan a landscape with the same feel to it, using plants appropriate to the region.

Can you mix styles? Yes, if you do it with care. Suppose you love Japanese gardens but have a 1770 colonial. A Japanese garden won't look odd if you plant it at a distance from the house, reached by a mossy path, or if you simply apply the Japanese aesthetic to a naturalized planting of native shrubs and trees near the house, avoiding anything that would look incongruous such as stone Buddhas or a pagoda. You might want to do some research on historical gardening styles and tasteful ways to use them.

Very often an older home in a formal style looks best with plantings and walkways that are geometrically laid out and rather symmetrical, like those in the plan in Figure 14. There is a strong central axis to this property, starting at the sidewalk and running through a series of sharply defined spaces: the terrace, the lawn and gardens, and the pool. A design like this need not be rigid, and its regularity can be softened with the placement and textures of the plantings. But there is a solidity and regularity about it that echoes the feeling of the architecture.

Compare this plan to the one for a more informal contemporary home in Figure 15, in which there is no axis at all. The landscape contains many of the same features as the other plan; both are on 135- by 200-foot lots that slope gently down to the west, with the front of each house facing east. But the second plan has free-form shapes and meandering paths. More space has been devoted to play areas and to growing edibles. This is not to say that a traditional house might not have a more naturalistic landscape surrounding it, or a contemporary home a formal geometric one, but these plans do illustrate two extremes of design. Note that in both at least a portion of the plan is devoted to wilder areas where wildlife can feel protected and the natural world can stake at least a bit of a claim.

Your house may not be at either extreme, but somewhere in the middle, and it may require a landscape plan that combines formal and informal features. Or it may be very rustic, or in a rural setting where there are large wild areas to develop in attractive ways. Your property may be much smaller or much larger than that considered in these two plans, which are for suburban lots two thirds of an acre in size. But these will serve to illustrate how different landscaping needs might be reconciled within a limited space.

Landscape Plan for a Traditional Home

FIG. 14

street

lawn   brick path   lawn

parking area

trees and ground covers

brick path

seat

front door

garage

native shrubs, trees, and wildflowers

house

screened porch

back door

sun room

herb garden

dwarf fruit trees

shade tree

stone terrace

steps

stone wall   flowers

stone wall   flowers

fence

woodland paths

flowering shrubs

lawn

lawn

hedge

arch

low

vegetable garden

stone wall   flowers

steps

stone wall   flowers

utility shed   compost

climbing roses

rose garden

seat

stone terrace

swimming pool

grape arbor

evergreen hedge

Landscape Plan for a Contemporary Home

Fig. 15

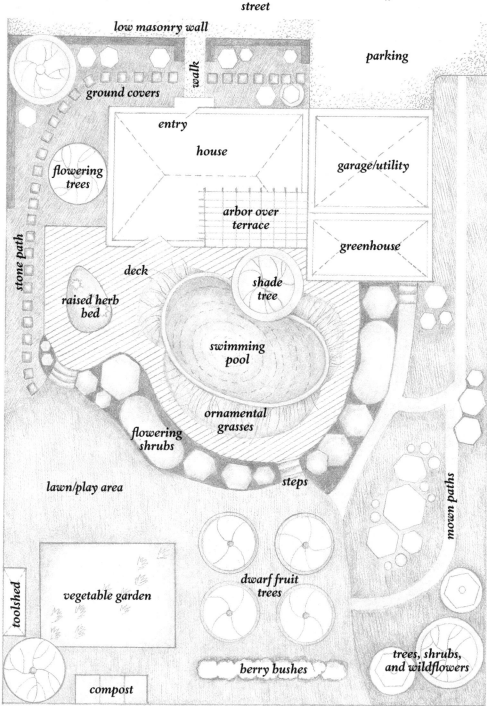

street

low masonry wall

parking

N E S W

ground covers

walk

entry

flowering trees

house

garage/utility

arbor over terrace

greenhouse

stone path

deck

shade tree

raised herb bed

swimming pool

ornamental grasses

flowering shrubs

lawn/play area

steps

mown paths

toolshed

vegetable garden

dwarf fruit trees

trees, shrubs, and wildflowers

berry bushes

compost

Drawing Your Own Plan

WHEN YOU'RE READY TO DO YOUR own landscaping plan, you will be dealing with a whole set of unique requirements: your household's specific needs, the spaces you have to work with, and the amount of landscaping you can afford. Ready-made plans such as the ones shown here are never carried out in their entirety. They must be adapted to the situation. Nor are plans usually executed all at once—more often they evolve in stages. I would start, for example, by planting the trees and shrubs in front of the house and taking care of some basic immediate needs such as lawns and play areas. Unless money were no object, I'd save such features as pools, terraces, and rose gardens until I had the time and money to tackle them. If I could foresee the need for these features now, however, I would set aside appropriate spots for them.

It may take you quite a while to figure out how to put all the pieces of a landscape plan together. I find it helps to lay sheets of tracing paper over the plan and sketch different layouts to see what might work. Keep going out and looking at the actual site as you work, seeing things from different angles to help you visualize them, and staking out lines where features like gardens or pools will go. If you have trouble seeing how your bird's-eye-view plan will look in real life, you can take photographs of the house, enlarge them, trace the general outlines onto tracing paper, and draw in your proposed plantings or construction projects to see how they'll look. If you prefer the digital route, there are computer programs suited to this kind of work. Or you can simply shoot various views with a digital camera and print them out, then make collages using images of plants, trellises, stone walls, and other features you've downloaded from one source or another and printed out. This can be enormous fun.

Principles of Garden Design

EACH PART OF THE PROPERTY WILL present a different kind of design challenge. Specific tricks for using roses, shrubs, ground covers, and other plant groups are discussed in their individual chapters. But certain principles hold true for all phases of garden-making. They are balance, contrast, and unity—basic elements of art. In fact, what you're doing in landscaping is painting a picture using plants instead of brushstrokes. Try to imagine each glimpse of your property and the areas within it, framed as if they were pictures, and try to make that picture both interesting and harmonious.

BALANCE

If you've ever assembled the furniture in a room, put together a still life, or created any kind of composition at all, you know that balance is necessary. Picture a room in which all the tall furniture is at one end and the low pieces are at the other—it doesn't work. Plants must also be balanced in a composition. In a formal garden design the balance has a lot of symmetry, as in Figure 14, where twin lawns, walls, and flower beds flank the center path. In a more informal plan the balance is more subtle: instead of duplicating a form on one side with a mirror image on the other, you provide masses of equal weight on each side, even though their contours are not the same. What kind of contours your plant picture will have will depend on the sizes and shapes of the individual plants and on how they are grouped. An example might be a doorway planting in which the groups of plants on each side of the door have equal weight visually, even though several different species with different forms—cone-shaped, columnar, low and spreading—are used.

Balance is not achieved with contours alone. You also need to think about a balance of color, of light and dark tones, and texture. A bed of brightly colored round flowers like zinnias and dahlias will be more beautiful and interesting if there are some spiky blue veronicas, gray-leaved artemisias, and ferny-leaved yarrows mixed in. Sometimes a single dramatic accent plant can be effective—a large yucca, for example, or a weeping birch. But such selectiveness is more effective if it's balanced by a harmonious, democratic approach to the composition. A great deal of harmony can be created by repeating a theme at intervals throughout a garden bed, or the yard as a whole. This might mean choosing a repeated thematic element for each season—say, white dogwoods in spring, pink phlox in late summer, and the yellow foliage of spice-bush in autumn. Even in a formal setting, this harmony grows out of its naturalness. In wild landscapes, certain conspicuous plants and plant colors unify the picture at every moment of the year.

CONTRAST

One of the things that makes any garden design interesting is contrast. Just think

how varied plants are, how many different ways flowers are colored, how many different textures evergreens can have, how trees can vary from the huge dense head of a maple or beech to the open branches and small leaves of a birch or an aspen. As you get to know plants better, you'll find contrasts you never thought of: leaves that have a red tinge to them when they first emerge in spring, say, next to others that are green from the start. Or trees with pale bark in winter that stand out against dark evergreens behind them. You'll find ways to combine similar plants that differ slightly—mixing several types of ground covers to make a richly patterned carpet, for example, or planting three different ferns, like three different patterns of lace. Some contrasts will become your favorites—perhaps pink roses against a background of dark hemlock, or yellow goldenrod and purple asters together in a "wild meadow."

UNITY

Giving your plant pictures a feeling of unity is something that simply takes practice. One thing that will help is to use repetition at the same time you're using contrast to arouse interest. A single element used throughout the composition may help tie it together. In a flower garden this might be clumps of white Shasta daisies dotted throughout the bed. In a shrub planting it might be a ground cover that unifies the whole. It might even be a construction material, such as the stone and brick used in Figure 14.

Very often the trick of a unified design lies in not planting too many different things. I find that the more I learn about plants, the more different ones I want to try to grow and the more I risk letting the yard become a motley jumble of this and that. It's hard to be a designer with plants and a collector of plants at the same time. Look at the living pictures in your gardens with this in mind. Are they designs or collections? And if you're an inveterate collector, perhaps there is something—like a ground cover or edging or background hedge—that you can use to unify your design. Plants can become like stray cats that you can't turn away, but a yard that is a horticultural orphanage will not be visually satisfying. If you have too much of something, give it away or feed it to the compost pile. It is not a federal crime to kill a garden plant.

THE LONG VIEW

Another factor to keep in mind is the element of time. A garden may be a picture, but it's one that changes from day to day, hour to hour. The flowers that bloom in your yard in May will not necessarily bloom in August, so you'll want to plant others to enjoy then. The red autumn leaves on your Japanese maple will be handsome at 4:00 P.M. but spectacular at 6:00 P.M. when the sun is setting behind them—if you plant the tree to the west of where you view it the most. The swimming pool will look attractive and inviting in summer, but less so in winter with the cover on it; if this bothers you, site the pool at a distance from the house. And always keep in mind the ultimate size and spread of everything you plant, whether it's a tree that will grow tall, a shrub that will become very broad, or a creeping perennial that will eventually range merrily throughout the garden.

USING YOUR IMAGINATION

As you drive through the residential areas of American towns you'll see a sameness to them, especially in their front yards. I would like to say that there is no law that each house must have a mown lawn before it and a row of clipped shrubs marching across the facade, but it would not surprise me to hear of places where such things are legislated. Often the only glimpses of individuality are in garden ornaments, and even these tend to look off-the-shelf, or silly. It would be great to see more people developing landscapes that avoid clichés (some tips on this can be found within individual chapters, especially the one on shrubs).

There also seems to be an ironclad division between the formality of the front yard and the anarchy of the back one. The front yard is assumed to be the face you present to the world, a sign of respectability and some sort of good citizenship. The backyard is where you really live. It's where you express your household's collective personality, its various interests, and whatever makes it unique. It is considered an American right to do whatever you want in your backyard as long as it doesn't hurt or annoy anyone. Though there may be some logic to all of this, I think life would be more interesting if some of our creativity were to spill out in front, in full view.

Despite the standardization of American yards, it is in these very plots that some of the most interesting innovations might occur. The relationship between human habitation and the rest of the natural world is a fluid one in yards, which lie midway between the rural countryside, where Nature tends to stake her own claim, and cities, in which one must take great pains to introduce and protect nonhuman life. I see two significant ways in which the stereotypical yard has begun to change a bit.

Planning for wildlife. The first change is a new awareness of wildlife, an interest

WHAT TO DO YOURSELF

WHETHER YOU TACKLE A GARDEN-ing job yourself will depend on many things: how much strength you have, how much knowledge, how much time, and how much interest in taking on the project. The following list may help you to make the decision.

Good do-it-yourself tasks:

Minor grading and terracing

Correcting minor drainage problems

Erecting unmortared masonry walls up to 1 foot high

Drawing a landscape plan

Planting and tending a vegetable garden

Installing a small ornamental pool

Pruning small trees

Building raised beds

Transplanting bare-root shrubs and trees

Planting balled-and-burlapped trees if the ball is not too heavy

Sinking fence posts

Constructing simple fences and gates

Building good garden soil

Installing simple above-ground irrigation systems

Making compost

Planting a new lawn or restoring an old one

Training vines

Designing and planting a perennial garden

Making compost bins

Building a cold frame

Laying an informal fieldstone walk and establishing creeping plants between the stones

Learning to monitor insect populations, both harmful and beneficial

Usually best done by a pro:

Major grading and terracing

Making tree wells

Correcting major drainage problems

Erecting masonry walls higher than 1 foot

Felling trees

Pruning, spraying, and cabling large trees

Removing large stumps and boulders

Diagnosing disease problems and certain insect pests

Soil testing (although you can easily take the samples for testing)

Planting balled-and-burlapped shrubs and trees with heavy root balls

Digging and balling a shrub or tree for transplanting

Sinking posts in very rocky or compacted soil

Building large arbors

Large-scale spraying, even with low-toxicity products

Planning and/or carrying out woodlot management

Installing underground irrigation systems

Building retaining walls to hold up earth on a steep slope (Whether of wood or masonry, such walls must be properly anchored, and drainage systems must be built into them; otherwise, they will be pushed outward.)

Digging out large tree stumps

in observing it, and concern about safe-guarding it. People are now much more conscious of the accelerated loss of species diversity—so necessary in maintaining healthy, resilient ecosystems—and the need to provide more habitats for threatened species of both animals and plants. It might be hard to imagine what your own tiny patch of the planet could do to further this effort, but if everybody joined in, all those yards could make a big difference.

Throughout this book I suggest ways in which homeowners can plant more native species and make their yards more friendly to wildlife, and yet still have a landscape that's comfortable for humans and pleasing to the eye. The two landscape plans included in this chapter have wild corners set aside where birds, mammals, insects, reptiles, and amphibians might coexist with the owners. But even more formal areas can include native shrubs and trees whose fruits are popular with birds, flower gardens that nurture insects and other pollinators, and native grass lawns. Some gardeners are taking the idea even further and turning their yards into small patches of wilderness. Even if this concept isn't for you, you can still be aware that wildlife favors interconnected plantings of shrubs and trees. These wildlife corridors, as they are called, provide cover for wild creatures and allow them to move safely and confidently from place to place in search of food, shelter, and nesting spots. Making water available—even if it's just a shallow birdbath set on the ground—is a great help to many species. This approach may go against our traditional ideas about keeping a tidy yard, but leaving a dead tree for birds to nest in, or a pile of brush and some rot-ting logs for small mammals, are acts with more value than hauling these materials off to the town dump. For excellent information and inspiration on this subject, I recommend Sara Stein's book *Noah's Garden* (see page 781).

Although there is an ecological mission to this form of gardening, its reward consists less in wearing a mantle of virtue than in the day-to-day pleasure of living in surroundings where the natural world is welcomed in all its variety. A yard without humming bees, birdsong, and the occasional glimpse of a fox, toad, or harmless snake is, to my mind, a poorer one. In planning and arranging my own home landscape, I often feel less like the director of a pageant than a sort of assistant stage manager who helps set the scene, then waits for the characters to play out their roles. They enter and exit at will, with no cues from me, and I consider that a big part of the enjoyment.

The fruitful yard. The second change is in the attitude toward food gardening. People grow much less of their food than they did a hundred years ago, and in recent decades the decline has been precipitous. A tiny percentage of what our citizenry eats is grown at home. But I've seen an increase in the number of people who ask me questions about food crops. During both World Wars the amount of food grown by home gardeners increased dramatically, and I think a small surge is beginning now. Part of this is due to anxiety about how safe our food supply is, and what we might do if it were interrupted, especially since so much of our food comes from afar. If the transportation system were ever impaired, or became difficult to fuel, you'd see the lawns of America converted very quickly to kitchen gardens and even to small plots of farmland. It would not be at all difficult to do.

Meanwhile, a renewed interest in food growing is being driven by a new interest in food, period. People are starting to put more value on what they eat. They're discovering that fresh-picked vegetables and fruits are tastier and more nutritious than the much-traveled alternatives they can buy at the store. More on this subject can be found in the chapters on vegetables, fruits, and herbs. In this chapter, food-growing areas have been designated in both of the landscape plans. But be aware that food can be incorporated into any kind of planting, whether it means a hedge of blueberries, a grapevine atop your arbor, or parsley used as a garden edging. It is astonishing how much food you can produce—even in a small yard—if you're determined to do so.

How Much to Tackle Yourself

THIS AND OTHER ASPECTS OF landscape design may seem a bit overwhelming if you're still unfamiliar with plants and the way they grow. You may decide you need to get help from someone skilled in the art, either to start you off with an overall plan or help you with specific areas. But as you learn more you'll enjoy trying your hand at these projects, which will give you the satisfaction of creating your own little world of color, fragrance, light, and shade.

You need to make similar choices when it comes to the physical work of gardening. Don't take on more than you have the time, money, strength, or expertise to handle, either in the initial preparation or the yearly maintenance. Perhaps you are one of those people who believe they can and should do everything themselves, even if it means learning the hard way. You may genuinely enjoy this process. But most of us eventually sort out which things we cannot do, cannot do well, or don't want to do. Perhaps you've learned to farm out dry-wall construction, tree felling, terrace building, and all forms of lawn care. Or you may shine at some of these tasks but have no patience with weeding or digging a bed. Most people with gardens like to do at least some of the work themselves because it's fun. It's also good for them physically and takes their minds off things that cause them stress. Others find that what they want most after a long, hard week is to take the time to smell the flowers—flowers planted by someone else. This is fine, too.

In short, use common sense in scheduling your projects. When you're sitting by the fire in winter, ordering plants and seeds, don't plan a monster. Plan gardens you will *enjoy* getting to when they need attention. After all, that's the whole point.

CHAPTER 3

Gardening Gear

MOST GARDENERS HAVE A CLOSE relationship with their tools, even though that relationship may take different forms. Some have a whole wall of specialized implements displayed on nails and pegboards, where they can reach like surgeons for the one that is perfect for the task at hand. Others have only a few simple tools to which they're very attached. Each handle fits their hands like a familiar glove, and woe betide the friend, spouse, or child who borrows and loses one. There are also gardeners who long to form such attachments but fear to, because they lose at least two shovels and three trowels each season.

Whether you're the pack rat or the minimalist, it's important to have a few simple, well-made, versatile tools that you feel very comfortable using. There's a wide range of prices, from cheap to exorbitant, but there are few real bargains—you get what you pay for. If you buy too cheap a tool, chances are the handle will break or the working end will bend or fall off; and the tool may not even be well designed for efficient performance. Begin by purchasing a few basic ones that will give you the most for your money, such as a shovel, a spade, a hoe, a rake, and pruners. Choose quality over quantity, and buy top-of-the-line products if you can. You can always collect some more specialized ones over the years, perhaps picking them up here and there at tag sales.

But what if you're the inveterate tool loser? Here's a suggestion: we all know tools can masquerade as sticks, or hide under piles of weeds to be composted, or wander over into someone else's yard. Why not paint all the handles bright blue? (Red-and-yellow handles work well up until fall, when they start pretending they're fallen leaves.) Tell everyone that your tools are the blue ones, then guard them with your life.

Deciding Which Tools to Buy

A BEGINNING GARDENER CAN WASTE a lot of money buying the wrong tools, so it's worth finding out something about which ones are available, what they do, and which will help you perform the jobs at hand. The list of basic tools that follows will acquaint you with most of the important ones and help you to choose among them. But first, some generalizations about quality.

When you go to buy tools, you'll notice that even within a specific brand there is usually a range of prices for a single type of tool. There might be a cheap version and an expensive version, or maybe three or four versions, each with a different price tag. Usually the one to buy is the best or next-best tool. Paying a lot of money for something does not always guarantee that you'll get quality, and there are other important considerations such as size, style, and weight to consider. But the cheapest tools are usually not economical. And there are certain things to look for that will make your choice less blind. Each specific tool has certain construction features that make it function best, and you'll come to recognize these with experience, but here are some criteria that you can apply to most tools in general.

What metal is used? The best tools are

of good steel that is labeled tempered, or heat-treated, and has been forged or drop-forged, as opposed to stamped out of sheet metal. Stainless-steel tools are even better because they don't rust, but they are usually very costly. The better tools have a solid feel to them because they're made out of heavier-gauge metal than cheap ones. A lighter-weight tool may be the right choice for you—just make sure it is light because of its design (a smaller blade or shorter handle, for example), and not because it has been made of flimsy materials.

Look at the handles. Some tools, especially small ones, have metal, plastic, or fiberglass handles, but for the most part tool handles are made out of wood. Wood is light and durable, and most people like the feel of wood-handled tools—I know I do. Look for handles made of ash, not just an anonymous "hardwood"; ash is a strong wood with a lively, springy feel to it. Make sure the grain is straight, not veering off to the side (that's the point where a break will occur), and check to see that there are no knots or other flaws. Avoid tools with handles that have been painted. That paint may be concealing faults in the wood. Better to add your own coat of paint if you like.

Sometimes there's a choice between a long-handled and a short-handled version of large tools, especially shovels. A long handle is often more comfortable to use because it enables you to remain more upright and it gives you more leverage, but in certain close-in situations it can get in your way.

In general, short-handled tools should come about to your waist when placed upright on the ground. Long ones should come at least to your nose, or even beyond that if the motion will require much of a reach (as with a rake). Tall gardeners should replace too-short handles with longer ones; short gardeners can simply cut them down to size.

Check the sockets. The way in which the working end of the tool is joined to the handle is very important. Generally what I look for here is called solid-shank construction. Most tools have a socket that the handle fits into; this socket and the working part should be all one piece, not two pieces of metal welded together. In some types of tools the wood is held in the socket simply by a tight fit. (See the mattock in Figure 16 for an example.) But the majority of tool heads have some piece of hardware, such as a rivet, that keeps them on. Look for solid, heavy-duty hardware. A wood screw is not adequate to hold a tool onto its handle, and a rivet should go all the way through the handle to the other side.

Evaluate size and weight. If you're a beginning gardener I strongly recommend that you visit either a good old-fashioned hardware store or an agricultural-supply store. You may end up buying some of your tools from a mail-order supplier since some carry specialized or particularly fine tools that are hard to find elsewhere, but I think it's important to actually hold in your hand some different kinds of tools, in different weights and sizes, and find one that matches your strength, your height, and the size of your hands. A tool that is too heavy will wear you out and slow you down. The handle length may also make a difference. Sometimes holding a tool in the store won't tell you what using it is like; if so, try borrowing one from a friend and using it for a while. Tools that last a lifetime are worth little if they're the wrong ones for you.

Basic Tools

MANY GARDEN TOOLS ARE VERY simple yet very versatile. Lots of different tasks can be performed with each one, so it's not necessary to own that many of them. But for the purpose of discussion, the following tools are grouped according to their chief function.

TOOLS FOR DIGGING AND PLANTING

Much of gardening consists of making holes in the ground so you can put plants in them. How you make those holes, and what you make them with, depends on what your ground is like, what's going to go into the holes, and the sizes and shapes of the holes you'll need to accommodate those plants. Because digging is the most tiring gardening task, it makes sense to dig with something that's sharp, efficient, and just heavy enough to do the job. You don't need to be lifting a too-heavy tool along with all that soil. Of the tools listed below, the ones I find essential are the trowel, the spade, and the digging fork.

Trowel. This indispensable little tool is used for digging small holes for planting and transplanting annuals, perennials, vegetables, and other relatively small plants. You not only dig the hole with it, but also lift the plants and move them to their new locations. Trowels are also used for weeding and cultivating, and are handy for mixing small amounts of soil and soil amendments. The broader one in Figure 16 has the widest range of uses, but the narrow one is handy for making smaller holes, for digging out an individual weed, and for working among plants that are close together. I own both,

and I usually take both with me when I go out to the garden, but you might begin with just the larger one. Other trowel styles include one in which the blade is at a right angle to the handle, excellent for making small planting holes. It's used with a dagger motion that is easier on the wrist than a digging motion if you're setting in a lot of transplants. It works best in fluffy, well-improved soil. Developed in Switzerland, its German name translates as "plant hand," since it imitates a hand scooping a hole in loose soil.

Look for trowels that have been forged or cast. Cheap trowels will bend at the tip or the handle as soon as they encounter a stubborn rock.

Bulb planter. I plant small bulbs with a trowel and large ones with a spade, but many people feel that a bulb planter is a quick way to make a lot of holes for bulbs, all exactly the right size. Use the dibble, or dibber, shown in Figure 16 if you don't have to go too deep, but for larger bulbs like narcissus and tulips, use the long-handled model also shown. It is used by pressing down with the foot to create a plug of earth, which you can then replace over the bulb. I find that extracting this plug is a nuisance, and I prefer a bulb planter that opens out to release the soil. (So far, unfortunately, I have not found this type in a long-handled version.) The dibble is also used for making holes to accommodate large seeds such as peas and corn, or skinny, deeply planted seedlings such as leeks.

Spade. When I need a bigger hole than I can make with my large trowel, I reach for either a spade or a shovel. They have slightly different uses, but first let's be clear about which is which. A spade has a relatively flat, usually rectangular blade; a shovel has a curved, scooped-out blade that can be a number of shapes, the most common being a round arc that comes to a point. For a typical spade see Figure 16; for a standard round-point shovel see Figure 18.

I use a spade to make holes with straight sides for planting trees, shrubs, and big clumps of perennials, and to dig up those same plants in order to transplant them. I also use it to edge a bed cleanly, dig a straight-sided trench, and slice through sod, weeds, and even tough shrub roots. It is the only tool that will dig up a shrub with a root ball around it, keeping the earth intact. A spade is more of a precision digger than a shovel is. It won't lift and carry soil as efficiently as a shovel, but it can lift enough soil during planting jobs that you often don't have to change tools. If you're digging with your spade and encounter something you cannot drive the spade through with your foot, take the handle in both hands, lift the spade vertically till your hands are just above your head, and plunge the blade straight down so that it slices through the stubborn obstacle. It's amazing what you can cut through this way (see Figure 10)—but be careful of your toes!

In order to perform such feats, a spade should have a D-shaped handle—the kind shown in Figure 16. It's also handy to have a foot rest on your spade—a narrow strip on top of the blade where you can place the sole of your boot while digging, for less wear and tear on your foot. I think a spade is important enough to warrant spending extra money for a good one and taking the time to keep it clean and sharpened.

Transplanting spade (Figure 16). This is a long, skinny version of the standard spade. It will dig a deep, steep-sided hole, and since it is narrow it will get in among tightly planted clumps where you want to disturb only the roots of the plant you're digging up. There is also a smaller version that's very useful for working in a crowded bed.

Edging tool (Figure 16). This is handy for putting a tidy edge on a bed. It's not as heavy as a spade and will not cut as deeply, but if you have a lot of beds to edge, and if neither the grass nor the earth is very hard to slice through, you might want a light tool like this on hand.

Digging fork (Figure 16). This tool has four thick tines with flat surfaces. I use it to loosen the soil and incorporate amendments when preparing a bed. I'm especially apt to reach for the fork instead of a spade when I'm hand-tilling soil that is firmly packed. The tines of a fork will break up clumps more efficiently than the blade of a spade will, because the digging motion alone breaks them without additional chopping. It's also excellent for loosening the soil in an established bed without disturbing the soil layers and turning up weed seeds. All you need to do is drive the tines in and wiggle them forward and back.

I use a fork when I want to lift a clump of plants (such as daylilies) that I'm moving bare-root, without taking a lot of soil with it. It's also excellent for removing weeds (such as clumps of long-rooted meadow grasses) when it's tricky to get out all the roots without breaking them. I lift the weed clump with the fork and shake it hard to make the soil fall off. (The daylily clump I would shake *gently*.) I keep two of these forks on hand to use back-to-back when I divide large, dense perennial clumps (page 185).

Forks come in a number of styles and weights, some of them with narrower, sharper, more lightweight tines, but if I

(continued on page 96)

Tools for Digging and Planting

FIG. *16*

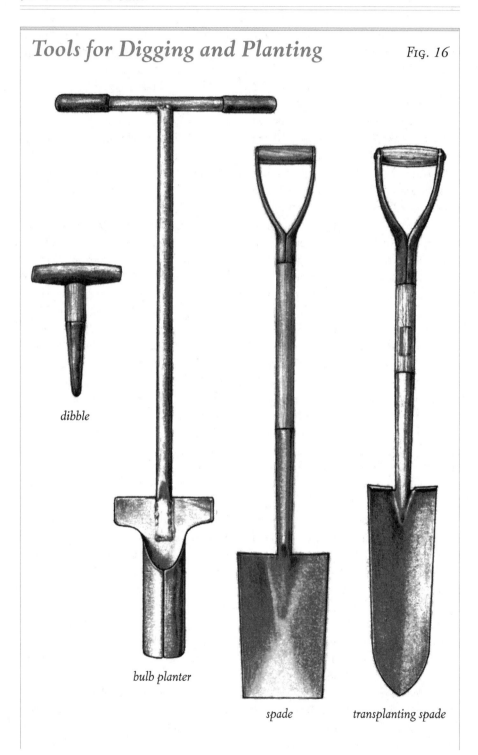

dibble

bulb planter

spade

transplanting spade

mattock

right-
angled
trowel

digging fork

edging tool

trowel   narrow trowel

(continued from page 93)

were to choose just one I would make it the heavy-duty model shown, to ensure that the tines stand up well in any encounters with rocks, roots, or compacted soil. It's not worth buying a cheap one, because the tines will soon get bent out of shape.

Mattock. This tool is useful for breaking up hard, stony soil that a digging fork cannot handle. It's also good for severing roots and for making planting holes, especially if you're standing on a slope, where a chopping motion is easier to make than a digging motion. There are several different kinds, but I prefer the one shown in Figure 16, which has a broad blade on one end and a pick (like that of a pickax) on the other. The pick will take care of extremely hard soil, and it's handy to have both tools on one handle so you can switch back and forth if need be. (A single-bladed mattock is easier to use because it is lighter, but unfortunately it's hard to find.) The joint of head and handle is not a socket but an eye attachment (in fact the tool is very similar to one called an eye hoe). Make sure the handle is good and strong and is set into the eye with a good tight fit.

TOOLS FOR LOOSENING THE SOIL

Almost any soil can benefit from being loosened and aerated. Air stimulates the activity of soil organisms and, in general, makes life easier for plants' roots. There are ways to accomplish this without having to use a power tiller, and without bringing weed seeds up from the soil layers below. The simple digging fork shown in Figure 16 does a pretty good job. Just by plunging the fork straight into the soil with your foot

and pulling the handle toward you, you're loosening and aerating. Pull out the fork, take a small step back, and plunge it in again about 6 inches from the first thrust; then keep going until you've done the whole bed.

The broadfork, shown in Figure 17, does the exact same thing only deeper, and it covers more ground. It is a larger, heavier tool with two upright handles. You plunge it into the ground with your foot, then simply rock it toward you with the tines still in the ground. This easy motion is enough to open up channels in soil without disturbing the soil layers. There are a number of versions on the market. Look for one with wooden, not metal, handles (which are unnecessarily heavy), and one in which the teeth curve away from the horizontal

Using the Broadfork

FIG. 17

Tools for Lifting

FIG. *18*

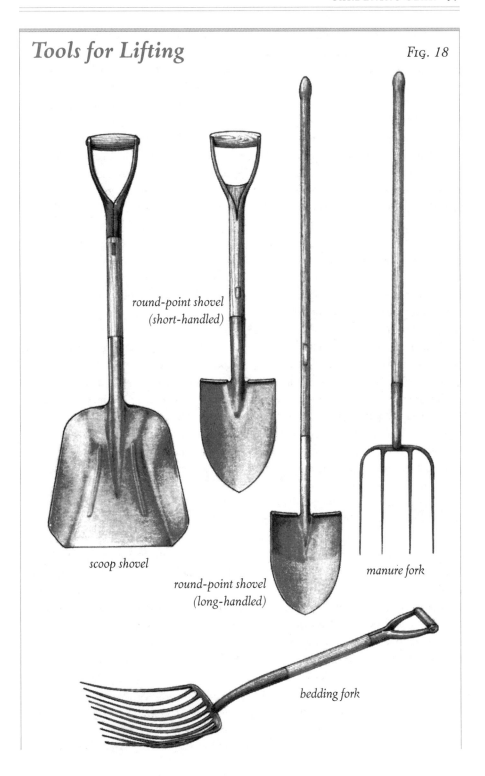

round-point shovel
(short-handled)

scoop shovel

round-point shovel
(long-handled)

manure fork

bedding fork

bar before pointing straight downward. This curve gives the tool an easy action that makes it more relaxing to use than a straight-tined model.

TOOLS FOR LIFTING

There are many lifting tools in gardening, each designed to handle materials of different textures and weights. The one essential is a round-point shovel. Whether you need any others depends on what you need to lift.

Round-point shovel (Figure 18). No manual tool moves earth quite as efficiently as this one. I use it for turning soil over, for making planting holes with rounded sides, for removing soil that I've loosened with some other tool such as a fork or spade, and for filling in the soil after I've set a tree or shrub into the hole. I load soil, compost, sand, gravel, and other materials into a wheelbarrow with it. I use it when I'm grading, to move and distribute soil, which I then even out with a rake. I use it to mix together soil, fertilizer, and other materials in a wheelbarrow. I use it to mix concrete in a wheelbarrow and then put the concrete mixture where it's needed.

There are shovels with short D-handles, but usually a long-handled one is the most versatile and the most comfortable to use. Once again, since this is an important tool I use all the time, I make sure that I buy a good one.

Scoop shovel. This shovel is much larger than the round-point and is squared-off rather than rounded (see Figure 18). I use it for picking up materials such as sawdust, which are lighter and more loosely packed than soil. It does not have a heavy, sharp blade that is angled for slicing through soil, but it holds a lot, so you can move material quickly with it.

Bedding fork. I'm very fond of this ten-tined fork (Figure 18) because I often mulch plantings with shredded bark, and this tool is perfect for lifting bark off a truck or storage pile and into a wheelbarrow. It will not, however, hold mulches that fall through the tines, such as small wood chips. This is why it's used to clean the bedding in horse stalls: clumps of manure stay on the fork while you shake the finer bedding material back onto the stall floor. I sometimes use it to move manure that's not too densely packed for the tines to penetrate, and it can handle light materials when I'm turning a compost heap. It can be found at farm-supply stores.

Manure fork (Figure 18). A manure fork with just three or four slender tines will only move something light and bulky, like loose hay or straw, but it does this beautifully and lets you avoid having to wield a heavier tool. You may only need to move loose hay for mulch occasionally, but if you can pick up this common item for a few dollars at a yard sale, it will save you some labor.

TOOLS FOR WEEDING AND CULTIVATING

You can weed your garden without having to buy any special tools. In fact, I'll often head out to weed the garden with just a trowel for the weeds I can't pull up with my hands and a digging fork for really stubborn clumps. But there are some tools that can make the job much easier, and one of them—the hoe—I consider essential if I'm growing vegetables in rows.

Garden hoe. No garden tool comes in more shapes and sizes than the hoe, because so many specialized ones have been designed for various purposes. Often these pertain to

Tools for Weeding and Cultivating

Fig. *19*

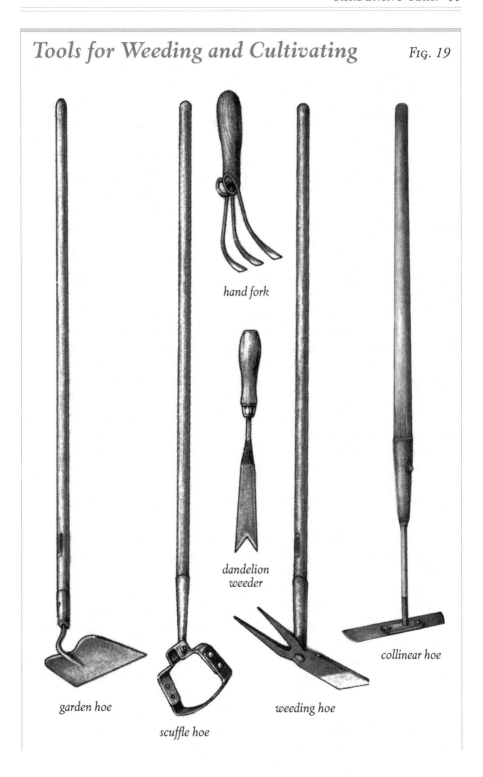

hand fork

dandelion
weeder

garden hoe

scuffle hoe

weeding hoe

collinear hoe

specific crops, so the list of traditional hoes almost sounds like a produce market: onion hoe, beet hoe, grape hoe, potato hoe, and so forth. Some gardeners like to own several hoes, each dedicated to a different task, but if you're going to invest in just one, the basic garden hoe is the most versatile. The 6-inch one shown in Figure 19 is probably the most familiar. It's used for chopping annual weeds so they can't regrow, and for moving soil around in the garden. You can use it to push soil up around a plant or draw the soil away. By holding the blade at an angle you can make a furrow for planting seeds. You can also cultivate the soil with it, breaking up the surface to let in air and moisture; in fact, when you use a hoe you're weeding and cultivating at the same time. (If you mulch your garden you won't be able to hoe it, except when a crop is newly planted and mulch has not yet been applied.) Hoes don't get the rough treatment that some tools do, but I still buy good ones that won't bend, and I always keep them sharpened.

Collinear hoe (Figure 19). If you can manage to keep after the weeds while they're still small, you'll probably use this hoe more than any other. Designed by my husband, Eliot Coleman, it is a draw hoe, not a chopping hoe. Its blade, a mere 6½-by-1-inch sliver of steel, is drawn toward you through the soil just below the surface, neatly dispatching small weeds before they become big ones. One of its biggest advantages is that it does not bring up new weed seeds from below. Another is its ergonomic design. "Collinear" means that the blade is right in line with the handle, focusing the force where it is needed. You grasp the handle with your hands in a thumbs-up position, standing fully upright, slithering the blade through the soil with a motion that is very easy on the back, even after long hours of hoeing.

I find that the blade can be used like a surgical instrument to get in and around closely spaced plants, whether they are vegetables or flowers, and the collinear is the only hoe I use in the flower garden. I even have a modified version with an extra-long handle with a right-angle grip at the end and the blade turned around. Using one hand, I push the hoe far into the bed where I'd rather not put my feet. I use a collinear hoe for vegetables as well, keeping a scuffle hoe handy for weeds in trodden paths.

Scuffle hoe. Scuffle hoes come in many different shapes, but the principle on which they work is always the same. Instead of just pulling them toward you, you can both pull and push them because they're sharp on two sides. You "scuffle" the hoe back and forth just below the soil surface, severing the weed stems. The first time I tried this hoe I knew I'd found a really efficient tool. Since most scuffle hoes are not good at hilling or furrowing, you'll probably want to own a regular garden hoe as well. Many scuffle hoes look like the one in Figure 19, also called a stirrup hoe. This is a heavy-duty tool that will even slice under mature weeds in hard soil, and it is of the type called an action hoe, oscillating hoe, or hula hoe, because the hinged blade swings forward and back as you work it, to give extra cutting power. A larger version, called a wheel hoe, has a rubber front-mounted tire, useful for big gardens with lots of paths.

Weeding hoe (Figure 19). I grew up using this hoe, which has a hoeing blade on one end and a forked weed puller on the other. To some degree it will pull out stubborn perennial weeds by the roots (if you just chopped them they would resprout).

It's an advantage to be able to do this as you encounter these weeds while hoeing, and not to have to bend over and dig them out with a hand tool.

Hand fork (Figure 19). Also called a hand cultivator, this tool is for weeding and cultivating while you're kneeling or sitting on the ground. It works faster than a trowel but less precisely, and I find it's easy to be careless and zap a valuable plant. It can also damage surface roots. Nonetheless, I mention it because so many people do like it, and it's always included (along with a trowel and a dandelion weeder) in sets of "essential small tools." A larger long-handled version with curved flat tines can be useful because it both cultivates the soil and lifts out the weeds. That one is also very good for working soil amendments into loosened soil.

Dandelion weeder. This long, skinny, notched tool (Figure 19) is also called a dock digger, a daisy grubber, and an asparagus knife. It's used for getting long, thin roots or stems out of the ground in one piece—both those you don't want, such as taprooted dock and dandelion, and those you do, such as asparagus (if you want to cut the stalk below the surface). The dandelion weeder is useful as a taproot weeder only if you follow the line of the root precisely, because if you miss and cut it, it will break off and regenerate. I usually take a chance on either pulling taprooted weeds out or digging them with a trowel or digging fork, but your aim may be better than mine. This tool is, however, excellent for extracting weeds or grass growing between flagstones and rocks.

TOOLS FOR RAKING

Dragging the tines of a rake through the soil can do many things: take something out of the soil, work something into it, or change its contours. Those tines will also remove plant debris, such as dead stems and leaves, from the surface of the ground. Rakes vary in their weight and construction according to how deep the tines need to go.

Level-head rake (T-rake). The simplest kind of rake is made of steel, has a long handle, and is flat on top, as shown in Figure 20. It's an important tool if you're creating new beds or lawns—use it for grading and smoothing the soil. Moving large amounts of earth is laborious with a rake, but for changing the contours by several inches the tool is highly efficient. Soil can be pulled toward you by using the rake with the tines down, or it can be pushed away from you if you keep the tines up. Bringing the tines down hard on the surface can break up compacted soil that will not yield by just drawing the rake across it. You can incorporate fertilizer or lime into the top layer of soil with a push-and-pull motion of the tines, or you can drag the rake through the soil to remove sticks, stones, and even small weeds. Use it to cultivate vegetable rows that are spaced far apart. Some gardeners even drag it through wide rows of seedlings to thin them.

Bow rake. This rake is the same as the one above except that it has a bow across the top (Figure 20). I prefer the level-head rake because I can turn it upside down for finer smoothing, but some people like the lighter weight and springy action you get from a bow rake.

Lawn rake (Figure 20). Also called a leaf rake or a fan rake, this tool is used to remove leaves, clippings, and sticks that have fallen onto lawns from nearby trees. But it's just as useful for clearing surface

Tools for Raking

FIG. *20*

level-head rake

lawn rake

bow rake

debris off the soil of a garden bed to make it look tidy after you've been working there—it even erases handprints and footprints. And it's extremely valuable for cleaning out debris from perennial beds in fall. Lawn rakes are made of either bamboo, metal, or plastic. Bamboo is the most attractive and has the most spring, but the strips don't last forever, even when gently used and stored under cover. The tines of metal lawn rakes get bent out of shape very easily. And both of these can come apart where the tines are joined together unless they're of very good construction, so if you buy these bamboo or metal types, buy good ones. The plastic rakes are much more durable—the tines rarely break or bend even when used by overzealous children, though the handle can get loose in the socket. Once I bought a plastic rake in a garish shade of pink, so it couldn't get lost no matter where someone abandoned it.

TOOLS FOR MOVING ROCKS

For me, rocks turn up most often when I am digging, so I'm apt to tackle the rock first with whatever digging tool I'm using, whether it's a trowel, a spade, or whatever. If I can't pry it out with a spade or shovel, even after uncovering it, I'll see if I can wiggle it with a crowbar, and then I decide whether to bother getting it out. I know that if the rock wiggles I can get it out if I have to, but it is important to know when to abandon lighter tools and move on to heavier-duty ones. Digging tools can be dulled and damaged by using them as mining tools, and there are better

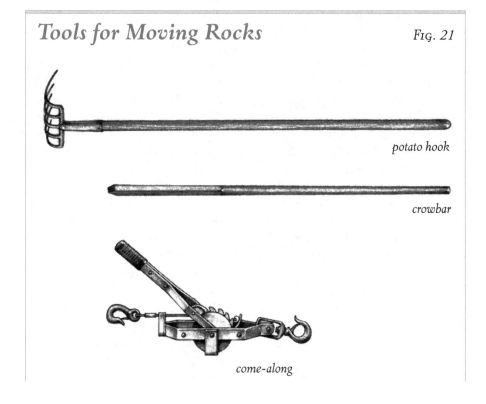

Tools for Moving Rocks   FIG. 21

potato hook

crowbar

come-along

things to use on rocks. (The mattock is an exception.)

Potato hook (Figure 21). Also called a potato hoe, this tool is designed to lift potatoes out of the soil without scratching them. It has long, curved, hooklike tines that wrap around the potato. It's a good tool to have even if you don't grow potatoes, because it will scoop potato-size rocks out of a garden or field.

Crowbar. A crowbar is used to pry rocks up out of the ground and roll them out of the way. It works as a lever and needs a fulcrum. If the rock is sitting at the bottom of a hole, the edge of the hole may work as the fulcrum, but often the best thing is to put another, smaller rock next to the one you want to move and get leverage from that. Crowbars come in different sizes—the heavier ones can lift more weight. Buy one with a chisel-shaped end (Figure 21) to help it slide underneath a rock. Unless you can't do heavy work of this sort, or just prefer not to do it, a crowbar is a very handy tool to have around. By lifting it up with both hands and then plunging the point into the ground, you can make holes for bean poles, tomato stakes, and posts for pillar roses—or holes for deep-feeding the roots of shrubs and trees.

Come-along (Figure 21). This little device will turn even the most petite gardener into Paul Bunyan. I've used it to remove huge boulders from gardens. By attaching one end of it to the rock and another to a tree or other stable object, you can winch the rock along. Rocks too large for the come-along will break its metal cables; for them you must move up to a power winch. But ultimately, some rocks are just not worth removing. Plant around them or cover them with extra soil instead.

TOOLS FOR PRUNING AND CUTTING

This is one area where I especially like to have fine-quality tools. Cutting tools are often more complicated mechanically than the kind used for jobs like digging. Good ones can be quite expensive, but if cared for properly they'll be your friends for life. I make sure I have a succession of implements that cut stems and branches of increasing sizes, so I don't damage any by asking them to do a job that will overtax them. Formulas that specify twig and branch diameters that these tools will cut do not take into account how an individual tool is made or the density of the stem that is being cut. Therefore pay attention to the way a tool is reacting. If you feel you're forcing it, go get the tool that will do the job easily.

Pruning knife (Figure 22). This is a small, curved knife that folds up and can be carried easily in a gardener's pocket, taking up a lot less space than your hand pruners. It will always be there to cut off a dead twig, poke into a woody stem to look for borers, and perform a host of handy little tasks during the course of the day—if you keep it sharp. It's great for cutting dead stems off perennials, and for trimming the tips of evergreens.

Hand pruners. Also called secateurs, these are among the most important tools a gardener can own. They cut herbaceous stems, woody twigs, and small branches, and are used for such jobs as pruning roses and other shrubs, cutting back perennials, and harvesting herbs. If I were to be extravagant about only one tool, it would be this one—and good pruners *are* expensive. If you treat yourself to a good pair, get them with bright-colored handles so you don't lose them.

Two kinds of pruners are generally available: the anvil type and the bypass type (Figure 22). Anvil pruners have one moving blade that closes against a fixed piece of softer material in the same plane. Bypass pruners have two moving blades that bypass each other just like those of scissors, except that the blades are curved. Both are good and do pretty much the same job, so you don't really need both. Gardeners usually have their preferences—I like a bypass pruner because it fits into tight places better.

It is important to keep your pruners free of dirt when they're not in use, and to keep them moving smoothly with an occasional squirt of fine lubricating oil. They also need to be sharpened periodically.

Loppers (Figure 23). If your hand pruner won't cut something, use long-handled pruners, also called loppers. These are larger and heavier than hand pruners, with two long handles. They will cut twigs and small branches of shrubs and trees. I have an ancient pair of wood-handled loppers that work fine, but metal-handled ones are sturdy and easy to use. Loppers come with both anvil and bypass blades, although I see

Tools for Pruning and Cutting   *Fig. 22*

pruning knife

hand pruner (bypass type)

hand pruner (anvil type)

hedge trimmer

short-handled grass shears

More Tools for Pruning and Cutting FIG. 23

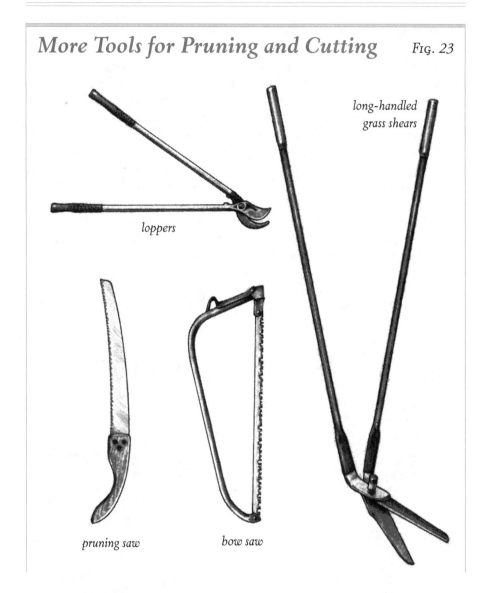

long-handled
grass shears

loppers

pruning saw   bow saw

the bypass type most often. Sometimes loppers are geared or ratcheted, to make them more powerful. They also come in various sizes. The smaller ones are good for getting into tight spaces—when you're pruning rose bushes, for example. The larger ones will cut branches of greater diameter.

Bow saw (Figure 23). If my loppers can't cut a thick branch, and if there are not a lot of other branches in the way, I might reach for a bow saw—an efficient hand saw that holds the blade at two ends and will charge through quite a bit of wood quickly. I use it to cut tree saplings and the annual Christmas tree.

Pruning saw (Figure 23). If there are a lot of branches in my way, I reach for a pruning saw because its curved blade, held at one end by a small wooden handle, can fit in among the branches and cut effectively. I sometimes use it to cut big, tough roots that defy my loppers or mattock when I'm removing a stump from the ground. Pruning saws come in varying lengths from about 9 inches to well over 20. If you're a serious tree pruner you'll probably have several sizes, including one on a long pole for pruning up high.

Obviously there are branches, trunks, and roots beyond the capability of a pruning saw, and when you get to one, you reach for an axe or a chain saw. These two are more in the realm of woodsmanship than gardening, but an axe is especially handy for severing really stubborn roots. Though a pruning saw will do this job, the soil around the root will dull the saw's blade.

Grass shears (Figures 22 and 23). These are useful for trimming grass at the edges of lawns and flower beds, but you must keep them dry, rust-free, sharpened, and well oiled or they'll be useless. Both long- and short-handled shears are available. The short-handled kind shown in Figure 22 has a nice spring to it, but my advice is to try working several in the store, to see which one you feel will do the job without tiring your hand. If you have a lot of trimming to do, you might want to invest in battery-powered shears or a string trimmer (see page 113).

Hedge trimmers (Figure 22). These are similar to grass shears but have longer blades that can cut twigs of shrubs. They're useful if you have a hedge that must be kept within bounds, but I don't like to use them to prune freestanding shrubs because they give the plants a severe, formal look. Sometimes this look is appropriate, but most gardeners overuse their hedge trimmers (see page 616 for ways to give a shrub a more natural look). They're quite handy for deadheading and cutting back perennials in fall, however, because you can cut more stems at a time with them than you can with hand pruners.

TOOLS FOR WATERING

Watering equipment has become so complicated that you almost need to be an engineer to understand it. If you live in an area where serious drought is rare, or if you follow some of the water-wise tips on pages 28 to 29, you may be able to stick to a few very simple devices.

Watering can. I use my watering can a lot: for starting seeds indoors, for taking care of houseplants and container-grown plants on the terrace, and for planting perennial clumps or annual and vegetable seedlings in the garden. It's often much easier to moisten a few planting holes with the can than to uncoil several lengths of hose and drag them across the lawn. A long-spouted can will reach under plant foliage to avoid wetting it, but I find it's more apt to spill when you carry it than a short-spouted can, so I generally use that (Figure 24). I use my can most often without the rose attachment so the water will flow faster, but I put on the rose to give newly planted seeds or delicate seedlings a gentle spray. Storing the rose inside the can is a good way to keep it from getting lost.

Hose. A garden hose (Figure 24) is like a lover that you can't live with and can't live without. No scientific advance, to my knowledge, has yet tamed its willful nature, and hoses will continue to knock over plants, get kinks in them, and get run over by cars for as long as there are gardeners. I've never had good luck with hose-coiling devices.

Tools for Watering

FIG. 24

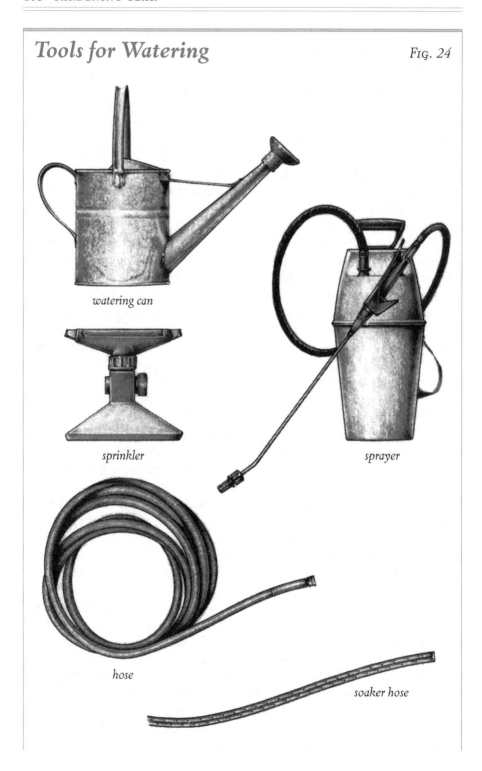

watering can

sprinkler

sprayer

hose

soaker hose

They either tip over or fail to hold all the hose you need. I prefer to coil my hoses on the ground in a figure-8 pattern instead of a circular coil (see Figure 25). This way they unwind easily without kinking.

Life with hoses is less of a living hell if you observe a few simple rules. Coil them up when not in use so they won't be damaged. Drain them and store them indoors in winter. Try not to run over or otherwise damage the couplings, since leaky couplings make the hose useless. And buy good-quality rubber hoses with brass couplings. These are expensive and sometimes hard to find, but are worth the investment, not only because they'll last much longer, but because a good hose handles better. Plastic hoses are less supple, won't coil up as easily, are more apt to kink, and may crack in cold weather. Another tip: any hose can be coiled more easily when it's warm from the sun.

Nozzles. These come in a variety of forms. Some are simple switches that allow you to turn the hose on or off at a distance from the faucet. Others have an adjustable spray.

Others have a trigger device that gives you a very long stream. Years ago, for my birthday, my son gave me a nozzle that combined the spray and the trigger and locked in any position I wanted it to. I loved it because I could stand in one spot and give most of my vegetable garden just the right amount of water without moving an inch. I am also very fond of the "wand" type (see Figure 25), which emits streams of water at the end of a metal shaft, and is great for soaking the soil underneath plants without wetting their leaves. Choose one that makes a nice gentle spray for watering newly sown flats or small, delicate seedlings. I have also had good experiences with the various click-together systems that are quick and easy to use.

Sprinklers. These have several drawbacks as watering devices. They waste a lot of water, both because of evaporation and because of wind that tends to blow the water where you don't need it. They also deliver water to the plants' foliage rather than directly to the ground. So does rain, however, and sprinklers can be very handy, especially for lawns and other large areas.

Hose Coiled in a Figure 8, with Watering Wand

FIG. 25

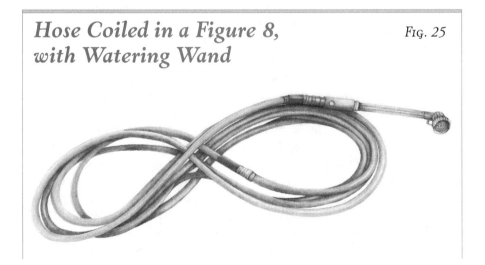

Avoid using them in windy weather. There are many kinds, from the simple whirling device shown in Figure 24 to sprinklers that walk around your lawn by themselves. Some sprinklers rotate in a full circle; others oscillate back and forth and can be set very precisely to water specific areas. Some are metal, some are plastic—either is fine as long as it is sturdy and well made.

Irrigation systems. The systems used to water large areas at a time are too varied and numerous to cover here, but they're worth investigating if you have need of them. In some areas they mean the difference between having and not having a garden. Irrigators can be as simple as a single length of soaker hose (Figure 24) that slowly leaks water into the area where you place it, or as complex as a large system of interconnecting hoses that emit little jets of water through holes or tiny nozzles. Some of these devices can be buried in the soil; others must lie on top, or under a layer of mulch. Some are very expensive while others come in kit form to cut costs and make them more adaptable to your needs. Often gardeners invent their own systems, using whatever ingenious combinations of hardware they can find. Try to find gardeners who have different systems and go watch them in action before you invest in an elaborate one. Not only will you learn what type of system will best fill your needs, but you'll be alerted to brands that really work and those that are not worth their price.

Sprayers. Even if you avoid using chemical sprays in your garden, you'll probably need to use some kind of sprayer from time to time, whether for applying a natural repellant or for foliar feeding. In choosing one, consider the volume of spray you need to use and the kind of stream you want the sprayer to deliver. The simplest type is just a pump bottle—for this you can use an empty window-cleaner bottle for small jobs such as dousing a houseplant. The old-fashioned "flit gun" will also deliver an atomized spray efficiently. Ones of this type are also used for applying a dusting of a powdered product, such as dried blood to repel deer. Though they look similar, the mechanisms inside differ for liquids and powders.

For larger jobs you can use either a trombone sprayer, which you operate by sticking one end in a bucket of solution you've mixed and then spraying, or a compressed-air sprayer, which forces water out in a stream because you've compressed the air inside with a pump. These come with various capacities, from about 1½ to 5 gallons, some of which can be carried on your back. There are even power sprayers, although these are far beyond the needs of the average gardener (remember that even 1 gallon of water weighs 8 pounds and is heavy to carry around). If you want to spray something at a distance (up in a tree, for example) and hit it with deadly accuracy, get a trombone sprayer—but be careful not to loosen the tip too much when you adjust the spray.

TOOLS FOR HAULING

Gardening always involves moving around a lot of bulky and/or heavy materials: soil, compost, bags of lime, large bales of straw or peat, rocks, gravel, piles of weeds, tools. It's important to have something to carry all this around in that you feel comfortable using. The two most common haulers available are wheelbarrows and carts. Each has slightly different uses and virtues, as you will find if you're lucky enough to own both.

Wheelbarrow (Figure 26). A wheelbarrow's greatest virtue is its maneuverability. Because it has only a single wheel, you can guide it along a narrow path, around obstacles, even along a plank laid over a muddy spot or leading up into the bed of a truck. You can mix soil in it, or even concrete for jobs like sinking gateposts. You can load all your tools, fertilizers, and pots or flats of plants into the wheelbarrow and then head for the garden. I've always used a metal contractor's wheelbarrow with a 4½-cubic-foot capacity. The plastic version of the same thing is lighter, though sturdy, so you might like to try that one.

But I do recommend buying a professional-quality barrow rather than a "garden" model unless you have a small yard or cannot wheel heavy loads. As with many pieces of equipment, the home version is often of less sturdy construction. The bed will rust out faster, the underpinnings will be less firmly attached, and the tire (which should be pneumatic) will be less tough and buoyant. A 5½-cubic-foot wheelbarrow may be the answer if you're stronger than I am, but I find that I cannot wheel it easily if it's full of anything heavy. There are also wheelbarrows with two wheels, which are more stable but less maneuverable.

Tools for Hauling

Fig. 26

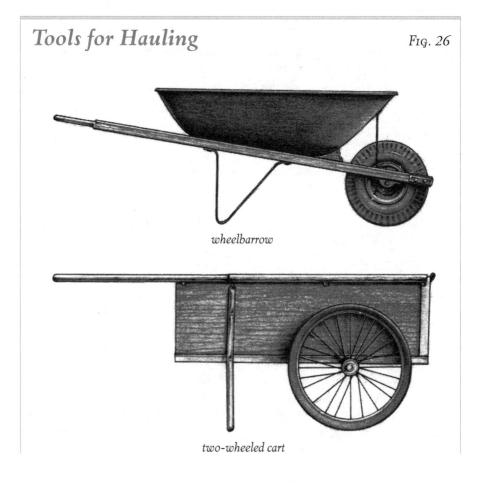

wheelbarrow

two-wheeled cart

Two-wheeled cart (Figure 26). A large, box-shaped wooden cart will allow you to carry a much larger, heavier load than a wheelbarrow will, because the weight is distributed over the two wheels. There are many of these carts on the market, and they're extremely popular. You can fit a great deal more bulky matter, such as leaves or bales of mulch hay, in a cart than you can in a wheelbarrow. The disadvantages: most of them are harder to dump with, so you may have to shovel out your load when you arrive at your destination (though some models have fold-down or removable ends). And carts are far less maneuverable than wheelbarrows, since you have to get those big wheels and that big box around things.

Carts are also inconvenient, if not downright hazardous, on steep ground. I once put a load of gravel in a garden cart and headed downhill with it. The load felt deceptively light on level ground, but on the incline the center of gravity shifted suddenly and the cart literally ran away from me. With a wheelbarrow, you'll feel the weight of a too-heavy, potentially tippy load right away and be less likely to overfill it. You cannot mix concrete or haul sloshy, soupy mixtures in a wooden cart, but you can get a lot of working gear in it to take to the garden, and you can use it as a nice flat work station when you get there. It even makes a good potting bench. There are also many smaller garden carts on the market, many of them plastic or metal. But beware of flimsy construction, and buy a small, lightweight cart only if you're doing very light hauling.

Baskets and buckets. Alas, they don't make as many bushel baskets, peck baskets, and bean baskets as they used to. These were my favorite containers for picking up weeds and for other tasks when I wanted a light, not too large container I could throw on the compost heap when it finally wore out. Plastic buckets, though not compostable, are the modern substitute. These come in sizes from about a gallon on up to garbage-can size, and are great for storing and toting soil amendments. I like to set paper fertilizer bags in them before the bags can rip and spill their contents.

Plastic tubs and buckets are also good for making potting-soil mixes or stirring up batches of liquid fertilizer. I often use the 2-gallon size for carrying out to the garden just the amount of lime or bone meal I need, so I don't have to put the whole bag in the wheelbarrow. For weeding, I use the large plastic pots that shrubs come in—the biggest and lightest ones I can find.

Power Equipment

I'M THE KIND OF GARDENER WHO prefers hand tools to power tools. They don't make a loud noise and vibrate, they're simple to use and take care of, and they're less expensive to buy and repair. If properly chosen, hand tools make work lighter—but not so light that I don't get the good physical exercise that is one of my reasons for gardening. I've built up some strong muscles from my years as a gardener, all from using hand tools.

But there are times when a power tool can save so much tedious work that even I break down and use one. I have mown lawns with a hand-pushed reel mower, cut down trees with an axe, and sawn up logs with a bow saw. But when these jobs start to take up too much of my time, I switch to a power lawn mower and chainsaw, even though I don't really enjoy using either.

Selecting power equipment for the garden is a tricky matter that's beyond the scope of this book. Home gardening machinery has long been a major source of air and noise pollution, and the best choice would be to avoid using it altogether. If there's something you think you must have, make a research project of seeking out the most environmentally friendly model. The trend is toward battery-powered electric machines that are quieter and less polluting than gasoline-driven ones. Here are a few brief comments about which machines are most useful to the gardener.

Lawn mower. If you want to mow your own lawn, invest in a *good* power mower. They are made in an enormous range of sizes and prices, from the simplest rotary mower to big ride-on lawn tractors that can perform other jobs as well, depending on what attachments you buy for them, such as tillers and brush hogs (heavy-duty mowers that cut brush). Some mowers have a mulching feature—they chop up the grass so you can leave it on the lawn, returning nutrients to the soil. Some mowers float on a cushion of air like a hovercraft, and thereby avoid obstacles such as rocks and edgings. Electric mowers are quieter, more maneuverable, less polluting, easier to start, and more pleasant to use than gas ones.

String trimmer. This handy tool is a pole with a small engine at the top, which powers a whirling string made out of tough plastic monofilament at the bottom. As the string whips around at high speed, it cuts grass and weeds. The machine works efficiently and weighs 10 pounds or less. It's useful for edging lawns or giving weedy areas a tidier look. Don't use it close to

tree trunks, especially young ones—it can nick and even girdle the trunks, thereby damaging or killing the trees. Although I favor hand tools for trimming, I sometimes employ a string trimmer that is electrically powered for easier starting. Larger string trimmers can cut brush, sometimes with a nylon string, sometimes with a circular saw blade, but are more dangerous and should be used with great caution.

Rotary tiller. This machine is standard equipment for many people with large vegetable gardens and even for those who do a lot of yard work. They have revolving tines that can cultivate the soil to varying depths, depending on the condition of the soil and the size of the tiller. With most you can adjust the depth of cultivation. Some have a hilling and furrowing attachment, which is handy at planting time. Their chief uses are for tilling a garden in preparation for planting, and for incorporating lime, fertilizer, and organic matter into the soil. They're also good for turning under cover crops (page 13) and can be useful in breaking up the soil for new lawns and gardens. The best rototillers have the tines in back and are operated by standing off to the side. This way neither the wheels nor your feet compact the soil after tilling.

I've used rototillers quite a bit and have liked them, but I have also discovered their limitations. Contrary to what most people believe, the tiller is not always the best tool for creating a new bed, especially if there are weeds and sod growing on the site. It does not cultivate deeply enough, and it breaks up the roots of perennial weeds and grasses, which only makes more of them come up. If tillers are overused, they can pulverize the soil too finely, destroying the structure so carefully built up by the soil organisms. Tillers can also create a hard-pan at a certain depth, which can interfere with drainage and good root penetration. With all this in mind, you may decide that this is a machine to rent, borrow, or share, and only for occasional use.

Shredder. Some zealous composters love this machine. They can chop up materials such as leaves and thereby greatly speed up decomposition. There are both electric and gasoline-powered models. The ones big enough to really do the job are noisy and expensive, and they take up enough storage space to make you wonder if they're worth the use they get—often just a week or two in autumn at leaf time. It might be better to rent a shredder in fall, or just make compost the old-fashioned way (see pages 14 to 18).

Other Aids

A MULTITUDE OF ITEMS CAN BE FOUND in gardeners' tool sheds in addition to tools, some of them essential, some of them necessary only for specific gardening situations you may or may not encounter—netting to keep birds off fruit, for example. Some, such as devices for starting seeds, are dealt with in other chapters of this book. Others are items that, while essential to the gardener, are really part of the carpentry or household-tool department, such as a 100-foot tape (Figure 27) for measuring beds, and a screwdriver (to slip through the tab at the end and then into the ground) to hold it in place. Scissors are in constant use, perhaps to snip twine for tying tomato plants—and to snip off a few ripe tomatoes while you're at it. I keep an ordinary

house broom in the toolshed to sweep off stone paths after I've messed them up by weeding.

A "garden line" or "planting line" is also helpful. There are several types. One entails a pointed piece of metal to insert into the ground, with a long cord attached for laying out nice straight rows for vegetables. Another type has twine with a toothed end for wrapping around a wooden stake, and a little hand crank that winds up the twine neatly inside the casing when you've finished with it. One-inch by 1-inch wooden stakes with pointed ends can be purchased in various lengths, to mark out the corners of a bed or other key landmarks. And it's great to have a big rubber deadblow mallet for hammering them in.

You will no doubt accumulate your own collection of miscellaneous paraphernalia. I try to keep mine to a minimum. Catalogs arrive with hundreds of suggestions about "gardening aids you cannot do without"—most of them expensive, brightly colored, and made of plastic. I usually flip through and decide I can do without all of them. My advice is to keep gardening simple. Buy a few good implements and treat them well.

100-Foot Tape Measure   FIG. 27

Maintaining and Storing Gear

TAKING CARE OF TOOLS MEANS NOT leaving them out in the rain, remembering to clean off the dirt when you've finished using them. This will keep the metal parts from rusting, the mechanisms moving smoothly, and the wood handles from deteriorating. Power equipment should always be stored out of the weather and kept clean and dry. Wheelbarrows and carts should also go under cover. If you have to keep them outdoors in rain or snow, upend them so that water doesn't sit in them and rust the metal or rot the wood.

It's much easier to take care of tools when you have a convenient place to store them. This will encourage you to put them away after use, and you won't waste time searching for them when you're ready to begin a job. If you have a large toolshed or a spacious area in your garage where you can put them, all the better; but even a tiny shed or a corner of the garage can work if you organize it well. You can get by with just a pegboard or row of nails from which to hang small hand tools, and a barrel in which to stick long-handled tools—handle down and working end up for quick identification. Figure 28 shows how a modest-size storage area might be organized by putting long tools in a barrel, hanging tools with a D-grip on the wall, and arranging small tools on a pegboard. The workbench provides a surface for jobs like marking plant labels, sorting packages of seeds, and even starting seeds in flats without having to bring the mess indoors. Shelves underneath it provide space for pots, soil amendments, and other supplies. And there's space on the floor where bagged supplies can sit upright in their containers. If the area is large enough to accommodate big items like lawn mowers, all the better.

Tools, from hand pruners to spades and hoes, will also do a faster, cleaner job if they're sharpened from time to time. For most large tools, I use a mill bastard file (a type used for filing metal, with an intermediate degree of roughness and teeth in parallel lines rather than crisscrossed), drawing it repeatedly across the side of the tool that's making the cut. Look at the blade first to see which side was sharpened originally (sometimes both sides are sharpened) and at what angle. For cutting tools such as pruners, a whetstone is best. Some gardeners who put their tools to heavy use invest in an electric grindstone to keep them in working order.

What to Wear

ONLY A WOMAN WOULD BRING THIS up, right? Wrong. In my experience, male gardeners are forever discussing the best boot, the best pants. The best gardening clothing for you is just as much a matter of personal taste as the best tools, and you'll end up wearing what feels comfortable.

Boots. Good, sturdy work boots with leather soles are long lasting and are the best to wear if you're out spading all day. They make the spading easier on the soles of your feet. But rubber boots are best for general work if it's wet, and insulated winter boots if it's very cold. Sneakers may feel right if it's hot and you're not spading a lot. I've also become a great fan of gardeners' clogs. These are made of plastic and can be ordered from a number of garden-supply catalogs. I find them durable, comfortable, and lightweight, but their best feature is that they don't become wet and soggy the way sneakers do. Most come with removable, quick-drying cork inserts. Both shoes and inserts can be hosed off with ease.

Pants. Heavy-duty cotton trousers sold as "work pants" are sensible—they're sturdy and long wearing, if not exactly flattering to the female form. Overalls have nice big pockets for items like pruners and fence staples, but I've given up on them, mainly because you have to undo the straps to shed an extra sweater or shirt, and if you wear those garments on top you have to shed them to get to the straps. I'm most comfort-

Organizing Your Storage Area

able in stretch jeans, or in old corduroys that are soft and supple from many washings.

Shirts. In my New England climate gardeners like the layered look because the temperature can change so drastically during the course of the day. I might start out wearing a T-shirt, a flannel shirt, a sweatshirt or sweater, and maybe even an old parka on top of that, then shed all but

Fig. 28

the T-shirt as the sun and my work heat me up. (Though even in heat there are times I leave on the long-sleeved shirt as protection against thorns, poison ivy, sunburn, or mosquitoes.)

Hats. Many gardeners like to wear a big-brimmed hat for shade. A wide hat also discourages gnats and certain other insects that are reluctant to venture under the brim. A bandanna helps to keep hair off your face, and you can soak it in water to keep your head cool when it's very hot. There are also hats—and shirts as well—that enclose you in netting if the blackflies are biting.

Gloves. Gardening gloves (Figure 29) are essential. They keep your hands from getting rubbed raw from very long, hard jobs, and are crucial if you're dealing with thorny plants like roses and scratchy ones like junipers. Leather gloves give you the most protection (a company called Womanswork sells excellent ones sized for female hands). Lightweight cotton ones are fine for weeding. If you prune a lot of prickly shrubs, buy a pair of leather gloves long enough to cover your wrists, or heavy fabric ones with leather palms and fingertips.

Frankly, I hate to wear gloves, because they're hot and because I garden so much

Gardening Gloves

Fig. 29

by touch: how the soil texture feels, how moist the soil is, where a weed's root system begins. But there are times when I want to keep my hands warm, or clean, or when I'm working near poison ivy. Then I force myself to wear gloves.

An important note about poison ivy, poison oak, and poison sumac: all parts of the plants are toxic, even the roots, and at *any time* of the year. Even dead leaves will give you the rash. The irritating oil will stay on your gloves, shoes, pants, shirt, and tools, so handle all these with as much caution as the plant itself if you've been working in a spot where it is growing. Many people think their rash is spreading when they are just reinfecting themselves every day by putting on contaminated gloves or sneakers. Throw them all into the washing machine with a strong detergent.

Whatever clothes you wear for gardening, be advised that they'll be permanently grubby, and that you really need a separate wardrobe for gardening and other outside chores. Getting dirty just goes with the territory.

CHAPTER 4

How to Buy Plants

Y OU'VE DECIDED WHAT KINDS OF gardens you want and where you want to put them. You've gained some understanding of how plants grow, where they need help, and what kind of equipment you're going to need to give them that help. You've prepared your soil, and now you're actually ready to go out and buy those plants and seeds and see them through life.

This is where you can get a case of cold feet. Throughout this book I tell you to "choose the right plant" for your climate, "choose the right plant" for our soil type, "choose the right plant" for the setting. You have some idea of what to buy. But now it's real life, and you're standing in a crowded nursery surrounded by green leaves, and they all look alike, except that they have different labels on them, mostly in Latin.

Plant Names

T HREADING YOUR WAY THROUGH THE nursery circus needn't be a nightmare, and I'll give you a brief "survivor's guide" to plant nurseries in a minute; but first a few words about those Latin names, because there they are, and ignoring them won't make them go away. In fact, they're very useful and can save you a lot of trouble.

If you only grow basic vegetables and fruits, you'll come across Latin names much less often than you will if you grow ornamental plants; nevertheless, plant nomenclature is worth understanding regardless of what you grow, because sooner or later you'll probably have to deal with it. All the plant descriptions in this book give Latin

names as well as common names and can be used as references when you're planning your garden. In many cases the Latin name has become the most common way to identify the plant. And having both written down will help you know exactly what you're getting.

A plant's botanical name usually consists of two Latin words written in italics. The first designates the genus (plural, genera) to which the plant belongs—a group of plants with similar characteristics. The second designates the plant's species—a smaller group within the genus. The species name usually describes one outstanding characteristic of the plants in that group.

For example, let's take a familiar plant, the Johnny-jump-up. Its common name suits it well, because after going to seed it jumps up all over your garden. Its Latin name, *Viola tricolor*, tells you that it belongs to the genus *Viola* and that its species name is *tricolor*, describing its petals, which are marked with three colors: purplish blue, white, and yellow.

Since few of us speak Latin, why not stick with a perfectly good name like Johnny-jump-up? While that might work fine for Johnny-jump-up, it gets confusing when a plant has several names. For example, *Monarda didyma* is commonly known as bee balm, or bergamot, or Oswego tea. *Stachys lanata* is variously called lamb's ears, woolly betony, and Saviour's flannel. And for an even more complicated example, consider the common purple lilac. Its botanical name is *Syringa vulgaris*. But there is another plant, a shrub with fragrant white flowers, whose common name is sometimes syringa (I don't know why) and sometimes mock orange (because the flowers look and smell like orange blossoms).

That plant is neither a lilac nor an orange, and its Latin genus name is *Philadelphus*. If you went shopping for what you called syringa (meaning *Philadelphus*), you might end up buying a lilac by mistake, since the plant could well be labeled with its Latin name, *Syringa*.

The best way to avoid muddles like these when you go to buy a plant is to call it by the name that does not vary—the Latin one—or at least have it handy should any confusion arise. (Sometimes the Latin names change too, when botanists reclassify plants, but this does not happen often.) You may feel awkward or downright pretentious using Latin names, but they will save you from getting the wrong plant. A rose by any other name may smell as sweet, but if you're not careful it may turn out to be a hellebore (if it's a Christmas rose) or a hibiscus (if it's a rose of Sharon). Besides, the botanical names can be just as descriptive and informative as the common ones once you know what they're telling you about a plant. Take *Chamaecyparis pisifera* 'Filifera Aurea,' a shaggy dwarf evergreen tree whose yellow-tipped needles hang in rather spidery fronds. Its common name is gold-thread false cypress. Its Latin says that it looks like (*chaemae-*) a cypress (*-cyparis*) and is pea-bearing (*pisifera*), thread-bearing (filifera), and gold-colored (aurea). Species named *divaricata* or *procurrens* are likely to spread widely in your garden.

And what is *Syringa vulgaris?* A vulgar lilac? Actually, *vulgaris* just means "common" or "ordinary." A friend of mine is still kidding me about the vulgar plant I put in his garden—*Calluna vulgaris*, or common heather. For some other species names and their English translations, see page 122.

Cultivars

SOMETIMES THE GENUS AND SPECIES names are followed by a third name denoting a subdivision within the species, composed of plants that differ from other members of the species in minor ways. If this third name is in Latin, and in italics, it is either a subspecies or a variety that has simply appeared in nature without human intervention. It could be the result of plants cross-pollinating in the wild or of a chance mutation. (Sometimes you will see the abbreviations "subsp." or "var." preceding the word.) More frequently, this third name is written in normal (not italicized) type, capitalized, enclosed in single quotes—as in *Syringa vulgaris* 'Alba,' the white version of the common (normally purple) lilac. This means that it is a "cultivar" (a contraction of "cultivated variety") and was produced by human efforts. Sometimes cultivars are created by cross-pollinating (hybridizing) two different species or two pure, inbred cultivars possessing different traits, in order to produce an entirely new plant. (See page 125 for a further discussion of hybrids.) Other times it is done by finding a naturally occurring specimen with some unusual characteristic—a mountain laurel with deeper pink buds, for example, or a more strongly flavored mint. This process is called selection, and it occurs in nature all the time as plants adjust, through evolution, to their surroundings. The plant breeder then produces quantities of this new selected plant, not by growing out its seeds but by propagating it vegetatively— that is, by dividing the original clump, by taking cuttings and rooting them, or by a

(continued on page 124)

GUIDE TO BOTANICAL NAMES

THE FOLLOWING LIST CONTAINS SOME OF THE COMMON LATIN (AND OCCASIONally Greek) descriptive words found in plant names (generally the epithet for the species), with their translations. The endings may vary; for example, words ending in -a can also end in -us, those ending in -is can also end in -e. But you'll always be able to recognize the root word, which stays the same.

aestivalis—of summer
alba—white
alpinus—alpine
alta—tall
amara—bitter
amethystina—violet
angustifolia—narrow-leaved
annua—annual
aquifolia—sharp-leaved
arborea—treelike
arenaria—of sandy places
argentea—silver
armata—armed
arvensis—of the fields
atropurpurea—dark
    purple-red
aurantica—orange
aurea—gold
auriculata—with ears
australis—southern
autumnalis—of autumn
azurea—sky blue
baccata—berrylike
barbata—barbed, bearded
biennis—biennial
blanda—mild, pleasant
borealis—northern
caerulea—blue
caesia—blue-gray
caespitosa—tufted
campanulata—bell-shaped
campestris—of the fields
canadensis—of the New
    World, of North America

candida—white
capitata—headlike
cardinalis—red
centifolia—many-leaved
cerea—waxy
chinensis—of China
chrysos—gold
cilians—fringed
cinerea—light gray
citrina—yellow
citriodorus—lemon-scented
coccinea—scarlet red
coelestina—sky blue
compacta—compact
concolor—of one color
conferta—crowded
conica—cone-shaped
contorta—twisted
cordata—heart-shaped
cordifolia—with heart-
    shaped leaves
cornuta—horned
coronata—crowned
crassa—thick, fleshy
cristata—crested
crocea—yellow
cruenta—bloody
cyanea—blue
damosa—bushy
decumbens—lying down
decussata—at right angles
disticha—with two rows
divaricata—spreading
diversa—varying

edulis—edible
elata—tall
elegans—slender, elegant
excelsa—tall
eximia—distinguished
fastigiata—compactly erect
filifera—slender, threadlike
flabellata—fan-shaped
flava—yellow
flore pleno—with double
    flowers
floribunda—flowering freely
foetida—strong- or
    ill-smelling
fragrans—fragrant
glauca—grayish white
glomerata—clustered
gracilis—slender
granda—large, showy
grandiflora—large-flowered
helix—twisting
herbacea—herbaceous,
    not woody
heterophylla—with leaves
    of different shapes
hortensis—of gardens
hyemalis—of winter
incana—gray
insularis—of islands
intermedia—intermediate
    in color, shape, habit
lacianata—fringed, jagged
lactiflora—white-flowered
laevigata—smooth

lanata—woolly
lanceolata—lance-shaped
latifolia—broad-leaved
liana—climbing
lignea—woody
littoralis—of the shore
lobata—lobed
lutea—yellow-orange
maculata—spotted
marginalis—margined
maritima—of the sea
meleagris—spotted
microphylla—small-leaved
minor—small
mollis—soft, hairy
montana—of the mountains
moschata—musk-scented
mucronata—pointed
multiflora—many flowered
mutabile—changeable
nana—dwarf
nigra—black
nivalis—white, or growing
  near snow
nivea—white
nodulosa—with nodules
nummularia—round,
  coin-shaped
nutans—nodding
obtusa—blunt, flattened
occidentalis—western
odorata—fragrant
officinalis—medicinal,
  of the apothecaries
orientalis—eastern
palustris—of swamps
paniculata—with loosely
  branched flowers
parvifolia—small-leaved
patens—open-formed,
  spreading
patula—spreading
pendula—weeping, hanging

perennis—perennial
pilosa—shaggy
pinnata—feather-shaped
pisifera—pea-bearing
platyphylla—broad-leaved
plena—full, double
plicata—with pleated petals
plumaria—plumed
plumosa—feathery
praecox—early
praestans—excellent
pratensis—of meadows
procumbens—trailing
procurrens—extending
prostrata—prostrate
pulchra—beautiful
pulsatilla—shaking in the
  wind
pumila—dwarf, small
punctata—dotted
pungens—sharp, pointed
pura—pure, clean
purpurea—purple
pusila—small and
  insignificant
pyramidalis—conical
quinquefolia—with five
  leaflets
radicans—rooting as it
  creeps
regalis—stately, regal
repens—creeping
reptans—creeping
reticulata—veined, netted
riparia—of river banks
rivala—of brooks
rivalara—of brooks
rosea—rose-colored
rotundifolia—round-leaved
rubra—red
rufus—ruddy
rugosa—wrinkled
rupestris—growing on rocks

saccharata—sweet
sacramentosa—having long
  runners
sagittalis—arrow-shaped
salicifolia—with willowlike
  leaves
sanguinea—red
saxatilis—living among
  rocks
scaber—rough
scariosa—thin, shriveled
sempervirens—everliving
  or evergreen
serpyllum—mat-forming
simplex—undivided
speciosa—showy
spectabilis—spectacular
spicata—spiked
spinulosa—spiny
spuria—false
stelleriana—starlike
stolonifera—with rooted
  runners
suffruticosa—shrubby
superba—magnificent
tectorum—of roofs
tenua—thin
tomentosa—woolly, hairy
uliginosa—of marshy places
variegata—irregularly
  colored
vegetus—of vigorous
  growth
verna—of spring
vernalis—of summer
verticillata—arranged in
  a whorl
violetta—violet-colored
virgineus—pure white
virginiana—of Virginia,
  of the United States
viscaria—with sticky
  stems

(continued from page 121)

sophisticated process called tissue culture. These new plants will all be identical to the original one.

The propagation of plants to obtain new varieties is a complex topic, but it's useful for the shopper to know a few simple things. The human hand has produced thousands of new plants that not only grow better in our gardens, but also make gardening more fun. Some, such as rust-proof asparagus, have been developed to resist specific diseases. Others better withstand climatic problems: spinach that is less apt to go to seed in hot weather, for example, and tomatoes that set fruit even when it's cold. We have created giant fruits and flowers and miniature fruits and flowers. We search for colors never found in nature, as in the elusive blue rose, and even for the absence of color, as in the quest for the white marigold—surely a search as long and obsessive as Captain Ahab's. Sometimes these advances are welcome, and sometimes they seem questionable. It's a subjective thing. From time to time I'll mention cultivars I consider outstanding in the chapters dealing with individual plants.

CULTIVARS VS. SPECIES

A wild plant from which garden cultivars have been derived is often referred to as "the species." The common lilac I mentioned is a good example of a species that is still as familiar as the named varieties that have been produced from it. Usually this is not the case. Hybrid roses, for example, are more familiar to us than most species of wild rose. Species plants vary greatly in their suitability to the garden. Among vegetable cultivars, most have undergone extensive

selection and hybridization to give them greater productivity, better flavor, bigger size, disease resistance, and other desirable traits. Even most "heirloom" vegetable varieties are hybrids that were bred long ago, not original species (for more on this subject see page 250).

Original species of ornamental plants are more commonly grown, but they're still far less available than cultivars. Often you must go to a source that specializes in native or unusual plants. That said, some cultivars are closer to the original species than others. Often the choice is simply a matter of taste. For instance, I prefer the red-and-yellow columbine (*Aquilegia canadensis*) that is native to the eastern United States rather than the large, showy bicolored hybrids. I prefer single hollyhocks (*Alcea rosea*), which are old-fashioned cultivars, to the modern powder-puff doubles that collapse of their own weight when it rains, then lie on the ground like soggy Kleenex.

Species plants are often more fragrant than hybrids as well, an example being the tall white *Nicotiana alata*. The fragrance has almost been bred out of many modern rose and sweet pea varieties in favor of other factors such as size, color variation, and length of bloom. Some heliotropes, plants once prized for their sweet scent, now have no fragrance at all. On the other hand, I'm always delighted to find a hybrid aster that doesn't flop, or a new chrysanthemum that is actually hardy in my region. So I check to see what is new and better each year, but at the same time keep an eye out for original species or great-but-forgotten hybrids that have become newly available.

Often these can only be obtained by mail order, and often only as seeds. But another advantage of original species and many heirlooms is that you can save their seeds and grow plants that will "breed true."

Saving Seeds

Acquiring plants isn't always about shopping. The seed business in America may have been flourishing for several hundred years, but that's a mere moment in the history of human seed use. For millennia, farmers and gardeners have saved seeds from their current year's crop to plant the following year, and many still do. They do it not because progress has passed them by, nor necessarily for economy—although clearly money is saved. Seed saving is a skilled craft, and one on which our agricultural history rests.

Seed saving is based on the process of selection (as described above on page 121), and it's a way you can improve your plants from one year to the next. Here's how it works. By letting a few of your biggest, healthiest, most perfect beets stay in the ground over the winter and go to seed, then collecting that seed and planting it for the new crop, you improve the chances that those admirable traits will show up again. Each year that you select for those traits, the chances are even greater. What you're doing is developing your own strain of that variety, one that is better adapted to your own particular soil and climate.

The majority of seed packets commonly sold are patented F_1 (first-generation) hybrids produced by crossing two parent varieties. If you save and plant seeds from these hybrids, they will *not* produce offspring reliably like themselves. For this you must obtain open-pollinated varieties.

These more or less mimic the plant from which the seed was collected. Many companies do sell open-pollinated seeds, and will indicate this in their catalogs. But the most enjoyable thing to do is to save and swap the seeds with friends, or pass them down from one generation to the next in your family.

Some seeds are particularly easy to save—peppers, for example. You just remove the seeds from a pepper, dry them on a plate or paper towel, and store them in a closed jar to completely exclude moisture. Keeping the jar in a cool, dark place will also help insure seed viability. Tomato seeds are a little more work. I ferment them in a glass of water until their pulp dissolves and they sink to the bottom. Then I dry them on a screen and store them the same way as the peppers. Other easy crops to save are beans (just dry the seeds in the pod), garlic (replant individual cloves in the fall), and potatoes (choose the nicest tubers from the best plants at harvesttime, and store them over the winter for spring planting).

Some crops are tricky. Corn varieties, because corn is wind-pollinated, must be grown at a large distance from one another to keep them from crossing. If you save squash seeds, you must pollinate the flowers by hand to keep the strain pure, lest bees bring in pollen from another variety. Biennial crops such as carrots and beets must, as described above, be left in the ground to make seed the following year (or stored, then replanted).

Seed saving is intriguing and fun, once you're drawn into the habit. It becomes part of the rhythm of growing your own food and flowers, and gives you a fine sense of self-sufficiency. It also fosters food sufficiency for the planet. With food crops, a handful of hybrid varieties of a few mainstay crops are fast replacing the thousands that people have so long grown. These thousands are the genetic foundation on which modern varieties rest, and if they're lost we won't have that foundation to dip into when we need them. Home gardeners who grow and save heirloom seeds can play a big part in keeping crop diversity alive. The sources listed starting on page 777 can give you guidance and inspiration in this endeavor.

Where to Buy Plants

THE BEST WAY TO BUY PLANTS IS ALMOST always to go to a well-established nursery that guarantees its plants and actually grows much of its own stock. It can be a large nursery or a tiny one—the important thing is the quality of its plants. Ask the proprietors if they grow their own. Most places "buy in" at least some of their material, either because of crop failures or because it's hard to grow everything for which there is a demand unless you sell a very specialized range of plants. But if you do find a place where the owner is a grower, chances are good that she or he can give you more dependable, disease-free plants, and ones better adapted to your particular region. These plant sellers also tend to be more knowledgeable about their stock. Most nursery owners, and their staff, do know Latin names and can discuss the relative merits of different varieties. Even if the person who waits on you is there more for brawn than expertise, someone can usually be found who can enlighten you about what to buy and how to grow it.

Today plants seem to be sold everywhere—supermarkets, big-box stores, roadside stands. They often cost less at places like supermarkets than they do in nurseries, and it's tempting to toss a box of petunias or an African violet into the grocery cart along with the chicken parts and yogurt. Sometimes these plants work out fine, but you're always taking a chance. Even if they've been well grown, plants at these stores are at the mercy of a staff who may not water them regularly. The azaleas and roses standing outside next to the shopping carts may or may not be hardy in your region, and no one is likely to know for sure. Nevertheless, it's sometimes worth giving them a try *if* they're labeled as a variety that you know, and *if* they appear to be healthy, bushy plants.

One place where I do tend to trust the plants is at a church fair or benefit plant sale. Plants at such affairs are usually grown by local people—good gardeners who either are standing right there or can be found if you have a question. Garden clubs and plant societies are also great places to swap plants and knowledge with other gardeners.

What to Look For

YOU MIGHT HAVE TO POKE AROUND nurseries for a while before you feel confident about judging the quality of the plants you see, but if you look closely you can easily tell what to avoid:

Plants with yellowed leaves. A number of things can cause yellowing, all of them bad. In general, a bright green or dark green leaf color is a sign of health, but even here you can never be quite sure. The plants might have been pumped up with a big dose of quick-fix high-nitrogen fertilizer but still have a weak, undernourished root system. If it's a flat of annual vegetable or flower seedlings, look at the seed leaves—the little pair of leaves closest to the ground, which were the first to emerge. If these are a good green, it means the plant had a good start and has been cared for since.

Plants with wilted leaves. A good watering might perk them up. *Might.* But you don't know if they've been neglected often, thus permanently weakening the plant.

Tall, spindly plants. Whether you're buying annuals, perennials, or shrubs, you generally want compact, bushy plants with many stems. Taller is usually not better and often indicates that the plant suffered from lack of light during growth, was not pinched or pruned enough, or has been growing in a pot for too long.

Plants in bloom. Many nurseries display these most prominently, because blooming plants lure the most buyers. But if you have a choice between a plant in flower and one that hasn't bloomed or even budded yet, choose the latter. Dormant shrubs and trees, perennials a few inches high or barely showing, and annuals no more than 6 inches high are all preferable. Let them do their growing in your garden, not in nursery pots. If the nursery grows its own plants, ask if you can buy younger plants in the greenhouse that they haven't put out yet.

Signs of bugs or disease. Look for insect bodies, stickiness, oddly distorted leaves or crowns, blackened areas, mushy or rotten places, spots, blotches, streaks, holes, or jagged bites taken out of the leaves. Not only will the plants have been weakened by the problem, but the insect or disease may spread to other plants in your garden.

Weeds in the pots. Weeds rob the plant of water and food and show neglect by the nursery.

Potbound plants with roots crawling out of the bottom. These are often starved, and may contain girdling roots that have wound their way around the pot and can strangle the main root years later. They may well respond to good care, but try to loosen the root systems before you plant them.

Plants with small, underdeveloped root systems. These plants will come out of the pot if you pull only slightly. Look for a pot in which the plant seems more rooted-in. Damaged or rotted roots indicate weakened plants.

Nicks, scars, and cracks in woody trunks and stems. These may have weakened the plant, and they can be an entry point for disease. They also point toward general neglect.

Balled plants where the ball is dry or damaged. Balled-and-burlapped trees and shrubs must be kept watered and handled very carefully. If the ball of earth is broken up so that it feels like a bag of loose soil when you tip it, do *not* buy the plant. The roots will surely have suffered and are a poor risk for transplanting.

Taking Your Plants Home

MAKE SURE YOU HAVE A GOOD LEVEL place on the floor or in the trunk of your car, where the plants can sit upright without their tops bending over. Wear something you can get dirty (plant shopping is an extension of gardening), and bring newspaper or a sheet of plastic to put under the plants if you're fussy about your vehicle. If you're carrying them in the open bed of a truck, put the plants near the cab, out of the wind, or better yet put a cap or tarp over them to protect them from drying and breaking, especially if it's a long ride home. And drive slowly! If you do seventy, that's a hurricane-force wind on your plants. Plants that have just leafed out are the most vulnerable (another reason to buy dormant ones). If you must tilt the tall plants, lean them toward the rear of the truck. Leaning with—not against—the wind, they'll be less battered. Putting annual and vegetable seedlings and potted perennials in cardboard boxes is a good way to protect them—better than a tarp, which can flap against their foliage and injure it.

Try to have sites chosen and planting areas ready for the new plants before you go shopping, so they don't sit around for a long time unplanted. People—myself included—often buy too much at one time, just because good plants are so hard to resist. If you must hold plants over, set them in shade or semishade. Put them close to a water source so you can keep pots and root balls well moistened. Water root balls carefully; the force of a hose can damage the ball. Better to turn a gentle sprinkler on the plants for several hours each day. Piling mulch around balled plants also helps to keep them from drying out.

Mail-Order Plants

S HOPPING BY MAIL IS AN ACCEPTABLE alternative once you know a little more about what you want. The best reason to order by mail is that a greater variety of plants is available, especially after you've amassed a good collection of catalogs or online sites. (See page 764 for information on plant sources.) You can sometimes buy younger plants in greater quantities, grow them to greater size yourself, and save money.

Read the plant descriptions in the catalogs very carefully. It's important to know not only the Latin names of the plants you're ordering, but something about their age and size as well. The more reputable the supplier, the more it will tell you about its plants. If perennials are described as seedlings or cuttings, expect something much smaller than plants that are called large divisions. Among woody plants, one-year grafts will be smaller than two-year-old plants. Specific plants sometimes have their own terminology. A peony division might be described as having three eyes or five eyes. New shoots will emerge for each eye, and the five-eyed division will be a larger, more expensive plant than the three-eyed. A daylily might be described as having one, two, or three fans (each fan is a spray of foliage that will eventually send up a flower stalk). Sometimes the size of the pot it comes in will be the key piece of information in determining the size of a mail-order plant: 2¼-inch, 4-inch, quart, gallon, and so forth.

The plants that arrive in the mail will often be dormant, because that is the best way to ship most of them. That's fine, since it is best to plant them at this stage, anyway; there will be less transplanting shock than there would be if plants had leafed out. But be prepared for something that may look rather insignificant at first. I once ordered a hundred young rugosa rose plants for a client's hedge, knowing they would make a fine show eventually. I could wrap one hand around the whole bundle. Planted, the roses looked like a row of little sticks—if you got up close. If you moved back a few steps they were invisible. "They grow really fast," I reassured neighbors passing by. At the end of the day I had fears that my client would feel a little shortchanged and decided to give her some older plants. The next day I dug up the sticks and planted them at my own house, and at my client's I put in a row of 2½-foot potted roses that were bushy and leafed out. Some were even starting to bloom. That night I got phone calls asking me where I had gotten the Amazing Fast-Growing Rose, and although I told everyone the whole tale, I fear I still bask in some undeserved glory on that street. The "sticks" at home did fine, and caught up to the others within a few years.

Try to place your mail order well before planting time, to be sure of getting the varieties you want. Usually the nursery will ship at the best time to plant what you've ordered, for your particular area; they may even ask you to specify a date when you'll be there to receive the plants.

Some mail-order companies do a great job of packing and some don't—and you may not be able to predict this in advance. Usually plants are shipped bare-root—i.e., without soil. When you get your order it's important to open the package right away, water the plants, and either plant them or store them in the proper way. For bare-root woody plants, heel them into the ground (page 40) and keep them watered until you can plant them. For herbaceous plants it's a good idea to pot them up in compost or in rich, light soil and set them outdoors in semishade to harden them off (get them used to outdoor conditions) for a week or two before you plant them. Protect any tender new stems and leaves from the burning sun. Then plant them along with their new compost or soil after they've made some growth. They'll appreciate the easy transition.

The biggest drawback to mail-ordering is the exaggerated claims made by many of the catalogs, both in pictures and text. The giant blossoms in heightened colors, the hedges spilling over with thousands of blooms, could only have been photographed on a distant planet discovered by the starship *Enterprise*. Sometimes catalog plants have made-up names, presumably more evocative than the real ones, common or botanical, that leave you guessing. (Just what is "Gilded Twinkles," anyway?) This is more of a problem in the big soup-to-nuts catalogs than in those of the smaller, more specialized nurseries; but I look through them anyway and sometimes turn up a real find even among those gaudy pages. Shopping on the internet has made it much easier to locate hard-to-find plants but, again, buyer beware. When in doubt, I consult websites that publish reports of other shoppers' experiences.

Much of plant shopping is trial and error, but it does help you to learn about plants, and it can also be fun. In addition to nurseries, there are many places to learn about new plants by actually seeing them: friends' gardens; botanical gardens and arboretums; public parks and private gardens that are periodically open to the public; flower shows and other exhibitions. Also try to notice plants when you travel. That fern growing in a Florida park may be a houseplant at your home in Detroit, but you might learn something about how it grows by observing it in a more natural setting.

One word of caution: as the plant trade, like all trade, becomes more complex and more global, gardeners should be aware of certain ethical issues. It has become increasingly clear that certain plants that occupy an appropriate niche in some ecosystems can be devastating to others, usurping the space occupied by native plants that in turn nourish the animal species that depend upon them.

Gardeners can do their part by avoiding plants known to be trouble in their area, and also by being cautious about growing exotic (nonnative) plants about which not enough is known. There is no foolproof master list that will tell you what you can plant and what to avoid. For one thing, no one knows the long-term effects of all the plants currently in commerce. For another, the problems are region-specific and site-specific. Purple loosestrife might be safe for your dry meadow, but strangle a nearby wetland if its seeds were to drift. For plants to avoid in your area, consult your local Extension Service or native plant society.

Another issue is the illegal harvesting and selling of wild plants, bulbs, and seeds, some of them endangered. It is essential to always buy from responsible nurseries that either propagate their own stock, or buy from those that do.

CHAPTER 5

Annuals

HAVE YOU EVER NOTICED HOW certain personality types are drawn to specific types of gardening? Take the vegetable grower: a fine, upstanding soul if there ever was one, the sort who'll always stop to help change your tire. Perennial gardeners are notorious overachievers who are as apt to run a marathon as they are to double-dig their grand herbaceous borders. If you're very close friends with a rose gardener you know that she's a romantic who wears lace in places that will never show. You'll forgive your neighborhood alpine-plant collector his touch of snobbery and the dwarf-conifer enthusiast his touch of arrogance, because both are so erudite, and they can always help you finish your crossword puzzle. Lawn fetishists wash the dishes between courses and pick white lint off their white suits, but you can count on them for anything.

No doubt I've pinned some unfair generalizations on your fellow gardeners. But I'm sure that you will accept without argument that all who favor annuals are hedonists. Not only do they seek sensory delights with abandon and without guilt, but they manage to escape any form of drudgery that might take time away from those enjoyments. They will only ski if there's a chairlift, and have no problem eating their ice cream before dinner.

The reason annuals are perfect for them is that annuals give such spectacular results with such little effort. Nothing else blooms with such profusion and for such a long stretch of time. If you want a riot of color, annuals are the answer, and gratification is, if not instant, then certainly not long delayed. You can have mature plantings in a matter of weeks. Your senses never become jaded with annuals because you can create a totally different color scheme or a whole new look each season. And best of all, these are about the easiest plants to grow. If you have insecurities about how you'll pan out as a gardener, try annuals. Your success will fill you with the courage to go on to some of the trickier plants—unless of course you're such a pleasure-seeker that you simply stick with annuals for good.

There's a bit of the hedonist in all of us, so most gardeners grow at least some annuals every year, even if their main focus is elsewhere. There are just so many ways to use them! A mixture of annuals in a bed by themselves is glorious, but they're also a fine addition to a perennial border, and they can provide a touch of summer color in front of evergreen or deciduous shrubs. Because so many annuals are ideal for bouquets, many people have an annual garden just for cutting. Annuals also make great container plants, set on a patio, next to a pool, in window boxes, or on windowsills indoors. Some even make good houseplants.

What Is an Annual?

A TRUE ANNUAL IS A PLANT THAT completes its entire life cycle in one season. Typically it grows from a seed in spring, quickly becoming a mature plant and quickly producing a great abundance of flowers. It does this because its only, or primary, means of reproducing itself is from seed. So an annual makes as many seed-producing flowers as it can. That's why, if you pick the flowers, even more will come—one reason why they're grown for cutting. After producing and dropping the seeds, the plant dies, although often, in cold climates, it is frost that arbitrarily ends the growth period. If the annual has been in a climate and soil that suit it, the seeds that have fallen by season's end will winter over on the ground and sprout in spring, starting the cycle over again.

There are also a number of plants that are technically perennials but are often spoken of as annuals simply because they are grown the way annuals are. These plants are perennial only in warm climates, because they won't withstand winter temperatures in cold ones. So a new crop is started each year. Not surprisingly, these "tender perennials" are chosen for this role because, unlike most perennials, they grow to flowering size the first season and then bloom for a particularly long time, so you don't mind having to replant them each year. Some perennials, such as geraniums (*Pelargonium* species), impatiens, nicotiana, coleus, and wax begonia, are grown as tender annuals. Others, such as alyssum, pansies, snapdragons, and lantana, are grown as hardy or half-hardy annuals. But don't count on any of them to winter over in regions where there is severe frost.

A few common plants we often treat as annuals are actually biennials—plants that take two years to complete their growth cycle and normally produce flowers and seeds in their second year. Forget-me-not (*Myosotis sylvatica*) and sweet William (*Dianthus barbatus*) are two examples; they can be sown in fall for spring germination or in late summer to produce seedlings that will winter over in mild climates. (For more information about biennials, see page 167.)

There are also several different kinds of "true annuals." The terms can be a little confusing, but you'll find it's worth taking the time to understand them, because if you know which kind you're growing you'll be better able to grow it successfully.

Tender annuals. These are plants that cannot take frost, either as young seedlings or as mature plants. Many common annuals belong in this category, including nasturtium, ageratum, portulaca, red salvia, and zinnia. These plants cannot be sown in the ground or set out as transplanted seedlings until after the danger of frost has passed. Hence they are often started indoors, so that by the time it's safe to plant the seedlings they are at least several inches tall. However some tender annuals, such as zinnias and nasturtiums, grow so quickly that they're often sown directly in the ground after the frost-free date.

Hardy annuals. These can take some frost, the amount varying from one plant to another. This means that you may be able to sow them directly in the garden in early spring as soon as the ground can be worked, or even the previous fall, especially in milder climates. It also means that they will not be cut down by the first frost in fall but will bloom awhile longer. This is a great advantage, for you'll often have one early frost followed by weeks of frost-free nights, and the blooming period of your garden will thus be substantially lengthened. Some hardy annuals are bachelor's button and calendula.

Gardeners sometimes start hardy annuals indoors, just to give them warmer, more controlled growing conditions in which they can attain a relatively large size before transplanting. But these must be hardened off (page 37) if they are to be set out while it is still cold.

Half-hardy annuals. These are plants that may take a few degrees of frost, but not as much as hardy annuals will. They cannot be fall-planted in cold areas. Some examples are cleome, snapdragon, cosmos, and petunia.

Warm-weather annuals. These are annuals that grow and bloom best during warm weather. More often than not they are tender annuals such as zinnia, but this is not always the case. Sunflower, for example, is a hardy annual but it likes warm weather. And many of the perennials grown as annuals prefer warm weather, including lantana, geranium, and blue salvia.

Cool-weather annuals. These are usually hardy annuals such as bachelor's button, or else perennials treated as annuals such as sweet alyssum. But some tender annuals, such as nasturtiums and African daisies (*Arctotis*), are also cool-weather plants—in other words they can't take either frost *or* extreme heat. They may stop blooming or even die in the heat of the summer, especially in warm climates. Gardeners in these regions either choose warm-weather annuals instead, grow the cool-weather ones in partial shade, or plant a second crop of them for fall or winter bloom. With some cool-weather annuals, day length is as much a factor as heat. They succeed better in northern regions where summer days are long than they do in the south where summer days are shorter.

Growing Annuals

A NNUALS DO NOT HAVE COMPLICATED growing requirements, but paying attention to a few simple needs will ensure a better show. Probably some do better in your climate or soil type than others. You can learn which ones by trial and error—experience is easy to get, since you're starting with new plants each year—or you can ask the advice of local nurserymen and fellow gardeners.

PLANTING SCHEDULE

When you plant and what you plant are very important. When you're growing perennials it's important to know the minimum winter temperature in your area and the coldest temperature zone a given plant will tolerate. With annuals the vital statistics are the first and last average frost dates for your area and whether a given plant will tolerate frost. Individual species' requirements are given in the List of Annuals in this chapter, but you can easily see that your planting will fall into several distinct tasks. First you'll start some plants from seeds indoors in early spring and start others in early spring directly in the garden. Then, after the last likely frost, you'll set out the seedlings you've raised indoors and perhaps sow a few other types directly in the bed.

Another alternative is to buy started seedlings in a nursery. Many gardeners do this, since the plants are fairly inexpensive, and if this is your first garden you may want to try this approach. (For advice about buying annual seedlings, see page 127.) The cost of started plants can mount up if you're growing a lot of plants, however; and if you have the time and space to do it, there is much satisfaction in starting your own annuals from seed. It's fun to do, for one thing. For another, there's a much wider selection in the annuals available from seed catalogs. Many of these offer hundreds of different species and varieties, as opposed to the dozen or so standbys you see in every garden center, and I always make a point of trying a few new ones each year.

Some years, if I'm just too busy to grow annuals from seed, I seek out the local nurseries that have the vision to see beyond the standard petunias and offer unusual annuals. Fortunately this is a growing trend. Nonetheless, when I buy started plants I always feel that I've missed out on something, and the plants I buy are rarely as vigorous as the ones I start at home. There I can move them up to a larger pot the minute they are ready, whereas nursery-grown seedlings can get rootbound while they're waiting around for you to buy them. The little soil cubes are inevitably white with matted roots, so I tear them apart a bit as I tuck them in the ground, vowing that next year I'll be a do-it-yourselfer once again. (For more advice on shopping, see pages 126 to 128.)

Because of space limitations, most of the annuals included in the list in this chapter are the tried and true, but don't let that stop you from searching out the unexpected. Annuals native to your region are also a wonderful idea because they look appropriate and are often easier to grow. This is especially true in areas with low rainfall. Local native plant societies, and nurseries that specialize in natives, can help you make your selection.

The practical advice that follows will help you to grow most annuals. For special issues, consult the nursery where you bought the plants. If you're growing them from seed, refer to the directions on the seed packet or in the catalog; usually these are quite explicit. I've also found that if I phone the customer service department of the companies I buy from, they're happy to give complete directions.

SOIL REQUIREMENTS

In a bed of annuals the soil does not have to be dug as deeply as it does for perennials, because most true annuals are fairly shallow rooted. But soil should be prepared to a depth of at least 8 inches. Keep in mind that the more thoroughly you loosen the soil and lighten it with organic matter, the more it will retain moisture and the more easily the plants' roots will reach down into it. Since the whole point of annuals is achieving rapid growth and early bloom, giving these plants the fluffy soil that roots love to probe is a huge help. Remove all obstacles, such as rocks, and competitors such as perennial weeds.

For the most part annuals need a richer soil than perennials do. Some are quite greedy for nutrients—zinnias, pansies, and marigolds, for example. But certain others, such as nasturtiums and portulacas, prefer a slightly poor soil. And I find that some of the larger ones, such as cosmos and cleome, can become almost treelike and a nuisance to stake if conditions are too luxurious. My advice is to try to please the majority that fall in between when you prepare your bed. Digging in plenty of well-matured compost before planting is the best policy. If growth is slow, a balanced liquid organic fertilizer can be applied.

You must also consider whether your soil is acid or alkaline. Most annuals are comfortable with a pH between 6.0 and 7.0. (See page 21 for information about pH and how to adjust it.)

PLANTING ANNUALS

Be sure to give sun-loving annuals a site that gets at least six hours of sun a day. And don't plant any annuals in a spot where tree roots take up space and rob the soil of moisture and nutrients. If drainage is poor, plant in raised beds. For information about planting techniques in general, see page 38; for specifics about individual plants, see the second half of this chapter.

How closely you space your annuals is fairly important. It is tempting, in that impatience we all feel in springtime, to plant them very close together so the bed will look lush and filled-in more quickly, and there will be less bare ground to weed. But although a sparsely planted bed will never make a good show, an overcrowded one can be just as bad, with great heavy clumps falling all over each other. As you get to know your plants, you'll be able to visualize how wide each one will become when mature, and you'll give the bushy ones more space than the skinny ones.

If you're sowing seeds directly in the garden, make sure the soil surface is particularly smooth, fine-textured, and free of even small stones and debris. I usually premoisten the patch of ground where I'm sowing, then scatter the seed in a random pattern unless I'm planting rows in a cutting garden. Unless the seed is one of the relatively few that needs direct light for germination, I cover the patch with about a quarter inch of very fine soil, pat lightly, and then water with a fine spray. I mark the variety clearly with a label at the beginning of the row or in the center of a free-form patch.

GROWING REQUIREMENTS

While annuals are growing they must be kept well weeded. Sometimes I'll mulch them with a few inches of a light mulch such as buckwheat hulls or finely shredded bark. Bear in mind that some annuals, particularly petunias, will rot if the mulch is right up next to the stems. It's also very important to keep the plants from drying out. Most annuals need to be watered more than perennials do, and newly sown seeds must be kept continually moist to insure germination. (For more on watering, see page 29.)

Some of the tall annuals, alas, need to be staked. In a natural setting they'd be held up by companion plants such as meadow grasses; in a garden, unless you have planted very cleverly, you may need some of the mechanical supports described on page 188. Short annuals that flop are particularly infuriating because it's so hard to stake them attractively, but many of them can be made sturdy and bushy by pinching the growing tips to make them branch (page 190). This will also make them more free-flowering. Ageratum, coleus, snapdragons, and petunias all respond very well to pinching. If you're starting them indoors, pinch them when they're a few inches high. You can also pinch plants you've sown directly in the garden when they are 4 to 6 inches tall.

Another big favor you can do for your annuals is to pick them. With most annuals, the more you pick, the more flowers you'll get. You can also deadhead the plants, removing spent blooms. This will not only make them bloom more, but your border will look tidier. Don't, however, deadhead all the blooms on plants that you hope will self-sow. You'll also need to draw your own personal line when it comes to deciding how much deadheading you're going to do. With a large garden, the task could drive you mad, or at the very least ruin your summer. I usually just pick my battles, going after really unsightly spent blooms such as those of the larger cosmos, or ones—calendula, for example—where deadheading ensures prolific bloom. With those the birds favor, such as sunflowers, I make a point of letting the seed-laden heads stay put throughout the winter.

VOLUNTEERS

The type of gardener who likes to start with a plan and stick to it finds self-sown annuals a nuisance in the garden. To me they're part of the adventure and give the garden a more natural look. A great many annuals—alyssum, cleome, love-in-a-mist, snapdragons, petunias, and portulaca, to name a few—will drop their seed and come up next year. This is how they play their role in nature, as colonizers of disturbed ground. Whether they do this in your particular plot, and how much, depends on how happy they are with your particular soil, moisture level, and winter climate. Needless to say, they do not always come up where they're wanted, but you can usually weed them out or transplant them, while still small, to a spot that suits you. Managing volunteers in this way enables you to let certain species flow around in drifts, in a graceful way, reappearing here and there as a recurring theme in the bed. Many annuals are hybrids that do not breed true to seed and will not be the same as the parent plants— a good argument for seeking out the old-fashioned types that are either the original species of the plant or are open-pollinated hybrids (see pages 124 to 125). But in the case of some plants, such as sweet William or gloriosa daisy, it is this variability that makes them fun—the color combinations are kaleidoscopic and you never know what will appear next.

PESTS AND DISEASES

In my experience, annuals are not often damaged very badly by insects or by disease. In a year when there are a lot of slugs or cutworms, young plants can be vulnerable. In hot, muggy summers diseases such as mildew, rust, and leaf spot can be a problem. For some safe strategies, see page 68. In general, I find that the best course is to choose annuals that are appropriate for the spot, then give them excellent growing conditions. Often just trying a different variety, such as one of the mildew-resistant zinnias, will do the trick, or adjusting the timing of your garden. In a hot climate where the growing season is long but disease problems can be acute, try growing cool-weather annuals in fall, winter, and spring, and replacing them with the hot-weather types in summer. This may be done either by having separate beds, or by growing the next season's plants in pots, to be set in when the old ones come out. If you don't mind a short hiatus, just clear the bed out when warm weather looms and direct-sow some quick growers like zinnias and nasturtiums.

Designing with Annuals

FOR MANY GARDENERS, ANNUALS ARE their most creative outlet because they can achieve so many different effects quickly. You might start by imitating something you've seen in someone else's garden or patio, or follow some of the suggestions here. But in future seasons you'll probably come up with your own unique flower combinations.

ANNUAL BORDERS

Whether an annual border actually *borders* something (like a path, a house wall, or the edge of a lawn) or is a freestanding "island border," such a collection of annuals massed together can add spectacular color to your surroundings. A garden of summer annuals is not difficult to plan because you don't have to worry about blooming periods. All the flowers will bloom at pretty much the same time—usually from early or mid summer up until frost. The only factors you have to keep in mind, then, are color combinations, heights, and plant forms—that is, upright plants versus bushy ones, broad leaves versus fernlike ones, and different flower shapes: flat umbels, spikes, big round clusters, daisy shapes, airy bunches of tiny flowers, and so forth. The more you combine different forms, and the more careful you are not to hide a short plant with a tall one, the more effective the picture will be.

Plan for an Annual Garden with Bright Colors (12' by 5')

FIG. 30

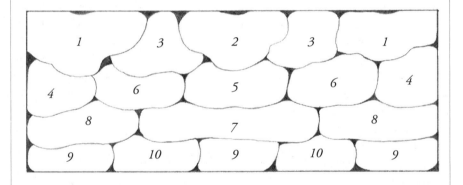

1. tall dark red cosmos
2. tall white cosmos
3. tall salmon zinnia
4. bronze snapdragon
5. yellow snapdragon
6. dark blue salvia
7. red-orange *Cosmos sulphureus*
8. calendula mix
9. blue multiflora petunia
10. marigold 'Lemon Gem'

Planning the Garden

Low Plants	Medium Plants	Tall Plants
yellow marigold	calendula	white cosmos
blue petunia	blue salvia	dark red cosmos
	red-orange cosmos	tall salmon zinnia
	yellow snapdragon	
	bronze snapdragon	

Color choice is a very personal thing. Some people want annual beds to be full of very strong, hot, bright colors, and since many of the most readily available annuals are vibrant tropical species, this effect is not hard to achieve. For many people, hot colors are what annuals are all about, and this is understandable. They are a great way to celebrate the coming of summer after a cold gray winter. And unlike many of the more subdued annuals, most perform relatively well in the grilling summers of warmer climes.

Some gardeners, on the other hand, like a more subtle, muted look. They prefer flowers in pastel colors, with more natural, old-fashioned shapes. For this kind of scheme you might have to do a bit more shopping around. Find a nursery with a very wide selection or, better yet, collect seed catalogs that specialize in the unusual. But even among the tried-and-true annuals, you can find many varieties in all those misty-English-garden colors, with blooms of modest size. Look for "single" rather than "double" in the descriptions, unless cheerleader pompons are what bring you to your feet.

The garden plans in Figures 30 and 31 show how you might arrange a 12-foot by 5-foot bed of annuals, one with a warm bright color scheme, one with a cool one. For each I made a list of some flowers I particularly liked together, then divided them into three groups based on height. I made sure I had at least two choices for each category, with most of them falling into the midheight range. I checked to make sure I had a wide variety of flower shapes and a good mix of colors. Then I started arranging them on the plan, making sure that plants in front would not hide the ones behind. In the process I discarded several choices and found others that would work better.

It's not always easy to combine bright colors, but bear in mind that nature does it all the time. I find it helps to include some cooler tones such as deep blue, lavender, pale yellow, or even white. I also like to use in-between shades for blending, for example using peach, salmon, or bronze to bridge the contrast between the purple/pink tones and the red/orange/yellow ones. Sometimes a foliage color such as burgundy or chartreuse is useful for blending. This particular garden is as gaudy as a Mardi Gras parade, but the snapdragons and the salvias help with the blending, as well as providing some spiky shapes to contrast with the rounder shapes of the other flowers.

In a "cool" garden, sometimes the problem is just the opposite—to avoid making it all too much the same, a wimpy sweep of pinks, lavenders, and blues. Here I tried to avoid that with contrasting patches of pure white, and very dark red, nearly black scabiosa in a key central position. I also included several commercially available mixtures—cosmos, scabiosa, and *Salvia viridis*. All contain some garnet or deep violet shades. If the garden were in part shade I might also have worked in some early-blooming pansies and forget-me-nots, followed by impatiens, wax begonias, and dark red coleus as a foliage accent.

BEDDING PLANTS

One traditional way to use annuals is as bedding plants. This generally means planting a large number of a single species, usually in a single color, and usually in a formal arrangement. Often several contrasting plants are used this way, in concentric rings, for example. The shape of the bed tends to be very regular and geometric, and is often outlined with a hard material such as brick, or a very low clipped hedge such as box or germander. In Victorian times this style of gardening was very popular, and bedding plants would be nurtured in greenhouses so they'd all be exactly the right height, and in full bloom, at the time they were needed for the display. Spring plants such as pansies would be ripped out after warm weather had slowed down their flowering, and would be replaced by summer annuals. In fall these might in turn be replaced by chrysanthemums.

Such a program is usually considered too wasteful and labor-intensive for modern times. The style, as well, has yielded to the more naturalistic "cottage garden" look. Nonetheless, formal garden beds are

Plan for an Annual Garden with Cool Colors (12' by 5')

FIG. 31

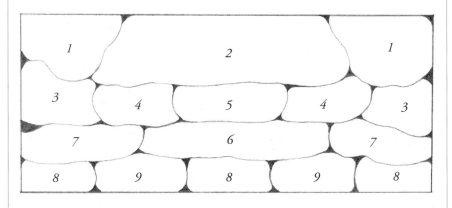

1. lavender cleome
2. tall cosmos mix, Versailles series
3. tall blue bachelor's button
4. scabiosa mix, Olympia series
5. deepest purple scabiosa 'Black Knight'
6. tall blue ageratum
7. *Salvia viridis* mix
8. white alyssum
9. blue edging lobelia

Planning the Garden

Low Plants	**Medium Plants**	**Tall Plants**
blue edging lobelia	*Salvia viridis*	cosmos
white alyssum	ageratum	lavender cleome
	scabiosa	
	bachelor's button	

sometimes appropriate for public or institutional plantings, and they can still effectively adorn a Victorian home, or even just a rather formal house and yard. Tastefully done, this kind of bed can be charming. If you're choosing plants for such a design, look for annuals of low or medium height that will be tidy and uniform in shape, such as wax begonias, small marigolds, ageratum, alyssum, verbena, lobelia, and foliage plants such as annual dusty miller (*Cineraria maritima*). The effect will be best if the plants are set quite close together, to avoid gaps in the design. It's also helpful to keep extra potted ones in reserve as fill-ins, in case some are injured.

ANNUALS IN CONTAINERS

Annuals make perfect container plants for outdoor use in cool climates. You can just discard them at summer's end and not have to worry about finding a place to overwinter them indoors. (On the other hand, many annuals can be brought inside and grown as houseplants if you're so inclined; see page 144.) Finding ways to use annuals in containers can really get people's imaginations going, often in bizarre directions. No empty receptacle is safe from a gardener on the prowl for a place to plant petunias, whether it's a wheelbarrow, an old sled, or a chamber pot. I personally can do without most forms of front-lawn cuteness, including these. But I do enjoy scouting out attractive containers for annuals—a rectangular terra-cotta pot, a wooden box that has weathered to a gray color, a shiny dark brown ceramic jar. For big containers, the modern terra-cotta or stone look-alikes made of fiberglass or plastic are a good substitute because of their low cost and the ease with which you can move them around.

What makes this kind of gardening fun is not only choosing the containers and plants but also finding artful ways to place them, either alone or in attractive groupings, and then choosing combinations of plants that will go well together in each one. Each pot, box, or trough becomes a tiny garden in itself. Let's take the classic wooden whiskey barrel, cut in half, available at many garden centers. You might put two or three pink geraniums in the center, then plant some dusty miller around them, and then add four or five variegated trailing vinca plants that will hang over the edge. Or you might start with the geraniums, then surround them with white annual baby's-breath, and add a trailing flower such as verbena or vining nasturtiums. I also love to mix in some culinary herbs as well—beautiful bright green curly parsley, dark purple basil, and bright blue borage flowers to use as garnishes. You can even throw in the surprisingly versatile salad crops; arugula leaves, for example, may be too strong to eat once the plant has gone to flower, but the cream-colored blooms are both charming and edible.

Success with container-grown annuals depends a lot on the initial preparation. For information on potted plants in general, see page 721. For larger containers such as the whiskey barrels mentioned above, I've come up with a formula that has worked very well. First I drill about six drainage holes in the bottom of the barrel with a ½-inch drill bit. Then I spread ¾ inch crushed stone over the bottom to a depth of a few inches. I cover this with a piece of spun-bonded polyester fabric—the kind sold as "floating row cover"—to keep soil from mingling with the crushed stone. (This keeps the soil from washing away, and also makes the stone easier to reuse.) I assemble my own potting mix in a wheelbarrow, using one third garden soil, one third compost (homemade if possible), and one third peat moss (or a commercial soilless potting medium whose main ingredients are peat and perlite). For each wheelbarrow full I add a half cup of rock phosphate or colloidal phosphate; a cupful of a nitrogen source such as cottonseed meal, alfalfa meal, or dried blood; and a half cup of lime (omit the lime if your soil is alkaline). After mixing these very thoroughly with a shovel, I fill the container to within a few inches of the top, then moisten the whole thing very thoroughly before planting.

It may take you a year or two of trial and error before you know just how much of each plant you need for a given container, and which combinations work best for you, but I guarantee you'll enjoy doing it. Upkeep of these mini-gardens is minimal because of their size, but deadheading will keep them more attractive. And regular watering is very important—they can dry out quickly in hot weather.

CUTTING GARDENS

Annuals are ideal plants for cutting gardens since they produce so many flowers, and cutting makes them more productive. When your regular flower garden is in bloom you can usually rob enough flowers from it for bouquets without spoiling the display, especially if you add a few wildflowers as well. I always make a point of letting a succession of seasonal wildflowers bloom somewhere on the property, whether in the garden or in a few "wild" areas (for some ideas, see the wildflower chapter). But if you need so many cut flowers that you'd spoil your ornamental plantings by

taking them from there, a separate cutting garden is the answer. I'll sometimes plant one if there's a special occasion coming up—a family wedding for instance—for which I know I'll need a wide selection. It may also turn out that the varieties you want to grow for cutting are not the same ones that work well in flower borders.

A cutting garden is not always grown to look good, though it is never an unattractive sight. Often the flowers in it are raised like a vegetable crop, in rows. These may be either straight single rows or wide ones, but not so wide that you cannot reach in easily from either side for cutting. One of the most popular ways to grow cut flowers is to sneak them into the vegetable garden itself. I sometimes do this, just as added insurance that I'll always have some flowers to cut. It makes them easy to mulch and to weed and, most important, easy to stake. Generally I have little patience with flowers that need staking, but with cut flowers it can be quite important. Flower stems that fall or blow over will start to grow up again at an angle, making them almost impossible to arrange well in bouquets. Often just lengths of twine tied to stakes and stretched taut along either side of the row will be sufficient. Or you may do what commercial flower growers do and let your flowers grow up through a special 6-inch plastic mesh netting, held parallel to the ground and supported by stakes at the corners.

If you plan to grow flowers for cutting, choose ones that have long stems and last a long time in water, such as zinnia, bachelor's button, larkspur, sunflower, salvia, stock, ageratum, and snapdragon. Avoid dwarf or compact varieties of these. There are also a host of annuals whose flowers can easily be dried for winter displays, among

TIPS FOR CUT FLOWERS

HAVING VASES OF CUT FLOWERS IN the house is certainly one of the joys of keeping a garden. Here are some tricks that will help the arrangements look their best and stay fresh longer.

• Cut flowers first thing in the morning or late in the day if the weather is hot and sunny.

• Choose flowers when they are almost open, or have just opened.

• Take a bucket of lukewarm water to the garden with you; strip lower leaves off as you pick, and immediately plunge in the stems. A plastic bucket is best because it is lightweight and nonreactive.

• Make clean, angled cuts, using sharp tools. For thick, tough, or woody stems, use your shears to give them "split ends," but don't mash them.

• Immediately seal the cut ends of "bleeders" such as poppies with a lit match or very hot water, to keep their juices in.

• Let flowers sit for an hour or two or overnight before you arrange them, to let them take up water.

• A teaspoon of vinegar in the picking water and the vase water, to acidify it, will make it easier for the flowers to take up and will kill decay-causing bacteria.

• Keep buckets, vases, scissors, and clippers clean with soap and water.

• Change the vase water every day or two, to prevent bacterial decay. This will help the flowers smell fresher; it will also keep stems from clogging. Recutting stems and removing any subsurface leaves will also minimize decay.

them statice, strawflower (*Helipterum roseum* and *Helichrysum bracteatum*), globe amaranth (*Gomphrena globosa*), and immortelle (*Xeranthemum annuum*).

OTHER USES FOR ANNUALS

There are many special situations where annuals can provide a quick—and pretty—fix. Let's say you have an ugly, slightly sandy patch of soil where weeds and crabgrass are going to grow unless you get there first. Let some trailing nasturtiums ramble over it. Perhaps you've had to put an ungainly fence around your swimming pool. Plant tall cosmos in front of it; even if they don't totally hide the fence, your eye will be drawn not to the fence but to the flowers. When you're planting near the pool, choose annuals that will tolerate what is, in effect, a hot microclimate within your yard. Heat and sun reflected from decking, stone coping, and the pool water itself can really bake plants. Choose species such as portulaca, marigolds, gloriosa daisies, and the various dusty millers that are relatively comfortable in these conditions.

Is your vegetable garden in the front yard because that's the only sunny part

BRINGING ANNUALS INDOORS

Many of the flowers we grow as annuals make fine houseplants. Some you can simply dig up and bring indoors before frost; others you would do better to start from cuttings you take from your plants while they're growing in the garden. To bring whole plants indoors, choose younger, smaller plants if possible, pot them up in a good soil mix (page 722), then condition them for indoor life by keeping them outdoors in their pots for a few weeks before the frost. But be sure to bring them in if frost is imminent.

What better consolation on the morning that the first hard frost has blackened your garden than to know that healthy plants are coming along on a sunny windowsill indoors? They may not be as long-lived as other houseplants, but they will provide a cheerful show in winter, and you can take cuttings again if the plants start to become tired. If some are still thriving by spring you can set them out in the garden again, or else take cuttings, root them, and plant those. (Among annuals that should last all winter are geraniums, impatiens, and coleus.) Here are some of the plants that respond well to indoor culture.

Alyssum. Dig up a clump, pot it, and bring it inside. Or divide a large clump into several; each will become larger.

Coleus. Whole plants may be dug up, cut back to a few inches tall, and regrown in a pot. Or take stem cuttings and root them. Pinch plants to make them bushy.

Geranium. Dig the plant up and cut it back at least by half, then fertilize with a fish-based liquid fertilizer. Or take stem cuttings and root them.

Impatiens. Taking stem cuttings is the best method and works well for all types of impatiens. Pinch plants to make them bushy. New Guinea impatiens is especially popular as a houseplant.

Lantana. The whole plant may be dug up and brought indoors. Usually it's best to cut it back hard and let it put out fresh growth. You can also take stem cuttings and root them.

Nasturtium. Take stem cuttings and root them.

Pansy. Try pansies only if you keep your house cool. Dig them up, pot them, and bring them inside. Cut back to encourage fresh new growth, and fertilize with a fish-based liquid fertilizer.

Petunia. Dig up, pot, cut back, and bring inside. You might have luck taking stem cuttings and rooting them.

Portulaca. Dig up and pot, or take stem cuttings.

Verbena. Dig up, pot, and bring inside.

Wax begonia. Transplant to pots or take stem cuttings.

of your property? Make it an ornamental garden by alternating vegetables with tidy rows or blocks of zinnias and calendulas, and plant tall sunflowers along the north side of the fence where they won't cast shade on your crops. Annuals look lovely in herb gardens, too.

And finally, never underestimate the power of annuals tucked into a perennial border. The perennial purist (the overachiever, remember?) would probably consider this cheating, but I find annuals very helpful in filling gaps here and there and providing dependable continuous color in an all-summer garden. This can be a little tricky, just because perennial clumps may get quite large and wide before the newly planted annuals have a chance to take hold. I have three strategies that help me solve this problem. The first is to choose hefty annuals that are tall and showy such as the taller zinnias and cosmos. I start them way ahead and grow them in pots, so that by the time they go in, after frost, they can easily hold their own. The second is to direct-sow some very low annuals such as alyssum or dwarf zinnias in the front of the bed. That band of color really helps to make the bed look full and showy. And the third strategy is to just toss around some seeds in the front and middle sections, in early spring or even the fall before, that will germinate early and just come up at random between the perennial clumps as "fillers." Two that work particularly well this way are Flanders poppies, which add bright spots of red color, and panicle larkspur, with its airy clouds of purple-blue. Both will self-sow, and perpetuate the process. I've also had good luck broadcasting seeds of the lovely blue Chinese forget-me-not (*Cynoglossum amabile*) and white annual baby's breath as fillers.

You might also plant a garden of permanent plants for spring and fall in which you've left plenty of spaces for temporary ones in summer. Thus spring-blooming bulbs such as tulips and daffodils, and early perennials such as bleeding hearts and primroses, would be followed by annuals; after frost the show would consist of fall-blooming perennials such as asters and tall sedums.

List of Annuals

THIS LIST NO DOUBT CONTAINS many annuals that are familiar to you. Most are popular plants commonly seen in gardens because they make a colorful display and are easy to grow. In some cases I mention specific varieties or series of varieties that you might try, but bear in mind that these come and go as the trade dictates. As new ones appear, try them and see how they work for you.

AGERATUM
Ageratum houstonianum

Description: I like this plant, sometimes called floss flower, because its masses of intense violet-blue, fuzzy flowers show up even from afar and do not recede into the background as blue flowers often will. A tender annual, it is often used as an edging plant, and many of the common varieties form the low, compact mounds described by flower authority Allan Armitage as "little blue meatballs." I am more apt to grow the 1½- to 2-foot, more informally shaped varieties such as 'Blue Horizon' that are great for cutting. Some ageratum varieties are white or pink.

How to Grow: Plants are usually started indoors six to eight weeks before the last frost, then set out into the garden after all danger of frost has passed. They are slow to get going, so the short varieties are most effective when planted closely—about 8 inches apart. They prefer full sun but do fairly well in light shade, especially in hot climates. Give them a light, well-drained soil.

ALYSSUM (SWEET ALYSSUM)
Lobularia maritima

Description: A perennial usually grown as a hardy annual, alyssum may grow as tall as a foot but is often no more than 6 inches tall; when closely planted it forms a beautiful carpet. The tiny, profuse flowers are usually white but sometimes purple, pink, cream, and even a few peachy tones. Alyssum is a good edging plant, one you can transplant in clumps to fill bare spots—even the spaces between paving stones. The flowers are fragrant and have a long period of bloom, from spring till after the first hard frosts, although they do not look their best during the heat of summer. Shearing them back when hot weather comes will sometimes promote regrowth. Where summers are very hot you might even resow at summer's end for a fall display.

How to Grow: I sow alyssum directly in the garden in early spring, without thinning. I find the plants are stronger, and will rebound more successfully after summer's heat when direct-sown. Alyssum may also be started indoors; press the seeds lightly into the surface of your planting medium since they need light to germinate. Transplant them into the garden in clumps, unthinned. They will often self-sow.

BABY'S BREATH

Gypsophila

Description: As its name implies, this plant gives an impression of sweetness and delicacy, which explains its popularity in bridal bouquets. The airy clouds of white flowers are also beautiful in the garden when used as a filler, woven in between stouter clumps toward the front of the border. The two species most commonly sold are *Gypsophila elegans*, which grows about 18 inches tall and can be either white or pink, and the much shorter *G. muralis*,

which is pink and has very tiny flowers. Of the two, the taller one is the most versatile for cutting. My favorite variety is "Covent Garden Market," which has larger-than-usual flowers.

How to Grow: These cool-weather hardy annuals are best sown directly in the garden, without thinning, in early spring, fall in mild climates. Successive sowings will provide a steady supply of flowers. They do best in full sun, in a well-drained, limey soil. In some areas baby's breath can self-sow, and can be invasive.

BACHELOR'S BUTTON (CORNFLOWER)

Centaurea cyanus

Description: I find a spot for this hardy annual every year because it keeps right on blooming long after most annuals have turned into frost-killed heaps, and adds a touch of true blue to autumnal bouquets. Varieties range from foot-high dwarfs up to the taller cut-flower types that can grow to 3 feet, with long grayish leaves. Flowers are usually about the size of quarters, their petals arranged in a loose, circular tuft that once earned them the name ragged sailor. Besides the usual bright blue, you can also find white, pink, lavender, purple, mauve, and even a stunning deep garnet. Mixtures are available, sometimes with a white "frosting" on the petals. Other *Centaurea* species include the yellow *C. moschata* (sweet sultan) and the white-leaved *C. cineraria,* one of the plants called dusty miller.

How to Grow: Bachelor's buttons are cool-weather plants that can be sown directly in the garden in early spring. You can also try sowing in fall for spring bloom, especially in warm climates. Plants may also be started indoors. Grow in full sun, 8 to 12 inches apart. In some areas bachelor's buttons self-sow and can be invasive.

CALENDULA
Calendula officinalis

Description: In colonial times this hardy annual was called pot marigold because of its use as a cooked vegetable. I grow it

for its intense shades of orange and yellow, and because it blooms after frost. The daisy-shaped flowers, usually up to about 2 inches wide, can also be shades of cream, apricot, and bronze; some are single, some double, though I prefer the simplicity of the single ones. Heights also vary, from 10-inch miniatures to 2 feet. All are long-lasting as cut flowers and will produce abundantly if they are snipped often.

How to Grow: Calendulas are easy to grow from seed. Sow early in spring indoors, or sow directly in the garden as soon as the soil can be worked, ¼ inch deep. Gardeners in warm climates can sow seeds in late summer for bloom all fall and winter. The plants may mildew in muggy weather. They like cool days, full sun and fertile soil, and do best planted about a foot apart.

CLEOME
(SPIDER FLOWER)
Cleome hassleriana, C. spinosa

Description: This half-hardy annual is prized for its huge heads of pink, white, or purple blossoms, with long wavy stamens. These heads renew themselves continuously along ever-lengthening stems.

Cleome grows between 3 and 5 feet tall, and manages to seem both monumental and dainty at the same time. Blooms are strongly fragrant, bordering on smelly, and are truly elegant in the rear of the flower garden.

How to Grow: Sow indoors about eight weeks before the last average frost, or outdoors in the garden after danger of frost has nearly passed. Thin to about 18 inches apart. Cleome is a sun-loving warm-weather plant, moderately drought tolerant. It will often self-sow.

COLEUS

Solenostemon scutellarioides
(Coleus blumei)

Description: A tender perennial grown as a tender annual, coleus is loved for its dramatically variegated leaves in contrasting shades of red, green, yellow, white, gold, apricot, chartreuse, and nearly black. Both the shapes of the markings and the shapes of the leaves vary widely from one cultivar to another. The plants can be effective both in mixtures and in uniform plantings. Coleus is often used in planters, pots, and window boxes as well as in beds. Tall varieties can grow as tall as 3 to 4 feet, shorter ones as low as 6 inches.

How to Grow: It is easiest to buy started plants in the colors and leaf forms that please your eye. Growing coleus from seed is slow. If you want to try it, sow indoors as early as ten weeks before the last expected frost. Sprinkle the tiny seeds on top of the soil and gently press them into it so as not to exclude light, and keep the soil moist and warm during germination. Transplant seedlings into their permanent location, in average soil, after danger of frost has passed. Coleus plants should be spaced at least a foot apart; they can become quite broad. With most of the tall varieties it is helpful to pinch the stems (page 191) to make them compact and bushy. A warm-weather plant, coleus can grow in sun or shade in most climates, but part shade will prevent wilting in hot weather and may produce stronger colors. A light mulch will help keep the soil moist, but should be kept away from the stems of the plants.

COSMOS

Cosmos

Cosmos sulphureus   *Cosmos bipinnatus*

Description: The most common varieties are hybrids of *Cosmos bipinnatus*, with daisylike flowers sometimes as large as 4 inches across, in shades of pink, red, maroon, or white. Plants have airy, threadlike foliage and grow between 2 and 5 feet tall, depending on the variety. The taller ones are ideal for the back of the annual garden, or for filling in gaps between clumps of tall perennials. Shorter ones, such as the Sonata series, are wide, bushy plants. Hybrids of *C. sulphureus* grow between 1 and 2½ feet. The red, yellow, or orange flowers, which bloom very profusely, are up to 2 inches across and sometimes semidouble. They perform well in hot climates. Both species are half-hardy annuals and are good for cutting.

How to Grow: Sow seeds outdoors after the last expected frost, or indoors about six weeks before it. For optimum bloom, plant in full sun or part shade in soil that is not too rich or too moist. Too much fertility can prevent or delay flowering. Plant at least 1 foot apart, up to 2 feet for most *C. bipinnatus* varieties. The tall ones often need staking, and all varieties bloom longer and better if deadheaded, however tedious this task may be.

FORGET-ME-NOT

Myosotis sylvatica,
Cynoglossum amabile

Description: Both these plants are members of the borage family, not surprising since their shining glory is their intensely blue flowers. *Myosotis sylvatica* varieties are typically bright blue but sometimes pink or white, and usually no more than a foot tall. They are early bloomers, often grown among spring bulbs or naturalized in woodland and water gardens. They also make good edging plants. *Cynoglossum amabile,* generally known as Chinese forget-me-not, bears flowers that are almost turquoise in color, on stems that elongate as successive blossoms are borne, until the plants are about 1½ to 2½ feet tall.

How to Grow: There are several ways to grow forget-me-nots. Easily raised from seed, they may be sown in fall when spring bulbs are planted, to germinate in spring for spring and early-summer bloom. They may be sown in late summer in a cold frame to produce seedlings that will overwinter in a protected setting. Or they may be sown indoors in March and transplanted outside later in the spring. *Myosotis sylvatica* does not need thinning. Both species self-sow under their favorite conditions: moist, humusy soil in light shade. These cool-weather plants may not bloom during the heat of August, but plants self-sown in summer may bloom in fall in warm climates. I often set out transplants of Chinese forget-me-not in spring and sow seeds among the plants at the same time, to ensure a late flowering as well.

GERANIUM

Pelargonium

Description: Tender perennials grown as tender annuals north of zone 9 or 10, these are the immensely popular bright geraniums seen on windowsills, on terraces, and in gardens everywhere. Most are varieties of *Pelargonium* × *hortorum* (zonal geranium), which forms a large, shrubby plant in mild climates but grows about 2 feet tall in colder ones. The large flower clusters can be red, pink, purple, lavender, salmon, orange, or white. Martha Washington geraniums (*P. domesticum*) are shorter, and are mostly used in containers. The flowers in each cluster are large, rather like those of azaleas, often with a blotch of a darker shade. Ivy geranium (*P. peltatum*) is a trailing plant often used in window boxes. There are also a number of species grown less for their flowers than for their leaves; these have various scents such as apple and lemon and are popular in herb gardens.

ivy geranium

zonal geranium

How to Grow: Seeds can be sown indoors in late winter or early spring in soil kept warm for better germination. Growing from seed can be slow, and therefore many gardeners prefer to buy a few plants the first year, then take cuttings each year for next year's crop or for a supply of bright houseplants in winter. Geraniums are warm-weather plants and relatively drought tolerant, but intense heat can be fatal to them, and cool nights are best. Martha Washington geraniums need a period of cool weather to bloom and thus are not satisfactory for hot climates. All like full sun but can take a bit of shade, especially in hot areas. Plant in not overly fertile, well-drained soil, 12 to 15 inches apart in the garden. Cut them back to half their height in late winter or early spring in climates where they are perennial. Give pot-grown geraniums plenty of light so they will not be leggy. Frequent deadheading will keep the plants looking more attractive.

GLOBE AMARANTH

Gomphrena globosa, G. haageana

Description: This increasingly popular tender annual is excellent for cutting, for drying, and in the garden, where it yields multitudes of fat, cloverlike blooms all summer long. Plants are upright but compact and branching, growing up to 2 feet tall. Hybrid varieties are available in many colors—pink, purple, lavender, white, and red. 'Strawberry Fields' is a striking red-orange. One of globe amaranth's greatest virtues is its tolerance of heat and drought.

How to Grow: Best started from seed indoors, six to eight weeks before the last expected frost. Plant 8 inches apart in a sunny spot in average to dry soil. Pick flowers for bouquets or drying when they are fully open but have not begun to elongate.

IMPATIENS
Impatiens

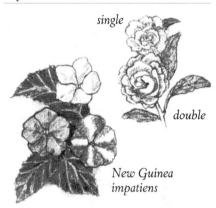

single

double

New Guinea
impatiens

Description: The most familiar species is *Impatiens walleriana*, which is also, paradoxically, called patience plant or patient Lucy. This tender perennial grown as a tender annual will always come to the rescue of the gardener who wants plenty of color but whose house is surrounded by shade (it will sometimes do well in full sun too, in cool climates). Plants are sometimes upright, reaching as tall as 2 feet, but are more typically low and sprawling, and each plant may cover a wide area before summer's end. Colors include almost everything in the flower spectrum except true blue, and some varieties are bicolors. Some have double flowers like tiny camellias. All are good container plants, even indoors.

New Guinea impatiens (*I. hawkeri*) is a tender annual with equally varied flowers, often larger than those of the usual impatiens. It also has strikingly variegated leaves and is often grown as a container plant or houseplant. Both species tend to be used in rather gaudy ways. Perhaps it's the names the breeders give to these flowers, lipstick names like 'Tempo Peach Frost' or 'Mega Orange Star,' that egg us on and drive us to plant the whole rainbow, or perhaps it's just the urge to light up all those shady corners. But these are pretty flowers when used with discretion, and hummingbirds love them.

How to Grow: New Guinea impatiens is grown from cuttings or from purchased plants, but *I. walleriana* can also be grown from seed; sow indoors six to eight weeks before the last frost. Press seeds gently into the soil surface so as not to exclude light, and keep soil moist and warm for faster germination. These are tender, warm-weather plants that will not take any frost, but they do like the soil to be somewhat cool and moist; make sure they have plenty of organic matter worked in. Impatiens stems are very soft and fleshy and will be obliterated by any foot traffic, so they should not be planted in a spot well traveled by dogs or people. Plants can be pinched (page 190) to make them more compact and bushy.

LANTANA
Lantana

Description: Lantanas are perennials grown as half-hardy annuals in most climates, or wintered over indoors. *Lantana camara* is a biggish shrub in very warm climates, where it can be distressingly weedy and even invasive. Elsewhere it grows to a well-behaved 1 to 3 feet depending on the variety. The small round flower heads are clusters of tiny blossoms in shades of red, pink, yellow, orange, lavender, and

white, sometimes with many colors all in one cluster. Trailing lantana (*L. montevidensis*), slightly less hardy, has trailing stems and pink or lavender flowers. Both types make excellent container plants but are also grown in gardens, the trailing kind as a ground cover. Butterflies love them.

How to Grow: Lantanas are warm-weather plants. Sow seeds indoors in late winter because they take a long time to germinate. In mild climates sow outdoors in the garden. Many gardeners buy plants and then take stem cuttings when they need new ones to bring indoors for winter display and for a source of new cuttings for the following season. Plants can also be dug up, cut back to 5 or 6 inches, and kept dormant in a frost-free basement until early spring with just enough water to keep them alive but not enough to produce new growth.

LARKSPUR
Consolida

Description: If you love delphiniums but don't have the patience it takes to grow them, these hardy annuals may cheer you up. Their flower spikes look like those of delphiniums (with which they are often confused in the trade) but are shorter and more delicate. Heights vary, but 2 to 3 feet is common. Commercially available varieties are hybrids of several species (chiefly *Consolida ambigua* and *C. regalis*), in shades of blue, lavender, pink, purple, salmon, carmine, and white. Dwarf varieties are also available. Plants have attractive, fernlike foliage, and are usually narrow and upright, although the type called panicle larkspur (varieties such as 'Blue Cloud') are luxuriantly branched; these have a beautifully open, airy look in both bouquets and gardens. Larkspur's bloom period is not as long as it is for some annuals—flowers may peter out before summer's end—but it makes an excellent, long-lasting cut flower.

How to Grow: Seeds can be sown directly in the garden as early in spring as you can work the soil or, in mild climates, in late summer to produce plants that will bloom next spring. Seeds started indoors must be transplanted with great care. Larkspur likes full sun but will take part shade, which it prefers in hot climates. Plants in the garden should be a foot apart, in fertile, well-drained, slightly alkaline soil. Keep roots cool with a light mulch, especially in hot climates. Tall plants may need staking.

LOBELIA (EDGING LOBELIA)

Lobelia erinus

Description: Lobelia is a hardy annual, rarely taller than 8 inches, whose flowers are dark, medium, or light blue and sometimes white. Some are among the most intense blues of any garden plant. In varieties such as 'Crystal Palace,' the foliage is tinged with red. Some have trailing stems and make good container plants. Lobelia is also used as an edging plant in flower gardens.

How to Grow: Sow seeds indoors in late winter or early spring, ten to twelve weeks before the last expected frost. Sprinkle them on top of the soil and press gently so as not to exclude light. After danger of frost is past, transplant in unthinned clumps a few inches wide, and set clumps about 6 inches apart. The plants grow best in cool areas and appreciate full sun except in hot climates, where they do best with some afternoon shade. Soil should be fertile and moist, but well drained.

LOVE-IN-A-MIST

Nigella damascena

Description: This is one of those flowers that you can establish in your garden and never have to plant again. A hardy annual, it self-sows charmingly, sprouting ferny foliage and bright blue blossoms a bit like large bachelor's buttons, weaving itself into spaces between your other plants and nicely tying them all together. Handsome burgundy-colored seedpods, prized by flower arrangers, follow the flowers. Varieties in shades of pink, purple, mauve, and white are also available, usually in mixtures.

How to Grow: Direct-sow in early spring in full sun in well-drained soil, thinning if crowded. Love-in-a-mist does not like to be transplanted—you can make successive sowings for longer bloom. It prefers cool weather.

MARIGOLD

Tagetes

Description: It's hard not to admire the sunny profusion of these pungent-smelling half-hardy annuals. The commercially available varieties are derived from several South American species. *Tagetes erecta*, called African marigold, is actually from Mexico. The ball-shaped flowers are often large, up to 4 inches across, on plants as tall as 4 feet. Colors range from cream to yellow and orange. *T. patula*, French marigold (also from Mexico), is usually between 6 and 18 inches high; flowers are yellow, orange, and red, often bicolored, and either single or double. *T. tenuifolia* varieties are dwarf marigolds with a similar color range, quite small flowers, and attractive fernlike foliage.

African marigold

French marigold

How to Grow: Sow seeds outdoors on or just before the last average frost date in average soil, and in full sun except in very hot climates. Seeds can also be started indoors six weeks or so before the last frost. Plant tall varieties 12 to 18 inches apart, short ones 8 to 12 inches. Marigolds are warm-weather plants that make bushy growth quickly and are fairly drought tolerant. Deadheading will keep them more healthy and productive.

NASTURTIUM
Tropaeolum majus

Description: This tender annual is a garden favorite because it is so easy to grow. The flowers are about 2 inches across, with ruffled, spurred petals in shades of red, orange, yellow, gold, orange, cream, salmon, pink, and mahogany. The stems are long and curving but rather breakable, the leaves light green and round. Both flowers and leaves are edible in salads or as garnishes. There are many varieties, most of them hybrids of this and other species. Some varieties, such as the Tom Thumb series, are dwarfs that grow no more than 9 inches. Others, such as the Jewel series, have trailing stems that can attain great lengths in warm climates. These look great in hanging baskets, spilling onto paths or terraces, or as a covering for banks or stone walls. The Alaska series is distinguished by variegated foliage, while that of the variety 'Empress of India' is a deep blue-green, with red flowers. The Whirlybird series has flowers that face upward and are less likely to hide under the leaves.

How to Grow: Sow the large seeds directly in the ground a few weeks before the last frost, at about half the distance apart that you want them to grow (6 inches for dwarfs, and up to 12 inches for larger types), then thin. Give nasturtiums full sun (part shade in hot climates). They will tolerate a dryish soil fairly low in nitrogen. In fact, too much fertility will result in big leafy plants that hide their flowers.

NICOTIANA (FLOWERING TOBACCO)
Nicotiana

Description: Related to *N. tabacum*, from which smoking tobacco is derived, are several species of *Nicotiana* grown in gardens. The *N.* × *sanderae* hybrids are the most common, bred for compactness, a wide red-pink-purple-white color range, and a tendency to keep their trumpet-shaped flowers open even on bright days. I'm more apt to grow the original species, which are much taller, with huge, broad leaves—a bit awkward for the small garden. They are profuse self-sowers. They also open their blooms mainly to night-flying moths, and on cloudy days may not be that interested in adorning your garden. But their luscious evening fragrance, to my mind, more than makes up for these traits. You can choose among *N. alata* and *N. sylvestris* (both have white trumpets, those of the second in spectacular drooping clusters) and *N. langsdorffii*, whose adorable trumpets are tiny and chartreuse-green. *N. alata* is a perennial grown as a tender annual; the rest are tender annuals. All of them self-sow.

How to Grow: Start seeds indoors six to eight weeks before the last expected frost, then transplant to the garden after frost danger has passed, spacing short varieties 10 to 12 inches apart, tall ones 12 to 18. Nicotianas like an alkaline soil and plenty of moisture in dry weather. They are warm-weather plants that prefer full sun but will tolerate part shade.

PANSY
Viola × *wittrockiana*

Description: Pansies are perennials but are short-lived in many areas, so they're often grown as hardy annuals or biennials. Hybrids come in just about every color imaginable, even black, with varying flower size (the common name "viola" usually refers to the small-flowered kind). Many are bicolored or tricolored, with the familiar "faces" that most people remember fondly from their childhoods. Most plants are less than 9 inches tall. They're used in window boxes and planters as well as in gardens. Like most gardeners I find the spring pansy show a welcome sight, but boy, can they sulk in hot weather! Fortunately most of them revive when it gets cool at summer's end, and there are all those little faces again. In mild climates they'll bloom all winter. *Viola tricolor*, commonly called Johnny-jump-up, has a tiny flower with purple, yellow, and white markings and, unlike hybrid pansies, it breeds true from seed. It is a welcome self-sower in my garden.

How to Grow: Pansies can be sown indoors ten to twelve weeks before the last average frost, but be sure to sow them shallowly, keeping the seed tray dark, moist, and cool. Transplant them into the garden in the spring in fertile, humusy, moist, well-drained soil; you should move them early enough so they can establish good root systems before the weather gets too warm. A more reliable method is to start plants in summer or fall for bloom the following spring. In cold climates they are best held over in a cold frame, or under a heavy mulch. Frequent picking or dead-heading will give you more compact plants and profuse bloom.

PETUNIA
Petunia

ruffled

single

double-ruffled

double

Description: Petunias are half-hardy annuals, related to the potato and other members of the nightshade family (page 233). Their familiar trumpet-shaped flowers come in many shapes, sizes, and colors, from the old-fashioned singles to modern hybrids that are striped, doubled, ruffled, and sometimes very large—4 inches across for some of the grandifloras. Multiflora petunias are small and single and bloom very profusely; they are also disease resistant. Because petunias make compact plants with masses of color, they are excellent in flower borders. I find that the more modest, simpler petunias are less harmed by humidity, heavy rains, and other natural disasters than are the larger, more flamboyant ones; the latter, however, are fine as container plants in sheltered locations. Cascading types are especially effective in pots, planters, and boxes. Petunia colors are virtually unlimited. Heights vary, but most plants are between 9 and 12 inches tall. Almost all that are sold are hybrids of several species, but true species such as the trailing purple-hued *P. integrifolia* or the night-fragrant white *P. axillaris* are well worth growing if you can find them.

How to Grow: Sow seeds indoors eight to ten weeks before the last frost, dropping the tiny seeds onto the soil surface and pressing gently with your fingers so as not to exclude light. Transplant into the garden after danger of frost, spacing at least 12 inches apart, more for spreading types. Petunias like full sun and well-drained soil. They are warm-weather plants but sometimes do poorly in hot weather. If they look straggly and aren't blooming well, cut them back to a few inches tall, feed them liquid fertilizer or compost tea, then water thoroughly. Petunias self-sow readily, but the offspring rarely look anything like the parents.

POPPY

Papaver

Description: I love all the annual poppy species for their luscious colors, their simple and graceful forms, and their unbridled urge to perpetuate themselves. When I plant a new garden I scatter seeds in spring; in subsequent years the poppies do it for me. Iceland poppies (*Papaver nudicaule*) are the most subtle, with papery blooms in a wide pastel color range. I've enjoyed low-growing mixtures such as 'Hazy Days' and 'Oregon Rainbows.' But I also like the exuberance of bright red Flanders poppies (*P. rhoeas*); the more varied Shirley types; and the sturdy, upright *P. somniferum*— opium poppy (or breadseed poppy if that name makes you nervous). Of these three, Iceland poppies seem to be the longest blooming and the most persistent as plants (they are, strictly speaking, perennials grown as annuals, whereas the other two are hardy annuals). The native California poppy, *Eschscholzia californica*, belongs to a different genus but has a similar blossom—generally bright orange—and fernlike foliage.

How to Grow: Annual poppies are cool-weather, cool-climate plants best direct-sown in fall or very early spring. They can also be started indoors, from seeds germinated in darkness, but seedlings must be transplanted very carefully since they are taprooted. Grow poppies in full sun in fertile, well-drained soils.

PORTULACA (MOSS ROSE)

Portulaca grandiflora

Description: Portulacas are often thought of as rock-garden plants because they do so well in hot, dry locations. They are tender annuals with succulent, needle-shaped leaves and trailing stems 6 to 8 inches long. Flowers are bright and papery-textured in shades of pink, red, yellow, salmon, orange, purple, and white. They are usually sold in mixtures, not as single colors. Portulacas close at night and on cloudy days, although some varieties have been bred to remain open. Since they are gloriously drought tolerant, I put them in pots, window boxes, or any container that I might forget to water from time to time.

How to Grow: Portulacas may be started ahead indoors but it's best to wait until the soil has warmed up and danger of frost has passed, then sow them in the spot where you want them to grow. Thinning is usually not necessary. A warm, sunny exposure is essential. They will tolerate poor soil but it must be well drained. In a spot where they are happy, they will self-sow generously.

SALVIA (SAGE)

Salvia

Description: A number of annual sages are grown in gardens. By far the most popular is *Salvia splendens*, scarlet sage, which is actually a tender perennial grown as a tender annual. Despite its name it comes in many colors besides scarlet, among them pink, purple, salmon, and white, in heights that range from about 9 inches to 2 feet. But the brilliant red ones have made it famous, or infamous. This is such a controversial plant that I have even heard of an Anti-Red-Salvia League. It is often grown in masses and as such *can* be too much of a good thing. I'm not such a salvia snob that I'd pass over it altogether, but I do like it best in small groups with other plants.

Of the other salvias, one of my favorites is *S. farinacea* (blue salvia, or mealy-cup sage). A tender perennial grown as a half-hardy annual in most climates, it has blue (or white) flower spikes that are as attractive and long lasting in the garden as they are in bouquets. Heights vary; I tend to choose the ones that are at least 2 feet tall, since they are best for cutting, and I consider this an essential plant for summer bouquets. I also love *S. viridis* (*S. horminum*), a 1- to 2-foot half-hardy annual distinguished by its papery bracts in shades of pink, purple, and sometimes white (often sold in mixtures). A champion self-sower, I like to naturalize it in informal drifts or as a filler in a perennial bed; it's also outstanding for cutting.

How to Grow: Most salvias are warm-weather plants best started indoors in warm soil about ten weeks before the last average frost. Transplant after danger of frost is past, in full sun (light shade in hot climates), spacing about a foot apart. They like warm but not excessively dry weather and need to be watered in drought unless they're well mulched. *S. viridis*, which does best in cool climates, may be direct-sown.

SCABIOSA (PINCUSHION FLOWER, SWEET SCABIOUS)

Scabiosa atropurpurea

Description: Beautiful dome-shaped, fuzzy flowers on long, sturdy stems make this half-hardy annual an excellent cut flower, and its wide color range is another big asset. Blossoms can be blue, lavender, mauve, pink, carmine, white, and a deep almost-black garnet shade that's a wonderful accent in bouquets. On top of all that, they're fragrant, long blooming, and favored by butterflies. There are excellent mixtures, in heights ranging from 18 to 36 inches.

How to Grow: Seeds may be started indoors four to six weeks before the danger of frost has passed, or direct-sown outdoors after frost danger. Grow in a sunny spot in well-drained, fertile, slightly alkaline soil, spacing plants 1 foot apart. Tall varieties may need staking. Frequent cutting or deadheading helps to keep the plants in bloom.

SNAPDRAGON

Antirrhinum majus

Description: Snapdragons are perennials grown as half-hardy annuals. The broad flower spikes grow in plants of varying heights, from 6 inches to 3 feet. Colors include pink, red, yellow, orange, purple, bronze, and white. There is always a place for their strong, vertical accents in the flower garden, and I find they bloom long after frost and the shortening days have brought other annuals' season to an end. As a bonus, they're a long-lasting cut flower—so grow extras.

How to Grow: Sow seeds indoors eight to ten weeks before the last frost, without covering the seeds since they need light to germinate. Transplant into the garden, 8 to 12 inches apart, after danger of frost has passed, pinching plants to make them branch (see page 191). The plants like full sun and will also thrive in light shade, though bloom may be diminished. Give them a rich, well-drained soil. These are cool-weather flowers that do not thrive in hot summers; in warm climates sow them in August for fall bloom, or in fall for early-spring bloom. They like fertile, slightly alkaline soil. Cutting the flowers helps to keep them coming. Plants may overwinter and/or self-sow.

STATICE

Limonium sinuatum

Description: If you're only going to grow one flower for drying, statice is the one. A biennial grown as a tender annual, it keeps its shape and color very well. In fact, the same qualities that make it dry well give it an exceptionally long life in fresh bouquets. The plant grows 2 to 2½ feet tall on strong stems, and bears flowers in an extremely wide range of colors. I particularly like the intense blues, and an excellent series called the Sunset mix, which has subtle shades of apricot, salmon, peach, yellow, and rose.

How to Grow: Start seeds indoors about eight weeks before the last expected frost, then set out in the garden 12 inches apart after danger of frost has passed. Plants tolerate heat and drought. Grow them in full sun in fertile, well-drained soil. Pick them when all the blossoms in the spray are colored but not all of them have fully opened.

STOCK
Matthiola

Description: Stock is an old-fashioned plant that is grown less than it used to be. It deserves a comeback. The common garden stocks, which are hybrids of *Matthiola incana* and other species, are biennials grown as hardy annuals. Plants are 1 to 3 feet tall, depending on the variety, with spikes of small, fragrant flowers in shades of blue, purple, pink, yellow, and white. *M. longipetala* (*M. bicornis*), evening or night-scented stock, is a hardy annual that grows up to 1½ feet tall and is a powerhouse of fragrance at night. The small single flowers, which are purple, lavender, or white, grow

on straggly plants and are never very showy even when they're open—which is only at night or on cloudy days. But I would never let a year go by without growing it. I sow it amidst a bushier plant such as *Zinnia angustifolia*, near a patio or open window, where even a small patch of it will perfume the entire yard from dusk onward.

How to Grow: Sow seeds indoors eight to ten weeks before the last expected frost, or outdoors after danger of frost has passed. Stock is a cool-weather plant that can also be sown in late summer in hot climates for winter and spring bloom. It likes fairly rich, well-drained soil and full sun (evening stock will tolerate part shade).

SUNFLOWER
Helianthus annuus

Description: There has been such an explosion in the number of sunflower varieties available that there's now one for every purpose—10-foot giants planted as substitute shade trees, 1-foot dwarfs edging the front of beds like rows of well-mannered

schoolchildren, heirlooms with pale yellow or deepest mahogany blossoms, flowers with seeds the birds love, flowers without the pollen that tidy housekeepers dislike. This smorgasbord of choice, coupled with the incredible ease with which sunflowers can be grown, has led to a great surge in their popularity.

How to Grow: Sunflowers, which are hardy annuals, are almost always sown directly in the garden, after danger of frost has passed. Sow about twice as thickly as you need to, ½ inch deep. When seedlings sprout, thin to 1 to 2 feet apart, depending on the size of the plant. These hardy annuals like full sun and light, well-drained soil.

VERBENA

Verbena

Description: Most garden verbena hybrids are tender annuals grown for their clusters of tiny, fragrant flowers in shades of red, pink, purple, lavender, and white. These are less than 18 inches tall, some upright and some with trailing stems. The trailing kinds are especially good in hanging baskets and other containers. *Verbena bonariensis,* a tender perennial, is becoming widely grown as an annual in cold climates, because it is such a good "see-through" plant in borders—tall as it is (up to 5 feet), its framework is so slender that it never hides what grows behind. Its beautiful tufts of purple flowers are great for cutting and attracting butterflies. Its only fault is its extreme tendency to self-sow.

hanging

low-growing

How to Grow: Sow seeds indoors very early in a light, warm, slightly dry starting mix, covering the seeds to keep them in darkness. Germination can be slow and difficult, so many gardeners buy started plants. Transplant into the garden, 8 to 12 inches apart, in average soil after danger of frost has passed. These are warm-weather plants that prefer sun, but light shade is a blessing in hot, dry areas.

WAX BEGONIA

Begonia semperflorens-cultorum hybrids

Description: A tender perennial treated as a tender annual, the wax begonia is grown partly for its pink, red, salmon, and white flowers and partly for its fleshy

leaves, which can be green, red, or bronze. It grows 8 to 12 inches tall and is a good source of summer color for either shaded or sunny gardens. Combining several different varieties can be particularly effective. These are tough little plants that you can count on to be covered with flowers all summer, and in conditions they like, each plant will make a large clump.

How to Grow: Begonias are very slow to grow from seed (they are sown at least 12 weeks before planting out), so most gardeners purchase nursery-grown seedlings. Plant in the garden, 8 to 12 inches apart, after danger of frost has passed, in fertile, well-drained soil. Light shade is ideal for healthy leaves and abundant bloom.

ZINNIA

Zinnia

Description: Zinnias are tender annuals that all gardeners love because they make a great show and, apart from certain disease problems, are easy to grow. Flowers are flat or rounded heads of petals like overlapping scales, in every color except blue. Height and flower sizes also vary. Modern hybrids are derived from *Zinnia elegans, Z. angustifolia,* and *Z. haageana,* and range in height from 12 inches to 4 feet. Large, tall zinnias such as the Benary's Giant series are good for the back of the garden, and for cutting. Other mixtures such as Cut and Come Again or Sunbow zinnias are bushy plants of more moderate height that are full of buttonlike flowers and bloom all the more if cut (though this might be said of almost any zinnia). The Profusion series are outstanding short zinnias that are always covered with flowers, in shades of orange, white, or red. I'm also very fond of the narrow-leaved zinnias (*Z. angustifolia,* also called *Z. linearis*), which are compact and bushy, with small single flowers in orange or white; they are notoriously trouble free. All zinnias bloom until frost, and only the tallest need occasional staking.

tall-growing double

tall-growing single

short-growing

How to Grow: You can sow zinnia seeds indoors about four weeks before the last frost, then set out in moist, fairly rich soil, 8 to 14 inches apart depending on the size of the variety. Large zinnias will not branch properly if planted too close, and too-close planting may also lead to mildew and other diseases. Because zinnias do not like to be transplanted, and because they germinate and grow so quickly, I often sow them directly in the garden after danger of frost has passed. Water during drought, but keep water off the leaves to avoid fungus diseases. If such ills are a problem, seek out resistant strains that will do well in your area. True to their tropical origins, zinnias are warm-weather plants, and make excellent long-lasting cut flowers.

CHAPTER 6

Perennials

A S WITH MANY POPULAR ENDEAVors, gardening has its fads and changing currents, and every decade seems to bring a passionate horticultural revival. When I was a child in the fifties it was terrariums, a craze that came and went in our household, leaving moldy globes and fish tanks in our cellar as a reminder of those mossy little tabletop gardens. In the seventies, every living room, bar, and real-estate office was a jungle of houseplants; but before long, hardware and grocery stores that could barely restock spider plants fast enough had gone back to selling hardware and groceries. The eighties brought us perennials, the nineties bonsai and native plants. For a while, topiary animals were rising up above the style horizon like floats at the Macy's parade. Were they there to stay? No. Does it matter? No. The wonderful thing about all these enthusiasms is that as they pass through our world of commerce, they leave a bit of new knowledge in their wake.

In the case of perennials, the tide of favor on which they were swept into our lives has never really ebbed. One reason for this is sheer economics. It's possible to grow these plants with little or no expenditure of fuel, by overwintering them outdoors or in cold frames. And the proliferation of small perennial nurseries attests to their ease of culture. Many a business owes its beginning to that point in time when the garden simply got too big. There were many large clumps to be divided, seed-grown plants of which there were "extras"—and not enough neighbors to adopt them all. So suddenly there was a small backyard nursery, perhaps with a specialty in a certain type of plant, such as rock-garden perennials or daylilies. That very same ease of cultivation in turn lures the buyers that keep these enterprises going.

There's truly something seductive about growing perennials. A bed of them in full bloom, with its glowing patterns of color, is as gorgeous as a stained-glass window. But it's more than that. The garden's performance changes with every day, every month, every year, and one can easily become totally absorbed in it, both as a viewer and as a creator. Such a garden is not so much a display as it is a process.

What Is a Perennial?

A PERENNIAL IS A PLANT THAT DOES not die after a season's growth but renews itself each year. (People sometimes speak of a certain perennial being an "annual" in their gardens; but this only means that the plant does not survive their cold winters, their hot summers, or some other vagary of their climate.) Strictly speaking, many types of plants are permanent in this way, including trees, shrubs, hardy bulbs, the lawn, several vegetables, and many houseplants. But generally, when we talk about perennials we mean a large group of nonwoody garden plants grown for ornament, often for their flowers. Most are "herbaceous" perennials, which means that their stems are green and soft, not brown and woody like those of a shrub. This soft growth usually dies in fall, especially in cold climates, but the roots are alive and well underground. In early spring you can see signs of life all over your perennial bed. At the base of dried brown stems appear little bumps of new growth that turn into green sprouts, a different shape for each plant. As you learn about perennials, you come to recognize them even at the bump stage, and it's exciting to watch them all come to life.

Biennials and perennials are often grouped together. A true biennial is a plant that takes two years to complete its growth cycle. If started from seed it will produce foliage the first year, but will not flower until the next, and after flowering once it will die. A biennial's growth cycle is, then, more like that of a hardy annual than it is of a perennial, since hardy annuals are often sown in fall for bloom the following season (see page 133). But the plants we call biennials are generally sown earlier in the season than hardy annuals, and biennials can winter over even in cold climates as fair-sized plants. It is thus easier to grow them in a permanent perennial bed than in an annual bed that's tilled up after the frost. Some of the standard garden biennials are Canterbury bells (*Campanula medium*), hollyhocks (*Alcea rosea*), foxgloves (*Digitalis* species), and sweet William (*Dianthus barbatus*). But even among these the category is fluid. I've grown some hollyhocks that flower the first year from seed, and others that persist for years as perennials. Certain foxglove varieties also have been bred to flower the first year.

Some common perennials that most people recognize are chrysanthemums, daylilies, peonies, and irises. But these fine old standards are only the beginning. There are hundreds and hundreds of garden perennials for you to discover and combine in color pictures that are yours alone. This is why gardening with perennials can become—let me warn you—addicting. By the time my perennial bed is starting to show signs of life in early April, I always have a list of new things I want to try in it, and ideas about rearranging it to make this year's show even better than the last one.

"Now wait," you may say. "I thought the whole point about perennials was that they're permanent—that you can plant them once and then never have to touch them again." Well, to some extent this is true. You can find daylily and peony clumps that have been growing untended for a hundred years or more, next to very old houses or cellar holes. But a mixed perennial bed does not have this sort of longevity, and if a maintenance-free flower garden is your chief goal, you'd best forgo perennials. They not only need some yearly care—such as feeding, staking, and cutting back the dead growth—but many of them must also be divided every few years to keep the clumps healthy and vigorous, or to keep them from overspreading their bounds. You must also experiment a bit to see which ones do best in your climate, your soil, and all the odd little conditions of your particular yard, discarding some and trying new ones.

Another common misconception about perennials is that they bloom all season long, the way annuals do. Not so. Most of them bloom for a few weeks, some even less. A few, which you'll come to cherish, might bloom from a month to six weeks or longer. Many will come up with a second flowering or a scattered continuous one through the rest of the season if you remove dead blossoms or cut back the flower stalks after bloom. Moreover, by combining plants that flower at different times, you can ensure that there's always plenty of color. Doing so takes a lot of planning, and you'll always have spots where nothing is happening at the moment. This is where the skill comes in. Planning such a garden is like conducting an orchestra that won't sit still. By the time the violins show up, the flutes have wandered off; when you finally get the trumpets' attention, the oboes have broken for lunch. But when you do manage to pull off a symphony, the effect is glorious!

If you doubt this, look at photographs of the great herbaceous borders in full bloom on the country estates of England. These perennial gardens have a monumental quality that you cannot achieve with annuals. Granted, there are few places in the United States, or even the world, that are as favorable for this sort of gardening as England, where winters are mild, summers are cool, and the air is filled with the moisture that is so flattering to both faces and flowers. But there are many ways in which the perennial garden concept can be adapted to other regions. It is particularly suited to cold areas such as Maine, where I live and garden. Here most annuals do not bloom profusely until at least early summer and they're cut down by the first frost, whereas many perennials bloom in the spring or fall months during which night frosts are common. As I write this, a heavy April snow is falling on my perennial bed full of spring flowers, with no ill effects at all. In warm-climate or dry-climate areas, perennials can be made to work well too; it's just a matter of choosing the right ones (see page 174).

What Kind of Garden?

THERE ARE MANY DIFFERENT WAYS of using perennials, some of them very simple. An effective planting can be designed with just one type of plant. Take daylilies, for example. If you've ever seen the wild orange ones growing along the road in early summer, you know that their bloom lasts only a few weeks. But if you were to plant the old-fashioned lemon lily, which blooms earliest of all, along with a succession of hybrid varieties that bloom at different times, you could have a daylily bed in bloom from spring well into the fall. (Catalogs with a wide daylily selection usually specify blooming times.) A daylily display like this might edge a lawn or a driveway, and would work very well as a naturalized planting on a steep bank, where the vigorous roots would help keep the soil from eroding.

You might plant an all-iris bed for a late spring display, an all-chrysanthemum bed in fall. Or site an all-hosta bed in a shady spot; this stalwart perennial is grown not so much for its flowers, nice as they are, but for the varied shapes and colors of its leaves— large and blue-green, small and wavy with white markings, green edged in yellow, yellow edged in green, and many others. When different species and varieties of hostas are combined, the effect is lovely.

In fact you might take any one of the plants in the List of Perennials and plant it in a mass to lend color to a spot even briefly. Globeflowers (*Trollius*), for example, have blossoms that look like giant yellow or orange buttercups with lights glowing inside them. A bed of these in part shade, blooming in late spring or early summer, will be so beautiful that you won't mind having to look elsewhere for your color later in the season. For summer you might also try a bed of feathery astilbes or, like my former Connecticut neighbor Jean Orr, grow a profusion of tall rose and purple foxgloves against a barn. For fall you could plant a bed composed of tall and short asters or a bed of tall, late-blooming sedums in mixed shades.

Combining two species can also be very effective. Try a bed of yellow yarrow and blue veronica together. Or mass columbines and lupines together; both are early-flowering self-sowers that will naturalize together in harmony if they like the conditions in your garden. You might even mingle a few particularly fast- and low-growing species such as perennial geraniums, foamflower, and catmint together to make a flowery carpet. Or combine a few native plants such as blazing star, butterfly weed, and coneflowers in a tamed mini-prairie.

Then again you might want to try your hand at an old-fashioned perennial border. It need not be large, grand, and formal like those English showpieces I mentioned above, and you won't need a squadron of hired gardeners to keep it beautiful. It might even have a naturalistic feel to it, with lots of plants native to the fields and woodland clearings of the region in which you live. (After all, aren't flower gardens really just our adaptations of these? See the wildflower chapter for more on the subject.) Picture a continuum with a wild meadow at one end and a highly controlled bed where every plant stays in its designated space at the other. In between lie the old-fashioned cottage gardens, characteristic of the English countryside or the dooryard gardens of our own colonial days, where favorite plants intermingle in a charming confusion. Or beds in which the outlines are quite formal but the plants have an intended exuberance, spilling out over the tidy edging or self-sowing here

and there to create a look of spontaneity. You will find that when these gardens are successful, there is still a firm hand at work. The sedum has only been allowed to creep a certain distance into the gravel path. The mauve breadseed poppies that "volunteer" are only allowed to remain if they make a harmonious combination with their neighbors.

Even with the most casual gardens you need two things: careful planning and excellent preparation for your bed. Both will pay off in less work and a better effect later on.

Planning

THE FIRST THING YOU NEED TO DECIDE is in what season you want your garden to be effective. Here are some of your choices:

A GARDEN FOR SPRING AND EARLY SUMMER

The mainstay of this garden might be irises, columbines, lupines, Oriental poppies, pinks, bellflowers, gas plant, coral bells, and perhaps some of the early veronicas. (If the bed were in partial shade, you'd eliminate the irises, poppies, pinks, and gas plant and add some more shade-tolerant perennials such as bleeding heart, foxgloves, wild blue phlox, globeflowers, primrose, and perennial geraniums.) To extend the blooming season, you might start the show with spring bulbs such as crocus, grape hyacinth, and miniature narcissus, whose foliage would later be hidden by the perennials. Then in the gaps between the perennials you'd plant bushy annuals such as snapdragons and low-growing cosmos, which would take over after the perennials have finished blooming. You might also plan to have your summer bloom elsewhere on the property. If you go away for the summer, and only care about spring bloom, you can forget the annuals altogether.

A SUMMER GARDEN

By planning carefully you can keep a border in bloom for several months in the summer. In the north, prime time would be mid June through August; in a warmer part of the country, you might focus on June and July or even May and June, before the intense summer heat gets the best of your plants.

The first part of the show is the easiest—early to mid summer is the favorite blooming time for most perennials, such as yarrow, bellflower, butterfly weed, delphinium, pinks, coreopsis, most veronicas and daylilies, scabiosa, balloon flower, Shasta daisies, and phlox. Following these you will need some of the late summer bloomers that make such good "bridge plants" between the midsummer and fall bloomers—great stalwarts like purple coneflower, false sunflower (*Heliopsis*), blazing star (*Liatris*), the various rudbeckias, and the late daylily varieties. A number of the early bloomers, such as pinks, coreopsis, and delphiniums, will rebloom if their flower stalks are cut back right after their heaviest flowering. And then there are those few heroic perennials that never really stop blooming from early to late summer, such as fringed bleeding heart (*Dicentra eximia*), and those, like hostas and ferns, whose foliage is effective all season.

There's no reason why you cannot extend your summer garden's season by including spring- and fall-blooming perennials. I do this. But remember that any space occupied by those plants will diminish the space available for the summer-blooming perennials. One solution is to tuck into the border a mixed collection of tulips that will bloom over a period of several weeks in late spring (see page 515), but treat them as annuals. Tulip foliage is rather ugly after the plants have bloomed, and the flowers are often at their best only the first year. They're also relatively inexpensive to replace. So if you can bring yourself to do it, simply dig them up after they bloom and plant some annuals you've potted up and have kept ready to take their place. Choose ones like calendulas and snapdragons, which will keep blooming even after a few frosts in the fall.

A FALL GARDEN

A garden planted for fall display might start with some of the bridge plants, combined with the real fall bloomers such as sneezeweed (*Helenium autumnale*), autumn monkshood, late sedums such as 'Autumn Joy,' asters, Japanese anemones, goldenrod, chrysanthemums, and some of the very late blooming lilies (*Lilium*) and daylilies (*Hemerocallis*). A fall garden can be quite beautiful, with many of the flowers displaying the same hues as autumn leaves but with the contrast of pink chrysanthemums, the blues of monkshoods, the wonderful rose and deep purple of asters, and the crisp accents of white asters and mums. Incorporating shrubs with bright fall foliage, such as spicebush, Virginia sweetspire, and oakleaf hydrangea within the garden is another tactic. And don't overlook the fall foliage of the perennials themselves. Some, such as certain peonies, sundrops, and geraniums, turn glorious shades of red or gold.

It may be that having different gardens for different seasons works best for your landscape. For example a spring garden might be sited close to the house and easily seen from indoors, a summer garden near a pool or patio where you spend your summer hours, and a fall garden at the far edge of the lawn where its blazing colors will stand out from afar.

If you have limited time and space and can only have one garden, try planting one with spring bulbs and perennials followed by summer annuals, followed by fall perennials that bloom even after frost. This solution is particularly useful in cold climates where annuals have a short season.

Site

MOST PERENNIALS ARE SUN-LOVING plants that, were they growing in the wild, would choose open meadows and prairies, or bright clearings in the woods where trees have fallen. Most of them need at least six hours of sun per day to grow and bloom well. So the first question asked in planning a border is usually, "Where is a good sunny spot?" Keep in mind that afternoon sun is stronger than morning sun. Thus in cool climates a garden that faced south or west would be ideal, and an eastern exposure would be preferred in hot climates where afternoon sun is too strong. But an ideal exposure will not do you much good if the spot is one you will never see. Another factor: some flowers, such as daisies, daffodils, and sunflowers, will actually turn to face the sun. With in-

the-round flower shapes this is not a consideration: astilbes, for example, look the same from any direction. And with some sites it may not matter. I once had a planting of daffodils far across the lawn, where I couldn't tell that they were facing the other way, only that the sun backlit them beautifully and made them glow. With pansies near the kitchen window it makes more of a difference. A pansy with its back to you is not much fun.

If you lack a sunny site, don't feel deprived. There are many perennials that actually prefer shade during part of the day, or better yet, filtered light such as that provided by a tree that lets some sunlight in. Often these are spring-flowering perennials that would be woodland plants if they lived in the wild, blooming before the trees are heavy with leaves. If you try some of these out of necessity, you'll probably decide you are fortunate to have a spot like this for your garden. Flower colors sometimes look more vibrant in dappled shade than they do in strong sunlight, which can wash them out. (See page 25 for more on gardening in shade.)

It is crucial, however, that the site have good drainage. Most perennials will rot if water collects around them and sits there, especially in winter. If your choice site is wet, you can build a garden around moisture-loving plants, but for a more typical garden you'll need to correct the problem either by draining the site (see page 27) or by creating a raised bed. This can sometimes be done just by mounding the soil 6 inches or so, but if the problem is severe you'll need to raise the bed further with a retaining wall.

The site will also need to be free of encroaching roots from trees and shrubs.

Most perennials will not tolerate competition from those roots, which not only take up space but also rob the soil of moisture and fertility. If the problem is unavoidable, you may have to pour an underground concrete barrier about 2 feet deep, to restrict the roots' growth.

Size of the Garden

IF YOU HAVE ONLY A SMALL AMOUNT OF time to spend in your perennial garden, stick to one of moderate size, say between 10 and 25 feet long. Figure that you may need to spend several days on the initial preparation and then a few hours each week maintaining it. In subsequent years you'll not only have to do the regular maintenance, but you'll have to spend at least a full day in spring and in fall dividing plants and putting things in order. If, for you, the point of gardening is in the doing, a large perennial garden will be a joy.

Deciding how wide to make the bed is tricky: if you make it as narrow as 3 feet, it will be easy to tend, and you will not have to worry as much about plants' hiding one another as you would with a wide border. On the other hand, the wider the border, the more you'll be able to give the effect of continuous bloom, since you can view a number of overlapping groups of plants with several of them in bloom at any given time. This not only makes the bed more colorful when seen as a whole, it also allows you to create smaller plant "pictures" within it, in which adjacent plants are combined in interesting ways. You

might start with a narrow border, then try a wide one after you become experienced with more plants and know their relative heights and periods of bloom.

Expense is less a consideration than you might think. True, to fill a 50- by 8-foot bed with big clumps of nursery-grown perennials will be quite costly. But you can also buy only a third of the full number of plants and then wait for them to form larger clumps, filling in the gaps with annuals in the meantime. In a few years you'll be dividing some and even giving extras away. You may also fill your garden up with friends' donations, though keep in mind that these gifts are usually plants that love to take over the garden. Spreaders such as purple coneflower or bee balm are only worth growing if you're prepared to weed out the excess from time to time (see the box on page 194).

Shape of the Garden

A "PERENNIAL BORDER" USUALLY JUST means a "perennial bed," though often the plot does border something: a lawn, a path, a fence, a wall, a building. It can also be a freestanding, or "island" bed, surrounded by lawn, ground cover, or paving. Beds can have formal geometrical shapes or they can be free-form, with sweeping S-curves. The important thing to remember in planning them is that an island bed will be seen from all sides; thus the tall plants will go in the center, the medium-height plants on either side of them, and the low plants along the entire edge. In a bed that backs up to a building, hedge, or other such feature, the tall plants will go in back, and the others will descend in height toward the viewer. Which shape you make your bed is partly a matter of style. Is the property formal or informal in feeling? If informal, meandering free-form beds would be appropriate. It's also a matter of how the bed will best be viewed. Often the view from the end of a long border is dazzling, because telescoped in this way the color is so concentrated—but only if the site is level or sloping slightly upward from the viewer. Beds with lots of curves can also be tricky when viewed end to end.

Backdrops and Edgings

A TRADITIONAL PERENNIAL GARDEN often has a "frame" around it like a picture. If you're lucky enough to have a tall stone or brick wall in the right location, this will be an excellent backdrop as long as it does not cast too much shade on the garden. It's also a good idea for the rear plants to start at least 3 feet out from the wall, for good air circulation. A house, barn, or garage can also be a backdrop, as can a tall wooden fence.

A tall hedge is also very effective—evergreens such as yew, holly, hemlock, or boxwood are traditional choices, because their rich dark green sets off the color of the flowers so beautifully. But a deciduous shrub hedge such as lilac or viburnum would also work. I also love to see perennials planted in front of a mixed hedgerow of shrubs and small trees of varying sizes, for the sort of "sunny forest clearing" effect you might actually see in the wild, in which plants of varying heights arrange themselves in layers so that all can be exposed to the sun.

Sometimes I have had a bed that faces the sun, and is meant to be viewed from the sunny side, but will sometimes be seen from the rear. In this case I like to cover the rather ugly bare legs of the tall plants at the rear of the border. I find a row of fairly tall, shade-tolerant ferns is a great solution, as long as they're not a spready sort that will invade the bed.

An edging provides visual definition in front of the bed. It also can be a helpful physical barrier between the lawn and the garden. Your lawn grass and your pinks or creeping veronica will not, by themselves, stay on the correct side of an imaginary line you call the edge of the garden. But for the most part, they'll respect an edging of flagstones, cobblestones, or bricks sunk vertically on end. A metal or plastic edging strip will also keep them in check but without the pleasing visual effect, and these devices have a way of not staying put. And an added benefit of a stone edging is that you can run one wheel of the lawnmower along it; if it is wide enough, foreground perennials can spill out attractively onto the edging and still not be cropped by the mower. I've also had great success just keeping a neat edge with a sharp spade, by cutting a 4-inch-deep V-shaped trench along the front of the garden. I might have to recut it once or twice a year, but it's a low-cost solution and one that leaves me the option of changing the shape of the bed easily if the mood should strike me. At present I have two long perennial borders, edged in cobblestones, with a wide gravel path between them.

Choosing the Plants

The List of Perennials at the end of this chapter describes 50 common, easy-to-grow plants, and in most cases specifies a few good species and/or varieties of each. As you come to realize how many different kinds there are, you'll understand how difficult it was to narrow the list down to this number in order to profile each as fully as possible. These should give you a good start, but I urge you to poke around nurseries and try some new ones each year. Seek out knowledgeable growers, salespeople, and gardening friends in your area and get the benefit of their experience. There are also societies devoted to the culture of specific types of plants (see page 758). Their newsletters often list members whose gardens are at times open to the public. Visiting these wonderful gardens will alert you to new varieties to try, even within a plant group that is familiar to you.

I cannot emphasize enough how important it is to have your plant choices appropriate to your particular region. Most of the plants I have suggested are very widely grown, but even among these some will do better for you than others. In the plant descriptions, I have indicated a few that are not especially suited to hot climates, but even these are often grown by southern gardeners. Some, like delphiniums or lupines, can be planted in fall to overwinter and give a showy early-season display. They are then replaced as if they were annuals. With others it is just a matter of giving them a spot that is shaded during the hottest part of the day. This is often true in parts of the midwest and in the mountain climates of the west as well.

Some perennials grow and bloom more abundantly and earlier in warm climates. Those that perish in the moist winters of the north may flourish in the aridity of the southwest; there a good many of the best flowering plants are more woody or shrublike. And in frost-free areas there is a whole other world of luxuriant bloomers. Both tropical and desert climates have a wide range of suitable plants that are too specialized to list here.

Finally, do not hesitate to use as perennials plants from the lists in other chapters in this book. The wildflower chapter contains numerous plants that might just as well have been included in this one, both for sunny or shady gardens. Summer-blooming plants that grow from bulbs, corms, and tubers are also extremely useful, whether they're hardy ones such as lilies and alliums, or tender ones such as dahlias, cannas, and tuberous begonias that must be overwintered indoors or treated as annuals in cold climates.

Perennial herbs such as oregano, marjoram, and sage are highly ornamental in perennial gardens—the last for its foliage as well as its flowers. In fact the subject of foliage plants in the border could fill a volume on its own. Silver-leaved plants such as artemisias or *Veronica incana* have long been favorites as plants that blend, soften, or generally tie the stronger-colored elements of the garden together visually by means of a subtly recurring theme. Dark red or purple-leaved plants such as orach, dark-leaved cannas, certain varieties of coral bells, or penstemon 'Husker Red' also harmonize well with flower colors. Often the foliage texture of certain perennials is what wins you over, whether it is the fernlike grace of astilbe and snakeroot, the grassy leaves of Siberian iris, or the smooth, fat pale green leaves of the tall sedums.

Note also the discussion of ferns in the wildflower chapter. Ornamental grasses, too, have become extremely popular in recent years and their availability in nurseries is a welcome trend. Some are invasive and it is wise to avoid those that can be a pest both in our own gardens and in the surrounding countryside.

Shrubs can also be combined well with perennials, either in a mixed border where they are used in large numbers, or as the occasional shrubby mass in an otherwise herbaceous plot. Shrubs can lend solidity to a border (especially a large one), and are an excellent way to give the scene year-round beauty. Some that work well are potentilla, roses, hyndrangea, viburnum, azalea, daphne, fothergilla, mock orange, and those with colorful leaves such as smokebush or purple-leaf sand cherry. Dwarf evergreens are also good for contrast and winter interest. If there is a building or trellis at the rear of the garden, vines such as sweet peas, morning glories, and clematis can add a whole other tier to the scene.

In some instances, of course, your choices will be influenced by the nature of the site. If your garden is partially shaded, look in the descriptions for shade-tolerant plants. If the garden spot is moist, select plants that will thrive there such as bee balm, Japanese primrose, Japanese iris, meadowsweet, snakeroot, sneezeweed, globeflower, and astilbe. If it is very dry, look for those that tolerate dry soil (see page 192). If your property is very windy, you might want to avoid tall plants such as delphiniums, which blow over easily. If your soil is either very acid or very alkaline, this might influence your choices, but since soil pH is easily brought within the ideal range for most perennials, which is 5.5 to 6.5, pH is only occasionally a critical factor (see page 21).

Winter hardiness zones (pages 756 to 757) provide some guidance, but remember that they are not hard-and-fast categories. Have you ever wondered why the zones assigned to a plant might differ drastically from one book or catalog to another? This is probably because peoples' experience with plants varies so much from garden to garden, even within a given zone. From year to year an individual garden may go up or down a zone. You might hear a zone 5 resident say, "We just had a zone 6 winter." Remember, the USDA zone numbers refer merely to the degree of winter cold a plant can take. The survival of perennials actually depends on many other factors, such as soil moisture levels at various times in the year, the amount of heat or humidity in summer, the fertility of the soil, and so forth. Furthermore, planting in a sheltered spot or applying a winter mulch may allow you to grow plants that are said to be too tender for your zone. And even if some are short-lived in your garden, they still will have served a purpose; it's not like losing a 20-foot tree.

When all is said and done, your garden should be composed of plants that please you. If the lordly and the majestic excite you, plant hollyhocks and plume poppies. If the soft and the fluffy comfort you, grow pink astilbe. If you're drawn to the eccentric and prickly side of life, choose globe thistle and sea holly. Perhaps it's nostalgia that moves you forward ("Mother always had foxgloves"), a preference for fragrant flowers, or a desire for both you and your garden to participate more fully in the rest of the natural world. For this, take your cues from the birds, the bees, and the other creatures that work there. Perhaps you just have a general idea of what the garden should look like, such as green and restful or bursting with color (both good ideas)—or exactly like Sissinghurst (too ambitious).

Making a Plan

ONCE YOU'VE DECIDED ON THE general concept of the garden, as well as its site, shape, size, and season, you'll need some kind of plan. Start with a list of possible plants. I find it helpful, when making such a list, to leaf through a book or two and some nursery catalogs, just to remind myself of what is out there. In order to make my final selection of flowers for a specific garden, I have to keep several things in mind at once: color, height, blooming period, and any other relevant features such as "attractive basal foliage" (which should not be hidden), or "unsightly foliage after bloom" (which should). Since it's difficult to keep all these things in mind at once, make the list as descriptive as possible.

Planning the Sunny Perennial Garden   FIG. 32

Plant Height in feet	Period of Bloom			
	June	July	August	September
	blanketflower			
1'	coral bells			
	Salvia 'May Night'			
		daylily 'Stella d'Oro'		
	catmint			
		Coreopsis 'Moonbeam'		
		Veronica 'Sunny Border Blue'		
2'		yarrow 'Fire King'		
			blazing star	
			Sedum 'Autumn Joy'	
			Rudbeckia 'Goldsturm'	
3'	Siberian iris			
		Shasta daisy		
		Phlox paniculata		
		purple coneflower		
			Aster 'Alma Potschke'	
4'			Helenium	
5'		meadow rue		

The next step is to make a chart like the one shown in Figure 32. Let's say I am choosing plants for the sunny border shown on page 180, which is 25 feet long and 6 feet wide. I'd like it to bloom for as much of the summer as possible, but with a bed this size my best bet is to aim for peak bloom in July and August, with some of it starting in June and some still left in September. To this end I have deliberately selected some of the most long-blooming varieties I could find.

I take each plant from my list and place it on the chart according to its blooming period (indicated at the top) and its height (indicated at the left side). Both of these statistics will be approximate, especially with plants I'm trying for the first time. Plant height varies drastically from one part of the country to another and is also affected by soil type, moisture level, sun, fertility, and the age of the plant (some plants are shorter the first year). Blooming periods are affected by much the same factors and may be quite different in your garden from what is indicated on the chart. Also, "bloom" on my chart is not always synonymous with "period of interest," since in some cases the plant is grown for its leaf color, berries, or some other feature.

Planning the Shady Perennial Garden   Fig. 33

Plant Height in feet	Period of Bloom				
	May	June	July	August	September
			bellflower, short		
		Geranium 'Lancastriense'			
			Astilbe 'Sprite'		
		Geranium 'Johnson's Blue'			
1'	bleeding heart, short				
		lady's mantle			
	Phlox divaricata				
	columbine				
		hosta			
2'	globeflower				
		bellflower, tall			
	foxglove				
3'	bleeding heart, tall				
		astilbe, tall late			
4'				Anemone 'Robustissima'	
		meadowsweet			
5'			snakeroot		

I always write down more plants than will fit into the bed, then eliminate some. I might find I've too many plants in the middle height range. Or perhaps I've picked too many white flowers, or too many pink ones. In fact I often make the final choice on the basis of color combinations that have worked for me in the past. For example, in the plan on page 180, the scheme for early summer gives me the blues and violets of Siberian iris, salvia, catmint, and veronica, overlapping with the sunnier hues of blanketflower, and the golden yellow of 'Stella d'Oro,' a long-blooming daylily. A bit later, Shasta daisies introduce a crisp white note and a red yarrow, *Achillea* 'Fire King,' adds pizzazz. Pink is excluded in order to achieve strong primary-color look for midsummer. Later in summer the scheme takes on more of a flamboyant richness with a foretaste of autumn, mingling the rust red of *Helenium* 'Moerheim Beauty' and the rosier red of *Aster* 'Alma Potschke' with the purples of blazing star, meadow rue, and purple coneflower.

The fine-tuning of the plan takes place when the bar graph is translated into the actual plan. Here I use paper marked with a light blue grid, letting each square represent 1 square foot. Working from the back of the bed to the front, I draw in areas where each plant should grow, usually in irregular patches that run fairly parallel to the front of the bed, but most of them sloping slightly to the back, all in the same direction, as if I were weaving a pattern in cloth. This shape allows me to overlap as many plants as possible, for the appearance of saturated color, but it means that I have to pay a lot of attention to the height each will be when it is blooming, so that nothing will be hidden. This can be especially tricky with long-blooming or reblooming species. The Siberian iris, on the other hand, blooms early and then quits, so that I can plant something tall in front of it for late color.

I also pay very close attention to how each plant group will look in combination with the ones adjacent to it. I not only look for harmonious color combinations, but also interesting contrasts in flower shapes. I always make sure there are some spike-shaped flowers (in this case veronicas, salvias, and blazing star). These balance the flattops (like yarrow), the daisy shapes (like gaillardias), the big blobby clusters (like phlox), and the airy-cloud shape of meadow rue. I also look for variety in foliage—the poufs of thread-leaved coreopsis mixed with meaty-leaved sedums and grasslike daylilies. The entire shape of the plant should also be taken into account. The front of a bed, for instance, is less interesting if it is a row of mound shapes; it's better to alternate these with skinny, upright plants and low, flat carpets.

At this point I often discard a few plants and perhaps add a few, to make it all work. Further fine-tuning, of course, will take place when the garden is no longer on paper but in the ground and blooming. The whole thing can be rearranged. But if I use some plants that are harder to move than others—balloon flower, butterfly weed, and gas plant, for example—I'm extra careful about putting them in an appropriate spot for their height.

As you build your border always imagine that you're looking at it from the spot where you will most often view it. Try to space out your plants for each blooming period so that you can see color dotted throughout the whole border at any given time, not just a big lump of it in one spot. I wouldn't make a bed perfectly symmetrical, but it should have a balance to it. Repeating plants or plant combinations throughout a long border is a good way to achieve this.

Sometimes it's helpful to make several different border plans, one for each part of the blooming season, just to check for large gaps in the flow of color. You can do this by placing several pieces of tracing paper over the original plan, one at a time, and drawing on them only the plants that will be in bloom together.

Another thing to keep in mind is what the foliage of each plant will look like after it has finished blooming. Will it be attractive like that of a Siberian iris? Or will it look messy and dried out like that of an Oriental poppy? In the latter case you'd try to arrange for a bushy mid- or late-season plant such as phlox to grow up and hide the unsightly early-blooming one.

You do not *have* to do all this on paper. If I'm starting a garden from scratch, I will sometimes just set out all the pots where I think they should go, then stare at them, think about them, rearrange them, and plant them only after I'm sure of the right position for each. But if you are new to laying out perennials, a plan is very helpful, especially since you need to know what heights, colors, and bloom periods you'll need before you go shopping. Even if yours is an "accumulation" garden, with many plants scavenged from friends, it is nice to have a master scheme to refer to, which you update from time to time.

The second plan shown (Figure 35) is for a semishaded garden in which one or two sides are bounded by a fence, a building, or taller woody plantings. I designed it

to span a long season, despite the fact that so many shade-loving plants are early bloomers. There are, after all, some late ones you can grow, as well as many that are of interest for their leaves alone. I also think that sparse or spotty bloom is easier to carry off in a shaded spot. Like the natural woodland it imitates, a shade garden is meant to be green, the better to highlight the glowing blooms that do appear.

This little garden's display begins in May or June with pink bleeding hearts, the almost electric lavender blue of *Phlox divaricata*, dainty red-and-yellow American columbine, and the large buttercup-like orbs of a globeflower. The low-growing fringed bleeding hearts (*Dicentra eximia*) contribute not only season-long bloom, but also the fernlike beauty of their season-long foliage. The taller bleeding hearts in the rear—*Dicentra spectabilis*—will, as their botanical name implies, dominate the bed with their bold, arching stems and striking dangling blooms. Later the whole plants will die down and other foliage will fill in around them. Early and mid summer bring the gentle pastel shades of perennial foxglove (creamy yellow), bellflowers (blue), and the dainty pinks of a perennial geranium. Later blooms include tall, plumelike meadowsweet, the white candles of snakeroot, and pale pink Japanese anemones.

In a garden like this, foliage plants could also be the key players. I've suggested several varieties of hosta, one with green leaves edged with pale green, and one whose leaves are gold-colored throughout. (Their late bloom is also a plus.) Ferns such as the native maidenhair would also be a welcome addition. Other excellent choices for this garden might be coral bells, annual

Plan for a Sunny Perennial Garden (6' by 25')

FIG. 34

1. *Iris siberica*, purple variety
2. *Iris siberica*, white variety
3. *Iris siberica*, blue variety
4. *Phlox paniculata* 'David'
5. *Phlox paniculata* 'Franz Schubert'
6. meadow rue (*Thalictrum rochebrunianum* 'Lavender Mist')
7. *Helenium autumnale* 'Moerheim Beauty'
8. *Aster novae-angliae* 'Alma Potschke'
9. Shasta daisy (*Leucanthemum* × *superbum* 'Becky')
10. purple coneflower (*Echinacea purpurea*)
11. *Rudbeckia fulgida* 'Goldsturm'
12. *Sedum* 'Autumn Joy'
13. blazing star (*Liatris spicata* 'Kobold')
14. *Veronica* 'Sunny Border Blue'
15. *Coreopsis verticillata* 'Moonbeam'
16. yarrow (*Achillea* 'Fire King')
17. catmint (*Nepeta faassenii* 'Blue Wonder')
18. blanketflower (*Gaillardia* 'Goblin')
19. daylily (*Hemerocallis* 'Stella d'Oro')
20. coral bells (*Heuchera*), brightly colored variety
21. *Salvia* 'May Night'

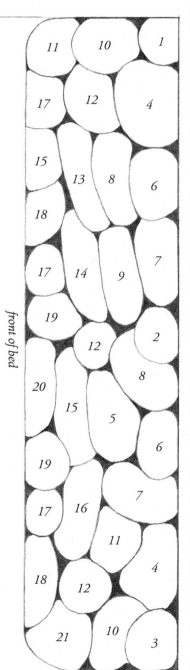

Plan for a Shady Perennial Garden (6' by 12½')

Fig. 35

1. snakeroot (*Cimicifuga racemosa*)

2. meadowsweet (*Filipendula rubra* 'Venusta')

3. globeflower (*Trollius europaeus* 'Lemon Queen')

4. globeflower (*Trollius chinensis* 'Golden Queen')

5. bellflower (*Campanula percisifolia* 'Telham Beauty')

6. bellflower (*Campanula percisifolia* 'Grandiflora Alba')

7. bellflower (*Campanula carpatica*)

8. foxglove (*Digitalis grandiflora*)

9. bleeding heart (*Dicentra spectabilis*)

10. bleeding heart (*Dicentra eximia*)

11. *Anemone vitifolia* 'Robustissima'

12. columbine (*Aquilegia canadensis*)

13. *Hosta sieboldiana* 'Frances Williams'

14. *Hosta* 'Gold Standard'

15. *Hosta sieboldiana* 'Elegans'

16. *Phlox divaricata*

17. *Geranium* 'Johnson's Blue'

18. *Geranium sanguineum striatum* 'Lancastriense'

19. lady's mantle (*Alchemilla mollis*)

20. *Astilbe simplicifolia* 'Sprite'

21. *Astilbe* 'Red Charm'

22. *Astilbe thunbergii* 'Ostrich Plume'

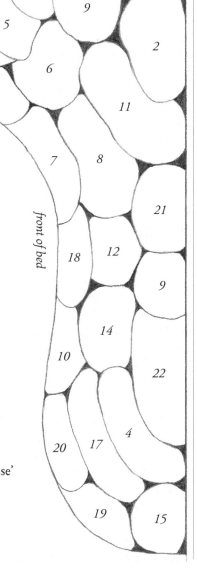

or perennial forget-me-nots, lungwort (*Pulmonaria*), primroses, lilies, and almost any of the native woodland wildflowers described in the wildflower chapter. Small spring bulbs and violas might also find a place. Some of the plants, notably trollius and astilbe, appreciate consistent moisture, and substitutions should be made if the site is a dry one.

You will find that your garden, over time, will take on a personality all its own. Groups will blend with one another. Plants will self-sow, and tall specimens may appear toward the front of the bed. Allow for some of this rule breaking. As long as you set a few limits, such serendipity can only make the garden more interesting, and more like a woven fabric.

Preparing the Bed

IDEALLY A PERENNIAL BED SHOULD BE prepared in fall, then planted in spring. This allows the loosely dug soil to settle, and any newly added amendments a chance to mellow into it. It is also best to do your digging and mixing at a time when the soil is not all clumpy from spring moisture. I admit that I've sometimes violated this rule out of necessity or sheer impatience. But if you can muster the foresight, fall preparation is better, especially if you're giving the bed first-class treatment and digging it deeply.

When you get a perennial bed ready, you're providing space for long-term residents, not short-term tenants. Thus while you might prepare your vegetable or annual garden hastily one year, vowing to better it the following season, with perennials you have one chance to make good.

Once you've made a firm decision about where the bed will be sited and what size and shape it will have, mark it. If it is straight-sided, lay it out with strings and stakes. If it is curved, use a garden hose on a warm, sunny day when the hose is limp and pliable. Then edge the bed with a sharp spade. Remove all grass sod and weeds— roots and all. I try to remove rocks bigger than an egg. If sod must be removed, the ideal would be to lay black plastic over it for up to a year to kill all vegetation, then incorporate the refuse into the soil. If this is not possible, remove the sod by skimming just below the surface with a sharp spade, then compost the sod. I've sometimes gotten away with tilling the sod under, but there's always a risk that it will regrow, especially if it's composed of deeply rooted, rhizomatous meadow grasses.

Picture what your perennials will want: a weed-free soil that has been loosened to a good depth, with a great deal of organic matter added to it for perfect tilth, and nutrients for proper growth. Even though you'll be amending the top layer every year, the bed will be more luxurious if you loosen and enrich the bottom layers as well. If you double-dig the bed, using the technique described on page 23, you can improve the soil to a greater depth than that of your digging fork or shovel, and this will certainly give your plants an excellent start. And it may be necessary to do this if there is a hardpan—that is, a hard, compacted layer just below all your nicely fluffed up soil. It is rarely practical to double-dig very large areas however, unless it is part of your training for the Olympic weight-lifting team. And to be realistic, digging the soil to a depth of 10 inches or so is adequate for most situations.

For specific information on soil fertility, see Plants Need Good Soil on page 5 and Feeding the Soil on page 10. Generally when I'm preparing a bed I dig in about 2 inches of compost and/or manure and about 2 inches of peat moss, as well as some rock phosphate, lime, and greensand (for amounts, use a soil test and the information on pages 8 to 22 as guidelines). I work it in with a rototiller if the bed is large, with a digging fork if it's small enough that the task is manageable. (Tillers, handy as they are, are somewhat destructive of the soil's natural structure.) When I'm done the soil looks dark and rich, like chocolate cake mix, and the surface is much higher than it was before I started (though it will later settle to almost its original level). It feels so loose and fluffy that I can dig it with my hands, without even using a trowel.

If I have done my job right, I do not really need to add any more fertilizer to the soil when I set in the plants. In subsequent years I might top-dress the bed with an inch or so of compost or manure in fall, letting it mellow in over the winter. I'll dig or scratch it into the soil a bit, but usually I try not to disturb the plants' roots; besides, plenty of digging and scratching goes on in the course of regular weeding and dividing, so it all eventually gets worked in.

In spring I might also add a liquid organic fertilizer such as fish emulsion to certain plants like delphiniums, which are heavy feeders and need that extra boost to grow strong, healthy stems—or any plants that are looking feeble and might need that extra kick. Since my soil is acid, I also work in some lime around plants such as pinks, which do best with an alkaline soil.

But again, all these are practices that are best adjusted to your own soil's particular needs. I tend to be conservative about feeding perennials, because I've found that too much high-nitrogen fertilizer can lead to tall, leafy, weak-stemmed plants that are hard to support and even short on bloom.

Planting and Dividing

PERENNIALS REPRODUCE VEGETATIVELY —that is, by sending up new stems from the roots, rhizomes, or tubers. Those same plants also reproduce by seeds, but many of the commonly grown ones are hybrids, and therefore their offspring will not look the same as the parent plant if you save and grow their seeds. Also, since most perennials take longer to attain flowering size than annuals, most gardeners grow them from plants they buy in a nursery or obtain from friends. Nevertheless, growing perennials from seed is a fun and challenging activity, and some are quite easy. Blanketflower, coreopsis, delphinium, and a number of others will grow to flowering size in one season.

I also like to grow a few self-sowers— plants that will reseed themselves in my garden—such as foxgloves, lupines, and columbines. They may not always breed true to the parent or come up where I want them to, but the seedlings can be moved or eliminated. Working with them gives the garden a controlled but natural look, as if things were allowed to happen accidentally. As permanent as a perennial garden is, I enjoy having, say, 25 percent of it in flux. There should always be a few places where I can try out new plants, tuck in some annuals, add a striking foliage plant or a useful and attractive herb.

The best time to plant perennials is when they are just starting to show signs of life. If you order them by mail, they will be shipped in this near-dormant state and, with any luck, they'll arrive at the proper time for planting: when the ground has thawed but is no longer too damp for digging—April to May in my climate. If you place your order as soon as you receive the catalog, you stand a better chance of getting your delivery on time, as well as a better shot at finding the varieties you want.

Planting Perennials *Fig. 36*

Plant fibrous-rooted perennials with the roots spread out and the crown at soil level.

Plant Oriental poppies in a hole deep enough for the taproot, with the crown an inch or two below the soil surface.

Plant bearded irises with the rhizome right at soil level; mound slightly if drainage is less than perfect.

Plant peonies in a deep hole with compost, firmed well, in the bottom. The pink "eyes" (buds) should be 1 to 2 inches below the soil surface.

Plant daylilies in groups by spreading the roots over a cone-shaped mound of compost in the center of the hole; keep crowns at soil level.

Often the plants arrive with some fresh new growth on them. These young shoots are very soft and tender because they have emerged under greenhouse conditions or even in transit, and may be vulnerable to excessive cold, wind, or strong sun. They can be planted in the garden right away if you first soak the roots thoroughly and then shield them with some sort of covering for several days to acclimate them.

But I prefer to pot up mail-order arrivals in a rich potting medium (say, one-third compost, one-third soilless mix, and one-third soil) and then harden them off in a protected, partly shaded spot. After a few weeks I plant them, along with their potful of loose, rich soil.

Mail-order sources offer a wonderful selection of often hard-to-find plants, but whenever possible I try to shop close to

---

Dividing Perennials   FIG. *37*

Pull apart fibrous-rooted perennials with your fingers.

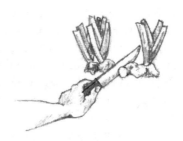

Use a sharp, clean knife to divide bearded irises, making sure there are buds on each division.

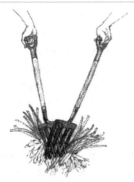

Pry apart large daylily clumps with two digging forks intertwined back to back.

Some plants, such as asters and chrysanthemums, become woody and unproductive at the center of the clump. Pull off fresh side shoots at the edge of the clump and replant them, discarding the center.

home. I find that even in my remote part of the world local nurseries try very hard to keep up with new varieties, and have a good awareness of what will perform best in my climate. I also just like the idea of supporting local businesses, and I love the interchange with salespeople and fellow customers that goes on in such places. I usually have to make several visits, because it takes a while for the nurseries to pot up all those perennials in springtime. I also like to wait until the roots have become a little established in the pot and the growing tips are all visible. I look for ones in which the new growth is healthy, with many shoots, not ones that have grown tall and may even be flowering in their pots. If I cannot plant them right away, I place them in a partly shaded area and keep them well watered. I save the pots and return them to the nursery for reuse.

Wherever you obtain your perennials you should plant them carefully, according to the instructions in Figure 36. Water them in well, then watch for signs of wilting in the days to come, making sure they do not dry out while becoming established. Nursery-grown plants in containers can be planted at almost any time, so you can take advantage of those late summer sales, but if they've been in their pots too long you'll need to loosen the hard, potbound mass of roots with a sharp knife before planting. It's also a good idea to cut back any tall, luxuriant foliage, especially if the weather is hot and dry, and pay careful attention to watering. A mulch for winter protection is advisable if you're planting in fall in a cold climate (see page 55).

There is no hard and fast rule about how closely to space perennials. If I'm filling a large space I might space them far apart and give them a chance to fill in— something that will take a long or short time depending on whether a plant is a "spreader" or not. Overcrowding is neither healthy for them nor economical. In general, I leave about 18 to 24 inches between large, tall-growing perennials, 12 to 18 inches between medium-size ones, and a foot or so between short ones.

After your garden has been growing for a year or two, some plants will need dividing, either because the clumps are crowding others or because they're not blooming as well as they used to. If you notice a dead spot in the center of a clump, it is time to divide. Follow the instructions in Figure 37. Often you will not have to dig up the whole clump, just pull or dig away pieces of it for replanting. I add a few handfuls of compost to each new hole and work it in thoroughly before I set the new divisions in the ground.

In cold climates it is best to divide in spring, when plants are just breaking dormancy and there is at least a month of cool weather ahead in which they can become established. Fall planting is possible only if you can ensure a few months of rooting-in time before hard frost; newly planted clumps might otherwise be frost-heaved. In warm climates, on the other hand, fall planting is ideal, in order to avoid stressing young plants with summer's heat.

Some perennials are customarily divided or planted in late summer or fall regardless of climate, poppies and peonies for example. Certain early bloomers such as coral bells and bleeding heart can be done right after blooming. Irises are divided just after flowering.

Division not only keeps plants healthy, it also provides you with lots of new plants.

In fact, this is the easiest way to obtain them. You can also propagate new plants from your garden by taking stem cuttings (page 733) and by saving seeds from non-hybrid varieties after the plants have flowered (page 125).

Maintenance

K EEPING A PERENNIAL BED PRETTY does not have to be arduous. It consists of a series of small tasks that end up being easier if they're performed regularly.

WEEDING

The weeds are worst in spring when the soil is moist; seeds are germinating, and there's lots of bare ground for them to fill. Once you survive this phase the work is minimal, because the perennial clumps fill in and compete easily with the smaller weeds. In a well-established garden your job mainly consists of tending the front of the bed, where the plants are shorter and less able to shade weeds out, and yanking the occasional tall weed that raises its head farther back. I find it essential to choose front-of-the-bed plants that are vigorous and well adapted to the site. Struggling plants will just leave nice sunny spots where weeds can gain a foothold.

A mulch can also help to keep the bed weed-free, and conserve moisture at the same time. If you've removed all traces of perennial weeds from the soil during preparation, a 2-inch layer of mulch will usually keep annual weeds from germinating. I like something light such as very finely shredded bark, buckwheat hulls, root mulch (chopped-up roots, sold in bags), or leaf mold. Pine needles also make a nice mulch if you have a source. I water the soil very thoroughly, then apply the mulch carefully, dropping shovelfuls between the clumps and spreading it around carefully with my fingers. I try to keep it an inch or so away from the crowns of the plants (the place where the stem joins the root) because this is the part that is most subject to disease and rot, and it needs to dry out between waterings.

A light mulch will have to be replaced or added to each year, since it will decompose and since you will disturb it when you weed, divide plants, or put in new ones. But this is not a bad thing; incorporating the mulch adds organic matter to the soil.

WINTER PROTECTION

Mulching for winter protection is another matter entirely. It is necessary to protect plants that are not quite winter hardy in your area, or to keep fall-planted perennials from being heaved out of the soil by alternate freezing and thawing. By concentrating on plants that can survive my winters, and by planting in spring, I usually manage to avoid the use of any winter protection. Where I live, winter mulches tend to attract voles, which burrow under them, using the garden for both housing and food. Mulch can also cause moisture-susceptible plants to rot. And in the end, applying and removing it adds to my labors.

But when mulching must be done, my material of choice is evergreen boughs, which don't lie flat on the ground, but catch the snow beneath them and hold it there as a protective blanket. I wait until after the ground has frozen. With luck, the voles will have already found their winter quarters by then, and besides, what I want to do is not prevent the soil from freezing but to prevent it from alternately freezing and thawing. Boughs from discarded Christmas trees, available at just about the right time in the season, are a great resource and are easy to remove in spring. Straw is also effective. Autumn leaves raked into the bed will catch and hold the snow to some degree, but avoid flat leaves such as maple, which can mat around the plants. Dead oak leaves, with their crisp, curly shape, are a better choice. Another solution is a cold frame (page 39). You can dig up perennials that may not survive your winter, keep them in the frame until early spring, then replant them where they were before.

STAKING

Staking is my least favorite garden job, probably because it's so difficult to accomplish in a timely, effective, and attractive manner. If I stake a plant too late (in other words, after it has flopped), the clump usually looks like an armload of tangled stems, awkwardly gathered up and pointing in all directions (which is exactly what it is). If I have the intelligence and foresight to stake each plant that I know will need support, well before the ruinous moment, I fare much better. But I have to look at all those supports before the greenery grows up and hides them.

Staking Perennials FIG. 38

Twiggy brush can be stuck in next to perennials in spring; as the plants grow, their foliage will hide the brush that helps support them.

Clumps of perennials can be supported by several bamboo stakes connected with soft green twine.

Tie tall perennials loosely to a bamboo stake with soft green twine.

Metal peony rings are set in the ground in spring; peony stems grow up through the ring and are kept from flopping on the ground.

Furthermore, they are not always successful. Strings can sag. Upright stakes can lean under the weight of heavy clumps. Handy "linking" stakes soon become unlinked by the action of wind, soil movement, and plant growth. Wands with a loop at the end can relinquish their grasp. Circular rings and grids, although I make frequent use of them, are never quite the right diameter, or height. There are countless styles of garden supports, most of them in my garden shed right now, expensive and awkward to store, in every shade of unnatural, unconcealable green. It is possible to spray them black which, oddly enough, is less conspicuous among foliage than green is. I've also found that old rusty fencing can be used in clever ways, and look surprisingly unobtrusive. You can make a cylinder out of a heavy-duty mesh—rather like a low, wide tomato cage—any diameter or height you need. Or you may cut a flat circle of rusty chicken wire and support it on bamboo stakes, wrapping cut strands of the wire around the stakes, so that the plants stems can grow up through the grid. In general, grids are good, especially with clumps that open up at the center and flop outward. Sometimes just a perimeter of bamboo stakes with string crisscrossed between them is enough to do the trick; but you may have to do it twice, as a tall clump outgrows the first grid.

Someday the perfect staking system will be invented. But meanwhile, here are a few helpful strategies.

1. Grow plants that don't need staking, especially in a windy site. Even within a single species, some varieties have better posture than others, either because they are more compact or because they have simply been bred for strong stems.

2. Minimize the need for staking. Choose plants that grow well in your climate; delphiniums and lupines, for example, will be weak-stemmed where summers are hot. Giving plants the amount of sun, fertility, and moisture they prefer will help make them strong-stemmed—and these requirements will not be the same for all species. Space them adequately. With some plants—asters and Shasta daisies, for example—you can cut the clumps back early in the season so the clump will grow shorter and bushier.

3. Go with the flow. Sometimes you can allow the front of some lax-stemmed clump to flop gracefully into the more rigid stems of the clump in front of it, though it takes some planning, skill, and luck to make this work. Some plants, such as asters, can even be pegged down at the front of the clump and allowed to grow upright from the point where the stem is tied to the ground, resulting in a split-level clump. How much you stake sometimes depends on how informal you want the look of your garden to be.

4. Use natural materials whenever possible. Homemade supports made of bamboo and twine are more work to put together than prefabricated gadgets, but they are cheaper and blend in better. Some techniques are shown in Figure 38. Staking with brush is an interesting alternative. You'll need to find a source of strong but twiggy branches (such as birch) that can be stuck in the ground while the perennials are still small; as the stems grow, they'll hide the brush. You'll see bare branches for a while, but at least they look natural. Various brush-staking techniques include upright branches, branches stuck an angle facing the back of the bed, and straighter branches bent over at their tops toward the center of the clump, forming a grid. Often just a pair of crisscrossed sticks or bamboo stakes will lift a plant just enough to show it off and keep it out of the path or off its neighbor.

WATERING

A well-established perennial garden is much more drought tolerant than a bed of annual flowers or vegetables. Many of the plants are deeply rooted, and the big, bushy clumps shade the soil and help reduce evaporation. Certain species are more vulnerable than others however, and any newly planted ones will need extra water while they're rooting in. If it's very dry I water thoroughly and deeply from time to time, even if I don't see obvious signs of stress like wilting or browning of the leaves—by then some damage has already been done. If you live in a hot and/or dry climate, perennial gardens often do not look their best during dry spells, and I cannot emphasize enough the importance of choosing plants that can weather them, and/or providing midday shade. Gardens that need constant watering waste a precious resource.

It's best to water plants at soil level, either by standing there with a hose or water wand and letting the water flow onto the soil at the base of the plant, or by laying down a soaker hose (page 108). An adjustable oscillating sprinkler is a handy way to direct water directly to the garden, but on a windy day much of the water can blow away. Too much moistening of the plants' foliage in hot weather can also make them more prone to mildew and other fungus diseases.

Whatever technique you use, it is better to water thoroughly once a week or so than to water shallowly every day. Make sure that "the moisture meets"—that is, that the new moisture you've applied goes all the way down and joins the moist layer underneath the soil surface, with no dry layer in between.

CONTROLLING PESTS AND DISEASES

I rarely have any serious problems with insects on my perennials. The occasional aphid or leaf miner infestation seldom does much damage, and I avoid using even the relatively nontoxic sprays on them, for fear I will harm other insects in the garden.

Diseases are occasionally a problem in muggy summer weather when I sometimes see fungus diseases such as powdery mildew or leaf spot. I combat these by destroying the debris of diseased plants, then trying to give the plants everything I can think of to make them strong and healthy. I enrich the soil with compost, and I give them plenty of air circulation by spacing them adequately and siting them in a spot that is not too enclosed. Keeping the soil moisture fairly constant by using mulch and by providing good drainage is also a deterrent to disease. Sometimes the best solution is to look for a more disease-resistant variety of that plant, or to try a different species altogether.

More tactics for controlling pests and diseases can be found on pages 60 to 72.

PINCHING AND CUTTING BACK

Pinching (Figure 39), in which just the growth tips of a plant are removed, will encourage some plants to become bushy, more compact, and more floriferous by making them branch. (Chrysanthemums are a good example.) You may want to do this several times at the beginning of the season. The longer you do it, however, the later the plant will bloom, so you have to adjust your pinching program according to the length of summer in your climate.

Cutting back involves removing more than just the tip. Sometimes cutting a plant back by a third or so in June will make a dramatic improvement in the growth habit of a plant that flowers later on. Cutting back all or part of the flowering stems of certain plants after they've bloomed—delphiniums, catmint, and yarrow, for instance—will cause them to bloom a second time.

Sometimes it's just a matter of looks. A floppy veronica or geranium may need a drastic trim whether you expect to get a rebloom out of it or not; often just a fresh flush of green foliage on a nicely mounded plant is all you need. For the fine points of pruning perennials, *The Well-Tended Perennial Garden* by Tracy DiSabato-Aust is an excellent resource.

DEADHEADING

This task is certainly not necessary for the plants' survival or health, it just makes them showier. "Deadheading" means cutting off flowers that have finished blooming. This will not only make the garden look tidier, but it will also cause the plant to put energy into growth and not into seed formation. Some plants, such as Shasta daisies, will keep blooming longer if you promptly remove spent blooms. Others must have their seed heads removed to keep them from self-sowing, either because the seedlings will be so numerous or because they will not be true to the parent.

As you get to know your plants, you'll learn how each one should be deadheaded. Just snipping off the dead flowers might be an improvement, but it leaves an awkward stem. I often remove more of the stem, cutting back to just above a bushy set of leaves.

If your garden is large and your time is limited, you may want to omit deadheading altogether, or at least concentrate on the ugliest, most conspicuous offenders—those slimy daylily petals, for example. And there are times when deadheading should certainly be avoided. A flower is "dead" only in the sense that its petals have wilted, and what is left is busily forming mature seed. Leave it alone if you want it to

Pinching to Produce Bushy Growth
FIG. 39

Pinching the tip of the stem of an herbaceous plant will prompt it to produce two new stems. Pinch those and they in turn will branch. This creates a bushier plant with more flowers.

scatter its seeds for next year's plants. With some, such as coneflowers, turtleheads, and *Sedum* 'Autumn Joy,' the seed heads are beautiful to look at in wintertime. The seeds of false sunflower, bee balm, coneflower, and blazing star provide needed winter food for the birds.

WINTER CLEANUP

If you leave all the brown stems and leaves on your perennials after they die in fall, the

---

PERENNIALS FOR DRY SOIL

OF THE PERENNIALS TREATED IN this chapter, the following are the ones best suited to a moderately dry site. All of them need plenty of water when they are first planted, and while they're rooting in.

Artemisia
Bearded iris
Blanketflower
Butterfly weed
Catmint
Coneflower
Coreopsis
Geranium sanguineum,
    G. macrorrhizum
Lychnis
Pinks
Poppy
Salvia
Sea lavender
Sedum
Sundrops
Veronica prostrata
Yarrow

---

new growth will come up though them in spring, just as it would in a wild setting. Gardeners usually remove this growth for the sake of tidiness, unless it is a very informal planting—a bank of daylilies for example. Typically this is done in the fall, after everything has stopped blooming, and there is a certain satisfaction in putting the garden to bed by cutting back all those stalks, raking the leaves out of the beds, making sure there are no weeds, and having the ground bare so that you can top-dress it with compost.

But there are good arguments for doing a spring cleanup job instead. In addition to nutrient-rich seeds for the birds to eat, all those bushy clumps can provide birds with winter cover and shelter. Dead stems also catch the snow, for a sort of winter mulch. And perennials can look beautiful with ice or snow on them, especially the ones that remain strongly upright, like the taller sedums, turtleheads, and Joe-Pye weed. Try leaving all of them uncut one winter and see which ones look best; watch to see which ones are visited by birds.

I usually compromise by cutting back the tumbledown, vole-attracting plants such as Siberian iris, and leaving the more upright ones until spring. I like going out on those first really warm days and starting to cut the garden back, one section at a time, removing any dead leaves that are left and seeing what's coming up. It's important to do this cutting before the new growth on the plants is more than an inch or two high, so you don't injure it. With many plants I use a hand pruner; with some, a set of sharp hedge shears does the job more quickly. The debris makes good compost, but for perennial stems that are tough or woody, which take a long time to decompose, I make a separate pile where they can sit for several years until they break down. Then they can be added to a more active compost heap along with softer wastes.

Making Changes in the Garden

A S YOU WORK WITH A PERENNIAL garden, it's enormously satisfying to watch the picture as it unfolds from week to week, day to day. You get to know the plants so you can recognize them by their foliage and growth habit, even when they're not in flower. And you'll see that the look of the garden changes from one year to the next.

Sometimes old perennial gardens start to look depleted, with more chaos and less bloom. Perhaps a few things have taken over. This may be true of an old bed you inherited when you moved to a new home, or it may be that watching the yearly return of all these old friends, you've simply started to take them for granted. At this point you need to roll up your sleeves and renovate. If the garden is really a mess, the best thing to do is remove all the plants in early spring and temporarily heel them into a nursery bed (page 40). Then loosen the soil in the bed just as if you were starting from scratch. Many of the clumps will need to be divided or discarded anyway, and you'll now have a good chance to remove any perennial weeds and grasses that have worked their way in among the roots. Either sacrifice large taprooted plants that can't be moved

successfully, or work around them. It may be that you can get away with reworking only certain sections of the bed.

Use this as a time to take stock of what has worked well and what hasn't. Perhaps a plant that has never quite lived up to its potential never will. It's too tall or too floppy, the wrong color, or too prone to disease. Compost it, or give it away. Even without taking such drastic measures, there's almost always something that needs to be changed in the garden. Sometimes it can be done as soon as you spot it: a phlox you bought was not the color you expected, and clashes with something; dig it up with as much soil around it as possible, move it, and water it well. A veronica you thought would grow to 2 feet tall is 3, and is hiding the yarrow behind it; move that as well.

On the other hand it might be a hot week in August, and both you and the plant need to wait till a cooler, moister time of year. Make a note of this and other things to do at a future time. A "spring reminders" list might read: "Move the tall veronica. Bed needs more blue and less purple. 'Miss Lingard' phlox is spindly; move it to a sunnier spot. Balloon flower is being engulfed by bee balm. Shasta daisy looks lonesome at left end of bed; buy two more. Try some snakeroot this year."

Taking frequent photographs is also a good way to keep records, shooting each section of the border at various intervals throughout the season. And this way when you tell friends, as every perennial gardener does, that they "should have seen the border two weeks ago when it was *really* gorgeous," you can actually prove it!

PERENNIALS THAT SPREAD

MANY PLANTS START OUT FINE IN your garden, then are too much of a good thing. Some are wild species; some are "civilized" cultivars. Often there's a legend about whatever villain introduced them to the region where they now grow. A spready plant may have been brought here by foreigners; in other cases, an infamous past member of the Garden Club did the deed. Sometimes it's a native plant that becomes more rampant than usual because of the high level of fertility or moisture you've provided in your garden. Or it may be a plant whose role in nature is to colonize bare, newly disturbed soil.

The line between "vigorous" and "invasive" is often a fine one. Some of these plants are beautiful if used in the right way. Some can go in the perennial bed if you weed out the extras, or contain them by planting them in a metal or plastic tub or bucket, punched with drainage holes in the bottom. Others are fine if you give them a spot to themselves where they can't cause trouble—naturalized in a meadow, or used as a ground cover. Still others may pose a threat to your local ecosystem however they are used, and if so, they shouldn't be grown at all (see page 130). None of these plants are intrinsically "bad"—just troublesome in the wrong place.

Bee balm. *Monarda didyma, M. fistulosa.* Bees, butterflies, hummingbirds and most gardeners agree that this plant has its place in the garden despite its spreading roots. The more rich and moist your soil, the more bee balm you'll have to remove each year; if your garden is very small, make another choice. Excellent in a wild meadow.

Bouncing bet. *Saponaria officinalis.* Considered a wildflower, bouncing Bet was brought to North America in colonial times and has naturalized. It has pretty pink flowers that are night fragrant, but creeping by means of stolons (underground stems) it may bounce all over your garden.

Chinese lantern. *Physalis alkekengi.* The little papery orange "lanterns" are beautiful in dried arrangements but it is stoloniferous, like the plant above, and usually a nuisance in gardens.

Creeping bellflower (rampion). *Campanula rapunculoides.* Rampant it is, creep it does. This blue-flowered herb was the source of Rapunzel's woes; her father harvested its edible roots in the wrong spot—a garden belonging to an evil sorcerer. Those same roots may end up in *all* the wrong spots if you grow it in your garden. Many of the low-growing bellflowers are also creepers but are so attractive that gardeners make peace with them.

Goldenrod. *Solidago.* This ubiquitous native wildflower has its own ideas about where it should suddenly start to grow in my garden. I let it have its way—up to a point—pulling up poorly sited clumps and dividing ones that grow too large. It is, finally, indispensible for fall color and for cutting. For the best goldenrods to grow, see page 706.

Goutweed (bishop's weed). *Aegopodium podagraria.* This plant has attractive, often variegated foliage like that of astilbe. The flowers look like Queen Anne's lace and some flower arrangers like to have them nearby. Resist the temptation. It makes a good ground cover for a spot more distant (such as Europe, where it is native).

Loosestrife. *Lysimachia* species. Yellow loosestrife (*L. punctata*) is an attractive plant for early summer but too invasive for small gardens, as is the white-flowered gooseneck loosestrife (*L. clethroides*). Two other plants called loosestrife, *Lythrum salicaria* and *L. virgatum*, are the gorgeous, tall, spiky magenta plants you see in wet meadows. Alas, both of these are catastrophic colonizers of wild areas, crowding out native species and the fauna that depend on them. It is illegal to sell them in many states. They spread both by seed and by their roots, and even the "sterile" cultivars pose a threat.

Obedient plant (false dragonhead). *Physostegia virginiana.* This hardy native plant is prized for its tall bright pink flowers in late summer. Would that it were obedient. In rich, irrigated garden soils it flops *and* spreads. Grow it anyway, but dig it up every year or so and replant only what you need.

Ox-eye sunflower. *Helianthus helianthoides.* This vigorous prairie native is one of the great joys of my garden for many weeks in late summer and fall, with its tall stands of golden-yellow flowers. Like most of the perennial sunflowers it is weedy. I find the trick, as with so many spreaders, is to recognize the foliage of its "babies" as soon as it goes to seed, and remove them while they're small.

Perennial pea. *Lathyrus latifolius.* The flowers of this climbing or scrambling beauty are long-blooming clusters in shades of pink, lavender, and white. Some gardeners do fine with it, but this and others of the perennial pea species have thick, ropelike roots that can be very hard to remove from gardens.

Plume poppy. *Macleaya microcarpa* (*Bocconia*). The British love to plant huge stands of stately plume poppy, with its handsome leaves and frothy pink flowers, at the back of their 20-foot-deep borders, but it can rapidly overrun a smaller garden. The aggressive roots can be confined if you plant it in a large, well-draining container such as a tank used for watering livestock. *M. cordata* is somewhat less invasive.

Purple coneflower. *Echinacea purpurea.* I once eradicated this plant from my garden in a huff, its runners were threaded under and around so many of my other plants. But I missed its beautiful purple flowers, so attractive to pollinators that they look like butterfly dinnerware. I now let it grow here and there but am more vigilant about curbing its wandering.

Ribbon grass (gardener's garters). *Phalaris arundinacea* 'Picta.' This attractive grass has white stripes. Ornamental grasses can be fine additions to the perennial border, but many are invasive, especially this one, which can escape and do ecological damage as well.

Other grasses that can pose problems both in the garden and in the surrounding environment, in some parts of the continent, are *Imperata cylindrica* and its cultivar 'Red Baron' (which can revert to the original species), pampas grass (*Cortaderia selloana*), giant reed (*Arundo donax*), feathergrass (*Pennisetum* species), and maiden grass (*Miscanthus sinensis* and its early-flowering cultivars).

It's a good idea to check with a local horticultural society or Cooperative Extension Service before you invest in grasses whose habits you're unsure of.

Sulfur cinquefoil. *Potentilla recta.* Unlike native cinquefoils, this low-growing yellow-flowered species has led to ecological devastation in many areas. There are "tamed" cultivars for gardens, but these too can be weedy and I would view the species in general with caution.

Sundrops. *Oenothera pilosella.* Often passed from one gardener to another, this species has straight 2-foot stems with clusters of bright yellow flowers at the top and little rosettes of leaves at the bottom. I like it for its color and just pull out the extras; they spread close to the soil surface and are easy to remove. Some of the other sundrops or evening primroses, such as the pink-flowered *O. speciosa*, are also creepers.

Tansy. *Tanacetum vulgare.* This herb is another escapee that was brought over by the early settlers and spread from the meadows of New England to the Wild West. With clusters of buttonlike flowers atop 3-foot stems and attractive, pungent, fernlike foliage, it looks great planted along a split-rail fence. But it's too much of an outlaw for the small garden.

Valerian. *Valeriana officinalis.* This tall, vigorous plant bears pinkish white flowers in midsummer that are almost nauseatingly sweet smelling. It, too, was imported by the colonists and will gladly colonize your garden.

Violets. *Viola odorata.* People love the common "sweet violet," but like most violets it self-sows everywhere. Often, in the right setting, this is just what you want it to do. Confederate violet (*V. papilionifera*) is a lovely white violet streaked with blue. It will march through your garden faster than Robert E. Lee.

List of Perennials

THIS LIST OF 50 PERENNIALS WILL give you a start in planning your garden. Many of them are familiar favorites; some may be new to you. Most are among the easiest perennials to grow. For each plant the entries describe only some of the species and cultivars available. (For the distinctions between species, varieties, hybrids, and cultivars, see pages 121 to 125.) Most will thrive in the sort of average loamy soil we try to provide when we must accommodate a large number of different plants in one bed. But when a plant has a distinct preference, I've noted it.

ANEMONE

Anemone

Description: There are many types of anemones for the garden, but my favorites are the tall, graceful Japanese anemones,

most of which are hybrids of various species. The graceful pink or white flowers, waving atop 3- to 5-foot slender stems, are a bit like those of cosmos, but slightly cupped, with showy gold stamens in the center. They tolerate shade (as well as sun, in reasonably cool climates) and bloom in late summer and fall when shade-loving flowers are scarce. The exquisite hybrid forms such as the white 'Honorine Jobert' and the pink 'September Charm' may need the protection of evergreen boughs during cold winters. Zones 5 to 8 or 9. Pale pink *Anemone tomentosa* 'Robustissima,' from China, is the most cold tolerant, hardy to zone 4. All can spread to the point of invasiveness in some gardens.

How to Grow: Give Japanese anemones a rich soil with plenty of organic matter to retain moisture, but keep them well drained in wintertime. Protect from hot afternoon sun. Weed out excess growth; division for propagation purposes should be done in spring. Some varieties may need staking.

ARTEMISIA

Artemisia

Description: Named for the moon goddess Artemis, the artemisias are treasured by gardeners for their white or silvery aromatic foliage. Their flowers are relatively uninteresting, but the pale leaves are

Artemisia 'Silver
Mound'   Artemisia stellerana

effective all season long to lighten and soften
the look of the garden. They vary greatly in
leaf shape and in their growing habits, which
tend to be annoying in one way or another.
But this does not seem to stop people from
growing them. *Artemisia schmidtiana* 'Silver
Mound' makes a low silvery cushion. When
you stroke it, it feels like a soft, fluffy cat;
when the wind blows, it undulates as if it
were dancing. When the weather gets hot
it turns brown in the center and has to be
cut back. Zones 4 to 7. Southernwood (*A.
abrotanum*) makes a large mound that can
be rather sprawly if not clipped. Zones 5 to
9. *A. ludoviciana albula* 'Silver King' has 2 to
3 foot plumes that flop a bit late in the season and is invasive in rich soil. Zones 3 to 8.
'Valerie Finnis,' a related variety, has wider,
very showy leaves. Zones 4 to 8. Beach
wormwood (*A. stellerana*) is the whitest of
the group; its foliage toothed and woolly. Its
stems are 2 feet and rather trailing. Zones 4
to 8. *A. absinthium* 'Lambrook Silver' (zones
4 to 9) and *A.* × 'Powis Castle' (zones 6 to
8) are popular feathery varieties. The latter
is shrublike and not reliably hardy in cold
climates.

How to Grow: Provide all varieties with
good drainage, especially in winter. They
need sun but dislike hot, muggy summers.

If possible, give them a dryish, not-too-
fertile soil. All are easily divided. Most types,
if they become floppy and unkempt, can be
cut back in summer; fresh new growth will
start to appear right away. Pinching to prevent bloom is also helpful. Shrubby types
should be cut back in early spring and again
in midsummer if needed, but not in fall.

ASTER

Aster

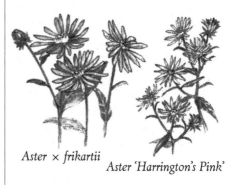

Aster × frikartii
                      Aster 'Harrington's Pink'

Description: The glory of the fall garden, asters are called Michaelmas daisies
in Britain, after the September 29th feast
day to which they lend color. They range
in height from under a foot to 6 feet tall,
and bloom in shades of purple, lavender,
pink, red, blue, and white. In zones where
they are hardy, the plants tend to be very
vigorous and sometimes invasive. Most
garden hybrids are derived from one of two
native species. Varieties derived from *Aster
novae-angliae* (New England aster) include
the towering pale rose 'Harrington's Pink,'
(up to 6 feet), the stout-stemmed 3- to 4-
foot 'Alma Potschke,' which is a strong
warm pink-red, and the richly colored 1½-
foot 'Purple Dome.' From *A. novi-belgii*
(New York aster) come numerous varieties including 'Marie Ballard,' light blue,

3 to 4 feet; 'Crimson Brocade,' reddish pink, 3 feet; and 'Eventide,' purple, 3 to 4 feet. Dwarf varieties include the 10-inch white 'Snowball' and the excellent blue-violet 'Professor Kippenberg.' Most asters are hardy in zones 4 to 8 or 9. *A.* × *frikartii* is a very long-blooming aster that bears gorgeous lavender-blue flowers in summer and grows 2 to 3 feet tall. Short-lived in both the far north and far south, it is still worth growing; best staked with brush. Native species that are less well known but well worth growing are the white: *A. divaricatus, A. ericoides, A. umbellatus,* and *A. lateriflorus* as well as the lavender *A. oblongifolius.*

How to Grow: Asters like moist but well-drained soil and plenty of sun. Most form big clumps that are best divided every few years by replanting shoots from the outside of the clumps. Tall varieties must often be staked, but the stems can be pinched early in the season to make the plants more erect as well as more compact and free-flowering. (This will, however, delay bloom.) Some varieties are spreaders; the tall hybrids often self-sow and are best deadheaded to preclude dissimilar offspring. Asters can be prone to disease. Destroy blackened foliage and uproot plants that die of unknown causes. It's wise to find disease-resistant varieties that thrive for you.

ASTILBE

Astilbe × *arendsii*

Description: What would I do for summer bloom in my shade garden without astilbes? The plants have delicious, plumelike flowers and attractive fernlike leaves, and bloom from early to late sum-

mer depending on the variety. Colors are shades of pink, red, lavender, purple, salmon, and white; heights range from 8 inches to 4 feet. Of the numerous fine varieties, early-summer bloomers include pale pink 'Europa,' white 'Deutschland,' and dark red, bronze-leaved 'Fanal,' all about 2 feet tall. Midsummer bloomers include 'Ostrich Plume,' deep coral and 2 to 3 feet, and 'Avalanche,' white and 2½ to 3 feet. The purple-pink *Astilbe taquetii* 'Superba' grows up to 4 feet tall and blooms in late summer (earlier in the south). The dwarf *A. chinensis* 'Pumila' is lavender-pink, about a foot tall, blooms in midsummer, and forms a spreading ground cover. Another popular low grower for midseason, *A. simplicifolia* 'Sprite' is pink and about a foot tall. Most are hardy from zones 4 to 8 or 9.

How to Grow: These vigorous, trouble-free plants will grow in shade, part shade, or even sun in cool climates, as long as they are kept watered. They require no staking, are salt tolerant and even deer resistant! Astilbes prefer fertile, fairly acid soil that is moist but well drained, especially in wintertime. They may self-sow; deadhead only if this is a problem, otherwise leave the attractive seed heads in place. Clumps can be divided in spring or just after bloom to maintain vigor. The woody little roots must be cut apart with a sharp knife.

BALLOON FLOWER

Platycodon grandiflorus

Description: This is a fine old-fashioned plant with bell-shaped, occasionally double flowers in colors that are never garish—blue, pink, or white. It's perfect for the English garden look. Blooms open in midsummer from fat, balloonlike buds on stems about 2 to 3 feet tall. 'Mariesii' is a shorter blue variety with single flowers. 'Shell Pink' is a popular pink; 'Albus' is white. Zones 3 to 9.

How to Grow: Though sun loving, platycodon will tolerate part shade and prefers it in hot climates. Provide slightly acid, light, well-drained soil. Sandy soils are more suitable than clay. The plant forms long-lived clumps that do not require division, though it may be done in spring if you dig deeply to get as much of the deep, fleshy taproot as possible. Watch for the emerging shoots in spring—they're slow to appear. (You can mark the spot in fall as a safeguard.) Deadheading flower by flower prolongs bloom. Some varieties require staking.

BEE BALM (BERGAMOT)

Monarda

Description: Bee balm, native to eastern and central North America, is a bit over-zealous but still a good, dependable perennial for the back or middle of the border. Strong upright stems bear bright blooms 2 to 3 inches across that are clusters of tiny tubes. These are beloved by hummingbirds, bees, and butterflies and worth growing for this feature alone. Flowers, which appear in midsummer, are shades of red, lavender, pink, mahogany, or white. Hybrids of *Monarda didyma* such as the old-fashioned 'Cambridge Scarlet' and 'Croftway Pink' grow 2 to 4 feet tall. Mildew-resistant cultivars include purple 'Blue Stocking,' red 'Jacob Cline,' and the foot-high pink 'Petite Delight.' *M. fistulosa* (wild bergamot) has lavender flowers and may get as tall as 5 feet in the garden. It's a bit more drought tolerant and is quite rampant; best grown in a semiwild planting. Zones 3 or 4 to 9.

How to Grow: Bee balm spreads just under the soil surface by runners. Unless you're allowing it to naturalize in a spot with plenty of space, you'll need to weed out the excess every year or so. But the plant is widely grown because it's beautiful and easy to establish, especially in cool climates. It prefers sun or partial shade, and a rich moist soil. Soil moisture, in fact, is the key to fighting the powdery mildew that plagues bee balm. Badly infested plants should be cut back to promote fresh growth. Clumps that die out in the center should be broken apart and replanted. Deadheading will extend bloom.

BELLFLOWER
Campanula

Campanula persicifolia

Campanula carpatica

Description: Whatever style of flower garden you have, there's a bellflower for you. The flowers vary considerably in shape and size; though most are blue, some are violet or purple, and some are white. They're beautiful in pastel gardens, with roses, or just anywhere you want a blue accent. Some grow on plants of mid-border height, others on low cushions, others on long, trailing stems. Most bloom in early summer but often will continue to flower, though less heavily, throughout the season. *Campanula persicifolia*, the popular peach-leaved bellflower, is available in blue varieties such as *C. p.* 'Grandiflora' and 'Telham Beauty,' as well as white ones such as *C. p.* 'Grandiflora Alba.' It grows 2 to 3 feet tall. *C. glomerata* also grows up to 2 feet; the variety 'Superba' is a wonderful rich purple, and 'Crown of Snow' is white. Low-growing bellflowers include *C. carpatica* 'Blue Clips' and 'White Clips,' 9 to 12 inches tall; *C. garganica*, blue, 6 inches; *C. poscharskyana*, lavender, 12 to 18 inches but sprawling; *C. rotundifolia* is blue and 1

to 2 feet, but the variety 'Olympia' is more compact. This last species can be weedy in some gardens. Most bellflowers, aside from the more tender *C. garganica*, are hardy in zones 3 to 8. The beautiful, old-fashioned Canterbury bells (*C. medium*) is a biennial.

How to Grow: Bellflowers like sun but will do well in light shade, especially in hot climates. Provide moist, moderately fertile, well-drained soil. Tall ones often need some support. Some self-sow, but this is often a plus because individual plants can be short-lived. Cut back after flowering to encourage rebloom. Sometimes slug control may be necessary (see page 63).

BLANKETFLOWER
Gaillardia × grandiflora

Description: Gaillardias resemble large daisies, but with the bold, bright markings of an American Indian blanket, in patterns of red, yellow, and gold. Most grow about 2½ feet tall, but there are also dwarf varieties. They bloom in summer over a long period and are an especially good choice if your climate is hot and dry. Tall varieties, which may need staking, include the variably colored Monarch strain and solids such as dark red 'Burgundy' and 'Maxima

Aurea.' Multicolored 'Goblin' and 'Baby Sun' grow a foot tall or less. Gaillardias grow in all zones, but are generally short-lived.

How to Grow: In moist, humid areas the plants may develop fungus diseases in summer or succumb to rot from winter moisture. Avoid mulching, and give them light, well-drained soil, preferably on the sandy side. Gaillardias can be grown fairly quickly from seed, and will flower the first year. In spring, watch for new shoots that may appear quite a distance from the original clump. If the center of the clump dies, discard it and replant the side shoots.

BLAZING STAR (GAYFEATHER)
Liatris

Description: These native American wildflowers, usually pinkish purple but sometimes white, look like little bunches of wavy string tied along a tall spike. They grow anywhere from 2 to 6 feet tall and most bloom in late summer and early fall, attracting butterflies in droves. They are suited to a variety of habitats, depending on the species. But all are vigorous growers that do well in gardens and can be naturalized as meadow flowers. Gardenworthy species include the 3- to 4-foot *Liatris scariosa,* the 3- to 5-foot *L.*

ligulistylis, and the ever-popular *L. spicata.* *L.* 'Kobold' is a compact 2-foot variety with midsummer bloom. Zones 3 to 9.

How to Grow: Blazing star grows from tuberous roots, which are planted 4 to 6 inches deep. The soil need not be very fertile, but it should be deeply cultivated and well drained. Choose a sunny location. Plants may be propagated from seed sown in spring or from division in spring. One plant is sufficient to form a sizable clump in the garden, which can be divided early in the spring. To divide, cut the tubers with a sharp, clean knife, making sure each piece has an eye (growth point) before you replant it.

BLEEDING HEART
Dicentra

Dicentra eximia

Dicentra spectabilis

Description: When most people think of bleeding heart they picture an old-fashioned spring perennial with long, arching stems from which dangle small pink, heart-shaped flowers. This is *Dicentra spectabilis,* well named because it truly puts on a grand show. After the plant blooms, its yellowing foliage courteously disappears until the following spring. It grows about 3 feet tall and equally wide, but can be planted with later-blooming plants that will fill the gap it leaves behind. Several long-blooming short species have recently become popular; these have attractive, fringed grayish green foliage and deep pink flowers. (White forms of both tall and short are available, though these are somewhat less vigorous than the pink ones.) *D. eximia* and *D.* × *formosa* grow 12 to 18 inches and bloom from spring to fall. 'Bountiful' and 'Luxuriant' are popular varieties. For *D. cucullaria* (Dutchman's-breeches) see page 705. All are zones 3 to 9.

How to Grow: All bleeding hearts prefer partial shade. The short ones may thrive in full sun in cool climates, but the flowers may appear a bit scorched and untidy if the sun is too strong. Regular watering can help keep the foliage of *D. spectabilis* going well into the summer. Give both types moist, fertile soil with plenty of organic matter and good drainage, especially in winter.

BUTTERFLY WEED

Asclepias tuberosa

Description: One of several species of native milkweeds, this showy meadow wildflower attracts not only the milkweed (monarch) butterfly, for which it is an important larval food, but many other butterflies, bees, and pollinators as well. It blooms for about a month in midsummer and is prized for its bright orange flower clusters, ease of cultivation, drought tolerance, and of course the butterfly show. As with other milkweeds, its large seedpods spill forth handfuls of white

fluff in fall. Stems reach 2 and sometimes 3 feet as the clumps become well established. Most plants sold are the original species, or selections with minor color variations. The related swamp milkweed (*Asclepias incarnata*) is pink, slightly taller, and naturally prefers moist soil. Both are zone 3 or 4 to 9.

How to Grow: Butterfly weed prefers a light, sandy soil, but will grow fine in most soil types as long as it has good drainage. Because of its deep taproot the plant withstands drought well. If you must move young plants, do it carefully, lifting all of the taproot; established clumps are best left alone and will often self-sow. The plants may be grown easily from seed sown in sandy soil, or propagated with cuttings in deep pots to accommodate the taproots. The shoots are late to appear in spring.

CANDYTUFT

Iberis sempervirens

Description: Perennial candytuft is one of my favorite edging or front-of-the-border plants, because its dark evergreen foliage is so handsome on its own. This is also a good plant for rock gardens and wall gardens. In early spring it covers itself with small pure white flowers, and a few varieties even rebloom in fall if cut back after

the initial flush. Varieties vary in height but are generally less than a foot tall. 'Autumn Snow' is a rebloomer. Zones 3 to 9.

How to Grow: This is essentially a sun-loving plant, but it will also do fine in part shade. It must have a well-drained soil. Shear the stems halfway back after blooming, even with nonrepeaters, for tidiness' sake. Division is not necessary, though I do divide mine in spring in order to have more of these useful plants.

CATMINT

Nepeta

Description: Catmint is indispensable in my garden, for its long-blooming lavender-blue flowers, its attractive gray-green foliage, its graceful, cascading habit, and its ease of culture. I use it to soften the front edges of my beds, where it is rarely without

flowers in summer, blending beautifully with the brighter blooms of coreopsis, gaillardia, yarrow, and other fellow sun lovers. It is not to be confused with catnip (*Nepeta cataria*), an herb famous for driving cats wild. *N.* × *faassenii* is a widely sold sterile hybrid about 1 to 1½ feet tall. If it goes to seed in your garden it is more likely to be *N. mussinii*. Good catmint cultivars include 'Blue Wonder,' 'White Wonder,' and 'Walker's Low,' which is not—as some assume—a dwarf (it's named for a garden in England). It is roughly the same size as the spectacular 'Six Hills Giant,' which produces a 30-inch fountain of arching flowers. Catmint blooms all summer long, and is always quivering with the work of countless bees. Zone 3 to 8.

How to Grow: Catmint prefers sun but can be grown in very light shade. It is drought tolerant and grows well in most soils as long as they are well drained. The length of bloom varies from garden to garden, as does the amount of sprawl. I've found that mature plants, especially those of 'Six Hills Giant,' tend to open up at the center in an unattractive way in midsummer, smothering other plants in the vicinity. At this point I shear them back by about two thirds even though they're still blooming; the new growth that has already begun to appear in the opened center immediately starts to fill it in, and usually reblooms well.

CHRYSANTHEMUM

Chrysanthemum × *morifolium*
(*Dendranthema* × *grandiflorum*)

Description: There are "mums" of many shapes, from little pompons the size of a nickel to huge "spiders." Some are shaped like daisies; some, called spoons, are nests of little spoon-shaped petals. The most familiar are the large round ones with many petals, which are classified as decorative mums, and the easy-to-grow cushion mums, which grow up to 15 inches tall. Colors include everything but blue, and heights range from less than a foot to 4 feet tall. The mums you see for sale in fall are pinched repeatedly to create great balls of bloom. Most are not reliably winter hardy in cold climates, and are treated as annuals or fall fillers for the late-season garden. But there are hardier sorts you can find if you seek them out, such as the pink 'Clara Curtis.' I've had great success with the lovely 'Single Apricot Korean' in my zone 5 Maine garden.

spider

decorative

daisy-flowered

pompon

How to Grow: Tender mums can be mulched with evergreen boughs. You can also divide them in spring (or fall, in warm climates) discarding the centers of the clumps and replanting the side shoots either in a cold frame or the garden. Pinch repeatedly until early summer (later in warm climates) to get bushy plants and abundant fall flowers. Mums need sun and fertile, moist but very well-drained soil.

COLUMBINE
Aquilegia

Description: Both the flowers and leaves of columbines have a dainty, airy quality. Many of the flowers have long spurs, and they come in every color, including bicolors in which the inner row of petals is one color, the outer petals (sepals) and the spurs another. Heights also vary. Most bloom in mid spring to early summer. *Aquilegia canadensis* (wild columbine) is yellow and red and grows 1 to 2 feet. *A. caerulea* (Colorado or Rocky Mountain columbine) is blue and white and grows up to 3 feet tall. Both are native American wildflowers. *A. chrysantha* is yellow, 2 to 3 feet. *A. alpina,* a Swiss species, varies from 1 to 3 feet. *A. vulgaris* is shades of blue and rose and grows up to 3 feet. *A. flabellata* (Japanese fan columbine) is as short as 6 inches (though sometimes as tall as 1½ feet), with bluish leaves; available varieties are usually white or blue and white. In addition there are many hybrids: McKenna and Dragonfly hybrids in mixed shades are medium height; Biedermeier strain columbines are mixed and shorter. In general, the species are hardy in zones 3 to 9, most hybrids in zones 5 to 9.

How to Grow: Columbines do best in part shade, and will tolerate full sun if summer heat is not severe. They only transplant well when small, and are sometimes short-lived, but they have a strong tendency to self-sow, and volunteer seedlings can be moved to the desired location. They interbreed charmingly. All prefer a rich, moist but well-drained soil. Leaf miners, which make white tunnels in the leaves, spoil their looks in some gardens; affected foliage can be cut back. *A. canadensis* is the most resistant.

CONEFLOWER

Rudbeckia, Echinacea

Description: These are cheerful bright flowers and among the easiest perennials to grow. The common black-eyed Susan (*Rudbeckia hirta*) is the most familiar coneflower, and many garden hybrids resemble it. Others have double, pompon-shaped flowers. Purple coneflower (*Echinacea purpurea*), an excellent native prairie plant, is irresistible to butterflies and bees. It grows as tall as 4 feet and is usually purple with a raised, iridescent rust-colored center.

Most coneflowers bloom from mid to late summer until frost, a time when it's hard to find good choices for the garden, so it's possible to overlook their tendency to spread.

One solution is to naturalize them in a place where they can't get into trouble. Some of the *R. hirta* varietes such as the Gloriosa daisies are grown as self-sowing annuals. Of the perennial types, *R. fulgida* 'Goldsturm' has single yellow flowers and usually grows 2 to 3 feet. Zone 4. *R. laciniata* 'Gold Drop' is a double that grows 2 to 3 feet. *R. nitida* 'Goldquelle' is a 3- to 4-foot double. Most coneflowers are hardy in zones 3 to 9.

How to Grow: These vigorous plants form clumps that are best divided every few years. They prefer full sun or very light shade and are undemanding as to soil.

CORAL BELLS

Heuchera

Description: These plants form mats of leaves close to the ground and send up wiry stems from which dangle tiny bells, usually in shades of pink and red. Though not large and showy, those little dancing blooms are a welcome addition to the garden in early summer, and will often continue throughout the season with proper care. The foliage is evergreen in most climates. Garden varieties are hybrids derived from a number of North American species. The Bressingham hybrids are famously floriferous, in mixed colors and heights. Others, such as 'Palace Purple' and 'Pewter Veil,' are grown for their bronze, purple, or silvery, often variegated foliage. Heucherella, a cross between coral bells and the beautiful *Tiarella cordifolia* (foamflower, see page 706), is a spreading pink-flowering perennial, 12 to 18 inches tall. Zones 3 to 8.

How to Grow: Coral bells need moist, fertile soil enriched with organic matter. They like moisture but require good drainage, especially in winter, when alternate freezing and thawing can heave them right out of the ground. (Planting with the crowns just beneath the surface and mulching will help to alleviate this problem.) Either full sun or part shade is suitable, but those with richly colored leaves will often fade in bright summer sun. Easy to grow, they are best used at or near the front of the border. Divide after several years, especially if heaving has occurred. Deadheading, and irrigating in dry weather will help to ensure long-season bloom.

COREOPSIS

Coreopsis

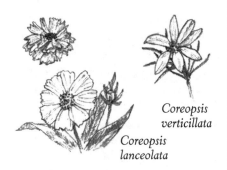

Coreopsis verticillata

Coreopsis lanceolata

Description: These summer-blooming natives usually look like slightly ragged yellow daisies. I like them because they're easy to grow and have a long flowering period. *Coreopsis lanceolata* is generally 2 feet tall. The variety 'Sunray' has double flowers. 'Goldfink' is 12 inches tall or less. 'Baby Sun' is 12 to 20 inches. Zones 4 to 9. *C. verticillata* (threadleaf coreopsis) is a real find. It has rather spidery foliage and a very long bloom period. The variety 'Moonbeam' is 1½ to 2 feet tall and has pale yellow flowers that fit wonderfully in gardens where a strong yellow would be too much. 'Zagreb' is 18 inches or less. 'Golden Showers' is about 2 feet and bright yellow. The pink-flowered *C. rosea* makes a low mat, covered with pink flowers. Most threadleaf coreopsis are zones 3 to 9.

How to Grow: These plants tolerate relatively infertile soil, self-sow, and are very easy to divide. They are all sun loving. *C. verticillata* and *C. rosea* spread by runners and must be periodically weeded out.

DAYLILY

Hemerocallis

Description: Daylilies are among the most satisfying plants you can grow because they're very easy and very colorful. They grow from rhizomes and are not at all the same plant as the true lily (*Lilium*), which grows from a bulb. Most people are familiar with the orange daylily that blooms along roadsides for a few weeks early in summer; but not everyone knows about the modern hybrids, derived from several different species, which bloom at different times from late June well into September and even October, in colors ranging from darkest purple, bright red, pink, lavender, and peach to orange, gold, yellow, and cream. There are also bicolored flowers, fragrant ones, double ones, and huge meaty ones called tetraploids, as well as tiny miniatures. Flower stems range from under 2 feet to a towering 6, but the foliage remains a fairly low mound. *Hemerocallis* means "beautiful for a day," for each blossom lasts one day only. But each stem bears many buds that will open even after cutting.

'Hyperion' is an old-fashioned, fragrant, summer-blooming yellow hybrid. 'Evergold' is a standard gold one. 'Prairie Sunset' is a good peach shade. But there are thousands of hybrids to choose from, with scores of new ones appearing each year. 'Stella d'Oro' is widely grown because of its low, compact habit, extra-long bloom, and golden blooms that remain attractive even after they fade. The fragrant, old-fashioned lemon lily (*H. lilioasphodelus*, or *H. flava*) is still as popular today as it was in colonial times. Most daylilies are hardy to zones 3 to 9.

How to Grow: Daylilies like well-drained soil of average fertility with plenty of organic matter. In general they are sun lovers, though they will grow in part shade, especially in hot regions, and pastel colors will sometimes be more vivid in a partly shaded situation. Some varieties are much more vigorous than others. Clumps that become very large will often bloom well without division, but can be more easily divided for propagation before they become huge. See Figure 36 for planting, and Figure 37 for dividing. Deadheading the slimy spent blooms, though not fun, will make the plants much more attractive and in some plants promote longer bloom.

DELPHINIUM

Delphinium

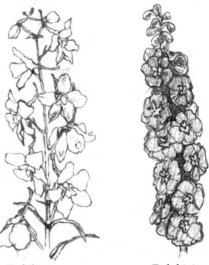

Delphinium
'Belladonna'

Delphinium
elatum

Description: My idea of luxury is to always have plenty of delphiniums. They are not maintenance free, but I put up with this for their magnificent flower spikes in the garden and for summer bouquets. The most spectacular ones are hybrids of *Delphinium elatum*, which are tall and grand—usually upward of 5 feet and as tall as 7. Among these are the Pacific series, which come in many shades, from true blue to rich purple, mauve, and white. Some are bicolored—each flower along the spike having the center, or bee, in a contrasting color. Despite their height, these are not really back-of-the-border plants. Since their late summer rebloom is invariably shorter, they are best used as a vertical accent in midborder position. The dwarf strains such as Blue Fountains and Connecticut Yankee grow to only 3 feet tall, and are easier to deal with because they are much less apt to need staking. All of these do best in cool-summer areas such as northern New England.

Many gardeners have better luck with the beautiful dark blue *D.* × *belladonna* 'Bellamosum,' which grows 3 to 5 feet with flowers in more loosely shaped branches. Chinese delphiniums (*D. grandiflorum*), which grow less than 2 feet and are very intense blue, are also fairly easy to grow. Most delphiniums are hardy in zones 3 to 7, but short-lived where summers are warm.

How to Grow: In climates with cool summers delphinium stems grow tall and strong, and are more apt to remain disease-free. Even so, a muggy spell can blight the foliage, either blackening it or turning it white with powdery mildew. But there are things you can do to help keep the plants strong and resistant. Give them a very fertile soil, well drained and rich in organic matter. Apply compost or manure in fall and a liquid organic fertilizer in spring. They like a high pH, so dig some extra lime into the soil at planting time and scatter a bit around the plants in future years as needed if your soil is acid. After the initial flush of bloom, cut off the dead flowers and any diseased foliage, and top-dress with compost or liquid fertilizer. When new growth appears at the base of the plants, cut back the whole stems to encourage rebloom.

Delphiniums need a sunny location, if possible one with good air circulation but protected from the wind. Even there they will probably need to be staked. A stake that is too rigid will just make the flower snap off in the wind, unless you literally support the entire flower. If there are many flower spikes, try creating a little thicket of stakes, linked at intervals with twine, within which the stems can sway freely, shaking off rainwater that can weight them down and break them. Avoid mulching around the base of the plant, which can lead to rot. Thinning out some of the stems can also be beneficial. Delphiniums are grown from seed or cuttings, and will often bloom the first year from seed.

FALSE SUNFLOWER
Heliopsis helianthoides

semidouble

double

single

Description: This tall plant with daisy-like yellow flowers is wonderful for bridging the gap between summer flowers such as phlox and fall flowers such as asters. Some are double; some are single. Most grow 3 or 4 feet tall and have a long flowering period. Hybrids include 'Karat,' a 4-foot single, and 'Summer Sun,' a 3- to 4-foot gold-colored double. My favorite is 'Prairie Sunset,' a 5-foot-tall single with red markings at the base of the petals, and burgundy-colored stems. Zones 4 to 9.

How to Grow: The plants need sun to be strong, upright, and free flowering. Soil need not be very rich. Division is not a necessity but is easily done for propagation. These are easy-to-grow plants that usually do not need staking. Leave some seed heads on the plants in winter for the birds.

FOXGLOVE
Digitalis

Description: Gardeners who love romantic, old-fashioned flowers can rarely resist growing foxgloves, even though some of the species are not reliably perennial in all climates. Most are biennials, forming rosettes of foliage the first year, blooming the second, and becoming unproductive after that. They are happy to self-sow, however, if conditions suit them. Flowers

occur on tall spikes in shades of rose, purple, yellow, or white, depending on variety. The spikes rise in early summer from a low mound of broad leaves. I like to place them so the spikes emerge from clumps of ferns in partly shaded corners.

Digitalis grandiflora (D. ambigua) is the longest-lived species; it has pale yellow or cream-colored flowers, and grows 2 to 3 feet tall. *D. × mertonensis* has 3- to 4-foot spikes of pink flowers. Zone 4 to 5. *D. purpurea* is a tall rose-colored biennial; the tall Excelsior hybrids derived from it, in mixed shades of pink, purple, and white, are particularly stately and spectacular. Foxy, a shorter strain, will bloom from seed the first year and is usually treated as an annual. The taller Camelot series also blooms the first year. All are zones 3 or 4 to 8.

How to Grow: Give foxgloves fairly fertile, moist but well-drained soil containing plenty of organic matter. Plant in partial shade except in climates with cool summers. Cutting the stems of spent flowers may promote rebloom, but leave some if you want them to self-sow. Dividing established clumps will prolong vigor.

GAS PLANT
Dictamnus albus (D. fraxinella)

Description: This old-fashioned flower is a good thing to establish in your garden. It takes a few years to make a good show, but after that it will stalwartly produce airy pink or white spikes on tall stems in late spring or early summer. The name derives from a gas produced by the plants on humid summer nights that can, some claim, be ignited with a match, though I've yet to meet anyone who has managed to perform this feat. Touching the plant incites an allergic reaction in some people. The species is white, but *Dictamnus albus* 'Purpureus' is pinkish purple, and 'Rubra' is red. All are usually 3 feet tall. Zones 3 to 8.

How to Grow: Gas plant will eventually form thick, permanent clumps that live a long time and will not require division (in fact they may not always survive dividing). The plants are taprooted and like a moist, well-drained, fertile, humusy soil. Sun suits them best but they'll bloom in light shade. They are grown most successfully by taking root cuttings or by sowing seeds in flats outdoors in fall; these will germinate the following spring. Nursery-grown plants can also be purchased.

GERANIUM (CRANESBILL)

Geranium

Description: These are the hardy geraniums as distinguished from the plants commonly called geraniums, which are tender perennials of the genus *Pelargonium*. Hardy geraniums grow in a mound anywhere from a few inches to a few feet tall, with five-petaled blossoms in shades of pink, crimson, purple, lavender, blue, and white, usually about an inch wide but sometimes larger. Depending on variety, they bloom in late spring and early summer. Some also repeat sporadically throughout the season, especially if deadheaded. They are vigorous, easy, and pest-free. Many even have colorful red fall foliage! Once you discover this fine family of plants you will wish you could grow them all.

Here are just a few of the many attractive species and varieties you can try. The low-growing pink *Geranium dalmaticum* and *G. macrorrhizum* 'Ingwersen's Variety' are both spreaders, as is the bright shrimp pink *G. endressii* 'Wargrave Pink.' These all make good ground covers and look good following bulbs or underneath roses. *G.* × 'Johnson's Blue' grows to 12 inches, with lovely violet-blue flowers. *G. sanguineum* forms a big mound a foot high but much wider, with magenta blooms that often repeat. The long-blooming variety *G. s. striatum* 'Lancastriense' is lower growing, its flowers pale pink veined with red. *G. endressii* is a pink variety that grows 12 to 18 inches. *G.* × *magnificum*, one of my favorites, bears large, intensely violet-blue flowers on 2-foot stems in early summer; it needs some support. I also love *G. renardii* for its exquisite leaves, like a soft, pebble-weave upholstery fabric. Other winners include the delightful pink, red-veined *G. cinereum* 'Ballerina,' the lushly blooming *G. clarkei* 'Kashmir Purple,' and the fabulous 3-foot *G. psilostemon*, its blooms richly magenta with black centers and veins. Our charming native *G. maculatum*, with its pink flowers, is always welcome in my garden. Almost all varieties are hardy from at least zone 4 to 8 or 9.

How to Grow: Most of the hardy geraniums will thrive in sun or light shade—the latter in climates with hot summers—but *G. sanguineum* is especially sun tolerant. They do best in moist, well-drained soils enriched with organic matter. Most form large clumps that need not be divided but that can be increased by carefully pulling a small clump away from the parent plant. Deadheading and/or cutting back will usually prolong bloom.

GLOBEFLOWER
Trollius

*Trollius
europaeus*

*Trollius
ledebourii*

Description: These lovely flowers look like large, round versions of the buttercups to which they're related. Colors range from light yellow to deep orange. Bloom is in late spring or early summer but will sometimes repeat throughout the summer. *Trollius*

europaeus is a bright yellow species that grows about 2 feet tall. Zone 4. *T. chinensis* (*T. ledebourii*) is taller gold-orange, and blooms a bit later. The native *T. laxus* is a pretty low-grower for moist, shady gardens. These are not plants for hot climates. They do well in zones 3 or 4 to 7.

How to Grow: Globeflower can do well in full sun but does best in partial shade. Give it fertile, moist soil with plenty of organic matter. It is slow to make big clumps. Established plants rarely need to be divided, though for propagation this can be done in early spring or fall.

HOLLYHOCK
Alcea rosea

Description: Hollyhocks are usually classified as biennials. The majority of them are grown from seed one year, then bloom the next. However, there are varieties that bloom the first year, and sometimes they are quite reliably perennial. I've found that regardless of the type, they are persistent in most gardens because they tend to self-sow close to the original plant in a sort of "hollyhock area" that lasts from year to year. Hollyhocks are often the tallest thing in your garden; they'll be at least 5 or 6 feet, and can tower to 8 and more.

Aside from a disfiguring rust disease that can appear on the leaves in late summer, these are splendid plants. Flower forms range from the old-fashioned singles (which I prefer) to doubles, some of them in dense balls like powder puffs. The traditional shades are red, pink, and white, but lately the yellow-copper-peach range has entered the mix. The parentage of these varieties seems to carry some rust-resistance as well. Dark purple-black types sold as 'Nigra' or 'The Watchman' are wonderful accents in a border. The yellow *A. rugosa* is rust-free and does not need to be staked, despite the fact that it often becomes a huge, tall, bushy plant. Zone 3 to 8.

How to Grow: Space hollyhocks about 2 feet apart, in rich, deeply dug, well-drained soil. Support must usually be provided. Using soft twine, tie the stalks to a wall or trellis, or to stout bamboo stakes. The huge leaves are great for hiding stakes and twine, though you may find yourself removing them, one by one, as the march of rust ascends the stems. I plant something bushy and of medium height just in front, for camouflage. Hollyhocks have thick, meaty roots that make them difficult to move. When I have second-year seedlings that I wish to transplant, I dig them up when they're just leafing out, replant them immediately, and water thoroughly and regularly until they are well estab-

lished. The flower stalks may become quite ungainly, long before they deliver their last, late-autumn gasp of bloom. If so, cut them back to the basal leaves.

HOSTA

Hosta

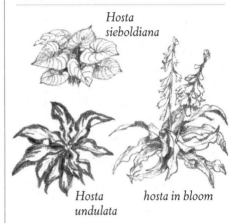

Hosta sieboldiana

Hosta undulata

hosta in bloom

Description: These plants are grown for their unusual leaves, which vary greatly in size, shape, and markings. Colors range from pale green to deep blue-green, and many have attractive markings in white, yellow, or a paler shade of green. Some leaves are very large, some are wavy, some smooth, some crinkly. The flowers—white or lavender bells dangling from erect stems several feet tall—are less showy than the leaves but are a welcome addition to the shade garden in late summer when few other shade-loving plants are blooming. Many of the white-flowered species are fragrant. Hostas make good edging plants, and those with pale foliage are great for lighting up shady corners of the garden.

Though the hostas are far too numerous to list, here are a few good ones to try. *Hosta sieboldiana* 'Elegans' forms big clumps of huge bluish leaves. *H. s.* 'Frances Williams' is edged in lighter green. *H. fortunei* 'Albo-picta' has yellow-green leaves edged in dark green. The common *H. undulata* has a small wavy leaf with cream-colored markings. Many of the bright yellow-leaved varieties such as 'Gold Standard' are sun tolerant and sometimes need some sun in order to truly shine. All are zones 3 to 8 or 9.

How to Grow: Hostas are easy, vigorous plants that will thrive in light or even full shade. They like rich, moist soil but need good drainage in winter. Slugs can be a problem, especially when plants are emerging, so spring is the time to bring out your beer traps (page 66). Division is easy and is usually done in spring.

IRIS
Iris

bearded iris

Japanese iris

Siberian iris

Description: The most familiar member of this group is the bearded iris (sold as *Iris × germanica*) that blooms in late spring. The large, handsome flowers are composed of three ruffled petals called standards, which stand upright, and three petals called falls, which hang down. The range of color is extraordinary in every color except bright red; sometimes the falls and standards are of different colors. The swordlike gray-green leaves are attractive until after bloom, when they start to yellow. These can be cut back to several inches tall and in a mixed bed they can be hidden with other plants as long as they are not too heavily shaded. Many feel they look best in a bed by themselves. Heights range from 2 to 4 feet. Zones 3 to 10.

The flowers of Siberian iris (*I. sibirica*), which appear in early summer, are more elegant than those of bearded iris; shades include blues, purples, rose, and white, some with exquisitely veined markings. The grasslike foliage is also beautiful, especially in motion. Zone 3 to 9. Japanese iris (*I. kaempferi*, also called *I. ensata*) is similar but the flowers are much larger—spectacular even—and bloom later still (June in warm climates, July in cold ones). Zone 4 or 5 to 9. (For irises that grow from bulbs, see page 509.) Other interesting species to grow include the native *I. cristata*, a spring-blooming woodlander, which is light blue and less than a foot tall; wild blue flag (*I. versicolor*), 1 to 3 feet tall, which is found in bogs or wet, sunny meadows (both zones 3 to 9); and the Louisiana iris—hybrids of various native species that thrive in moist gardens in the south.

How to Grow: The roots of bearded iris are fat rhizomes, prone to rot and to infestation by root maggots. The best prevention for both is simply to give the plants the conditions they need to thrive—sun, a rich neutral soil, and perfect drainage. This means planting the roots so that their tops are just visible, and even planting them on mounded soil if drainage is iffy. They are traditionally planted just after bloom time, because this is when they make their root growth. It's important to remove and destroy debris from around the plants before winter sets in, especially if there are any pest or disease problems. Divide established clumps from time to time to promote good health, cutting out any mushy roots or those with the small holes made by borers. If you find the creatures inside, squoosh them.

The roots of Japanese and Siberian irises are long and stringy. The plants like moist, slightly acid soil that is rich in humus. Divide Japanese iris every few years. Siberian clumps can be left undisturbed until bloom starts to decline. Pull the roots apart carefully if you can. The roots of old clumps become densely matted together but can be pried apart with two digging forks worked back to back (Figure 37). If too dense even for this trick, cut through them with a sharp spade. Both species like wet summers and dry winters, if you can imagine such a thing. Japanese iris, especially, needs to be kept moist in time of summer drought.

LADY'S MANTLE

Alchemilla mollis, A. vulgaris

Description: Of all the perennials grown for both flowers and foliage, this is near the top of the list. Lady's mantle makes a lush mound of scalloped, slightly felted leaves that hold raindrops as if they were jewels. The frothy yellow-green flowers are also a delight in early summer, especially when planted with the blues of veronica and cat-mint, and as cut flowers they are among the best fillers for early summer bouquets. Zones 3 or 4 to zones 7 or 8.

How to Grow: Lady's mantle thrives in both sun and part shade, and does best in cool climates. It prefers a fertile, moist, well-drained soil. Though very easy to grow, it presents a few maintenance tasks to the tidy gardener. Self-sowing can be a slight problem, though an advantage if you're using the plant as a ground cover. I like the way the brown seed heads look, and am willing to put up with the population explosion that results. When a plant becomes large and mature it tends to flop over and smother its neighbors. When this happens I cut back the stems soon after flowering, especially those at the outer edges. I also remove any leaves that become scorched and brown as the season progresses. The plant continues to make fresh new leaves.

LEOPARD'S BANE

Doronicum

Description: This plant has yet to become a household word among gardeners but it is worth discovering. Blooming so early that it joins the spring bulb show, it sends up beautiful yellow daisylike flowers on

upright stems. The foliage remains fresh and bright green in my garden, but may die back and go dormant in warmer zones. The botanical names are rather confused in the trade. Expect the cultivar 'Little Leo' to be about 12 inches tall, but 'Miss Mason' and 'Magnificum' to be closer to 2 feet. Some of the original species, when available, are taller and spread by rhizomes, with a later flowering period. Zones 4 to 7 or 8.

How to Grow: These plants, even when dormant, need adequate soil moisture to survive the summer. They will take full sun in areas with cool summers, but otherwise need some shade. They flourish best in cool climates.

LUPINE

Lupinus

Description: These tall, spikelike flower clusters can be truly spectacular in a garden that suits them. With most species this means in a cool climate where the stems grow thick and sturdy. They can, how-ever, be grown as fall-planted annuals in the south, and there are also some species well suited to warm parts of the country. Bluebonnet, the state flower of Texas, is an annual lupine. Other native lupines, the Washington lupine (*L. polyphyllus*) and the eastern lupine (*L. perennis*), also have blue flowers; those of California's tree lupine (*L. arboreus*) are yellow. Those most commonly sold, the Russell hybrids, cover a full range of blue, purple, red, pink, yellow, rust, cream, and white, with many bicolored combinations. These grow 2 to 4 feet and may need staking. Most lupines are zones 4 to 8 but may be short-lived.

How to Grow: Most hybrid garden lupines prefer a sunny spot (part shade in hot climates) and deep, rich, slightly acid, moist but well-drained soil. Fertilize well when they are planted, then top-dress each year. Mulching will help to keep the roots cool and the plants vigorous. They are short-lived in most gardens, and best treated as fall-sown annuals in warm climates. They tend to self-sow, but may not resemble the parent plant. Easy to grow from seed, though you'll need to soak the seeds overnight or nick them with a file to hasten germination. Saved seed should be sown in fall or cold-stratified (given a chilling period) if sown in spring. Best sown directly in the garden or in pots since the seedlings do not like to be handled. The foliage gets quite ugly soon after bloom; cutting back to the basal leaves will promote fresh new growth and may even cause the plant to rebloom.

LYCHNIS (CAMPION, CATCHFLY, MALTESE CROSS)

Lychnis

Description: The genus *Lychnis* encompasses a number of very diverse and useful garden plants. Maltese cross (*L. chalcedonica*) is about 3 feet tall with very brilliant scarlet flowers (cross-shaped, in clusters), that I love to splotch in among the misty early-summer blues of delphinium, salvia, catmint, and geranium. Though reliable and long-lived, it needs support, especially for the stems on the outside of the clump. Its foliage soon becomes unsightly on about the bottom third of the stems, and needs to be hidden by the lush growth of another, lower plant. Catchfly (*L. viscaria*) bears unabashedly magenta flowers along

its stems, on a tidy 1½-foot plant; it is valuable for its very early bloom and easy care. Rose campion (*L. coronaria*) is one of those can't-live-with-it-can't-live-without-it plants. The flowers are a glowing magenta made downright acceptable by the nearly white, woolly-leaved plants supporting them; the contrast is beautiful, and bloom continues from early to late summer. Growing 2 to 3 feet tall, it is a rampant biennial self-sower, casting its little white seedlings throughout any bed it inhabits, and the lawn as well. I dutifully weed it out, saving the ones for which I know I'll be grateful when they bloom next year. A new sterile variety called 'Gardener's World,' with double carnation-like blooms, may need staking but does not go to seed. All zones 3 to 8 or 9.

How to Grow: Apart from needing decent drainage and the tidiness issues mentioned above, these are simple plants to care for. Maltese cross needs a rich, moist soil. All *Lychnis* species prefer full sun.

MEADOWSWEET (FALSE SPIREA)

Filipendula

Description: It has taken this group of plants a while to catch on with American gardeners, despite the fact that a number of them are native to our meadows. Though typically found growing in wet places, they adapt well to garden life. The stately Queen-of-the-prairie (*Filipendula rubra*) grows 6 to 8 feet tall, with pale pink feathery plumes—a perfect back-of-the-border plant. The variety 'Venusta' is a deeper pink and shorter, as is Japanese

meadowsweet (*F. purpurea*). There is also a white form of the latter. Queen-of-the-meadow (*F. ulmaria*) is a 4-foot plant, with white flowers in loose panicles; though not native, it has naturalized widely in North American fields. Dropwort (*F. vulgaris*), another nonnative, is 2 to 3 feet tall; it is widely available in its double form 'Flore Pleno,' which has cream-colored flowers and grows to 1½ feet. All bloom in mid to late summer and thrive in zones 3 or 4 to 8 or 9.

How to Grow: Give all the meadow-sweets plenty of soil moisture; only drop-wort is drought tolerant. Meadowsweets like a neutral or slightly alkaline soil with plenty of organic matter, and do well in full sun or light shade (the latter in warm climates). Some of the tallest forms may need staking.

MEADOW RUE

Thalictrum

Description: These towering plants are easy to place in gardens, lending the airy grace of their flowers wherever that effect is needed, often without hiding what's behind them. Their foliage is so decorative that they're an asset even before or after their bloom. *Thalictrum aquilegifolium* is an early bloomer with bluish leaves like those of columbines; its fuzzy purple, pink, or white flowers, on strong 2- to 3-foot stems, are followed by attractive pale seed heads. The other species bloom in mid-summer. *T. rochebrunianum,* 'Lavender Mist' is my favorite, growing up to 5 or 6 feet (and more!) with huge, open clusters of small lavender blooms. The gorgeous purple stems need little or no staking. *T. speciosissimum* (*T. flavum glaucum*) is tall with fuzzy yellow blooms. I've found the stems impossibly weak and unstakeable in shady situations, strongly upright in sunny ones. Early pruning may also lead to more easily supported stems. All from at least zone 5 to 7 or 8.

How to Grow: Meadow rues grow in full sun but appreciate light shade in warm climates. They need a fertile, moisture-retentive soil. They do not need to be divided, but you may do so in fall for propagation purposes.

MONKSHOOD
Aconitum

PEONY
Paeonia

double   *Japanese*

single

Description: These plants produce tall spikes of flowers, usually blue, which do look like a throng of hooded monks— hence, the name. They are a fine plant for the middle or back of the border in late summer or fall. Beware: all parts of the plant are poisonous. Monkshoods for the garden come from a number of different species. Some good varieties include 'Bressingham Spire,' a 3-foot, strongly erect plant with lavender-blue flowers; 'Bicolor,' a slightly taller plant with blue-and-white flowers; and 'Spark's Variety,' which grows to 4 to 5 feet and blooms late in the season with dark purple-blue flowers. Zones 3 or 4 to 8.

How to Grow: Monkshood prefers part shade in hot climates but otherwise grows best in full sun if the soil is kept moist. Soil should also be moderately fertile, light, humusy, well drained, and deeply culti- vated to accommodate the extensive root system. Monkshood does best in cool cli- mates where the stems grow strong and are less likely to need staking. The clumps should not be disturbed once they're established.

Description: The classic hybrid gar- den peony is a stalwart plant that thrives from zone 3 to 7 or 8, depending on the variety. Peony flowers are classified as doubles (huge round balls with many petals), semidoubles (with fewer petals), singles (with one sparser row of over- lapping petals surrounding a handsome cluster of gold stamens in the center), and Japanese (single, with a nest of showy, petallike stamens in the center). Colors range from dark maroon to bright red, pink, white, and occasionally yellow. Many, especially the pale ones, are fra- grant. They grow on long, arching stems in a mound of dark green foliage about 3 feet high and 3 feet wide.

The plants do not bloom for long, although you can choose varieties that bloom for several overlapping periods, and the foliage is attractive all sum- mer and into fall, when many variet- ies turn a pleasing gold or bronze color. *Paeonia tenuifolia* (fern-leaved peony) is low growing and admired for both its handsome foliage and its dark red flow- ers. "Tree peonies" are really shrubs that grow into a mound about 5 feet high and 5 feet wide; there's a wider range of flower colors among the tree peonies than with the typical herbaceous kind, including the yellow-to-bronze range. Zones 4 to 7 or 8.

By choosing a selection of early, midseason, and late varieties you can keep a peony bed in bloom for as long as six weeks; this is a good idea because they make a good cut flower as well as a grand show in the garden. Some of the many hybrid peony varieties are 'Kansas,' a bright red double; 'Festiva Maxima,' a beautiful variety over 100 years old, which is a white double flecked with traces of red; and 'Krinkled White,' a single variety suitable for the south.

How to Grow: Peonies are planted in fall in deep, well-drained soil enriched with organic matter. Plant as shown in Figure 36, making sure the "eyes" are no more than 2 inches below the soil surface, because planting too deep may result in failure to bloom. Peonies usually do very well when planted right, even though they may take a few years to get established and bloom well. They're not suitable for climates with very mild winters, although some early-blooming varieties may thrive there. Staking with peony rings (Figure 38) will keep the blooms more attractive, especially when it rains.

If you've planted your peonies correctly and they still do not bloom after several years, other conditions may be at fault, such as excessive moisture or drought, too much heat or too much shade, too much fertility or too little, as well as various pests and diseases. To keep plants healthy, always clean up dead foliage at the season's end.

PHLOX
Phlox

Phlox
paniculata

Phlox
subulata

Description: Most people are familiar with *Phlox paniculata*, the tall garden phlox that is the glory of the summer garden, with its big, fragrant clusters of red, pink, salmon, lavender, purple, or white blossoms. It grows 2 to 4 feet tall and looks especially well massed in large clumps of one color each. Good varieties include the bright red 'Starfire,' pink 'Bright Eyes,' lavender 'Franz Schubert,' and white, admirably mildew-proof 'David.' The earlier blooming *P. maculata* varieties, such as the white 'Miss Lingard,' are shorter with looser flower clusters. Low-growing phlox include two native woodland species: the wonderful, highly fragrant spring-blooming wild blue phlox (*P. divaricata*), and creeping phlox (*P. stolonifera*), with pink, blue, or white blooms. The widely planted moss phlox, also called moss pink (*P. subulata*), has a color range similar to that of creeping phlox. Most phlox are zones 3 to 8 or 9.

How to Grow: All but the woodland species prefer full sun or very light shade, and all phlox like light, fertile soil with ample organic matter to retain moisture; they must also have good drainage. Provide adequate air circulation around the plants by not crowding them. Thinning to about five vigorous stems is said to help forestall the white mildew that often disfigures the leaves of the tall garden phlox, but in the end you may have to seek out resistant varieties if this proves to be a problem. Dividing clumps of tall varieties every few years and replanting the side shoots will help to keep them vigorous. Remove spent blooms to prevent plants from going to seed; seedlings will usually revert to a vivid magenta, or to lavender.

PINKS

Dianthus

Dianthus alwoodii 'Alpinus'

Dianthus 'Doris'

Dianthus deltoides

Description: These flowers are often pink but are sometimes shades of red or white, and sometimes marked with several colors. Some are shaped like small carnations (to which pinks are related); others have fewer petals, often with ragged edges. Some have a pleasant, clovelike scent. The foliage is often very pretty, usually in shades of grayish or bluish green. Pinks are generally short—many grow close to the ground in matlike carpets. The tallest are rarely more than 1½ feet high. They usually flower in spring or early summer, but some continue to produce blooms throughout the season, especially if cut back.

Maiden pink (*Dianthus deltoides*) produces tiny, single dark pink or white flowers on short stems in late spring, and self-sows. Grass pink (*D. plumarius*) is usually about a foot tall, with bluish foliage and multicolored flowers. Cheddar pink (*D. gratianopolitanus*, also called *D. caesius*), is a low-growing, spreading pink flower with grayish leaves; the variety 'Tiny Rubies' is very low and abundant with bright pink flowers. In general, all these are zones 3 to 9. Hybrids such as salmon-colored 'Doris' and red 'Ian' have larger flowers and are hardy only to zone 5 or 6, but the low-growing variety *D. alwoodii* 'Alpinus' is hardy to zone 3. In warm climates you can grow carnations, also called clove pinks (*D. caryophyllus*). Zones 8 to 10. Sweet William (*D. barbatus*) is a tender perennial best treated as a biennial or self-sowing annual.

How to Grow: All pinks need excellent drainage and prefer slightly alkaline soil. They grow best in cool climates. Do not mulch the crowns. Remove spent flowers to encourage rebloom, and cut back long-stemmed varieties if they get dry and scraggly in midsummer. Mat-forming varieties can be left alone unless they take up too much space, but clump-forming ones such as carnations and the larger-flowered hybrids may need to be divided every few years to keep them attractive and vigorous. They can also be increased by layering or taking cuttings.

POPPY

Papaver orientale

PRIMROSE

Primula

Primula × polyantha

Primula japonica

Description: The Oriental poppy's showy flowers appear for only a week or two in late spring or early summer in gorgeous shades of red, pink, orange, and salmon, as well as white. They are borne on stems 2 to 3 feet high above foliage that looks, alas, quite messy as summer wears on, then disappears. They can be grown in a bed by themselves, or tucked in among later-blooming plants whose foliage will fill in and provide cover for the poppies' untidy exit. There are many varieties from which to choose, including the long-blooming pink 'Helen Elizabeth,' the enormous 'Barr's White,' and the bright red 'Beauty of Livermore.' Zones 3 to 7.

How to Grow: Poppies are planted in late summer or early fall. They rarely need division, and propagation is best done by taking root cuttings several inches long. They prefer sun, except in hot climates where some light shade is best during the hot part of the day—if they survive at all, for they are essentially cool-climate plants. They like a fairly fertile soil, but poor drainage will cause them to rot, especially during the winter.

Description: I'm not sure why Shakespeare had his primrose path lead to "easy dalliance," but a primrose path is certainly a colorful way to lead a visitor to your door. The most characteristic primrose color is yellow, but there are many other colors available. All the species have cheerful, low-growing, spring-blooming flowers, and most are easy to grow. Some have evergreen leaves, and some will rebloom a little in fall.

The most commonly sold primroses are hybrids of *Primula × polyantha;* these come in just about any color you can name, many of them bicolored. Zones 3 to 8. Some primroses, such as the Japonica hybrids, have a tiered candelabra shape. These bear clusters of pink, purple, or white flowers atop stems as tall as 2 feet in late spring. Zones 5 to 8. Japanese star primrose (*P. sieboldii*) is shorter, in rosy shades. Zones 4 to 8. The Barnhaven strain is particularly vigorous.

How to Grow: Primroses prefer part shade and humusy, moisture-retentive soil that is not allowed to dry out in summer. Some candelabra types need downright boggy conditions, and are beautiful planted next to a stream. But most primroses, despite their need for spring and summer moisture, can be done in by winter wet. Most also fail in very hot climates. They can be grown from seed and are also propagated easily by division, which renews their vigor. Do it right after they've finished blooming.

SAGE

Salvia

Description: Though the culinary sage described on page 405 is itself a highly ornamental plant, there's an excellent tribe of sages grown for their looks alone. Among the ones hardy in cold climates, the most garden-worthy are cultivars of mixed parentage. Among my favorites for roughly zones 3 to 8 are the sages usually listed as cultivars of *S.* × *superba* (*S. nemorosa*) such as deep blue, long-blooming 'May Night,' the purple 'East Friesland,' and the true blue 'Blue Hill,' all of which grow about 1½ feet tall. The equally compact *S. verticillata* 'Purple Rain' has a rosier hue. Gardeners from zones 7 south have more choices, including the bright red autumn sage (*S. greggii*), pineapple sage (*S. elegans*), and Texas sage (*S. coccinea*) as

well as the shrublike white Mexican bush sage (*S. leucantha*).

How to Grow: All the sages are sun loving, and tend to be drought tolerant. They like a moderately fertile, well-drained soil. Deadheading can extend their bloom. Divide in spring as needed.

SCABIOSA (PINCUSHION FLOWER)

Scabiosa caucasica

Description: These lacy blue or white flowers do look something like a pincushion. You need a good mass of them to create a showy effect in the border, but they are easy to grow, long blooming, and good for cutting. Most grow 1½ to 2½ feet tall and bloom from early to late summer. Some good varieties are the 'Isaac House Hybrids,' which are mixed shades of blue and white, and 'Butterfly Blue,' which has an especially profuse and prolonged bloom. All zones 3 to 7 or 8.

How to Grow: Scabiosa prefers sun except in hot climates. It needs moist, light, slightly alkaline soil with good drainage. Division is rarely needed, though this may promote flowering; it should be done in early spring. Scabiosa is also a good perennial to grow from seed. Deadheading will produce longer bloom.

SEA LAVENDER
Limonium latifolium

Description: This plant is not grown as often as it should be. It is a good front-of-the-border plant with a flat rosette of dark green leaves and airy lavender-colored flowers on long, thin stems. It gives much the same effect as baby's breath both in the garden and in flower arrangements, and it blooms for a long period in summer. Grow either the original species or the variety 'Violetta,' which has darker flowers. Zones 3 to 9.

How to Grow: The plant needs sun (part shade in the south) and a deep, sandy loam that is well drained but not too fertile or the stems will flop. Give it plenty of air circulation. It's slow to establish, but once it gets going you can take divisions from the sides of the clump for propagation. An excellent seaside plant.

SEDUM (STONECROP)
Sedum

Description: Sedums are succulents—they have thick, fleshy leaves filled with water. There are many kinds, most of which are good rock garden plants, especially the low-growing ones. Some of these are also good ground covers. The taller species are very effective in borders. Most sedum species have attractive flowers; some are also grown for their leaves, which are colorful and/or variegated.

Sedum acre (gold moss) is a bright yellow, spring-flowering prostrate creeper that is ideal as an edging, in rock gardens, and even in cracks between paving stones. *S. spurium* forms a 6-inch mat of pink or white blooms in late summer. *S. kamtschaticum* forms clumps a foot high or less and bears yellow flowers in the latter half of the summer. Good border types include the 2-foot *S. spectabile*, whose varieties 'Meteor' and 'Brilliant' bear reddish pink flowers in late summer, and *Sedum* 'Autumn Joy,' whose pink flowers turn a deep mahogany in fall and leave seed heads that are pretty all winter. Most sedums are zones 3 to 9.

How to Grow: Sedums need good drainage, especially in winter, but are otherwise not fussy about soil requirements. Give them sun in the north, part shade in hot-summer climates. They are very easy to propagate by stem or leaf cuttings, from seed, or by division. Otherwise there is no need to divide them. The taller types, when mature, may flop open in the center. This problem can be solved by staking with strong brush or circular grid-style supports. It can also be prevented by pinching the stems or cutting the whole plant back in June to make it more compact.

SHASTA DAISY

Leucanthemum × *superbum*
(*Chrysanthemum* × *superbum*,
C. maximum)

single

double

Description: Shasta daisies are always white but can be either single or double, tall or short. They generally bloom for a long time in summer, especially if the flowers are picked and/or deadheaded, and they are a great white accent in the border. 'Alaska' and 'Becky' are among the hardiest tall varieties; both single, about 3 feet tall, zones 4 to 9 (most others to zone 5). 'Marconi' is a 3-foot semidouble variety, 'Miss Muffet' a single that grows about a foot tall.

How to Grow: Provide sun in cool climates, part shade in hot ones. The plants need fertile, moist soil that is well drained, especially in wintertime. Water in very dry weather. Pinching the stems in early summer will make the tall varieties bushier and less in need of staking. Clumps are sometimes short-lived; divide established

ones every few years to keep them vigorous and flowerful.

SNAKEROOT (BUGBANE)

Cimicifuga

Description: This woodland plant, native to the eastern United States, is not widely known but truly a delight to grow. Its flowers are tall, fuzzy white spikes (occasionally pink). The leaves are attractive and fernlike, rather like that of astilbe. *Cimicifuga racemosa*, native to eastern North America, grows 5 to 6 feet tall, sometimes even taller, and flowers in mid to late summer. The fragrant *C. simplex* grows at least 3 to 4 feet tall and blooms quite late in fall. Snakeroot's luminous candlelike flower spikes are as beautiful in the back of shaded borders as they are in woodland plantings. Various cultivars are available with very dramatic dark foliage, such as 'Hillside Black Beauty' and 'Brunette.' Zones 3 to 8.

How to Grow: Both species prefer part shade, though they will grow in sun in cool climates if watered sufficiently. They like a moist, rich, acid, woodsy soil. Consistent moisture is essential for good growth and bloom, and to prevent the foliage from browning. Division is not necessary, but the stems may need to be staked up to where the flower begins. Do not deadhead, since the seed heads are attractive.

SNEEZEWEED
Helenium autumnale

Description: Don't be put off by this plant's name. I've never known it to produce sneezes, only admiring looks. Always an essential part of my late-summer garden, the gold, terra-cotta, or mahogany tones of its little daisylike flowers provide a harmonious bridge between the phlox and coneflowers of summer and the asters and goldenrods of fall. My favorite is the 3- to 4-foot burnt orange-red 'Moerheim Beauty.' The 4- to 5-foot 'Riverton Beauty' is bright yellow. All have dark, raised centers. Zones 3 to 8.

How to Grow: Sneezeweeds need sun and reasonably moist, well-drained soil. All but the most compact varieties need staking, but tall varieties can be pinched early in the season to promote bushier, stronger, shorter growth. Keep in mind that this will make them bloom even later in the season. The clumps are best divided every few years to maintain vigor.

SUNDROPS
Oenothera

Description: The sundrops commonly found in gardens are mistakenly called evening primroses; some *Oenothera* species do bloom at night, but not these. They resemble large, spread-open buttercups and bloom in early to mid summer, with some repeat bloom later on. Two excellent species are commercially available. One is *O. tetragona*, usually sold as *O. fruticosa*, of which there are several cultivars. The long-blooming 'Fyrverkeri' (fireworks) is one of the best. It grows 1½ feet tall with showy yellow blooms and a gorgeous red fall color. The other, *O. missouriensis*, has 4-inch-wide flowers and grows low to the ground on trailing stems. It can be a bit wilty in afternoon sun, even in cool climates. All are North American natives and, in general, thrive in zones 4 to 8.

How to Grow: All are sun loving and tolerant of dry, infertile soil. They require good drainage but are otherwise trouble free. Some species are a bit invasive, and must be weeded out from time to time. Easily divided in spring or early fall.

VERONICA (SPEEDWELL)
Veronica

Description: Veronica's spiky flowers are usually blue but sometimes lavender, pink, or white. The plants range in height from a few inches to 4 feet. Blooming period varies from early to late summer. *Veronica spicata* 'Blue Peter' grows up to 2 feet and flowers in midsummer. 'Icicle' is the same height, white, and a long bloomer. 'Red Fox' is a bit shorter and fairly early. *V. prostrata* 'Heavenly Blue' is low and mat forming, and early blooming. *V. incana,* 12 to 18 inches tall, has striking silvery leaves as well as blue flowers; like all gray-leaved plants, it requires excellent drainage. *V. teucrium* 'Crater Lake Blue,' an early bloomer, has a floppy habit but the intensity of its blue flowers makes you forgive all. Several hybrids such as the foot-tall 'Goodness Grows' and the 18- to 24-inch 'Sunny Border Blue' are very long blooming. Most are zones 3 to 8.

How to Grow: These plants like sun but will take part shade. They need adequate moisture but good drainage as well. The soil should be moderately fertile. Plants are easily divided in spring or fall. Cutting back spent blooms may encourage rebloom, as well as keep the plants more presentable for the remainder of the season.

YARROW (MILFOIL)
Achillea

Achillea 'Fire King'

Achillea 'Coronation Gold'

Description: Most people are familiar with the wild white yarrow with its flat clusters of flowers, a European plant long ago naturalized in the American landscape. Garden specimens are most often yellow, sometimes pink or red, and most recently a rainbow of wonderfully in-between shades such as peach, ochre, salmon, rust, and sand (look for mixtures such as 'Summer Pastels'). All have ferny leaves, sometimes with a grayish cast. They are easy to grow and bloom for a long time in summer. Garden varieties are derived from a number of species, including *Achillea millefolium, A. filipendulina, A. taygetea,* and *A. clypeolata.* 'Moonshine' is lemon yellow with gray leaves and grows about 2 feet. 'Coronation Gold' is bright yellow with greener leaves and grows to 3 feet. 'Fire King' is 18 to 24 inches, pinkish red and very long blooming. 'Gold Plate,' among the tallest, is a soft yellow. *A. tomentosa* is a very pleasing low variety that forms a mat of whitish leaves and has flowers less than a foot tall. I love it both in the rock garden and at the front of the border. Generally zones 3 to 8 or 9.

How to Grow: Yarrows are sun loving, drought resistant, and easy to grow, but must have good drainage. They rarely need staking, though stems can be lax if the soil is too rich. Deadheading and/or cutting back to basal foliage will extend the bloom period. All benefit by division every few years in early spring or in fall. (Spring is best in cold climates.) Yarrow can also be grown from seed.

CHAPTER 7

Vegetables

Why Grow Your Own Vegetables?

IN SOME PEOPLE'S MINDS, VEGETABLE gardening *is* gardening. When they parcel out the limited time, space, and resources they have for this activity, the vegetable garden comes first (with a nod, perhaps, to the obligatory lawn). This is a passion. Even as a veteran rose-sniffing, tree-hugging grower of ornamental plants, if I had to choose between growing food and growing flowers, food would win.

Why, with ample fresh produce available year-round in the supermarkets, is this tradition still alive and well? Sometimes the initial goal is to save money. If gardeners are efficient and diligent they do so, but I've heard beginners joke in fall about the tomatoes that cost them a dollar apiece to grow—after figuring the price of the fence, tools, and soil amendments plus the cost of their normally well-paid time. Yet the following spring, undaunted by these economics, they're back in their gardens.

The desire to feed ourselves from our home ground is something that is rooted firmly in our cultural history, maybe even in our genes. For much of the world, growing food is the only way to obtain it. Even for the rest of us, a commercial food supply is not something we should take for granted. But I grow my own vegetables for two very good reasons: the quality of the crops I can produce myself, and the quality of the time I spend doing it. There's no question that food picked fresh from my garden tastes better than food that is picked thousands of miles away, then rides in a truck for days, sits in distribution centers, waits in display bins in the store, rides home in the car, then idles in the refrigerator until it's the right item for the menu. Vegetables ripened in the garden and eaten right away have many more vitamins, too. I also appreciate the fact that I alone decide whether chemical fertilizers are used to grow my food and whether it's sprayed with pesticides and other controversial substances. I believe that the quality of the food we eat is extremely important in keeping us healthy, and I know that the food I grow myself is fresh, safe, wholesome, and alive.

Furthermore, the selection of vegetables available to me as a home gardener is so much wider than that in the produce department of a store. Market vegetables are usually bred for ease of transportation and storage, uniform size and color, and the ability of the crop to bear all at once for a profitable, large-scale harvest. In choosing what to grow in my garden, on the other hand, I look for better flavor and nutrition, new and unusual varieties to try out, and quite often a crop that does *not* mature all at once, so that I can pick it over a long period of time.

All these are benefits I have discovered during the course of growing vegetables, but they're not what motivated me in the first place. Initially it was simply the itch to get out there in the spring, to smell the warm earth, and to grub around in the garden all spring, summer, and fall in the sunshine, feeling fit and contented, watching my bounty ripen. I think there is a basic satisfaction in growing food for the table, and that most of us who do it enjoy the activity of gardening itself just as much as the result.

What Is a Vegetable?

Botanically, the term "vegetable" means nothing. When we speak of vegetables we mean an odd assortment of plants, mostly annual and soft stemmed, that we grow for food. Generally we exclude those that taste very sweet and most of the grain crops such as rice and wheat. A few vegetables are perennial, such as asparagus, rhubarb, horseradish, Jerusalem artichoke, and (in tropical climates only) tomatoes and peppers.

The distinction between a "fruit" and a "vegetable" is an unscientific one. "Fruit" is the botanical term for the part of a plant that contains the seeds. Thus the tomato plant is grown for its fruit, as are the eggplant, the pepper, and the squash. But vegetables vary widely in terms of which part of the plant is eaten. Often it is the leaves, as with lettuce, spinach, cabbage, Swiss chard, and all the crops we call greens, cooked or otherwise. Onions are also, strictly speaking, a leaf crop, even though the bulbs (actually leaf bases) grow partially underground. Other vegetables such as rhubarb and celery are stem crops, and oddly enough, kohlrabi is a stem too, although a greatly enlarged one. True root crops include turnips, carrots, parsnips, and beets. Potatoes are tubers formed on underground stems called stolons. Crops grown for the seeds inside the fruits include peas and corn. Some grown for the edible flower buds are artichoke, cauliflower, and broccoli.

Frequently gardeners group vegetables together according to their botanical families. You can grow prize vegetables without ever knowing their Latin names, but it does help to know something about vegetable families for practical reasons. Many of the plants within these main groups have similar characteristics, are subject to the same problems, and are grown in similar ways.

Organizing your garden by plant groups will help you to rotate crops from year to year and thereby avoid some of the diseases that plants within the same group share. Also, the family names crop up quite frequently in garden literature. Use the list on page 232 as a reference, so when someone mentions, say, the brassicas, you'll know what they are talking about.

Which Vegetables Should You Grow?

The first criterion should be your appetite and that of the people you live with. A friend of mine used to grow a bumper crop of pumpkins every year, no small feat in the north country. Stacked in crates from floor to ceiling each fall, they provided his large family with months of the nutritious pumpkin pudding he took pride in making. Unfortunately, no one in his household could stand pumpkin pudding except him, so he finally admitted defeat and settled for a few pumpkin plants for jack-o'-lanterns. If your tribe loves beets, plant beets. If they like lettuce, plant lettuce. You might even get them involved in taking care of the garden that way (always worth a try).

Even though I've advised planting

VEGETABLE FAMILIES

KNOWING WHAT FAMILY A VEGETABLE belongs to has little to do with botanical erudition and lots to do with how the plant grows. The members of a given family usually share the same soil requirements, like the same climate and weather, and are subject to the same pests and diseases. If you know how to grow one member of a family, this will help you to grow the others.

The other reason to know vegetable families is so that you can rotate your crops properly. If you grow members of the same family repeatedly in the same spot, the diseases that afflict them can persist in the soil and pests can overwinter as well, ready and waiting the following spring. Also, different crops deplete or improve the soil in particular ways. By alternating families on different patches of your garden, you reduce repeated stresses and spread benefits around.

Chenopodiaceae. These include spinach, Swiss chard, and beets. Spinach tends to bolt in heat, but by and large these are problem-free plants.

Compositae (Asteraceae). These plants are so named because what we regard as their "flowers" are actually inflorescences—flower composites in which a ring of elongated ray flowers generally surrounds a cluster of small, round disk flowers. A daisy illustrates the type perfectly. In this family are some salad plants, notably lettuce, endive, and chicory, and the root crops

salsify and scorzonera. These easy crops like cool weather.

Cruciferae. Most are in the genus *Brassica*, often called cabbage or mustard vegetables, brassicas, or cole crops. Besides cabbage and mustard greens, the Cruciferae (sometimes called crucifers) include broccoli, Brussels sprouts, cauliflower, kale, collards, turnips, rutabagas, kohlrabi, cresses, arugula, and radishes. All are cool-weather crops that like a moderately rich soil, with plenty of organic matter to maintain a steady supply of moisture. Root maggots, cutworms, and cabbage worms can be a problem. They share a number of diseases such as blackleg.

Cucurbitaceae. Called cucurbits or the cucumber family, the group includes squash, pumpkins, melons, and gourds as well as cucumbers. All are warm-weather plants and most produce vigorous, fast-growing vines that need fertile soil amply supplied with organic matter. The cucumber beetle afflicts them all, as do certain diseases.

Leguminosae. Called legumes or the pea family, these are all the peas and beans, including soybeans and peanuts. Clover, alfalfa, lupines, and locust trees are also legumes. Rich in protein, they are good for you and good for your soil; nodules growing on their roots make the atmospheric nitrogen in the soil available for plant use. Cold tolerance varies, but all legumes have large, fast-germinating seeds that are usually sown directly in the garden. They share certain diseases that can spread if you move among their leaves when wet.

Liliaceae. The lily family contains all the onion-type vegetables and also asparagus. Members of the onion group like to be started in cool weather. They need a rich soil, plentiful moisture, and good drainage.

Solanaceae. Called the tobacco or nightshade family, it includes not only these but also tomatoes, peppers, potatoes, and eggplants. (I call them ratatouille vegetables, because so many of them go into that summer dish.) Some Solanaceae are toxic, have toxic parts (like potato sprouts), or are slightly toxic for certain people. But as a group they are rich in vitamin C. All are warm-weather plants that like rich, moist soil. They tend to be disease prone, so it's important to rotate them.

Umbelliferae. Carrots, parsnips, and celery belong to this family, as well as many edibles grouped under "herbs," such as parsley, cilantro, chervil, and dill. They all have an "umbel" flower cluster (umbrella-shaped, like that of Queen Anne's lace). All are cool-weather crops with few diseases or pests. They like a deep, loose soil. Their germination can be temperamental— all need a pulverized, moistened soil to sprout. They also have a tendency to bolt (go to seed) in warm weather.

vegetables you know and like, I still think that a vegetable garden is a golden opportunity to try the new and unfamiliar. Often having a garden is the only way you can eat certain delicacies: skinny little French string beans, zingy Italian salad greens, crisp and colorful Asian radishes. Perhaps the cook in your household craves ordinary vegetables in "baby" sizes ("small-fruited" varieties as opposed to varieties where the plant itself is dwarf or compact). Some of these novelties may be experiments you never repeat again; others may become permanent features in your garden. Mail-order and Internet sources (page 764) can supply you with seeds for unusual crops, together with more detailed descriptions and growing instructions than I have space for here.

WORKING WITH YOUR CLIMATE

In deciding what to grow, you'll have to take your climate into account. Each region has a set of vegetables that are easier to grow than others. Southerners have no trouble with okra, sweet potatoes, eggplant, and peanuts. Northerners have an easy time with cool-weather crops such as broccoli, peas, lettuce, and cabbage (as do southerners if they wait for cool weather). Gardeners in wet climates excel at celery; those in dry ones succeed with sweet potatoes.

If you're a beginning gardener, my advice is to start with the crops that thrive in your area. Ask your neighbors what grows well for them, or ask local nurserymen or your Extension Service. It is also helpful to start with some crops that are notoriously easy to grow anywhere because they are not fussy plants: lettuce, radishes, beets, summer squash, cucumbers, and Swiss chard. Then, with a few gardening seasons behind you, try anything, even vegetables that are more of a challenge in your climate. The gardening magazines are full of stories about people who have grown the "wrong" vegetable against improbable odds with a few tricks and attention to detail. Often it's just a matter of choosing the right variety, such as a heat-resistant spinach or a short-season eggplant.

Individual vegetables, how to grow them, and what varieties to grow are discussed on pages 266 to 382 of this chapter. But it is important to get an overview of how vegetable gardens are planned in relation to climate—how the growing schedules vary from one region to the next. In the north, where I live, my gardening fortunes rise and fall on my observation of two important dates: the last frost in spring, and the first frost in fall. Unfortunately, I never know exactly what these dates are going to be. All I know is that the *average* last frost in spring for my locality is May 17, and the average first frost in fall is October 3. By keeping my mind on these dates, my eye on the weather, and my ear tuned to the forecast on the radio, I can at least set up a gardening schedule. In my case it will mean starting the seeds of some crops indoors in March and April, and then setting the young plants into the garden after the danger of frost has passed. Other crops will be sown directly into the garden as the weather becomes right for each one. Some spring crops will be harvested early. In their place I will plant successions of summer vegetables. Some of the ones planted in spring and harvested in summer will then be followed by fall crops. When that fateful first frost threatens, some vegetables will leave my garden and go into the freezer, into canning jars, and into the cellar, or they'll be hung on strings in the kitchen. But a lot of rugged ones will keep right on producing despite the frost. And some will even stay in the ground over the winter, to be harvested in early spring, or in cold frames or a simple greenhouse for continuous harvest.

If I lived in a hot climate, I might preserve some of my food, but I would not be as concerned about it as my northern locale obliges me to be. In mild-winter areas it is possible to eat a wider variety of vegetables fresh from the garden all year long. Instead of one or two successions of most crops, I could have three successions of many of them. I would still keep an eye out for frost, since some vegetables cannot tolerate even a touch of it, but my main worry would be the summer heat and/or drought, which would bring much of my vegetable production to a standstill. While some of my crops would thrive during the hot stretch, for many it would be the fallow season. For those I would make the most of the more temperate days of winter, spring, and fall.

Temperature and moisture are not the only factors that vary from one part of the country to another. With certain vegetables you must also take day length into account. In the north, days start to shorten dramatically at summer's end, an effect that is much less pronounced in the south. This makes cauliflower, for example, a better crop in the north, because the heads start to develop when the days become noticeably shorter. The ability of onions to form bulbs is also affected by decreasing day length. There are actually "short-day" onions more appropriate to southern gardens than the "long-day" onions that thrive up north. Questions of how day length influences growth are considered in more detail under specific vegetables.

The number of sunny days is another factor. Some parts of the country, the Pacific northwest for example, have so many rainy, cloudy, or foggy days during the growing season that gardeners there have to choose vegetables that will tolerate the relative lack of sun. In general most vegetables prefer full sun, and with fruiting crops such as tomatoes, peppers, and eggplant it is essential. None will do well in true shade. But some will tolerate more cloudy days than others, or a yard that is semishaded beyond remedy. The leafy crops are the most shade tolerant; these include lettuce, endive, cabbage, kale, Brussels sprouts, chard, and many herbs such as parsley. Certain other early, cool-weather crops such as asparagus, broccoli, and peas may also succeed. Less tolerant than these, but still worth a try, are onions, and root crops such as beets, radishes, parsnips, leeks, and turnips.

How Big a Garden Do You Need?

THIS IS AN IMPORTANT DECISION. I think the most common mistake made by new gardeners (and often old ones) is that they plant too much—too many crops, too many seeds, too many plants. Either the upkeep overwhelms them and much of the garden succumbs to weeds, bugs, or drought, or the harvest is too bountiful and they cannot keep up with the picking, let alone the eating and preserving. If you're really sure that you want a large garden and will spend the time needed to bring it to harvest, by all means plant one. But I would hate to see you discouraged forever by a garden that failed because it was too ambitious. You'll probably find it more fun and rewarding to start small.

In fact you may want to stay small. I've had many different kinds and sizes of vegetable gardens, depending on where I was living, how long I expected to stay there, how many people I was feeding, and how overcommitted I was in other areas of my life at the time. One garden, in a hayfield next to a rented apartment, was about 6 feet by 6 feet and contained two cherry tomato plants, two rows of lettuce, and some basil. It served its purpose perfectly. By alternating the two lettuce rows I had good salads all summer, and when frost threatened I picked all the cherry tomatoes and marinated them in jars of vinaigrette in the refrigerator (even with two plants I had a surplus of tomatoes).

Another year, living in a more permanent residence, I planted a 45- by 60-foot garden—enormous, considering the fact that I was only feeding two people. It was elaborately fenced against intruders (with moderate success) and had thirty-five or forty crops, from snow peas to corn to about five kinds of dried beans. I canned a number of crops and stored root crops in the basement in winter. It took three months to clear land for that garden—to dig it, condition its soil, fence it, and plant it—and during that time I did nothing else, though I certainly enjoyed it all. It required considerable upkeep all summer, even with mulches, and when canning time came I again did nothing else. The following year I was working for a nursery and had far less time for the garden. So I planted only a quarter of the area. Even without the big initial task of preparation, I knew that was all I would be able to manage in a few daylight hours after work each week.

Now, many gardens later, I'm feeding a lot of people, and am again tending a large garden (along with my husband), one that includes many storage crops and protected winter crops as well. In addition, we have a market garden from which we sell produce. But our home garden only requires about half a day's work each week, if properly managed on a regular basis. And because of the season extension techniques we use, there is less of the food-canning frenzy that used to fill my autumn days (for more on this subject, see pages 258).

As this history illustrates, there are a number of ways to have a vegetable garden, and certain questions to ask yourself in order to plan yours. How many will you be feeding (account for company, too, if you do a lot of entertaining)? Will you be canning, freezing, or drying a lot of your harvest, and if so how much? Do you have a place for winter storage where the vegetables will stay cool but not freeze? How much space do you have for a garden—and that means sunny, well-drained space close enough to the house to be tended and watered. Realistically, how much time will you have to care for it? Will it be a food garden only, or one that combines food and flowers?

Allotting the right amount of space for each crop can be a little tricky. I tend to be mistrustful of formulas for specific crops that predict your yield "per 100 feet of row" or some such figure. This varies according to soil, climate, and care from one garden to the next (or one year to the next), and different vegetable varieties produce different yields as well. Even the size at which you're picking a crop may vary. Planting styles these days are also less uniform than they used to be. We don't always plant in rows, and plant spacing varies depending on whether you're using an intensive method. I have tried to give a few guidelines in the individual vegetable sections, but you'll want to experiment to some degree, to see what works best for you. When in doubt, plant less, not more.

These days more people seem aware of different possibilities for laying out vegetable gardens. Twenty-five years ago garden geography was pretty standard: a large rectangular plot tilled up each spring and planted in parallel rows. Gardeners are becoming more resourceful about using small spaces for vegetable growing or perhaps having several different gardens: a salad-and-herb garden near the house, and a large garden for big crops at some distance. Or a vegetable garden with flowers in it, either tucked in as ornaments or planted in rows to be cut for bouquets. Or even a vegetable garden grown entirely in containers, either for ease of cultivation or for lack of tillable ground.

Choosing the Site

D ECIDING WHERE TO PUT THE GARDEN is a matter of juggling several different needs, some of them yours and some the garden's. A committee composed of your vegetables would unanimously select the sunniest spot on your property, a place where water never collects in puddles after a rain but always drains away nicely, where the ground slopes slightly toward the south. The soil there would be neither porous sand nor heavy clay, neither full of stones nor tightly compacted—and of course, it would be fertile.

Rarely is a garden site perfect, but almost every site problem can be corrected. Trees can often be cut down to let in more light. Tree roots below the surface are a big problem, but growing vegetables in high raised beds can make even a root-ridden site a possibility, as long as sun shines in under the branches. Poor drainage can be corrected by raised beds (Figure 41) or drainage systems (page 28). Poor soil can always be improved with compost, and slopes can be terraced.

What if the perfect site for the vegetable garden is the front lawn? This could work! If the garden would truly detract from the formal look you want for your home, it can be hidden by an attractive hedge or rose-covered fence. Or conversely, you can turn the lawn into a garden jewel box that you'll display with pride. You might begin by planting it in tidy rows or blocks with ornamental paths of brick or flagstone, and by edging beds of edibles with flowering annuals. Even without such decoration, vegetables can look beautiful combined if they are staked as needed and weeded regularly. Look for colorful varieties such as the multicolored chards, crimson-leaved beets, and bronze fennel. The usual repertoire even can look glamorous. I consider a healthy stand of corn, backlit by the late-day sun, as handsome as any other "ornamental grass," and a row of well-grown,

mature red cabbages with their beautiful blue leaves as gorgeous as full-blown roses.

Styles of Vegetable Gardening

AFTER YOU DECIDE WHERE TO PUT the garden, figure out what kind of layout it will have. Traditional single rows, wide rows, or blocks? Raised beds or flat ones? Paths in the garden or just wide spacing between rows? Mulch or no mulch? The answers depend partly on your own climate, soil conditions, and other site considerations, but they are also very subjective. My advice is to try gardening in different ways from year to year or even in one part of the garden at a time, and find the style that suits you.

Here are the results of my own experience:

Rows. I often plant vegetables quite close together within a 30- to 40-inch-wide bed, either in blocks, broad rows, narrowly spaced single rows, or on a grid (see Figure 40). I find that if I get larger yields in a smaller space, I'll have more left over for paths, experimental plots, rows of cut flowers, a nursery bed for perennials, or whatever extra projects find a home in the prime real estate of the vegetable garden. This method, as opposed to widely spaced single rows that you can walk between, is called intensive gardening. To make it work the beds must have deeply loosened soil, well enriched with compost and other organic matter, and never be trodden upon.

I don't plant all my crops intensively, however. I find that certain plants such as tomatoes, for example, no matter how clever and industrious you are about staking or trellising them, don't do well if crowded together. They need sun all around them. Their vines are also very rampant and are never far from total chaos. Crowding them creates a jungle. Vining squash or sweet potato vines, which ramble over the ground, would make a mockery of tidy little beds.

It's also easier to mulch a garden that is planted in more widely spaced rows. The theory behind intensive planting holds that the lush growth of the plants will form a "natural mulch" that will shade the ground, force out weeds, and conserve moisture. But this does not always happen, especially with skinny plants like onions, and plants whose foliage is never very lush like carrots and onions.

Raised beds. At times I have used raised beds in my gardens. They take a lot of work to build, but they save time in subsequent

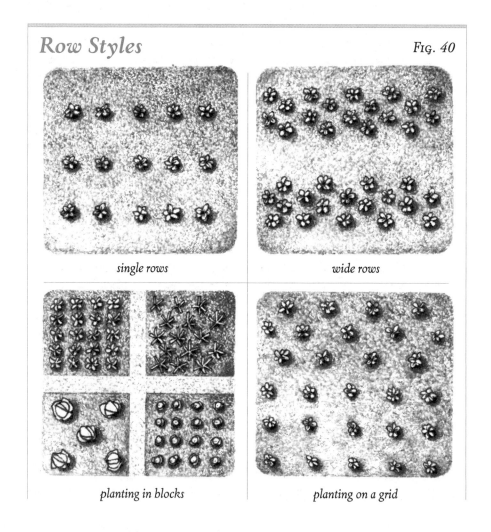

Row Styles

FIG. 40

single rows

wide rows

planting in blocks

planting on a grid

Using Raised Beds

Fig. *41*

Build bottomless boxes out of pressure-treated 2-by-6 lumber.
Set them on the ground, with straight paths between them at least 2 feet wide.

Dig all the topsoil out of the paths and put it into the boxes.

Fill the paths with gravel and/or shredded bark to the original soil level.
Lighten and enrich the soil in the boxes as needed, and plant your crops.

years because these tidy beds are easy to tend. You can sit in the paths between them and don't have to lean over very far to weed. I make them small enough (not more than 4 feet wide) so that I can reach into the middle from either side and never have to step on the soil inside them—helpful in keeping that ideal loose and fluffy texture. The soil also warms up faster in these beds, giving my spring crops an earlier start. Simply because I have *created* these garden structures with the sweat of my brow, I find I'm always trying to make the most efficient use of them and so I plant them rather intensively.

I've learned the hard way not to let raised beds get out of hand. Crops thrive in these little plots of warm, luxurious soil, and unless I'm careful about how many plants I put into them, my tidy arrangement can become an unruly mess. I make them as simply as possible (Figure 41) out of lumber (stone or brick can also be used), digging out the topsoil between them, putting it into the beds, and then filling these corridors with the most inert substance I can find. I have tried builder's sand and gravel, but found that these are exhausting to move and that weeds will eventually grow in them, especially after several years of my spilling the soil out of the beds and onto the paths while I work them. Some weeds, such as horsetails, will grow in anything; my own self-sowing chives are another culprit. A thick bark mulch is a better material for paths. It can be easily removed and tossed on the compost pile if it becomes full of soil, or more bark can be added on top of it. A layer of gravel covered with a thick layer of bark mulch is a good compromise.

For a large garden with a number of space-consuming crops such as corn, squash, potatoes, and beans, a raised-bed system is just too ambitious. In this case a good solution is to make half the garden raised beds and half of it flat. You may find that if you live in a very warm climate, raised beds will not work for you at all. Even where I live I have found that they dry out much faster than flat ones, and with some crops I have to be extra careful about keeping the beds moist. Since they are relatively small plots, this is not difficult, but if you find yourself engaged in a constant struggle to keep your garden soil moist and cool, raised beds may not be for you. You might even consider planting in rows that are actually shallow trenches, which will collect more rainwater and partly shade the plants' roots (Figure 42).

Another good arrangement (and one I presently use) is to make beds that are slightly mounded, but not edged with any hard material. You might shovel a bit of the topsoil in the garden's paths into these beds, but most of their mounded structure results simply from the fact that you do not walk in the beds but you do walk in the paths. The beds will also grow higher over the years as you add compost and other amendments, or if you use organic mulching materials that eventually are dug into the soil.

Paths. I consider garden paths very important. I like to have a lot of them, and I make the main ones, the "avenues," at least 3 feet wide so I can wheel a wheelbarrow through them, set a weed bucket down anywhere on them, and sit in them while I work. Smaller paths between individual beds—the "side streets"—can be as narrow as 12 inches. In an elegant ornamental *potager*, these might be permanently laid in brick or stone throughout the garden, in a

Raised Rows

Sunken Rows FIG. 42

basketweave or herringbone pattern. But most of us settle for simpler solutions that are easier to install and easier to maintain. (Remember, grass and weeds can grow between all those cute little bricks.) Grass strips that can be mowed like a lawn are one solution, but the grass tends to encroach on the beds. Gravel, too, is difficult to keep separate from beds that are not edged with wood or stone. I usually settle for plain old soil, either mulched with bark or straw, or left bare and weeded with a scuffle hoe or wheel hoe (see page 100).

Mulch. I have had good success with mulch in the vegetable garden. It does not totally deter weeds, but depending on what kind of mulch you use, it can cut weeding time down by as much as 75 percent. You'll need to do much less watering, too. But mulch is not for everyone. Some people have more problems with garden pests such as slugs when they use mulch. In some gardens it provides nesting sites for meadow voles, which can be highly destructive.

My favorite mulch material used to be salt hay, a type of hay that grows wild by the seashore and contains no seeds that can germinate in garden soil. But it is now a protected resource, and largely unavailable. Straw is a pretty good substitute. Regular hay is risky because of the amount of weed seeds it can contain. I've also used shredded bark.

Black polyethylene plastic mulch has many devotees. Gardeners carpet their vegetable beds with it, then cut slits or × s in the sheets for the transplanted seedlings, and bury the plastic's outer edges in the soil. It seems to absorb the sun's heat to warm up the ground, then helps keep it moist and weed-free. My chief objection to plastic is the way it looks—I prefer a more natural style in the garden. But I have used black plastic occasionally. It is almost indispensable for growing certain heat-loving crops such as sweet potatoes and melons in cold climates. There are even specialized mulch plastics available—a red one that inspires tomatoes to produce greater yields, and a brown IRT (infrared transmitting) plastic that lets in a wider spectrum of the sun's rays, without fostering weed growth.

Remember that any mulch keeps garden soil cool in spring. You want it there in hot weather, but not in early spring when you're eager to have the soil warm up. I apply straw mulch around transplants if the soil is sufficiently warm, and around direct-sown plants when they're about 6 inches tall. I also spread straw very thinly over newly sown seeds such as carrots, which need very steady moisture for germination.

Planning the Vegetable Garden

I THINK IT'S A GOOD IDEA TO DRAW A sketch of your garden, even before you order your seeds. You may end up deviating from that neat plan for one reason or another, but the garden will be a more successful one if it has been well coordinated at the beginning. I love drawing my garden plan, especially if it's 10 degrees outside with a foot of snow on the ground. The plan makes spring seem like a distinct possibility. And I find I buy seeds more judiciously if I have the dimensions of the garden foremost in my mind. Instead of buying everything in the catalogs that catches my eye, I consider more realistically how many crops I'll actually have space to grow.

There are a lot of factors to consider in planning a vegetable garden, even after you've decided how large a garden you want, what you want to grow in it, and how much of each crop you want to produce. When you draw your plan you'll need to know how to space the plants, where to place crops so they can be grown

Building a Garden Fence and Gate   FIG. 43

1. For the fence, use cedar, locust, or wood treated with a preservative. Posts should be 8 feet long (or 10 feet to keep out deer) and sunk at least 2 feet into the ground. Sink corner posts in concrete and/or brace as shown. Use heavy-gauge wire mesh and bury the bottom at least 6 inches deep to deter animals from digging under.

3. For the outer frame, sink 4-by-4 posts 2 feet into the ground, anchoring them in concrete and checking with a level to make sure they're upright. Nail on temporary braces as shown. At the same time, sink a pressure-treated 2-by-4 in concrete for the doorsill, making it flush with the surface of the ground and using a level to make sure it is perfectly horizontal.

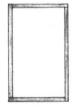 

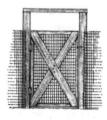

2. To build the gate, make an inner frame of 2-by-4s nailed together. Nail boards across it diagonally to keep it square.

4. When the concrete is thoroughly dry, remove the bracing lumber and attach the inner frame to the outer frame with hinges. Use a heavy metal hook and eye as a latch, and stretch a section of mesh across the gate, stapling it in place.

conveniently and with the proper degree of light, how to interplant one crop with another, how to plant crops in succession to ensure the maximum harvest, and how to rotate groups of vegetables year by year to ward off disease. I will explain, one by one, how these decisions are made. The list may seem a little daunting at first, but none of these principles will be difficult to follow if you plant only as much garden as you have the time, space, and experience to handle. After a while much of the planning will start to seem automatic. The garden may sometimes resemble a jigsaw puzzle that will never quite fall into place, and sometimes it will just not be possible to reconcile all the requirements with one another—to plan for a succession of crops but still practice crop rotation, for example. Usually your plan will result from a series of compromises.

There are an infinite number of vegetable-garden schemes that could be devised according to your own preferences and climate, and it seems very arbitrary to present only two suggested plans. But since this is the easiest way to illustrate the principles involved, try to see these two plans as examples of what one might do, not as strict models to follow.

The small garden in Figure 44 is the kind you might plan if you have a small yard or little time for gardening, and not many people to feed (though it will produce more than you might expect). It is also a good garden to begin with if you're not very experienced. It is surrounded by a fence to keep out critters, and is divided into small beds, some of which run the length of the fence and contain crops that the fence will support. The beds can be raised or flat, according to your preference.

The second garden (Figure 45) is laid out the same way, but some of the beds are larger. Again, the beds might be raised, flat, or a combination of the two. The area at the eastern end of the garden is for perennial crops. Both gardens are designed to reduce the possibility of taller crops shading shorter ones. The larger garden produces many more vegetables and more varieties; consequently, it requires more care.

What if you would like to start small but graduate to larger gardens as you gain experience? Does this mean that you have to fence and refence each year? Not necessarily. You might fence a big area but leave it untilled, or till it and plant a cover crop (page 13) or plant it with annual flowers until you're ready to fill it with more vegetables. Or you might use a simple, inexpensive fence on metal posts that is easy to reconfigure later on.

For both of these gardens you would probably want to make a number of changes based on your own needs. For example, the early peas in the large garden will be fine for a few tasty early-summer meals, but if you'd like a freezer full of them you would have to devote a larger area to them, perhaps eliminating the limas. You might have no interest in growing escarole but want to include something I have not, such as cauliflower. You might have a particular interest, such as Asian vegetables. You might need additional space for flowers (though with this plan you can still tuck them in the corners of the beds or fill in a vacant row with them here and there). You might want to change the layout as well, allowing for more large blocks of space with traditional rows in them, especially if you're growing more large-space crops such as shell beans, winter squash, sweet potatoes, or corn.

Plan for a Small Vegetable Garden (20' by 24')

FIG. 44

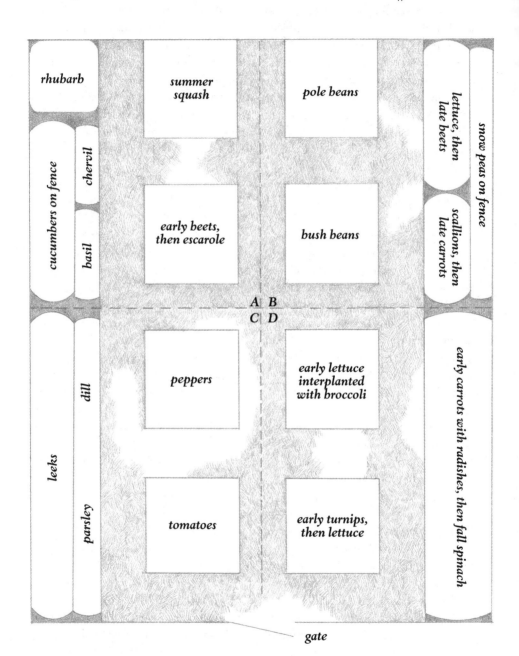

rhubarb

summer squash

pole beans

lettuce, then late beets

snow peas on fence

cucumbers on fence

chervil

basil

early beets, then escarole

bush beans

scallions, then late carrots

A B
C D

dill

peppers

early lettuce interplanted with broccoli

early carrots with radishes, then fall spinach

leeks

parsley

tomatoes

early turnips, then lettuce

gate

In the section on individual vegetables I suggest the proper spacing for each one. Sometimes I give one figure for traditional-row planting and one for wide-row or block-style planting. But these are not hard-and-fast rules. Close planting may produce smaller plants but more of them, so that in many cases the yield will be greater per square foot.

Succession Planting

Planting crops in succession is a good way to make the most of your precious garden space. Sometimes it means planting one or more repetitions of the same crop. In the small plan there is a spring carrot crop (planted together with radishes, which shade the carrot seedlings), then a late-summer carrot crop planted in another spot to mature in fall, for late-fall and winter harvest. There are also early and late beet and lettuce crops in different locations. The longer the growing season in your area, the more successions of the same crop you can have.

Planning successions also means having a late crop of one vegetable follow an early crop of another. Cool-weather spring crops such as peas, lettuce, or baby turnips can then be succeeded by ones that do well late in the season such as escarole, cabbage, or broccoli. Many gardeners don't realize how many vegetables can be planted in mid to late summer to mature in time for a fall or winter harvest: broccoli, Chinese cabbage, kale, kohlrabi, carrots, radishes, turnips, spinach, Swiss chard, and numerous salad greens, just to name some. Occasionally you can find started plants in garden centers in summer, but for good variety you usually have to grow them from seed starting in June or July. In warm climates you can sow seeds of certain crops just before frost so they'll be ready to sprout when the ground thaws, even if it's too wet to be worked. Lettuce, radishes, beets, onions, spinach, peas, and carrots are some you might try this way.

In the large garden plan there are many such successions, and you will no doubt find good combinations of your own. You'll notice that some crops stay in the same place all season, such as eggplant and peppers. But even these crops that take a long time to mature can be part of successions in a climate with a more extended growing season. Pay attention to the needs of each vegetable as outlined in the section on each, and allow plenty of time for the crop to mature before frost if it is not frost hardy, or before hot weather if it is not heat tolerant. For example, if you live in a very warm climate, you can grow your cool-weather crops such as lettuce, peas, radishes, spinach, Brussels sprouts, cabbage, cauliflower, kale, and Swiss chard right through the winter, then follow them with warm-weather crops like okra, sweet potatoes, eggplant, and tomatoes.

Interplanting

Interplanting means growing two crops in the same spot. You can do this with alternating rows, or in a grid pattern (Figure 46). Usually a small, fast-maturing crop is interplanted with a large, slow-growing one that will take a while to use

Plan for a Large Vegetable Garden (40' by 60')

FIG. 45

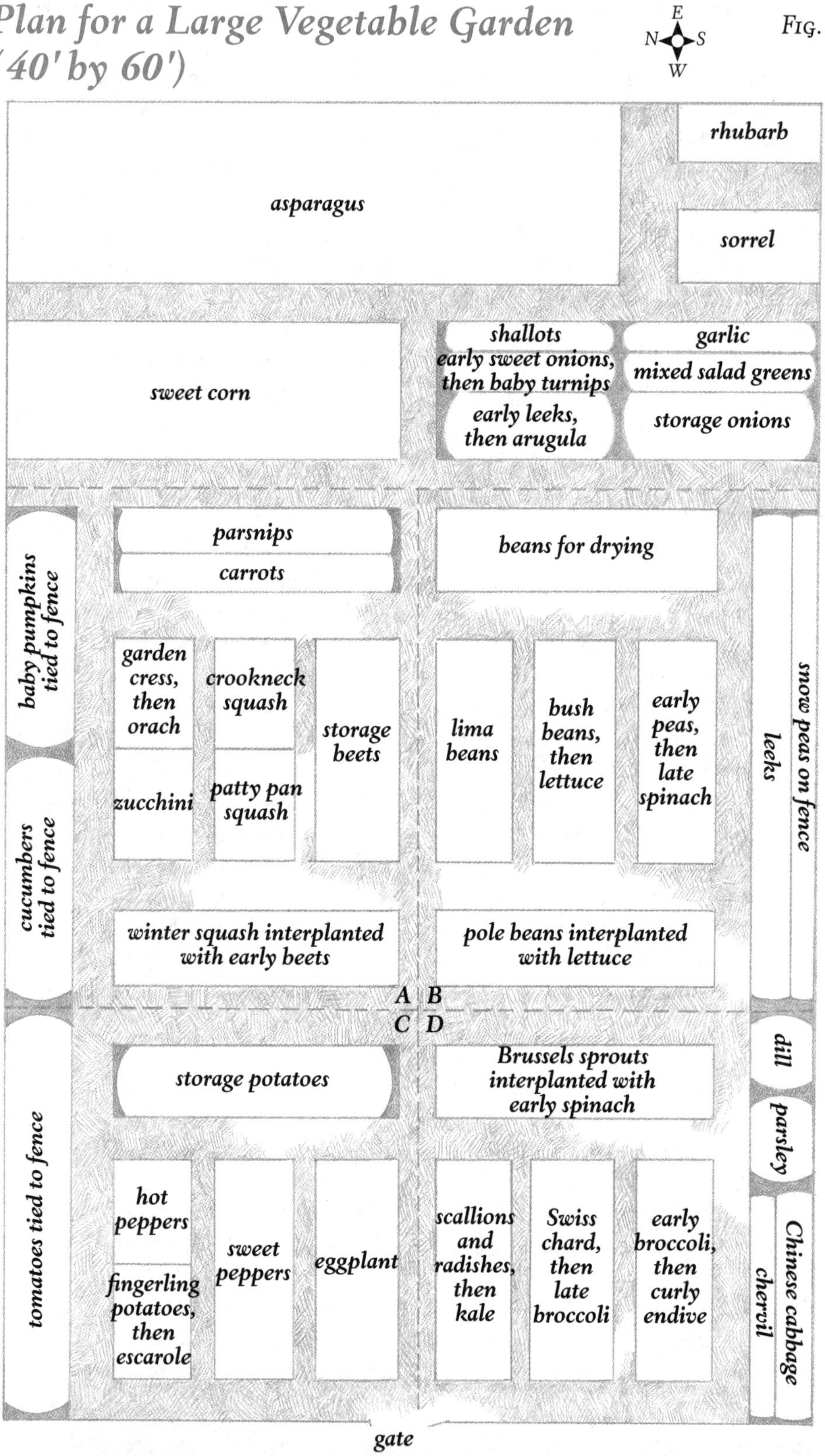

rhubarb

asparagus

sorrel

sweet corn

shallots

early sweet onions, then baby turnips

early leeks, then arugula

garlic

mixed salad greens

storage onions

baby pumpkins tied to fence

parsnips

carrots

beans for drying

garden cress, then orach

crookneck squash

storage beets

lima beans

bush beans, then lettuce

early peas, then late spinach

snow peas on fence

zucchini

patty pan squash

cucumbers tied to fence

winter squash interplanted with early beets

pole beans interplanted with lettuce

leeks

A B
C D

tomatoes tied to fence

storage potatoes

Brussels sprouts interplanted with early spinach

dill

parsley

hot peppers

fingerling potatoes, then escarole

sweet peppers

eggplant

scallions and radishes, then kale

Swiss chard, then late broccoli

early broccoli, then curly endive

Chinese cabbage

chervil

gate

up the space allotted for it in the garden. So, for example, the large winter squash patch in the big garden has early beets in it that are pulled long before the squash vines are long and the leaves large. The Brussels sprouts are interplanted with early spinach that must be harvested before the heat of summer. The broccoli in the small garden has a few heads of lettuce growing among it. You'll find that there are several crops—lettuce, scallions, radishes, the cresses, and other small greens, for example—that can be stuck in odd corners of the garden so conveniently that you'll always have them somewhere, ready for picking. You may not even need to include them in your original plan. Another trick is to interplant some-

thing that dislikes the hot summer sun, like lettuce or arugula, with a tall vegetable like pole beans. The greens will tolerate the partial shade cast by the beans, and their tendency to bolt may be lessened.

Crop Rotation

Crop rotation is the practice of changing the location of the crops from one year to the next. There are several reasons to do this. One is that the diseases and insect larvae that affect a particular crop during the summer and then lie in wait for it in the soil over the winter will not find that crop in spring and peter out. This practice will not, by itself, totally prevent diseases or pests in your garden, but it will help, and the longer you can wait before repeating a crop, the better. Another reason is that crops vary in their nutritional needs, and therefore deplete the soil in different ways. If you grow one crop in the same place each year, the soil may become deficient in certain elements. While these nutritional deficiencies could be corrected by fertilizing, rotating is just that much easier on your soil, and you will find that you need to fertilize less.

Not all of the effects that a crop has on the soil are negative ones. Some are particularly good at smothering out or shading out weeds, for example. Also, the roots of various crops behave in different ways, occupying different levels in the soil, extracting different minerals from deep in the soil, breaking up the soil in different ways, and altering its chemistry and types of microbial activity. Legume crops such as peas and beans are particularly beneficial because of

Interplanted Crops Fig. 46

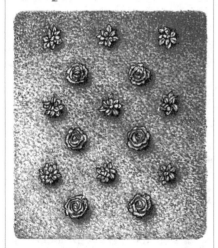

Planting a small-head variety of lettuce between Brussels sprout plants is a good way to increase your garden space. By the time the Brussels sprout plants are full grown, the lettuce will have been harvested.

the nitrogen-fixing nodules that form on the roots when the crops are grown well. Rotating crops through the garden spreads all these benefits around.

Although crop rotation is practiced a great deal in commercial agriculture, home gardeners tend to be careless about it because it can be confusing. Following a whole field of beets with a whole field of corn is not hard to keep track of. But what if you're growing 30 little crops in one garden? It requires pretty careful record-keeping as well as skillful jigsaw puzzle-making.

Unfortunately, the problems that afflict one vegetable often afflict all the members of that vegetable's family, as mentioned above. They share some diseases and pests with other families, but not as many as they share with each other. So to properly rotate your tomatoes, you have to avoid not only a spot where tomatoes have grown recently but also peppers, eggplant, and potatoes. This also makes the possibilities for succession planting more limited. For example, you might be tempted to follow an early bean crop with broccoli, only to find from your records that broccoli grew on that spot the past year. This is the point at which most people give up.

It is still worth trying, though, and there are ways to make it work. I've worked out a four-quadrant method, by which I can rotate my garden by plant groups. In the two plans shown on pages 244 and 246, I have divided most of each garden into four quadrants: A, B, C, and D. In each one I have segregated the vegetables from the four large vegetable families that benefit the most from rotation. Thus the A section contains the cucurbits (cucumbers, squash), B contains the legumes (peas, beans), C contains the cabbage family (Brussels sprouts, broccoli, rutabaga, etc.), and D contains tomatoes and their relatives. Each family is rotated clockwise as a group each year, so that four years will elapse before any family returns to the same spot.

There are other vegetable crops that can benefit from crop rotation but do not belong to these families—lettuce, carrots, and onions, for example. To make the scheme perfect you'd have to create more sections, or attach each of these to one of the other quadrants. But I find it easier to just make these free-floating crops, inserting them where they fit in well, trying not to repeat them in the same spot two years in a row. Lettuce and onions, for example, are so handy to stick in here and there.

You also may find that you want to grow much more from one family than another, and that four more-or-less-equal quadrants will not work unless you leave extra space in each one, as I have done. This space can be either filled up with the main family, used for the free-floating crops, or planted in annual herbs and flowers. The space at the upper right is also useful for any overflow.

Companion Planting

MUCH HAS BEEN SAID ABOUT THE powers of one plant to repel the pests that attack another, and I often see long lists of companion plants that if planted side by side will help each other out. Radishes are said to repel the squash-vine borer. Marigolds are supposed to repel nematodes, and there have been scientific studies that seem to bear this out. I'm sure there are countless beneficial plant associations in nature, and if you've found some combinations that work for you, by all means use them. I find that with so many other considerations to think about in planning the garden, this one usually comes last—though it certainly can't hurt to scatter plenty of onions and marigolds throughout the garden just in case.

Vegetable Varieties

C HOOSING VEGETABLE VARIETIES FROM catalogs can be bewildering. There are so many of them, full of glowing descriptions of every plant. It takes a while to realize that "vigorous" sometimes means "rampant" and that "sweet" might mean "not quite as bitter as the other varieties." Shop around until you find a few reputable companies that will reward your loyalty with good seeds and good service.

I like to have a number of different catalogs on hand, to get a good composite picture of what is available. In any category there are always some tried-and-true favorites that everybody sells. If you stick to those instead of experimenting with the latest rage you can't go too far wrong. But some new varieties are genuine improvements over the old ones; perhaps they bear more abundantly or quickly, withstand cold or heat better, taste better, store better, look prettier, bear smaller or larger fruits, grow on a more compact plant, or resist certain diseases. Bear in mind that these traits are often geared to specific gardening needs—cold climates, for example, or lack of space.

Sometimes you'll see a vegetable variety labeled AAS. This means it is an All-America Selection, having been selected by a large group of experts who have grown it in many trial plots across the country, and that it has beaten out all the rest in its field. But it still may not be the one for you, since those bred for limited parts of the country rarely win the award. Sometimes you can find a seed company that specializes in growing seeds for your own particular region, and will therefore give you the most trouble-free plants and abundant harvests. But of course the final test is how they taste to you when they finally make it to the table. You might not like supersweet corn; or you might find that the extra-early pea (like many other extra-early crops) is not as flavorful as the one for which you have to wait another two weeks. Or that a particular bush squash is not as tasty as a less convenient vining one.

You can of course buy seeds in a nursery or a hardware store. But you will not have as many varieties to choose from as you would by mail. This also applies to flats of plants started in the garden center. Most of us end up buying started plants at some point in our lives. Perhaps we haven't had time to start seeds indoors early, or there was no bright, warm spot in which to do it. But if you cannot experiment with interesting varieties, you do miss some of the fun of gardening. Most of the information about specific varieties can be found in the individual vegetable sections of this chapter. Refer also to the list of heirloom varieties on page 250, and the list of varieties for small spaces on page 256.

(continued on page 253)

HEIRLOOM VEGETABLE VARIETIES
YOU CAN GROW

MANY OF THE VEGETABLES OUR ancestors grew have been abandoned in favor of modern hybrids, which are in one way or another "improvements" over the old standbys. In some cases these improvements reflect home gardeners' needs—earlier production, disease resistance, a more compact habit, or some such trait. In other cases the advances have been made to satisfy the needs of commercial producers who want crops of predictable, uniform quality that will mature all at once (for ease of mechanical harvest) and have thick skins or sturdy leaves for easy shipping and long storage.

Many of the old favorites, on the other hand, are better suited to home production, because of the very fact that they do produce over a longer period of time. They are often more flavorful and nutritious as well, since these traits have not been sacrificed in the breeding of a more profitable, industrial-style crop.

The term "heirloom vegetable" is a broad one. Some heirlooms are original species no different from those that might be found growing in the wild in the places where they are native or naturalized. More often, they are old garden crops that have been selected over the years for desirable traits, by gardeners who have saved their seeds from the specimens that performed best in their gardens that year. These open-pollinated, nonhybrid varieties have often been passed down

through the generations by family farmers or from friend to friend. Still others are old-time hybrids that do not breed true to seed and must be purchased, but which possess valuable traits and have remained old favorites.

The richness inherent in the vast number of plant varieties that have been grown over the years—often in adaptation to local soils and climates—cannot be overemphasized. Their value lies not only in each variety's uniqueness and worth, but also in the diversity they present as a whole, in contrast to the relatively narrow range of commercial crops being grown in the world today. This enormous gene pool, which was necessary to produce today's crops and will be necessary to produce tomorrow's, is unfortunately not something we can take for granted. Planting heirloom seeds, saving them from your own crop, and sharing them with others enables you to participate in a chain that has been going on for millennia. In many cases you'll even be doing your part to preserve some valuable resources from extinction. You will also be putting some delicious food on your table.

Precisely because the array of heirloom crops is so vast, it's difficult to narrow down one's choices. Fortunately, most seed companies that sell to home gardeners now include a decent number of heirlooms—some obscure, some well known. I have listed a number of them here, but it is only a tasting menu. I urge you to wander through the encyclopedic array offered by the Seed Savers Exchange in Decorah, Iowa (see page 773), and to participate in the delightful game of seed-swapping with gardeners both near and far. William Woys Weaver's excellent book *Heirloom Vegetable Gardening* (see page 780) is a good introduction to the subject of old varieties.

Arugula. Try the Italian fine-leaved *Rucola selvatica*, sometimes sold as the variety 'Sylvetta.' The classic arugula is itself an heirloom vegetable; this is an entirely different species, *Diplotaxis erucoides*.

Beans. *Pole Beans:* 'Kentucky Wonder' and 'Blue Lake,' for great flavor. 'Scarlet Runner,' a colonial variety with beautiful red flowers. 'Lazy Wife,' a stringless bean. 'Fin de Bagnol,' an old French "filet" type. *Limas:* 'White Dutch Runner' ('Oregon Lima'), for the Pacific northwest. 'Hopi' ('Bandy') lima, a Native American strain for southern areas. 'Henderson's Bush Lima,' an old bush lima. 'King of the Garden,' an old pole lima. *Shell Beans:* 'Jacob's Cattle,' white with maroon blotches, native to the American southwest. 'Speckled Cranberry' ('Wren's Egg'), with red-speckled pods, was imported from England in 1825 and is good fresh-shelled or dried. 'Black Turtle,' an old-fashioned soup bean. 'Swedish Brown,' a good bean for baking, early 1800s.

Beets. 'Detroit Dark Red,' the old standby, dates from 1892. 'Winter Keeper,' long keeping and vigorous. 'Bull's Blood' is great for roots and greens. 'Golden' dates from the early 1900s. 'Chiogga,' the beet with bull's-eye stripes, is an old Italian variety.

Broccoli. 'Calabrese' ('Italian Sprouting') and 'De Cicco' are valuable because of their continuing sideshoot production. 'Romanesco,' an old Italian variety with spectacular yellow conical heads, flowers in a spiral pattern (it's sometimes considered a cauliflower).

Brussels sprouts. 'Catskill' ('Long Island Improved'), an old semidwarf. 'Early Dwarf Danish,' early, with short plants.

Cabbage. 'Early Jersey Wakefield,' large, matures early (dates from 1840). 'Late Flat Dutch,' dependable, with good flavor and slightly flattened heads (1860). 'Danish Ballhead,' good for storage (1887). 'All Seasons' ('Wisconsin'), yellows resistant.

Carrot. 'Danvers Half-Long' (1871). 'Early Scarlet Horn,' an old "baby" carrot. 'Nantes' (1870). 'Oxheart,' short and fat (1884).

Cauliflower. 'Early Snowball,' an early producer (1888). 'Autumn Giant,' very large (1885).

Celery. 'Giant Pascal,' the old favorite. 'Golden Self-Blanching,' does not need to be blanched.

Corn. *Sweet Corn:* 'Country Gentleman' ('Shoe Peg'), small, sweet white kernels (1890). 'Golden Bantam,' small ears (1853). 'Black Mexican,' a blue-black corn (1863). 'Stowell's Evergreen,' a fine old late white corn with a long harvest (1840). *Corn for Meal:* 'Taos Pueblo White Flour,' a pre-Columbian corn that makes very fine white flour. 'Nothstine Dent,' an early, tasty cornmeal corn. 'Mandan Bride' and other Mandan strains are multicolored Indian corn; also attractive as an ornamental corn.

Cucumber. 'Long Green Improved,' a slicing cucumber (1870). 'Straight Eight' and 'Marketmore 76,' both old slicing favorites. 'Boston Pickling,' an old pickling cucumber (late 1800s). 'Lemon,' with its crisp, lemon-shaped fruits, needs no peeling.

Eggplant. 'Black Beauty,' the old favorite for warm climates. 'Early Long Purple,' better for cooler areas (1880s). 'Louisiana Long Green' has long, mild-tasting fruits. Those of 'Pingtung Long' are a beautiful glowing lavender-purple.

Garlic. 'German Extra Hardy' is an excellent, vigorous hardneck type.

Kale. 'Green Scotch Curled,' very hardy (1865). For sheer gorgeousness grow the old 'Red Russian' and the deep green-black Tuscan 'Lacinato.'

Leek. 'Giant Musselburgh,' grows very large (1850–70). 'Prizetaker' is a fine old English leek; 'Blue Solaise' is an old-time French one.

Lettuce. 'Black-Seeded Simpson,' a fast crop (late 1880s). 'Parris Island White,' an old favorite cos. 'Mescher,' a fine old butterhead. 'Prizehead,' leaves tipped with red (1880). 'Four Seasons' ('Merveille des Quatre Saisons'), both heat- and cold-tolerant (1880). 'Iceberg,' the standard crisphead (1894). 'Deer Tongue,' an old mild Bibb type. 'Forellenschuss,' a speckled Austrian variety (also known as 'Freckles' and 'Trout Back'). 'Lolla Rossa,' an Italian red-tipped beauty.

Okra. 'Clemson Spineless.'

Onion. 'Red Wethersfield' and 'Yellow Globe Danvers' (1850) are old reliables. 'Ailsa Craig,' a big, early Spanish type, huge and an excellent keeper. 'Borretana,' a classic Italian *cipollini* type.

Parsnip. 'Hollow Crown' (1850). 'Guernsey.'

Pea. 'Alaska,' cold tolerant. 'Thomas Laxton,' 3-foot vines (1897). 'Alderman' ('Tall Telephone'), large peas, tall vines (1861). 'Little Marvel,' early and a heavy bearer (1908).

Pepper. 'Bullnose,' the oldest green bell pepper (1759). The flavorful Italian 'Corno di Toro' is curled like a bull's horn and just barely hot. Old hot varieties include 'Long Red Cayenne' (1828), 'Anaheim,' and 'Tabasco.'

Potato. Heirlooms include 'Green Mountain,' 'Irish Cobbler,' the yellow-fleshed 'Fingerling' and 'Russian Yellow Banana.'

Pumpkin. 'New England Pie' ('Small Sugar'; from 1863). 'Connecticut Field' (1700s). 'Rouge Vif d'Etampes.'

Radish. 'Round Black Spanish' (1824). 'China Rose.' 'French Breakfast' (1885).

Spinach. 'Bloomsdale,' vigorous and slow to bolt.

Squash. *Summer:* 'Yellow Crookneck.' 'White Bush Scallop' ('Patty Pan'). 'Cocozelle,' the original zucchini (1856). The old Italian black zucchinis such as 'Milano Black.' *Winter:* 'Table Queen,' the classic Acorn. 'Delicata,' small and striped. 'True Hubbard,' large and green (1857). 'Turk's Turban,' edible ornamental (1800). 'Long Island Cheese,' a tan-colored baking squash shaped like a cheese wheel. 'Mouscade de Provence' is tan and deeply indented. 'Queensland Blue' and gray-blue 'Jarrahdale' are old-time squash from Down Under.

Swiss chard. The great old standard is 'Fordhook Giant,' but try the highly ornamental 'Ruby Red' (also called 'Rhubarb'), with dark green leaves and red ribs. The super-hardy 'Argentata' is an Italian heirloom.

Tomato. 'Ponderosa,' old, large-fruited variety. 'Yellow Pear,' small, yellow, sweet and pear-shaped (1852). 'Marglobe,' red and juicy (1900). 'Earliana,' an early variety (1900). 'Brandywine,' a much-celebrated delicious Amish variety with pinkish flesh. Orange 'Striped German' is yellow marbled with red. 'Stupice,' an old Czech tomato, ripens early then keeps on going. 'Red Cherry,' an old red cherry tomato (1865). 'Principe Borghese,' an Italian cherry type. 'San Marzano,' the classic old Italian paste tomato. 'Red Currant' and 'Yellow Currant' have tiny fruits.

Turnip. 'Purple Top White Globe,' the old standard, still grown (1890s). 'Golden Ball' (1859).

(continued from page 249)

Getting the Garden Ready

IF I'M STARTING A NEW GARDEN I TRY TO prepare it the year before. In the ideal situation I would till under any sod and weeds, amend the soil, grow a cover crop on it for a season, till it again in fall, then let the plot rest over the winter, giving all the plant matter plenty of time to decompose, the soil amendments time to mellow in, and all the soil microorganisms time to rebuild the soil structure. At the very least, I'd have the soil tilled and amended by the fall before spring planting so that I don't have to do it in spring. It takes a long time for the ground to dry out after the winter snows and spring rains, and by the time it is ready for any serious tilling it would be too late to plant early crops such as peas. If this were the case, I would just start with the summer crops such as tomatoes.

Even with an established garden there's a lot to do in spring, but first you must wait until the ground can be worked. This phrase sometimes puzzles new gardeners. When *can* the soil be worked? In most regions workable soil comes when the ground is not only free of frost but also sufficiently dry to prevent your seeds from rotting. Even more important, the soil's structure can be damaged by working it while it's still mucky and compacted. Digging it while wet will compact it all the more, preventing the free movement of water and air that's necessary for plant growth.

You can tell that soil is too wet if it forms a firm ball when you squeeze it, but frankly the best way to learn what good soil is, is by working some wet soil and seeing what happens to it. Always picture good soil structure in your mind and try to achieve it whenever you can. Good soil is light and fluffy. Thrust your fingers into the soil, pretending they're roots that have to grow through it, and try to make that job as easy for them as possible.

What your soil needs in general and how to provide it is discussed starting on page 5. You may want to begin by having a soil test done for your future vegetable plot (page 10). The test results will come with recommendations about what to add to give your soil the right pH and amount of nutrients for basic vegetable gardening. I always ask for organic recommendations.

One thing that may confuse you is the fact that various vegetables have different requirements with respect to soil texture, soil fertility, and soil pH. How, if you are continually changing the location of the crops in the garden, can you provide

precisely what each one needs? You can't always do this. The best you can do is to establish soil with a good structure by adding plenty of organic matter; keep the soil moderately fertile and well balanced, without an overabundance of any one element; and try to maintain the pH somewhere between 6.0 and 7.0.

It is still helpful to know which little preferences each crop might have, however. This way if your soil has a particular condition—very acid, very sandy, very low in an essential nutritional element—you'll know which crops will need special attention. You can make careful seasonal applications of lime, sulfur, fertilizer, or whatever a particular crop needs for its growth period, but don't add excessive amounts that the next crop growing in that spot might not appreciate. Potatoes, for instance, will be prone to a disease call scab if the bed has been recently limed.

Sometimes you'll be told to top-dress or side-dress a crop if it is a heavy feeder, or if you need to hasten it along in order to bring it to maturity before frost or before hot weather. One method is to lay manure or a balanced fertilizer on top of the soil next to the plant, and allow it to slowly leach down into the soil. A faster-acting method is to top-dress with a liquid fertilizer. Some gardeners make a "manure tea" for this purpose by steeping manure in buckets of water. The same can be done with compost, dried blood, fish emulsion, and other soluble materials. Some crops that feed heavily and profit by this kind of attention are asparagus, cabbage, celery, corn, eggplant, rhubarb, squash, and tomatoes.

In discussing individual vegetables, I have occasionally specified amounts of a given nutrient to add for a crop at a particular stage in its life. But please keep in mind that the usefulness of such advice is limited by the fact that I do not know what your soil is like—what nutrients are already there, whether your soil is a clay that holds nutrients well or a sand that lets them leach away. It's better if you familiarize yourself with the simple basics of plant nutrition, then *watch* how your plants grow, looking for signs of excess or insufficiency until you know what you can safely add, and when.

Planting the Crops

THE BASIC TECHNIQUES OF PLANTING, transplanting, and thinning are discussed in detail beginning on page 32. Specific information about planting individual vegetables is covered later in this chapter. Here I want to give you some advice about planting vegetable gardens in general.

Vegetable crops vary in how and when they are planted. This makes your job easier, because it means that not all the work of planting has to be done at one time. You can plan your labors more easily if you keep the following chronology in mind.

Some vegetable seeds can be sown directly in the ground as early as you can work the soil; these include peas, beets, lettuce, onions, radishes, spinach, and turnips. Others, such as corn, beans, and squash, are sown directly in the garden but not until the danger of frost has passed. In cool climates with shorter growing seasons, many crops such as tomatoes, Brussels sprouts, cauliflower, celery, eggplant, and cabbage are sown indoors and then set out in the garden when there is little or no danger of frost.

With quick-growing crops that are planted in succession, you have a considerable choice of planting times and will probably evolve your own schedule for each one. For example, if you want to harvest a crop toward the end of the season, just find out how long the plant will take to mature and count backward from the ideal harvest time to find the ideal planting time. This may take a little practice at first.

Seed companies tell you how many days each variety takes to grow from sowing to harvest, but these estimates can vary from one seed seller to another and can vary even more from garden to garden. Much depends on where you live, what kind of weather you're having, and whether you have direct-sown your seeds or started them indoors. The numbers are not useless, however, since they do give you a general idea, and also a means of comparing one variety with another. For example, if you live in a cold climate and want to grow hot peppers, choose the ones in the catalog with a short "days to harvest" rating, so they'll color up before frost.

Even after the danger of spring frost has long since passed, you may want to start your late crops in a separate place, either indoors in a sunny spot, in a greenhouse, in a cold frame, or even in a separate nursery-bed corner of your garden. This way they only take up a tiny bit of space while they're small, freeing up the garden for early crops that need it more. Later, when they're ready to be transplanted to a permanent place, there will be gaps waiting where the early crops have been harvested.

(continued on page 258)

VEGETABLES FOR SMALL SPACES

THERE IS AN INCREASING DEMAND for edible crops that do not require a large space for growing. People have smaller properties, smaller families, and more often than not, a smaller amount of time available for gardening. A lot of space can be gained just by using techniques that maximize the amount of space you have—intensive planting, interplanting, succession planting, cut-and-come again harvesting, and season-extension strategies that spread the harvest out over more of the year. Some crops just by their nature are space-savers. Others are big space-consumers for which you must seek out space-saving varieties.

Many vegetable varieties grow on dwarf or compact-shaped plants, which makes them good choices for small-space or even container gardens. In some cases they are bush varieties of vegetables that are more commonly grown on long vines. Some of them produce small or "baby" fruits as well, but in most cases the fruits are average size. For baby vegetables look for appropriate varieties, or just pick regular varieties when they are very young (this technique does not work for vegetables such as winter squash or tomatoes that only taste good when fully ripened).

Beans. Pole beans, though long-vined, can be space-savers since they produce heavy yields over a long period and are grown vertically. The flat-podded heirloom 'Garden of Eden' is a winner because it can be eaten at any stage— young pod, old pod, shell bean, or dried.

Beets. Beets are a good small-space crop in general. 'Little Ball' and 'Pronto' are quick early crops that are harvested while small, then pulled to make room for something else.

Broccoli. Broccoli 'Raab' (also 'Rabb' or 'Di Rapa') grows on small plants and so takes up less space than the heading types; 'Cima di Rapa' is especially compact. For regular broccoli, grow a variety like 'De Cicco' that is compact to begin with and produces small heads followed by a continuous harvest of side shoots.

Cabbage. Look for small-headed varieties such as 'Dynamo,' 'Gonzales,' and 'Arrowhead 11' (green), 'Primero' and 'Red Express' (red), or 'Savoy Express' and 'Kilosa' (savoy types). Of the Chinese cabbages the napa and michihili types are more compact than the open-headed ones. The pac chois are also great space-savers, especially the small-headed 'Mei Qing Choi' and 'Riko.'

Carrots. Carrots are a small-space crop in general. For tiny ones, try the 4-inch 'Kinko' or the little round 'Parmex.'

Cauliflower. 'Snowball.'

Celery and celeriac. Both good for small gardens in general.

Corn. Corn is not a likely candidate for a small garden, but there are miniature corn varieties such as 'Bonus,' and 'Tom Thumb,' a popping corn.

Cucumber. Cukes grown vertically take up little room in the garden. Compact bush varieties include the short-vined 'Bushy' and 'Miniature White.' 'Bush Baby' and 'Bush Pickle' are recommended for containers.

Eggplant. 'White Egg,' 'Modern Midget,' 'New York Improved,' 'Early Black Egg.' For growing in containers try 'Bambino,' which bears clusters of tiny round fruits.

Herbs. Many of the perennial herbs get very large over time. Starting new plants each year, or growing them in containers, is your best bet if space is limited. For annual crops, plant successions of crops like parsley and chervil. Choose small varieties of basil such as the Thai basils or 'Spicy Globe.'

Lettuce. Any lettuce is a space-saver, especially if grown as a cut-and-come-again crop. Avoid varieties with huge open heads; the romaine types are more compact. 'Little Gem' and 'Tom Thumb' are popular petite varieties. 'Tennis Ball' is a compact butterhead.

Onions. Most onions are good small-space crops, especially scallions and the cipollini types. Also grow garlic and shallots.

Parsnip. In general a crop that takes up little space as long as the soil is deep.

Peas. 'Little Marvel' is a good, compact variety. Also try the short-vined 'Knight' and 'Sugar Sprint,' a sugar snap type.

Peppers. Most peppers take up little space and do well in containers, though some, such as 'Tequila Sunrise' and 'Vidi,' are more compact than others. Any of the hot ones are particularly ornamental in pots, and there are a number such as 'Nosegay,' 'Aurora,' and 'Jingle Bells' that seem designed to look like edible bouquets.

Pumpkin. Although pumpkins are generally not suited to small gardens, 'Cheyenne,' and 'Trickster' are among the small-fruited, short-vined varieties.

Radish. All are good for small spaces, especially the small, quick crops. The daikons and large black types occupy more garden space and for a longer stretch of time. The edible-pod type needs vertical space and must be staked or trellised so it doesn't flop onto other plants.

Salad crops. In general, most greens are space-savers. The smallest, such as mâche or the cresses, can be tucked in anywhere a space opens up.

Squash. *Summer:* 'Gentry' is a compact yellow crookneck; also try the Italian 'Milano Black' and 'Lebanese Clairmore,' both zucchini types. *Winter:* 'Gold Nugget,' 'Table King Bush Acorn,' 'Table Ace,' 'Early Butternut,' 'Sweet Dumpling,' and 'Bush Delicata.' 'Small Wonder' is an orange-fleshed, small-fruited spaghetti squash on a semibush plant.

Tomato. 'Patio' is the standard pot tomato. Try 'Tumbler' for hanging baskets. 'Tiny Tim' is a cherry tomato suitable for containers.

(continued from page 255)

Moving seedlings from indoors to the garden can be very hard on them, because plants grown indoors tend to have soft, tender stems and leaves that are easily injured by either extreme cold or hot sun. You'll need to "harden off" your plants before moving them permanently to the garden. This means bringing the seedlings (still in their flats or pots) outside and exposing them gradually to cold, sun, and wind. The best way is to start about two weeks before transplanting time, leaving the plants out for a few hours each day and increasing the time as weather permits. Always bring them back in if frost threatens. By planting time you'll notice that the leaves and stems look tougher, thicker, and better able to withstand the elements on their own.

Season Extension

FEELING THE WAY I DO ABOUT THE importance of fresh, homegrown food, it's not surprising that I'm willing to make an extra effort to have it available all the time. This presents a challenge when you live in the northernmost tier of the United States, where the trees are leafless for seven months of the year, and where April is a winter month.

In our household we tackle this problem head-on. First of all, we've developed systems by which we can grow food crops in our climate year-round. Second of all, we've taken the idea of seasonal food and made it an essential part of our lives. Simply put, there are some foods that grow best and taste best in warm weather, and others that are at their prime when the weather is cool.

I've come to think of the modern supermarket, in which you can buy any food you want on any day of the year, as a false luxury—one that fails to fulfill its promise of true food quality. To me, luxury is being able to eat each fruit or vegetable at its own moment of perfection, and not only for its exquisite flavor, but also for its seasonal associations. The taste of the first peas is all about standing in the garden barefoot and eating along the row, gorging on that fresh taste and tossing the empty pods on the ground. The first corn is about husking it on a stool in the garden, then boiling up a big pot for my friends and eating it at the picnic table, with butter dripping down our chins. In fall, butternut squash is about a soup that simmers on the back of the stove while I work at my desk, drawing me back to the kitchen now and then with its rich scent, to add some garlic or bay. And the winter carrots are like finding gold under a snowbank. As long as the soil is kept soft enough to dig, they are there for the pulling, their sweetness and crispness enhanced by the cold. With the year a succession of moments like these, I've no desire to eat a tomato in January.

In moderate climates a year-round food supply is a simple matter, in cold ones you need a bag of tricks. There are numerous devices on the market such as cloches, hot caps, grow tunnels, or portable cold frames and mini-greenhouses that allow you to get a head start on early crops. The general purpose of all of them is to capture the sun's warmth absorbed by the earth during the day and radiated back by night. Cold frames can also be used to cover mature plants in fall or winter to extend the harvest.

A System of Frames to Protect Your Garden

FIG. 47

You can build a series of simple wooden frames, all the same size, that can serve a variety of purposes in your garden. The ones shown are pieces of 2- by 4-inch pressure-treated lumber nailed together at the corners, all of them 4 feet by 4 feet. Various materials are then stapled or nailed over them.

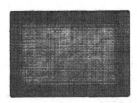

Floating row cover over the frame wards off insect pests and also provides some frost protection.

Black plastic keeps weeds from growing in a bed that is not being used.

Stacked frames can provide several kinds of protection at once; for example, you might cover your summer lettuce crop with chicken wire against the rabbits, and lath for shade. Spacers (empty frames) can be stacked under the protecting frames to make them taller as plants grow. For long beds, set a series of frames next to one another.

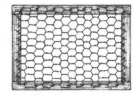

Chicken wire over the frame protects against rabbits, deer, and other predators. Use plastic netting or metal screening to keep birds from eating newly planted seeds. Screening will also keep out mice.

Clear plastic is stretched over a frame as protection against frost.

Lath (narrow strips of wood) protects plants from excessive sun in summer. Shade cloth works well too.

Originally these devices were made of glass; modern versions are usually plastic. They vary in cost, ease of assembly and use, durability, and stability against wind. Generally they work well, though most make weeding and watering difficult if left in place for any length of time. The biggest worry is ventilation. The air can get too hot inside the covering and bake the plants. Those with vents to let heat out and rainwater in give less protection from cold; those that are opened and shut manually take a bit more time and vigilance. Some of the relatively lightweight frames on the market have self-venting mechanisms so they can lift their own lids if necessary. Usually, the heat-holding devices that cover the largest area provide the greatest protection from frost.

I recommend that unless you live in a frost-free climate you keep some form of protection on hand in case an unexpectedly late spring frost is forecast, or an early fall one that might prematurely do in the tomatoes and basil. For small individual plants you can use plastic gallon jugs with the bottoms cut out. Either stick them into the soil around the plant, or partially cut the bottom to make a flap, which you can anchor with a stone. If you leave the jug on during the day, be sure to unscrew the top in case it gets hot. You should also have some big sheets of clear plastic (or even tarps or old blankets) that you can throw over a large number of plants, weighted at the sides with stones. (On a still night no weighting is needed, and in fact, it's usually on still, clear nights that frosts occur). Use these for fall frosts as well.

I have also had good luck with the fabric made of spun-bonded polyester that is sometimes referred to as floating row cover or as Reemay (the name of a prominent brand). This not only affords a few degrees of frost protection for plants of any size, but also keeps out most insect predators during the growing season. This material lets in water and sunlight, and traps a certain amount of heat. Usually a strip of it is placed over an individual row, and held up by wire wickets placed every 4 feet or so. But the stuff is so lightweight that most plants can grow to their full height under it even without the wickets, pushing up the fabric as long as you leave enough slack. The edges of the fabric must be anchored to keep the wind from blowing it off. This can be done by burying it or by weighting it. Stones work, but a long piece of something is easier to remove. Try using 2-by-4s or long pieces of reenforced metal bar (rebar). Sandbags are better yet. You'll have to remove the fabric not only for harvesting crops but also for weeding them, and to allow them to be pollinated by bees.

If you want to go in for more elaborate protection devices, I recommend building a series of wooden frames all the same size that you can use for a variety of purposes (Figure 47). Pick a specific size, say 4 by 4 feet or 4 by 6 feet, and plan your garden so that rows or blocks of plants will fit under the frames. Then just nail, staple, or weight down whatever material you need over the top. This might be floating row cover or fiberglass screening to keep out harmful insects or slugs, chicken wire to keep out rabbits and other nibblers, and plastic netting to keep out birds. Some can be fitted with heavy clear plastic or storm windows for frost protection (but make sure you remove them or vent them when the sun is out, to let out excess heat). The frames might also hold lath, snow fence, or shade cloth to shield plants that bolt in summer heat, or black plastic to keep an unplanted area weed-free. These frames are easy to build and light enough to transport, but heavy enough to stay put. They can be stacked on top of each other to cover tall crops. This system works particularly well if you garden in raised beds. Just make the frames exactly the same size as your beds and keep some extras around for quick use.

The most versatile season-extender is a permanent cold frame (see Figure 7). It's similar to the bottomless boxes described above, but is built so that its transparent top slopes toward the sun, for the best solar effect. The ideal spot to place one is at the foot of a south-facing wall (the side of a building, usually) to take advantage of the extra warmth and wind protection the wall affords. Better yet, build a row of them so as to take advantage of their many uses. They're great for hardening off seedlings in spring; the more cold-tolerant ones such as the brassicas might even be started there, then set out in the garden after the soil can be worked. Tender herbs and flowering perennials can be overwintered there in pots. Mail-order plants can be heeled in there to protect and acclimatize them before planting.

Best of all, a succession of crops can be grown there for cold-weather eating. No matter how severe your climate, you can use a cold frame to stretch the season for salad crops: lettuce, spinach, arugula, beet greens, mâche, Swiss chard, and numerous Asian greens such as tatsoi—just to name a few. Root crops such as carrots, radishes, leeks, and turnips can be grown there for fresh winter harvest. The hardiest of these—such as spinach, mâche, leeks, and carrots—will survive the winter with the most ease, espe-

cially if you bank the frame with bales of straw. When a row has been harvested, try planting a new one. You'll probably be amazed at what you can produce, and will enjoy experimenting with new varieties. The reward will be fresh food that often tastes milder and sweeter than the same crops grown in the more stressful conditions of your hot summer garden. Just make sure you vent your frames by propping them open on days when there is any possibility at all that bright sun might overheat them and "cook" the veggies inside.

Some gardeners feel a sense of exhaustion after spring planting, summer growing, and fall harvesting and want to take the winter off. This is fine too. But bear in mind that a few simple cold frames require very little tending. For one thing, there's very little weed growth in wintertime. For another, winter is a moist time, with the sun at a low angle and not much evaporation of soil moisture, so not much watering is required.

You may even decide to take the idea a step further and erect a simple greenhouse. This seems to be quite a popular idea, judging by the number of companies that advertise them in the back of gardening magazines. But I have a feeling that in many cases they are used more as sunlit potting sheds than as a place to grow cold-season food. For one thing, most of them are too small for this purpose. To be worth the trouble, a greenhouse should really be at least 12 by 20 feet, both in terms of growing space and heat retention—and at this point you start to encounter considerable expense. One alternative is to build a small commercial-type hoophouse, or high tunnel as it is sometimes called, made from aluminum pipes covered with plastic film.

This type gives you plenty of sunlight and wind protection, for relatively little money. You can even set a row or two of cold frames inside it, or beds covered with floating row covers, to double the amount of protection.

But the major drawback of the commercial-style Quonset hut greenhouse is its appearance. Its semicircular shape is also not the best for shedding snow. A better option might be to just frame up a simple peaked-roof building and cover the frame with plastic sheeting. The wood can be painted to blend with the style of your home. If plastic film still seems too ugly, you can use plexiglass panels instead, but these are quite expensive and can also scratch easily if you're not careful with them. Be sure you include doors and windows that can be opened for ventilation, or an automatic venting system. A greenhouse that adjoins your home is the most efficient. On warm sunny days you can open the door that separates them to take advantage of that lovely solar-heated, earth-fragrant air. On cold nights the door can let warm house air into the greenhouse to help protect the crops.

Taking Care of the Garden

MAINTENANCE IS THE HARD PART— not because it requires a great amount of skill, but because it is so easy to neglect. I know I always have more time, energy, and enthusiasm for gardening in spring, after being indoors for much of the winter, than I do in summer when there are so many other fun things to do outside. This is why it's so important to plant an area that you can realistically, not hypothetically, take care of. It also helps to know what the maintenance priorities are.

WEEDING

In maintaining the garden, the most important activity is weeding, especially early in the season. Weeds compete with garden plants for all the necessities: light, nutrients, water, air. It's difficult to have your garden produce much of anything if you don't keep weeds down.

One way to minimize weeds greatly is to mulch, but even a mulch will let some weeds sneak by. Some annual weed seeds already in the soil will poke up through the mulch or fall into it and sprout. Roots of perennial weeds that have not been eradicated from the soil will sprout and push up through it valiantly. But your labors will be greatly lessened if you mulch, especially since some weeds are easier to pull from nice moist, friable mulched soil. It may also be worth taking the trouble to remove all the vegetation from a strip several feet wide around the outside of the garden, and apply a thick layer of mulch there to prevent weeds from sending in runners or dropping their seeds. Keeping your feet out of the beds will also help, since it's harder to pull weeds out of compacted soil.

Your biggest weed battles will be in early spring—I think of it as "weed season"—when so many of the annual weeds are sprouting. At this point mulch won't help because most of your crop seedlings are so small that mulch would smother them. Mulch may also prevent the ground from warming up and in so doing hinder both germination and growth. The best way to deal with these early weeds is by repeated, careful cultivating—that is, by disturbing the soil with a hoe, a hand culti-vator, or whatever works best for you—so that the tiny weed roots are dislodged, exposed to air, and killed. You must be careful not to uproot the young seedlings sprouting among them. You'll sometimes find yourself pulling weeds with your fin-gertips where they are close to the plants, which is picky work but necessary.

Even after weed season, and even with a well-mulched garden, you must still weed. You'll benefit the garden and save your-self much labor if you catch weeds when they are *tiny*. Try to get yourself to weed an hour here, an hour there, instead of ignor-ing the garden for a week or two or three and then treating it to an all-day marathon housekeeping session. Going in to weed often forces you to notice other problems as well and catch them before they get out of hand.

Another way to control weeds is by not tilling too deeply once the garden is well established. As you gradually cultivate the top few inches of the soil, year after year, the weed seeds there will sprout and promptly be dispatched—by you. Let the sleeping ones lie. If you need to loosen the lower soil layers, do so by inserting a digging fork into the soil and wiggling it forward and back without turning the soil over or by using a broadfork (page 96).

HARVESTING

The second most important maintenance task is picking. Most vegetables have an optimum time when they should be picked, and some, such as edible-pod peas, are at their best only for a day. Corn must also be picked promptly or the raccoons will do it for you. With many crops, such as snap beans, cucumbers, broccoli, summer squash, and okra, you must keep picking continuously or the plants will slow down their attempt to bear fruit and even stop altogether. And with some vegetables such as salad greens, the harvest starts long before the plant is mature. You can eat even the smallest thin-nings, then thin some more the week after and eat those. Most leafy greens taste bitter as they are going to seed, and frequent pick-ing can help to postpone this.

WATERING

There are no hard-and-fast rules about watering vegetable gardens. The traditional wisdom holds that a garden needs an inch of water per week during the growing sea-son. If it doesn't get that inch from rainfall, the moisture must be provided by water-ing. If the weather is very hot, however, either because of your climate or because of a heat wave, your garden may need more than that inch, but if you mulch the garden it may need less.

I don't like to waste water. I give sup-plemental water when it is dry, but try not to go overboard. When I encounter a par-ticularly wet summer, and watch the gar-den turn into some sort of macabre Mold World, I realize that nature invented dry Augusts for a reason. On the other hand, most vegetables are annuals, which by nature are less drought tolerant than more deep-rooted perennial plants. Those that are composed largely of water (like cucum-bers and tomatoes) will need more mois-ture than others. The consistency of the water supply is also a factor with tomatoes. If this is an important crop for you it may be worthwhile to use soaker hoses (page 108) or a drip-irrigation system. It is espe-cially important to wet the soil thoroughly after planting any seeds or setting out any transplants. I will sometimes make little circular dams of earth around individual plants so they sit in saucers that catch and hold water.

The most important thing is to water deeply. Merely wetting the surface causes plant roots to come up to the surface where sun will burn them. Don't stop watering until the surface moisture meets up with the groundwater.

PEST CONTROL

Deer, rabbits, raccoons, woodchucks, skunks, porcupines, voles, gophers, coyotes, dogs, cats, livestock, and children can all interfere from time to time with your desire to have a vegetable garden. I've even found a bear in mine. Usually a good fence is the answer, one specifically designed to keep out what wants to come in. (In the case of voles, traps are the answer.) For specifics, see page 71.

Insects and other small predators such as slugs can also give gardeners fits. The solution, however, is not to reach for a can of bug-killing spray. I avoid even the kinder, gentler arsenal of "safe," "benign," "nontoxic," "green," "all-natural," or "organic" products that are for sale. Even if I waited the required number of "days to harvest" that is specified on the can of spray, I would worry about the stuff straying to plants nearby that I might be picking and eating before that time. I also worry about the effect of these sprays on creatures that are presently doing useful work in the garden, such as bees, birds, butterflies, and ladybugs.

Some better remedies are discussed on page 60, as well as in the sections on individual vegetables. But most of the time I just concentrate on giving the plants whatever they need to keep them as healthy and robust as possible—great soil, weed-free beds, and water as needed—and this seems to give them the vigor they need to resist most infestations.

The same goes for diseases—well-grown plants are less susceptible. I also try to clean up garden debris promptly, rotate crops to avoid predators or pathogens that might overwinter in the soil, and select disease-resistant varieties. Often just trying a different variety does the trick, as some are simply better suited to my garden than others.

If you're intent on grappling with a pest problem, try to find out exactly what the problem is. If you can't identify it, take a sample of the plant (and/or the bug) to your local Extension Service. There is nothing worse than gardeners who at the first hint of anything odd say, "I've got to *spray*," without knowing what they're dealing with—an insect, a disease, a soil deficiency, or just rotten weather. I once spoke with a couple who bragged about their war against tomato worms. "We killed all the mothers!" they crowed. "They were covered with little white eggs that were about to hatch out and devour all our tomatoes!" I explained to them that the eggs had been laid on the tomato worms' bodies by parasitic wasps, who were actually helping to keep the worm population in check. Usually nature is way, way ahead of you.

OTHER CHORES

There is not much else you need to do to keep your garden in good shape. Some crops do require special kinds of attention. The tall or sprawling ones need to be staked or trellised, as discussed in the individual sections that follow. And a number of vegetables can be partly covered to blanch (whiten) them, tenderize them, or make them less bitter. The most common vegetables that are blanched are celery, leeks, asparagus, cauliflower, escarole, and endive. Blanching is variously done by putting boards over the plants, tying the plants' own leaves over the edible portions, having them wear hats, or mounding earth over the parts to be blanched. With some vegetables, such as cauliflower, this is almost always done; with others, such as asparagus, it's optional. In recent years the view has been that unblanched vegetables have more nutrients, and so blanching is somewhat out of fashion. Just as with flour and rice, the trend has shifted away from whiteness and toward natural color and greater health benefits. If you do blanch vegetables, make sure you peek into their dark hideaways from time to time to make sure they're not rotting, mildewing, or being eaten.

HOUSEKEEPING

One more task: cleaning up. This should begin as soon as you have a crop you're finished with. Pull it up and put it on the compost pile. This will help keep the garden free of disease and insect pests, add to your store of composting material, and often provide space for a succession crop. By the time the ground has frozen, everything should be out of there except the perennial vegetables, any crops you're overwintering in the ground for spring harvest, seed you've sown for spring sprouting, or any cover crops you may have planted.

If your winters are mild, your cleaning up and replanting will go on all year long. If your winters are severe it's time to hibernate along with your garden. Even if you have crops under protective coverings, they will need little care. You'll have plenty of time to read the seed catalogs as they arrive, reevaluate the year's work, and decide what to try next year. The fantasy will be a much more enticing one if the garden is all tidied up and ready for those first seeds to go in.

Artichokes

European artichoke

globe artichoke

FEW HOME GARDENERS GROW ARTI-chokes because they have never been included among those easy annual crops adaptable to most gardens. And in fact this perennial Mediterranean vegetable has only been grown domestically as an important commercial crop in one area between San Francisco and Los Angeles, where it never gets too cold or too hot. But don't be daunted by this fancy, presumably fussy vegetable. While you may never produce the huge, high-yielding plants of Castroville, California, you can certainly grow a respectable harvest in much colder climates, thanks to a few tricks of the trade.

The artichoke is essentially a type of thistle. Its buds are harvested before they open into gorgeous purple, fuzzy blooms—unless of course you're growing them for their flowers. Under normal circumstances they do not produce these buds until they're two years old—which is why they've been considered a mild-climate crop. Though only moderately frost hardy (temperatures below 20 will kill the roots), they are traditionally wintered over to bear the second and subsequent years.

Determined cold-climate gardeners have always devised ways of producing second-year plants by growing them under the cover of cold frames or a greenhouse, by growing them in pots that are moved indoors, or by digging up the roots or suckers and storing them in the basement. In somewhat milder areas they often can be left outdoors, protected by large overturned pots mounded with straw mulch.

But the cleverest—and simplest—method in cold climates is to fool first-year plants into thinking they're two years old and ready to bear "chokes." This is done by "vernalizing" them—that is, by giving them a six-week period of indoor warmth followed by a six-week period of outdoor cold. When the weather outdoors starts to warm up in early summer, the plants think they're going into their second summer. New "annual" varieties have been developed that play this game particularly well, so it's now quite easy to produce artichoke-bearing plants in one growing season.

SITE

Choose a sunny, well-drained spot. If your climate is mild and you're growing artichokes as perennials, site them in a permanent location where the large plants will not shade smaller crops. If grown as annuals, avoid planting them where lettuce and chicories have recently grown.

SOIL

The soil should be very fertile and rich in organic matter to help it retain moisture and drain well. Till it deeply to accommodate the plants' long taproots.

PLANTING

My own experience has been with seed-grown artichokes, but it is sometimes possible to buy them as one-year plants, as with asparagus. Seed should be started very early (mid February in my Maine climate) in order to give the plants a good six weeks of indoor warmth and another six of outdoor chilling. When the seedlings are about ten days old transplant them into 4-inch pots, or into the long, skinny ones designed for tree seedlings.

For their artificial "winter," set the plants out in a protected spot such as a cold frame, but make sure you vent it during the day to keep the plants cool. You can also just set them next to the door and whisk them inside on nights when temperatures below freezing are predicted. A south-facing house wall is also a good spot. Another alternative is just to have some sheets of heavy plastic or old blankets handy to lay over them gently on very cold nights.

After the danger of serious frost has passed, plant the artichokes about 2 feet apart in a row in cool climates, but at least 3 feet apart in warm climates, where the plants can get very large. Mulch to conserve moisture and top-dress as needed with a high-nitrogen liquid fertilizer such as fish emulsion.

GROWING

Water at ground level as needed to keep the soil consistently moist. Doing this will often mean the difference between success and failure in hot climates. For perennial plantings, remove suckers that form near the original plants, except for the ones needed to renew the crop. Plants become less productive after four or five years, and can be replaced by digging up the best suckers and replanting them in a new, well-prepared bed.

PESTS AND DISEASES

Artichokes are usually a healthy crop. Aphids, though a common pest, can be hosed off if they start to cause damage.

HARVEST

Buds start to form in mid to late summer. It's important to harvest them before they start to open (before the scales start to pull away), otherwise they will be tough. In cooler climates this often happens before the buds are as large as the giant ones available in markets. But the small ones are very tasty. If picked at baby size (up to about 2 inches at the base) they are nearly chokeless and, apart from trimming the tips, can be eaten whole. Harvest them with a sharp knife, leaving several inches of the stems, which, when cooked, are delicious scraped or peeled.

Since artichokes are a cool-weather crop they will bear after frost, and some varieties, especially the purple ones, will carry well into fall. In Italy, which is artichoke heaven, they are a winter crop.

VARIETIES

The best variety for vernalizing is 'Imperial Star,' though other early-bearing varieties such as 'Grand Beurre' can also be manipulated in this way. For perennial crops the large-budded 'Green Globe' is the standard. I'm also very fond of the slender purple European varieties, such as 'Violetto' and 'Orlando.'

Asparagus

I THINK THAT PLANTING ASPARAGUS IS one of the best investments a gardener can make. It is a crop that asks a great deal of you at first: a lot of space in your garden, a lot of work preparing the bed, and a three-year wait before you can harvest your first full crop. But provided you pay attention to a few rules of good maintenance, nothing you can grow will give you such a good return.

Asparagus is one of the few perennial vegetables—that is, one of the few that comes back each year without being replanted. A well-established bed can produce for decades, giving you a delicacy that, if you had to buy it in the store, would be expensive and never as savory as those fresh-picked, home-grown spears. Asparagus doesn't keep its flavor well after cutting, but freezes well, and much of the fresh taste and bright green color will be retained. I have come to view it as one of those crops that I'd rather eat only in season, to preserve the specialness of this spring treat. I also like looking at the plants, with their tall, fernlike foliage—bright green in summer, then yellow-orange in fall.

SITE

To grow enough asparagus for a family of four—about 50 plants—you need 250 square feet of land. The spot should be sunny, if possible. Even though asparagus will tolerate some shade, full sun will give you more vigorous plants that can better ward off disease. It's also very important that the site be well drained, and not just at the surface level. The plants are deep-rooted and will not be happy in a spot where the water table is only a few feet down. Asparagus is generally grown in a separate plot by itself, for it is so tall that it easily shades most plants growing next to it. The first year, before the ferns are tall enough to cast much shade, you can plant crops such as beans between the asparagus rows. In subsequent years you might, if you're very short on space, interplant with early crops such as radishes and lettuce, which are harvested before the ferns reach their full seasonal growth.

SOIL

Because asparagus is a perennial, the bed it grows in will be a permanent one. The only chance you'll have to give your asparagus the luxurious soil preparation it needs is before you plant, so do it then. This means removing all grass and weeds from the bed, including any pieces of perennial weed roots that might resprout. When mature, the asparagus will form a dense mat of deep roots from which you cannot disentangle these invaders. Perennial grass, especially, can quickly destroy the bed if it is neglected. Just to be safe, I never rototill a new aspara-gus bed unless I've removed all the grass and weeds first with a digging fork.

Asparagus is a relatively hungry plant, so I dig a lot of fertilizer into the whole bed—at least a 4-inch layer of rotted manure and/or compost if I have it, plus some rock phosphate and greensand. If you're using fertilizer in pellet form, make sure you also add plenty of organic matter, such as peat moss, too. A 4-inch layer, spread on the bed and dug in thoroughly, should be plenty unless the soil is heavy. (Asparagus prefers a sandy loam.) Double-digging the bed (page 23) would also benefit this deep-rooted crop. Add lime as needed to bring the soil pH up to the preferred 6.5 to 7.0.

PLANTING

Most gardeners grow asparagus from one-year-old roots, or crowns, from a local nursery or mail-order supplier. Some parts of the country have had problems with an airborne fusarium wilt of asparagus. Check with your local Extension Service, and if fusarium wilt is a problem in your area, be sure you order disease-free roots from a reputable nursery in a part of the country that has not been affected, or else—better yet—grow your plants from seed.

Asparagus roots are long and whitish, and hang like the tentacles of an octopus from the center of the crown, where you can see little white tips ready to sprout. When I first saw a bin of these crowns for sale I was surprised to find them lying exposed to the air. Up to a point asparagus roots will withstand exposure to air, but the less stress the roots encounter, the more vigorous the plants will be. If they arrive by mail and you cannot plant them right away, keep them in their package or wrap them in damp sphagnum moss or newspaper. Try to plant them as soon as you can.

If you live in a warm climate, the best time to plant asparagus roots is fall or winter. In a cooler one the proper time is early spring, about four weeks before the last average frost date. It's best to prepare the bed the previous fall, to give it a chance to settle.

I plant asparagus in rows, leaving a good 4 to 5 feet between them, partly because they need a good root run and partly because I like to be able to walk between the rows without compacting the soil around the plants or stepping on the young shoots. For each planting row I dig a series of shallow trenches about a foot wide. I add a few inches of mature compost to the bottom of the trench, then make mounds of compost or light, rich soil, one for each plant, spacing them 18 inches apart. The top of each mound should be about 3 inches below the soil surface.

I drape the "tentacles" over the mounds that I have made (Figure 48), then I start to fill the trench with soil, firming it gently

Planting Asparagus

FIG. 48

around the roots and covering the tips with 2 or 3 inches of soil. As the spears grow, I gradually fill the trench up with soil. In subsequent years the crowns will work their way closer to the surface.

Growing asparagus from seed is the method some gardeners prefer. It is a bit more trouble, and it can take up to a year longer to produce plants of harvestable size. But they will generally be more vigorous and healthy, and produce higher yields. Growing from seed also costs less. Seeds should be started indoors anywhere from three to five months before planting (with an earlier sowing you may be able to harvest them sooner) and set out as small plants after danger of frost has passed. Plant them in trenches the same way you do the roots.

GROWING

Keep a new bed well watered and cultivate very lightly to keep it free of weeds, being careful not to damage the emerging shoots. Do this in subsequent years as well. Many an asparagus bed has succumbed to summer neglect after the excitement of spring harvesting has passed. A mulch is particularly helpful with this crop in order to keep it weed-free; mulch will help keep the bed moist, too. Volunteer seedlings from the asparagus plants should be removed.

A few puny spears will come up the year that you plant. Don't pick them! If the whole plant is to mature, you must let the first spears grow into the foliage that makes food for the long roots to store. Do not cut the foliage down until late winter or until it dies down by itself. Even as it turns yellow, it will be helping the plant to grow. Besides, that bright color is a cheerful sight in winter when so much looks dead and brown. After the color fades it's a good precaution to cut down the old stems and leaves since they can harbor diseases or the eggs of the asparagus beetle.

The second spring there will be more spears than there were the year before. If they have been grown from roots you may pick a few per plant, for about two weeks, but only those that are as thick as your finger. Just keep waiting, watering, and mulching; and top-dress at least once a year with compost or manure. I apply this in fall in my cold climate and let it sink in over the winter. In a very warm climate, however, it's better to withhold food in fall, and even water (except in extreme drought), to encourage the plants to turn yellow and go dormant. They need the rest that winter provides in order to yield well in spring. A spring feeding with liquid fertilizer will also give the plants a boost.

PESTS AND DISEASES

The chief insect plague is the asparagus beetle. These can be controlled in all but the direst cases by picking them off when they appear. If beetles have been a problem, destroy the dead stalks in fall.

Asparagus rust is a common disease, especially in the south, but most of the good modern varieties are rust resistant. Fusarium wilt can be fought by obtaining disease-free roots or by growing from seed—and by burning any diseased plant debris. Also, do everything you can to raise a vigorous crop that will do its own part in resisting disease.

HARVEST

The third spring there will be many more spears. You may now pick any that are finger-size, but stop after a month or six weeks. I usually pick for two months in the years following.

How you pick asparagus is a burning issue with some people. There are the snappers, and there are the cutters. Nature has arranged for the asparagus spear to break off at a point where it starts to be tender and cook nicely, so snapping works fine. So does cutting, as long as you use a sharp knife and try not to injure the emerging shoots nearby, especially if you're cutting just a bit below the soil surface in order to get a longer spear. The spears should be cut when they are about 8 inches above the ground, but the size is less important than the appearance of the tip; the spears are tastier and more tender when the scales are flat against the stalk and have not yet begun to open.

VARIETIES

The old favorite is 'Mary Washington.' This and the other Washington varieties have been bred for rust resistance, as have 'Early California 500,' 'Hybrid Waltham,' 'Jersey Centennial,' 'Jersey Giant,' and the other excellent Jersey varieties from Rutgers University. These were also bred for the production of predominately male plants, which concentrate on poking up more spears, not on forming the bright red berries that, though beautiful, are superfluous to the crop and can be a nuisance when they fall and sprout in the bed.

Beans

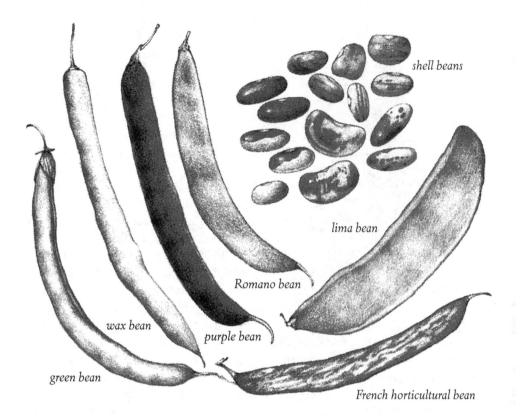

shell beans

lima bean

Romano bean

wax bean

purple bean

green bean

French horticultural bean

YOU CAN GROW BEANS IN A SMALL garden, but there are so many interesting kinds that they may lure you into planting a larger garden just so you can include them all. The most familiar are string beans, so called because they used to have inedible strings running down the spines before this trait was bred out. These are also called snap beans because they snap in two when ready for picking, and are eaten pods and all. They can be green, purple, or yellow; if yellow, they're called wax beans. Varieties that grow short are called bush beans, and varieties that grow

on long vines are called pole beans. Those that are raised just for the beans inside the pod are called shell beans. Some of these, such as limas, are eaten fresh; others, such as navy beans, kidney beans, and soybeans, are usually dried. Broad beans, also known as favas, are a staple in Europe, and eaten as a fresh shell bean, without the pods. They are not to be confused with the wide Italian Romano type, which are more often eaten at the snap bean stage.

Beans have a way of twining their way out of these categories, though. Many a snap bean that has grown past the tasty

bush beans

pole beans

ites. I'm partial to the Romano type for fresh eating, but my curiosity about the world of shell beans is insatiable. I eat the dried ones all winter and love to see rows of them in glass jars on my shelves, in all their gorgeous shapes and colors.

All beans are rich in vitamins and fiber, and the shelled kind are rich in protein, too. Soybeans are popular as a meat substitute (I probably have had one soyburger too many at vegetarian tables to be a true fan), and also make a good green manure (page 13).

Beans are a fast, easy, abundant summer crop that needs plenty of sun but will produce little but mildew in very foggy climates. Too much intense heat in summer will cause the blossoms to drop; and cold, heavy, wet soil in spring will rot the seeds. But given a reasonable three-month summer, you should be able to grow most beans if you choose varieties geared to your region.

SITE

Plant beans in a spot where they will get full sun and good drainage. Early crops will benefit from soil that warms up quickly in spring. These factors make beans good candidates for raised-bed culture. This is not always practical if you're growing a

pod stage can be picked for the bean inside it, and any shell bean can be eaten either fresh or dried. Green beans, wax beans, and limas can all be either bush or pole. Half-runners, popular in the south, are somewhere between a bush and a pole type. There are also a number of southern beans such as black-eyed peas, which are actually beans. "Pea" and "bean" are rather loose terms that describe a number of different legumes, all closely related. But generally the word "pea" denotes plants in the genus *Pisum*, which includes the common green garden pea that is eaten fresh. Southern "peas," which comprise several species, are sometimes eaten fresh and sometimes dried.

My advice is to try a lot of different beans—a few new ones each year. Most people wind up with their particular favor-

number of different kinds of dried beans and want to give them a lot of space (you'd need to build a lot of beds). But for an early, quick crop of snap beans, raised beds are great. I make sure I give pole beans a spot where they won't cast shade on other crops, unless they are such crops as lettuce, which need a bit of midsummer shade.

SOIL

The soil in which beans grow should have a neutral to slightly acid pH (6.0 to 7.0). Beans like any good loam with plenty of organic matter added, and a moderately rich soil. Usually they leave the soil better than when they found it because of certain "nitrogen-fixing" bacteria in the nodules that form on beans' roots. These bacteria enable the roots to convert atmospheric nitrogen into nitrogen compounds that the plants can use for growth. When parts of the bean plants are left in the soil they enrich it and pass nutrients on to the next crop. Dusting the seeds with the proper bacterial inoculant for that particular bean—although not a necessity—will help to jump-start this process. If you're using a prepared fertilizer, choose a balanced one that is not overly high in nitrogen.

PLANTING

Bean seeds are sown directly in the garden, usually after danger of frost has passed. If you want to start eating them early—as soon as six weeks after the last average frost—plant some bush beans, either green or wax. They will produce all at once, which is handy for both the commercial grower and the home gardener whose chief goal is to fill the freezer. You can also sow new plantings every ten days or so for succession crops.

Pole beans take longer to bear—10 or 11 weeks—but their advantage is that they then keep bearing continuously until frost. Thus they are the joy of the gardener who wants to pick and eat fresh beans over a long period of time. Pole beans are also great space savers because they will ultimately produce about three times the yield of the bush types in the same amount of garden space. Except in very warm climates, they are generally sown in one planting.

Lima beans take a long time, so choose "early" varieties up north. So do soybeans, but these can make fast progress in spring even if it's a bit chilly. Fava beans are a cool-weather crop and respond well to early sowing. In southern France I've seen them growing in January. But most of the typical garden beans we grow are not frost hardy, and they will make a very slow start if the soil is colder than 65 degrees.

Plant beans 1 inch deep. Moisten the soil well when you plant, and make sure that the seeds will be coming up through fine soil, patted firm but not hard and crusty. If the soil in your garden tends to be lumpy, rub the lumps between your hands, letting the soil fall onto the seeds.

Bush beans can be planted either in single rows about 30 inches apart or, in a more intensive bed, in two rows 18 inches apart. Seeds spaced about 4 to 6 inches apart will not have to be thinned. (Germination with beans is usually good, but if you have plenty of seed you may also sow more thickly, then thin to the right spacing.) Planting pole beans is a bit more complicated, because you first have to decide what kind of support you're going to give the vines (Figure 49). You can use single unpeeled saplings—8 to 10 feet long if possible and about 2 inches in diameter—or groups of three thinner ones placed 3 to 4 feet apart in a triangle or square, and joined tepee-style on top with a stout string. (If it's difficult to find saplings, use cut lumber or thick bamboo poles.) For extra stability I also place poles horizontally so they connect all the tepee tops. This also gives the long vines something else to climb along when they reach the top.

Either way, I make sure I sink the poles deep enough in the ground so that they won't blow over (at least a foot for tepee poles, and at least 18 inches for single uprights). Sow six seeds in a circle around each pole, about 6 inches away from it, then later thin these to three strong seedlings per pole. The vines will twist their way up the poles as they grow.

Another good way to support pole beans is on a trellis that runs the length of the row. Trellises work if they are sturdy enough to support what will be a pretty heavy crop. Wires or untreated twine can be hung vertically within an upright frame as shown. You could also use a very open plastic mesh. One advantage to using the twine is that you can compost your trellis along with the dead vines at the season's end. Install the trellis before you plant, then sow a row of seeds on one side of it. Once the bean plants are up, thin them to 6 inches apart.

GROWING

Mulch is good for beans because they are shallow rooted and can easily be damaged by cultivating and weeding. They also are more prone to disease when wet, and mulch cuts down on the need for watering. I try not to mess with beans when they're wet because the wet plants can spread disease from one to another. But I also make sure they don't get too dry. Bean plants that have dried out produce pods that start out with a few beans and end in a squiggle.

Successive feedings may be necessary if your yields tend to be small, or if you notice that the leaf color is not a rich dark green. The plants can be side-dressed with a liquid fish fertilizer, or with compost or manure tea. This step is more important for long-bearing pole beans and for heavy feeders such as limas.

PESTS AND DISEASES

Beans can get anthracnose, bacterial blight, rust, mosaic, and other ills, but these are rarely a problem if you use healthy seed, rotate your crops, and keep the garden free of debris. If diseases still recur, seek out resistant varieties. I like to save my own seeds for the following year, so I try to make sure I save only the cleanest, most pristine ones and store them under dry conditions.

About blossom time you might be visited by Mexican bean beetles, which look like large brown ladybugs. Pick off the adults, the fuzzy yellow larvae, and the yellow egg masses under the leaves, as well as any Japanese beetles that arrive. Hose off aphids with a stream of water.

HARVEST

When should you pick? For snap beans, wait until they're about pencil size, but harvest before the beans inside the pods have become lumpy. Then keep picking! Otherwise they will stop producing. I can still remember my mother complaining every summer about "keeping up with the beans." But she did it, and there were never any complaints from us about her freezer full of 'Kentucky Wonder.' This is especially important for the vining types that can produce all season. Even if some have "gone by," pick those and add them to the compost heap or let them all go to the shell bean stage and harvest them. Pick the skinny little French "filet" types while they are still skinny—every day if possible.

For fresh shell beans, let the lumps in the pods get good and fat. For dried shell beans, let the pods get brown and dry on the plant, then pick them before they can split open and spill out the beans or before they can mildew. If it's getting near frost time or the weather is very moist or humid, you can pull up the vines and finish off the drying process indoors. When dry, the beans can be shelled by hand or threshed by putting them in a feed bag, stomping on them, then spreading them out in a windy place. Make sure they are dry and free of chaff and debris before storing them. Pouring the beans from one bowl to another in front of a fan is a quick way to remove chaff.

VARIETIES

Everybody has their favorites. For flavor in a green bean it's hard to beat some of the old timers like 'Kentucky Wonder' and 'Blue Lake,' which also come in bush form. The Italian flat-podded 'Romano'

Ways to Grow Pole Beans

FIG. 49

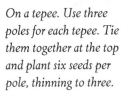

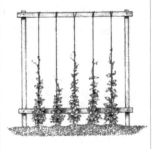

On poles. Sink pieces of lumber or saplings, 8 feet long and 1 inch in diameter, a foot apart. Plant several seeds at the base of each.

On a tepee. Use three poles for each tepee. Tie them together at the top and plant six seeds per pole, thinning to three.

On a trellis. A wooden frame made with pressure-treated 2-by-4 posts is sunk 2 feet into the ground at each end; smaller pieces of lumber are nailed horizontally to support vertical wires 4 to 6 inches apart. Grow one plant per wire.

and the newer 'Kwintus' are both excellent. 'Garden of Eden,' from Johnny's Selected Seeds, is a great heirloom bean with big flat pods that are tender even when mature. I always grow at least one wax bean such as 'Roc d'Or,' and a purple such as 'Trionfo Violetto' or 'Royal Burgundy.' The pods of the purple ones turn green during cooking, but look great raw on a crudité platter next to a green and a yellow variety. There are also white-streaked-with-red ones such as 'Dragon Tongue.' 'Nickel' is a stringless bush form of the tiny, tasty French filet bean, or *haricot vert*. 'King of the Garden' is a good pole lima. Good bush limas include the Fordhook varieties and 'Henderson Bush Lima,' a good baby lima or "butter bean."

I also grow a few vining beans that I choose more for their looks than their flavor, such as hyacinth bean (*Dolichos lablab*) with it's huge, gorgeous purple pods and contrasting pink flowers. Another is 'Scarlet Runner,' whose bright red blooms are a favorite of hummingbirds. Its large seeds, which make very good eating, are black splashed with magenta.

Shell beans are so varied and numerous that my best advice is explore at will, consulting some of the specialty catalogs or trying some of the wonderful heirlooms offered by the Seed Savers (page 763). I love the large, fat white beans with dark red speckles called 'Jacob's Cattle,' which not only taste good but look pretty, either in jars or on the plate. Many of my choices are determined by dishes I like to cook. 'Black Turtle' is a good soup bean for cool climates. 'Dark Red Kidney' and 'Vermont Cranberry' make good chili. I grow the Italian white 'Cannellini' to serve at room temperature with olive oil, tomatoes, and fresh sage. 'Navy' is for Boston baked beans. In warm, dry climates you can grow chickpeas (garbanzo beans) and many of the wonderful southwestern beans developed by the Native Americans. And I would surely grow the luscious French *flageolets* if I had a longer growing season— they take at least 100 days to mature.

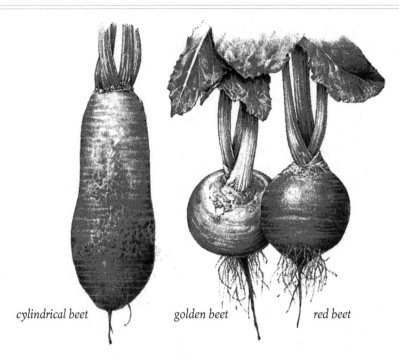

cylindrical beet · golden beet · red beet

Beets

THE BEST REASON TO GROW BEETS is to make homemade borscht. They're also great steamed at baby size and served with butter. For a winter treat you might roast them whole the way the French do, peel and toss them in vinaigrette while still warm, then set them on a bed of fresh mâche greens. The tops are lovely in salads if cut at 3-inch height, or used as a cooked vegetable when mature.

I savor beets from the first tops in spring to the last-dug roots in December, just before the ground freezes solid. And it's easy to preserve them long after that by canning, freezing, or storing in the root cellar. To top it all off, they are an easy, fairly quick-maturing crop. Few bugs or diseases bother them, and almost any climate suits them.

Beets are biennials that in the wild would winter over in the ground, then send up seed stalks the following spring from the nutrients stored in their fleshy roots. The plants are very cold tolerant, and even the seedlings are frost hardy, though the roots keep best if you harvest them before the first hard freeze. Beets can be grown in spring, summer, and fall in cold climates, and in fall, winter, and spring in hot ones. Summer-grown beets in hot climates will be neither tasty nor tender.

SITE

It's easy to find a place for beets. They will tolerate some shade, and you can even grow them between rows of tall crops such as Brussels sprouts. They do not take up much room. You can even grow an extra-early or extra-late crop in a small cold frame. The greens can be harvested as a cut-and-come-again crop all winter in a cold frame, even in very chilly climates.

SOIL

The best soil for beets is a sandy loam lightened and enriched with compost or aged manure (fresh manure makes the root grow side shoots instead of forming one nice round beet). Beets do not like acid soil. Use lime to raise the pH to between 6.5 and 6.8. The soil should be luxurious; lighten and enrich it to a depth of at least 8 inches, pulverizing it and ridding it of rocks, roots, and other obstacles. Dig in plenty of organic matter if your soil is clay. Make sure your soil has all the trace elements it needs (a soil test will tell you). In particular, beets grow and taste poorly in a soil low in boron; a light dusting of borax powder will correct this.

PLANTING

Sow the seed as early as you can work the soil, for an early crop. Try planting a small row every two weeks or so until late summer for a nice succession of greens or baby beets. Storage crops are started in early summer in cool climates, late summer or early fall in hot ones. Soaking the seeds first will help them germinate, especially if the weather is dry. (So will spreading a very sparse covering of hay or straw to shade the ground after sowing.) Plant the seeds ½ inch deep in rows a foot or so apart for small beets or beet greens, and up to 18 inches for large storage beets. Try to sow the seeds about an inch apart. If they are any closer they will be hard to thin later; but if they are too sparse you'll have gaps in the rows. Water the seed bed thoroughly.

GROWING

When your seedlings emerge, remove any straw or hay mulch that is covering them. If you have planted in rows, add mulch between the rows. Keep the bed moist and thin the seedlings when they are about 2 inches tall. If you get behind and don't have a chance to thin them early, it is not a disaster. The thinnings are delicious in salads when young. Thinned roots are also a treat. Just be sure to give maturing roots space in which to grow without crowding. Beets grown as baby beets can be as close together as 2 inches; large storage beets do best at about 4 inches apart.

The main idea in growing beets is to get them to mature quickly so they're tender and not hard and woody. This is done by giving them the kind of soil described above, a steady water supply, no weeds to compete with, and proper thinning. Mulch is especially beneficial in hot, dry climates, though I'd avoid using it in an area where voles are a problem. Beets are fairly heavy feeders and appreciate a topdressing with compost or a balanced fertilizer when about half grown. Hilling the soil around the shoulders, especially for the cylindrical types, will give them a better appearance.

PESTS AND DISEASES

A few flea beetles might show up but probably will not decimate the crop; neither will the small yellow leaf miner. Both are spring pests, and can be foiled by laying down floating row covers on early crops. Cutworms, which come out at night, can destroy young seedlings; the best control is to probe the soil near the plants with your finger, find the fat, sleeping worms, and crush them. Voles, which look like fat, furry mice, can be devastating; they love to gnaw on the sugary roots. Avoiding mulch and leaving extra space between rows can help because the voles have less chance to hide in the bed and are more exposed to predators.

Beets occasionally get a fungus disease that gives them a spotted or mottled appearance. Remove debris promptly and rotate the crop. Some varieties are resistant.

HARVEST

While the beets are growing you can pick up to a third of the leaves off each plant and use them as cooked greens. (If you're a real beet-green aficionado, you can just pick all the greens and forget the roots.) Beets can be harvested at baby size—as small as an inch across—or grown as large as possible for storage. Pull them up, give a yank and a shake, then cut off the stems. Leave on an inch of stem if you're storing the roots. In warm climates beets can be pulled from the ground as needed all winter, but har-vest them all before they start to regrow in early spring.

VARIETIES

The basic tried-and-true red beet is 'Detroit Dark Red,' good for spring or fall. I grow the newer hybrid 'Red Ace' for an all-purpose beet, and sometimes 'Winter Keeper' if I want a very large storage beet. For baby beets try 'Pronto,' 'Early Wonder,' or 'Little Ball.' I like 'Bull's Blood' for its gorgeous maroon foliage, especially good when cut as small, tender salad greens in cool weather. The long, tapered types such as 'Cylindra' or 'Forono' are a nice shape for slicing. 'Chioggia' has a striking red-and-white bull's-eye appearance when cut. 'Golden' is a beautiful red-orange beet root that does not turn everything purple when cut. This is a plus if you're adding it to potato salad, unless, for you, beets should be like real madras—guaranteed to bleed. Especially if you're making borscht.

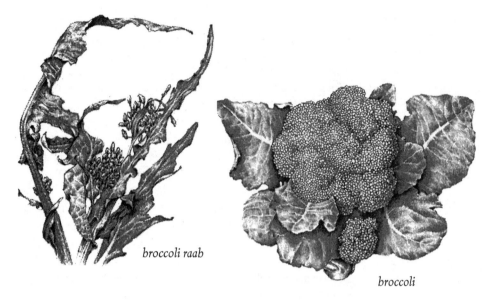

broccoli raab

broccoli

Broccoli

I HAVE A GREAT APPRECIATION FOR broccoli because it tolerates the cool climate in which I live. In a summer with little sun, or a fall with no Indian summer, there is always broccoli, and all it asks is that I keep up with the picking. Gladly. I can make a whole meal out of broccoli, olive oil, and garlic. Gardeners in warmer areas love it for it's all-winter freshness.

Our basic green broccoli, sometimes called sprouting broccoli and *calabrese* in Europe, came originally from Italy. It makes a big plant with deep spreading roots. The big broccoli "bunch" that you buy in the grocery store, really an immature flower head, is usually only the beginning for the home gardener. After the central cluster is cut back, side shoots develop that can be harvested for a long time if the summer is not blistering hot. In warm-summer climates the tight buds will rice, or open as flowers too soon, thus ending the crop, so southern gardeners plant a fall crop that will bear well into the winter instead.

SITE

Choose a spot with good drainage and air circulation where broccoli and other members of the genus *Brassica* (page 232) have not grown for several years. Full sun is best, but partial shade will also sustain broccoli. The plot need not be large. Even though the plants get fairly sizable (2 to 2½ feet tall and spready) each one produces a lot of food. Six plants in a 4-foot by 6-foot plot is a good number to start with. Passionate broccophiles will want more.

SOIL

Soil should be fairly rich to begin with. As a leaf-and-stem crop, broccoli needs plenty of nitrogen. I dig in a shovelful of compost or well-rotted manure for each plant. Calcium is important; you can make sure it is there by adding lime. Keep in mind that this will also raise the pH—something you'd want to do anyway if your soil is acid. The ideal pH for broccoli is a neutral 7.0. It is even more important to add organic matter to the soil, to help it retain the steady moisture supply that the crop needs.

PLANTING

In planting broccoli there are several schedules you can follow. To grow a spring crop you can start seeds indoors in a sunny but cool place, six or seven weeks before the last average frost date, and set the seedlings out as 5- to 6-inch plants, two or three weeks before the last expected frost. Or you can sow directly in the garden; in a cool climate do this a month or so before the last frost; in a warm one do it in very early spring. But usually broccoli is grown from transplants. Set them a few inches lower in the ground than they were in their pots or flats, watering them and firming the soil around them. Cover the young plants with floating row covers (page 260) if you think there might be a really hard freeze. Space seedlings about 18 inches apart each way if you're using a grid, or 18 inches apart in rows with 2 to 3 feet between the rows.

For direct-seeding in the garden, sow several seeds in hills (clusters) and later snip off all but the strongest plant in each. Space the hills the same distance apart as you would transplants. Cutworms like young broccoli plants, so it's a good idea to use collars to foil them (page 65), and check for the sleeping worms in the soil near the plants each morning.

I usually plant several spring broccoli crops in succession, just to keep a good supply coming along. I keep the last one going as long as I can by keeping up with the harvesting, then get ready for a fall crop or two, which I set out as transplants in late June and July. In a warm climate, you might follow a similar program, but plant the first spring crop as early as February and the fall crop in August or early September; you could even sow a crop in fall for winter or early spring harvest.

To save space the early crops can be interplanted with something smaller, such as baby lettuce or spinach, if the plants are wide enough apart.

GROWING

A good mulch will help the plants retain moisture, but in times of drought give them a good long soaking if the soil is dry. Extra enrichment is really needed only when you're trying to hasten maturity. In this case a side-dressing of blood meal or fish emulsion soaked in (not dug in) is effective.

PESTS AND DISEASES

Apart from the cutworms mentioned above, the only pest that ever bothered my broccoli was the small green cabbage worm, which is very common. It never did much damage to the plants, but it had a way of turning up as a surprise garnish at the dinner table. Well camouflaged by its color even after picking, the worm turns white when cooked. "Good protein!" a polite dinner guest may exclaim diplomatically, but unless your diners have an unusually good sense of humor, you'll want to check carefully for worms before cooking and before serving, or soak the broccoli in salt water to kill and dislodge them. If cabbage worms do more damage in your garden, lay down floating row covers before the white butterflies that flutter above broccoli in spring have a chance to lay their eggs.

Spray off aphids with a hose. Root maggots can be a problem in some gardens. A traditional way to keep the maggot fly from laying her eggs is by placing small tar paper mats on the soil around spring transplants; modern floating row covers are also effective. Most bugs won't bother your later crops, except in the south where cabbage loopers are a pest (best avoided by growing in cool weather). Diseases like blackleg, black rot, and clubroot are best prevented by crop rotation. In the case of clubroot (puny yellowed plants with misshapen roots), boost the pH to 7.0 with some lime.

HARVEST

When the first nice bunch has formed in the center of the plant, cut it off with a sharp knife above any new buds that may be forming. If you don't keep picking, the green heads will send up tall yellow flowers. A row of blossoming broccoli may look pretty and provide great nectar for bees, but it means that the plants will stop producing edible stalks. So keep up with the picking, even if you cannot keep up with the eating or freezing. You can cook and eat stalks with flowers that have started to open, but the swelling buds turn brownish when cooked and look almost as unappetizing as cooked cabbage worms.

VARIETIES

'Green Comet' is a fast-maturing early broccoli that forms large heads, good for efficient freezing; 'Arcadia' is a good late one. For continuous harvest look for ones like 'DeCicco' that are noted for good side-shoot production. 'Green Duke' and 'Cleopatra' are good varieties for the south. Another kind of broccoli, more recently popular, is broccoli raab, or *broccoli di rapa*, as the Italians call it. This is grown by direct-seeding. It never forms a head at all, just small branches, and the leaves and open flowers are more appetizing than those of regular broccoli, though with a bitterness many people enjoy. If cut regularly it will produce for up to a month. It tastes mildest in cool weather.

Brussels Sprouts

S OME VEGETABLES, LIKE LETTUCE and asparagus, are grown for the thrill of an early harvest of fresh-tasting produce for the table. Brussels sprouts are a late thrill. The ultimate cool-weather crop, their flavor is actually improved by a touch of frost. So plantings are timed to mature just when days are still warm and sunny but night frosts have just begun. The plant is slow growing but makes up for it by being frost hardy. Picking continues well into fall and even winter. The mature plant looks like a palm tree with big floppy leaves on top and little round sprouts growing tightly all up and down the "trunk." Each plant should yield over a quart of sprouts, which freeze well.

SITE

Grow Brussels sprouts in a sunny, well-drained plot. Since this crop takes a long time to mature, reserve it a spot for the whole season. You can interplant small and/or early crops between the rows. If there's a way to shield Brussels sprouts from the wind without shielding it from the sun, do so. The tall mature plants can blow over.

SOIL

Brussels sprouts have the same soil requirements as broccoli and the other "cabbage" vegetables: average pH; and a deep sandy loam, well worked and fertile. Organic matter in the soil will help it to retain the steady moisture the plants need. Traditionally, Brussels sprouts are grown in a compacted soil, but just a moderate firming with the hands after planting should be sufficient. (Do this even if planting in raised beds.) "Firm" soil doesn't mean "heavy" soil, however; good drainage is important.

PLANTING

How you time your planting depends on the climate. In a cold-winter area you grow one crop, starting seeds indoors and setting out the transplants so they have 90 to 100 days to grow before hard frosts. By contrast, if you live in a warm climate where the plants would have trouble getting through the hot summer, you're better off planting a fall crop, set out as transplants in midsummer. In all cases, keep the plants well watered.

It might take you a season or two to work out the right Brussels sprout schedule for your area and for the varieties you want to grow. Be aware that the plant can take frost, but enough hard freezes will eventually turn it to mush. And in a totally frost-free area you might not have luck with it at all.

Plants should be spaced about 2 feet apart each way if you're using a grid, or 18 inches apart in the row with 3 feet between rows. Dig a shovelful of compost into each hole, and water very thoroughly. Make collars to foil cutworms (page 65). If you are direct-seeding, keep the bed moist, and thin to the above spacing.

GROWING

A mulch will help keep the soil evenly moist, and an occasional side-dressing of liquid fertilizer may be helpful. Since the plant is tall but shallow rooted, it tends to be a little tippy; it helps to make a soil mound around the plant as it grows, firming with your foot or the back of a hoe.

PESTS AND DISEASES

Pest control is the same as for broccoli. Diseases are best controlled by crop rotation.

HARVEST

Each sprout grows in a leaf axil and matures from the bottom of the stalk upward, so start picking at the bottom. I prefer to pick them small, like large marbles—not like the golf balls you sometimes find in the market. I like to wait until after the first few frosts, because the delicious flavor that frost imparts is one of the things that distinguishes homegrown sprouts from supermarket ones. Try to pick before the tight little balls open. To detach them, use a twisting motion.

You can extend the season a long time by piling straw or other loose mulch around the plants as high as possible and covering plants and mulch with clear plastic. I prefer to pull them up roots and all, and store them in a cool place where I can pick them for about three more weeks. In fact it's a tradition in our house to do this so that we can serve Brussels sprouts with our Christmas dinner. Another trick to hurry things up, if frost seems to be coming and the sprouts are still immature, is to pinch off the top of the plant. This makes all the sprouts mature together, though there will be fewer of them.

VARIETIES

The two most commonly grown varieties of Brussels sprouts are 'Jade Cross Hybrid' and 'Long Island Improved.' Both are dwarf and short-season (roughly 90 days to harvest). 'Valiant' is an excellent European variety, though it takes longer to mature. 'Rubine' is both tasty and highly ornamental; both the leaves and the sprouts are a deep, velvety reddish purple.

Cabbage

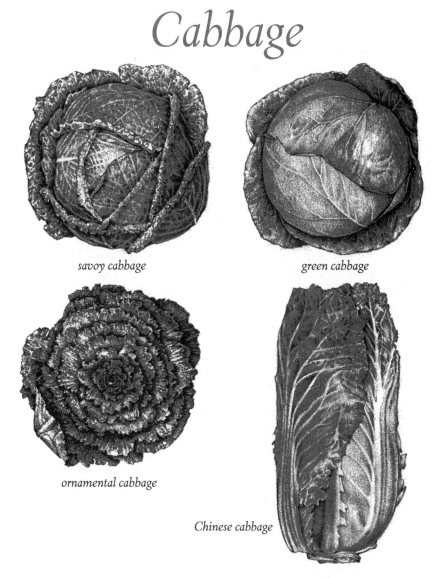

savoy cabbage

green cabbage

ornamental cabbage

Chinese cabbage

CABBAGE ISN'T GROWN AS MUCH as it used to be. Why? Perhaps it's because in gardening, big is no longer beautiful. Long rows of huge cabbage heads to be stored in cellars, then boiled up in soup cauldrons for large families, no longer have their place in the backyard plot—often no more than a cross-stitch sampler of baby eggplants, patio tomatoes, and finger-size carrots. Perhaps it's because of the strong smell cabbage has when it's cooking—an honest vegetable smell in my view. Maybe gardeners read up on cabbage diseases like blackleg, clubroot, and the yellows and lose their appetites.

But for the same reasons that cabbage has always been such a good staple, it will always be grown. There will always be a sauerkraut, a cole slaw, or a red cabbage simmered in bouillon and laced with sour cream. For those who demand a bit more panache there are the savoy types—mild, tender, and crinkled—and the many and succulent Chinese cabbages. Whatever you may have heard, cabbage is also easy to grow, hardy in any climate, and one of the few leafy vegetables you can store for months in a cold cellar.

Two crops are possible with cabbage, an early one started indoors to mature before the heat of summer becomes intense, and a late one set out in early summer to mature in the fall. In warm areas cabbage can be grown through the winter. If you only want to grow one crop, I suggest growing the fall one, to take advantage of a time when the lush, quick-growing spring and summer produce has been cleared out, and the relatively bug-free days are upon you. For the early crop you'd choose a fast-maturing variety (65 days to harvest or less); for the second, the large tight-headed kind that takes a longer time to mature (often 100 days or more) but keeps better in storage.

SITE

Most kinds of cabbage prefer a sunny site but will tolerate some shade. Grow them in a spot where other cabbage-family plants have not grown for three years. Allow 2 to 3 square feet for each head of cabbage you want to produce, less for Chinese cabbage. If you're serious about storing them for the winter, plant more for your late crop than for your earlier one.

SOIL

Cabbage is a heavy feeder and likes a rich soil with plenty of organic matter dug in. A good compost is best, supplemented if necessary with a balanced organic fertilizer. A balance of nutritional elements will help to produce cabbages that are healthy and resist cracking. Add lime if the pH is below 6.5.

PLANTING

For an early crop, start seeds indoors. Plants can be set out three to four weeks before the average last frost date, so do your sowing four to six weeks before that, giving them a warm spot for germination, a cooler place for growing on. Harden them off outside with protection before planting; they need to be fairly robust and leafy before they go into the soil. After what you hope is the last hard freeze, set them out deeper than they were in their pots, right up to the first leaves, and firm the soil around the plants. Small-headed cabbage can be set as close as 12 inches apart.

Late crops are started from May through July, depending on the climate and the variety. For winter crops in the south, they can be started even later. Either sow seed directly in the garden, to be thinned later, or sow it outdoors in flats or a separate seedbed and then transplant it. Doing this saves precious garden space when you're overlapping crops. Late seedlings should be spaced a little farther apart than early ones and can be shaded from very hot sun with lath or shade cloth as needed (Figure 47), or by a tall neighboring crop like pole beans. Chinese cabbage is usually grown as a fall crop, planted ten weeks or so before the first average frost date.

GROWING

Moisture, for cabbages, needs to be steady and consistent—always enough, but never so much that drainage is poor. Keeping the soil evenly moist during a drought can help to prevent cracking. If you're trying to hurry a slow crop along in order to harvest it before hot weather or before a hard freeze, a light topdressing of a balanced organic fertilizer will help. Be careful when you cultivate or weed around the cabbages, since their roots are shallow. Mulch helps. The Chinese cabbages are grown in the same way, except that they can be planted closer together and they mature more quickly; they respond well to topdressing.

PESTS AND DISEASES

Pests and diseases, and their treatment, are much the same as for broccoli and Brussels sprouts. If a fungus disease called cabbage yellows is a problem, grow a resistant strain such as 'Golden Acre' next time around. Try to catch diseases in the seedling stage by watching for blackened stems or lumpy roots. Throw these seedlings out. They are not likely to succeed, no matter what you spray them with, and they will only contaminate your garden soil. Southern gardeners can avoid some of the insects that plague cabbage and other brassicas by growing a very early and a late crop that bypass the worst of the bug season.

HARVEST

Cabbages are harvested when they look completely formed but while they are still firm to the touch. Leave the big outer leaves and cut the head free with a sharp knife. Store them in a root cellar or other room where the temperature stays above freezing but below 45 degrees. You can even store cabbages in a pit outdoors, with several feet of straw mulch piled over them and topped with a layer of soil.

Chinese cabbages can be stored whole, though for a shorter length of time. Unlike the western types, they can be harvested quite young and used for stir-fries or as a raw salad vegetable. With the pac choi (also known as bok choy) types you can also pick the outer leaves and let the rest of the plant keep right on growing.

VARIETIES

There are a lot of cabbage varieties to choose from. The best-known early green one is 'Early Jersey Wakefield.' Others are the yellows-resistant 'Golden Acre,' and a number of very early and/or compact varieties such as 'Dynamo.' Later ones include 'Danish Ballhead' and the heirloom 'Late Flat Dutch.' 'Red Acre,' 'Ruby Perfection,' and the nice, small, early 'Primero' are good red cabbages; 'Savoy King' and the early 'Savoy Express' are good savoys. Among the Chinese cabbages the pac choi varieties include the delectable 'Joy Choi.' These have wide white stems that are joined at the base and open up like a vase on top.

The heading types, illustrated on page 287, are known as napa cabbages, michihili, or pe-tsai ('Mei Qing Choi,' a baby pac choi, is shown on page 334). In addition, there are the loose-headed types. These form a lettucelike head if left to grow to maturity, but I prefer them grown as a cut-and-come-again baby leaf crop. 'Tokyo Bekana,' is a beautiful bright yellow-green variety. There is also a wonderful Portuguese loose-headed cabbage called *couve tronchuda*. It's the key ingredient in a famous hearty soup, *caldo verde*, whose name translates as "green broth."

Carrots

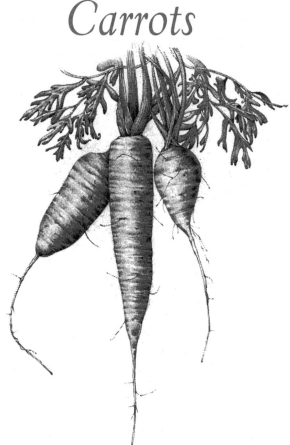

IF YOU PULL UP A QUEEN ANNE'S LACE plant growing along the side of the road, you'll find that its root is a little white carrot. This wild carrot (*Daucus carota*) is the species from which our modern hybrid carrots were developed. Indians ate the wild ones, and so can you. But for most gardeners—and cooks—carrots have come a long way. The main goal in breeding has been to develop better flavor, color, and sweetness. The central core, where once less color, sugar, and vitamins were found, is now almost indistinguishable from the rest. As a result, the typical modern carrot is a rich red-orange—crunchy, sweet, and packed with nutrients.

Carrots now come in all shapes and sizes: long tapered ones, short stubby ones, tiny fingerlike ones, even little round ones. Such variety does more than just make life interesting. Carrots of different lengths are suited to different soils and different lengths of season.

Carrots do not grow well in very hot weather. Coolness keeps them from turning woody and seems to bring out their color and flavor, too. So in warm areas you must grow them during fall, winter, and spring. In cooler areas you can plant them in early spring, then start more every few weeks until early August, so there are carrots in the ground even in wintertime.

A few hard frosts actually makes the roots sweeter and tastier. Carrots are one of the few vegetables that you can actually leave growing straight through the hard freezes of winter, to dig in early spring. To a northern gardener these seem like buried gold. At our house we harvest them most of the winter, either from a cold frame with a thick layer of straw between glass and soil, or in an unheated plastic growing tunnel under a layer of floating row cover.

SITE

The best possible site is sunny and well drained, but carrots will grow in partial shade. I've grown them in raised beds with great success—it's the best way to maintain the fluffy soil they like. But I find I must be extremely vigilant with my hose, since carrots need consistent moisture, and these beds dry out quickly.

SOIL

Carrots like a deep, loose sandy loam—the classic Beautiful Soil. But there is some latitude here. If your soil is a little heavy, even after adding organic matter, you can still grow the shorter carrots (usually an early crop). If your good topsoil is shallow, these shorter ones are also the right choice. For midseason crops you can get by with poorer soil, and a little less moisture and coolness, by growing the longer carrots that root well below the hot, dry soil surface. But for the carrots to get down that far with any kind of grace, the soil has to be light and airy to the full depth of the carrot root. If the soil is not free of obstacles—stones, roots, clay lumps, old horseshoes, etc.—the carrot will bend, fork, twist, or even stop cold. The closer to the surface, the more the soil should be pulverized.

Soil moisture is essential. Digging in organic matter such as compost, peat moss, or very well rotted manure will help the soil to stay moist, but in the case of manure, dig it in at least six months before you plant the seeds. (Fresh, or even well-rotted manure if recently applied, can cause carrots to fork and send out side roots.) Mulching will also help to keep the water content steady.

Since carrots are a root crop, the soil should be relatively low in nitrogen, higher in phosphorus and potassium. Use rock powders such as rock phosphate and greensand. The ideal pH is around 6.5.

PLANTING

Carrot seeds are always sown directly into the garden. The first ones can go in about three or four weeks before the last expected frost, and even earlier in a cold frame. I prefer single rows about a foot apart because they are much easier to mulch, so as to maintain the moist soil surface carrots need. I try to space the seeds about an inch apart, although this is very difficult to do because they are so tiny. Some people say that mixing them with sand or coffee grounds makes for easier distribution. You can also buy pelleted seeds of some varieties; these are a joy to sow. Cover the seeds with a half-inch of loose, pulverized soil made airy with organic matter. The seedlings won't come up through a hard crust. You can cover them with sifted compost, a nonsoil medium such as vermiculite, or whatever mixture suits you, as long as it is very light.

When the seeds are in, I water the bed thoroughly with a fine spray every day—twice if the weather is sunny and/or dry—and sometimes lay a very thin layer of straw over it to shade it and keep it moist.

You might lay wet burlap over the seeds, especially if you plan to be away for a few days and won't be able to water, but be sure to remove the burlap as soon as the seeds have germinated. Another trick is to sow them together with a "nurse crop," such as a fast-growing radish variety. The radish seedlings will emerge first and shade the slow, spindly carrot seedlings. They will also mark the rows and help break any crust that might form. The radishes will be harvested long before the carrots produce their major root growth. But like it or not, carrot seeds just take a long time to germinate, and the best thing to do is keep them moist (without washing them away) and be patient.

GROWING

It's best to thin carrots several times, first when they are 1 to 2 inches high, then later on whenever they're starting to look crowded. In the first thinning eliminate any seedlings that are closer than half an inch to another seedling. Snipping them off with scissors is one way to do it without damaging the seedlings still growing. The second thinning is more fun, because you're pulling up tiny carrots to toss in salads. When you're finished thinning, each plant should have a space to grow in that is at least the size of a mature carrot, plus a bit more.

So far I have probably made carrot culture sound like pretty picky work. It is at first, but once the carrots are off to a start they take care of themselves quite well. The only supervision they might need is weeding, watering in dry weather, and perhaps a topdressing when they're about 6 inches tall. The last succession crop—protected in winter by a straw mulch and/or a cold frame in cold climates—really repays you for your trouble because the roots are so deliciously sweet once they experience a few good frosts. They stay this way right up until the time they start to regrow. Carrots are biennials which, left to their own devices, would normally go to seed the second summer of their lives. When they begin their second-year growth, they start to use up their stored sugars and their flavor diminishes. This happens at about the time the days become ten hours long— early February at our latitude, some time in January for most of the country. If you see flowers resembling Queen Anne's lace in your carrot patch, these are from overwintered carrot roots. It's important to pull the carrots before this happens—unless of course you enjoy picking Queen Anne's lace.

PESTS AND DISEASES

Carrot problems are usually minimal. Carrot diseases are not common, but most, including carrot yellows, can be avoided by crop rotation. Rotating the crop will also deter the one serious pest, the carrot rust fly. Using floating row covers on the early crops will also solve the problem; the fly will not bother your late plantings.

HARVEST

Pull carrots up by grasping the shoulders and giving them a bit of a wiggle or twist when you pull them up. If they don't come easily, stick a digging fork into the soil, parallel to the row, and waggle it to loosen the soil's grip; then pull. Once the carrots are out, cut off the stems right away, leaving an inch or two of green for looks (you can cook them with the green sprig attached). Carrot tops look beautiful, but they will keep right on growing. This draws moisture and nourishment out of the roots and leaves them limp, wrinkled, and tasteless.

Carrots keep a long time in storage, either in the root cellar or the fridge. You can freeze the small tenderest ones, but use the heavy-duty "keepers" in soups and stews or simmered with butter and a little honey until all the cooking liquid has evaporated.

VARIETIES

Good short early varieties include the Chantenay varieties such as 'Royal Chantenay.' I love the sweet Nantes types such as the early 'Mokum' and the later 'Scarlet Nantes.' Good long-storage carrots are the Imperator types such as 'Orlando Gold' or 'A-plus,' which is especially nutritious. For fun, grow one of the little ball-shaped carrots such as 'Parmex,' or the purple-red 'Nutri-Red,' which is very high in beta carotene and better cooked than raw. The best cold-weather carrot is 'Napoli.' It is everything that a commercial carrot is not. It lacks the tough shoulders developed for machine harvesting, and it's too crisp and juicy to resist shattering when dropped on the floor. That's why it's so good.

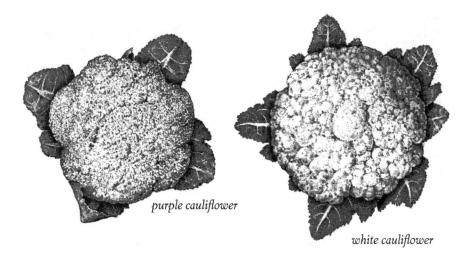

purple cauliflower

white cauliflower

Cauliflower

AULIFLOWER REALLY IS A FLOWER. The big, lumpy white "head" that we eat is a cluster of flower buds nested inside a cabbagelike plant. I think that cauliflower is the sweetest, mildest-tasting member of the cabbage family, but home gardeners grow it far less often than the other brassicas. Why? Probably because it won't tolerate either very hot or very cold weather, so there is only a short season before and after the summer heat in which it thrives. Also, most varieties need to be blanched—their heads covered with leaves while they are maturing. Unblanched heads turn green and don't taste as good as white ones. It's a tricky crop that requires a little extra effort.

Yet cauliflower certainly has its place in the garden. It is a good source of calcium and other vitamins. It freezes well. It is fairly expensive to buy in the store. And it can be grown well if you time it right, respect its need for consistent moisture,

and take the trouble to blanch it. Even the so-called self-blanching varieties need to have some of the leaves pulled over the developing head to keep it white, tasty, and tender. There are also purple-headed varieties that look like broccoli when cooked but taste nonetheless like cauliflower and do not need blanching.

SITE

Choose a sunny, well-drained spot where other cabbage-family vegetables have not grown recently. Space requirements are the same as for cabbage.

SOIL

Provide the same soil conditions that you would for other brassicas. The soil should be fairly rich, especially in nitrogen and potassium. The pH should be 6.5 to 7.0. And plenty of organic matter should be incorporated into the soil, so that it will retain moisture. It's best to dig compost or well-rotted manure into the soil the fall before planting.

PLANTING

Cauliflower plants can take a little frost at the very beginning and the very end of their lives, but not much, and they won't form nice heads in long, cold springs. In short-season areas cauliflower usually works best as a fall crop, of which there can be several successions, each a week or two apart. Plant these from late May to early July, depending on how cold your climate is. The idea is to allow two to three months between the time you set it out and the first frosts. Purple-head cauliflower takes longer—about 85 days to harvest. In hot climates you can plant it in fall for a winter crop.

For spring crops start seeds indoors, four to six weeks before setting the plants out. Keep the seedlings at about 70 degrees, with a steady supply of moisture. The roots don't like to be disturbed in transplanting, so use peat pots or soil blocks. When they're about 6 inches tall they can be planted outside, as long as it is no earlier than three or four weeks before the last expected frost. You can set the plants outside in a protected spot to harden off a week or two earlier.

Space plants about 18 to 24 inches apart. Build a saucer of earth around each plant to help it hold water (page 43), and use cutworm collars (page 65). Fall crops of cauliflower can be sown directly in the garden, but to save space you can start them indoors, outdoors in a cold frame, or in a nursery-bed section of your garden, then transplant them to their growing place. Otherwise sow them in hills (clusters) and thin them to one seedling per hill.

GROWING

The most important thing about raising cauliflower is to keep the growth going. It cannot sit out a hot dry spell. If the weather is dry, give the soil a good soaking until the surface moisture meets up with the ground moisture. A mulch will help keep the water from evaporating. If the heads are still not growing bigger, top-dress the plants with a balanced liquid organic fertilizer.

The white flower head that emerges is called a curd or a button. When it is egg-size, blanch it by bending over the big leaves that surround the curd so they cover it; then tuck them in on the opposite side, breaking the ribs of the leaves to keep them from springing back. If the head still doesn't stay covered, tie some leaves together at the top with a string or rubber band. The idea is to keep light and moisture out but let some air in, and also leave some space in which the head can grow. The heads should not be covered when the plant is wet, or they may rot. Water the ground *around* the plants and keep the soil water constant.

PESTS AND DISEASES

For pests and diseases treat cauliflower the way you would broccoli, cabbage, or Brussels sprouts. As usual, good growing practices help thwart both pests and diseases; floating row covers can be an aid for the former, resistant varieties for the latter.

HARVEST

Check the heads from time to time to see if they are large enough—about 6 inches across but still tight, with the buds unopened. Some varieties have larger heads—up to 12 inches or more—so consult the information on the seed package or in the catalog.

When they're ready, cut them right away at the base and either use them or freeze them. Alternatively, you can pull up the whole plant, roots and all, and store it in a cool cellar where it will keep for at least a month.

VARIETIES

The Snowball varieties, such as 'Snowball' and 'Snow King,' are large-headed late crops. The early 'Snow Crown' is more dependable, and one of the best cauliflowers to start with. You might also experiment with some of the nonwhite varieties such as 'Purple Head,' or one of the green, chartreuse, or gold-colored ones, to avoid the whole issue of blanching. The Romanesco types are a wonder of natural geometry, their yellow-green heads actually clusters of spirals within spirals; two varieties are 'Tower' and 'Minaret.'

Celery

Few GARDENERS TRY TO GROW celery because they think of it as cheap to buy and fussy to grow. But it does taste good and fresh if you grow your own, and frankly, traditional methods of growing celery are fussier than they need to be. Blanching the celery to produce a white stalk is no longer considered to be a necessity. All that mounding of soil and shoring up of plants and tying of collars and what have you got? A plant with fewer vitamins. The green celery we buy in the store is proof that today's green varieties do not need blanching to taste good.

You can grow celery in any climate if you time it right. Some of the older varieties take a long time to grow—four months or more from seed to harvest—and all dislike hot summers. So sow it in the fall in hot areas, and in early spring in cold ones. The short frost-free season in very cold states is compensated for by relatively cool summers. Celery likes those.

If growing celery still seems uninspiring to you, consider celeriac, also called celery root or celery knobs. This gourmet celery produces a large, gnarled root that is hard to find in stores and is much easier to grow than ordinary celery. It doesn't replace celery, since the tops are tough and only good for flavoring stocks and broths. (Botanically they are the same plant, but one has been bred for an enlarged stem, the other for root.) But the roots have a mild celery flavor. Encountered in the market for the first time, celeriac looks ugly and intimidating. People are always asking me, "What do you *do* with it?" Well, I use it in soups and stews, in a purée, mashed together with potatoes or layered with them in a scalloped or gratin dish. I include it in stir-fries and in mixed roasted vegetables with garlic. One of my favorite ways to use it is raw, marinated in a vinaigrette or rémoulade dressing. Another is to parboil it, slice it, bread it, fry it in butter, then squirt it with lemon juice and garnish it with parsley. And so on.

SITE

If you have mucky soil or a high water table, you have an ideal place for celery and you owe it to yourself to grow it. Celery by choice grows in marshes. But if your soil is of average moisture, you can still grow it, and it will also tolerate partial shade. You don't need a lot of space for a celery crop. An 8-foot row will yield about ten bunches of celery, or the same number of celery knobs.

SOIL

Celery is a heavy, even gluttonous feeder; it needs very rich soil. It is an equally

voracious drinker. Large amounts of well-rotted manure tilled into the bed are great, as are compost and peat moss. Plenty of organic matter will help to keep the soil moist as well as enriching it and making boron (an element especially important for this crop) more available to the plants. Calcium is important too, in order to avoid a sinister-sounding disease called black heart. The best pH range is 6.0 to 7.5. Adding lime to boost the pH may take care of the plants' calcium needs as well.

PLANTING

Given a choice, it's easier to buy seedlings than grow celery from seed. The seeds are tiny, take about two weeks to germinate, and need plenty of light, warmth, and moisture. But local nurseries seldom have a good range of varieties, and they may not have celeriac at all. So you may want to raise a seed crop anyway. For a spring-planted crop, start seeds indoors about ten weeks before the last average frost date. For a late crop, start in May or June. Sow in soil blocks or flats in a light potting medium, just pressing seeds lightly into the surface. Keep perfectly moist, 70 to 75 degrees.

Spring transplants go in around the time of the last average frost—but only if the soil and the weather have started to warm up—and they should not be set outside in the cold to harden off. The plant is a biennial, and if the temperatures are still in the 40s during the day the celery may think it is going into its first winter, then set seed when temperatures begin to climb. This will cause it to form a tough flower stalk at the center of the bunch. Celeriac seedlings can bolt if it is cold also. The plants should be about 5 to 6 inches tall and spaced about 10 inches apart. Set the crowns a bit below soil level. Even if the soil is already fertile, giving each seedling a cupful of liquid fertilizer at planting time is a good insurance policy. You might use manure tea (water in which manure has been steeped) or fish emulsion that has been diluted according to the directions on the bottle. Periodic doses every few weeks or so will keep them growing vigorously. Mulching at planting time will help protect them from chilling and moisture stress.

GROWING

Water well, especially in a drought. This is really the key to celery, as with other vegetables whose edible parts are filled with water. Keep the bed weeded. The finely branched, hungry roots will not tolerate competition. Celeriac is grown the same way. It is less affected by heat, cold, or dry weather, although watering in a serious drought is necessary to keep the centers firm and tender.

celeriac

PESTS AND DISEASES

Good seeds, good soil, and steady watering will ward off most diseases. Early blight and late blight of celery are fungus diseases best fought with a tidy, debris-free garden and well-grown plants. Celery worms can be picked off, but do consider that they will turn into the black swallowtail butterfly if not destroyed, and that the damage they do is minimal.

HARVEST

Pick outside stalks as you need them, or harvest a whole plant, cutting it off at the base when it looks like a proper mature bunch of celery. Cut promptly, before the stalks have a chance to turn pithy. Sometimes you can prolong your harvest past the first frosts in fall by mulching heavily with straw.

Celeriac roots can be dug as soon as they are a few inches in diameter, but you'll want to leave many of them in the ground to attain full size. They can sometimes get as big as a small grapefruit. They will take some frost but should be dug before a hard freeze. I loosen the soil with a digging fork, then yank up the plants and cut off the tops, leaving an inch or so of stem. I store them with all the dangling side roots still attached. (In the store these are sometimes cut off.)

Celery can be stored for several weeks, and sometimes several months in a cool cellar—pretty good for a green crop. But even in this respect celeriac puts it to shame. I have kept fall-harvested roots as late as the following June in our root cellar.

VARIETIES

Among the most reliable celery varieties are 'Ventura' and 'Utah 52-70.' The Pascal types are bolt resistant. Years ago, strong-flavored red celery was popular. It's perhaps a more nutritious vegetable, but better suited to cooking than eating raw. An improved variety called 'Redventure' has a lot of the assertive flavor of the old types but less stringiness. Southern gardeners will have good luck with the Florida series. For celeriac, try 'Diamant' and 'Brilliant.'

Cooking Greens

curly kale

Swiss chard

flowering kale

mustard greens

collard greens

"COOKING GREEN" IS USUALLY A leafy vegetable that is commonly considered too tough to be eaten raw the way you'd eat lettuce. Swiss chard and kale are typical examples. But just about any cooking green can be enjoyed raw when the leaves are young and tender. And lettuce can also be cooked—it is braised by the French and stir-fried by the Chinese. Eating raw greens, in fact, is a relatively modern practice. In colonial times almost all greens were called pot herbs because they were cooked in a pot. A colonial salad, or sallet, was usually a dish of boiled greens. So let's substitute a more positive definition for cooking greens: they are leafy crops that have enough substance to hold up well in cooking.

I happen to think cooked greens are underrated. They don't have to be overcooked, bitter, or boring. Try Swiss chard cooked in bouillon and served with lemon wedges, or collards simmered with small cubes of good slab bacon. Often the simplest treatment is best. I like any green steamed lightly and buttered. Or sautéed in a big skillet with olive oil and garlic. And remember that all sorts of surprising plants can be cooked vegetable dishes if you experiment a bit. For instance, I once grew a long row of borage in my garden. I enjoyed the brilliant blue flowers but forgot what you were supposed to do with the leaves (make a broth to instill courage in the soul, tradition says). I simmered them, ate them with butter, and found them quite good. If you don't mind eating leaves that are slightly furry, give borage a try. My sister Anne once served me lamb's quarters, a rampant weed most gardeners grow whether they want to or not. She made them the way you would make creamed spinach, and they had a good, fresh-tasting flavor.

The following greens are more usual choices. All are very easy to grow and outrageously nutritious, with high levels of vitamin A, vitamin C, calcium, and folic acid. Furthermore, they're cool-weather crops that you can really appreciate after the avalanche of summer harvests is over. The tomatoes have been canned, the beans are all in the freezer, but kale, collards, mustard, and Swiss chard are still fresh in the garden and just starting to taste their best. Some even winter over!

Kale

KALE, AS A GREEN, IS REALLY SOMEthing of a rainbow. The type we call Siberian kale is more blue than green. Scotch kale (also called curly kale) is gray-green. Tuscan kale is green-black. Certain others have maroon or red ribs. Flowering kale is so named because its multicolored heads look like giant blooms in combinations of white, green, and vivid pink. It is useful as a fall annual in the flower garden or some other spot in the ornamental landscape, and is as edible as the more subdued types, though perhaps not as tasty. Used

raw as a garnish it adds bright color to a plate. Other kales are used for garnishing too because they are so handsome to look at and because they're slow to wilt.

Kale matures in two months or less, so you can grow a spring crop before summer weather toughens the leaves. But its greatest value is as a fall crop you can plant at your leisure, after the great spring rush. Start fall kale anytime from June till about two months before the first frost (frost will actually improve the flavor). Give it a rich, humusy soil and side-dress it with manure tea (page 20) or an organic liquid fertilizer if you want to speed up growth. Kale, collards, and mustard like a pH above 5.5, so add garden lime if your soil is very acid; limestone also contains the calcium that kale needs.

Kale can be started indoors, or sown directly in the garden in early spring, ½ inch deep. When the seedlings come up, thin them so they're about 18 inches apart. Don't crowd them. If you're growing them from transplants, set them in the soil a few inches deeper than they were in their pots.

Keep the moisture constant by mulching and watering as needed, because the roots are shallow and the plant can easily dry out. A good mulch will also help to extend your harvest into the winter. In warm climates kale is sown in late summer for a continuous winter harvest. And even in my cold Maine climate, the roots often survive over the winter and regrow in spring! Pests and diseases are the same as for the other brassicas, but tend to be minimal.

Pick the outside leaves while they're still tender, and the plant will continue to produce from the inside out. Just keep picking until frost starts to diminish the leaf quality. Kale freezes well, but my neighbor Chip Wadsworth taught me another trick: just pick the leaves before the first hard freeze and store them in a big plastic bag in the root cellar or in an unheated shed. Even if they freeze they may keep for many weeks.

I like the curly varieties such as 'Dwarf Blue Curled Vates' ("Vates" is an acronym for the Virginia Truck Experiment Station) or the ultra-hardy 'Winterbor.' I sometimes grow flowering kale but I appreciate the subtle beauty of the standard eating types more. 'Red Russian' is especially glamorous in the garden; its blue leaves are richly veined in rose-red. I also love the deep maroon 'Redbor.' My favorite is Tuscan kale, also called black kale or dinosaur kale. This plant makes a big vase of narrow, deep green-black, pebbly textured leaves. I've seen it sold as 'Toscano,' 'Lacianato,' and 'Cavolo Nero.'

Collards

COLLARDS BELONG TO THE SAME genus and species as kale, but the two plants grow differently. Collards look like cabbages that have failed to form a head, sitting on top of an upright stem. They are especially popular in the south, where they are grown as a winter crop, usually from transplants, but I have grown them from seed in northern Connecticut as a summer-to-fall crop and found them very easy. They can take some heat and some early frosts. They like the same growing conditions as kale but can be planted a little closer together. A shot or two of fish emulsion will help produce good, healthy dark green

leaves. Harvest them the same way you do kale (the inner leaves are the tastiest).

'Georgia' and the shorter 'Vates' are standbys; 'Georgia' is tall and might even need staking. 'Champion' and 'Hicrop' are compact and heat tolerant. I've also enjoyed growing a beautiful red-stemmed heirloom collard, shared by a friend, from which I now save seed.

Mustard Greens

THE MUSTARD SEED FROM WHICH hotdog mustard is made comes from several different plants. This green is not one of them. Sometimes called Chinese or Indian mustard, it is grown not for its seeds but for its foliage, which has a sharp flavor when raw, a milder one when cooked. The young leaves are wonderful raw, used to pep up salads.

Mustard greens mature fast—sometimes in as little as thirty days! But they need a fairly light, rich, sandy loam and constant moisture to perform this neat trick. A cold-weather plant, mustard is a good bet for spring or fall—easy to do with such a quick crop. Direct-sow the seeds as early as possible, ½ inch deep, in either blocks or rows. Thin the seedlings to 4 to 6 inches apart, munching the thinnings as you go. Harvest the plants before they go to seed. You can plant a succession of mustard crops, up until 6 to 8 weeks before the first frost, or you can cut the whole plant to just above the soil surface and wait for it to put out a whole new set of leaves.

Mustard has no serious pests or diseases to speak of; flea beetles can be controlled with floating row covers. Good varieties are

'Giant Southern Curled' (for fall), 'Green Wave' (a bolt-resistant variety for spring), and 'Tendergreen' (an especially quick, mild crop). 'Florida Broadleaf' is mild and bolt resistant. Asian types include 'Giant Red,' with beautiful red/pink/pale leaves, or the darker 'Osaka Purple.' I love both in salads and stir-fries.

Swiss Chard

THIS GREEN DOES NOT BELONG TO THE cabbage family. Essentially, it is the same plant as the beet. As with celery and celeriac, different parts of the plant have been bred for different purposes. With regular beets (which the Europeans call beet-roots), it is the underground part we prize, as well as the greens. With chard (which the Australians call silverbeet), the action is all aboveground, and it is the leaves and stems that have been taught to grow to a magnificent size. Since the stems, when mature, take longer to cook than the leaves, the two are sometimes used separately. I use both in stir-fries, but add the leaves toward the end. The fresh young leaves of chard—less then 4 inches long—are referred to as "butter chard" in our household because of their softness and tenderness. They are delicious in salads and we harvest them continuously from the cold frame or greenhouse in wintertime.

Swiss chard does not bolt in hot weather the way spinach does. Though not as cold tolerant as kale, it will often survive a cold winter and resprout in spring. But since it is a biennial, those second-year plants will soon go to seed, so you really need to sow a new crop each year.

Swiss chard is not fussy about soil, but given carte blanch it would choose a loose, rich loam with a pH between 6.0 and 7.0. For a summer crop, sow it directly in the garden in spring—two or three weeks before the average last frost. (If you grow from transplants, set them out when the weather has warmed, to prevent bolting.) Sow in midsummer for a fall crop and in fall for a winter crop in warm areas. The "seeds" are actually little pods containing several seeds, as with beets. This makes them easy to space an inch apart when you plant them. Later you'll need to thin them gradually (eating the thinnings) until the plants are the desired spacing. For baby-leaf harvest, you can thin to 2 to 4 inches apart; for full-size plants, 10 inches. With large plants it's best to pick the outer leaves and let the inner ones keep growing, though you can also chop off the whole plant, just as for mustard, and let it regenerate. Top-dressing with a liquid fertilizer will ensure robust, productive plants. Few pests will bother them.

'Fordhook Giant' is a tried-and-true variety, good for both butter chard or a full-size harvest. 'Perpetual Chard' regrows well when cut back. I also grow 'Rhubarb Chard' (also called 'Ruby Chard'). It is dark green with brilliant crimson stems and veins, and I'm always a sucker for plants that look beautiful in the garden. 'Bright Lights' is a marvelous seed mixture that produces plants with veins in neon shades of red, pink, orange, and yellow.

Corn

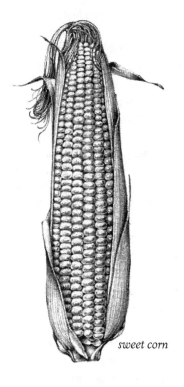

sweet corn

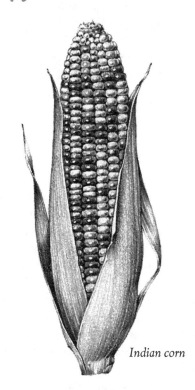

Indian corn

WHEN I WAS A KID, HARVESTING corn was a triathlon. First you picked the ears, then you ran back to the house from field or garden at full speed, then you husked the ears quickly so they could be plunged into the waiting pot of boiling water. Total time from stalk to serving plate was not supposed to exceed 20 minutes, lest the sweetness be lost as the kernels' supply of sugar turned to starch. Nowadays, high-sugar corns have been developed that hold on to their sweet taste, and the triathlon is rarely run anymore, except by diehards like me. I think the freshest corn is still the best.

Growing corn is so much a part of our heritage that our folk wisdom is full of advice about it. "Put one fish head in each hill, as the Indians did," we are told. "Plant the seeds when the oak leaves are the size of a squirrel's ear." The corn should be "knee high by the Fourth of July." Corn culture is now far more scientific than it used to be, but the old basic advice still holds up well, and no red-blooded American gardener should have much trouble producing a stand of corn.

There are so many different corn varieties that it's hard to know which to choose, but this leads the gardener to experiment. A popcorn patch is fun, especially if you have children. I have enjoyed raising an ancient Native American flint corn to make cornmeal for real homegrown cornmeal muffins. Most gardeners choose to grow sweet corn.

I enjoyed the new "sugar-enhanced" and "supersweet" corn varieties at first. They stay sweet for days after being picked or cooked. Even if they've gotten so old they're tough as cow corn, they still taste like sugar. And even the yellow varieties, which are the most vitamin-rich, are sweet, while in the old days it seemed only the less nutritious white ones were. But the super-sweets are watery rather than creamy, and with both I find the sweetness too cloying. I also don't like the fact that they make me lazy about cooking up a fresh batch each time. Leftover vegetables are never as nutritious or flavorful. And the supersweets are also trickier to grow and less resistant to pests and diseases.

Indian corn, with its multicolored kernels, is rewarding to grow for fall center-pieces and house decorations. You can also grind it into cornmeal for cooking. The dwarf corn varieties might be the best choice if your space is very limited. You can even find Asian "baby corn"—those tiny ears you eat whole, cob and all. They grow on short stalks, but there are five or six ears on each one, as opposed to the one or two that most corn stalks bear.

SITE

A corn plant is really just a huge stem of grass. It takes up a lot of room vertically but not horizontally, so even a fairly modest vegetable garden can have a place for it. All it needs is a sunny spot where it won't shade what is next to it (unless you're deliberately using corn as a screen to protect a crop from hot sun). If your property is very windy, find a sheltered spot for your corn if you can, because it can blow over.

If you have the space to really make a project of corn, you can span a long season with it. Instead of planting one variety that you pick for a week (or all in one day, if you are in a race with the raccoons), plant some early-, middle-, and late-season corn. Or plant one variety in several plantings, two weeks apart. Most varieties take two to three months to grow from seed to harvest, so there's usually time for several overlapping crops between the last spring frost and the first fall one.

This is where site selection comes in. You cannot put different varieties next to one another while they are pollinating. As an annual grass, corn is wind-pollinated; even the slightest breeze brings pollen from the male tassels down to the female silks, each of which, when pollinated, grows a kernel. Pollination will occur whether the pollen falls on the silks of the same plant or on those of one near it, and cross-pollinating can be a problem. The flavor and texture of sweet corn can be affected if it is pollinated by feed corn, cornmeal corn, popcorn, or ornamental corn, because the kernels are, of course, the seeds that result from cross-pollination. This is especially true with modern hybrid corn, particularly the sugar-enhanced and supersweet. One way to avoid this is to time your plantings so that your varieties mature at different times. Another is to separate them physically by a minimum of 25 feet (150 is better). This is possible only if you have plenty of room in your garden. A third solution is to grow only open-pollinated varieties (page 125), which are more stable. A beginner is best off starting with these, or with only one kind of hybrid corn, and getting a good sense of the plant's life cycle before trying a lot of combinations.

SOIL

Corn is a heavy feeder and needs rich soil that is renourished each year at planting time and often while the plant is growing as well. Nitrogen is especially crucial—the Indians knew what they were doing with those fish heads. Dig in well-rotted manure or compost, at least a 1-inch covering each spring.

Corn looks like a shallow-rooted plant, because you can see short roots spreading out on the surface around the plant. But these side roots exist partly to support the tall stalks. The feeder roots go deep, so tilling fertilizer in deeply before planting is beneficial. Lime should be applied in fall as needed to raise or maintain the proper pH, which is between 6.0 and 7.0.

PLANTING

Corn is traditionally sown in the garden around the time of the last average frost, but I wait awhile after that if the weather is cold, to ensure germination. Untreated corn seeds simply will not germinate in soil colder than 65 degrees and even seeds treated with a fungicide (which I prefer not to use) need soil that is above at least 55, and 60 or 65 is better. Treated seeds are usually bright pink in color. If your patch is just a small one, you might push up the date of that first delicious harvest by germinating some seeds indoors in peat pots or soil blocks a week or so before planting. Transplanting or sowing into a cold frame or in a protected spot will help, and you can also use salt hay or straw to keep the soil warmer at night, pushing it aside during the day to let the soil warm up. Or cover the seedlings at night with a plastic sheet. This may sound like an absurd amount of trouble to go to, but some gardeners really have a fetish about early corn.

There are as many "best" ways to plant corn as there are gardeners. You might plant 6 inches apart, then thin to a foot, with the rows 2 feet apart. Or plant on a grid, dropping two seeds in together every 12 inches each way. Or plant six seeds in a hill (cluster), every 2 to 3 feet, then thin to three seedlings. What kind of geometry you use does not make too much difference as long as you sow some extra seeds (because some will not germinate), then thin to the desired spacing. And you need to make sure that stalks are not too close together, to give each plant its share of the light and nutrients. Early and midget varieties that grow 4 to 5 feet tall need less space per plant than do the tall, late-season varieties. Planting in blocks of at least two rows helps to ensure successful pollination.

Corn "seeds" are just kernels of corn. I plant them stretching out a tape measure in the row as a guide, then poking my finger in the ground and dropping one kernel into each hole. I make the holes an inch deep if it is very wet weather, because kernels planted deeper may rot. I might plant them a bit deeper for a late crop in warm or dry weather, when it is important to keep the seeds moist. The deeper they are, the harder it is for the crows to find them and pull them up. (For super-sweet varieties, make the seedbed extra moist and keep it that way until the seeds have germinated; they need twice as much moisture for sprouting.) If your climate is hot and dry, plant in furrows that will catch and hold the rain or the water from your hose. If your climate is cold, plant in raised or slightly mounded beds that warm up quickly. Do not plant past midsummer, because corn does not ripen well in cold weather.

GROWING

As the corn grows, the main thing is to keep it fed and watered. Top-dress with a high-nitrogen fertilizer when the corn is about 8 inches tall, and again when the stalks have tassels. Liquid fish emulsion makes a good topdressing for corn; water well to soak it in.

Keep an eye on the leaves. If they curl up on the sides, it means that the plants are thirsty and you need to give the bed a thorough soaking. Don't let weeds compete with the corn's big appetite for nutrients. Discourage weeds by cultivating around the corn until the shoots are about 6 inches tall, then apply a mulch. After the shallow side roots have formed, it is easy to damage them by cultivating, so a mulch can be very helpful.

Remove any puny stalks because they will not bear corn and will only take up room. With tall varieties, mounding earth around the stalks will provide some extra support and may help them withstand wind better. Don't let an old-timer convince you to remove either side shoots or tassels; the plant needs both. Not *all* folk wisdom is accurate.

PESTS AND DISEASES

The worst threat to corn is usually your local wildlife, starting with crows. Even the biggest, noisiest, tin-can-laden scarecrow will not deter them if they find out that tasty corn kernels are buried in your garden. If this is happening, just replant the seeds and protect them with a chicken wire cover, placed 6 inches off the ground. Remove it when corn shoots reach that height.

Raccoons are the most disastrous. They are ready to harvest your corn for you the minute it is at peak flavor. People put out flashing lights, blaring radios, barriers of thorns to keep the raccoons out. They smear oil on the corn ears and tie plastic bags over them. They lay plastic sheeting, mesh, and aluminum foil along the ground near the corn on the theory that the critters won't walk on it. Sometimes these tricks work, often they don't. Electric fences are the only dependable solution, though they are laborious to install, can short out if weeds touch them, and can do odd things to people's heart pacemakers. An outdoor dog can be very effective—or not, depending on the dog. Humane traps that catch the raccoons are another solution if you keep trapping them and releasing them miles away, but you're just giving your problem to someone else, and other coons will move in to take the old ones' place.

Another deterrent is the trick of growing long-vined winter squash among the corn. If you give the soil some extra nourishment and plant the corn a bit farther apart than usual, the squash will not compete. The raccoons presumably do not like to walk on the leaves, and this interplanting is a good way to use garden space. The huge leaves also act as a mulch. I have had good luck with this method, but perhaps it was just that—luck. My husband thinks the idea is useless.

Squirrels can be a problem also, though they've never bothered my corn. I have heard that slipping small paper bags over the ears can deter them.

European corn borers can attack the leaves, stalks, and the base of the ears. If you find signs of their damage you can poke a knife into their little entrance holes and destroy them. After harvest, destroy or compost corn stalks promptly to prevent the borers' larvae from wintering over, and never try brushing the worms off because they will just lay eggs on the ground.

If you plant late corn in order to avoid the borers, you might be just in time for a late infestation of corn earworms. These munch on the silks, causing incomplete pollination, then crawl in through the tips of the ears where they devour kernels and often each other. Even in a really bad earworm year there are plenty of good ears if I pick them promptly, and I don't even mind cutting out some of the bad parts of each ear. But an industrious gardener who notices the problem early can prevent a good deal of damage by squirting a bit of mineral oil into the tip of the ear with an eyedropper when the silks start to wither, signaling that pollination is complete. Then when the silks are brown, open up the husks just enough to pick off the worms and crush them. Do not allow them to pupate over the winter in the soil. Certain corn varieties, such as 'Silver Queen,' have ears that are more difficult for the worms to penetrate.

Corn smut is an unappealing grayish black mass that sometimes appears in corn ears. A fungus, it is filled with spores that spread when the mass bursts. Catch it and burn it before it does so, preferably in its earlier white stage. Or buy a good Mexican cookbook—this edible fungus, called *huitlacoche* south of the border, is a great delicacy in soups and other dishes.

HARVEST

When do you pick the corn? "Just before the raccoons do" is the usual country retort. Beat them to their raid by watching for big dark green ears whose silks have turned brown. The ears should feel firm and the tip should feel rounded, not pointed. If in doubt, peel back just enough of the husk to reveal a few kernels to check for ripeness; they should be up to size and squirt milky juice when pricked with your fingernail. Don't let them stay on the stalk after ripening, unless they're being grown for cornmeal, for ornament, or for popping. Popcorn should dry for a month on the plant, then a month or so on the picked cob. Only when it is thoroughly dry will it pop. Corn yields vary, but most early corn produces one ear per stalk; most late corn produces two.

VARIETIES

Of the open-pollinated (nonhybrid) types, some old favorites are 'Improved Golden Bantam' (midseason) and the white 'Country Gentleman.' Open-pollinated types for cornmeal include the beautiful multicolored 'Mandan Bride' and the Yellow Dent types such as 'Nothstine.' Of the hybrids, 'Early Sunglow' makes a nice early crop, perhaps followed by the midseason old favorite 'Butter and Sugar.' For late corn the old standby is 'Silver Queen,' but life is often more interesting if you shop around.

Indian corns are usually sold as Ornamental Indian Corn mixtures, but some named varieties are 'Painted Mountain' and 'Strawberry,' which is actually a popcorn. Other named popcorns include 'Japanese Hulless' and 'Robust.'

Cucumbers

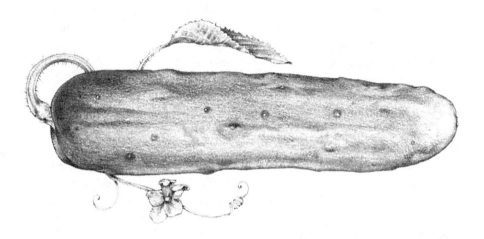

C UCUMBERS HAVE COME A LONG way. If you grew them 20 years ago and gave up because they got diseases, or they turned out great but gave you indigestion, or they just didn't seem all that interesting, try again! Today there are many good disease-resistant varieties, less bitter ones, even "burpless" ones that you don't have to peel. There are also ones with interesting shapes, such as the skinny "yard-long" cucumbers, and the little pale yellow ones shaped like lemons. Some of these are the result of new breeding; others are dependable, rediscovered heirlooms.

There are also "gynoecious" varieties that produce more predominantly female flowers than male for a bigger yield. Seedless cucumbers, which do not need to be pollinated, are fine as long as they are designed for outdoor culture and do not have to be protected from the pollinating types. There are also bush types (really just cucumbers with short vines), but they tend not to be as healthy or productive, and space-saving is best accomplished by vertical culture.

SITE

Native to the tropics, cucumbers like warm weather but not intense, dry heat. They are not frost hardy, but since they grow and mature quickly (55 to 60 days, usually), it is easy to get a crop even with a short season as long as you plant them in full sun.

Before you decide where to put cucumbers, you need to think about how they're going to grow. The plants have long vines that take up a lot of room. They can be allowed to sprawl on the ground as they grow, but this way you will need to allow about 9 square feet per plant—that's a 6-foot by 9-foot plot if you grow six plants, an ample number unless you're doing a great deal of pickling; one plant can produce a *lot* of cucumbers.

It usually makes more sense, in a home garden, to grow cucumbers vertically.

Getting cucumbers off the ground not only saves space, but it gives you healthier, cleaner fruits. I have often just planted them at the edge of the garden and let them climb up the fence, tying them as they grow. This way I don't have to erect a separate support structure. But supports are not difficult to provide. Some people grow them up stakes or up trellises hung with string, wire, or netting, pinching the growing tip when it reaches the top and pruning side shoots to reduce the weight of the vine. Remember that you'll have a big, heavy vine, so whatever support you provide must be a good strong one.

SOIL

Clay soils with plenty of humus in them give the highest cucumber yields, but sandy loam that warms up quickly will produce an earlier, faster crop. Prepare the soil by adding plenty of organic matter, preferably a rich compost or well-rotted manure, because cucumbers like fertile soil. The pH should be about 6.0 to 6.5.

PLANTING

Cucumbers are often started indoors two weeks before planting to extend the season, but don't bother unless you can keep your seeds at 70 to 80 degrees by day and no colder than 60 degrees at night. Otherwise it's better to wait until the soil has warmed up. If you do sow indoors, keep the planting medium moistened but well drained. Soil blocks or peat pots work best because you can later set them out in the garden without even having to disturb the roots— something cucumbers particularly dislike. I sow a few seeds to a pot without firming the soil and thin to the tallest seedling— snipping, not pulling, the discards.

If you sow directly in the garden, you can either plant in hills (clusters) or rows, about ½ inch deep. Rows work better if you're using a vertical support. When the seedlings are a few inches tall, thin to a foot apart in the row, with rows about 3 feet apart. Enrich the rows before you plant. A good way to do this is to dig a trench, put a few inches of rotted manure in the bottom, then cover the manure with an inch or two of soil so it cannot come in contact with the seeds.

If the ground and the air remain cold, protect them with cloches or some other heat-conserving device such as floating row covers. The latter are a good idea anyway, to prevent cucumber beetles from moving in on the new plants. Be sure to remove the covers when the female blossoms appear, so that they can be pollinated. The female flowers are the ones with a small swelling at the base, which will eventually become the fruit. Once the covers are off, you can set up your vertical supports and gently start the vines upward by winding them around your chosen device. They will catch on to the idea right away.

GROWING

Mulch is especially worthwhile for cucumbers, for several reasons. Any that lie on the ground are better protected from disease and rot if there is mulch for them to lie on. Also, since the fruits are mostly water, the plants need an extra-big, consistent water supply, and mulch will help keep the soil evenly moist. Mulch will also keep down the weeds. This is important because weeding can damage cucumber roots to the point where the whole plant dies. (Careful weeding and cultivating are fine when the plants are small.) When they get to be about a foot high, give them a good topdressing of manure tea or a liquid seaweed fertilizer. This can be repeated from time to time as needed.

You'll still need to soak the plants in dry weather. If you have planted in hills, you might like to try the coffee-can method—putting a can with holes punched in the bottom in the center of each hill. For rows, try a soaker hose or drip system along the row. But try not to brush against the plants when they are wet—either from watering or from rain—this is how disease spreads. And do not confuse "steady moisture" with "standing water." The plants need good drainage.

PESTS AND DISEASES

The worst cucumber pest is also the culprit behind some of the cucumber diseases. The cucumber beetle (striped in the east, spotted in the west) can damage the plants by chewing but does even more harm by spreading bacterial wilt and mosaic. Pick off any beetles you find, checking for them inside the flowers as well as on the leaves. It's easiest to do this in the early morning when they move more slowly. Removing them with a vacuum cleaner, using the slot attachment, is another great trick. You can also protect the young plants by covering them with floating row covers (page 260). Another safeguard is to make several plantings several weeks apart in case one whole planting is destroyed. If all the plants make it, then you'll just have an extra-large harvest.

Cucumbers are prone to certain fungus diseases such as anthracnose, downy mildew, and powdery mildew. The best defense is to buy resistant varieties ('H19

Little Leaf' is one) and give them the growing conditions they need to keep them healthy.

HARVEST

Cucumbers are one of those vegetables that *have* to be picked, whether you have too many of them or not. Feed them to the neighbors or the compost pile, or the pig, but don't stop picking. If they yellow on the vine, the plant will stop producing altogether. Check the seed packet or catalog to see how big each variety is supposed to get, and don't let them exceed that size. In fact many are best picked when small, especially if you're planning to pickle them. Twist them off gently or snip them off with clippers, but use two hands, and be very careful not to break the fragile vines.

VARIETIES

Most cucumbers are either the smooth slicing types (for salads or cooking) or the pickling types. The pickling ones are smaller, faster producing, and have little knobs all over them. Good slicing varieties include the open-pollinated Marketmore series and the popular, mild, burpless 'Sweet Slice' and 'Burpee Hybrid II.' (They should have named one of them 'Burpee Burpless'!) 'Diva' is a good modern variety.

For pickling cucumbers try 'West India Gherkin' and 'Parigno Cornichon.' It's also fun to experiment with the long, twisted, striped Armenian types, which are big on flavor. 'Suyo Long' is a good heirloom variety. I also like the little round 'Lemon,' a crisp, tasty heirloom cuke, good for both pickling and fresh eating.

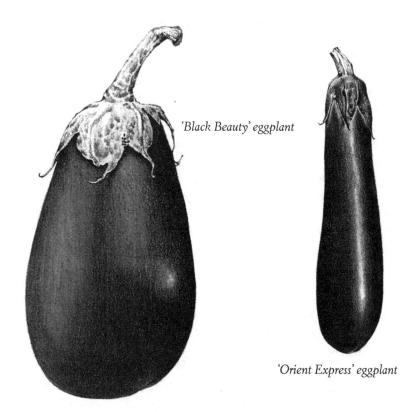

'Black Beauty' eggplant

'Orient Express' eggplant

Eggplant

GGPLANT IS HAPPIEST IN A GARDEN with five months of hot weather, which certainly does not describe mine. It's not as nutritious as some vegetables, having relatively few vitamins and little protein, despite its frequent use as a main-course meat substitute. But I love eggplant. I love to fry it, broil it, stuff it, bake it. So I grow it anyway, and the more effort I put into it, the more successful I am.

The plant gets its name from a small white Asian variety that is seldom grown in this country. We're used to seeing the large, shiny purple kind, although the long, skinny purple Asian ones are becoming more and more popular. Cold-climate gardeners buy seedlings from a nursery, or start their own indoors anywhere from 8 to 12 weeks before the last average frost date. Sowing eggplant is sometimes the first garden job I do in the new year, crossing my fingers that it will be a sunny one, for a certain amount of eggplant culture is sheer luck.

SITE

Grow eggplant in the sunniest spot you can find, where other plants in the same family have not grown recently (page 247). It does well in raised beds, because the soil there will warm up more quickly than in flat ones. Raised beds will also give the plants the good drainage they require; they will not thrive in soggy soil. Garden writer Nancy Bubel even recommends growing them in large containers, to warm up the soil. Actually, growing eggplants in containers is a good design trick as well. The plants are quite beautiful with their dark green foliage, luminous purple blossoms, and handsome glossy fruits. Imagine one in a terra-cotta pot, surrounded with trailing nasturtiums in sunny colors.

SOIL

A heavy feeder, eggplant likes rich soil, made porous by the addition of humus to promote quick growth and good drainage. Dig in well-rotted manure or compost the fall before, if possible. A pH of about 6.0 is ideal.

PLANTING

Germination will be slow (10 to 12 days) unless you soak seeds overnight and keep the soil very warm—in the 80s if possible (see page 34). The only other alternative is patience, and if you let the soil get below 50 degrees, your patience will be sorely tried. Sow the seeds in a loose, fine potting medium and transplant when seedlings are 2 to 3 inches tall to 4-inch pots filled with a loose, rich soil mix.

Set out plants after danger of frost, but not if the soil still feels cold and the weather is chilly. Hardening them off and bringing them in at night will give them a good start, but do not plant them unless the weather is really starting to warm up. It does help to warm the soil with black plastic before you set out the plants, and then put a portable cold frame over them. There's nothing wrong with transplanting them up to larger and larger pots until the weather is more auspicious.

When you do set them in the ground, the plants should be spaced about 2 feet apart each way. Eggplant is not a crop to grow too intensively; the plants will be more vigorous and disease free with ample space, and the fruits will ripen faster if the sun can get in between them. Enrich each planting hole with a shovelful of compost or a cup or two of liquid fertilizer, water well, and firm the soil gently. Put cutworm collars around the young plants if these pests are a problem in your garden.

GROWING

Do not cultivate around the plants, or you may hurt the shallow roots. Pull weeds carefully instead, or use a mulch. You can even plant a quick early crop around the young eggplants, such as lettuce or chervil, or even a flower like alyssum, to provide a living mulch and make use of all that wide spacing. Pour more liquid fertilizer around the plants when they're starting to bloom, and at least once a month until harvest. Keep the soil moist.

Some people pinch the stems' growing tips, the bottom suckers, and even some of the blossoms to get better production. I don't know whether this is worth doing. The main thing is to get your crop started early, choose early varieties if you have a short, cool season, and make sure the plants do not suffer a serious setback at any time, from seed to harvest. They may seem to bounce back after a chilling, a drying out, or a pest plague, but even so you may get little or no fruits.

PESTS AND DISEASES

Watch out for Colorado potato beetles and pick them off; better yet, watch for their yellow egg masses on the underside of the leaves and squish those before they hatch. Tomato worms can also be picked off. Aphids and red spiders can be knocked off with a hose. Flea beetles are the worst pest. They're the ones that suddenly riddle the young plants with tiny holes until there's nothing left of them. Covering the plants with floating row covers (page 260) during that early flea-beetle stage will prevent most damage.

Verticillium wilt, a fairly common eggplant problem, can be averted by using resistant varieties and crop rotation. Fungi such as phomopsis blight are also best avoided by planting resistant strains if needed.

HARVEST

You do not have to wait until eggplant is mature to pick it. It can be a third of its mature size and still be worth eating. This is its saving grace. If frost threatens and the fruits are still small, just pick them and serve up a feast of baby eggplant. You'll be *au courant,* and no one will be the wiser. If you have brought the fruits to full size, pick them while the skins are still shiny; if they reach the dull-skin stage they will not taste as good, and if you wait too long, production will slow down as well. To harvest, cut the stems; don't twist them. You can store eggplants a week or two in a cool place.

VARIETIES

The old tried-and-true eggplant variety is 'Black Beauty,' which is open-pollinated and a long-season crop. 'Burpee Hybrid' and 'Dusky Hybrid' are reliable standards and somewhat earlier. For even earlier crops or for short seasons, grow the long thin types such as 'Orient Express.' 'Florida Market' is a standby in the south. The long pink 'Ping Tung' is notably heat resistant. 'Easter Egg' and 'White Beauty' are small white "egg" types. 'Round de Valence' and 'Small Round Italian' are (you guessed it) small round eggplants. In addition, there are eggplants in glowing colors such as the lavender 'Neon'; some are violet streaked with white, some are white streaked with violet. 'Louisiana Long Green,' conservative as to hue, is in the opinion of some the best tasting eggplant.

Boston lettuce

iceberg lettuce

'Black-Seeded Simpson' lettuce

romaine lettuce

Lettuce

SOME LETTUCES ARE FOR LAZY cooks; others are for lazy gardeners. Lazy cooks like 'Iceberg,' that classic American lettuce with the big, tight, firm head that needs little washing and keeps for weeks in the refrigerator. It is the joy of the commercial grower, shipper, or marketer, and of the bachelor who buys it once a month to eat two leaves at a time in his BLT.

For the home gardener, however, such crisphead, or cabbage-head, types can be tricky to bring successfully through a hot summer without bolting (going to seed). Lazy gardeners choose the fast-growing looseleaf types like 'Salad Bowl' and the soft, tender butterhead types, also called Bibb or Boston lettuce (originally these were variety names, but now they usually refer to the type). Gardeners also like the narrow, upright, firm-leaved romaines. As cooks they might complain about the extra effort of washing them, drying them, and keeping them fresh. But as gardeners they give these softer lettuces the prize for easy growing—and for flavor and nutrition, too.

There are so many good lettuce varieties to select from, and they're all so different! Whether planted in contrasting rows and blocks in your garden or tossed in a salad bowl, they are beautiful to mix together. The colors go from pale to dark green, and there are handsome reds and even some with speckles. With some the heads spread wide open, with others they curl tight or stand upright. The leaves can be crinkled, ruffled, or smooth. Tastes differ from mild to strong, and textures from soft to crisp.

Bolted Lettuce

FIG. 50

In growing lettuce you are usually not fighting frost; you're fighting heat. To grow lettuce in the summer you need to either shade the plants or find heat-tolerant varieties. In hot climates you may not be able to grow them in summer at all—only in fall, winter, and spring. Heat makes the plants bolt, each sending up a tall stalk with small, bitter-tasting leaves and a seed head on top (Figure 50).

SITE

Finding a spot for lettuce is easy because you can harvest it so soon after you plant. This means that you can grow it in the spaces between slow-maturing crops such as cabbage, cauliflower, eggplant, and peppers, harvesting it before the slow crops get big. It doesn't even need full sun and will appreciate the shade cast by stands of corn, staked tomatoes, pole beans, or cukes, thus utilizing space that would otherwise go begging. It's also great for tucking into empty spots in the garden where another crop has been harvested. You can even grow it in containers on the terrace or indoors. Better yet, build an insulated cold frame and harvest it into early winter, or longer if your climate allows.

SOIL

Soil for lettuce should be rich, especially in nitrogen. For once, it doesn't matter if the nitrogen makes the crop "all leaf"—that's exactly what lettuce is. Tilling in well-rotted manure or compost is the first step to provide an airy, moisture-retentive texture as well as nutrients. Later on, top-dressing with blood meal, cottonseed meal, or fish emulsion will sustain the quick, steady growth lettuce needs. The ideal soil for a spring crop would be a little on the sandy side, because sandy soil warms up quickly, but heavier soil is just as good for later crops. Lettuce also likes soil that is rather pulverized, just as carrots do, so you might follow an early lettuce crop with a carrot patch. The ideal pH is between 6.0 and 7.0, so lime is sometimes needed.

PLANTING

Sometimes I start lettuce indoors early and transplant it outside, but because where I live so many other things *have* to be started indoors and then transplanted, I'm grateful for crops I can sow directly in the garden if I want to. Nonetheless, it's great to get a jump on the lettuce season by putting in some transplants, especially if you grow the crisphead types that need a long, cool season. Iceberg lettuce will bolt if temperatures are much above 70 degrees for a few days, and can take up to 95 days to mature, so you have to start it early. Even the quicker butterheads and romaines can benefit from this treatment. Looseleaf types need it the least, because they mature in 40 to 50 days.

To start lettuce indoors, sow as early as ten weeks before the last frost, keeping the flats cool (below 70 degrees) and moist. Hardening off for a few days outdoors is worthwhile. Then set the young plants out in the garden as soon as the soil has thawed and dried out a bit. (They will withstand temperatures as low as 20 degrees.) Space them a foot apart each way—less for the more upright or compact varieties.

Lettuce seeds can be sown directly in the garden as soon as the soil can be worked. Try to space the seeds about ½ inch apart if possible—lettuce is a nuisance to thin. Buying pelleted seeds that are easier to space widely will make life simpler. An initial thinning to 2 inches apart will give you some "micro-greens" for garnishing. A second thinning could be made when the leaves are a few inches high—just right for a lovely tender salad—leaving plants spaced a foot apart to grow into full heads. Cut-and-come-again rows of "baby leaf" salads are thinned to just an inch or two apart and can be of either single varieties or a lettuce mixture for instant gourmet salads.

After sowing, cover the seeds with only a fine sprinkling of soil. I rarely sow a whole seed packet; instead I divide it into halves or even less. I do plant several varieties at the same time, though—say, 'Black Seeded Simpson,' 'Summer Bibb,' and 'Red Sails'—so I can have mixed salads. Then I plant all of them in succession throughout the season—small plantings every two weeks if I'm well organized. During the summer you might want to plant a few heat-tolerant varieties such as 'Slobolt,' 'Salad Bowl,' or 'Green Ice,' then at summer's end sow some more quick-growing, cool-weather types like the ones you sowed in spring.

Some years you'll get lettuce well into late fall, even in cold climates, but it is wise to sow some in a cold frame too, for a sure-fire late harvest. This works best with lettuce harvested at baby-leaf size, when it's hardier, not as large heads. Fall sowing can be made as early as mid August in my climate, since growth starts to slow down in the cool days soon to follow. You can also make sowings in the cold frame throughout the fall and winter; these lettuces will often begin a timid growth in February as the days begin to lengthen and give you an early spring crop. Some of the hardiest, such as 'Red Oak Leaf,' will winter over in outdoor beds and regrow in spring, even here in Maine. Baby leaf lettuces can be sown much more closely than head lettuce—½ inch apart in the rows, with the rows as close as 2 inches apart.

GROWING

While lettuce is growing, try to maintain constant moisture. A mulch not only serves this purpose but also keeps down weeds, keeps the lettuce cleaner, and helps ward off fungus diseases that can rot the lower leaves. Even if you've used a mulch, you should soak the ground if the plants seem limp, for the roots are shallow and dry out easily. Lettuce that is watered well also tastes less bitter.

Topdressing from time to time with a nitrogen-rich fertilizer like blood meal, fish emulsion, or manure tea will help keep growth going. To keep lettuce from bolting in warm weather, screen it with shade cloth or lath stretched across frames and placed on vertical supports (page 259). The same apparatus could double as a frame for clear plastic covers for frost protection in fall. You can also sow warm-weather lettuce in a part of the garden that gets dappled shade.

PESTS AND DISEASES

Not much bothers lettuce. Occasional pests include cutworms (use collars if necessary), aphids (hose them off), slugs (trap them or pick them off), and leafhoppers, which spread disease (keep nearby weeds to a minimum and use a garlic spray). Several soil-borne fungi can cause leaf rot. Prevent this by mulching, rotating your crops, and cleaning up all debris promptly. If mil-dew is a problem, plant resistant varieties. Certain varieties will also resist mosaic, but because this disease is spread by aphids and leafhoppers, you can also control it by dealing with them. Tip burn, a disease of the leaves, is sometimes the curse of hot weather; prevent it by giving the plants consistent moisture and some shade, or seek out resistant varieties such as 'Ithaca.'

HARVEST

Lettuces are harvested in different ways, depending on the type. You can pick leaf lettuce from the outside, letting the inner leaves continue to grow, or you can crop the whole thing an inch above the soil and let it resprout. Heading types are usually cut whole, head by head as needed, but these can also be picked outer leaves first. And frankly, any lettuce is worth cutting back to the base if you don't need the space for another crop. There's always a chance you'll get a few tender leaves for salads when there's no other fresh-picked lettuce around. For cut-and-come-again crops, harvest by grasping the tops of the leaves gently and cutting along the row about an inch above the soil with a small serrated knife.

VARIETIES

There are so many new lettuce varieties appearing each year, some of them improvements on the old standards, others more exotic, that it's hard to choose. In the crisphead category, old favorites are 'Ithaca,' 'Burpee Iceberg,' and the heat-tolerant 'Great Lakes' and 'Vanguard.' 'Crispino' is early and easy to grow. Popular butterheads include 'Buttercrunch' and the reddish 'Four Seasons'; in the south grow 'Summer Bibb' for its heat tolerance.

Favorite looseleafs are 'Salad Bowl' and 'Oakleaf' (both come in green or red), 'Red Sails,' and the compact, super-early 'Black-Seeded Simpson.' I try to grow a few of each, but the last is so reliably good that I always include it. The most popular cos, or romaine type, is 'Parris Island Cos,' which grows well in hot or cold climates. In addition to the romaines mentioned below, I also like the delightfully spotted 'Freckles' (also called 'Troutback').

In the north, plant cold-tolerant lettuce varieties like 'Winter Density,' 'Rouge d'Hiver' (both are romaines), and the red oakleaf types for your early and late crops. I've also used the beautiful, frilly 'Lolla Rossa' (red) and 'Tango' (green) for winter salads. In hot climates try 'Sierra' and any other heat-tolerant varieties. On the west coast grow varieties marked "MI," which are mosaic resistant. For small spaces, a good bet is 'Little Gem,' a miniature romaine.

Okra

ROWN FOR ITS EDIBLE SEEDPODS, okra is a handsome plant to have in the vegetable garden. It has showy pale yellow flowers with red centers—not unlike a hollyhock. Okra haters are not impressed by this. They remark that the pods are prickly on the outside and slimy on the inside, and that if they want showy flowers they can grow petunias. Okra lovers, most of whom live below the Mason-Dixon line, point out that modern "spineless" varieties aren't prickly at all, and that the viscous inside is the magic ingredient that thickens the good hearty stew known as gumbo. ("Gumbo" is also another name for the plant itself.)

Okra is popular in the south because it is a warm-weather crop that won't bolt, yellow, die, or otherwise misbehave in midsummer. It just gets taller, lusher, and more productive. It's hard to get started up north, and I've had no success with it in Maine's cool summers, but in more favorable north-ern areas it redeems itself by being, unlike eggplant, a fast-maturing crop once warm weather settles in. So even if you don't plant until late June, you can still pick okra two months later if you urge it along a little. You only need a few plants for the home garden (I'd start with six), though any extra pods can be frozen sliced or whole. Dwarf varieties are available for small spaces. Okra is rarely bothered by pests or diseases.

SITE

Choose a sunny site where the ground will warm up quickly (or even raised beds in the north). Otherwise assign the whole plot to okra for the season. If you grow it each year, rotate the crop, but planting okra where members of the Solanaceae family (page 233) have just grown is not advised. In warm climates where the plants grow as much as 5 to 6 feet tall, they should go in a place where they won't shade other crops (unless of course you want them to). Dwarf varieties that grow to 3 or 4 feet are often more convenient for the home garden.

SOIL

Okra prefers a light, well-drained loam with plenty of organic matter. Avoid heavy soils that warm up slowly, especially up north. A pH of 6.0 to 7.0 is best, and moderately high fertility. I suggest a healthy shovelful of compost or aged manure worked into each planting hole.

PLANTING

Buy new seed each year and speed up the normally slow germination process by soaking the seeds overnight in tepid water. In short-season climates they will need to be started four to six weeks ahead indoors. Sow in soil blocks or peat pots, keeping the soil at 80 to 90 degrees if possible; thin carefully to one seedling. Where the climate permits, direct-sow after the danger of frost has passed. The air temperature should be consistently above 60 or even 70 degrees and the soil no longer wet or cold.

The seeds should be planted ½ inch deep and thinned to 12 to 18 inches apart, in rows spaced 2 to 3 feet apart. In cool climates where the plants do not grow so large they still should not be crammed too close together, to allow as much sun as possible on the pods to ripen them.

GROWING

It's important not to let growth lapse. Gardeners use various warm-up devices to bring the young plants along if it's chilly— raised beds, hot caps, grow tunnels, portable cold frames, and sheets of black plastic slit with an × to allow the plants to grow through them. Keep plants well watered in dry weather; using a mulch will help to conserve water. And top-dress every few weeks with a balanced liquid fertilizer.

PESTS AND DISEASES

Pest and disease problems are usually minimal. Occasional pests such as corn earworms, cabbage loopers, and stinkbugs can be picked off. Aphids can be knocked off with a hose. Diseases such as fusarium and verticillium wilts are best dealt with by crop rotation.

HARVEST

Okra pods are ready for picking several days after the flowers drop but before they are fully mature. If you wait until the pods reach full size, they will be tough. The stems should still be soft and easy to cut, the pods 2 to 3 inches long. Some varieties can be picked at 4 to 5 inches. When the plant is in full production it needs to be picked every other day. If some pods have gone too far, pick them anyway and feed them to whatever will eat them, even if it's the compost pile. Otherwise the plants will stop producing. Use gloves when you pick if your skin is sensitive to the prickles on the pods.

Okra plants, if picked regularly, will continue to produce until frost. In the south growers sometimes cut the plants back almost to ground level in midsummer, top-dress them, and let them resprout for a whole second crop.

VARIETIES

The old standby is 'Clemson Spineless.' 'Annie Oakley II' and 'Cajun Delight' are both compact, early, spineless varieties that are good choices for cool climates. There are also varieties whose stems, leaf ribs, and pods are a beautiful rich burgundy color—highly ornamental in the garden.

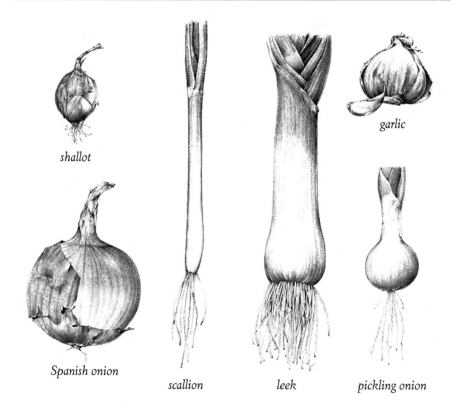

shallot

garlic

Spanish onion

scallion

leek

pickling onion

Onions and Family

THE ONION TRIBE ARE THOUGHT of as nature's great repellers. Depending on whom you talk to, you'll learn that they will ward off garden bugs, vampires, heart disease, and (if you eat them raw) your friends. I'm willing to keep an open mind about all of these, but I know the onions that come out of my kitchen win me more friends than they send away. They are the cook's greatest ally, whether they're yellow storage onions, big red salad onions, little white boiling onions, scallions, leeks, garlic, shallots, or chives.

Most of them are raised for their bulbs (swollen leaf bases), which are pungent or sweet in varying degrees, some for their green tops, and some for both. Although they are grown in somewhat different ways, all onions like pretty much the same conditions: a sandy, fairly fertile loam; plenty of moisture but good drainage; cool weather to grow the tops; and warm weather to ripen the bulbs. They do not require much space, are easy to grow, and are relatively disease- and pest-free as vegetables go.

Onions

SOME GARDENERS FIND ONION CULTURE a bit confusing because there are so many kinds of onions and often several growing methods for each one. But choosing the right onion and the right method really is not that hard once you know a few simple facts.

There are three ways to grow onions: from seeds, from purchased seedlings, and from sets. Growing from seed can take a long time and in northern gardens may not bring onions to the bulb stage in time for warm, bulb-ripening weather. So some people start seeds indoors and transplant the seedlings. They also buy started seedlings, either from local nurseries and feed stores or by having them shipped up from the south, and they transplant these into their own gardens in early spring to mature at summer's end. Or they buy onion sets— tiny, immature bulbs that have been harvested and dried and are ready to plant in early spring to complete their interrupted growth. This is the easiest way to grow onions, but unfortunately very few varieties are available as sets. So unless you just want basic yellow storage onions that are usually the harder-to-peel flat type, it's tempting to try seedlings or seeds. Seed also produces better quality onions.

Which onions you grow depends partly on your cooking and eating needs. If you want long-storing, pungent onions, grow the small, firm American type, either yellow, white, or red. If you want the tiny, round white type, grow pearl or pickling onions. If you want the very large, sweet type that are sliced for hamburgers, grow Bermuda or Spanish onions (also yellow, white, or red). If you want scallions you can either harvest other onions while they're still scallion-size (before they form a bulb), or grow bunching onions, which don't ever form a round bulb but keep the scallion shape even when mature.

Different parts of the country favor different varieties. If you've never grown onions before, I'd suggest starting with the most standard variety for your area. Ask around to see what grows best where you live. The major regional distinction is between "northern" and "southern" onions. With most vegetables this simply means a short, cool versus a long, hot growing season, but with onions there is yet another factor. The point at which onions start producing bulbs is a function not only of temperature but also of day length. In the north days are much longer in summer than in winter. In the south day length varies less from season to season. "Short-day" onions are suited to the south; they bulb too soon in the north as days lengthen. "Long-day" onions are suited to the north; they don't bulb properly in the south because the days don't lengthen enough. When shopping for seeds, seedlings, or sets, try to find out whether the varieties are recommended for the north or south.

Generally speaking, storage onions are often grown in the north from sets, Spanish or Bermuda types from purchased seedlings, and smaller types, such as pearl onions or scallions, from seed. This is the program most gardeners start out with.

SITE

In choosing a site for onion beds, look for a sunny spot and one that is the least likely to sprout a crop of weeds, either from pieces of perennial weed roots or from dormant annual weed seeds. Often this is a patch that had either a thick mulch or a weed-less crop on it the previous year. Onions may perform poorly on a bed that has just grown brassicas (such as broccoli, cabbage, and cauliflower).

SOIL

Lime the soil if the pH is below 6.0, and dig in plenty of organic matter. Well-rotted manure is fine as long as it has been dug in the previous year. A well-made compost with all the necessary trace elements is probably the best insurance for good growth. If in doubt, add a good balanced organic fertilizer to make sure everything the crop needs is there. The soil needs to be fairly well pulverized, but not to any great depth, since the plants are shallow-rooted.

PLANTING

Onion seeds should be new and fresh, because they usually are not viable for more than a year or two. If you're starting seeds directly in the garden, sow them in very early spring or else in fall for a win-tered-over crop. (Wintered-over crops, unless protected by a structure, are chiefly for warm-climate gardens.) Make a wide furrow, soak it thoroughly, sow the seeds, and then cover with ½ inch to an inch of fine soil. As the plants come up, gradually thin them to 3 to 4 inches apart, depending on how big the onions will be. Eat the thin-nings as scallions.

If you're starting seeds indoors, plant them very early. Keep them at a tempera-ture of about 60 degrees and keep them moist. When they're about 6 inches tall, trim the tops to 5 inches to help them stay upright, and set them in a moistened fur-row in the garden, poking a hole for each

one with a pencil or your finger, and allow-ing the same spacing as for thinned onions (above). They can also be sown in a cold frame, then transplanted in similar fashion. Scallions can be sown in the garden as a spring crop, a fall crop, or a wintered-over crop. They do not need thinning, nor do the little round pearl or cipollini onions.

Onion sets are purchased by the pound. If you have a choice, pick the smaller (but not the tiniest) ones in the bin. Plant them 2 to 4 inches apart with the tip up and just barely showing, and water them well. If you're really ambitious and want to grow your own sets from seed, sow the seeds thickly in midsummer so that the tops die down while the onion bulbs are still very small—under ¾ inch—and don't thin them.

GROWING

While the onions are growing, it's impor-tant to keep the soil moist and free of weeds, which can choke them out. A mulch, applied when the plants are about a foot tall, will help with both. If you do mulch you may find that planting in rows is best because it's hard to get a mulch in between the plants otherwise.

Side-dress with a balanced organic fer-tilizer every now and then if the soil needs enrichment, but don't go overboard on the nitrogen or you'll get all tops and no bulb; and stop feeding as the summer wears on for the onions you'll be storing. Cut off any seed heads that threaten to develop, and watch for signs that the tops have matured. They will yellow and start to fall over. Do not mistake this yellowing for signs of drought—it happens only when the bulbs are pretty much grown, and you should stop watering at this point. A common practice is to bend over the onion tops manually to hasten ripening, but this is not a necessity, and you can harm the plants if you don't do it carefully. Better to let them fall naturally unless you're trying to hasten maturation for a special reason such as imminent frost or wet soil that you fear might rot the bulbs.

PESTS AND DISEASES

Onion thrips can be a problem in the south, where they suck onion leaves. They can be hosed off with a stream of water or washed off with a soap spray. The onion maggot can rot the bulbs; an oil or soap spray applied to the ground is said to be effective. It's said that onions repel pests with their strong odor, and in fact none has ever bothered mine. Diseases are rare.

HARVEST

After the tops have fallen, I pull up the onions to dry and cure them. If the weather is dry and sunny, I let them cure right there on the ground, but if it threatens to rain I move them to a warm, dry place with good air circulation. Drying onions on screens works very well. When I visited Plimoth Plantation, in Plymouth, Massachusetts, I saw how the Pilgrims cured their onions— on the roofs of low sheds and chicken coops. You might give that a try.

Don't cut off the tops! They should be left to dry too, until the necks of the onions are thin and no longer green. I like to braid these dried tops together in a French braid (one in which new strands are added as you go), weaving a stout piece of twine through the braid to give it strength. I then bring them out of storage one braid at a time to hang in my kitchen. If not braided, the tops should be cut off an inch above the bulb.

All types of onions can be harvested and stored this way, or in mesh onion bags like the ones used in stores, or in those open-grid plastic storage boxes. Do not put them in a moist cellar with your other storage crops. Scallions are usually not cured but used green as you need them, for as long as they last.

VARIETIES

'Buffalo' is a good, very early onion to grow from seed. The yellow 'Copra' is the best-keeping onion for storage; some like the old favorite 'Yellow Globe.' For a good early red try 'Mars'(red onions store less well, as a rule, but 'Mars' is not bad). The Granex types are the classic short-day onions for the south (made famous by the ones grown in Vidalia, Georgia). 'Walla Walla Sweet' is the northern equivalent, for a spring-planted or overwintered crop. We have had great luck at our place overwintering them in a cool greenhouse from a fall sowing. I'm fond of the little white 'Cipollini' (which means "little onion" in Italian). 'Barletta' is good for pickling. 'Evergreen White Bunching,' which sometimes winters over, is the best all-around scallion. Onion varieties commonly sold as sets include 'Stuttgarter,' 'Ebeneezer,' 'Yellow Globe,' and 'Yellow Danvers.'

Leeks

THESE ONION RELATIVES LOOK LIKE overgrown scallions. They do not form bulbs but develop into fat cylinders that are delicious if grown well and blanched to make them white and tender. They are a wonderful, flavorful, mild-tasting vegetable—cold tolerant, easy to grow, and for some odd reason, expensive to buy. All the more reason to produce your own. Unless they are dug at scallion-size, they're eaten cooked. They like everything that other onions like, including plenty of water and a rich soil.

I like to grow two separate crops—summer leeks and winter leeks. Since I live in a cold climate with a short growing season, I start both of these in the greenhouse or a cold frame in early March (you can also buy leek transplants at a nursery if you don't have adequate seed-starting space). Later on in the spring I transplant them into rows in the garden, spaced 6 inches apart. Usually I plant two varieties, one early-maturing one for the summer harvest and a later variety for winter. In long-season climates leeks are direct-sown. You can also direct-sow leeks anywhere to harvest at baby size.

Traditionally leeks are blanched, either by planting them in a trench that is gradually filled with soil as the leeks grow, or by mounding them with soil. An easier method is to make a deep hole and drop each seedling in. Dibbles are often used for this, but I prefer my husband's trick of plunging in a trowel and pulling it toward you, to make a tidy hole in which the soil is not compressed. The holes are not filled in; we let the rain do that for us. But additional soil can be mounded up from time to time to produce that beautiful, long, white shank that cooks so dearly love.

I start harvesting whenever I want a few leeks, and finish off the summer variety by fall. By then the winter ones are nice and fat and can be dug as long as the ground remains unfrozen. By erecting a plastic A-frame tunnel over the row, we then dig them all through the winter. Leeks that winter over in frozen soil can often be dug and eaten in spring, before they start to go to seed.

Leeks are harder to dig up than bulb onions. I pry them loose with a digging fork, then gently pull them up by grasping them at the base. They can be stored for several weeks in the root cellar or refrigerator.

'King Richard' is an excellent summer and fall leek. 'Tadorna' and 'Laura' have proved successful for winter. Varieties have also been developed for eating at scallion size.

French Shallots

THE DELICATE FLAVOR OF SHALLOTS is, to my mind, indispensable in cooking. You cannot make Béarnaise sauce without them. This is another "onion" vegetable that is inexplicably expensive to buy. Few plants are easier and cheaper to grow. All you do is buy a few shallots (the *last* you will ever have to buy) and pull the clusters apart to make sets. Plant them with their points up as you would onion sets, but just a bit deeper and 6 inches apart. Plant in early spring in cold climates, mid to late fall in warm ones. Instead of forming big bulbs like onions, each set will form a whole new head of shallot bulbs.

These take three to four months to mature. Harvest them when the leaves die down, and do not leave them in the ground or they may resprout. Braid the tops and hang them up, or store them in mesh bags. Save a head or two for next year's crop. Be sure you've bought the true French shallots, not multiplier onions, which have their virtues but do not taste like shallots.

Garlic

THIS STRONG BULB WILL SURELY finish off any vampires—or fastidious company—that the other onions may have left unscathed. Garlic can be planted in spring if you can find the appropriate variety at the appropriate time, but for most of the available ones, fall or winter planting is standard. Even though theoretically you could go to the store and break apart a head of garlic and plant the cloves, it's best to find out which varieties are best for your climate and order them from a catalog. (In addition, garlic in the store may have been treated to prevent sprouting.) The softneck types, whose tops can be braided, and the huge "elephant" types are less hardy than the smaller, milder hardneck types, which form a hard stalk at the center of the head. The hardnecks tend to have a circle of large cloves, without a lot of tiny ones at the center; they are also easier to peel. The scapes (seed stalks) they send up in summertime are delicious sautéed or roasted in olive oil.

Plant each clove separately just as you do shallots, pointed end up, and late enough in fall that the tops will not start to grow (just as you would tulips and daffodils). Mulch to protect them over the winter and keep them from heaving, but remove the mulch in spring to let the ground warm. During the following spring and summer keep them moderately watered and weed-free. To harvest, dig up the heads when the tops have started to die down in summer but there are still six green leaves left. These leaves are connected to the bulbs' protective coating. Cure the bulbs in a dry, warm, airy place out of the sun, then store them in a cool, dry place. Set aside some of the biggest, firmest heads to plant next year.

Other Onions

CHIVES, THE TINIEST ONION, ARE considered on page 396. In addition there are a number of unusual onions that you can explore. White multiplier onions and yellow potato onions form clusters underground. Mild-tasting Egyptian onions (also called tree onions and top onions) form exotic-looking plants with clusters at the tops. All of these can be used as green onions or in cooking the same way shallots are. Welsh onion (*Allium fistulosum*) is a nonbulbing type.

radicchio

Belgian endive

watercress

garden cress

arugula

escarole

curly endive

Other Salad Plants

WITH ALL THE THOUSANDS OF green-leaved plants growing in the world, what makes some of them salad-worthy? They need to be flavorful, somewhat crisp, not too bitter, and of course nontoxic. For commercial production, they must be economical to grow, ship, and store. Lettuce is the standard by which we tend to measure them, but lettuce can get boring after a while, and some greens such as the peppery arugula or the Italian radicchio, which is not even green—are favored precisely because they are not like lettuce. Both gardeners and cooks are expanding their salad repertoires, rediscovering some old-fashioned leaf crops and trying new and unfamiliar ones, often from other countries. Here are some that are worth trying.

Sorrel

THIS IS ONE OF THE EASIEST PLANTS you can grow—a stalwart perennial that takes care of itself. I put the young leaves, sliced in thin ribbons, into salads to give them a lemony zing. I also like to make sorrel soup in early spring, when fresh garden tastes are so well appreciated. Sorrel is used in sauces and purées, especially with strong-flavored fish. Because it is a perennial planting for which the bed is not tilled up each year, I keep it in a patch off by itself. All it needs is a good loam with fairly high fertility and a pH of around 6.0. Like most greens it will take light shade.

To start a new crop, sow sorrel in early spring; thin to 12 inches apart and eat the thinnings. Keep cutting the plant back so it will send forth fresh young leaves. By the time warm weather comes and the flower stalks appear, the leaves have become tough and too strong-tasting to eat. Clean up the debris in fall and look for new foliage as soon as winter is over. You can divide the plants in the patch every few years and give the extras to friends. For salads I'm partial to a type called French sorrel (*Rumex scutatus*), which forms a big clump of dainty, rounded leaves with a particularly fine flavor. But the ordinary garden sorrel (*R. acetosa*), also traditionally grown in France, is useful too and easier to find. This type has larger leaves, with a strong flavor; I will use slivers of it in salad but it lends itself best to cooking. Richter's Herbs has a variety called 'Profusion,' which, because it is sterile and does not send up seed stalks, holds longer in summer. You probably already grow wild sorrel, also called sheep sorrel (*R. acetosella*), an unwelcome weed of wide distribution. Curse it as you may, it is tasty in salads too.

Arugula

ALSO CALLED RUCOLA, RUGULA, ruchetta, rocket, and roquette, this is a traditional European green that has now become fairly common in our produce markets. But if you want it fresh for picking right before dinner, grow your own, even if you have only a big pot on the terrace or in a very sunny window. Arugula leaves have a very sharp, pepperlike tang to them, and a unique flavor. Most people use it sparingly as a salad seasoning (the way you would a fresh herb), or mixed in generously with other greens. I eat it all by itself, by the bowlful, and I stuff handfuls of it into BLTs. It can also be used cooked—tossed with pasta, for example, or as a bright green bed under meat or fish. Arugula has few problems or special requirements, and is grown like lettuce. It is a member of the brassica family (page 232).

Direct-sow arugula 1 inch apart in spring or fall, when the leaves are more tender and mild (I eat hot, bitey summer arugula too, but as you can see, I'm a strange case). Sown too thickly it will go to seed too soon. Hot weather causes it to bolt rapidly, but the edible cream-colored flowers make a beautiful garnish. You can grow arugula as a cut-and-come-again crop, or make succession plantings. It is excellent picked at baby leaf size as part of a mesclun salad mix. If larger plants are desired, thin to 6 inches and eat the thinnings. This is a good crop for the winter cold frame or cool greenhouse, with a hardiness about like that of lettuce. Winter sowings will produce in early spring.

Arugula's botanical name is *Eruca sativa*. It has an Italian relative (*Diplotaxis tenuifolia*) known as wild arugula and sold as 'Sylvetta.' The plant tastes like arugula but has finely dissected leaves and is a bit more cold resistant.

Escarole and Curly Endive

BOTH BELONG TO THE GROUP OF plants called chicories (various forms of *Cichorium endivia* and *C. intybus*), which have over the centuries provided fresh winter greens to Europe, where they are native. They are biennials, and if given any chance to winter over in the ground and go to seed, the flowers will look just like those of the blue chicory you see growing along the roadside in summer. Both are easy to raise, frost hardy, and grown much like lettuce, except that they are even more cold tolerant, and sometimes more heat tolerant as well. Curly endive has light green leaves with thick, crisp ribs and narrow, frilled edges. It has a touch of bitterness that many people love. Escarole has darker leaves that may be wavy but not frizzy. It is good raw, or cooked Italian-style with garlic and olive oil.

Both can be spring-planted for a summer crop, but taste best as a fall or winter crop sown from midsummer on. If you're growing them as heads, they should be thinned to a foot apart (less for some types) since they can grow quite large. Sow more thickly for baby leaf salads. Though the centers will be somewhat pale and tender naturally, you can also blanch them during the last week to ten days of growth. Traditionally this is done by tying the leaves together or by laying boards over them, supported by bricks. This should be done on a day when the leaves are dry, and the plants must be monitored for signs of rot. More recently I have seen a better method practiced in France in wintertime. Each head wore a little white plastic hat, pegged at the sides with stout wire. When the hats were removed, the heads had gorgeous pale golden, mild-tasting centers. In a salad, both the color and flavor contrast was wonderful, and the inclusion of some darker leaves no doubt made it more nutritious.

The plants can be cut at ground level when full size. When cut at baby leaf size (about 3 inches) they are more tender, mild, and cold hardy; they will speedily regrow and you can get a number of cuttings off one planting. Curly varieties include 'Green Curled,' the bolt-resistant 'Salad King,' and the traditional French type 'Très Fine Maraîchère.' For baby leaf salad my first choice is the wonderful yellow-green curly endive called 'Bianca Riccia.' For escarole, 'Natacha' and 'Batavian Full Heart' are good choices.

Belgian Endive

MORE PROPERLY CALLED WITLOOF chicory (*Cichorium intybus*), these are the expensive little white pointed heads you can buy in the store. But you will not get those little heads in your garden simply by planting their seeds and harvesting the plants. The process is more elaborate but worth the extra effort.

Sow seeds outdoors around the date of the last average frost in the same kind of stone-free soil you'd use for carrots. (Do not worry about the top layer being very finely pulverized, because germination is not as difficult as it is for carrots.) Long, carrotlike roots will grow, which need to be carrot-distance apart or a bit farther, about 4 to 6 inches. With no attention beyond weeding and adequate water, they will sprout some bitter-tasting greens. In fall, after a long season of growth, the roots will have attained the ideal diameter of 1½ to 2 inches. Harvest them by prying them up carefully with a spading fork. At the same time, cut off the leafy tops carefully with a sharp knife, being very careful to spare the growing tip at the base, just above the root. Compost the leaves you have removed.

These long, thin roots are sometimes used as a coffee substitute or additive. But to get the little heads, or *chicons*, as the French call them, you have to force the roots to produce new growth, and blanch this growth to make it white, sweet, and tender. To do this, cut off the root tips (and any side roots) so that all are a uniform 8 inches long or so, then store the roots in a dark place that is cold but above freezing. They must be kept in absolute darkness (a black plastic bag will work as long as it has no holes in it) and should be damp but not wet. Take about a dozen roots at a time and "plant" them upright in a 2-gallon bucket, or similar watertight container, filling the container with sand up to the root tops and firming gently so there are no air pockets. You can either fill all your buckets at once and leave them in cold storage, ready to be brought out one by one for forcing, or you can pot up one bucket at a time as needed. The roots can also be forced in just a bucket

of water; in this case you'd fill the bucket at the time you're ready to force it.

To force, bring a planted bucket into a warm, dark place, fill it with water to the top of the sand, and cover it with a heavy-duty black plastic bag or an upside-down black bucket that will exclude *all* light. Perfect darkness is important, because even a tiny amount of light can cause the emerging leaves to color up and turn bitter. A closed cupboard makes a good storage spot.

In a few weeks you'll have snow white heads about 4 inches long. They will not have quite the perfect pointed shape that commercial growers achieve by having the heads grow beneath the surface of the growing medium, but this doesn't matter. Harvest the heads at the base, as needed, with a sharp knife. They can resprout, but

Blanching Belgian Endive
FIG. 51

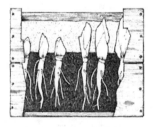

Belgian endive can be blanched by simply planting the roots in a bucket or flowerpot and keeping them in the dark. But by using a box filled with soil to the top of the roots, and 6 inches of sand on top of that, you don't have to worry about the light. The little heads will grow up through the sand, to be harvested when the tips show.

you'll get numerous tiny heads from each root instead of one nice big one. When I finish a bucket I compost the roots and start on the next bucket. Both white and red varieties are available.

Radicchio

THIS PLEASANTLY BITTER ITALIAN crop is also a form of chicory; in fact its British name is red-hearted chicory, since it sometimes resembles a small green cabbage head with a red center. Many varieties are bright red all the way through, with striking white veins in the leaves. Radicchio is eaten raw in salads, and also grilled or braised. Generally it works best as a fall crop in areas with cold winters, and as a spring crop in areas with mild ones where you can sow very early. But at our farm in Maine, we have grown it in every season. Our cool summers make summer crops possible, and we have even wintered it over in cold frames inside an unheated greenhouse. The outer leaves are injured by the cold but the red hearts stay crisp, red, and delicious. It's not too fussy about soil fertility, soil texture, or even water, though it should not get either waterlogged or bone dry.

Either direct sow or start indoors. When the seedlings are about 4 inches tall, thin or transplant them to about a foot apart. When the plants are mature, you can harvest the outer leaves or cut the whole head, which will sometimes regenerate. In mild winters, fall crops may winter over. You also might experiment with indoor forcing as you would Belgian endive—which is essentially the same plant. For this the Treviso types are best.

Many of the old-time varieties bear the names of the towns in northeastern Italy that are famous for radicchio culture—'Castelfranco,' 'Chioggia,' 'Treviso.' All form heads as beautiful as giant roses, in various combinations of red and light or dark green. If you have not grown radicchio before, start with the modern improved varieties that head up easily. 'Indigo' is currently the most reliable one for home growers. It colors up well and resists boting.

Watercress

WATERCRESS IS ONE OF THE FEW greens that will grow right in the water. If you have a cool, slow-flowing, unpolluted brook, or can dam up your fast-flowing brook to form a slow one, you could grow watercress there as a spring crop. It likes a spot in semishade and will withstand light frosts. If your winters are fairly mild, you might establish it as a perennial by planting seedlings shortly before the last frost, just above the water line. Tuck the roots under stones to keep the plants from washing downstream.

Watercress can also be grown right in the garden if the bed is kept moist all the time. It also grows surprisingly well in the moist, cool atmosphere of a cold frame or greenhouse in winter. It prefers a fertile, humusy soil with a pH around 7.0, and is quite happy in partial shade, especially if the weather is warm.

Another possibility is to grow it in pans or saucers of water. Start it either from seed or by rooting the watercress bunches you buy at the food market. Just put the stems in a container of water with the leaves above the surface, and change the water often. Wherever it is growing, keep it well fed with a liquid or readily soluble high-nitrogen fertilizer, and keep picking it for your salads or garnishes to encourage it to produce more. 'Improved Broad-Leaved' is a good variety.

Garden Cress

ALSO CALLED CURLY CRESS OR PEPPER-grass, this dainty green is so quick, easy, and satisfying that it is a good first crop for a child to grow. You'll be able to start eating it in a few weeks. You can even plant it in a window box, indoors or out.

Sow the seed in spring, or anytime indoors, and feed it liquid seaweed or fish fertilizer. When it is 3 inches tall, thin it a bit, using the thinnings to spice up your salads. Harvest it when it's about 6 inches tall, cutting it with scissors. It will regrow, but in the meantime start another row or pot. There are both broad-leaved and fine-leaved varieties. 'Wrinkled Crinkled Crumpled' from John Scheepers Kitchen Garden Seeds is extra curly.

Mini-Greens

THE LAST DECADES OF THE TWENTIETH century saw an explosion in the popularity of mixed salads composed of many different kinds of leaf crops cut small—anywhere from an inch to 3 or 4 inches long. These "baby leaf" mixtures adopted the name *mesclun* from the Provençal word for "mixture"—a type of salad served in spring in the south of France, much of it from wild-harvested greens. (A similar one, *misticanza* is enjoyed in Italy.) Once when I mentioned *mesclun* to a French grower he remarked with amusement, "You Americans all want to talk about mesclun, but it's not a big crop here. It's something eaten for a few weeks in spring near Nice."

Whatever you want to call them, these dainty salads seem to be here to stay, not just in America but in many parts of the world, and their popularity is not surprising. From the diner's perspective they're tasty because so many different flavors, textures, and colors are combined on the plate. From a nutritional standpoint they give you a wider range of vitamins than a traditional salad, since they usually include members of several plant families—the crucifers (mustards, cabbages), chenopods (beet, chard), composites (lettuce, endive), and perhaps others if you count the edible flowers that people sometimes toss in. For the gardener, they offer crops that can be harvested after a very short growing period, then often cut and recut after that. They take up little space in the garden, and are more cold hardy picked at this stage than if grown to full size. Add to that the fact that there are always so many new ones to try in this ever-expanding corner of horticulture, growing them is never monotonous. Every year might yield a new mix planted to suit your taste, and each day's picking might combine them in different ways.

The following list is just a sample of some I like best. The greens I've described, in this section—arugula, curly endive, Belgian endive, radicchio, and the cresses—are also obvious choices. In addition, many vegetables I discuss in other sections of this chapter are used in these mixes when cut at baby size, namely spinach, loose-headed Chinese cabbage, kale, Swiss chard, mustard greens (chiefly the red Asian varieties), and lettuce (especially the oakleaf types and the romaines).

All of these are cool-weather crops that are best direct-sown from early spring on, as either succession or cut-and-come-again plantings. Give them a rest during summer's heat, then start sowing again in late summer and early fall. Most can be grown and harvested all winter long, though in cold climates they will need the protection of floating row covers, cold frames, a simple greenhouse, or a combination of these. For sowing, growing, and harvest see the section on lettuce page 315.

Asian greens. Some of the best Asian greens for cool-weather baby leaf salads are discussed elsewhere—namely, the loose-headed Chinese cabbages and the red mustards. Baby pac choi, especially the delectable 'Mei Qing Choi,' are among my favorites. Another delicious green is tatsoi, which makes a broad, flat rosette of dark green, spoon-shaped leaves when mature. It's delicious and tender at any stage and perfect for salads when cut between 1 and 3 inches long. Mizuna, with long, feathery light green foliage, is also valued in salads as a textural accent. All of these have a very mild cabbagey flavor. Another green called mibuna has long narrow leaves that are not as feathery as mizuna's. Komatsuna's are broader and fleshier. Autumn poem and hon tsai tai are both good in salads at baby size; left to mature they are eaten at the flowering stage, the way you would broccoli raab. Hon tsai tai has narrow purple stems.

All of these are fine in combination with small European greens, but are especially effective when mixed with one another. Their leaves tend to be a bit more substantial, keep longer, and hold up to dressings well without wilting. They are a nice change from the usual cast of characters.

'Mei Qing Choi'

tatsoi

mizuna

hon tsai tai

claytonia

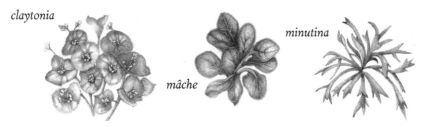

minutina

mâche

Claytonia. Not to be confused with plants whose proper botanical name is *Claytonia,* this little gem is *Montia perfoliata,* usually sold either as claytonia or miner's lettuce (in Europe, it's winter purslane). During the gold rush in the American west, prospectors munched on this mild, tasty, nutritious California native. The plant, as the species name suggests, is "perfoliate," which means that the leaves encircle the stems, making them look like miniature inside-out umbrellas. The stems are long and slender, and are harvested by making a bouquet with your hand, much the way you would a bunch of violets. I usually leave on an inch or two of stem—none if I'm picking for a garnish and want the leaves to lie flat.

As the plant matures it develops a tiny, fragrant white blossom cluster in the center of each leaf. Divine as the scent of a bed of flowering claytonia may be, it should not be left to progress past this point. The flowers rise from the leaf on an extended stem, the leaf starts to toughen, and the plant prepares to go to seed, which it does with a vengeance. Unless you're deliberately letting the crop self-sow, don't let it become a weed and wear out its welcome. The plants are very easy to remove while young but more difficult if they've become overgrown. They can be cut and recut over and over again for successive harvests, but go to seed very rapidly in hot weather and are best grown as a spring, fall, or winter crop. Sow about an inch apart if you can (the seeds are tiny, so it's hard to be precise), in rows 6 inches apart.

Mâche. Other names for mâche include lamb's lettuce and corn salad. The second one sounds confusing until you learn its origin: the crop is a common weed in grain fields in Britain, where all grains were traditionally known as corn (and did *not* include the New World corn known as maize). It is one of the cold-hardiest salad crops.

Unlike most mini-greens, mâche is allowed to form heads, which are tiny rosettes of cupped dark green leaves, perfectly designed to hold a dressing. They have a very mild flavor and are equally good in mixed salads and on their own. Mâche can be sown very thickly—about an inch apart in rows 2 to 3 inches wide. Harvest the heads at 2 to 3 inches in diameter for use in mixtures, or let them grow to 4 inches (pretty much their maximum) to serve by themselves. The best harvest method is to grasp the leaves of several plants gently with one hand and run a sharp knife along the soil surface, severing the heads from the roots while keeping the heads intact. It takes a little practice but is easy once you do it a few times. You'll need to give them a good washing.

Minutina. Narrow leaves with sparsely toothed margins earned this plant one of its common names, buck's-horn plantain. The French call it *cornu de cerf,* which

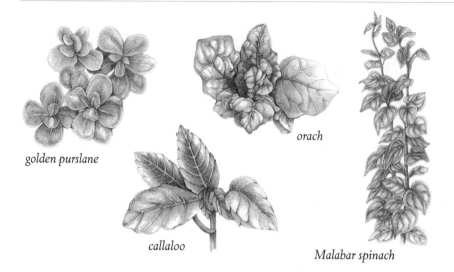

golden purslane

orach

callaloo

Malabar spinach

also denotes its antlerlike shape. Minutina is from the Italian, as is the alternate *erba stella*, which refers, I suspect, to the starlike clumps. Though firmer than other mini-greens, it is far more tender than the fibrous wild plantains to which it is related, and it's such an unusual shape that I include it in salads as much for variety's sake as anything else. Cut it when it's very young, no more than 3 inches tall. The leaves that regrow from the center of the plant are the best for a second harvest, but cut all of them, to keep the clump producing. Plants go to seed in hot weather, sending up tiny green cattail-like seed heads, so they're best grown as a spring, fall, or winter crop.

Warm-Weather Greens

THE FUN OF GROWING UNUSUAL COOL-weather salad greens led me to experiment a bit with the heat-tolerant ones. Golden purslane was a winner, a pumped-up version of the purslane that is known to garden weeders everywhere. New Zealand spinach, also called tetragonia, is prized for its young leaves, which can be harvested at times when spinach would bolt from the heat. Malabar spinach, a vine, plays a similar role; some varieties of it have red stems. A low-growing form of amaranth called callaloo or vegetable amaranth (as opposed to the type grown for the seeds) forms beautiful rounded leaves with red-and-green markings somewhat like those of a coleus. The flavor is rather indifferent but it's a nice accent in a salad. Even better was a selection of orach varieties in shades of brilliant chartreuse, light green, and magenta-purple. These are tender, mild-tasting, and glamorous on the plate, either in a salad or as a garnish. As the stems elongate I even use them in bouquets. Shungiku, aka edible chrysanthemum, also has a lot of visual personality; both the leaves and the flowers resemble those of garden chrysanthemums. There are also heat-tolerant strains of some of the cool-weather greens mentioned, such as komatsuna and mustard.

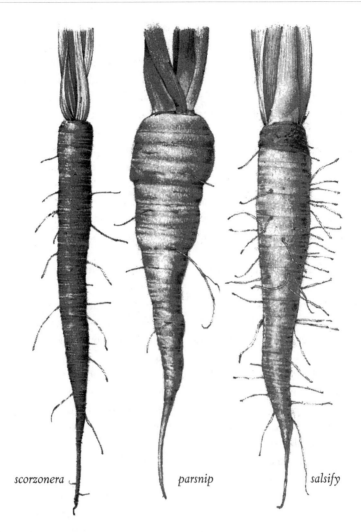

scorzonera   *parsnip*   *salsify*

Parsnip, Salsify, and Scorzonera

ARSNIPS TAKE SOME PATIENCE. The seeds are slow sprouting, the plants are slow growing, and the whole crop can take a good year to produce the tastiest roots. But they are easy, pest-free, and well worth the wait. Parsnips look like white carrots but are fatter on top and skinnier on the bottom. Their texture is somewhat potatolike, and they are rather caloric as vegetables go, especially since they absolutely demand, in my mind, to be smothered in large amounts of butter.

They are also sweet and flavorful in soups and stews.

Parsnips are biennials that would send up flower stalks and bloom the second season if you let them, but you don't. You plant them in spring, dig some in fall after a few freezes make them sweet, and leave them in the ground for an early-spring harvest. Since it is the cold that turns parsnips sugary, and since they overwinter beautifully in the soil without rotting, it makes sense in this case to make the garden bed your root cellar. With parsnips, as I said, patience pays off.

Salsify, or oyster plant, is often grouped with parsnip because it's closely related and is grown the same way. It looks like a slightly shorter, thinner parsnip. Black salsify, or scorzonera, is not even closely related to either, though it looks like a black-skinned, white-fleshed salsify. It is grown like salsify and parsnip, so it's convenient to put it next to both of these in books and seed catalogs— as well as in gardens. All three vegetables are more popular in cool climates than hot ones, but you can succeed with them in warm areas by growing them over the winter, and harvesting them early in the spring.

SITE

The site and space requirements for parsnips, salsify, and scorzonera are the same as for carrots, except that they will occupy their plot for the whole growing season.

SOIL

The soil should be deep, moderately rich, and not too sandy, heavy, or stony— exactly what you would prepare for carrots except that you should pulverize the soil a bit deeper. Obstacles will cause distortion of the roots. Very sandy soil will encourage large, unnecessary side roots to form, and heavy clay soil will be hard for the roots to penetrate. To correct either condition, add plenty of organic matter until the texture is that of a good average loam (page 6). If you still suspect the soil is too heavy, make a large, parsnip-shaped planting hole for each plant by plunging a crowbar into the soil, waggling it back and forth, and filling the hole with a more hospitable material such as aged compost or light rich soil. Avoid too-fresh manure, or soil that is very rich in nitrogen, which will cause branching of the roots.

Being taprooted, these vegetables will accept slightly dry soils better than most other plants, since they can reach water well beneath the surface. They also tolerate slightly poorer soils. But don't ask the impossible from them. What you want to give them is a moderate but consistent supply of water and nutrients for a long, slow, steady season of growth. The pH can be anywhere between 6.0 and 8.0.

PLANTING

In cool climates, sow the seeds outdoors in the garden in early to mid spring. If you wait too long, the plants may not get the full growth they need before cool weather slows down the growth in fall. In warm climates, where mild winters make winter growth possible, you can wait till the cool weather of fall for planting. Parsnips take at least three and a half months to mature; salsify and scorzonera take four.

I recommend direct-sowing in traditional rows, to make mulching easier. Make the rows 12 to 18 inches apart. You can make this crop better pay for its year-long stay in one spot by interplanting the rows with an early crop of baby salad greens.

Use fresh new seeds. Soaking them overnight in warm water will help shorten the two- to three-week germination period. Seeds can be mixed with sand or coffee grounds for easier planting. Make a furrow and moisten it well, then sow seed thickly because germination of parsnip and salsify is sometimes sparse, even with brand-new seed. (This is less of a problem with scorzonera.) Cover the seeds with a half-inch of very light, fine soil, or even vermiculite, because they will balk at a surface crust just as badly as carrots will. Pat the soil lightly.

As with carrots, it's very important to keep the seedbed moist during the germination period. If you're like me, you can very easily forget to do this, but there are some tricks to make up for lack of vigilance. Put wet burlap, sphagnum moss, or a light scattering of hay over the seeds till they come up. Another trick is to plant the seeds with radish seed mixed in. When the fast-sprouting radish seedlings break the surface, they'll mark the spot where you have planted so you can cultivate confidently. They'll also shade the spindly young parsnip seedlings, keeping them from drying out. By the time you're pulling the radishes, the parsnips should be tall enough to thin—4 inches tall or more. If you have made crowbar holes, thin each cluster to one plant, snipping the extras with scissors.

GROWING

While they're growing, the plants cannot take much competition, so cultivate and weed often unless your mulch is keeping the weeds at bay. Make sure the soil does not get too dry, especially if the bed is unmulched. If growth is slow, an occasional light topdressing during the summer will speed it up, but don't overdo this.

PESTS AND DISEASES

Neither insects nor diseases should be a problem. A few leaf miners may tunnel into the leaves, but neither these nor any other insects are likely to set the crop back very seriously. My parsnips sometimes get canker, which produces patches of brown rot on the roots. Canker is best fought by raising the soil pH a bit (if yours is acid), providing good drainage, rotating the crop, and choosing a resistant variety.

HARVEST

If you're harvesting in fall, dig the roots and store them as you would carrots. For overwintering in the ground, pile on at least several inches of leaves or straw or some other loose mulch, as soon as the ground threatens to freeze in earnest. This way you can always pull a few up during winter thaws. As soon as the ground has really softened in spring, harvest all of them before the tops start growing again or you'll ruin the roots' flavor.

VARIETIES

The canker-resistant 'Harris Model' is an old standby; the newer 'Lancer' is an improved version. 'Hollow Crown,' a quicker crop, is also very popular. The standard salsify is 'Sandwich Island Mammoth.' For scorzonera, grow whatever variety you can find—there's not a wide selection.

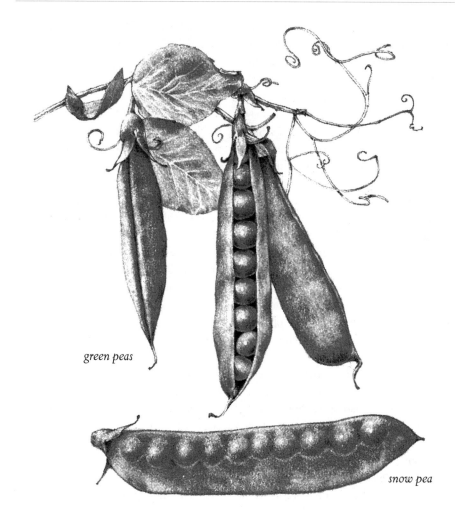

green peas

snow pea

Peas

A PEA CROP IS A LOT OF VINES AND a lot of pods, but when you come right down to it, not very many peas. They are sweet, succulent, miraculous if you can harvest them in May for that first garden feast. But high volume they're not.

On the plus side, peas are easy to grow, they're good for your garden's soil, they don't take up much space, and they're an early, quick crop that can be over and done with in time to free up space for something else—a fall cabbage crop, perhaps. They also freeze very well if picked and processed just at the point of sweetness. And you can take your pick from a wealth of varieties. There are super-early smooth-skinned peas; early-, middle-, and late-season wrinkle-seeded ones; and even a few heat-resistant ones to take you into the summer. You can choose between the bush kinds that need little or no support and the tall climbers that do need trellising but earn that right by producing far more peas. There are also, increasingly, varieties that resist the diseases with which peas are sometimes plagued. All these types fall into the category of green peas or English peas—to distinguish them from peas grown for drying and ones whose pods are eaten as well.

Personally, I don't mind if shelled peas don't fill bushels, so exquisite is their taste if fresh and homegrown. I snack on them raw in the garden all the time, and the ones that do make it indoors are sublime simmered briefly in butter, or tossed raw into the first potato salad of the season, made with the first tiny spuds I dig. If you typically feed a big crowd, go for the snow pea types, whose tender pods taste as good as their contents, raw or cooked. We can thank the Chinese for this great leap forward in pea culture—not only for developing them but for putting them into dishes at Chinese restaurants so we'd know what they were for.

For an even bigger haul, grow the sugar pod types, which are also eaten pod and all. Although snow peas are picked while the pods are still flat, sugar pods are sweetest when the peas are fully round. Some of them, the original 'Sugar Snap' being one, have strings running down each side of the pods that must be removed before you eat them; if this bothers you, look for those that are "stringless." Some edible-pod peas are tall and some are dwarf, but whichever one you choose, you can count on a much bigger harvest by weight. As a result, many gardeners now grow only these kinds.

The most important thing to know about growing peas is that they cannot stand hot weather. If temperatures are consistently above 70 degrees the plants slow their growth, dry out, turn brown, then die. Since the seeds will tolerate frost well, they are an ideal early-spring crop, but don't think this necessarily makes them an ideal fall crop as well. The maturing pods do not tolerate frost at all, so unless your climate affords you a two-month stretch between muggy summer and frost, a fall crop is not dependable. But peas are—face it—so little trouble that it's sometimes worth the gamble if you can shade them behind the corn or pole beans while it is still hot. Before I knew any better, I once planted an unshaded second crop of snow peas in late summer in Connecticut and got a fine harvest.

If you live in a warm climate, fall and even winter planting can be fine. Some southern gardeners sow in fall and let the seeds lie dormant in winter so they can sprout as early as possible in spring in order to beat the heat. Do keep your climate in mind when you choose your varieties, though. If your spring is short, plant an early, fast-maturing variety or a heat-resistant one. If you have a cool growing season, you can plant several varieties at once that mature at different intervals (early-, mid-, and late-season) so you can pick peas over a longer period.

SITE

Peas will grow both in full sun and in a partly shaded location. In choosing the right spot, take into account the need to support long-vined varieties. I've grown snow peas on the garden fence, but erecting some sort of a trellis is the more conventional technique. Early peas like growing in raised beds that warm up quickly in spring. Pea crops should be rotated from year to year, both to avoid disease and to benefit other crops by nitrogen fixation (page 247).

SOIL

In the cold, wet days of early spring the ideal soil for peas would be a light sandy loam that warms up quickly. For a later crop a clay soil will help keep the plants' roots cool—though it should not be so heavy that it slows growth and delays the harvest till hot weather. But most gardens have either one type of soil or the other. Either way, the soil should have plenty of organic matter incorporated into it, because peas always need a good supply of moisture to germinate and grow well. At the same time, good drainage is necessary to keep the seeds and plants from rotting. If you have either very sandy or very heavy soil and cannot easily change its composition, adjust the timing of your planting accordingly, and experiment with varieties to find the one that works best for you.

The soil's pH should be around 6.5, and should be limed if it is more acid than that. Soil fertility is important because peas do feed heavily even though, as legumes, they also return nutrients to the soil (page 275). Nitrogen fixation takes a while to really alter the soil. Lots of compost or well-rotted manure applied the fall before will create pea heaven. Using a bacteria inoculant powder, though not a necessity, can be helpful in starting the process of nitrogen fixation; you might order the appropriate one at the same time you order pea seeds, then coat the seeds with it. (It's also sold at garden centers.) But this will not work if the peas have been treated with a fungi-cide—and they often are. That is why the pea seeds are often bright pink when you take them out of the packet. It's a signal for you to be careful not to let your children or pets eat the seeds, for the fungicide is toxic. I avoid treated seeds whenever possible.

PLANTING

A standard-size packet of peas doesn't go very far because the seeds are so big, so I buy them in 1-pound packages. There are so many different ways to plant peas that you may want to try several before you decide which you like best. I've often grown the climbing types on a wire mesh fence around my garden, for simplicity's sake. The fence is already there, so I don't have to erect another structure. Even dwarf varieties appreciate its support. But if I do this I make sure that I weed a strip a foot or so wide along the *outside* of the fence and cover it with mulch as if it were a part of the garden. If the weeds that normally border my garden were to start encroaching (as they always do), the fence bed would not be a very choice spot. (In fact, it's not a bad idea to have a cultivated, mulched strip along the entire outside of the garden fence, whatever you're growing.)

One thing to bear in mind with peas is that the vines are rather delicate. It's best not to fool with them in any way until it's time to pick them. Even cultivating and weeding can hurt the vines. A wide row or block is one way to grow a lot of low-growing peas together. You'll get a big harvest, while the peas help to support one another and also shade the ground so that few weeds can grow. You can make this row or patch as wide as you want it to be, but if it's no more than 3 feet wide, you can reach into the patch easily from either side to pick. My father, who always planted a gigantic pea crop for freezing, used to follow a tip from gardener writer Dick Raymond: he'd plant extra-wide patches, then set a stool in the middle of them and sit on it to pick, doing no damage to the crop. But you may find it easier just to plant in linear rows, or bands several inches wide, with mulch in between, and several feet of path in between the rows for squatting and picking—and munching. Brush cuttings stuck into the ground every foot or so along the row, while not essential, will help lift the peas off the ground and into the sunlight, as well as making them easier to pick. A low trellis works well, too.

If you're growing tall peas, you'll definitely need something for them to climb on. My father always grew them on "pea brush"—well-branched sticks he placed in the ground so they were at least 4 feet high. (For most tall varieties, 6 feet is better.) It gave his garden a more natural look than a man-made structure would, and he just discarded the brush at the end of the season. Nevertheless, planting a row on either side of a man-made vertical support is still a great method. This can be wire fencing stretched between wood or metal posts, or just horizontal strands of wire with perhaps some twine crisscrossed among them for extra support. You can also build simple wood or metal frames—single vertical types or double A-frame types—that can be reused each year (Figure 52). Or lash stout bamboo poles together, as in the section on beans.

Some garden catalogs carry a type of nylon mesh with 6-inch-square openings. It makes a wonderful support for vining crops, especially peas. Not only is it simple to use—you just erect a simple frame and hang the netting from nails driven into the frame, or weave the supports through the netting—but it's also easier on the fragile vines than metal mesh, because it doesn't get hot from the sun.

If your bed has been prepared the fall before, poke the seeds in as soon as the ground has thawed and dried out sufficiently. If you want super-early peas, you can start them in soil blocks a couple weeks before planting time, but an even easier trick is to sow them in a cold frame—a microclimate in which spring has magically advanced by at least a few weeks (page 39). A raised bed will also speed planting up by a week or so, because of the good drainage and warmer soil.

Plant the seeds 1 inch deep, and 2 inches apart for bush peas, 4 inches for tall ones. In warmer weather or drier soil, planting in a slightly sunken furrow is helpful. Make the furrow 4 inches deep with a spade or wide hoe, moisten it thoroughly with a hose, and plant the seeds in it, covering them with an inch of soil. Then moisten it some more with a fine spray. Keep the soil well moistened while the peas are sprouting. Planting a succession of pea crops, or planting varieties that mature at different times, will give you many weeks of early summer peas. For fall crops, sow about two months before the first expected frost.

GROWING

Once peas are planted, there's not much you need to do with them. A topdressing when seedlings are about 6 inches tall is beneficial if you feel the soil is not sufficiently rich, or if you're trying to hurry up the crop before hot weather. At about this time you should mulch if your crop is planted in rows, since the weather is now warmer and the soil is apt to be drying out. (Mulching at planting time will keep the soil from warming up.) Fall crops can be mulched lightly as soon as they're planted, and more heavily as soon as the seeds are up an inch or two. Broad rows or blocks are not mulched at all. Sometimes you'll need to guide pea vines gently toward their supports if they're leaning in the wrong direction. You might even need to tie a piece of twine horizontally from one end of a vertical support to the other, to keep them upward bound.

PESTS AND DISEASES

There are a lot of things that *can* bother peas, but often nothing does. So don't let this list discourage you. Pea aphids can suck juice from the plants and spread mosaic disease. Hose them off. Pea weevils, whose tiny brownish, black, or white larvae burrow into the peas themselves, are common in some parts of the country. If you have them, dusting your crop with lime can help. Any debris from infected plants should be destroyed, not tilled under.

Birds sometimes eat the seeds or young seedlings. If your birds are this hungry, cover the bed or row with nylon mesh or chicken wire stretched over small stakes, hoops, or the wooden frames as shown on page 259.

Mosaic virus, which makes the plants yellow and stunted, is best fought by curbing the aphids that spread it. If mildew afflicts the plants in damp, warm weather, avoid overhead watering and destroy infected vines after harvest. Root rot is a fungus that makes the leaves turn yellow and the stems rot. Fusarium wilt distorts the leaves and stunts the plants. Both are best controlled by rotating leguminous crops and growing resistant varieties.

Garden hygiene is especially important with peas. Even though it's a common practice to turn under pea crops because they enrich the soil so well, this should *only* be done if the crops have been healthy ones.

HARVEST

Pick peas promptly! If you wait even a day too long they can lose their sweetness and flavor because the sucrose in them will turn

Ways to Grow Peas　　　　　　　FIG. 52

On brush. Tall varieties need support. Cut some twiggy branches and "plant" them in the ground alongside your row. The plants will twine around the brush, which can be discarded after harvest.

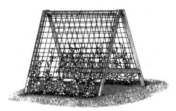

On a trellis. Make lightweight wooden frames or use old window frames. Cover with wide-mesh wire and lean two together, joined at the top with wire or hinges.

to starch; and if you wait several days too long you can also slow down production. Pea vines produce from the bottom up, so look for mature peas at the bottom first.

Traditional green peas are picked when you can feel full-size round peas inside the pods but the peas do not feel hard. You can also open up a pod, look at the peas and taste them. I always make sure I pick them when the skin of the pod is still smooth. Once it feels rough, the peas are no longer sweet and tender. But these should be picked anyway and composted, to keep production going. Most edible-pod peas are picked before the peas form, when the pods are full size but still flat. The exception is the sugar pod type, which are picked when the pods are full of round peas.

As soon as you pick garden peas, the sugar in them will start to turn to starch. So pick just before dinner. If you're not eating them right away, at least refrigerate them promptly or freeze them. They will stay sweet when frozen. If you've let any kind of peas go too far, you can leave them on the vine to harden and dry, then harvest, thresh, and store them as dried peas.

VARIETIES

For early peas, a good succession might be 'Dakota,' 'Knight,' and 'Maestro'; the last makes a good fall pea also. 'Lincoln,' a good main-crop pea, is delicious, reliable, and heat tolerant. All of these have fairly short vines. 'Sugar Snap,' the original sugar pod pea, is a tall one that tastes good even when mature. There are a number of shorter varieties, some of them stringless. 'Snow Green' and 'Mammoth Melting Sugar' are tasty, dependable snow peas.

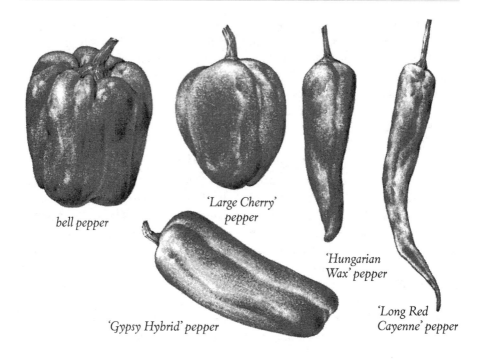

bell pepper

'Large Cherry' pepper

'Gypsy Hybrid' pepper

'Hungarian Wax' pepper

'Long Red Cayenne' pepper

Peppers

YEARS AGO I USED TO THINK OF peppers as a slightly boring sidekick for tomatoes. I'd buy the started plants along with tomatoes, and plant them exactly as I planted tomatoes, at the same time, in the very next row. At harvesttime I'd pick them together and try to think of things to cook with both tomatoes and peppers in them. That was all right, but I did gradually learn that peppers have their own needs and are fun on their own, especially if you experiment with the many different kinds you can grow from seed.

There is nothing wrong with the typical fat, blocky peppers usually found at garden centers. They are versatile vegetables, excellent stuffed, roasted, sliced for salads, or diced up for use in numerous cooked dishes.

Some people automatically pick them while the peppers are green. This is fine for those first early harvests or for when you want them to keep longer in the refrigerator. But let them get red on the plants and you will have sweeter, prettier, more nutritious peppers (though fewer of them, since the fruits' ripening slows the plant's production). The sweetest of all are the bell peppers that turn yellow when ripe (these also keep the least amount of time in the fridge).

Most diverse are the hot peppers, which come in numerous shapes, sizes, colors, and degrees of fieriness. Those who can tolerate the real firebombs claim that the more apparent damage to the tongue, the more harmful bacteria they will destroy in the rest of your body. But it's your stomach lining, so you decide whether to heed this counsel or not. I assume that most of the bacteria in my body are there for a purpose, so I grow just a few hots, lots of sweets, and always some ancho/poblanos. These last are one single type of pepper, traditionally called poblano when they are fresh and green, and ancho when they have ripened to a red color and been dried for storage. They have just the right amount of fire so that you can add a lot of peppers to a dish to enjoy the flavor, without incurring agony.

Peppers are easier than tomatoes in one sense: they are much less apt to need staking. But they are even fussier than tomatoes about needing warm weather to grow and ripen, and they are harder to bring to maturity before frost in cold climates. You can do it easily, though, if you pay attention to a few details. The hot ones are generally easier to ripen simply because of their smaller size.

SITE

Give peppers a very sunny spot that they can occupy all season long, where peppers or other members of the same family have not grown recently (see page 232). Growing them in raised beds, in which the soil warms up more quickly, will hasten ripening. I always plant some in an herb garden near the house that is sheltered from wind and traps the sun's heat. It also has many heat-absorbing granite paths. Those peppers ripen before any others except the ones we grow in an unheated greenhouse.

SOIL

Peppers like a sandy loam of moderately high fertility, but too much nitrogen will produce big, vigorous plants that are all leaf and no fruit. Some extra phosphorous can be beneficial, and the plants will suffer if the soil is low in calcium or magnesium. A pH of 6.5 is about right. But the really crucial factors are warm temperatures and an ample, steady supply of water.

PLANTING

Seeds should be started indoors at least eight weeks before the last average frost date. Since the seedlings do not like to be transplanted, soil blocks are ideal; or you can sow them in peat pots, several seeds to a pot, then thin to the strongest one. For big, sturdy plants, transplant one more time before setting out by carefully peeling away some or all of the peat pot, then setting them in half-gallon milk cartons, which in turn can be peeled away at planting time. Or just use 4- to 6-inch plastic pots and knock the plants out very gently (see page 41).

If possible, keep the soil mix at 80 to 90 degrees while germinating, then keep the plants about 75 degrees. There's no sense in planting them out in the garden unless it is warm enough—65 degrees by day and 55 degrees at night. Even if the danger of frost has passed, wait until the soil has warmed so growth will not be checked. In the case of peppers, hardening the plants off outdoors in pots is *not* a good idea. Remove any flowers that appear until about a month after setting out, so the plant will work on developing a good root system, and have more energy for producing a good yield later on.

If you can stand the idea of black plastic, laying it on the soil several weeks before planting peppers will help the soil to warm up. Cut an × where each pepper should go. A good planting distance for peppers is 15 to 18 inches apart, depending on variety. Hot pepper plants are generally smaller than sweet ones and can go closer together. Collars are good insurance against cutworms. A balanced liquid fertilizer in the hole will help to start them off. Water well when planting.

GROWING

Top-dress each plant with liquid fish or seaweed fertilizer if the leaf color is too pale or growth seems to be slow. Repeat this again in two weeks. Keep the soil evenly moist. After the ground has really warmed up, you can lay down a straw mulch if you've not already mulched with black plastic.

Warm but not beastly hot weather will ripen the fruits properly, and there's not much you can do but wait for it. If the weather is too hot or cold, flowers may drop; when the weather changes, flowering and fruiting should resume.

PESTS AND DISEASES

Peppers are less susceptible than tomatoes are to both pests and diseases. Aphids can damage pepper plants and slow down growth as well as spread mosaic virus, so they should be hosed off. Flea beetles and leaf miners can be controlled by using floating row covers at planting time, which will also help keep the plants warm. Late planting also reduces infestations. If whole peppers rot, you may have corn earworms. Find these borers and kill them so they will not breed in the soil.

Prevent disease by rotating crops and by watering at ground level to keep the foliage dry.

HARVEST

Picking can be done anytime. Once peppers mature, it's important to pick them or production will slow down. Cut carefully with a knife or clippers rather than yanking the pepper off the plant, which would damage the stems. Production will eventually start to slow down in cold weather, even without a frost. Pick off small peppers that are not likely to ripen, and the larger ones will have a better chance of maturing. Green peppers will usually color up after picking if brought indoors and kept in a warm, dry, sunny spot.

VARIETIES

In the wide world of peppers the early and reliable 'Ace,' with its large yield of huge, perfect red fruits is my favorite. I also like 'Vidi,' an early, elongated sweet pepper. 'California Wonder' is thick-walled and good for stuffing. 'Golden Summer' is a good large yellow. 'Sweet Banana' and 'Cubanelle' are both good peppers for frying and roasting. Look for varieties described as "early" if your summers are short and cool.

Growing all the hot peppers would be a lifelong project (and I could think of worse ones). In addition to 'Ancho,' mentioned above, the Anaheim types and 'Robustini' are good if you like them just barely hot. 'Hungarian Yellow Wax,' a medium hot variety that does well in the north, is a favorite for pickling. If you want to play with fire, all the Serrano, Habanero, and Jalapeno types guarantee serious pain.

The long, slender, hot Cayenne types are great for drying and stringing up as *ristras*. I enjoy drying peppers, either in a dehydrator or just by spreading them out in a warm spot on screens or cookie sheets. It takes very little time. For wonderful, rich homemade paprika you can use any red pepper, sweet or hot, but the ones with "paprika" in the name have an especially dark, rich red color and pungent flavor. When fully dry, spin them in a blender or electric coffee grinder and store the powder in tight containers in a dark place.

Peppers are an important part of the "rainbow revolution" now going on in vegetables, from the dark browns of the "chocolate" peppers to the bright purples of 'Aurora' or 'Numex Twilight,' which bear in shades of yellow, orange, purple, and red simultaneously, all on the same plant. The ornamental qualities of peppers have not been lost on flower gardeners. The ones that make upright clusters are great in decorative arrangements, both fresh and dried. And many peppers are both pretty and productive when grown in containers.

white potato

fingerling potato

red potato

Potatoes

A LL ROOT CROPS ARE SATISFYING to grow, but potatoes are the most fun. They are buried treasure, a revelation at harvesttime. I love fishing through the soil at summer's end to see how many each plant has produced—minus any I've stolen for summer use.

Many people think that new potatoes are a specific type of potato, and in fact some varieties, especially the red-skinned ones, are best harvested as new potatoes. But in truth a new potato is any early, immature one. When I was a child our local farm stand used to sell these as small, medium, and large, ranging from pea-size to mothball-size, to golf-ball size. Such labor-intensive luxury is rare in markets now, but if you grow your own you can have some wonderful early meals either by digging up a whole plant before its prime or by robbing here and there around the edges of your hills—a practice once known as grabbling. And there is more dif-

ference between the taste of a fresh-dug, home-grown new potato and the stored commercial equivalent than with any other vegetable. Serve them simply—just steamed briefly and buttered heavily. At least that's my formula.

There are some wonderful potatoes out there, though they can sometimes be elusive. I once drove all over Vermont asking farmers about a local potato variety I had tasted. It had a very crisp skin when baked and a flavorful, fluffy inside. I never did find it or learn what it was, and I would welcome any clues. Nor have I yet seen, in American markets, the mealy yellow-fleshed potatoes I enjoyed eating in Peru. But in the last 15 years or so the European "fingerling" potatoes—tiny, yellow, and shaped like fingers —have been rediscovered, and are a delicious gourmet crop for a small garden. Even blue-skinned, blue-fleshed potatoes have become readily available, so who knows what may yet appear as time goes by.

Sweet potatoes are not closely related to regular potatoes. They are vine plants of the morning glory family and while the two have some things in common, they are grown rather differently, and are discussed on page 370.

When we talk of potato "seed" we do not mean seed in the usual sense, though potatoes have those, too. Seed potatoes are mature potatoes that are planted in the ground, either whole or cut into pieces. You know what happens to a potato when it has been in your kitchen too long. Its "eyes" send out long white stems, which if left to grow would produce leaves and flowers. A potato planted in the soil will produce these too, and it will also grow long underground stems (called stolons) on which more potatoes (tubers) will form. The foliage grows first, as the weather warms, then as cooler weather approaches the tubers start to grow. They are dug up after the rest of the plant has finished growing and the foliage has died.

In the north potatoes are a summer crop, but in warm climates they're planted in late winter for spring harvest, or in late summer for a late fall one, so they will not mature during hot weather. (Nature has designed them as a storage organ to get the plant through the winter.) The crop can take two to four months to mature, depending on whether you're growing it for early new potatoes or a high-yield storage crop. In any climate you can do both with one planting, harvesting some potatoes early and letting the rest grow. You can also plant two separate varieties, early and main-season. Or you can make two separate plantings in succession, both of them for early potatoes, if you have no interest in storing any.

SITE

Choose a sunny spot where potatoes, tomatoes, and other related crops have not grown recently. You also want a spot that has not been limed heavily and recently, since potatoes prefer a more acid soil than do many vegetables (between 5.0 and 6.8 is the tolerable range). Alkaline soils are more conducive to a disease called scab, which produces rough spots on the tubers but seldom ruins the crop, and is not the end of the world for the home gardener.

SOIL

Good soil is especially important to potatoes, since they are a root crop. Potato soil should not be extremely rich but should be very well drained and well aerated. Heavy clay soils not only make it hard for full-size tubers to develop, but they drain poorly and cause tubers to rot. As usual, plenty of organic matter is the best medicine. Beware of fresh manure, though. A well-rotted compost is best, along with some rock phosphate for phosphorous (if needed) and greensand for potassium. Avoid wood ashes, which are alkaline.

PLANTING

Always buy "certified disease-free seed potatoes" from a reputable source. I once grew a crop by simply cutting potatoes I bought in the supermarket and planting them, but I was probably just lucky. Store potatoes have often been treated with a chemical that keeps the eyes from sprouting, and this may take weeks to wear off.

You can plant potatoes several weeks before the last average frost date in spring, but only if the soil has dried out sufficiently. The potatoes may be cut so that each piece has one to three eyes in it, and enough potato flesh to give the young sprout some nourishment to start it off. If your seed is in the form of cut pieces, you need to cure them by letting them sit for a few days in a fairly cool, dry place so their cut surfaces will harden. I save my seed potatoes from the previous year's harvest and plant them whole, selecting the best, healthiest potatoes of moderate size. This is a good way to adapt a variety to your soil and climate in subtle ways, but it only works as long as the crop remains healthy and vigorous. If quality starts to decline, buy fresh certified seed.

The conventional way to grow potatoes is to plant them in a shallow trench that is filled partway with soil. Then as the plants grow, you gradually mound soil up around them to give them more and more underground space in which the tubers can grow under cover and away from the light. Light turns potatoes green, and these green areas are poisonous (as are the white sprouts from the eyes).

If you use the trench method, make the trench about 6 inches deep and place the

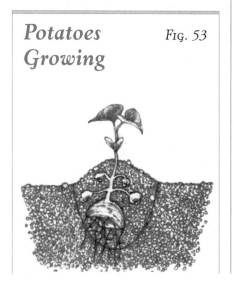

Potatoes Growing

Fig. 53

pieces of potato a foot apart. Some compost in the bottom of the trench will get them off to a good start. Plant the potato with the root end down—you'll see a little bump on one end—and the eyes facing up. (Don't worry—a potato will still grow if it's upside down.) Cover with 3 to 4 inches of soil. Then rake soil in from the sides as the potatoes grow. You can also just plant the potatoes in individual holes made with a shovel or trowel.

Hilling with soil is a nuisance, and also requires a lot of space between rows to provide all that soil. If you have access to a good mulch material such as weed-free straw, mulching is a better technique because it helps to keep the soil cool and moist. Potatoes must have a consistent supply of soil moisture to grow and stay healthy, and mulching is so useful in achieving this. I have even tried growing potatoes right on top of the soil, covering them with layers of mulch as they grow. The only trouble with that method is that it attract voles and mice, who eat potatoes and love to burrow in mulch. So I compromise by planting in soil with a heavy layer of mulch on top. Rodents do appear, but their burrowing can be kept to a minimum by trapping (see page 71).

Another clever planting method, especially if you have little space, is to grow the plants in large containers that you gradually fill with soil. Gardeners talk of bounteous harvests in garbage cans, plastic tubs, and barrels. Once when I was turning my compost bin I found it chock full of potatoes, from top to bottom, that had grown there from discarded kitchen scraps!

GROWING

After the potatoes are bedded down there's little to do unless pest or predator problems appear. Watering is necessary in dry weather.

PESTS AND DISEASES

You may play host to Colorado potato beetles, flea beetles, leafhoppers, aphids, or wireworms, but the first one is the main pest to watch out for. It can quickly wipe out a crop. The adults are yellow with black stripes, and the larvae look like bloated pink ladybugs. Almost every potato patch has potato beetles sooner or later, but they are not hard to hand-pick and drop into a jar of soapy water. Vacuuming them with a shop vacuum cleaner is another option. (The attachment with the slot opening works best.) Be sure to rub off the reddish egg masses that you find under the leaves as well. Aphids and other insects can spread disease and should be hosed or picked off. Floating row covers, set up at planting time, are also very effective.

The worst disease of potatoes is late blight, the cause of the great Irish potato famine that brought waves of immigrants to our shores in the 19th century. Alas, the Irish are no safer from potato blight here. If your potato foliage becomes blackened, then moldy, it has this blight. Remove it, burn it, then wait a few weeks to dig any potatoes that are under the soil. Fight blight with clean seed and crop rotation, then hope that you don't run into long spells of the cool, damp weather that seems to foster it.

HARVEST

Potatoes for immediate consumption can be dug as soon as they are formed and anytime thereafter. (Look for the beautiful purple or white flowers that appear—these are a good indicator that there's good eating down below.) But for good storage potatoes, leave them in the ground for at least a few weeks after the foliage withers and browns, to thicken up their skins. They should be dug if hard frost threatens, but otherwise I leave them in the ground as long as I can so I don't have to store them in warm weather.

Dig *carefully* with a digging fork or potato hoe, starting from the outside of the hill and getting down under the potatoes so you don't spear or scratch them—the potato hoe, with its curved tines, does this just right. (If your soil is light and fluffy, you can even do this with your hands.) Make sure you get all the potatoes down deep and out to the sides. Dig on a dry day, when the soil is dry as well.

Ideal storage conditions are dark and cold but above freezing, lightly humid but not damp, and well ventilated. Do not wash the potatoes before storing, and don't pile them more than a foot or so deep.

VARIETIES

'Red Pontiac' is a fairly heat tolerant, all-purpose potato for north and south alike. But you should also seek out the ones that gardeners favor in your own particular area—then perhaps branch out and try some new and exotic ones, or some heirlooms. Among the early potatoes, I love the red-skinned yellow-fleshed 'Rose Gold.' The yellow-skinned, yellow-fleshed 'Yukon Gold' and the red-skinned white-fleshed 'Red Norland' are also excellent. The Russet varieties are the most popular for baking. 'Kennebec' and 'Katahdin' are very good for storage, but my favorite storage potato is the delicious yellow-fleshed 'Charlotte.' 'All Blue' and 'Purple Peruvian' have ardent fans. Of the fingerlings, 'Russian Banana,' 'Bintje,' and 'La Ratte' are all excellent.

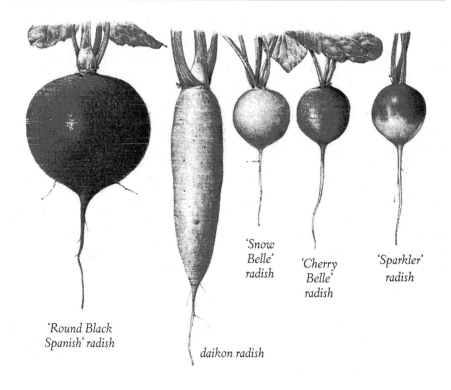

'Snow
Belle'
radish

'Cherry
Belle'
radish

'Sparkler'
radish

'Round Black
Spanish' radish

daikon radish

Radish

Radishes earn their keep in the garden. They germinate fast, mature fast, and take up less space than almost anything you can grow, and you can easily interplant them between rows of slower crops. They are so compact they can be grown easily in containers, even indoors in a sunny window. Sown in the garden as a nurse crop, with slow-sprouting parsley, carrots, or parsnips, they help mark the row and shade these more delicate seedlings from the hot sun until they're robust enough to make it on their own. A "sacrifice" radish row will report-edly lure root maggots away from the more time-consuming, less expendable plants in the cabbage family, of which radish is a member.

But these are subsidiary reasons for growing radishes. We grow them because they are crunchy, juicy, zippy, pretty on the plate, and stimulating to the digestive juices. Radishes are not known for being versatile in the kitchen, but this is the fault of both the gardener's and the cook's imag-ination. For the gardener's part, it's worth experimenting with some of the lesser-known radish varieties. The familiar round red balls are great, but have you ever eaten the skinny white ones? Or tried "win-ter" radishes, including the various Asian types? The larger ones are good cooked in stews, and any radishes are as delicious stir-fried as they are eaten raw. Japanese cooks are highly adept at pickling them. You can even let some of your radishes go to seed and eat the little seedpods, peppery when raw, mild when cooked as a green vegetable. Even tender radish greens are good in soups, stir-fries, and salads.

If you did any gardening as a child, you were probably handed a packet of radish seeds. This is a perfect crop for kids because the seeds are just big enough to plant singly, and they germinate in about five days. An impatient young grower can check the row from time to time, watching the little red roots become more and more like radishes, then eat his or her prize crop in as little as three weeks.

But though radishes are in some ways a quick and simple crop, you must obey a few rules to order to grow them well. They are a cool-weather vegetable that does best in spring and fall, and depends on regular watering and prompt picking to taste mild and sweet. The winter radishes take up to two months to mature but keep well in storage for months of fall and winter eating. In the south, radishes are often a winter crop.

SITE

Radishes will tolerate some shade, and in fact it will be a help in warm weather. But normally sun is better, since the main goal is to get them to grow quickly so they'll be mild, tender, and crisp. A radish crop that sits in the ground and matures slowly is apt to taste too strong and have a tough, woody texture.

It's easy to find a spot for radishes, though, because they take up so little room. Just 1 or 2 square feet will probably grow as many radishes as you need

in one harvest. But don't plant them where radishes or their cabbage family relatives have grown recently. Succession crops (see below) help to spread the supply out over the season.

SOIL

The best soil for radishes is a very fertile sandy loam that warms quickly and presents no obstacle to root development, with plenty of humus for moisture retention. If you have a clay soil, you'll have better luck with winter radishes than with the early ones. The late ones like a deeply cultivated, deeply enriched soil. Use rock phosphate if a higher phosphorous level is needed. Wood ashes, in moderation, are a good potassium source that will also help keep root maggots at bay if sprinkled on top of the soil or dug in an inch or two.

PLANTING

Radishes are sown directly in the garden, not transplanted, but they may be grown very early in a cold frame if you like. Sow early varieties as soon as the ground has dried out sufficiently. Successive plantings can then be made every week or two to ensure a steady supply, since early radishes don't store well either in the ground or after harvest. Fall radishes started in early or mid summer can be either the fast-maturing types or winter radishes grown for storage.

If you have found one radish variety that is definitely "your radish," buy several packets of the seed and plant in succession. But if you're still exploring, it's more fun to buy several different kinds, especially if you are not sure which ones will do best in your garden.

Work mature compost into a single row, a wide row, or a broad patch, bearing in mind how deep your roots will go for that variety. Moisten the soil and sow the seeds ½ inch deep and 1 inch apart. Single rows can be anywhere from 4 to 18 inches apart, depending on the variety and your space requirements. When the plants are 1 to 2 inches tall, thin them to 2 inches apart for small radishes, and up to 8 for the large ones.

GROWING

Mulch if possible and keep the plants consistently watered for the best mild flavor. They should not need topdressing unless your soil is very poor or sandy. Cultivate very carefully to keep weeds down if you have not used a mulch.

PESTS AND DISEASES

Root maggots and flea beetles are the two common radish pests. They are active early in the season, and best avoided by placing floating row covers over the crop at planting time. (With flea beetles it is only the foliage that is attacked, though root growth can be affected if the damage is severe.) Good soil fertility, ample moisture, and rotating your cabbage-family crops are all good assurances of vigor and pest resistance, and this may be all the help you need.

HARVEST

Harvest spring and summer radishes the minute they're full grown, and store extras in the fridge. Winter radishes should be pulled before the first hard frost, then stored in damp sand, sawdust, or peat in a root cellar or another area that can be kept just above 32 degrees. They will last at least two months.

VARIETIES

For a quick, round red variety, 'Cherry Belle' is a good choice. Follow with 'Champion' and 'Crimson Giant,' which are larger and somewhat heat-resistant. The small cylindrical varieties include the charming French Breakfast types, which are red with white tips. 'White Icicle' is one of my favorites; even the greens are tasty. It can grow to 5 inches long but I usually pull it while it is smaller.

For the long white daikon type, 'April Cross' and 'Summer Cross' are popular standbys. For black winter radishes 'Round Black Spanish' is the standard. There are also the hard-to-find golden-colored radishes among the Asian varieties, and some, such as 'Beauty Heart,' that are round with bright red centers—elegant for slicing in a salad or cut in rounds as a vehicle for a dip. I love to add them to stir-fries as well for a gorgeous red note. 'München Bier' is a large white, turnip-shaped radish that the Germans love to eat slathered with butter, as a companion to dark beer. There are even radishes bred for their seedpods, borne on tall, upright stems. Do try those whimsically curled green-and-purple pods borne by the 'Rat Tail' radish. They're tasty either raw or cooked.

Rhubarb

EVEN IF YOU'RE NOT A BIG RHUBARB eater, it's nice to have a plant or two because they are so undemanding. One of the few perennial vegetables, rhubarb just keeps coming up every year, sending out long, celerylike stalks for rhubarb pies, steamed rhubarb, rhubarb jams, jellies, syrups, juices—even wine. If you did absolutely nothing nice for it at all, it would still give you some good pies each season. With a little extra attention it will produce all the more—indeed, you might well become a fan if you have such a handy supply. It freezes well for winter use; you can even force a plant indoors, for fresh winter rhubarb. And it also provides a fruitlike dish in spring and early summer when other fruits are not yet bearing. If you do become so addicted, you can divide and replant rhubarb to increase your supply.

A rhubarb plant is a big mound almost 3 feet wide and almost as tall. Its huge leaves are supported by stalks that are usually crimson, but are sometimes green like a thick stalk of celery. I prefer the red because it's more tasty, more tender, and more beautiful to look at, both in the garden and on the plate. The poisonous leaves are never eaten because they contain large amounts of oxalic acid (in fact, all parts of the plant *except* the stalks are toxic), but the stalks are rich in vitamins and flavor. They are very acid, and so are cooked with sugar or honey. Thus they're classified with fruits, even though the fruiting part of the rhubarb plant is not the part we consume.

Rhubarb is ill-suited to hot, dry climates. The plant will grow, but not vigorously, and it will go to seed too easily. But certain varieties will grow well in relatively mild climates such as that of northern California.

SITE

Choose a spot that is out of the way, like the back row of the garden. Since the planting is permanent, it will not be part of your annual turning-under or crop-rotation program. Planting it on the sunny side of your asparagus patch is a good idea (unless you're in a warm climate, and then the shady side is better!). The two crops are planted, grown, and harvested in much the same way, and it's convenient to work on the two together. In my garden the rhubarb is right next to the sorrel, another perennial crop.

SOIL

Like asparagus, rhubarb needs a deep, fertile, well-drained soil. The large roots will spread several feet out and several feet deep, so cultivate the whole area. If you can, dig in a half-bushel or so of well-rotted manure or compost for every plant you expect to grow. The pH should be slightly acid—between 5.0 and 6.5.

PLANTING

Rhubarb is not generally grown from seed, but from divisions of existing clumps. Divisions have one or more buds, or eyes. Rhubarb seeds cannot be trusted to breed true and they also take a long time to produce mature plants. If you already have an established clump of rhubarb, divide it in half where it grows. Hold a sharp spade over the clump with two hands and plunge it straight down the middle. Leave one half in the soil, where it will keep growing, invigorated by this pruning. Divide the rest into many one-eyed pieces if you want many immature plants, or several larger pieces if you want only a few plants that will bear soon. If you don't have a plant to divide, buy divisions from a nursery or mail-order company.

Plant in early spring as soon as the ground has dried out enough to be worked (in milder climates plant in fall). Make a deep, wide trench as for asparagus and dig rich organic matter into the bottom. If you're planting only one division, just make one deep, wide hole about 2 feet in diameter. Rhubarb has

big, thick, hungry roots that will spread out farther than the circumference of the part above ground and deeper than the plant is tall. Also remember, this is a permanent bed that you won't redig each year, so make sure a large enough area has the proper enrichment and good soil texture.

Make a mound of soil in the bottom of the trench and spread the roots over it, with the crown (the place where the leaves and roots join) just barely below the surface. Three feet between plants is a good distance, but size varies from one variety to another, and plants grown in cold climates are always larger than those in warmer ones.

GROWING

The following spring, top-dress the young rhubarb plant with compost, manure, or an organic fertilizer. The more water and nutrients you give rhubarb, the more stalks it will produce and the thicker they will be. There is little danger of overfeeding. But make sure that water can drain into the soil around the plant, not collect around the root, stems, and leaves, because standing water can rot them. Mulch after the ground has warmed up, drawing the mulch away in early spring to let the sun warm the soil around the crowns and coax them into early-spring production.

Later on in the summer, the plant will send up very tall, thick, round stalks that look different from the leaf stalks and produce whitish, plumelike flowers. Cut these stalks near the base, before the flowers form if possible. If the plant sends up a lot of these, it will produce fewer and thinner leaf stalks, or even stop producing altogether.

To force a rhubarb plant in your cellar for winter eating, dig one up before the ground freezes in fall, trying to get as many of the roots as possible and leaving as much soil around them as you can. Put it in a large container and fill in around it with light soil, moistened peat moss, or moistened sawdust. The crowns should be cut back almost to the roots and covered with several inches of whatever potting medium you're using. Leave the container outdoors and let it freeze at least once. A month to six weeks outdoors is even better. Then bring it into a cool, dark place (about 40 degrees) if you are going to keep it dormant for a while. Keep the soil moist but not soggy wet. When you want it to start growing, bring it into a somewhat warmer area (about 60 degrees), but keep it covered with something that will exclude the light. Soon the plant will start sending up tender, edible stalks. When it has finished producing, you can either throw it away or replant it in the spring. Production may be set back for a while, but the plant will regroup eventually.

Rhubarb plants are not easily discouraged! A clump will thrive almost indefinitely without being divided, though dividing will benefit the plant. When a plant is old, the stalks will be very numerous but thinner.

PESTS AND DISEASES

If you see black spots on the stems or your plants, they probably have rhubarb curculio, also known as rusty snout beetle. It bores into the stalks, crowns, and roots and can be kept in check by constant picking off. These insects are very attracted to dock, a common weed. So make sure you don't have any of that growing in or around your garden.

Occasionally the plants get foot-rot, causing the stalks to rot at the bottom. Dig up the whole plant and burn it if this happens, and if you've been mulching the rhubarb patch, stop. Give the plants plenty of air circulation, and if they're in a shady location, find them a sunnier one. Replanting in a new spot will help to avoid rot the next year, too.

I always notice a few dead leaves at the bottom of my rhubarb plants from time to time throughout the summer. This is normal, not a sign of a grave disease. The leaves rot because they're resting on the ground. I just pick them off and get rid of them, the way I would any garden debris.

HARVEST

The first year you plant rhubarb you should not harvest any of the edible leaf stalks, but do cut back the flower stalks. The second spring you can pick some leaf stalks that are at least an inch thick, but most of them should be left on the plant to form leaves so that the roots can grow. (Keep removing the flower stalks, though.) The third year you can pick the thick leaf stalks for about a month. From the fourth year on, pick as many of the thick ones as you like. I have cut near the base with a knife without any problems, but the usual way is to twist the stalk and give it a tug. This is said to leave the stalk less receptive to disease and rot. I pick mine until midsummer or so, and stop when the stalks are coming in thin.

VARIETIES

The standard green rhubarb is 'Victoria,' a big, vigorous plant. Favorite red varieties include 'Ruby' and 'Valentine,' the last especially resistant to disease. 'Cherry' and 'Giant Cherry' are recommended for areas with mild winters, but for best results check local suppliers for those that do best where you live.

Spinach

S PINACH USED TO BE THE KIND OF vegetable you joked about. Kids wouldn't eat it unless you could convince them that spinach, and spinach alone, made Popeye strong. Its popularity surged when grownups started eating it a lot in salads. I still love it best cooked just long enough to wilt it, with some olive oil in which I've crushed a clove of garlic.

This is not a hard crop to grow, and it's also a quick one—40 to 50 days to harvest, even less if you pick it at baby size. The problem most gardeners have with spinach is that they try to treat it like lettuce. It's a cold-weather crop, like lettuce, but even more so. It bolts in hot weather just as lettuce will but does so more quickly. Spinach is really a spring or fall crop, though you can edge a bit into the summer months if you grow a "long-standing" type. Though heat and dryness are factors, it is day length that causes spinach to bolt—that is, to send up a tall seed stalk and stop produc-

ing. The lengthening days approaching midsummer tell the spinach it's time to go to seed. In warm climates it is grown in late fall, winter, and early spring. In the north, plants will winter over in the ground even in quite cold areas.

There are two kinds of spinach, the dark green, crinkly leaved (savoyed) sort and the smooth-leaved version. Neither "New Zealand spinach" nor "Malabar spinach" are really spinach, though both taste something like it when cooked, and are sometimes grown as spinach substitutes in warm climates or warm weather.

SITE

Plant spinach in full sun or part shade—the latter if the crop will be growing in warmish weather. You might start a fall spinach crop between rows of a tall crop such as corn or beans, which will shade it in summer and then be harvested once cool weather comes. Baby-leaf spinach for salads needs only a few square feet of space for the whole crop. For growing spinach to cook or freeze, however, I recommend a good 40 square feet at least, because it will lose so much volume.

SOIL

Spinach prefers a light soil, but a heavy soil has its merits too—it is cooler and holds moisture better, so the plants are less quick to bolt. In either case add plenty of organic matter to increase moisture retention. As a leafy crop spinach thrives in very fertile soil, and it is almost impossible to overfeed it, but make sure the soil has a balance of all the nutrients and trace elements essential to growth. If you're using commercial organic fertilizer, 10-10-10 is a good choice, though a well-made compost is ideal. You do not need to fertilize the soil to a great depth, because the plants are shallow-rooted. They're a little fussy about pH, preferring the 6.0 to 7.0 range, so add lime if your soil is acid (this will contribute much-needed calcium as well), but don't go overboard because spinach doesn't like very alkaline soil either.

PLANTING

Sow spinach directly into the garden or cold frame. For spring planting you can start as soon as there is some ground in your garden that has thawed and dried out. Some gardeners even get the furrow ready in the fall, so all they need to do the following spring is drop the seeds in and not worry about working the soil while it's still muddy. If your fall crop has overwintered, just pick off the frost-damaged leaves and watch the plants spring to life.

Plant spinach either in single rows, multiple rows, or blocks with a grid pattern. How you space the plants will depend on whether they will be harvested as baby spinach, which can be as close as 4 inches apart in rows spaced 6 to 8 inches apart, or as large heads, which might need as much as a square foot of soil per plant. Seeds should be ½ inch deep, and if possible 1 inch apart. They will germinate in five to nine days, or a bit more if it is very cold. When there are two true leaves on the plants, thin to the desired spacing, and use the exquisite little discards in salads.

Unless you want a great deal of spinach all at once for cooking or freezing, it's best to save half a packet or so, then sow one or more extra crops at intervals of about ten days. But stop sowing around mid May (earlier in warm climates). The idea is not to have spinach maturing during the long, warm days of July and August. May sowings should be of a long-standing type, as an extra safeguard against bolting. Start fall sowings in late August, even later in warm climates. These should be sown a little thicker and deeper than spring crops, because germination is less reliable in warm weather. It helps to keep the soil moist with frequent watering. Crops sown in early fall in a cold frame can be harvested all winter.

GROWING

Mulching will help to keep the soil moist, but I would avoid a very acid mulch such as sawdust, bark, or peat moss because these can lower the pH to below the plants' tolerance. Straw is better. If you are overwintering a crop by keeping young plants dormant, it's best to mulch them heavily after the ground freezes to keep it frozen evenly. Alternate freezing and thawing can damage the plants.

Cultivating or weeding is important if you do not mulch, but do it carefully so as not to harm the spinach plants' shallow root systems.

PESTS AND DISEASES

Home gardeners generally do not have many problems of this sort. Spinach leaf miner larvae burrow inside the leaves and produce tan patches. The easiest control is to pick off affected leaves and destroy them. Keeping the garden free of debris and weeds will help. By growing very early or late crops, you might avoid this bug's season. You can also cover young plants with floating row covers so that the fly that lays the eggs that produce these larvae cannot land on the plants.

Spinach blight, or yellows, is a mosaic virus spread by aphids. The leaves turn yellow, and the plants are stunted. You can control the virus by controlling the aphids, or you can grow resistant varieties. Also practice good garden hygiene. If there are yellow spots on the leaves and a moldy substance underneath, the problem is the disease called blue mold. It appears occasionally in very wet weather. Best defenses are weed control, good drainage, and vigorous, well-fed plants. If they still get blue mold, throw them out and try again in better weather and in another spot. Fusarium wilt can affect spinach, but there are resistant strains.

HARVEST

You can reap your spinach two different ways—by cutting the outside leaves and letting the centers keep producing, or by cutting the whole plant just at soil level, like a head of lettuce. I choose the leaf-by-leaf method unless warm weather is approaching, or if I have a fresh young crop coming along.

VARIETIES

'Long Standing Bloomsdale,' a savoy type, has long been the most popular bolt-resistant spinach, and for late crops 'Winter Bloomsdale.' I've also had excellent success with the very hardy, smooth-leaved 'Space' and the crinkly, bolt-resistant 'Tyee.'

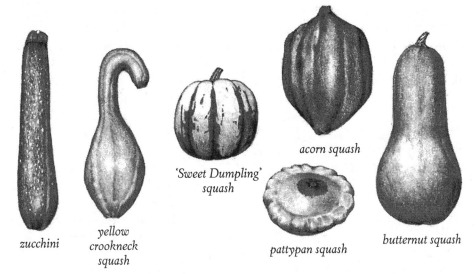

acorn squash

'Sweet Dumpling'
squash

zucchini

yellow
crookneck
squash

pattypan squash

butternut squash

Squash, Pumpkins, and Gourds

 NATIVE AMERICANS WERE GROWing gourds, squash, and pumpkins when the European settlers arrived. These members of the cucurbit family are all closely related and like most of the same growing conditions, but they all look very different. In fact, their odd assortment of shapes is one of the fun things about growing them. Wherever you live, there are a number of excellent ones that will suit your climate.

Summer Squash

THIS GROUP INCLUDES THE FAMILIAR green zucchini squash, the equally familiar yellow crooknecks and straight-necks, and some less familiar ones that are spherical or scallop-shaped. All are extremely easy to grow, unless your summers are very cold and rainy. All you need is 50 to 60 days of good warm weather.

A few summer squash plants don't take up much room in a small garden, since most are bush type, but some people are slow to realize that they only need a few. I once fed three families from one zucchini plant, though two or three per family is a more realistic number, more if you intend to freeze some. Some people think that summer squash does not freeze well, but my mother froze them sliced with diced onions, and they tasted wonderful cooked together. If you grow too many you'll soon find yourself making squash soup, squash bread, squash ice cream, squash compost—or surreptitiously leaving them on doorsteps. I'd rather plant just one green, one yellow, and maybe one experimental plant of a new variety than have people say, "Uh-oh, here she comes with her zucchini."

SITE

Find a sunny spot with good drainage, where other cucurbits have not been growing recently. Allow 9 to 16 square feet per plant.

SOIL

All squash like fertile soil with plenty of organic matter to retain moisture. They are heavy feeders and drinkers, because they produce big stems, big leaves, and if left to mature, big fruits. Their ideal pH is around 6.0 to 6.5. The old bushel-of-manure-per-plant trick is great for them, if you have access to this precious stuff, but a shovelful would do. A well-made compost is excellent. Or dig in a lot of moistened or composted peat moss and an application of a balanced organic fertilizer with a good range of trace elements. Distribute this enrichment throughout the planting area so that the plants' far-ranging root systems will be sure to find it.

PLANTING

The seeds of squash and its relatives should be purchased, not saved from previous crops, unless you can be certain they have not cross-pollinated with another variety. Otherwise you'll get some very odd-looking, inedible fruits. With summer squash I always plant seeds directly in the garden as soon as the danger of frost has passed, and the soil has dried out and started to warm up. You can also start them inside if you want to get a jump on the season, but this is best done in soil blocks or peat pots to save them from transplanting shock.

I plant the seeds six to a hill (cluster) and 1 inch deep, thin to the best three seedlings, and then thin to one seedling when the plants are a few inches tall. I put summer squash plants 3 to 4 feet apart. Closer planting will lead to lower yields, and I would rather have a few big bushy plants with space around them. I like to be able to walk around them easily and peer under the big leaves to look for ripening squash.

GROWING

Usually the first pretty yellow flowers that appear are male. You should eat them. Squash blossoms are good in salads, good sautéed, and good stuffed and deep-fried as fritters. There will be plenty of them to spare, because you only need a few male ones for pollination. The female flowers soon follow, and can be recognized by a small bump of "squash-to-be" at the base. You can eat some of the female flowers too, and the plant will just keep producing more. (If the females appear first they will wither and fail to form fruit, but fruit set will begin as soon as there are males.)

Weed the plants when they are young. Later the big leaves will shade the ground and keep weeds down. This will also keep the soil moist, but water the plants anyway if the weather is very dry, and top-dress from time to time if, despite your best efforts, your soil is still poor.

PESTS AND DISEASES

I find that healthy, well-fed squash plants repel pests well, but if you have had a problem with striped cucumber beetles in the past you should put down floating row covers (page 260) at planting time. (I would use the heavier weight if there is a need for frost protection as well.) Mulching can also be effective. These insects, which are yellow with black stripes, can also spread mosaic and bacterial wilt diseases. Remove the covers once the male and female flowers have appeared, so that pollination can take place. Any bugs that arrive after that can be picked off, but by then the plants will probably be big enough to resist them. Another pest, the squash bug, lays red eggs on the underside of the leaves. Scrape these off and destroy them.

Squash can contract a number of diseases: fusarium wilt, powdery and downy mildew, bacterial wilt, mosaic virus, and blossom-end rot. The best defense is to keep the plants as vigorous as possible with plenty of water and fertile soil. Burn any debris and always rotate your crops.

HARVEST

When my summer squash are really producing I try to pick them every day. They are delicious when tiny—about 3 to 4 inches long for the long ones, and 2 to 3 inches in diameter for the round types. These are best cooked whole or even raw as crudités. Larger ones are good too, either sliced or stuffed, but I try not to let them get more than about 7 inches long, or 3 to 4 inches in diameter for the scallops. Large, mature squash can be stuffed and baked, but frankly the plants' energies are best put to use in making lots of delectable little ones. If you forget to pick, or go out of town for a week, you'll find huge green zucchini monsters hiding under the leaves—and believe me, the green ones are good at hiding (perhaps an argument for choosing yellow squash). Making big squash causes the plant to slow down its production.

When I pick summer squash I cut them off with a serrated knife such as a grapefruit knife. Pulling or twisting them may damage the plant. I harvest the blossoms first thing in the morning when they are wide open, so they're fresher, firmer, and easier to stuff with a mozzarella or goat cheese filling.

VARIETIES

I've always liked 'Gold Rush,' a compact bush squash that looks like a yellow straightneck but is actually a yellow zucchini. I also like 'Zephyr,' whose prolific, healthy yellow fruits are tipped with green. You might experiment with one of the dark green-black Italian heirloom zucchinis, or one of the pale green globe-shaped squash like 'Ronde de Nice,' very tender when picked small. The pattypan types come in a range of colors—off white, pale green, deepest green, and bright gold. They're highly decorative for steaming or stuffing. If you don't mind trellising it, try out one of the Italian *tromboncino* types, such as 'Zuchetta Rampicante.' These grow on vigorous vines and bear long, ribbed, firm-fleshed fruits.

Winter Squash

FEWER PEOPLE GROW WINTER SQUASH than summer, which is a shame because they're richer in vitamins and, to my mind, tastier. They also keep a long time in storage, for those who like to eat their own produce all year. But since winter squash are eaten mature, not very young like summer squash, they generally take twice as long to bring to harvest, and you need a good, long warm season in which to grow them. Many are vine types too, and as a consequence need a good deal of space. Squash vines can grow 20 feet long, though 10 or 12 is more usual. Nonetheless I have enjoyed growing them in the north, especially the early-maturing varieties, and there are ways of managing them in relatively small gardens. Some varieties come in bush form.

Butternut, acorn, and buttercup are good traditional garden types that are still popular and are easy to bring to maturity even in regions with cool summers. Butternuts are smooth-fleshed, and so make wonderful purees and soups. Hubbard squash are quite enormous, but great keepers. The acorn and buttercup types are great for baking.

SITE

Choose a sunny site if possible. I've grown winter squash between rows of corn to save space, but crops grown that way are probably not quite as prolific as they would be without the shade cast by the corn stalks.

Winter squash production will not run away from you in terms of sheer numbers of fruit the way that of summer squash will, but the vines will run across the garden and beyond. There are several solutions to this problem. One is to let them head out through the garden fence and into the weeds or onto the lawn, as long as they won't be in the way. (They can even be useful in smothering the weeds on the outskirts of a garden.) Another trick is to turn the tips of the vines gently back the way they came; they'll keep going just as if returning to the garden were their idea

in the first place. Still another solution is to snip off the fuzzy tips of the vines once they've produced a few squash. (This will make the fruits mature faster anyway.) I've also trellised winter squash vines successfully on a sturdy wire mesh garden fence. This works best with the smaller varieties. To do this with the very large heavy types you'll need to support them individually with slings.

SOIL

Soil requirements are the same as for summer squash.

PLANTING

Winter squash seeds can be sown the same way as summer squash, but in short-season climates you may need to start them indoors or in a cold frame four to six weeks ahead. Using soil blocks or peat pots will make transplanting more painless, since the seedlings do not like to have their root systems disturbed. If sown directly in the garden, seeds are usually sown in hills, as above, then thinned to one plant. The plants should be placed 4 feet apart in rows 6 feet apart, or in a grid pattern with plants 5 feet apart each way. Compact varieties can be planted closer together.

GROWING

Winter squash generally lie on the ground a long time while they're maturing. If conditions in your garden cause them to rot on the bottom, it may help to put mulch under them, or something you can slide under each fruit such as a piece of wood or plastic, or a shingle.

If your growing season is short, cut off the late-appearing flowers after you've some nice fruits on the vines—anywhere from one to six per vine, depending on how prolific the variety. All the plants' energy will then go into the production of those fruits.

PESTS AND DISEASES

Squash-vine borers generally do the most damage to winter squash—a nice long vine will suddenly die, wiping out the fruits. Look for a little telltale pile of excrement (it resembles sawdust) and find the little white grub inside the stem by making a lengthwise slit with a sharp knife. Remove the grub and bury that section of the vine. Squash vines root readily in the soil, and this may help any fruits remaining on the unaffected stretch of vine to mature. Squash with particularly hard, tough vines, such as butternuts, are resistant. For the striped cucumber beetle, see page 311.

HARVEST

You should leave winter squash on the vines till they're mature. Squash will not ripen after picking the way tomatoes will, and unlike summer squash, most winter kinds do not taste good young. How do you know when they're mature? Some varieties, such as the buttercups, are ripe when their stems turn dry. But the only really sure way to tell with most of them is to see what the ripe ones look like in the market or in pictures on seed packets or in catalogs. If you're trying a new variety and you can't find a picture of it, you may have to simply use trial and error. Eat one early, let another one go late; you'll figure it out. But be sure you harvest them before frost. If "the frost is on the pumpkin," your pumpkin—or squash—has no business being in the garden. If some of the squashes are still unripe and a frost is coming, pick all the ripe ones and cover the unripe ones with something like a heavy straw mulch. Or very carefully gather all the vines together without breaking them and spread a large blanket or tarp over them. Newspapers anchored with rocks might also work. But remove any of these covers in the morning so the fruits can get sun.

When you pick winter squash, cut off a few inches of stem along with the fruit, using a sharp knife. Tearing the stem leaves a jagged wound that is more open to rot than a clean cut is. Do not use this stem as a handle for picking up the squash. Winter squash look like hard, tough fruits, but actually they need to be handled carefully. Nicks and bruises will prevent them from keeping well. Before storing them, it's a good idea to cure them for a week or two in the sun or in a warm room to toughen the skin. Then place them in a reasonably dry, cool, permanent storage place. About 50 degrees is ideal, but I've seen squash keep quite a long time at room temperature. Some varieties store longer than others. The butternuts are especially good keepers.

VARIETIES

If your space is limited or if you're new to squash growing, I recommend that you grow one of the smaller, earlier varieties. Some good ones are 'Buttercup,' which matures in about 95 days, the semibush acorn 'Table Ace' (90 days), or a slightly flattened Kubocha type called 'Sweet Mama' (85 days). 'Jersey Golden Acorn,' which can be picked very small, also has its ardent fans.

'Early Butternut' (a semibush) matures as early as 82 days, and I'm fond of the old standard butternut called 'Waltham,' which is a fantastic keeper and has a nice thick neck for more uniform slicing. (I like to fry slices of butternut squash—and nothing beats it for velvety soups.) Two varieties that are very popular despite being long-season are the little round 'Sweet Dumpling' and the cylindrical 'Delicata' (of which there is a bush variety). Both look very decorative in a basket in the kitchen, and are small enough to serve stuffed as individual portions.

I also love 'Vegetable Spaghetti,' whose flesh separates into spaghetti-like strands when scooped out of the skin with a fork. It is heavenly baked or boiled whole, then scooped out and slathered with butter and parmesan cheese.

If you want a good big squash that keeps for most of the winter, grow the various Hubbard types, or the big tan French heirloom 'Muscade de Provence.' And for sheer beauty try 'Turk's Turban,' a red-and-green turban-shaped squash so beautiful you can use it as a centerpiece—and eat it as well.

Pumpkins

large pumpkin   pie pumpkin

PUMPKINS ARE SIMPLY ONE KIND OF tough-skinned winter squash, but they've earned a category of their own because of Halloween and Thanksgiving.

Once a kitchen staple for soups, stews, and puddings, they appear now in time for jack-o'-lanterns and pumpkin pies, then fade back into obscurity. If you grow them, no doubt you'll find more long-term uses for them. You can serve a stew or soup inside the pumpkin shell, for instance. And they are delicious pureed in soups. Some varieties now have edible-shelled seeds that are more rewarding to eat than the usual hard-shelled kind.

Grow pumpkins exactly as you would any other winter squash. The only thing you might do differently is try to get some huge ones for Halloween. The best way to do this is to space the plants widely apart in extra-fertile soil, then pinch off the tips of the vines when they have a few small pumpkins on them. Then remove all but the best pumpkin per vine and let the remaining one get all the plant's energy. Remove all flowers as well. Water the vine often, and top-dress it every two weeks or so, not only at the base, but also wherever it may have touched the ground and rooted. Turn your prize gently from time to time so that one side does not get flat from lying on the ground.

Your chances of growing the biggest pumpkin around will be increased if you've chosen a large variety such as 'Connecticut Field' or 'Big Moon.' For baby ones grow 'Jack-O'-Lantern' (aka 'Halloween') or the even smaller 'Baby Bear.' For pies and other cooked dishes grow a fairly small, good-tasting variety such as 'Small Sugar' ('New England Pie'). 'Lady Godiva,' appropriately, is one of the "naked seed," or edible-hull, varieties. And I personally love the glamorous 'Rouge Vif d'Étampes,' also called 'Cinderella.' This French heirloom is brilliant red-orange with the classic Cinderella's-coach shape and rich-orange flesh.

Gourds

*'Turk's Turban' squash
surrounded by gourds*

YOU CANNOT EAT MOST GOURDS, BUT you can do almost anything else with them. I loved to grow them as a child. We used the dipper type to make birdhouses, with a small hole cut in the fat part. Sometimes the skinny "tail" curved around in curlicues, and we just hung them on something as ornaments. We had a huge round one several feet wide that our grandmother had grown in her long-season Louisiana garden. We used round gourds as various kinds of containers, with a circle cut to make a lid and a bit of stem left on for a lid handle. All these types were the tan-colored *Lagenaria siceraria*.

The small multicolored gourds are the *Cucurbita pepo* species. They're grown for fall decorations, and are often sold in mixed-seed packets. This makes growing them more fun because you never know what shapes or colors you'll end up with. I grew a variety recently called 'Crown of Thorns' that had a consistent, crown-topped shape but with variously colored markings. I drilled a hole in the top of each

and used them as candleholders for a family wedding.

Plant and grow gourds just the way you would winter squash, but allow a long maturing period for the biggest ones—as much as 140 days. Since gourds weigh less than other squash, trellising is very successful, and it keeps them from flattening on one side. (Of course you might want to flatten one side to grow a container that won't tip over—round-bottomed gourd bowls work best if you're living in a hut or tepee with a sand floor.)

Gourds are heavy feeders, and should be top-dressed if needed. Ripen them on the vine until the stems are brown, but pick them before the first frost or they'll go soft and not keep. Handling them very carefully, wash them in a mild chlorine solution or with rubbing alcohol to prevent mildew, then dry them very thoroughly in a warm, dry place with good air circulation. This may only take a week for the little ones, but large gourds may have to sit for months before the sound of rattling seeds tells you they're done. The outsides can be coated with paste wax or clear shellac, but only if thoroughly dry.

Pick the club-shaped luffas when they are young and green if you want a soft sponge, when they're brown and mature if you want a very scratchy one for scrubbing. You'll need to peel off the skin. It is easier to do this when they're mature, and freezing them makes it easier still. Cut off one end and shake out the seeds, then wash in soap, water, and bleach, squeeze thoroughly, and spread out to dry.

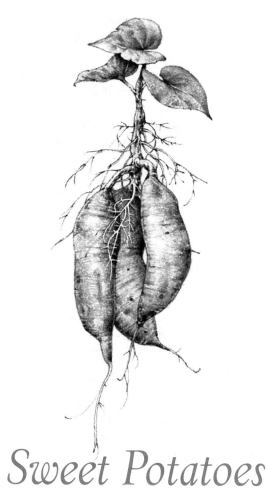

Sweet Potatoes

SWEET POTATOES GROW UNDER THE ground just as regular potatoes do, but there the resemblance ends. Aboveground the plants are sprawling vines that can take up a lot of room in the garden. And unlike standard potatoes, sweet potatoes are a warm-weather crop, often needing four months of fairly high temperatures to mature. Nonetheless, gardeners can grow them in northern climates. You can also adapt them to small gardens, either by choosing bush-type varieties or by growing them in containers.

They are sometimes referred to as yams, but this is a misnomer. The sweet potato is *Ipomoea batatas*, a close relative of the morning glory. The Chinese yam is *Dioscorea batatas*.

SITE

Choose a warm site in full sun where sweet potatoes have not grown recently. The drainage must be very good.

SOIL

The best kind of soil for sweet potatoes

is a light, sandy loam, slightly acid, with sufficient phosphorus and potassium, and rich in organic matter. Too much nitrogen can produce rampant vines and distorted tubers.

PLANTING

Sweet potatoes are not grown by cutting up the potato and planting it, but by planting "slips"—sprouts from the large, swollen root. These slips can be obtained by placing a root, or just the round end of it, in moist sand, or by suspending it in a glass of water (three toothpicks will hold it there). Perhaps you did this when you were a child, just to see the sweet potato sprout. Change the water often, and when the slips are about 8 inches long, pull them off the root with a twisting motion. They are then ready for planting.

Southern gardeners either save sweet potatoes from their fall crops and sprout them during the winter, or else they buy the slips and plant them in early spring. In the north, where this is not a commonly grown crop, it's hard to find roots to sprout that are good cold-climate varieties, so they're usually ordered by mail. When they come they should be opened right away and removed from their wrapping. They come in bundles and don't look very promising—just long white stems with a few puny leaves. But don't worry—they'll be fine. Put the stem part in a jug or bucket of water to keep them fresh.

Ideally, you'll plant your slips as soon as they arrive, but it's important for the soil to have warmed up—usually about two weeks after the last frost. (Try to time your order accordingly if you're having them shipped.) The warming process can be hastened by using raised beds or just

mounded-up rows. (These improve drainage, too.) The soil may also be warmed by laying black plastic over it; the slips are then planted through slits cut in the plastic. Still another shortcut is to root the slips in sand or some other potting medium, so that they'll have developed good root systems by the time they're planted. This is also a handy way to hold them if they arrive in the mail before the soil is warm.

Plant them about a foot apart (more if the crop is very vigorous in your area), with about 3 or 4 feet between rows. Plant them deeply, covering as much of the stem as possible, but making sure most of the leaves are aboveground. Premoistening the planting hole, and swishing the stems in a thin mud slurry, will help them to establish well without drying out.

If you have more slips than you need, choose the biggest, leafiest ones and give the others away. They may look very modest at first, but eventually cover the space with their creeping vines.

GROWING

Once in the ground, the slips should be kept well watered to keep them from wilting. A cupful of organic liquid fertilizer per plant, especially one high in phosphorus that is designed for transplanting, will also help get them off to a good start. You will not see a lot of lush foliage right away; the plants are working on their root systems.

While the roots are developing they need a steady water supply, but heavy soaking during drought can cause the roots to crack. Keep the beds weeded and cultivated until the vines cover them, topdressing them with a liquid organic fertilizer as needed, but not one too high in nitrogen.

PESTS AND DISEASES

The most important ways to avoid the rot diseases to which the plants are prone are to provide very good drainage and to rotate the crop. But don't expect a lot of problems from sweet potatoes, especially with northern crops. Nematode infestations are avoided by rotation and by obtaining pest-free plants from a reliable source. If nematodes have plagued any of your solanaceaous crops (tomatoes, potatoes, etc.), do not follow these with sweet potatoes.

HARVEST

Dig sweet potatoes when the foliage turns yellow and dies, or when frost cuts it down. The roots should not be allowed to freeze. Use a digging fork, and lift them very carefully. Any that are nicked or bruised should be used right away. But the rest will store well, especially if cured for about two weeks—if possible at around 85 degrees—to harden the skins. Then store them at 50 to 60 degrees or so in a moderately humid environment. Keep a few for sprouting if you want to repeat the same crop next year. Mine keep for most of the winter.

VARIETIES

The best varieties for small spaces are 'Bunch (or Bush) Porto Rico' and 'Vardamon.' 'Jewel' is a popular variety, as is the old standard 'Centennial,' which matures fairly quickly and does well in the north. The early 'Georgia Jet' and 'Beauregard' have been the champions in my Maine garden. 'White Yam' is an unusual, sweet white-fleshed variety.

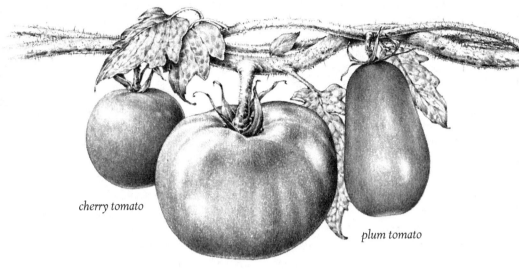

cherry tomato

plum tomato

large red tomato

Tomatoes

Tomatoes are the seductive vegetable—bright red, bursting with juice and flavor, fruitful to a fault. Had they been native not to Peru but to Asia Minor, a tomato—not an apple—surely would have caused our fall from grace. Tomatoes, it seems, have always engendered strong emotions. In the Renaissance they were called love apples and thought to be deadly poison. But now they're America's undisputed favorite vegetable (not to mention Italy's), and the gardener's pride and joy. My father once grew a tomato so enormous that he placed it on a platter and carved it as if it were a crown roast. At harvest and canning time they are so bounteous that they're almost too much of a good thing, as the poet Marge Piercy noted in her poem "The Engulfing Garden":

> . . . tomato seeds
> in my hair, tomato skins
> in my teeth, the surfaces
> of the kitchen heaped with
> tomatoes, tomatoes in buckets,
> tomatoes lined up on the window
> sills. . . .

Even if you don't reap buckets, tomatoes will reward you in flavor, versatility, and vitamin C that lasts long after picking, especially if the fruits are ripened on the vine. They have become something of a symbol for the current shift toward real, fresh, home-grown or locally grown produce, because the difference in taste between a supermarket tomato and a vine-ripened homeboy is such a dramatic one. When you decide which tomato to plant and how to grow it, you do not have to ensure that it has a thick skin for safe shipping, or pick it green in anticipation of its long journey. You can concentrate on flavor and nutrients—which is what food is all about.

Success with tomatoes depends in part on choosing varieties that are right for your climate. Sometimes the names give you the clues you need. Tomatoes called 'Seattle Best of All' and 'Frisco Fogger' are predictably suited to misty weather. 'Heatwave II' clearly suits the dry, blistering summers of the south. One way to locate those adapted to your region is to find a local nursery that takes the trouble to choose and sell seedlings with the local climate in mind. Also read the descriptions in a variety of seed catalogs; many make regional recommendations. There may even be a mail-order nursery that grows its own seed in and for your area. Or best of all, use seeds saved by successful gardening neighbors.

Climate is not the only factor in deciding which varieties to grow. "Determinate" tomatoes are short, bushy and set all their fruit at once—then stop producing. "Indeterminate" ones are long vines that keep growing and fruiting indefinitely—or until frost puts an end to them. Determinates are easier, because you don't have to deal with all those long vines. They're handy if your goal is canning tomatoes and you would just as soon process them all at once. But with indeterminate plants you can have your fresh summer eating spread out over more of the season. Because of their greater ratio of leaf to fruit, resulting in more photosynthesis, they are tastier as well.

There are also early and main-season types you can grow in succession. Then there's the plum or paste types, good for sauces and canning. Or the round, sweet cherry tomatoes, or the delicious little oval yellow ones—not to mention all the fabulous heirloom varieties. The only way to find your favorite tomatoes is to try different ones each season.

This is where seduction comes in. Looking over the seed catalogs at all those enticing choices, you're bound to order— and grow—too many tomatoes. Even those of us who know better usually have too many plants. Unless you do a lot of preserving, six is ample. You can still grow several varieties—just save part of the packet for next year. Tomato seeds are remarkably long-lived and resilient. When you feed tomatoes to your chickens, the seeds can go through the chickens' digestive systems intact, survive in the manure, survive in the compost bin where the manure is placed, survive in the soil after the compost has been spread in your garden, and come up as volunteers among your eggplants four years later. If they can do this, surely they can survive in a seed packet stored in a cool, dry place. When buying started plants from a nursery, try to buy them singly or in packs of two instead of in six-packs, so you can try more different kinds.

SITE

Choose a very sunny spot where tomatoes and plants in the same family have not grown recently (see page 232). Tomatoes do very well in raised beds because the soil there warms up fast and gives the young plants a good start. But when growing them this way, give them plenty of room or trellis them (see Figure 54).

SOIL

The soil should be loose, friable, and full of organic matter. Tomatoes feed rather heavily, so it should be rich, with a pH of 6.0 to 7.0. I incorporate peat moss and other organic matter throughout the bed, but often I'll add a shovelful of well-rotted manure to each hole before I set in the young plants, mixing this in thoroughly and watering the plants well. The soil should stay moist but not soggy, because good drainage is important.

PLANTING

Tomato seeds are usually best started indoors, six to eight weeks before the last average frost date. Use your warmest, sunniest windowsill or, better yet, wide-spectrum fluorescent lights (see page 35). It's essential that tomato plants not get leggy as they grow, for lack of light.

Either use the soil block system or sow the seeds ¼ inch deep in flats, then transplant to peat pots after about ten days. I move them up into 4-inch pots after they start to outgrow these, so that I have big, vigorous plants ready to go into the ground when the danger of frost has passed. But "big" does not mean "tall and leggy." You want your seedlings to be short, bushy, well-grown plants with good dark foliage.

Ways to Grow Tomatoes Fɪɢ. 54

Letting them sprawl. Vines, especially determinate varieties, may be grown without staking. Mulch helps keep fruits dry and disease free.

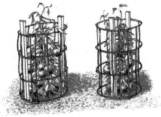

Caging. Wire cages will support tomato vines without tying. Use wire mesh with openings large enough to put your hand through for picking.

Staking. Use metal or 2- by 2-inch wood stakes, 6 feet tall. As vines grow, tie them to the stakes with soft twine, strips of cloth, or old stockings.

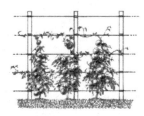

Trellising. Use horizontal wires or wire mesh attached to stout stakes. Tie vines to the trellis with soft twine or cloth.

Since tomatoes take a long time to ripen, it's tempting to set the plants out as early as you can. But there is no sense in setting them out before the air and the soil are starting to warm up. Covering them with cloches to ward off frosts and trap more sunlight will help to some degree, but for the most part tomatoes set out prematurely just sit there and do nothing. I find that later-planted ones always catch up to the early ones anyway. Some gardeners warm up the soil with black plastic and leave it on as a moisture- and heat-conserving mulch, planting the tomatoes through x-shaped slits. Special red plastic designed for growing tomatoes can also be used.

Tomatoes suffer more shock in transplanting than do most vegetables, but you can minimize this by hardening them off for a week or two first. This means setting them outdoors in their pots in a protected place so they get some warm sun, a little gentle wind, and even some cool (not freezing) nights. Then they'll have

adjusted to some of the stresses of real life in the garden before they're hit by the additional stress of having their roots set in the cool ground.

If your tomatoes are the long-vined, indeterminate type, you'll need to decide whether or not to give them a vertical support. If you just let them flop on the ground the plants will take up more room, and the fruits will be vulnerable to splattering mud, diseases, insects, and assorted small scurrying predators. I have grown tomatoes on the ground successfully, especially the bush types, by using a salt-hay mulch that keeps them dry while they ripen. On balance, however, I've decided that using some sort of support is almost always the way to go.

There are many different ways to support a tomato plant—stakes, cages, and trellises are illustrated in Figure 54. Oddly enough, supporting tomatoes is a very sentimental topic for me because I first met my husband, Eliot Coleman, when he was doing that very thing. He was with his Maine neighbor, the late Helen Nearing who, with her husband Scott Nearing, wrote the back-to-the-land bible *Living the Good Life*. They were standing in Helen's little unheated lean-to greenhouse, cleverly built against a section of the heat-retaining stone wall she had built around her garden. Eliot was training Helen's tomato vines around strands of ordinary garden twine that hung from the greenhouse roof, along the warm stone wall. It was July 9 and the plants were already quite tall. Well into November they were still bearing fruit.

In our commercial greenhouses Eliot and I use a similar system, minus the stone wall, and with the addition of fancy little plastic clips that hold the vines to white

Pruning FIG. 55
Tomatoes

Training a plant to just one main stem. Use pruning shears or scissors to remove the suckers, the small shoots that grow in the angle between the leaf stalks and the main stem. This will prevent side branches from forming.

nylon string suspended from above. But at present, in my home garden, my usual method is a simple one that I'd recommend to any home gardener—homemade tomato cages made of 6-inch concrete reinforcing wire mesh. I cut lengths of it and make cylinders about 16 inches in diameter and sink them firmly into the ground to keep them from blowing over in our windy yard. (You can drive in a metal stake on one side for extra rigidity but I haven't found this to be necessary.) The 6-inch openings are just right for a plant's branches to protrude through (making it self-supporting), and for me to reach my hands through to pick the fruit. At season's end I store the cylinders behind the compost pile. (You can also buy ready-made tomato cages, but these are flimsy and expensive.) I even use a shorter version of these homemade cages for bush-type tomatoes.

If you grow tomatoes in cages they should be planted up to 30 inches apart. Vining types can be pruned at the bottom, by removing the first two suckers—the little stems that grow out of the leaf axils (Figure 55), but after that they can just sprawl within their supports.

Those grown on strings or stakes, or on a vertical mesh trellis, can be planted closer together—about 16 inches—but need to be trained more severely. Prune them to one stem and cut out all the suckers that grow in the leaf axils. If they need tying, use a strip of cloth or soft twine in a figure-eight loop (Figure 56) so you don't break the stems. Pinch the growing tips when the stems reach the top of the support.

Whether bush type or vining type, tomato plants should be set into the ground much deeper than they were in the pot. Don't cover any flower clusters, but it is all right to bury the stem so that the first pair of leaves is under the soil. Water thoroughly.

GROWING

Tomatoes need a steady water supply to help them ripen well. Drought will slow them down, and an excess of water after drought can cause them to crack or develop blossom-end rot (recognized by round black spots on the fruits). A mulch (applied after the soil has warmed up), plus a moderate watering during drought, helps to keep the moisture level more consistent. I have never had to top-dress tomatoes, but you might apply an inch of compost around the plants or dose them with some liquid fertilizer once or twice in the season if growth seems slow or the plants lack that glow of health. This can either be done by drenching the soil around the plants with your fertilizer solution or by foliar feeding (spraying the leaves).

It seems to take forever for tomatoes to get red. Some people spray them at

How to Tie FIG. 56
a Stem to a Stake

the flower stage with a fruit-setting hormone spray. But ripening is largely up to the weather. If it is a cold, cloudy summer, well, everyone else will be staring at green tomatoes too. The best remedy is to make at least one or two of your plants early varieties to assuage your impatience.

PESTS AND DISEASES

In addition to blossom-end rot, described above, tomatoes get several diseases, notably verticillium and fusarium wilts and mosaic virus. The solution to these problems is to choose resistant varieties, which will have a "V," an "F," or an "M" next to their names, or all three. "N" means that the variety at hand also resists nematodes, small wormlike organisms that inhabit the soil and can injure plants. Rotating crops and removing debris is also important.

Aphids, tomato hornworms, and other insects bother tomatoes but don't usually do much damage. Far more serious are raids by chipmunks and their ilk, but vertical growing usually foils them.

HARVEST

When is the romance finally over? You can protect the fruit from the first light frosts by covering the plants with tarps or sheets. If it's really going to freeze, however, you'd best get everybody out there and pick all the tomatoes. Put a few on the kitchen table, and let the rest ripen in a cooler, darker place. Arrange them in one layer, and check often to see if any have holes, cracks, or even a small spot of rot. Remove these before they start to go, for go they will, transmitting moisture and rot to any others they are touching.

Even if your late tomatoes are spared from freezing, the flavor will decline as the days grow colder. If you've taken a few suckers from a healthy, small-vined plant before the freeze, you can root them and grow them indoors. A few gallons of soil each will sustain potted plants in a warm, sunny spot. The harvest won't be bounteous, but it is a treat to have a few vine-ripened tomatoes in winter.

Tomatoes are a very popular vegetable for canning and drying, but I've come to prefer a quick-freezing method. I harvest paste tomatoes at the peak of ripeness and just wash them off, cut out the little hard cores at the tops of the fruit, and toss them whole into plastic bags in the freezer. I can then reach for them individually for use in soups and sauces. The skins slip right off if I hold them under the hot water faucet while still frozen hard. If I let them drain in a colander all day they'll even reduce themselves to a nice thick paste. The clear liquid that collects below can be chilled as a beverage or saved for soups.

VARIETIES

It is impossible to even begin to survey the hundreds of tomato varieties now available to gardeners. The array, not to mention people's preferences, changes every year. There has certainly been a color revolution. I always used to look for brilliant red color in a tomato because it looked so great on the plate, but the wide color range of this wonderful vegetable is also beautiful to display—the pinkish red of the popular heirloom 'Brandywine,' the almost murky purple of 'Black Russian,' the orange of 'Persimmon,' the green of the striped 'Green Zebra.' There are yellow varieties too, and ones with mottled yellow-and-red flesh such as 'Big Rainbow.' In fact I love nothing more that a huge platter of mixed, sliced heirloom tomatoes in various colors, sizes, and shapes, dressed only with olive oil and salt so the different flavors come through.

Certain up-to-date varieties bring improvements, for example the reliability of the early 'First Lady II,' the productivity of Burpee's 'Brandy Boy' over that of the old 'Brandywine,' and the crack resistance of some of the successors to the old favorite cherry tomato 'Sweet 100.' The little heart-shaped 'Tomatoberry' is especially crackproof. 'Sungold' is a top-notch yellow cherry. For a main-season tomato I love the French hybrid 'Carmello.' For a paste type I have most often grown the big, meaty 'La Rossa'—a bit pale on the inside, so I'm still looking for The Perfect One. The old 'Amish Paste' comes close. In fact, I always find a few new tomatoes to try each year. It's only the "few" part that's difficult.

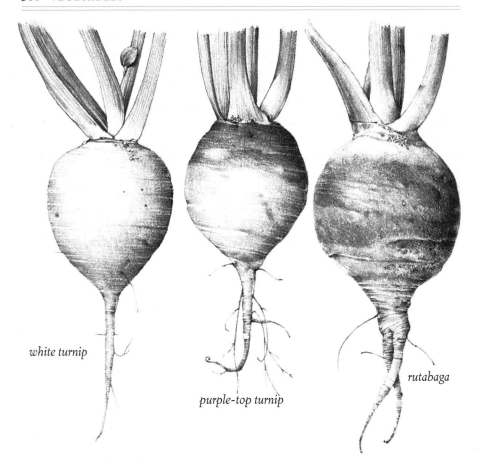

white turnip

purple-top turnip

rutabaga

Turnips and Rutabagas

To most people's minds, there is nothing in the garden quite as unromantic as a turnip, unless perhaps it's a rutabaga. Strong-flavored, good-storing root vegetables, they are rarely invited to sit at formal tables, but are good earthy peasant food nonetheless. Tradition dictates a bowl of buttered mashed turnips at a family Thanksgiving dinner, and they're also good cut up in soups.

Most turnips are smallish and white, and have no necks (rather like the children in *Cat on a Hot Tin Roof*). The leaves, which are green and slightly fuzzy when mature, sprout right from the root itself and are an excellent, nutritious cooked green—especially tasty with pieces of ham, salt pork, or slab bacon added. Some turnips have yellow flesh. Some varieties are grown for the root, others for the greens, still others for both. Many people don't realize that when harvested very young, turnips are exquisite—so sweet and tender you can eat them raw.

Rutabagas, sometimes called Swede turnips or just Swedes, are typically 5 or 6 inches in diameter and purplish in color. They look somewhat like a rounded sweet potato. The flesh inside is usually yellow. There's a neck or crown 1 or 2 inches long, from which sprout smooth blue-green leaves. I once got through a lean winter on my rutabaga crop. The tubers, stored in the basement, kept fine until spring.

Both turnips and rutabagas are cool-weather plants that get tough and woody and go to seed in hot weather. Which to grow? If you want an early-spring crop, or want to grow cooking greens, choose turnips. Then plant fall turnips as well for an even tastier treat. For a fall crop that will keep a while in the ground as well as in your cellar, rutabagas are a better choice. But bear in mind that turnips are twice as fast to mature, 35 to 60 days compared to rutabagas' 90 days. Both improve in flavor when grown in cool weather.

SITE

A sunny location is appreciated but not essential. A 4-foot by 4-foot bed will give you up to 25 rutabagas or up to 30 turnips. Since both are members of the cabbage family, try not to plant either where other cabbage vegetables have recently grown.

SOIL

Soil texture is important for both turnips and rutabagas, as it is for any root crop. Make the soil loose, well drained, and well ventilated by incorporating plenty of organic matter into it. Use well-rotted manure, compost, or peat moss, and dig it in to a depth of at least 7 inches, especially for rutabagas, whose tubers are larger and

whose root systems can go down several feet. Both of them like a neutral pH.

Make sure your soil has adequate phosphorus for root development. If you're growing turnips primarily for their greens, some extra nitrogen can be beneficial.

PLANTING

Spring turnips should be planted as early in spring as you can work the soil (late winter in warm climates) for a quick crop of small roots that mature before summer's heat and are eaten fresh-dug. Storage turnips are started in midsummer in the north, late summer in warmer climates. Successive sowings can also be made throughout late summer and fall for delicious quick crops of baby turnips, sweetened by a nip of frost. You can even sow them in a cold frame or cool greenhouse for winter consumption. In the south, sow all through the fall and winter outdoors.

Plant rutabagas in early summer in the north, allowing three months before the first average frost. You can plant them in mid to late summer farther south, to be sure the tubers are forming in cooler weather.

Seeds are sown directly in the garden. They are very tiny, but try to get them about an inch apart. They should be sown ¼ inch deep in spring, but ½ inch deep in warm weather, in well-moistened furrows. The seeds germinate quickly but do not like to come up through a crust, so just sift some compost or fine soil over the furrow and then keep it moistened.

Rows should be about 6 inches apart for baby turnips, and at least 12 inches for storage turnips and rutabagas. When the seedlings are 3 to 5 inches high, thin them to 2 to 3 inches apart for baby turnips, eating the thinnings as greens (young turnip leaves are even good raw in salads). Thinning is not as important if you're growing just for greens. Rutabagas should be thinned to at least 6 inches apart to permit good root development.

GROWING

Both crops need careful but frequent cultivation to keep the weeds down. Turnips appreciate a good, deep soaking with water once a week if the weather is dry. Rutabagas are drought tolerant within reason, since the roots go so deep. Topdressing should not be necessary with either turnips or rutabagas as long as your soil is moderately fertile, except perhaps with spring turnips or turnip greens. Use a high-nitrogen fertilizer only if you're growing turnip greens, not tubers.

PESTS AND DISEASES

For the most part the same ills that beset cabbage and other members of that family afflict rutabagas and turnips. Flea beetles, aphids, and root maggots are best controlled by the use of floating row covers at planting time.

Clubroot and blackroot are occasional problems. Rutabagas can rot in the center from insufficient boron in the soil, an affliction known as brown heart. If this condition appears, get a soil test done and ask for organic recommendations.

HARVEST

Dig turnips when they are 1 to 2 inches in diameter for a "baby" crop or 3 to 6 inches for large turnips, depending on variety. A few light frosts may improve the flavor of both tops and roots, but don't let them freeze solid. Cut off the tops and store the tubers in a cool place, just above 32 degrees if possible. Harvest rutabagas while the ground is still soft enough to dig, and cut off the tops and any long roots projecting from the tuber. Store them the same way you do turnips. Burying them in a container of barely moist sand will help keep them from drying out if the humidity in your storage area is low.

Turnip greens can be eaten as early as you do your thinning, and as late as a month or so after planting. If you're growing a root-turnip crop, you can still harvest a few outer leaves from the plants occasionally to make a meal of greens. But don't cut off all the greens if you want to harvest the tubers, at least not until it's time to dig the tubers up.

VARIETIES

For baby turnips my favorite variety is 'Hakurei.' 'De Milan Rouge' is a nice one for small white turnips with rosy tops. 'Tokyo Cross' is also good for a quick, early crop. 'Purple Top White Globe' is the standard variety for storage turnips.

The standard rutabaga varieties are 'American Purple Top,' 'Laurentian,' 'Long Island Improved,' and 'Macomber,' a white-fleshed type that keeps very well.

CHAPTER 8

Herbs

IT'S EASY TO GET THE WRONG IMPRES-
sion about herbs. Leafing through
those gorgeous books with color pictures of English herb gardens, you might
assume herbs are exceptionally tidy plants
that grow in little mounds, hummocks,
and intricate knot patterns, respecting the
careful geometrical shapes to which they
are confined. What you're seeing in those
handsome gardens, however, is herbs
on their best behavior. Left to their own
devices herbs are the anarchists of the garden. To sustain such elegant geometries
someone has tended them diligently.

Like many gardeners, I learned the les-
son about herbs the hard way. Planted in
little square raised beds, each 4 feet square,
some of my herbs after a few years really
considered themselves shrubs. My oregano plant had completely usurped a bed
of its own, the sage and my tarragon very
nearly did so. The neat little "chive edging"
was a forest so dense I could hardly dig up
the plants. Their flowers were bending
over the wooden sides of the beds, sowing
volunteer seedlings all over the path. Even
the lacy chervil plants that succumbed so
swiftly to heat or frost had colonized the
walkway with volunteers.

None of this discouraged me from herb
gardening. The experience did teach me
something about the best way to go about
it, though. Perhaps the formal herb plot
evolved, in part, as a way of curbing these
plants' assertive natures. After all, how
much do you need of any one herb? If I
wanted to dry a lot of tarragon, say, or make
a big batch of pesto sauce with my basil, I
would certainly raise a large crop of each.
But often all I need are small herb plants
that I can snip a few leaves from here and
there for cooking. Compact herbs also seem

to bear leaves with more flavor than large,
sprawling ones, and sometimes I've even
started afresh in spring with new plants for
this reason. Fortunately, using your herbs
is one way to keep them the proper size:
the more you snip them, the more bushy,
healthy, and flavorful they become.

I think you have to be realistic about
herb growing and consider why you're
doing it in the first place. To begin with,
how are we defining "herb"? Botanically,
an herb is any plant with a soft stem as
opposed to a woody one, not just the ones
we cook with. (The term also disqualifies
most of our common perennial "herbs,"
such as sage, lavender, rosemary, and
thyme, all of which are woody.) Our idea
that herbs are useful plants has also narrowed. To the colonial housewife, herbs
included a great many plants that were put
to household use—for cooking, for treating
illnesses and wounds, for dyeing fabrics,
for sweetening musty drawers or rooms
with their aromatic foliage—and for a host
of other tasks. Herbs were powerful instru-
ments that could heal, kill, and even work
magic spells. The now-outdated image of
the witch throwing assorted herbs into a
pot is based on the practical power women
once derived from their herb gardens, especially older ones with years of experience in
the ways of using nature.

Some modern herb growers are strongly
drawn to this tradition and explore the very
real medicinal uses of many herbs. Others
grow them for dried bouquets and pot-
pourris. Others simply enjoy their attractive appearance and scent. (Weeding an
herb garden is more a treat than a chore,
because your hands moving among the
plants stir up such pleasant odors.) But
for most herb gardeners today, the prime

motivation is to produce fresh seasonings for the kitchen. I enjoy my herbs' nostalgic associations as much as anyone, but not enough to grow herbs that I don't like to cook with, look at, or use to attract wildlife—even if they have great old-fashioned names like costmary or woad. My witchcraft largely consists of tossing bay into my cauldron of bean soup, snipping chervil sprigs into a salad, stuffing sage, tarragon, or rosemary leaves under the skin of a chicken, or brewing a fragrant bright green lemon verbena tea. I share the sentiments of Elisabeth Morss in this verse about bee balm (*Monarda didyma*) from her book *Herbs of a Rhyming Gardener:*

Monarda, or Oswego tea
First gladdened Indian and bee.
Then came the English, French,
    and Dutch,
I wonder if they liked it much.
It paid no tax to King and Crown,
And so our forebears gulped it down.
To patriotic zeal I bow,
Delighted not to drink it now.

With the need to avoid the British tea tax now well behind us, I grow bee balm not for tea but for its handsome flowers, which lure hummingbirds and butterflies as well as bees. You'll find it in the chapter on perennials rather than here. I love the way many other herbs look, too, and I've grown them in many different kinds of gardens, always being a bit more vigilant with my pruners and spade than I was in that first herb plot. And while I have narrowed down the list of herbs in this chapter to a modest 17 basic culinary herbs, I love to experiment with new ones and I urge you to do the same.

Ways to Grow Herbs

YOU DO NOT HAVE TO PUT ALL YOUR herbs in one spot. For one thing, herbs vary in the way they grow. Some, such as dill, basil, chervil, and coriander, are annuals. Many, such as tarragon, sage, chives, mint, oregano, and thyme, are perennials. Others, such as parsley, are biennials. Many perennial ones are hardy but others, like rosemary and bay, do not survive cold winters. Some you want a little of, some a lot of. So you may wind up choosing several of the following options for growing them.

HERBS IN THE VEGETABLE GARDEN

I always have a few herbs growing with my vegetables, usually the annual ones I use in quantity, such as basil, parsley, and dill. I plant these crops in rows or blocks, to snip as needed during the summer, and I harvest them before frost for pesto or herb vinegars.

You could, of course, grow all your herbs in the vegetable garden. (If your habit is to till the whole garden under as a whole at the end of the growing season, you'd want to place perennial herbs such as sage in a separate, defined area.) But if that garden is at a distance from the house it might be better to keep most of your herbs close at hand for snipping. To me it's very important to be able to rush out in the middle of fixing a meal to pick what I need.

One compromise might be to put the herbs you need most in pots near the kitchen door. Another might be to have a large vegetable garden for space-consuming crops like corn and beans, and a smaller kitchen garden or salad garden closer to the house. The kitchen garden might combine herbs with an eye-catching array of lettuces in different colors, some peppers, and even some compact tomato plants.

One of the advantages of growing some annual herbs with the extra space a vegetable garden supplies is that you can grow them in succession. Certain of the annual ones—dill, chervil, and coriander in particular—go to seed readily, especially when the weather becomes very warm. It's great to be able to sow a fresh crop and have it coming along as you're approaching the cooler weather of fall. Some herbs, such as chamomile, are such dependable self-sowers that they replenish themselves each year. Of course, this means keeping them in the same bed and not working them into a crop rotation.

GROWING HERBS WITH FLOWERS

It is also possible to grow some, or even all, of your herbs in the flower garden. Most of them have at least one ornamental feature. Often it's the flowers, as in dill's lacy yellow umbels, mint's purple spikes, or borage's little bursts of true blue. But herb foliage is often decorative too—the leaves of common sage are a beautiful gray-green, rue's are blue. Those of 'Dark Opal' basil are such a rich purple color that they'd earn their keep even if you never ate a leaf. So would the feathery dark strands of bronze-leaved fennel. Both work especially well next to blue flowers and plants with silvery leaves such as artemisias, which are themselves aromatic herbs (not used in cooking).

Low-growing herbs such as thyme or prostrate rosemary make good edging plants. And many herbs are particularly effective in the rock garden, their various foliage colors and textures blending beautifully with the colors and textures of stone. You can even tuck them in crevices between the pavers of a terrace or in the chinks of walls. The ones of Mediterranean origin such as rosemary and thyme actually appreciate the relatively dry, well-drained soil found in such situations.

These examples only begin to describe the ornamental uses of herbs, and you'll enjoy coming up with your own. In planning these gardens, refer also to the design principles discussed in the chapters on annuals and perennials.

HERB GARDENS

If you want to put together a garden just for herbs, there are a number of ways to go about it. Your garden might be an entryway planting, for example—a formal one for the front door or a more casual one for the door leading into the kitchen. The area around the kitchen door is a particularly good site because the herbs are then easily accessible for cooking. Another good spot might be along a fence in a back or side yard, especially if you want to grow a lot of tall herbs such as dill, angelica, and lovage, and if your goal is to produce large bunches of them for drying. There you can give them plenty of room to grow tall and broad, and tie them to the fence if they flop.

Herb gardens are not hard to plan (see Figure 57 for an example of one). If it is a border, meant to be viewed from one side, put tall herbs in back, medium-height herbs in the middle, and short ones along the border for edging—or plant an edging of annual flowers or alpine strawberries. With herbs you don't have to think so carefully about bloom times, because bloom is largely incidental. In fact, you may be cutting many of your herbs just before they bloom, when their flavor is at its peak. But if it's important for you to keep the garden looking pretty, plan some successions to take care of post-harvest bare spots. A chamomile or dill patch can look pretty barren, for instance, after it has been harvested and the stalks have started to yellow in late summer. Try surrounding them with a sprawling annual such as portulaca or trailing nasturtiums that can wander among old, dead stems and shine in summer's second inning.

Give vigorous plants like mint plenty of room, or grow them in a container, sunk in the ground to keep them under control. An old bucket or plastic tub with holes punched in the bottom for drainage would work fine. In the case of mint, it often makes better sense to find a moist spot for it in some other part of the yard. Mine is spreading happily in a drainage ditch.

In choosing the site, do keep several things in mind. First, most herbs need plenty of sun (though a few, such as chervil, parsley, and mint, will grow well in part shade). Second, most herbs absolutely require good drainage, and you may have to provide it by growing them in raised beds. And third, most won't tolerate competition from tree roots (again, raised beds might be the solution).

GROWING HERBS IN POTS

I always have some herbs growing in the house in winter. Not only does it spare me the work of drying or freezing them in the summer, but they taste better when freshly picked. In some busy years I've even taken to growing almost all my herbs in large pots or boxes year round. Annual herbs can be sown in long window-box-type containers. For perennial herbs I look for attractive pots or boxes, one plant to each. Potted herbs are great on a terrace next to the house, where they're not only handy but also decorative, grouped with geraniums, lantana, and other flowering plants. I find that perennial herbs in containers need to be divided less often than those grown in the ground. Constraining their root systems keeps them compact and flavorful. Indoor annual herbs must be resown from time to time; I pinch off the flowers to keep them from going to seed, but sooner or later the crop starts to peter out. By then I might have another crop of seedlings started in another container.

One thing to remember about herbs in pots is that the soil dries out very quickly, especially if the pots are clay ones. Although some herbs are quite drought tolerant, you still may have to water them every day in hot, dry weather. If this is difficult for you, try sinking the pots in the soil of the vegetable garden or some other bed, after you bring them outdoors in spring. They'll need watering far less often this way.

GROWING HERBS INDOORS

Even if you live in an apartment, you can grow most of the herbs discussed in this chapter in containers. All you need is either a very sunny window (one that gets at least five to six hours of sun a day) or else a growing light (page 35). In fact, if the only outdoor space you have is shady, herbs are better off indoors in a sunny window or under a light. And herbs are attractive indoors, not only to the eye but to the nose as well. Trailing ones such as thyme and sweet marjoram can even be used in hanging baskets.

Plan for an Herb Garden (18' by 18')   FIG. 57

1. sweet basil
2. purple basil
3. lemon basil
4. broadleaf parsley
5. curly parsley
6. leaf fennel
7. chervil
8. lemon verbena

9. sweet marjoram
10. dill
11. rosemary
12. coriander (cilantro)
13. sage
14. French tarragon
15. chives
16. oregano

17. bay
18. lavender
19. thyme
20. Johnny-jump-ups
21. calendula
22. nasturtium, compact variety
23. 'Lemon Gem' marigold
24. 'Orange Gem' marigold

Though almost any herb is worth trying indoors, you'll find that some do better than others. Rosemary is a clear winner; it even blooms indoors in wintertime! Bay is also excellent. Sage may be sparse indoors but even a few of those fresh leaves for soups or pasta will make it earn its keep. My program with the less successful ones like basil is to keep them there for as long as they're healthy. Once they succumb to whitefly or the indoor blues I just bid them farewell.

A PLAN FOR AN HERB GARDEN

The herb garden shown in Figure 57 is my idea of a somewhat formal one in an old-fashioned style—a garden that is decorative yet practical, supplying you with the basics for cooking with herbs. I've combined annual and perennial herbs, and tossed in some edible flowers both for looks and for use. At the center is a large, attractive pot with a bay plant in it, to serve as a focal point. (I put the bay in a pot because in my climate I must always bring my bay indoors for the winter, but if your winter temperatures do not go much below freezing you can grow yours right in the ground.) You might want to plant your rosemary in a pot too, if it's not hardy in your area. The centerpiece for the garden might also be a statue, birdbath, sundial, or some such ornament.

The perennial herbs will be dug up and divided or replaced from time to time as they get large, sprawling, and woody, but probably not all at once. They do need to be cut back, though, and sometimes twice a year. For example I might make one cutting of the tarragon in midsummer for drying, another in early fall for tarragon vinegar. I've left out a few herbs that I normally plant in a plot where I can assign them more space, such as mint and lovage. Thyme is used as an edging here, along with Johnny-jump-ups, which are grown for their edible flowers, and which will persist from year to year. The four beds at the corners are planted with a mix of annual and perennial herbs, with some annual flowers—all edible!—added for color.

The garden is 18 feet square, but could be a half or even a third that size and still provide you with plenty of herbs for cooking. You may not want as many different kinds, and you might want more of some, less of others, depending on your taste. I've made the paths 24 inches wide—enough to let the herbs sprawl just a bit without impeding foot traffic. I think brick paths look great, but flagstones, flat fieldstones, cobblestones, gravel, or simply grass would also be attractive. (Where you use brick, make your dimensions in multiples of four, since most bricks are 8 inches long by 4 inches wide.) You might also plant the paths with a carpeting herb such as Roman chamomile (*Chamaemelum nobile*) or thyme. The outside of the garden could be edged with another path, more bricks, a row of stones, a fence, or a lawn.

Growing Tips for Herbs

THE CARE YOU GIVE YOUR HERBS depends in part on where you decide to grow them.

OUTDOORS

Once you have found the right site, you'll discover that most herbs aren't fussy about growing conditions. Some people will tell you that herbs like poor, dry soil, and it's true that since many of our favorites come from the Mediterranean region, they're relatively tolerant of drought. They may even lose flavor if grown in very rich soil. But frankly, I grow herbs much the way I grow most everything else, in a soil of average fertility with a pH between 5.5 and 7.0, enriched and lightened with plenty of organic matter. I give them water when they seem to need it. The recommendations in the List of Herbs in this chapter will give you some special pointers about which need that extra dose of fertilizer and which shouldn't get too much, or which ones benefit from a sprinkling of lime. But if your soil is good, and if it's well drained, the only real problem I think you'll encounter is that some herbs might succeed *too* well, and some might not survive the winter.

Seeds of hardy annual herbs like chervil are sown as soon as the ground can be worked in spring, or even in fall for spring crops. Tender annuals like basil are sown after the danger of frost has passed. Some perennial herbs that are easy to grow from seed are sweet marjoram, oregano, chives, and thyme, but you'll probably want to start these quite early indoors. Many perennial herbs are planted and divided like any perennials (see page 185)—except those that become woody shrubs, such as sage and rosemary. Tender perennial herbs can be protected with a cold frame. In Maine, we have also been able to winter over many tender herbs by placing a simple plastic A-frame tent over the bed.

Winter survival can be perplexing with herbs, however. Lavender and tarragon always survive in my garden but not in my neighbor's. Thyme is supposed to be a reliable zone 5 plant, but I lose it every year. I have a feeling that winter drainage is a critical factor in many cases. Adding plenty of organic matter to the soil will help it to drain, especially if your soil is heavy. I also think the stone-and-gravel paths that separate all my herb beds help them to drain better year-round. A mulch of evergreen boughs, which do not mat and become soggy, is also good winter protection for herbs. Some people have good luck spreading chicken grit (made from ground-up oyster shells or granite meal) on the soil surface around the plants.

INDOORS

If you're growing herbs in the garden and want to bring some indoors, you have several options. Many herbs can be dug up and brought inside, to be potted in a container of ample size in a good potting medium for houseplants (page 723). Perennial herbs respond especially well to this treatment though some, like tarragon and chives, do best if you give them an artificial "winter" by letting them go through a few weeks of freezing night temperatures outside. When brought back indoors, these will end their period of dormancy by sending up fresh new growth. This trick will often revive housebound perennial herbs that have not been doing well; just set them outside for a while, protecting any tender ones from hard freezes.

But bringing entire herb plants indoors may not always be worthwhile. The annual ones may be at or near the end of their growth cycle, and the perennial ones may be at the point where they're too old, too woody, and—unless you have a pot the size of a small armchair—too big to be potted. Any established herbs you do dig up should be pruned back a bit before their trip indoors. Often it's better to take stem cuttings (page 733) or to layer plants (page 620) in the garden, and then pot up those that grow where the layered stem takes root. You could dig up and transplant some self-sown seedlings of chives or sage. Or see if the local nursery still has some small ones in pots. To learn which technique is best for which herb, read the growing instructions in this chapter under individual herbs.

Herbs grown indoors need plenty of light and water and an occasional feeding (fish emulsion works well). A little extra humidity not only helps their growth but keeps the foliage succulent and tasty. If the air in your dwelling is dry, place the pots in a tray of stones and keep the tray filled with water just up to the bottom of the pots; this helps to keep moisture in the air. Except for rosemary, which appreciates it, I don't like to mist herbs—it encourages fungus diseases. But they do like to be washed off in the sink from time to time.

Regular washing will also discourage pests. Although the strongly aromatic nature of most herbs helps to repel pests outdoors, there are some that bother indoor herbs, simply because indoor plants live under more stressful conditions (less light, less humidity, no cleansing rains) and are more susceptible. You might sometimes find mealybugs on your indoor rosemary, whiteflies on your chives or basil, and scale on your potted bay. Use the soapy-water treatment and other safe pest repellents described on page 66. Also refer to the houseplants chapter.

Harvesting Herbs

I DON'T HAVE A FIXED PROGRAM FOR harvesting herbs. When I need some of the leaves I pick them. I go easy on very young plants, because I don't want to set them back. But when plants get very big and bushy I try to think of ways to use the leaves, such as making up a batch of herb vinegar or drying some of the stems in bunches. The basic idea behind preserving herbs is that their leaves contain volatile oils that produce the scents and tastes we prize. Herbs should be preserved in a way that keeps these oils in their potent state. There are several ways to do this.

DRYING HERBS

When herbs are dried, the moisture leaves the plant but the oils do not, so that dried herbs sometimes have a more concentrated flavor than fresh ones. The trick is to dry them quickly and thoroughly, but not in such a way that you cause the oils to volatilize (escape into the air).

Pick herbs you want to dry on a day that is neither rainy nor humid, just after the dew has dried on the leaves. The age of the plant is also a factor. The ideal time is immediately before the plant starts to bloom—then the oils are at their strongest. With most herbs you can cut back as much as two thirds of the plant, but you'll probably want to discard parts of the stems you've cut if the foliage on them is sparse (stems retain a lot of moisture). To dry the plants you can hang them upside down to let the oils run down into the leaves, putting them in a paper bag to catch any leaves and seeds that fall. If you keep them out of the sunlight the oils stay stronger.

Another method is to lay the herbs on trays or screens. You can even put them in a warm oven for a few hours, but I find this risky—I'm afraid of losing the oils. After the leaves are dry and crumbly, strip them off the plant and put them in airtight jars, boxes, or plastic bags. Check every now and then to make sure no moisture is accumulating on the jar or box lids, or on the sides of the bags; if it does, take out the herbs and dry them some more.

Herbs grown for their seeds, such as dill, caraway, and coriander, should be harvested when the seeds have turned light brown or gray. Hang the branches in bags (as above) or spread them out to dry. Then, after they've dried somewhat, shake the seeds out of the plants and dry them some more. Thresh away the hulls by blowing on them gently, by using a fan, or by letting the seeds fall through a colander, screen, or hardware cloth.

OILS AND VINEGARS

The most decorative way to make herb vinegars is to put sprigs of fresh herbs in glass bottles filled with white wine vinegar. I like to make several kinds: tarragon (always), lovely rose-colored basil vinegar if I've grown 'Dark Opal,' and also some bottles with mixed herbs. They make great presents. You can also warm herbs in the vinegar and put it through the blender or food processor for an even stronger brew, strain it, *then* add a few sprigs for looks.

Herb oils can be made the same way, but sometimes sprigs that float to the top of the oil can turn moldy. You can also whiz the herbs and oil in a blender, let the mixture sit awhile, then strain it. Use it up promptly.

FREEZING

There are several ways to freeze herbs. One is simply to put them in plastic wrap or plastic bags and stick them in the freezer, but this does not work for all herbs. (Basil, for instance, will turn to black mush.) Another is to put them in oil, butter, or water, puree the mixture, and freeze that. The oil and butter purees don't freeze quite solid, and some can be scraped off as needed if you freeze them in jars or plastic boxes. My favorite method is to freeze any of these pureed mixtures in ice-cube trays, then remove the cubes and store them in a plastic bag in the freezer. This gives me handy little portions to drop into a soup or a sauce whenever I need them.

List of Herbs

THE HERBS LISTED HERE ARE ONLY a snip and a taste of the vast world of herbs, but they are all good for cooking and handsome to look at. Added to any other favorites you might have, they'll give you the makings of a kitchen herb garden.

BASIL
Ocimum basilicum

Description: Every summer the basil in my garden produces tall, lush plants with big bright green leaves. I put the leaves, whole, into salads, especially salads of sliced ripe garden tomatoes. I chop the leaves and put them into sauces, soups, and eggplant casseroles. And I puree great handfuls of them in the food processor along with Italian parsley, olive oil, pine nuts, garlic, and Parmesan cheese to make pesto, that glorious Italian sauce that turns a simple bowl of pasta into a feast.

Basil is avidly cultivated, and even grows wild, on the frost-free Ligurian coast of Italy—the area around Genoa. In the tropics it flourishes year-round. But every fall the basil in my garden gives me the first unmistakable sign of winter's approach. A few maple leaves just *might* be turning orange because those particular trees are stressed, or because it's been dry lately. The geese just *might* be flying south to escape encroaching suburbanization. Yet there's no mistaking the blackened mess that is my basil after the first frost. Basil, for all its summer bravado, is a tender annual, and if frost is predicted some evening you might find me out there in the dark, picking basil by the armful and making emergency batches of pesto.

The commonest kind of basil is called sweet basil and can grow as tall as 6 feet in warm climates. For pesto I grow a large-leaved sweet basil 'Genovese,' which approaches 3 feet. It has small white flower spikes, beloved of bees. There are many other, exotic basils such as anise basil and cinnamon basil, and a bush form (*Ocimum basilicum* 'Minimum') that is recommended for indoor culture. 'Spicy Globe,' pungent and small-leaved, makes little topiary balls—great for growing in a pot or a small garden. Of the red-hued basils, the wonderful purple 'Dark Opal' has a particularly intense color, nice for garnishes and for tinting herb vinegars. But 'Red Rubin' and 'Purple Ruffles' have proved more vigorous in the garden, at least for me. These and many other varieties have pink flowers. I also like the complex-flavored Thai basils. My favorite of all is lemon basil ('Citriodorum'), which combines a strong lemon flavor with basil's characteristic minty taste. I use it constantly all summer.

How to Grow: Grow basil in full sun if possible, in rich, loose, well-drained soil a little on the limy side. Sow seeds outdoors after all danger of frost has passed and the ground has warmed up, thinning plants to about 10 inches apart. They are also easily started ahead indoors, about six weeks before the last frost date. When the plants are about 6 inches tall, pinch them to make them bushy. When the plants start to bloom, pinch the flowers off to keep the foliage productive and flavorful, leaving a few to feed the bees, or to self-sow if you live in a warm climate (or just because the flowers are beautiful!). To grow an indoor crop in winter, either sow seeds or root some stem cuttings from your summer garden. Give the plants plenty of warmth and light. Indoors or out, your basil will tell you whether its soil is rich enough. If so, the leaves will be a rich dark green; if not, they will be pale.

Harvest: Pick basil leaves—or whole branches—as needed. I'll often combine this with deadheading the spent blooms, making a bouquet for the windowsill with the flowers and leaves. The leaves can be preserved by cutting them before bloom and drying as quickly as possible on trays or screens in a dark, well-ventilated place. But I've never found this very satisfactory. I prefer to puree them in oil and freeze them, as described above. Since this is essentially making a pesto, I just make a simplified pesto version with olive oil alone, add-

ing other ingredients like nuts, garlic, and cheese later on during cooking.

BAY
Laurus nobilis

Description: Like many cooks, I once thought of bay as a single dried leaf you put in soups, stews, and other dishes to simmer along with a bunch of other herbs like parsley and thyme. I have since come to think of it as one of my favorite flavors—one that can stand perfectly well on its own. I use fresh bay rather than dried, and I add it to quick dishes as well as long-cooking ones. I'll often drop a leaf into some chopped vegetables I'm sweating in a covered skillet, and notice the wonderful aroma right away. (I usually remove the leaves, which never entirely soften, before serving.) Unlike the flavor of many herbs, bay's is stronger fresh than dried. It is sometimes called sweet bay or sweet laurel, and is the same plant used to crown poets, scholars, athletes, and other honorees. The native mountain laurel, whose leaves are poisonous, is an altogether different plant.

How to Grow: Bay is difficult to propagate, both from seeds or from cuttings, so I always buy started plants. This may seem like an expensive way to grow it, but the plants can attain a considerable size and live indefinitely, so the purchase is a good investment.

Only gardeners in moderately mild climates (zones 8 to 10) can grow bay outdoors year-round without protection, although a selection from the National Arboretum, simply called 'Hardy,' is said to be less tender. I grow bay in pots that I keep outdoors in summer and bring in for the winter.

If I lived in a climate warm enough to grow bay outdoors in pots, I still might pot up a plant or two and bring them in for the winter, because even where it is hardy it is not always evergreen. If your outdoor plant sheds its leaves, it will nonetheless resprout when warmer temperatures return. Pruning the plant back a bit in spring will prompt it to put out fresh new growth. Plant it in a sunny spot and give it fertile, well-drained soil. In very warm areas it may attain the status of a tall shrub or small tree.

Sun, adequate drainage, and a monthly fertilizing with fish emulsion constitutes basic care. (I feed biweeekly in late winter and spring when the longer days encourage fresh growth.) The plants like high humidity, but should never be overwatered. Indoors, mine are quite prone to scale insects, which can be recognized by the stickiness that forms on the leaves. They are rarely life-threatening but can set back leaf production. I wash the leaves with insecticidal soap, scraping the little hard scale bodies off the stems and undersides of the leaves with my fingernail. Spraying with alcohol also helps.

Harvest: Cut fresh leaves with scissors as needed for cooking. Whole branches can be cut and dried very easily, just by laying them in a warm, well-ventilated spot out of direct sun. When thoroughly dry, remove them from the stems and store in jars or bags, out of the sunlight. A package of homegrown bay makes a nice gift.

CHERVIL
Anthriscus cerefolium

Description: Chervil looks like parsley but is even more feathery. It has a very mild, subtle, slightly licorice-like flavor that tastes like spring itself in a green salad, as long as you don't overpower it with stronger herbs. It is also sublime in an omelet. It keeps its flavor best if used uncooked, or cooked only briefly. Rarely much more than a foot tall, dainty chervil is nonetheless a rugged plant, a hardy annual that will withstand some frost. Though it germinates slowly, it self-sows with abandon. Much of my chervil harvesting consists of plucking little clumps that have come up in the wrong place (but at just the right time for a meal).

How to Grow: Chervil will grow in full sun but prefers part shade, especially in hot climates. Grow it in nice, light, moderately rich soil. Direct-seeding works best. Sow seeds outdoors as soon as the soil can be worked in spring, being careful not to cover them. When seedlings come up, thin to 4 to 6 inches apart. My chervil goes to seed and succumbs to hot weather in midsummer, but by then it has either self-sown its replacement or I have sown a succession crop in a semishaded spot. Interplanting it with a taller, bushier plant such as basil will also give it some shade. You can grow chervil indoors in winter by sowing it in a long box, then sowing a new crop in another box before the first one peters out. In mild climates you can keep it going all winter long in the garden. It's also a good cold-frame crop.

Harvest: Snip upper foliage as needed; this may also help to retard bolting. Chervil can be dried by cutting the leaves before the flowers open, but will lose most of its flavor. Freezing it, using the ice-cube trick described on page 392, is more successful.

CHIVES

Allium schoenoprasum

Description: Almost everybody likes chives. If you have grown only one herb in your life, it was probably chives. If you have eaten only one herb in your life, it was probably chives. When my son Chris was

little and my mother complained that he didn't like a single vegetable, he replied, "That's not true. I like chives."

Chives are hardy perennial bulbs that belong to the onion family. A clump of them is essentially a dense mass of tiny onions that never make bulbs and never get big. In early summer they are covered with beautiful purple flowers a bit like those of clover, which can be used as garnishes, in bouquets, or just as a lovely presence in the garden. Bees and butterflies love them too. In addition to the common kind are garlic chives—sometimes called Chinese chives (*Allium tuberosum*), which taste stronger and grow about 2 feet tall. Garlic chives are often grown as ornamental plants because of their attractive, flat gray-green leaves and fragrant white flowers in mid to late summer. I always have a pot of plain old chives indoors or on the terrace, for whenever I want a fresh, oniony but not overpowering taste in something, and I plant both species outdoors in the garden as well.

How to Grow: Grow chives in full sun or part shade, in rich, fairly moist but well-drained soil. You can grow them easily from seed sown in early spring, but chive plants are so readily available that they are usually grown from a piece of someone else's clump—either from a neighbor or the garden center.

If well mulched, both types of chives will often stay green outdoors all through the winter. I seem to remember that when I was living in frigid Vermont, where 4 feet of snow kept them well blanketed, I had lovely fresh green chives as soon as I was able to dig the snow away from them. They are a good herb to winter outdoors in a cold frame, too.

Aside from the occasional aphid plague, chives don't have many problems, but sometimes an indoor clump will start to look very dried out and not very productive. If this happens, cut the plant back to an inch or two and try to pull out some of the dead leaves. Then put it outdoors or in a cool spot for several weeks. This artificial "winter" should shock the clump into new "spring" growth. Then start feeding it gradually with a liquid fertilizer.

Outdoors, both species can be a pest because of their enthusiastic sowing—especially garlic chives. The best way to control this is to deadhead the blossoms before the seeds can scatter.

Harvest: Snip foliage as needed, cutting the leaves at the outside of the clump. Chives are best fresh; frozen is second best; dried chives are better than nothing but definitely in third place. If you can't keep a fresh pot indoors, grow them in the garden, then chop them up and freeze them in plastic bags or boxes. Or make chive butter and freeze that.

CORIANDER (CILANTRO)

Coriandrum sativum

Description: This hardy annual herb, widely used around the world, has upper leaves that look like dill and lower ones that look like parsley. The leaves have a pungent flavor all their own, which people tend to either love or hate, and the seeds are also very flavorful. Generally speaking the word "coriander" refers to the seeds, and the leaves are called cilantro, the name given to the herb in Spanish-speaking countries,

where it is often used fresh. It is called *dhania* in India, and is used in many other parts of Asia as well, such as Vietnam, Thailand, and China. Sometimes it is called Chinese parsley. There has been something of a coriander renaissance of late because there is so much interest in the cooking of foreign countries, and chances are, if you scratch a foreign cuisine you'll find coriander. The flowers are flat umbels, usually white but sometimes pale pink or lavender.

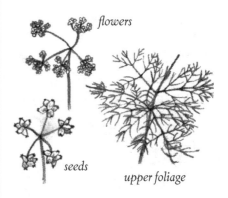

flowers

seeds

upper foliage

How to Grow: Grow coriander in full sun or part shade, in very well drained, moderately fertile soil. Using fresh seed, sow after danger of frost is past in spring, and in late summer for an early fall crop. Thin to about a foot apart. Like all the Umbelliferae (page 233), it has a long taproot and does not like to be transplanted. But unlike some members of this family it germinates fairly quickly, so it's easy to make successive sowings later on. Since the plant tends to bolt in hot weather, it's great to have a late-sown planting coming along as temperatures start to cool. (Some varieties such as 'Santo' are more bolt-proof than others.) Plants will also self-sow, persisting for years in the garden on their own. To grow indoors, sow seed in deep pots that will accommodate the roots, and cut frequently.

Harvest: Leaves can be cut anytime for seasoning. For drying cut them just before bloom. The dried leaves do not retain their flavor well and they are better preserved frozen, as cilantro butter. To dry the seeds, cut the plants when the seedpods start to turn brown and aromatic, and will crack if you pinch them, but before the seeds start to drop. Hang the bunches in paper bags to catch the seeds as they fall. Rub the pods between your fingers to get them all out.

DILL
Anethum graveolens

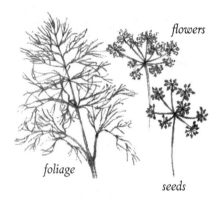

flowers

foliage

seeds

Description: Dill has very pretty, wavy, threadlike leaves that are bluish in color, and its flat, umbrella-shaped yellow flowers produce pungent seeds. I use the leaves in many dishes, especially in salads and with fish. Dill is a tall plant, sometimes growing to 4 or 5 feet. A half-hardy annual, it self-sows readily and is very easy to grow. Usually the foliage is called dill weed.

How to Grow: I have grown dill indoors, so as to always have a bit of its fresh-tasting leaves for seasoning. But the plant does get very gawky in a container, even when snipped regularly, and is not long-lived. Outdoors it makes a big stand of attractive plants. When it starts to go to seed, I cut the big flowers to lend an airy touch to bouquets.

Dill can be either direct-sown or started indoors, but if you do the latter, use peat pots or soil blocks since transplant shock will make it bolt. Plants should be set out, or thinned to, at least a foot apart. They need full sun and a steady water supply, but the soil should be well drained, slightly acid, and moderately fertile. Seeds can be direct-sown in early spring, or in fall for the following year's crop. (My plants usually do this themselves, by self-sowing.) Always use fresh seed. Plants do tend to bolt in hot weather, even with frequent snipping, so you may want to make repeated sowings for a steady supply. They may need staking; brush stakes work well (see page 188). Do *not* kill the caterpillars that feed on the leaves—they'll turn into black swallowtail butterflies.

Harvest: Dill leaves taste best fresh, but can be dried or quick-frozen in plastic bags as ice cubes or as herb butter. The seeds hold their flavor better than the spidery leaves do. Cut the flowers when the seeds are brown but not yet dropping, then hang them in a paper bag till the seeds fall.

FENNEL
Foeniculum vulgare

Description: Fennel is a plant used a lot in Mediterranean cooking. It is reputed to stave off hunger when chewed, and its mild licorice-like taste is often used to balance the strong taste of fish. Sometimes fish is grilled or roasted on a bed of its stalks, which bear feathery fronds. There are two

leaf fennel   *bulb fennel*

kinds of fennel. One, usually called leaf fennel, is grown for the ferny foliage, the stems, and the seeds. It can grow quite tall, anywhere from 3 to 7 feet depending on soil and climate. The plants look a lot like dill. There are beautiful bronze-colored varieties that are often grown for ornament as well as for seasoning. Bulb fennel is similar except that it forms a large, flat bulb just above ground, at the base of the plant, formed by the overlapping stalk bases. Both types can be used much the way you would celery, to flavor various dishes, but bulb fennel also stands on its own as a main vegetable. I love it braised in olive oil and garlic; it caramelizes nicely, the way onions do. It is also delicious raw, and is often added to salads, sliced fine. 'Zefa Fino' is a favored variety.

Since the plants are biennials, the attractive yellow flower umbels appear the second year and form seeds that are used to flavor breads and other dishes. The flowers and sometimes the pollen alone are used as a very aromatic, highly prized flavoring.

How to Grow: Fennel is a cool-weather crop best grown in spring and fall. In climates where it overwinters (zone 7 and warmer) it can go to seed and sometimes be invasive. It has naturalized in Virginia and California. It can also cross-pollinate with coriander and dill.

Direct-sow in spring or start indoors six to eight weeks ahead. Fennel likes plenty of sun, and a light, well-draining soil. Space plants 10 to 12 inches apart. If growing as a perennial, divide in fall.

Harvest: The leaves and stems of both forms of fennel can be used anytime they are needed. The bulbs can be cut at the base at tender baby-size, or allowed to grow to maturity (several inches across), but should be harvested before they become woody. Harvest the flowers when just open, and the seeds just before they're fully ripe.

LAVENDER
Lavandula

Description: Lavender is usually thought of as an aromatic herb, used to scent soaps, sachets, and the like, but it can be put to culinary use as well. The flowers make a lovely seasoning for desserts such as ice cream, sorbet, puddings, and frostings. The stronger-flavored leaves are used in the same way but in smaller quantities.

They also are used with roasted meats and other dishes.

Even if you never get around to cooking with lavender or tucking it in among your nighties, it's a beautiful plant to have in an herb or flower garden, with small, narrow grayish leaves and flower spikes that are sometimes pink, yellow, and other hues but more usually, well, lavender. There are many species and varieties of this perennial Mediterranean plant, most of them ill-suited to cold climates. But the standard English lavender, *Lavandula angustifolia*, is often winter hardy to zone 5. The variety 'Munstead,' named for Gertrude Jekyll's home, is hardier than most. I sometimes grow the more tender ones as annuals, or bring them indoors for the winter. I'm fond of Spanish lavender, *L. stoechas*, with its tufts of showy pink-purple bracts atop each stalk.

How to Grow: It's easiest to grow lavender from started plants, set out in spring when the weather has warmed up. Though essentially an evergreen shrub, with a nice silvery-bluish cast in winter, the plant can suffer a lot of dieback in cold climates. Prune out the deadwood as new growth is starting to appear, but don't cut into the older woody stems unless it is really necessary for the shape of the plant. Deadheading the flower spikes after bloom will also help to keep the shape tidy.

Lavender needs sun and must have good drainage. It prefers an alkaline soil of moderate fertility. Too much nitrogen can make plants susceptible to disease and winterkill. Avoid soggy mulches (evergreen boughs laid over the plants make the best winter protection), and water only when the weather is quite dry.

Harvest: Fresh leaves and flowers can be snipped as needed. To use the flowers, pluck or snip the tiny petals, leaving the tougher calyxes behind. To dry the foliage, harvest whole stems on a warm, sunny day before they bloom. Flowers for drying should be picked when about a third of the blooms on the spike have opened.

LEMON VERBENA
Aloysia triphylla

Description: If you order a cup of herb tea (*tisane*) in France, chances are it will be lemon verbena (*verveine*). The fresh taste of this lovely herb is more than that of lemon alone, and it imparts a beautiful green color to the tea. Try it for seasoning sorbets and other desserts. When young and tender the leaves are good in salads, savory sauces, and cooked vegetable dishes as well. Its flowers are not showy, and the lanky plant is not graceful, but the scent of the long, narrow leaves when touched or rustled by the wind make it a great asset in the garden.

In climates where it is hardy (zones 8 to 10), this deciduous perennial can grow up to 10 feet tall. Normally it is between 3 and 5 feet, with most of the growth being made in one season.

How to Grow: Best grown from purchased plants, or from cuttings. Set the plants out in a sunny spot in the garden, in fairly moist, fertile soil. Give them plenty of room. If grown in a cold frame and/or mulched heavily in winter you can extend the hardiness range. Wait awhile before you conclude that a plant has succumbed to the cold, because the new growth can be slow to emerge. Plants can also be brought indoors in wintertime, though they will generally shed their leaves. Let them go dormant, giving just enough water to keep the soil from drying out completely.

Harvest: Snip leaves as needed, then dry your winter's supply before the leaves wither in fall. Remove whole branches and spread them out on screens in a warm, dry room. Store the leaves in any airtight container, out of the sunlight.

LOVAGE

Levisticum officinale

Description: Lovage is a rugged perennial that grows so vigorously I almost think of it as a tall shrub, despite the fact that it dies to the ground each year. It towers above me in my garden, hardly justifying the space it occupies, since just a few leaves is enough to contribute a strong, celerylike flavor to a soup or a stew. It digs in for the long term, and though it doesn't spread, its deep roots make it difficult to banish. I appreciate its resilience, and think of it as a stately garden accent. Oddly enough, one of its old names was "smallage."

How to Grow: Lovage can be grown easily from seed but it may be easier to buy one plant, since that's all you'll ever need. Choose a sunny or partly shaded spot with deeply dug, moist, well-drained fertile soil. The large yellow flower umbels are beautiful, but unfortunately the foliage starts to turn yellow, (and eventually brown) as soon as the plant begins to bloom. On the other hand, if you cut the flower stalks back before the flowers form, fresh new growth will spring up at the base of the plant. Plants can be divided in spring or fall. If you find caterpillars on the plant, leave them alone. Chances are they are the larvae of swallowtail butterflies, which will do little harm: there is plenty of lovage to go around.

Harvest: Lovage is harder to dry than most herbs, so I just snip the leaves for fresh use during the growing season. The stems can also be eaten cooked like celery. Freezing is more successful than drying, and the aromatic seeds can also be shaken into a bag when they start to brown, and used for seasoning.

MINT

Mentha

Description: Mint is such a strong flavoring that I don't use it for very many

things; but when I need it I'm very glad I have some around. I stuff large handfuls into jugs of iced tea (*before* it's iced, so the tea will absorb more flavor) and sprinkle small snippings of it into cold mixed fruit or on homemade ice cream, sherbet, and ices. As a tea by itself it is excellent for settling the stomach.

Mint is a very hardy, vigorous perennial that grows 1 to 3 feet tall depending on the species and conditions. Most species have crinkly leaves, an upright growth habit, and attractive purplish flowers.

As with the basils, thymes, scented pelargoniums, and certain other genuses, the mints are many and varied, with subtle and complex flavorings. Of the numerous mints in commerce, spearmint (*Mentha spicata*) is the one most often grown. The strong-flavored peppermint (*M.* × *piperita*), with dark pointed leaves, is also very popular. I'm partial to a strain called black mint, with very dark stems and dark foliage. Apple mint (*M. suaveolens*) is more subtle; its leaves are rounded, gray-green, and somewhat hairy. The variety 'Variegata,' called pineapple mint, has white-marked leaves and is more compact, making it a good mint for container growing. Most mints grown as herbs are hybrid varieties that do not breed true to seed. It's wisest to buy plants rather than seeds. Mints tend to cross-pollinate promiscuously and so are best not grouped together in a single bed.

How to Grow: Having some mint around is never a problem; having just a *little* mint is harder. If you don't restrain the plant in some way, your herb garden will simply be a mint garden. Gardeners devise their own schemes, the more successful of which will involve a barrier not only around the mint but also under it—generally a stout container such as a bucket, with some holes for drainage. Mint roots will, eventually, snake themselves over the top and through the holes, but you can buy yourself a lot of time this way. I prefer to find a spot where mint can spread to its heart's content. This way I can have plenty of it to dry for tea.

Mint will grow well in full sun but prefers partial shade and a rich, moist soil. It's a great thing to grow in a spot too moist for other food plants. Pinching back the stems and snipping off flowers as they form will make the plants bushier. Even if cut right to the ground, it will regrow. Mint may be easily propagated to increase your supply. "Why?" you ask. Answer: to give some to a friend or bring indoors. Just dig up a plant with runners attached, cutting the stems back, or root a runner or stem in moist sand. Before bringing a pot of mint indoors for the winter, cut it back and keep it outdoors for a few weeks of freezing nights.

Harvest: Snip as needed. Mint can be sheared off several times during the season and more will regrow for the next harvest. To dry, pick before flowering. (I also pick mine before the leaves are disfigured by a rust-colored disease in late summer.) Keep the leaves on the stems until they're dry, crumble them off, and dry them some more; then store in airtight jars. The leaves may also be frozen.

OREGANO
Origanum

sweet marjoram

wild oregano

Description: I've always felt a bit confused on the subject of the oreganos and the marjorams, but I don't feel too bad, because many others are too. Various common names are matched with various species and subspecies—often depending on what country you're in. The plant we generally call oregano (*Origanum vulgare*) is the available plant that most closely resembles the herb they put on pizza, though I'm told the jars of oregano you buy in the market are really a blend of several different "Italian" herbs. Sweet marjoram has a milder flavor, and its botanical name is *O. majorana*. Oregano is a big, sprawling thing that will make it through harsh winters; sweet marjoram is a lower, more trailing plant that, though perennial, is not hardy except in warm climates. It has oval leaves and knotlike nodes along the stems, which is why it is sometimes called knotted marjoram. I grow oregano in the garden, mainly because bees and butterflies love its lavish display of pinkish flowers.

For kitchen seasonings I'm more apt to use my sweet marjoram, which does better as a potted herb than oregano. In addition, there are varieties grown mainly for decorative purposes, such as the beautiful *O. laevigatum* 'Herrenhausen,' a hardy perennial whose purple flowers are particularly showy and long-blooming; it makes a great edge plant in the flower garden.

How to Grow: Both oregano and marjoram need full sun. They prefer light, well-drained, slightly alkaline soil. Both benefit by being cut back, especially oregano, which should also be divided every few years after it becomes very woody. In addition to division, you can propagate it from stem cuttings—or from seed, though germination is fairly slow.

Harvest: Both oregano and marjoram have better flavor if cut just before they bloom. They dry very well hung upside down in a paper bag or in a dark, airy place. Crumble the leaves off the stems when they're completely dry.

PARSLEY
Petroselinum

Description: Through history, parsley has had powerful symbolic connotations, death and fertility among them. What a comedown to wind up in the twentieth century as the world's most boring garnish. I do remember that among my girlhood classmates, eating parsley was believed to increase the size of the breasts, and nary a plate was sent back to the kitchen at lunch hour with parsley still on it. And health-conscious folk always extol parsley as a

flowers

seeds

curly parsley *Italian parsley*

source of vitamins A and C, as well as iron. Some of its aura has also returned with the resurgence of Italian broad-leaved parsley, which is actually cut up and used in food instead of merely sitting next to it. We now encounter parsley pesto on spaghetti, soups green with parsley, and parsley as a key ingredient in tabbouleh—that flavorful Middle Eastern salad of bulgur wheat, lemon, olive oil, and tomato. But gone are the days when you could just wave parsley in front of an advancing army and cause the soldiers to retreat in terror (if you believe Plutarch).

I would not be without it, nonetheless. A hardy biennial, parsley sometimes overwinters, but will soon go to seed as the days lengthen. Since it also tends to self-sow, new plants may await you in early spring. In warm climates (or in a cold frame in chillier ones) you can harvest it all year, for it actually prefers cool weather. I grow both the foot-high curly parsley (*Petroselinum crispum*) and the slightly taller Italian (*P. crispum* var. *neapolitanum*). There's also a type called Hamburg parsley, or turnip-rooted parsley (*P. c.* var. *tuberosum*), which is grown for its long, fleshy taproot. I have

forced it in winter by potting it up in a container of soil, where it sends forth tasty foliage.

Parsley is an important butterfly plant. Watch for some particularly gorgeous caterpillars on it, green-and-black-striped with yellow spots. In return for a small share of your parsley crop, they'll turn into black swallowtail butterflies that will hover around the flowers of your other herbs, especially the pink and purple ones.

How to Grow: Parsley likes full sun or light shade. Soil should be rich, well lightened with organic matter, and moist but well drained. Parsley seeds are short-lived and must be fresh. Sow early in the spring or in fall, soaking the seeds overnight to speed up germination, which can take up to three weeks. Or buy started plants for an earlier harvest. Thin to about 6 to 8 inches apart. Plants can be dug up in fall and brought indoors for winter use, but this is only moderately successful—it's easier to sow new ones.

Harvest: The leaves can be used fresh, frozen, or dried, although unlike some herbs, parsley has a weaker flavor preserved than fresh. Cut stems close to the ground on the outside of the clump. Plants cut back will regrow.

ROSEMARY
Rosmarinus officinalis

Description: Rosemary is an evergreen perennial in zones 8 through 10. Up north it could, I suppose, be grown as an annual, but a far more satisfactory method is to keep it as a potted plant. It will never achieve the

grand scale of the 6-foot hedges you find in warmer climates, but you will get a handsome shrublet with dark green, needlelike leaves that smell pungent if you so much as touch them. In late winter it will even produce pretty little lavender-blue flowers. There's also a trailing, prostrate form.

I use rosemary a lot in cooking, particularly in Mediterranean meat dishes and with cooked vegetables. I may not be able to smell the rosemary miles out from shore, the way sailors do in Greece, but I can smell it all through the house (mingled with the scent of garlic) when I'm roasting chicken or lamb.

How to Grow: Grow rosemary in full sun. It will tolerate soil that is slightly dry, rocky, and poor, but drainage needs to be excellent (use a raised bed if necessary). A slightly alkaline soil is preferable, so if yours is very acid, plant it with a handful of lime.

Rosemary is rarely grown from seed. It's easier to just buy a small plant from a nursery, or to get a friend to layer some for you (page 622), or to root a soft stem cutting in wet sand. Grow it right in the ground in warm zones; in borderline zones, try mulching the plant heavily and you might be able to overwinter it. I simply set my potted rosemary out in spring and bring it inside in fall, being careful not to let the soil in the pot dry out. After a while the plant gets very woody and outgrows even a large pot, so I replace it with a young one.

Harvest: I prefer to use rosemary fresh, but it also dries well. Cut some stems and dry them on screens or hang them in a paper bag. Then strip the leaves from the stems and store them in jars.

SAGE

Salvia officinalis

Description: Sage has long, pointed, pebbly textured leaves. Usually they're gray-green (sage green, no less, like all those sweaters) but there is also a wonderful yellow variety called 'Golden Sage,' and one called 'Tricolor,' which is purple, green, and white. Sage plants always have beautiful flowers in early summer; usually they're purple, but those of pineapple sage (*Salvia rutilans*) are bright red. Those of clary sage (*S. sclarea*) are very fragrant. Most plants are 1½ to 2½ feet tall and get rather broad and woody after a few years. (My 'Golden Sage,' however, stays quite compact.)

How to Grow: The plants like full sun and very well drained soil that is not overly rich. Most gardeners just buy a plant, but you can grow sage from seed, starting it indoors in very early spring. You can also take stem cuttings from an established plant, or root its stems by layering (page 622). These are also good ways to obtain an indoor sage plant, or to renew an overgrown one that has a lot of deadwood in the center of the clump. Cutting back sage plants at the beginning of the season keeps them from taking up too much space, and produces nice fresh growth. It also rejuvenates tired house-grown plants.

Harvest: Pick fresh sage leaves whenever you need them. Cut sprigs for drying just before the plant flowers. It's sometimes hard to get enough moisture out of sage leaves to store them in jars; if so, you can just leave them hanging in bunches. I prefer to grow a potted sage plant in addition to the ones I have in the garden and bring it in for winter use. The foliage is not lush indoors, but it gives me just enough to poke under the skin of roast chicken, and the fresh leaves are much tastier than dried ones. And even in my cold climate the leaves on my outdoor plants last well into winter. They are also the first herbs to leaf out in early spring.

TARRAGON

Artemisia dracunculus

Description: In some climates this hardy perennial becomes a woody shrub between 1 and 3 feet tall. In my northern garden it dies back to the ground in winter, but comes up lush and bushy each spring.

Its long, slender dark green leaves have a strong, slightly licorice-like flavor that you either enjoy or you don't. I love it—in salads, in béarnaise sauce, in vinegars, and many other ways too. Ideally I like to have a big tarragon plant in the garden so I can harvest great gobfuls of it in summer, plus one or two potted plants inside for winter. You should buy only plants labeled "French" tarragon. The tarragon market has been infiltrated by a Russian variety that, while a vigorous plant, has little or no real tarragon flavor.

How to Grow: Tarragon prefers full sun but will take some shade. It grows best in very well drained, slightly sandy, alkaline soil. If your soil is heavy and wet, make a raised bed and mix plenty of organic matter into it. It needs good air circulation and should not be crowded in the bed. In very hot climates the plants may go dormant in summer. In cold climates cut the plants back in fall. If it gets extremely cold where you live, mulch with evergreen boughs. Unlike Russian tarragon, French tarragon is not grown from seed, so if you see seed offered you know it's the wrong kind. Purchase a plant or obtain a division or a stem or a root cutting from a friend.

Dividing your plants every few years will keep them vigorous and also keep the flavor strong. To bring tarragon plants indoors, pot them up and let them sit through the first few light freezes.

Harvest: Cut sprigs or branches for drying at a time when it is not rainy or humid, then hang them upside down in an airy place, out of direct sun. Store the leaves in airtight jars. Freeze in ice cubes or as tarragon butter. Make tarragon vinegar. But *try* to keep a pot of fresh tarragon around all the time if you are a tarragon lover, because it tastes best fresh.

THYME
Thymus

Description: Thyme is a low, woody plant, sometimes shrubby, sometimes prostrate. It has tiny little round leaves and is beautifully aromatic—if you walk across a bed of thyme, you scent the air around you. The flowers, usually borne in early summer, are shades of pink and purple and attract butterflies and bees. Thyme is an excellent landscaping plant, especially useful for filling in cracks between paving stones. It is one of the most useful culinary seasonings, too. There are dozens of different thymes you can collect, with different scents and often with strikingly different foliage colors. All are hardy perennials (though the culinary thymes can be a bit tender). No wonder there's a sort of thyme cult out there, and herb nurseries that take pride in having long lists of thymes in their catalogs.

Cooks generally grow *Thymus vulgaris* —variously known as common thyme, garden thyme, and black thyme—because it has the best flavor. The French type has narrow leaves, the English has broader ones. There is also lemon thyme (*T. citriodorus*) and creeping thyme, also known as wild thyme or mother-of-thyme (*T. serpyllum*). Both common thyme and creeping thyme have yellow-leaved and silver-leaved forms that are beautiful in the garden, but usually the thymes sold for ornamental features are not good for cooking.

How to Grow: Thyme needs full sun and prefers sandy, very well drained soil. If your soil is heavy, lighten it with organic matter. Gardeners usually start thyme from divisions; they propagate it by dividing when the center of a clump dies, or by layering. In cool climates it's better to cut plants back in spring than in fall (heavy cutting in fall produces tender growth that will only be winterkilled), and sometimes a mulch is needed to protect against ice damage. In addition, don't let the soil around the plants get too soggy in winter. A layer of grit or fine gravel on the soil surface can help the plants' chances of survival.

Harvest: Just before the plant blooms, cut sprigs and hang them upside down in the dark. Strip off the leaves when dry, and store in a jar.

EDIBLE FLOWERS

FRESH FLOWERS OR FLOWER PETALS lend color and a festive or romantic atmosphere to dishes, but not just any flowers will do. They won't get by on their looks if they're bitter-tasting, and you certainly wouldn't want to garnish your meal with any that are toxic or have been sprayed with a pesticide, even a "safe" or "natural" one. Don't use purchased flowers—use only those picked from a garden you know well. And explain to children that not all flowers can be eaten, just special ones.

Many kinds of flowers are safe to eat. Some are tasteless or inoffensive at best, while others are quite delicious, especially if their nectar has not yet been gathered by bees and other pollinators. The flowers of culinary herbs often have the same flavor as the leaves; sometimes the taste is even stronger in the flower. I usually plant edible garnishes in the herb garden because I use them the way I use herbs, snipping them just at the time they're needed. They should be picked when they are just opening, and full of nectar. If you must hold them for a while, make a bouquet and put it in water in the refrigerator. Flowers are very fragile and best added to the plate at the very last minute, unless they're being preserved or cooked. Add them to a salad only after it is dressed, because oil tends to drown them.

Here is a sample of some edible flowers and some of their uses.

Anise hyssop. The mild licorice flavor is delicious in fruit desserts and teas. Put a flower spike in a glass of iced tea.

Arugula. After arugula starts to bloom the leaves may be too strong-tasting to eat, but the cream-colored, four-petaled flowers are pretty and flavorful in salads or on hors d'oeuvres.

Basil. Use the whole flower spike as a garnish, the tiny white individual florets for seasoning.

Bee balm. The petals, especially red ones, are striking in salads both for their color and for their strong, minty taste. Sometimes they are dried and added to tea.

Borage. The intense blue of borage blossoms makes them an irresistible garnish. Remove the fuzzy green sepals if the flower will actually be eaten. They're beautiful on salads, fruits, desserts, and drinks—either floated on the surface or frozen in ice cubes. You can also float them on soups. Sometimes they're candied.

Calendula. This is one of the most popular culinary flowers; I've even seen it sold in salad mixes. The bright yellow or orange petals are strewn over numerous dishes. Cooked, they impart a yellow color that has earned them the nickname "poor man's saffron." Try coloring rice with it. The flowers are sometimes dried for later use.

Chamomile. Soothing, relaxing chamomile tea is made from the flowers of both the annual German chamomile (*Matricaria recutita*) and the perennial Roman type (*Chamaemelum nobile*). The flower heads are picked when just opened and dried whole, spread out on screens. The flowers can also be used fresh.

Chives. The round purple flower clusters have a very strong, oniony flavor, more pungent than that of the leaves. Used whole they make a pretty garnish but a powerful mouthful—I prefer to pull them apart and scatter individual florets when using them as a seasoning. They can also be steeped in vinegar.

Chrysanthemum. With ordinary garden chrysanthemums, only the flower petals are edible. A Chinese plant called *Shungiku*, which is sold as "edible chrysanthemum," has bright yellow flowers. These can be eaten separately or cooked along with the leaves and stems.

Coriander. The savory little flowers are used in Latin dishes.

Dame's rocket. Pretty pink-purple flowers of *Hesperis matronalis* are used as a garnish in salads and other dishes.

Dandelion. Dandelion wine is made from the flowers. I've also used the buds in fritters.

Daylily. This is one of the very best edible flowers. The petals have a sweet taste, and a gently crisp texture. I love to strew a few of them over a salad. They're firm enough to scoop up a light dip.

Dill. The yellow flower umbells make an attractive garnish. Individual florets lend a dill flavor to salads.

Elderflower. The white flowers of the elderberry bush are used to make jams, jellies, syrups, and cordials. You can also swish them in a thin batter to make fritters or tempura.

Fennel. The flowers make a delectable garnish or seasoning. They're incredibly flavorful dried. Sometimes just the pollen is used, and is considered a great delicacy.

Geranium. There are many varieties of annual geranium (properly called *Pelargonium*), with diversely scented and flavored leaves—rose, lemon, apple, mint, and so forth. The attractive flowers (usually pink) carry this flavor as well. Remove the bitter white base of each petal before using it.

Hawthorn. The blossoms are traditionally steeped in brandy or wine.

Hollyhock. Used as a garnish and in tea. Cut off the bitter base of the petal.

Honeysuckle. Used in salads and other dishes. Pick when just open and still full of nectar.

Jasmine. The fresh flowers are a beautiful garnish. Dried, they are mixed with black tea, and can also be used as a flavoring in cooking.

Lavender. The flowers are strongly flavored and often used in desserts and teas. Individual florets, with the green calyxes removed, are wonderful sprinkled over a salad.

Lilac. Use as a garnish or dip in batter for fritters.

Marigold. The petals make a colorful garnish. Varieties such as 'Lemon Gem' and 'Orange Gem' have a mild citrus flavor.

Mimosa. Use in the same way as lilac, above.

Nasturtium. This is a very popular garnish or salad flower because the flowers are gorgeously colored, and have a nice mildly peppery taste and a velvety texture.

Orange. Orange blossoms are used in many ways, including jellies, syrups, cordials, and fritters.

Pinks. Pinks and carnations (*Dianthus* species) often have a clovelike flavor and have long been used to flavor foods and drinks. They make an attractive, tasty garnish. Cut off the bitter, spurlike base before eating.

Primroses and cowslips. Used in vinegars, teas, and salads, and for garnishing. Cowslip flowers are made into cowslip wine.

Rose. Roses have been used extensively in cooking throughout history, for syrups, sauces, sorbets, puddings, vinegars, candies, and so forth. They

are sweet tasting, and look beautiful and romantic sprinkled over salads and desserts. The old-fashioned ones tend to have the most flavor.

Rosemary. The tiny blue flowers taste just like the leaves, but with a sweet touch of nectar. Delicious!

Sage. The very showy flowers, in shades of purple, blue, and red, are used for garnishes and sometimes for flavoring.

Squash. The large golden flowers of squash and pumpkins can be simmered in soups and used as garnishes or in salads. I love them the Roman way, stuffed with mozzarella cheese and anchovy, dipped in a light batter, and fried in olive oil.

Sweet woodruff. This charming creeping plant (*Galium odoratum*) has small white, starlike flowers that are used to make May wine. Steep them in a German white wine such as a Rhine or a Moselle.

Thyme. The tiny white flowers make a dainty but pungent seasoning.

Violet. Violas, violets, pansies, and Johnny-jump-ups are all used as garnishes, especially in salads where they lend color and a velvety texture. Violets are sometimes candied and used to decorate cakes and other desserts. Johnny-jump-ups are so cold tolerant I've even harvested the blossoms from an unheated winter greenhouse.

CHAPTER 9

Fruits

W HEN I THINK ABOUT GROWING fruits I sometimes imagine the walled "paradise gardens" of ancient Persia, filled with pomegranates. I remember my Louisiana grandfather plucking ripe persimmons off a tree and eating them. I picture a sensuous California garden filled with avocadoes, loquats, lemons, and figs, or a hacienda in the tropics where luscious exotic fruits like cherimoyas grow. Speaking as a northern gardener, my idea of luxury would be a glass-roofed orangery in which I could pluck all these treasures from indoor trees.

Such things are possible—but for most of us out of reach. In coastal Maine I must be content with sweet strawberries and raspberries in early summer, followed by blueberries, then the few hardy peaches and grapes we can ripen, and lots of crisp fall apples to store through the winter. Add to those the melons we grow, a few patches of wild blackberries here and there, and it all adds up to a rich harvest! Wherever you live, there are fruits that do best not in some faraway place but in your own backyard. If you choose varieties based on those that feel at home where you live, you can grow them without a struggle.

Fruit crops vary a great deal. Small fruits such as grapes and berries are grown quite differently from tree fruits. Since most fruit crops take up more space than flowers or vegetables, however, they are alike in that you have to plan for them carefully. Hence "the vineyard," "the orchard," and "the berry patch." Fruits are almost all perennial crops, so they must be planted in a spot that has been carefully chosen for their needs—then left there to stay. "But wait," you may say. "I can't have an orchard or a vineyard. I own a third of an acre in sub-urban Minneapolis." No problem. Most fruits can be grown on a small property in a way that not only fits the space but also beautifies it. For gardeners who plant grapes on arbors, apples as small shade trees, or cherries just to enjoy their romantic blossoms, the fruits are often extra.

The following pages give an introduction to some popular fruits for home culture. Refer to the chapters on trees and shrubs for more information on topics such as planting, growing, protecting, and pruning trees, and to the first chapter for general advice on how to deal with pests and diseases. Although fruits may often seem more prone to pests and diseases than other plant groups, many of these can be minimized by selecting appropriate varieties and siting them well, giving them good care, removing and destroying diseased or infested material, and surrounding your crops with a biologically diverse collection of plants that attract helpful insect predators. Home gardeners are more willing to overlook minor damage since large, cosmetically perfect crops are not always a necessity. For serious ills, bring a sample to the Extension Service for identification of the problem, then request an organic solution.

Refer to the first section of this chapter, the one about apples, for some specific topics that concern fruits in general, such as training and pruning for a better harvest, thinning fruits, the advantages and disadvantages of dwarf trees, the best site for an orchard, and why some fruit trees bear only in alternate years. You should also keep in mind, when dealing with any fruit, that some are "self-fertile" and can pollinate their own flowers, whereas others need a second variety of the same fruit to ensure pollination—one that comes into bloom at the same time. Espaliering fruit, that is, training them so they grow in a two-dimensional plane (such as flat against a wall), is beyond the scope of this book. But it is not a skill beyond the grasp of the beginning gardener.

Most of the important lore about fruits is local. Talk to people in your area—friends and neighbors, owners of orchards and berry farms, nurserymen, and people at the Extension Service or local agricultural research stations run by the state or by colleges and universities. And try to give the fruits you grow the taste test first. No matter how highly rated a fruit may be, it's important that something you spend so much time bringing to bear be tasty to you and worthy of inclusion in your own backyard paradise.

crab apple

'Delicious' apple

'McIntosh' apple

Apples

THE POET D. H. LAWRENCE, WHO wrote about country matters in general, had much to say about apples. In his poem "Beautiful Old Age," he compares people who have had rich, full lives with mature apples hanging on a tree:

> If people lived without accepting lies
> they would ripen like apples, and be
>   scented like pippins
> in their old age.

This might not be quite how you picture growing old gracefully, but the poem, as it continues on, is a gratifying tribute to ripeness—even over-ripeness. I also happen to think that the trees on which apples grow are particularly good at aging. We talk of the grandeur of mature oaks or spruces, but apple trees look their best when they are *ancient*. Each old tree acquires a shape quite its own, the branches gnarled and craggy, the trunk thick and covered with rough bark. In spring old apple trees still cover themselves in a froth of pink-and-white flowers, like six-year-old ballerinas, but under a heavy, wet snow they're like old men with white hair, beards, and eyebrows. Probably a few frozen apples are still hanging high up where nobody can reach. Ever pick one? Sometimes there's fermented syrup, like applejack, inside those dark red ice globes. And the trees' old limbs make the best firewood, perfuming the room with a faint apple scent.

Although I admittedly have a special liking for the way apple trees look, their enormous popularity is a result of their usefulness, not their beauty. No fruit is more versatile for both cooking and eating fresh, and few fruits grow as vigorously in so many parts of the country. Although in general, apples do best in areas where the winter temperature does not stay below 20 degrees for very long stretches and is not above 40 degrees for more than 40 days throughout the winter, there are varieties that can be grown even under these conditions (in zones 9 to 3). Apple trees usually live up to about 60 years, but you can often find trees much more ancient than that. At ages 10 to 30, they are at their most productive.

The traditional way to grow them is in an orchard with other apple trees, mainly because of the simple fact that you can never have too many apples, though there is the pollination issue as well. Most apples are not self-fertile, so several varieties are needed to ensure pollination. In most cases, practically speaking, you only need two trees. To be perfectly sure of fruit, you might arrange for both to be early-, mid-, or late-flowering varieties, but the bloom times of most apples will overlap. A crab apple, or even an apple tree in a neighbor's yard less than 100 feet away, will fill the bill. Varieties that are particularly good pollinators, called "rooster trees," include 'Golden Delicious,' 'Cortland,' and 'Jonathan.' Triploid varieties (those with three sets of chromosomes) such as 'Baldwin' and 'Winesap' cannot pollinate typical apples, which are diploid (with two sets), although diploid varieties can pollinate them.

Generally the early-bearing apples are eating apples ("dessert apples," which are sweet and tasty but don't keep well). Late-bearing apples are the good winter keepers, usually best for cooking. Midseason apple varieties can be either good eating or good cooking. So with roughly three seasons and several apple varieties maturing at

each season, it's easy to fill a small orchard. That's fine if you have the space. After all, there are so many ways to use apples—in pies, apple crisp, applesauce, apple butter, apple jelly, cider, apple wine, dried apples for winter nibbling, and of course eaten fresh—and there are so many fine apple varieties to try, that you might well want an orchard full of them.

Even if you don't, apples make great landscaping trees. Placed in the right spot they can grace your yard as well as provide fruit. Since the tallest ones rarely exceed 40 feet and are often half that, apple trees—and especially the crab apples—make excellent small ornamental or shade trees. And you don't need the traditional field or large block of orchard space. They also look lovely lined up along a fence or next to a driveway, providing an attractive welcome in any season.

Although the trees themselves are easy to grow, it is not all that easy to get a big harvest of perfect-looking apples like those that come wrapped in plastic at the supermarket. A number of diseases and insect pests plague apples, many of modern origin. While few do much harm to the general health of the tree, the fruits you grow yourself will probably be blemished unless you live in a part of the country where problems are rare or unless you take measures to combat them. In the past, the traditional advice to home apple growers was to embark on a massive spray program that had them in protective gear all summer, spraying poisons that drifted all over the property—something I do not advise. I think you can enjoy home apple production much more if you set your sights on less than total cosmetic perfection and employ a few effective and safe means of dealing with apple problems (see pages 421 to 423).

Even if you're growing apples as shade trees, you may not want them to attain a height of 40 or even 20 feet. Maintenance tasks such as pruning, thinning, or using an oil spray, not to mention harvesting, will be more difficult the larger the tree; and you won't be able to plant as many trees if you grow big ones. Fortunately for the owner of a small property, apple trees don't have to be so large. They can be grafted onto dwarfing rootstocks to produce trees as small as 6 feet tall in the case of miniatures, though most dwarf apple trees are about 8 to 12 feet, and most semidwarfs 12 to 20. Almost all apple trees are grafted, partly because they rarely breed true to seed, and partly because the vigorous rootstocks onto which they are grafted resist diseases that apple roots might otherwise get.

Dwarf trees have other advantages over standard-size varieties as well. Fruit that drops from a dwarf does not fall far and is less apt to bruise. Dwarfs also bear at a younger age. And since neither the roots nor the branches spread as widely, you can grow as many as nine dwarf trees in the space it would take to grow a large standard-size one. On the other hand, dwarfs are more short-lived, and their root systems less securely anchored. As a result they need to be staked heavily, sometimes permanently. They can also be espaliered (trained flat against a wall) or grown in rows supported by horizontal wires. Dwarf varieties are not suitable for very cold climates where the roots can be winterkilled, although ones on the hardier rootstocks such as 'Budagovsky' and 'Ottawa 3' may be worth a try. Semidwarfs fare better in harsh climates and need less staking, but

even they cannot take very cold winters. In zones 3 and 4 it's best to stick to standard-size trees.

Dwarfs' lack of sturdiness can be overcome by complex grafting. Sometimes dwarf trees are grown on an "interstem" graft—a double-grafting technique whereby a piece of main stem imparts the dwarfing habit but is in turn grafted onto sturdier roots. These trees will often withstand harsher conditions than single-grafted dwarfs can. Also bear in mind that trees can be kept smaller by pruning, often without lessening the yield. Soil conditions will also make a difference; trees grown in soil that is very rich may grow larger than you'd like even if they're on dwarf rootstocks. There are also trees in which the scion (the main part of the tree that is grafted onto the rootstock) has a dwarfing habit. An example of this would be a "spur-type" strain, which has very plentiful fruiting spurs (the twigs on which apples grow). These trees put their energy into the buds that produce fruit, not the ones that produce growth. There are spur strains of many popular varieties, and often it makes sense to buy them so you'll have a large harvest of fruit that is also close to the ground and thus easy to pick.

Another thing you need to know about apples is that some bear heavily only in alternate years. (It can happen with other tree fruits as well.) This is because apples form buds at the tips of the fruiting spur for the new crop the year before the spur bears. A heavy crop takes much of the tree's stored food, so that new fruiting buds cannot form, and the tree must rest a year before it has the resources to produce a full crop again. Some varieties bear quite consistently each year. Others will bear annually if soil conditions are particularly good.

Those that do not can be made to bear annually by thinning the fruit, an option that gives you a choice between a bumper crop every other year and a smaller one annually. To have the desired effect, thinning must be done before the little apples are bigger than grapes, leaving a spacing of about 6 inches on the branch. Where there are clusters of fruit, only the best in the cluster should remain. Thinning can also improve the health and vigor of the tree. It gives you the opportunity to reduce the numbers of pest- or disease-ridden fruits, and takes a load off stressed branches.

SITE

Apples like a sunny site with good drainage, preferably a slope, with no more than a 20 percent incline. (On a steeper slope the trees are hard to tend.) If you do have a slope, don't plant the trees near the bottom. Despite the fact that valleys are sheltered from cold winds and tend to be warmer than higher areas in daytime, cold air can flow down into them at night so that they become frost pockets. This is a problem in spring when the trees are setting fruit, because buds or flowers can be nipped by frost before pollination can take place. Planting in a frost pocket can also hurt trees in late fall, when apples can freeze before ripening. On the other hand, trees growing at the top of the hill may be exposed to harsh, cold winds that can break branches, cause fruit to fall, or winterkill the trees. If you have a choice, partway down the hill is best, and the absolute ideal is on a slope overlooking a body of water, which will always moderate temperature. As with most plants, a south-facing slope will promote the best growth and ripening. However, if your trees are at risk

for frosts after the blossoms have opened, a northern slope that retards bloom time is better. In a climate with late-spring frosts, planting late-flowering varieties can help. If early frost in fall is also a problem, plant midseason varieties.

If a site is very windy, planting a windbreak of other trees may be necessary. It's said that apples do not do well in seaside areas where the winds are strong and salt-laden, although I have seen many thrive there. Coastal gardeners should make a point of seeking out locally adapted apple varieties.

When you plan your orchard, even if it's only two or three trees, be sure to allow enough space between them. Though apple trees are often planted closer than this, I recommend leaving at least as much space between them as the ultimate height of the tree. If you're setting out a lot of trees, plant them in rows with enough distance between them to let you bring in a pickup truck or other equipment for removing limbs, harvesting, mulching, and other tasks. The more room between trees, the more sun they will get, too.

SOIL

Soil for apples should be deep—that is, unobstructed by bedrock or other obstacles. If you're planting on land you have cleared of trees, the stumps and major roots should be pulled out. The water table should be at least 3 feet below the soil surface. Though apples do not require an extremely fertile soil, they do appreciate some richness, and they need plenty of organic matter to hold moisture and at the same time facilitate drainage. If you have a heavy clay soil, don't just dig pockets and fill them with lightened soil. Water will collect there. Try to improve the soil throughout the planting area. A pH above 5.5 and slightly below 7.0 is best for apples.

PLANTING

Apple trees are best planted in early spring in the north; in warm climates they can be planted anytime they are dormant. You can buy them by mail order or at a local nursery. Buying by mail will give you a wide choice of varieties, but by shopping locally you may be able to get advice from the seller about varieties that suit the climate, your particular site, and your particular needs.

When you plant a fruit tree, buy it young. Not only will it establish itself better, quickly catching up in size to trees that were older when planted, but you also have more control over the way the tree grows and can give it that very important early pruning that will determine its final shape. It's probably best (and least expensive) to start out with a one-year-old "whip," also called a maiden. This is just a central stem that hasn't branched yet. Most mail-order fruit trees are sold bare-root as whips. If you're buying locally you can also start with a two-year-old tree. A whip should be about 4 feet tall. A two-year tree should have three or four horizontal branches spaced well apart on a nice straight trunk; the branches should come out at wide angles, not narrow ones, and should be well distributed around the trunk's circumference like the spokes of a wheel. If you're shopping in a nursery you should also check for signs of disease, damaged branches, and a poorly developed root system.

Before you plant, trim off any damaged roots. Heel the tree into a spot with well-drained soil if you cannot plant it right away (see page 40 to learn about heeling in). All the information on planting trees in the tree chapter applies to apples, and note page 71 about protecting them from animal damage. Plant apples so that the graft is at least 2 inches above the soil surface, especially if the tree is a dwarf or semidwarf. If it's lower, the wood just above the graft may root, thus circumventing the dwarfing effect created by the rootstock and causing the tree to grow tall. Even standard-size trees should be staked initially to keep them from blowing over if they are planted in a windy spot (see pages 659 to 660).

A young tree should be cut back when it is planted. By doing this you accomplish several things. You compensate for the loss of roots the tree has suffered when it was dug, you encourage the tree to start branching low enough on the trunk so that harvesting will be easier, and you start to create a scaffold of branches that is shaped in such a way that the tree will look good and bear well. If you've planted a whip, cut it back by about a third, just above a bud. If it has branches, cut these back by about a quarter of their length to an outward-facing bud. Save only the three to five branches with the best placement and crotch angles, rubbing off buds between them with your thumb. Branches that are growing vertically, with narrow crotches, should be removed. The uppermost branch that you keep will become the central leader. If all the branches are too high up, beginning 3 feet or more above the soil surface, you can start over again by removing all of them to make a whip and cutting it back just above a bud.

Be sure that you water your young tree well when you plant it, building an earthen saucer to contain the water (page 43).

Spread a circle of mulch 3 feet in diameter around the tree, leaving 6 inches between the mulch and the trunk, and apply a mulch of gravel or crushed stone in this inner circle to deter rodents.

GROWING

While the young apple tree is growing, keep it watered and mulched. A mulch is especially important with trees that are young or dwarfed. It protects the trees from winter injury, loss of moisture, and competition from grass and weeds. Thick straw is a good mulch; so is about 3 inches of shredded bark. Some growers just let grass grow around the trees, and many an apple tree has done perfectly well with this treatment, but they do better with the mulch. Don't have either grass or mulch right near the trunk, since both can encourage damage by voles, who use it as cover.

Assuming that the soil in the planting area is reasonably fertile to begin with, I wouldn't start feeding your young tree until a year after you set it out. After that some topdressing will help it to grow, to bear earlier, and even to produce more fruit in its "off" years if it's an alternate-year bearer. Spreading an inch or two of rotted manure or compost on top of the soil under the tree's whole canopy works wonders. You'll have to rake aside the mulch to do it, but it's worth it. A phosphorus source like bone meal or rock phosphate is also important, but it's best added to the soil initially before you plant the trees, to help get it down to where the roots are. Young apple trees, and older ones that are not producing well, need an extra supply of nitrogen. If you don't have manure handy, purchase some cottonseed meal or blood meal and water it into the soil thoroughly, or apply a pound of a balanced organic fertilizer such as 10–10–10 throughout the root zone for every inch of the trunk's diameter. Feeding is best done early in the spring so that the new growth it produces can harden off before winter.

During the tree's early years, continue the training program you began when you planted it. If it started as a whip, prune it the second year as described above for a new two-year-old tree. In the third year of its life you'll be encouraging the next set of well-placed lateral branches to form from the main trunk, creating more of a framework, and you'll be choosing the best side branches that form on them. Keep the ones that grow outward rather than back toward the center of the tree. The more vigorous the side branch, the more it is cut back; this will keep all the branches in balance.

Your goal in pruning apples is to let light into the tree from above so that more fruits will be produced and ripen well. Everything I say about pruning trees in the tree chapter applies to fruit trees, but the need for pruning is greater with them than with the others because you're producing not only a pleasing shape, but also a shape that will help the trees to bear fruit. Eliminate branches that cross one another or grow right under the branch above them. Imagine branches coming out like the spokes of a wheel and at the same time ascending like a spiral up the trunk of the tree, letting in light and air.

Some tree pruners simply remove the top third of an apple tree to let in sunlight. Even if you don't want to take such drastic measures, at least keep the center fairly open, and head back branches so that those on top are short and those below them increasingly long. That way, the tips of all branches receive light.

Training and Pruning Apple Trees

FIG. 58

(green lines indicate pruning cuts)

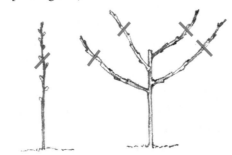

one-year-old whip two-year-old tree

three-year-old tree

mature tree

Regular maintenance pruning also entails removal of water sprouts, which spring up vertically along the branches, and suckers, which come up from the base of the trunk. Overpruning a tree may lead to the formation of many water sprouts and may dwarf the tree and reduce the fruit yield. This is where experience comes in. As you work with your trees you'll learn to balance growth with fruitfulness and achieve just what you want from them. Spur-type strains, because they put more energy into fruiting than growing upward, need less pruning than other types but profit from thinning the fruits.

Crab apples also need less pruning than most other apple trees and can become covered with water sprouts if overpruned. Thinning them is rather impractical too, since the fruits are so numerous and tiny. If they are alternate bearers, and many crabs are, you can try top-dressing them with manure, but usually you just have to be content with blossoms and fruit in alternate years.

People often have old, neglected apple trees on their property. Picturesque though they are in this untamed state, you may want to give them some restorative surgery to improve their health, prolong their lives, and encourage them to bear. And as long as the trunk is not hollow or many of the limbs are not lost to breakage or disease, they may well be worth the effort. Even if they have fruit, chances are it's way up at the top of the tree where you can't reach it, and the lower branches are too shaded to bear. If the tree is tall, it's best to enlist a professional's aid for safety's sake.

The best way to tackle the job of restoring an old tree is in stages. The first year remove any dead branches, suckers, and water sprouts. The second year remove the worst of the crossing or inward-leading branches and some of the top branches, to let in light. The third year do the same thing, but more completely. Work from the bottom of the tree up, and from the trunk outward, thereby opening up some room for you to work in, and taking care of the major cuts first.

The traditional time to prune apple trees is in late winter or very early spring when they are dormant, but when most of the very hard freezes are finished. It's also a convenient time because it gets you outdoors when nothing else is going on in your gardening life except misting indoor ferns or bringing pots of forced bulbs out of darkness. Be aware, however, that winter pruning has the effect of producing vigorous new growth, because when spring comes the tree will respond to your stimulus with gusto, and you may end up with a lot of thick new growth toward the inside of the tree where you don't want it. If you're renewing an old tree in stages or trying to keep a rapidly growing younger one within bounds, you might try pruning in midsummer instead, when growth is slowing, especially in a warm climate where new growth can be particularly rampant. Then when you have the tree tamed, so to speak, do some winter pruning toward the end of the branches to encourage fruiting.

PESTS AND DISEASES

What discourages gardeners from apple growing is not the intricacies of pruning, pollinating, and picking. These are all pretty simple tasks, really, and if you follow even half the advice I've given you'll probably do all right. Most woes are caused by critters that gnaw and girdle the trunks, and by insects and fungus diseases that disfigure the fruit and make it unappetizing. Damage to foliage by pests and disease can also set back growth and fruiting. The trunk-nibblers are the most deadly—a rabbit or a vole can decimate your precious young apple tree in minutes—but fortunately they're also the easiest problem to deal with. Just follow the advice for protecting trunks below and on page 70.

Apple borers can also kill the tree outright just by tunneling in through the trunk. The beetles lay eggs in the trunk, usually near the base, by making little slits. The larvae hatch out inside and go to work eating the wood. Check for these frequently. Painting the trunk with white latex paint diluted to 50 percent will make it easier to spot the sawdust residue produced by the larvae's tunneling. If you find the little slits, scrape them clean with a knife. They are easy to miss, and it may help to squirt cooking oil into the holes with a turkey baster as well. Fiberglass screening wrapped around the trunk and tied at the top can help to prevent borers from entering in the first place. A circle of crushed stone around the base, anchoring the screen, is also a deterrent. But it is important to unwrap the tree and check twice yearly nonetheless. Trees are especially susceptible to apple borers when they are young.

The fruit spoilers are less of a problem if you're growing cider apples and perhaps some for baking—the ugly parts can be cut out and discarded. Some pests, however, such as apple maggots, do so much damage that often there are no good parts to keep at all.

Of course, most of us like to have some "pretty" apples, to put in a bowl on the kitchen table and bite into confidently without fear of surprises. If you live in a part of the country where apple plagues are *rampant*, I can only offer you protective measures that will help to give you *some* pretty apples, while urging you to settle for less than perfection. Let's start with the apple maggot, also called the railroad worm because in its larval stage it tunnels through the fruit, leaving little brown tracks. The maggot is also called the apple fly because it looks something like a housefly in the adult stage. It starts its fruit-tunneling journey in mid June in warm climates, early July in colder ones. Planting late-maturing apple varieties may help to outfox the apple maggot, but for your early crops be ready for him with the red sticky ball traps described on page 66. Hang the balls two weeks after the petals fall so that they dangle visibly, about six per tree for standard trees, three or four for semidwarfs, one or two for dwarfs. You won't get all the maggots, but enough will be gummed up on your ersatz apples that you'll probably reduce the damage quite a bit. Hanging out jars of molasses and water spiked with ammonia and soap (which lure and then kill the flies) also helps. Picking up apples that fall to the ground and composting them far from the tree will also help minimize infestations from one year to the next.

The codling moth, which makes a larger hole than the apple maggot and goes straight to the core of the fruit, is another serious apple pest. Long ago the remedy was to build a bonfire in the orchard to lure the moths. The customary bonfire— probably an excuse for a good party on a summer evening—was later displaced by the use of insecticide sprays. Modern non-toxic methods of control include wrapping the trees in collars of corrugated cardboard with the bumpy side next to the tree, letting the moths spin cocoons in the collars, and destroying the cocoons regularly until after harvesttime. You can also scrape loose bark from the trees—this dislodges cocoons. (Scrape carefully, lest you injure the tree.) Pheromone traps may also help control codling moths.

Using a dormant-oil spray on your apple trees can be effective against a number of problems including scale, leaf rollers, mites, aphids, and even apple-scab disease. It should be applied just before the flower buds open. A blast of organic insecticidal soap spray may help to control some insect pests. Using a device that attaches to your garden hose will make spraying your trees a lot easier. Your local Extension Service and other sources close to home can give you more details about coping with individual pests, many of which may be specific to your part of the country. (Be sure to ask for organic solutions.) But keep in mind the importance of cleaning up debris such as fallen fruit, fallen leaves, and rotted portions of the tree, which may harbor insect larvae from one year to the next. Growing lots of flowering plants in and around your orchard will attract not only helpful pollinating insects but also those that eat insect pests. Needless to say, avoiding all poison sprays on your property will protect the safety of these and insect-eating birds as well.

Diseases are a bit less discouraging to the home apple grower than insects because of the development of so many disease-resistant varieties. While some are suggested below, I recommend that you research the subject further, finding out from your Extension Service what diseases you can expect in your locality, and what apple varieties that do well in your area can best resist them. Beyond this the best prevention, as always, is tidiness—raking up dropped fruit and dead leaves and cleaning out any infected parts of the tree.

The most annoying and prevalent disease of apples is apple scab, which causes dark spots to form on the leaves, twigs, and fruit. It overwinters in fallen leaves and is especially active in rainy weather. Clean up all debris, plant resistant varieties whenever possible, and if these measures fail, try dormant-oil spray.

Cedar apple rust, which produces rust-colored spots on the leaves, especially during wet spring weather, occurs only when you have red cedar trees (*Juniperus virginiana*) nearby. The disease spreads from the junipers to the apple trees and back again, but not from juniper to juniper or from apple to apple. Break the cycle by growing either junipers or apples but not both. If your neighbors won't part with their junipers, grow resistant apple varieties.

If your trees get fire blight (the ends of the branches will look blackened and burned), prune out the diseased portions and burn them, sterilizing your tools with a bleach solution after every cut you make, and grow resistant varieties. A wettable sulfur spray applied weekly in warm weather may help save disease-prone apple crops, but the best prevention is removal of all debris.

HARVEST

How do you know when an apple is ripe? A ripe apple looks and tastes the way it's supposed to look and taste. Its seeds are black. It picks easily, hanging onto its own little stem but parting without resistance from the fruiting spur, which must remain on the tree to produce more apples next year. Late-maturing apples can be picked a little bit before they're ripe so they can ripen off the tree and keep longer, but the flavor may suffer.

When you pick, it's important to use both hands. If you yank, you'll break off the spur. I start by picking the ones I can reach easily from the ground, then climbing into the tree to get the higher ones, then shaking the branches to loosen those I still can't reach. Falling can bruise the apples, so an apple picking tool, with a long handle and little basket attached, is better yet; just jostling the fruit inside the basket should make it fall if it's fully ripe.

If you've just planted your first collection of apple trees, you'll no doubt be impatient for your first harvest, but it may take as much as ten years before you have a crop. When your trees are mature you might get anywhere from seven to twenty bushels for a standard-size tree but as little as one bushel or less for the smallest dwarfs.

"Keeping apples" should be stored at a temperature just above freezing, if possible, in a fairly moist atmosphere, and they should not be piled too deep. More than half a bushel deep invites rot. Inspect them from time to time—one rotten apple can, as they say, ruin the whole barrel. You should not try to store apples that are nicked or bruised. Nor should you store them in the same room as carrots and other root crops. The ethylene gas that apples give off in storage can ruin root vegetables by causing them to resprout.

Apples that are not "keepers" should, of course, be eaten or made into preserves right away.

VARIETIES

Choosing apple varieties can be daunting because there are so many good ones and because you want to be sure the ones you've selected are worth the wait—and the work. First, order some catalogs or go online and see what varieties exist. Read the descriptions carefully—not just phrases like "irresistibly flavorful and juicy," but remarks about suitability for different purposes, how the tree grows, for what climates it is appropriate, when in the season it bears, and which diseases it resists, if any.

The nursery catalogs will help narrow down your choices somewhat, but what tastes wonderful to some may seem uninteresting to you. Therefore, I suggest you also try to find a pick-your-own orchard located nearby, where you can taste a number of different apples, observe how they grow, and even get advice from the owner about their culture. In the meantime, here is a sample of what is out there.

Old standbys. While many of these apples have been improved upon by hybridization, they have nonetheless stood the test of time and are still grown. Look for "improved strains" with superior characteristics such as better keeping ability, color, flavor, or disease resistance, as well as a spur-type, dwarf, or semidwarf habit if that is what you require. Heirloom apples are sought after today for their distinctive flavor, but since many were used chiefly for cider, they might seem tart to modern palates. Here are some of the more versatile ones, which are often the standard against which newer apples are measured.

'Baldwin.' A large red, late-season apple, long considered a good all-purpose apple for cooking or eating. Good keeper. Sterile pollen.

'Delicious.' This is the popular variety's original name, though it is often called 'Red Delicious' to distinguish it from 'Golden Delicious.' Though still very popular because of its sweetness, many find its taste bland. Ripens late. Not for the far north.

'Cortland.' A good all-purpose midseason apple that doesn't turn brown when cut. Dark red, with fine eating quality.

'Cox's Orange Pippin.' This old English apple is famous for its flavor. Lovely yellow-and-red color, all-purpose use. Midseason.

'Golden Delicious.' Also called 'Yellow Delicious,' it is like 'Delicious' only in that both are very sweet. This one is rounder and grows on an extremely vigorous tree that bears while young. A late-season apple for fresh eating, not for baking. It does not need a pollinator. Ripens late. Not for northern zones.

'Golden Russet.' On the tart side, this is prized as a cider apple. Greenish gold color with russeting (rough skin). Late season, good keeper. Hardy and disease-resistant tree.

'Granny Smith.' A mid-nineteenth-century Australian apple that has had a recent resurgence in popularity, this green apple is a classic late-bearing one, excellent for storage. Although it's rather tart, it is popular for both eating and cooking. Needs a long season; not for northern zones.

'Grimes Golden.' A tasty midseason variety, popular in the south, that is yellow inside as well as out. Very aromatic but not good for baking. Hardy, disease resistant, and self-pollinating.

'Jonathan.' A red midseason apple, tart and aromatic, that is good for eating fresh or for cider, less good for pies or storage. The tree bears young and heavily. Popular in the midwest.

'McIntosh.' Best for eating fresh, with outstanding tart flavor. It grows on a hardy, vigorous tree but may be susceptible to scab and other diseases. Early. Popular in New England.

'Northern Spy.' An all-purpose late apple. Fruit is large red-and-green striped, juicy, tart and tasty. A great keeper. Hardy tree takes a long time to bear. One of the best apples for cold climates.

'Rome.' This very large red apple is excellent for baking, bears young, and is quite disease resistant. Late-season, good keeper. 'Red Rome' is an improved variety.

'Summer Rambo.' No relation to the movie hero, this is an old French apple originally called 'Rambour.' In late summer it bears big, healthy apples on a large, hardy tree. Sterile pollen.

'Wealthy.' A crisp, hardy old-timer that bears early in the season and is popular in the midwest. All-purpose apple, yellow striped with red, some pink in flesh. Hardy tree that bears young.

'Winesap.' A classic, all-purpose, late red apple with exceptional flavor good for cooking, cider, and storage. Tree bears young, and heavily. Sterile pollen.

'Winter Banana.' A large, late variety with a unique flavor, good for fresh eating but also a keeper. Yellow blushed with pinkish red. Midwestern apple that fares well in warm climates.

'Yellow Transparent.' A very early, hardy, and vigorous yellow apple that does well most anywhere. This old favorite is sweet and good for applesauce.

Newer apples. Some of these are brand-new and excellent, while others have been around somewhat longer and have acquired a fine reputation.

'Arkansas Black.' This late apple is very dark red, golden inside. A fine cooking apple and an outstanding keeper. Sterile pollen.

'Empire.' This popular apple is a cross between 'McIntosh' and 'Delicious.' Ripens midseason, with excellent flavor for eating, juicy and sweet. Dark red with white flesh. Hardy tree that bears young.

'Fuji.' Yellow-and-red late apple, crisp and juicy. Excellent keeper. Needs a long growing season.

'Gala.' Light red-and-yellow, crisp fruit, great for fresh eating. Ripens early but also keeps well. Hardy.

'Honeycrisp.' Red, fairly early apple, very sweet and tasty for fresh eating, with a fine, crisp texture. Hardy.

'Idared.' A late, very red apple with tart, white, crisp flesh, fine for both eating and cooking; an excellent keeper. Tree bears young.

'Jonagold.' Large red-and-yellow dessert apple. Bears heavily in midseason. Not for warm climates. Sterile pollen.

'Macoun.' One of my favorites. A mid-season apple rather like McIntosh but larger and a better keeper. Very fine flavor. Hardy tree, benefits from thinning.

'Mutsu.' This Japanese introduction is a big yellow-green, late apple, slightly tart but tasty, crisp and a very good keeper. Sterile pollen.

'Red June.' This very early apple is deep red and great for cider or eating.

'Spigold.' A cross between 'Northern Spy' and 'Golden Delicious.' Yellow with red stripes, crisp and tasty. Ripens late. Sterile pollen.

Disease-resistant apples. One of the best recent developments in apple culture has been the breeding of apples that resist the major apple diseases. Here are some of the best.

'Freedom.' A hardy, late apple on a vigorous tree. Large, crisp red fruits are good for both fresh eating and baking.

'Liberty.' A midseason, all-purpose, dark red apple. Crisp, juicy, and tart-sweet. Stores well. Hardy tree.

'Macfree.' Similar to McIntosh. Grows on a vigorous tree. Keeps well and tastes best when stored awhile.

'Prima.' Large red-and-yellow fruits in late summer. Slightly tart.

'Priscilla.' Red, with a bit of yellow. Crisp white flesh, good for fresh eating. Matures in early fall and keeps well.

Low-chill apples. The following is a special group of apples developed for areas that never get cold enough for most apples to set fruit. (Apples suited to the cold winters and short growing seasons of the northern states and Canada are noted above as "hardy.")

'Anna.' A big pie apple developed in Israel, it is a heavy producer and will grow even in zone 10. Crisp, tasty green-and-red fruits ripen early. Not a keeping apple.

'Dorsett Gold.' A good yellow apple, sweet and crisp. Keeps better than most southern apples. Self-pollinating.

'Ein Shemer.' Also from Israel, it is similar to 'Golden Delicious' but more tart. Popular in the south. Early, not a good keeper.

HISTORICAL APPLES

THOUGH MANY POPULAR APPLES are very old, there are many other old-time varieties that are less apt to be in general circulation. These have been the subject of historical preservation in recent years—some for nostalgic reasons, others because they really are fine old apples. Some have been passed by because they don't ripen as uniformly or ship as well as modern varieties do, but for the home gardener these drawbacks are not important. Some have skins that might appear funny-looking to the average supermarket shopper; they might have a strange color inside or out, or they might show a rough brownish speckling, called russeting, a trait that is actually a sign of a good keeper. Here are some apples that have stood up best over the years. They are available in the specialty nurseries listed in the back of the book, and now even in some more general nurseries.

'Wolf River.' This large midseason apple is very hardy, grows on a strong tree, and is valued for pies.

'Snow Apple' ('Fameuse'). A dark red apple with very white, juicy flesh. Exquisite, but not a keeper. Midseason.

'Esopus Spitzenburg.' A late-midseason Baldwin type that Thomas Jefferson considered the tastiest eating apple. Many still agree. It is yellow-fleshed and an excellent keeper.

'Cox's Orange Pippin.' A very flavorful yellow-fleshed midseason apple, long a favorite in England.

'Golden Russet.' A very sweet russeted apple that bears late and keeps extremely well.

'Westfield Seek-No-Further.' This late-fall apple is very hardy and has especially fine flavor for eating.

'Pound Sweet.' An enormous midseason apple—one is said to be enough for a pie. It is yellow, very sweet, hardy, and vigorous.

'Calville Blanc d'Hiver.' A late-bearing European apple especially rich in Vitamin C.

'Sops of Wine.' A medieval variety, good for all purposes, it is dark red with streaks of red running through the white flesh, and it bears early in the season.

'Lady Apple.' This tiny apple dates back to Renaissance France. It has red-and-yellow skin and tasty, crisp white flesh. It bears late in the season.

Crab apples. Crab apples are most often planted as ornamental trees, but many (especially the white-flowered ones) have fruits that are both beautiful and fine to eat or to use in jellies. There is a bewildering array of varieties on the market, some of them prone to scab and other ills, some not. Here are some of the better ones.

'Bob White.' Red buds followed by white flowers. Yellow fruits stay on the tree a long time.

'Dolgo.' Early purple-red fruits, borne on a vigorous, spreading, hardy tree, make exquisite jelly. White flowers may bear in alternate years.

'Donald Wyman.' White flowers followed by abundant bright red fruit. Large, spreading tree.

'Profusion.' Vigorous, with purple-red flowers and fruits. Bronzy foliage.

'Red Jade.' White flowers and long-lasting, bright red fruit. Fairly small tree with a graceful, weeping habit.

'Snowdrift.' Vigorous variety with white flowers and small red-orange fruits.

'Sugar Tyme.' White flowers, then abundant, long-lasting red fruits. Vigorous, upright, scab-resistant tree.

Apricots

Apricots are native to the mountains of Asia and need freezing weather during their dormant period. Though quite cold-hardy, they are happiest in the long-summer areas of zones 6 to 8, especially the west coast. Since they bloom very early in spring, they don't thrive in areas such as New England where spring weather is erratic and can kill the tender flower buds, thus keeping the trees from fruiting. Nonetheless, zone 5 gardeners often give the hardier varieties a try if they have a suitable microclimate. Similarly, there are low-chill varieties developed for areas where winters would otherwise be too mild. The tangy fruits are very rich in vitamins and are grown on 20-foot trees that are very long-lived in favorable climates.

SITE

Though southern slopes are good in mild climates, avoid them in areas where early bloom can be frost-nipped, choosing a northern exposure so bloom will be delayed. Don't plant apricots near tomatoes or any other members of the Solanaceae (page 233), or near melons, raspberries, or strawberries, all of which can harbor diseases to which apricots are prone. (It's best to avoid sites where these plants have recently grown.) Plant the trees a good 25 to 30 feet apart unless they are dwarfs. The branches spread wider than the tree is tall.

SOIL

Soil should be deep, with no interference from subsurface rock. Fertile, well-drained loam is ideal. Clay soils are all right if not too heavy. Sandy soils, because they warm quickly in spring, can cause too-early bloom.

PLANTING

Buy one-year-old trees and plant in early spring while dormant (fall in mild climates). Cut the top back to 2½ feet.

GROWING

Apricots need to be thoroughly watered, especially when the fruiting buds are developing. Don't overfeed them, though. Too much growth, too fast, can produce weak branches. Avoid high-nitrogen fertilizers, which can produce soft fruit with pit burn.

Thinning is not always necessary but if the crop is very heavy, thinning will produce larger, more disease-resistant fruit and reduce strain on the branches. Often late frosts will thin the tree for you, or the tree will drop some fruit on its own later on. If needed, thin fruits to about 3 inches apart when they are thumb-size. Prune apricots as you would apple trees but more lightly, heading back the top when it reaches the desired height and keeping it open enough to let in sun to ripen the fruit. Fruiting spurs that have stopped producing should be pruned out to favor new growth. The right time to prune apricots depends on the

locality and the prevalence of certain diseases. Consult local authorities.

PESTS AND DISEASES

A number of diseases can plague apricots. Brown-rot fungus, which covers the flowers with gray spores, occurs east of the Rockies in warm moist weather. Some growers treat it with sulfur sprays or with Surround, a product made with kaolin clay. But just sitting trees for good air circulation, keeping them pruned in an open shape, and thinning the fruit is often protection enough. Remove any injured fruits and debris. Some varieties are resistant. Bacterial canker (black spots on fruit, purplish spots on leaves) should also be pruned out. Black heart, a verticillium fungus, may appear as wilting leaves in early summer and as black streaks within the wood. Avoid growing apricots with the plants mentioned above.

Many apricot diseases can be thwarted by spraying with a horticultural oil while the trees are dormant, but note that most sulfur sprays, though sometimes approved for organic use, are toxic to apricots. Some problems can be minimized just by choosing appropriate varieties for your area, giving them the best care and removing and destroying infected plant parts. Keep the roots cool with mulch in hot weather, and avoid overfeeding. Wounding trunks with the lawn mower can lead to a number of problems, so take care to avoid it. Fight borers by promptly removing all dead or diseased wood, including any lying on the ground. Some pests that bother plums and peaches, such as plum curculio (page 470) and peach-tree borer (page 434), also affect apricots. If any problems become serious, it's best to take a sample to your state Cooperative Extension Service for identification. Ask for the recommended organic control.

HARVEST

You can expect to start harvesting some fruits three or four years after planting. A healthy, mature tree can produce as much as 250 pounds of apricots. Pick when fruit is ripe and can be picked easily, but before it loses its firmness.

VARIETIES

Most apricot trees are self-pollinating, so the time of bearing is less important in select-ing varieties than is the area in which you live. Though single trees will bear, yield is often greater when more than one variety is grown. 'Moorpark' and 'Blenheim' are pop-ular in prime apricot country. Other good varieties include 'Rival,' 'Early Golden,' and 'Perfection' (the last is not self-fertile). In colder climates you will do better with 'Alfred,' 'Chinese,' 'Sungold,' and a series bred for both hardiness and disease-resis-tance that includes 'Harcot,' 'Harglow,' and 'Hargrand.' Low-chill varieties such as 'Erligold' and 'Katy' are suitable for warm areas like southern California.

Blueberries

Blueberries are wonderful plants. Not only do they live for decades, bear delicious fruits, and need little care, but they are also beautiful in themselves, with white bell-like flowers in spring and handsome oval leaves that turn orange-scarlet in fall. The berries are pretty, ripening slowly so that clusters are green, red, and blue all at once. Even the bare reddish stems (on first- and second-year growth) are eye-catching in winter. As shrubs, they are assets to the home landscape whether the owners enjoy eating the berries or not (if they don't, the birds certainly will). They look good as hedges, at the edge of a pond or even near the house as specimen plants.

There are several different blueberry species. The one most commonly grown for fruit and for ornament is highbush blueberry (*Vaccinium corymbosum*). It is hardy to zone 4, and is native all along the east coast (except Florida) and some inland areas, including all of New York State. It grows from 6 to 12 feet tall if unpruned. Lowbush blueberry (*V. angustifolium*) stays under 2 feet tall and makes a fine ground cover. It is hardy to zone 2 and grows wild in the northern tier of the midwest, all of New England, and south through Pennsylvania (farther south at high elevations). Rabbit-eye blueberry (*V. ashei*), native to the southeastern United States, is a highbush species that, unlike *V. corymbosum*, does not need to be thoroughly chilled in winter and will bear well even in Florida and the Deep South. It is best suited to zone 8 and below. *V. ashei* is a very tall, vigorous shrub that ripens later than northern blueberries; the fruits are generally not as sweet but are large and good for baking. With the northern species I think the wild ones are the best if you judge by flavor alone, even though the fruits are smaller than the cultivated ones and "picking a pie" may take hours. And what better way to spend a few hours in a sunny summer meadow? But I would not want to be without some nice fat hybrid berries right in my yard for a handy treat.

SITE

Selecting a blueberry site by observing the plants in the wild can be misleading. The highbush ones often grow in swamps, and while it may look as if they were growing with their feet submerged, they are actually perched above the water, their roots pulling it up from the moist soil below. Lowbush blueberries appear to scramble over bare, rocky mountaintops where there seems to be hardly any soil at all, let alone water. But their long roots are actually snaking down into fissures in the rocks, finding both. (Roots of both highbush and lowbush blueberries spread vigorously underground.) You should give your blueberries a site where moisture is ample but where prolonged flooding does not occur. Other important factors are the full sun they need for ripening, and good air circulation to prevent disease.

SOIL

Soil should be loose and light, but the most important factor in growing blueberries is acidity. Blueberries like a pH of about 4.5 and will grow in anything from 3.5 to 5.5. If you're not sure whether the soil is acid enough in your area or in the spot where you want to grow them, have it tested. If the soil is alkaline you may want to grow something else instead, but if you are hell-bent on blueberries, you'll need to acidify the soil. The best way is to dig in a lot of acidic organic matter such as peat moss, rotted leaves, or composted pine bark. These will also help the soil to retain the moisture that blueberries need. Avoid both lime and wood ashes, which are alkaline.

PLANTING

Buy dormant plants that are two or three years old—those any older are difficult to transplant. You can order them by mail or pick them up locally. Planting bare-root is fine and gives you a chance to see whether the plants have a good, healthy, fibrous root system rather than just a few stringy roots. But be sure to keep the roots moist up until the time they go into the ground; this is crucial.

Plant blueberries in early spring in cool climates, late fall in mild ones, in holes 18 inches deep and equally wide. If the planting area has poor soil, enrich it throughout with compost and well-rotted manure, but I wouldn't add fertilizer or manure directly to the planting hole. Highbush berries are best planted 6 feet apart (further for rabbiteyes), so the whole bush can be sun-ripened, but if you're making a hedge, then 3 to 4 feet apart is acceptable. Dwarf highbush varieties can also go this close, or they can be planted in containers. Set lowbush berries 2 feet apart.

Plant blueberries at the same depth at which they were growing previously or an inch deeper, spreading the roots out in the soil, firming lightly, and watering well. Apply a thick mulch (4 inches or so) of an acidic organic material such as pine needles or shredded bark. Sawdust is all right if it is old and well rotted. Fresh woody materials can rob the soil of nitrogen as they are decomposing.

Rub off the flower buds the first year, to encourage the bushes to put energy into growth.

GROWING

It is very important to keep the plants moist the first year they're growing and anytime fruit is forming. They should be fed fairly heavily each year at blossom time by top-dressing with compost, well-rotted manure, or a commercial fertilizer designed for acid-loving plants. You can use high-nitrogen materials such as cottonseed meal, blood meal, and fish meal, but don't overdo them or you may get vigorous plants with sparse fruit. You can feed again as fruits are forming, but don't feed past June in climates where late new growth may be winterkilled. It's best not to dig amendments into the soil, since this may injure surface roots. Just remove the mulch, apply nutrients to the soil surface, water well, and replace the mulch. The mulch will break down and do its part in acidifying and lightening the soil, and it's fine to add some more each year. Mulch will help keep weeds at bay, but weeds and grass should be pulled out as needed.

Blueberries, especially highbush species, benefit from pruning to keep the plants a size you can pick easily. Pruning also lets sun into the bush to ripen fruits, and keeps a good supply of fresh new growth coming along. Berries develop on fruiting spurs produced the previous season, on side branches of old main stems. You probably won't have to start pruning until bushes are three or four years old, but then start thinning them once a year while they are dormant. Just when they are about to leaf out is a good time because you can then remove any winterkilled wood. Thin out old gray canes (stems) with lots of little twigs that have grown beyond bearing age and have no fruiting buds visible, cutting them at the base of the plant. Remove prostrate canes and short, weak ones. Favor the newer redder canes, keeping six or eight good bearing ones on the bush. Tall, straggly canes can be headed back, and weak, short, twiggy growth can be removed from tips. Note, while pruning, that fruiting buds are fatter than leaf buds; avoid removing twigs with a lot of these.

PESTS AND DISEASES

If you buy healthy bushes and take good care of them, you'll probably have very little trouble with blueberries. There are some diseases, but most modern cultivars have been bred for resistance. If you live in an area where the berries are more disease-prone, apply fresh mulch each year, prune out debris promptly, and go easy on the fertilizer. If bushes succumb to botrytis in wet weather (the berries shrivel and the tips die), or stunt diseases (which are spread by leafhoppers and stunt the plants), destroy them and start over in a new place. They might occasionally get yellows disease if drainage is poor and the pH too high. Mummy berry, a fungus that makes the berries shrivel and harden, is often caused by wet weather and poor air circulation. Remove all debris, especially dead berries, hold off on fertilizer, and replace the mulch in early spring.

The most troublesome pests of blueberries you'll have to deal with will be birds. You might have to cover the bushes with plastic netting or cheesecloth extending clear down to the ground to avoid losing much of your crop. Spreading the netting on a lightweight metal or wooden framework with a flap you can lift to enter the "cage" will make picking easier. Other pests include blueberry maggot (the larva of the blueberry fruit fly), which enters the fruit and rots it. Clean up dropped berries and fight the critter by catching it in the fly stage with yellow sticky traps (page 66). If blueberry stem borers get into the stems in early summer, causing them to wilt, remove the stems and burn them. Pick off Japanese beetles or use milky spore disease (page 67).

HARVEST

Blueberries bear very young, and you'll be getting abundant crops by the time they are four or five years old—as much as six quarts per bush. You should pick at least twice a week, just tickling the berry cluster with your hand and letting the ripe berries fall into a container held under them. (I use a large yogurt container hung from my neck with a string.) Picking this way is important, because berries that look blue are not always ripe. They should really sit on the bush for a week after they are blue, until they fall off easily. The fact that the clusters ripen a little at a time means that you can pick from a single cluster for up to a month and enjoy the berries over a long period. If you plant early, middle, and late varieties, you might be able to harvest berries for two months.

VARIETIES

Most blueberry varieties do not self-pollinate well. It's necessary to plant several different ones in order to achieve complete pollination and have berries of good size. Popular early varieties include 'Earliblue,' the short-growing 'Northland,' and 'Collins,' which bears in long, uniformly ripening clusters. For midseason you might grow 'Blueray,' 'Bluecrop,' and 'Berkeley,' all of which bear abundant crops of large berries. For later berries there's 'Jersey' (the shrub is especially handsome), the sweet, dark 'Herbert,' and to wind up the season, 'Coville.' Good varieties for the north are 'Northland,' 'Earliblue,' 'Blueray,' the early 'Patriot,' the late-bearing 'Elliott,' and 'Northblue,' which is a self-fertile dwarf variety. 'Tophat' is a hardy dwarf that can be grown in tubs. For rabbit-eye varieties the standard favorite is 'Tifblue,' a vigorous, upright bush that bears fairly late. For an early one try 'Climax' or the lower-growing 'Woodward.' For midseason try the compact 'Southland' and for late-season the sweet-tasting 'Delite.'

Cherries

CHERRIES ARE BEAUTIFUL TREES to have, whether you grow the purely ornamental kinds or those bred for their fruits. Cherry trees have a pleasing shape and distinctive smooth, shiny bark, and they bear clouds of delicate pink or white blossoms in spring. The tasty fruits are among the earliest tree fruits to appear—usually in June or July.

There are two basic types of edible cherries: sweet and sour. The distinction seems to blur at times, because some of the sour cherries can taste quite sweet if left on the tree long enough to fully ripen, and some of the sweet ones are a bit tart. But in general, "sweet cherries" are best for eating fresh and "sour cherries" are used mostly

for cooking or preserves—in fact the latter are often called pie cherries.

Sweet and sour cherries are two distinct species and differ quite a bit. The sour ones are easier to grow. They're hardy, generally speaking, from zone 4 to zone 7, and they are less bothered by insects and diseases than sweet cherries are. They are more compact trees (most attain about 15 feet) and well suited to small properties or intimate landscape settings. Most sweet cherries are hardy in zones 5 through 8. They do well in roughly the same climates where peaches thrive. They average about 25 feet tall. Dwarf varieties of both sweet and sour cherries are available, as well as bush types such as Nanking cherry. Some dwarfs and bush types are so small they can even be grown in tubs for terrace gardens.

The purely ornamental cherries are sold as "flowering cherries," despite the fact that those grown for their fruits also bloom beautifully. They are very fine landscaping trees bred mainly for their showy flowers, and they require the same growing conditions as fruit cherries.

SITE

Cherries like a sunny spot, and those grown for fruit are often planted on south-facing slopes. Avoid cold valleys where trees can be winter-injured and the early blooms nipped by late frost. Allow enough room between trees to permit ripening—about 12 feet for most dwarfs, 20 to 25 feet for sour cherries, and 25 to 40 for sweet, depending on the size of the variety.

SOIL

The most important requirement is that the soil be very well drained. Cherries will not thrive in soggy soil, especially in cold climates where it can contribute to winter injury. Both sweet and sour cherries prefer a light, rather sandy soil, though sour cherries can take soil a bit heavier than sweet ones can. Soil for cherries should be reasonably fertile and also deep, especially if the ground is dry. Cherries need moisture at flowering and fruiting time, but can get by with a dryish soil even at these times if the roots can get down deep enough to find moisture. The ideal pH for cherries is about 6.5, but a range of 5.5 to 8.0 is acceptable.

PLANTING

Almost all cherry trees you buy are grafted, usually on cherry rootstocks. Buy one- or two-year-old dormant trees 4 to 5 feet tall, and cut them back by a third. Cherries are best planted in early spring before buds swell, except in warm climates, where fall planting is fine.

It is very important when planting cherries not to let the roots dry out at any time. Cut off any that are either damaged or long and straggly. Organic matter such as compost or moistened peat moss should be dug into the general planting area. The soil should be well loosened in the bottom of the planting hole and for several feet around it. Set the young tree at the depth at which it grew in the nursery or just a bit deeper, and be very sure to firm the soil around the roots to avoid having any air pockets, which might cause the roots to dry out. Apply a mulch, especially if you're planting in the fall, to protect roots in winter and conserve moisture in summer. Protect the trunk against mice with wire mesh. It is also helpful to paint the trunk with white tree paint to prevent sun scald.

GROWING

Water cherry trees deeply if the weather is very dry at flowering time or just as the fruits are ripening. The trees do not need a lot of feeding; in fact too much can lead to diseases and a sparse harvest. Nonetheless an annual topdressing can be beneficial if your soil's fertility is low. Don't feed trees after early summer, though, or they may form new growth that will not harden sufficiently before winter. Weed control is important; again, a mulch will help.

Cherry trees need only a little pruning. Prune them as you would an apple tree, opening up the top to encourage the fruits to ripen well. Take care to eliminate narrow crotches when you're selecting lateral shoots for the main structure. Narrow crotches are characteristic of cherry trees and can produce a tree with very weak branches, especially if cropping is heavy. Sweet cherries are more upright in their growth, while sour cherries are more open and spreading, making them much easier to pick. Sweet varieties can be cut back hard on top to make them more manageable. Pruning is best done when the trees are dormant.

PESTS AND DISEASES

The biggest challenge with cherries, especially sweet cherries, is beating the birds to the crop. Hanging noisy objects like pie tins in the trees is of limited value. About the only thing that really works is netting. Covering a small tree with netting may well be worth the effort. For a tall tree you might try to cover the bottom branches and let the birds have the cherries on top, which are hard to pick anyway. If you have a large number of trees, there may be enough fruit to go around. Or you can plant mulberries as a "trap crop": the birds like them better than cherries. Make sure, however, that the cherry varieties you've chosen ripen at the same time as the mulberries—otherwise the birds will just get a two-course meal.

The other serious pest of cherries is the tent caterpillar, described on page 66. Breaking up the caterpillars' nests, and then quickly squishing or stomping them, is the best remedy. (Use rubber gloves if you find this too gross.) A shop vacuum cleaner also does the job. If a nest is in a fork toward the end of a branch I'll sometimes just prune that part off, then stomp on the nest. You can also spray the larvae with insecticidal soap when they're crawling on the tree trunk or chewing the leaves. Another pest is the cherry fruit worm. Bt (*Bacillus thuringiensis*) is one treatment. Wormy cherries can also be the work of cherry fruit fly larvae. If you're not sure which you have, get the Extension Service to identify it for you. Cherry fruit flies can be foiled in the adult flying stage by the red sticky-ball traps described on page 66. Another common pest is cherry aphid. (Doesn't it sometimes seem as if every plant has its own special aphid?) Fight it with soap spray and dormant oil. Since cherries and plums are close cousins, you also might encounter plum curculio and black knot (page 470).

Cherry leaf spot is a typical leaf-spot disease in which purple-edged spots develop on the leaves and often fall out to produce a shot-hole effect. Leaves then turn yellow. Bordeaux mixture (a concoction of hydrated lime and copper sulfate) applied at the time blossoms drop may help. It's also important to clean up fallen leaves in autumn. Cherry fruits can also crack in rainy weather. If that's a problem in your area, seek out resistant varieties.

HARVEST

From a good, vigorous sweet cherry tree you might get three bushels of fruit; from a sour cherry, two to two and a half bushels; from a dwarf of either, perhaps one bushel. Pick when the cherries seem to be the right size, color, and taste and are easily picked. Cherries keep best with their stems on, but if you're going to use them right away, try to pick them without the stems to spare the fragile spurs. Otherwise, pull the stems off the spur gently with a twisting motion. Sweet cherries might keep a few weeks if refrigerated; sour ones should be made into rich jams or pies as soon as possible.

VARIETIES

The most recognizable cherry, to most people, is 'Bing.' It is vigorous, productive, tasty, and moderately hardy, and it grows on compact trees. Like many sweet cherries it's also disease-prone. Other dark sweet cherries include 'Schmidt's Bigareau,' 'Black Tartarian,' 'Lambert,' and the hardy 'Sweet Black Kristin.' Of the dark sweet type, 'Hedelfingen' and 'Van' are somewhat crack-resistant. Some other interesting sweet cherries include the compact-growing, self-pollinating dark red 'Stella,' and the yellow cherries, which are a bit more disease- and bird-resistant. These include the classic 'Royal Ann' (known in the east as 'Napoleon'), the delicious 'Ranier,' and the very hardy 'Yellow Glass.' It is important to investigate which varieties will do best in your immediate area, as well as which combinations of varieties are needed for pollination.

Sour cherries are usually self-pollinating. The classic is 'Montmorency,' a big red, all-purpose pie cherry that is crack-resistant. If you live in a very cold climate—even zone 3—try the semidwarf 'Meteor' (under 15 feet) or the dwarf 'North Star' (well under 10 feet). Also worth noting are the Duke types, such as 'Royal Duke,' 'May Duke' (early), and 'Late Duke' (late). These are sweet-sour crosses and bear big dark fruits in zones 5 through 8.

There are a number of fine ornamental flowering cherries, too numerous to list here. Of special note are Kwanzan cherry (*Prunus serrulata* 'Kwanzan'), which bears heavenly double pink blossoms on a compact tree (usually about 15 feet), the striking purple-leaf sand cherry (*P.* × *cistena*) and the elegant weeping Higan cherry (*P. subhirtella* 'Pendula'), whose willowlike branches brush the ground. Ornamental cherries aren't good for eating with the exception of the Nanking cherry (*P. tomentosa*), a hardy, easy-to-grow shrub that's good for hedges and bears small edible fruits.

lemon

lime

orange

grapefruit

Citrus Fruits

I F YOU LIVE IN THE RIGHT PART OF the country, you'll probably want to have some citrus trees on your property. Not only do they bear tasty, vitamin-rich fruits, but the trees themselves are beautiful—compact broad-leaved evergreens with a pleasing, rounded shape and waxy white flowers that fill the air with fragrance. Some citrus fruits can be grown outdoors year-round in California, Florida, the Gulf coast, and parts of Texas and Arizona, but if you have a warm, protected spot on your property, you just might get away with some varieties farther north. And citrus trees on dwarfing rootstocks also make fine container plants in cooler climates. The houseplants chapter tells you how to grow them indoors, but you can also grow them as small trees in tubs on your terrace in the summer, moving them to a spacious, sunny spot inside the house to spend the winter.

Citrus fruits vary in their hardiness. Limes can't take any frost at all and can be grown only in zone 10. Lemons are almost as tender but can survive in the warmer parts of zone 9. (Meyer lemons, which are hardier, are not true lemons but a hybrid of lemon, orange, and mandarin.) Sweet oranges, the kind most commonly grown, can survive temperatures in the low 20s. Grapefruits have the same hardiness as oranges, though they produce the tastiest fruits where it is hot. They are grown the same way oranges are in most respects.

Conditions in the "citrus regions" are not at all uniform. Florida is quite moist and humid, whereas the southwest and the west coast can be very dry. Each locality has citrus varieties best suited to it, and while some popular ones do well in all citrus regions, it's advisable to get advice from local experts about which thrive best where you live. In addition, commerce among various citrus regions is restricted in order to avoid transmission of disease, so it is generally advisable to buy plants locally unless you're an out-of-state gardener growing them indoors.

Lemons and limes both bloom and fruit year-round. Oranges and grapefruits are spring-blooming and experience a dormant period in winter if temperatures go down into the 50s, but the fruits keep well on the tree for so long that oranges and grapefruits may often seem like all-year crops. Valencia oranges can take more than a year to ripen in some climates. As a result you may have the crops of two separate years on the tree at the same time. Orange trees can grow as tall as 25 feet (sometimes Valencias grow even taller), and are rather upright. Grapefruit trees are a comparable size but more spreading. Lemons and limes grow on open, spreading trees up to 15 feet tall for limes and up to 20 feet for lemons. One of the nicest things about citrus trees is that most of them are self-pollinating, and while you might well want a number of varieties, one is all you need to get fruit.

SITE

Where you grow your citrus fruits depends on local conditions. All citrus like plenty of sun and heat, so if you live in the cooler edge of their range make sure they get your sunniest, warmest, most protected exposure. If your area is very hot, however, some partial shade will be appreciated, especially at midday and especially if you live in the desert. Drying desert winds can also be a problem, and a windbreak should be provided. In Florida you need to make sure that the site where you plant a citrus tree is very well drained.

Container-grown citrus trees do best on a sunny terrace. Containers should be at least a foot tall and a foot wide, larger if you're letting the trees grow over 4 feet tall. But if you are wintering the trees indoors, don't make the containers too heavy to move. When transporting plants indoors or outdoors, it's a good idea to make the transition gradual. In spring, move them into partial shade first before exposing them to bright outdoor sun. In fall, give them a bit of shade before moving them back inside, and do it before temperatures are very chilly, to minimize the shock. You'll have more patience with this program if the containers are not too large and heavy.

SOIL

Citrus fruits are not too fussy about soil, but the moisture level must be right. There should be sufficient moisture for growth, but drainage must be good—in fact it's best if the soil gets slightly dry between soakings, especially if it's clay. Oranges like a light, sandy loam; heavy soils should be lightened with plenty of organic matter. Lemons have more tolerance for heavy soils, but only if they're well drained. The pH should be slightly acid—between 5.5 and 6.2 if possible. In the dry areas of the west, soils are often too alkaline and must be corrected. Salty soils will not grow most citrus fruits.

PLANTING

Lemons and limes can be planted at any time of the year; oranges and grapefruits are best planted in cool weather. Plant citrus trees bare-root in moist climates, balled-and-burlapped in dry ones. Oranges and lemons should go 20 to 30 feet apart, depending on the size of the variety, lemons and limes 10 to 15 feet apart, and dwarf trees 6 to 10 feet apart.

Citrus trees are almost always grafted, and it's important that the graft be about 6 inches above the soil level. This often means planting the tree a bit higher than it was growing in the nursery. Water thoroughly and keep the soil fairly moist after planting and during the tree's first season.

GROWING

The roots of citrus trees are fairly shallow and extend quite a bit beyond the spread of the branches. Keep this in mind when you're feeding and watering. In dry climates you'll probably need to irrigate them, giving them a deep soaking, not a steady trickle. In fact, it's fine if the soil dries out to a depth of 6 inches or so between waterings. The same applies to watering in other regions. If the soil remains saturated with water, poor growth and disease may result, but too much drought will affect the juiciness of the fruit.

Citrus trees need a good nitrogen supply. Top-dressing with compost, well-rotted manure, blood meal, or cottonseed meal works well, or you can apply a slow-release organic fertilizer several times a year. Trees will need heavier feeding in

sandy soils where nutrients leach out easily, but in dry climates they may not leach out fast enough, so avoid using inorganic fertilizers whose residues can accumulate and make the soil too alkaline.

Keep the area around the tree free of weeds that can compete with the shallow roots; even mowed grass can rob them of nutrients. Using a mulch is best, but keep the area right around the trunk free of mulch to avoid brown-rot gummosis. Citrus bark is thin, and the trunks should be protected against sunscald with white latex paint or tree wraps, especially in the desert.

Your trees won't need much pruning. In fact, it's best to keep pruning to a minimum—ample foliage will protect the fruits and lead to greater yields. While they're young, train the trees to have a nice, balanced scaffold shape, just as you would any tree, removing excessive water sprouts. Then in future years just cut back the occasional over-vigorous limb that unbalances the shape of the tree, and remove branches that grow too low on the trunk. Lemon trees may need a bit more cutting back to keep them round and compact and thereby protect the fruits from sun, wind, and cold. Old citrus trees can be rejuvenated by heavy cutting in early spring after danger of frost has passed. And always remove any dead, damaged, or diseased wood as soon as you notice it. Container-grown trees should be root-pruned every few years (page 618).

PESTS AND DISEASES

Aphids, mealybugs, and red spider mites can all attack citrus trees. They are controlled to some extent by spraying with a strong stream of water or with insecticidal soap. An oil spray may also be needed for these insects, as well as for scale infestations. (Consult your Extension Service for advice about types of oils and the proper timing of their use in your area.) Gophers can destroy citrus trees by girdling the roots. Avoid mulch if gophers are a problem, because it gives them a good hiding place. You may need to resort to trapping them.

Citrus trees are much more prone to diseases in humid areas such as Florida than they are in the drier western regions. Lemons in humid climates can get scab, which makes the leaves and fruits blemished and distorted. Fight it with good sanitation. Destroy all plant debris, and cut off suckers that grow from the roots; these can harbor the scab fungus. Brown-rot gummosis (also called foot rot) is as distasteful as it sounds; the bark on the lower trunk gets gummy after a stretch of wet weather, and a bad case of it can girdle and kill the tree. Seek out plants with resistant rootstocks, plant the tree a bit high, keep the trunk as dry as possible, and remove any mulch and even the top few inches of soil. Destroy all plant debris, and make sure soil drainage is excellent.

HARVEST

Pick lemons, limes, and Valencia oranges year-round, navel oranges and grapefruits in winter and spring. All citrus fruits must be fully ripe on the tree before you pick them. It is sometimes hard to tell if they're ripe, because color depends more on the time of year than on ripeness. It's best to cut one open and taste it to be sure. Picking carefully with a gentle twist or snipping with shears will help you avoid damaging the twigs.

VARIETIES

The most popular oranges are 'Washington Navel' and 'Valencia,' but others may be better suited to your region. You might also want to try the strong-flavored blood oranges, which grow on small trees and are ruddy inside if grown in sufficiently cool parts of the orange's favored temperature range. Blood orange varieties include 'Moro' and 'Sanguinelli.' The tiny calamondin orange is described on page 743. It is often grown as a houseplant as well as an outdoor tree, and is not a true orange but a hybrid of obscure origin.

'Eureka' is the standard lemon variety. 'Lisbon' is slightly more cold hardy, growing on a large, vigorous tree. 'Meyer,' as noted above, is not a true lemon (it's more compact and hardier), and 'Ponderosa' bears huge fruits; both are also discussed on page 743. The seedless 'Redblush' ('Ruby Red') is an excellent grapefruit. For limes you have a choice between the large-fruited, 15-foot 'Bearss' (also called 'Tahiti' or Persian lime) and the more compact, fine-leaved key lime, which grows in the Florida Keys. Small and thin-skinned, the latter is the essential ingredient in key lime pie. When grown elsewhere it is called Mexican or West Indian lime.

Figs

IF THERE IS A FRUIT MORE SENSUOUS than the fig, I haven't tasted it yet. To begin with, the tree itself is glamorous—wide and spreading. Its huge bright green, deeply lobed leaves spread out like giant hands. Inside this foliage jungle the figs emerge at the nodes where the leaves are joined to the upright branches. While they're growing they extend from the branch horizontally, but as they ripen their necks relax and they start to droop, plumped up with moisture. By the time they're ready to drop into your outstretched hand they are soft and pillowy, dripping a honeylike syrup. Most are the size of small plums, in colors that range from pale green or yellow to brown and deepest purple.

The insides can be creamy white, pinkish tan, or deep rose.

Unless you live in a warm climate—zones 8 to 10—you might never have seen or tasted fresh figs, let alone seen them growing on a tree. Few edibles are as poorly suited to storage and long-distance transport. Unlike pears or cherries, the fruits don't ripen off the tree; and after they're picked they keep only a few days, even in the refrigerator. Figs are easily bruised or broken when handled. I do see them in markets but they're very expensive, and many people have to settle for them dried. Southern, west coast, and southwestern gardeners have long known the joys of having a fig tree in the yard for fresh eating or making into tarts, puddings, jams, and other delights. Until about ten years ago these pleasures dangled far out of my own reach, living as I do in New England. But I've since learned that with a little effort and planning, the practical range of the fig is greater than you might suppose, as long as you choose the right variety and protect it from cold.

There are several different kinds of figs. One that is widely grown commercially in California, the Calimyrna fig, is poorly suited to home culture because it can only be pollinated by a certain specialized wasp. Instead, look for varieties of the "common fig," of which there are many. These bear without pollination, by means of a complex process that takes place inside the "fruit"— which is really just an enlarged, fleshy stem enclosing the flowers.

Many figs bear two crops a year. The first, called the breba crop, appears early in the summer on wood that was formed the previous year. The second, in late summer and fall, appears on new wood from the current season. Whether a variety bears one crop or two, and whether it is the early or late crop, depends on both the variety and the climate.

One note of caution: figs are invasive in parts of California and care should be taken to prevent them from escaping into the wild. Consult your local Cooperative Extension Service for specific information.

SITE

Figs are sun-loving trees. They prefer sun all day, and eight hours is usually needed to produce and ripen fruits. The farther north you are from zone 8, the more important it is to find a protected spot for them. In zone 7 a hardy fig variety will rarely be lost, even in an especially harsh winter during which it dies back to the ground, and I have even seen an unprotected fig resprout from the roots up north after a subzero winter. But bearing well after such a winter is another matter. If you can find a sunny place protected from winter winds, you greatly increase a tree's chances of coming through unharmed. Spraying with Wilt-Pruf—an antidessicant spray made from pine resin—is sometimes all that is needed.

One strategy is to grow a fig up against a sunny structure that holds the heat. I've seen this done in England, where trees are espaliered in a fan shape on stone or brick garden walls. Be careful which wall you choose, though. The sunny south wall of your home might be kind to the fig, but the fig might ill repay you, undermining your foundation and your plumbing with its powerful roots. These roots are also stiff competition for other plantings. People have been known to wall them off underground with concrete barriers.

Figs do very well in containers. Any variety can be grown this way, though some respond better than others. Fortunately the tree doesn't have to be either large or old to bear fruit. The pot or planter should be at least five-gallon size—larger as the tree matures—and it helps to mount it on wheels or casters in cold climates so you can bring it indoors in wintertime. Because edible figs are deciduous they don't make very exciting houseplants, and in fact a tree will sit out the winter much better in a cool cellar, garage, or outbuilding where the temperature stays above 15 degrees. Warm-climate gardeners also grow figs in containers, especially if garden space is limited or if there are soil problems such as nematodes (see page 447).

Many gardeners wrap their fig trees in winter to protect them from cold and drying winds. This may be all you need for a hardy variety in a zone 6 garden. The trick is to tie the branches up and stuff them with straw, then wrap them well in burlap, carpeting, blankets, fiberglass insulation, canvas—whatever comes to hand. You could also encircle the tied-up tree with a cylinder of chicken wire, stuffed with straw or leaves. (Clear or black plastic wrapping may cause overheating if the sun is strong.) It helps to cut the tree back to 6 feet in height, shortening the branches partially but leaving some of this year's growth if you want a breba crop next year. Mounding the base of the tree with soil and mulching it will also help. Another technique is to cut through the tree's roots on one side, tie up its branches in a bundle, lay it on its side, and bury it in a trench filled with mulch; then blanket it with a covering, weighted with bricks or stones. This sounds like an enormous production to me, especially since fig roots can be hard to sever.

I have had excellent success growing an 'Italian Honey' fig tree in a plastic greenhouse in Maine where the temperature can dip to 15 degrees below zero. When the greenhouse was heated to just above freezing, the tree bore two crops the following year—the second one quite heavy. The year I kept the greenhouse unheated and wrapped the tree I still managed to get one good crop. If you wrap a tree, make sure you remove all its coverings promptly in spring before growth starts.

SOIL

Figs are not demanding as to soil, and will put up with moderately dry and moderately infertile conditions. The ideal pH is around 6.0. If your soil is truly poor and/or sandy, it's a good idea to work plenty of organic matter throughout the planting area. (Lime can be added also if a soil test shows it is needed.) Organic matter such as manure and peat moss will also help to retain moisture. Even though the trees are drought tolerant, they need adequate water in order to bear well. Good drainage is extremely important too; they will not abide standing water or continually soggy soil. Overly fertile soil will cause rampant growth at the expense of fruiting.

PLANTING

Since figs bear very young (sometimes the first year after planting) and are vigorous growers, you should start with a one-year tree. Plant while dormant in early spring. Ten feet apart is adequate for trees pruned to a compact shape (see below), but 15 to 20 feet is required in warm climates if a full-size shade tree is desired. Dig a hole that will accommodate the root system, then set the tree a bit deeper than it grew in the nursery or in the pot. Do not add any soil amendments. Fill the hole, making sure there are no air pockets, then water thoroughly.

GROWING

Figs can be very effective as shade trees, though you can't expect other plants to thrive beneath their heavy canopy. In warm climates figs are often grown in a tree rather than a bush form, with a central trunk. The young tree is cut back by a third at the time of planting, then several main stems are allowed to grow in an open-vase shape, in order to let in light for ripening fruits. These stems are then headed back at the ends to make them branch. In the future little pruning may be needed, though you may want to thin the tree for more light by removing several main stems each year, or to control its size for ease of harvesting by heading back the branches. Remove dead branches or ones that cross one another. Suckers that grow from the bottom are removed, unless you are using them to produce new plants. (Suckers often form roots on their own but you can also layer them as shown on page 620.) Pruning is usually done while the tree is dormant in winter, just before it breaks dormancy. Some people must wear gloves while pruning because their skin is sensitive to the sap.

Figs also do well if allowed to grow in a bush shape, with main stems arising from the base of the plant. In colder climates this is often necessary so that the tree can regenerate better if winterkill occurs. But even in warm areas, maintaining a bush shape has its virtues. It makes the fruit easier to pick, and helps keep the ground beneath the tree moist in time of drought. Young trees tend to form low growth on their own, but you can encourage this by planting 4 inches deep and by cutting out the main stem after a year or two, when the tree is well established.

Water young trees liberally until a root system is well developed; after that, water deeply every two weeks or so in very dry weather. Drip irrigation can be helpful if the tree is refusing to bear. A mulch is also beneficial. Tree roots are best kept dry in winter to discourage out-of-season growth. The trees are much hardier when fully dormant.

Don't fertilize unless poor soil has resulted in stunted growth or lack of fruit. The usual rule of thumb is that 6 inches of shoot growth in one season is adequate; over 2 feet of growth may be considered excessive. If feeding is needed, scatter compost or a nitrogen source such as blood meal or alfalfa meal beneath and somewhat beyond the tree canopy. But proceed cautiously, since overfeeding can prevent fruiting and make the tree more susceptible to cold. Figs grown in containers need regular watering throughout the growing season, and periodic feeding during spring and early summer. If overwintered indoors, water very occasionally—just enough to keep them from being bone dry.

If excessive fruit drop occurs, the cause might be drought, cold damage, too much shade, nematode damage, overfeeding, or trying to grow one of the few varieties that need a pollinator.

PESTS AND DISEASE

Figs are generally healthy trees without severe disease and pest problems. Root-knot nematodes are a threat in some areas, especially in the south. These microscopic worms form growths on the roots that inhibit the uptake of water and nutrients. Though it is best to avoid nematodes by planting clean figs from reputable sources, in uninfested soil, their effects can also be alleviated by feeding, watering, and mulching, and by pruning to reduce the mass of vegetation to be sustained.

Souring, a yeast fermentation caused by insects who crawl into the "eye" of the fruit (an opening at the bottom end), is best avoided by growing resistant varieties such as 'Excell,' whose closed eyes keep insects from entering. Birds are sometimes a serious enough pest to warrant netting the trees.

Persistent foliage diseases are best avoided by growing resistant varieties and by promptly cleaning up fallen fruits, leaves, and other debris.

HARVEST

Figs become very soft when ripe. Try to catch them just before they fall—otherwise the fall could split them open. If a fig is ripe but doesn't fall into your hand when touched, you can snip the slightly wilted stem with kitchen shears. With practice you'll pick them at just the right fleeting moment—unfortunately, immature figs are inferior to ripe ones for both cooking and fresh eating.

Figs are easily dried and will keep a long time in that state, but will eventually harden and be less delicious. When figs are not in season, simmering dried ones in water or port wine will make them plump up so that they make a fine garnish or stuffing for roasted pork, poultry, or lamb.

VARIETIES

Fig varieties are numerous and often confused; there is much debate about whether certain varieties are synonyms for one another. Selection is also tricky. For example, when choosing one for the north you must look not only for winter cold hardiness but also for the ability to ripen in a short, cool growing season. Among mild climates the needs of different regions vary—California, southeast, southwest, northwest. It's always wise to check with the Extension Service and other local sources of information.

Among the hardiest varieties are 'Celeste,' 'Brown Turkey,' 'Sal's Fig,' 'Tennessee Mountain,' 'Hardy Chicago,' 'Magnolia,' and 'Italian Honey' (also called 'Lattarula'). Some that lend themselves well to container culture are 'Violette de Bourdeaux' ('Negronne'), 'Petite Negri,' 'Black Jack,' 'Brown Turkey,' 'Italian Honey,' and 'Hardy Chicago.' Figs for warm climates include 'Kadota,' 'Mission,' 'Alma,' and 'Conadria.' Also of interest are the variegated 'Panachée' and the disease-resistant 'LSU Purple,' which sometimes bears three crops in a season.

Grapes

GRAPE GROWING ISN'T WHAT IT used to be. No more do carefree *bacchantes* run wildly through the forests of Greece, celebrating the fruits of the vine. And I wonder if village lads and maidens anywhere still roll up their pantaloons and hitch up their petticoats to tromp on the newly picked bunches. Modern grape culture is such a serious, scientific business that I'm happy to be a modest home gardener when it comes to this wonderful, earthy fruit.

For me, grapes will never quite lose their romance. When I was a child I spent hours swinging from the wild vines that grew high into the trees in my parents' woods. Some years later I made grape jelly from those same vines, throwing in some pectin-rich wild crabapples to make the jelly set. As I write this, some vines I planted a few years ago now cover a 60-foot-long iron arbor that I had built for them. In fall we have farm lunches in their shade, reaching up at the end of the meal to pluck dessert.

Grapes are among the most beautiful of plants: the vines, the broad leaves, the tendrils, the ripe bunches of fruit. And the harvest gives you so much—jams and jellies, tarts, juice, syrup, grapes for fresh eating, and wine too if you're adventurous. Grapes grow on immensely vigorous and sturdy plants that, if you plant them correctly and give them good basic care, will probably outlive you. They are easy to grow if you choose ones that are right for your climate.

The best wine regions of the world are warm, sunny places with long growing seasons, but there are grapes native to cool, short-season areas as well. After all, when Leif Eriksson landed in North America, he named the new continent Vineland because of the abundance of wild grapes he found growing there. These were native species such as fox grapes (*Vitis labrusca*), whose skins slipped off the flesh easily, quite different from the grapes brought over in colonial times. These were of the species *V. vinifera*—the great European wine grape. The imports failed to thrive in the New World, largely because of the climate, but fine varieties emerged from the native grapes, such as the famous 'Concord,' which began as a seedling in Concord, Massachusetts. The American types are the best for the cooler climates of most of North America. There are also "French hybrid" wine grapes, which are crosses between American and European grapes. But the pure European *vinifera* varieties grow splendidly in California. Gardeners in the southeastern and Gulf states can grow hybrids of the native muscadine grapes (*V. rotundifolia*), which are tasty and grow on extremely vigorous, heavy-bearing vines.

Most grapes are self-pollinating, so only one variety is needed. Some of the muscadines are exceptions; for those you must plant a suitable variety as a pollinator.

SITE

Where you grow your grapes depends partly on what you're growing them for. Two vigorous vines might be ample for the table-grape consumption of a household, since each can produce up to 15 pounds of grapes. Table grapes can be made part of your landscaping plan. They might be trained against an existing wooden fence, along a stone wall or even as an "eyebrow" for a window so that the grapes dangle down and are visible from indoors. You might also grow several vines, as I did, on a sturdy arbor over a terrace, forming a canopy that you can sit under. Bear in mind though, that grapes grown overhead are harder to take care of. If your goal is strictly grape production, not *la dolce vita*, it's better to use a trellising system closer to the ground, such as the one shown in Figure 59. If you're making a lot of juice or wine, or if you just want to try a lot of different varieties, you'll want to create a vineyard. It needn't be a large one, but you would need to have a cleared area with plenty of sun.

Grapes need full sun to ripen, so the best spot for them is a gentle slope that faces south or southwest. (Sometimes grapes are planted on a north slope so as to delay spring growth and thus forestall damage from late frosts.) The site should also have good air circulation. That's crucial for grapes and can mean the difference between a disease-ridden crop and a healthy one. You should also protect vines from strong, cold winds. Having the rows run in the direction of the prevailing winds will cut down on their impact and will allow the winds to blow down between the rows to circulate the air freely.

SOIL

In many parts of the world grapes can be seen growing in perfectly dreadful soil—dry and gravelly. I once saw a successful vineyard in France where they appeared to be using a stone mulch. No . . . that was the soil. Grapes' long, deep roots allow them to adapt to conditions such as these. A soil on the sandy side that warms up well in spring is preferable; it will also give grapes the good drainage that they require. But it must be deep, and if possible, well supplied with organic matter to retain the moisture the vines need when they're getting established. In general, grapes like a fertile soil, but too much richness can weaken the vines and make them more vulnerable to disease. The ideal pH is 6.0 to 6.5.

The soil must be well prepared, preferably starting in the fall before spring planting. Since grapes are a permanent crop, be sure to remove large rocks and any perennial weeds that will compete with the vines and be difficult to remove after the grapes start growing. Dig or till organic matter into the soil throughout the planting area, not just in the spots where individual vines will be planted. The roots will eventually spread out in a radius of at least 8 feet from each plant.

PLANTING

Buy first-grade, one- or two-year-old stock (older plants will not produce grapes any faster), and plant them while they are fully dormant in early spring, as soon as the ground is workable. Fall planting is done only in areas where there is no danger of winter injury. The root system should be healthy and fibrous. (Snip off any damaged roots.) The top of the plant should be cut back so that only two nodes are left on the stem (Figure 59). A node is the slightly enlarged point on a stem where leaves or branches are attached (or just a bud if the plant is dormant).

Even though your vines will be quite small the first year or two and will need fairly minimal support, it's wise to figure out at the beginning how you're going to support the mature vines and set up the appropriate structure, so you don't have to disturb the plants and their roots with future construction. There are many ways to train and support grapes. (See page 580 for methods of supporting vines in general.) The four-arm Kniffin system shown in Figure 59 is a common setup for grapes grown as a food crop. While it might seem complicated at first, it is quite logical once you get the hang of it, and the trellis used would make a beautiful vine-covered fence with which to define your yard. At each end of the row, set a stout 4- by 4-inch post, at least 8 feet long and set 2½ feet into the ground. Brace each end post with a diagonal piece of wood. Then set posts in a row between the end posts, spaced no more than 24 feet apart. The posts set in between need not be buried as deeply—in fact they could be those metal fence posts that are easy to drive in—but all the posts should extend about 6 feet above the ground. Then string two strands of heavy wire (10-gauge is fine) tightly along your row of posts, stapling it securely at the ends and running it through screw eyes attached to the row posts. Put the first strand 2½ to 3 feet above the ground, the second 5½ to 6 feet above the ground. It's useful to install a turnbuckle on each wire near an end post so that wires can be tightened as needed in years to come. If you're planting more than one row, make the rows at least 10 feet apart.

Now you're ready to plant. Space vines 8 feet apart. More vigorous varieties might need as much as 12 feet, muscadines as much as 20. For each vine, dig a hole a foot deep and wide enough to spread out

Training and Pruning Grapes

FIG. 59

trellis with newly planted grapes, cut back to two nodes

after first spring pruning

after second spring pruning

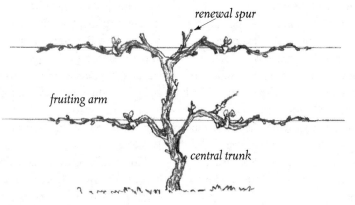

renewal spur

fruiting arm

central trunk

mature vine after annual spring pruning

all the roots. Place a 2- by 2-inch stake about 4 feet tall in the hole as a temporary support for the young vine—if the vine grows upright it will produce better in the future—or tie a string from the young plant to the first wire. Spread out the roots in the planting hole and fill it with soil, watering when the hole is half full and setting the vine at the same depth at which it originally grew, or an inch or so deeper. If the vine has been grafted, be sure not to bury the graft (the lump where the vine and rootstock are joined). After filling the hole, firm the soil gently and water again. If rabbits are a problem in your area, either fence the whole planting or use the guards described on page 70. Mulching the whole planting with an organic material like straw, hay, or shredded bark will keep weeds down and conserve moisture.

GROWING

While the grape vines are growing they will not need much feeding or watering. A good mulch, by minimizing evaporation, will reduce the need to water, though if you need to warm up the soil early in spring to promote growth, you may want to pull the mulch aside at that time and put it back in early summer. It's important to give young plants consistent water while they're becoming established. In general, try to avoid overhead watering of grapes, which can increase the risk of fungus diseases.

Although some growers never feed their grapes at all, grapes do in fact like some nitrogen, especially if the soil is poor. Top-dress the soil with well-rotted manure or a fertilizer in early spring, gradually widening the dressed circle to about 8 feet for a mature vine.

The most important things to do for your grapes are the initial training and, after that, annual pruning. Grapes that are left untrained and unpruned turn into a mass of tangled vines that are mostly old and unproductive wood. You'll get a much better crop if you prune regularly. Even a vine grown on an arbor for ornament will be healthier and more attractive and will put less strain on its support structure if it's pruned each year. Pruning is done while the plants are dormant. In warm areas, prune anytime during dormancy. In cold ones wait till after the vines are no longer frozen. Spring pruning will also let you see wood that has been winterkilled, so you can remove it.

There are a number of different ways to train and prune grapes. All of them depend on the fact that fruit is borne only on shoots that sprout from one-year-old stems. In the system I describe here, you maintain a sturdy main stem (the "trunk") and four side branches "arms" from which new lateral fruiting stems ("canes") are allowed to develop each season. Since the grape crop will sprout from buds on year-old canes, you need both a supply of bearing canes, trained along horizontal wires, and some renewal canes coming along for next year.

With a brand-new grape vine the initial training, to establish the framework, is begun in the winter following the first summer's growth. That little stick you planted will have grown canes from those two buds and probably some other side shoots as well. Choose the strongest cane—this will be your trunk—and tie it loosely to the supporting stake. (Cut back the other one, leaving at least one bud on it as insurance.) When the trunk is tall enough to reach the first wire, let two good canes (with at least four buds each) develop at a height just below the wire. (If the trunk doesn't get as high as the wire the first season, prune it back to two or three buds the following spring and let it start over.) Tie the two chosen canes to the wire, one to the left, one to the right, as shown in Figure 59. If the trunk has reached the second wire, do the same thing there—select two canes and train them horizontally. (If it hasn't grown that far, do this the following spring.) Prune off any other shoots that have sprouted from the main trunk, leaving only the four canes that have formed the new arms. For the first few years—until the framework is well in place—it's best to remove flower clusters so the vine will put its energy into growth.

Subsequently, your annual spring routine will be to select one of the long, one-year-old canes from each arm. These will be the "fruiting arms" for the growing season and should be cut back so each has about ten buds. (Choose canes that are vigorous but have buds spaced close together, as opposed to lanky ones with sparser buds.) In addition you should select another cane, close to the base of each arm, near the trunk. These, which are pruned back to two buds, are your "renewal spurs." They will produce fruiting arms for the following year from one of those two buds (the other is just for backup). During the third growing season you can allow clusters of grapes to grow on the fruiting canes, and allow each renewal spur to form a nice long cane for next year's crop. When you prune in spring, always remove the old canes that have just borne, and any growth other than the four fruit-

ing canes and the renewal spurs—as well as any new shoots that might emerge from the main trunk. This will seem drastic, but persevere!

Grapes grown on an arbor are grown in much the same way, except that the main trunk must be long enough to climb to the top, then branch out along the horizontal supports there. You can follow the same practice of pruning to selected fruiting canes and renewal spurs.

If you're interested in grape-growing, it's worth learning about other methods of pruning as well. Different ones may be better for specific varieties, and in specific climates. For more information, see the list of books on page 778.

PESTS AND DISEASES

If you give your grapes good air circulation, keep them well pruned, clean up all prunings, fallen leaves, and fallen fruit, and don't overfeed them, it's quite likely that you won't have any disease problems at all. Nevertheless you might encounter some of the following troublemakers. The black-rot fungus turns the fruits hard, black, and shriveled. It can be a problem in warm, moist areas and is best fought by good air circulation. There are also rot-resistant grape varieties available. Anthracnose, which produces spots on the fruit, can occur in wet spring weather and is best prevented by the sound grape culture summarized just above. Downy or powdery mildews most often affect the European-type grapes, but any grapes can get them in areas where mildew is a problem. Growing grape varieties that are recommended for your particular area is a good way to keep disease problems to a minimum.

The grape berry moth is best identified by the little silken webs with which it ties leaves or grape clusters together. If you spot these, be sure to clean up all fallen leaves or fruit in fall; then from mid to late spring cultivate the first inch or two of the soil (carefully, since grapes have roots near the surface) to expose overwintering pupae to the air. Japanese beetles love grapes. They can be controlled with milky-spore disease, though in cool climates this takes a few years to work. In the meantime, it may be necessary to pick beetles off by hand to save your crop. Grape leafhoppers can also do considerable damage. Control them with insecticidal soap or by planting blackberries next to the grapes—these harbor a tiny parasitic insect that attacks the leafhoppers. Grape phylloxera is a serious insect pest that sucks the juices from the roots. You can see pea-size galls on the roots and on the undersides of affected leaves. Phylloxera infestation almost destroyed the entire European wine industry many years ago. It was saved, by using American rootstocks, which are largely resistant. You can avoid phylloxera for the most part by growing American grapes or by growing European grapes grafted onto American rootstocks.

HARVEST

Grapes must be fully ripened on the vine in order to reach the peak of flavor and sweetness. Don't go by looks—taste a grape near the tip of the cluster. If it tastes ripe and the seeds have turned brown, you can pick. Grapes should be cut off the vine with a sharp knife or a pair of grape shears, not pulled off. Pick them on a dry day and they'll store better. They don't keep a long time but can be held for a few weeks at just above 32 degrees. The European types store better than the American.

VARIETIES

The varieties of grape you will find listed most often in catalogs are of predominantly American parentage. Among these, some of the most versatile and easy to grow are 'Concord,' the classic blue grape, which matures fairly late in the season on a vigorous, healthy vine; 'Niagara,' sometimes called a white Concord, which is a bit earlier; 'Fredonia,' a big, early blue-black table grape on a vigorous, disease-resistant vine; 'Golden Muscat,' a late white; 'Steuben,' another good blue-black table grape; 'Delaware,' a good midseason red grape; and 'Catawba,' an excellent late red. In general these grapes do well in both warm and cold regions. Others do well only in the south, such as the sweet red 'Flame' and the muscadine types. Southern grapes include 'Scuppernong,' the classic muscadine that is bronze-green and tart-sweet. Most muscadines need a male and a female plant for pollination, but 'Carlos,' a big bronze-colored grape, and the large blue-black 'Cowart' are both self-pollinating. For short seasons try 'Swenson's Red' and the delectable dark 'Edelweiss.'

Seedless grapes do not always have the richness of flavor that the seeded, slip-skin types have, and so are not as good for cooking and preserves, but they are popular for easy eating. The hardiest are the white 'Himrod,' the pinkish 'Reliance,' and red 'Canadice.' Other good ones are 'Seedless Concord,' which is like 'Concord' but smaller, blue-black 'Venus' and 'Glenora,' and the moderately hardy red 'Suffolk' and white 'Interlaken.'

Wine can be made from any grape, but there are varieties bred expressly for wine. Wine grapes are a rather specialized topic about which much has been written. In general, gardeners in climates like that of California can grow just about any wine grapes, including the European ones; in the north you can grow French hybrids such as the red 'Foch' and 'Baco Noir,' or the white 'Aurora' and 'Seyval.' These are well suited to climates such as that of New England and New York State.

cantaloupe

honeydew melon

watermelon

Melons

HEN I WAS A LITTLE GIRL MY grandfather would take me out into his Louisiana melon field and show me how to thump watermelons. You struck the melon hard, then listened for the sound: if it was a resounding hollow thump the melon was ripe. When we found a ripe melon we took it back to my sisters, and then sat and ate it on the lawn, where we were allowed to make a mess, shooting the seeds at each other between two fingers. (No one needed to teach us how to do that.)

Even if I had a space big enough for a watermelon field now, I'd have trouble growing many varieties in New England. Most melons need at least three or four months of genuinely warm weather to produce well, especially watermelons and the "winter melons," so called because they ripen as it's starting to get cool (these include honeydews, crenshaws, and casabas). Muskmelons (commonly but inaccurately called cantaloupes) can be grown up to zone 4, but only with a lot of effort. Northern melon growers take a heroic pride about the endeavor—every bit of it justified. Their success is partly a matter of choosing early-ripening varieties and partly a matter of learning some handy tricks described below. Even watermelons and the winter melons can be worth a try if you grow short-season varieties and have enough space in your garden.

SITE

A site that gets full sun is crucial for melons, wherever you grow them. If it is also protected from chilling winds in spring and fall, all the better. But there should be plenty of air circulation to dry the plants quickly after rain and help ward off the diseases to which melons are prone. A gentle south-facing slope is ideal. Many gardeners grow melons in the vegetable garden because, unlike other sweet fruits, they are annuals and so are replanted each year, just as most vegetables are. In fact, they are grown very much like squash and pumpkins, with similar space requirements and pest problems. For these reasons you may want to make melons part of your garden-rotation scheme (see page 247), rotating them along with the squash. But bear in mind that a single melon plant needs at least a 2-foot by 4-foot space, and usually much more—a large watermelon plant might sprawl over 100 square feet if left unpruned. If space is limited you can try the compact "bush" melon varieties, or even try growing the standard types vertically on a fence or strong trellis. But if you do this you must support the ripening fruits or they'll fall. Use slings made from pantyhose, mesh onion bags, or less conspicuously, pieces of black nylon bird netting. Tie the vines loosely but securely to the support with soft strips of cloth.

If you have plenty of space on your property you may well find it easier to have melon patches away from the garden, rotating the melons with other space-consuming crops like corn, or with cover crops that will add nutrients to the soil when tilled under (page 13).

SOIL

Melons like a light, sandy loam. They do less well in heavy clay soils, so if that's what you have, be prepared to lighten it with a lot of organic matter. Even in sandy soils, adding organic matter is a good idea because it will help retain the steady supply of moisture that melons need, and will help to insure good drainage at the same time. The soil should also be high in nutrients in order to produce the fast, steady growth that will ripen the fruits before cold weather. If possible dig in some compost or well-rotted manure. A soil test will show whether other amendments might be required.

Having a deep, obstacle-free soil will cause the plants to root deeply, which is important in helping them to resist drought. Soil pH should be about neutral for cantaloupes; a range of 6.0 to 8.0 is acceptable. Watermelons can take greater acidity—a pH as low as 5.5.

It might seem from all the cautions I've given that melons are delicate plants in need of coaxing. Quite the contrary: they are big, vigorous vines. The problem is rather that they must be planted when the weather has warmed up, and that for the most part they won't ripen if the weather turns cold. So you need to give them good soil as well as the extra care described below so they'll mature within the limits of the season. This is true in hot climates too, where it's preferable to ripen melons before the intense, drying heat of summer. The heat can be almost as hard on melons as the cold, and summer humidity also takes its toll, increasing the threat of disease.

PLANTING

Young melon seedlings will not grow if the temperature drops below 50 to 55 degrees; in fact the vines may not even set fruit later on if they've been chilled in infancy. So you need to wait longer than "until danger of frost has passed" to plant them. The weather must be warm and the soil about 65 degrees. If this happens early enough to give the plants the number of days necessary to ripen the particular variety you're planting (the catalog or seed packet will tell you how many days this is), you can sow the seeds directly in the garden; if not, you must start them in a cold frame or indoors.

If you're sowing melons indoors, you may be tempted to do it very early in order to have large plants to set out, but resist this urge. Melons are not easily transplanted, and if the plants have more than four leaves and have started to produce little tendrils, the roots will be difficult to establish. It's better not to sow until two to four weeks before you plan to set them in the garden. Sow several seeds in large peat pots or soil blocks, ½ inch deep, and try to keep the soil temperature between 75 and 90 degrees—75 after germination. When the seedlings are about 2 inches tall, thin to the strongest one in each pot by snipping the others at soil level with scissors. Harden them off outdoors before planting. To start them in a cold frame, follow the same procedure, but be sure the frame is well insulated against cold nights.

Make sure your soil has been well prepared before you put either seeds or seedlings in the ground. Most varieties should be spaced about 2 to 3 feet apart in rows 4 to 6 feet apart, but spacing will depend somewhat on the variety and the climate. Watermelon rows should be about 10 feet apart. Bush varieties can go as close as 2 feet each way. Seeds planted directly in the garden should be sown in hills (clusters), then thinned. I'd leave two vines in the hill unless you are not sure they will ripen before frost—if so, thin to one to avoid competition.

A mulch is usually a good idea for melons, in order to keep the ground moist and the fruits clean and less prone to disease and rot. Melons are one crop where a black-plastic mulch can make a lot of sense, even if you don't like the way it looks. It really helps the soil to warm up in the spring in cold climates and keeps it warmer on cool days in summer, too. Put down sheets of it a few weeks before planting time, to pre-warm the soil, and make ×-shaped slits when it's time to set in your transplants. Anchor the plastic firmly on the sides by burying the edges or laying boards over them, then anchor it between plants with bricks, boards, or stones. If the plants are small, make sure the plastic doesn't shift position and cover them. If soil warmth is not an issue, use any good organic mulch like straw, hay, or chopped leaves.

Give the seeds or transplants plenty of water to help them get established. You can also spread some manure or compost on top of the soil in a circle around the plant about 2 feet in diameter, or top-dress with a liquid organic fertilizer. Some people keep the young plants warm and hasten their growth by using hot caps or clear-plastic grow tunnels. Do this only if you check them constantly, as these heat concentrators can bake melon seedlings if you're not careful. Self-ventillating slitted plastic row covers are another solution, as are floating row covers (page 260), which will warm the plants a bit and also keep out aphids and striped cucumber beetles. Guarding the young plants against these pests is important not only because of the damage the insects can cause by feeding on the plants, but also by the diseases they can transmit. Be sure to remove the fabric when female flowers start to form (recognize them by the tiny fruits forming at the base), so that bees can pollinate them. By then there will be less danger from both cold and pests.

GROWING

As melon plants grow they need a steady supply of water up until the time the fruits are ripening; but unless it's very dry you should hold off on the water the last week or two to give the melons better flavor. Try to keep the leaves and fruits dry when you water, to help prevent disease.

If your soil is rich you may not need to feed melons while they're growing. If it is poor or average, or if you're trying to hasten growth along, give them some liquid fertilizer (fish emulsion or manure tea is fine) just before the vines start to take off and just when the tiny fruits are forming. If you're trying to grow very big watermelons, top-dress them with a lot of manure.

Don't cultivate the soil, since roots near the surface can be injured; weeds that come up despite the mulch should be pulled carefully. You should also try to avoid walking on the vines, but by the time the vines cover the soil and make walking difficult, they'll be shading out the weeds. In very hot climates you may need to shield ripening fruits from sunscald; often all you

need to do is draw the vines over the fruits so big leaves shade them a little.

If you want your melons to be large, or if you're trying to hurry up the crop, remove all but two to four melons from each vine. Watermelon vines will produce at most two fruits anyway, but if you want a very large watermelon, leave only the one closest to the base of the plant. After midsummer it's a good idea to remove all blossoms and small fruits that won't ripen in time; this will make the vine put its energy into those that are left. Pinch off the tips of the vines at the same time.

PESTS AND DISEASES

The worst pest to watch out for is the striped cucumber beetle, described on page 311. If they're still a problem after floating row covers have been removed, a combination of hand-picking, vacuuming, and insecticidal soap may do the trick. Use organic pesticides only as a last resort, and only spray at the end of the day when bees aren't active. Squash-vine borers may also do damage (page 367).

A number of fungus diseases can attack melons, especially in warm, humid climates. That's the bad news. The good news is that many modern varieties are resistant to some or all of these diseases. Rotating crops is also a big help. Fusarium wilt is a fungus that lives in the soil. It occurs most often in the north, so crop rotation is especially important there (as is controlling the cucumber beetles that spread the wilt). If a vine suddenly wilts this may be the cause, so unless you can find evidence of squash-vine borer, the vine should be destroyed. Mildews are more common in warm climates in wet weather. Powdery mildew, which gives the leaves a dusting of white, can ruin a crop. It is fought by keeping the vines' foliage dry. Diseased shoots should be cut out and destroyed. Next year rotate the crop and plant only resistant varieties. Downy mildew (described on page 69) can sometimes be controlled by standard garden fungicides but is best fought by growing resistant varieties. Mosaic virus makes the foliage yellow and mottled and is best controlled while the plants are young by controlling the aphids that spread it, either by hosing them off regularly or by using an organic insecticidal soap.

HARVEST

Melons won't ripen much off the vine, so it's important to know just when to pick them. You can usually smell that wonderful rich aroma when muskmelons are ripe. Another sign is that the stem slips off the fruit easily when you press the base of the stem with your thumb; also, the color of the background underneath the "netting" that covers the fruit turns from green to tan. With some melons it's a bit harder. The stems on honeydews, crenshaws, casabas, and the French Charentais do not slip off and must be cut with a sharp knife. Charentais turn slightly golden in color when ripe and may crack slightly at the blossom end. With honeydews that end may soften slightly.

For watermelons, thump them and listen: a "ping" is unripe, a "pong" means it's ready. A dull thud means "sorry, you're too late." You can also turn a watermelon over and look at the light-colored patch on the bottom where it rested on the ground; when this turns a gold or orange color the melon is likely to be ripe. Harvest the thin-skinned "icebox melons" promptly. (These are small watermelons developed specifically for household use.) Storage time for melons varies. Muskmelons may last only a week, even in a cool place, and taste best without refrigeration. Casabas can be kept much longer.

VARIETIES

Among the best muskmelons to grow are the vigorous 'Burpee Hybrid' and the green-fleshed, disease-resistant 'Ambrosia.' I'm very fond of 'Athena' and 'Gold Star.' Heirloom varieties such 'Jenny Lind' and 'Pride of 'Wisconsin' have great flavor. You might grow the spectacular 'Moon and Stars,' in which the deep green-black skin is spangled with tiny starlike gold dots and larger gold "moons." My favorite melon is the Charentais type; you're best off growing one of its disease-resistant cultivars such as 'Savor.' Ask local growers for regional recommendations for all these types, and for watermelons as well. For best success in the north, grow a small-fruited, small-vined icebox watermelon like 'Sugar Baby.' If you live in a warm climate and want to grow big whoppers, try 'Black Diamond' (also known as 'Cannonball') and 'Florida Giant.' There are a few seedless watermelon varieties, notably 'Burpee Seedless Hybrid.' Seedless watermelons actually have rather inconspicuous white seeds and do best in warm climates. Of the heirloom watermelons I especially adore the small, delicious 'Blackfoot Mountain,' which has very dark skin and brilliant red flesh.

Peaches

PEACHES HAVE THE REPUTATION of being hard to grow. It's true that both the trees and the fruits are fragile and the ideal growing range is limited. But if you can find a variety that does well for you, and if you manage to get some peaches to that perfect tree-ripened moment, you'll find it was all worth the trouble. There's a world of difference between store-bought and fresh-picked peaches, and in some ways they are a more trouble-free crop than apples.

To start with the good news, most peaches are self-fertile ('Hal-Berta' and 'J. H. Hale' are two exceptions), so that even if you grow just one little tree you'll get peaches. They are also early-bearing as fruits go; you can have them ripening from July to September if you plant a succession of varieties. Peaches grow on attractive trees about 20 feet tall that have pink flowers in spring and bear when they're as young as three years old. As fruit trees go, they are quite short-lived, but the early-bearing habit helps to make up for this drawback. It is a good idea to have some replacement trees coming along as yours are aging. Many modern varieties are disease resistant, and while a few serious pests attack them, they are less apt to blemish the fruit than are pests that attack apples.

The tricky part of growing peaches is temperature. Most of the best peaches won't take winter temperatures colder than minus 10 degrees, although many fine varieties have been developed that withstand lower winter temperatures. On the other hand, peaches tolerate warm climates better than many other fruit trees, such as apples, pears, and plums. In warm areas you just need to be sure to plant low-chill varieties or they will break dormancy only sporadically in spring. Consult local growers or your Extension Service office for advice on peaches that do best where you live.

Peaches are usually grafted on peach stock. There are dwarf varieties, but I would start with standard-size ones, which are more reliable and can be kept low and easy to pick by pruning. You might try some "genetic" dwarfs, however, such as 'Compact Redhaven' or 'Compact Elberta,' which are true semidwarf trees, not standard trees on dwarfing rootstocks. (They grow 8 to 10 feet tall.) You might like to grow nectarines too, especially if you live west of the Rockies, where they do best. The nectarine is not a different fruit, but simply a fuzzless form of the peach.

SITE

The ideal site for peach trees is on a slope above a body of water, which will tend to draw off the cold air and keep the temperature even. Never plant them in a frost pocket where cold air collects at night. Usually a south- or southeast-facing slope is best, but in cold areas you might want to plant on a northern slope to avoid too-early bloom. Full sun is crucial for the ripening of fruits. The site must also be perfectly well drained—perhaps more important for

peaches than for any other fruit, because they can develop moisture-induced problems such as crown rot.

SOIL

Peaches like a light, fertile soil that is sandy or even gravelly, so it will warm up well. The soil should be well supplied with organic matter, and have a pH as close to 6.5 as possible.

PLANTING

Peaches are generally planted in spring while dormant. Buy vigorous one-year-old trees and plant them 20 to 25 feet apart (10 to 12 feet for dwarfs). The graft should be just 2 inches above the soil surface, and the trunk should be protected against rodent damage (see page 71). It's also a good idea to guard the lower bark against sunscald, either with white tree paint or by wrapping it in a white opaque plastic tree protector. When planting the new tree, cut it back to 2 to 3 feet tall, removing any lateral branches that have formed. Water the tree well and mulch it, but not close to the trunk.

GROWING

About six weeks after planting you can scatter some compost around the young peach tree, then each year feed in spring and again in early summer. It is important to fertilize peaches with a light hand. Too-rapid growth can produce weak-limbed trees. Avoid fertilizing beyond early summer, so as not to stimulate growth that won't harden before winter. For the same reason you should not prune after early summer, or even water too heavily unless the soil is very dry. If your soil is very rich you might even want to grow grass around the trees to slow their growth. Otherwise keep a mulch on the ground, especially if you're trying to forestall early bloom in cool climates.

Peach trees need careful pruning. In warm climates do it when trees are dormant; in cool ones wait until you can tell which wood has been winterkilled, if any. With peaches, it's important not to prune when temperatures are still very cold. Unless the tree is a strongly upright-growing variety, it is best pruned with an open center—i.e., without a central leader. Allow three strong lateral branches to develop. As other laterals and side branches grow in, eliminate downward-growing ones and those that turn back into the center, always trying to let sunlight into the middle of the tree. Fruit is produced on lateral twigs formed the previous season—you want these to be vigorous shoots at least 10 inches long.

Peaches are pruned more severely than other fruit trees, unless they've suffered a lot of winter damage and so need a lot of foliage with which to recover. Yearly pruning should not only eliminate weak or misdirected branches but should also serve to lighten branches, because fruit-laden ones can easily break. (Some may even need to be propped up with posts from below.) Thinning the fruit is also very important with peaches. Wait and see how much the tree will drop by itself, then about a month after bloom carefully pluck off enough of the small fruits with your fingers so that there are 5 or 6 inches between those that remain, eliminating any that have been damaged by insects or other causes.

An old, neglected tree can be gradually renewed by cutting back, each year, one or more of the older upper branches, opening up the center, and making room for productive new growth to develop lower on the tree.

PESTS AND DISEASES

Among the diseases that plague peaches are brown rot (page 430) and plum curculio (page 470). Nectarines are particularly prone to both. Perennial canker is a fungus that can get into the tree if you prune it while the weather is very cold, so don't prune until spring weather has settled in. Bacterial leaf spot causes spots to appear on the leaves that may then turn into holes, and it also produces sunken spots on the fruits; but many modern peach varieties are resistant. Yellows causes the fruits to discolor and the tree to eventually die. Since it is contagious, you'll have to destroy the tree as soon as it is diagnosed.

The peach-tree borer gnaws into the trunk, usually near the bottom, leaving a gummy secretion. It can girdle the tree and kill it. These borers are easier to find and remove than apple borers are, but it is important to dig them out as soon as you discover them. The peach-twig borer overwinters in the bark of the twigs. Encouraging beneficial insects will help to control it; if the problem is severe enough to threaten the crop, a dormant oil spray (page 66) can be used.

HARVEST

A peach tree, if you're lucky, might give you ten years of good bearing. The two most important things to know about harvesting peaches are that they *must* be ripened on the tree, and they *must* be picked carefully. When you look at most peaches you'll see that they have a background color (usually yellow) and a rosy "blush" on top of that—just like the blush on someone's cheek. A blush does not in itself indicate ripeness—you must wait for the background to lose its green color. Only then will the peach taste ripe and sweet. It should still be slightly firm but should come off the twig with just a slight twist. Picking before this moment will also result in bruises from your fingers as you try to remove the peach against its will. Always handle these delicate fruits with great care and store them in a cool spot so they don't get overripe before you can eat them.

VARIETIES

There are two kinds of peaches: freestone and cling. Cling peaches, the kind you usually see in cans, have firm yellow flesh that holds its shape well. Although these are good for canning, their texture is not as good for fresh eating, and of course the flesh *clings* to the pit. Most peaches grown for the home orchard are freestone, with delicate flesh that comes away from the pit easily when you eat it.

There are many fine peach varieties; here is a sampling. The old standby is 'Elberta,' a big, hardy peach that keeps and ships well and grows on a vigorous, disease-resistant tree. 'Redhaven' is probably the best early variety; it's red and almost fuzzless, freezes well, doesn't brown when cut, and has excellent flavor. 'Cresthaven' is an excellent disease-resistant peach. The old 'Indian Blood Cling' is dark red both inside and out. The old-fashioned 'Belle of Georgia' is a hardy, sweet peach with white flesh and skin that is also white but flushed with pink; and there are many other fine white peaches such as 'White Lady' and the hardy 'Polly.' Low-chill peaches include 'Earligrande,' 'La Feliciana,' and the white 'Babcock.' In very cold regions try 'Reliance,' a super-hardy peach that grows on compact trees that are great for small yards.

Among the most popular nectarine varieties are 'Mericrest,' which is red, hardy, and disease resistant, the early 'Nectared' and 'Hardired' (both red), and the white 'Snow Queen.' Good low-chill nectarines include 'Redgold,' 'Fantasia,' and the early disease-resistant 'Durbin.' 'Southern Belle' is a miniature variety.

'Seckel' pear

'Bosc' pear

'Bartlett' pear

Pears

Pears are wonderful trees to have in your yard. Sturdy and deep-rooted, they can live and bear for as long as seventy-five years. They will take less cold than apples but more than peaches, and often have fewer pest and disease problems than either. No other fruit goes quite so well with cheese.

On the negative side, the pear's brief, early bloom can result in the flowers' being killed in cold areas, and can lead to inadequate pollination. Even if the flowers appear when it is warm enough for bees to be active, they are not as fragrant as those of other fruits, and bees may pass them by. Pear trees are not self-fertile either, though most varieties will cross-pollinate each other well. (The combination of 'Bartlett' and 'Seckel,' which are incompatible, is one exception.) Most do badly in very warm zones, since they need a winter chilling to break dormancy. But with the right tree in the right place they're splendid. Check with local growers or the Extension Service for the best pears for your area.

Pears are upright growing, usually reaching at least 25 feet. Dwarfs can be grown successfully, usually on quince rootstocks.

SITE

Plant pear trees in a sunny spot except in climates where the sun is very strong. Protect them from winds that are cold or salt-laden. In cold climates planting on a northern or eastern slope will help to forestall too-early bloom. It is very important to give pears good air circulation to ward off fire blight, the most troublesome pear disease. Plant standard-size varieties 20 to 25 feet apart, dwarf ones 12 to 15.

SOIL

Pears are deep-rooted and need a deep soil. They will do better in a heavy soil than a light one, since they need plenty of soil moisture. (Sandy soils also warm up too quickly in spring, producing frost-vulnerable early bloom.) Pears growing in dry soil will bear their pretty flowers and then drop unripe fruit all over the ground. On the other hand, too-rich soil will make them more susceptible to fire blight and may produce rapid growth that splits the bark. Best pH is about 6.5, but a wide range is tolerated.

PLANTING

Plant while dormant in fall in warm areas, otherwise in early spring. Buy one-year-old whips and cut back to 3 or 3½ feet. Set them out at the same height at which they grew in the nursery, but with dwarf varieties make sure the graft is about 2 inches above the soil so the tree won't root above the graft. At planting time dig in organic matter such as peat and perhaps some bone meal, but no nitrogenous fertilizer. You have a vigorous tree, and can kill it with too much kindness.

GROWING

As the tree is growing, you can top-dress it lightly with compost or whatever it takes to keep leaf color a healthy green and the tree productive, but you may not need to feed at all. It is more important to make sure the tree has plenty of moisture, especially at blossom time and when the fruit is ripening. A heavy mulch not only will conserve moisture but also may help to forestall too-early flowering. You may also grow grass around the tree to defer flowering and restrain growth. But beware heavy applications of lawn fertilizer.

Pear trees are pruned very much the same way as apple trees, but lightly so as to avoid producing vigorous new growth that will be susceptible to blight. Like apples, they bear for many years on long-lived spurs. It is, however, a good idea to keep the top pruned low while the tree is young so it will not grow too tall to pick. Cutting it back later is harder to do and will invite blight. Old trees can be renewed in the same way as apples (page 421). Thinning will benefit the tree and the crop, though pears are notorious self-thinners, often dropping half their crop in early or mid summer.

PESTS AND DISEASES

The biggest pear plague is fire blight, a bacterial disease that blackens the leaves and twigs so they look burned. They may also curl over in a shepherd's crook shape. Cankers (sunken places) can be seen at the base of the blackened parts. The disease is carried by insects that enter the flowers in spring, and is best prevented by growing resistant varieties and by giving the trees good air circulation and judicious light pruning. If your trees still get fire blight, prune out the affected shoots at least several inches below the damage, sterilizing your clippers in a chlorine solution between cuts and destroying the debris by burning it. Badly damaged trees may need to be destroyed.

Other diseases include brown rot (page 430) and pear canker, a fungus that produces sunken areas on the twigs. Take them to the Extension Service to see if pear canker is the trouble. If so, just prune it out and improve drainage in the area where the tree grows. Pear scab produces spots on the fruit in warm, wet weather. Prune out and destroy any twigs that are affected. Rake up leaves and other debris. Grow resistant varieties.

Pear psylla, a plant louse, is the most serious insect pest. Both leaves and fruit are blackened in midsummer from the sooty mold that grows on the sticky "honeydew," which the lice secrete. Dormant oil spray, applied in spring before buds swell, will help to control it; follow this treatment with insecticidal soap spray, as needed, later in the season. Aphids, which also secrete honeydew, are also controlled by dormant oil followed by soap. Even if neither psylla nor aphids do great damage, both can introduce fire blight into the tree. Pears are also injured by the codling moth (page 422), and by pear slugs, which can be done in by dusting them with lime.

HARVEST

Pears are best picked before maturity. Left to ripen on the tree they become grainy and can go very quickly from ripe to rotten. Pick when the skins are light green, when the seeds inside are brown (open one pear to check), and when the pears can be severed from the branch easily with an upward-twisting motion. If possible, store pears in a dry room where the temperature is just above freezing; they'll keep this way for several months. Then bring them into a warmer room when you want them to ripen. But handle them carefully at all stages because they are easily nicked and bruised. Standard trees bear a good crop in about six years, on average, and dwarfs in three or four. Expect up to five bushels per tree from standards, up to a bushel and a half from dwarfs.

VARIETIES

'Bartlett' is the best-known pear, the standard commercial variety that keeps and ships well. The tree is vigorous but prone to blight; the fruits are early. 'Clapp's Favorite' is the standard late variety, hardier for the north than 'Bartlett' but also susceptible to blight. So is the exquisite 'Bosc,' that wonderful little brown, long-necked pear, and the sumptuous old-world 'Flemish Beauty.' Less risky is the wonderful old 'Seckel,' or sugar pear, which is small, brown, and very sweet; it grows slowly but vigorously on a compact tree and is quite hardy. Unlike other pears it should be left to ripen fully on the tree. Modern choices include the early and dependable 'Moonglow,' or for canning and cooking, 'Kieffer,' a big, crisp yellow pear that matures fairly late and keeps very well. Another good bet is 'Magness,' a good blight-resistant pear for the south and west that is very sweet, keeps well, and grows on a nice, spreading tree. (Two additional varieties are needed to ensure pollination, because 'Magness' cannot pollinate other trees.) You might also try the great-keeping 'Red Anjou' or the trouble-free 'Starking Delicious.'

Western gardeners owe it to themselves to try the 'Comice' pear, an old, choice French pear considered the *crème de la crème;* it bears late, has exquisite flavor, and is blight-resistant. Many climates favor the hardy and popular Asian pears. Huge and crisp, they are something like apples in texture. These are good keepers and grow on large, self-fertile trees. Good early-bearing varieties include 'Chojuro' and the dwarf 'Hosui.'

The Callery pear (*Pyrus calleryana*) is an ornamental tree that is frequently planted as a street tree, especially the variety 'Bradford.' It has a tidy lollipop shape that, to my mind, makes it uninteresting as a landscape tree. But it is resistant to fire blight and bears profuse white flowers in spring and handsome dark red foliage in fall. The tiny fruits are not edible.

Plums

This Is Just to Say

I have eaten
the plums
that were in
the icebox

and which
you were probably
saving
for breakfast

Forgive me
they were delicious
so sweet
and so cold

—WILLIAM CARLOS WILLIAMS

PLUMS ARE A GOOD FRUIT CROP for the home gardener. In areas where they do well they have relatively few problems. Since they grow on small trees, it is usually unnecessary to plant dwarf varieties. Even if you have only a supermarket education in plums, you know that they come in many sizes, shapes, and colors. The big, fat, juicy red ones are Asian. These do best in moderate climates, anywhere that peaches thrive. The trees are more delicate, bloom earlier, and require more care than other plums. European plums are the smaller, oval blue or purple ones. They are hardier than the red plums and do well in the north. They include Italian plums, prune plums (which are simply plums that have a high enough sugar content that they can be dried without removing the pits), and the tart but hardy damson plums, which are used for jams and jellies.

There are also a number of native American plums such as the beach plum of the northeastern coast, which tolerates seaside conditions, and the hybrids of *Prunus americana*. These are very cold hardy and can be grown where other plums cannot. They are not as delicious as European and Asian plums, however.

With many Asian and American plums you will need more than one variety for pollination. Although most European plums are self-pollinating, you'll get a better crop if you grow several varieties, provided they're in the same color group. Consult your nurseryman to make sure the varieties you buy are pollination-compatible.

SITE

Plant plums in full sun and away from any frost pockets. Since plums bloom early, it's best to plant them where the soil will warm up slowly in spring. That way, flowers will not appear so soon that they'll be frost-nipped. This is especially important if you live in a cool climate and grow the red plums. Allow about 20 feet between trees, less for dwarfs, bush types, and damsons.

SOIL

Plums aren't fussy about soil, though a slightly heavy soil will suit them better than a light sandy one (except for beach plums). Blue-skinned plums need deep soil. All types prefer well-drained, fertile soil that is well supplied with organic matter. Ideal pH is about 6.5.

PLANTING

Plant one-year-old dormant trees in early spring (late fall in mild climates). Cut back to about 3 feet tall. Plant trees at the same depth they grew at in the nursery, or slightly deeper; protect the trunk (page 70) and apply a mulch to conserve moisture, but take care to keep the mulch away from the trunk.

GROWING

Top-dress plums annually with compost or well-rotted manure. Make sure the trees have adequate water at the time they are flowering and fruiting. Prune young trees to three strong lateral branches, allowing the trees to develop multiple trunks only if, as some plums do, they have a bush habit. Asian plums are pruned to an open center, as with peaches (see page 464). The more upright European varieties do better with the central leader system. As a rule plums don't require a lot of pruning, but you should let light into the tree to promote fruiting and ripening. Remove water sprouts (weak, nonfruitful stems that shoot straight up from the branch). Some moderate pruning will also encourage the tree to bear annually. Red plums need more pruning than blue ones, because they fruit on wood formed the previous year as well as on older wood. Pruning some of the year-old wood will help to prevent the tree from over-bearing. The fruits of red plums are also heavier than others and so are more apt to need thinning.

PESTS AND DISEASES

Plum curculio is a beetle that lays eggs in the fruits when they are small, making a little crescent-shaped cut. The grubs hatch inside the fruits and rot them, secreting a gummy ooze that you can see on the outside. Some growers apply sulfur or Surround, a kaolin clay product, to combat this and other fruit pests from petal fall until a week before harvest. However, shaking the beetles out of the trees onto sheets laid on the ground at blossom time is a time-honored way of dealing with them without spraying. It works even better if you can turn chickens loose in the orchard at the same time. (You can tap hard-to-reach branches with a long padded stick.) Do this daily until they no longer fall, disposing of the beetles in a bucket of soapy water before they can breed. Later on, destroy all fallen fruit containing grubs. (Red plums are not susceptible.)

The fungus disease called black knot produces hard black lumps on the twigs and branches. Prune out by cutting the wood several inches below the knot, then burn the cuttings. Wild cherry and wild plum trees can harbor and spread black knot, so monitor these if you have them on your property, destroying affected trees if need be.

HARVEST

Blue plums generally start to produce in about five years, red ones somewhat sooner. Yield is two to three bushels from a productive tree. Plums are ripe when they come off the branch with a slight twist. Red ones should be ripe when you pick them. Most of the others will ripen off the tree and so can be picked when they're a bit firmer.

VARIETIES

Nurserymen and the Extension Service can advise you as to the best plums for your particular area, as well as the best rootstocks and how individual ones are best planted. Popular red plums include the early, purple-red 'Santa Rosa,' the vigorous red 'Ozark Premier,' and the sweet yellowish 'Shiro.' Also try 'Elephant Heart,' a very big purple-red plum, 'Burbank,' which grows on compact trees, and 'Methley,' which ripens over a long period and is a good low-chill variety for warm climates. In cold areas try the hardy 'Superior,' an Asian-American cross, and 'Tecumseh.' 'Wade' is suited to the south.

'Stanley' is the most popular blue plum. Fairly late-bearing, it is good for preserves and grows on a vigorous, productive tree. Also try 'Fellenberg' (Italian) and the late 'Blue Damson' ('Shropshire Damson'), which is also great for jellies. 'Mount Royal' (from Montreal) is hardy enough even for the far north. 'Bounty,' an American plum, is also extremely hardy—best used for cooking and preserves. The old-fashioned 'Green Gage,' a greenish, sweet, all-purpose plum, does well in most regions.

Raspberries and Blackberries

raspberries

blackberries

I F I COULD GROW ONLY ONE FRUIT, it would be raspberries. They're my favorite to eat, and they're almost unaffordable in the markets, even during berry season. Fortunately they're very easy to grow in my climate, and for the most part they're trouble-free. If I lived in the south where raspberries do less well, I'd grow some gorgeous fat blackberries, which like hot climates.

Raspberries and blackberries are known as bramble fruits because they are so thorny—surely a deliberate move on nature's part to make them harder to pick. Like roses, they are an exquisite prize that you earn only by putting up with a little aggravation.

Bramble fruits are perennial plants that bear on biennial stems called canes. This means that the roots live indefinitely and send up canes each year; these generally fruit the second season, then die. By removing dead canes that have finished fruiting and letting the new ones grow, you can maintain a berry patch for many years. Since the patch is a permanent planting, it's worth spending some time at the beginning to figure out just which berries you should grow.

Red raspberries appear in early summer, usually in July, although there are some fall-blooming varieties (see below). They bear for a few blissful weeks during which you gobble as many fresh raspberries as you possibly can, since they don't keep well, then freeze the rest or make them into jam. You can stretch this early-summer nirvana to a month or more by planting several varieties that ripen at slightly different times. Yellow raspberries are excellent for home growing too. They are very sweet but not quite as appealing to birds as the red ones are. You rarely find yellows for sale in markets, since they don't ship well, so they make a special home-grown treat to serve alone or mixed with red and black raspberries. They grow exactly like red raspberries, on sturdy, erect plants, and many are hardy even in zone 3. Both red and yellow raspberries send up new canes from the crowns and also from the roots as suckers, so even if you plant only a few you'll soon have many. Raspberries and other brambles are self-fertile, so you need only one variety to ensure pollination (though some growers maintain that their yield is greater if they grow two).

Black raspberries, also called black caps, are quite different from red ones. Their canes are arching or trailing, and send out vigorous fruiting side branches, whereas red raspberries are borne mainly on the long, slender canes. Black raspberries don't produce the multitude of suckers that red raspberries do. Most are hardy only to zone 5 or 6, but unlike the red ones, black raspberries will tolerate a fair amount of heat. Their flavor is also a bit more tart and rich, making them a superb choice for baking, for ice cream, or for jams. Purple raspberries, a cross between black and red, grow much like the black ones, though they are often more hardy.

You can also plant ever-bearing raspberries for a fall harvest (they can be either red or yellow). These don't really bear all summer, as their name implies. Rather, they have two crops, one borne in fall on the tips of new canes produced that season and another, on the same canes, borne the following summer. I prefer to grow them only as a fall crop, as described on page 476, and just grow a standard summer-bearing variety for the early crop. But in areas where fall is short, cold, and wet the two-crop system may work better.

Blackberries (not the same as black raspberries) are larger than raspberries and a bit less sweet. They are also less cold-hardy and do best in moderate or warm climates. The plants are extremely vigorous and vary as to their growth habits. Some have strong, erect canes; others are trailing and will lie on the ground unless supported; still others are semitrailing. Some varieties are thornless. Boysenberries and loganberries—both of which are large and wine colored, growing on trailing plants—are simply blackberry varieties.

SITE

The best site for bramble fruits is a slightly sloping, sunny hillside where cold air drains away. They will take a bit more shade than other fruits, but a sunny location will provide a better yield, especially in cool climates. Avoid sites where any of the Solanaceae have grown in recent years (see page 233), since members of this family share with brambles a susceptibility to the verticillium wilt virus. It is also best to separate red and black raspberries by 300 feet, if possible, since seemingly healthy red plants can transmit diseases to the less-resistant blacks. Wild raspberries and blackberries can also transmit diseases, so it is wise to eradicate any you have on the property. Be sure to pick a well-drained site; none of the bramble fruits will grow where it's mucky.

SOIL

Most soil types will grow bramble fruits as long as drainage is good. Moderate fertility is sufficient, though the bed should be carefully prepared initially, with some rotted manure or compost worked into the soil. The more organic matter in the soil, the better—it will help the soil to hold moisture. Add bonemeal or rock phosphate if the soil is low in phosphorus, and greensand for added potassium and trace minerals. The soil should be slightly acid. About 6.0 is ideal, but a range of 5.5 to 7.0 is acceptable. Remember that this is a permanent bed, and all weeds, rocks, and other obstacles to good growth must be removed at the beginning.

PLANTING

It's very important to buy certified virus-free plants. Your neighbors will tempt you with offers of free raspberry plants when it's time to weed out the suckers between their rows. Turn them down, or there's a chance you'll start out with diseases you'll never get rid of. Root nematodes can also get started in your garden this way, and the nursery you buy from should be able to guarantee their stock to be free of these too.

Planting time is early spring, except in zone 6 and southward, where fall or even late-winter planting is possible.

You don't have to buy very many plants of each variety, especially red raspberries. (Keep in mind that in a few years you'll be throwing out extras.) A dozen plants, spaced 3 feet apart, will soon give you a large harvest, with each foot of row producing, ultimately, up to a quart of berries. Plant blackberries and black raspberries about 4 feet apart, trailing blackberries 5 to 6 feet apart. If I'm planting more than one row, I make sure that the rows are pretty far apart—8 to 10 feet is best—for more comfortable picking. If you're using a trellis system (below) and maintaining it well, you can space the rows more closely, but with less air circulation the plants may be more vulnerable to disease. It's best not to grow brambles right next to other permanent crops such as asparagus, lest the brambles invade their root systems.

Make sure that the roots do not dry out between the time you buy them and the time you put them in the ground, and moisten your planting holes thoroughly. Plant raspberries a few inches deeper than they were growing in the nursery, blackberries at about the same level. Cut red raspberries and blackberries back to 6 inches, then water the plants some more.

GROWING

It's very important to give all bramble fruits a constant water supply while they're growing, and especially when they are forming fruit. A good thick mulch of an organic material such as straw or shredded bark will help a lot, and it will also keep down weeds, which might otherwise work their way into the berry plants' root systems. In addition, mulch will keep you from having to cultivate the soil. This is an important advantage, as cultivating can nick the plants' shallow roots, which, in the case of red raspberries, can promote excess suckering. Even with a mulch, you should watch soil moisture. If it's dry weather and a crop is ripening, laying a soaker hose along the rows will definitely increase your yield. Top-dress each year in early spring, pulling aside the mulch and applying at least a shovelful of compost or rotted manure for every foot of row.

The most important job in growing bramble fruits is keeping the plants

Ways to Grow Raspberries

Fig. 60

using the hedgerow system

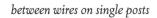

between wires on single posts

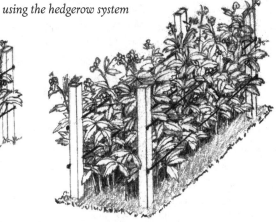

between wires 2 feet apart on double posts

between wires 2 feet apart on crosspieces

properly pruned so that the bed does not become an impenetrable tangle of thorny canes. Each berry type has a different way of running rampant, but run rampant it will.

Red and yellow raspberries, as I explained above, don't branch much but they do send up lots of canes. Every year in early spring you should go out to the raspberry patch, wearing a long-sleeved shirt and leather gloves, and prune out any winterkilled canes at ground level. After the harvest, cut back at soil level all the canes that have borne fruit. If the plants have just fruited it's easy to tell which these are, because you can see what remains of the little berry clusters after the berries have been removed. If you've let the job go until winter or early spring, you'll still be able to distinguish the old canes because they are darker, with peeling bark. Any part of the plant that looks diseased should be removed at whatever time you spot it.

With red and yellow raspberries, because the stiff canes support themselves so well, it's not strictly necessary to trellis them. I have used the hedgerow method, by which you just let the row fill in with new plants until it gets about 1½ to 2 feet wide. Any wider than that, and it's hard to reach and pick. Every spring you would pull up *all* the suckers that come between the rows (and later in the season too, as they appear). One trick is to mow the suckers down from time to time with a sturdy power mower between the rows, but they'll come back sooner if you don't at some point yank out the suckers completely. If you catch them while they're young, you can usually just slice along the edge of the legitimate growing area with a sharp spade, then pull up the emerging suckers by their tips.

It's also a good idea to thin the plants within the rows, pulling up some of the new canes so that the remaining canes are about 6 inches apart. Weak, thin canes should be eliminated in favor of strong, vigorous ones. A good time to do this is in late winter or early spring when you're removing last year's fruiting canes.

These days I use a trellis system, rather than a hedgerow, because it makes picking easier and keeps the plants better restrained. It also helps me to keep track of where the bed begins and ends. See Figure 60 for several trellising styles. I prefer the type at bottom, where the plants are boxed in between parallel wires and held by crosspieces nailed to posts, as on a telephone pole. You can also just set metal stakes in two parallel rows, 2 feet apart and string wires along those. Brace the end posts to keep them from bending.

Ever-bearing raspberries produce fruit the first year in fall, at the tips of the canes, as noted above. If you want a second crop, cut off the tips after harvest. The following season they'll bear on the uncut portion in early summer. Then cut back the whole cane after it finishes fruiting. Both crops will be smaller than that produced by ordinary summer-bearing raspberries. To get one big fall crop instead—and simplify your pruning job as well—cut *all* the canes back to the ground after the fall harvest. The plants will put all their energy into the fall crop, and you won't have to prune them twice.

Black raspberries don't sucker freely, but grow in fixed clumps. Their way of running amok is to bend over their long canes so that the tips root in the soil between your rows. If you let them do this, pretty soon you won't have any rows, just a forest of berry bushes. Instead, in midsummer cut off the new canes to 2 feet tall for black caps, 2½ feet tall for purples. This will cause them to form lateral branches, which will bear fruit next year. In late winter or early spring cut back each of those laterals to about 12 inches long. At the same time, thin the clump at the base, leaving only thick, strong canes. (Ideally, you'll have about five canes over ½ inch thick.) After harvest cut back the canes that have fruited, just as you do with red raspberries. If you prune them this way you can keep the plants fairly short and erect, so you shouldn't need to trellis them.

If you're growing blackberries, cut the first-year canes back to 3 feet in midsummer to encourage lateral branches, which will bear fruit. Then in late winter or early spring, cut each lateral branch to about half its length. After harvest, cut back at soil level those canes that have borne fruit. Thin the new canes so that they're about 6 inches apart. Whether or not you trellis blackberries depends on what type they are. If they have erect canes and you prune them well, they can stand alone like raspberries. If they are trailing or semitrailing, they'll need some kind of support. You can bunch the canes together and tie them to stout stakes, but they'll enjoy better air circulation if you train them on wires. Either use the four-armed system shown for grapes on page 452, tying a number of canes to each wire, or use one of the box systems shown in Figure 60. With trailing varieties you'll have to tie the canes to whatever support you use.

Propagating new bramble plants is easy. Do it at the time you would normally plant them in your area. For red raspberries just dig up some suckers and replant them. For black raspberries bend a cane over and bury the tip in a pocket of enriched soil, anchoring the tip with a rock or a bent wire just as you do with a stem you are layering (as described on page 620). Blackberries can be propagated by replanting suckers, by rooting the tips of canes, or by digging up some roots on the edge of an established clump and replanting them. With all these methods, cut the stems back to the appropriate height when you replant.

PESTS AND DISEASES

There is a long list of diseases of bramble fruits, though yours may escape all of them, especially in cool climates. Fortunately there are a number of things you can do to keep berries healthy, even in areas where diseases are common. First, buy new, clean stock. Remove all plant debris—winterkilled stems, canes that have borne fruit, and any diseased parts of the plant—as promptly as possible, and either burn the debris or cart it away. Don't leave it lying around the property, even in the compost heap. If possible remove all wild bramble plants from the property. Try to provide the plants with good air circulation by choosing the right site, pruning and thinning the canes, and trellising them as needed. Provide good water drainage for the roots. Apply compost, water, and mulch as needed to keep the plants vigorous, but avoid giving them excessive nitrogen. Finally, seek out varieties that resist specific diseases that are prevalent where you live.

Some diseases that might affect the crop are mosaic, which makes leaves yellow and mottled; botrytis cane wilt, which makes new canes wilt; verticillium wilt, which causes canes to wilt suddenly in hot, dry weather; anthracnose, which produces purplish spots on the leaves, then grayish growth on the stems; powdery mildew, which covers the leaves with whitish powder; orange rust, which shows up as bright orange pustules on the undersides of the leaves; leaf-curl virus, which makes the leaves dark green and tightly curled; and spur blight, which produces brown spots on the canes.

Foil hungry birds with plastic netting if they're getting too much of your crop, though if you have lots of berries and pick often you may not find birds a big problem. The netting can be draped over the plants, but it is hard to remove for pruning and picking that way, so you may want to erect a lightweight wooden or metal frame to support it. This can be either box-shaped or constructed like an A-frame house.

Japanese beetles bother raspberries. Pick them off or use milky spore disease (page 67). Hose off aphids, which can transmit disease, or spray them with insecticidal soap. Prune out canes infested with borers (you'll be able to see the little holes where they've entered the cane), and remove plants with galls (tumorlike swellings on the stems, usually near the base of the plant) that indicate crown borers. Fruit worms, which eat the buds and the berries, can be picked off in a small planting. The soil should then be cultivated around the plants in late summer and early fall to expose the worms to predators and keep them from overwintering in the soil as pupae. A few raspberry varieties, such as 'Purple Royalty,' are insect resistant.

HARVEST

Pick berries only when they're ripe, and pick at least twice a week when they are bearing. Be careful not to squeeze the berries; just pull them off the stem gently. (Raspberry cores will stay on the stems.) Try to keep your pail or basket in the shade as you pick, and don't let the berries get more than a few inches deep in the container or they'll squash. Store in the refrigerator until you're ready to use them.

VARIETIES

For summer-bearing red raspberries, the old standby 'Latham' is fine, but there are other good choices too. My favorite, 'Taylor,' is hardy, vigorous, and especially fine tasting. 'Newburgh' is vigorous, hardy, productive, and disease resistant, with a big berry. 'Canby' and the very large 'Thornless Red Mammoth' have practically no thorns, for easy picking. 'Reveille,' 'Sunrise,' and the huge 'Titan' are extra-early. 'Willamette,' a large dark red berry, is recommended for the west coast, and the vigorous 'Dorman Red' is the one to grow in the south. The everbearing 'Fallgold' is the most popular yellow variety. Of the ever-bearing reds, 'Heritage' is the most universally grown, but the hardy, disease-resistant 'Fall Red' is well worth trying. 'Scepter' and 'Indian Summer' also have good disease resistance.

Popular black raspberries include the vigorous, upright standby 'Bristol,' and 'Black Hawk,' which is both disease and heat resistant. Especially cold-hardy varieties are the large 'Cumberland,' 'John Robertson,' and the disease-resistant 'Jewel.' 'Allen' is sweeter than most. For purples try the large, sweet 'Royalty,' which is hardy and both insect and disease resistant. 'Brandywine' is a good, fairly hardy, tart variety that people favor for jams. 'Lowden Sweet Purple' is anthracnose resistant and almost seedless.

Good erect blackberries for the south include 'Cheyenne' and the sweet, early 'Rosborough.' 'Darrow' and 'Ebony King' are hardy upright varieties. 'Boysenberry,' 'Loganberry,' and 'Lucretia Dewberry' are tasty trailing varieties. Among the thornless blackberries 'Chester' and 'Hull' are especially hardy, and 'Black Satin' and 'Thornfree' especially disease resistant. Also try 'Thornless Boysenberry.'

alpine strawberries

strawberries

Strawberries

I N GROWING STRAWBERRIES YOU MUST know what to expect. Yes, you'll get luscious red fruits for shortcakes and pies, and in a lot less time than you'd have to wait for tree fruits. Yes, strawberries are vigorous perennial plants that grow like crazy with very little encouragement. And yes, they take up relatively little space in the home landscape. But beds that are left to fend for themselves will become weedy and overcrowded, overruning other parts of the garden. Old plants, left alone, will bear less heavily, their crowns pushing out of the soil to incur winter injury. And what you assumed would be strawberry fields forever will be a strawberry mess. Yet none of this will happen if you apply a little supervision.

There are four different kinds of strawberries, each of them wonderful for different reasons. The classic strawberry plant bears for a few weeks in June (earlier in warm climates) and then quits. Strawberry festivals were inspired by this type, because the output during those weeks is so great that you need to either bake them, can them, freeze them, or open up your doors and feed the whole town.

Ever-bearing strawberries, the second kind, don't actually bear all season. They produce two crops, the first at the usual time and the second in late summer. Neither of those crops are as large as that of a June-bearer. Ever-bearing types also tend to be a little less hardy, but for gardeners who want two modest harvests rather than one big one they are just right.

Day-neutral strawberries are a more recent development. Because they are less sensitive to the difference between long and short days than the first two types, they bear most of the summer, letting up only in the very hottest weather. These are perfect if you're more interested in a steady supply of strawberries than an avalanche. Day-neutral varieties are often planted in fall and harvested the following spring even in relatively cool climates. Give this a try even if you live up north and see how it works for you. They are not suited for very warm regions, but in others they have been so successful that they've almost superceded the ever-bearing type.

Finally, there are the alpine strawberries, or *fraises des bois*—little elongated fruits from Europe that are similar to the tiny wild strawberries that grow in the United States, but are bigger and easier to pick. You have to grow a great many plants to have more than a sprinkling of fruit to top a bowl of cereal or a whipped-cream-covered cake or a pie, but a great many alpine strawberry plants is not a bad thing to have. I've had excellent luck growing them from seed. They don't spread by runners the way other strawberries do and so require less managing. They are also very pretty and can be used as decorative edgings in flower gardens as well as for a food crop. Best of all, they bear all season long.

SITE

First of all, you need a sunny spot for strawberries. It should also be a warm, protected place, to help the plants escape late-spring frosts. These can nip the blossoms, turning their centers black and preventing berries from forming. A gently south-facing slope is ideal. Avoid low pockets that trap cold air. You also need a spot with good drainage or the plants will rot or be prone to disease. If your drainage is not excellent, consider growing strawberries in raised beds.

The vegetable garden is a good place for strawberries if you can spare even as little as 60 square feet. If your space is very limited, you might grow a small crop spaced intensively in a raised bed. Those strawberry barrels, jars, or pyramids you see for sale might look charming on a terrace, but they don't give you much of a yield, and the plants dry out very quickly between waterings.

SOIL

In addition to needing a well-drained site, strawberries require soil that is fertile and very generously supplied with organic matter. Peat moss, compost, and well-rotted manure, thoroughly dug in, will accomplish both purposes. The pH should be a bit on the acid side, 5.5 to 6.5. Removing all weeds from the site is of *utmost* importance, especially if you want to keep a bed going for a few years. Like many gardeners, I've learned the hard way what perennial weeds, particularly grasses, can do to a strawberry bed. It's best not to plant on a spot where grasses or hay have been growing recently; instead choose a more established garden area. You might even prepare a spot by growing cover crops (page 13) and turning them under for the year or two preceding the crop.

PLANTING

Strawberries are usually planted in early spring, although in warm climates they can be planted in fall. (Fall planting will give you a crop the first spring.) Strawberries are available at most garden centers, where they're grown in flats, just like vegetables. But the most inexpensive way to buy them is in bare-root bundles. Strawberries may carry viruses that will ruin the crop and be hard to eliminate from your garden, so order strawberries from a reputable company that will certify them as disease-free stock. One-year-old plants will usually bear just as soon as older ones, and they're cheaper.

Start with 25 plants. Since you do have to fuss with strawberries a bit, it's best not to overextend yourself at the beginning. In any case, 25 plants may be all you'll need because each mature plant can produce as much as a quart of berries. (If you find you enjoy strawberry-growing a lot and want to freeze them or make jam, just add more plants, of several different varieties, in subsequent years.) If the plants arrive when you're busy, put them in the refrigerator, still wrapped, and keep the packing around the roots slightly moist. Try to plant them within a few days, or at least heel them into the ground (page 40). Take special care not to let the roots dry out at any time.

When your soil is thoroughly prepared, mark out some nice straight rows. Although there are several different ways to arrange a strawberry plot, depending on how you want to manage the subsidiary plants that form on runners, they all start with rows.

If you watch the way most strawberry plants grow, you'll see that the original plant that you put in the ground, called the "mother" plant, soon puts out long, thin stems; these are the runners. When they get to be about 9 inches long they put down roots, forming "daughter" plants. If left to their own devices the daughters send out their own runners and produce granddaughters, and pretty soon what you have is a thick, unproductive ground cover. So some form of birth control is needed.

For the laissez-faire gardener, the simplest method to use is called the matted-row system. The plants are set out about 18 inches apart in rows 3 to 4 feet apart, and are allowed to send out runners freely. To keep the pathway between the rows from filling up with plants as the season progresses, you get rid of the outermost plants on each side of a row, either by removing granddaughters individually by snipping the runners and digging up the little plants, or by running a mechanical tiller between the rows. When you're done, the row should be no more than 30 inches wide—a mixture of mothers and the daughters that will provide the bulk of the crop next year. In the future, older plants are thinned out as needed.

If you're a meticulous kind of gardener, you'll like the spaced-row system. Here, you set the strawberry plants at least 18 inches apart and remove some of the runners from each so that there are only four to six of them, spaced at least 6 inches apart. Some conscientious growers even reposition the daughters to make the spacing more even and perfect. In future years, you keep removing older plants so there's always at least 6 inches of space around each of the remaining ones.

The last method is for tidy gardeners. It is commonly (and rather misleadingly, I think) called the hill system. No true hills are involved, however. You simply set the plants fairly close together (sometimes in a cluster of several plants) and keep runners from forming. As the plants grow, remove any and all runners. This forces the mother plant to put its energy into fruiting rather than making runners, though it will form multiple crowns. In future years the mother clumps will get too dense, so if you're growing your own replacement plants you'll want to let a few runners grow and form new ones. The hill system can produce quite high yields, and works particularly well for ever-bearers, which do better if no runners are allowed to form, and for day-neutral strawberries, which tend to produce fewer runners anyway.

Set the plants into the ground with the roots spread out but pointing downward. The best way to do this is to dig a cone-shaped hole with a smaller cone of earth in the center of it, then drape the roots over the earth-cone, rather like the way daylilies are planted in the illustration on page 184, but with only one plant per hole. Be absolutely sure that the crown (the place where the roots join the stem) is just slightly above the soil surface—too deep and the crown will rot, but too shallow and the roots will dry out. Firm the soil well around the roots. Water thoroughly.

Sow alpine strawberries indoors in early spring; set out plants 1 foot apart.

GROWING

The first year, little spring-planted strawberries will produce some flowers, but if they are June-bearers their blossoms should be pinched off so that the plant will put its energy into growing and producing a fine crop for next year. (Ever-bearers can have their flowers pinched until the end of June, to produce a bigger late crop.) A mulch between the plants and between rows will help conserve moisture and keep down the weeds, and a winter mulch laid over the plants may be necessary from zone 5 northward. You can use the same material for both purposes. Not surprisingly, straw—for which the plant was named—works best. Apply the winter covering about Thanksgiving, or whenever hard frosts are a regular occurrence, then brush it aside to expose the plants at blossom time. Don't take the mulch away, though; leave it next to the plants and use it for a quick emergency cover if late frosts threaten or for covering the ground under ripening berries to keep them clean and rot-free.

Top-dress the plants at blossom time with rotted manure, compost, or a balanced organic fertilizer. If the weather is dry, make sure the plants get an inch of water per week, especially when flowering and forming fruit. And be sure to keep up with the weeds, removing them while they're still tiny, especially if you haven't mulched.

One decision you will have to make, no matter what planting pattern you use, is how long to keep a patch going. Day-neutral and ever-bearing strawberries are often grown as an annual crop to be started over each year. And even with June-bearers you may find that starting a brand-new crop in a different part of the garden every year will keep the plants healthier. That will mean having two patches going at once. While one patch is producing, another one will be growing to replace it the next year. On the other hand, if your plants are thriving you may prefer to just keep the same patch going for a while by removing the older plants each year. If so it's a good idea to renovate a bed of June-bearers by cutting off the foliage right after the harvest has finished. This must be done as soon as the crop has finished bearing, otherwise there won't be enough time for new leaves to grow and nourish the plants for the rest of the season. In a small patch you can cut plants down with shears, but the simplest way is to mow them with a lawn mower set to a height of 1½ inches. Weed and top-dress with compost, then water deeply. As new growth starts to emerge, thin the bed, removing more than half the plants. The plants that remain will fill the bed with runners during the rest of the season to produce daughter plants for next year.

PESTS AND DISEASES

You will assuredly have some problems with birds eating your ripe strawberries, and chipmunks and other creatures as well. If your crop is big you may not lose enough for that to make much of a difference, but if it's a small one you may need to protect it. Many pests can be deterred by plastic netting, cheesecloth, or floating row covers (page 260).

White grubs in the soil, especially those of June bugs, can eat the plants' roots. If your plants wilt suddenly, even when it's not dry, pull one up and see if the root system looks damaged. One way to prevent grub damage is to avoid planting in areas where grass sod has recently been growing.

Rotating your strawberries with other crops will help keep both insect and disease problems under control. It's also very important when growing strawberries to remove all rotting plant debris from the patch, because it can harbor fungus diseases. This includes berries that you don't pick because they are overripe or those that have been nibbled or otherwise damaged. Toss these into a separate basket and compost them.

Another disease to watch out for is red stele, a fungus that rots the strawberries' roots. Both verticillium and red stele are cool-climate, cool-weather diseases. Botrytis fungus and other rot diseases are best fought by good sanitation and thorough picking. Virus-infected plants must be destroyed, and the place where they have grown should not be used for strawberries for a number of years. In fact, it's best to wait awhile before growing strawberries anywhere following a virus attack. Virus diseases are difficult to identify, so it's advisable to consult your Extension Service if your plants are doing poorly and you can't pinpoint the problem yourself. Fortunately, there are varieties that resist specific strawberry diseases.

HARVEST

With the standard June-bearing strawberries, which are harvested the second year after planting, you'll have waited about 14 months for your first crop. Resist the urge, in your eagerness, to pick them underripe. Wait for the berries to be fully red, not green at the tip. They will not ripen as well off the vine. With alpine strawberries, make sure the undersides are bright red. Strawberries, despite their bright color, can be hard to find—lift the foliage up to see those hiding underneath. Never grasp the berry itself when you pick, because it is easily bruised; instead pinch or snip the stem. Collect and store the berries in shallow containers, in a layer no more than 5 inches deep, or the weight will crush those on the bottom.

VARIETIES

There are so many strawberry varieties available that it's sometimes hard to know which to choose. Some of the most popular June-bearing varieties are 'Earliglow' and the large-fruited 'Honeoye,' both early bearers, and the later 'Allstar.' I've had good results with 'Cavendish.' The most popular everbearing strawberry is 'Ozark Beauty,' good for most regions, even the north. Those with more disease resistance include 'Oglala' and 'Quinault.' The best day-neutral varieties are 'Tristar' and 'Tribute,' both fairly disease resistant. Consult your Extension Service for recommendations about varieties for specific areas. 'Alexandria' is a good alpine strawberry variety.

CHAPTER 10

Bulbs

SPRING BULBS MUST HAVE BEEN invented by some divine marketing expert to make life easy for beginning gardeners. A bulb is a prepackaged kit, complete with its own stored food. Put it in the ground in fall, and it will simply carry out the growing program that it came with, while you forget about it and go on with the business of winter. Then, lo and behold, in spring it presents you with a flower.

This is not to say that bulbs come with a money-back guarantee. Neither Mother Nature nor the bulb sellers are responsible if a mouse eats your bulb or if you plant it in soggy soil, and there are a number of little things you can do to make your bulb display more spectacular. But as plants go, hardy bulbs are among the easiest and showiest. They are also among the most rewarding. Perhaps it's because they are such joyous heralds of spring, bursting into bloom long after the labor of planting them has become a dim memory.

Usually when we speak of bulbs, we mean flower bulbs, as opposed to the kind you eat, such as onions. And when we think of bulbs we think of Holland, where most of the world's hardy spring flower bulbs are grown. So it might come as a surprise that virtually none of the bulbs sold commercially are native to Holland or anywhere near it. Most originated in the Middle East or southern Europe, particularly the area around the Mediterranean. But bulbs, both hardy and tender, have always been world travelers, prized by emperors and kings, traded in commerce, and brought back by soldiers and adventurers from exotic lands where the bulbs were growing as native plants. Many bulbs were first introduced to Europe by soldiers returning from the Crusades. The fact that they are so easily transported while dormant (that ingenious packaging!) surely has been a contributing factor to their international spread. Take the ranunculus, truly a citizen of the world. It is variously known as the Dutch buttercup, the Scotch buttercup, the French buttercup, and the Persian buttercup; but only the last name is appropriate. *Ranunculus asiaticus,* from which modern hybrids are derived, is native to Asia Minor.

Again, when bulbs are mentioned most people think only of spring bulbs. They don't realize how many excellent summer-blooming bulbs there are, and they forget that there are even a few fall-blooming bulbs as well.

What Is a Bulb?

ALL THE BULBS DISCUSSED IN THIS chapter are perennial—that is, they come up every year, assuming they're planted in a climate they can tolerate. They are also herbaceous—that is, they have soft green stems as opposed to woody ones. But bulbs are distinguished from the fibrous-rooted herbaceous perennials in the perennials chapter by the fact that they come up from a swollen mass of plant tissue of one sort or another (though these masses generally have fibrous roots at the bottom).

A number of plants that are discussed along with bulbs—and sold by the same people that sell bulbs—are not true bulbs but corms, tuberous roots, or tubers. These terms all refer to an enlarged portion of a plant that stays underground and stores food over the winter, for root growth in winter and for leaf and stem growth the following season. A true bulb, such as that of a tulip or daffodil, is a swollen underground stem consisting of scalelike leaf bases. These are filled with food that will nourish the upper part of the stem and leaves when they start to grow. The leaf bases are tightly wrapped around a bud in the heart of the bulb, and usually are surrounded with a hard protective covering. A corm, such as that of a crocus or gladiolus, is similar but has a bud on top and is replaced by a new corm each year. A tuber (cyclamen or tuberous begonia) is the swollen part of an underground stem. A tuberous root (dahlia) is a swollen root, not a stem, and must have part of a stem with a bud attached to it in order to produce a plant.

It is not important that you remember all these distinctions, and indeed, in this chapter I will sometimes use the word "bulb" to cover corms, tubers, and tuberous roots as well as true bulbs. What is important is that you understand in general what all these swollen tissue masses do. Their purpose is to enable the plant to survive the periods of cold and/or drought that it experiences in its native climate, then have enough nourishment to begin its growth properly when the growing season arrives. Bulbs and similar structures go through those cold or dry periods in a state of dormancy. If your climate does not give the bulbs that dormant period, then *you* must.

There are two major categories of bulbs, spring-blooming and summer-blooming. The few that bloom in fall include colchicums, autumn crocuses, and some of the alliums and cyclamens. Spring-blooming bulbs and summer bulbs are usually handled differently. (Fall-blooming bulbs are handled in various ways and are considered individually in the List of Bulbs.)

SPRING BULBS

This group is the most familiar and includes (among others) anemones, most crocuses, fritillarias, glory-of-the-snow, snowdrops, grape hyacinths, hyacinths, bulbous irises, daffodils, scillas, tulips, and winter aconites. Most spring bulbs, once planted, do not have to be dug up except for propagation purposes or to ease overcrowding. There are exceptions, however. In the north some, such as Dutch irises, are tender. Gardeners in these areas may elect to dig them up and store them over the winter in a protected place. But usually northern gardeners simply choose from the many hardy spring bulbs they can grow without this inconvenience.

In very warm climates, by contrast, spring bulbs can be a problem for gardeners because the winters are not cold enough to make many spring bulbs go dormant. They must dig them up in late fall and refrigerate them for a few months to simulate a northern winter—or grow tropical bulbs instead.

SUMMER BULBS

These include such bulbs as alliums, tuberous begonias, cyclamens, dahlias, gladiolus, lilies, and ranunculus. Most of these are tender and need warm, frost-free regions. The exceptions, which prefer a cooler, more temperate northern climate, are most lilies, most alliums, and some of the cyclamens. Gardeners in cold zones can grow the tender bulbs very successfully by digging them up and storing them over the winter in a place where they will stay cool but not freeze. (Even in warm areas many of these bulbs are dug up, divided, and replanted in order to renew their vigor.)

How to Use Bulbs

A S YOU CAN SEE, WE'RE TALKING HERE about a very diverse group of plants, united only by the fact that they grow from a swollen mass where normally you'd only find roots. Since as a group bulbs span a long blooming season, from winter or early spring to fall, you might conceivably create a bulb garden in which something was always in bloom. This would be an interesting project and could result in a pretty garden, but it is rarely the way bulbs are grown. Usually spring bulbs are grown by themselves or combined with early-blooming annuals and perennials, or with bushy later-blooming plants that will hide the bulbs' withering foliage. The summer bulbs are grown in plantings by themselves, in containers, or combined with summer-blooming annuals and perennials. Following are some of the ways I have particularly enjoyed using bulbs.

AN INTIMATE
SPRING GARDEN

I think it's very important to have some of the small, early bulbs close to the house where you can really enjoy the encouraging sign of winter's end that their flowers bring. In one place I lived, I planted them under some old crab apple trees near the back door (the one everyone used). I had winter aconites, followed by crocuses, scillas, grape hyacinths, and hyacinths, in that order. For this intimate planting I could also have added snowdrops, *Iris reticulata*, glory-of-the-snow, miniature daffodils, and some of the small early tulips.

Planted among these bulbs, in the same bed, were spring-blooming perennials: wild columbines (*Aquilegia canadensis*), foamflower (*Tiarella cordifolia*), wild blue phlox (*Phlox divaricata*), creeping phlox (*Phlox subulata*) in both blue and white, Jacob's-ladder (*Polemonium caeruleum*), *Pulmonaria saccharata* 'Mrs. Moon,' pale yellow primroses (*Primula* 'Moonlight'), and some lamiums with both silvery-white and golden-yellow leaves. These were all fairly low growing, and they were chosen not only because they complemented the bulbs well, but because they appreciated the dappled shade cast by the crab apples. All were vigorous enough to tolerate some competition from the tree roots; in fact, I had to weed out some of the extras each year. I stuck a few pansies in here and there, too, and tolerated the violets that volunteered, weeding some of them out whenever their population started to get out of control.

The garden was at its best in spring, but for later bloom there were about six different kinds of perennial geraniums, followed by four or five different astilbes, and I also tucked in some shade-loving annuals such as impatiens, coleus, and wax begonias. For fall there were hybrid Japanese anemones. Some of the bulbs left rather untidy foliage, especially the hyacinths, but the perennials growing around them helped to minimize the messy effect until the bulb foliage died down.

Some years later I achieved a similar effect by planting small bulbs under an old, spreading red maple tree. This was more challenging because the roots of maples compete for soil, water, and nutrients even more than crab apples do. Nevertheless I was able to naturalize a glorious array of *Tulipa tarda*—a low-growing species tulip whose yellow flowers opened wide like suns on bright days. These were followed by a mixture of small alliums. For later color I established in some vigorous summer-blooming perennials such as catmint (*Nepeta mussinii*) and a creeping perennial geranium (*Geranium macrorrhizum*).

Presently, most of my small bulbs are mixed in with my cooking herbs in a geometric garden I see from my kitchen window. They share the spring display with small early-blooming poppies and soft carpets of woolly thyme.

A DAFFODIL AND TULIP BORDER

During the time of the crab apple garden, I grew my taller bulbs at the far side of the lawn in a long sweep in front of an old stone wall. The daffodils were a mixture I had assembled, including many shapes and colors and periods of bloom (see the List of Bulbs), so the display lasted several weeks and overlapped with the slightly later tulip display. The tulips were likewise a collection of different shapes, colors, and times of bloom. (You can put together your own collections or buy preselected assortments.)

All the bulbs were planted in small clumps of about four or five, each clump a single variety, but they would also look good completely mixed up. I tried to make the swath of plants (roughly 6 feet wide and 200 feet long) look as natural and informal as possible. All the bulbs were growing in the lawn rather than in a bed, though admittedly, tulips are usually grown in beds and are probably at their very best that way.

Since I added new tulips each year and sometimes some daffodils, it wasn't easy to find planting spots where no bulbs were growing. By fall planting time the bulbs' foliage was gone without a trace. I tried marking bulb clumps with little plant labels too short to be chopped up by the mower, but they were impossible to find later. You may devise your own system. One trick is to plant some grape hyacinth bulbs among the larger bulbs (at a shallower depth, of course). Since these grow their leaves in fall they mark the spots!

NATURALIZING BULBS

When you naturalize, you group plants together informally in drifts or patches and let them multiply by themselves. Many gardeners find that this is their favorite way to grow bulbs. The best bulbs to choose for naturalizing are those that are the most at home in your area and have a vigorous habit of growth, for these will spread despite competition from grasses and other plants. A woman I know in Connecticut planted 10,000 daffodils, then added to them over the years, fertilizing them and occasionally dividing them when the clumps got very thick and the leaves started to flop over. Forty years later they carpeted acres of meadows, lightly shaded woodland, and the shores of a small lake. People come from miles around each spring to walk among the daffodils, admire them, and photograph them. An orchard is also a wonderful place to naturalize daffodils in this way.

Another bulb I often see naturalized successfully is scilla (*Scilla siberica*), which makes lawns look like blue lakes in springtime. Subsequent mowings will not impede the plant's growth, since the leaves are close to the ground, and the relatively short spring grass will not hide the flowers, which grow on 4- to 6-inch stems. Scillas are also charming when naturalized in woodland areas. Other good bulbs for naturalizing are *Anemone blanda*, colchicums, *Fritillaria meleagris*, glory-of-the-snow, grape hyacinths, bulbous irises, some of the lilies such as the Asiatic hybrids, snowdrops, camassias, and crocuses, which I have naturalized to great effect on a steep, scrubby bank. Make sure that the bulbs are in a setting where they will be seen. And remember, just because a plant self-sows, don't assume that it can hold its own among all grasses. Winter aconite, for example, will naturalize in beds or in rock gardens, but it would not survive in grass, even lawn grass. And keep in mind that when you plant most bulbs in grass, you won't be able to mow the grass until after the bulbs' foliage withers.

BULBS IN ROCK GARDENS

Most of the small and medium-size bulbs look beautiful in a rock garden and can be used to start off the season there. I especially like to see crocuses, the small bulbous irises, and the species tulips. Naturalize a number of spring bulbs on a rocky hillside, and it will look like a little piece of the Aegean coast. Even pockets between the flat stones of a terrace can host small, early bulbs. A combination of grape hyacinths, scilla, and American columbine (*Aquilegia canadensis*) is enchanting. Once introduced, the columbines will usually self-sow. Violets would do the same, especially in dappled shade.

BULBS IN HERBACEOUS BORDERS

Currently I use spring bulbs to extend the season of my perennial gardens, planting some tulips and daffodils toward the back.

Other plants grow up to conceal the spent foliage while I'm waiting for it to die back. I've also enjoyed using small bulbs with fairly unobtrusive foliage, such as glory-of-the-snow, in the front of a flower border. But the best bulbs for the herbaceous border are the summer-blooming ones. I've added gladiolus for vertical accents, dahlias to add color to that difficult late-summer blooming period, and many kinds of lilies just for their spectacular effect. Among the most successful lilies I've tried in the border have been 'Enchantment,' which forms indestructible clumps, and white regal lilies, which are grand and vigorous, but you may find others that become your favorites.

FORMAL USES FOR BULBS

Naturalizing bulbs is a relatively modern concept. Throughout history bulbs have most often been grown in tidy geometrical beds, whether in the fragrant courtyard gardens of ancient Persia, the carefully measured parterres of the European Renaissance, or the dooryard gardens of colonial America. In Victorian times bulbs were used in formal bedding patterns—a style that is still used today in parks and other public places.

In some situations a formal style may be exactly right, even for the average home. Next to a colonial-style home in Virginia, say, I might well choose to plant a courtyard garden in neat parterres edged in boxwood, with pink cottage tulips in every one. Tulips are the bulbs best suited to formal gardening, because they are so regular: all those stems the same length, all those symmetrical globes of color that don't, like daffodils, face every which way or turn toward the sun with their backs to you. Other bulbs also lend themselves to formal treatment if planted in a regular pattern: hyacinths, irises, and many of the summer bulbs such as lilies, tuberous begonias, and cannas. But don't plant bulbs in a rigid pattern unless the design of your garden makes it appropriate. Lines of tulips marching across the front of a curved bed or foundation planting often look too stiff for the style of the garden; free-form clusters would work better.

BULBS IN CONTAINERS

Just about any kind of bulbs can be grown in containers, on a terrace or patio, in a rooftop or balcony garden, or around a swimming pool. This is obviously a good solution if you don't have land for growing flowers—or not enough of it. But the most common use of container bulbs is as a way of growing summer bulbs in climates where they are tender. Growing ranunculus or tuberous begonias in pots will make it easier for you to dig them up in fall before frost. And summer bulbs such as these are often such special, showy plants that gardeners don't want them to get lost among the masses of a large planting. Gardening in this way may also encourage you to try exotic tropical or semitropical bulbs that are unfamiliar to you, and that I have not had the space to describe in the List of Bulbs— such as crocosmia, tigridia, lycoris, crinum lily, lily-of-the-Nile, and hymenocallis.

OTHER WAYS TO USE BULBS

You will no doubt find places for bulbs and ways of combining them that perfectly suit your own needs. You could plant them in front of shrubs, or along a fence or wall. You might grow them indoors in winter in addition to your spring and summer dis-

plays; or if there is no outdoors connected to the place where you live, you might make spring and summer displays indoors. Specific combinations will appeal to you as you start to learn which plants flower at the same time—red tulips planted with blue forget-me-nots, for example, or with blue grape hyacinths. Or try a succession of early, middle, and late lilies emerging from a bed of ferns. The tall lily stems will look less gawky with an understory of feathery ferns, yet the matlike roots of the ferns will not interfere with those of the deeply planted lily bulbs. In fact, they will help to give the lilies the "cool feet" they require. I have also grown lilies among peonies and roses to good effect.

How to Grow Bulbs

SPECIFIC GROWING INSTRUCTIONS FOR 21 bulbs are included in the List of Bulbs. But a few general comments apply to all of them.

CHOOSING A SITE

Bulbs, in general, are sun-loving plants. It's easier to find a sunny setting for the spring-blooming ones than it is for summer bulb plantings because most of the spring bulbs bloom and carry out much of their growth before there are leaves on the trees. Thus you can plant them almost anywhere except under evergreens. Growth will continue for a while after the trees leaf out, but the partial shade will not compromise the plants during that period. Most summer bulbs however, with the exception of tuberous begonias, need a spot that gets full sun.

When it comes to drainage, bulbs are fussier than most plants. If they sit in waterlogged soil they will simply rot and die. Sandy soil, or soil well lightened with plenty of organic matter, will make life easier for your bulbs, but if the topography itself is causing poor drainage, lightening the soil will not be enough. In that case you'll have to correct the drainage problem, or grow your bulbs in containers or raised beds.

Another site factor to consider is that the soil warms up faster in spring in a warm, protected location, thus producing earlier blooms. For example, the bulbs I have planted in an ell of the house facing southeast bloom a week or two earlier than the very same kinds of bulbs planted around the corner to the northeast. In the southeast-facing bed, the very first to open are the ones closest to the house, because the house itself gives off heat. Bulbs planted in raised beds will also bloom faster. Those growing in a dense ground cover such as pachysandra, or under a thick mulch, will come up more slowly and bloom later than those planted in unmulched soil or along with a sparser ground cover that lets in some sun, such as periwinkle. Of course you may not always want early bloom. I like to have the same plant in several locations with different conditions, precisely because they will not all bloom at the same time and I can enjoy their display longer.

SOIL PREPARATION

Summer-blooming bulbs, which are usually grown in beds or containers rather than naturalized, tend to have more specific soil requirements than spring-blooming ones. Individual soil needs are discussed under individual plants. With spring-blooming bulbs, apart from providing a soil with good drainage, there's not much you need to do to the soil unless it is poor. This is especially true for large-scale, naturalized plantings where you're not digging up the whole area but merely making planting holes here and there and digging in a little fertilizer. When planting in wild grassy areas, try to find spots that are not too rocky and avoid ground filled with extremely vigorous perennial weeds or grasses with dense, matted root systems that will compete too aggressively with the bulbs. For small plantings, or plantings in beds, I like to dig organic materials such as compost or peat moss into the soil, but I avoid manure unless it is extremely well decomposed. Most bulbs like a neutral pH; the soil can be limed as needed.

BUYING AND STORING BULBS

Spring-blooming bulbs become available in garden centers, hardware stores, and various and sundry places toward summer's end. It's a good idea to buy them as early as possible to get the best selection, but they should not be planted while the days are still warm; this can cause them to sprout prematurely. On the other hand, you do want them to start establishing a good root system before the cold and dryness of winter set in.

Often bulbs are sold prepackaged in mesh bags, but I prefer to buy them at a place where I can select each bulb myself and drop it into a bag, just as if the bulbs were onions in the grocery store. This way I can choose nice, solid, fat ones and squeeze them to make sure they're not mushy and do not have any soft spots. I can check them for

Which End Is Up?

FIG. *61*

Planting bulbs right side up will give them a better start in life. Corms and true bulbs are usually pointed on top and flatter on the bottom; often you can see the dried remains of last year's roots on the bottom, too. Round tubers are usually concave on top, round on the bottom. If a tuber has a flat side, place that side facing up; if there is a circular mark on one side, put that side up. Anemone tubers come in a number of shapes, depending on the species; plant clawlike ones with the claw facing down.

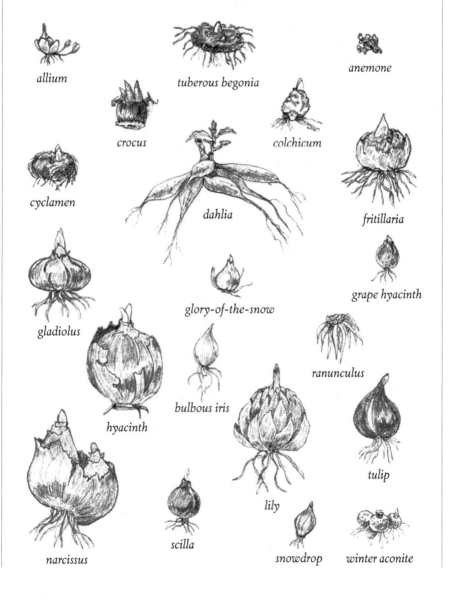

allium

tuberous begonia

anemone

crocus

colchicum

cyclamen

dahlia

fritillaria

grape hyacinth

gladiolus

glory-of-the-snow

ranunculus

hyacinth

bulbous iris

tulip

narcissus

scilla

lily

snowdrop

winter aconite

visible signs of disease, insects, or mildew and smell them to see if there is any sign of rot. With daffodils especially I took for the really big "double-nosed" bulbs, which are really two bulbs joined at the base—or better yet, three.

I also buy bulbs through the mail. They may not always arrive as early as the ones you buy in the store, and of course you cannot squeeze, smell, or look at them. But mail order enables you to choose from a greater selection of varieties and take advantage of more specials. If you order from a reputable supplier, the risk is not great.

Summer-blooming bulbs become available in nurseries and stores in early or mid spring. Order from mail-order companies in mid to late winter for spring shipping. Lilies are usually available in either spring or fall.

If I obtain spring bulbs before I'm able to plant them, I open the boxes to let them breathe and keep them in a dry, dark, cool, well-ventilated place where they won't freeze. To store bulbs in preparation for forcing, see page 496.

If summer-blooming bulbs arrive before spring planting time—which usually means after danger of frost has passed—they can be stored under similar conditions unless you're starting them indoors (see the List of Bulbs for growing specific plants such as tuberous begonias or dahlias).

PLANTING BULBS

Generally, I plant bulbs by making a hole large enough for four or five bulbs, digging some bulb fertilizer into the bottom of the hole, and then replacing the soil. If they are large bulbs such as narcissus, hyacinths, and tulips, I make a square-sided hole by making deep cuts with a sharp spade. If they're smaller bulbs that are planted more shallowly, I might use a large trowel. If I'm planting in grass I really have to heave the spade into the sod (Figure 10, page 53), and it is hard work—something I'm inclined to forget when I am happily ordering bulbs by the hundred. But once I have that nice hole, all I have to do is replace the soil and the sod lid, and the bulbs will come up through it. Some gardeners prefer planting in single holes, especially with large bulbs, using the bulb planters described on page 92.

Gardeners disagree about how deep bulbs should be planted. The rule of thumb is usually three times the depth of the bulb itself. It's best not to skimp on depth. If bulbs are buried deep, there is less chance of their sprouting in fall, being damaged by cold, getting heaved up by freezing and thawing, or being eaten by animals. Deeply planted tulips will produce flowers for more years than shallowly planted ones.

If you have a good supply of compost, dig some into the bottom of the holes. Otherwise, use an organic bulb fertilizer. These are high in phosphorus, for root development, but low in nitrogen. For specific planting instructions, see the List of Bulbs. If you're nervous about getting the bulb right side up, see Figure 61.

MAINTENANCE CHORES

Usually bulb plantings are low-maintenance gardens that can just be left alone. They benefit, however, by being top-dressed with compost or organic 5-10-5 fertilizer in early spring when the tips show, after the foliage dies down in summer, and again in fall. Some, especially daffodils, need to be divided from time to time. Deep watering is a good idea if you're going into winter after a long drought. But the most important task is to make sure no one comes along with a lawn mower and cuts off those "messy leaves" before they've turned brown.

Deadheading (page 191) is another favor you can do for your bulbs, since it keeps the plant from putting energy into seed formation. But don't do it with bulbs that you hope will self-sow, such as scilla or grape hyacinth. Some of the summer bulbs such as lilies have other maintenance requirements, such as staking.

GETTING READY FOR WINTER

If you've planted spring bulbs in late summer and have an unseasonably warm fall that causes the tips to emerge from the ground, don't panic. I have left sprouted narcissus unmulched, and the little green tips weathered the winter cold and snow just fine.

Summer-blooming bulbs that are not hardy for your region should be dug up, or their containers brought in, when the weather turns frosty. Most can be stored in bags of peat or some other dry, loose material in a dry place where they'll stay cool and dormant but will not freeze.

PESTS AND DISEASES

Pests, aside from the ones that dig up bulbs (like dogs) and eat them (like voles), are rarely a problem. Nor are there many diseases that plague them. Given the chance, deer will nibble my tulip plants when they're young and tender. I find a dusting of dried blood (available in feed stores and garden centers), reapplied after each rain, does the trick. If rodents bother your bulbs despite deep planting, plant them in cages made of wire mesh; the stems will grow up through the mesh (Even with many bulbs per cage, this is quite labor-intensive). I've read that hyacinths and daffodils are the only bulbs that animals do not find and dig up. But a puppy of mine once dug up a hyacinth and chewed it to pieces. So much for that bit of wisdom.

FORCING BULBS

IN CLIMATES LIKE MINE, WHERE winters are long and cold, there is a lot of enthusiasm for forcing spring bulbs. In bloom they are an encouraging reminder that the grayness of winter will end, that the roads will not be icy forever, that the heating bills will stop coming.

If you've ever been confused about what bulb forcing is all about, think of it as letting the bulb do what it naturally wants to do, but in a time period that you, the gardener, determine by manipulating the bulbs' natural growth cycles. You must start with a dormant bulb, as usual. You must give it a long, cold period in which it *thinks* it is buried in the dark, cold ground. Then, when you bring it out into the light and warmth of your windowsill, it will think spring has arrived, and it will bloom. You can make this "spring" happen at any time.

Buying and storing bulbs for forcing. Although all of the spring-blooming bulbs discussed in this chapter can be forced successfully, some varieties are better than others. Suppliers will sometimes make recommendations. Buy bulbs as soon as they are available, in order to get a good selection, and store them in the coolest spot in your house. When you put bulbs into cold storage, take into account that the bulbs' "winter" has begun. The best way to store them is potted up.

Planting bulbs. Many kinds of containers are sold for bulb forcing. I buy inexpensive clay pots that are about half as tall as they are wide, in a range of sizes, with saucers. I fill the pots partway with a soil mix that I make up, consisting of one part ordinary garden soil to one part soil lightener such as peat or a commercial peat-based potting medium (some gardeners use perlite). I might throw in a small handful of compost or very well rotted manure for each pot.

Then I place the bulbs in the pots and pack the soil mix gently around them so that just the tips are showing, making sure the soil comes up no higher than a half-inch below the rim. I water them well, using a weak solution of high-phosphorus, low-nitrogen liquid organic fertilizer. Strictly speaking, forced bulbs don't have to be fertilized. The nutrients stored in the bulb are sufficient to produce bloom. But if you want to keep them in the pot, let the foliage grow, and then replant them in the garden, they'll need to replenish themselves. Some bulbs, notably hyacinth and Paperwhite narcissus, are commonly grown in nothing but plain water, either in a special glass container so you can see the roots, or sitting on top of stones. If you do this be aware that you'll have to discard the bulbs after bloom, because they will be too depleted to be worth much in the future. Even forced bulbs you planted in potted soil, fed, and replanted outdoors will take a year or two in the garden to recover their vigor.

How many bulbs you put in a pot is up to you. I plant hyacinths one to a pot, because one makes a big flower that will perfume a whole room, and also makes a nice gift. Five daffodils look nice, or seven crocuses. I leave about an inch of space between bulbs.

Putting them to bed. On the average, bulbs need about 12 weeks of artificial "winter" in order to bloom properly, but this varies a great deal. Crocuses, hyacinths, and grape hyacinths might get by with as little as six or eight weeks; tulips and narcissus may need as much as 15. Logically enough, the earlier a bulb flowers outdoors, the less of an indoor winter it needs. On the other hand, the longer a bulb is kept in winter storage, the faster it may sprout and bloom when you bring it out (partly because as spring nears there is more light and warmth in the house).

Finding the right spot for this storage period is important. It must be dark, and the temperature must stay between 35 and 50 degrees (40 degrees is ideal). Perhaps you don't have the oft-mentioned "cool cellar" or "attached garage," only a cool attic full of bulb-eating mice. Use the attic, but wrap the pots with hardware cloth secured with bits of wire. A minimum-maximum thermometer is a help in selecting your storage spot and it's wise to check the temperature from time to time as the weather changes. Some gardeners bury their bulb pots outdoors, covering them with sand and mulch to keep them from freezing into the ground. You might store them in a cold frame filled with various mulching materials such as leaves, shredded bark, or hay. Cover the pots securely with wire mesh if mice or voles are a problem. The sooner you can get bulbs into a *consistently* cool environment, the sooner you can start counting the weeks till they are "done" and ready to bloom.

Waking them up. When you're ready to bring a pot of bulbs into play, you may see little shoots emerging, just as you would on a 40-degree day in early spring. Get these tender shoots used to the light gradually. Put them in a shaded spot for a day or two, then in a spot that gets bright light but not direct sun and stays at about 55 to 65 degrees. Keep the soil moist but not soggy, and give them a little liquid fertilizer. When the shoots are green and about 5 inches tall, put the pots in a sunny spot at a normal or slightly warm room temperature. When the buds start to show color, put the pots back in the cooler spot with bright, indirect light so the flowers will last longer—or just display them wherever they look best.

After blooming. When the show is over cut the flower stalks back, but let the leaves continue to grow, just as if they were in the ground. Feed them occasionally, but start to water them less and less. When the leaves die back, cut them off and store the bulbs in a cool, dry place till the normal planting time. You can even replant them in late spring, just to get them out of the way. Don't expect them to be their old selves for a few years. You'll need to start with fresh ones for the next fall's forcing.

Timing is everything. You will notice that I've not said a word about *when* to do any of these steps. That's because you have to look at the whole sequence. Forcing bulbs is easy to do, but it takes some careful planning to produce bloom exactly when you want it—Paperwhite narcissus for Christmas, for instance, or your mother's favorite blue hyacinth for her birthday in February. Or you may simply want to have something always in bloom throughout the winter. Just as the length of time needed for dormancy varies with the plants and with the place you store them, so the length of time it takes to bring the plant into bloom varies. If timing is important to you I would suggest keeping records, noting also where you kept the pots and for how long, so that in subsequent years you can manipulate bloom with greater accuracy. Usually it will take between three and five weeks to produce bloom after the pots are in the light. So just count backward from the desired blooming date, adding together the number of weeks in the light and the number of weeks in the dark. If you put up new pots every week or so, then remove some from the dark each week as they become ready, you should have an overlapping sequence of bloom.

The easiest way to keep it all straight is to write the name of the bulb and its planting date on a little wooden label and stick it in the pot. You can even use this as your permanent record, noting the wake-up date and blooming date on the same marker.

Bulbs that don't need a "winter." Tender bulbs that are native to areas with mild winters naturally don't need such a long cooling period. Paperwhite narcissus, for example, can be purchased when available, potted, and kept in a 50- to 60-degree spot in the dark or low light till they sprout; then they can be moved into the light to bloom. The whole process should take four to six weeks. Since there would be no point in planting them outdoors in a cold climate where they would not survive, they are discarded after bloom. As a result, Paperwhites are usually grown in water. I put mine on top of pebbles or rounded black stones in a low ceramic container, and keep the water level just below the bulbs so they don't rot.

This is so easy to do, and the fragrance of the flowers is so sweet, that Paperwhites and other Tazetta varieties of narcissus are probably the most popular bulbs for forcing. But do try some of the more subtle, less predictable ones too, such as a little pot of snowdrops or some blue scilla mixed with tiny yellow winter aconites (being sure to soak the tubers overnight first). Combining several bulb types in one pot for a forced "garden" is a lovely winter gift. Try to have some different little surprises each winter to bring in out of the dark.

List of Bulbs

ALLIUM (FLOWERING ONION)
Allium

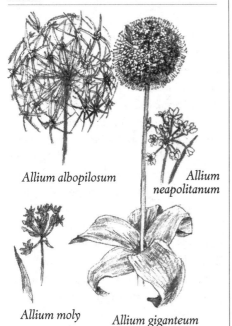

Allium albopilosum

Allium neapolitanum

Allium moly

Allium giganteum

Description: If you've ever seen chives blooming, you may have been surprised to find that the plant is as ornamental as it is useful in the kitchen. Most gardeners don't realize that many members of the onion family produce flowers pretty enough to grow in gardens. They are a very diverse group, with flower clusters in many sizes, shapes, and colors, and blooming times range from spring to summer to fall. The one thing they have in common is an oniony smell when the foliage is rubbed or stepped on, but this does not happen often enough to offend, and some of the flowers are sweetly fragrant. Most of them make fine, long-lasting cut flowers, and some even dry well for winter arrangements.

A wonderful allium to try is *Allium giganteum* (giant garlic). In early summer it sends up long stalks about 4 feet tall, topped with 5-inch balls, perfectly round, made up of tiny purple flowers. By the time they bloom there is little or no foliage around the stems, so grow them together with lower, bushy plants or behind a low wall. If you like big, round purple flowers, you'll *really* love *A. albopilosum* (*A. christophii*), commonly called star of Persia. Its flower cluster is looser than that of *A. giganteum* and up to a foot in diameter, with star-shaped flowers in late spring. Stems are shorter, about 2 feet. *A. aflatunense* has 4-inch purple balls in May or June and grows 2 feet or more. It is as showy as the other big purple-ball alliums, but less expensive; I love it in perennial gardens. Other handsome spring alliums include *A. moly* (golden garlic), with flatter clusters of yellow flowers, about a foot tall, and *A. neapolitanum* (daffodil garlic), which is roughly the same height and bears fragrant white flowers in April.

For late-summer bloom there's *A. tuberosum* (Chinese chives or garlic chives), which has fragrant white flower clusters. It is a strong self-sower. For fall try *A. stellatum* or *A. thunbergii*, both short stemmed and pink-flowering. Most alliums are hardy to zone 4; *A. neapolitanum* is hardy to zone 6.

How to Grow: Alliums like full sun, though *A. giganteum* will do fine in part shade. Soil can be of average fertility but it should be lightened with organic matter and be moist but well drained. They can be planted in spring or fall, from bulbs or from seed (though seed-grown plants may take a long time to reach flowering size, and named hybrid varieties must be bulb-grown). Plant the short ones about 3 to 4 inches apart and 4 inches deep, and the tall ones 8 to 10 inches apart, 6 to 8 inches deep.

A few things to watch for: some alliums must be deadheaded to prevent them from self-sowing all over the place. (They also propagate themselves by forming little bulblets on the sides of the bulbs, by which you can increase your stock if you so desire.) A friend of mine cautions me that his *A. giganteum* did not produce flowers the second year because its energy had gone into producing bulblets, although by the third year the bulblets were large enough to flower. So if your allium gives you foliage but no flowers, be patient; it may perform better in the future. Also note that many spring-flowering species are summer dormant, so don't be alarmed when the foliage vanishes.

ANEMONE (WINDFLOWER)

Anemone

Description: These are the tuberous anemones as opposed to the fibrous-rooted types such as Japanese anemone (*Anemone hupehensis* var. *japonica*). All are spring

Anemone blanda

Anemone coronaria

flowering. The most familiar kinds are the ones sold by florists, which are hybrids of *A. coronaria*. These have 3-inch, very brightly colored flowers in shades of red, pink, purple, blue, or white, often with striking black or yellow centers. They look a bit like small Oriental poppies and grow 12 to 18 inches tall. Popular strains are the single DeCaen hybrids and the semi-double 'St. Brigid' and 'St. Bavo.' None are reliably hardy north of zone 7. *A. × fulgens* is similar in flower and growth, bright red, and a little hardier. *A. blanda* (Greek anemone) is hardier still, though a bit less showy. Daisylike flowers on 6-inch stems in shades of blue, pink, lavender, and white carpet the ground and may survive as far north as zone 5 with a winter mulch.

How to Grow: Anemones like full sun but can take part shade, especially at midday. The soil should be well drained and can be lightened with organic matter for better growth. Add some lime if a soil test indicates acidity or if you have used an acid material like peat to lighten the soil. Soak the tubers overnight in water before planting. Both types can be planted 4 inches apart and 4 inches deep. If you live in the north you need not give up on the tender anemones altogether. Either grow them indoors or plant them outdoors in early spring, then dig them in late summer and store in a cool place in bags of peat.

BEGONIA

Begonia × *tuberhybrida*

camellia-form

hanging begonia

picotee

Description: Tuberous begonias are prima donnas compared to the relatively low-key plants in the rest of this chapter, but it is hard to resist them, especially if you're coping with a shaded or partly shaded situation. These are not grown as annuals, like the fibrous-rooted wax begonias described on page 162. Tuberous begonias grow from round tubers that persist from year to year if you care for them properly.

There are many types of tuberous begonias, all of them gorgeous. The most spectacular are the upright forms, which grow a foot or more tall and produce flowers as large as 10 inches across in vivid red, pink, salmon, apricot, yellow, orange, or white. Flower forms vary. Some are shaped like roses, some like camellias, some have ruffled edges, some have edges in a contrasting color. The Multiflora types are bushy

plants about a foot tall with smaller flowers, but they are easier to grow and are more tolerant of sun. The Pendula types have long, trailing stems that make them perfect for hanging baskets. All types bloom throughout the summer but are hardy only in frost-free zones.

How to Grow: The stems of all begonias are fragile and will not stand heavy dog, cat, or child traffic, so plant them in a safe spot. They can also be grown in containers, indoors or out. The leaves don't like to get too wet (they'll mildew) or sit in the sun (they'll scorch). The worst thing you can do to begonias is to get their leaves wet and let them sit in the sun—their leaves may die. Both the tubers and stems can rot if the soil is too wet. The flowers also have a tendency to drop off like runaway brides, just as they're reaching their peak of exquisite perfection. (But wait! You can float a dropped-off blossom in a bowl of water, and it will stay pretty for days.)

Put begonias in a spot where they'll get plenty of bright light to keep them from getting leggy, but little or no direct sun. Give them moist, light soil with plenty of organic matter, and make sure it is well drained. They like humid air, but it must circulate freely around the plant.

To plant begonias, start the tubers as early as February, setting them in trays of moistened peat moss. Simply press them gently, flat side up and round side down, into the surface of the peat. Water lightly and wait for them to sprout little pink buds if they've not done so already. Shoots will emerge from the buds, and roots will form at the sides of the tubers. When the tubers have sprouted, put each one in a pot about 5 inches wide on top, filled with a light potting mix such as one part loam, one part peat, and one part sand, with perhaps some compost or rotted manure worked in. As the plant grows, be sure it has plenty of light or you'll get leggy growth. (Stems should not be pinched.) Use fluorescent lights if you haven't a bright natural source out of direct sun.

When night temperatures are consistently 50 degrees or more and there is no danger of frost, you can move the pots outside or unpot the plants and set them in a bed of nice humusy soil, at least a foot apart. Keep feeding them liquid fertilizer every couple of weeks. A high-nitrogen fertilizer such as fish emulsion will give the leaves the rich dark green color you want to see. When frost threatens, bring the potted plants indoors but don't try to keep them blooming too much longer. Before fall is too far under way you should let them become dormant by withholding water and letting the foliage die. Then store the tubers in dry peat or sawdust until it's time to plant them again. Some people divide the tubers by cutting them, making sure there is one eye to each plant. I prefer to let each tuber get bigger and fatter each year, making larger, more magnificent plants, and then I take cuttings from these if I want to increase my stock. Cuttings should be rooted in moist sand.

CAMASSIA (CAMASS, INDIAN HYACINTH)

Camassia

Description: These beautiful plants are North American natives. They grow from rather large corms, which flower in May or June. The species sold for gardens are

indigenous to the northwestern states, although there are eastern ones as well. The Native Americans roasted the corms to make a molasses-like syrup, but the process is a time-consuming one, and much of the plant is toxic. The species known as quamash (*Camassia quamash*) bears deep blue flowers with striking yellow stamens. The flower slightly resembles a hyacinth but the florets are more delicate and less densely spaced. It is taller than hyacinth (2 to 3 feet) and not fragrant. *C. leichtlinii* and *C. cusickii* are similar but a paler blue, lavender, or white. *C. l.* 'Semiplena' is a double white form.

In the wild, camassias grow in soil that is wet in springtime—damp meadows, pond edges, moist woodlands. They have handsome grasslike foliage that dies down soon after bloom. Camassias look best in a natural setting and can compete fairly well with grasses.

How to Grow: Give these plants the conditions they favor—cool, rich, moist, fairly acid soil. They will tolerate a wide range of soil textures, from sandy loam to clay. They do not like to be flooded however, so if planting them next to a pond or stream, keep them above the water level. They will thrive and bloom well in an ordinary garden setting as long as they are watered in a dry weather. (They withstand dry conditions better when dormant.) A soil rich in organic matter will suit them best. They like sun but will do well in partial shade.

Plants grown from seed take a number of years to flower, so starting from corms is more usual. Plant in fall, 5 inches deep and 5 inches apart. They will often spread by going to seed. The foliage can be mowed down after it withers.

COLCHICUM (AUTUMN CROCUS)

Colchicum autumnale

Description: This is a very weird plant, and if you don't know what to expect it can really fool you. Its foliage comes up in spring, just like that of a spring bulb, but it doesn't bloom, and by summer the leaves disappear. In fall, long after you've probably said, "Oh, well, so much for *Colchicum autumnale,*" some stems come out of the ground with no leaves on them, just big pink, lavender, or white flowers that look sort of like large crocuses.

Nice as it is to have a fall-blooming bulb, or fall-blooming anything, you do have the problem of how to landscape those flowerless spring leaves and those leafless fall flowers. They're supposed to look great planted in front of shrubs, but I think this makes them look all the more gawky. Plant them in a natural setting, in sun or light shade, where there is a permanent evergreen ground cover such as periwinkle, which will de-emphasize both the leaves and their absence. They will also naturalize well in grass. Colchicums grow from corms and are hardy to about zone 4.

Hybrids of *C. autumnale* grow about 8 inches tall. Some colchicums sold are hybrids of *C. speciosum*. These are apt to be a bit taller. *C. speciosum* 'Album' is white. Despite the fact that these all resemble crocuses and are even called autumn crocuses in some catalogs, they are not the same as the fall-blooming version of the true crocus (see below), which are another species altogether and have their leaves and flowers well synchronized.

How to Grow: Colchicum corms are sold in summer. They should be planted in late summer or early fall in sun or part shade, about 8 inches apart. They're not fussy about soil, but add organic matter if yours is sandy or dry because they need a reasonable amount of moisture. Plant the large bulbs with the tops at least 3 inches below the soil surface. Bulbs usually multiply by themselves without human intervention.

CROCUS

Crocus

Description: Of all the small spring bulbs, the crocus is most people's favorite. It is not the earliest to bloom, but when it does, often poking up out of the snow,

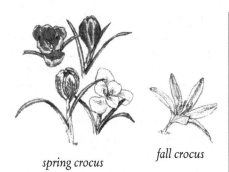

spring crocus

fall crocus

its bright colors seem to tell you that if *it* can get through the rest of winter and mud season so can you. Most of the crocuses we grow are hybrids of *Crocus vernus* or *C. chrysanthus* and have showy flowers in shades of yellow, purple, lavender, and white. Some are striped, and all have handsome yellow stamens. The large-flowered Dutch hybrids are the most popular, but if you search out other kinds of crocuses you may be able to stretch the blooming period. Some, such as the lavender *C. speciosus,* even bloom in fall. *C. sativus,* which is lavender or white, is the crocus from which the prized spice saffron comes. The bright orange stamens are dried to make this costly seasoning. Most crocuses are hardy to zone 3 and do best in cool climates. They grow from corms.

How to Grow: Gardeners like crocuses not only because of their spring message of cheer, but also because they are trouble-free, permanent plantings that multiply by themselves and needn't be divided. They can be naturalized in lawns, but as with any bulb with foliage that persists after bloom, they should not be mowed while the leaves are still green. Crocuses like full sun or part shade. I recommend planting some in a sunny, sheltered spot for early bloom and some others in a cooler or more shaded

spot for later bloom. Soil need not be rich but must be well drained. Plant them about 4 inches apart and 4 inches deep in early fall (5 inches deep for the large-flowered type). Plant fall-blooming crocuses as soon as they become available in late summer.

CYCLAMEN
Cyclamen

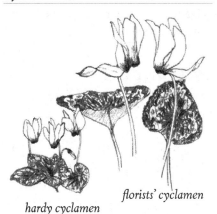

florists' cyclamen

hardy cyclamen

Description: Cyclamens are lovely, graceful plants. The flowers hover above the leaves like moths, on long wavy stems. The leaves are heart shaped and often handsomely variegated. Most are dormant in summer. The florists' cyclamen, *Cyclamen persicum,* thrives outdoors in places like California but is grown as a winter-blooming houseplant in zones colder than zone 9. Its flowers are as large as 4 inches across and rather flamboyant, in shades of pink, red, lavender, and white; often they are fringed or double. The plant blooms from late fall to early spring and grows about a foot tall.

Several cyclamen species are hardy in the north. They are shorter (4 to 5 inches tall) with pink, red, or white flowers about an inch across, and marbled or mottled leaves.

Many gardeners find them even more charming than their subtropical relatives. *C. coum* blooms in early spring. *C. purpurascens (C. europaeum)* and *C. hederifolium (C. neapolitanum)* are fall blooming and fragrant. They are all hardy to about zone 5 but may survive farther north with winter protection. They look charming in an informal, woodsy setting, but only if they're not overshadowed by larger, bolder plants.

How to Grow: Cyclamens grow from corms and are planted while they are dormant, usually in midsummer, about 2 inches deep and about a foot apart. (Plant florists' cyclamens outdoors in fall in zones 9 and 10.) They like soil that is rich and moist but not cold or wet. Give them part shade outdoors. Indoors, give them indirect, bright light.

DAHLIA
Dahlia

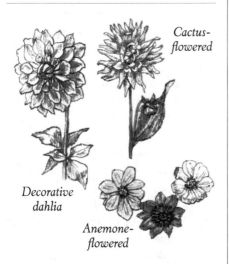

Cactus-flowered

Decorative dahlia

Anemone-flowered

Description: Dahlias are one of those plants with endless flower classifications. Some are Single, like daisies; some are like round balls; others are Cactus-flowered, Orchid-flowered, Anemone-flowered, or Peony-flowered (why do flowers always have to look like some *other* flower?). The flowers can be as small as an inch across and as large as 12 inches if you're growing them for exhibition. Heights range from 1 to 7 feet. There's a large range of colors, roughly the same as that of chrysanthemums. The thing I like about dahlias is their blooming period, which goes from midsummer to the first frost or a bit after. I use them to add some showy late bloom to perennial borders, but they are also very effective grown with annuals or in beds by themselves. They are colorful and long lasting as cut flowers.

How to Grow: Grow dahlias in full sun or light shade, in a soil rich in organic matter and nutrients, especially phosphorus and potassium. Add some lime if your soil is very acid. Dahlias have tuberous roots that must be dug up and stored over the winter in zones where there is frost, a chore that is not much of a bother once you get into the routine.

Dahlias can be grown easily from seed, although you will find a much wider selection of varieties if you order the roots by mail. Either way, they should be planted about a week before the date of the last possible frost. Seed-grown plants can be set into the ground at the depth they were growing in their pots. Bare roots should be laid horizontally in a hole 6 to 8 inches deep. If you're planting a tall variety, it's helpful to place a 5-foot bamboo stake next to the root and stick it firmly into the ground (if you stake later on you run the risk of piercing the root). The root should be covered with a few inches of soil; as the plant grows, the rest of the hole can be filled. When the stems become tall, tie them to the stakes; if you want shorter, bushier plants, pinch them when they are 10 to 12 inches tall (page 191). Pinching is less important with the short varieties. Deadhead the plants for more profuse bloom, and water them deeply during drought, or bloom will be sparse.

After the first few frosts, gently dig up the roots with a digging fork, cutting the stems back to a few inches. I've found that storing in a cool cellar (ideally 35 to 45 degrees) in a bag of barely moistened peat is a good way to hold dahlia roots over the winter. If mice are a problem, protect them with some form of wire mesh. (One year I stored them in trays of peat; come spring, the mice had eaten every speck of the dahlias.) When it's time to replant them in spring, you can divide them to increase your stock. Notice that the buds ("eyes") emerge from the base of the old stem. Slice through the stem vertically with a sharp knife, making sure that each piece of root has part of the stem attached and at least one eye. (Dahlias can also be propagated from stem cuttings.) I have gotten a head start on the dahlia season by starting mine in pots indoors in a rich, light soil; the only drawback is that pots large enough to hold the roots comfortably take up a lot of space.

FRITILLARIA

Fritillaria

Description: There are two kinds of fritillarias commonly grown in gardens, and they're like Mutt and Jeff. *Fritillaria meleagris* (called checkered lily or guinea hen flower) has flowers shaped like little

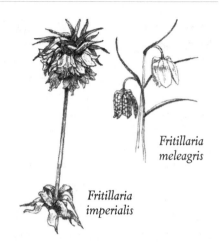

Fritillaria meleagris

Fritillaria imperialis

hanging bells, in muted, neutral tones like gray, purple, brownish, and white with an odd, checkerboard pattern. They grow at most to 12 inches, bloom in midspring, and often self-sow prolifically. They are best seen close up, in a natural setting, and are hardy to zone 3. *F. imperialis* (crown imperial) sends up a 3-foot stem topped by a huge cluster of hanging bells in shades of red, yellow, and orange (often two shades together), and the leaves stick up in a tuft on *top* of the flower. Grow it in a clump by itself or behind shorter bulbs. Combining it with contrasting tulips could be interesting (though it wouldn't produce the subtlest of effects). Fritillaria is hardy to zones 5 to 6 but may need some winter protection in zone 5.

How to Grow: Give fritillarias a gritty, humusy, moist but extremely well drained soil. It ought to be fairly rich. They grow well in full sun or light shade. Buy them as soon as they become available and plant them immediately. Their bulbs should not be allowed to dry out. Crown imperial bulbs should go 8 to 10 inches apart and 6 to 7 inches deep (measured to the top of the large bulbs). Checkered lilies should be 5 to 6 inches apart and 5 to 6 inches deep. Division is possible but not necessary; in fact the bulbs seem to do better if left alone.

GLADIOLUS
Gladiolus

gladiolus hybrids

Gladiolus byzantinus

Description: Gladiolus, or "glads," as they are sometimes nicknamed, are popular flowers. Their tall, brightly colored spires are showy in the garden and last a long time when cut, opening gradually from the bottom of the stem upward. Their name, which means "little sword" in Latin, refers to their long, bold leaves. Since I prefer to make relaxed-looking flower arrangements, I don't grow glads for cutting. But I have enjoyed them in a large flower border as vertical accents, and in the center of a small round bed filled with a tumble of bright annuals. I can imagine a fine gladiolus display with flowers growing in a bed by themselves along a fence. You might also plant them in rows in the vegetable garden if your main goal is to have them to cut.

Glads come in all colors except blue, and sizes vary from 6-foot spikes to the dwarf "baby glads." Most are modern hybrids bred from several species. There are also several gladiolus species that some find more natural in appearance, such as the 2-foot-tall *Gladiolus byzantinus*, with its loose spray of red-purple flowers. It has the added advantage of being hardy to zone 5, so you don't have to dig it up in fall in most climates. The white-flowered *G. callianthus* (also called *Acidanthera*) is less hardy but deliciously night-fragrant.

How to Grow: Glads grow from corms. They are planted in full sun and in rich, well-drained soil that should, ideally, be more sandy than clay. You can start planting as soon as the danger of frost is over, then plant in succession every two weeks until midsummer for a longer season of bloom. Group them in clusters, digging compost and a little bonemeal—or else some 5-10-5 organic fertilizer—into the soil. Plant the corms about 4 to 6 inches deep, 6 to 8 inches apart. Tall varieties are planted on the deep side for better support. Staking or mounding the stems with soil may also be necessary to keep stems upright. A site well protected from wind is also helpful.

Sprinkle a little more compost or fertilizer around the plants after they come up, and once again after picking. You should leave some foliage when you pick them so the plant can continue to grow and form new corms. Water plants deeply once a week during very dry spells.

Dig the plants up with a spading fork before the first hard frost, and cut the stems back to 1 inch. Clean the soil off the corms and dry them for a few weeks, out of the sun. Then break off the new corms that have formed on top of the old ones, which should be discarded. Save the new corms and any cormels (small, immature corms), storing them at about 40 degrees in paper bags in a well-ventilated spot. Even gardeners in frost-free areas dig up glad corms for the winter, since three months of cold storage during dormancy is necessary for flowering the following season. If thrips are a problem, grow only early plantings and dig them up before the thrips become active.

GLORY-OF-THE-SNOW

Chionodoxa

Description: These delightful bulbs have little bright blue, star-shaped flowers and grasslike leaves. They start blooming shortly after crocuses, which is handy, because the two look beautiful together. They are good bulbs for cool climates and are hardy to zone 3, but they don't do well south of zone 8. Naturalize them around a tree, in a rock garden, along a woodland path, or wherever they'll best be seen. *Chionodoxa luciliae* grows up to 6 inches tall and is typically blue with a white center, but 'Alba' is white, 'Rosea' is lavender-pink, and the large-flowered 'Gigantea' can be blue, purple, or pink. *C. sardensis* is dark blue without the white eye.

How to Grow: Full sun is best, but glory-of-the-snow will take part shade and in warm areas actually prefers filtered shade. Plant in early fall about 2 to 3 inches apart and 3 inches deep (a bit deeper in warm climates). It likes a soil that is rich, moist but well drained, and lightened with organic matter.

GRAPE HYACINTH

Muscari

Description: I can count on this bulb to bloom at the same time as my daffodils and tulips and provide me with some blue accents for bouquets. If you choose a variety with stems long enough to be stuck in among the larger flowers, the small spikes of tiny blue balls will provide a good contrast to the rounder shapes of the daffodils and tulips. Grape hyacinths are best grown in a spot where you can admire them up close, because the flowers are small and because blue flowers are hard to see at a distance. They are lovely in rock gardens.

Most of the hybrids sold are derived from *Muscari armeniacum*, which has large flowers and grows up to 8 inches, or from *M. botryoides*, which is a little taller and usually deep blue. There are also a few white or yellow varieties and some bicolors. The lovely 'Valerie Finnis' is an unusual pale blue. Most of these rugged little bulbs are hardy at least to zone 4. Foliage appears in fall and winters over, then dies after the flowers have bloomed.

How to Grow: Grape hyacinths like full sun or part shade and an average, well-drained soil. Plant 3 to 4 inches apart and 4 to 5 inches deep in late summer or as early in fall as possible. You can propagate the species from seed and hybrids from offsets (new bulbs that form next to the old ones), though they tend to multiply well enough on their own.

HYACINTH

Hyacinthus

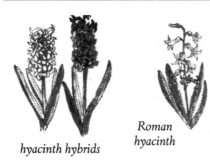

hyacinth hybrids

Roman
hyacinth

Description: I always grow at least a few hyacinths so I can pick them. I think they look prettier indoors in vases, where they can perfume the room, than they do in gardens. The leaves, which seem to stick around forever, are quite unsightly, and even the flower heads look rather lumpy among the more dainty shapes of the other bulbs. But grown with something to soften them, such as a sea of forget-me-nots or blue-flowering periwinkle, they are not hard to take.

There are hyacinths you can grow besides the common *Hyacinthus orientalis*, from which the big Dutch cultivars are commonly derived. Try Roman hyacinths (*H. o. albulus*) in blue, pink, and white. Roman

hyacinths have a looser cluster, with more stems per plant. Those called multiflora hyacinths are similar. Both common and multiflora hyacinths are hardy to at least zone 5, Roman hyacinth to zone 6 (but you can try it north of there if you give it some winter protection and plant it fairly deep).

How to Grow: In the north plant hyacinths in early fall, mid fall in warm areas. They like a sandy loam of moderate fertility that is moist but very well drained. Grow in full sun or light shade. Plant the large bulbs 6 inches deep and 6 inches apart, trying to create the effect of natural groupings.

IRIS

Iris

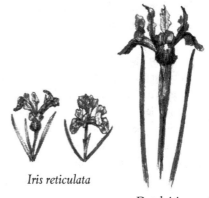

Iris reticulata

Dutch iris

Description: Some irises, such as bearded iris, grow from rhizomes; some, such as Siberian iris, have fibrous roots; and others, such as Dutch iris, grow from bulbs. Only irises that grow from bulbs are considered here. The others are treated as perennials and are discussed on page 214. Most of the bulbous irises are small, elegant plants that look particularly good in rock gardens but are effective in any intimate garden spot. My favorite is *Iris reticulata* (netted iris), which blooms even earlier than crocuses in shades of intense blue, lavender, purple, yellow, and white. Other "rock garden" types are the violet *I. bakerana*, yellow *I. danfordiae*, and the charming blue *I. histrioides* 'Major.' All are about 4 inches tall, have grassy foliage, and are hardy to at least zone 5. The so-called Dutch irises, which are hybrids of *I. xiphium* (Spanish iris) and other species, are much taller—about 18 inches—and bloom in late spring or early summer. They come in a wide range of colors and bicolors. When picked just as they're opening, they make very fine, long-lasting cut flowers and are often used by florists. Unfortunately they are not reliably hardy above zone 7, but if you live in the north and dearly love them you can try mulching them or even digging them up in late summer and storing them over the winter.

How to Grow: All the irises mentioned here should be planted as early in fall as possible, in full sun. They like a light, moderately fertile soil and need water during their growth period, although they absolutely must have good drainage. I would plant the smaller types 4 inches deep and 4 inches apart, the larger Dutch irises 6 inches deep and 6 inches apart.

LILY

Lilium

Description: These are the true lilies as opposed to the daylilies described on page 207, which grow from rhizomes. True lilies grow from big, fat white bulbs that are made up of scales and produce magnificent flowers in a very wide range of shapes, col-

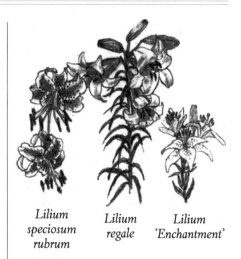

Lilium speciosum rubrum   *Lilium regale*   *Lilium 'Enchantment'*

ors, and sizes. They bloom at various times, from early summer to late summer and even into fall.

Everybody who has grown a number of different lilies has favorites—I mentioned some of mine in the introduction on page 490. I haven't the space here to describe many of them in detail, but here, at least, is a rundown of the basic lily groups, more or less in order of bloom:

The Asiatic hybrids bloom in June (some later), in many colors, with heights ranging from 2 to 5 feet and with several different flower shapes. The red-orange 'Enchantment' is typical of the upward-facing flower types and is a particularly vigorous plant that forms clumps. 'Connecticut Lemonglow' has an outward-facing flower; others have a pendent or "Turk's-cap" shape. The Martagon hybrids are a group that bloom in June, have Turk's-cap flowers, and are quite tall—up to 6 feet. Madonna lilies (*Lilium candidum*) are white (though some of the hybrids are cream or yellow), stand 3 to 4 feet tall, and bloom in June or early July. The classic Easter lily, *L. longiflorum*, is forced into bloom for Easter display but blooms in early summer in the normal course of things.

For later white blooms you might choose regal lilies (*L. regale* and its hybrids), most of which are tall, white, and very fragrant. The stately Aurelian hybrids (4 to 6 feet) are an important part of the midsummer lily show. They include such spectacular varieties as the dusty rose 'Pink Perfection,' and 'Black Dragon,' whose large flowers are dark red on the outside and white within. Tiger lilies (*L. lancifolium*), with orange, curled-back petals spotted with black, grow up to 4 feet tall.

The last lilies to bloom, in late summer and sometimes early fall, include the Oriental hybrids, such as the glorious gold-banded lily (*L. auratum* and its hybrids), the glorious 'Stargazer,' which is red edged in white, and the wonderfully fragrant white 'Casa Blanca.' The old-fashioned speciosum lilies, such as the red-spotted *L. speciosum rubrum*, the white *L. s. album*, and hybrids such as 'Uchida,' round out the season in August and September. Most lilies are hardy as far north as zone 4 or 5; *L. candidum* to zone 7.

Native lilies include the yellow Canada lily (*L. canadense*), the towering Turk's-cap lily (*L. superbum*), and the beautiful red-orange wood lily (*L. philadelphicum*). Always acquire these lilies from reputable nurseries that propagate their own stock. Never dig them—or pick them—in the wild. Some are endangered species that will not regrow if picked.

You have to think carefully about how to use lilies. They have tall stems with rather sparse foliage. Often they must be staked, which makes them look a bit like basketball players on crutches. I put some in perennial beds, and I grow the rest in a semishaded spot where a lush nest of ferns hides at least the lower half of the stems. Peonies also make a good understory. It is often said that lilies like to have "their heads warm and their feet cool," so that growing something around the base of the plants may help their health as well as their looks, but choose plants with shallow or self-contained root systems that won't crowd the lily bulbs.

How to Grow: The difference between lily bulbs and other bulbs is that lilies never really go dormant—their roots are always growing—and no hard protective covering forms around them. What this means for the gardener is that you must handle them very carefully so as not to break off the roots or the delicate scalelike pieces that make up the bulb, and you should keep them out of soil for as short a time as possible. Local nurseries often sell them potted up. If they're unpotted, or if you order them by mail, keep them in a cool place, in a slightly damp (not wet) packing medium such as peat moss until you can plant them.

Lilies do not need fertile soil. In the areas where they are native (generally in Asia), lilies often grow wild in poor, gravelly ground. Overfeeding causes them to have weak stems that always need staking. They need some moisture while they're actively growing, but drainage must be exceptional. Adding organic matter will help to provide both. Soil pH is not much of an issue except in the case of the Martagon lilies, which like soil slightly acid, and Madonna lilies, which like it slightly alkaline. Most lilies will do equally well in full sun or part shade—filtered shade is especially good because it keeps the colors from fading. Martagon lilies, wood lilies, and a few others really prefer some shade.

Lilies may be planted either in spring or fall. The only lilies I know of that are always planted in fall are Madonna lilies. Plant lilies 6 to 8 inches deep, measured from the top of the bulb (tiger lilies and Oriental hybrids require the greater depth). Madonna lilies, again the exception, are planted with only an inch of soil on top of the bulbs; you should start to see some of their foliage sprouting before winter. I plant most lilies a foot apart to allow for air circulation. I hold off staking the plants until I think something might knock them over if I don't.

Lilies can be deadheaded for tidiness, but cut off only the dead flowers, not the stems and leaves. These will continue to make food that the bulbs will store. One other word of caution: lilies can be slow to come up in spring, so be very careful that you don't dig around the spot where they're planted. If your memory tends to be fuzzy, mark the spot or draw a detailed plan. Expect to see either large pointed shoots or ones with little pointed leaves arranged in concentric layers, like a shaggy haircut. These get longer and longer, and are fragile, so try not to step on them and break them off. Don't be disappointed if your lilies fail to reach their full height the first year. This is often the case. It's best to refrain from picking them until the year they settle in and attain their full height. Pick only the top third of the stem so that the bulb will have the resources to replenish itself.

In recent years, an imported lily beetle has become a serious pest. Watch for the small bright red-orange beetles on the foliage as soon as it emerges in spring and squash them, or brush them off into a pail of soapy water. Remove the orange egg masses that appear on the undersides of the leaves the same way. If the larvae hatch (covered unappetizingly with black excrement), don a pair of rubber gloves and remove those larvae too. Persistence will keep the pest within bounds.

NARCISSUS

Narcissus

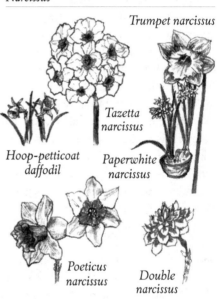

Trumpet narcissus

Tazetta narcissus

Hoop-petticoat daffodil

Paperwhite narcissus

Poeticus narcissus

Double narcissus

Description: First, let's establish what we're talking about. We all know what a daffodil looks like, right? Well, maybe. When I was a child I called all the yellow flowers of this type daffodils, and the white ones narcissus. I also know people who call the yellow ones jonquils. Well, botanically speaking, they're all from the genus *Narcissus.* But you're welcome to call them whatever you like. And of course, they all bloom in spring.

Narcissus, like many flower groups in which many different species and their hybrids are grown, have been classified into groups. Here are the major ones, which sound at times like a list of bra sizes. Keep in mind that the "cup" is the round, protruding part of the flower that is surrounded by the outer petals.

Trumpet narcissus produce one flower per stem, in which the cup is at least as long as the petals. The big yellow 'King Alfred' narcissus is a classic example.

Large-cupped narcissus have a cup that is as big around as a trumpet's but shorter. I especially like the ones with the pink cups, of which 'Mrs. R. O. Backhouse' was the first, and 'Salome' is a fine modern example.

Small-cupped narcissus are rather flat flowers with a short cup. With any of these, the cup may be one color, the petals another.

Double narcissus are any that have more than one row of petals. They tend to be very fragrant, with almost a jasmine scent, and there are often several on one stem. 'Cheerfulness,' which is white with some yellow deep in the center, is a popular double.

Jonquils are hybrids of the small, early *N. jonquilla*, and have as many as six flowers to a stem. No longer all-yellow, the colors vary.

Tazetta narcissus have many flowers on a stem and are fragrant, often with a small, darker colored cup. The Paperwhite types and the yellow-and-orange 'Grand Soleil d'Or,' both nonhardy narcissus that are excellent for forcing, belong in this group.

Those in the Poeticus group are fragrant and have only one flower per stem, which is white with a contrasting shallow cup. In 'Actaea' and 'Pheasant's Eye,' both old favorites, the cup is yellow edged with red.

In addition, there are a number of delightful species and their hybrids that produce miniature flowers on short stems, perfect for the rock garden or any other small-scale planting. Among these are N. *bulbocodium* (hoop-petticoat daffodil), which has a big cup and rather wispy petals; N. *triandrus*, which has little drooping flowers with pulled-back petals ('April Tears' is a lovely, fragrant yellow variety); and N. *cyclamineus*, whose petals look as if they were being blown back by the wind. It's important to buy species narcissus from a dealer who does not sell bulbs collected in the wild.

With the exception of Tazetta narcissus, most are very cold hardy but not all of them do well in very warm climates. Zone 9 gardeners do best with the Tazetta, Poeticus, and Jonquilla groups.

How to Grow: Give narcissus full sun or light shade. They prefer a well-drained sandy loam. Plant large varieties at least 6 inches apart and 6 inches deep. Small varieties can be a little closer and shallower. I dig some compost into the bed before planting, adding some rock phosphate or bonemeal for root development if a soil test indicates it's needed; I also add some lime. If I'm planting in the woods or in grass, I similarly amend the planting holes. It's very important not to cut the foliage down until it turns brown.

Established plantings will increase by themselves, but being dug up and divided every four or five years will increase their vigor. If a clump is dense and the leaves have started to flop, it's sign that division is needed. To do this, wait till the foliage has withered, then dig up the bulbs with a digging fork and pull apart the ones that separate easily. Either replant them right away or store them in a cool place until summer's heat has subsided.

RANUNCULUS (PERSIAN BUTTERCUP)

Ranunculus asiaticus

Description: Most of the ranunculuses available are the showy hybrids that you see in florist shops. The flowers, which are several inches across, are round globes made up of many papery-textured petals in bright, almost electric colors: red, pink, yellow, gold, white, and picotee—that is, with the petals edged in a contrasting color. They grow 18 to 24 inches tall. They are hardy only in warm climates, blooming there in late winter and spring and going dormant in the summer. Both the flowers and the attractive ferny foliage die back. In zones where there is frost, they are grown outdoors for bloom in spring and summer—until it gets very hot. They can be grown in beds, but they make a particularly fine show as container plants on a deck or terrace.

How to Grow: The plants like full sun and need moisture around the roots (perhaps this is why their Latin name means "little frog"). But they will rot if drainage is poor around their crowns. They are planted in late fall in warm climates. In cool ones they are started indoors two months before the last frost. Soak the claw-shaped tubers in water for a few hours before planting. Place them in the soil with the claw facing down. Start with small pots, filled with a light, rich potting soil, and move them up to larger pots as they grow, keeping them cool at night and keeping their soil moist. Bring them outdoors only after danger of frost has passed. After they stop blooming in summer, let the foliage die down and the tubers dry out. Store them in bags of dry peat moss at about 50 degrees until planting time.

SCILLA (SQUILL)

Scilla

Scilla siberica   *Scilla campanulata*

Description: Scillas have small bell-like flowers that dangle from thin 3- to 6-inch stems. Most of the ones I see in gardens are blue, but you can find purple, lavender, pink, and white scillas too. They are lovely in situations where their delicate beauty can be appreciated: planted in woodland gardens, under the light shade of a deciduous tree, in rock gardens, or naturalized in lawns. Modern hybrids come from a number of species, most commonly *Scilla siberica*, which is usually an intense bright blue but is sometimes white. Of the others, the pale blue *S. mischtschenkoana* (also called *S. tubergeniana*) has fewer flowers on a stem but more stems to a plant. *S. bifolia*, the twin-leafed squill, has airier flower clusters. All of these are about 5 inches tall. (Spanish bluebell, a larger plant formerly classified as *S. hispanica* or *S. campanulata*, is actually *Hyacinthoides hispanica*.) The hardiest scilla is *S. siberica*, which will survive as far north as zone 3; the others mentioned will grow up to zones 4 or 5. All are cool-climate plants, but if you live in zones 8 to 10, you can grow *S. peruviana*, which is a foot tall and lavender-blue. Like the names of many bulbs, that of *S. peruviana* is a geographical muddle; although both its Latin name and the common name, Cuban lily, give it a Latin American origin, it is native to the Mediterranean region.

How to Grow: Plant scilla bulbs in the early fall in sun or part shade in a nice sandy loam, 5 inches deep and 4 to 6 inches apart. Give them moisture during the growing season if it's very dry, but otherwise you can just leave them alone.

SNOWDROP
Galanthus

Description: These little white nodding flowers on stems up to 8 inches are the first bulbs to appear in early spring. Plant them where they will be noticed, or they'll just blend in with the snow. Try planting them with yellow winter aconite and blue *Iris reticulata*, which bloom at the same time,

for a colorful early-spring display. Since they like filtered shade, they do well under deciduous shrubs and trees. Plant a lot of them for best effect. Snowdrops will usually self-sow.

Galanthus nivalis is the most common and the best for cold climates (hardy to zone 3). There is also a double variety, *G. nivalis* 'Fiore Pleno.' *G. elwesii*, which has slightly larger flowers, is slightly less hardy. Snowdrops are sometimes confused with snowflakes (*Leucojum*), which are similar but have flowers that are more bell-like, with little green dots on the points of the bells. Snowflakes also bloom a bit later than snowdrops.

How to Grow: Plant in late summer, if possible, in a humusy, well-drained sandy loam. Bulbs should be covered with about 4 inches of soil and should be spaced 2 to 4 inches apart. They can be divided and replanted after blooming if you want to make a patch of them somewhere else, but they are also inexpensive to buy.

TULIP
Tulipa

Description: A yard erupting in lavish tulip blooms looks like a jeweled crown. There are so many wonderful tulips that

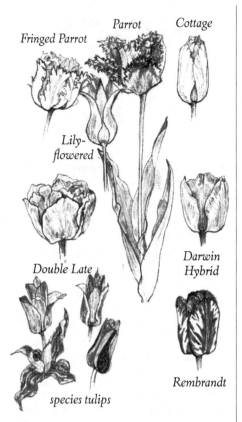

Fringed Parrot
Parrot
Cottage
Lily-flowered
Double Late
Darwin Hybrid
Rembrandt
species tulips

it's tempting to tuck them in everywhere. But if you do this, keep in mind that the broad, straplike leaves will be conspicuous long after the jewels are gone, becoming more and more unsightly as they start to turn brown. You'd have to either live with that or treat tulips as annuals by getting rid of the leaves after bloom and ending the plants' growth. Tulip leaves can be deliberately hidden by bushy annuals, perennials, or ground covers. My solution is to plant them far enough away that I can see all those bright spots of color but not the denouement that follows. I also find that the back of a perennial garden is an excellent spot. The tulips bloom early and are then quickly hidden as asters and phlox make their ascent.

Buying tulips bulbs can be confusing unless you know the different types. Here are the major tulip groups:

Early-flowering tulips. These start blooming soon after crocuses. They include single tulips that grow up to 16 inches and doubles that grow up to a foot. The gold-orange single 'General de Wet' is a fine example. 'Peach Blossom' is an appealing heirloom with double pink flowers.

Midseason tulips. These include the single Mendel and Triumph tulips, which grow 16 to 26 inches tall, and the big Darwin Hybrids. These grow to 30 inches, stand up well in bad weather, and are quite long-lived as tulips go. They come in many colors; 'Apeldoorn' is a bright orange-red.

Late-flowering tulips. This group includes Darwin tulips (not to be confused with the Darwin Hybrids), which are shaped like an egg that is slightly squared off at the bottom and grow 22 to 30 inches tall. The Lily-flowered tulips, such as the pink 'Mariette,' are shaped like a vase that comes in at the neck and then flares out again in points, and grow 18 to 26 inches tall. Cottage tulips have a compact egg shape. Parrot tulips, which grow 20 to 22 inches tall, are fantastically showy with twisted, ruffled, or fringed petals (plant the spectacular deep-purple 'Black Parrot' with some white parrots for a striking combination). The spectacular Rembrandt tulips are "broken," that is, striped or spotted; the colors are combinations of red, yellow, or white. For a lovely, more subtle effect, plant the Green tulips (also called Viridiflora), which are variations on pink and red or white with green streaks at the base of the petals. The Double Late tulips, also called Peony-flowered tulips, have big, many-petaled flowers and grow 2 feet tall or less. The pink-and-cream 'Angelique,' an old favorite, is in this group.

Botanical tulips. Somewhat closer to the original species than those described above, this group is composed of long-lived, fairly short stemmed, early-blooming hybrids, usually with decorative mottled foliage. These include Kaufmanniana, also called Water Lily tulips, which have open-spreading, pointed petals with bright, striking color combinations. They grow 4 to 8 inches tall. Fosteriana tulips, with very large, brilliantly colored flowers, grow 12 to 18 inches tall. Greigii tulips, which range from 8 to 20 inches tall, bloom later with bright yellow and red petals.

Species tulips. This group of small bulbs is a large one. There are well over 100 species of wild tulips growing in the world, and quite a number of them are sold commercially. Perhaps this reflects a growing interest in smaller, simpler, more natural plants as opposed to large, showy, extensively crossbred ones. Yet most of the species tulips offered are now selections or hybrids of wild forms, just as the Botanical tulips are, making them an even more diverse group, with a wide color selection. Nonetheless, they retain much of the wildflower look. Most species tulips are low-growing, though the flowers are often just as large, bright, and showy as the classic garden hybrids. Most (though not all) are early flowering. One of their main attractions is their permanence and ease of care. Easily naturalized, they tend to come back year after year and even spread. Some are fair-weather flowers, folding up their petals on cloudy days and at day's end, but they are colorful even when closed. They require well-drained soil (dry in summer) and do best without major competition from other plants. Many have several blooms per stem and look great in rock garden settings.

Tulipa tarda (and the very similar *T. dasystemon*) is one of the most long-lived tulips. The flowers are starlike and bright yellow, tipped with white. *T. batalinii* is also yellow but varieties are shaded with other colors. The various forms of *T. clusiana* (lady tulip) and *T. linifolia* tend to be red. *T. praestans* 'Fusilier' is a popular red-orange with multiple flowers on the stem. *T. bakeri* 'Lilac Wonder' is a popular rosy-lavender variety. The very low-growing *T. humilis* (*T. pulchella*) comes in many colors. Species tulips are very cold hardy. In addition, several with low chilling requirements do well in zones 8 to 10, notably *T. clusiana* and two that spread by stolons—the yellow *T. sylvestris* (Florentine tulip) and the lavender-pink *T. saxatilis* (Candia tulip).

How to Grow: Tulips like sun but will grow and bloom in part shade; in fact they prefer partial shade in warmer climates. Be sure to keep the bulbs cool if you are not planting them right away; in hot climates give them a month of refrigeration before planting time. Plant in mid fall in well-drained, sandy loam. If you're planting them in a bed, dig plenty of organic matter into it. Most garden tulips are a short-lived display. After a year or two the plants may come up, but bloom will be reduced or nonexistent. Many gardeners treat them as annuals, especially in warm climates. See the descriptions above for those with more of a perennial nature. These can be fertilized in fall to keep them vigorous. Plant tulips at least 6 inches deep (deep planting tends to increase their longevity). Small varieties can be planted more shallowly. In general, tulips are planted about 6 inches apart. Set them in underground wire-mesh cages if nibbling by rodents is a serious problem. Fencing or dusting with dried blood may be necessary to deter deer.

WINTER ACONITE

Eranthis hyemalis

Description: Among the earliest to bloom, this bulb sends up 4-inch stems topped with bright yellow rosettes, shaped like large buttercups. The leaves are a ruff-like collar just under the blossoms. Winter aconites are a welcome sight, and the snow does nothing to discourage them. They look best planted in casual drifts and will help add to the effect each year by self-sowing. They do fine in rock gardens but won't hold their own very well if planted in grass. They grow from oddly shaped tubers and are hardy to zone 4.

How to Grow: Grow winter aconites in full sun or light shade, such as that cast by deciduous trees and shrubs. The soil need not be very fertile, but it must be well drained. The plants need moisture in spring and early summer, then they go dormant. Plant in late summer if possible, 4 inches deep and about 4 inches apart. Soak the tubers in water overnight before planting.

CHAPTER 11

Roses

I'VE READ A BIT ABOUT THE HISTORY OF roses, and I am convinced there's a film in it. It has everything—sex, violence, romance, spectacle, intrigue. Cleopatra wading through knee-deep billows of rose petals to receive Mark Antony on their first date. Nero throwing a banquet with petals strewn on the floor, petals hanging in nets from the ceiling, petals in the food, petals in the baths, petals in the beds. Roman politicians hanging a rose from a conference-room ceiling to proclaim that a meeting was secret, or as they said, *sub rosa*. Persian poets or Mogul emperors luring doe-eyed maidens into perfumed rose bowers.

The plot takes a turn in the Middle Ages, when the Catholic Church holds a dim view of wallowing in roses. Medieval ladies are scattering roses daintily among the linens, bathing in rose water, dosing ailments with rose syrups, and weaving roses into garlands ("rosaries") in their cloistered gardens, which were set off like tiny paradises in a violent world. In great cathedrals light is filtering through rose windows in glowing colors. But the rose, once a symbol of luxury and sensuality, has now become symbolic of the Virgin Mary, the unity of creation, and pure Christian love—except when a daring poet like the author of *The Romance of the Rose* writes of stealing into a walled garden and capturing his rose (really a beautiful lady) as a prize.

Fast-forward to another rose garden, in the fifteenth century, where Richard Plantagenet plucks a white rose as an emblem of the House of York, and the Earl of Somerset, of the House of Lancaster, plucks a red one. Thus the Wars of the Roses begin. Forward again to the Napoleonic Wars. While Napoleon is off annexing countries, Josephine is raiding them for new rose varieties, trading cuttings with enemy horticulturists, and amassing the most vast and imperial rose collection in history in her garden at Malmaison. Even when French captains seize ships at sea, all roses on board are sent to Josephine.

And what great rose scenes can be played for modern times? Perhaps Francis Meilland dispatching cuttings of a hybrid rose on the last plane out of France before the Nazi invasion, then discovering after the war is over that rose growers around the world have propagated it as the great rose 'Peace.' Or U.S. Army Intelligence officers meeting—each wearing an arm patch with a rose surrounded by compass points, to signify secrecy. Perhaps the best scene is in a film already made, where Charlie Chaplin holds a rose to his nose and smiles shyly at the shop girl in *City Lights*.

Or perhaps it is a scene of you in your rose garden. The late-afternoon sun is backlighting the velvety petals in shades of salmon, crimson, and gold. Butterflies hover above the blooms, and there is a background hum of lawn mowers and bees. You are endlessly dropping Japanese beetles, one by one, into a large, kerosene-filled jar.

Two television movie critics debate the meaning of this scene: "It's fraught with irony," one says. "You want to participate in the romance of growing what Sappho called the Queen of the Flowers, but the truth is, roses are a pain to grow. The best ones aren't very hardy, you have to prune them constantly, and they attract every insect and fungus known to man." "No, you miss the point," says the other critic. "The flower is so sublime that just looking at it makes any struggle worthwhile. Ask Dante. Ask Josephine. Ask anyone who has made money on a rose patent."

Actually both critics are wrong. Contrary to current mythology, roses are not hard to grow. They are a stalwart shrub, one of the oldest plants known to man, and some even grow above the Arctic Circle. There are a few tricks you can learn that can make you more successful with roses, and you do need to choose the ones that will do best in your climate. You may turn out to be one of those people who must grow perfect roses. Or you may be like me, a grower of perfectly okay roses that are healthy, survive most winters, and provide blooms for bouquets all summer long. There is nothing else I can grow in my climate that is as showy and long blooming, and that comes up every year. This is why I grow roses.

Types of Roses

THERE ARE MANY WAYS TO USE ROSES in your landscape, because they have several different habits of growth: as small shrubs, large shrubs, hedges, climbers, and even ground covers. Let's take a look at the major types and how they can be used most effectively. Although I note some outstanding varieties, I urge you to investigate which ones do best in your own immediate area. In addition to local nurseries, your local chapter of the American Rose Society can best advise you.

HYBRID TEAS

This is the flower most people picture when they hear "rose." A typical hybrid tea flower is large, with many petals and a high center, opening from long, pointed buds (Figure 62). The typical bush (Figure 63) grows about 3 feet tall in cool climates,

taller in warm ones. The history of the hybrid tea rose dates back to 1867 when the first one, called 'La France,' was developed. This was a real revolution in rose breeding. Up until then the roses grown here and in Europe had red, pink, or white flowers and bloomed only once during the season, usually in June. By crossing these with the yellow roses of China that bloomed all summer long, breeders obtained long-flowering modern roses that bloomed not only in all the old shades but also in yellow and in mixtures such as orange, salmon, and peach. These were the forerunners of the hybrid tea roses we grow today.

Since the Chinese roses were native to warm climates, the hybrid teas that were developed from them are not as vigorous in the colder zones as their European predecessors, nor as resistant to disease. If you grow hybrid teas you must expect to pamper them a bit. While gardening in Connecticut I found that if I stuck to those that were the most reliable in cold winters, such as the huge creamy pink, lemon-edged 'Peace' or the coral 'Tropicana,' they might survive even if I didn't bother to protect them in winter. But sometimes I'd take a chance on some less hardy roses that are worth the extra effort. Some particularly popular and stalwart hybrid teas are 'Mister Lincoln' (dark red), 'John F. Kennedy' (white, fragrant), 'Fragrant Cloud' (orange, fragrant), and 'Blue Girl' (lavender). In Maine, hybrid teas are so risky that I concentrate on other categories, notably old roses, shrub roses, and hardy climbers.

Hybrid teas are generally compact shrubs that look best in a bed planted primarily with roses, though they do mix well with roses of other types if you give them their own section of the garden. A

Rose Flower Types

FIG. 62

single

semidouble

hybrid tea

floribunda

old rose

front edging of flowering annuals or low-growing perennials such as lavender will complement them well. The garden in Figure 64 shows how this might be done.

FLORIBUNDAS

These have the same color range as hybrid teas, but the flowers are usually less high-centered and are arranged in clusters. The bushes tend to be a bit shorter. Floribundas are easy to grow because they're hardier and more disease resistant than the hybrid teas and can be useful as landscaping plants—as low hedges, for example, or in the foreground of shrub borders. Pink 'Simplicity' and 'Betty Prior' are especially reliable for massed plantings. Other old favorites are the red 'Europeana,' white 'Iceberg,' and salmon-pink 'Fashion.'

GRANDIFLORAS

These are a group of hybrids bred by crossing hybrid teas and floribundas. The first grandiflora was a pink rose called 'Queen Elizabeth.' They are large bushes, occasionally as tall as 8 to 10 feet. 'Queen Elizabeth' is a wonderful old standby; I also love the salmon-pink 'Sonia.' If you have the room they are satisfying to grow because they are so vigorous.

CLIMBING ROSES

Climbing roses are not vines and do not climb the same way that vines do. Vines have tendrils or some other means of twining around or sticking to the thing they are climbing, to help them up. They also tend to have flexible stems so they can bend in appropriate directions. Roses, on the other hand, simply send up stiff woody canes in hopes of reaching the sunny air above the tops of other shrubs and small trees. The

only aid they have is their thorns, which hook onto vegetation. Once they're up in the light, they send out horizontal shoots that produce flowers, which is why a climbing rose that is only growing vertically may not bloom much, or at all.

I often wish I lived in a warmer climate where climbing roses were vigorous and I could send them up into the trees as Gertrude Jekyll did in Victorian England. (I wouldn't plant them right among the tree roots, however.) Apart from the indestructible 'William Baffin' and 'New Dawn,' there are not many climbers I can grow well. But good new roses appear all the time. Recently I tried a modern climber called 'Rosenholm,' with pale pink clusters and an old-rose look. It has proved very hardy and disease resistant in Maine. Gardeners in warmer zones, rejoice! Look at Jekyll's book *Roses* to see how she camouflaged unsightly tool sheds with them. Judging from the pictures, some look as if they might charmingly obliterate your house if you turned your back.

There are a number of different climbing rose types, but most of the ones available are called large-flowered climbers and have flowers in clusters, in a large variety of shades including yellow. Climbers do well on walls and trellises, supported in such a way that the branches can be trained laterally.

"Pillar roses" are either roses that don't climb as high as most climbers—about 8 to 10 feet—or ones that respond well to pruning at the top so that they remain at this height. They're traditionally trained vertically on a free-standing pillar, but they also look attractive and natural growing on a post supporting a porch or other structure. Cutting some of the stems back helps to maintain bloom along the length of the pillar. "Ramblers" are climbers that have very flexible canes and usually bloom only once, in early summer. 'Albertine' is a bright pink rambler; 'Ghislaine de Féligonde' is apricot-yellow. "Trailers" are low-growing roses with long canes that are very lax and tend to lie on the ground rather than grow upright. They make good ground covers. Many different types of roses fall into this category; the hybrid rugosa 'Max Graf' is one example.

MINIATURE ROSES

These roses are dwarf in every way: their flowers, their leaves, and their bushes. Sizes range from the tiniest microminis, as short as 6 inches, to the 3-foot macrominis. They have a broad range of flower types and colors. Miniatures are charming in small-space gardens where they can be viewed close up, in flower borders, in rock gardens, massed as ground covers, and in containers. Some even look good in hanging baskets. Many have rather cutesy names such as 'Wee Jock' and 'Little Buckaroo.'

OLD ROSES

This vast category encompasses many important types of roses, among them gallicas, albas, cabbage roses, moss roses, bourbons, damasks, hybrid perpetuals, teas, Chinas, and noisettes. Despite the fact that color range and blooming period are limited, these "historical roses," as they are sometimes called, have much to offer that modern roses lack, and they have recently experienced a comeback. Most are large plants, grown as shrubs. A number of specialty mail-order nurseries sell old roses, and garden centers frequently have a good selection.

Many things attract gardeners to old roses. They tend to be more fragrant than modern ones, which have been bred for such things as wide color range, large high-centered blooms, stiffer necks that don't nod and bend, and stiffer petals that don't crush when shipped, as well as disease resistance and vigor. But fragrance has often been sacrificed, even though there are some notoriously fragrant modern roses (such as 'Mister Lincoln,' 'Fragrant Cloud,' 'Sutter's Gold,' 'Chrysler Imperial,' and 'Double Delight'). But in a garden of old roses almost all exude fragrance. And there are wonderful flower shapes in the old ones that you rarely see in new. The heavy, luxurious cabbage roses, or centifolias (the name means "a hundred petals"), nod on their stems like sleepy courtesans. These and many other old roses have a flat, "button-eyed" flower whose petals all seem pulled in toward the center. On top of that the old varieties are rich in history. Their names alone are enough to seduce gardeners: 'Reine des Violettes,' 'Souvenir de la Malmaison,' 'Belle Amour,' 'Hebe's Lip,' 'Nymph's Thigh.'

WILD OR SPECIES ROSES

These roses are the ones from which all the countless hybrids, old or modern, have been derived. You will find some of them hard to obtain except through specialty nurseries, and their rarity makes them alluring. Unfortunately, some proved to be invasive when they were long ago transplanted into North American soil. The Japanese *Rosa multiflora*, for example, grows in many a New England meadow. In some areas, if you jog along the roads on a warm June evening, you're almost overpowered with the heady scent of its small white, clustered blossoms. It's lovely, but unfortunately you can't have just one or two multifloras, because birds eat the seeds and spread them everywhere. Local landowners are out there with their tractors and brush hogs every year, trying to stop *R. multiflora* from taking over their pastures. *R. rubiginosa* (the sweetbrier rose, or Shakespeare's "eglantine") is another that colonizes fields to the detriment of native vegetation. So is the dog rose (*R. canina*), a rose commonly used as a rootstock for grafted hybrids, which has escaped this supporting role and colonized on its own. Not all imported species roses are invasive, but it is important to check before planting one.

If you appreciate the simplicity and vigor of wild roses, it is far better to domesticate whichever ones are native to your area. These are less invasive because their role in the local ecosystem is a balanced one that has evolved over many years. In my neck of the woods, it's the pasture rose (*R. carolina*), and *R. virginiana*, both of which bear pink flowers. *R. virginiana*, fragrant and indestructible, makes an especially fine low hedge. In the midwest you find prairie roses such as *R. arkansana*, and *R. setigera* with its long, trailing habit. California has *R. californica*, often used in gardens, and the coastal *R. minutifolia* (the prickly Ensenada rose). Wild roses of the

How Roses Grow
FIG. 63

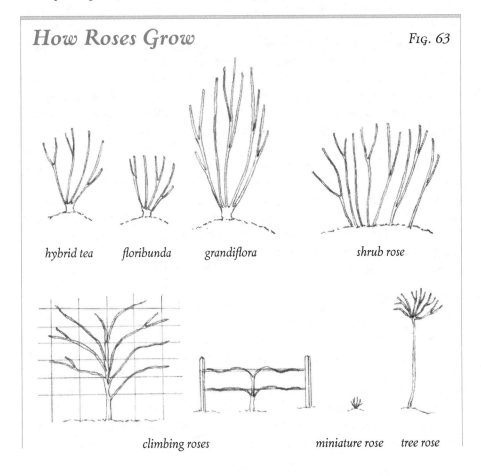

hybrid tea   *floribunda*   *grandiflora*   *shrub rose*

climbing roses   *miniature rose*   *tree rose*

Pacific northwest include R. *gymnocarpa,* R. *nutkana,* and R. *woodsii.* There are even desert roses such as R. *stellata,* native to the southwestern states. In the recent past it was nearly impossible to buy wild roses such as these, but that is changing. Thanks to a greater interest in habitat reclamation, nurseries are propagating them.

Wild roses tend to bloom profusely in early summer, then stop, but their bright, abundant hips (the fruits that follow rose blossoms), attractive foliage, and often showy fall coloring make them a multiseasonal asset in the yard. The small, simple, wide-open flowers vary in shades of pink, reddish pink, or white, and also in the number of petals. The open shape and the showy, upright stamens, loaded with ample pollen, make them extremely attractive to bees and other pollinators, unlike many highly bred roses. Nectar is also abundant. The hips provide sustenance for birds and other creatures. Thus they play an important role in the ecology of the garden and home landscape, as well as in that of wilder areas. They require little care, and gardeners enjoy their resistance to pests and diseases. Even the somewhat overenthusiastic ones can have a place—rambling along a fence for example. In a moist area, try the beautiful swamp rose, R. *palustris.*

SHRUB ROSES

This rather amorphous classification includes a number of rose types. Those of early origin, such as the fragrant white 'Blanc Double de Coubert,' are often listed under old roses. Others such as 'Bonica,' a pink rose, are modern hybrids. The rugosa roses, which originated in Japan, are important members of the group. They are very hardy and vigorous, with wrinkled leaves, and are remarkably tolerant of seaside conditions (too much so, in areas where they have supplanted native vegetation). Flowers are pink, red, or white and usually single, though there are some doubles. Rugosas bloom over a long period. The hips are particularly showy and rich in vitamin C. Among the many hybrid rugosas is 'Pink Grootendorst,' which has pink double flowers. Rugosas are extremely easy to grow and because they sucker freely, they're sometimes better off in a planting by themselves. Like many shrub roses, rugosas tend not to be grafted but are grown on their own roots.

Some other favorites classified as shrub roses are 'Harison's Yellow,' which bears small, fragrant yellow flowers once early in the season; 'Austrian Copper' (R. *foetida* 'Bicolor'), with striking early-blooming yellow-and-red single blossoms; and 'The Fairy,' a wonderful hardy rose with thick clusters of tiny pale pink flowers and delicately cut foliage on a low, sturdy, twiggy plant. A member of a small, largely early-twentieth-century group called the polyanthas, it looks as good in a perennial border as it does in a rose bed, and is a pretty accent plant next to a gate or doorway.

TREE ROSES

These are not really trees but roses grown to look like trees. They consist of three parts: the rootstock; the trunkstock, which is budded (grafted) onto the rootstock; and the top, which is budded onto the trunkstock. Many different types of roses are used for the top. If it is an upright, compact rose, the top will be a round head of foliage and flowers. If it is a long-caned type, the top will hang down and resemble a "weeping" tree. Tree roses require staking and special winter protection for the trunk and upper graft, and are not recommended for cold regions. Generally they are small, exquisite specimens except in very mild climates, where they can become quite large.

Plan for a Rose Garden

IN DISCUSSING THE VARIOUS TYPES OF roses, I have mentioned some ways to use them in the landscape. But if you're really attracted to roses, you may decide that you want a separate garden devoted solely to them. The phrase "rose garden" suggests many things: fragrance, formality, luxury, romance. Assuming that time, space, and money were no object, I could conjure up a rose garden in the old style, surrounded by ancient brick walls or boxwood hedges, to enclose you in a secret world of color and scent. Few of us have the means to achieve anything so grand. On the other hand, it is possible to plan a very modest rose garden that echoes the grand style.

The garden shown in Figure 64 is only 20 by 24 feet and contains no elaborate structures, but it captures something of the old-fashioned formal rose garden on a small scale. At the back is a dark evergreen hedge to set off the bright colors of the roses. One good, simple choice for the hedge would be sheared Japanese yew. Others would be hemlock, arborvitae, and Hinoki false cypress. In fairly mild climates you can use boxwood.

In the center, just in front of the hedge, is a simple arbor with a seat where you can sit and admire the roses. A climbing rose or pillar rose might be placed to grow on each side—or on just one side if your climber is a vigorous, heavy plant. A simple wooden fence or trellis borders the garden on each side. Here you could plant more climbers, some ramblers, and some old shrub roses (I would, however, avoid the very vigorous ones in this small setting). Any of the climbers and ramblers could be trained along the fence horizontally, and even some shrub roses look better when there's a sturdy fence to support their heavy branches.

The central part of the garden consists of two walkways that join at the bench and are separated by a small central bed shaped like an elongated ellipse. These are easy to mark out: all you do is take a garden line (or a screwdriver tied to a string) and, using it as a compass, make two concentric half-circles, one with a radius of 5 feet (for the walkway), the other with a radius of 2 feet (for the center bed). If you're working in bare ground, scratch the lines in the earth; if in sod, mark the circles with small wood or plastic plant markers every foot or so and lay a garden hose along them. Then edge the line with a spade. The side beds are planted with the smaller roses such as hybrid teas and floribundas; the central bed has small ones as well. In the very center is a tree rose. I haven't suggested specific rose varieties except for 'The Fairy' (in the center bed), because I would prefer you to select roses that are just the right ones for your area.

I sometimes mix other plants with roses, although if I'm growing roses that need winter protection I don't plant anything too close to them; this way there's plenty of room to place winter mulch or soil mounds around

Plan for a Rose Garden (20' by 24')

FIG. 64

arbor with bench underneath

path

fence

fence

1. yew hedge
2. climbers, ramblers, and shrub roses on fence
3. hybrid teas and floribundas
4. grandifloras
5. climbers
6. tree rose
7. 'The Fairy' rose
8. low-growing annuals and perennials
9. tall annuals and perennials

them. Certain kinds of plants go especially well with roses—old-fashioned, romantic flowers in shades of pink, red, blue, lavender, pale yellow, and white. Flower forms should be subtle and restrained too, and it's nice to find some with airy flowers, such as sea lavender or baby's breath, or spiky ones such as lavender, foxglove, and veronica, as a contrast to the round shape of the roses. I would avoid big flowers in hot colors, such as large-flowered marigolds or gloriosa daisies. You want to set off the roses, not overpower them. Some other plants that might go well with roses are perennial geraniums, heather, any of the bellflowers, columbines, coral bells, scabiosas, and yarrow (all of these grown as perennials). Or annuals such as larkspur, stock, violas, love-in-a-mist, lobelia, and Iceland or Shirley poppies. Foliage plants such as silvery-leaved artemisias, red-leaved coral bells, or blue-leaved rue can be lovely too. Use annuals, perennials, biennials, or a combination. If most of your roses are early blooming you might plant early-summer perennials. If it is an all-season rose garden, plant some that bloom later, mixed with annuals.

You don't want to let these companion plants steal the show from the roses. (Sometimes just a low edging is best.) But the floral diversity they provide can often justify a bit of competition from them. And their nectar attracts pollinating insects, some of which are also predators of insect pests.

The garden in Figure 64 is edged with flowers that will neither hide the roses nor interfere with winter protection of the hybrid teas. These might include artemisia 'Silver Mound,' alpine pinks, creeping baby's breath, and creeping thyme. You could also use annuals such as alyssum and love-in-a-mist. At the rear of the beds, some lilies, balloon flowers, and cosmos would do handsomely.

The path could be simply a grass strip—an extension of the lawn. Brick or stone would be more low-maintenance, since you would not have to worry about grass creeping into the beds. If you want to make this bed even smaller, you can cut off some of the bottom area, making the central bed a shorter ellipse or even a small circle with one exquisite tree rose or rose bush in the center.

Choosing a Site

ROSES GENERALLY LIKE A SUNNY location—at least six hours of full sun a day—but if your only good spot gets as little as four hours a day, roses are still worth a try. Southern and western exposures are fine, but an eastern one is best in most areas, especially warm ones and those with a lot of humidity, where disease is a heavy risk. The morning sun will dry the dew off the leaves promptly, and you will also avoid the hot afternoon sun that is apt to fade the color of the flowers.

In cold climates, try to find a sheltered location out of cold winter winds, but don't pick a spot where air circulation is really poor—this can foster disease. Your site should not have tree or shrub roots that can compete with the roses. Above all, it should have excellent drainage. Roses will not survive if their roots are sitting in water. If your only possible site does not drain well, build raised beds for your roses, or even have drainage pipes installed to lead excess water away from the area.

Preparing the Soil

R OSES WILL TOLERATE A FAIRLY WIDE range of soils. Many do better in clay soils than sandy ones because clay is more moisture retentive. The soil does not have to be very rich, but it should have plenty of organic matter worked in—compost, well-rotted manure, moistened peat moss, leaf mold, ground bark. The ideal pH is between 6.0 and 7.0. Lime may be needed if the soil is very acid. Adding lots of peat moss, bark, and other acid materials will help acidify the soil if it is too alkaline.

Since roses have long, deep roots, I like to dig a rose bed deeply for the initial preparation. For spring planting, it's best to dig the bed in fall and let it settle over the winter so you won't be working wet soil in early spring. Your bed will be all ready so that you can plant the roses early, while they are still dormant.

Buying Roses

I T CAN SOMETIMES BE FRUSTRATING TO buy roses, because you cannot always tell whether or not they're the best ones for your garden. The colorful picture on the tag beckons, and you buy. Consult a number of catalogs or online listings from mail-order suppliers and go through them carefully. Many companies will make recommendations based on climate. They may be a bit vague—saying only "winter hardy" or "not winter hardy" as opposed to giving hardiness zone numbers—but even such

minimal information is a start. Besides, a rose that is not quite hardy enough for your zone may survive fine if you plant it in a warm, sheltered part of the property and protect it well in winter. If you buy plants from a local nursery, they may or may not be the best choices for the area; but if it's a good nursery the staff will be able to tell you which ones people have the best luck with. I would start with some that are fairly safe bets so that a cold winter does not wipe out your new garden completely and discourage you from rose growing.

Most mail-order companies ship at the best planting time for your area—in general, early spring for cool climates, early fall where winters are fairly mild, and winter in very warm areas. Some suppliers of old roses ship in fall even to cold climates. This is because old roses are sometimes not grafted but grown on their own roots, and are thus very easy to establish. When you buy a modern rose you'll notice that there's a bulge at the bottom of the main stem where a bud of a hybrid variety has been grafted onto the rootstock of a very vigorous rose that will provide a good root system for the plant. The graft bulge is called the bud union.

Plants that are shipped by mail should be "dormant, two-year-old, No. 1, field-grown plants" (look for this designation). According to the official system of grading roses, "No. 1" means that the plant has at least three vigorous canes at least 18 inches high (15 inches for floribundas). Two other notations that may alert you to a good rose are "AARS" (meaning the rose is an All-America Rose Selection) or a high rating on a scale of 1 to 10 by the American Rose Society, as published in the magazine *The American Rose*. But don't go by these ratings alone, since there may be particular qualities in roses that you will come to prefer, and certain ones that will do best in your particular garden.

Unless they are miniatures, your roses will arrive bare-root (with no soil around them) and should be soaked in water for 24 hours upon arrival. Heel them in (page 40) or wrap them in damp sphagnum moss if you cannot plant them right away, but try not to hold them this way for more than two weeks.

If you buy your plants potted in a local nursery, look for No. 1 plants with healthy foliage. I would avoid bargain plants in places like box stores and supermarkets; even if you have an eye for a good rose bush and know your varieties, it is better to buy from nurseries you know, whose plants are usually healthy and who will replace the plant if it's not satisfactory. Potted roses can be held until you're ready to plant them if you keep them in a semishaded location and water them well.

Planting Roses

SOMETIMES PEOPLE PLANT HYBRID TEAS and floribundas very close together, especially in cooler climates where almost all the growth is the current year's, where the bushes never get very large, and where they may not always be covered with blooms. It does make for a better show, but I advise keeping the distance between the plants' outer branches at least 2 feet apart, and more in warm areas where disease is more prevalent. I'd rather be optimistic about the size the bush will attain and keep plenty of circulating air around each one.

Of course different types of roses have different spacing requirements. Miniatures can go as close as a foot apart, but many old roses, shrub roses, and climbers can become very large, even huge, and you need to allow room for their eventual spread. Try to find out as much as you can about the plants' growth habits before you decide on their spacing.

Planting roses is easy if you follow a few simple rules. Always dig a large enough hole, deep enough and—more important—wide enough to accommodate the roots. When you're planting a rose bare-root, it's important not to let the roots dry out. Don't leave them lying exposed to sun and wind. Better yet, puddle them by sloshing the roots in a bucket of mud slurry, and leave them in the bucket until the minute you're ready to plant them.

On bare-root plants you can see the root system and tailor your hole to accommodate long roots (don't prune them back unless they are damaged). The position of the bud union is important. In warm climates it should be just above the soil so the sun can reach it and cause it to send out new canes, but in cold climates it is safer to place it an inch or two below the soil—even more in severe climates—to protect it from cold.

Making a soil mound in the center of the hole and draping the roots over it is helpful, but don't try to crowd the roots into a tidy arrangement or wind them around in a circle. Firm the soil gently around the roots, water them when the hole is half full, let the water settle, then fill the rest of the way with soil, making sure there are no air pockets. After that make a soil saucer and fill it with water.

If your rose is in a pot, lift it out very gently, trying to keep as much of the soil around the roots as possible (see page 43 for more about planting shrubs). Roses that come in cardboard boxes are planted box and all, though you should peel off the part that sticks up above the soil. (Instructions on the box will usually guide you.)

If you have enriched the soil throughout the bed, you should not have to feed the roses at the time you plant them. You do not want to encourage a lot of new growth until the root system develops further and can sustain it. In fact, if the rose has canes longer than 18 inches it is best to cut them back to this length when you plant. Your last job is to remove the little metal tag that is usually wired to one of the canes. Attach it to a stake and stick it next to the plant if you want it for identification,

but don't leave it on the plant; if you do, it may girdle and kill the stem as it grows.

Rose Supports

A SMALL ROSE BUSH OR A TRAILING rose does not need any kind of support, but climbing types usually do, to keep them from sprawling awkwardly, getting in the way, and falling down (Figure 63). Roses that climb up pillars must be tied to the pillars; those on trellises can be tied on or woven through the openings.

Rose supports can also be used to encourage lateral branching and more profuse bloom. Roses can be grown com-

Planting Roses

FIG. 65

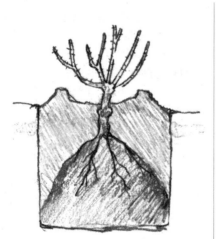

Spread the roots over a mound of soil. The bud union should be above the soil surface in warm climates, and just below it in cold ones. Fill the hole halfway with soil, watering thoroughly and firming the soil gently around the roots.

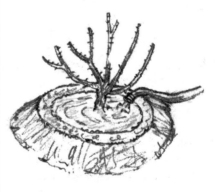

Fill the rest of the hole, then make a saucer of earth around the rose bush and fill it with water.

pletely horizontally along a fence, where they will send up lateral shoots along the canes. Or the canes may be trained upward to a certain point, then trained sideways along a wall or trellis. Gardeners also construct arbors and pergolas—open wooden structures like the frame of a house without the walls—for roses to climb on. Keep in mind that if a rose is the kind that only blooms well on horizontal canes, you don't want it to reach the roof before going sideways or you'll never see the flowers. With some roses you may have to watch them grow and see how they're going to behave before you figure out the best way to support them.

Taking Care of Your Roses

R OSES ARE NOT DELICATE CREATURES that must be fussed with every two minutes. If I have an exceptionally crazed summer and don't get to tend mine at all, they're still there in fall and have provided me with enough blooms to stick into flower arrangements for a touch of elegance among such peasant stock as coneflower and yarrow. But there are a lot of small favors you can do for your roses that will make them more than just "still there." They will be there in all their glory, and if you want to, you'll be able to gather bouquets that are nothing but roses, roses, roses.

WATERING

With their deep root systems, roses will make it through all but the most horrific drought, but will they bloom through it?

No. Even if your summer is not a particularly dry one, chances are it's noticeably drier than your spring was or your fall will be. And if you give your roses a thorough, deep soaking when the soil is dry, you will have more flowers. The best way is to water the soil, not the leaves, using a soaker hose (page 108) or a drip system. Watering in the morning is best so that you don't go into the evening with a lot of disease-fostering moisture sitting around on the ground or on the plants. If water is scarce, however, it is best to just let your roses take a break from flowering in high summer.

WEEDING

Any garden needs to be kept free of weeds, and roses are no exception. Try to remove the roots of all perennial weeds from the bed when you prepare it, then cultivate every now and then to prevent annual weeds from gaining on you. I don't advise using systemic herbicides, and be advised that roses are especially sensitive to them. A mulch will help keep the weeds down, and will also help keep the soil moist.

FEEDING

When it comes to feeding roses I'm like a mother who never lets her kids eat Froot Loops or Twinkies. "No rose food." I tell them. "I'm never sure what's in it—probably a lot of empty calories." I'm sure there are some good rose formulations out there, but mine just get a moderately enriched soil to start with, then a good topdressing with well-rotted manure or mature compost in very late fall or early winter. I tend to use a liquid fertilizer such as a seaweed/fish mix that delivers nutrients straight to the roots when they need it—say after unmounding in spring, after the first flush of bloom, and in early August to promote fall bloom. Roses should not have food just before bedtime: top-dressing with compost too early in fall before they have gone dormant will make them put out tender growth, subject to winterkill. In a warmer climate I would be a bit more indulgent, giving larger portions and perhaps a feeding in mid or late August. Rose enthusiasts who exhibit their roses often practice foliar feeding, a method of spraying soluble fertilizers onto the undersides of the leaves to promote flowering and give the leaves good color.

PESTS AND DISEASES

I feel the same way about "rose spray" and "rose dust" as I do about "rose food." They're supposed to take care of everything that might possibly afflict your roses. But I don't like all-purpose chemical concoctions that will wipe out insects indiscriminately—including those that feed on plant pests. My entire focus is on choosing roses that are happy in my climate, siting them where there is good air circulation, giving them great soil, mulching them, feeding them properly, watering them abundantly when it's needed, and keeping them pruned in a way that lets plenty of sun and air into the center of the bush. Every now and then I encounter a rose that is particularly susceptible to a pest or a disease. I make sure all the measures listed above are being taken, then evaluate whether the problem is seriously hindering my enjoyment of this rose. If the answer is yes, I usually discard it and go on with my life.

Roses in some parts of the country are chronically prone to blackspot, which you can recognize by black spots on the leaves; the disease haunts regions that are rainy or humid. Powdery mildew, which turns the foliage white, is another common rose disease that is often a problem in hot weather. Seeking out disease-resistant varieties for your area is a good first step. Improving air circulation, trying to keep foliage dry, mulching, and promptly removing all debris (especially dropped leaves) can reduce damage. Some gardeners have luck spraying the plants with a solution of 1 tablespoon of baking soda per gallon of water. If you're pruning diseased plants, dip the pruners in a disinfectant such as alcohol between cuts. This avoids spreading a disease from plant to plant.

Every region has its own insect predators, too. When I lived in Connecticut I decided that if mountain laurel was the State Flower, then surely the Japanese beetle was its State Pest. Some years they were very hard on the roses, some years not. I didn't use poison sprays and found pheromone traps of no benefit. Applying milky spore disease to the lawn to kill the beetles' larvae was one solution but an expensive one. I preferred my mother's remedy. When we were children she always kept a quart jar of kerosene in the garden, and the rule was that whoever went outside had to make a pass through the roses and drop any beetles they found into the jar. If you're vigilant about doing this, you can minimize the damage they cause. Picking them off with the slot attachment of a shop vac is another trick.

If you see a lot of ants in your rose blossoms, they're herding aphids—literally farming them so they'll secrete a honey-like substance the ants love to eat. You can usually just wipe out the whole operation with a blast of water from the hose. Rose scale (white spots on older canes) can be controlled with a dormant oil spray (page

66) applied early in the season before the plants leaf out. Remove badly infested canes, and clean up all debris. For spider mites, which make webs on the undersides of the leaves, spray with the hose and keep the bed free of weeds and debris. Rose galls, which are bulges on the stems, are caused by wasps and can be pruned out; crown gall, at the base of the plant, should also be cut out, or the plant destroyed if it is badly affected.

PRUNING

For serious rose enthusiasts, pruning is a complex topic about which few agree, but for the average gardener it's a fairly simple practice aimed at keeping roses healthy, well shaped, and free flowering. If you did no pruning at all—letting winter kill

off some excess canes, then simply cutting back stems in summer by picking roses for the house—you could get by. But you'll have nicer roses if these things happen in a more controlled way.

Some people cut back their roses in late fall or winter. This is fine in warm climates; just wait until the leaves turn their fall color, a sign that no more growth will occur. Spring pruning generally works best in colder areas. In fall I might snip off some long tips, and anchor the long canes of climbers to keep them from blowing around and getting broken by ice. Then I let nature take its course.

On the rare occasions when I grow hybrid teas or other roses I have had to wrap or mound for protection (page 537), I remove the coverings and mounded soil just when

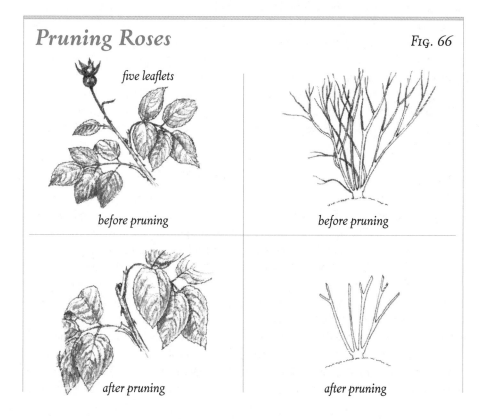

Pruning Roses   FIG. 66

five leaflets

before pruning

before pruning

after pruning

after pruning

the buds are swelling and about to leaf out. I can see immediately that some of the canes have died on the less hardy plants, or died partway. Wearing leather gloves, I take my hand pruners and go to work on anything that looks dead. Rose canes are deceptive: sometimes they look brown and lifeless when they are still alive. So I start at the tips and start snipping a few inches at a time until the centers of the pruned stems look white instead of brown. Then I start shortening the living canes, with the goal of giving the plant a compact, balanced appearance. The goal in pruning back rose bushes is not only to keep the bush nicely shaped and make it flower, but also to open up the center. This lets sun into the whole plant for better growth, promotes air circulation to ward off disease, and creates a vase-like shape that displays the flowers better than a dense, twiggy one would. If there are a lot of canes coming up from the bottom, prune out some of the older ones as shown in Figure 66. Remove dense, twiggy growth and canes that cross each other. Sometimes a tall, thick cane will shoot up quickly, with few buds on it. It will not flower well and should be removed at the base.

When cutting canes back partway, always try to cut back to an outward-facing dormant bud, because a branch will emerge there that leads away from the center of the plant. This applies to summer picking as well. Notice that a rose sprig is made up of a number of leaflets—always an odd number, in fact. When you cut the stem just above one of these sprigs, a bud will later appear there; if the leaf is facing outward, the bud will be too, and it will send out a new branch in that direction. So when cutting roses for the house it's a good idea to count leaflets. Cut back to a group of at least five leaflets, so that a bud will form. If you have a choice of blossoms (and enough patience!), choose one you can cut above an outward facing bud. Make your cuts on a slant to encourage water to drain off the cut.

These techniques apply to the types of roses that grow on fairly small plants. But even large shrubs and climbers need to have deadwood removed, old canes thinned out, and the center of the plant kept open. For these you will probably need loppers or even a pruning saw (page 106). Ramblers are pruned rather heavily to encourage them to form lateral branches for more flowers, and are often cut back entirely after they bloom; the new branches that grow will produce the following year's flowers. Old roses that bloom just once in early summer are generally pruned lightly in early spring to remove deadwood, then more drastically after flowering to improve shape and promote growth. Roses that sucker at the bottom (send out new shoots from below the soil surface) will often need to have those suckers dug out with a spade. Rugosa roses and rugosa hybrids are notorious in this regard.

DEADHEADING

Deadheading (page 191) is important with the smaller rose bushes and should be practiced just as if you were pruning, cutting back to an outward-facing bud above five leaflets as described above. All types of roses benefit from deadheading, but with climbers and large shrubs it may be impossible, and if you have a lot of roses in your garden it may not be possible to deadhead them all. I tend to choose my battles, focusing on ones that I view close up and can reach easily. It is a somewhat tedious housekeeping job, but it gives a rose garden a beautiful, refreshed look.

On the other hand, there are a number of roses that I would never, ever deadhead. All rose flowers are followed by fruits, called "hips," that are rich in vitamin C and can be used in jams and other dishes. They are also beautiful and hang on the bushes in wintertime, providing food for birds and mammals. The older roses seem to have the nicest ones, so I make a point of leaving all or most of them in place, then snipping them off in spring as part of the annual pruning. Some roses shed petals more gracefully than others, and if they are an unsightly mess (as with the beautiful old 'Blanc Double de Coubert') I'll often just remove the dead petals with my fingers but leave the part where the hip will form. A rose like R. rubrifolia whose oval red hips are striking against the blue-green foliage, should never be deadheaded. Besides, the exquisitely simple pink flowers leave barely a trace when they go.

WINTER PROTECTION

In late summer you should let your roses start winding down for the winter, especially in cold areas. You don't want to feed them, prune them, or even pick them heavily for fear of promoting new growth. If the weather is dry you'd best water them, however, so they'll have enough moisture around their roots after the ground has frozen.

In cold areas you should then cover any roses that are not hardy in your climate. Even those that are hardy will look less beat-up in spring if protected in some way.

The traditional way of protecting tender roses is to mound soil around the base of the plants, anywhere from 6 to 12 inches of it. The soil will not only protect against

extreme cold but also help to keep the roots from drying out. It is applied after there have been several hard freezes. In fact, I'd usually wait until just before the ground is too hard to dig—otherwise, the mounding may encourage new growth. The soil must be brought in from somewhere else, like the vegetable garden, not dug up from between the rose bushes (which would make the root systems all the more vulnerable). Mounding works best with the shorter roses, although tender climbers are sometimes removed from their supports, laid along the ground, and buried. Tender tree roses are sometimes dug up entirely, laid on their sides, and buried (or dug on one side and tilted over). If tree roses are left standing, the trunk and top are wrapped in burlap.

In spring, when you think new growth might be starting to appear at the base of the plants, dig away some soil with your fingers. If you find new growth, remove all the mounding soil very carefully and haul it back to the place it came from.

A less laborious method of protecting roses is to erect a barrier around the bushes, or around the whole bed, to make a sort of pen that is then filled with leaves, shredded bark, or some other loose material. To contain the mulch, people use tarpaper, snow fence, wire fence, bushel baskets, even newspapers. If your filling is the same material you're going to mulch with, you can simply spread all or most of it back over the bed in springtime. This method also helps keep ice and wind from breaking the branches. (Sometimes gardeners mound roses *and* surround them with mulch.) There are also "rose cones" you can buy, which fit down over the whole plant, though this method can be expensive if you have a lot of roses. Tall roses such as grandifloras or climbers can also be wrapped in burlap for some measure of protection if you don't mind looking at mummified rose plants all winter. I do mind, so I generally stick to roses that don't require extreme measures.

Whether you protect your roses, and how, will depend on what you grow and where you live. Sometimes roses winter over beautifully in regions where a heavy snowfall provides a natural mulch, keeping soil temperature constant.

Roses are among the most satisfying ornamental plants you can grow, and many gardeners get totally hooked on them. Since they are such a popular plant, it's fairly easy to find opportunities to see them growing and learn about different kinds.

The American Rose Society (page 759) can direct you not only to its regional branches but also to public gardens where you can see dozens of different roses on display. If you get involved in the rose world you'll meet many gardeners ready to share their enthusiasm and their expertise—and also budwood with which to graft new hybrids you may not have tried, or cuttings of old rose treasures that have nearly passed out of existence. You'll learn which varieties and which techniques succeed in your area and which don't. You may never get to wade knee-deep in rose petals, but as the little chores of rose growing become routine, you'll wonder how you could ever have a garden without at least a few roses in it.

CHAPTER 12

Lawns

LIKE MANY PEOPLE, I HAVE A LOVE-hate relationship with the lawn. So let's start with the positive side. The lawn is cool, soft, and green. It puts oxygen into the air. It doesn't reflect glaring sun the way a hard surface would. It absorbs dust and rain. As a foreground for landscape plantings it ties the whole picture together, setting off the bolder shapes of trees and shrubs and the multicolored hues of flower gardens. On bright days it is dappled with the moving shadows of trees and passing clouds. In low-angled sun, it glows like an emerald sea. It is a very useful surface because unlike most ground covers, it can be walked on, run on, and played on without its being injured. Under swing sets and jungle gyms it provides a soft landing. It invites you to play tennis, croquet, football, baseball, frisbee, badminton. It hosts barbecues, picnics, weddings, graduations. We like the smell of it just after it's been cut. Some of us even enjoy mowing it.

Then there's the negative side. Some of us *hate* mowing the lawn. It's a very high-maintenance part of the landscape, especially because of mowing, so as a result people have always looked for a quicker way to do the job, starting with Edwin Budding's invention of the rotary push mower in 1830. This gadget was followed by noisy, smelly, polluting gas-engine machines, then ride-on models that don't even give you the excuse of exercise. In search of an ideal of lawn perfection, tons of pesticides, fungicides, herbicides, and chemical fertilizers are spread on the land each year. To keep lawns green, water is lavished on them, especially in regions where water conservation is most needed. And their ability to absorb water runoff is often exaggerated—heavy rainfall flows off them into storm drains, carrying whatever chemicals have been applied, often polluting waterways and groundwater. Pretty as lawns may be, there are more environmentally responsible and generally more interesting ways to carpet the earth. Most lawn grasses are sterile collections of nonnative species, cut off before they have a chance to bloom. They do almost nothing to sustain wildlife. Regarding the standard chemical-dosed lawn, it might be more ecologically benign to lay down Astroturf.

Both of these views are true. Our fondness for lawns is a natural one. Perhaps it's a cultural memory—a flashback to times when we lived surrounded by meadows or prairies grazed by cattle, when the village green or common was nibbled by flocks of sheep. Some think the memory goes back to the dawn of man, when we lived in African savannahs—grassy areas dotted with clumps of shrubs and trees where we had a clear view of both predator and prey. (Sounds a bit like the typical yard, doesn't it?) So there's no need to discard the idea of the lawn, even though it could use some reform. Fortunately, home gardeners are thinking more seriously and creatively about how to have a lawn without its being a burden either to themselves and to the world in which they live. The result, I feel, is a lawn that is much more enjoyable than the obligatory great green carpet we once took for granted.

Do You Need a Lawn?

HOW YOU MAKE PEACE WITH YOUR own lawn depends on a lot of things, including who mows it. But before you decide on an approach to your lawn, you might ask yourself whether you want one in the first place, and if so how extensive it needs to be. In some communities a lawn may be a requirement—an implicit one if not an official one. Homeowners have been sued by their neighbors for growing wildflower meadows in their front yards instead of mowed turf-grass. I tend to admire people who do whatever they want with their yard, even though it's different from all the other identical yards on the block. I think we should have the right to our own personal standards of decor. But custom and tradition are powerful forces, so you may decide that the green patch in front of the house can stay, as long as there's room for a wilder area out back. On the other hand, you may be able to find other ways to cover the ground neatly and attractively in a way that won't offend your neighbors, such as the ground covers described in the following chapter. There are even a few ground covers, such as thyme, that will take minimum foot traffic, though most must have paths through them where walking is necessary.

Most lawns must be mowed at least once a week when they are actively growing (for more low-maintenance lawn grasses, see below). Ground covers, though more expensive to plant than lawns, require far less upkeep. They are also much more appropriate and easy to keep up in areas where mowing is difficult—slopes, tight corners, under overhanging branches of trees and shrubs or around their trunks, rocky areas, and near pools where clippings can get in the water. There are also places where grass simply will not grow because the ground is too shady or the soil is too wet or too dry. For all these problem spots there are ground covers that are just right.

Your choice of lawn or ground cover may also be based on visual considerations. Lawns do not provide the varied effects that you can achieve with ground covers. (See page 560 on designing with ground covers.) Don't assume that every spot that *can* have grass *must* have grass. Consider letting some of the property revert to a more natural state as a habitat for wildlife, with native shrubs and small trees. Or nurture a wildflower meadow on part of the lawn area (see the wildflower chapter).

In the end it may come down to how much lawn you want to take care of, and this may change at various points in your life. I reflect on how much my own lawn has shrunk over the past 15 years or so, to the point where it's little more than a series of broad paths between flower gardens, vegetable gardens, and orchard. But recently a small crop of grandchildren has sprung up and I've been thinking about having just a bit more greensward for them to run around on.

What Makes a Good Lawn

IF THERE IS GOING TO BE SOME LAWN on your property, you might as well have a good one. Notice I said "good," not "perfect." Since a lawn is something that most yards have, and its care is often the only form of gardening a homeowner does, there is enormous peer pressure about the subject. I find that men especially take great satisfaction in having the lawn look healthy and well tended (in other areas of gardening, male and female enthusiasm is usually about equal), and that they talk about their grass the way people talk about their hair. It is never thick enough or the right color. And heaven forbid it should have a weed in it.

Taking pride in a lawn is fine, but too often the quest for perfection leads to a lawn madness that causes people to overfeed and overmedicate, with little understanding of their lawn's real needs. I've heard of gardeners in the advanced stages of lawn madness who use dyes to make their grass greener and chemical growth retardants to keep them from growing too fast! My own philosophy, as with the other kinds of gardening discussed in this book, is that such a goal is not worth the chemical means used to achieve it. I believe that a healthy environment is more beautiful than an unblemished rose, tomato, or lawn, and that safer methods of lawn care can actually keep your lawn in better condition than the chemicals allow. Too often we reach for products simply because they are there. Marketing has convinced us of the need for them, when actually a low-cost or no-cost solution would have better results.

Lawn grasses are very tough, resilient plants that shouldn't need much care beyond mowing if you choose the right ones and give them the right growing conditions. Here are the steps that I consider most important to having a good lawn.

Preparing the Site

I F YOU HAVE NO LAWN AT ALL AND HAVE to start from scratch, you're lucky. You have a chance to start off right. While there are steps you can take to improve an estab-

lished lawn, they will make much less difference than those you take at the outset.

MAJOR GRADING

The first thing you need to do is take a look at the whole area where the lawn is to go, and see if it needs to have its drainage corrected (page 28). Grass planted in spots where water sits will not grow well and will be prone to disease. It might turn out to be simpler just to plant moisture-loving plants in low areas where water collects.

At the same time, look at the lay of the land and see what grading you need to do. Your lawn need not be perfectly flat unless you're constructing a very formal area, or one where sports that require a flat lawn will be played. Nevertheless, some major grading is usually necessary, if only to give the lawn a smooth, rolling appearance instead of a lumpy one. Whenever possible try to make your lawn slope away from, not toward, the foundations of buildings so that water drains away from them. Don't plan lawn areas on slopes that look too steep to be mowed easily and safely. Either terrace them to create flat sections that are mowable, or plant ground covers on the slopes instead. (You might also try one of the no-mow native grasses described on page 546.) If it is a large area, or if the grade problems are major, you may need to bring in a tractor or other large equipment. Otherwise use a shovel and rake to create the grade you want.

REMOVING OBSTACLES

You will also need to remove rocks from the lawn, wherever possible. I don't mean areas where rock outcroppings appear above the surface. These are interesting features that afford you the opportunity to create rock gardens. I wish I had some in my yard! Large rock formations just below the surface are another matter. While lawn grasses may seem relatively shallow rooted as plants go, their roots go down a foot or more. Also, soil with large rocks under it dries out much more quickly than a deeper soil, and will give you brown patches in the lawn. If there is ledge or large rocks you can't remove that are closer to the surface than, say, 6 inches, you should either uncover them and plant around them, spread more soil over them, or plant something other than grass in those spots. Even small rocks close to the surface can give the lawn a spotty appearance. I would say any rock larger than an egg in the top 2 to 3 inches of soil should go. Below this level you only have to worry about removing larger rocks, and the deeper you go, the larger the rocks you can ignore. Rocks may work their way up in time, but at least you'll have gotten the new grass off to a good start. Remove all debris as well, including buried stumps or logs, severed tree roots, old chunks of concrete, and pieces of lumber. Most likely you'll remove some of the rocks while grading and the rest later on when you till the ground.

IMPROVING THE SOIL

After you've finished the major grading, it's time to go to work on the soil. Everything I say about soil structure and fertility on pages 5 to 23 applies to the ground where you're going to put your lawn. Ideally, the topsoil layer should be at least 6 inches deep. (You can tell where it ends and the subsoil begins by observing a change in the color of the soil. Topsoil is usually much darker than subsoil.) If there is less than 6 inches of topsoil—either because it is naturally shallow, or because of recent construction or the grading you have just done—it's a good idea to add more topsoil and spread it evenly. If possible buy topsoil that has been screened to remove rocks, roots, and other debris. Just as in a garden, it is possible to create topsoil by adding enough organic matter; but if a lawn area is too large for this to be practical, you'll have to bring it in from elsewhere.

New homesites can be discouraging. Builders who are responsible first scrape off the topsoil layer in areas where digging and compacting will ruin the integrity of the soil. They stockpile it off to the side, then spread it back over the ground when the job is finished, or at least bring in new soil to remedy the damage. But often this is just a token gesture—as little as 2 meager inches of soil. Planting in skimpy soil, especially if the layers underneath have been compacted by heavy machines driving over it—is not worth doing. You'll always be struggling in vain to produce a healthy, self-sufficient lawn. Better to bite the bullet and till up the subsoil layer, incorporating organic matter such as peat moss into it and adding 6 inches of topsoil on top of that. If you can't do this right away, or can only afford to do it on part of the bare ground, use a thick straw or bark mulch to suppress weeds until the rest can be landscaped.

Even if there is plenty of topsoil, it will probably need some improvement. A soil test is a good first step (see page 10). The test will tell you not only what nutrients you need to add to help the grass grow well, but also the soil pH, which should be corrected if it departs too much from the pH that most grasses prefer—about 6.5. Remember, a lawn is a permanent planting, and creating good soil is the most important thing you can do to ensure that your lawn will be successful. Incorporate plenty of organic matter into the soil. Peat moss, compost, rotted manure, and leaf mold are all good materials. You may also need to add some mineral nutrients for long-term fertility. If the soil is low in phosphorus, some rock phosphate can be added. Greensand, for extra potassium and trace elements, can also be beneficial. For large areas a rototiller can be used. For smaller ones you can work the materials in with a rake or long-handled cultivator, removing rocks and debris as you go. If the soil deeper down feels compacted (and the area is not too large), spike it with a digging fork by driving the fork in and wiggling it back and forth; this will help air and moisture to penetrate.

After the soil is amended, go over the whole area with a rake, continuing to remove any rocks or debris in the top layer, and smoothing the surface. This is a lot of hard work but believe me, it will save you a lot more work in the future.

When the surface is smooth, it's time to plant. But first you'll have to give some thought to what kind of grass you'll need.

Choosing the Right Grass

WHICH GRASS YOU PLANT DEPENDS partly on what your lawn will be used for. For example, creeping bent grass is used for golf courses but it's too high-maintenance for lawns. Annual ryegrass is sometimes sown temporarily to prevent soil erosion, but it won't survive the winter, and too much of it in a lawn mix will result in bare patches where weeds quickly fill in.

If you want a permanent, all-purpose lawn that is partly for decoration and partly for play, there are many formulations on the market. You'll find that different grasses are suitable for different parts of the country and different degrees of sun and shade, and that lawn grasses fall into two major categories: cool season and warm season.

Most commercial lawn mixes are composed primarily of imported European grass species that were brought over when North America was settled. Though they serve some purposes well, they are high-maintenance, especially if used in climates for which nature never intended them. Some have escaped into the wild to the detriment of native ecosystems. As a result there is a movement to replace them with native grasses. I'll consider this option as well as the more traditional ones.

COOL-SEASON LAWN GRASSES

Cool-season grasses, used primarily north of zone 7, are hardy in northern winters. They stay fairly green in winter but are subject to stress in very hot weather, and may brown if the weather is very dry. They tend to be fine textured and are mowed relatively high (2 to 4 inches). They can be either grown from seed or started as purchased sod. Although you can buy different kinds of seed individually (in "straight" lots), northern lawns are best planted with lawn-seed mixtures that are made up of several grasses. A mixture helps ensure the health of the lawn, since a disease, an insect pest, or some other stress factor is more likely to wipe out a lawn composed of only one grass species. A mixture also helps a new lawn to become established, because different grasses germinate at different rates. To understand this, let's look at the grasses that might be contained in a typical cool-weather lawn seed mix:

Kentucky bluegrass. Not native to Kentucky, but a European introduction, Kentucky bluegrass is the most widely planted lawn grass in America, and makes up a large percent of most cool-season mixtures. There are many varieties, suited to different regions, so it may be worth seeking out a grass mixture approved by local turf experts. According to the USDA Natural Resource Conservation Service, Kentucky bluegrass is listed as an invasive weed in the Great Plains states and Wisconsin.

Fine fescues. These include red fescues (creeping fescues), chewings fescues, and hard fescues. Fine fescues are usually present in mixes because they are more shade and drought tolerant than Kentucky bluegrass. Their fine texture makes them very attractive, and they are quite disease resistant as well.

Perennial ryegrass. Up to 15 percent of the mix can be perennial ryegrass, but any greater percentage may keep the other grasses from developing. This grass becomes established much more quickly than the others, and thus it is often included as a "nurse grass," to shade the slower-sprouting species and help hold the soil as the others grow. Improved "turf-type" varieties don't turn brown at the tips after cutting, as older ones did. It can be invasive in California.

Bent grass. This very fine textured grass is best suited to cool, wet regions such as the Pacific northwest. It is widely used for golf courses and can be mowed much shorter than most cool-season grasses.

WARM-SEASON LAWN GRASSES

These grasses go dormant and turn brown in cool weather, so they are not suited to northern climates, but they keep a good green color during the long, hot summers of the southern zones. They tend to have a coarser texture than cool-weather grasses, and they are mowed short (1 inch for most). Usually they are not planted by seed but rather as sod, sprigs, or plugs (see below), and they are most often planted straight, not in mixtures. Here are some of the more common warm-season grasses:

Bermuda grass. This is a vigorous, popular southern grass. Its improved varieties need more watering, feeding, mowing, and dethatching than the old kind but are finer textured and do not brown as much in winter. None of them will do well in shade. Bermuda grass can be an invasive pest in some areas.

St. Augustine grass. I used to love to pull the runners of this grass out of my grandmother's Louisiana lawn because each came up in one seemingly endless strand, unlike the grasses back home. St. Augustine is coarse textured and difficult to mow; its chief value is its shade tolerance. But it needs lots of moisture and high fertility. It has poor insect and disease resistance, and needs frequent dethatching.

Zoysia grass. This extremely durable grass is quite fine textured and tends to have few problems, with the exception of thatch (see page 552). It does not need to be mown as often as most grasses. Though it will survive in cool climates it turns brown in winter and is not recommended for the north.

Bahia grass. This coarse-textured grass spreads by seed and may be hard to eradicate once established. But it is well adapted to hot, dry climates such as that of Florida's, and to sandy, poor soil. It is somewhat drought and shade tolerant. Mow it high (2 to 3 inches).

Carpet grass. A coarse but low-maintenance, disease-resistant grass, best for very warm, moist climates since it is neither drought nor cold tolerant. Mow it low (1 inch).

LAWN GRASSES FOR TRANSITION AREAS

If you live in an area where the winters are a bit too cool for warm-season grasses, and the summers too hot for cool-season ones (generally, zone 7), you may feel frustrated about finding the appropriate lawn grass. Try either the turf-type perennial ryegrass mentioned above or this one:

Tall fescue. Though rather coarse in comparison with other cool-season grasses, tall fescue makes a very durable lawn in transition states. It withstands hard traffic and playing, and newer varieties are finer textured than the old ones. It grows in bunches, takes some shade, is quite drought tolerant, and stays green all year. It is invasive in the moister parts of the western states.

NATIVE GRASSES FOR LAWNS

In the areas where they are naturally adapted, short-growing native grasses make an excellent substitute for more traditional lawn species. When they are well suited to the climate they need little or no watering, no chemical aids, and little other care. Some don't even need to be mowed, so that you can allow them to flower and complete their life cycles in greater harmony with other species. The use of these grasses is an emerging field—one that I expect will grow even more fruitful with time. When using native grasses it is advisable to remove all existing vegetation, including other lawn grasses, before planting. It can be grown from seed, sod, or plugs.

Buffalo grass (Buchloe dactyloides). This Great Plains native, a staple of the short-grass prairie, is an excellent substitute for standard lawn grasses in much of the western half of the country where rainfall is limited. It needs very little fertilizing except when it is first established. Watering needs are limited. It is disease resistant and fairly insect resistant. Controlling weeds by hand-pulling or by mowing is important until the grass is well established, but it will coexist well with certain low-growing plants such as small spring bulbs. A number of superior turf types have been developed, including all-female varieties that bear only short seed stalks. It turns a light golden brown in cold weather and does not tolerate much shade.

Blue grama (Bouteloua gracilis). This bunching grass is another from the Great Plains. It is sometimes used in combination with buffalo grass, which makes sense since they grow together in the wild. Though cold-hardy, it is a warm-season grass that goes dormant in winter. It is very drought resistant and in summer only goes dormant in extreme drought. It is low maintenance and disease resistant.

Native fescue (Festuca rubra). This cool-season grass is a good low-maintenance option for both the north and the upper south. It is a low-growing, fine-textured, bunch-forming grass with a soft, informal look. It can be mowed to a height of 3 inches in fall and spring, or left to grow to its natural height of 8 to 12 inches. It does best in fairly dry soil and is planted singly or used in no-mow mixes. Sheep fescue (*Festuca ovina*) and the blue-colored variety blue fescue are often included in these mixes as well. Though not native, these bunch grasses need little or no mowing and save energy.

Sedges. Sedges aren't true grasses, though they much resemble them. Their stems are triangular rather than round (the phrase "sedges have edges" will help you keep that distinction straight). There are over 2,000 sedges native to the United States, many of which make fine lawns or ground covers. Though many are moisture loving, some are quite drought tolerant. They tend to be clump forming; some are spreading. They are grown from plugs and require only occasional mowing to form a turf. A number of low-growing evergreen species have proven lawn-worthy, among them Pennsylvania sedge (*Carex pensylvanica*), which is spreading, drought tolerant, and fairly shade tolerant; Texas sedge or Catlin sedge (*C. texensis*), which is very adaptable and tolerant of foot traffic; and California meadow sedge (*C. pansa*), which performs well in a number of western areas. Many cultivars have been developed, among them a low, mop-headed sedge called 'The Beatles.'

THE VOLUNTEER LAWN

There are grass lawn areas on my property that I did not plant. In fact, nobody planted them—they just grew. These are spots where land has been cleared for vegetable gardening and other useful activities. Though some of this land is wild meadow, mowed yearly to keep trees and shrubs from taking hold, other parts of it are mowed regularly as pathways, or to keep the space around outbuildings accessible, or to give growing areas a tidier look. Around gardens they've been mowed so that crop-nibbling voles have no tall grass in which to hide from predators. Where once these were mixtures of tall grasses and broad-leaved plants, short grass now predominates. This is because repeated mowing has favored the growth of small grasses—these are not set back by mowing the way the other plants are, but come back stronger than ever. These "lawns" are not weed-free, but the weeds are not especially strong. Grass predominates, and most of the year the areas look as green and lush as any intentional lawn. I don't recommend this method if your goal is fine-quality turf without dandelions and plantains, and it might not work in every climate. But it is an interesting phenomenon.

Planting a Lawn

How you plant your lawn will naturally depend on where you live and what type of grass you intend to grow. The best time to sow cool-season grasses is late summer or early fall. The soil is warmer than it is in spring, helping the grass to germinate and get off to a good start. Annual weeds will soon be killed by frost, whereas in spring they are just starting to marshal their forces. Since these grasses do their growing best in cool weather, you're giving them a good long stretch of it before they have to face summer's heat, which is more traumatic to them than winter's cold. Still, try to get the seed in at least four weeks before the average first frost date (six weeks is better yet), to let them establish a root system. Warm-season grasses, on the other hand, are started in spring so they can enjoy a long stretch of the warm weather they like before they're subject to the stress of winter.

SOWING GRASS SEED

After you've prepared the soil, as described above, it is best to let it settle for a while.

If this is not possible, and the soil is very loose and fluffy so that your feet sink into it, you'd do well to use a lawn roller to roll it smooth. (These are easy to rent or borrow if you don't have one.) If you have your choice of days on which to sow, do it on a day when rain is in the forecast for later in the day. No sprinkler system does as perfect a job as a good soaking rain.

How thick you sow your seed is best determined by the directions on the package (3 pounds per 1,000 square feet is about average for a standard bluegrass mixture). I enjoy broadcasting seed by hand, especially in a small area, but many people find it easier and more accurate to use a spreader. For a small or medium-size lawn, the kind that drops the seed from a hopper as you wheel it along would do fine. For larger areas it's faster to use the barrel-type, which you strap to your chest. As you walk along, cranking the handle in a circular motion, it spins the seed out in broad arcs.

After the seed is sown it will grow even if left alone, but it will grow better if you do something to bring it into closer contact with the soil. If you have a bedding fork like the one shown on page 97, turn it upside down and drag the back of the tines lightly across soil so as to mix the seeds in very lightly—just to the depth of the tines. Dragging a lawn rake lightly across the seeded ground will also work, but be careful not to work the seeds in too deeply or some may not germinate. Don't worry about walking on the new seed; you'll notice that your footprints will be the very places where the seed germinates first! This is because the seed has been put in good contact with moisture in the soil. If you have a lawn roller, rolling the whole seeded area will accomplish this goal beautifully.

Watering is also a good way to work the seed in, as well as helping it to sprout (unless of course you're expecting that perfect rain). Put down a light mulch to keep water runoff from taking the seed with it (especially if the ground is sloping). It's very discouraging to see your carefully sown grass seed collecting in puddles. Weed-free hay, applied thinly enough so that you can see plenty of ground between the stalks, is the best mulch. Don't bother to remove it. When the grass is up you'll never even know the hay is there, and eventually it will rot. If you don't get any rain, keep sprinkling the seed whenever the soil is dry, until it has germinated. After that you can ease off a bit, making sure the new lawn gets at least an inch of rain per week (less for dry-climate grasses).

PUTTING DOWN SOD

Some of the warm-season grasses are best started from sod, and sod is also a good way of starting cool-season grasses as well. The advantages? One is that you get instant lawn. Another is the fact that sod is easy to lay down on a slope—you won't have to worry about seed washing off. Finally, sod is weed-free. Disadvantages are sod's cost and the fact that it is harder work to lay heavy sod strips than to sprinkle light seeds.

Sod usually comes in a big roll and is less than an inch thick when spread out. There is very little soil attached to the grass, so don't make the mistake of thinking you don't have to prepare the soil as deeply for sod as you do for seed. Lower the soil level next to walkways or other hard surfaces so the sod will lie flush with them when it's laid down. Try not to let the sod sit around more than a few days before you plant it, and be sure to keep it moist. Once sod dries out it dies—it cannot be revived with water the way established grass can.

To lay sod, water the ground thoroughly, then cut off blocks of sod in a size you can handle easily, laying them in staggered courses the way you would bricks, making sure the edges are fitted tightly together. Cut pieces to fit along curves and odd-shaped corners. Then water again. Keep the sod well moistened until the roots have taken hold and you can no longer pull up clumps with your hands.

PLANTING PLUGS AND SPRIGS

Some grasses are sold as little plugs of sod or individual bare-root sprigs. These can be planted individually, just as you would any small perennial plants. Set plugs out at the recommended distance apart (the supplier should give you guidance about planting the particular type of grass you have purchased) in a grid pattern or in staggered rows. The plugs will fill in the spaces between them fairly quickly, since most of the grasses planted in this manner are vigorous spreaders. Nevertheless, it's a good idea to sow some annual ryegrass along with them—it will deter weeds while the soil is bare, and the ryegrass will die out or be smothered out by the grass you have planted. Sprigs, which are individual rooted stems, are best planted in furrows, but it may be tedious to plant them this way if you have a very large area. In this case, just scatter the sprigs on the surface, mulch them lightly with a material like shredded bark or straw, and tamp or roll them. Whichever method you use, keep the sprigs watered until they take hold.

Maintaining a Lawn

ONCE YOU HAVE YOUR LAWN PROPerly installed, the amount of work it requires will depend partly on the type of grass you've chosen and its mowing, watering, or fertilization needs. It will also depend on your climate, current weather patterns, and your own personal standards. You may be satisfied with having a serviceable lawn that remains more-or-less green, or you may be fussier, insisting for example that all the green comes from bona-fide lawn grass and not from whatever weeds turn up. Though you will decide yourself just how much time or money you want to put into the lawn, you'll want to keep your priorities in order. The most important job is mowing.

MOWING

For many traditional lawn mixtures, mowing is crucial, and the way you mow it can make a big difference too. Use whatever type of mower suits you (page 113) and follow these general principles:

Mow grasses to the correct height. Each grass has a height at which it does best. Don't cut it too long or too short. Weather can also influence how high you should mow. Cool-season grasses can be mowed on the short side in spring to let the ground warm up but should be mowed higher in hot weather so they'll be less stressed. Mow any grass a bit higher if it is in a shaded spot. Most people tend to mow their lawns too short either because they think it looks tidier or because they think it will take longer to grow back and they won't have to mow it again so soon. Neither is true. Too-short mowing yellows the lawn and gives it a scalped look; and setting it back like that may only encourage it to grow faster, to make up the loss of blade surface. A taller lawn will also shade out weeds better. Unfortunately, many lawn mowers don't even have a high enough setting for most of the cool-season grasses—3 to 4 inches is ideal except in spring, when you want to encourage new, rapid growth by cutting a little shorter. (This also lets in more sunlight to warm the soil.) Even within grass types, mowing needs vary and it pays to follow the directions given on the package.

Mow the lawn regularly. This helps to control weeds by cutting annual weeds' stems before they can go to seed and by restraining the vigor of perennial ones. If you let the grass go too long between mowing, you will not only have a weedy lawn, but it will be hard to cut and may turn brown when you do mow it because you'll be exposing the part of the blade that has been shaded and isn't used to direct sun. Cutting tall grass will also leave heavy piles of clippings that can kill the turf. The rule of thumb is to cut no more than a third of a blade's length. If you have a bluegrass lawn that grows best at 3 inches, for example, you would mow before it got higher than about 4 to 4½ inches. Cutting too short, on the other hand, can keep grass from forming a good root system.

Often we end up mowing our lawns once a week regardless of factors such as these, simply because weekends are the only time we have to mow or because the person you hire to mow the lawn is on a fixed schedule. But if you or your lawn service can be flexible enough to mow more often when the grass is really leaping up (in spring or after a rainy spell), and hold off when it is growing slowly, the lawn will be better off.

Do not cut the grass when it is wet. Wet grass is not only harder to cut, it cuts raggedly.

Avoid mower damage. Be very careful not to bump up against the trunks of shrubs and trees. (Having a mulched area around them instead of grass is a good way to avoid this.) Laying down a brick, wood, or flagstone mowing strip on which to run one wheel of the mower is a handy way to edge flower beds without chopping up valuable plants or their flowers (page 54). But even with these tricks you'll need to use some kind of trimmer on areas that the mower is too large or clumsy to take care of (page 113).

Leave the clippings. It's not necessary to take up lawn clippings unless the grass is very high when you cut it (if it lies there in piles or thick clumps, it can smother the grass beneath). You can, of course, rake clippings up if you're collecting them to use as compost or mulch. But otherwise, just let them decompose and return nutrients to the lawn's soil. Some mowers have a feature or separate attachment that chops up the clippings and shoots them evenly onto the lawn as you mow.

Keep your mower sharp. Dull blades will fray and chew up your lawn. If you mow a lot, you may need to have the mower sharpened several times each season.

Research a mower carefully before you buy it. You want a mower that is easy to use and easy on the environment. At present a number of electric models are being sold. These are definitely quieter, easier to start, and often easier to handle than gas-powered ones. They are less polluting for your home environment, although the source of the electricity is another matter. Those that use rechargeable batteries are an option (you also avoid having to deal with a power cord). Solar-powered models are another. There are also lawn mowers that float on a cushion of air, and hence deal very well with rocks, hard edging materials, and other obstacles.

For small lawns, hand-push mowers do the job perfectly well and give you some healthy exercise at the same time. New models that are more lightweight and manageable make the job quite easy if you keep the mower sharp and don't leave it outdoors where the blades can rust. Some models can't be adjusted to cut high enough, so it's worth seeking out one that does, especially if you live in a transitional area where too-short grass in summer does poorly.

FEEDING

If you've prepared the soil well and chosen a grass that likes your climate, you'll need to feed your lawn only rarely, if at all. Probably more problems are caused by feeding lawns too much, or with the wrong material, or at the wrong time, than by not feeding them at all. Producing too much lush growth by overfeeding can make grass prone to disease and cause a thatch layer to build up (see page 552) because so much plant matter is decomposing. Putting chemical fertilizer on a lawn can burn it, and too-frequent applications can cause harmful salts to build up in the soil because rain and watering can't flush them away quickly enough. Even worse, it can harm the soil organisms, both visible and microscopic, that are so important to soil health. In addition, grass plants that exist on quick-fix fertilizer applications near the soil surface are not encouraged to form deep roots; they are puny plants that need to be fed more often than vigorous ones. Lawns on a regular diet of fast-acting chemical fertilizers can become chemical-dependent. They lack the strong root systems—and the healthy living soil system—to go it alone.

If you've tried to establish a good lawn but it still seems to need a boost from time to time, there are gentler solutions. The best one is to top-dress with compost. I use my own homemade stuff (see page 14) but you can buy it in bags if necessary. Dehydrated cow manure is also a decent substitute. I use a simple sifter that's just a square frame made of 2-inch by 4-inch lumber with a piece of ½-inch hardware cloth stapled to it. It's built to fit the top of my wheelbarrow. I just lay it on the wheelbarrow, put on a pair of thick rubber gloves, and rub the compost so that it falls through the mesh, leaving sticks and stones behind. Then I just fling it over the lawn using a long-handled shovel. Just a dusting does the trick, though I apply it more heavily over bare patches, to help them to regrow. If needed I sprinkle on some seed as well. Over the winter the compost will filter down to the plants' roots, providing a balanced, slow release of nutrients. If needed, you also give the grass an early-spring feeding, just as the grass is ready to start greening up, especially if you're growing warm-season grasses. It's best to do this just before a rain. If your soil is very sandy, nutrients will leach out of it quickly, and despite good soil preparation you may have to feed a bit more often. If you're not sure what your lawn's nutrient requirements are, a yearly soil test before feeding will be helpful. It is better, both for the lawn's health and for the environment, to feed too little than too much.

If you ever feel a quicker green-up is needed, apply a high-nitrogen natural material such as alfalfa meal, blood meal, or fish meal. Sprinkle it on by hand or use a spreader, then water it in well. Compost tea, applied with a sprayer, is also effective.

WATERING

Most of what I've said about feeding lawns applies to watering them as well. If you've built a good lawn with the right grass and plenty of organic matter in the soil, it should survive dry periods. Even if the grass goes dormant and looks brown, there's no need to panic and waste water if it's a scarce resource where you live. The lawn usually revives when wet weather returns.

The most important thing to know about watering is that you should either water deeply or not at all. A shallow sprinkling of water on the surface causes roots to grow toward the surface rather than down deep where you want them to go. It's best to water at the beginning or end the day when less of the water will evaporate, and on a still day when the wind won't cast it astray. Let the sprinkler soak the lawn until there is no gap between the water you have applied and the natural soil moisture level below. Deeper, less frequent waterings will help the lawn to resist disease.

In some parts of the country dry weather may make it very difficult to keep a lawn green. Some gardeners install underground sprinkler systems that do the job. My advice is to choose drought-resistant grasses in preference to laying out fancy irrigation systems. Then try using some of the simpler watering devices described on page 107 before you resort to more expensive measures. If you're watering a lot, you should probably have less lawn. Consider the ground cover options discussed in the following chapter.

DETHATCHING

Thatch is a layer of dead grass parts that forms just above the soil surface of a lawn. It is composed of dead plant debris—chiefly dead stolons and rhizomes by which the grass clumps have spread. There is always a thatch layer in grass, but sometimes it gets too thick and causes problems. Thatch buildup is more common with southern grasses and often results from feeding or watering too much or from mowing too infrequently. If thatch is more than a half-inch thick, it can harbor insect pests and keep water and nutrients from penetrating down to the grass roots. Some grasses are more prone to thatch than others. If your grass has a springy, spongy feel, like carpet with a thick foam-rubber pad under it, and if you're able to see the thatch if you poke down among the grass with your fingers, the thatch is too thick.

Try raking the grass with a heavy metal rake or a dethatching rake. You can pull a lot of it out this way. But if the thatch is too heavy or the lawn too large for this to be practical, rent a dethatching machine, also called a vertical power mower. This machine has tines that dig down into the soil and slice up the thatch. In cool climates you should dethatch in early fall so that you can spread fresh grass seed over the lawn. For warm-climate lawns do it in spring.

LAWN WEEDS

Weeds are not as conspicuous in a lawn as they are in a garden, because they blend into the green. Technically, a lawn weed is anything that is not part of the original grass formulation you planted, although there are usually some extraneous wild grasses and broad-leaved plants in purchased grass seed. Most intruders just appear from seeds already present in the soil, and often weeds are not very noticeable. It is only when a lot of broad-leaved plants or coarse-textured grasses start to intrude that the appearance of the lawn suffers. In the normal course of things, lawn grasses grow so vigorously that they crowd out most weeds. If anything weakens the vigor of your lawn grass, however, broad-leaved plant species may take over. If there are bare patches due to infertile soil, crabgrass will make itself at home. Compacted soil can also encourage weeds. In these cases the best course may be to renovate the lawn as described below, or even to start over again with better soil and new grass, although such drastic measures are seldom needed.

Traditional means of lawn weed control involve the use of herbicides: either preemergent weed killers that keep annual weeds like crabgrass from germinating, or products that kill only broad-leaved plants without harming grasses. I don't use either. Not only are they toxic to people and animals, they are also apt to drift or wash onto other plantings and damage them. As part of commercially prepared combinations of weeding and feeding formulations, herbicides are often applied indiscriminately and excessively. And sometimes herbicides contain unadvertised amounts of nitrogen fertilizer that can lead to unintentional overfeeding. Besides, herbicides don't really address the problem, which is that the grass is not growing strongly enough to resist weeds, which it would normally do.

My approach to lawn weeds is to tolerate many of them, especially those that bloom. Once I was working on someone's perennial garden and took a close look at the adjacent lawn, which the lawn service had abandoned for a week or two. It was starting to look like one of those "flowery meads" that you see in medieval tapestries, where little clumps of flowers are spotted here and there in a sea of green. Perhaps the lawn grasses suffered a tiny bit from such neglect, but I couldn't help but notice that the lawn looked just as pretty as the flower bed I was so carefully constructing. Flowers in the lawn encourage butterflies, bees, and other desirable insects, too.

It might surprise you to learn that the earliest lawns looked very much like that accidental flowering meadow. During the Middle Ages, the castle dwellers of Old Europe would cut squares of sod turf (turves), load them onto wagons and carry them through the castle gates to be laid down as little "plesaunces," or paradise gardens. They provided little pieces of wild nature in an age where it was not always safe (especially for women) to roam about the fields. Many of our lawn weeds, like the grasses themselves, are European imports that came over with European settlers.

Some lawn weeds that bloom nicely in lawns are ajuga, creeping veronica, ground ivy, pussytoes (with furry white leaves), dandelions, coltsfoot, violets, English daisies, and Quaker ladies (also called bluets, these make tiny bluish white masses in springtime)—and there are many more. Most are short enough to escape the mower much of the time, though if there is a fine stand of ajuga sending up bright blue flower spikes in the lawn I will mow around it. Spring bulbs such as scilla and crocuses can be allowed to thrive in spring lawns as well.

Dwarf white clover is another pretty lawn weed; in fact many, myself included, consider it a legitimate component in a lawn seed mix. It is a tenacious, low-growing plant with good green color and small leaves—and as a legume it enriches the soil (see page 13). I've even seen lawns composed entirely of clover. Most flowering lawn weeds bloom early enough that you can enjoy their brief show, then mow for the rest of the season. If you find you like a mix of wildflowers and grasses better than you like a lawn, investigate the prairies and wildflower meadows discussed in the wildflower chapter.

If there are a lot of less interesting weeds in your lawn, however, and if they really detract from its appearance, I would give hand-weeding a try. This may sound like a crazy proposition, especially if your lawn is a large one. But if you just do a section at a time when you have the energy for it, sprinkling some fertilizer and seed as you go to help the grass rebuild, you can make quite a bit of difference over the course of time.

Also keep in mind that regular mowing helps to keep weeds down. It lops off the heads of annual weeds before they can go to seed, and it sets back the growth of some perennial weeds. Few broad-leaved weeds benefit from mowing because they grow at the tips. Grasses, which continually send up new "tiller" stems from the base, remain undaunted.

Lawn Diseases

THERE ARE A NUMBER OF DISEASES that lawn grasses can contract. It is likely that if you establish and maintain the lawn well, none of these will ever appear. The microbes that are naturally present in healthy soil will usually outcompete those that cause problems for grass plants. Also, modern lawn grasses are increasingly resistant, as are most native ones. But here are a few you might conceivably encounter:

Brown patch produces roughly circular patches that are purplish and then turn brown, becoming several feet in diameter. It can plague bent grasses, fescues, and most southern grasses, especially in hot, humid weather, and can be cured by holding back on water and fertilizer and by improving drainage.

Snow mold is a grayish, stringy fungus that lives under the snow and appears as round dead patches in spring. Prevent it by raking leaves off the lawn in fall and avoiding too-late applications of fertilizer in fall. Mow late in the fall, since snow mold breeds in tall grass.

Dollar spot, which afflicts bent grasses, Bermuda grass, and others, causes whitish spots the size of silver dollars. Fight it with watering and applications of compost.

Stripe smut is a systemic disease of Kentucky blue and creeping bent grasses. The lawn will appear thin or patchy. Up close, the blades will show a yellow stripe that turns gray, then sooty black as the fungal spores mature. Holding back on high-nitrogen fertilizer may help. If necessary, replant with varieties that resist the disease.

Melting-out produces purple-bordered spots on grass leaves, which then die. If drainage is poor, try to improve it, and mow higher.

Fairy rings are caused by fungi, sometimes from woody matter such as stumps or pieces of wood buried in the soil. Large dark green circles magically appear on the lawn, often with mushroomlike growths. They are best fought with compost and lots of water, and by aerating the soil to let these penetrate. On the other hand, minor infestations of fairy ring mushrooms are quite charming.

Most lawn diseases are caused by fungi. If you have a truly serious problem, taking a sample to the local Extension Service office will help you identify it and decide on a solution. Apply extra water and fertilizer if this is indicated. However, if you have been feeding or watering *too much*, this may have been the initial cause of your trouble. Cutting the lawn higher or aerating it may help—you could either rent an aerating machine (see below) or spike the lawn with a digging fork as described on page 93.

Your Extension Service can also direct you to varieties that are the least susceptible to whatever plagues your lawn. If the problem recurs often enough you may want to start over with a new lawn, planting a resistant grass, but before you do anything this drastic make sure it really is a disease that is making the lawn unsightly. Insect damage, spilled gasoline or other chemicals, road salt, spilled fertilizer, or the urine of female dogs can all cause dead patches that look like disease symptoms. If you can trace the problem to a spilled toxic substance, flush the spot with water to dilute the harmful agent.

Lawn Pests

A NUMBER OF INSECT PESTS CAN CAUSE problems in lawns, but usually the damage is not serious. If you find damage in irregularly shaped patches and have ruled out chemical spills, look hard and see if you can find and identify the culprit. One of the best things you can do is to encourage birds and other insect-eaters to make themselves at home in your yard. Keep it poison-free and follow some of the pointers in the first chapter.

Grubs are often found in lawns. These are the larvae of beetles such as Japanese beetles and June bugs that live in the soil and feed on grass roots. You can diagnose the problem quickly by the fact that a dried-out patch of grass peels back like a carpet; the reason is that the roots have been severed. You can also see the white grubs themselves, curled up like commas. Milky spore disease, which is introduced through a purchased product, will combat them. (As a side benefit, you'll also reduce the local population of adult Japanese beetles.) But that treatment is expensive and may take a few years to be effective, especially in cool climates. If so you'll have to live with the problem for a while. Water the patches to revive the dry grass and get the roots to regrow.

Sod webworms are caterpillars that gnaw off the blades of bluegrass and drag them into little silk-lined tubes just above the soil surface, where they consume them. This causes small brown spots at first, then larger irregular patches in your lawn. The caterpillars turn into little tan-colored moths, which you can see fluttering above the grass at dusk, laying eggs. The caterpillars themselves can only be found at night, but you can detect their presence from tiny green, pellet-like droppings. Since the caterpillars like hot, dry grass, ample water will sometimes be enough to control them, or at least help the grass, dried out by their chewing, to renew itself.

Chinch bugs, which are tiny black-and-white creatures, live above the soil surface, feeding on the grass and creating irregular brown patches. The bugs themselves are found in the green grass on the edge of these patches. One way to see if you have them is to tap a bottomless coffee can into the soil a few inches, fill it with water, and see if any chinch bugs float to the top. Like sod webworms, they prefer dry grass and can be discouraged by watering, which also helps to restore the damaged grass. Some grasses, such as St. Augustine and zoysia, are bothered more than others by chinch bugs.

Most lawn insects are kept more or less under control by natural predators: the moles that eat grubs, the big-eyed bugs that eat chinch bugs, the birds that peck out the sod webworms. Gardeners and lawn services that dump insecticides on lawns kill these beneficial predators and also kill the earthworms that aerate the lawn's soil and the microorganisms that keep it fertile. Insecticides can also harm household pets. Poisons sprayed in large quantities on your neighbor's lawn can drift over to your place and be a hazard, so using them is best discouraged on a neighborhood basis.

Try to keep your lawn healthy and vigorous, the better to weather these brief insect invasions. If a thick thatch layer is harboring insects, dethatch the lawn. One relatively new development is the marketing of grasses that contain endophytes—fungi that repel insects such as chinch bugs and sod webworms and fight some diseases as well. Some tall fescues and perennial ryegrasses contain them. Though this is generally assumed to be a good thing, endophytes tend to be toxic to livestock, and I cannot accurately foresee what increased use of them will mean for the environment.

Renovating a Lawn

SOMETIMES, DESPITE YOUR BEST EFFORTS, your lawn remains a disappointment. Often this occurs with a lawn that's been inherited from a previous owner who didn't plant the right grass or prepare the soil adequately. If only parts of the lawn have problems you can sometimes just fix those, patching dead spots with clumps of new sod, or cultivating the soil there and reseeding it. Rolling the soil will often help if grass roots have been heaved out of the soil by insects or moles. (See page 72 for more information about moles.)

Sometimes the lawn is compacted and needs to be aerated, although this is not often the case in northern lawns, where the action of frost in winter moves the soil and breaks up hard clumps. But where compaction is a problem you might consider renting an aerator—a machine that rolls over the soil and extracts little cores of earth, which it then deposits on the soil surface. The best approach is to rake these up and use them to fill in low spots, then fill the holes you've made in the lawn by sprinkling on some good compost or other fertile organic material.

If the entire lawn is hopeless, use a tractor or rototiller to till up the whole thing, burying clumps of sod and adding whatever soil amendments are needed. Sod clumps that are lying on the surface should be raked up so that the surface is smooth. Then reseed as you would for a brand-new lawn. If the old grass is a kind that you want to keep from regrowing, strip all of it off or smother it with sheets of black plastic for about a year, or until it is completely dead and can be tilled without chance of regrowth.

CHAPTER 13

Ground Covers

IF YOU'RE AN AVID HIKER YOU KNOW about ground covers because you're so often looking down. Unless the path leads through very dense woods, small plants are doing their best to carpet the soil, protecting it from the erosion of wind and heavy rain, and keeping in the moisture that nourishes larger plants around them as well. Sometimes one species seems to dominate, but usually there's a mixture—a tapestry of leaves in different colors and textures. In a woodland you might find mosses, ferns, and lichens mixed in with low-growing wildflowers and creeping evergreens. Next to the ocean an assortment of gray- or silvery-leaved plants meander about rocks or dunes. On mountaintops, tiny tundra species colonize every crack and crevice between wind-whipped stones. In jungles the greenery, straining upward toward the light, is so thick it bars your way. In meadows and prairies, grasses share the soil with broad-leaved flowering species. With each bend in the trail, the tapestry changes along with the terrain. Whether the soil is dry, moist, rocky, sandy, or hard clay, something is working to cover it. Nature does not like bare earth.

Gardeners also recoil from bare earth, not just because we fear erosion but because we like some say in the matter of what shows up first to colonize the plot. Crabgrass? Poison ivy? Ragweed? Straggly canes of wild raspberries? Not in my backyard. Open spaces that I'd prefer not to fill with a lawn must be planted with something healthy and attractive that can hold its own. This is where ground covers come in. Though famous as problem solvers, many are very beautiful, and are an important element in the design of a harmonious landscape—just as they are in the wild.

Using Ground Covers

THIS VERY BROAD CATEGORY OF plants includes just about anything that will cover ground attractively, quickly, thoroughly, and permanently—without making problems for the gardener. Though usually the lowest plants come to mind, those that inhabit the space beneath shrubs and small trees, it's often low-growing shrubs themselves that play the carpeting role. Those discussed in the shrubs chapter include many suitable ground-cover shrubs—certain cotoneasters, daphnes, and forsythias for example. The creeping junipers described on page 637 are classic ground-cover plants, and there's even a terrific prostrate version of the native sumac called 'Grow-Low' that I've used with great success. In very dry climates such as the southwestern deserts, or even moderately dry ones in the west, the lowest plant layers are often shrubby. Two examples are indigo bush and coyote brush—both included in the List of Ground Covers in this chapter. California fuchsia, also called hummingbird's trumpet (*Epilobium canum latifolium*), is a popular shrubby ground cover on the west coast. There are also numerous ground-covering vines, such as the excellent native woodbine (*Parthenocissus quinquefolia*), which seems as happy creeping across a clearing as it is ascending the bark of a tree.

Among the common herbaceous perennials in the perennials chapter, candytuft, catmint, daylily, hosta, and lady's mantle make fine ground covers, as well as the creeping forms of phlox, veronica, baby's breath, sedum, yarrow, astilbe, geranium, and pinks. Sometimes just massing a single flowering perennial in large drifts works as a ground cover. Natives are especially appropriate, such as black-eyed Susan (*Rudbeckia hirta*, page 206) or the drought-tolerant blackfoot daisy (*Melampodium leucanthemum*, page 701).

Many of the native grasses such as prairie dropseed (*Sporobolus heterolepis*) or little bluestem (*Schizachyrium scoparium*) and the native sedges might be used, as well as spreading ferns such as lady fern (*Athyrium felix-femina*). And some of the very best ground covers for shade are woodland natives described in the wildflowers chapter: bunchberry, bloodroot, golden star, foamflower, May apple, and Solomon's seal. The genus *Vaccinium*, which includes lowbush blueberry and mountain cranberry (*V. vitis-idaea minus*), is full of beautiful native ground covers for acid soil. Native violets such as *Viola labradorica* make a beautiful spring-blooming carpet.

Certain herbs are commonly massed as ground covers too. The prostrate form of rosemary makes a wonderfully tough, drought-tolerant, and fragrant mat—excellent in western gardens. There are even two dainty-seeming herbs that are so resilient, they withstand foot traffic: low-growing Roman chamomile (*Chamaemelum nobile*), as opposed to the taller annual German chamomile (*Matricaria recutita*), can be grown as a lawn, as can creeping thyme, also called mother-of-thyme

(*Thymus serpyllum*). I'm especially fond of woolly thyme as a ground cover (*T. pseudolanuginosus*). Requiring perfect drainage, it can't wait to leave the beds where I've planted it and take up residence in my stone and gravel walkways. There it forms soft gray mats, as rugged as a broadloom rug. (For advice about growing thyme, see page 407.) Mint, a determined spreader, is a good ground cover for a moist spot as long as it doesn't intrude on other plantings.

Even annuals can be easy-care ground covers if they reseed themselves each year. I've kept beds of white alyssum, *Salvia viridis*, Chinese forget-me-not (*Cynoglossum amabile*), and purple perilla going for years just by letting them go to seed—with a bit of thinning as needed.

Most ground covers spread across the ground in order to propagate themselves (though they may also spread by seed as well). Many accomplish this feat by means of modified stems called rhizomes, which venture sideways underground and send up new shoots, or by stolons, which do the same thing but above the soil surface, putting down roots at intervals as they go. Others spread by means of branches that trail along the ground and put down roots along the way. In some cases the plants cover ground simply by being long-stemmed and floppy, like spreading cotoneaster (*Cotoneaster horizontalis*) or a "ground cover" rose like 'Max Graf.' Traditionally, the most popular ground covers have been low growing, perennial, and evergreen. Like grass, these are grown primarily for their foliage, though if a ground cover were to cover itself in blue flowers, as periwinkle does, who could object? And many are so perfect in their proper season that nobody minds if they take a winter break. The trick is finding the right one for the spot.

Designing with Ground Covers

N O MATTER HOW EAGER YOU MIGHT be to get something into that bare ground quickly, it's important to consider the look you want from a ground cover. By its very nature, it's in there for the long haul.

Only the evergreen ground covers like prostrate juniper, periwinkle, or pachysandra look more or less the same all year (and even some junipers have a different winter color). If such consistency is not essential, you have a much wider choice of plants. If the look you want is a flat carpet to set off other plantings, choose a very low growing one such as Irish moss (*Arenaria verna*), creeping thyme, or one of the prostrate sedums. On the other hand, if you'd like a large mass of foliage that will make a more dramatic statement, try the taller yellowroot or a stately stand of ostrich fern (*Matteuccia struthiopteris*). For a very tidy look, in a formal situation, a compact, well-behaved ground cover like wild ginger would be appropriate. In a more natural setting an informal plant like yellowroot is equally suitable.

How you site your ground covers in relation to other plants is important too. One that might be fine in a patch by itself, or weaving through a group of shrubs that can hold their own, might terrorize a collection of weaker perennials. Note that vines, given a chance, will climb, and you must expect them to head upward when they get to trees, shrubs, and smaller plants. (Some may not appreciate the onslaught.) See the chapter on vines for more about the management of them. Some creeping perennials spread so modestly that you can use them in the front of a flower garden with only a small amount of supervision. I've grown snow-in-summer (*Cerastium tomentosum*) this way, as well as creeping thyme, sedum, candytuft, pulmonaria, and many others. These help to keep weeds from sprouting in the front of the bed (which weeds tend to do), and they prevent that bare-earth look that gardens have in spring before other perennials have fully leafed out. I've even used ajuga in the front of a perennial border, idiotic as this may seem. Yes, it continually crept into the rest of the bed (not to mention the lawn that adjoined it). But since it bloomed like a blue river every spring at the same time as the tulips in the bed, and even made an attractive dark-leaved edging over which I could run the wheel of the lawn mower, I was willing to chop off its errant runners several times during the season.

The paradoxical thing about ground covers is that the very thing you plant them for may eventually disqualify them. Just because a plant is spreading and vigorous does not mean it's the one for the job. Goutweed (page 195) is often sold as a ground cover and makes an attractive one, but I think it is much too invasive for any garden. I also rule out Oriental bittersweet and Japanese honeysuckles (including Hall's), wintercreeper (*Euonymus fortunei*), English or Algerian ivy, *Houttuynia cordata*, and most members of the *Polygonum* genus such as fleeceflower. Be very careful that ground covers do not escape into the wild and displace native vegetation that wild creatures rely on. Some people even object to periwinkle, ajuga, lilyturf, and lily-of-the-valley on these grounds, although in most situations the risk is minimal. To ascertain the invasiveness of these or any other plants in your area, consult your local native plant society.

One of the best uses for ground covers is as a unifying theme. Let's say you have a shrub planting that runs across the front of your house. You've put a lot of different plants into it, either because you like variety or because you want to look at something interesting—foliage, flowers, bark, or berries—at different times of year. Planting the same ground cover in front of and around the bases of the shrubs will tie the collection together visually and give it the appearance of a designed border rather than a hodgepodge. The effect will be even better if you carry out the same ground-cover theme in other parts of the yard—around the trees in the lawn, for instance, or along the walk that leads to the front door.

The ground cover you choose might echo the foliage texture or color scheme of the plants it complements. Periwinkle might be grown as a foreground for other broad-leaved evergreens such as rhododendrons and Japanese holly. All have smooth, dark green leaves, though in different sizes—those of the periwinkle fall between the long, narrow leaves of the rhododendrons and the tiny, round ones of the holly. In other situations a contrast might be needed instead. You might combine the rounded leaves of wild ginger, densely crowded in a low carpet, with the lacy fronds of ferns.

Often the ground covers themselves are the whole show: a planting of spiky lilyturf next to a patio, a circle of epimedium beneath a maple, or several ground covers combined, like sweet woodruff, periwinkle, and ajuga mingling together under birches. I'd probably make the lilyturf planting a regular shape, edged neatly on the sides and mulched, whereas the planting under the birches would be more random, seeking its own shape. I might weed out some of one species if it threatened to crowd out the others—or just let them fight it out—but in either case I'd be happy if the planting had a free-form look.

Choosing Ground Covers

THE MOST IMPORTANT DECISION TO make in choosing any plant is whether it will thrive in your particular climate and soil. You would not plant a warm-climate sun lover like indigo bush in a shady Massachusetts yard. Nor would you attempt a woodsy plant like wintergreen in Arizona. Even your own yard has distinct microclimates, and there are ground covers for nearly all of them. In fact these plants, well-sited, excel at growing where fussier ones fail. Here are a few examples to get you started, but the more you can find out about the plant life of your own particular region, the more informed your choices will be.

Shady sites. Many ground covers will grow in shade, whereas most grasses will not. So shade is probably the situation where ground covers are most often used.

Among the shade-tolerant ones described in the List of Ground Covers are ajuga, epimedium, lamium, lily-of-the-valley, pachysandra, paxistima, periwinkle, pulmonaria, sweet woodruff, wild ginger, yellowroot, and wintergreen. But there are many others not on the list including the wild woodland species described on page 695. Do note how much shade the site has, however (see page 25 for different types of shade), and make sure that the light available is enough for the plants you choose. You may have to prune the lower limbs of some trees, since few plants will grow in full shade. Mosses are also splendid as ground covers and can sometimes be encouraged in shaded situations just by keeping the ground free of fallen leaves.

Sunny sites. Some sun-loving or sun-tolerant ground covers described in the List of Ground Covers are bearberry, heather, coyote brush, lilyturf, indigo bush, pussytoes, and yellowroot. But there are many other choices, both shrubby and herbaceous. Sedum, woolly yarrow (*Achillea tomentosa*), mat-forming pinks such as *Dianthus gratianopolitanus*, prairie grasses, creeping thyme, and moss verbena (*Verbena tenuisecta*) are good examples of ground covers that dote on sun.

Dry sites. Some good ground covers for dry places are coyote brush, bearberry, thyme, sedum, pyracantha, lavender cotton (*Santolina chamaecyparissus*), snow-in-summer, indigo bush, St. Johnswort (*Hypericum*), and any of the prostrate junipers. Bear in mind that "dry" is a relative term, however. The dry shade of a Wisconsin woodland bears little relation to a stretch of California high desert.

Moist sites. In moist soils you might try ground covers such as sweet woodruff, bunchberry, yellowroot, heather, sweet fern (*Comptonia peregrina*), wild blue phlox (*Phlox divaricata*), partridge berry (*Mitchella repens*), violets, heather, mint, bog rosemary (*Andromeda polifolia*), and forget-me-not (*Myosotis scorpioides*).

Banks. To keep a steep bank from eroding you need a vigorous ground cover that spreads quickly, with roots that go deep enough to really hold the soil. Bearberry is a good one, as are spreading cotoneaster, heather, sweet fern, 'Grow-Low' sumac, yellowroot, juniper, daylilies (especially the wild *Hemerocallis fulva*), and 'Arnold Dwarf' forsythia. It is best to plant permanent, perennial ground covers on a bank (rather than annuals ones) so that the soil will be held all year long.

Ground covers with bulbs. Ground covers and spring bulbs are a great combination because the foliage of the ground cover helps hide that of the bulbs once they have finished blooming. This is especially true if small bulbs such as crocuses or species tulips are used. But be sure to match the ground cover to the bulb. Pachysandra is so tall and thick that a short bulb like crocus, glory-of-the-snow, or winter aconite would be lost in it, and sweet woodruff is too low growing to hide the large, conspicuous leaves of hyacinths or tulips. Periwinkle looks good with all but the smallest bulbs, and since it is not a dense ground cover it lets enough sun come through to warm the ground beneath. This encourages bulbs to come up early. Ground covers are also excellent in combination with bulbs that bloom with no foliage. Fall-blooming colchicums, for example, look less naked when emerging from a bed of lilyturf than they do when planted all by themselves in mulched ground.

Establishing Ground Covers

FOR PERMANENT GROUND-COVER plantings prepare your soil well to a depth of at least 8 inches (preferably 12), following the general advice given in the first chapter and with the needs of the particular plants in mind. Some herbaceous ground covers are sold bare-root, as bundles of rooted cuttings. If not, it still makes sense to buy them in quantity—say, flats of 50 plants each—to make large plantings more affordable. In cold climates try to plant them in spring, so as to avoid having the roots heaved out of the earth by winter freezing and thawing. If fall planting is necessary, make it as early as possible. I have also found that a shredded-bark mulch several inches thick will help prevent heaving. In climates with hot summers, plant in fall or very early in spring. If you're unable to plant an area of bare soil right away—because of weather, lack of time, or the unavailability of the plants—put down a bark or straw mulch as described on page 58. Bark has the advantage of being without weed seeds, though it is harder to remove at planting time. Nevertheless, it's worth applying it, then raking it aside and putting it back as a permanent mulch after the plants are in.

How closely you space ground covers depends on how impatient you are to have them fill in, how quickly your chosen species is expected to spread, and how many plants you can afford to buy. If you set out periwinkle or pachysandra 6 inches apart, you'll have a nice thick bed within two years. But if a large area is to be planted, you may have to sacrifice patience for economy and space them as far apart as 12 inches, waiting three or four years before your bed has a good, lush growth. (It is said of ground covers such as these, "The first year they sleep, the second year they creep, and the third year they leap.") Most ground-cover shrubs can go between 2 and 3 feet apart—some even more. Plant in staggered rows, with all the plants equidistant from one another. The farther apart you space the plants, the more useful a mulch can be in preventing weeds from filling in the gaps. Interplanting with spring bulbs and annuals can help fill the space and allay your impatience while you're waiting for a ground cover to grow.

If you're planting on a bank, either terrace the slope or form little soil berms that will help the plants retain water. These look just like the water-catching saucers pictured on page 43, except that they're built up only on the downhill side of the plant.

While you're waiting for the planting to fill in, replace mulch as needed and remove any weeds that crop up. In established beds weeding can sometimes be difficult. It may be very hard, for example, to remove weeds with long, creeping roots from plants like pachysandra and lily-of-the-valley, which have that kind of root themselves. Or you might have a bed of junipers so thickly grown that it's almost impossible to dig down and pull up grass that has worked its way into the soil. If there are large weedy patches, sometimes it's necessary to dig them up, extract every bit of weed root, then replant the ground cover you have removed. Grass can be a problem. It pays to keep after it by vigilant weeding, and to clearly separate ground-cover areas from both lawns and wild grassy areas.

Propagating ground covers is usually easy, since they are naturally spreading plants. You can often divide them, layer them, root them from cuttings, or take clumps from a thick bed and transplant them to a spot where you'd like more of the same. More often than not, your best source will be a neighbor with a surplus. "We have a pachysandra *farm*," she'll tell you. "*Please* come and take some." A few ground covers, such as bunchberry, do not transplant well and are best purchased from a nursery that propagates them. *Always* refrain from digging native ground covers you find in the wild.

List of Ground Covers

AJUGA
Ajuga reptans

Description: This fast-spreading plant, sometimes called bugle, is useful because it can take more foot traffic than most ground covers and is hardy to zone 4. Once established, the rosettes of foliage form mats on the ground that are very good at discouraging weeds. Ajuga's handsome leaves are a rich, very dark green that turns to bronze in fall, and they last long past frost. (In zones 8 to 10 the plant is evergreen.) Some varieties such as 'Bronze Beauty' are bronze all season. Others are variegated, such as 'Burgundy Glow,' which is marked with white, purple, and pink. In late spring the plants send up lovely spikes of flowers, about 8 inches tall. Usually they're an intense blue, but you can also find white, purple, and red varieties. For some reason ajuga tends to appear, then disappear in lawns according to a secret program of its own. A related species, *Ajuga pyramidalis*, is attractive but doesn't have the spreading habit.

How to Grow: Plant in sun or shade in any good garden soil, but make sure it is well drained. The plants spread by surface runners and can be easily divided in spring for propagation.

BEARBERRY
Arctostaphylos uva-ursi

Description: This native American plant, also called kinnikinick, can be seen scrambling over sand dunes in seaside areas. Though the stems can be many feet long, they are prostrate, and the plant is only about a foot tall. The stems root as they go and are good for holding the soil on steep banks. They also look terrific hanging over a wall. The attractive 1-inch leaves are evergreen, turning a bronze color in winter. Tiny white, bell-like flowers appear in mid spring, followed by red berries in late summer that stay on the plant a long time, to the delight of the birds (and bears). Hardy in zones 2 to 8, the plant is widely grown on the west coast but will do well in many other areas. 'Point Reyes,' with good dark green foliage, is a popular variety.

How to Grow: Grow bearberry in full sun or part shade. It will do all right in good garden soil but is just as happy if the soil is rocky, sandy, dry, and poor. It does not like to be transplanted and is best purchased as sods, not bare-root. You can also grow it from cuttings or purchase small, nursery-grown plants and establish them while they're young.

COYOTE BRUSH

Baccharis pilularis

Description: This west coast native is part of the mixed shrubby vegetation known as chaparral. It has small, glossy evergreen leaves and spreads in billowy mounds. Because of its tenacious roots, it is effective against erosion on banks and slopes. Selections in the trade include 'Pigeon Point,' which generally grows under 2 feet high, making an attractive, dense cover. 'Twin Peaks' is another popular variety. Plants in this genus bear male and female flowers on separate plants. The females of this particular species bear white, cottony blossoms that are scattered by the wind. Since some regard these as messy, most varieties sold consist only of male plants, whose yellowish flowers stay put.

How to Grow: Coyote brush adapts to a wide range of soils and is salt tolerant,

fire resistant, and deer resistant. Though very drought tolerant, it will do better in most areas if watered deeply at least once a month in summer. Shearing it back in late winter before growth starts will result in thicker, tidier growth. It does best in sun, planted 6 to 10 feet apart. Hardy in zones 8 to 10.

EPIMEDIUM

Epimedium grandiflorum

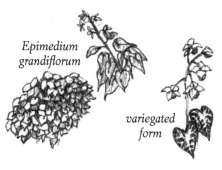

Epimedium grandiflorum

variegated form

Description: Epimedium, also called bishop's hat, is one of my favorite ground covers. It's one of those plants, like maidenhair fern, that looks dainty and delicate but is really as tough as they come—adaptable, easy to grow, and hardy to zone 3. The small spurred flowers are supposed to resemble a bishop's miter, but they look to me like miniature columbines. They come in many different colors, depending on the variety—white, pink, red, yellow, or lavender—and appear in late spring. 'Rose Queen' is a good red, and 'Niveum' has large, showy white flowers. The heart-shaped leaves are pinkish when they first emerge in spring. They overlap in beautiful soft-looking mounds and last even into early winter, after turning a reddish bronze color.

Epimedium grows slowly when first planted, but like the tortoise that beat the hare it slowly and steadily establishes large, vigorous clumps. It will grow well even around the bases of trees, where it is a graceful addition.

How to Grow: Epimedium prefers part shade but will grow in sun if you give it the moist, humusy soil in which it does best. Soil should be well drained and slightly acid. Since it is shallow rooted, try not to cultivate around it, but instead apply a light mulch to control weeds. Divide in spring, preferably while plants are dormant, cutting the tough roots with a knife.

HEATHER

Calluna vulgaris

Description: Heather is one of my favorite plants because of its spiky shape, the subtle variations in its foliage colors, and best of all, its profuse, long-lasting summer bloom. Some varieties bloom for as long as three months, starting in summer and going into mid fall. The plants vary in size but never exceed 2 feet. They bear their flowers along small spikes in shades of pink, red, purple, lavender, or white. The tiny scalelike leaves are evergreen, often with startling colors such as yellow, red, or gray, and it's fun to mix plants of different colors together. In fact, if you design a heather planting with different foliage colors, with each plant having a different winter color as well as flowers of varied colors, you'll have quite a tapestry.

While heather is outstanding in a bed all by itself, it also looks good as the foreground of a shrub border. Some good standard varieties are 'J. H. Hamilton,' a pink; 'County Wicklow,' with double pink flowers and bright green foliage; and 'H. E. Beale,' a double pink that blooms very late. Most heathers are hardy to zone 5.

How to Grow: Plant heather in sun or part shade. It blooms best in sun, but part shade in winter will help it to withstand winter burn. In cold climates lay evergreen boughs over it in winter; these will protect it from sun, wind, and cold, and will also trap the snow in an insulating blanket. In early spring you may still need to prune out winterkilled stems, but don't worry if the plants look beat-up at winter's end. As long as they're still alive, fresh new growth will appear after cutting. Give them acid, moist, well-drained soil, but don't make the soil too rich or the plants will be leggy. Heath (*Erica* species) is closely related and is also a fine plant; it is spring blooming, however, and has needlelike foliage.

INDIGO BUSH

Dalea greggii

Description: There are a number of native *Dalea* species but this one, also called trailing dalea or Gregg's prairie clover, is the one most often used as a ground cover, as it forms a mat about a foot high. Native to the Chihuahuan desert, it is a tough, resilient legume that grows in silvery-blue evergreen mounds—great for covering steep banks and for use in difficult, dry, rocky, or nutrient-poor spots. Its long, wandering stems root at the tips. In spring and early summer it bears tiny, fuzzy purple flowers that are attractive to bees.

How to Grow: Indigo bush is sun loving and very heat and drought tolerant, although occasional deep watering in summer will give it a better appearance and more rapid growth. It also tolerates infertile soil—in fact, both overfeeding and overwatering (especially in winter) will weaken it. The plants look rather modest when purchased but very soon make an attractive carpet. Plant 4 feet apart. Prune back just before spring growth if a harsh winter has killed stems, or if they've become straggly with age. Hardy to zone 8 (and sometimes colder areas, but with winter dieback). Resistant to rabbits.

LAMIUM

Lamium maculatum

Description: Lamium is an excellent ground cover for shade. The common name is often given as spotted dead nettle—far too unappealing a label for this very low growing carpet. Its rounded leaves have a stripe down the middle that can be white, yellow, red, or silver. Lamium is evergreen from zone 6 south and even in zone 5, where I grow it, the foliage persists well into the winter. The erect flower clusters

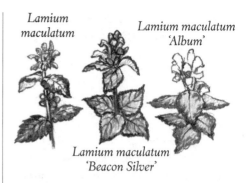

Lamium maculatum

Lamium maculatum 'Album'

Lamium maculatum 'Beacon Silver'

are long blooming, lasting from late spring to midsummer, and can be reddish purple, pink, or white depending on the variety. 'Album' has white flowers and white-marked leaves; 'Beacon Silver' has pink flowers and silvery leaves. The pale-leaved varieties are especially good at lighting up dark spots in a shade garden.

If you set out a little nursery-grown pot of lamium in spring, you'll have a lamium carpet by fall, and the following year you'll be able to give "starter plants" to all your friends. It spreads rapidly by aboveground runners and is hardy to zone 4.

How to Grow: Grow lamium in part or full shade if possible, but if the site is very sunny, make sure the soil has plenty of moisture. Other than that, lamium seems to have no special requirements and is easily propagated by division, cuttings, or seed. If you don't want to open a lamium nursery, and it's crowding other plants, weed some of it out or shear it in midsummer to promote more compact growth.

LILY-OF-THE-VALLEY

Convallaria majalis

Description: Most people recognize the little white, bell-like flowers of this plant.

Even the fragrance is unmistakable. The flowers are indeed beautiful, and naturalized in the right setting lily-of-the-valley is a useful ground cover, but it can be a disappointment in the wrong place. The leaves—two emerge to embrace each flower stalk—are not evergreen but start to turn brown in late summer and cannot be walked on at all. The roots are quite invasive, interfering with the growth of everything else in the plants' vicinity. Find a spot for it all its own. The plants produce orange berries after the flowers, but the berries are not profuse. The variety 'Rosea' is pink. Plants are hardy to zone 3.

How to Grow: Lily-of-the-valley does better in part or full shade than it does in sun, and will tolerate quite deep shade. It likes a fertile, moist soil. Plants can be divided easily for propagation. If your bed is flowering poorly, divide and replant, or donate the excess to your favorite charity. Lily-of-the-valley is a good plant for a Mother's Day fundraiser.

LILYTURF

Liriope

Description: Lilyturf is valued for its evergreen, grasslike leaves and for the blue flower spikes—rather like those of grape hyacinth—that it sends up in late sum-

mer. These are followed by black berries. Big blue lilyturf (*Liriope muscari*) grows to 18 inches, with fairly broad, arching leaves; its flowers can also be lavender, purple, or white depending on the variety. It is clump-forming and an elegant ground cover in areas where it is hardy (to zone 6). Creeping lilyturf (*L. spicata*) is a bit hardier (to zone 5, generally) and shorter (about 10 inches), with narrower leaves and a decidedly creeping growth habit. It spreads by underground rhizomes and bears pale lavender flowers in July and August.

How to Grow: Lilyturf will grow in sun or shade and prefers fertile, moist soil enriched with plenty of organic matter. It dies to the ground in winter in the northern part of its range. If it looks bedraggled at winter's end, mow or cut it to the ground and it will sprout fresh new growth.

PACHYSANDRA

Pachysandra terminalis

Description: Few ground covers make such a thick, dense evergreen bed as pachysandra. It doesn't do its job overnight, but

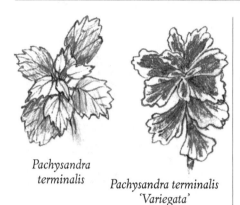

Pachysandra terminalis

Pachysandra terminalis 'Variegata'

just you wait! It is hardy to at least zone 4, and is an excellent solution to the problem of what to plant right around tree trunks where sunlight is scarce and mowing is difficult. It grows up to a foot tall with attractive dark green, tooth-edged leaves arranged in whorls. The white flower spikes in spring are neither numerous nor conspicuous; even less noticeable are the whitish berries that follow. The variety 'Variegata' has white-edged leaves that help to lighten up a dark, shaded area.

How to Grow: Grow pachysandra in full or part shade, but avoid sunny sites. Not only will the leaves yellow in the sun, but grasses will come up among the pachysandra and will be very difficult to eradicate. Any ordinary soil will do, but it should not be too dry and should be on the acid side. Plant pachysandra deeper than it was in the flat, so more roots will form along the stems. It roots very easily from cuttings. If you're planting some you have dug up at a friend's house, and are dismayed by all those long, tangled stems, separate them and tie each one in a loose knot, then plant them. (This makes the long stems easier to handle, and will not deter them from growing roots.) I always mulch newly planted

pachysandra, although once established it won't need mulch because it grows so thickly. If you have problems with leaf and stem blight, which begins with brown blotches on the leaves and spreads to the stems, don't use a heavy mulch, and rake fallen leaves and any diseased plants out of the bed. Euonymus scale is occasionally a problem with pachysandra; it's best dealt with by pruning out infested plants and spraying the others with dormant oil in early spring before growth starts.

PAXISTIMA
Paxistima canbyi (Pachistima canbyi)

Description: Paxistima is a woody shrub that grows along the ground, staying about a foot tall and rooting in the soil as it spreads. The narrow dark green leaves, less than an inch long, are evergreen, turning bronze-colored in fall. Hardy to zone 5, this is an excellent dense ground cover to use in shrub plantings.

How to Grow: Paxistima grows well in sun or shade but may need to be shielded from winter sun in cold areas. It likes a light, rich, acid soil and excellent drainage.

The best way to propagate it is by layering (see page 620), but it can also be grown from cuttings taken in midsummer, and by division.

PERIWINKLE

Vinca minor

Description: Also called myrtle, this popular ground cover, about 6 inches tall, sends out runners over the soil surface that root where they touch ground. The handsome dark green leaves are about an inch long, and the April-blooming flowers a cheerful blue. You can find varieties that are white or purple, but I like the old-fashioned "periwinkle blue" the best. There are also some varieties with variegated leaves. Periwinkle is hardy to at least zone 5.

How to Grow: Grow periwinkle in sun or shade, though some shade is preferable, especially in hot climates. Though it is not fussy about soils and will grow even in poor ones, it prefers soil that is moist and slightly acid. I value it for its rather open growth habit, which allows me to interplant it with spring bulbs, but it can be sheared to promote denser growth. In some gardens it is disease prone; if this is the case, substitute a better ground cover for your area. Do not plant it in areas where its aggressive nature would present a problem.

PULMONARIA

Pulmonaria

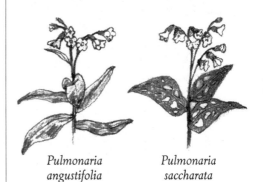

Pulmonaria
angustifolia
'Johnson's Blue'

Pulmonaria
saccharata
'Mrs. Moon'

Description: This plant used to be called lungwort because its spotted leaves resembled diseased lungs and it was reputed to cure lung ailments. Fortunately, the plant has more demonstrable virtues. It spreads vigorously by creeping rhizomes. Its broad leaves make it very attractive as a ground cover, and on top of that it bears beautiful clusters of tube-shaped flowers in spring. These generally open pink and turn to blue, resulting in both pink and blue flowers in the same cluster. *Pulmonaria angustifolia* is low growing (under 10 inches) and has leaves that are not spotted. Popular varieties are 'Johnson's Blue' and the white 'Alba.' *P. saccharata*, called Bethlehem sage, grows as tall as 15 inches. I like the variety 'Mrs. Moon'; both its blue flowers and its spotted leaves are large and showy. If you find you get along well with pulmonarias, there are a number of other, less familiar species worth trying.

How to Grow: Pulmonaria is a truly shade-loving plant and will wilt in sun. Even the morning sun that mine gets makes it wilt in hot weather. Soil need not be rich, but it should be full of organic matter to help it hold moisture. Plants are easily divided in early spring but should be watered well after transplanting.

PUSSYTOES

Antennaria

Description: This charming little plant has a low rosette of silvery-gray leaves from which it sends out stolons, creating a mat only a few inches high. In April, May, or June (depending on the location) stems arise, generally less than a foot tall, bearing little fuzzy upright flower clusters. These do look like a kitten's toes. The genus is widely distributed around the world. The USDA's Natural Resource Conservation Service lists 37 species in this country alone, with names like Rocky Mountain pussytoes, pygmy pussytoes, pinewood pussytoes, and so forth. Most sold in the trade are *Antennaria dioica* (stoloniferous pussytoes) although I have also seen offerings of *A. neglecta* (field pussytoes) and *A. plantaginifolia* (ladies' tobacco). This is a good ground cover for a sunny, dry-ish site with poor, sandy soil. It is highly favored for use among stone outcroppings, on rocky banks, and in rock gardens where drainage is excellent. I've used it in patches surrounding stepping-stones, although the plant itself cannot withstand foot traffic.

How to Grow: Hardy to zone 3, the pussytoes commonly sold do well in most regions, although it is important not to attempt them in moist, rich soil. Patches of it are easily transplanted to new locations as needed.

SWEET WOODRUFF

Asperula odorata (Galium odoratum)

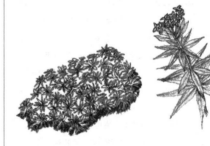

Description: Sweet woodruff carpets the ground with star-shaped whorls of bright green leaves, and blooms in frothy, fragrant white clusters in May and early June. It is the flavoring ingredient in May wine—something you can easily make yourself by steeping a handful of *Asperula odorata* in a good Moselle or Riesling. It can be depended on as a ground cover under trees, even shallow-rooted ones where it is difficult to get most ground covers to grow.

How to Grow: Plant sweet woodruff in part or full shade in fairly moist, well-drained, slightly acid soil. Divide it in early spring or early fall by simply picking up a clump and planting it somewhere else, then watering it well.

WILD GINGER
Asarum

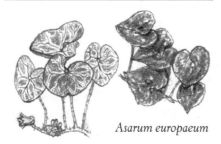

Asarum europaeum

Asarum canadense

Description: This is one of my favorite ground covers for shade, the rounded leaves crowding together in a dense, tidy, elegant mat. (It bears flowers too, but these are hidden by the leaves.) Wild ginger gets its name from the pungent smell and taste of its leaves and roots. One common native species, *Asarum canadense*, is deciduous, hardy to zone 3, and grows up to about 8 inches high. You can also choose from several evergreen species, including British Columbia wild ginger, *A. caudatum* (hardy to zone 4), and European wild ginger, *A. europaeum* (hardy to zone 5). The latter has smaller leaves and is more low growing. There are also a number of other native species, as well as various horticultural selections, some with mottled silvery foliage.

How to Grow: Wild gingers appreciate fertile soil, but the essential ingredients are shade, moisture, and plentiful organic matter. They will tolerate full or part shade. The creeping rootstocks are easily divided and transplanted.

WINTERGREEN
Gaultheria procumbens

Description: This very low growing native plant has shiny evergreen leaves that turn purplish in fall and have a distinctive minty flavor when chewed. It bears little, nodding white bell-shaped flowers in late spring, followed by bright red edible berries in fall, which last into winter. It is an elegant little plant with a fairly open habit, especially good in wooded areas, and is hardy to at least zone 4.

How to Grow: Wintergreen does best in part shade, in moist, acid, humus-rich soil. It spreads by creeping stems and is best transplanted from sods or nursery-grown clumps. Propagate it by division. I find that in areas where it is happy, it's as good as a ground cover gets, but it tends to be fickle, so I would not count on it for large areas.

YELLOWROOT
Xanthorhiza simplicissima

Description: Yellowroot will not bring traffic to a screeching halt if you plant it in your front yard. Its flowers are tiny purplish brown clusters that dangle from slender stems, its leaves a bit like those of astilbe but

larger. Nonetheless, I consider it a beautiful and useful ground cover for an informal setting—especially if you have a fairly large, shaded area you must plant without great expense. Fall color is a beautiful yellow-bronze.

One of yellowroot's great virtues is that it tolerates fairly deep shade. In the wild it chooses a shady, moist spot (such as along a woodland stream) although I have seen it do fine with sun and average soil moisture in areas where summers are cool. A woody shrub about 2 feet tall, it grows wild throughout the eastern United States. Both its common and botanical names are derived from the yellow aromatic roots. It provides cover and seeds for small mammals and birds.

How to Grow: Yellowroot prefers an acid, fertile soil. It will need watering in dry weather if sited in a sunny, dry location. Plants spaced 4 feet apart will spread by suckers and fill in rapidly to create a leafy mass. It can be planted as an understory for larger shrubs and the taller, more assertive ferns, but most herbaceous competitors will be crowded out.

CHAPTER 14

Vines

VINES ARE A LITTLE LIKE WILLFUL children. They set forth with a great sense of purpose, determined to climb as fast as possible into the light-filled air above them, using anything they can to help themselves up and often taking up more space than you want to give them. But watch a vine when it finds no means of support: the growing shoot just hangs in midair, looking disappointed, and then falls to the ground, ready to try again. For all their ambition, vines often need attentive guidance from the gardener, who helps and directs them in their climb and restrains them at the same time.

Working with vines can be fun if you understand their habits and know some attractive ways to use them in the landscape. And yet the reasons that gardeners plant vines often sound rather negative, because they frequently begin with a problem. A building has a bare, ugly wall—let a vine cover it. The house next door is an obtrusive presence—build a fence covered with vines that will hide it. A terrace is too hot to sit on in summer—build an arbor so that a dense vine can shade it. But there are many positive reasons to grow vines, too. Many have attractive leaves or flowers. Some bear fruit. And their twining, clinging, or reaching growth habits make them a good visual contrast with the other plants around them. Some vines in the garden are "working vines," and some are displayed for their beauty alone. Most can be functional and ornamental at the same time.

Some vines are truly low-maintenance plants that will go their own way with a minimum of nurturing and discipline; others you must fuss over. But all of them must be chosen carefully and placed carefully. Most troubles with vines come from using the wrong vine for a given spot. Some highly invasive ones are best not planted at all (see the box on page 577).

Vines are not a distinct, homogeneous category of plant. Some are annual, and some perennial. Some are herbaceous (soft stemmed), and others are woody. Some are hardy; others are tender. Some are vigorous and fast growing; others are more restrained. Vines also differ in the ways they climb. In fact, the only thing that all vines have in common is that they have long but weak stems that must be supported, either by your efforts, theirs, or a combination of the two.

Types of Vines

VINES ARE GENERALLY DIVIDED INTO groups according to their primary method of climbing.

VINES THAT TWINE

Some vines grow by twining their stems around an object, preferably a vertical one. In the wild their support is most often a tree; in your garden it could be a tree, a pillar, a fence post, a downspout, or anything small in diameter (a silo, for instance, would be too thick for a twining vine) yet sturdy enough to support the vine's weight. What support you provide will depend on the type of vine and the way it behaves in your climate. (See the individual descriptions in the List of Vines.) Wisteria is a typical twining vine.

A vine starts to twine when it touches an object. Sensitive tissues respond by producing cells faster on one side of the vine than the other, so that it bends as

INVASIVE VINES

Not all aggressive vines are considered threats to ecosystems, but many vines are among the plants that have spread beyond gardens in destructive ways. Here is a partial list of those known to be invasive, and the regions where they have caused the most concern so far. Check your own state's invasive plant lists to see which apply. Sometimes growing the plant in a container (if it does not go to seed) or as an indoor plant is a good compromise.

Asparagus vine (*Asparagus asparagoides*). California and Hawaii.

Bittersweet (*Celastrus orbiculatus*). Eastern United States.

English ivy (*Hedera helix*). Much of the United States, especially the northwest.

Five-leaved akebia (*Akebia quinata*). Eastern United States.

Japanese climbing fern (*Lygodium japonicum*). Southern states.

Japanese (or Hall's) honeysuckle (*Lonicera japonica*). Eastern United States. Substitute the native species noted on page 589.

Jasmine. A number of species have escaped into the wild in the southern United States, especially Florida. Brazilian jasmine (*Jasminum fluminense*) and Gold Coast jasmine (*J. dichotomum*), which seriously threaten woodlands, are the worst offenders. Carolina jasmine (*Gelsemium sempervirens*) makes a nice substitute.

Kudzu (*Pueraria lobata*). Southern United States but creeping northward.

Mile-a-minute (*Polygonum perfoliatum*). Chiefly mid-Atlantic states.

Morning glory (*Ipomoea purpurea*). This and a number of related *Ipomoea* species are proving invasive in a number of regions; it is best to check and see if yours is one of them.

Porcelain berry (*Ampelopsis brevipedunculata*). Eastern United States.

Silver lace vine (*Polygonum aubertii*). Mid-Atlantic and southern states.

Winter creeper (*Euonymus fortunei*). Eastern United States.

Wisteria, Chinese and Japanese (*Wisteria sinensis, W. floribunda*). Many regions. Substitute native wisterias.

Wood rose (*Merremia tuberosa*). Not a true rose. Southern Florida, Hawaii.

it grows and continues to bend round and round the object. Just as people are right- or left-handed, so are twining vines, which you will hear described as twining "from right to left" and "from left to right." I find this terminology confusing, since the direction of twist is different depending on where you stand when you view the plant. I prefer "clockwise" and "counterclockwise" to describe vines' twists. These directions are easy to see when you look at a honeysuckle, which goes clockwise, and a bittersweet, which goes counterclockwise. Sometimes the direction varies even within a given genus—some wisterias, for example, twine one way, and some the other. The only reason you'd ever need to know which way a vine twines is so you avoid trying to direct it the wrong way. But as soon as it starts up its support, you'll be able to tell and thus cooperate with it.

VINES THAT CLING WITH TENDRILS

These vines sometimes twine, but their chief means of support is little threads that grow out from the stem and wrap themselves around something. Sometimes tendrils are actually leaf stems. Examples of vines with tendrils are clematis and grape. When the vine touches an object, it produces these tendrils very quickly, but the object must be thin enough for the tendrils to wind around. Wire mesh or wooden lattice are both satisfactory supports for tendril vines, as long as they're strong enough to hold them up. A clematis will do fine on a piece of chicken wire, but a grape vine needs a strong wooden or metal trellis or arbor. In the wild, vines wrap their tendrils around the branches of other vegetation.

VINES THAT CLING WITH HOLDFASTS

Some vines, when they touch an object, can quickly produce appendages that will adhere to it. The two chief kinds are aerial rootlets, which are short, hairlike projections from the sides of the stem, and adhesive disks, which are little round plates at the ends of thin tendrils. The rootlets work by burrowing into even the tiniest fissures in the surface they're climbing, and the disks work by suction. Both devices enable vines to climb flat vertical surfaces, which would foil a twining vine or one with tendrils since they offer nothing for the vine or its tendrils to wrap around. In the wild, the support might be a tree trunk or a rock. In cultivation, a wall of brick, stone, or any kind of masonry can provide a support. Ivy is an example of a vine with aerial rootlets. Virginia creeper has adhesive disks.

VINES WITHOUT SUPPORTS

Technically, perhaps, the plants in this category are not vines, but they are grown like vines. They have long, arching branches or canes that grow up through the stouter branches of other plants and are thereby supported. Some, such as the climbing roses described in the rose chapter, have thorns that help them hook onto other plants; others just rely on the dense branching patterns of the shrubs and trees with which they keep company. The climbing jasmines are examples of this type. In the garden, vines without natural support must be given considerable assistance if you want them to grow upright—usually by tying them to something.

Landscaping with Vines

With these distinctions in mind, let's look at some of the vines that are available and the ways in which they can be used.

VINES ON FENCES

The most common request I hear for vines is from people with a fence they want to cover. Usually the fence is a necessary evil: the one the law requires you build around the swimming pool; the one that keeps children or animals in—or out of—a designated area; the property boundary that separates your yard from the yard next door. Often there's quite a bit of fence, and the gardener might be tempted to plant rather rampant vines that will cover it quickly. This is fine if the fence is a very sturdy one and can support a big, heavy vine, but many are not. And extra-vigorous vines can sometimes present more problems than they solve. I think it's best to plant ornamental vines that you especially like looking at. Even if they don't hide the fence entirely, they'll soften its visual impact. Let's say you have a split-rail fence around your pool with wire mesh attached to it. If you plant clematis, climbing roses, and hyacinth beans along it they won't totally disguise the fence, but your eye will be drawn to pretty flowers and foliage, not to the wire.

Let's say your neighbor has erected a tall wooden stockade fence on the property line. You hate the way it looks. It looms massively, as if you lived inside a fort. But if you plant the right vines, it will seem as if the fence were there just to display them. Even a tendril vine like clematis can be grown on it if you hang some heavy-duty black plastic mesh for it to cling to. Chicken wire, rusted to a natural nonshiny color, also makes a good vine support for a flat surface. For a heavier vine like trumpet vine, it's better to string lengths of heavy-gauge single-strand wire horizontally, and encourage the vine to climb from one to the next. Stems of leaning climbers like roses or hardy kiwi can be tucked between the wire and the wood. It is not, however, a good idea to grow vines that cling with rootlets or disks on wood fences. They injure the wood both by penetrating it and by keeping it too moist, causing it to rot. And you can never paint or repair a fence with a clinging vine on it.

A chain-link fence is one that you might want to cover entirely with vegetation, and fortunately this is easy to do. Plant big vines such as Dutchman's pipe on it, thereby turning it into a hedge. Whatever the vines' own means of support, you can guide them through the openings in the mesh or tie them to it, even if they don't do it themselves.

VINES ON BUILDINGS

A vine and a building can have a good relationship or a bad one—it's a matter of choosing the right vine. If it's a good match, the vine will profit not only from the building's support but also from its warmth, which will cause the vine to grow rapidly and perhaps survive the winter in a zone in which it is only borderline hardy. In return the vine will not only lend beauty to the wall, but often cool it in summer and even lend a bit of winter insulation of its own.

Some Ways to Support Vines

FIG. 67

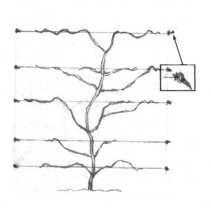

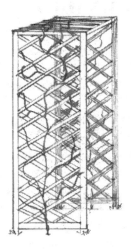

fishing line strung on screw eyes
attached to a wall

preassembled lath trellis nailed to a
wooden frame to make an arbor

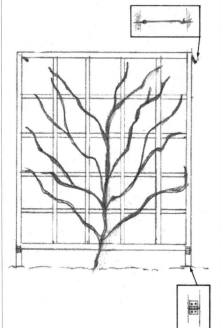

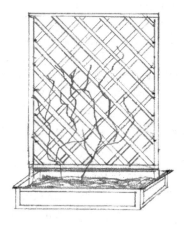

hinged trellis attached to a wall,
secured at the top by latches and
screw eyes

lath trellis nailed to a frame
attached to a planter

If the vines and buildings are badly matched, however, the vines can do real damage. Vines that cling with disks or rootlets (and sometimes even vines with tendrils) are unsuitable for wooden buildings for the same reason they're unsuitable for wooden fences. They can rot or pry off wooden shingles and clapboards. They can also damage vinyl or aluminum siding, wood shingles, and even masonry if the mortar is loose or crumbly. Such vines are often grown on masonry structures, however, including brick, stone, concrete, and stucco, and they will usually support themselves completely. Ivy on stone and brick buildings has become an established tradition, but watch out for window frames, shutters, and shingles, which these vines can damage. You might have to get up on a ladder from time to time and cut away parts of the vine that look like they mean mischief, and you'd need to provide wire supports if the surface is smooth and the vine very heavy.

If you have a wooden house but a large masonry chimney from the ground up, it could support a clinging vine such as climbing hydrangea, but again, keep it off the wood. People sometimes try to hide a large expanse of ugly concrete foundation with a clinging evergreen vine such as *Euonymus fortunei*, but it's a nuisance to have to clip it off continually when it reaches the siding. With freestanding masonry walls that are not part of a building, this is less of a problem. Even a tumbledown stone wall is a fine place for a vine.

You can grow twining vines on wood or masonry buildings, but you need to provide them with something to twine around. If the vine is a light one—a morning glory, for example, or a soft-stemmed clematis—you can tie horizontal lengths of transparent fishing line to screw eyes in the area you want the vine to climb. For heavier vines such as passionflower you can use copper wire, which will quickly weather to an unobtrusive green. For very heavy vines such as wisteria or trumpet vine, you'll need a stout wooden trellis. It is wise to position the trellis a foot or so out from the wall so that there's space for air to circulate. For walls that will need to be painted, make your support removable. The hinged trellis shown in Figure 67 is one solution.

VINES ON TREES

Vines are usually thought to be bad for trees. Often this is indeed the case. Heavy, large-leaved vines such as grape can cut off the light from a tree and kill it. Even soft little vines like ground ivy—a common weed—can creep into a specimen shrub and, by depriving some branches of light, distort its shape. But properly chosen and properly pruned, vines can enhance the appearance of trees that support them.

For example, a climbing hydrangea will cling to the trunk and gradually climb up into the tree without harming it. By growing a lightweight flowering vine such as a clematis or climbing rose on a small tree or shrub and letting it twine through the branches, you can add color at a season when the tree is a merely a green background. This will only work if the branches are open enough to give the vine sufficient sunlight to grow and bloom.

Just use common sense in your choices. Don't introduce a vine onto a tree if the tree, or its trunk, is better appreciated without the vine. I wouldn't let a vine hide the trunk of a white-barked birch or let one climb through the lacy foliage of a threadleaf Japanese maple. Sometimes a dead tree provides an appropriate support for a vine. I like to leave snags such as these for owls, woodpeckers, and other inhabitants. A Virginia creeper vine would look beautiful encircling its trunk and branches.

VINES GROWN ON SPECIAL STRUCTURES

While it may often be handy to use a free-standing support that is already in place, like a fence, a house, or a tree, very often the most sensible solution is to grow a vine on a support that you build for it and tailor to its particular needs. Ready-made decorative trellises for light vines such as morning glory are available in hardware stores and garden centers. You can also buy sections of lath or lattice trellis—thin wooden slats nailed together in a grid or diamond pattern—and nail them to supports that you provide. Lumberyards often sell such panels, but they're often too flimsy to support a substantial woody vine. For these you'll need to build, or have built, a sturdier support.

Vines can be grown on freestanding pillars sunk in the ground with crosspieces at the top, or on a series of posts connected with horizontal beams, wires, or chains that the vines then clothe. Arbors are more common, however. These are overhead structures that you can walk or sit beneath, the way you would a series of spreading branches (the word "arbor," after all, means "tree"). Some arbors are simple arches with a vine growing over them, and are especially beautiful at transition points in the yard—over a doorway, or the point where a path leads to the entrance of a garden, for example. These can be either round, flat, or pointed at the top. In other cases the arbor

is extended to form a pergola—originally a vine-covered passageway that linked one building with another, but now often a freestanding construction. In other instances the arbor projects from a building, creating a shaded outdoor room. Sometimes these are built with a series of connecting metal pipes; more commonly they are built of wood. It's important that they be solidly constructed and well anchored in the ground. I, for one, would not tackle the job of building an arbor or pergola but would hire a carpenter to do it. It is difficult to repair or shore up a failing arbor once it has become a leafy bower.

Arbors are a good way to support, display, and enjoy large vines, especially fragrant flowering ones. Sitting on a terrace under an arbor and smelling roses or jasmine is very pleasant indeed. You might add some annual vines to the mix as well, trying some different ones each year. The List of Vines in this chapter includes several, such as hyacinth bean and Allegheny vine—and there are many more you could grow, such as black-eyed Susan vine (*Thunbergia alata*), cup-and-saucer vine (*Cobaea scandens*), trailing snapdragon (*Asarina scandens*), and canary bird vine (*Tropaeolum peregrinum*). Besides beans, there are other vining food plants such as tomatoes, cucumbers, melons, and squash that could grow up the sides of such a structure, planted either in containers or in the ground. Decorative gourds are also a delight grown on an arbor.

A vine-covered terrace is a delightful place to sit on a hot day, and if it's next to a house wall, the vine will help to cool the house as well. If shade is the main goal, the best vines to use are those with large leaves or dense foliage that will block the light in summer, but that lose their leaves in winter to admit light and warmth. Grapes and Dutchman's pipe, described below, are good choices. The lovely pink-flowered *Bougainvillea spectabilis* is a popular choice in zones 9 and 10. The hop vine (*Humulus lupulus*) is also an attractive shade vine and is the larval food for the comma (or hop merchant) butterfly.

VINES ON THE GROUND

Many vines will scramble over the ground just as readily as they will climb. Virginia creeper is one you can use in an informal setting. Prairie rose (*Rosa setigera*) is another choice. See the chapter on ground covers for more information on this subject.

VINES IN CONTAINERS

You might not think of vines as good plants to grow in containers, but this is actually a very good way to grow ones that you fear may overstep their bounds. There are many ways to do this effectively. Smaller vines such as morning glory and the other annual vines are nice in hanging baskets. Many of the small-leaved "houseplant" ivies such as bird's-foot look good this way too, cascading out of, say, a hanging wire basket lined with sphagnum moss. You can also grow a vine in a large pot that's placed next to a support for it to climb. This is especially handy for plantings near the house where there are only paved surfaces and no earth. You can even erect a vine support that's part of the container itself, such as the wooden trellis attached to the wooden planter shown in Figure 67. Or set vine-filled planters on top of a wall and let the vines cascade down from there. Or build a double wooden fence that has soil-filled boxes set into the top, and have vines spill out of those.

Growing Vines

HOW TO PLANT, GROW, AND MAINTAIN specific vines is discussed under the individual entries in the List of Vines. The important thing to understand in general is that you can have control over what the vine does.

SUPERVISING GROWTH

Even though different vines grow at different rates, you can influence the growth rate of a vine to some degree. If you want it to grow in a hurry, dig plenty of compost or well-rotted manure into the general planting area, together with rock powders such as rock phosphate, greensand, and lime as needed; then top-dress regularly with a fish/seaweed fertilizer. If you'd rather the vine grew more slowly, go easy on the fertility and use peat to lighten the soil rather than a rich substance like manure. Feed it only the amount it needs to stay healthy and grow at a rate that suits you.

You can also influence growth by the way you prune a vine. Though there's no single way to prune all the various vines, it is a general rule that pruning in late winter or early spring will stimulate more growth than summer or fall pruning will. If you have a rampant vine that you're trying to control, prune it late in the season and make sure you thin out whole branches rather than just hacking away at the tips. Pruning large vines is a lot easier if you keep doing it each year instead of waiting until the thing is such a tangled mess that you want to cut it all down in disgust. This may sometimes be necessary, and even fruitful. Vines that are cut way back—in order to allow a building or porch to be painted, for example—often regenerate beautifully.

TRAINING VINES

Though all of the true vines will go their own way, given the right support, you often need to direct them, either to make them go a certain direction or because you're training them on a support that is not the one they would normally choose—for example, a twining vine grown on a flat wall. Training will almost always be necessary with vines that merely reach or arch upward without their own means of support. You will often need to tie vines to their supports, either permanently or until they use their own means to attach themselves. Even then you may sometimes have to anchor them if they become very heavy and look as if they might fall.

You can tie lightweight vines, or vines you are merely guiding temporarily, to their supports with soft twine, twist-ties, or whatever might be handy. Even a loop of masking tape will work if the need for its help is brief. With large vines it's best to use pieces of strong, plastic-coated wire. Again, never tie or staple a vine in a way that will constrict or girdle the stem as it becomes larger, because this can kill the stem. If a tie is a permanent one, make it large enough to accommodate the stem as it grows. Tie vines loosely in a figure eight, as with the tomato vine shown on page 377.

GOOD VINES GONE BAD

When growing vines it's important to be attentive; watch what the vine is doing, and be consistent in your attention to it. If you've picked the right vine, put it in the right place, given it the right support, and kept it pruned and tied, it should be fine.

But if you've chosen a vine that is too vigorous for the spot, you may well have created a monster—one that will be hard to banish. Even if kept pruned, some vines have aggressive root systems. I've seen people struggle with Asian wisteria vines, for example, whose underground offshoots keep coming up in flower beds and shrub plantings. Or ivy that clings to a house like a demon lover. Although I like hardy kiwi vines, I've learned that I can't plant them near my crab apples or hawthorns or other prized specimens; the vines persistently ascend into the branches, compromising both the appearance and the vigor of the trees. With some other vines, birds scatter the seeds. This is how poison ivy—that deadly native beauty—gets around. If you scan the common names of vines it's easy to read them as a tale of botanical mischief—bindweed, stickywilly, devil's gut, bushkiller, mile-a-minute, wood vamp, strangler fig. Many invasive plants overcompete simply by usurping space (and light, moisture, and nutrients) that other plants need, but vines often take the additional step of wrestling them to the ground.

When vines move from aggressive to invasive, they do far worse things than inconveniencing gardeners. Imports from other countries (or even different regions of our own), given relief from factors that might otherwise keep them in check, can invade and disrupt local ecosystems, preventing native plants from growing and thereby removing resources on which local wildlife depends. The classic example is kudzu. Imported to this country from Japan as a way of controlling erosion on slopes, this rampant vine escaped into the wild and now blankets a good part of the southeastern United States with its wide leaves and is steadily moving northward. Driving through Georgia you can see trees that rise up like prehistoric animals, totally smothered by kudzu. My Louisiana grandfather used to tell me that when you sit on a porch covered with kudzu, you can actually *hear* it growing. The problem is that kudzu was introduced into a climate where it did too well. And there are many others that pose just as great a threat. I've seen the same tree-smothering performance along the parkways near New York City, only this time it was porcelain berry. In other areas I've seen silver lace vine misbehaving almost as badly. Some vines, like the Asian wisterias, have the ability to roam underground and penetrate the interior of forests, emerging wherever a clearing allows the penetration of sunlight. The list of invasive vines on page 577 contains some of especially ill repute, but the problematic ones are too numerous to list here, and a vine that is fine in one part of the country might pose a threat in others. (A good example is American bittersweet, *Celastrus scandens*, which can be benign in cold climates but a tree strangler in warm ones.) With others the environmental impact has yet to be determined. I strongly advise you to check with your local native plant society or Extension Service before planting any vine.

List of Vines

THE FOLLOWING LIST INCLUDES some of the more popular vines, plus a few that are less well known. Most are perennial, a few are annual. Most are hardy in the north, a few only in warm or tropical climates. Because vines vary so much in their growth habits, depending on where they're growing and in what type of soil, I have not, in most cases, given the growth rate or the ultimate height of the vines described.

Seeds for annual vines can be obtained from local sources or through catalogs that sell seeds for annual flowers. Woody vines can be ordered from mail-order nurseries, but many are also available locally. For fruiting vines such as grapes, melons, and blackberries see the fruit chapter; for vegetable vines such as cucumbers see the vegetable chapter; for climbing roses see the rose chapter.

ALLEGHENY VINE

Adlumia fungosa

Description: If you don't recognize the name of this vine, perhaps you've heard it called mountain fringe or climbing fumitory. But most likely you've never encountered it at all, as I had not until about 15 years ago when a friend gave me some seeds. What a delightful surprise! A few dainty seedlings sprouted at the foot of a clematis, and the following year were making their way through the clematis's established scaffold, clinging to it with tendrils. The ferny, fringelike leaves and the tiny pale pink flowers (a bit like bleeding hearts) were a nice contrast with the clematis's large white blooms in summertime. As the stems elongated, more flowers kept appearing at the tips, a process that continued until frost!

How to Grow: My plants succeeded thanks to a moist, partially shaded location. They are biennials, happy to drop their seeds and come up in the same spot each year. Since this is a plant of mountain forests, it is happy climbing up through trees. The trees do fine, too, as this is a gentle vine, albeit a determined one. Rocky clearings are also a good setting. Allegheny vine is endangered in some states, and you'll do a good deed by saving its seeds and scattering them in suitable places. Give it moist, fertile soil and protection from wind. It grows wild from Maine down to North Carolina and west to Illinois, preferring areas with fairly cool summers.

CLEMATIS
Clematis

large-flowered
double clematis

large-flowered
clematis

seed head

Clematis paniculata

*Clematis
tangutica*

Description: This vine is cherished for its wonderful, long-blooming flowers and its manageable habit of growth. As if that were not enough, the flowers are followed by lovely plumed seed heads that are decorative in themselves. The leaf stalks, used as tendrils, twine around everything they can, and very rapidly—if you set two potted clematises next to each other, watch out! They will soon look like one clematis. In most species the vines never become very heavy.

There are many different clematis species, and their hybrids, in cultivation. Most are hardy to zones 4 or 5. They are generally divided into two categories, large-flowered and small-flowered. All can be grown on trellises, arbors, fences, and other common vine supports, but supports for the larger woody ones must be strong.

Large-flowered clematises have flowers up to a foot across in extreme cases, but usually 5 to 8 inches. *Clematis* × *jackmanii* is an old favorite, a vigorous climber with profuse purple flowers, and there are clematis hybrids of other colors—pink, lavender, mauve, purple, blue, bright crimson, deep maroon, white. Some have bicolored markings. Peak bloom is usually in June or July, with scattered blooms until fall. *C. lanuginosa* hybrids include the red 'Crimson King,' white 'Henryi' and 'Candida,' and lavender-blue 'Ramona.' *C. patens* 'Nelly Moser' is mauve with pink stripes.

Many of the small-flowered clematises are large woody vines. *C. montana* has little white, starlike flowers in late spring or early summer; the variety *C. m.* var. *rubens* has purple flowers. *C. tangutica* bears little yellow, bell-like flowers in June and thereafter. *C. texensis*, a splendid American native, has little red bells in June and thereafter. The fragrant *C. paniculata* (sweet autumn clematis) has small white, starlike flowers that appear in late summer and fall. *C. virginiana* (virgin's bower) is a very vigorous and hardy native with similar blossoms in late summer; it's best grown in a spot where it will not encroach upon other garden plants.

How to Grow: Clematis likes sun but will tolerate partial shade and prefers it in warm zones. The soil should be a light, slightly alkaline loam with plenty of moisture but very good drainage. The plants like to have their roots cool. To ensure this, gardeners sometimes put flagstones or pebbles on top of the soil around the plant. A mulch will also help, but if it's an acid one like shredded bark, add lime to the soil. In order to keep clematis roots cool, you may allow them to crawl under tree roots as long as these are not the tree's feeder roots, which would compete with the vine for food and water. Remember, too, that the rest of the plant must be able to grow quickly into the light and not be shaded by the tree.

Clematis is transplanted in early spring in most climates (those grown in containers can go in later if necessary). In mild climates fall planting is possible. Dig a hole at least 1 foot deep and 1½ feet wide, and work in plenty of materials that will lighten and enrich the soil. A good combination (depending on your soil analysis) might be a shovelful of rotted manure, a shovelful of peat, and a handful each of bone meal and lime. Plant with the crown 2 inches below the soil surface (it will form roots); water when you plant and when growth starts. Then have a little patience—the plants can be slow to establish and may not bloom for several years. Some gardeners cut clematis back for a year or two to prevent bloom and let the plant work on its root system. It's a good idea to feed young plants liquid fertilizer every six weeks or so while they're growing, and established plants can be top-dressed with compost in early spring and in fall. Some clematis die back to the ground in cool climates, so don't assume your plant has gone to clematis heaven just because you can't see it in spring. Before long you'll see fresh, little light green shoots.

The rules for pruning clematis are confusing to gardeners, because they tell you to prune different species in different ways even though you cannot always tell which species a variety belongs to. Often the seller does not know, and your clematis may be a hybrid of more than one species. The basic rule is: clematises that bloom on new

wood (stems formed during the present growing season) are pruned in early spring before growth starts; those that bloom on old wood (the previous year's growth) are pruned just after flowering. (Usually it is the early-flowering ones that bloom on old wood.) Try to notice whether your clematis is blooming on new or old wood and prune accordingly. If on new, just cut back in early spring to promote fresh growth (unless of course the plant has died back to the ground); if on old, prune after bloom as needed to keep the plant the size you want it or to promote new growth.

The one troublesome thing about clematis is a fungus disease called clematis wilt, which can turn your beautiful vine into a string of blackened, dead foliage almost overnight. There's not much you can do about it, although some people feel events like these are really the result of rough handling of the rather fragile vines. If you see rotted stems at ground level, it is too late to do anything. Sometimes one upper stem will die; if so you can try pruning it out below the blackened area. If the plant succumbs, it might be best not to grow another clematis in the same spot.

Buy two-year-old plants that have been grown on their own roots, not grafted. New ones are easily propagated from stem cuttings.

DUTCHMAN'S PIPE
Aristolochia macrophylla (A. durior)

Description: I can think of few plants better able to create cooling shade than this one. Its leaves, borne on a stout, woody trunk and branches, overlap to form a dark green blanket. No wonder it's such a popu-

Lonicera sempervirens

lar vine for arbors and porches. Because it is deciduous, there is no canopy to block the welcome sun in wintertime. Native to the Appalachian region, it is nonetheless very hardy and grows well even in northern New England. Its name derives from the quaint flowers that really do resemble the curved bowl of an old-fashioned pipe. Pipevine, another of its common names, is echoed by that of the pipevine swallowtail butterfly—a lovely creature whose caterpillars feed on this vine. There are other *Aristolochia* species native to various parts of the country.

How to Grow: Dutchman's pipe is a trouble-free vine that is also quite shade tolerant. It climbs by twining. Give it fertile soil and cut it back if it gets messy or overgrown. Don't worry about removing flowering shoots. The flowers hide under the leaves and are all but invisible.

HONEYSUCKLE

Lonicera

Description: One of my childhood memories is sitting with my sisters under a huge honeysuckle vine at my grandpar-

ents' Pennsylvania home, sucking the nectar out of the ends of the gold-and-white blossoms. It wasn't till long afterward that I realized that not all honeysuckles were vines, that just as many of them were shrubs, and that among the vining ones not all of them grew as lushly as that childhood bower. With the wisdom of adulthood, I came to understand this as a blessing. The Japanese honeysuckle my grandparents grew is now recognized as a highly invasive plant, and gardeners are strongly advised not to plant it. (Some of the shrub honeysuckles fall into forbidden territory as well.) Fortunately, there are several native honeysuckles that can be grown without offense. Though they lack the fragrance of the invasive kind, they are superior in other ways.

My favorite is the native trumpet honeysuckle (*Lonicera sempervirens*), hardy to zone 4, which bears bright red-orange flowers continuously from early summer until as late as December, even in Maine! I have never grown a more long-blooming plant. Like many plants with tubular red flowers it is pollinated by hummingbirds, which can reach down inside to extract the nectar. I once grew this vine so that it encircled a large window. From a window seat inside the house you could watch the birds feeding, inches away. It is a vigorous twining vine. Goldflame honeysuckle (*L.* × *heckrottii*), also hardy and long blooming, has flowers that are combination of yellow and coral-pink. Both these vines are gorgeous and semievergreen. They are quite vigorous, but if supported they do not send out runners along the ground or under it—nor do they seem to go to seed. Other native honeysuckles include yellow honeysuckle (*L. flava*), orange honeysuckle (*L. ciliosa*), and limber honeysuckle (*L. dioica*).

How to Grow: Honeysuckle vines will grow in most soils, and in sun or shade, but they bloom best in full sun and in soil that is fairly moist. Don't feed them unless your soil is truly deficient, since they are vigorous without much encouragement. I prune mine heavily in early spring, cutting about a third of the older stems back to the base. Sometimes I have to do a bit more pruning later in summer if the vine has made too many shoots and some refuse to stay on the trellis. Though mine have never had disease problems, it's wise to give the plants plenty of air circulation as a precaution.

HYACINTH BEAN

Lablab purpurea (Dolichos lablab)

Description: This fabulous vine is an herbaceous perennial in its native Africa and southern Asia, but is generally grown here as an annual because it is not cold hardy. Technically it is edible, and in fact the seed, pods, flowers, leaves, and roots are all eaten by people in some parts of the world, as well as fed to livestock. But I have never heard anything enticing about its flavor, and it is

said to make you ill if you eat too much of it. When the seeds are cooked they are boiled in several changes of water. Raw seeds should never be eaten. I grow hyacinth bean for its sprays of stunning bright lavender flowers, followed by reddish purple pods. Even the attractive leaves have a slight purplish hue. There's also a white-flowered, green-podded type. The plant looks beautiful on an arbor—perhaps combined with a more permanent vine such as a rose or clematis. Hummingbirds, butterflies, and bees are among its devotees.

Some of the more usual edible beans make fine decorative vines as well. I love the look of yellow- or purple-podded snap beans dangling from their vines. The 'Scarlet Runner' bean is the edible landscaping plant par excellence, with its brilliant red flowers, irresistible to hummingbirds. Its seeds make fine eating.

How to Grow: Nothing could be simpler to grow than a climbing bean. When the earth has warmed and the chance of frost has passed, sow the seeds in any soil of moderately high fertility. Keep the bed moist while the vine is getting established. Most beans need watering in dry weather, but hyacinth bean is quite drought resistant. Though sun loving, it can take some shade. As annual vines go it is quite vigorous and needs a sturdy support.

HYDRANGEA
Hydrangea petiolaris

Description: Hydrangea is another plant most people think of as a shrub, not a vine, and most hydrangeas are indeed shrubs. But this climbing form from the Far East is an excellent vine that ought to be more widely grown. Hardy to zone 4, it clings by aerial rootlets, is excellent on a masonry wall, and will even grow on a large tree without doing the tree harm. (It will harm the wall of a wooden building, however.) Make sure you give it a strong, permanent support. The plant is quite slow growing and may not bloom for as much as five years after planting, but once established it is a large, woody vine with beautiful, large white flower clusters in June, and handsome dark green foliage and peeling reddish bark that is attractive in winter. Even the withered flowers, which persist, are pretty. I like it on a fence, or spilling over a stone wall. If you have a pile of rocks you want to hide—rocks that are scarred from blasting, for example—climbing hydrangea is a beautiful way to cover them.

An American native vine also called climbing hydrangea is also well worth

growing. It is *Decumaria barbara*, also called wood vamp. A southern plant, it is hardy in much of New England. Faster-growing than the Asian species, its fluffy white flowers are less showy, and it is valued primarily for its attractive glossy leaves and its covering power.

How to Grow: Grow in full sun or part shade in rich, moist, well-drained soil that is a bit on the acid side. Feed and water until the vine is well established. You may never need to prune this plant if it is well sited, but errant branches can be cut back as needed in midsummer. If a plant must be removed from its support it can be cut back severely in early spring and will grow anew. Layering is the easiest way to propagate this hydrangea, but it can also be grown from seed.

PASSIONFLOWER
Passiflora

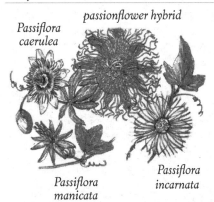

passionflower hybrid

Passiflora caerulea

Passiflora manicata

Passiflora incarnata

Description: Passionflower (also called passion vine) is a lovely plant. Most species are tropical, with dramatic, long-blooming flowers, many of them fragrant. These are typically a broad, flat circle of pointed petals with a raised, fringed corolla in the center.

Projecting from that are showy reproductive parts that later become oval, lemon-like fruits. Some of these fruits are edible. Colors vary widely. All cling by tendrils.

Blue passionflower (*Passiflora caerulea*) can actually be blue, pink, purple, or white with a purple center. Its hybrids produce flowers over 4 inches across that bloom most of the summer. There are many passionflowers to choose from; two of the red-flowered ones are *P. manicata* and *P. coccinea*. The hardiest passionflower is the native maypop (*P. incarnata*), which grows as far north as zone 7 and has a 2-inch lavender or white flower with a purple corolla.

In warm climates passionflowers provide shade in an attractive way when grown on trellises, arbors, or fences. In cool climates they are grown indoors.

How to Grow: Give passionflowers full sun and light, moist but well-drained soil. They will tolerate considerable heat, given sufficient water, and are bothered by few pests. Pruned back fairly hard in fall or winter, they will then bloom profusely on new wood. (They sometimes die back in winter on their own.) To grow indoors, cut back hard in winter and keep dormant but slightly moist, with no fertilizer. Feed and water in late winter to produce fresh growth. Plants may be propagated by division, from seed, or from cuttings rooted in moist sand.

SWEET PEA
Lathyrus odoratus

Description: This gem of a garden plant will win you over if you like old-fashioned flowers, especially fragrant ones. Though of Mediterranean origin, they were brought

to great horticultural heights in early-twentieth-century England and continue to be very popular there to this day. For a time, breeding seemed to sacrifice bigger, showier petals at the expense of scent, but it is now quite easy to find collections in which fragrance is emphasized. Colors range from white to deepest maroon, with shades of pink, lavender, purple, blue, and red in between. More recently, bicolors and colors in the yellow range have been developed (although the yellow ones, thus far, lack the intense fragrance). Usually sold as mixtures, you can order individual colors from nurseries that make them a specialty.

As vines go, this is a very manageable one. Nine feet seems to be about tops for its height, and 6 to 8 more usual. Sweet peas climb rapidly by means of tendrils, just like any pea or bean. As with edible peas, there are also bush types if your goal is to produce flowers for cutting, not to clothe a trellis, fence, or wall. Take note: sweet peas are not edible.

Modern varieties have a number of flowers clustered on slender stems. They make exquisite small bouquets. Do not confuse this species with the perennial

Lathyrus latifolius. I've found it to be quite rampant, spreading by underground stems and hard to eradicate when well established. But many gardeners consider it a joy to grow in the right spot. Its flower clusters are a handsome mixture of light pink, bright pink, and white florets.

How to Grow: Sweet peas will not grow in hot weather. If you live in a warm part of the country, sow them in late fall and let them make slow growth until winter just starts to break. They will then give you several months of bloom. In cooler climates sow them in early spring, as soon as the soil can be worked. It is simplest to sow them directly in the ground, but starting them indoors in small pots will ensure uniform germination. Space the plants about 8 inches apart, with a support already in place if they are the climbing type. Planting a row on each side of a free-standing trellis is a good way to grow a lot of them for cutting. They like a fertile, moist soil, and it's important to keep them watered during dry spells (a mulch will help keep the bed moist), but overwatering should be avoided. The only serious chore involved in growing sweet peas is keeping them picked. If you stop, they will cease bloom and make seeds. Even withered flowers should be continually removed. For this task, upright vines are easier than bush plants, since you don't have to stoop.

TRUMPET VINE

Campsis radicans

Description: The native trumpet vine is a perfect example of a hummingbird plant. Its red-orange, 2- to 3-inch, trumpet-

trumpet vine

'Madam Galen'

shaped flowers, which bloom in mid July, have evolved along with the long, slender bill of the hummingbird, which pollinates them. Even the color is a signal that attracts this bird. The vine clings with aerial rootlets and is very large and heavy. Even if you have a massive masonry chimney for it to grow on, you might need to wire it for additional support, and make sure the roots do not cling to the house if it is made of wood. An easier place to grow it would be on a very sturdy arbor or over a rock pile. (If you do not have a suitable spot and want a good hummingbird vine, grow the smaller trumpet honeysuckle instead.) The hybrid *Campsis radicans* × *tagliabuana* 'Madam Galen' has especially showy flowers.

Another American native vine called crossvine (*Bignonia capreolata* or *Anisostichus capreolatus*) bears similar red-orange trumpets in spring and is also a beautiful, useful vine. The variety 'Tangerine Beauty' is widely available in commerce. Both trumpet vine and crossvine are too rampant for small spaces but very rewarding in the right spot, and are hardy in most parts of the country.

How to Grow: Grow trumpet vine in full sun in moderately fertile, moist, well-drained soil. Prune it on top in winter or early spring as needed to lighten it and improve its appearance, especially if it is very heavy on top. You don't want the flowers—and the hummingbirds—to be too high for you to see, and top-pruning will encourage new bottom growth. Propagate by layering, by removing and replanting suckers, from stem cuttings, or from seed.

VIRGINIA CREEPER

Parthenocissus quinquefolia

Description: The Latin word *quinquefolia* means "five-leaved"—an important thing to know about Virginia creeper (what you see are actually five leaflets that make up one whole leaf). When I was a child the only way I could tell Virginia creeper from poison ivy, which it closely resembles, was to count these leaflets—if there were only three it was poison ivy. ("Leaflets three, let it be.") Virginia creeper, also called woodbine, is relatively lightweight for a vine that can grow to 50 feet, and it is very attractive

on a wall, fence, or terrace. (Avoid planting it on wooden buildings.) It would be one of my first choices if I wanted to view the wall behind a vine, since its growth is rather open. It also makes a good deciduous ground cover. The leaves turn bright red in fall, and the plant bears small blue-black berries. It clings with disk-tipped tendrils, is native to the eastern United States, and is hardy to zones 3 to 4.

How to Grow: Woodbine grows well in a loam of average fertility, lightened with humus (in the wild it chooses woodland soil). It will tolerate either sun or light shade. Plant in spring or fall. Prune only to keep it within the space allotted to it. Propagate from stem cuttings.

WISTERIA

Wisteria frutescens, W. macrostachys

Description: Mention wisteria to most people and they think of the Chinese wisteria (*Wisteria sinensis*) or the Japanese one (*W. floribunda*). They picture long purple flower clusters dangling from an arbor, exuding perfume and romance. Lovely as these are, they present so many problems that they are rarely a good garden choice.

Even in regions where they don't penetrate forests and smother trees, they have a rampant growth that can be impossible to control. And they often, frustratingly, refuse to bloom, even when the vines appear healthy—all *too* healthy. Better to try one of the native species instead, found in many parts of the eastern United States. Kentucky wisteria (*W. macrostachys*) is the one most like the Asian species. Though it lacks the delicious fragrance, it is less aggressive and does have lovely, dangling purple flower clusters. American wisteria (*W. frutescens*), which is easier to find in the trade, has flower clusters that are more upright and globe-shaped. Both are twining vines that bloom in late spring after the foliage appears, and are hardy as far north as Massachusetts. The cultivar 'Blue Moon,' developed by Rice Creek Gardens in Minnesota, is hardier still. 'Carol Mack' is a white-flowered cultivar of Kentucky wisteria.

How to Grow: Native wisterias will grow well in partial shade but need full sun to flower. Give them a strong support and a spot where air can circulate, but keep them away from strong wind. Young plants should have a deeply dug soil lightened with humus, then be fed, watered, and tied to their support for a few years until well established. In future years, prune out errant branches whenever they get in the way, removing main stems in winter as needed to control the shape. Remove any suckers that grow up at the base of the plant. Begin by purchasing a plant from a nursery, or by taking cuttings from a friend's vine.

CHAPTER 15

Shrubs

IF YOU'VE EVER BEEN CHEERED BY the sight of a forsythia in full bloom or been greeted by the fragrance of a lilac at the entrance to a house, you know what a few well-placed shrubs can do for a landscape. But you may not know their full potential, and how many different kinds of shrubs gardeners have at their disposal beyond the usual favorites.

No garden plants are grown as universally as shrubs except perhaps lawn grasses, and none are grown with so little imagination, not only in the choice of shrubs but in the way they are used. Shrubs have come to be something you are *supposed* to have—marching across the front of your house like Snow White's dwarves, clipped into the classic shapes: the Muffin, the Golf Ball, the Chicken Croquette. They are such unobtrusive fixtures in the landscape that often you only "see" them after someone cuts them down, just as with supermarket music you only "hear" when somebody turns it off to make an announcement. That's a pity, because shrubs are too versatile and too beautiful to be taken for granted.

A shrub is, generally speaking, a woody plant that is smaller than a tree—usually less than 15 feet tall—with more than one stem. Some shrubs can be grown as trees (that is, with one trunk), and some trees are shrublike (that is, grown with several trunks). Sometimes extremely short, ground-hugging plants are described as shrublike or as subshrubs, because they have more or less woody stems that do not die back each year in wintertime.

Shrubs vary not only in their size and habits of growth but in many other ways, too. Some are deciduous, losing their leaves in winter or, in some climates, during the dry season, while others are evergreen. Of the evergreen shrubs, some have needles (these are often short versions of plants that normally grow as trees), and still more, like rhododendron, have broad leaves. Many shrubs are grown for their flowers, some for their berries. Some shrubs have a particularly lovely shape, or their leaves have an interesting color or texture. Many have leaves that turn bright hues in fall in regions where cool nights bring good fall coloration. One of the pleasures of growing shrubs is finding ways to combine the different variations so that they complement one another. They are also an important class of plants for wildlife, who often depend on their fruits, foliage, buds, or twigs for food, and on their branches for nesting and cover. In the woods shrubs form the understory beneath the trees and above the herbaceous ground covers. In arid climates, they are often the main plant group in the ecosystem.

Ways to Use Shrubs

THE LIST OF SHRUBS BEGINNING ON page 621 describes some of the many shrubs appropriate for home landscapes and will give you some ideas about which to grow. If the choice seems overwhelming, try pinpointing what you want from a shrub—the things you would like it to accomplish in the location you have in mind for it, what times of the year its appearance is especially important, whether showy flowers or fruits are a requirement, and any other wishes you have.

FOUNDATION PLANTINGS AND ENTRIES

You don't *have* to install a foundation planting just because every other house on the block has one. True, they do have their uses. If the house foundation is made of an unattractive material or is very high, a shrub planting can camouflage it. Perhaps the house simply needs some plants growing along the base to anchor it to the ground visually and give it solidity. In cold, windy areas shrubs near the house can provide insulation, especially on the side of prevailing winds. In hot climates they can lend cooling shade. But these plantings can often be too much of a good thing, oppressing the house both visually and physically, excluding too much light and fostering mildew and other ills. If so, the same protective, enhancing features described above can be provided a little farther from the structure. And finally, the foundation planting is all too often a cliché, put there without much thought because we think it's expected.

Visually, I find the idea of an entry planting more interesting. A group of plants that defines an entrance to a house (it could be a side or rear entrance as well as the front one) gives the house a welcoming appearance. The planting is a foretaste of hospitality to come and should be chosen as carefully as the carpet on the floor and the flowers on the table. It should reflect your own taste, and it can be as interesting as you want it to be.

The plan shown in Figure 68 is just one example. Two things make it different from entry plantings you usually see. First, the planting does not hug the foundation, but rather its main focus is farther out from the house. Instead of just admiring a planted facade as you approach,

you have the feeling of walking through a small garden. Second, instead of the usual needle evergreens, such as yews, junipers, and sheared hemlocks, I've used primarily deciduous shrubs. I can understand why people often stick to evergreens in climates where other trees lose their leaves in wintertime. They feel that somehow this makes the landscape seem less "dead" in winter. And evergreens used well can certainly contribute winter interest to the landscape. However, evergreens pruned into formal shapes can produce the opposite effect—they seem more like sculpture or furnishings than living things. And they are high-maintenance as well, since they require frequent shearing. Sometimes formal, clipped topiary is quite appropriate, but it depends on your personal taste and the style of your home.

Whichever plants you select, it's important that they be the right size for the spot. By this I don't mean the size they were when you bought them at the nursery. Many of those adorable little fuzzy bushes will someday be giants. It's important to note the ultimate height and width of any shrub you buy (if the tag doesn't tell you, ask a salesperson), and especially important for those sited near the house. The most common landscaping mistake people make is to plant shrubs and trees that outgrow their setting, turning their home into Sleeping Beauty's castle—obstructed and darkened by greenery. The plants are constantly being hacked back to a reasonable height and breadth, rather than being allowed to express their natural form. Often people just give up, yank them all out, and start over again every ten years.

The house in Figure 68 is entered by way of a winding path with plantings on

Plan for an Entry Planting (24' long) FIG. 68

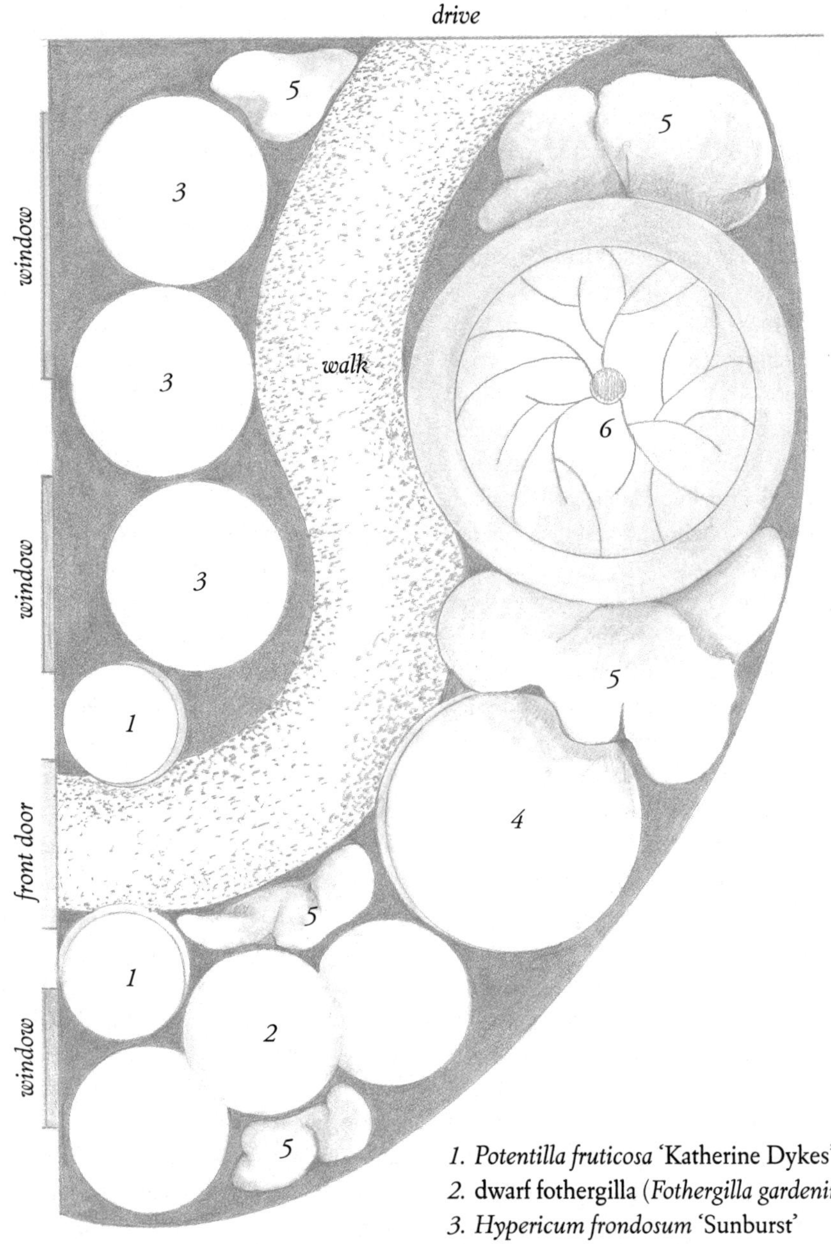

drive

window

window

walk

window

front door

window

6

5

5

5

5

5

3

3

3

1

1

2

4

1. *Potentilla fruticosa* 'Katherine Dykes'
2. dwarf fothergilla (*Fothergilla gardenii*)
3. *Hypericum frondosum* 'Sunburst'
4. *Viburnum* 'Mohawk'
5. *Juniperus horizontalis* 'Bar Harbor'
6. birch tree

either side, none of which will hide the house from view or block its windows. To your left you pass a multistemmed birch that, though ultimately tall, has an open pattern of leaves and branches and will eventually cast a bit of filtered shade. Its white bark has year-round interest. Of the shrubs specified, only the 'Mohawk' viburnum is likely to exceed 3 or 4 feet tall. (See the List of Shrubs for individual descriptions.) All of them flower in spring or summer and the viburnum's intense fragrance is a good way to welcome a visitor. The low-growing fothergillas give an excellent fall foliage display. I've indicated low creeping junipers as a ground cover to tie the composition together. Heather or lavender—which also have year-round color—would work as well, if your climate is not too severe. All of the plants were chosen for a sunny location. If your house entrance is partly shaded, you'd want to find a substitute for the hypericums and junipers, and you'd want to consider all the wonderful broad-leaved evergreens at your disposal such as mountain andromedas, dwarf evergreen azaleas, and the many fine low rhododendrons such as *Rhododendron impeditum*. Broadleaf evergreen ground covers such as paxistima or periwinkle would be appropriate. Gardeners in arid climates, or very warm ones, will want to make appropriate substitutions.

Included in the List of Shrubs are a number with low, compact growth habits that might also be appropriate to an entry planting. Naturally, if you're not planting shrubs next to a building with windows you'd be free to use larger specimens. My feeling is that if a shrub like forsythia can't become the great weeping fountain that nature intended, there's no point in growing it. It won't flower as well if you keep chopping it back, anyway. Usually the best way to deal with a forsythia, or any large shrub, is to set it apart, surrounded by lawn or next to a windowless garage where it can have your undivided attention. Shrubs of varying sizes can also be combined in a shrub border.

SHRUB BORDERS

A shrub border is a planting that displays a group of shrubs in a harmonious way. Often it borders a lawn, terrace, parking area, or some other landscape feature, and it can be used as a hedge to create privacy or seclusion. But it is meant to be beautiful in itself, just the way a flower border is. Designing a shrub border is in some ways like designing the perennial gardens described in the perennial chapter, because you're orchestrating heights, flower colors, foliage, plant shapes, and blooming periods. But now you're dealing with larger—and generally fewer—plants. As with herbaceous perennials, you might strive for a border that is in its full glory during a particular season—usually spring, when most shrubs bloom. Or you might try to stretch the border's interest over the seasons by using late-blooming shrubs, those with colorful fall foliage, evergreens, and shrubs with winter berries. If you do this you'll never have the whole border in bloom at once, but since each shrub presents a large color mass that can stand alone visually, it won't matter. In fact, a fine shrub border can be built around plants with no conspicuous flowers at all, just graceful shapes and beautiful leaves.

The plan shown on page 602 is for a shrub border planted for all-season interest, from the witch hazel blossoms in late

Plan for a Shrub Border (50' by 12')

Fig. 69

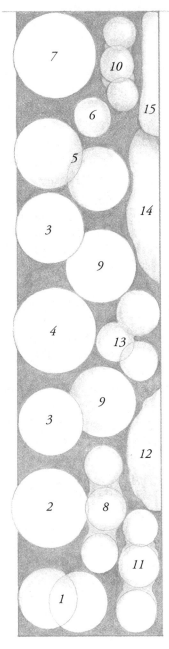

front of bed

1. oakleaf hydrangea (*Hydrangea quercifolia*)

2. vernal witch hazel (*Hamamelis vernalis*)

3. Hinoki false cypress (*Chamaecyparis obtusa*)

4. double-file viburnum (*Viburnum plicatum tomentosum*)

5. winterberry, female variety (*Ilex verticillata*)

6. winterberry, male variety

7. American cranberrybush (*Viburnum trilobum*)

8. Oregon grape (*Mahonia aquifolium*)

9. roseshell azalea (*Rhododendron prinophyllum*)

10. *Spiraea* × *bumalda* 'Anthony Waterer'

11. *Caryopteris* × *clandonensis*

12. heather (*Calluna vulgaris*)

13. *Potentilla fruticosa* 'Katherine Dykes'

14. catmint (*Nepeta* × *faassenii*)

15. lavender

winter to the red fruits of winterberry and American cranberrybush that are showy through fall and beyond. Spring-flowering shrubs include viburnums and roseshell azalea, followed by heather, catmint, lavender, potentilla, 'Anthony Waterer' spirea, caryopteris, and oakleaf hydrangea. The latter has excellent fall color. Burgundy-leaved mahonia, the winter hues of heather foliage, the gray-green leaves of potentilla, and the dark evergreen needles of Hinoki cypress are also part of the tapestry.

To plant this collection you'd need a space 50 feet long and 12 feet wide. It's important that the plants have room to spread out as well as up. To some extent they can mingle their branches with those of their neighbors and still look attractive, but you do need to give each one room for its branches and roots to grow without too much competition. (Even so, you will have to monitor them as time goes by, removing suckers from the base of one plant or trimming off errant branches from another.)

I've found that the best way to plan a border such as this one is to make a list of the shrubs you like along with their heights, widths, and best seasonal features. Using graph paper, draw a plan (see pages 78 and 83 for advice), placing the tallest shrubs in the rear of the bed and the more compact ones in front. Foreground areas might be tied together by using just one species, such as heather or the creeping junipers in the entry plan (Figure 68). A mixture of different heathers would also produce a pleasing effect. Here I've also added some shrubby perennials (catmint and lavender) that contribute long-lasting summer color. For more about catmint see page 204; for more about lavender see page 399. For the rest, see the List of Shrubs in this chapter.

Obviously there are many plants you might include in a border like this, and you'd probably want to incorporate special favorites. If fragrance is important to you, shrubs like mock orange, lilac, and daphne could be included. I've tried to exclude anything that might become enormous, so that none would monopolize the whole bed, but plants perform differently in different climates. Oakleaf hydrangea, for example, may stay quite small in cold zones, even dying back to the ground. Southern gardeners have choices not available to northern zones, such as nandina, oleander, camellia, and the tender daphnes. Gardeners in California and the southwest might substitute natives such as carpenteria, fremontia, apache plume, and toyon, as well as some rugged ground covers described in the ground cover chapter. If the site is a shaded or partly shaded one, you have the opportunity to introduce broad-leaved evergreens such as inkberry, rhododendrons, and andromeda (*Pieris* species).

MIXED BORDERS

In the wild, shrubs usually don't grow in shrub-only plantings except in certain ecosystems like scrub, chaparral, mountaintops, and rugged seacoasts. Normally they have trees above them and smaller herbaceous plants at their feet. A mixed border mimics this composition. Even though it may seem like the normal course of things, it's not always an easy project for the gardener—albeit a fascinating one. To transform the border described above into a mixed one, for example, you might introduce some small trees such as shadblow, redbud, or dogwood, then weave some patches of self-sufficient perennials in the foreground—rudbeckias, tall sedums, and liatris for instance. Tall ornamental grasses would be effective as well. This makes for a rich mix of colors and textures, with even more contrast than you'd find when shrubs, trees, or perennials are planted alone.

SHRUBS IN ROCK GARDENS

Many shrubs, especially the smaller ones, are excellent rock-garden plants. The best are those like junipers and potentilla, which don't need a great deal of moisture or deep, rich soil. The dwarf conifers (evergreens with needles) are particularly appropriate, not only because of their small size, but because of the variety of their foliage colors and textures. Some of them are described in this chapter under false cypress and juniper, but there are also dwarf spruces, firs, arborvitae, hemlocks, and pines. The important thing is to make sure the shrubs you buy are really dwarf. Whoever sells you the plant should be able to tell you how tall it will ultimately grow and how quickly.

If you have a large rock garden, with either big boulders or extensive natural rock outcroppings, you can use larger specimen plants—a full-size azalea or Sargent's weeping hemlock for example. But in a garden of modest size with smaller rocks, look for spreading and creeping plants such as junipers, cotoneasters, and some of the dwarf azaleas and rhododendrons. Plant them so they'll flow around the rocks or cascade over them from a spot above.

HEDGES

Hedges can serve many purposes, often all at once. A hedge can give you privacy so that you won't have to look at the neighbors' yard, or they at yours. The same hedge can minimize noise and be a barrier against wind and even sun. A tall hedge can help to shade people and herbaceous plants in summer or protect broad-leaved evergreens in winter. It can keep out roving pets and children, and even, if thorny enough, be a deterrent to burglars. It can also define a space in a number of ways. An impenetrable hedge might say, "This is my space—keep out," but a hedge with an enticing opening in it might say, "There is a secret world in here—come in and take a peek." It might be a frame or a backdrop for a garden, statue, seat, or some other special feature, in which case it might say, "Now, may I present—the rose garden!"

Hedges can be formal or informal. We all know what a formal hedge looks like. It is closely sheared to a uniform width and height or even shaped to a specific geometric figure (such as a squared-off rectangle or a triangular wedge). Certain short-needled evergreens such as yew, and small-leaved shrubs like box, both of which put out dense twiggy growth when sheared, lend themselves best to this type of hedge. But don't use shrubs valued for their showy flowers, such as forsythia, weigela, or spirea, in a formal hedge because as you shear you will constantly be cutting off flower buds. Make these into informal hedges instead. An informal hedge can be a row of a single type of plant, such as spirea, or a mixture like the shrub border in Figure 69. For even more casual hedges, see the section on hedgerows, below.

Hedges come in all sizes and shapes. The tallest ones are simply a row of trees planted fairly close together and left unpruned; they might be pine, spruce, hemlock, or arborvitae. These serve well as windbreaks, and make a dramatic statement in the landscape. Trees that take well to shearing, such as hemlock, beech, and yew, are often planted as clipped hedges, as can shrubs like Japanese holly, box, and privet but they require an immense amount of upkeep, and it is often more practical to plant a shrub that will reach the desired height and width and stay that way, with no effort on your part. One with an upright growth habit such as enkianthus is useful when a narrow hedge is needed. If more space is available you can choose a more billowy plant such as viburnum or spirea. Clethra makes a wonderful informal hedge that rarely gets more than 6 feet high. For a low hedge you might try hypericum or potentilla. Tiny edgings for formal gardens can be created with low shrubs like germander (*Teucrium chamaedrys*) or lavender cotton (*Santolina chamaecyparissus*). For information about pruning hedges, see page 616.

HEDGEROWS

If you really like informality, grow a hedgerow, which is simply a long thicket bordering a field or yard and containing a number of shrubby plants growing together. Trees and herbaceous plants are often included. The idea is something like a "mixed border" composed of perennials, bulbs, and shrubs, but there is more serendipity involved. Traditionally hedgerows divided one field from another and kept wandering livestock out or in. Most of the European landscape once consisted of fields divided by hedgerows. Now the consolidation of farms has made them an increasing rarity, and there is a strong movement to restore or reinstate them. They were once rich centers of biological diversity. Wildflowers sprouted there at will, with the attendant insects that pollinated them or fed from

their nectar. Small animals made their homes in these thickets, which were also prime habitat for birds who nested and fed there, especially if the shrubs bore fruits and berries.

Hedgerows definitely have a place in the home landscape. Sometimes too informal for a front yard in an urban setting, they're perfect in a backyard or side yard where it's fine for the landscape to be more natural. How casually you maintain a hedgerow is a matter of preference. I try to exclude brambles and poison ivy, establish native ground covers such as bunchberry, and introduce native perennials such as aster and goldenrod that naturalize well without coddling.

NATIVE SHRUBS

Some of the shrubs traditionally used in home landscapes have come into disfavor because of their invasive tendencies. A few prime examples are burning bush (*Euonymus alata*) and Japanese barberry (*Berberis thungergii*). Both are imported plants that have escaped from gardens and taken over woodlands to the detriment of native species. Some others are Russian olive (*Elaeagnus angustifolia*), autumn olive (*Elaeagnus umbellata*), tamarix, privet, broom, *Euonymus fortunei*, some forms of butterfly bush (such as *Buddleia davidii* and *B. alternifolia*), alder, buckthorn (*Rhamnus frangula*), European cranberrybush (*Viburnum opulus*), English holly (*Ilex aquifolium*), multiflora rose, and a number of bush honeysuckles (*Lonicera tatarica, L. morrowii, L. × bella*). Not all of these are a problem in all areas, but it's wise to consult your local native plant society or Extension Service and find out which exotic shrubs are a problem in your area.

I would probably feel disappointed about not being able to safely plant so many old garden favorites if there were not so many other shrubs, both native and imported, that fill the bill just fine. And so many excellent natives are coming into the trade each year that gardeners have yet to explore. A number of the shrubs recommended in the List of Shrubs in this chapter are natives (they are so noted), but there are many I did not have space to include: sumac (a number of species), bayberry (*Myrica pensylvanica*), bog rosemary (*Andromeda polifolia*), drooping leucothoe (*Leucothoe fontanesiana*), Carolina allspice (*Calycanthus floridus*), black pussy willow (*Salix melanostachys*), flowering raspberry (*Rubus odoratus*), bottlebrush buckeye (*Aesculus parviflora*), groundsel bush (*Baccharis halimifolia*), American beautyberry (*Callicarpa americana*), ocotillo (*Fouquieria splendens*), silverberry (*Elaeagnus commutata*), Labrador tea (*Ledum groenlandicum*), American snowbell (*Styrax americanus*), red osier dogwood (*Cornus sericea*), and elderberry (*Sambucus canadensis, S. caerulea, S. pubens*), to name just a few.

LEAF COLOR

Usually when you think of fall color you think of trees, but many shrubs are at their best in fall. Spicebush turns a dazzling yellow, Virginia sweetspire a brilliant red. Fothergilla and oakleaf hydrangea both go out in a blaze of multihued leaves. Other shrubs with great fall color are chokeberry, blueberry, bridalwreath spirea, cotoneaster, enkianthus, witch hazel, sumac, swamp azalea, flame azalea, summersweet, hypericum, and double-file viburnum.

Not all shrubs have green leaves in summer either, and those that don't can make an interesting contrast with those that do. Purple-leaved sand cherry (*Prunus × cistena*) is a good example of a shrub with deep red leaves all season long. Many of the Japanese maples—some so dwarf in habit that they are grown as shrubs—have beautiful dark red or bronze leaves as well. There are also some red-leaved forms of normally green plants such as weigela. A number of shrubs, such as elderberries, have been developed with yellow-leaved forms, or variegated ones as in the case of *Kerria japonica* 'Picta.' Others have very showy coloration when they first emerge in spring, as with the red-tipped branches of *Pieris × 'Brouwer's Beauty.'* Others have a whitish cast, like the shrubby artemisias and many of the desert species, or a bluish hue as with snowberry or *Rosa rubrifolia*.

Notorious for their rainbow-hued foliage are the heathers and heaths, and the various species of dwarf evergreens—bred specifically for this trait (see the entries for juniper and false cypress for some examples). It's fun to play with all the combinations of colors you can achieve by combining oddly colored shrubs. It's also easy to get a little carried away. Somehow I don't mind the carnival atmosphere of a bed of colorful flowers, but when too many leaves get into the act it sometimes seems bizarre. Perhaps that's just my own idiosyncratic reaction. If it pleases you, enjoy!

FRAGRANT SHRUBS

When the eighteenth-century poet Thomas Gray wrote ". . . many a flower is born to blush unseen / and waste its fragrance on the desert air," he had it all backward. Plants have fragrant flowers in order to attract specific pollinators, not to please us—although this feature certainly encourages us to plant them. We'll often tolerate the brevity of a shrub's brief bloom and the lankiness of its branches—lilac and mock orange come to mind—just to get that yearly fix of swooningly sweet scent. (With lilac you can sometimes throw mildewy foliage into the mix.) In fact, for some gardeners fragrance is everything.

Fortunately, the list of scented shrubs is long and diverse. The fragrant viburnums are among the most potent (see page 650). For the Deep South there's even one called *Viburnum odoratissima*, which translates as "most fragrant." Warm-climate gardeners can also wallow in *Daphne odora* and *Osmanthus × fortunei*. The plains states have their native clove currant (*Ribes odoratum*), with its sweet-scented yellow blossoms. As for the "desert air" of the American west, it is perfumed not only by fragrant flowers, such as those of the native acacias, but also by a host of scented herbal leaves—sage, bay, and others whose oils are easily volatilized by the warm dry atmosphere. In my own northeastern garden the scent season starts with the subtle fragrance of vernal witch hazel and *Daphne mezereum*, intensifies when *Viburnum* 'Mohawk,' mock orange, and swamp azalea come into flower, reaches a heady pinnacle with August-blooming summersweet, and ends with sweet autumn clematis (*Clematis paniculata*), a woody vine, and common witch hazel. When I want something more earthy, less flowery, I can always finger the leaves and twigs of my spicebush.

Where you site a fragrant shrub is important. Placing it beneath certain windows brings the scent indoors. If you have a deck, particularly one built high off the ground, surrounding it with shrubs will conceal the underpinnings; if you choose fragrant ones, they will scent the air above them. It's also fun to tuck fragrant plants in odd corners of the yard where people stroll, barbecue, or play games. They'll often stop to figure out where the aroma is coming from.

SHRUBS IN WINTER

Another wonderful way to use shrubs is for winter interest. In this, evergreens do have their virtues. It's lovely to look out on the mixed greens, blues, grays, and purples of yews, spruces, and junipers frosted with ice or snow. Some of them, such as Andorra junipers and heathers, have a special winter color. Broad-leaved evergreens such as mountain laurel are also a pleasing sight in winter, although in the case of rhododendrons, the way they curl up their leaves in the coldest weather (to conserve moisture) can be a little depressing. My favorite winter broadleaf is mountain andromeda (*Pieris floribunda*). Not only do the leaves stay fresh-looking and glossy, but the flower buds, formed during the summer, are held erect above the leaves as a cheering promise of spring.

Personally, I also enjoy looking at deciduous shrubs after they've shed their leaves. Each one has a different branching pattern and catches the snow in a distinct way. Some bare twigs even have interesting color and textures, such as green-stemmed kerrias and the red-stemmed shrub dogwoods (page 671). Many shrubs, such as winterberry, keep their colorful berries for a long time during the winter, too.

SHRUBS ENJOYED BY BIRDS

If you like to attract birds to your garden, leaving seed heads on flowering plants and growing shrubs with tasty fruits is far better than putting out bird feeders, in my view. I try to site food plants in parts of the yard where birds feel protected. The shrubs also offer concealment from predators, as well as nesting sites.

What plants will attract and sustain birds naturally varies a great deal from one locale to another. Regional wildlife organizations or the Audubon Society can help direct you to wise choices. Native shrubs are a good place to start. Shadblow, for example (a shrubby native tree) grows wild all through my neighborhood and the ones I have planted near the house are full of hungry birds as soon as the small red fruits ripen in summer. My crab apples, though not native, are just as eagerly devoured in winter, especially by grosbeaks and grouse. I also plant snowberries, blueberries, chokeberries, and viburnums for them. Hungry birds will eat just about any fruit in winter, starting with the most tasty ones. It seems fortunate that some are less delicious, in fact, so that there's still something hanging on the branches in late winter when other food is scarce. One thing to be careful about is invasive shrubs like multiflora rose, Japanese barberry, and tatarian honeysuckle. Their seeds are spread by birds who no doubt appreciate the gift, but you wouldn't be doing the local ecosystem a favor.

SHRUBS FOR
SPECIAL SITUATIONS

One excellent use of shrubs is to plant them on a steep bank. Many are good at holding the soil, and they'll also provide something decorative to look at that won't have to be mown. In fact, if such a planting is well mulched, it should not need any maintenance at all beyond pulling occasional weeds. Some of the best shrubs for banks are low and spreading and will, within a few years, merge together to form a mat. Ones that have worked well for me are shore junipers, which hold even the sliding dunes at the seashore, and spreading cotoneasters. (The latter should be avoided in areas where they are invasive in the wild.) Other possibilities include 'Grow-Low' sumac, the dwarf forsythias, toyon, apache plume, and the shrubby ground covers described in the ground cover chapter such as indigo bush, coyote brush, bearberry, and yellowroot. Taller choices include clethra, snowberry, and ceanothus.

Choosing Shrubs
That Will Thrive

WHEN SHRUBS DON'T DO WELL, IT'S usually because they have not been chosen with an eye to climate and site. Here are some factors to take into account.

WINTER HARDINESS

Before buying any woody plant it is important to find out the minimum winter temperature it can stand, because it usually costs quite a bit more than an herbaceous plant, and you want it to be around a long time. Sometimes it's worth taking a chance on a shrub's hardiness if you can give it a protected location. You might get lucky; then again, you might see it thrive for years only to have one severe winter finish it off. Use the hardiness ratings given in this chapter as a guide, but note the qualifying remarks on page 31. And see the comments on winter protection below.

If you live in a very cold climate, there are a number of shrubs you can grow with reasonable assurance that they will survive: potentilla, common lilac, sheep laurel, and red-twigged dogwood for example. If you live in a warm climate, your choices are bounteous. The list in this chapter includes several shrubs for mild areas that do not fare well up north.

SHRUBS FOR DRY PLACES

Many shrubs that do well in climates with average rainfall can thrive in dryish conditions as well, such as juniper, potentilla, oleander, quince, smokebush, hypericum, rosemary, sage, yucca, and New Jersey tea (*Ceanothus americanus*) to name just a few. If you live in a western area where dry conditions prevail but nights are cold, eliminate oleander and other tender shrubs from the list. In a dry area you can still grow plants that need an average amount of moisture if you're prepared to irrigate them. But with a growing awareness of the preciousness of water, there is a serious movement toward the use of drought-tolerant plants. Taking care of them requires less time and money and they look more appropriate in the landscape, too. Many gardeners in California and the southwestern states are skilled at landscaping with palms, cacti, and other succulents that those of us in cooler, moister regions can only grow as houseplants. Wonderful dry-climate flowering shrubs abound; I can only dream about having a *Ceanothus cyaneus*, with its cascade of blue flowers, in my yard. This is not to say that all western areas are dry, however. As always, the most important thing is to match the plant to the site.

Many drought-tolerant shrubs thrive by the seashore, too, assuming they are hardy for the region and the site chosen really is dry. Seaside gardeners face the triple challenge of sandy soil (which drains quickly and fosters dryness); strong, constant winds; and salt—either in the ground or wind-borne. Shrubs with grayish foliage such as potentilla are especially seaworthy. The tiny hairs on the leaves that give them their gray look protect them from wind, salt, and dryness. (Desert shrubs often have a similar appearance.) Other good shrubs for shore plantings include groundsel bush (*Baccharis halimifolia*), shore juniper, heather, red chokeberry, beach plum, rugosa roses, sweet fern (*Comptonia peregrina*), lavender, inkberry, and bayberry.

SHRUBS FOR MOIST PLACES

If it rains a lot where you live, or if the spot where you want to grow shrubs is moist from springs, streams, pond edges, or poor drainage, there are some shrubs you can plant that tolerate a great deal of moisture, such as clethra, blueberry, and others for which drainage can be less than perfect— red-twigged dogwoods, elderberry, pussy willow, many native azaleas, spicebush, sweetspire, mountain laurel, inkberry, winterberry, red chokeberry, drooping leucothoe, and some of the viburnums such as American cranberrybush and arrowwood. If you have your heart set on growing shrubs that don't like moist feet, consider some of the ways to improve drainage (page 28), but so many beautiful plants thrive in wet places that I look on an area such as this as a great opportunity.

SHRUBS FOR SHADE

Many shrubs do well in a spot that gets sun for only part of the day, or in sunlight that is filtered through tree branches, or in the "bright shade" cast by trees with branches that are high off the ground. Some of these are camellia, holly, fothergilla, coralberry, snowberry, mahonia, leucothoe, clethra, the shrub dogwoods, *Pieris* species, skimmia, pittosporum, and nandina. Some shrubs will do well in full shade, too, although those grown primarily for their flowers—such as rhododendrons, azaleas, mountain laurel, and viburnums—will flower less profusely in shade. Consider shade lovers not only for the usual "shady side of the house" situation, but also for woodland settings and for areas under trees where it might seem as if little gardening were possible. In some suburban or urban areas the yards are all so shady that this is the only kind of gardening people do. Remember, though, that shallow-rooted trees such as maple, apple, beech, poplar, and elm will compete with shrub roots. Deeper-rooted trees like oaks, pines, and sweet gums present less of a problem.

PREVENTING WINTER DAMAGE

A few shrubs, such as caryopteris and some hydrangeas, can die back to the ground in winter but make enough new growth in summer to bloom satisfactorily and keep us happy. In most cases, however, we expect the woody stems of popular species (and the foliage, if evergreen) to withstand cold air, snow, and ice. The amount and kind of winter damage a shrub will receive is sometimes hard to predict because several factors are involved. Soil temperature is one. Each plant has a lower limit for the temperature its roots can stand—or can stand over a protracted period. Plant roots may also be affected by how constant the soil temperature remains. Alternate freezing and thawing can damage roots. Have you ever noticed

how food becomes mushy if you repeatedly thaw and refreeze it? Something similar can happen to plant roots, and the freeze/thaw cycle can also break them and heave them out of the soil. Mulches (discussed in detail on page 55) can keep the soil temperature above a plant's danger zone, and also work to maintain frozen soil at a more constant temperature. This is why a good snow cover can be so beneficial to shrubs. The snow acts as a protecting mulch.

Soil moisture in winter is very important too, especially with evergreens. Evergreen leaves that remain on the plants transpire (that is, give off water) in winter, albeit at a slower rate than in warm weather. If conditions have been dry prior to the time the ground freezes, the plant will not have stored enough water to get it through the winter. There's no way for it to replace the lost moisture until spring, so its leaves will inevitably dry out. If you live in a cold climate and are having a dry fall, it's good insurance to give your evergreen shrubs a thorough soaking once or twice a week as you head into winter.

Some evergreens are better adapted to winter than others. Needle-leaved shrubs transpire less than broad-leaved ones, and plants such as rhododendrons, whose leaves curl up when it's cold, also save moisture. But most broad-leaved evergreens are quite vulnerable to winter drying, and you often see their leaves turn yellow or brown in February or March, when the roots have lost the race to replace their moisture. (Frozen ground makes this job harder.) Drying winds in winter can cause moisture loss, too, and the situation is further complicated by sunlight: the sun shining on the leaves causes them to lose water more quickly than they would in shade. On top of that, leaves can get a sunburn from the strong sunlight reflected off snow. Certain shrubs like box and Japanese holly are particularly susceptible.

Thus, while mulching and fall watering can help to protect broad-leaved evergreens in winter, their location is equally important. It might seem to you that a warm, sunny, south- or west-facing spot would offer the most protection, but with broad-leaved evergreens the opposite is true. The ideal location is a north- or east-facing spot (since morning sun is less strong than afternoon), where the plants get bright shade and are protected from wind. If you can't give them a site like this, some may have to be wrapped in a protective material such as burlap, which air and moisture can penetrate. (Support the fabric with wood or metal stakes.) Or use a covering of snow fence to create partial shade. An antidessicant spray like Wilt-Pruf, made from pine resin, can be applied in fall and is very effective in preventing winter damage to broadleaf evergreen foliage.

Planting Shrubs

GENERAL ADVICE FOR BUYING WOODY plants can be found on page 127, and for planting them on page 43. Following are a few more things to bear in mind about shrubs in particular.

WHEN TO PLANT

When you plant shrubs depends, in part, on where you live. In cold climates the best time to plant most shrubs is early spring while they are still dormant. This gives them a long time to establish new roots

before winter. In warm climates the greatest stress on a new plant is not winter cold and dryness but summer dryness and heat. In these areas fall planting, or even winter planting in frost-free regions, is preferable. The shrubs need to get well established before summer.

This does not mean that gardeners never plant shrubs in fall in the north. Nurserymen who wish their fall sales were as strong as their spring ones (and are trying to sell all their woody plants before winter) urge gardeners to plant then; landscapers eager to stretch their work out over the season plant then; and even busy home gardeners like to make use of those nice fall days, after other projects are over for the season. Fall planting can make a lot of sense, as long as you stick to plants that are easily moved and established. Most needle-leaved evergreens take fall planting well, as do a number of deciduous shrubs such as lilacs. Those at greater risk, including most broad-leaved evergreens, are best planted in spring. A responsible nurseryman will advise you about individual species.

In cold climates, shrubs that you do choose to plant in fall should be in the ground at least by late October so that some new root growth is possible before the ground freezes. Make sure you water the plants very well during and after planting, and give them a 3- to 4-inch mulch.

In warm climates spring planting is possible too, especially for plants with needles, since needles transpire less than broad leaves do in hot weather. Be sure to water them well, mulch them, and soak them deeply when it is hot and dry. Even very drought-tolerant species become better established if you water them from time to time the first season.

When you plant also depends on whether the plant is bare-root, balled-and-burlapped, or container grown. Most bare-root plants require spring planting, especially in cold areas, to give them time to reestablish their root systems before winter. You have greater flexibility with balled-and-burlapped plants, which have been dug while dormant. Because there is soil around their roots, they have suffered less shock. Most can be planted at any time except in very hot summer weather (especially in the south) or in very late fall (in the north). Container-grown plants carry the least risk of all, since their intact root systems have been growing inside the pot. But find out whether the shrubs you buy really are container grown and not dug bare-root, stuck in a pot, and immediately put out for sale. If you're not sure, have the nurseryman pull the plant out of the pot partway so you can see its root system. If it pulls out too easily and the soil does not cling to the roots, it has not been in the pot very long. I wouldn't necessarily reject the plant but I'd look around and see if the nursery has some that are better established.

SPACING SHRUBS

How far apart you place shrubs depends on how wide the plant will spread. Unless I'm planting a screen or windbreak, I like to give a plant enough room so that I can see its shape when it is mature and not have its growth impeded by other plants. Sometimes I don't know precisely how wide the shrub will become. My rule of thumb is to figure that it will spread about as wide as it will grow tall, unless (as is often the case) it is described as being "broad" or "spreading" or, on the other hand, "narrow," "fastigiate," or "columnar."

For hedges, the common advice is to plant shrubs 1 to 2 feet apart. I find that usually this is too close: most shrubs get wider than that very quickly and will be healthier if given more space. Planting 3 or 4 feet apart—or more—will make a long hedge more affordable, too, if you're willing to wait a few years for the space between the plants to fill in. But of course it depends on the plant. I would space narrow shrubs like 'Skyrocket' juniper much more closely than I would a row of big, fat spireas or viburnums, or a plant like clethra or rugosa rose that will soon sucker and fill in the gaps from below.

When planting low shrubs to hold a bank, I place them in staggered rows so that all the plants are equidistant from one another, usually about 3 feet apart each way. If the plants have been purchased in one-gallon containers, they will take a while to fill in and cover the bank, though in the meantime a mulch will help keep the bank from eroding. Those in five-gallon containers, planted 3 feet apart, will give a thick planting in as little as two years, depending on how fast that particular species grows.

Pruning Shrubs

IN THE FIRST CHAPTER I STRESSED the importance of understanding how plants are structured and how they grow, so that you can identify their needs and give them what they want. But sometimes, as a gardener, you want to make a plant do what *you* want. Pruning is a case in point. For example, a shrub may be naturally inclined to grow tall and leggy in order to compete with other plants for light, whether or not such competition is in fact at hand. So up it goes, not caring what it looks like—whether it has a nice filled-out shape, or whether it has plenty of flowers or berries at eye level. But you care. So armed with pruners you take it in hand and give it some gentle guidance.

Plants do get pruned in the natural course of things—dead branches fall off, deer nibble twigs and cause them to branch—but it's a pretty haphazard pruning and one that you can improve on if you understand how pruning works. Shrubs are pruned for a number of different reasons: to give them a more attractive shape; to keep them from getting too tall or wide for the space they occupy; to induce fresh new growth for more flowers, fruits, or colored bark; to ease the shock of transplanting; to remove dead, diseased, or damaged wood; to let light into a dense plant in order to improve its health; and to rejuvenate an old plant that no longer looks good, flowers well, or bears plentiful fruit. Individual shrubs often have special pruning requirements, and these are mentioned in the List of Shrubs. But here are some general guidelines.

WHAT PRUNING DOES

It may seem at first that the chief reason to prune is to stop growth. Sometimes it is. If you remove an unwanted, mature branch from some kinds of woody plants the branch will not regrow. But just as often we prune to induce growth, paradoxical as this may seem. If you look at the twig in Figure 70 you'll see that there is a bud at the tip, called the terminal bud, and also side buds along the twig's length. The terminal bud is responsible for the length-

ening of that twig and actually produces hormones that keep the side buds from developing, which they are quite capable of doing if something should accidentally happen to the terminal bud and the secretion of the growth-inhibiting hormone should cease.

In pruning you cause this "accident" to happen by making a clean, slanted cut just above a side bud and getting rid of the terminal bud. The side bud will then start to send out a new shoot. Often the other buds on the stem will do likewise, and you may then choose whether to leave them all growing, perhaps cutting them all back to a side bud to make *them* branch or, kingmaker that you are, you may choose a single shoot that grows in a direction that suits you and eliminate the rest.

Often you won't see any side buds low down on a branch, where the wood is old and thick. Severing the branch at this point may not produce any new growth. In some plants it may, however, because of the existence of invisible dormant buds beneath the bark, or because the plant is capable of producing brand-new (adventitious) buds in a spot where a branch is cut.

Usually, when we prune a shrub, we are doing one of two things: thinning it by removing some branches altogether, or cutting back stems to side buds to induce branching. It is important to understand the difference between thinning and cutting back, because they produce different results and are used in different situations. Cutting back is sometimes referred to as heading back, and can be done in varying degrees. If only the tips of the branches are cut, the process is called shearing; if a great deal of the branch is removed, it is called cutting back hard. Cutting back produces

Pruning Shrubs FIG. *70*

terminal bud

side bud

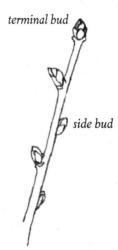

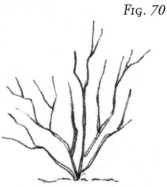

shrub before cutting back

shrub after cutting back

twig before cutting back

shrub before thinning

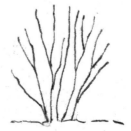

twig after cutting back

shrub after thinning

new growth. Thinning by removing whole branches may produce new growth in some shrubs, even if done at soil level; but its initial purpose is generally to diminish the plant—to remove thick, overgrown sections and let in air and light.

PRUNING NEW SHRUBS

When shrubs are planted bare-root, they are usually cut back by from one third to one half their height. The main reason for this is to compensate for the loss of roots, especially feeder roots, that takes place during transplanting. The smaller the root system, the more the top of the plant is removed. If you buy plants bare-root, especially if they come by mail, this will often have been done for you, and you'll be able to see where recent cuts have been made. But if the plants come with long, wandlike stems you'll need to do this yourself. Plants that are container grown or balled-and-burlapped do not need to be cut back, because their roots have suffered much less than those of bare-root plants. But if a shrub's stems are long and straggly, they will still benefit by being cut back in order to cause branching and give the plant a better shape. (This is not the case for trees grown with a central leader, which must remain intact.)

The most important pruning you do is often this early pruning of newly acquired shrubs, because it starts to establish the basic framework. A plant like an azalea, for example, whose branching structure will always be very visible, will be much prettier if you control its branching from the start and don't let tall, awkward shoots develop. And certain plants like junipers can never be brought back to a pleasing shape if you let them go too far without pruning.

It's especially important to cut back hedge plants while they are young, so that the bottom of the hedge will grow thick and bushy. The standard practice is to cut the newly planted shrubs back by at least a third, then each year cut back half of the plants' new growth until they reach their desired height. This may seem like excruciatingly slow growth if you want "instant hedge" for screening purposes, but if you don't do it you may wind up with a hedge that is bare at the bottom. The only real shortcut is to buy and plant a row of tall, bushy mature plants.

MAINTENANCE PRUNING

Once a shrub is established you may not have to prune it at all. If you've selected the right shrub for a given spot, you won't have to worry about its getting too tall, and you can often let it simply achieve its natural shape. Unfortunately, many gardeners regard shrubs the way they regard lawns—as something that must be cut regularly. So each year they go around giving them all crewcuts, not only ruining their grace but often preventing flowers and berries from forming.

How you prune is partly a matter of taste. Here is the way I go about it. For most shrubs I just watch the plant grow and remove any long, leggy shoots or branches that head out in an awkward direction. If a shrub is growing very thickly with lots of twiggy growth so that no light can reach the center, I might remove some of the twiggy ends or thin out some of the main stems at the base of the plant (Figure 70). I would cut back to a bud that faces outward (see page 613 for more discussion of this) so that the shrub will open out like a bouquet. On the other hand, if it is too open and lax (a straggly looking quince, for example), I might cut back to an inward-facing bud so that new branches will grow toward that gappy center and fill it in. Once you try this kind of sculpture pruning you'll realize how easy it is and will enjoy controlling shrub growth in a way that you consider beautiful.

One thing to keep in mind is that needled evergreens cannot be cut back as hard as broad-leaved evergreens or deciduous plants, because most of them do not regenerate from old wood that has been cut. Most of the long-needled ones such as pine and spruce don't even take shearing well. These should be pruned very selectively. Eliminate only branches that you don't want to regrow, or don't prune at all. Pines can be kept compact by pinching the "candles"—the little projections that shoot up from the tips of the branches—when they have just started their spring growth. If you pinch a candle while it is still small, new little candles will grow up around its base, creating a bushier appearance.

Sometimes you want a plant to have a more geometrical, "shaped" look, whether for a formal garden or for a hedge that you want thick, close-cropped, and tidy. Frequent shearing with hedge trimmers will give you this smooth effect, but unless a plant or hedge is very large, I prefer to use hand pruners and give the plant a softer, less regular outline. I take a protruding twig and cut it several inches shorter than the ones around it so that the cut is hidden. I keep doing this until the size of the plant has been reduced a bit, but I leave it with roughly the same outline and with its surface more shaggy than smooth. (For very large hedges, I admit, this would take forever and an attack with the hedge shears would be more practical.) I make sure that I prune hedges in such a way that the bottom is wider than the top. In this way the bottom receives enough sunlight to keep it green and growing, not bare.

I am also always on the lookout, in any shrub, for wood that is dead, diseased, or dying, for this is neither healthy for the plant nor attractive. I cut bad wood back to a branch or bud, being careful not to leave a stub, which will only die and decay. If the plant is not in leaf and I'm not sure whether a branch is dead or alive, I scratch it just a tiny bit with my fingernail—if there is green under the bark, it's alive. I try to pick the right tool for the size branch I am cutting. When dealing with diseased wood it's wise to disinfect the tool between cuts with alcohol or a weak chlorine bleach solution to avoid spreading the problem to healthy tissue.

REJUVENATING OLD SHRUBS

Old shrubs often become progressively less attractive because they have too many main stems, too much twiggy growth, and/ or weakened branches that don't produce many leaves, flowers, or fruits. They can also become too leggy at the bottom, or produce a nest of nonflowering suckers at the base. Some shrubs simply get too large. I spoke disparagingly a moment ago about the forsythia with a crewcut, but at the opposite extreme is the forsythia that ate the yard—the one that is almost as large as your house and out of scale with the rest of the property.

If left alone, many of these shrubs would eventually weaken and die (except some, like lilacs, that can go on for hundreds of years). But you can prune them in a way that will make them more attractive and also prolong their lives. In a few special cases, such as potentillas and some hydrangeas, you cut old shrubs back hard to a few feet or even to the ground. But the basic and more usual technique of pruning old shrubs is to cut out some of the main stems at the base to let light in, sometimes cutting out some of the twiggy tip growth as well to promote flowering and shorten a plant that has grown too tall. Often this is enough; but if the shrub is really a mess, or severely weakened, you can make pruning it a three-year program, cutting back a third of the old stems to the ground each year until all that is left is new young growth that has emerged from the base (this is less of a shock to the plant than doing it all at once). You can recognize old stems by their thickness and their shaggy, rough bark. New ones are thinner and smoother. With plants that already have a lot of suckers, as lilacs often do, you can prune out all but a few strong ones and let these replace the old stems that you cut.

WHEN TO PRUNE

Pruning at the wrong time of the year will rarely kill a plant, but doing it at the right time can make it more attractive and productive. Each plant has its own requirements, but here are some general principles.

Thinning a shrub to improve its looks or rejuvenate it is usually done in late winter or early spring while it is dormant. This is also the time to prune if you are trying to produce a lot of new wood; those buds will be primed to burst into action as the weather warms. (In hot, dry climates where there is no cold winter, you should prune at the end of the dry season when the plants' dormancy is about to end.) A hedge is usually pruned just after it has made its major spring growth, then as

often as needed throughout the season to keep it looking tidy.

If you're pruning to control the growth of a vigorous shrub, prune in summer or fall. Fall pruning is generally risky in cold climates, however, because new growth that results will not have time to harden off before winter and may be killed. In these areas, stop summer pruning soon enough to let any new growth harden.

The most common mistake people make is cutting back the tips of flowering shrubs at the wrong time. These shrubs can be divided into two categories: those that bloom on new wood (twigs produced during the same growing season as the flowers) and those that bloom on old wood (that is, twigs produced the season—or seasons—before). Those that bloom on new wood usually don't bloom until after June, because they're spending the first part of the season growing the wood. They should be pruned in late winter or early spring before that growth starts. Plants that bloom on old wood usually bloom in spring, and they should be pruned right after they bloom so that they can spend the latter part of the season making new growth unimpeded. So you see how great a mistake it would be to prune all your flowering shrubs at the same time. Unless they are all the same type, you would end up sacrificing some bloom. Shrubs grown for their fall foliage or berries are pruned after the show is over and the plants are dormant—usually late winter—or just thinned instead of cut back, so as to sacrifice as few berries as possible. Another trick with flowering plants such as lilacs is to deadhead them, removing the spent flowers after blooming. This not only puts more energy into plant growth but may also counteract the tendency of some plants to flower and fruit heavily only in alternate years.

ROOT PRUNING

Sometimes you want to prune a shrub's roots, for a variety of reasons. One is to restrict the shrub's growth if there is too much of it. Another is to prepare it for transplanting. Root pruning prospective transplants is done a whole season ahead and consists of severing the roots in a circle around the plant, at the point where you will dig a ball of earth when you come to move the plant. It causes the roots to branch and form a more extensive system of feeder roots, so the plant will suffer less root loss when moved. Root pruning is practiced frequently by nurserymen, less by the beginning gardener, who is usually better off not trying to move large, well-established shrubs and should hire a professional for such work. Still, root pruning is good to know about.

There are many other, more specialized forms of pruning, such as creating espaliers (training shrubs or small trees in a two-dimensional plane, either freestanding or against a wall), topiary (shearing to produce a specific shape, from a cube to an elephant), disbudding stems to produce huge blooms on one bud, and selective pruning of pine candles to affect direction of growth. Bonsai, by which woody plants are kept exquisitely small and graceful, is the supreme pruning art. These are all techniques that you may research further once you're comfortable with the fundamentals of pruning.

As you prune your shrubs, keep the needs of your specific climate in mind. In general you can be more drastic with your pruning in areas that are mild and moist, and indeed you have to be, since plant growth there tends to be lush. In cold or dry areas, and especially in ones that are *both* cold and dry, you should be cautious about how much you prune and when you do it.

Other Maintenance Tasks

APART FROM PRUNING, MOST SHRUBS require very little care. If you've planted them with good soil amendments to start them off right, they usually do not need any additional feeding—unless they have suffered some stress, such as a severe pruning, or unless you want to produce rapid, vigorous growth for some reason (establishing a hedge quickly, for example). Usually, fertilizing can be done just by top-dressing with some well-rotted manure or liquid fertilizer just before growth begins in spring. The need of shrubs for nutrients also varies from one to another.

A mulch will help to promote root growth and keep the plant moist during dry weather as well as afford the winter protection described above. But some shrubs will still need a good soaking in severe drought, especially newly planted ones. Specific pests and diseases afflict specific shrubs; refer to the List of Shrubs and to the advice offered on page 60 and following. In general, though, I try hard to select shrubs that are suited to my area, site them well, and give them the nutrients and water they need. This gives them the strength to defend themselves against most ills.

Propagating Shrubs

SOME PROPAGATING TECHNIQUES, SUCH as grafting, are beyond the scope of this book. The ambitious can grow shrubs from seed if the shrubs are not hybrids, or they can take cuttings—often a simple task, but one whose rules vary from plant to plant and are best learned by consulting more specialized sources. Here are a few easy propagating techniques that anyone can master.

TRANSPLANTING SUCKERS

To propagate shrubs that send up rooted suckers near the base, such as weigela, clethra, and lilac, expose the roots around a sucker and cut off the whole thing from the stem that produced it. Replant it as you would any bare-root plant, making sure that the roots do not dry out. If a shrub has been grafted, don't replant suckers that grow from below the graft; these will be like the understock, not like the plant grafted onto it.

DIVIDING SHRUBS

Some shrubs can be increased simply by dividing their crowns, just as you would divide the crowns of herbaceous perennials (page 185). With some all you need to do is slice the crown with a sharp spade or axe, making sure there is a stem coming out of any section you replant. With others, it is a matter of clearing away the soil from the roots to expose them, and severing sections of rooted stem with loppers or a pruning saw. How you tackle the job is pretty much a matter of common sense:

you'll see what you need to do when you look at the plant and see how it is constructed. But it only works with plants that are very easy to transplant and so can be planted bare-root. Some of these are Japanese quince, lilac, azalea, clethra, glossy abelia, viburnum, winterberry, and holly.

Just to give you an idea of how easy dividing can be, I once dug up a Japanese flowering quince next to the front entrance of a restaurant and planted a rhododendron in its place. Since the quince was in bloom at the time, with beautiful flowers in a coral shade, we took all the little pieces we'd hacked up to my boss's nursery and planted them. They grew into fine plants in a row we marked "coral quince." Ten years later I happened to stop at that restaurant for breakfast and noticed that the rhododendron was looking rather peaked, but that shoots of "coral quince" had sprouted up all around it from bits of rootlet in the ground. On the way out I said to the waitress, "You don't know me, but I planted that rhododendron, and perhaps it should be taken out, because the quince loves the spot!" I'm sure it's still there now.

LAYERING

To layer a plant, you simply bury part of a low-growing stem in the ground and wait for it to send down roots. Many plants grow roots this way without any help (ivy is a prime example), but you can initiate the process yourself if you want new plants from an established shrub. It works best for deciduous shrubs with long, flexible stems such as forsythia, quince, cotoneaster, daphne, and some viburnums.

In early spring or fall, when the weather is cool, take a section of stem about 1 foot from the tip and bury it about 6 inches deep with the tip protruding (Figure 71). Set a flat rock over the soil to keep the stem down and the soil moist. With easy-to-layer shrubs this is all you need to do, but for extra insurance, and for shrubs that are more difficult to root, slice off a small section of the underside of the stem and dust the wound with a powdered rooting stimulant to make the stem root faster. Working organic matter and bone meal into the soil under the stem will help, too. Tying the new shoot to a stake will help it to grow upright.

After a year or so, you can sever the plant from the old stem at ground level and transplant the newly rooted plant to a different location. Another method that makes transplanting easier is to layer directly into pots that you have buried up to their rims in the soil. While the plant is rooting you can feed it liquid fertilizer to hasten its development.

Layering a Shrub

Fig. 71

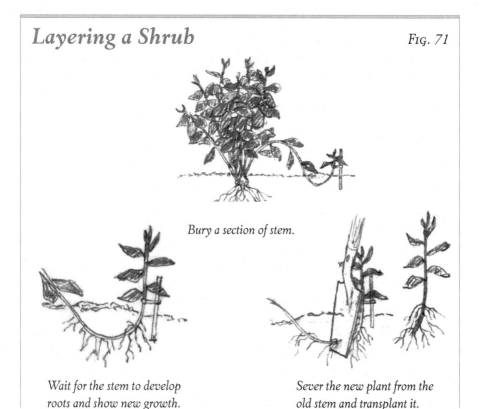

Bury a section of stem.

Wait for the stem to develop roots and show new growth.

Sever the new plant from the old stem and transplant it.

List of Shrubs

T HE FOLLOWING LIST CONTAINS some easy-to-grow shrubs, chosen for their usefulness in the home landscape. Most are old favorites, others might be new to you. Most can be grown throughout the country, though a few are listed with only warm-climate and/or dry-climate gardeners in mind. In addition to species in this list and in other parts of this chapter, other chapters in this book describe shrubs masquerading in other guises. Roses, for example, are shrubs, though it's often said that the rose is a great flower but a poor shrub; its flowers are prized, not the rather sparse, lanky plants on which many of them grow. Some of the woody perennial herbs such as lavender, sage, and rosemary are essentially shrubs, as are a number of garden perennials like artemisias. Many tree genuses include shrublike species, as noted in the tree chapter: arborvitae, dogwood, fir, hemlock, spruce, and willow, in addition to yew, holly, juniper, and false cypress, which are considered here.

Typically, shrub purchases are made at local nurseries where you can see the foliage and form of the plant, even if it is a small specimen. You can also order shrubs by mail and patiently wait for them to grow. This is helpful if you're looking for something obscure, and it can save you money if you're looking for shrubs in quantity. They will usually come bare-root.

Note the advice given on page 655 for teaching yourself about trees. Arboretums and botanical gardens often have fine shrub specimens, and these are good places to observe them in their mature form and better judge what their effect would be. Do you like their shapes? Is their scale right for the setting? Will they fit the spaces where you plan to use them? Your visit may inspire you to try something new and wonderful in your next shrub planting.

ANDROMEDA
Pieris

Description: The garden plants most commonly called andromeda are not members of the *Andromeda* genus but of the genus *Pieris*. Of these the most familiar is known as Japanese andromeda (*Pieris japonica*). In New England where I live it is held in great esteem as "the only shrub the deer do not eat." Whether or not this is categorically true, the plant also has other things to recommend it. The long evergreen leaves hang down in clusters, but new ones in spring are perky red-tinted rosettes. Flowers, in early spring, are dangling creamy-white bells. This shrub grows fairly tall if not cut back, and can be rather lanky if not pruned occasionally for shape. It goes well with rhododendrons and laurel in the woods or near the house, and seems to appreciate partial shade. I've noticed that hot afternoon sun can make it look wilted, but it soon revives. Full shade will reduce bloom.

I like the native mountain andromeda, *Pieris floribunda*, even better. Also called fetter bush, it has a more compact, nicely shaped growth habit, although I'm always surprised to see it described as very low growing. It may grow slowly but I have plants that are at least 6 feet tall. The foliage is beautiful in winter if protected from strong sun; better yet it holds its spring-blooming flowers on erect twigs, well above the leaves. The showy white buds are formed the previous season and are thus visible all winter long. A hybrid between these two species, *Pieris* × 'Brouwer's Beauty,' is compact and easier to propagate than mountain andromeda.

Of the true andromedas, *Andromeda polifolia*, or bog rosemary, is a nice garden plant if you live in a very cold part of the country (it's hardy to zone 2!) and have a moist, acid, humusy location for it. It grows less than 2 feet tall and bears pretty pink or white flowers.

How to Grow: Both *Pieris* species do best in light, humusy, slightly acid soil. A mulch will help keep the soil sufficiently moist. Plant in early spring and prune after flowering to encourage branching, since plants bloom on old wood. Overgrown plants can be thinned gradually at the base or even cut to the ground. Do this in early spring to give the plant a full season to make new growth.

APACHE PLUME
Fallugia paradoxa

Description: This desert shrub, native to moderately high elevations in the American west and southwest, is an excellent land-scape plant for dry climates. Though fairly cold hardy, it does not thrive in regions with humid summers, even when grown in dry, sandy soil. The compact size is a plus—between 3 and 6 feet, with at least as great a spread. Single white flowers, shaped like those of wild roses, are held on erect stems above the small dark green leaves. These are good for bees and butter-flies, appearing continuously throughout the spring and summer when it rains or when the plant is irrigated. Beautiful pink-ish purple fluffy seed plumes follow the flowers in late summer and fall, and a plant often displays both flowers and plumes together. The foliage is evergreen in warm areas, the bark rough and shaggy.

How to Grow: Seeds can be direct-sown in appropriate regions, but nursery speci-mens are commonly available. You'll need both male and female plants to produce seed. Give plants full sun. They respond well to cutting back in winter to make them more shapely or compact. Soak them thoroughly once a month during very dry weather. Do not fertilize them.

AZALEA

Rhododendron

Description: Azaleas are a group of plants that belong to the genus *Rhododendron.* The other members of the genus are simply called rhododendrons. While both can be either evergreen or deciduous, there are more deciduous azaleas than there are deciduous rhododendrons (almost all rhododendrons are evergreen). The main thing to remember is that all azaleas are rhododendrons, but all rhododendrons are not azaleas.

There are so many azaleas to choose from, one almost wonders where to start. Some bloom in spring, with flowers appearing even before their leaves, while others bloom as late as early July. The color range includes red, pink, lavender, salmon, orange, yellow, and white. Heights also vary a great deal; some azaleas are nearly prostrate and some grow to over 12 feet. Your choice of azaleas will depend in large part on your climate. Some are cold hardy, some not. Most azalea hybrids come from Asia, but there are also many beautiful native American azaleas, almost all of them found in the east coast states from Florida to as far north as Maine. Listed below are just a few groups of azaleas that are widely grown, each containing many cultivars. But the world of azaleas is so vast and overwhelming that it's best to consult a good local nurseryman who knows the subject and can recommend the best ones for your purposes. Sources of further information can be found on page 779.

Exbury and Knap Hill hybrids. These showy deciduous plants, hardy to at least zone 5, can grow as tall as 12 feet. Colors include the whole azalea range. They are a good choice for northern gardens.

Kurume hybrids. These are evergreen, small leaved and small flowered, and grow 4 to 6 feet tall—shorter when trained as container plants. They can be sheared closely and still produce profuse flowers in shades of pink, red, lavender, salmon, and white. Most are hardy to zone 7.

Indica hybrids. These tall, large-flowered evergreen azaleas are relatively sun tolerant. They are popular in the south.

Torch azaleas (Rhododendron obtusum kaempferi). These are low-growing deciduous plants about 3 feet tall, with red, pink, or salmon flowers in spring. They are hardy to zone 5 or 6.

Mollis hybrids (R. × kosteranum). These grow 5 to 8 feet tall with yellow, red, orange, pink, or white flowers in spring. They are deciduous and most are hardy to zone 6.

Gable hybrids. These are evergreen, 3 to 4 feet tall, with pink, red, or white flowers. They are generally hardy to zone 6.

Girard hybrids. Most of these are evergreen, showy and large-flowered, and winter hardy. The Glenn Dale and Robin Hill hybrids are other popular groups.

Native American azaleas. These are my favorites! All of these are deciduous, and some have showy fall foliage as well as handsome flowers. Some of the best are the fragrant swamp azalea (*R. viscosum*), which usually grows in wet places, has sticky white flowers in early summer, and is hardy to zone 3; sweet azalea (*R. arborescens*), which bears very fragrant white or pink-tinged flowers in late spring on 9-foot plants, and is hardy to zone 5; pink-shell azalea (*R. vaseyi*), which is found in moist places, has pink flowers in spring and red foliage in fall, and is hardy to zone 4; pinxterbloom (*R. nudiflorum*), also known as pink honeysuckle, which grows 6 feet tall, bears pink flowers in spring before the leaves and is hardy to zone 3; rose-shell azalea (*R. prinophyllum*), whose pink flowers are quite showy; and flame azalea (*R. calendulaceum*), which bears stunning yellow, red, or orange flowers on plants 9 feet or taller in late spring, and is hardy to zone 5 or 6.

Azaleas can be used in many ways—in shrub borders, as specimen plants, near terraces or entryways, and in containers indoors or out. Their colors are so dazzling that an array of the brightest ones can be too much of a good thing. I like them best in an informal or woodland setting, mixed with plants like laurel and dogwood where the intensity of the colors is softened.

How to Grow: All the advice in the section on rhododendrons (see page 644) applies to azaleas. Remember that the native azalea species are indigenous either to sunny clearings or open woodlands with filtered light, so this is what they like best—too much sun can fade the blossoms of most natives, and too little can result in sparse bloom.

Azaleas vary in their need for pruning. Many deciduous ones benefit from being cut back to encourage branching when they're young and then whenever they become leggy. Cutting back new shoots that emerge at the bottom of the plant will produce branching and fill in bare spaces near the ground. And all kinds of azalea will bloom more heavily if the tips of the stems are pinched. Both pruning and pinching are best done in early spring while the plants are still dormant, or just after flowering if you prefer not to sacrifice the flower display. Leggy stems can be removed from the bottom in summer as well.

BOX (BOXWOOD)
Buxus

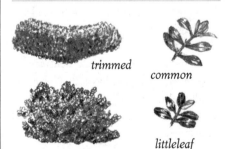

trimmed

common

untrimmed

littleleaf

Description: My climate, alas, is not kind to boxwood, which grows in lush evergreen mounds in the mid-Atlantic states on plants often several hundred years old.

I can remember playing hide-and-seek as a child among the gnarled trunks and fragrant billows of foliage while visiting my grandparents in Pennsylvania. Dwarf varieties such as 'Suffruticosa' or 'Green Pillow' are good for edging a formal bed.

Common box (*Buxus sempervirens*) is extremely slow growing but can sometimes grow as tall as a small tree; it is hardy to zone 5 or 6. Littleleaf box (*B. microphylla*) is more compact. 'Wintergreen' and 'Chicagoland Green' are less apt to brown in winter than most; 'Vardar Valley' and 'Welleri' are compact, slow growing, and particularly hardy. 'Green Beauty' and 'Justin Brouwers' are among the best of the more recent boxwood introductions.

How to Grow: The biggest problems with box are winter cold and winter dryness. It is prone to winter burn and should not be planted in exposed, sunny areas in cold climates. If you're a box lover you may not mind wrapping your precious specimens in burlap for the winter or mulching their shallow roots to keep them cool and moist in summer and warm in winter. An antidessicant may also be applied (see page 611).

Aside from this, box is not difficult to grow except in regions where root nematodes are an intractable problem. It tolerates a wide pH range and needs feeding only while becoming established. Occasional ills such as root rot, leaf spot, stem canker, and leaf miners are best dealt with by removing the affected parts and, if necessary, transplanting to a different location.

Box can be sheared as a hedge and also tolerates severe cutting back if damaged or overgrown. Generally all it needs is to have deadwood removed, however. Prune in early spring.

CAMELLIA
Camellia

semidouble

double

Description: Camellias were a wonder to me as a child because they bloomed in winter. My maternal grandmother used to grow many of them in the Deep South, and one Christmas sent us a box of the beautiful flowers packed in dry ice (with minimal success). Camellias, alas, cannot take frost and are grown outdoors dependably only to zone 8; but gardeners farther north often grow them in containers, keeping them indoors for all or part of the year.

The most common species is *Camellia japonica*, of which there are hundreds of hybrids. The plants, which are handsome, glossy-leaved evergreen shrubs, can get very tall when mature and are sometimes grown as small trees. From October to April they bear flowers that are usually 2 to 5 inches wide in several different forms—single, semidouble, double, peony form, anemone form, and rose form—and in colors ranging from white to pink to dark red. *C. sasanqua* hybrids, which are smaller, more open-branched shrubs with smaller flowers, bloom from September to December. Camellias are equally effective as landscaping plants and in a natural woodland setting.

How to Grow: Camellias need to be protected from direct sun and drying winds. Give them moist, well-drained, slightly acid soil, and mulch the roots to keep them cool until the plants are well established. The plants will need to be watered while they're young; even the leaves appreciate a sprinkling. Pruning young plants will help to achieve a compact shape; cut back after blooming to just above where the current year's growth begins. Old, overgrown plants can be thinned at the base in two stages, one year removing the lower branches to produce bottom growth and the following year cutting the tops back hard.

mid summer, are a bit larger—rather like white anemones with vivid yellow stamens in the center. The leaves, growing in pairs, are long and pointed, glossy and evergreen. Oddly enough, the plant is valued in England and Europe but far less well known in the United States.

How to Grow: Carpenteria tolerates fairly dry soil but may need minimal irrigation in very dry weather for the foliage to look good. It benefits from a well-drained soil with average moisture and fertility, in sun or part shade. It can grow up to 10 feet tall, more typically 6 to 8. It does fine in a container and is hardy in zones 8 to 10.

CARPENTERIA (TREE ANEMONE)

Carpenteria californica

CARYOPTERIS (BLUEBEARD)

Caryopteris × clandonensis

Description: This beautiful endangered plant is native to only a few sites in the foothills of the Sierra Nevada in Fresno County, California. But it is available in nurseries and makes an adaptable landscape plant in mild climates. Related to mock orange, its fragrant flowers, which bloom in early to

Description: I value this shrub for its fuzzy true-blue flowers and the lateness of its bloom. I use it mainly in perennial gardens as a contrast to the bright red, orange, and yellow shades that dominate August and September—heliopsis, helenium, chrysanthemum, and such. It is also beautiful next to a swimming pool, or in the foreground of a mixed shrub planting. 'Blue Mist' was one of the early cultivars so it sometimes goes by that name. There are a number of others now, including 'Dark Knight' and 'Longwood Blue.' There are also varieties with yellow leaves, such as 'Worcester Gold.' Normally, the small, slender, aromatic leaves have a gray-green color. The plant is compact and very twiggy, growing up to 4 feet tall, usually less in cold climates.

How to Grow: Don't be dismayed if the plant dies back almost to the ground after a cold winter. I often cut it back anyway, even before I know how much of the plant has been spared, since this produces healthy new growth and a good compact shape (it blooms on new wood). Like many plants with grayish foliage, this one is sun loving and tolerant of dry soil—although I find it also does fine with the fertile, well-moistened soil of my garden, and also tolerates some shade. Do not overwater or overfertilize. Hardy to zone 5.

CEANOTHUS (WILD LILAC)

Ceanothus × delilianus

Description: There are 50 species of this native shrub, most of them in California. There they are indispensable plants for the dry-summer landscape. Most are evergreen, and are attractive even when not in bloom. With some the spring flower clusters are lilac-shaped, with others they are smaller and rounder, the colors sometimes white, pink, or lavender but most gloriously a brilliant true blue, in tones ranging from

light powder blue to deep indigo. Growth habit ranges from prostrate to large and sprawling. A large blue-flowered ceanothus in full bloom is a dazzling sight to anyone, especially easterners encountering one for the first time, for we have nothing comparable. Western gardeners should investigate which species might be native to their region, and which of the many hybrids do well where they live. Much of the breeding work has been done in Europe where these plants are much prized. The low-growing species make fine ground covers, and all are good for stabilizing banks and hillsides, since they naturally prefer the well-drained soil these sites afford. Most are hardy only to zone 8, although some of the hybrids, crossed with eastern species, are hardier and better adapted to the moister conditions of the eastern U.S. As a group, ceanothus are among the best plants for butterflies, bees, and other insects, as well as providing fruits and cover for birds.

The 3-foot New Jersey tea (*Ceanothus americanus*) bears white, upright, lilac-shaped flowers in spring and is an excellent shrub for dry, infertile soils. It is a bee and butterfly magnet, hardy to zone 4 or 5. Its name comes from its use as a tea substitute during the American Revolution.

How to Grow: Grow ceanothus in full sun. Give it a light, well-drained soil. Plants should not be irrigated—in fact it's best not to let water from sprinklers drift onto the leaves. Too much water can cause root rot in the western species, so they don't do well in areas with moist or humid weather, even where they are cold hardy. The plants can be propagated by layering or cuttings. They don't need much pruning but can be pinched to encourage bushiness, and cut back or thinned at the base if overgrown. Suckers at the base can also be removed.

CHOKEBERRY

Aronia

Description: These wonderful native shrubs are finally catching on with gardeners, thanks to their multiseason interest and ease of culture. Two species are commonly available in the trade. Red chokeberry (*Aronia arbutifolia*) produces clusters of small white blooms in spring, followed by bright red berries and brilliant red fall foliage. Black chokeberry (*A. melanocarpa*) is similar but with black berries and fall foliage that is a deep maroon. *A. × prunifolia* is a natural cross between the two, with purple berries. Nurseries sometimes offer cultivars selected for particular traits; 'Brilliantissima' is a red chokeberry with especially showy fruits and very vivid red fall leaves. Aronias vary in size depend-

ing on where they're grown. In my gardens they have been very upright, and about 8 feet tall. The clumps tend to sucker and are best in shrub borders and informal plantings. Since the flowers and fruits appear toward the top of the plant, atop leggy stems, they look best with lower shrubs or perennials growing in front of them. Though not sweet, the berries do sustain birds in winter after tastier ones have been consumed, and cold weather has made them more palatable.

How to Grow: Though chokeberries usually choose moist sites in the wild, they will tolerate a wide range of soil types and degrees of soil moisture. Apart from occasionally thinning out clumps for tidiness or to promote new growth, and removing suckers as needed, there is little care involved—none, in fact, in a natural setting.

CLETHRA (SUMMERSWEET)

Clethra alnifolia

Description: This native of the American northeast is a useful shrub for several reasons. It blooms at a time when few other shrubs do—late summer—and it tolerates very wet soil. It also withstands the salty winds at the seaside. Flowers are very fragrant spikes about 5 inches long, and there are also some pink varieties. The shrub can grow as tall as 9 feet, though it usually attains around 5 or 6. It is hardy to zone 3 or 4.

How to Grow: Clethra prefers moist, acid soil, though it will also grow in soil of average moisture if there is sufficient organic matter. It thrives in sun or light shade, but too much shade will retard bloom and make the plant leggy. It makes spreading clumps, and suckers can be removed and replanted for propagation. Clethra is best left to grow in its natural shape but can be thinned at the base or cut back at the tips if clumps get straggly. Do this in early spring, since it blooms on wood of the current season.

COTONEASTER
Cotoneaster

Description: The name of this plant is pronounced "cah-*toe*-nee-*as*-ter," not, as you might think, "cotton-Easter." Many species and varieties are used in gardens. Most are deciduous with small, rounded leaves that turn red-orange in fall, tiny pink or white flowers in spring, and red berries in fall that last most of the winter. The plants have long, graceful, arching stems with many side branches and are attractive for their shape alone. Spreading cotoneaster (*Cotoneaster divaricatus*) can grow to at least 6 or 7 feet tall and wide, making a big mound of weeping branches. But many others are low growing, even prostrate, and are used as ground covers, on steep banks (where they grow quickly to hold the soil), or in the foreground of shrub plantings. Cranberry cotoneaster (*C. apiculatus*) and rockspray cotoneaster (*C. horizontalis*) stay under 3 feet tall (the latter is semievergreen in mild climates). Creeping cotoneaster (*C. adpressus*) is slow growing and only about a foot tall. All are tolerant of dry soil and the salty winds of seaside areas. Most are hardy to zone 5. Several species have become naturalized and are considered to be invasive in parts of California and in Hawaii: littleleaf cotoneaster (*C. microphyllus*), silverleaf cotoneaster (*C. pannosus*), milkflower cotoneaster (*C. lacteus*), and Franchet cotoneaster (*C. franchetii*).

How to Grow: Give the plants full sun and well-drained soil. They do not transplant easily; it's best to buy container-grown plants and leave them in one spot. They attract spider mites in some areas, which can be hosed off, and fire blight, which blackens the ends of the branches and should be pruned out. The plants should be grown in their natural shape, but long, awkward branches can be cut back to a side branch (early spring is the best time), and dense plants can be thinned at the base.

DAPHNE
Daphne

Description: Daphnes are small shrubs, mostly evergreen and mostly very fragrant;

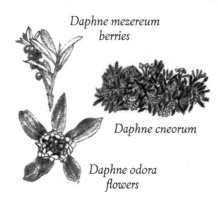

Daphne mezereum berries

Daphne cneorum

Daphne odora flowers

they should be planted in a spot where they can be easily seen and sniffed. *Caution:* all parts of the plant are poisonous, especially the berries. Daphne should *not* be grown where children have access to the plant. Most bloom very early in spring. The deciduous February daphne (*Daphne mezereum*), hardy to zone 4 (semievergreen in some climates), has purple flowers in February or March (later in very cold regions), followed by red berries; *D. m. alba* is white-flowered with yellow berries. February daphne is an upright plant, growing up to 5 feet tall. Lilac daphne (*D. genkwa*) is about the same size, has fragrant lilac-blue flowers and white berries, and is hardy to zone 5. Winter daphne (*D. odora*) is evergreen, about 4 feet tall (sometimes taller), bears fragrant purple flowers in early spring, and is hardy to zone 7. Rose daphne (*D. cneorum*) is a creeping evergreen mat less than a foot tall, with fragrant pink flowers in May, and is hardy to zone 4.

How to Grow: Give daphne full sun or light shade. It likes well-drained, humusy soil and a mulch to keep the roots cool in summer. Difficult to move, it should not be planted bare-root; it is propagated most easily by layering. Daphnes do not often need pruning, though they will tolerate

severe cutting back. Awkward shoots are best dealt with by picking them for the house while they're blooming, in order to enjoy their perfume.

DEUTZIA

Deutzia

Description: For a few weeks in late spring, deutzia is covered with a froth of white flowers (in some varieties they're touched with pink, but I like the pure white ones best). I appreciate its compact growth and use it in the front or middle of shrub plantings. It makes a good low deciduous hedge. In cool climates grow slender deutzia (*Deutzia gracilis*), which usually stays as short as 3 feet and is hardy to zone 5. Lemoine deutzia (*D. × lemoinei*), hardy to zone 4, can grow to 7 feet, though there are some compact varieties. Fuzzy deutzia (*D. scabra*), hardy to zone 5 or 6, blooms in late June and can grow 8 feet tall.

How to Grow: Deutzia is very easy to grow in most soils and will take either sun or part shade. In cold climates the low-growing varieties often die back considerably in winter. Prune out the dead growth carefully in early spring, being careful not to snip live shoots that are about to flower, since deutzias bloom on wood formed the previous season. After bloom you may cut back more severely, especially in the case of the taller deutzias, where you want to encourage lower branching. Old branches that no longer bloom can be cut out at the base, and branch tips can be sheared in order to promote more bloom the following season. Plants are easily propagated from softwood cuttings.

ENKIANTHUS

Enkianthus campanulatus

Description: Sometimes called red-vein enkianthus, this handsome shrub has tiny, dangling yellow flowers tipped with red that appear just before the leaves in spring. As a bonus the leaves turn bright red in fall. There are also white- and red-flowered varieties. The plant usually grows to about 8 feet tall (sometimes as tall as 12). It is hardy to zone 4 or 5.

How to Grow: Enkianthus does well in full sun or part shade. It likes the same kind of soil that rhododendrons do: well drained, slightly acid, and rich in organic matter. It doesn't transplant easily and is best propagated by layering. The upright-arching plants don't need pruning to look shapely, but can be cut back after flowering if more branching is desired, or thinned at the base if they're too dense.

FALSE CYPRESS

Chamaecyparis

*Chamaecyparis
pisifera 'Filifera Aurea'*

Description: This evergreen tree usually goes under its Latin name, which is pronounced "cam-uh-*sip*-ar-is." It is a varied genus with many garden-worthy species, the most popular of which are native to Japan. Though all species grow to be large trees, most of the ones sold in nurseries are compact or dwarf varieties suitable for shrub borders, plantings near the house, and even rock gardens. The shapes and colors of the needles are often unusual and make the shrubs effective as specimen plantings and in rock gardens.

Hinoki false cypress (*Chamaecyparis obtusa*) is very tall if you grow the original species. It has dark green needles like overlapping scales, arranged in a fan shape. The columnar varieties such as 'Erecta' are elegant alternatives to arborvitae either in a hedge or in a spot where you need a tall, narrow evergreen. The compact varieties grown as shrubs have the same lovely foliage. 'Gracilis' is broadly pyramidal and grows to 7 or 8 feet tall; 'Nana Gracilis' grows slowly to 4 feet. The *C. pisifera* varieties include many that are strikingly colored, such as

'Boulevard,' which is very blue and grows to 8 feet, and 'Filifera Aurea' (gold-thread false cypress), which is a pyramid of long, bright yellow, threadlike needles. While the latter can ultimately become a tall tree, it grows very slowly and should be pruned to keep the form graceful.

Three American natives are also grown: *C. thyoides*, a swamp tree found in the northeastern and southern states, and two from the northwest, Lawson's false-cypress (*C. lawsoniana*) and the Alaskan *C. nootkatensis*. The first of these has a number of shrublike cultivars. All of the species mentioned are hardy to zones 4 or 5.

How to Grow: These plants do best in areas with some moisture in the air; they do not like hot, drying winds. They also appreciate a mulch as many of them are shallow rooted. Varieties with yellow foliage should grow in full sun to bring out the color. Branch tips may be pinched in spring or late summer to maintain a compact, bushy shape, but cutting back into old wood will not produce branching.

FORSYTHIA

Forsythia

Description: Few plants herald spring quite as loudly as forsythia does; no wonder people love it. It does best in a spot where it can form a big mound and its long stems can arch and spill over without interfering with anything. It can be a hedge if there's room for a very wide one, with the plants spaced 5 or 6 feet apart. Forsythia often affords a good way to block the view from the road, because even when it's bare of leaves you can't really see through it. The

most familiar forsythia is *Forsythia × intermedia*, of which there are many varieties ranging from pale to dark yellow. 'Spring Glory' is a popular variety because of its profuse bloom; its low chilling requirement makes it a good choice for the south. Weeping forsythia (*F. suspensa*), and particularly the variety *sieboldii*, is excellent for slopes and banks. It forms a huge fountain, the lax stems bending over and rooting along the ground. 'Arnold Dwarf' forsythia, 4 feet tall or less, is a fast-spreading creeper that is also good for banks, though its flowers are nothing to brag about. All these are hardy to at least zone 5, though cold winters may sometimes nip the flowers in the bud. Extra-hardy hybrids such as 'Northern Sun' and 'New Hampshire Gold' bloom more reliably even in zone 4.

How to Grow: Forsythia will tolerate almost any growing conditions, though it prefers moist soils and needs plenty of sun for flowering. It is not bothered by diseases or pests. Plants can be propagated easily from suckers or cuttings and by layering. Pruning forsythia is the trick. I sometimes think there should be a Forsythia Protection Society to make sure gardeners do it right. Shearing the plants into compact forms ruins the flower display, which is, to be honest, the only reason to grow most forsythias. If you must tackle a plant that has become a monster, you have no choice but to crawl into the middle of it and remove the older stems (they look darker and rougher than the newer ones) to thin the plant out and let in light. As new growth develops at the base, more old stems can be cut out each year until there is a whole new compact plant, produced without loss of bloom. The whole plant can also be cut back to a foot or less, and it will eventually regrow. Pruning should be done after bloom, since flowers are made on the previous year's wood.

FOTHERGILLA

Fothergilla

Description: Also known as witch alder or bottle-brush, these wonderful shrubs offer so much to the gardener that it is surprising they're not more widely grown. In May they bear creamy white flowers that look like bottle brushes (what you see are not petals but many prominent stamens) and have a spicy fragrance. In fall the leaves turn beautiful shades of yellow, orange, and red. Large fothergilla (*Fothergilla major*) can grow as tall as 10 feet; the 1- to 2-inch flowers appear at the same time as the leaves. Dwarf fothergilla (*F. gardenii*) is usually about 3 feet tall; its slightly smaller flowers appear before the leaves. It is one

of the best compact shrubs, very versatile in the landscape. The excellent cultivar 'Mount Airy' grows 5 to 6 feet tall. Though native to the southeastern United States, all are hardy at least as far north as zone 5.

How to Grow: Fothergillas are easy to grow and are usually pest-free. Plant them in full sun or part shade (afternoon shade in hot climates). Soil should be moist but well drained, and moderately acid. Fothergillas rarely need pruning, but old wood can be thinned out at the base of the plant in late winter or just after bloom.

FREMONTIA (FLANNEL BUSH)

Fremontodendron californicum

Description: One of the showiest of the California chaparral shrubs, fremontia is an explosion of yellow flowers in late spring, much the way forsythia is in other parts of the country. It grows large and bushy, the branches reaching upward and outward toward the sun. Though usually about 12 feet tall, it can become treelike. Flowers are 1 to 3 inches across, and the evergreen leaves are leathery with pale, fuzzy undersides. Related species include Mexican fremontia (*Fremontodendron mexicanum*), whose flower display is somewhat less showy, and *F. californicum* var. *decumbens*, which grows only 3 to 4 feet tall. Commercial varieties such as 'California Glory' are hybrids. Fremontia is often planted with ceanothus, which likes similar conditions.

How to Grow: Fremontia needs full sun and a dry, very well drained soil. It is not long lived, but is fast growing and blooms at a young age, so specimens are not difficult to replace in plantings. It may need to be staked while becoming established. Plants should not be fertilized, and need to be dry in summer. Prune after flowering as needed to control size and shape. Hardy in zones 8 to 10. In areas with very hot summers it does better in partial shade.

HOLLY
Ilex

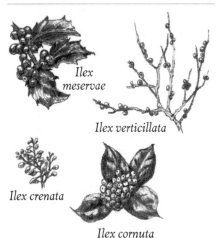

Ilex meservae

Ilex verticillata

Ilex crenata

Ilex cornuta

Description: Some hollies are grown as trees, but a number of them, both deciduous and evergreen, make fine garden shrubs. Among the evergreen types the Meserve hybrids (*Ilex × meserveae*) are noteworthy because they are hardy as far north as zone

5; they grow as tall as 12 feet. Some have names like 'Blue Angel' and 'Blue Prince' because of their lustrous dark blue-green leaves. With most hollies it's necessary to have both a male and a female plant that bloom at the same time, in order to ensure pollination of the female plant and the production of red berries. Japanese hollies (*I. crenata*) have small, shiny leaves rather like those of boxwood. Their black berries are not showy but their slow, compact growth habit makes them desirable in many landscaping situations. Most are hardy to zone 5 or 6 but often need protection against winter burn. Size varies widely among cultivars. Inkberry (*I. glabra*) is a native evergreen holly hardy to zone 4. Its variety 'Compacta' usually grows 4 to 5 feet tall. I find this species performs better than Japanese holly does. Chinese holly (*I. cornuta*) is popular in the south and is hardy to zone 7. Longstalk holly (*Ilex pedunculosa*) is an Asian species with red berries, very hardy in the north.

A number of deciduous hollies native to the United States are fine garden plants. One is winterberry (*I. verticillata*), also called black alder, which is hardy to zone 3 or 4 and bears bright red berries that remain on the twigs a good part of the winter, for the birds to eat and for you to admire. I've had good luck with the varieties 'Winter Red' and 'Sparkleberry.' You must also grow a male such as 'Southern Gentleman' to insure pollination. Smooth winterberry (*I. laevigata*) doesn't need a male, is more compact, has bigger berries, and turns a nice yellow color in fall. Possum haw (*Ilex decidua*) is a better choice in warmer climates and more alkaline soil.

How to Grow: Most hollies need moist soil. Even those that are hardy in cold climates must be well watered before winter to prevent winter burn, and sometimes need to be screened with burlap or sprayed with an antidessicant. Inkberry and winterberry will both grow in very wet soil, though average soil suits them too. Most hollies benefit from a mulch year-round. There are no very serious pests or diseases, and plants rarely need pruning but can be cut back to lateral branches in late winter or early spring for more compact growth.

HYDRANGEA

Hydrangea

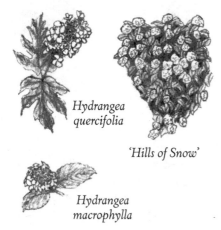

Hydrangea quercifolia

'Hills of Snow'

Hydrangea macrophylla

Description: If you like to grow a lot of large, showy flowers with a minimum of effort, hydrangeas are for you. Peegee hydrangea (*Hydrangea paniculata grandiflora*), named for the initials of its Latin name, will grow to a large treelike plant with big balls of white flowers in July when few other shrubs are blooming. The flowers dry nicely right on the plant for winter bouquets. It is hardy to zone 4. The native *H. arborescens*, often referred to as wild hydrangea, is a smaller shrub, usually about 4 feet tall. It often dies back during

the winter, though it is root-hardy to zone 4. Popular varieties are 'Annabelle' and 'Hills of Snow.' Bigleaf hydrangeas (*H. macrophylla*) are sometimes sold as houseplants. Hardy only to zone 6 or 7, they do best in warm climates, generally growing less than 5 feet tall. Colors vary according to the many varieties, but most hydrangeas have the odd trait of turning pink in alkaline soils and blue in acid ones, just like litmus paper. (Add lime if you like pink hydrangea blossoms, and peat moss or other acidic organic matter if you like blue.) The flower clusters also vary as to their form. Even within *H. macrophylla* cultivars, some have large balls of bloom while others (called lacecaps) are flat on top, with a clear contrast between the showy outer ray flowers, which are sterile, and the tiny fertile flowers at each cluster's center (the ray flowers guide pollinators toward this nectar payload). 'Endless Summer'—a blue ball-of-bloom type—is an especially hardy bigleaf variety for cold climates.

Oakleaf hydrangea (*H. quercifolia*) is a native shrub, blooming in early July. Though technically hardy to zone 5 it frequently dies to the ground, resulting in foliage regrowth but no bloom that season. The flowers are white. In a more favorable climate it forms low, wide-spreading clumps, and sports a spectacular medley of red, orange, and purple in fall. If I could grow it in Maine it would be my hydrangea of choice.

How to Grow: Give hydrangeas fertile, humusy, moist but well-drained soil and they will take care of themselves unless it is very dry, in which case they'll need watering. Mulch helps. Either sun or part shade is suitable. Peegee and 'Hills of Snow' hydrangeas bloom on new wood, so can be cut back as needed in early spring. French and oakleaf hydrangeas should be pruned after flowering, though winter-killed wood can be removed in early spring. Plants are easily propagated in spring from softwood cuttings.

HYPERICUM (ST. JOHNSWORT)

Hypericum

Description: The hypericums are a wonderful group of low-growing shrubs that should be used more in home landscapes. They are compact, with attractive blue-green foliage and sunny yellow flowers like large, open buttercups. They do especially well in New England and the Pacific northwest, where summers are not excessively hot and humid. *Hypericum frondosum* is probably the most adaptable, with the variety 'Sunburst' widely available in the trade. 'Hidcote' is a popular hybrid. It dies back to the ground in winter in my garden, but the blue-green foliage sprouts anew in late spring and produces showy yellow blossoms. *H. prolificum* is rugged and small-flowered.

How to Grow: Plants seem to tolerate light or heavy soils, but must have good drainage. They are fairly drought-tolerant and thrive in sun or light shade. Prune out any winter-killed growth in spring.

JUNIPER

Juniperus

Juniperus chinensis 'Pfitzerana'

Juniperus sabina 'Tamariscifolia'

Juniperus scopulorum 'Gray Gleam'

Juniperus horizontalis

Description: Some junipers are trees (what we call red cedar is really a juniper). But many others are shrublike and as such are extremely useful in landscape plantings, especially since they'll tolerate poor soil. They do well by the seashore as well as in hot, dry places, and they cover banks beautifully. There is great variety in their shapes, foliage textures, and foliage colors. Many make fine specimen plants, and the smaller ones look good in rock gardens, either as accents or trailing down over rocks. The low, spreading junipers make excellent ground covers.

Many varieties of Chinese juniper (*Juniperus chinensis*), such as the bluish 'Hetzii' and the flat-topped 'Pfitzerana,' may grow as tall as 10 feet and just as wide, sending out long, irregular horizontal branches. They are usually misused because people rarely understand how big they will grow. Given the right space, the big ones can be effective, but a compact juniper is more appropriate for most landscaping situations. The variety called Sargent's juniper forms a low, bluish mat. Varieties of common juniper (*J. communis*) include 'Depressa,' which grows under 4 feet tall, and 'Compressa,' a little gem of a plant that grows upright with a pointed top and never exceeds 2 feet. Tam juniper (*J. sabina* 'Tamariscifolia') is much used because it forms a low, wide, tidy mound of rich green. Varieties of creeping juniper (*J. horizontalis*) are the most prostrate of all: 'Wiltoni,' also called 'Blue Rug,' forms a blue mat just a few inches high that spreads widely and is excellent for the foreground of a shrub planting or in a rock garden. 'Bar Harbor' is gray-green and turns purplish in winter. Andorra juniper (*J. h. plumosa*) is taller than 'Bar Harbor' (under 2 feet) but also has a distinctive purplish winter color. Shore juniper (*J. conferta*) has a slightly bluish hue and an attractive bristly look; it does very well in seaside conditions. It's a bit less hardy than the other species.

How to Grow: Junipers like full sun and a soil that is rather dry, sandy, well drained and slightly acid. They rarely if ever need feeding. They should not need much pruning if you've chosen the right one for the spot—in fact they're appreciated for the irregularity of their branching patterns. But you can remove awkward shoots in spring or summer, trim recent growth in early spring if more bushiness is needed, or cut all of the season's growth in summer to limit size. Cutting back hard to bare wood will not, however, produce branching.

KERRIA

Kerria japonica

Description: Kerria makes a showy display of yellow flowers in April or May. The original species has single blooms and grows about 5 feet tall, but the more common 'Pleniflora' has many-petaled flowers like little yellow balls and can grow as tall as 7 feet, with a somewhat gawky habit. The plants are vigorous almost to the point of being rampant, but in the right spot they can cheer you in two seasons, for the stems remain bright green year-round. Some have variegated leaves and make very pretty specimen plants; 'Picta' has white markings and 'Aureo-variegata' yellow ones.

How to Grow: Kerrias like shaded sites but will grow in sun. They favor a soil that is rich in organic matter, but most soils will do as long as they are well drained. Plants can be propagated by dividing the roots, by layering, or from cuttings. The major care involved is pruning tall shrubs yearly, removing stems at the base so new ones can replace them. Stems can also be cut back partway, and they will branch. Prune after flowering.

LILAC
Syringa

Description: Most lilacs are not very graceful; they get tall and leggy, and their leaves are a magnet for mildew in late summer. But for many the fragrant flowers redeem them, and they will always be a favorite with gardeners. The common lilac (*Syringa vulgaris*) is the one most often grown; it has spawned hybrids by the hundreds in shades of lavender, purple, rose, and white. It's very hardy (to zone 3), and I have seen it grow as tall as 20 feet.

The adventurous can experiment with other lilac species and their hybrids for different flower shapes, more compact growing habits, and the opportunity to stretch out "lilac time" to as much as six weeks. The early Korean lilac (*S. oblata dilatata*) is fairly tall and has large, fragrant lilac-pink flowers. Cut-leaf lilac (*S. laciniata*) is a short shrub (7 feet or less) with pale lilac flowers and finely cut leaves; it is mildew resistant. Littleleaf lilac (*S. microphylla*) is also short but very wide; the variety 'Superba' has deep pink flowers. Persian lilac (*S. × persica*) is also very wide and spreading; the pale lilac flowers are small but very profuse. Meyer lilac (*S. meyeri*) is short with deep purple flowers; it is mil-

dew resistant. For late bloom try late lilac (*S. villosa*), which has long lilac or pinkish flowers (less fragrant than some), and Japanese tree lilac (*S. reticulata*, also called *S. amurenesis* var. *japonica*), which can grow as tall as 30 feet and bears long white flowers in mid June. *S. patula* 'Miss Kim' grows to 8 feet with lavender-blue flowers and purple fall foliage. Most lilacs are hardy to zone 3 or 4. They do not do well in warm climates, although some low-chill cultivars have been developed.

How to Grow: Lilac likes a light, fertile, well-drained soil with a neutral pH. If yours is very acid you'll need to dig in some lime. Lilacs are easy to transplant, even bare-root, but should not be dug while the new leaves are emerging. The powdery mildew they get is unattractive but generally harmless; scale infestations can be controlled with dormant oil. The loss of branches can sometimes indicate borers in the lower stems—look for little holes with sawdust beneath them, and cut the stems and burn them.

Prune lilacs only after they've become well established. Remove the oldest stems and let a few new suckers grow up to take their place, but don't leave too many suckers—they can rob the plant's energy and reduce the number of flowers. Carefully pinching off spent flowers just to the first leaves can result in more blooms the following year. Old plants can be cut as far back as 4 inches from the ground and still come back as bushy, rejuvenated plants, but this is best done over a period of three years, cutting back a third of the old stems each time. Severe pruning can be done in early spring before buds swell, lighter pruning just after bloom.

MAHONIA
Mahonia

Description: The mahonias are closely related to the barberries, with whom they are sometimes grouped, but they do not have barberry's thorny stems. Most are very compact, versatile shrubs for the landscape, with much multiseasonal interest. Although some Asian species are grown, such as the tall leatherleaf mahonia (*Mahonia bealei*) and *M. lomariifolia* with its frondlike foliage, most are native to the American west. Mahonias bear bright yellow flowers in spring, followed by dangling clusters of bluish berries.

The species most often seen in gardens is Oregon grape (*M. aquifolium*), which has stiff, sharply toothed, hollylike leaves. It typically grows to 3 feet tall, sometimes much taller, and spreads slowly by underground stems. It is evergreen in moderate climates. Though hardy to zone 5, it may die back to the ground in the north in areas without consistent snow cover, but new stems resprout from the base. Fall and winter color ranges from burgundy to red, and emerging spring foliage is also reddish. The flowers are fragrant, the edible fruits blue. Longleaf mahonia (*M. nervosa*) is a

low-growing version and creeping mahonia (*M. repens*) is prostrate and creeping—often used as a ground cover. Agarito (*M. trifoliolata*) is a southwestern plant with attractive blue-green foliage year-round, fragrant yellow flowers, and bright red berries. Red barberry (*M. haematocarpa*) is a taller, drought-tolerant southwestern species with small evergreen leaves and red berries. There are a number of other desert or coastal species worth investigating.

How to Grow: Mahonias vary in their needs. *M aquifolium, M. nervosam,* and *M. repens* like moist but well-drained, acid soil and need protection from winter sun. Spring pruning may be needed to remove winterkilled stems, and maintain a pleasing shape. Those suited to drier regions need very good drainage, and benefit from occasional watering in summer.

MOCK ORANGE
Philadelphus

Description: This lovely old-fashioned shrub bears clusters of fragrant white flowers, 1 to 2 inches wide, in June. Some are single, some double; the height and shape of the plants also vary, and the right size should be chosen to fit the spot. Often they have interesting peeling bark. (An old common name for this plant is syringa, not to be confused with the botanical name of lilac.) Sweet mock orange (*Philadelphus coronarius*) grows as tall as 9 feet, with single flowers. *P. × virginalis* can be equally tall and rather leggy, but some varieties are more compact, and the flowers are usually double or semidouble. 'Albatre' is about 5 feet tall; 'Minnesota Snowflake' is tall

single flowers

double flowers

banded

freckled

but bushy and very hardy in cold climates. The Lemoine hybrids are among the choicest, growing 4 to 6 feet tall. 'Avalanche' and 'Belle Etoile' are compact singles; 'Boule d'Argent' a double; 'Mont Blanc' is an extrahardy single. Most mock oranges are hardy to zone 5. There are a number of native species including the very fragrant western mock orange (*P. lewisii*), native to the American northwest and western Canada, and littleleaf mock orange (*P. microphyllus*), a compact, fragrant plant that's more tolerant of dry soil than most.

How to Grow: Mock oranges are very easy to grow, with no serious pests or diseases. Give them sun or part shade. They like moist, well-drained, humusy soil but they aren't fussy. They can be propagated by layering or by removing and replanting suckers. Their chief drawback is their shape, which often consists of long, straggly shoots, but they can be trimmed back after bloom to keep them compact. Old plants can be renewed by thinning at the base or cutting back the whole shrub close to the ground.

Description: Unlike the bay tree (*Laurus nobilis*), this American native is not a true laurel. But it is a very handsome broad-leaved evergreen that looks good as a specimen shrub, in group plantings, or naturalized in a woodland setting. Most of those found in the wild have white to pale pink flowers, but there are many fine varieties (originally developed by Dr. Richard Jaynes at the Connecticut Agricultural Experiment Station) with bright pink or red buds, and with flowers blotched, freckled, or banded in vivid red, pink, or purple. Even when the red-budded ones open to white, the gradually opening flowers give the whole cluster a rosy look. Varieties also vary in habit from nearly treelike to low and bushy to almost prostrate. Mountain laurel's glossy dark green foliage is beautiful year-round. It grows in the woods from southern Maine to Florida (near water in the southern states).

A related plant, sheep laurel (*Kalmia angustifolia*), is another favorite of mine. Both it and mountain laurel are planted right next to the north-facing entrance to my home. Sheep laurel is low growing and gradually spreading, its bright pink flowers emerging just below the new foliage in springtime.

How to Grow: Mountain laurel needs a moist but well-drained, acid, humusy soil just like it would choose in the forest. Incorporating peat moss and compost into the soil, then mulching with an acid material such as pine bark, will help to achieve this. Plants will grow even in full shade, though they flower better and grow more vigorously in sun. It's important to protect them from strong sun and drying winds in wintertime. An ideal site is one where the sun is high enough to reach the plants in summer, but dips below a building or evergreen trees in winter. Plant in early spring. Mountain laurel is prone to leaf spot, which is usually just a cosmetic problem. Wash lacebugs off with a hose.

Mountain laurels often don't need pruning, but they can be cut back to forks or lateral branches—or even to the ground—to counteract a tendency to legginess. Those transplanted from the woods should be cut back in this manner. Drastic pruning should be done in early spring, but if you're pinching off recent growth to limit size or make plants bushy, do it after flowering, as plants bloom on old wood. Sheep laurel seems to need no care, although I do give it some water in very dry weather.

NANDINA

Nandina domestica

Description: Popular in the south and on the west coast, this plant is sometimes called heavenly bamboo because of its bamboolike

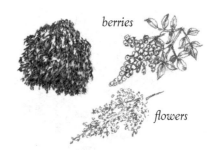

berries

flowers

foliage. It bears large clusters of small white flowers in July, followed by even showier red berries. The foliage is evergreen, the new leaves reddish when newly emerging in spring and reddish again in fall and winter. Plants grow up to 8 feet tall, but there are a number of dwarf varieties such as 'Nana Purpurea' and 'Compacta.' 'Alba' has white berries. If protected with a mulch it can grow in zone 7 and even farther north, though the tops will be winter-killed.

How to Grow: Nandina prefers sun but it will take part shade. Although the plants will tolerate drought, a moist, light soil will produce more flowers and berries. Few pests or diseases bother it.

Large plants grow vigorously in warm climates and can become leggy. They're best pruned in early spring or after bloom, by removing some stems at the base each year and letting a supply of shorter new ones continually replace them. Old plants can be renewed by cutting half the stems to the ground one year and the rest the following year—or even by cutting all of them at once.

OLEANDER

Nerium oleander

Description: This southern plant actually blooms from spring to fall; its 1- to 2-

inch flowers are shades of red, pink, yellow, orange, purple, or white, depending on variety. Some are fragrant, some have double blooms. The leaves are evergreen and rather like those of bamboo. Oleander tolerates a wide variety of conditions including heat, drought, partial shade, salt, and highway pollution. Now for the bad news: all of oleander's plant parts are poisonous to people and animals. If you grow them you might warn your children against them the way my grandmother did, telling us the story of Leander's death upon eating the plant, and the exclamation of his lover, who discovered him: "Oh, Leander!" My grandmother kept the leaves and flowers out of harm's way by training the plant as a tree. It can grow as tall as 20 feet in the Deep South but is more typically 4 to 10, depending on the variety and the amount of winter dieback.

How to Grow: Generally oleander favors a sunny site with well-drained soil. To contain its vigorous growth you may root-prune it or cut the branches back to a fork in early spring. Deadheading the flowers will produce more bloom. Cutting the whole plant back to 6 inches will rejuvenate an old one. To grow as a tree, remove all stems but one, and all suckers; keep removing lower branches as they start to sprout. Hardy to zone 8.

POTENTILLA
Potentilla fruticosa

Description: Potentilla has gained a firm place in the gardener's repertoire. It's easy to grow, it's not at all fussy about soil, and most varieties keep a compact shape (4 feet or less), although I have seen old plantings where potentillas have attained great heights. The bright yellow 'Farreri' (also called 'Gold Drop') and the white 'Everest' are very low growing. Potentilla blooms most heavily in early summer, but you can expect a lesser display all summer and into fall, especially if the weather is cool. Flowers are about an inch wide and typically bright yellow, but varieties include pale yellows such as 'Katherine Dykes,' whites such as 'Abbotswood,' and the occasional orange, peach, or pink. Even without flowers the plants are attractive, with delicate gray-green foliage. I like to use potentilla near swimming pools for its summer color and because it can take the heat. It's also excellent in a foundation planting because it is both low and showy, and because of the way its foliage contrasts with that of other shrubs. Hardy even in the far north, it is unsuitable for warm climates.

How to Grow: Potentillas like fertile, sandy, slightly alkaline soils but will grow in almost any that are sufficiently well drained. They like full sun but do better in part shade where summers are warm. They are pretty much pest-free. They can be propagated by layering, root division, or softwood cuttings. They look fine without pruning, and it's best to plant them where their shape needn't be restrained. Prune long or awkward shoots in spring while the shrub is still dormant, and thin old shoots at the base if your plants seem overgrown.

PYRACANTHA

Pyracantha coccinea

Description: A common name for this plant is firethorn—appropriate because of its thorny branches and bright red or orange berries. The species listed here is the most popular, scarlet firethorn, and its most common variety is 'Lalandei,' which usually grows to about 6 feet. Some pyracanthas grow very tall; others are low growing and used as ground covers. Most are hardy to zone 6, with some more hardy, some less so. Pyracantha is evergreen in warm climates. A favorite way to use it is to let it climb up against a wall, but it also makes a good freestanding specimen plant. All kinds can be pruned as trees by removing the lower branches. They also makes good hedges, especially if you want a thorny barrier.

How to Grow: Plants do fine in part shade but full sun produces showier fruits. They are fairly drought proof, and require well-drained soil. They are susceptible to fire blight, which can blacken the branches. Remove affected branches a foot below the blackened part, but never leave a stub or it may rot. I think the plant looks best in its natural shape, but new growth can be pinched back to control the plant's size, and long or awkward branches can be cut back to a side branch after the fruits have fallen.

QUINCE

Chaenomeles

Description: The growth habit of flowering quince is often described as picturesque. Its irregularly shaped, prickly branches are twiggy and angular in form, evoking the branches portrayed in Chinese and Japanese paintings. Woody-plant expert Michael Dirr's word for the shrub is "ratty," and in fact flowering quince rarely has a well-behaved shape that would make it useful for foundation plantings. Most people grow it for the five-petaled flowers, which are about 1½ inches across in shades of pink, red, salmon, and coral as well as white. The flowers can be single, double, or semidouble, appearing just before the leaves unfold. Blooming on old wood, they often appear, annoyingly, toward the bottom of the stems, deep within the thicket the plant creates. Nonetheless, they do bloom quite early in spring and are excellent for forcing indoors as long as you cut down far enough on the branch.

Flowering quinces are not to be confused with the large tree-size quinces grown for their fruits (*Cydonia oblonga*). These have pale pink blossoms and fruits that resemble lumpy pears—good for jellies. Flowering quinces (which sometimes bear a few tiny fruits) are landscape shrubs, best given a spacious spot at the edge of the lawn or in a shrub border; a row of them forms a fine, barrier-like hedge. Shopping for them can be complicated. There are two common species. One is Japanese quince (*Chaenomeles japonica*), sometimes just called japonica, which supposedly grows only 3 or 4 feet tall and has bright red-orange flowers. The other is common flowering quince (*C. speciosa*, also called *C. lagenaria*), which can become a 10-foot plant, though low-growing hybrids have been developed. I have found size estimates in quinces quite unreliable. It's best to ask the nurseryman for his or her best guess as to the ultimate height and spread, then plan for excess, just in case. Both species are hardy to zone 4 or 5, although flower buds may sometimes be killed in the north by spring frosts.

How to Grow: Quinces are very easy to grow. They will tolerate any reasonably good soil and are drought tolerant. Sun is preferred, but they will take some shade. Plants can be set out bare-root, though container-grown or balled-and-burlapped plants are best. Quinces are easily propagated by dividing the plant with a spade, especially if suckers have formed at a distance from the plant. They can also be layered. You may prune after the flowers have faded, to keep the plants compact and promote bloom. On compact plants this is rarely necessary, but some of the large ones can send out long, lanky stems that are best cut back to a side branch to make them more graceful. Old plants may be thinned at the base in winter.

RHODODENDRON
Rhododendron

Description: The genus *Rhododendron* includes nearly a thousand species and an immense number of varieties (including the azaleas, described on page 623). The ones you select will depend in large part on which do well in your region. The plants are grown almost entirely for their spectacular flower clusters, which come in every color except true blue. The foliage, which is usually evergreen, is handsome during the growing season, but in cold weather the leaves droop and curl at the sides to conserve moisture—something I find rather disheartening on a day when I feel like drooping and curling up myself.

Many gardeners find rhododendrons addictive, especially if they live in a climate that suits them, because there are always so many new ones to try. What climate suits them? One that is enough like the temperate woodland mountainsides where they grow wild (most are from Asia, but some are native to the United States): where the air is moist but the soil drains well, leaf fall makes the soil acid, and summers are not too hot and winters not too cold.

Three American natives you might grow are rosebay rhododendron (*Rhododendron maximum*), a huge, treelike shrub hardy to zone 4, the lovely, low-growing Carolina rhododendron (*R. carolinianum*), and catawba rhododendron (*R. catawbiense*), hardy to zone 5. The last has produced many notable hybrids such as the hardy white 'Catawbiense Album' and the purple 'Roseum Elegans.' Other major groups include the Dexter hybrids, such as the lovely pink 'Scintillation,' hardy to zone 5, and the Caucasian hybrids, including the very hardy and compact white 'Boule de Neige,' which is more sun tolerant than most. The Korean rhododendron (*R. mucronulatum*) is deciduous, hardy to zone 5, and bears lavender flowers before the leaves. 'PJM' is a hybrid with fairly small leaves that have a nice purplish color in winter and rosy-purple flowers; it is hardy to zone 4. Bloom times for rhododendrons can be as early as early May for Korean rhododendron, and as late as late June for rosebay rhododendron. Most fall in between. It is worth shopping around and experimenting with new varieties that may be improvements on the old favorites.

Most rhododendrons should not be planted in front of windows or anything else you don't want obscured, for most grow at least 6 or 8 feet tall, many as tall as 15 feet and taller. They are all too often planted in spots where the owner must prune them drastically every year just to keep them in check. For sites like these, choose a rhododendron like the exquisite *R. yakusimanum;* hardy to zone 5, it slowly forms a 3-foot mound that is covered with big pink-white flower clusters in spring. Or plant some of the charming small-leaved rhododendrons such as *R. impeditum* or 'Purple Gem.'

How to Grow: Give rhododendrons a light, moist, but very well-drained soil with plenty of organic matter. Peat moss is the perfect thing to incorporate into the soil, because it is also acid. The plants are shallow rooted and don't need deep soil preparation, but a mulch such as shredded bark is an excellent idea to protect the roots and keep the soil moist. Plant rhododendrons where they will not be exposed to drying winds or strong sunlight in winter, especially in very cold or very hot climates. A northern exposure in sunlight filtered through deciduous trees is excellent, though no varieties bloom quite as well in full shade.

Plant rhododendrons in early spring in cold climates, fall in warm ones. They cannot be planted bare-root. They generally do not need to be fed, though some liquid fertilizer or a topdressing of manure will help if growth is slow or if drastic pruning is anticipated. Well-grown plants do not often suffer diseases, and there are not many pests to worry about. Lacebugs will sometimes suck the undersides of the leaves, producing a stippled, yellowed look; the bugs can be rubbed off with your fingers while they are active in late spring and early summer. Stems attacked by borers should be removed and burned.

Pruning is often not needed if the right site has been chosen, but sometimes plants are lanky and need some attention. The terminal buds (found in the center of a leaf rosette) can be pinched to cause side buds to develop and branches to form, or stems can be cut back to a leaf rosette; both are best done after flowering. Removing spent flowers at their base, just above the new buds, will produce heavier flowering the following year. For overgrown, leggy plants, cut back in early spring to produce lower growth. If possible, cut back to a leaf rosette, but if the stems are bare try to find the faint mark of a growth ring where dormant buds may be induced to grow. To rejuvenate gangly old plants, you can cut a third of the stems back to a foot or so each spring; sometimes a whole plant cut back at once will regenerate, but this is risky.

ROSE OF SHARON

Hibiscus syriacus

Description: The chief value of this shrub, also known as shrub althaea, lies in its late-summer bloom, usually coming in August. It is not a true rose, and does not grow like one. There are a number of varieties, in shades of pink, purple, blue, lavender, red, and white. Flowers are usually 3 to 5 inches in diameter; extra-large ones can be produced by cutting stems back to two buds after blooming. These are tall, bushy plants reaching as high as 15 feet and can be grown as trees by eliminating all but one stem and removing lower branches. They make good specimen shrubs, given enough space, and can also be used as informal hedges, though close shearing is detrimental both to bloom and to the shape of the plant.

How to Grow: Plants should be set in while still young, and protected with mulch until well established. Even so, until they are mature, they are susceptible to winterkill. They will grow in sun or part shade, and they like moist, humusy soil with good drainage. Pruning need only be done if you want a smaller, compact plant, or to produce larger flowers, as above. Cut back stems to laterals to control size and produce vigorous growth, and remove dead or damaged wood. Prune in winter in mild climates, early spring in cold ones.

SNOWBERRY

Symphoricarpos albus

Description: Snowberry is an old-fashioned plant, native to eastern North America and grown since colonial times. My great-aunt had one next to an old stone wall at the entrance to her yard and I always marveled at its large, heavy white berries in wintertime, dangling ghostlike from the spindly twigs. There is nothing refined about this plant—its shape is straggly and it spreads rapidly and persistently from suckers. Its tiny pinkish flowers are barely noticeable. But in an informal settling where it won't

bother anybody, it's wonderful. The small blue-green leaves are handsome, especially as a backdrop for the berries, which attract birds. The closely related coralberry (*Symphoricarpos orbiculatus*) has larger leaves and clusters of dark red berries. There are a number of western species, including *S. albus* var. *laevigatus,* as well as several hybrids such as chenault cranberry (*S.* × *chenaultii*), and some cultivars with variegated foliage. Most grow about 5 feet tall, sometimes taller in sun and rich soil; there are also low-growing, creeping types.

How to Grow: These rugged plants, hardy to zone 2 or 3, do well in almost any soil, in sun or in shade, and are quite drought tolerant. They can be pruned back for a more compact shape, but this is less important in the informal situations that suit them best. Their tenacious root systems make them excellent for covering a steep bank.

SPICEBUSH

Lindera benzoin

Description: The aromatic compounds inherent in all this plant's parts inspired its common name. Crumble a leaf in your fingers or bite into a twig, and if the scent

doesn't identify it immediately the taste will. Native to the eastern half of North America, spicebush pleases the visual sense as well. The stems are an attractive green, the small, clustered yellow flowers a subtle early-spring treat. The leaves often turn a spectacular bright yellow in fall; when they drop, bright red berries are revealed, but only on female plants, and they are rapidly consumed by birds. Spicebush can grow as tall as 12 feet, though 6 to 8 is more typical. It is the larval host plant for the beautiful spicebush swallowtail butterfly.

How to Grow: This shrub, which grows naturally in damp woods, does best in moist, well-drained soil, but average-to-dryish soil will suit it if there is sufficient organic matter. It can be grown in part shade but fall color is showier in full sun, and the plants are fuller and better shaped. Since flowers form on old wood it's best to prune after bloom. Hardy to zone 4 or 5; difficult to transplant.

SPIREA

Spiraea

Description: There are two very different groups of spireas. The first consists of

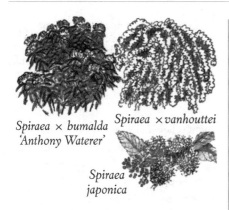

Spiraea × bumalda 'Anthony Waterer'

Spiraea × vanhouttei

Spiraea japonica

a number of fairly large spring-blooming shrubs with profuse white flowers. One of these is bridalwreath (*Spiraea prunifolia*), which grows as tall as 9 feet and has stems covered with buttonlike flowers in May and foliage that turns red or orange in fall. Thunberg spirea (*S. thunbergii*) grows to about 5 feet, bears clusters of flowers before the leaves, and has fuzzy foliage with some fall color. Vanhoutte spirea (*S. × vanhouttei*) grows up to 8 feet and has gracefully arching stems laden with small flower clusters in late May and some fall color. *S. nipponica* 'Snowmound,' a more upright and compact form than most, has flatter flower clusters. All are hardy to zone 4, though twigs on some, particularly *S. thunbergii*, will often be winter-killed.

The second group blooms in summer, with flat pink or red flower clusters, and includes the fairly low-growing bumalda spirea (*S. × bumalda*), of which 'Anthony Waterer' is a popular variety, and Japanese spirea (*S. japonica*). Some varieties are very low and compact, others as tall as 6 feet. Ask your nurseryman how tall a plant will get before you choose a spot for it. These spireas, too, are quite hardy although some winterkill may occur. Japanese spirea is considered invasive and disruptive to ecosystems in parts of the eastern U.S. Many

of the native spireas such as steeplebush (*S. tomentosa*) and mountain spirea (*S. splendens*) are beautiful, although it's best to note which are, like steeplebush, rampant colonizers before placing them in the home landscape.

How to Grow: Spireas will be happy in almost any soil, though they do like it a bit moist if possible. They will grow well in part shade but bloom best in full sun. Give the big ones plenty of room to spill out in their lovely, arching shapes, because pruning them to a compact shape defeats their reason for being there. All the spring-blooming species bloom on old wood, so prune awkward shoots after flowering, unless you want to pick them for bouquets. Thinning at the base to remove old stems can be done in early spring; so can trimming to remove winter-killed twigs. The summer-blooming spireas can always be pruned in early spring since they bloom on new wood. They really do look better and flower better if old wood is thinned out regularly; this will also help to keep them low growing. Most spireas can be cut back almost to the ground and they will regrow.

SWEETSPIRE

Itea virginica

Description: This little-known native shrub is finally coming into its own, mainly because of its wonderful fall color. It's also fairly compact (especially some of the new cultivars), and bears lovely spikes of fragrant white flowers in early summer, attractive to butterflies, bees, and other pollinators. The foliage is evergreen in mild climates and even in its northern limit (zone 5) slow to

for birds—and Christmas decorations for western gardeners.

drop. Fall color is a range or blend of scarlet, crimson, maroon, orange, and gold.

How to Grow: Though found growing wild in moist or swampy areas, sweetspire tolerates a wide range of conditions, even dryish soil. Sun, high fertility, and organic content will give it a more full, luxuriant shape than it usually displays in its more wet, shaded natural habitats. It is easy to transplant. Prune as needed if it becomes lanky and you insist on a more civilized form.

TOYON (HOLLYWOOD)

Heteromeles arbutifolia

Description: Before "Hollywood" signified large-budget movies with predictable endings, it was a shrub, also known as California holly or toyon. A chaparral plant originally native to that fabled town, toyon still grows wild in southern California and is a versatile landscape plant throughout the state and beyond. It is large and often treelike, with lustrous evergreen leaves, small white blossoms in early summer, and glamorous red berries in fall and winter. These provide winter sustenance

How to Grow: Plant in full sun or part shade. Though drought tolerant, toyon looks better if watered occasionally as needed. It is not fussy about soil type. Prune only as needed for a shapely silhouette. The root system is tenacious and good for supporting the soil on slopes and banks.

VIBURNUM

Viburnum

Description: I've always considered viburnums a joy to grow because they are so trouble-free and because they offer so much. Most bear white flowers in mid or late spring, some of them very fragrant. These are followed by berries, many of which are showy and either red, black, or yellow. In addition, many have colored foliage in fall, some of it quite striking. Sizes vary, so choose the right one for the site. Alas, in recent years a European pest called the viburnum leaf beetle has spoiled the party for many viburnum lovers, although at the time of this writing not all parts of the

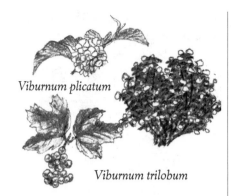

Viburnum plicatum

Viburnum trilobum

country have been affected, and some species are more resistant than others. Your local nursery or Extension Service can offer advice on the situation in your area, and tell you how to spot signs of the pest for prompt removal of eggs and affected leaves.

Among the fragrant viburnums are Burkwood viburnum (*Viburnum × burkwoodii*), whose flower clusters are 3-inch pinkish white balls, and fragrant snowball (*V. carlcephalum*), which is similar and grows to 9 feet. Korean spice viburnum (*V. carlesii*) is only 5 feet tall, its variety 'Compacta' even smaller. I'm fond of a hybrid called 'Mohawk,' whose buds are a showy dark red before they open, thus extending the floral display. All are hardy to at least zone 5. In warmer climates the Chinese snowball viburnum is popular (*V. macrocephalum*), with its big white floral pom-poms. Because of its large size it needs plenty of room—a statement that applies to all the viburnums to a greater or lesser degree.

Other favorite viburnums include the supremely elegant double-file viburnum (*V. plicatum tomentosum*), a tall and broadly spreading shrub. Each of its horizontal branches bears a double row of wide, flat flower clusters; in the variety 'Mariesi' they are especially showy. Linden viburnum (*V. dilatatum*) has very showy red berries as well as rust-red fall foliage and grows to 9 feet. Both are hardy to zone 5. American cranberrybush (*V. trilobum*) has flat flower clusters and red berries that are edible and good for preserves if you can snatch them before the birds do. It is hardy to zone 3. (I avoid planting European cranberrybush, *V. opulus*, because of its potential for invasiveness.) The most common wild viburnum where I live is witherod (*V. cassinoides*). It grows quite tall and its berries change from pink to red, then blue, then black; the fall foliage is dark red. It's worth investigating which wild viburnums inhabit the countryside near you—a sign that they might do well in your yard. Other good natives include the forest-dwelling mapleleaf viburnum (*V. acerifolium*) and the bird-friendly arrowwood (*V. dentatum*) and nannyberry (*V. lentago*).

How to Grow: Though not particular, viburnums appreciate a good light, moist loam. They are shallow rooted and a mulch will help to keep the roots moist and protected in winter. All will tolerate some shade, though full sun produces the best flowers and fruits. Viburnums can be propagated by layering. They rarely need pruning, though old plants can be thinned at the base. Since the buds are formed the year before, shrubs should be pruned right after flowering, if needed.

WEIGELA
Weigela florida

Description: Formerly classified in the genus *Diervilla*, this old-fashioned plant has only one trick, but it's a good one—

WITCH HAZEL
Hamamelis

producing small, bright flowers in May on long, arching stems. Typically red, they are little open-mouthed tubes designed just right for feeding the hummingbirds that suck their nectar. Old varieties generally grow 6 to 9 feet tall and quite wide; many modern ones are more compact. Their hardiness varies too, with older ones zone 5 but many newer ones zone 4 or even 3. 'Vanicek' ('Newport Red') and 'Bristol Ruby' are typical of the red varieties; there are others in shades of pink, magenta, salmon, cream, and white. The Dance series, with names like 'Polka,' 'Minuet,' and 'Samba,' are low growing and especially cold hardy. (A related species, *Weigela middendorffiana*, is yellow.)

How to Grow: Weigelas bloom more profusely in full sun, but they put on a fairly respectable show even in shade. Most soils suit them fine, though they appreciate some moisture and need good drainage. They look best unpruned, with the arching branches spilling out like a fountain, but some clipping must sometimes be done in spring in cold climates if tips have been winter-killed. Any pruning to shape is best done after flowering.

Description: Every spring it happens. Somebody who has driven by my place tells me "Boy, your forsythia is blooming early!" It's no wonder that people don't recognize my vernal witch hazel (*Hamamelis vernalis*), because it is not frequently grown. *That's* the wonder, for it's one of the most satisfying shrubs, decking itself out in fragrant yellow, threadlike blooms long before any other plant displays color. Common witch hazel (*H. virginiana*), which I also grow and love, is no less of a tour-de-force, producing similar blossoms in late fall. (Modern breeding has worked to provide specimens that drop their leaves in time to reveal these subtle blooms.) Between the two they make our long winters seem shorter. Common witch hazel is the taller of the two—often a treelike 20 feet or more—with vernal witch hazel usually topping out at 6 to 10 feet. Both have an open shape and handsome, fairly large leaves that turn a glorious yellow in fall. Some *H. vernalis* varieties turn a more orange or red-purple color, and there are some with coppery, pink-purple, or red flowers. Both species are native to North America and very hardy. Chinese witch hazel (*H. mollis*), although the most fragrant, is barely hardy to zone 5. *H.* × *intermedia* is a cross between *H. mollis* and *H. japonica* (Japanese witch hazel); many cultivars have been developed for flower and foliage color as well as fragrance. 'Jelena' and 'Arnold Promise' are popular favorites.

How to Grow: Though not easy to transplant, witch hazels are easy to grow. They like moist, acid soil, do well in average soil with plenty of organic matter, and fare poorly in dry areas. All will grow fine in part shade, and prefer it in very warm areas, but bloom more profusely in sun. I try to position them near enough to the house so that the charm and scent of their blooms can be appreciated.

YEW

Taxus

Description: Most yew species are trees at maturity, not shrubs, but they're often used as shrubs, either by pruning them to keep them low, or by using compact varieties. No other evergreen responds quite so well to shearing, so yews make excellent evergreen hedges, possessing a fine dark color that is the perfect backdrop for pale flower colors such as those of many roses. Female plants have showy red berries, as long as there is a male plant around to pollinate them. Yews are trouble-free plants, but they are absolutely the first food choice of our local deer. *Caution:* yew berries are poisonous.

Most yews grown are derived from two species: English yew and Japanese yew. The English yew (*Taxus baccata*) is generally not hardy north of zone 7, though some of its varieties, such as the low, flat-

forms of Taxus cuspidata

topped 'Repandens,' are hardier. Growth habits vary widely, from the tall, columnar Irish yew, 'Fastigiata,' to the 3-foot 'Nana.' Japanese yew (*T. cuspidata*) is hardy at least to zone 5 and also comes in many forms. One of the best is 'Densa,' which grows no more than 4 feet high but can spread a lot wider than that, with very dark green needles. Concern has been expressed about the invasiveness of Japanese yew, but in most areas the deer seem to keep unprotected plants in check! Canadian yew (*T. canadensis*) tends to be low growing and is a good informal plant for relatively cold climates. It has a reddish tinge in winter.

How to Grow: Yews will grow well in sun or shade but too much winter sun can leave them scorched-looking. They appreciate moist but well-drained soil, and are at a particular risk of winter burn if they go into winter with dry roots and then are subjected to drying winds. A mulch will help to keep the soil moist. Yews may be sheared anytime there is too much new growth, but it's best to keep young plants shaped the way you want them as they grow. Plants cut back severely look like victims of a Pruning Shears Massacre; they will slowly grow back, but may never quite develop a pleasing shape.

CHAPTER 16

Trees

PEOPLE GET ATTACHED TO TREES. They seem to feel more affection for them than they do for any other kind of plant. Perhaps this is because we once lived in trees, before we evolved from simian tree-swingers to human tree-planters. If you doubt the significance of that, look at children. As soon as they outgrow climbing all over their mothers, they're out there climbing into the trees—if they're country children—or into jungle gyms and monkey bars if they're city kids. Having grown up doing both, I can say that trees are much more interesting. My favorite climbing trees were old friends whose branches I'd hide in. Even in college, I found a favorite tree in which I liked to sit and read.

Even if all you do is look at your trees or pick up after them in the fall, they take on individual personalities. Your rock-solid sugar maple cools your house in summer, eases you cheerfully into fall with the brightest and earliest color on the place, and holds up your child's swing, all without asking anything in return. Your irresponsible weeping willow, on the other hand, loses limbs in high winds and is trying to get its roots into your septic system. But when it leafs out yellow in early spring like a long-haired blond, then does its dance of the seven veils in a summer storm, you're hooked again and let it stay another year.

Another reason we feel so strongly about trees is that they last so long. Usually they outlast us, if not in years, then by nature of the fact that we move from place to place and they remain. I have an old photo of me as a small girl, planting a young pine tree in our yard with my father. I'm wielding a mattock over my shoulder, and he is holding a shovel. Before our house was eventually sold we both saw that tree tower above it—something that happens less and less as people move about more. When we do manage to live with a tree for a long time, it is sad indeed when it falls or must be cut down. It's like losing a companion. Even when a new tree doesn't work out and must be removed, its end is painful. Mature trees give a sense of grandeur even to a modest homesite, and add considerable value to a property. Yet there's no shortcut—trees take a long time to attain their full size.

Growing trees is much trickier than growing smaller plants. Years may pass before you realize you've made a mistake in your choice of tree, your choice of site, or the way you planted. Problems don't always develop right away, and even when there are solutions to these problems, they get harder to implement as the tree gets bigger. If the tree must be replaced—well, usually you can't replace it, except by waiting years for a new one to grow.

Choosing the Right Tree

THERE ARE A LOT OF WONDERFUL trees available to home gardeners. Choosing the right ones will give you years of pleasure and help insure their health and longevity.

ORNAMENTAL FEATURES

Often the choice of a tree begins with a mental picture of a species you particularly like, either because of nostalgic associations or because it's attractive to you in some way. There are many different traits that make certain trees garden-worthy—not necessarily the same traits that make them good for populating a forest or for producing lumber, or firewood. A tree might be handsome because of its overall shape or because of its leaves—their color, shape, or texture. It might bear showy flowers or fruits, or nuts. Its bark might be beautiful. Or it might just provide welcome shade. Most often a tree has a combination of several features that attract. For example, a copper beech is prized not only for its dark red leaves, but also for its massive, spreading form and smooth gray trunk. A paper birch has not only striking white bark, but also foliage that lets some light through—for part-shade gardens—and turns bright yellow in fall.

Which tree you choose will depend partly on how it looks in a specific place. The beech is an impressive sight when you drive up to a house, if placed on the front lawn. The birch might look best in front of some dark evergreens that set off its white trunks.

It's very important to give a tree plenty of room. Although it is fine to arrange some trees in groves, or in rows as a windbreak, they will neither grow well nor look good if crammed in too tightly among other trees. If you plant a tree where its branches will eventually interfere with foot or vehicle traffic, or with power lines, you'll end up pruning it in ways that mar its shape. Make sure that when you select a tree you take into account both its ultimate height and its ultimate spread. Keep scale in mind, too. So often a gardener plants a tree like a blue spruce next to a modest-size home. That tidy little cone grows into a 80-foot specimen that dwarfs the house and seems to bear no relation to it. Such a tree might complement a larger structure, but even

then it would probably look better planted at a distance, as a background plant. Large deciduous trees often work well near to a house, however, because they shade it in summer, then let light through in wintertime. Their overarching branches seem protective, sheltering. Even so, it's usually wise not to plant them any closer to the house than 20 feet or so. It's best if their branches do not hang over the roof.

If you have a small home, you may want to pick one of the many small ornamental shade trees, such as magnolia, hawthorn, paperbark maple, silverbell, hornbeam, or some of the ornamental fruit trees described in the fruit chapter, such as crab apple and flowering cherry.

Trees vary enormously in their sizes and shapes. One might never get taller than 20 feet, another might grow well over 100. Their heads (the leafy part) may be round, wide spreading, pendulous (weeping), broadly pyramidal, pointed like a church spire, or even straight like a column. Try to visualize which shape will look best in the place where the tree will grow. It's unfortunate that gardeners do much of their thinking while walking through a nursery, looking at infant trees. The best way to educate yourself about them is to visit a botanical garden or an arboretum, preferably one in the same climatic zone as yours, to see what various trees look like when they are full grown. You might even photograph some so they don't all blur together in your memory after you get home. This sounds like a lot of trouble to go to, but not when you consider how long you'll be living with those trees. Driving around an older neighborhood can also be helpful. Notice which mature trees match their site and which don't.

Try not to be taken too much with novelty. It's great to discover new plants that are outside of the usual run of things, but too much quirkiness or drama can look cluttered or clownish. Just how many trees can you have with variegated leaves, weeping branches, and peeling bark? Accent trees such as these should be used judiciously. You may feel that planting your yard with basic old green shade trees is like having a wardrobe with nothing but business suits. Maybe so. But build on the basics, then accessorize. As I said before, those trees will be there a long time.

Think about how your trees will look at different times of the year. Many are interesting during more than one season—with spring flowers and bright fall foliage, for example, in addition to summer greenery. And winter is just as important, especially in climates where deciduous trees are leafless for half the year or more. A number of trees, such as European mountain ash and many of the crab apples, have fruits that stay on the tree through fall and into winter. Others have bark—less visible in summer—that is a handsome color, or that peels to reveal patches of another color beneath: river birch, Amur chokecherry, paperbark maple, kousa dogwood, Chinese elm, lacebark pine, and Japanese stewartia to name a few. Evergreen trees can be all the more effective when the leaves are off the others, for different species have needles of varying textures, in shades of blue, gray, or green. I love to look at all the different shapes of bare deciduous trees in winter, too.

USEFUL TREES

Sometimes you plant a tree for a specific job. Say you want a tree that will shade a house, lawn, or terrace in hot weather but let in the sun when it's cold. You'd choose a deciduous tree and plant southwest of the site to be shaded, to block the sun for as much of the hot part of the day as possible. To provide shade heavy enough for this purpose, you'd need a tree with a dense head of leaves like a maple or a beech. If you're not so much concerned with blocking the sun as you are with providing dappled shade for certain plants, choose trees such as birch, shadblow, or redbud.

Trees make highly effective windscreens. They break the force of the wind by absorbing it rather than by rerouting it up over the barrier the way solid walls and fences do. Evergreens such as spruce, fir, cedar, arborvitae, and pine are often used as windscreens, but some deciduous trees planted close together, such as beech, linden, or hawthorn can also block the wind when they are in leaf.

For visual screening, the best trees are those that have branches growing all the way to the ground. Often the most effective ones are the fastigiate or columnar trees such as 'Sentry' ginkgo, Hinoki false cypress, columnar English oak, Irish yew, 'Armstrong' red maple, or 'Skyrocket' juniper.

Plants that take hold quickly are used to hold banks and keep soil from eroding. While this can be done with ground covers or shrubs, trees such as pines also serve the purpose, especially when a screening effect is desired as well. Generally when you're looking for a useful tree, you want one that will be ornamental as well. But sometimes you just want to reforest an area that has been cleared or to plant a large number of trees, prevent soil runoff, and keep the area from growing up with undesirable species. In this case the trees you choose do not have to be the same kind you buy as landscaping specimens, and you don't have to buy them in large sizes. Your local Soil Conservation District or Forestry Service can advise you on the best trees to choose for reforestation or erosion control in your climate and the specific site. They may even sell you tree seedlings at an affordable price.

If your land has woods on it, it's a very good idea to find out which trees are growing in them and learn how to manage them. Forests go through many changes in the course of time. Some trees crowd out others, and trees die and are replaced by new ones. You can control this process by eliminating less-desirable species and by thinning the better ones to give more room to those that remain. Don't just go out into the woods with a chainsaw and start cutting, however, unless you've consulted with a forester or tree service first—they can mark trees to be eliminated or do the work itself for you. It takes a long time for a forest to grow, and only a short time for a thoughtless person to undo nature's work. It would also be a mistake to destroy all the understory plants (shrubs and small trees) in an effort to "clean up" your woods. These provide food and shelter for wildlife. You can make paths and remove some of the standing deadwood or fallen logs if you like, but I choose to leave most of this alone. Hollow trees and logs are home to many wild creatures, and are part of the beauty of a true woodland. Don't feel you need to achieve the "parklike" grounds that realtors so often speak of in describing land. Find out what treasures your woods have to offer before you take control of them.

CHOOSING TREES THAT WILL DO WELL

Finding a tree that will look good is useless if the tree will not survive. One impor-

tant factor is winter hardiness. Hardiness zone numbers are not always a good guide to how trees will fare in a given locale, for the reasons given on page 31, especially in areas where the climate varies because of changes in elevation or other conditions. For a major purchase like a tree, ask knowledgeable people in your own area to find out which ones do well. If the tree is an obscure one, buy it from a source that can advise you on its suitability. If you're taking a chance with a tree, even a slight chance, plant it where it will not be subjected to drying winds, especially in winter. Until it has weathered a few winters, you might even wrap it in burlap. Warm climates are also bad for some trees, such as larch and hemlock. Other trees are best suited to areas with high or low rainfall.

The amount of soil moisture on a specific site can also be a factor in a tree's survival. Most will die if their roots sit in very wet soil. Unless your wet soil is easily corrected (page 28), choose moisture-loving trees such as red maple, larch, willows, arborvitae, black tupelo, and bald cypress. For dry soils choose trees like red cedar and other juniper species, honey locust, golden rain tree, white ash, and paloverde.

If your lot is very shady, either from large trees of your own or your neighbor's, or from shade cast by a building, plant trees that naturally survive in forests, such as Carolina silverbell, moosewood, shadblow, redbud, and hemlock. If you are by the sea, Japanese black pine, Monterey pine, white spruce, arborvitae, and red cedar should do well.

Trees planted in cities must endure especially difficult conditions: soot and other air pollutants, dry soil, reflected heat from buildings and sidewalks. If they are street trees, add to this list such possibilities as damage from vandals or from vehicles striking the trunks, and poisoning from road salt and dog urine. Trees that tend to survive life in the city include magnolia, ginkgo, crab apple, linden, hawthorn, honeylocust, red oak, catalpa, white ash, and Bradford pear.

Another thing to consider in choosing a tree is the risk of diseases or insect pests. Specific trees are susceptible to certain problems but often only in some parts of the country. I've mentioned some of these in the List of Trees, but consult your Extension Service or state university to find out which species are at risk in your area.

Finally, you should be aware that some trees are simply more long-lived than others. In general the faster a tree grows, the shorter its life will be and the more susceptible it will be to damage. Trees such as willows, poplars, birches, and silver maples are short-lived and have brittle branches that break easily during storms. If you want large trees in a hurry, or if you simply like these trees very much, you can certainly plant them, especially if you have more long-lived trees as well. But you should be aware of their relative fragility and of the fact that fast-growing tree roots are often invasive, snaking their way into septic systems and drains in their quest for moisture. It's a good idea to keep any tree roots away from drains and leaching systems, but it is especially important with the species mentioned.

Getting Started

G IVING TREES A GOOD START IN LIFE is important. All of the advice about woody plants beginning on page 40

applies, but there are a few things to keep in mind about trees specifically.

BUYING TREES

For general information on buying woody plants see page 127. When purchasing trees, the gardener is faced with the decision of how large a tree to start with. Often it makes sense to buy very small specimens, especially if they're fast growing or if you are buying a large number of them. As a rule, the younger the tree, the easier it is to establish. Some young trees can even be planted bare-root, which enables you to order them through the mail and perhaps obtain varieties that are not available locally. Smaller trees are also much easier to plant than big ones—an important consideration if you're doing the work yourself. If you can patiently wait for them to grow you will have saved yourself both labor and money.

On the other hand, if you want one large specimen, or only a few, sometimes it makes sense to invest in larger stock. Perhaps you have a brand-new house on a lot devoid of trees or with no trees close by. The house looks stark and lonely sitting there by itself and may need the protection of shade trees in summer, or a line of trees to break the winter winds. In a situation like this it might make sense to invest in a few large trees rather than spend money on many smaller ones. How large is large depends on your budget and also on the type of tree you're considering. (Some that are best transplanted while young are so noted in the List of Trees.)

PROTECTING YOUNG TREES

After you've thought very carefully about where a tree should go, allowing for its ultimate size, plant it according to the directions beginning on page 40. Since most trees, unlike shrubs, only have one trunk, it is important to protect that trunk from damage. A tree trunk has a very thin layer of cells beneath the bark called the cambium, which is necessary for the tree's survival. It cannot be replaced if lost, and thus if a tree is girdled—the bark cut in a complete circle around the tree—it will die (though an expert can sometimes save a girdled tree by a procedure called bridge-grafting). The chief threats to young tree trunks are animals such as rodents, rabbits, and deer that nibble on the trunk, especially in winter, and often girdle it. A cylinder of hardware cloth, buried a few inches deep (or less, depending on what the tree's roots allow)

will foil rodents. Extended well above the anticipated snow level, it will foil rabbits and deer as well. But as trees grow, these collars should be removed so they themselves do not girdle the trunks.

Another danger to the trunk in winter is sun scald—a burning of the trunk on its sunny side. Yet another is the cracking of bark caused by sunny winter days followed by very cold nights. Both sun scald and cracking are less a problem in older trees with many branches, because even leafless branches provide some measure of shade for the trunk and because the bark of older trees is thick and tough. You can protect younger trunks from winter sun and wind by wrapping them in burlap or painting the trunks with white latex paint.

Staking Trees

FIG. 72

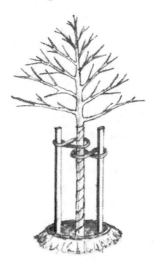

Tall wooden 2-by-4 stakes on each side of the tree, sunk 2 feet deep, provide the most support. Attach them with heavy wire threaded through sections of garden hose to protect the trunk.

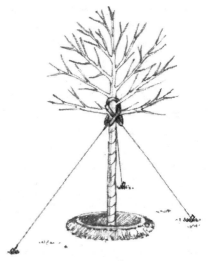

Short wooden 2-by-4 stakes may be all you need. Sink these 2 feet into the ground, then attach them with guy wires looped around the lower branches and threaded through sections of hose.

Another form of protection is a commercial tree wrap, such as the white plastic guards that are easily wrapped in a spiral up the tree. These give some protection against animals, too, but should be removed during the growing season so the trunk can get light and air.

Another frequent misfortune is jokingly referred to by landscapers as lawn-mower disease. Trees are often badly damaged when struck during careless mowing. The best solution to this problem is to mulch the area around the tree so that there's no need for the mower to come close. If trees are planted near a parking area, driveway, or road, you may need a barrier to keep vehicles from striking them. Sometimes just a row of stones or railroad ties that defines the driveway area will do the trick.

Staking new trees used to be a commonplace procedure, but the advisability of using tall stakes has recently come into question. Studies have shown that the play of an unstaked tree in the wind helps it to develop a sturdy, tapered trunk that doesn't need support. (There's even a name for this phenomenon: "thigmomorphogenesis.") Usually a tree that is planted correctly, with a large enough root ball, won't need staking. If it is in a windy site, however, and it's a tall tree with a good, full head on it, stakes may be necessary, at least for the first year. If you're not sure whether a tree needs staking, compromise by using the short stakes shown in Figure 72, which will allow some swaying but will prevent the tree from tipping or pulling out of the ground in strong winds. Or use tall stakes for the first year but attach them loosely. If the tree is growing straight and well the following year, and seems firmly anchored, you can then remove the stakes altogether.

Taking Care of Trees

MOST TREES, ONCE ESTABLISHED, don't need much care. But while they're building new root systems and canopies of leaves to provide themselves with food, they usually need some help.

WATERING

It is crucial to keep young trees thoroughly watered. A deep soaking once a week in dry weather is much more valuable than a daily sprinkling that only wets the top inch or two of the soil and never gets down to root level. If you have built a dirt saucer around the tree when you planted it (page 43), you can simply put the end of a garden hose into the saucer, turn it on partway so a trickle runs out, and leave it there for an hour or two. Or you can do the same with a soaker hose that you lay in a circle around the tree. Another way to water a tree is by filling a five-gallon bucket whose bottom has small holes punched in it; set it next to the tree and water will trickle down at a slow enough rate for the soil to absorb it. A 3- to 4-inch mulch of a material such as shredded bark, shredded leaves, or wood chips will help the soil around the tree stay moist. In cold climates mulch will also give the roots some winter protection (see page 55). So that voles and other rodents don't hide or nest in the mulch, it's best to leave about 6 inches of unmulched ground around to the trunk and substitute a gravel mulch in that area.

FEEDING

Established trees don't usually need to be fed, but a young tree will benefit from a yearly feeding in late fall. Fall application will give the fertilizer time to work its way down to the roots by the following spring. Compost has worked best for me. Make sure you apply it at the outermost circle of the tree's root system, where the feeder roots are. A mature tree's root spread is very large and reaches even farther out than the branches, whereas a tree that has only been in place a year will not have roots extending very much past the original root ball. In between it's a guessing game, but to be safe put some fertilizer out at least as far as the tree's branches reach (the "drip line"). With deep-rooted trees you can remove the mulch and scratch fertilizer into the soil; with shallow-rooted ones it's better just to scatter or spread it on the ground. Some gardeners deep-feed tree roots by making holes with a crowbar or by using an injection device, but I feel this is something you only need to do if a tree is badly stressed and needs fertilizing in a hurry. And even in cases like these I prefer to just spread a layer of manure or compost or give the tree periodic feedings with a liquid fertilizer and water it in well.

PESTS AND DISEASES

This subject is treated in general terms beginning on page 60. When you're dealing with trees, pest and disease control is more complicated than with smaller plants. You certainly can't hand-pick all the bugs off a tree, unless it's a very small one. One alternative is to spray, but this is also difficult with a large tree, and is something best tackled by a professional. Consider, also, whether you need to spray at all. A great deal of spray is needed to treat a tree, and the spray must cover a vast area. The hazard to animal life from spraying trees even with relatively benign chemicals can be enormous. It's something you want to think through carefully. If you have valuable trees that are prone to scale insects, for example, you might hire someone to spray them with dormant oil (page 66) before they leaf out, as protection. Also consider that many insects that attack leaves may cause the trees to look unsightly and even defoliate them. But this may not happen every year (many insect infestations come in cycles), and in many cases trees recover quite quickly from an insect attack. Borers, which attack trunks and branches, can be a serious threat. These are controlled by placing screen barriers around the lower trunk (the most vulnerable spot) and by digging the larvae out and destroying them (see page 422).

All in all, the best way to deal with insect damage is to prevent it. Avoid planting trees that commonly attract certain bugs in your area, or ones that will struggle because they're not right for the climate. Try to keep your trees as healthy and vigorous as possible by giving them good soil, water, mulch, extra nutrients if they need them, and the right amount of sun.

With diseases, control is similar: it is partly a matter of choosing trees that are not disease-prone where you live, and partly a matter of keeping trees vigorous. If possible, infected parts of the tree should be removed. Ends of twigs that are blackened by fire blight and stems infected with canker should be cut off, if you can reach them safely. Crown galls (knobby growths on the trunk and branches) can be cut out. If fungus diseases such as anthracnose or leaf spot appear on the leaves, promptly rake up any that fall and destroy them, so that the disease will not overwinter in the soil.

It is difficult to diagnose tree diseases. The best approach is to put a sample of the diseased tissue in a plastic bag and bring it or mail it to your Extension Service for diagnosis. And don't give up on a tree too soon. It may surprise you and survive a plague that appears to be quite deadly. In a few cases where a serious disease threatens all trees of a certain type in your area, it's necessary to remove the afflicted ones to prevent the plague's spread, but these situations are rare.

WATCHING FOR SIGNS OF STRESS

Often when a tree is in poor condition, no disease or insect is at fault. Many situations can cause trees simple physical stress. So before you start hunting for a bug or microbe, try asking yourself these questions about the tree.

Is the soil around it dry? If leaves look scorched or wilted, it may be that the roots aren't getting enough water. The tree may also drop some of its leaves to prevent them from giving off too much water through transpiration. Soak the ground thoroughly and mulch the tree if possible.

Is the soil too wet? Leaves that turn brown or the appearance of dieback (in which branches die at the top of the tree) is a sign of general decline and may mean that a tree's roots are not getting enough oxygen because the soil is poorly drained (see page 28). If the tree is small, consider moving it to a drier spot; if not, try to correct the drainage problem.

Is the soil compacted? If there is general decline, determine whether the soil around the roots is receiving vehicle traffic or heavy foot traffic, or if it has been compacted by recent construction. Can the traffic be rerouted? If construction has caused problems, try to dig some organic matter into the soil as deeply as possible without damaging the roots so that air, water, and nutrients can circulate freely. Then apply a thick mulch, about 4 inches deep. The spread of a tree's roots may seem like a very large area to mulch heavily, but mulch can often save a stressed tree, perhaps because it provides a cover so much like that of the forest floor.

Have the roots been damaged? If there has been construction near a tree—even outside the reach of the branches—the roots may be severely affected. Even digging a trench to lay a pipe can cause the death of a tree that is close by. If you suspect root damage, feed and mulch the tree as described above.

Trees can also suffer from construction that changes the grade of the soil around the tree, even by a few inches. Removing soil can bring the roots too close to the surface and even expose them; in these cases the soil should be replaced. Adding soil to a tree's site, on the other hand, can rob the roots of food and air. Anytime the soil level must be raised around the trunk of a tree, a tree well should be constructed. This involves digging down to the original soil level around the trunk (if it has already been buried), building a circular retaining wall to keep the excess soil away from the trunk, and installing drainage tiles that will carry water and air out to the root tips. Ideally this should be done *before* the grade is changed; it is a job for professionals.

Are there enough nutrients? If the leaves are pale and small, flowers few or nonexistent, and the tree spindly, the tree may need fertilizing.

Is the climate too cold or the site too unprotected? Even if a tree is hardy enough to survive your winters, leaf and flower buds may be killed in winter or by early-spring frosts that nip them after they start to open. The result may be poor leaf growth as well as lack of flowers and fruit. The best spot for a tender tree is one protected from winter winds and also from bright spring sunshine that will cause buds to open too soon. If the tree is well established and too big to move, you might try planting some sturdy, fast-growing evergreens such as white pines near it, to shield it from wind or afternoon sun.

Have toxic materials affected the tree? If your trees are being poisoned by toxic elements in the environment, the cause of the trouble may be hard to diagnose, since different toxins produce different symptoms. But if deciduous leaves are scorched, glazed, or streaked, and if evergreen needles of recent growth are falling, air pollution may be the problem—one you can do little about. An evergreen tree's dropping needles, however, is not *necessarily* a cause for concern. Even though they do not shed all of the present year's growth the way deciduous trees do, evergreens do shed some needles each year. Some species hold on to their needles longer than others. While three years is about average, pines shed some needles the second fall after they appear, and junipers can hold them ten years or more.

Trees that look as if they were suffering from drought may be contaminated by ground pollution; here you may be able to track the source and remove it. Injury to roots from herbicides used on weeds usually produces distorted new growth (twisted needles, puckered leaves). Use of the herbicide should be discontinued. Road salt is a very common culprit, causing branches and even whole trees to die.

If the salt is from your own driveway or walkway, use mechanical means to remove ice and snow instead, or choose trees that are salt-resistant, such as oak, hawthorn, honey locust, and the trees suggested above for seaside plantings. If the situation is beyond your control, you may need to avoid trees like white pine, which are very susceptible to salt.

MAKING TREES FEEL AT HOME

In taking care of trees always think of the woods in which they grow naturally, in the company of other trees and certain understory plants with which they often have longtime associations. They would not choose to grow in the middle of lawns, surrounded by grass, a covering that affords the roots little shade or protection and competes with them for water and nutrients. Before planting a tree in the middle of your lawn, consider these alternatives.

Plant it at the edge instead. Often a tree on a house lawn sticks out like a sore thumb, especially a large tree that is not in scale with the house. Planted at the edge of the lawn, with other trees of varying heights, the same tree may fit in much better. A shade tree that must be fairly near the house can be visually tied to it with a foundation or entryway shrub planting and by using the same type of mulch or ground cover under it as you use for the shrubs (see the ground cover chapter).

Create a grove. Try planting several trees together as if they were a tiny woodland. Each tree should be given enough room for a comfortable spread, but branches can overlap. These trees might be grouped in a distinct area that's not treated as lawn but is rather mulched and underplanted with groups of bulbs, ferns, and woodland wild-flowers. Grass does not grow well under trees anyway.

If you must plant a tree alone, at least mulch it. A thick layer of mulch will cool the soil and encourage feeder roots to come up to the topsoil where nutrients are most plentiful. Even raking the leaves from the lawn in fall but leaving some of them under the tree will help. (Don't do this, however, if the fallen leaves are known to harbor disease or pest organisms.) In planting ground covers under trees I try to avoid those with thick, matted, hungry root systems such as pachysandra.

Pruning Trees

M ANY OF THE SAME PRINCIPLES explained in the section on pruning shrubs (page 612) also apply to trees. By cutting back twigs or branches, you can induce branching and increase flower and fruit production. You can also thin trees by removing upper branches to let more light into the center of the tree, and you can stimulate the growth of lower branches by selective pruning. A tree's branches must occasionally be thinned to lessen its wind resistance in very windy areas.

A tree will have a better shape when mature if you remove branches that grow in toward the center, or straight up, or straight down, and branches that criss-cross one another either in a horizontal or vertical plane (Figure 73). Branches that simply look awkward or give the tree an asymmetrical appearance can also be removed. Eliminate branches with weak crotches—those that are tight and vertical

as opposed to open and U-shaped. If a tree is of the type that should have a "leader"— a central trunk that continues up to the top of the tree—but instead has two competing leaders, you should eliminate one of them early on. Multiple trunks can be thinned at the base to just one as needed. If horizontal branches develop water sprouts (small branches that stick straight up) or suckers (branches that sprout from the bottom of the trunk), these too should be eliminated. Lower branches can be removed to expose an attractive trunk, let light into the landscape, or allow you to walk under the canopy—though it is wise to wait until at least several years after you plant the tree to do this, to keep the young trunk shaded against sun scald and to avoid reducing the number of leaves too much.

In general a tree will not look its best if you prune it in a way that interferes with its natural shape. If it's a round-headed tree, don't try to make it columnar. If it's a wide-spreading tree, let it spread, eliminating only branches that are too long or heavy and threaten to break.

It is important to do major shaping while the tree is young, for two reasons. First, early pruning for shape will start the tree off on the right road by giving it a pleasing form, something that cutting a large tree back will never accomplish. Second, you'll do the work while it can still be done safely. Small trees can be pruned with precision by using pruning shears, loppers, and short-handled pruning saws while you stand on the ground. As they get larger you can still prune and stand on the ground by using a pruning saw on a pole, but this becomes more and more difficult to do well as time goes on. I will sometimes sit on a lower branch and lop

Pruning Trees

FIG. *73*

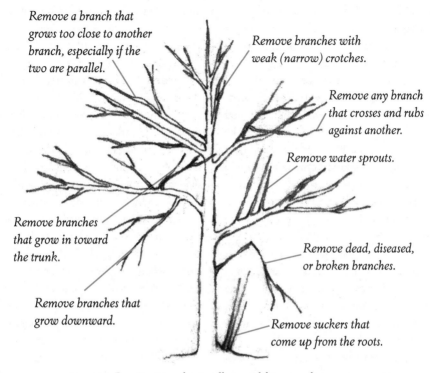

Remove a branch that grows too close to another branch, especially if the two are parallel.

Remove branches with weak (narrow) crotches.

Remove any branch that crosses and rubs against another.

Remove water sprouts.

Remove branches that grow in toward the trunk.

Remove dead, diseased, or broken branches.

Remove branches that grow downward.

Remove suckers that come up from the roots.

Pruning to make a well-spaced framework.

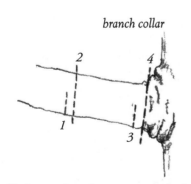

branch collar

2   4

1

3

Undercut a branch to prevent the bark from tearing (numbers indicate the right order in which to make the cuts). The final cut should be flush with the branch collar but should not damage it.

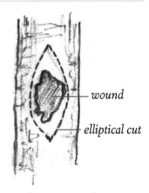

wound

elliptical cut

To repair a wound in a tree, make a vertical elliptical cut after cleaning out the cavity.

off water sprouts or awkward branches, as shown on page 653, but believe me, in that picture I am not very far from the ground. Climbing high into trees is dangerous, and I would *never* climb up into a tree with a chainsaw. Pruning tall trees is, as far as I'm concerned, the work of a tree surgeon.

Sometimes there are pruning jobs that must be done on mature trees. Any deadwood should be removed. Branches that break should be cut back either to the trunk or to a healthy side branch. Prune large branches yourself only if you can do it with both feet on the ground. And cut the branch back gradually so that its weight will not tear the bark all the way to the trunk when the branch falls (Figure 73). In severing a branch, when you make your final cut, don't cut so close to the branch that you destroy the "branch collar"—the circular ridge that runs around the base of a branch. This collar will help the cut to close over and heal.

Wounds in a tree that are made by disease or physical blows should be cleaned out with a knife so there is no dead, rotting tissue. Then make a vertical elliptical cut (Figure 73) around the wound; this will heal better than an irregular or horizontal cut. Hollow cavities in trees do not need to be filled. As tree expert Alex Shigo so admirably demonstrated, trees naturally compartmentalize their wounds, so there's no need to coat them with tree paint. It's best to let a tree heal itself.

It's important to know your limitations when working with trees. There is a lot to learn about them, and each kind of tree is a bit different from all others in the way it grows and the way it should be cared for. Unless you're an expert you will not know when a tree needs to be cabled to prevent breakage, for example, let alone be able to do it safely and successfully. That's where the experts come in. Good tree surgeons can be expensive, but I put them in the same category as doctors and vets—they are not something to skimp on when they're needed. Remember, you are not Paul Bunyan. You are not even Tarzan, even though you may once have loved to climb trees.

List of Trees

HE TREES INCLUDED HERE ARE special because of their beauty and their general usefulness in the landscape. While some are native American forest trees valuable for lumber or fuel, it is not their use for these purposes that has put them on the list. Nor were trees selected for their edible fruits, though many fruit-bearing trees are commonly grown as ornamentals. (Some are described in the fruit chapter.)

Narrowing the list down to 22 trees was difficult. The result is merely a selection of popular trees that do well in a significant percent of the country. Do try some of the more unusual ones not on the list, such as smoke tree (*Cotinus americanus*), with its flowers like puffs of smoke, or franklinia (*Franklinia alatamaha*), which has white flowers and brilliant red-orange fall leaves and was named after Benjamin Franklin. Give thought to trees that are associated with your particular part of the country— the wonderful madrones and mesquites of the west coast, for example or the fragrant Roemer acacia (*Acacia roemeriana*). And consider growing some nut-bearing trees such as hickory, hazelnut, or pecan. Some other excellent landscape trees I was tempted to include are Carolina silverbell (*Halesia tetraptera*), American yellowwood (*Cladrastis lutea*), snowbell (*Styrax* species), horse chestnuts and buckeyes (*Aesculus* species), golden rain tree (*Koelreuteria paniculata*), fringetree (*Chionanthus vir-*

ginicus), hornbeam (*Carpinus caroliniana*), stewartia (*Stewartia* species), black tupelo (*Nyssa sylvatica*), and Amur chokecherry (*Prunus maackii*). The list could go on at some length.

In making a selection, it is important to avoid trees known to be invasive and a threat to native woodlands. The worst include Norway maple (*Acer platanoides*), tree of heaven (*Ailanthus altissima*), Russian olive (*Elaeagnus angustifolia*), and smooth buckthorn (*Rhamnus frangula*). It's a good idea to check with your local Extension Service about any tree of which you are unsure.

The figures given for ultimate size and spread are approximate and will vary widely from one locale to another. Hardiness zones are also approximate. Whenever there is a choice, you should try to buy trees that have begun their lives in your particular area. Usually they are better adapted to the region, and have a better chance of thriving than those grown in another climate.

ARBORVITAE
Thuja

Description: Arborvitae is a good tree to use if you need a tall vertical evergreen either for an accent or for a hedge. A row of them planted 4 to 5 feet apart will grow into a dense barrier that will screen out sights, sounds, and wind year-round. The trees are fairly slow growing and have flat, scalelike needles. The most popular species is American arborvitae (*Thuja occidentalis*), which grows as tall as 60 feet with a church-steeple shape, reaches about 15 feet across on the bottom if grown by itself, and is hardy as far north as zone 2. Unfortunately it tends to turn brownish in winter, although some of the more garden-worthy cultivars overcome this trait, notably 'Techny' ('Mission'), 'Nigra,' and 'Emerald' ('Smaragd'). These are also smaller and more slow growing than the original species. There are cultivars with weeping, globe-shaped, dwarf, or strictly columnar shapes, as well as a number with gold-colored foliage. All are very cold hardy and do best in cool climates.

Western arborvitae (*T. plicata*), also known as giant arborvitae or western red cedar, stays green in winter. It is hardy to zone 5, magnificent in the northwest but adaptable in other regions. Oriental arborvitae (*T. orientalis*, also called *Platycladus orientalis*), hardy to zone 6 or 7, is best suited to the south and the west coast.

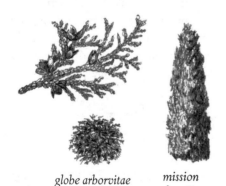

globe arborvitae   *mission arborvitae*

How to Grow: Plant arborvitae balled-and-burlapped or container-grown, in full sun or part shade. In nature it chooses moist sites and should be given fertile soil

with adequate moisture. Plants are susceptible to red spider mite and bagworm in some areas, but usually pest problems are not severe. Since the plant makes a rather tidy shape on its own it doesn't often need pruning, but it can be sheared lightly in late winter to shape or contain it. Upright forms are usually trained to one leader. Cutting back to bare wood will not produce branching, which is unfortunate, because these trees are hungrily browsed by deer. It may be necessary to wrap or fence the bottom 6 feet if winter deer predation is a problem.

ASH

Fraxinus

Description: Ash is a useful tree because many kinds of plants can be grown in the dappled shade that it casts. Varieties of several native American ashes are used as garden trees. White ash (*Fraxinus americana*) can reach 120 feet; it is hardy to zone 4. Fall foliage is yellow and/or purple, and in varieties such as 'Autumn Purple' and 'Rosehill' the fall color is especially showy. Green ash (*F. pennsylvanica*), sometimes called red ash, is a smaller but fast-growing tree, hardy to zone 3. It is very adaptable and often used where other trees are hard to establish. Autumn foliage is yellow. It can self-sow profusely, but there are male varieties such as 'Marshall's' ('Marshall's Seedless'), which are less of a nuisance in the garden.

Flowering ash (*F. ornus*), hardy to zone 6, is a European species that bears profuse, fragrant white flowers in late spring. A flowering ash native to the American southwest, *F. cuspidata*, is also very fragrant. It is a much smaller tree. For mountain ash (*Sorbus*), see page 679.

How to Grow: Ash trees are easy to establish and can be planted bare-root. White ash likes full sun and prefers a deep, fertile, moist soil. This and green ash are sometimes bothered by scale insects, borers, and other pests, but established trees usually weather most problems. Green ash wood tends to be more fragile, so it is important when pruning to eliminate branches with weak V-crotches and leave those that will grow strong. Ash trees tend to grow with one central leader. *F. cuspidata* is tolerant of dry, rocky soils but also performs well in a garden setting.

BEECH

Fagus

Description: Beeches are monumental trees that are long-lived and beautiful year-round. Though fairly slow growing they eventually form huge, round, spreading heads whose branches often sweep the ground. The oval, toothed leaves turn dark gold in fall; the smooth gray bark is striking in winter. These trees need a large space all their own. The overhanging branches create an enclosed world of deep shade where nothing will grow, and the shallow roots emerge from the soil, forming great snakes along the ground.

The American beech (*Fagus grandifolia*) grows up to 90 feet tall; at that height the spread would be about 60 feet wide. It is hardy to zone 4. Fall color is bronze, and young beech trees in the forest often hold on to their tan or pinkish leaves in wintertime. It is a reliable tree in both the north and the south. The European beech (*F. sylvatica*) is similar, and most of the cultivars sold come from this species: the weeping 'Pendula,' the fern-leaved 'Asplenifolia,' the upright 'Fastigiata,' the variegated ones such as pink-bordered 'Roseomarginata,' and those that have deep red leaves year-round such as 'Riversii' (these are often referred to generically as copper beech).

weeping beech

Rivers' purple beech

leaves and burrs

How to Grow: Give beeches a deep, well-drained, acid, fertile soil, well supplied with organic matter. They prefer full sun but will grow well in part shade. Plant them balled-and-burlapped, taking care not to plant too deeply or pile too much soil over the roots, which like to be near the surface. Young trees should be trained to a central leader, and branches with weak crotches should be removed since the wood is brittle and the branches grow long and heavy. Lower branches may be removed, if you like, so that you can walk under the tree and so that the handsome trunk will be visible.

BIRCH
Betula

Description: Birches are not long-lived trees, but they are graceful ones, and they are valued for their open branches that cast light shade, their yellow fall color, and their splendid bark, which varies from species to species. They are fast growing. Their flowers, born in spring, are fuzzy, dangling catkins. Birches look particularly fine with a background of evergreens, and are attractive planted in groves.

When most people think of birches they think of the paper birch, or canoe birch (*Betula papyrifera*), with its white bark marked with black bands and blotches. This native tree grows as tall as 90 feet, usually forming clumps. It is more long-lived when trained to one trunk, but the clumps are pretty, and it may be your choice to grow them that way. Paper birch is very hardy (to zone 2) and resistant to borers, though like most birches its trunks

and branches are easily broken by winter storms. Sweet birch (*B. lenta*) is another native, hardy to zone 4, with attractive dark bark and good fall color. I am especially fond of river birch, also called red birch (*B. nigra*), probably the most problem-free of the birches. Its bark does not retain a white color into maturity but it is still handsome, peeling off in shreds to reveal a cinnamon color. The variety 'Heritage' is the one most commonly sold, with the whitest bark of any birch while young. River birch is hardy to zone 5 and requires a fairly moist site.

Most of the fancier birch hybrids come from the tree called European white birch or silver birch (*B. pendula*, also known as *B. alba* and *B. verrucosa*). It grows up to 50 or 60 feet and has white bark that tends to darken with age. European white birch is more or less weeping in habit, especially 'Youngii,' a popular variety. Others include 'Purpurea,' with purple leaves; 'Fastigiata,' which is narrow and upright; and cutleaf European birch ('Gracilis'), which is slightly weeping and has very fine foliage. The trouble with European white birch is that it is especially susceptible to both the bronze birch borer, which eats the wood underneath the bark, and the birch leaf miner, which can defoliate it (though trees are rarely killed). Paper birch is more resistant to both. A Japanese birch with white bark, *B. platyphylla japonica*, is susceptible to birch borer, especially when stressed, but the variety 'Whitespire' has shown good resistance.

How to Grow: Birches are not easily moved and should be planted balled-and-burlapped or container-grown. They like full sun and fairly moist but well-drained, moderately fertile soil. Prune while young to form a single trunk (if one is desired) and to remove branches that are awkward, have weak crotches, or grow low on the trunk and would obscure the handsome bark. Try to restrict later pruning, as cuts do not heal easily. Birches ooze sap in spring from which birch beer is sometimes made. Pruning at this time can be messy, and cuts made then will not heal well. It's best to prune just after the leaves have dropped in fall.

DOGWOOD

Cornus

Cornus kousa   *Cornus florida*

Description: The dogwoods comprise a varied group of trees and shrubs, useful for different purposes. The flowering dogwood (*Cornus florida*) is the most familiar—an extremely graceful tree with horizontal branches that tilt upward at the ends. Most are about 20 to 25 feet tall, though they can grow taller, and are hardy to zone 5. Little fat, pointed buds that perch on the branch tips bear showy white or pink flowers (actually leaflike structures called bracts) in spring before the leaves appear, and are followed in fall by red ber-

ries. Fall foliage is a handsome dark red. There are numerous varieties. Kousa dogwood (*C. kousa*) has similar flowers, usually white, and the bracts are pointed rather than notched. Their flowers appear several weeks later than those of *C. florida*, along with the leaves, and are followed by red, raspberry-like fruits. The tree is somewhat less graceful in form and often has several trunks, though it can be trained to one. It is less affected by the disease problems that have devastated so many flowering dogwood trees in recent years, especially in the mid-Atlantic states and the northeast. Pacific dogwood (*C. nuttallii*) grows over 40 feet tall and is hardy to zone 7; it has very large, showy white flowers in spring and sometimes reblooms in fall.

Cornelian cherry (*C. mas*) grows to about 25 feet with a spread of up to 15 feet, and bears fluffy yellow flowers in very early spring followed by edible red berries. Leaves are red in fall, and there are some variegated varieties. It is hardy to zone 5 and resists drought, pests, and diseases.

In addition, there are two shrubby dogwood species grown for their bright red stems—especially striking in winter against the snow—and valuable for their extreme hardiness (to zone 2 or 3). Tartarian dogwood (*C. alba*) usually grows to about 6 feet but can get as high as 10, with white flowers in spring followed by whitish berries in late summer. Variegated varieties include the yellow-edged 'Spaethii' and white-edged 'Elegantissima.' 'Sibirica' has stems that are a very bright coral red. Red osier dogwood (*C. stolonifera*, also called *C. sericea*) can grow equally tall but is sometimes low and spreading. The variety 'Flaviramea' has bright yellow stems and can be planted with the red-stemmed varieties for a dramatic effect. Pagoda dogwood (*C. alternifolia*) is a beautiful shrub or small tree for the northeast. Gray dogwood (*C. racemosa*) is an attractive shrubby species, good for naturalizing.

How to Grow: Dogwoods like moist, well-drained soil, though red osier dogwood will grow in very wet sites as well. Soil should be slightly acid and fairly rich, and should contain plenty of organic matter. Plant dogwoods balled-and-burlapped in early spring while plants are young. Kousa dogwood does best in full sun but will take some shade. Flowering dogwood does best along the woodland edge in the wild, but in areas where fungus diseases such as anthracnose and powdery mildew are serious problems, a more open site may be preferable. In general, *C. florida* is quite disease prone, though its resistance can be bolstered with a fertile soil and watering in dry summers. The tree is shallow-rooted and especially susceptible to herbicide damage. Flower buds, which are formed the year before blooming, can be killed during harsh winters. Borers can be dug out and cankers pruned out.

Flowering dogwood should be pruned as little as possible. Like birch, it bleeds sap in spring and its wounds heal slowly. Prune in late summer or early fall to remove injured or awkward branches as needed. Kousa dogwood and cornelian cherry can be pruned at the bottom to train them to one trunk, or left as tall shrubs. Tartarian and red osier dogwood should have old stems that have lost their red color cut out at the base regularly to promote bright red new growth. In addition, suckers that come up from underground stolons should be removed if you need to restrict the plant's spread.

FIR

Abies

Description: Firs are imposing forest evergreens with fragrant needles. Like any tall evergreen they are handsome in the right spot, where their size and form are in scale with their surroundings. They are best suited to cool climates. The concolor fir (*Abies concolor*), also known as white fir, is a western species and the one most often sold for landscape use. It looks rather like a blue spruce but with longer needles (about 2 inches). It will eventually grow over 75 feet tall, is hardy to zone 4, and resists heat, drought, and city conditions. Noble fir (*A. procera*), also from the west, is a very tall fir, hardy to zone 5. Korean fir (*A. koreana*) is small as firs go (about 30 feet), with fat, upright cones, and is hardy to zone 5.

How to Grow: Plant firs balled-and-burlapped or bare-root in moist, well-drained, slightly acid soil. They do not tolerate wind well, especially if it is hot and dry. Firs can be shaped while young by cutting back the tips in late winter or early spring, but cutting back hard will not induce branching. Trees should be trained to a central leader. If the leader is lost, a side branch can be pulled over and tied to the trunk to make it upright. The branch will become the new leader.

GINKGO

Ginkgo biloba

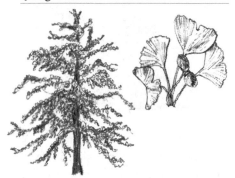

Description: The ginkgo is also called maidenhair tree, because the fan-shaped, two-lobed leaves look something like fronds of maidenhair fern, to which the ginkgo is, oddly enough, related. Like ferns, ginkgos are ancient—among the oldest plant species known. The ginkgo comes to us from China and is hardy to zone 4. The tree will sometimes grow 100 feet tall or more in old age, but it grows quite slowly. Plenty of space should be allowed for it as its spread can be 40 feet wide. One of the ginkgo's greatest virtues is its ability to adapt successfully to city conditions. The branches shoot out at odd, irregular angles, giving it an interesting appearance, then fill in as the tree grows older, to form a dense round mass. Fall color is a glorious yellow. There are male and female trees, males being much preferred because the females produce foul-smelling fruit. (A reputable nursery will specify the sex of the tree it sells you.) There are a number of varieties with distinctive growth habits. 'Princeton Sentry,' for example, is columnar.

How to Grow: Plant ginkgos balled-and-burlapped in any reasonably fertile soil, but make sure the soil is well drained. They are easy to establish but should be thoroughly watered after planting. There are no serious pests or diseases. Usually ginkgos are not pruned but are left to go their eccentric way; nevertheless, pruning can be done in early spring if needed.

HAWTHORN

Crataegus

flowers

berries

Description: Hawthorns are among the best ornamental trees, especially when a small one is needed. By and large they are hardy to zone 4. They have thorns, as the name suggests, and fruit called haws, which are an important food for wildlife. The English hawthorn (*Crataegus laevigata*) is the "May tree" about which there are so many folk traditions in the British Isles. Its clusters of small white spring flowers have such lighthearted associations as the Queen of the May, and a dark side as well. An English friend's grandmother considered it a curse to bring a branch indoors. Growing to about 15 feet, English hawthorn bears red berries in fall but the fall foliage is not colorful. 'Crimson Cloud,' named for its fruits, is a noteworthy variety.

Washington hawthorn (*C. phaenopyrum*) is rather upright but becomes more rounded as it ages, growing as tall as 30 feet. The white flowers generally bloom in June, the leaves turn red-orange in fall, and the red berries last till spring. Glossy hawthorn (*C. nitida*) is similar, with earlier flowers. Lavalle hawthorn (*C. × lavallei*) is May-blooming and about 20 feet tall, with red fall color and red-orange fruits. All these mentioned are hardy to zone 5. The cockspur thorn (*C. crus-galli*) can grow to 30 feet, but is multistemmed and is often grown as a shrubby hedge prized for its vigor, its orange fall foliage, and its deep red fruits. *C. crus-galli* var. *inermis* is thornless.

How to Grow: Hawthorns are best planted while they are small, because their long taproot makes them hard to move. Plant them balled-and-burlapped in early spring. They like full sun and will tolerate drought and rather poor soil, though a fine organic loam suits them best. They make good city trees. Leaf blight can spoil their appearance and even defoliate them, so sweep up and destroy all diseased leaves. Prune in winter or early spring while the trees are dormant, thinning to let in light, to remove low branches, and to shape the tree—remembering that some irregularity and even shrubbiness is appropriate in a hawthorn. Suckers can be cut at any time.

HEMLOCK
Tsuga

Description: Hemlocks are tall, stately forest evergreens that adapt better than most to garden sites. One reason is the hemlock's graceful appearance: its slightly drooping branches and feathery needles seem to soften the tree's impact even when it is large,

making it suitable as a specimen plant. Another is the ease with which hemlocks are sheared to a compact shape, allowing them to be used as hedges, either for screening or as a background for other plants. The most commonly used species for either purpose is Canadian hemlock (*Tsuga canadensis*), which grows as tall as 90 feet and is hardy to zone 4. The unusual weeping variety 'Sargentii' forms mounds of drooping greenery in very picturesque shapes; it does not grow tall but spreads outward, cascading onto the ground. Carolina hemlock (*T. caroliniana*) is a denser, shorter tree, hardy to zone 5. Japanese hemlock (*T. diversifolia*), hardy to zone 6, can get very tall but grows slowly and often remains shrublike, with multiple trunks.

How to Grow: Hemlocks are best planted balled-and-burlapped or container-grown if possible. They will be bushier, more filled-out plants if grown in full sun, but they will also grow in part or full shade. Hemlocks need a deep, moist but well-drained soil and suffer in windy, dry, hot, or polluted sites. They sometimes fall prey to hemlock scale, which is treated with a dormant oil spray, but a far worse pest is the hemlock woolly adelgid, an imported insect that is decimating populations in much of the eastern U.S. It is important to buy from nurseries with a good record of selling pest-free stock, and in some areas it is best to forgo Canada and Carolina hemlocks in favor of other trees.

Hemlocks will put out new growth even when cut back hard. When used as hedges they should be sheared regularly from the time they are young. Shear each year in early spring before growth starts, and again in midsummer. Specimen trees are routinely sheared by nurserymen to make them denser and bushier, but you may prefer the more open shape of the tree's natural growth. If so, the tree will need little or no pruning, except that it's best to train it to a single leader.

KATSURA

Cercidiphyllum japonicum

Description: This tree is not nearly as well known as it should be. It has rounded leaves up to 4 inches across, similar to those of an aspen or a redbud. When they first emerge early in the season, they have a wonderful reddish color, especially beautiful with the sun behind them. In summer they become blue-green, then turn yellow-orange or red in fall. Flowers and fruit are insignificant. Katsura can be hard to estab-

lish but you shouldn't have much trouble if you plant it young and give it plenty of water. Since it is fairly fast growing, this is an economical way to acquire a beautiful tree for your property without having to wait endlessly for its welcome shade. Ultimate height is generally about 60 feet. Trees with multiple trunks are quite broad. If you purchase a single-trunk specimen it will be more columnar.

How to Grow: Katsuras are generally pest and disease free, but will suffer in dry climates. Give them fertile, moist but well-drained soil. Hardy to zone 4.

LARCH

Larix

Description: Larches look for all the world like evergreen trees. Their long, waving twigs have tufts of small needles. They even have cones. But come fall those needles turn bright yellow and fall off, just like the leaves of any deciduous tree. The wood is more like that of deciduous hardwoods than the softer-wooded evergreens. Larches are beautiful in the woods. A stand of them will turn a hillside a pale tender green in early spring when the needles start to grow, and bright yellow in fall. But I have also lived with a larch on the lawn, as a specimen tree, and I found it a handsome, unusual accent. The native American larch (*Larix laricina*), also called eastern larch and tamarack, grows in an open pyramid as tall as 90 feet in the wild (usually much less in a home landscape). It is fast growing and one of the hardiest trees known. It will even live in zone 1, regions of which are simply referred to as the tamarack because that's about all that grows there. European larch (*L. decidua*), hardy to zone 2, is even taller and is perhaps best known for the variety *L. d.* 'Pendula,' a shorter variety whose limbs have gracefully drooping side branches. Japanese larch (*L. kaempferi* or *L. leptolepis*), hardy to zone 4, is also pendulous, with peeling bark. It grows very fast and is more resistant to canker than other larches.

How to Grow: Larches need a cool climate. They prefer a sunny location and deep, fertile, rather acid soil that is moist but well drained. They are not tolerant of pollution. They are easy to transplant and are best planted balled-and-burlapped in fall or early spring. Larches rarely need pruning. Lower branches can be removed for headroom or if they are weak and straggly. This is best done in summer. The trees should have a central leader; if that is damaged, replace with another branch as described in the entry on fir.

LINDEN
Tilia

Description: Lindens are tall and fairly fast growing, with an attractive dense shape. They are used as shade trees and often as street trees. They bear dangling clusters of fragrant pale yellowish flowers in early summer. Littleleaf linden (*Tilia cordata*), a European tree, is among the best. In the British Isles, where it is sometimes called lime tree, it is often sheared into ornamental shapes—a process to which it adapts readily. It grows up to 90 feet tall in a dense, compact pyramid and is hardy to zone 4. Small, heart-shaped dark green leaves turn yellow in fall in cool climates. 'Greenspire' is a particularly well-shaped, fast-growing variety. American linden, or basswood (*T. americana*), is a bit shorter and a bit hardier, but it lacks the good fall color. Its large leaves give it a coarser appearance and it is prone to a number of insect pests. Silver linden (*T. tomentosa,* also known as *T. alba* and *T. argentea*) has leaves with whitish undersides that give the tree a silvery look when the wind blows. It is hardy to zone 5.

How to Grow: Grow lindens in deep, fertile, moist but well-drained soil in sun or part shade. Plant them balled-and-burlapped. Young trees should be pruned in late winter to develop a strong central leader, and lower branches can be removed to allow movement under them; but in general lindens develop a handsome, symmetrical shape on their own. Old trees can be thinned to remove deadwood and admit light.

MAGNOLIA

Magnolia

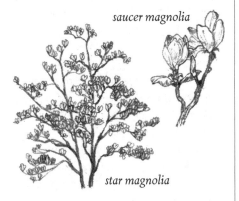

saucer magnolia

star magnolia

Description: Magnolias are handsome ornamental trees, with their showy flowers, their dark green leaves, and their relatively small size. They are generally thought of as southern plants, but there are species that will do well in the north even if they don't make you feel like Scarlett or Rhett. Saucer magnolia (*Magnolia × soulangiana*) grows about 25 feet tall, usually with several trunks, which have smooth dark gray bark. The large flowers, white streaked with pink and purple, sit upright at the tips of the branches before the leaves appear. Star magnolia (*M. stellata*) is a smaller tree. The fragrant flowers, which appear quite early in spring before the leaves, are like large, fragile white stars. (Some varieties have a pink color.) The foliage is much finer textured than that of saucer magnolia. Both are hardy to about zone 5, but in cold climates are best grown in a partly shaded site to retard bloom—early flowers can be killed by cold, and late snowstorms can turn star magnolia blossoms into tattered shreds. *M. × loebneri* is a cross between star magnolia and the Japanese *M. kobus*. The variety 'Leonard Messel' is especially beautiful.

Southern magnolia, also called bull bay (*M. grandiflora*), is a native evergreen, single-trunked tree that can grow as tall as 90 feet, though it is usually a good bit shorter. It is hardy to zone 7, though it may survive farther north if grown in a sheltered location. It has huge, glossy dark green leaves and fragrant white flowers that can be as large as a foot across. Its seedpods, which open in fall to reveal red seeds, are also ornamental. Other worthy native species include sweetbay or swamp magnolia (*M. virginiana*), cucumber tree (*M. acuminata*), and umbrella magnolia (*M. tripetala*).

How to Grow: Magnolias generally like full sun, except in the situation described above, and except for southern magnolia, which is fairly shade tolerant. All like fertile, loose, well-drained soil that is rich in organic matter, with a slightly acid pH. Magnolias do not transplant easily and should be planted balled-and-burlapped or container-grown in spring. The roots are shallow, and care should be taken when cultivating around them; most ground covers do not perform well beneath their canopy. Keep the soil moist while the trees are becoming established, and mulch them. Magnolia scale can be treated with a dormant oil spray. Magnolias do not respond well to pruning because the wounds do not heal easily, so any shaping should be done while the tree is young. Nonetheless, any dead or diseased wood should be removed, and you may also take out water sprouts, suckers, and any undesirable branches while they are still small. Prune in early summer, right after flowering. The shorter kinds can be trained to one trunk or allowed to be shrublike.

MAPLE

Acer

sugar maple

silver maple

Japanese maple

Description: Everyone knows what a maple leaf looks like, right? It's the leaf on the Canadian flag, the one that lends its shape to maple sugar candies. Well, yes and no. While most maple leaves do have a three-lobed outline, they vary enormously in size and shape. With some the lobes are barely indented; others are so deeply cut that they look like lace. Some even have three separate leaflets the way poison ivy does. Size of the tree also varies, and it's easy to find a suitable maple whether you want a large shade tree or a small ornamental one for a city yard. Most maples have especially fine fall color, and seeds with wings on either side that children love to spread apart and stick on the bridge of their noses.

Of the large maples, one of the most magnificent is the sugar maple, also called rock maple (*Acer saccharum*). It is a fine shade tree that can grow over 100 feet tall (usually up to 75 feet in yards), with a big, round, dense head and leaves that turn shades of red, yellow, and orange in fall. Collecting and boiling down the sweet sap to make maple syrup takes a long time (it must be reduced to less than a thirtieth of its original volume), but it's a good way to get outdoors at the end of winter. Named cultivars often emphasize fall color, and there are narrow, columnar ones such as 'Newton Sentry.' Hardy to zone 3.

Red maple, also called swamp maple (*A. rubrum*), is nearly as popular as sugar maple because its showy red flowers are such a welcome sight amid bare branches in early spring. Like sugar maple, it turns color early in fall, but in this case the leaves are blazing red. It is a bit less sturdy than sugar maple but will tolerate wet sites and less fertile soil. Silver maple (*A. saccharinum*) is often planted because of its very fast growth, its graceful, pendulous branches, and its finely cut leaves with silvery undersides, which cast a dappled shade. It is also hardy to zone 3. Silver maple has weak, breakable wood, however, and its roots can clog drains and septic systems if the tree is planted near them.

Of the smaller ornamental maples the choicest is Japanese maple (*A. palmatum*) and its hybrids. The original species, which can grow to 20 feet and more, has fine, deeply indented green leaves in summer that are reddish when they first emerge and turn red again in fall. It's hardy to the milder parts of zone 5, but it is wise to plant it in a spot well protected from harsh winter winds. It self-sows freely. Varieties such as 'Bloodgood' are dark red all season. The very slow growing cutleaf, or laceleaf Japanese maple (*A. p. dissectum*), can grow to 12 feet but is often much smaller. An exquisite mound of cascading branches is supported by a twisted, picturesque trunk, with lacy leaves often sweeping the ground. Certain varieties such as 'Garnet' may hold their red color all season, especially when grown in sun. In addition there are variegated varieties and some with leaves so fine they look like threads, such as 'Filigree.'

Among smaller maples those also worthy of note include paperbark maple (*A. griseum*), which grows about 25 feet tall, has leaves with three distinct leaflets, and is valued most for its bark, which peels off in papery strips to expose a rust-colored layer beneath. It is hardy to the warmer parts of zone 5 if planted in a protected location. Striped maple (*A. pensylvanicum*), also called snake bark maple or moosewood, is a lovely native tree found in cool, moist regions. It does best in a naturalized setting with other trees. Its best features are the bright yellow color of its leaves in fall and its bright green bark, striped with white. The hard-to-find variety 'Erythrocladum' has bark vividly striped with coral.

Norway maple (*A. platanoides*), a big, round tree, casts a very dense shade and is fast-growing. It has become highly invasive in forests, crowding out more desirable trees, and its shallow roots prevent anything from growing beneath it. For this reason it is a difficult landscape tree as well. I don't advise planting it.

How to Grow: Maples in general are easy to grow and have few pests or diseases. Most of them, especially red maples, need soil with adequate moisture. Most need plenty of sun, and if they're to develop a good fall color, they need a climate that is cool in winter. Give cutleaf Japanese maple a fertile, moist, well-drained soil with plenty of organic matter and some light shade in hot climates. It should be staked until the trunk is well developed. Twiggy growth may be removed from the center as needed, though the tree is usually allowed to assume its own eccentric form. Maples in general are pruned in late summer or fall when the sap is no longer running. They need only occasional attention to remove dead, awkward, or crossing limbs. But silver maples should be pruned to eliminate narrow, weak crotches and water sprouts. Paperbark maple should have lower branches removed to display the trunk.

MOUNTAIN ASH

Sorbus

Description: Though vulnerable to pests and diseases in some areas, mountain ashes are still popular ornamental or shade trees because of their size (mostly under 50 feet), their rapid growth, their flat clusters of white flowers in spring, and in particular their beautiful, long-lasting red-orange berries, which the birds love. Mountain ash even has showy red-orange foliage in fall. In short, it is worth trying, though perhaps not a safe bet for mass plantings. There are a number of garden-worthy

mountain ashes, some of them native to the U.S, such as the eastern *Sorbus americana* and the western species *S. sitchensis* and *S. scopulina*. European mountain ash, or rowan tree (*S. aucuparia*), is the most widely grown, however. It is hardy to zone 3 and generally grows to about 40 feet, with rather fernlike leaves. 'Fastigiata' is an upright variety, and 'Xanthocarpa' has yellow-orange berries. Korean mountain ash (*S. alnifolia*), hardy to at least zone 5, can sometimes grow as tall as 60 feet and has a rounded head that can extend all the way to the ground, though you might want to remove lower branches to view the smooth gray bark of the trunk. Both the berries and the autumn leaves are very showy, though the foliage is not as finely cut as that of European mountain ash.

How to Grow: Plant the trees balled-and-burlapped in full sun and a moist but well-drained, fairly acid soil. They do best in cool climates. Newly planted trees benefit from staking. Fire blight may blacken the ends of branches, especially in the south. Affected branches should be pruned out. Young trunks may need to be protected from sun scald in the north. Borers may be found in the trunk near the ground in some regions in the east and can sometimes be destroyed by probing their burrows with a wire—laborious, but a labor of love if you have a fine tree. (Korean mountain ash is somewhat resistant to borers.) Older trees rarely need pruning, but young ones can be pruned in winter or early spring to produce one central leader and to remove crossed or vertical branches or ones with weak crotches.

OAK

Quercus

white oak

red oak

Description: Oaks are very sturdy, deep-rooted, long-lived trees. Most are deciduous, but a few are evergreen. They tend to have round, spreading heads and cast a shade that is less dense than, for example, that cast by maples. The leaves are quite acid but make good compost or mulch because their leaves curl, and so don't mat down as much as other leaves do. All oaks bear the familiar acorns and some hang onto their dead leaves in fall after the leaves of most other trees have fallen.

White oak (*Quercus alba*), the classic "mighty oak," can grow to 90 feet and more, with a large, round head and purplish red leaves in fall. It is fairly slow growing, so it's tempting to start with a large specimen: however the tree is taprooted and hard to move, so it is best planted while young. Older specimens should be dug by a competent nurserymen, after a root-pruning the previous year, and balled-and-burlapped. White oak is hardy to zone 3. Red oak (*Q. rubra*, also called *Q. borealis*) is somewhat shorter but grows quite a bit faster and is easier to transplant. Though named for its red heartwood, it also has red leaves in fall. It resists pollution well. Hardy to zone 3 or 4, it is best grown in cool climates. Scarlet oak (*Q. coccinea*) generally has even brighter fall foliage. Pin oak (*Q. palustris*) has small, very indented leaves, a spire shape, and dense, rather drooping branches that are attractive when planted with enough space to display them without interference. Leaves are red in fall, and the dead ones cling to the tree all winter. It is fast growing, easy to move, and hardy to zone 4.

English oak (*Q. robur*), hardy to zone 5, lacks the colorful fall foliage of most oaks and is known mostly for its unusual ornamental varieties, such as the columnar 'Fastigiata' and others that are purple- or cut-leaved. Willow oak (*Q. phellos*) has fine, almost willowlike foliage that is yellow or bronze in fall. It is fast growing and hardy to zone 6. Like pin oak, it tolerates wet soil. If you live on the west coast you can grow the splendid California oak, also called coast live oak (*Q. agrifolia*), a glossy-leaved evergreen that can grow quite tall but is more often 50 feet high or less, spreading widely on gnarled, twisted branches. Hardy only to zone 9, it tolerates moderately poor soil and drought. Southerners can grow the southern live oak

(*Q. virginiana*), a large, wide-spreading tree that is evergreen in the Deep South, where it drips with Spanish moss. It grows fairly quickly to 60 feet or so, with an even larger breadth, and is hardy to zone 7 or 8.

Both the leaves and the acorns of oaks are important food for numerous species of wildlife.

How to Grow: Oaks like full sun and average, slightly acid soil. Unfortunately they are rather like a big strong man who constantly has a cold. They get various diseases, including a fungus that enters the trunk and creates gaping cavities. Borers and gypsy moths love oaks. The best way to keep an oak healthy is to choose the right one for your climate, then give it a site with sun, good air circulation, good soil, and mulch. Oaks can be pruned while young to develop a strong central leader. They have a tendency to get twiggy. Side branches can be cut to induce longer branches to form, but they should be cut back to the main branch since stubs left will produce more dense twigs. Mature oaks seldom need pruning. The strong wood resists breakage, but dead branches should be removed.

PALOVERDE
Cercidium

Description: Gardeners in hot, arid climates need not long for sugar maples or blue spruces when they have excellent native trees that thrive and look appropriate in the setting. The paloverde, the state tree of Arizona, is among the best. Most paloverdes grow to between 15 and 30 feet and are drought-deciduous—that is, they

shed their leaves in dry weather to conserve moisture, then sprout new ones when the rain comes (cold may cause leaf drop as well). In addition, their green trunks, branches, and twigs are able to carry on photosynthesis to help them through prolonged dry spells, and even when the trees are in leaf this process continues. Their deep root systems help them to find water as well. Both the foliage and the bare twigs produce a filtered shade that is useful in the landscape. (In the wild this shade and the somewhat thorny branches provide a nursery for baby saguaro cacti.)

The trunk of the beautiful blue paloverde (*Cercidium floridum*) is a blue-green color. That of the smaller foothills or littleleaf paloverde (*C. microphyllum*) is yellow-green. Both are hardy to zone 8 or 9. Sonoran paloverde (*C. praecox*) and Mexican paloverde (*Parkinsonia aculeata*) are also widely planted. Paloverdes bear yellow flowers in spring. Those of blue paloverde are earlier, bright yellow, and fragrant. These are important wildlife trees and the seeds, which can be ground up into flour, were once an important native food source.

How to Grow: It's fine to allow this tree to grow into its naturally wide-spreading, multistemmed shape, but as a landscape specimen it is often more useful if some lower branches are removed so that understory plants may grow beneath them. These trees are generally trouble-free and can survive neglect in most southwestern areas. A deep watering once a month, however, will produce taller trees, better foliage and flowers, and less leaf drop. Paloverdes prefer a sandy, well-drained soil.

PINE

Pinus

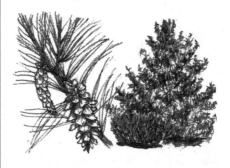

Description: There are many pines suitable for use in the landscape, from small rock-garden specimens to towering forest trees, and most are easy to grow. Most have longer needles than other evergreens. Their branches generally have an open appearance, largely because most species shed needles that are as young as two years old, so that eventually only the ends of branches have foliage. A grove of pines with a carpet of fallen needles—even a small grouping with only three or four trees—is a lovely thing to have on your property.

Eastern white pine (*Pinus strobus*) has particularly long needles and a rather bushy, pyramidal shape. It is fast growing and reaches a height of 150 feet in the wild. Hardy to zone 3, it makes a fine specimen plant as well as a good screen or hedge. There are columnar and weeping forms of white pine, as well as the dwarf, globe-shaped 'Nana,' which typically grows to about 5 feet with a wider spread. Scotch pine (*P. sylvestris*) is even hardier (to zone 3), with bluish needles and reddish bark. Because of its attractive dense shape it is often grown for Christmas trees. There are several dwarf varieties of Scotch pine. Japanese black pine (*P. thunbergii*) is a tall tree, hardy to zone 5 and valuable in seaside plantings. Being battered by strong winds only seems to make the shape more interesting. It has long dark green needles and dark brown bark. Mugo (or mugho) pine (*P. mugo*) is a garden standby, especially the dwarf varieties that behave like shrubs, with a dense, compact shape and long, thickly bunched needles. It is hardy to zone 3. Try to determine the ultimate size and width of a specific mugo variety before you site it in the landscape.

In the west, if you have the space, you can grow ponderosa pine (*P. ponderosa*), a stately, fast-growing tree that can attain a height of 100 feet (more than twice that in the wild) and is hardy to zone 4. Another fine western species is Monterey pine (*P. radiata*), which can grow very quickly to 60 feet and more and is hardy to zone 7 or 8. As a seaside tree it has the same virtues as Japanese black pine, and is especially beautiful perched on the rocky headlands of the California coast.

Japanese white pine (*P. parviflora*) is another picturesque tree, especially the variety 'Glauca,' which has short bluish needles growing in tufts. It is hardy to zone 4. One of the choicest species is bristlecone pine (*P. aristata*), native to the American southwest. In the wild it often grows, windblown and stunted, on mountaintops; tiny specimens have been found that are thousands of years old! Although it may eventually grow to 40 feet, it is so slow growing that it is best to consider it a very special rock-garden plant, with densely bunched needles, each plant having a shape all its own. An 8-foot specimen might be considered very large. Bristlecone pines look like gnarled old men, stunted by wind, drought, and age. They are hardy to zone 4. Other smaller pines favored for landscape use include the columnar, dense-needled Swiss stone pine (*P. cembra*), hardy to zone 4, and lacebark pine (*P. bungeana*), which has beautiful peeling bark like that of a plane tree and is hardy to zone 5.

How to Grow: Most pines seem to prefer a rather dry, sandy, well-drained, acid soil, though mugo pine will tolerate alkaline soil too. All like full sun. Most are easily transplanted and can be planted bare-root while young. White pine can be killed by a blister rust that is carried by gooseberries and currants; don't plant either if you or your neighbors grow white pine.

Pines can be pruned to promote bushiness by pinching their new shoots, or candles, in half before the needles on them develop. This will both restrain growth and promote branching. You can treat the candles in two ways: pinch only the central candle in each bunch, or for an even bushier effect, pinch each candle. Branches can also be headed back to a cluster of twigs or side branches. As long as there is a cluster of needles, new shoots will then form.

Cutting back to the part of a branch that has no needles will kill the branch.

Pines are trained to a central leader, and all dead branches should be removed where they join the trunk, including the lower branches, which tend to die as the tree ages.

REDBUD
Cercis

Description: Redbud trees are a national treasure, opening their brilliant pink flowers in early spring before the leaves appear. They may be naturalized in a woodland setting or grown as specimen landscape trees in the yard, where their small size is an asset. They rarely exceed 30 feet tall, and are usually smaller. Some white-flowering forms exist. Redbuds possess the unusual trait of "cauliflory"—the ability to produce flowers even on the thickest, most mature trunk wood—and often a tree seems utterly plastered with bloom from top to bottom. Leaves emerge with a purplish color, a hue retained all summer in the variety 'Forest Pansy,' provided the summer temperature remains fairly cool. Generally, redbud foliage turns yellow or yellowish in fall.

Eastern redbud is the most common species sold, and the most treelike. Others can be more shrublike in habit. *Cercis texensis* is a southwestern redbud better suited to a dry locale. *C. occidentalis*, western redbud, hardy to zone 8, is even more drought tolerant. In addition there are several Chinese and one Mediterranean species (*C. siliquastrum*) sometimes found in commerce.

How to Grow: Although eastern redbud is hardy to zone 4, it does not do well where summers are cool, needing a good long stretch of warm weather to make adequate woody growth. Redbuds are fairly fast growing, given adequate moisture, and can be grown from seed or planted balled-and-burlapped in early spring. Give the eastern species a moist but well-drained soil and provide regular watering as needed while it's getting established. Trees are shade tolerant but flower best in sun.

SHADBLOW (SERVICEBERRY)
Amelanchier

Description: This excellent tree is yet another example of a native American specimen that is neglected here but widely praised and planted abroad. Fortunately, that is changing as gardeners discover the virtues of this multiseasonal plant. Often the shadblow's are the first blossoms you notice in early spring, in fields and at the edge of woodlands, with clouds of dainty white flowers conspicuous among the gray

trunks of wintry, leafless trees. (Some are pinkish-colored before the buds have fully opened.) The small oval leaves, attractive in summer, turn bright yellow, orange, or dark red in fall. The small summer fruits, which usually emerge red, then turn to purple or black, are sweet and delicious for baking or preserves, once valued by Native Americans and settlers alike. But you must be quick with your harvest, lest the birds get first pick.

Usually the trees are multistemmed, growing to about 20 to 25 feet tall. *Amelanchier canadensis* is apt to be a suckering thicket, more shrublike than *A. arborea* and *A. laevis* or the western species *A. alnifolia*. Running serviceberry (*A. stolonifera*) is an even lower-growing thicket. All of these tend to be confused in the trade, however, so you may have a few surprises. Never mind—they are all beautiful and rewarding to grow. Plant them in a natural setting that suits their rather informal growth habit and enjoy them. All are hardy to at least zone 4.

How to Grow: Most shadblows prefer moist, well-drained soil but are quite adaptable, though not very tolerant of pollution.

They are best suited to acid soils, except for *A. alnifolia*, which tolerates some alkalinity. *A. canadensis* is more salt-resistant than the others. They all grow well either in sun or part shade. Transplant them balled-and-burlapped or container-grown in early spring. Prune only to remove weak or broken branches.

SPRUCE

Picea

Description: Spruces are tall, fast-growing evergreen trees with symmetrical spire shapes. You can distinguish them from firs, which they resemble, in two ways: spruce needles can be rolled between the fingers, whereas the needles of fir (as with hemlock) feel flat; and spruce cones hang from the branches rather than sit on top of them. Colorado spruce (*Picea pungens*) is a popular tree with a classic Christmas tree shape and smell. On healthy specimens, the branches extend all the way to the ground in dense, graceful layers. Blue spruce (*P. p.* 'Glauca') is very widely grown—perhaps too much so, as it is often out of scale with the average house and yard, and planted too close to buildings. Needles of blue spruce have a bluish cast, but the degree of blueness varies from one tree to another. Certain varieties such as 'Koster' or the semidwarf

'Fat Albert' show a more dependably blue color. White spruce (*P. glauca*) likewise forms a tall, dense spire with a bluish cast. The variety 'Conica' (dwarf Alberta spruce) is a striking tree, growing slowly in a soft, fuzzy pale green cone—an excellent accent plant, though not as dwarf as people often suppose. I've seen older specimens that are well over 10 feet, planted in spots where such height was clearly not expected.

Norway spruce, whose botanical name, *P. abies*, literally means spruce fir, forms a broad, dense dark green pyramid with distinctive upward-lifting branches and drooping side branches. It too is a massive tree that can dwarf a home, but there are several small ornamental varieties of this spruce, such as 'Nidiformis' (bird's-nest spruce), which grows to a mere 3 feet, with a flat top. All the spruces mentioned are hardy to zones 2 or 3, and are cool-climate trees.

How to Grow: To counteract their tendency to lose their lower branches, give spruces plenty of sun and don't crowd them. They will tolerate heat or cold and most soils, including dry ones, but the site should be well drained. Norway spruce likes a bit more fertility and moisture, and all species need to be watered while they are becoming established. White spruce tolerates seaside conditions well in the northeast. Norway and Colorado spruce can be planted bare-root while young. Pests that afflict stressed trees include spruce gall aphids, spider mites, and scale; dormant oil sprays can be effective against them, though hard to apply on large specimens.

It's difficult to prune large spruce trees without ruining their shape. They can be trained to one leader while young.

Awkward branches can be cut to a side branch if necessary. But for the most part pruning consists only of removing dead branches.

WILLOW
Salix

Description: Willows, some of whose vices and virtues are noted on page 654, are lovely trees in the right spot. Of all the species, the weeping willows are the most popular and are best planted by a pond or stream or where you want a pretty, fast-growing specimen tree. But avoid sites where the roots will wreak havoc with your plumbing, septic system, or storm drains. This means several tree widths away from any structure that might be affected. The botanical names of the weeping willows are somewhat confused in the trade, but the tree sold as Babylon weeping willow (*Salix babylonica*) is the best one where it is hardy (to zone 6). It grows to about 40 feet, with long branches that sweep the ground and fine-textured leaves. In zone 5 you can grow the Thurlow weeping willow (*S.* × *elegantissima*), which is similar, or one of the varieties of white willow (*S. alba*), which is hardy to zone 2. It normally grows rather upright, but the one called 'Tristis' (golden weeping willow) is pendulous, with fine fall color.

Pussy willows are different plants altogether. The native pussy willow, *S. discolor*, is a rather weedy, upright shrub that produces the familiar furry gray bumps along its stems just before the catkins break out in yellow bristles. It can grow to 15 feet and is hardy to zone 3. Goat willow, or white willow (*S. caprea*), is an import that grows considerably taller and has larger, showier "pussies" (which, by the way, are produced only on the male plant). There are pink-flowered and weeping varieties. Also of interest is coyote willow, a shrubby grayish-leaved species that grows wild in wet places over much of the U.S., especially in the west. I am also fond of black pussy willow (*S. melanostachys*), a tall, vigorous shrub that spreads out like a giant bowl from the base of the plant. Its pubescent catkins, which are black and rather bristly, develop bright red anthers, followed with bright yellow pollen. I planted it next to spring-flowering witch hazel and the effect is striking.

How to Grow: Willows will grow in most average soils but prefer moist, even wet conditions. You may need to water them during dry spells until the root systems are developed. They grow best in full sun, though native pussy willows also thrive in the woods. They are among the easiest trees to establish and can be planted bare-root. They are easily propagated by cuttings or just by sticking a willow stem into moist soil. Weeping willows benefit from careful pruning, which encourages them to develop a strong central leader and strong upper branches—the idea is to get the branches to grow tall and arching so they can support the long, weeping twigs. While the tree is young, prune to one central stem with a few good side branches, but keep removing the lower ones. Do this in late summer or fall, since willows bleed sap in spring. Keep removing any upright water sprouts from branches, and any suckers at the base of the plant. If you remove a branch, remove all of it—cutting back partway produces twiggy growth that will mar the overall effect. Trailing branches may be pruned at the ends, however, if they're in the way.

Pussy willows are pruned like shrubs and should be cut back hard to produce fresh new stems. This will restrain the vertical growth and keep the twigs within reach for picking. You can cut out the old stems at the base, or even cut back all of them to force the whole plant to regrow.

CHAPTER 17

Wildflowers

THROUGHOUT THIS BOOK I'VE been telling you to look to nature for gardening advice: to see how nature fertilizes plants; to note how nature provides leaf mulches; to respect the balance of power that nature maintains among insects and plants; to take from nature ideas about grouping plants and designing gardens. With wildflower gardening this principle is especially important. Some wild plants adapt to a wide variety of situations; some have an extremely narrow range of adaptation. But all plants have certain conditions under which they grow best, and even when these conditions are met they still may need some supervision to remain a part of your landscape. When you see a plant growing in the wild, it is because it has chosen that particular spot—at least for now.

Because people see wild plants doing fine without being planted or tended, they may assume that these are somehow more rugged, more indestructible that garden specimens, and that consequently they can be planted—then ignored. As a result their wildflowers fail to thrive, and the gardeners become discouraged about growing them.

This is too bad, because if it's done right, growing wildflowers is one of the most satisfying forms of gardening there is. The bare spots in the lawn where shade once kept grass from growing can be a miniature woodland glade spotted with foamflower and Virginia bluebells in spring. The unmown grassy area out back could have patches of goldenrod, milkweed, and other meadow flowers for color all summer. The boggy place where it seems nothing worthwhile could ever grow might nurture clumps of red cardinal flower and pink turtleheads in late summer. None of these lovely pictures can be counted on to happen by accident—but gardeners can create them. Certainly nature might put black-eyed Susans in the meadow, but she might also decide on burdock and poison ivy instead. As a gardener you can gently change her mind.

What Is Wildflower Gardening?

FIRST, LET ME EXPLAIN A FEW THINGS that wildflower gardening is not.

It is not gardening with weeds. Both weeds and wildflowers grow wild, but a weed, by definition, is unwelcome. Interestingly enough, some of the worst weed pests are not native to the country in which they are growing, but have been introduced either intentionally or by accident, their seeds mixed in with grain seed or hiding in the mud on visitors' boots. Without the ecological checks and balances that exist in their native lands, they become rampant. Some weedy imports can be both pretty and harmless in a landscape if allowed to grow in a spot where they're fairly self-contained—say, tansy along a fence, or jewelweed in a boggy part of the yard. But most of the wild plants best suited to your yard are native not only to your own country but also to the specific area in which you live. The less you have to adjust a site to make a plant feel at home— or to protect other plants against it—the more rewarding your attempts will be.

Furthermore, with local indigenous species you can often go and see these plants growing in their favorite habitats and so better understand their needs.

Wildflower gardening is not digging up plants from the wild. If you go out walking in the woods or fields and see flowers you like, then dig them up, bring them home, and replant them, there is an excellent chance that they will die. For one thing, the time of year when wildflowers are showiest, prettiest, and most recognizable is generally the worst time to move them. For another, even if you mark the spot where they grow and dig them later on when they're dormant, you may not be able to transplant them successfully. Just because a plant is growing happily in the woods without anyone's help does not mean that it's easy to grow at home, or easy to transplant. Some wild plants are extremely particular about how much sun or shade they get, how much moisture, what the soil texture or pH is, even what specific microorganisms inhabit the soil. Pink lady's slipper is a prime example of a plant that is very difficult to domesticate (although its relative the yellow lady's slipper, *Cypripedium calceolus*, is a good plant for a gardener to grow if purchased from a responsible nursery). A certain fungus must be present in the soil for the pink lady's slipper to thrive, and it would be extremely hard for anyone but an expert to provide just the right conditions for it at home.

The last and most important reason for not digging up wildflowers in the wild is that many are becoming endangered by this very practice. Even species that seem quite plentiful are being depleted, often by nurseries that collect plants from the woods and fields rather than propagate them.

The smartest—and most responsible—course for a beginning wildflower gardener is to start with a few species that are known as being easy to grow, and adaptable to the home setting. These should be seeds or live plants. Your local nursery may sell some wildflowers potted up, and for a wider choice you might eventually want to order dormant plants from mail-order companies. Some reliable sources are listed beginning on page 764; but if you're buying from a place whose propagation policies are unknown to you, you should ask them to tell you what they are and avoid those that rely on collection from the wild.

If you really get involved with native plants you'll probably want to learn how to grow them from seed. You can join a society that, as part of its membership program, has a seed exchange. Both collecting and growing wildflower seeds can require considerable knowledge and skill—as well as patience. (The books listed on page 780 offer guidance.) With some species you must wait many years between the time you sow the seeds and the time they bloom. For these reasons a beginner is usually better off starting with dormant clumps of mature perennial plants. In nurseries these are usually in pots. (They will sometimes arrive in the mail as "sods"—matted clumps with soil attached.) But if you enjoy this kind of gardening you might want to join a local native plant society, not only to learn more, but to meet other enthusiasts and to swap plant divisions and seeds with fellow gardeners (page 761).

Wildflower gardening is not maintenance-free. Often it is low maintenance, but sometimes not. A colony of wildflowers will not maintain itself unless conditions are right. If you've successfully matched the plant with the right setting and planted it with care, it may look after itself, especially if it is a vigorous spreader. But many wildflowers, though easy to grow, will not withstand competition from other wild plants, including grasses. In addition, plants in nature often simply come and go. A wildflower you find in one spot may not be there the next year for a variety of reasons, and you'll probably want to help ensure the survival of those you plant by protecting them better than nature does—weeding, mulching, and feeding them as needed.

In short, wildflower gardening is much more like gardening with standard garden material than you might have thought. It involves buying plants from nurseries, planting them in prepared soil, weeding them, mulching them, watering them, and performing other tasks to help keep them alive and productive. If you understand this, you'll save yourself a lot of disappointment.

Original Species Versus Hybrids

"WILDFLOWER GARDENING" AND "naturalizing" are closely related topics, but they are not precisely the same thing. "Naturalistic" or "naturalized" plantings are designed to look as if they were the work of nature, not man. They are most convincing when you use local wild species, but you can also achieve a natural, informal look by using species native to other parts of the country or the world, and even by using garden hybrids. The drifts of spring bulbs mentioned so frequently in the bulb chapter are a good example of this: all are hybrids of species native to other lands, but sprinkled here and there, even growing in grass, they make themselves at home without much help and often look as if they belong there. The same natural effect can be achieved with garden annuals and perennials that are planted where they can increase by self-sowing or by creeping rootstocks. Take bee balm, for example. You might choose to exclude it from your more formal garden because of its spreading habit but allow it to form large colorful clumps in a moist spot at the edge of the lawn. In doing so you might use either a hybrid bee balm or a wild species such as *Monarda fistulosa*—the effect would be much the same. I find no reason to be a purist in this regard. At times I do prefer the unadorned simplicity of an original wild species. But if a hybrid or an improved selection of a plant is readily available and known to be a good garden subject, I might use it just as readily in a wild setting as I would the original.

Wildflowers in Gardens

ON OTHER OCCASIONS YOU MIGHT want to do just the opposite—take a wild species and place it in a conventional garden setting. A large number of the perennials that we use for sunny herbaceous borders are simply native meadow flowers, usually in a hybrid or selected form but occasionally the wild species. Some of these are New England or New York aster, butterfly weed, gayfeather, coreopsis, and blanketflower. All these, and many more, are discussed in the perennials chapter. Even goldenrod and the towering Joe-Pye weed might be suitable, in the right garden. Other wildflowers that are attractive in a sunny perennial border are the feathery meadow rues, pearly everlasting (*Anaphalis margaritacea*) with its white buttonlike flowers so useful in dried arrangements, bright purple ironweed, and all those superstars of late summer with *helios* (the Greek word for "sun") in their name— *Heliopsis, Helianthus, Helianthemum.* And let's throw in *Helenium,* named for Helen of Troy.

The many native species that can be used in shaded perennial gardens include fringed bleeding heart, wild columbines, and wild blue phlox (all are discussed in the perennials chapter). There are many more, including a large number included in the List of Wildflowers in this chapter, such as bottle gentian, Virginia bluebell, and cardinal flower.

For the most part, this chapter deals with native plants naturalized in a wild setting, or planted in well-supervised "wild gardens" that look natural but are collections of native plants carefully grouped together and conscientiously maintained. But keep in mind that many of these plants can be managed in tamer, more formal settings as well. In the List of Wildflowers, I've selected natives that are easy to grow. I hope that if you find these plants rewarding, you'll do some exploring on your own in this very large, fascinating, and challenging field.

Matching the Plant to the Site

WITH WILDFLOWER GARDENING THE choice of plant, soil preparation, planting, and maintenance are all keyed to the site. Rather than creating a "lowest common denominator" soil that will support all the plants you decide will look good in the garden, as you would in a more conventional flower bed, you're dealing with small microenvironments that sometimes need to be prepared and tended in specific ways.

One of the smartest things you can do as a wildflower gardener is to explore the countryside in the area where you live and see which native species thrive. Take along with you a good wildflower field guide, such as one of those listed in the back of this book, to help you identify them. Note which sites they choose in the wild and how they grow. Is a particular wildflower in small clumps or does it carpet the ground? Is it in full sun or part shade? Is the soil dry, average, damp, or wet? What company does it keep? Often there are "companion plants," which appreciate the same conditions and might also look good in your plantings.

WOODLAND GARDENS

Woodlands are different everywhere you go, and in every kind of woods there are certain plants that will do well. Each region has its own combinations of trees that predominate and its own understory plants— the shrubs and small trees that grow in the shade of larger ones. Remember, each woods has soil conditions that are greatly influenced by the depth of the tree roots and the materials that the tree leaves add to the soil when they fall. Some woodland soils are very rich and moist, while others are rather dry and not as fertile. Some have extremely acid soil, others less so. These factors must all be kept in mind when you're choosing which plants to grow.

The light requirements of woodland plants also vary. Some like to grow where a clearing in the woods admits some sunlight. Others are happy with just the sun they get in springtime before the deciduous trees leaf out and shade the forest floor. Many of these, called "spring ephemerals," actually go dormant in summer and disappear from view until the following spring. Virginia bluebell is an example—don't be dismayed when it does this in your garden! A few, such as bunchberry, will even tolerate the all-season shade and highly acid soil of evergreen forests, although even here, they're likely to appear in a clearing where a tree has blown down. But it's much easier to find plants for deciduous woods. Conifers such as spruce and cedar, and arborvitae in particular, are very difficult to garden under; not only do they cast deep shade, but their needles are chemically hostile to herbaceous plants.

You do not need woods to grow woodland plants, but if there are woods on your property you have the ideal situation. You can put plants in one specific spot among the trees where they can be admired together in an informal grouping. Or you can create a path that meanders through the woods, with wildflowers planted here and there, sited so that they can be admired from the path. Look for areas where there is dappled shade, or the partial shade you find in a small clearing. Paths can be simply

renewed periodically by mowing, scything, and clipping individual woody plants with loppers. Or they can be mulched to deter unwanted growth more permanently. One trick you might try is to lay down newspapers about six sheets thick, then place about 4 inches of shredded bark on top of them. The newspapers will decompose after a year or two, but by then they will have permanently smothered much of the plant growth that might otherwise have poked up through the mulch. Frequent foot traffic will take over from there.

To prepare the woods for planting, you'll probably need to do some clearing to make them a bit tidier and to allow you to view your plantings better—but don't do too much. Remove unwanted trees or saplings to open up the woods and create the dappled shade that so many woodland plants prefer. You can remove fallen trees and spindly underbrush to create paths and planting areas. But leave some understory plants, especially if they're attractive ones, and keep enough fallen trees and old stumps for woodland creatures to live in. You may even want to plant some native shrubs such as azaleas and mountain laurel, or small flowering trees such as shadblow or dogwood. It's often helpful to remove some of the lower limbs from surrounding trees to let in a bit more light. But the woods should still look more like woods than a landscaped area.

In the spots where you're going to plant your wildflowers, look to see if there are existing plants—small woody shrubs, herbaceous flowering plants, or foliage plants such as ferns—that you can incorporate into your scheme. You can leave clumps of bunch grasses (those that do not spread by rhizomes), sedges, and mosses—anything that looks woodsy and natural but won't compete with your new introductions. If you need to remove existing herbaceous and woody plants to make room for others, dig them up by the roots so they won't reestablish themselves. A trick I learned from Garden in the Woods, a wonderful public garden and native-plant nursery in Framingham, Massachusetts, is to lay down newspaper and mulch, as described above for paths, and then make planting holes right through these layers for new plants.

If the soil is lovely woodland soil, enriched and lightened by years of leaf fall, you won't have to do anything to it—in fact, it should not even be tilled as you would an ordinary garden. Just dig holes large enough to accommodate your new plants, perhaps mixing a handful of bonemeal into each hole to encourage root growth. Set the plants in the holes, spreading the roots out and then replacing the soil. Water the plants well and either replace the ground litter of decaying leaves that you found there or add some additional light mulch of shredded leaves, salt hay, decaying straw, buckwheat hulls, grass clippings, or finely shredded bark. (If the mulch looks too artificial you can scatter some leaves on top.) Moistened peat moss can be used as a mulch if another material such as leaves is spread on top to keep the surface from drying out and crusting over. For plants that like very acid soil, a mulch of pine needles is beneficial as well as beautiful. Apply any of these mulches carefully, making sure you don't cover the leaves and crowns of the plants, and don't forget that your mulch will be augmented by the leaves that fall from the trees. Many plants will rot if they are smothered with mulch.

How you arrange the plants in your woodland garden is important. You'll want a less formal look than a perennial border might have, of course, but the same principles apply. Don't place tall plants where they will hide shorter ones. Try to achieve interesting foliage contrasts—combining the fernlike foliage of Dutchman's breeches with a broad-leaved plant like galax (*Galax urceolata*), for example. And be mindful of what blooms when, so you can visualize the various color combinations that will emerge as the plants flower. Try to think of what small pictures you can create in this or that corner of your woods, so you'll come upon them as you walk the paths. One of my favorite pictures is made with white foamflower, wild blue phlox, and red-and-orange wild columbine, but the possible combinations are endless. Try a colony of Jack-in-the-pulpits emerging from a nest of maidenhair ferns; or plant trilliums with ferns. In other spots you might want to highlight just one kind of plant—a patch of shooting star, for example—so that nothing else will distract from its subtle beauty.

Many of the plants included in the List of Wildflowers make good woodland ground covers, such as bloodroot, bunchberry, May apple, Solomon's seal, foamflower, and golden star. If you combine them with other plants, make sure that those can hold their own against the spreaders. Or else plant the ones with invasive roots in containers sunk in the ground so they'll be restrained. A bucket with the bottom either perforated or removed works well for this. Plants that spread by self-sowing too abundantly can be somewhat controlled by snipping off the spent flowers before seedpods can form and scatter their seeds, though this will be laborious if there are a lot of them.

If you don't have woods on your property but are creating a woodland garden beneath or in the shade of ornamental trees, you may have to work harder at preparing your site. If there is lawn grass you must remove it (page 54) as well as any other competing plants, or use the newspaper and mulch trick described above. To create good woodland soil, you might need to scratch some well-moistened peat moss, compost, or other organic matter into the top few inches to lighten it. If your soil is heavy clay, it might even be better to start from scratch by replacing the clay with soil that you mix yourself. Build raised beds to contain it, and edge them informally with stones or old logs. Raised beds will also help if the soil is too wet for the plants you want to grow. The garden can then be designed and planted in the same manner as the shaded perennial garden described on page 179, except that you'll aim for a more informal look, with creeping plants like foamflower drifting across some areas and taller accent plants like snakeroot and turtlehead highlighting others.

The plants described as woodland species in the List of Wildflowers will do fine in the shade of most deciduous trees. Some others you can try are herb-Robert (*Geranium robertianum*) and other wild geraniums; native lilies such as Canada lily (*Lilium canadense*); the *Erythronium* species, which are variously called trout lily, fawn lily, and dogtooth violet, and which have small, dangling, lilylike flowers. Consider the various species of wild violets; partridgeberry (*Mitchella repens*), a creeper with beautiful white-veined leaves and bright red berries in fall; win-

tergreen (*Gaultheria procumbens*), a woodland ground cover with evergreen leaves and red fall berries; Oconee bells (*Shortia galacifolia*), with its dainty white, bell-like spring flowers; shooting star (*Dodecatheon meadia*), with flowers like little rosy cyclamens; pink-flowered spring beauty (*Claytonia virginica*); and wild ginger (*Asarum canadense*), which carpets the forest floor with its shiny round leaves. I've also enjoyed growing red baneberry (*Actaea rubra*), with its clusters of red fruits, and fringecups (*Tellima grandiflora*), with their arching wands of fragrant, bell-shaped flowers.

For woods that are very deeply shaded, try miterwort (*Mitella diphylla*), also called bishop's cap, with dainty white flowers borne high above the spreading foliage, or plant bluebead (*Clintonia borealis*), noted more for its fat bright blue berries than its dainty yellow flowers. Most woodland flowers bloom in spring, although you might spot your woods with some summer and fall color by planting wood lily (*Lilium philadelphicum*), turtlehead, cardinal flower, and snakeroot (*Cimicifuga* species).

MEADOW FLOWERS

Woodland gardening is the easiest type of wildflower gardening for the beginning gardener because so many of our native plants are woodland species. Before our country was settled, much of it was woods, with only occasional sunny clearings. So a large proportion of our native herbaceous plants are shade lovers. Moreover, many of our towns consist of tree-shaded yards, for which this kind of gardening is so appropriate. On the other hand, there are some parts of the country where sun-loving plants were always prevalent—the high meadows of the Rocky Mountains, for example, and the midwestern prairies, kept treeless by the hooves of bison. In the mountain meadows, wildflowers do well because competing grass is rather sparse, giving them a chance. On the prairies certain flowering plants have adapted to coexist with prairie grasses. But the acres and acres of fields cleared for crops or pastureland are a recent development, and so are many of the wildflowers that populate them. Often these are species, brought in by settlers, that are now naturalized. Furthermore, fields that have been plowed and fertilized support many tall, vigorous grasses with creeping roots that can quickly crowd out broad-leaved flowering plants not adapted to this type of competition.

For this reason the recent popularity of growing "wildflower meadows" has resulted in some very discouraged gardeners. While grassy fields sustaining a number of flowering species are sometimes seen in nature, they are not easy to duplicate, despite the great number of wildflower-seed mixtures on the market. If you scatter these seeds in a grassy meadow, few if any will grow because they cannot compete with the established plants that are already there. If you start from scratch with bare ground you will have more success, but it may be short-lived. Mixes with annual wildflower seeds will give you something like an instant meadow the first year, but there's no guarantee that any will self-sow in subsequent seasons. Even mixes that contain seeds of perennial flowers may contain many plants that are unsuitable to your particular climate and terrain, and the perennials that do bloom could be crowded out over time by one or two of the more rampant wildflowers, by grasses,

or by undesirable weeds. Your best bet is to obtain seed from a nursery that specializes in prairie plantings and has formulated mixes that include native grasses and flowering plants known to coexisit well together. Even with these there is maintenance involved, and it may be several years before you see permanent results from your labors. But by following the supplier's directions, you may well have a meadow you can be pleased with.

Another approach is to establish clumps or even large drifts of perennial meadow flowers and then maintain them as if they were part of a garden. In fact, the more you think of your meadow as a garden and not as a self-sufficient environment, the more successful your attempt will be. Try creating a minimeadow in some spot on your property that is readily accessible, and that you can keep an eye on during the course of your regular activities. A perfect spot would be a corner or strip of the back lawn—or even a curbside strip in front of your home. Select several perennial wildflowers that will naturalize, such as goldenrod, New England aster, butterfly weed, and gayfeather. If the area is a bit moist you might also try turtlehead, bee balm, cardinal flower, gentian, or Joe-Pye weed. Remove the grass and prepare beds for these plants. Put just one species in each bed, but plant at least three clumps or divisions of that one species. They can all be set out in early spring, or you can start the early-blooming ones the previous fall. Water them well, mulch with a material like straw or shredded bark, and then keep checking them—weeding out grass and other competing plants around them until they become fully established. Even after that, they may need some protection against competition.

Yet another approach is to take a grassy field and establish plantings of appropriate meadow flowers within it. You'll have to be all the more vigilant about your little planting beds, watching to see that they don't get swallowed up by the growth of the other vegetation. The best way to handle the meadow is to keep some paths mowed through it leading to the planted areas, so you can not only take care of the plants but also admire them—and the insects and birds that visit them. You might even put mulch on the paths if you like to walk there often, using the same method as I've described for woodland paths.

As your clumps become established and spread out they may need much less care, especially the most vigorous ones and those best suited to the soil and climatic conditions of your particular meadow. But there will always be a few tasks to perform. As your meadow grows, keep removing any plants that you don't want there, such as burdock, wild raspberry brambles, and thistles. Mow or burn the entire meadow once a year after the last species has finished blooming and dropped its seeds. (If you choose to burn, consult the wisdom of someone who has experience with this technique and knows how to do it safely.) Some people mow or burn only half the meadow yearly, to preserve the chrysalises of overwintering butterflies and moths. Mowing or burning will keep woody plants (shrubs and trees) from growing up. You might, of course, want to have some woody plants in your meadow, either ones you've planted or ones that occur there naturally, such as sumac, blueberries, sweet fern, or bayberry. If so, just mow around them. You might even want to encourage a few tree seedlings. Those that are considered too "weedy" to be ornamental specimens, such as wild cherry or field junipers, might be just right in your meadow.

Watch and see what nature contributes to the scene: milkweed and wild roses, perhaps. And keep thinking of new plants that you can add as well. The meadow will always be in flux and will never be quite the same from one year to the next. And of course it will vary according to what part of the country you live in. Out west your meadow might include penstemon, Indian paintbrush, blue mountain beardtongue, or one of the columbines such as western red columbine or the yellow *Aquilegia chrysantha*. In Texas the yearly highlight might be bluebonnets (*Lupinus subcarnosus*). If you live in the midwest, for example, you'd grow one of the gayfeather species native to the Great Plains—*Liatris punctata* or *L. pycnostachya;* in the south you'd grow the southern species *L. elegans;* in the northeast *L. scariosa* or *L. spicata.* Even if a plant is adaptable to a number of different regions, it will usually have more fruitful interactions with indigenous wildlife if it is growing in its place of origin. Wherever you garden, consult a local native plant society for more ideas.

WILDFLOWERS FOR DRY AREAS

Nowhere is the principal of local knowledge and local plant sources more crucial than in the drier parts of the American west. There the concepts of "woodland" and "meadow" might often seem as relevant as microclimates on Mars. Trying to establish New England or Appalachian wildflowers there would be, if not futile, then certainly wasteful of resources. If you're a newcomer, allow yourself to fall in love with all the gorgeously diverse cactus blossoms, California poppies (*Eschscholzia californica*), and California asters (*Lessingia filaginifolia*). Investigate the numerous penstemon species, the western evening primroses (*Oenothera*) and monkeyflowers (*Mimulus*), and the wonderful purple owl's clover (*Castilleja exserta*). If they're right for your terrain, grow hummingbird sage (*Salvia spathacea*), desert marigold (*Baileya multiradiata*), sand verbena (*Abronia villosa*), and hummingbird's trumpet (*Epilobium canum latifolium*). If you already know the territory, you need only look to see how native plant communities form in the hills and plains around you.

Even in parts of the country that are not habitually dry, gardeners are becoming more aware of the need to conserve water and not site thirsty plants where they will need frequent irrigation. A sunny south- or west-facing hillside, for example, might be especially drying for plants, especially if the soil is sandy or rocky and the site exposed to drying winds. Some good choices for a spot like this would be blanketflower, gayfeather, various salvias, asters, butterfly weed, brown-eyed Susan, and the delightful prairie coneflower (*Ratibida columnifera*).

WILDFLOWERS FOR WET AREAS

The woodland stream where I played as a child was a perfectly landscaped water garden. In early spring skunk cabbages poked up their purplish flowers all along it—odd bulbous things that came to a point and smelled like skunks if you bruised them. Later their leaves would open into wide green cabbagelike rosettes. Bright yellow marsh marigolds appeared right down next to the water, and ferns unrolled their fronds, forming a lush carpet in summer.

Many attractive wild plants grow like this in wet spots all by themselves, in stream beds, marshes, bogs, the banks of ponds, woods, and fields where the soil is soggy, or just roadside ditches where the water sits after rain. If there's a wet place on your property, you may have had some unkind thoughts about it. You can't walk through it or drive through it. You couldn't build anything on it without great difficulty, even if the local wetlands commission would let you. You suspect it's full of snakes and mosquitoes, and you're considering having it drained at great expense.

Do not! Your wet spot is a valuable resource that many gardeners would envy. Chances are it's full of wildlife, including frogs that eat those mosquitoes. It might host nesting waterfowl, or even fish. If you look closely you may find that it has already been "landscaped," just as my old stream was, with native plants. I happen to love marshes, swamps, and boggy places. For one thing they're beautiful to look at; for another it's important to have some parts of the landscape that people can't walk in easily, so wildlife can be protected there. I tend to resist even the idea of damming up the rich ecosystem of a swamp to create a pond, unless most of the swamp is left intact.

Finding plants for your wet spot is not at all difficult. You go about it just as you would for any of the environments I've been talking about. See what plants are there already that you'd like to encourage. Find other species that are either native to your area or will do well without displacing natives. Plant them carefully in designated spots, then maintain them, both while they're becoming established and thereafter. Inform yourself about the needs of the plants you use. While some moisture-loving species like blue flag iris can grow right in the water with their roots submerged, others like Canada anemone cannot, and merely prefer damp soils to dry ones. The beautiful and rare swamp pink (*Helonias bullata*) will naturalize along a pond edge, but only if you keep its roots free of competing grasses.

Some other plants you might consider for moist sites are the dainty meadow rues (*Thalictrum* species), frothy white goatsbeard (*Aruncus dioicus*), the *Monarda* species, and vervain (*Verbena hastata*), with its tall blue spikes so lovely for cutting. Welcome cattails (*Typha latifolia*) to the edges of your pond and the beautiful native sedges (*Carex* species) wherever you find them. And don't forget all the wonderful native ferns, such as the dainty maidenhair (*Adiantum* species), the wood ferns (*Dryopteris* species), the magnificent ostrich fern (*Matteuccia pensylvanica*), the tiny spleenworts (*Asplenium* species), and the evergreen Christmas fern (*Polystichum acrostichoides*). But be sure you distinguish between moist but well-drained sites and those that are sometimes flooded. A cattail will tolerate having its roots submerged, but a fern will not.

Trees to frame your water garden might include swamp maple, river birch, and sycamore. Moisture-loving shrubs include summersweet, blueberry, spicebush, and witch hazel (see the shrubs chapter for more on these, and others).

When you're working in wet soil, remember to take care that it does not become compacted. Don't till it or cultivate it, just do what is necessary to keep it free of too-vigorous weeds or grasses, and try to avoid walking on the areas you've planted.

ROCKY AREAS

Rocks are almost always an asset in wildflower planting. Rocks that occur in woodland plantings blend beautifully with the plants, especially if they are covered with lichens and mosses, and they can help you to highlight your favorite specimens. Site tall plants behind rocks so that they stick up above them when they flower, or flow down over them. Put a special plant in front of a rock so the rock forms a background for it. If you're creating a woodland garden or small shade garden where no rocks exist, you might even consider bringing some in. If you do, place them carefully so they look natural, burying the bottom third of the rock in the soil so it looks as if it "grew" there. Use types of stone that occur in your area for a more natural look—granite rocks if those are typical, limestone ones if those predominate. And if you have boulders or ledge outcroppings already, by all means make the most of them.

An old friend of mine named Bluie Piel, then in her seventies, once led me out the front door of her home to admire her semishaded yard. The grass was fighting it out with slabs of New England granite, which broke the soil surface like the backs of half-submerged whales. It was spring, and drifts of self-sown blue scilla had spread through the grass, blending exquisitely with the clumps of red-and-yellow wild columbine that had also self-sown there, taking hold even in tiny soil pockets in the rocks. It looked like a miniature alpine meadow, Connecticut-style. "Now, dearie," Bluie said, "God didn't do that. I did that." And so, I might add, can you. That's what wildflower gardening is all about.

List of Wildflowers

THIS LIST IS A SAMPLING OF COM-mon, herbaceous flowering plants of woods, marshes, and fields. All of them are native to North America. Start with these easy-to-grow favorites, then experiment further, exploring wild shrubs and trees, ferns, and other foliage plants as well. Most states have native plant societies (see page 761). They can steer you toward species that can be grown successfully in your area.

BLACK-EYED SUSAN
Rudbeckia hirta

Description: Even most nongardeners recognize this bright wildflower with its yellow, daisylike petals and raised dark brown center. It generally grows 2 to 3 feet tall, usually in sunny meadows or by the side of the road. It blooms a long time—from June to September—and I find it a good cut flower for summer bouquets. Sometimes it is called brown-eyed Susan, a name usually associated with

Rudbeckia triloba, a smaller-flowered spe-cies—though in my view it doesn't matter which name you give to either. Black-eyed Susans are biennials or short-lived peren-nials that may persist for a few more years if cut back after bloom, but more often than not they bloom once from seeds dropped in late summer.

How to Grow: Black-eyed Susans are prairie flowers that will compete fairly well with other meadow flowers and even with grasses if the latter are sparse and without long, vigorous roots. They like a sunny spot best but will tolerate part shade. Soil need not be moist or fertile. In fact, in the rich soil of a garden the plants may rapidly become too much of a good thing—grow them in a meadow or in a spot all their own. They are easily grown from seed sown in late summer or early fall, then let them self-sow over the years.

BLACKFOOT DAISY
Melampodium leucanthemum

Description: Blackfoot daisy is a low-growing evergreen with silvery foliage. Growing less than a foot tall, it is a won-derful plant for the dry-climate garden or landscape. Its small white daisylike flowers bloom all spring and summer—even spo-radically in winter in mild climates. The plant has a creeping habit, and is beautiful

dormant in late summer if it is very dry.) The plants are also attractive in smaller groups in a shade garden. Bloodroot rarely grows more than 8 inches tall and is hardy to zone 3. A very showy double variety is also available.

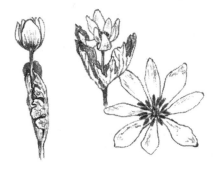

naturalized at the base of shrubs or among rocks. It also has a delightful fragrance and is attractive to butterflies.

How to Grow: This southwestern native is a highly adaptable plant and will grow in a wide variety of soils as long as they are well drained; in true desert conditions it needs some watering to bloom well. Blackfoot daisy is fairly winter hardy in dry climates. Prune in fall to a more compact shape if it becomes straggly. The plant is not a rugged one—it has fragile stems and cannot take rough treatment—but its self-sowing habit makes it gratifyingly persistent.

BLOODROOT

Sanguinaria canadensis

Description: Bloodroot's starlike white flowers emerge from the forest floor or next to streams in early spring, opening like little cups, then flat saucers, to reveal yellow centers. The flowers last only a few days, but the large, attractive light green leaves, which wrap around the stems, then unfold, last all summer, and make a good ground cover for shady areas. (Bloodroot may go

How to Grow: Bloodroot needs soil with adequate moisture, but the soil must be well drained. The ideal is a fertile woodland loam with plenty of humus. The pH level is not especially important, but if the soil is poor in nutrients, a topdressing of compost will be beneficial. But don't apply a heavy mulch or stem rot may result. The plants need some filtered sunlight to bloom in spring but should not have hot sun in summer. The roots are rhizomes that bleed red when cut. Plant in fall or in spring if the plants are dormant, with the rhizomes lying horizontally just below soil level. They will send up new shoots. Plants can be divided for propagation, but dense clumps can also be left alone. They will spread by self-sowing as well as from the root system.

BLUE FLAG

Iris versicolor

Description: These small, elegant irises have flowers that are blue marked with gold, and appear from late spring to midsummer. They look something like a Siberian iris, but the leaves are sword shaped, like those of bearded iris. Plants grow 2 to 4 feet tall. Blue flag grows wild in wet meadows and can survive with its roots submerged beside ponds and streams and in marshes. Crested iris (*Iris cristata*) is another good wild iris for the home landscape; it grows from bulbs and forms a low carpet in moist areas, with small blue flowers.

How to Grow: Blue flags prefer full sun but will tolerate part shade. They are grown very easily in any fertile soil, including that of a perennial border, as long as it is kept reasonably moist by watering or mulching. They are not fussy about soil pH. Plant them either in early spring or in late summer or fall. Some people's skin is sensitive to the roots; if yours is, wear gloves. Dividing every few years after bloom will promote flowering. To do this cut the plants back to about 6 inches, and divide the rhizomes into clumps with leaves attached. Replant each piece of the rhizome horizontally just below soil level with the crown at soil level. The plants will spread themselves by means of the creeping rhizomes and also by seed.

BOTTLE GENTIAN
Gentiana andrewsii (G. clausa)

Description: These late-summer bloomers are also called closed gentians, because the petals of the violet-blue flowers appear to be tightly closed. They aren't, though— bees do get inside to pollinate them. Bottle gentians grow 1 to 2 feet high, with a cluster of flowers on top of the stems and a whorl of leaves just below them. Often there is another flower cluster and leaf whorl further down the stem. One plant can form a large clump, sending out thick roots from the crown. Usually bottle gentians are found in moist meadows or next to streams, sometimes in bogs. In warmer climates they grow in the mountains in open woods. Hardy to zone 3, this is the easiest of the many gentian species that wildflower gardeners grow. It's the one to start with, therefore, but you can explore others, including the beautiful, elusive fringed gentian (*Gentianopsis crinita*). It is a biennial that must be grown from seed, and you never know where it will turn up in the wild from one year to the next.

How to Grow: Bottle gentians can either be naturalized in a wild garden or grown in a more formal one. Give them full or filtered sun. They cannot take strong competition from other perennial plants, and it's best to weed around the clumps from time to time, and mulch them. Although they like moist soil, a soil that is only moderately moist will usually do, especially with a mulch. A rich, sandy loam is best, with plenty of organic matter and a neutral or slightly acid pH. Plant them in early spring or fall, while they're dormant. Plants do not need to be divided to stay vigorous, and they resent root disturbance, but you can try dividing and moving them as long as you keep plenty of soil around the roots. The crowns should be set at soil level.

BUNCHBERRY

Cornus canadensis

Description: These shrubby little woodland plants hug the ground, growing no more than 8 inches tall, yet they're closely related to dogwood trees. The white flowers, in fact, look very much like those of flowering dogwood, though smaller. They start blooming in late spring, followed by clusters of red fruits, and bloom is staggered so you'll often see plants in summer on which flowers and fruits are displayed together. The showy white blooms (like those of the tree dogwoods) are actually leaflike bracts surround-

ing the tiny true flowers; these bracts remain long after the true flowers have withered. The leaves are a handsome glossy green, turning a bluish purple in fall and persisting through the winter. In short, this plant is attractive almost year-round, making it an ideal ground cover in climates where it does well. Only in early spring, when the new leaves are slow to appear, does it look bare and untidy.

Hardy to zone 2, bunchberry grows wild in the whole northern tier of the United States and some high elevations in the southwest, as well as Canada. The plants favor open woodlands, the roots extending along the soil surface just under the leaves littering the forest floor. They will do well as a ground cover even south of their native range if given enough moisture and a partly shaded spot. They will also grow in an open, sunny location where summers are cool.

How to Grow: There's not much to growing bunchberry—just make sure the plants are shaded and the moisture around the roots is fairly constant. Beyond that they like an acid soil, lots of organic matter, and a light mulch to cover the spreading roots. They are very hard to establish bare-root, and it is best to purchase sodlike clumps, setting them out in spring or fall with the eyes (buds) just below the soil surface. Divide in early spring or late fall, making sure each piece of rhizome has an eye. They can also be propagated from seed.

CARDINAL FLOWER

Lobelia cardinalis

Description: Cardinal flowers are about the most intense red of any flower I know.

As perennials they tend to be rather short-lived, but will persist in a spot they like, and I can remember my great-aunt's delight when they came up every year without fail next to her brook. The ideal situation is a sunny, damp spot that never dries out completely, even in summer. I saw them naturalized next to a pond at Garden in the Woods in Framingham, Massachusetts, and the effect was stunning. But you can also grow cardinal flowers in the herbaceous garden, as long as you keep the plants watered. The flowers are in spikes, as tall as 5 feet, with little tubelike petals from which hummingbirds love to sip. They bloom for a month or more in late summer. They are lovely grown with another wild lobelia species, great blue lobelia (*Lobelia siphilitica*), which flowers at the same time.

How to Grow: Cardinal flower likes light, humusy soil of average fertility and a slightly acid pH. Grow it in sun or part shade, but in sun take extra care to make sure soil moisture is consistent. Plant in spring in cold climates, spring or fall in mild ones, with the crowns at soil level. In the wild they spread by seed and by making offshoots—little rosettes at the base of the plants. They can be divided in spring and the individual rosettes replanted. Keeping the plants free of mulch or leaves in winter will help ensure their survival.

DUTCHMAN'S BREECHES

Dicentra cucullaria

Description: These plants are closely related to bleeding hearts. They have the same deeply cut, fernlike foliage and long, arching stems. But instead of flowers like little hearts dangling in a row from the stems, they have flowers like a Dutchman's pantaloons hanging upside down. Flowers are generally white or pinkish. They grow in large spreading colonies, but don't work as an all-summer ground cover because the leaves go dormant not long after the early-spring flowers have faded. They are most effective naturalized in the woods where they can spread freely or mingle with ferns and other vigorous plants.

How to Grow: Dutchman's breeches are best grown among deciduous trees, where the sun shines through the bare branches in early spring. A light, humusy, slightly acid soil suits them best—moist but well drained. A fertile soil will promote flowering, and a light organic mulch such as shredded leaves will best duplicate natural forest conditions. Plant or divide the small white tubers in summer after the plant's natural period of dormancy sets in, and up until late fall. Don't be discouraged if new plants fail to bloom; they will when they are well established.

FOAMFLOWER
Tiarella cordifolia

Description: This is one of my favorite shady ground covers. Its maplelike leaves spread on runners that just seem to touch the soil lightly and then move on. Small fuzzy pyramids of white flowers appear in spring atop short, upright stems. Despite the apparent fragility of the runners, there are sturdy underground roots beneath the crowns once the plants are established. En masse, foamflowers are spectacular, looking just like waves flowing through the woods and around rocks and trees. In warm climates the plants are evergreen. Cool weather often gives the foliage a purplish hue. Their natural habitat is fertile, moist woodland. There is also a clump-forming type (usually listed as *Tiarella wherryi*), which does not spread by runners.

How to Grow: Foamflowers prefer part shade in cool climates but can take full shade in warm ones. They are not fussy about pH but like moderately rich soil and mustn't dry out at any point. A soil rich in

organic matter, and a light mulch, will help keep them happy in warm weather. Plant or divide in spring or fall. New plants, formed where the runners touch down, can be transplanted by cutting the runners and replanting the new crowns at soil level. Clumps of *T. wherryi* can be divided and replanted.

GOLDENROD
Solidago

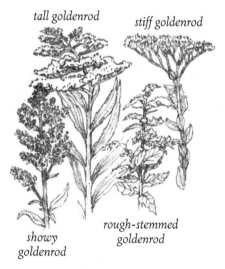

tall goldenrod

stiff goldenrod

showy goldenrod

rough-stemmed goldenrod

Description: Most people are familiar with goldenrod, with its bright yellow plumes in late summer and fall. For years it has been blamed for the hay fever that plagues people at that time of year, perhaps because the fuzzy goldenrod flowers *look* so pollen-laden. In fact it is the sly, less-conspicuous flowers of ragweed, which bloom at the same time, that cause most of the trouble. Ragweed's pollen is light and easily airborne; goldenrod's (transported by insects) is too heavy to fly.

People also don't realize that there are about a hundred species of goldenrod.

Hybrid forms are even sold. Most are hardy to zone 3. (In Europe goldenrod is much admired, and often grown as a garden plant.) The best goldenrods to grow are probably the ones native to your area, though goldenrods are very adaptable. Most are typically found in rather infertile meadows. (In fact, farmers often surmise that the soil of an abandoned field needs work if they see goldenrod growing there.) Canada goldenrod (*Solidago canadensis*) is a common species that likes meadows slightly moist in spring and dry in summer, and grows up to 4 feet. It is too spready for the flower garden. Wrinkled, or rough-stemmed goldenrod (*S. rugosa*), is similar though sometimes taller, and there is a cultivar of it called 'Fireworks' that is not invasive. Showy (or noble) goldenrod (*S. speciosa*) has particularly fine gold, poker-shaped flower clusters that bloom late in fall. Seaside goldenrod (*S. sempervirens*), also late-blooming, is semievergreen, and is the best species to grow in coastal locations. Gray goldenrod (*S. nemoralis*), with gray-green foliage, thrives in poor, dry soil.

How to Grow: Goldenrods prefer full sun. Many can be very invasive, spreading by creeping rootstocks and self-sowing, especially in moist, fertile soil. They may need to be controlled in a garden setting but are good flowers for a meadow garden. To propagate, divide and replant when the ground first thaws.

GOLDEN STAR

Chrysogonum virginianum

Description: This plant's other common name is green-and-gold, perhaps because

the flowers are bright gold with a bit of green in the center. The leaves are an attractive, rather dark green, the plants about 8 inches tall. I often wish golden star were more easily available, for few plants are longer blooming. It usually starts flowering in April, with great profusion, then throws out sporadic blooms all summer and into fall—and even through the winter in warm climates! The leaves are also evergreen in warm areas. I have not found it reliably hardy in zone 5, though there is purportedly a northern and a southern strain and I may have wound up with the latter. In areas where it does very well it makes a fine ground cover, but also try it in flower gardens or in a rock garden.

How to Grow: The plants seem to do well either in sun or shade, though filtered shade is best (too much shade will restrict flowering). They like a fertile, moist but decidedly well-drained soil, rich in organic matter. A mulch may keep them too moist and also impede self-sowing, which they generally do prolifically. They also spread by runners. (For winter protection you can try using a noncompressing mulch such as evergreen boughs, but remove them promptly in early spring.) Plants can be divided in late winter, early spring, or late fall by cutting the rhizomes with a knife, making sure each one has a crown with a rosette of leaves visible. Replant and water thoroughly.

HEPATICA
Hepatica americana

Description: Generally called round-lobed hepatica, this plant sends up clumps of little flowers in very early spring, before the new leaves appear. The flowers are usually white, sometimes pale blue and sometimes (in alkaline soil) pink. They only flower on sunny days and close at night. The leaves stay on the plants all year, though in winter they turn a brownish green color and are replaced by fresh leaves after the plants flower. Native to open woodlands, hepatica works fine as a ground cover for partly shaded areas, as a specimen in the woodland garden, or in a rock garden. It is hardy to zone 3. Sharp-lobed hepatica (*Hepatica acutiloba*) is very similar, but the leaves have pointed lobes rather than rounded ones, and the plant prefers soil with a neutral pH.

How to Grow: Give round-lobed hepaticas humus-rich, slightly moist acid soil. Plant with the crowns at soil level and mulch lightly. Clumps will enlarge by

themselves and will often self-sow, but they may be propagated by dividing in fall. Don't remove the leaves, though, since they should remain during the winter.

JACK-IN-THE-PULPIT
Arisaema triphyllum

Description: I used to love to find these plants in the woods when I was a child. In mid to late spring they send up a stalk about 2 feet tall with a strange flower that flops like a canopy over an enclosed "pulpit." Inside the pulpit is a small protuberance called a spadix (that's Jack). The pulpit, or spathe, is usually green-and-brown striped. In late summer a cluster of red-orange berries forms where Jack once stood. The root is a corm once valued by the Indians as a cooked food—hence the plant's other name, Indian turnip. But the corm is poisonous if eaten raw, and in some individuals all parts of the plant cause a skin irritation. (Handle them with gloves if your skin is sensitive.) This plant thrives in rich, moist woodlands, or places like seasonal stream beds that flow only in spring and dry out in summer.

How to Grow: Giving Jack-in-the-pulpits a humus-rich soil is more important than finding them a moist spot. They like full or part shade but not full sun. Soil should be rather light and acid. Plant nursery-grown specimens at the same depth they were in the pot. Corms can also be dug and moved from one spot to another after the foliage dies down in fall. Plant about 6 inches deep, or about 3 times the depth of the corm itself. Once established, the plants can take care of themselves very well, often forming large colonies.

JOE-PYE WEED

Eupatorium fistulosum and other species

Description: There are a number of species of Joe-Pye weed, named for a Native American herbalist in colonial times, who, as the story goes, used the plant to cure typhus. You'll also find it sold as *Eupatorium purpureum* and *E. maculatum.* All are fairly similar—tall, erect plants on sturdy stems. The flowers, their nectar irresistible to bees, are muted pinkish purple in large, open clusters. They appear in late summer and last for many weeks. This is a monumental plant, often found in moist areas in the wild. I treasure it in the garden since it blooms late, never needs staking, and doesn't spread aggressively, although the odd plant will show up in a new spot from time to time, identifiable by its vigorous eruption of large, pointed, toothed leaves and purple stems. It has several interesting relatives, one being the wild boneset (*E. perfoliatum*), which is shorter and white-flowered, and white snakeroot (*E. rugosum*), a pretty plant with small white flowers and handsome dark green foliage. Both of these spread by rhizomes —too aggressively for a garden situation but appropriate if naturalized.

How to Grow: The Joe-Pye weeds are among the easiest plants for the sunny garden. Given moist-to-average soil they need no particular care. In fertile garden soil they might become too giant for your taste, but this is easily remedied by cutting them back in June. They will then branch and bloom at a lower height, with numerous, smaller flower clusters that are great for cutting. Give each plant plenty of room, and watch for it in springtime. Its new purple-colored shoots are late to emerge.

MAY APPLE

Podophyllum peltatum

Description: This is a charming plant if used in the right way. In late spring each plant sends up what looks like two little, closed-up beach umbrellas. These unfurl as two broad, parasol-like leaves under which you have to peek to see the small white or pinkish flowers. I like them just for the foliage. An established clump forms a large mat that hoists a solid mass of umbrellas

all summer long, shading out other plants beneath them. In May a small yellow fruit (the "apple") forms where the flowers were. The fruit, when fully ripe, is purportedly edible, but toxic when immature, as are the roots or leaves, and touching the roots can cause a rash. (If this happens, wear gloves when handling the plant.) Another name for the plant is wild mandrake.

How to Grow: Hardy to zone 3, may apple grows naturally in open, damp, deciduous woods. It appreciates a rich, moist soil and a fairly acid pH, but it will persist in dry conditions. It makes an excellent ground cover for shaded or semishaded sites. Plant or divide the rhizomes in fall, leaving at least one bud on each division for faster growth, and spreading out the rhizomes 1 inch below the soil surface.

PENSTEMON (BEARDTONGUE)

Penstemon species

Description: There are about 250 different native penstemons from which American gardeners can choose. You'll find them in a wide variety of colors, in heights that range from a few inches to at least 4 feet. All have tube-shaped flowers, flared at the ends, arrayed along slender, waving stems. Lest this bounty seem daunting, be advised that the whole key to growing penstemons is to narrow down the ones best suited to your part of the country. Regional wildflower handbooks or native plant societies can help steer you toward the most suitable, as can the American Penstemon Society (see page 759).

The best-known penstemon for gardens is a white-flowered selection called 'Husker Red.' It has very handsome dark red foliage that turns green as summer progresses. In the wild, white *Penstemon digitalis* is a familiar sight to easterners. Southeasterners will know the rosier *P. smallii.* In the Rocky Mountains look for blue-violet *P. strictus,* and in the northwest the taller *P. serrulatus* with a similar hue. On a dry California hillside, *P. heterophyllus* might be the penstemon of choice; in the southwest, the fire-engine-red *P. eatonii.*

How to Grow: Since all these species are suited to specific habitats, their care requirements vary greatly. Choose one that is known to do well in your part of the country and research its particular needs.

Some like moist soil, some dry. Some are hardier than others. Perhaps the one thing all of them have in common is that they need good drainage. This is especially true of the many western species.

SOLOMON'S SEAL

Polygonatum biflorum

Description: Another favorite woodland plant, Solomon's seal has arching stems about 2 feet high with two rows of lance-shaped, drooping leaves. From their axils (where the leaves join the stem) hang yellow-green flowers, usually in pairs, in late spring. In summer blue-black berries appear and are eagerly consumed by small mammals and birds. Solomon's seal makes a good shade-loving ground cover, eventually forming big clumps. A close relative, great Solomon's seal (*Polygonatum biflorum* var. *commutatum*) can grow to over 5 feet and is very showy and vigorous. Make sure you have adequate space to accommodate it. Both are hardy to zone 3.

How to Grow: The ideal spot for this plant is shady, with moist, acid soil; but it will tolerate sun, neutral soil, and even some dryness. Mulch will benefit it, as it will most woodland plants, by keeping soil moisture relatively constant. Divide the rhizomes in spring (fall in warm climates), with at least one bud per division, and lay the pieces horizontally 1 inch below the soil surface.

TRILLIUM

Trillium

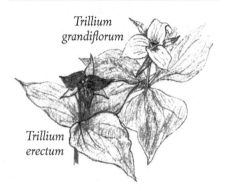

Trillium grandiflorum

Trillium erectum

Description: The trillium I grew up with was *Trillium erectum*, variously called purple trillium, wake robin, and stinking Benjamin. (Its flowers smell putrid, but that's not a problem if you keep your nose out of them.) The name "trillium" refers to the fact that there are three leaflets in each leaf cluster, as well as three purple petals, alternated with three green sepals. These May-blooming flowers are followed by large dark red berries, which birds and small mammals relish. Plants are a little over a foot tall and hardy to zone 4. They grow in wet, cool, fertile woodlands.

There are many other species of trillium for the wildflower gardener to grow. The white trillium (*T. grandiflorum*), also called snow trillium and great white trillium, has beautiful white flowers several inches across. Like purple trillium it is easy to grow; hardy to zone 3. There is also an exquisite form of white trillium with double petals. A number of southeastern trilliums such as the deep red *T. cuneatum* and yellow trillium (*T. luteum*) have beautifully mottled foliage. Western white trillium (*T. ovatum*) is appropriate for the Pacific northwest.

Although these and certain other trilliums are easy to grow, propagating them for the trade is another matter. Some can take seven years or more from seed to salable plant size. As a result there is a good bit of poaching from the wild—a practice that threatens to reduce their numbers. Purchase trillium plants only from a nursery that you trust to behave honorably and sell only propagated plants. If you're buying from a mail-order source and are not absolutely sure, order the double white trillium, which is always nursery-grown and is not found in the wild.

How to Grow: Trilliums have bulblike rhizomes with stringy roots attached that extend deep into the soil. They like sun in early spring, then dappled shade as the trees leaf out. Give them a rich, moist soil with plenty of organic matter and a mulch. Their pH requirement varies from one species to another. *T. erectum* likes acid soil, whereas *T. grandiflorum* is more lime-loving. Topdress with a little compost annually, especially if your soil is poor. They are planted or divided in fall, with the rhizomes about 2 inches below the soil surface. Handle the fragile root system with care.

TURTLEHEAD
Chelone lyonii

Description: This rather showy pink-to-purple flower is native to the south but has naturalized throughout the east. It grows about 3 feet tall and is one of the few good shade-tolerant wildflowers for late summer,

blooming anywhere from July to September. The flowers, clustered atop a spiky stem, look like, well, the heads of turtles. It is found in boggy places. *Chelone obliqua* is very similar, with narrower leaves. A related species called snakehead (*C. glabra*) has white flowers and similar growing habits. It is a larval food for the black-and-orange Baltimore butterfly. Both species are hardy to zone 3.

How to Grow: These are wonderful easy-to-grow plants. You may site them in full sun if the soil is moist all summer; otherwise, light shade is best. Plant in rich, light, humusy, acid soil and mulch to keep soil moisture constant. They may need supplemental water during drought, and are not well suited to typically dry locations. You can divide the fibrous roots in early spring for propagation, but they usually spread well without your help—though rarely enough to become a nuisance. They further endear themselves to the busy gardener by never needing staking. Turtleheads are beautiful naturalized in a moist spot or beside a pond.

VIRGINIA BLUEBELL
Mertensia virginica

Description: This plant is a typical spring ephemeral, sending up broad apple-green

leaves in early spring and pretty bell-like flowers that progress from pink to lavender to vivid blue as they open, mature, and finally fade. Because individual flowers in a cluster open at different times, all these colors are present at the same time. After blooming, the entire plant simply disappears, to reemerge the following spring. It is helpful to mark the spot where Virginia bluebells grow while they are blooming so you don't disturb the roots later on when the plant is dormant. They choose to live in moist, semishaded places. There are several western species of *Mertensia* that, conversely, prefer dry, rocky soil.

How to Grow: Give Virginia bluebells rich, fairly acid soil that is moist but well drained. Though hardy to zone 3, and very easy to grow, they may benefit from a light winter mulch. The tuberous roots do not need to be divided, but for purposes of propagation you can do it carefully after the plants go dormant, replanting them 2 inches deep. Keep new plants watered well. This is another oft-pilfered wildflower, so be sure that any you buy are nursery-grown, not collected in the wild.

CHAPTER 18

Houseplants

IT USUALLY STARTS WITH ONE PLANT. You're a nongardener until your Valentine gives you an azalea. Or your mother brings over a philodendron when you move into your new apartment. Or you go to the hospital with pneumonia and come back with a streptocarpus. Much to your astonishment, the new plant doesn't die. In fact, after you follow a friend's advice about its care, it thrives, blooms, and puts out new growth. Encouraged, you buy another plant to keep it company, then another, and another. Pretty soon your apartment looks like the set of a jungle movie. You're hooked.

There are a lot of reasons why people get started with houseplants. Plants make the indoors look like the outdoors, softening the lines of the architecture and making any place look more hospitable. With their flowers and foliage they bring spring and summer into our rooms in the dead of winter. They also make us healthier. Plants give off moisture that's a good antidote for a dry, central-heated atmosphere, and they emit oxygen that enriches the air we breathe. Also, there's an emotional benefit to having other living things around us, and even something as uncommunicative as a plant can help fill that need.

Often indoor gardening is the only way a person can satisfy the gardening urge. Perhaps you live in an apartment, or a house with a yard that's too small, too shaded, or otherwise unsuitable for plants. Perhaps you like to garden year-round but live in a cold climate. Growing plants indoors is the simplest answer. While houseplants can be fussy about specific things and are less self-sufficient than outdoor plants growing in the ground, they are also less time-consuming to grow as a rule (fewer weeds!) and require less physical exertion. You can turn them into a hobby if you like, experimenting with new ones and propagating them, or you can just let them be decorative. It's your choice.

Best of all, houseplants open up a whole world of variety. While there are many species to explore in any kind of gardening, houseplants offer a particularly wide range of choices. It's exciting to grow the beautiful, often weird specimens of the tropical rain forests or the desert—environments that may be so different from your own that the plants that grow there seem like exquisite works of art. Setting a bromeliad on your table, its jewellike flower emerging from a circle of spiny leaves, is like setting a priceless vase there, except that the bromeliad is affordable. Hanging a staghorn fern on the wall is even better than hanging a painting, because its shape changes as its "antlers" grow.

If your interest in this field grows, you may want to acquire a structure like a greenhouse that will let in more light, allow you to grow plants in a more carefully controlled environment and give you a better place to perform messy tasks like potting. Small models are available that can be added on to a house easily; there are even miniature greenhouses you can attach on the outside of a window so plants can be grown with maximum light. For the purposes of this chapter, however, I'll assume that you're working with whatever resources your living space already provides.

Ways to Use Houseplants

Any plant can be displayed singly like the ones just mentioned. The more interesting the plant, the more it lends itself to this treatment. But sometimes plants work better in groups. For one thing, each will benefit the others by giving off moisture, thus making the air a bit more humid around the plants than it is in the rest of the room. For another, you can create lovely decorative effects, massing plants to resemble an outdoor scene, be it a cool-climate woodland "planted" with ferns, trailing ivy, and Norfolk Island pine; a tropical rain forest with spider plants, Christmas cacti, and bromeliads; or a desert of cacti and succulents.

You needn't be a purist about grouping plants according to their origins. Simply combining a diverse group, with foliage of different shades, shapes, and textures, is always effective. You might assemble them by using a few complementary foliage types or flower colors. Or you might make a composition of one plant type alone, but with species and varieties that vary slightly—such as a windowsill of cacti with different shapes, a miniforest of different dracaena species, or a tray of rex begonias with different foliage patterns.

Let's face it, though: with indoor gardening there is the temptation to be a collector. If you've succumbed you probably violate the rule of design that insists on using masses of a few plant types rather than "one of this, one of that." So be it. There is, after all, limited room in which to put plants without having asparagus fern dripping into your tea or hoya vines crawling into your bed. So collect as many different ones as you have the space and interest to try.

Finding the Right Location

While you're being creative with your plants, you must always remember that while they may be artworks, they are also alive, and they have specific individual needs. Where you put a plant is not just a matter of deciding where it looks good; also crucial is picking a spot where it will get the amount of light it needs to do best, where it will have the right temperature and the right degree of humidity. Sometimes this is a matter of choosing the spot to fit the plant, but sometimes it means choosing a plant to fit the spot, especially if your surroundings do not offer an unlimited choice of conditions. Fortunately there are plants that do well even in the most unlikely spots. You'd need a sunny window if your passion is passionflower, orange blossoms, and *Phalaenopsis* orchids. But if your home is on the dim side you can still grow a host of foliage plants like ivy, philodendron, schefflera, and dieffenbachia. Many houseplants appreciate a humid atmosphere; but if your heating systems renders your winter air bone-dry, you can still do fine with dracaena, many cacti, peperomias, and aloe. The List of Houseplants includes a description of the specific needs of each of the plants covered. When you are trying others, you can usually obtain information on culture from the nursery that sells them to you.

One thing to keep in mind when placing plants in your home is that some are toxic to humans and/or pets. I would never let children or pets nibble on *any* plant that is not a known, safe food plant. But with some common houseplants, special care must be taken to display them out of harm's way. These include philodendron, spider plant, dieffenbachia, oleander (*Nerium oleander*), croton (*Codiaeum*), mistletoe (*Phoradendron serotinum*), poinsettia (*Euphorbia pulcherrima*), and Jerusalem cherry (*Solanum pseudocapsicum*).

After you find the right spot for a plant, you must care for it in just the right way. It must be in the right pot, have the right soil, and be given the right amounts of water and fertilizer. Various maintenance needs such as dusting, washing, and pruning must be met, and any insect or disease problems must be taken care of. Unfortunately, a number of different houseplant problems have very similar manifestations. Rather than give you a confusing list of symptoms and their possible causes, I suggest the following approach. Whenever a plant is not doing well, review the kind of care you're giving it in the three areas discussed below—light, temperature, and humidity—and make sure the plant is getting what it needs. Note the ways in which the factors are interrelated: the kind of pot and the potting medium affect how much water the plant needs; the more light a plant gets the more fertilizer it needs; the time of year affects a plant's needs—many plants "rest" in winter. Always look at the total picture.

LIGHT

Few homes are lit as well or as uniformly as the great outdoors. Our plants tend to cluster on windowsills, sunning on one side at a time like beachgoers on a row of lounge chairs. To be sure, modern homes have more light than traditional ones, where windows are small. Nowadays many houses have picture windows, or entire glass walls, or skylights and bubbles that let light in from above. Homes are lit with more artificial light as well. Instead of lamps perched on end tables there's now track lighting, spot lighting, and more convenient and attractive versions of the fluorescent lights that plants dearly love. You can even buy fixtures specially designed to light plants.

But it's very important to give a plant exactly the right kind of light. Some will tolerate very low light, others need a good four hours of sun each day, and yet others, the great majority in fact, prefer bright light that is not direct sun. Bright light might be sunlight that fills a room with a glow so that even plants set back from the window are lit. It might be light reflected off white walls. It might be sunlight filtered by a gauze curtain or a fiberglass screen. Or it might be the morning sun from an east window or late-afternoon sun from a west one, neither of which is as strong as direct midday sun from a south window. An excellent site for some plants is a north window where there's no direct sun at all; but in that case there should be no trees or other obstructions to keep the outside light from flooding in.

Plants often do splendidly in offices that are brightly lit throughout with fluorescent lighting. As long as the plants get 14 to 16 hours of light each day, they need not be very close to the lights themselves. If you have fluorescent lights in the bathroom or kitchen and can keep them turned on all day, these can be good spots for plants too. But if your dwelling is dimly lit and you want to grow flowering houseplants, you may have to put together the kind of fluorescent-lighting apparatus shown on page 35 to suit their greater need for light. Try setting the lights about 18 inches above the plants; then watch to see how they react and adjust the distance accordingly. Even if you don't find such a setup an attractive way to display plants, you can bring them into flower under lights and then remove individual plants at their peak to grace a table. This is a good solution to the problem of having no bright light at all—often the case in city apartments. Incandescent light is not as good as fluorescent light for plants, chiefly because it gives off more heat. To get the leaves close enough for them to benefit from the light, you risk scorching them.

Foliage plants in general are tolerant of low light conditions, while flowering ones tend to need brighter light (though not always direct sun). If a plant is not getting enough light, the leaves will be thinner than normal—the result of the plant's having used the sugars and starches stored there in order to grow. (With enough light to carry on photosynthesis actively, it can replenish the supply.) The leaves of light-deprived plants may also be smaller, and the stems will have long stretches between the nodes where leaves form, resulting in a gangly, leggy appearance. The plants may also be bending toward a light source in order to get more light, and may drop leaves. Light-starved plants will usually not bloom. On the other hand, if a plant gets too much light the leaves turn yellow, then brown between the veins or on the edges.

TEMPERATURE

While some houseplants can tolerate a wide temperature range and probably prefer about the same degree of warmth that you do, others are rather fussy and may not thrive in your environment. Many apartment buildings are kept very warm in winter, even at night. If you live in warm rooms, and the temperature is out of your control, you may have trouble with "cool-room" plants such as cyclamens and camellias, or with plants such as clivia and Christmas cactus that need a period of winter dormancy (during which they are kept cool) in order to bloom. On the other hand, if you can control your environment and are one of the many homeowners who once considered 72 degrees "room temperature" but now, in an energy-conscious, economy-conscious age, put it closer to 65 (and even lower at night), you had best bypass "warm-room" plants such as African violets and certain orchids. In many houses some rooms are cooler than others. Even parts of a room can vary drastically in temperature. Unless you have in-floor heat, the floor is cooler than a spot atop a bookcase. A windowsill might be warm during the day but very cold when the sun goes down. A minimum/maximum thermometer is a wise investment. It will let you find out exactly how cold the living room gets at night, or how hot your plants will be if you set them near a heat register, or how much a spot is affected by drafts. Plants that are too cold will grow very slowly, if at all. Those that are warmer than they like to be will wilt, or their leaves will look scorched or dried out (though many plants will tolerate high temperatures if you keep the air moist).

HUMIDITY

Apartment buildings and houses with central heating often have very low humidity—as low as 5 to 10 percent, especially in winter when the heat is turned up—causing dry skin for both you and your plants. If they are cacti they'll shrug it off, but if they're ferns they'll turn brown and perhaps even die. Most plants prefer a humidity of 50 to 60 percent. (Some like it even higher, but these are best grown under greenhouse conditions.) Humidity is measured by a device called a hygrometer—not an essential tool for the average gardener, but if you're curious, you might borrow one just to see what the humidity in your living space is on an average day.

If the air is too dry for a plant, its young leaves may be small and yellowed or may not even form. Old leaves may dry out, brown, and drop off. If the air is too humid, plants can get mold or mildew; the leaves may have soggy spots or rot altogether. Buds may form, then decay.

If the humidity is low there are several things you can do to help your plants fare better. You can group them together, for the reason explained above. You can mist them, using an inexpensive plastic bottle or an empty window-cleaner bottle filled with warm water. The trick is not to wet the leaves but to envelop them in a cloud of mist by spraying around them. Try to mist at least once a day. Ferns especially love misting, but don't mist fuzzy-leaved plants such as African violets. Another good trick is to set plants on a "humidity tray." To set one up, just get a tray of some waterproof material such as plastic or metal at least 2 inches deep, and fill it with pebbles. If you use attractive pebbles the tray can be a decorative asset. Set your potted plants on the pebbles and fill the tray with water that almost covers the pebbles but does not quite come up to the level of the pots. To create even more humidity throughout the room you can set a tray of water on the radiator, heat register, or woodstove and let it evaporate into the air. You may find that there's a room in your house that is more humid than the others—the bathroom because people shower there, perhaps, or the kitchen because people cook there. You can also create some "jungle air" in one room by means of a humidifier, and put all your humidity-loving plants in there.

Sometimes there's too much humidity in a house—in summer perhaps, or in rooms that are below ground. This can be remedied with a dehumidifier and sometimes with just a fan to increase air circulation. If this fails try another spot for the plants or grow plants that love high humidity such as bromeliads and ferns.

Buying Houseplants

SEE CHAPTER 4 FOR A GENERAL DISCUSsion of how to buy plants. When you're buying houseplants, you should be especially careful to examine them for signs of insect infestation or disease, because both spread more readily indoors than out and can infect your healthy specimens. Look for compact plants with good foliage color. To make sure they have not been weakened by being grown in the same pot for too long, turn the pot upside down and see if roots are coming out.

There are new houseplants appearing on the market all the time, and even if you're familiar with the field, many may be new to you. Try to find a salesperson who can tell you what growing conditions each plant needs. Often plants come with labels that give you directions for their proper care.

Houseplants can also be ordered by mail. You may find this is the best way to acquire an interesting collection, since a wide range of varieties is available from catalogs. Generally they will arrive bare-root (see page 128 for information about buying plants through the mail).

Potting Your Plants

AFTER YOU'VE BOUGHT YOUR PLANT, check out the pot it's in. It may look fine to you or it may need to be replaced, either because the pot doesn't have the look you want, because it's a temporary container made out of pressed peat or some other short-lived material, or because it's too small and the plant is outgrowing it. It is important to get the plant off to the right start with the right kind of pot and the right kind of soil, and then pot it up correctly.

PLANT CONTAINERS

The right plant container is one that will keep just the amount of soil around the plant that it needs. In a too-small pot there will be little soil, and the plant will be "potbound" or "rootbound"—its roots will fill the pot so there's not enough room for soil, water, or nutrients. In a too-large pot with too much soil, excess water will be held around the plant's roots, depriving them of air and killing them. A good rule of thumb is to give the plant a pot that is an inch wider than its root ball.

Make sure the pot provides for drainage. If water is to drain away, obviously the pot needs to have at least one hole in the bottom, and the pot must be set on a saucer or some sort of tray to receive the excess when you water the plant. The humidity tray described above serves this purpose as well.

When you bring home a new houseplant, chances are it will either be in a plastic pot or a standard, reddish brown clay one. Each has its advantages. A plastic pot is light and holds moisture better, so the plant does not have to be watered so often. This can be a drawback, however, because if you overwater a plant in a plastic pot the water will take longer to drain away. Clay pots, on the other hand, are of a porous material that releases excess water over the pot's entire surface, not just at the bottom, and also lets air in and out. The soil in them dries out faster, so they need to be watered frequently, but there's less danger of overwatering. Clay pots are heavier than plastic—a problem with a large pot full of heavy soil, but a plus if a pot contains a top-heavy plant in a light soil mix, which might tip over in a light pot. Clay pots often have white deposits on their outsides after they've been used a while. These are salts from fertilizers that have leached through the pot's porous sides. The stains might seem unattractive to you, but they are useful as a way of monitoring the amount of fertilizer you give a plant. If a lot of white appears soon after you clean off the pot and flush out the soil (see below), you have overfertilized.

Both kinds of pots have their uses. Clay pots are, to my mind, the more attractive. I especially like to group a collection of them in different shapes and sizes. But if you prefer to use plastic pots, you can always hide them inside something more decorative.

Plants look good in many types of containers: glazed ceramic, wooden, straw, metal, and so forth—you can experiment to suit your own taste. By monitoring my watering very carefully, I've grown certain plants successfully in pots that were not designed for holding them and hence had no drainage holes, but I don't advise this unless you know exactly what you're doing. Nevertheless, if you want to try because you have a beautiful plant container with no holes, and you cannot drill holes without damaging it, put an inch or two of stones on the bottom and set the plant in a plastic or clay pot on top of them. Excess water will drain safely into the stones, but don't let so much collect that it reenters the pot.

There are also decorative planters you can buy called cachepots (from the French for "hide the pot"), which are made specifically to hide a utilitarian container. If the decorative planter is a basket, put a water-catching saucer inside so the basket doesn't rot.

Plant containers should be kept clean, not only for appearance' sake but to get rid of disease organisms. When reusing a pot, wash it out first with soap and water and a mild chlorine-bleach solution (about 9 to 1), scouring it to remove all dead leaves, algae, and fertilizer deposits. If the pot is made of clay, soak it in water for a while so it won't draw water out of the soil when you pot the plant.

Various containers are available for hanging plants, often with holes in the rim so that cords or wires can be attached. If there are no holes, you'll have to sling something around the bottom of the pot that will support it, such as those macramé supports. (I think the simpler ones, without a lot of dripping tassels, look best.) If there are holes in the rim and the pot is not too heavy, try this trick: use heavy transparent fishing line to support the pot. It will be almost invisible, so the plant will appear to float in midair. (Using a soilless mix inside the pot will make it lighter.) Another option is to get a wire basket and line it with moistened sphagnum moss (not peat moss, which would fall through the holes), then fill this with your soil mix. Wire baskets are too messy to use indoors but they're pretty and natural looking on a porch or terrace, or in a greenhouse, and plants drain well when growing in them.

Make sure that there is something to catch the excess when you water a hanging plant. Many pots come with a saucer attached, but you still must water carefully so the saucer doesn't overflow onto the floor. A hanging planter without holes in the bottom works fine if you put an inch or two of pebbles in the bottom, then set a conventional pot on top of them. It's helpful if the plant hangs within easy reach for watering. If not, you can water it by setting ice cubes on the soil surface and letting them melt into the soil—although the best way is to just take down the pot and give the plant a good soaking in the sink.

SOIL

The kind of soil that you use for your houseplants is very important. A plant in a pot needs soil that is lighter in texture than soil for an outdoor plant, because drainage is crucial. Ordinary garden soil may work fine for some potted plants, but it holds too much moisture for many of them. It's usually best to use a mixture of soil and soil lighteners, and there are many different formulas for soil mixes. A typical "standard potting mix" might be one part soil, one part peat, and one part sand. For the soil I usually dig some up in fall before frost, so I can have it handy during the winter. Some people feel it's a good idea to sterilize garden soil in a 180- to 190-degree oven for at least an hour to kill disease organisms and weed seed, though I confess I don't bother. I don't like the idea of "dead" soil. If you haven't access to garden soil you can buy bags of potting soil. But try to get "real" soil if you can; I find the bagged kind has a pulverized, uniform texture that does not drain as well as what I dig up. Natural soil has particles of more varied size, including little stones. For peat, use a medium-textured type if you can find it, not the fine, powdery kind. For sand, use sharp builder's sand, never beach sand, which is rounded and has salt in it. Beware of sand provided for use on icy roads, which also may contain salt.

Other nonsoil ingredients might also go into your mix. Vermiculite, which is made from mica deposits, is a light, very absorbent material. If you want your mix to hold water a bit longer, you might substitute this for the sand, which drains very fast and makes for a rather heavy pot when combined with soil. Perlite, a natural mineral product that looks, nonetheless, like little pieces of white styrofoam, is almost weightless and is good for lightening and aerating a mix. Composted bark is another good organic soil lightener. Charcoal is sometimes added to soil mixes as well because it absorbs toxic agents.

With many plants you may decide that you don't want any soil at all, just a soilless mix—say, equal parts of perlite, vermiculite, and peat. Such mixes can be bought in bags and usually contain some lime to counteract the acidity of organic materials like peat and bark. Soilless mixes usually include some fertilizer as well, and are sterile. I find a soilless mix very handy and I keep a large bag of it around. I use it for adding to garden soil, or I use it by itself for starting seeds and for plants that like a very light, well-drained potting medium. Remember, though, that if used straight, a soilless mix may make the pot so light that a top-heavy plant will tip. For hanging baskets, however, it's often ideal. Always moisten a soilless medium thoroughly before you use it so it will not draw moisture away from the plant's roots. You may also have to water and fertilize the plant more often.

Each plant has its own requirements as to growing medium. Cacti and succulents, for example, need particularly good drainage and prefer either a soilless mix or one to which a large amount of sand has been added. Ferns like a more moisture-retentive mix, such as one containing soil, vermiculite, and peat.

Any growing medium you use should be replaced from time to time if possible, for several reasons: it can become compacted, the organic matter in both soil and soilless mixes eventually breaks down, and fertilizer salts can accumulate in any medium. If a plant has been diseased, it is wise to unpot it, shake the soil out of its roots, and put the plant in fresh soil that does not harbor the disease organisms. Start with fresh soil whenever you pot up a plant, whether for the first time or when moving it from one pot to another. If a plant needs to remain in the pot for years with its roots undisturbed, you can still do it a favor by removing and replacing the top inch or so of soil every so often, because this is where the greatest concentration of salts, debris, or algae will be.

POTTING UP

When you're all set with the right pot and the right growing medium, you're ready to pot up the plant. Do your potting on any hard surface where you can make a mess. If you have a table you can use, that's great. I pot outdoors if weather permits, or on the linoleum floor of our utility room. While you're getting a pot ready, make sure the roots of the plant do not dry out. If the plant has arrived in the mail bare-root, open the carton but leave the plant in its packing material till the last minute. If it's in a pot, leave it there till you're ready for it. Take a fresh, clean pot and put a piece of broken clay pot over the hole in the bottom (several if there's more than one hole), laying its concave side down; this will keep soil from falling through the hole. Then put some of your soil or mix in the bottom, suspend the plant over it with the roots where you want them and carefully start to add soil at the sides, poking it gently with your fingers to firm it as you go. Every now and then whack the pot down solidly on your floor or table to settle the soil—it's important not to have air pockets in the soil as they will cause the roots to dry out. Fill to within an inch or two of the top (the bigger the pot, the more space you should leave), whacking and poking as you go. With most plants the crown should be

just at the soil surface so the foliage is not covered with soil but the roots are. When you're all done, water the plant until water runs out the bottom hole. A little soil will come with it, at first, but this will lessen as the soil settles.

Sooner or later, as the top grows and the root system gets too big for the pot, you'll need to repot the plant. When a plant is potbound you may see roots on the soil surface, or they may literally crawl out of the top of the pot or through the hole in the bottom. Water may have trouble sinking into the soil, or may drain out very quickly because organic matter in the soil mix has broken down and been replaced with roots. The pot may also feel abnormally light. If you're not sure what's going on in there, lift the plant out and see if many roots are visible along the outside of the soil.

Here's how to remove a plant from a pot: hold it upside down and rap the rim on a hard surface as shown on page 41. Support the plant with the stem between your fingers so you can catch it when it slides out.

When you have the plant out of the pot, look carefully at the roots. If any look rotted or mushy, remove them; in fact, if the roots look badly damaged and other signs have also led you to suspect a disease that might spread to other plants, it's probably best to throw the plant away. If the plant is very potbound and the roots are matted or circling the pot, try to pry them apart with your fingers. If necessary make a few slashes with a sharp knife. By forcing them to repair themselves, you're ensuring that they will strike out into their nice new soil; otherwise they might stay in a matted lump.

When repotting plants, take their individual needs into account. Some plants such as clivia enjoy being potbound. Some grow quickly and need frequent repotting. Others grow very slowly, but even these like to have their soil replaced periodically.

Taking Care of Your Plants

MAINTENANCE IS THE PART OF houseplant care that confuses most people, but it's really a pretty simple business. There are some dos and don'ts, which I'll describe below, but one thing to remember is that although you're giving plants a very consistent environment in which factors such as temperature fluctuate much less than they would if the plant were outdoors, the plant is still conscious of the seasons. Unless its environment is totally controlled by artificial lighting and a carefully monitored temperature, it will respond when fall comes and the days are shorter, the light weaker, the humidity less, and the drafts cooler. Many plants will do best subjected to natural seasons, because they are biologically designed to go through a resting period in winter. Some plants even go completely dormant, and all their aboveground growth dies back. These should be left alone almost completely, usually with nothing more than a tiny amount of water. Others simply grow more slowly or not at all in winter, and just need to have less water and less fertilizer. If you feed and water them to produce active growth when there is too little light, the growth will be weak and leggy. Plants' individual needs are discussed in the List of Houseplants.

If you can bring your plants outdoors in summer it will benefit them greatly, even if you only set them on a balcony. You'll need a spot that gives the plants the degree of light they like (sun, part sun, bright filtered light, low light, etc.). And you'll need to water them when they are dry, remembering that they'll dry out much faster after a rain than plants in the ground will. If they are on a surface where they still require saucers, you'll need to go around and empty the saucers after a heavy rain so the roots don't rot. Another trick is to bury the pots up to their rims in the soil. This usually takes care of the plants' watering needs, and you can even go off for a month or two and leave them. But don't forget to dig them up again in fall! And bring any frost-tender plants inside as soon as a frost threatens.

WATERING

Everyone knows that houseplants need to be watered, but it's a classic case of a little knowledge being a dangerous thing. More houseplants are killed by faulty watering than by any other cause, and it's usually overwatering, not underwatering, that does it. If a plant is underwatered it shows its dissatisfaction very quickly by wilting or, in the case of succulents, by wrinkling—obvious signals that most people respond to immediately, and unless the plant stays wilted a long time it will usually recover as soon as it is watered.

It's much harder to tell when a plant has been overwatered. People try to be too kind to their plants and end up drowning them—the roots can't get enough oxygen in overwatered soil, and so they start to die. If roots are drowning, they can't absorb nutrients, and this failure eventually makes itself visible in poor growth of the plant, though usually not until the roots are damaged beyond repair. As this point the plant will also wilt, since the dead roots cannot absorb water, and so the hapless gardener rushes up with *more* water, thereby finishing the plant off altogether. Watching for earlier, easier to recognize signs of overwatering—such as failure to produce new leaves, darkened, mushy leaves and stems, and leaves that curl, yellow, or brown at the edges—is one way out of the dilemma, but frankly the best course is to be attuned to each plant's individual needs for water. When in doubt, or when you're learning the ways of a new plant, underwater, just to be on the safe side.

The best way to water is to really soak the plant with tepid or room-temperature water until it runs out the bottom of the pot. You need to get water to the roots at the bottom of the pot, not just those near the surface. If a plant has become very dry, it's a good idea to immerse the entire pot in water until it stops bubbling. This way you're letting it drink up as much as it can hold, especially in a porous pot, which could otherwise drain moisture from the soil if the pot itself has dried out. But never let the plant sit indefinitely, either in the sink or in a saucer full of water. If the water in a saucer has not been absorbed after half an hour or so, pour it off. If the pot is too heavy to lift, use a turkey baster to remove the excess. Then leave the plant alone until it needs water again. This will usually be when the soil surface has been dry for a day or two. Plants that need soil that is "evenly moist" prefer to be watered just as the surface is starting to dry out, but even most of these will take a day of dryness, and if in doubt it's best to give them one.

The best way to tell if the soil is moist is to feel it with your finger. To see how far down the dryness goes, stick your finger down into the soil. This is especially important to do with nonporous pots, in which the surface can be dry but the rest of the soil quite wet. (The soil in porous clay pots dries out more uniformly.)

There are certain factors you should be aware of that will help you to anticipate a plant's water needs. A plant will need to be watered more often if it's in a sunny spot, if the room is warm, if the air is dry, if it's in a small pot, if it's in a clay pot, if the pot contains light soil or a soilless mix, if the plant is a large, fast-growing, or lush-leaved specimen, or if the plant is at a stage when it is actively growing, flowering, or fruiting.

For watering a potted plant, a watering can with a long, thin spout that you can poke under the leaves is ideal. Bottom-watering (submerging the bottom of the pot in water and letting the plant absorb it) spares the leaves and is efficient, and is sometimes recommended for fuzzy-leaved plants such as gloxinias, whose leaves do not like to get wet, but it must be closely monitored. Don't let the plant sit in water for more than half an hour. Also, any plant should be top-watered every now and then to flush out fertilizer salts.

If you have to leave your plants, don't make other people responsible for watering them unless they are gardeners or have been fully instructed about your plants' needs. If the weather is mild and you have an outdoor area, bury the pots up to their rims in the ground in a shaded spot until you get home. Another trick, indoors or out, is to soak the whole pot, then encase the entire plant in a transparent plastic bag—a food-storage bag for the small ones, a dry-cleaner's bag for the large ones or for a group of plants. The air inside will be very humid and will recycle lost moisture back to the plant's leaves. This will get most of your plants through a week or two of neglect. But always keep bagged plants out of the sun or they will bake. There are also wick watering devices you can purchase that will water your plants for you when you're away.

FERTILIZING

It's a natural impulse to overfeed a growing plant. "Have another helping," you say, adding a tad more than it says on the label, figuring that the little bit extra will give your plant just that much more encouragement, especially if it isn't looking good.

This is not the right approach to fertilizing houseplants. For one thing plant food, unlike chicken soup, does not cure everything. Feeding will not make a plant flower—light will. Feeding will not necessarily make a sluggish plant grow if what it needs is more or less water, or more or less light. Even a nutrient-starved plant won't respond to fertilizer if there's not enough light for photosynthesis to take place; or if it does respond, it will produce growth that is weak and spindly.

A potted plant can use some fertilizer at certain times but probably less than you'd think. It needs it at the time it is actively growing, because nutrients are required for leaf, stem, and root production. If a plant has gone through a period of winter dormancy it will benefit from feeding during the growth spurt with which it emerges from dormancy and produces a lot of new leaves, lengthens its stems, and enlarges its root system. But don't feed it right away. In most cases it's best to let a plant break dormancy on its own by showing new growth, then give it light and water to encourage it, and *then* feed it.

It's easiest to feed your plants a formulation specially designed for houseplants, feeding not more than, and preferably less than, the amount specified on the label. Plants grown chiefly for their foliage need fertilizer relatively high in nitrogen. (Fish emulsion has given me good results.) Those grown for their flowers usually prefer a formula lower in nitrogen but higher in phosphorus. Pay attention to the needs of individual plants described in the List of Houseplants, or by the greenhouse or store where you bought them.

Moisten the soil thoroughly before you feed, especially if you're applying a dry fertilizer. Roots cannot absorb fertilizer unless they are thoroughly moistened. Don't feed a plant if it's diseased or has been severely damaged by an insect invasion, because the roots may not be able to absorb the fertilizer and it will only collect in the soil, leaving excess salts. Don't feed plants heavily if they are growing in low light. Don't feed plants that have gone into dormancy or are resting. And don't feed newly purchased potted plants for, say, two months—they've probably been given a good shot of slow-release fertilizer in the nursery. Plants you have repotted yourself should also be given a rest from feeding. Just let light, warmth, and water do their work until there's enough of a new root system to absorb extra nutrients.

If a houseplant is starved of nutrients you'll see the leaves turn pale or yellow; usually these are old leaves that are suffering at the expense of new growth, which is getting whatever resources the plant has.

Overfed plants may show vigorous growth initially, with large, crisp dark green leaves. But eventually the leaves will brown as salts accumulated from overfertilizing diminish root growth. You may see white salt deposits and green algae on the pot and on the soil surface. If you think that you've overfed a plant, the best thing to do is flush it with water. This means watering until the water runs out of the pot, waiting till it stops, and doing it again. Do this about four times.

INSECT PESTS

Dealing with insects on indoor plants can be aggravating. You can't depend on other creatures in the environment to help you out, because except for a few spiders, they aren't there. You certainly can't bring bug-eating birds and toads into the house. To be sure, gardeners with greenhouses and even some windowsill gardeners have had excellent results with bringing in natural predators—they are, after all, a captive crew and won't disperse into the countryside the way they do in your vegetable garden. But someone in your household may object to your releasing swarms of ladybugs, lacewings, and ichneumon flies in the living room—probably the same person who leaves for the day when you sterilize soil in the oven.

It is also more difficult to ignore even a few insect pests indoors, since a few can rapidly become an infestation and spread to other plants. Furthermore, you should be even more reluctant to use toxic sprays and dusts or other toxic materials inside your home than you are outside, since contact by breathing or touching is even harder to avoid. But fortunately there are some simple, safe means of controlling insects on houseplants. And the fact that houseplants are relatively small can sometimes make control easier than it is on large outdoor specimens. (Nevertheless, I notice that many houseplant ills magically vanish as soon as I bring the pots outdoors in summertime.)

Start by keeping your plants as vigorous as possible by siting them properly and giving them proper care, as described above. Good health will make them better able to withstand any insect damage they receive. Keeping the area free of dead leaves and other debris where insects can hide or lay eggs will help, and washing plants with insecticidal soap as part of your regular maintenance program can be very beneficial.

One of the most important things to understand here is that few houseplant pests originate in the house. They have to come in on a plant, either one you've bought or have been given or one that has summered outside. Therefore any new arrival should be isolated from other plants for a week or two while you examine it for possible problems. Putting it in a separate room is often sufficient, but you may even want to tie a plastic bag over it to be really sure new bugs don't leave the plant and roam at large. Examine the whole plant daily, especially the undersides of the leaves and the places where leaves and branches join the stem.

If you do see injured plant parts or a lack of vigor that suggests insect damage, be sure to identify the pest correctly. Don't just reach for a pesticide spray. The problem may be due to a disease or some other form of stress. Even if it is an insect that's causing the trouble, you'll need to apply the controls that work best against it. Some insects, such as whiteflies, are visible and obvious; some, such as scale, may be best identified with a magnifying glass (a handy tool for any gardener to have); others, like mites, may be too small to see at all, and you'll need other clues (see below).

Always try to use the safest, least toxic means of control. Even a relatively safe organic poison like pyrethrum should be applied outdoors if at all possible, and any safety precautions given on the container should be observed. Prune out badly infested parts of the plant and get them out of the house right away. If the plant is badly afflicted it's sometimes wise just to discard the whole thing. If a certain type of plant is routinely infested, I will often conclude that life in my home does not provide it with appropriate living conditions, and abandon it in favor of species that are more trouble-free.

Here are some of the visitors you might sometimes receive:

Aphids. These are visible as clusters of tiny dots, usually green but sometimes red or brown. They are most often found on new growth, at the tips or forks of branches, and in buds or flowers. Look for new growth that is stunted or distorted, and for yellowed leaves. Aphids do harm not only by sucking plant juices, but also by spreading viruses. And they secrete a sweet, sticky substance called honeydew, which in turn attracts the black sooty mold fungus, which is both unattractive and harmful. Wash aphids off by spraying with insecticidal soap, which will also remove honeydew. Dabbing with a cotton swab soaked in alcohol will also help.

Mealybugs. These strange little bugs look like tiny spots of white cotton and are often found in the forks where two stems meet. Leaves may look yellow, or plants stunted. If you watch mealybugs long enough you'll see that they move—but not much, and very slowly. Mostly they just sit there sucking plant juices, secreting honeydew and toxins that harm the plant. I have been able to control them by dabbing with alcohol but find that you have to repeat the treatment several times till the bugs are gone. Insecticidal soap also helps. Use pyrethrum if all else fails.

Scale. A number of scale insects afflict houseplants. Crusty-looking patches along the stems prove under the magnifying glass to be tiny oval objects, usually whitish, tan, or brown. They too suck sap, causing discolored leaves and stunted plants, and they secrete honeydew—in fact the most noticeable symptom may be stickiness. Best treatment is to spray with insectidal soap and rub them off with a soft cloth. You may have to do this a number of times. Alcohol applied full strength may be effective.

Spider mites. If your plants' leaves have pale-colored, almost transparent spots, and there are fine webs on the undersides, they have spider mites, which scrape away the leaf tissue and then suck up the sap that accumulates. The mites will probably be too tiny to see, even with a magnifying glass. Since they like hot, dry air, you may be able to prevent infestations by misting or raising the humidity in the room and at the same time giving the plants plenty of fresh, free-circulating air. A soap spray, or just a forceful spraying with water in the sink or the shower may eradicate them, but be sure to spray the undersides of the leaves. If spider mites are on wide-leaved plants, wiping them off with a soft cloth can also help to control them.

Thrips. These are very small, narrow insects with feathery wings. They can be yellow, brown, or black. They attack plant parts in the same way that spider mites do, and the damage looks similar. They like buds, especially those of white flowers. Best treatment is to remove infested buds and use insecticidal soap on the whole plant. Use organic sprays only if necessary.

Whiteflies. These tiny flying insects are annoying to deal with because they don't sit still. As soon as you put your hands near the plant they fly up in a cloud. You can try spraying the remaining ones with insecticidal soap, or you can wave strips of flypaper around the plant and then spray with soap. Or hang a yellow sticky trap nearby (page 66).

Cyclamen mites. These are invisible, but their damage appears as a pronounced twisting and deforming of new plant growth. They afflict cyclamens and a number of other plants, including African violets. You may be able to prune out affected parts, but the surest control is to immerse the entire plant—pot, leaves, and all—in water that is at exactly 110 degrees for 30 minutes. If this is difficult for you to do, it is best to discard the plant before others are infested.

HOUSEPLANT DISEASES

Houseplant diseases are hard for the average gardener to identify and even harder to treat. The best course is prevention. Houseplants will usually ward off diseases by themselves if you give them proper care to keep them vigorous. Giving them fresh air is also important, either by opening a window from time to time, or by simply making sure that air circulates in the house. Use a fan if necessary or just put the plants in an airier spot rather than in a corner or a room whose door is seldom opened. While misting usually benefits plants, don't mist a plant that is fighting a disease, and when watering, try very hard to keep its leaves dry. Changing a sick plant's soil may also help, or at least changing the top inch or so.

Giving new plants a quarantine period and close scrutiny during that time is as important for detecting diseases as it is for finding bugs. You must also isolate a plant with a disease so the problem won't spread. Diseased parts should be pruned out and destroyed, and you should be prepared to throw out the whole plant if necessary. Don't let a dead or dying plant sit around until you can get around to removing it.

Most houseplant diseases are caused by fungi. Leaf-spot diseases, which prompt brown, black, or tan spots to appear on the leaves, are among the most common. Affected leaves later drop off. Leaf spot and like diseases are best fought by reducing humidity, improving air circulation, and pruning out affected leaves or stems. Bacterial leaf-spot diseases (in fact, most bacterial diseases) cause watery-looking patches to appear and are dealt with in the same way.

Powdery mildew makes leaves whitish; just remove affected leaves and improve the air circulation. Virus diseases such as mosaic are much harder to control. Plants with mosaic are stunted, with mottled, deformed leaves. If aphids have transmitted the disease, destroy the aphids and remove infected parts; the plant may recover. But generally a plant with a virus is best destroyed before it affects others.

If you're not sure what's wrong with the plant, first check for bugs, then ask yourself if you're giving it the location it likes. Perhaps you should try it in another spot, and of course, make sure it's getting the proper care. If you still suspect a disease, take a sample of the affected parts to your Extension Service to have it diagnosed, then try the control methods described above.

OTHER MAINTENANCE TASKS

You can forget about talking to your houseplants. Whatever people tell you, a plant is no more ready to hear what you have to say than is a puppy who would rather sniff things than proceed down the street. But hovering over plants does seem to make them grow better. One theory is that in standing over them a lot you breathe enough carbon dioxide on them to improve their general vigor. Perhaps. But in any case, the more ways you find to fuss over your plants, the more apt you are to notice bugs or other small signs of trouble and deal with them before they become big trouble. In addition to hovering, here are some other good things to do:

Pinching and pruning. Pinching indoor plants is the same process as pinching outdoor ones, as described on page 190. In some cases it is done to make the plant bushier, with a more graceful, compact shape; in others it's done to keep the plant a manageable size. Often the biggest problem with a thriving houseplant is keeping it from outgrowing its confined quarters and turning into a monster. Unfortunately, pinching doesn't work on single-stemmed plants like palms and dracaenas, but on other large ones such as schefflera, citrus fruits, and *Ficus benjamina* it works fine. Pinch the ends of stems that have several sets of leaves on them, just above a node.

If a plant has already gotten out of hand, a more drastic pruning may be in order. Prune as illustrated on page 614, cutting back to a node and being careful not to leave a stub. Some plants can even be root-pruned by removing the plant from the pot and cutting off the tips of the roots (leaving at least two thirds of the root system intact), then repotting in the same size pot, with soil added where the old roots were. The plant should have a third of its top growth removed at the same time. The best time to do both types of pruning is spring, when plants are actively growing and can recover well.

Washing. It may seem odd to give plants a bath, but they love it. Plant leaves get dirty, and even if you dust them, they can still accumulate grime that will keep them from producing food efficiently. Wash them outdoors if you can, or in a sink or bathtub, using a teaspoonful of mild liquid soap (not a detergent) in a quart of water—or use one of the insecticidal soaps designed for plants. Either kind of soap will also help to keep the plants pest-free. Rinse with a stream of water. Indoors a hand-held shower nozzle at the end of a hose is ideal. Or just let the shower rinse them. Outdoors use a hose, adjusting the nozzle so that the spray is forceful enough to do the job, but not forceful enough to break the stems or wash the soil out of the pot.

Turning the pot. Just giving your pots a quarter turn each week will do wonders for them if the light they receive is strongest on one side (as from a window). Turning will ensure that all the leaves get the full benefit of the light and grow better, and it will keep the plant from growing more on one side than another, making it lopsided. You needn't turn plants grown directly beneath artificial lights, but even then you may need to change their position to give them uniform light. The center of a fluorescent light tube gives more light than the ends.

Tidying up. Be sure to remove any dead leaves or stems from the plants promptly, and any plant matter that falls into the pots, saucers, and trays, or onto table surfaces or floors. Such trash not only looks a mess, but it can harbor insects and disease organisms.

It may be a good idea to set a particular day aside for these small maintenance tasks each week. But don't let such a schedule cause you to feed and water improperly. Many plants need to be watered more or less often than once a week, and feeding schedules also vary from plant to plant. If your plants are surrounded by many gardeners, whether in a home or in an office, make sure that only one person is in charge of feeding and watering. Otherwise the plants will be either fed and watered too little or too much—usually the latter. Here's a typical office conversation:

"The plant is dead."

"But I've been watering it!"

"So have I."

"So have I."

"So have I."

Plant care, like so many other things in life, is better done by one than by a committee.

Propagating Houseplants

EVERYONE WHO BECOMES ENTHUSI-astic about growing indoor plants winds up propagating them. It's so easy to do! If you like a plant, you can propagate it and have several or give some to friends, swapping them for plants that *they* have propagated. If a beloved plant has overgrown its spot or just gotten too big to be beautiful, propagate it, and by the time you have a nice, compact new plant you can chuck the old one without remorse. The only thing you shouldn't do is propagate a diseased or otherwise unhealthy plant. The propagation may not even work if the mother plant (the plant from which the new plants are made) has been weakened, and if it is diseased or buggy it can just pass on the problem to its offspring.

There are several ways to propagate houseplants. Sometimes one method works better than the others for a particular species, sometimes you have a choice of several methods.

DIVISION

Dividing indoor plants is no different from dividing herbaceous perennials that you grow outdoors, as described on page 185. Houseplants that can be divided are those with multiple crowns. With these you can pull or cut the plants apart to produce smaller plants, each with its own root system and at least one stem or an "eye" where a stem will form. Some plants that divide well are streptocarpus, bromeliads, aloe, snakeplant, ferns, clivia, and some begonias.

Many plants that grow from bulbs can also be divided. A plant like amaryllis can be divided after its rest period by breaking off a bulblet that forms at the side of the main bulb and replanting it.

ROOTING PLANTLETS

Some houseplants have a charming habit of making "babies" by themselves, often without the benefit of soil. Spider plant is the perfect example: the tufts of leaves that grow at the end of the long stems are little plants that need only a bit of soil and moisture to induce them to root. If you set the mother plant on a table surrounded by small pots, you can root the plantlets without even removing them from the stem, then cut the stem when new growth on the subsidiary plants indicates that they have rooted. But I've had equally good luck just taking off a plantlet and sticking it in a moist planting mix.

STEM CUTTINGS

This is the most common way to propagate houseplants (Figure 74). You simply cut a section of stem and root it in a medium such as sand, perlite, vermiculite, peat moss, or a combination of these. It's easiest to use a commercially prepared soilless mix. Usually the growing end of the stem is cut, in which

Making New Plants from Stem Cuttings

FIG. 74

1. Cut stems just below a set of leaves.

4. Cover them with plastic wrap supported by stakes.

2. Dip each cut stem into rooting hormone powder.

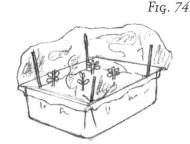

5. Wait for new growth to appear.

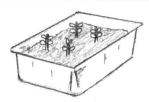

3. Stick the cuttings in moistened soilless mix.

6. Then remove the cuttings and transplant them.

case it is called a tip cutting. Middle sections of stems can also be used, though. It is best to take your cuttings while the plant is actively growing, because a fresh young shoot will root best, but don't try rooting a shoot so immature that it's very limp and tender.

The night before you take the cutting, water the plant so the stems and leaves will have plenty of moisture in them. Have your potting mix all ready before you take the cuttings. Sterilize it, if it is not a material sold already sterilized, and put it in a container such as a shallow clay pot or a small plastic flat (the kind annual seedlings are sold in). It doesn't much matter what you use, but the container must be thoroughly cleaned and have drainage holes in the bottom.

Using a clean, sharp knife or razor blade, cut a stem 4 to 6 inches long, one that has several sets of leaves on it. Make the cut at a slant, and cut just below a node (the point where a leaf joins the stem). Remove the leaves from that node. You can remove the next set, too, but there should be at least one set of leaves left on the cutting. You'll give the rooting process an extra boost if you dip the end of the cutting in a rooting compound—a white powder containing rooting hormones, available at stores that sell plant supplies. Don't dip the cutting into the container of compound; take out whatever you'll need, and if there is any compound left after you've treated the cutting, discard it. Then make a hole in the potting mix with a pencil. It should be an inch or two deep, depending on the length of the cutting. Stick the cutting in so the end is at the bottom of the hole. Firm the mix lightly around the cutting and water it gently but thoroughly.

Now all you have to do is cover your container with plastic film to keep the air inside humid, and wait for the cuttings to root. You can either put the container in a plastic bag or spread plastic wrap over it, supporting the wrap with wire hoops or sticks inserted into the mix so the plastic doesn't touch the plant. Or just put your flats and pots in a large transparent plastic box. While they're rooting, the cuttings should have plenty of light but not direct sun, and should be kept at a temperature of 65 to 75 degrees. Check regularly to make sure that the potting mix and the air around it do not dry out. The plastic should look moist or foggy. Water as needed, or let air in if it looks too sodden in there or if you see mold. Cuttings of fuzzy-leaved plants like the air to be drier. These should have the soil moist but not the leaves.

Your cuttings should root in two to five weeks. Usually you can tell they've rooted by the fact that they stand up in a perky way with good color and even fresh new growth, but if you're not sure, tug on the cutting ever so slightly. If it resists, it has rooted. Dig up the rooted cuttings very gently using a spoon or fork, and plant them individually in small pots using a similar potting mix or one with a larger percentage of soil. Don't fertilize the cuttings at all until about a month after they root—the roots aren't ready for it yet.

LEAF CUTTINGS

For fleshy-stemmed plants such as gloxinia, African violets, streptocarpus, rex and Rieger begonias, peperomia, jade plant, and sedum, leaf cuttings are an excellent way of propagation. It may take a bit longer to get full-size plants with this method than with stem cuttings, but since each leaf makes several plants you'll have more of them. In spring or summer (or anytime if you're growing under artificial light), cut a healthy young leaf (a clean, sharp razor blade works best) with 1½ to 2 inches of stem attached, making a slanted cut. Rooting compound is not always used with leaf cuttings, although I always figure it can't hurt. Insert the stem ½ inch into the soil and lightly firm the medium around the stem. With some plants, such as rex begonias, the stem or the underside of the leaf vein is split lengthwise; plantlets grow from this wound. With large-leaved plants such as these you can also cut the leaf into a wedge-shaped section that includes the central vein, and plant that.

Some plants, such as jade, geraniums, and Christmas cactus, are so easy to root from leaves that all you need to do is stick the bottom end of the leaf rather unceremoniously into the ground. Succulents also like to be left for a day or two to callus the cut a bit. Leaves of nonsucculents must be set in the medium right away, however, so they don't dry out.

One advantage of propagating with leaf cuttings is that you can watch the result aboveground—little plantlets form around the leaves. Keep the soil and air moist, as above, and remove plantlets from the mother leaf when they are large enough to have adequate root systems. (You'll learn easily by experience.) Then plant each one in a small pot (a peat pot is fine).

Making New Plants from Leaf Cuttings

FIG. 75

1. Cut leaves from the mother plant with a razor blade, making a slanted cut.

3. Wait for new little plantlets to form.

2. Insert the stems in moistened soilless mix so that they lie almost flat on the soil surface.

4. When the plantlets have developed root systems, transplant them to individual pots.

OTHER METHODS OF PROPAGATION

Some of you are probably asking, "When is she going to talk about the glass of water?" To many people, plant propagation is a jelly glass on the windowsill with a cutting inside it growing roots that you can *see*. Yes, you can see them, but relatively few plants can sit with their roots in water without rotting. It's always fun to try, however, and in the case of some plants such as philodendron, coleus, impatiens, and the tall cane-type begonias, rooting in water works very well. But if you try it, be sure to pot the cuttings soon after they develop roots and before they turn to mush.

At the opposite extreme of complexity is a sophisticated technique of propagation invented by the Chinese, called air-layering, in which a plant stem is cut partway through, then enclosed in a material like damp sphagnum moss with plastic film wrapped around that. The moss should be kept moist. In a few weeks roots will grow, making a new plant, which is then removed and replanted. Air-layering is useful if you have a plant that has grown too tall. Simply air-layer it at the desired height. If it then branches in an attractive way, you'll have two plants.

I've been describing methods of propagation that don't require plants to flower and produce seed. Many houseplants can be grown from seed as well. Some of the choicest varieties of African violets, gloxinias, and cyclamens, for example, are available as seeds.

List of Houseplants

A LMOST ANY PLANT CAN BE A houseplant if you want it to be— even a tree if it's grown as a bonsai or in a very large container. Other chapters have covered some plants that can be grown indoors, such as the herbs in Chapter 8, some annuals such as impatiens in Chapter 5, vines like passionflower in Chapter 14, perennials like sedum in Chapter 6, bulbs that can be forced indoors for winter bloom (page 496), and even vegetables like patio tomatoes or lettuce. If you've ever watched a sweet potato plant grow in a glass of water, or carefully nourished an avocado pit even though you knew it would never produce avocados, you know the fun of growing something green even when it's not gardening season.

In growing houseplants the limitations are the space and light available, but the plant choices are almost infinite. The following list includes many old favorites, some plants that are becoming old favorites, and a few exotic-but-easy plants you might not have heard of. But please explore further! I have ignored many succulents, such as *Echeveria, Euphorbia, Kalanchoe,* aloe, and agave. Consider the many fine hanging or vining plants, such as *Mandevilla,* grape ivy (*Cissus trifoliata*), Swedish ivy (*Plectranthus australis*), wax plant (*Hoya carnosa*), and wandering Jew (*Zebrina pendula*). And foliage plants such

as *Fatsia japonica, Aspidistra, Monstera,* and *Sansevieria* (snake plant). And those that bloom! What about the ghostly white *Spathiphyllum,* the papery-flowered *Abutilon* (flowering maple), the flamboyant *Strelitzia reginae* (bird of paradise), spectacular gingers, and the incredible orchids—many of them not at all hard to grow. Use the catalogs in the List of Mail-Order Sources to experiment further.

A word about gift plants. Sometimes you might get lucky and receive a plant as a gift that is perfectly suited to your living room or office. But frequently the plants sold as gifts are specimens designed to express a certain sentiment in the showiest possible way. "Merry Christmas!" carols the poinsettia. "Happy Easter!" announces the Madonna lily. "Get well soon!" chortles the bright red azalea. Your relationship with the plant will probably go downhill from there, ending with its final words, "You've killed me. Don't you feel bad?" It's important to accept the fact that many of these cheerful gifts have been forced into magnificent bloom under lights in commercial greenhouses and were never meant for long life in your home. Even the shrubby ones like hydrangeas and azaleas might not thrive even if replanted outdoors in spring, because they may not be varieties that are hardy in your climate. Often it's best to just acknowledge them as seasonal pleasures—and then move on.

AFRICAN VIOLET

Saintpaulia species

Description: If you only have patience for one little houseplant, this might be the perfect one. It blooms almost all the time, even in winter. It's tidy and compact, with pretty, oval, fuzzy leaves surrounding the flowers, which grow up in the center, making the plant look like a bouquet. (Sometimes the leaves are bronzed or variegated.) Hybridizers have produced thousands of varieties whose flower colors range from a wonderful intense blue to purple, magenta, lavender, pink, coral, and white. There are also some red, yellow, pale green, and multicolored ones. The flowers are usually about an inch wide; some are ruffled or fringed. All have bright yellow stamens in the center. Standard-size plants grow up to a foot tall, and semiminiatures are 6 to 8 inches, as are the true miniatures,

which have tiny flowers as well. There are also trailing varieties. Though they do come from Africa, none are related to the true violet (*Viola*) species.

The Optimara, Ballet, and Rhapsodie series all contain excellent varieties. If your interest is sparked you'll want to investigate the wider world of African violets. If you do not have much light and your rooms are on the cool side, you won't have good luck with them unless you grow some of the newer varieties bred for low light and cooler temperatures. Consult the African Violet Society (see the List of Plant Societies) for more information.

How to Grow: Most African violets do best in a warm room where it's at least 70 degrees during the day and no colder than 60 degrees at night. Light should be bright but not blazing direct sun. Fluorescent lights and special broad-spectrum growing lights designed for plants seem custom-made for African violets, and many enthusiasts use these alone. The plants prefer quite humid air (especially the trailing ones) and soil that is kept evenly moist, never drying out for more than a day at most. Yet they respond very poorly to overwatering and poor drainage. Use water that is at room temperature, and try to keep the leaves dry to avoid leaf-spot diseases.

The easiest way to give African violets the soil they like is to buy a bag of commercial "African violet soil." Or you can make your own mix using one part peat or leaf mold for organic matter, and one part sand or perlite for good drainage. Feed about once a month with an organic fertilizer (one that is not too high in nitrogen, or you'll get lots of beautiful fuzzy leaves and no flowers). Overfeeding is a grave error, causing the leaves to turn gray and the leaf stems to rot. Flush out excess fertilizer salts regularly.

Use fairly small, shallow pots, keeping the plants a bit rootbound, and turn the potted plants from time to time if most light comes from one side—otherwise your flower display will be lopsided. Crowns can be divided, but leaf cuttings are the best way to propagate African violets. Use a medium-size leaf and dip the stem in rooting powder. African violets don't last forever; after they become woody they often decline. That's the time to take leaf cuttings.

BEGONIA

Begonia

Rieger
begonia

rex
begonia

Description: There are many kinds of begonias you can grow indoors, all of them very different from one another in the way they look and grow, and all with their own special virtues. The fibrous-rooted wax begonias, which are grown most often as outdoor annuals, make fine ever-blooming houseplants (page 162). Tuberous begonias (page 501) also can be grown as houseplants, though they'll only bloom in summer. Angel-wing begonias (*Begonia coccinea*) are fibrous rooted, cane-type begonias that grow up to 4 feet and more and bear dangling clusters of small red flowers almost year-round. Iron-cross begonias (*B. masoniana*) are foliage plants, growing 1½ feet tall from rhizomes; they are valued for their crinkly apple-green leaves, which are marked in the center with a dark green cross.

Probably the most spectacular and popular begonias grown as houseplants are rex and Rieger begonias. Rex begonias (*B. rex-cultorum*) grow from rhizomes and have small pink or white flowers in spring, but they are most prized for their large, magnificent leaves, which are an intricate brocade of green, red, bronze, pink, or silver. They make a lavish mound a foot tall or a bit more; miniature varieties are 6 to 8 inches. Rieger begonias (*B. × hiemalis*) often have colored leaves but are grown for their profuse, showy flowers at least 2 inches across, in shades of red, pink, orange, and yellow, which provide months of color in winter. They are fibrous rooted.

How to Grow: Begonias, in general, like plenty of light, and the flowering types should have several hours of sun each day for best winter bloom. Daytime temperature should be in the 65- to 75-degree range (a bit cooler for Rieger begonias), and not below 50 degrees at night. All, especially rex begonias, like humid air, but the air must circulate well to avoid mildew, especially with the large-leaved types. Soil should be a nice, light, organic mix, like that sold for African violets, and should be kept evenly moist, or just slightly dry between waterings. But drainage *must* be excellent, and you should avoid wetting the leaves. Fertilize lightly with a balanced fertilizer about every two weeks while plants are in active growth, or in the case of Rieger begonias, all year. Fibrous-rooted kinds should be repotted in spring as needed; those with rhizomes go in shallow pots and should remain rootbound until you can see rhizomes all over the soil surface.

Rieger begonias that stop blooming can be cut back to several inches to produce fresh flowering growth. Stems of rex begonias should be cut back to the base if they start to get leggy. Wax begonias also benefit from being cut back, and stems of angel-wing begonias without leaves should be cut back in early spring to make new growth. All begonias can be propagated easily by stem cuttings. With rex and Rieger begonias, leaf cuttings are also a good method.

BROMELIAD
Many genera

Description: These fascinating plants are among the most exotic houseplants a gardener can grow—and also among the easiest! Not a genus in themselves, but a large group of genera, they include *Aechmea, Billbergia, Cryptanthus, Dyckia, Guzmania, Neoregelia, Nidularium, Tillandsia,* and a number of others. Bromeliads come from the jungles of South America. Some are terrestrial, but more are air plants (epiphytes), living high up in the trees without any soil and taking nourishment only from whatever organic matter washes their way. (They are not parasitic and do not draw

Guzmania lingulata

Aechmea fasciata

nourishment from the trees themselves.) Tree-growing bromeliads catch rainwater in cuplike urns of leaves.

Bromeliads are grown mainly for their spectacular flowers, but the leaves are often particularly handsome too. A typical bromeliad has a rosette of leaves, sometimes soft and green, sometimes stiff and spiky, with variegated markings. A flower stalk usually emerges from the center of the rosette. The showiness of these flowers really lies in the brilliantly colored bracts that surround them, though the tinier flowers are also beautiful. A plant blooms only once, but the flower is often extraordinarily long lasting, and bromeliad plants readily produce offshoots. You may remove these from the mother plant and repot them, or cut out the spent mother plant and let the cluster of new ones bloom together.

If you're looking for a bromeliad to start with, try *Aechmea fasciata.* You might find it marketed under various names such as urn plant or silver vase, but you'll recognize it by its vase of stiff, tooth-edged green leaves, marked horizontally with silver bands. The flower spike has toothed bracts of a bright pink color, and little blue-purple flowers that nestle among the pink spikes. Best of all, this colorful spectacle lasts about six months. The plant grows 1 to 2 feet tall.

Another gorgeous, long-blooming bromeliad is *Guzmania lingulata*, which is about the same size, with long green, straplike leaves (sometimes striped with purple), and a red-orange cluster of bracts enclosing white flowers from late winter to summer.

How to Grow: Bromeliads with stiff variegated leaves like good, bright light and often will take some direct sun (but don't expose them to strong midday sun in summer); those with softer green leaves are fairly shade tolerant. They do well under artificial lights. They are happiest in warm rooms (65 to 75 degrees) that can be as low as 50 to 60 degrees at night (even lower for *Aechmea fasciata*). Give them humid air and a very light, porous organic soil or soilless mix—remember that many bromeliads are air plants, and their roots don't normally grow in soil. Some gardeners grow the ephiphytic types on pieces of tree branch wrapped in moistened sphagnum moss, but a shallow clay pot will do fine. You can allow the top inch or so of the pot to dry out between waterings (overwatering can lead to fungus diseases), but always keep the cup inside the leaves filled with water. Feed lightly—a balanced liquid fertilizer added to the soil and cup twice a month in spring and summer (less in fall and winter) is about right. (Avoid adding fish or seaweed-based fertilizers to the cup, as bad odors may build up.) Propagate by dividing offsets with a knife and repotting them.

CACTUS

Many genera

Description: Cacti are fun to grow because of their eccentric, even comical shapes. They're also beautiful, especially

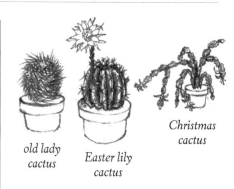

old lady
cactus

Easter lily
cactus

Christmas
cactus

when they bloom. If your air is dry and you have trouble growing plants that like high humidity, put away your mister and pebble-filled trays and try cacti instead. They also need less attention than other houseplants. They are part of the large group of desert plants called succulents, which store water in their fleshy leaves to get them through the long dry spells their native climates are known for. Cacti don't have conventional leaves, just stems, which are often jointed. They also have "areoles"—small holes from which tufts emerge. Sometimes the tufts are soft, like hairs; sometimes they are sharp and spiny. (The tufts shelter them from the sun and, if sharp, against creatures who might bite them to get at the water inside.) The flowers, which appear in spring and summer, also emerge from the areoles.

Cacti are a large family, with many genera that make good houseplants. Here are some good ones to start with. *Mammillaria* cacti are sometimes called pincushion or nipple cacti. Most look like small round globes covered with nipples and bear clusters of small, pretty flowers in a crown around the top. Good ones to try are old lady cactus (*M. hahniana*), which is covered with long white hairs, produces red flowers, and generally grows less than 10 inches tall; the tiny golden star cactus (*M. elongata*), which is composed of a cluster of long projections with yellow spines and white flowers; *M. zeilmanniana*, which forms a little round ball and produces pinkish red flowers even at a young age.

Easter lily cactus (*Echinopsis multiplex*) is a little round cactus with vertical ribs and large pink flowers borne on tall stems; these open in the evening and have a lovely fragrance. Hybrids, which are crossed with species of *Lobivia* cactus, come in other colors such as red and orange, and may be day-blooming. Among the many other good flowering cacti to try are species of *Opuntia* (prickly pear), *Aporocactus* (rat-tail), *Echinocereus* (hedgehog), *Ferocactus* (barrel), and *Rebutia* (crown).

One of the most popular is the Christmas cactus (*Schlumbergera truncata*), a jungle epiphyte that sends out long, arching, jointed stems. Lovely red or white tube-shaped flowers dangle from the tips around Christmastime. The variety known as Thanksgiving cactus blooms a few weeks earlier and can be distinguished by the fact that the last joint on a stem has two prominent teeth. A similar plant, Easter cactus (*Rhipsalidopsis gaertneri*), is spring bloom-ing. All these are long-lived and can grow as tall as 3 feet and at least as wide.

How to Grow: Most cacti prefer full sun, so give them as much of it as you can. Some will do all right in bright light or under fluorescent lights. They like warm temperatures during the day but can tolerate 40 to 45 degrees at night (don't let them freeze, though) and may even bloom better if you turn down your thermostat at night. They like dry air but will take average humidity. In spring and summer, when growth is active, they should be watered thoroughly.

During the winter they go dormant for a time, a period they need in order to bloom. They probably won't need water at all during this time, unless they wrinkle. If your water is softened, water them with bottled water, since they cannot tolerate salt.

The spiny cacti are best planted in small, shallow clay pots, with a light, sandy soil; among the exceptions are rain-forest species such as orchid cacti (*Epiphyllum oxypetalum*) and the Christmas cacti described below. Repot in spring if you see roots in the drainage hole. Don't feed new plants for a year, then feed about once a month during the growing season with a weak concentration of low-nitrogen liquid fertilizer; don't feed cacti at all while they're dormant. They love to be summered outdoors, in fact the cooler days and shorter nights at the end of summer can help to trigger bloom, but bring them indoors when temperatures start to get down into the 40s. Propagate them by transplanting offsets that have developed their own roots.

Christmas and Thanksgiving cacti need more water and fertilizer than other cacti, and they need a soil with more organic matter. Feed them twice a month in spring and summer, and let the soil dry out a bit between waterings. But starting eight weeks before the time you want them to bloom, give them a rest. Keep them in a cool place that gets no light at night (50 to 60 degrees), give them no fertilizer and just enough water to keep them from wrinkling, and don't repot them during this time (do it in spring). Gradually introduce them to warmer temperatures. The shortening days will trigger bloom (or lengthening days, in the case of Easter cactus). Water while blooming, then keep the cacti on the dry side until spring. They are propagated easily by stem cuttings.

CITRUS
Citrus

Meyer lemon   Calamondin orange

Description: You may not think of citrus fruits as houseplants, but some of them make excellent ones! If you've ever dropped an orange or lemon seed into a pot you know they grow easily, producing handsome bright green foliage and even fragrant white flowers. If you buy grafted plants of specific citrus types, you can grow fine fruits as well, even on plants that are quite young. Citrus are broad-leaved evergreen plants that can be a bit fussy to grow, but are ultimately very resilient. Even if they drop all their leaves they can pull themselves together and regroup.

The hardiest lemon is the Meyer lemon (*Citrus limon* 'Meyer'), which bears 3-inch fruits. This is a good one to start with, but also try the ponderosa lemon (*C. l.* 'Ponderosa'); just one of its 5-inch fruits yields enough juice and rind for two pies. Both can be kept to 4 feet or less with a little pruning. For a good indoor orange, try calamondin (× *Citrofortunella mitis*), which bears, continuously, a multitude of little bright orange fruits an inch or two wide. Too tart and seedy to eat out of hand, they are good for marmalades and glazes. The plant flowers freely and can be kept

very compact. Others to try include Meiwa kumquats, Satsuma mandarins, and Kaffir limes. When buying indoor citrus plants, look for those specified as dwarf varieties.

How to Grow: Citrus plants are sun loving and should get at least four hours of direct sun a day. In summertime set them outdoors. They do best with fairly warm temperatures by day—around 70 degrees—but prefer about 55 at night, especially in winter. Give them fairly humid air. Citrus are best potted or repotted in early spring just when new growth is starting. Grow them in a well-drained, all-purpose potting mix a bit on the acid side. Keep plants pot-bound and let the soil get almost dry, then water thoroughly. Feed every two weeks from early spring to late summer with an acid fertilizer, then feed about once a month, skipping December and January altogether. Pinch the tips whenever you want to control growth and make the plants bushy, and propagate from stem or tip cuttings anytime from mid summer to late fall. Scale and spider mites can be a problem indoors (see page 729 for treatments), but they disappear as soon as the plants are brought outdoors in warm weather. The light and humidity of a greenhouse will also make a difference.

CLIVIA
Clivia miniata

Description: Clivia, also called Kaffir lily, grows from a thick-rooted bulb. It looks something like the more familiar amaryllis to which it is related, but its clusters of orange, red, or gold flowers are smaller and more subtle. Flowers can appear anytime from December to April (most often in

March), rising on 18-inch stalks from the tidy dark green, straplike leaves and opening over a period of several weeks. Most plants get about 2 feet tall, but there are more compact varieties.

How to Grow: Clivias are very easy plants to grow once you understand them. They will take morning or late-afternoon sun, but too much midday sun will scorch the leaves. Bright indirect light all day is best. Give them average room temperature and humidity by day, but cool temperatures at night if possible. During the dormant period before bloom, a temperature of 50 to 55, day and night, will help to induce bloom. Clivias like an organic soil like that used for African violets, and need to be potbound in order to flower. Repot only when the roots are crawling out of the top of the pot. A heavy pot is often necessary to keep them from tipping over.

In spring and summer keep the plants evenly moist, fertilizing every two weeks. A summer outdoors in filtered sun will do your clivias good. Bring them in before frost, and stop feeding them. Starting around Thanksgiving, give them little or no water, and if possible keep them in a cool room that gets no light in the evening. When a flower

stalk emerges, bring the plant into a warm, light place and start feeding and watering it again. Plants may be propagated by removing and replanting side bulbs in spring when new growth starts.

DIEFFENBACHIA
Dieffenbachia

Dieffenbachia amoena

Dieffenbachia maculata

Description: This plant's common name is dumb cane, because the sap irritates the tongue and causes it to swell so you can't talk. It is highly irritating to the eyes as well. Dieffenbachia is a large plant from the American tropics, grown for its wide leaves. There are many species and cultivars to choose from, many with attractive markings in shades like chartreuse or cream. Usually they are single stemmed. The most common species is *Dieffenbachia maculata*, which often has striking yellow or white variegations. *D. amoena* has large dark green leaves with white blotches. Both can eventually reach the ceiling. Their leaf variegations make them good plants for brightening up a corner, though they will grow best if the corner is not a very dark one.

How to Grow: Among the most easy-to-please of houseplants, dieffenbachias like bright, indirect light but will tolerate much lower light conditions. *D. amoena* especially prefers shade. All dieffenbachias grow best in fairly humid rooms that are warm during the day and no colder than 50 degrees at night. Plant them in a light, organic potting mix that drains easily, and keep them fairly potbound to control their size. Repotting, if needed, can be done at any time. Water thoroughly, then let the soil dry out before watering again. (Don't ever overwater, or both roots and stems will rot.) Feed once or twice a month in warm weather but not in winter, and be careful not to overfertilize.

Leggy plants can be cut back to within 4 to 6 inches of the soil and will sprout new growth (this is best done in spring). Propagate by tip or stem cuttings. It is best to wear gloves and eye protectors when you're working with these plants so that the sap cannot get in your eyes or mouth. Keep children away from dieffenbachias for the same reason.

DRACAENA

Dracaena species

Description: Among the tallest of houseplants, the treelike dracaenas are perfect when you need a strong accent. They have swordlike leaves, often with attractive variegations. Although they are single-stemmed, several plants of different heights can be grown together in the same pot for a bushier look. They are easy-to-grow plants, very tolerant of indoor environments.

Dracaena fragrans 'Massangeana,' sometimes called corn plant, has leaves that resemble those of corn, with a yellow stripe down the middle. *D. marginata* (dragon

dragon tree

striped-leaf dracaena

gold-dust plant

tree) has a cluster of red-edged leaves atop a tall stem that twists in picturesque ways. In the variety 'Tricolor' the leaves are green, red, and yellow. *D. deremensis* 'Warneckii' has rather stiff leaves, striped with white. All these can grow to the ceiling eventually. If you want a more compact dracaena, grow *D. surculosa* (*D. godseffiana*), called gold-dust plant, which only grows a few feet tall. The flat oval leaves are dark green with cream-colored spots; in the variety 'Florida Beauty' the leaves are so spotted that they're almost all white. There are also some compact forms of *D. deremensis.*

How to Grow: Dracaenas will tolerate quite low light, though brighter light will bring out foliage variegations better. They will also tolerate low humidity to some degree, and they do prefer warm rooms. Plant them in an average potting mix, repotting anytime they look crowded. Water freely from spring to fall, keeping the soil evenly moist but never letting them become waterlogged. In winter let the soil dry out a bit between waterings, but not to excess or the tips will die back. Feed every two weeks or so during the growing season.

Plants can be cut back to 4 to 6 inches, and new growth will sprout. New plants can be propagated by removing and replanting suckers that form at the base, or by cutting sections of the canes that have at least one node and laying them on moist sand.

FERNS
Many genera

Description: Ferns give a better softening effect to an indoor environment than any other type of plant. They are easy to grow if you have a fairly humid room, and many kinds make good houseplants. Most people are familiar with that old favorite, the Boston fern (*Nephrolepis exaltata* 'Bostoniensis'), a very easy indoor plant with rich green, arching fronds; it can grow very large over time. In the variety 'Fluffy Ruffles,' the fronds are rather upright and have frilled edges. Even more foolproof is its relative the Dallas fern (*N. e.* 'Dallasii'), which grows less than a foot tall. Bird's-nest fern (*Asplenium nidus*), a type of spleenwort, has wide, shiny, wavy-edged fronds that look more like leaves and can grow 2 to 3 feet tall. Holly fern (*Cyrtomium falcatum*) also has leaflike fronds (a bit like large holly leaves) and is extremely adaptable as an indoor plant. Indoor plant expert Elvin McDonald says that it was the first fern he was ever able to grow successfully, and it gave him the courage to try others.

If you want something a bit unusual that's also very easy to grow, try rabbit's-foot fern (*Davallia fejeensis*), a beautiful feathery fern from the South Pacific. Its long rhizomes look like furry brown paws and can be seen crawling out of the pot and hanging from its rim. When supplying an

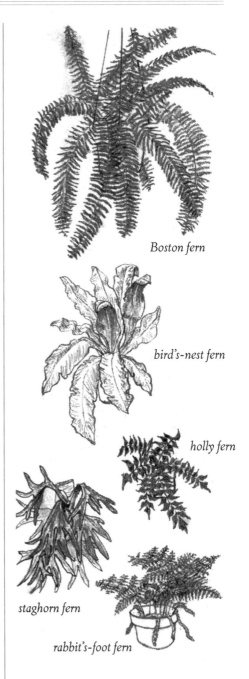

Boston fern

bird's-nest fern

holly fern

staghorn fern

rabbit's-foot fern

office with plants I once set one of these on a woman's desk, and the fern made her so nervous that she couldn't sit next to it. But most people find *D. fejeensis* charming, myself included. Another exotic that is not terribly hard to grow is the staghorn fern (*Platycerium bifurcatum*), whose gray-green fronds look like antlers (I'd say more like those of a bull moose than those of a stag). It is an epiphyte, generally grown on a piece of wood or bark, with its roots wrapped in moistened sphagnum moss.

How to Grow: Few ferns can toler-ate much, if any, sun, and most grown indoors don't like deep shade either. Give them bright indirect or filtered sun and an average room temperature. The one thing they are really fussy about is humidity. Generally, the more feathery its fronds, the more moisture in the air a fern needs. Ferns with leaflike fronds are more drought toler-ant. Misting or using a humidity tray may make the difference for you.

Ferns are shallow rooted and should be grown in shallow pots in a light soil mix that contains plenty of organic matter. Keep the soil evenly moist but not soggy (the phrase "like a squeezed-out sponge" is often used to describe the right degree of wetness). The surface can be permitted to dry out a little between waterings in winter, however. Water the base of a staghorn fern when it feels dry. Indoor ferns do not need a period of dormancy, though they may go dormant if the temperature is below 50 degrees; and they can be fed at least once a month all year. With many, such as Boston fern, a light dose of fish emulsion once a week is better than a heavier dose monthly. You can move them outdoors in sum-mer but not into direct sun. Ferns spread by runners, which can be severed and replanted for propagation. To propagate rabbit's-foot fern, pin the tip of a "foot" to the surface of moist sand with a hairpin.

FICUS
Ficus

weeping
fig

rubber plant

Description: One of the most popular indoor plants for an institutional setting is the weeping fig (*Ficus benjamina*), usually just called ficus. Though related to the edi-ble fig, it does not bear fruit, but it makes a beautiful display in an office, a sunny lobby, a shop, or a showroom—and in a well-lit home. A bushy tree that might grow to 50 feet in its native Malaya, it can easily be kept to 6 feet or so or allowed to grow to ceiling height, which it may do within a few years. Its 3-inch, shiny pointed leaves tol-erate low humidity well—one reason why ficus is such a favorite. Another oft-grown ficus is that old standby the rubber plant (*F. elastica*). It looks almost like an artificial plant, with its large, oval, shiny dark green leaves, and it can grow to the ceiling if you don't pinch its tip. Though currently out of fashion, *F. elastica* is still a good plant to grow if you need something big and green in a spot with little light. (It will grow in bright light, too.) The variety 'Decora' has very broad leaves, and there are variegated varieties as well, though these need more light in order to show their colors.

How to Grow: Ficus plants like fairly warm rooms but will tolerate low humidity because their leaves are rather leathery. *F. benjamina* needs more light than *F. elastica*—full sun, part sun, or at least bright indirect light. With too little light, *F. elastica* will get leggy and *F. benjamina* will drop its leaves. With the latter, sudden changes in the environment, such as a move or exposure to drafts, may also cause a sudden leaf drop—what I call a leaf tantrum—making it seem like a delicate, fussy plant. But it will usually recover promptly with new growth.

Soil for both species should be evenly moist; avoid overwatering. Feed both regularly except in fall or winter, and wash the leaves with warm water. The plants like to be rather potbound, and their size can be controlled by root-pruning them and putting them back into the same pot. Stems can also be cut back to the desired height and will produce new, compact growth.

GLOXINIA

Sinningia speciosa

Description: A gloxinia is a beautiful plant when in bloom, and this is when you're apt to receive it as a gift—a cluster of large, bell-shaped flowers rising out of a circle of large, fuzzy dark green leaves. After the blossoms fade the plant goes into a dormant state during which the leaves and stems die and there's nothing left but a little, flattish tuber. At this point most people throw the thing away, not realizing that they can keep growing it and reflowering it for decades. Native to Brazil, gloxinias come in colors as vibrant as a Mardi Gras costume—chiefly red, purple, pink, and white but sometimes salmon or orange; some are spotted or edged with a contrasting color.

How to Grow: You can purchase a gloxinia at any point in its life. If it's in bloom you can see what the flowers look like, of course, but often it's easier and less expensive to purchase a tuber in midwinter, planting it about ½ inch deep, concave side up, in either a soilless mix or a light, humus-rich potting soil. Water it sparingly while it's starting to root, then keep soil evenly moist but not soggy while the leaves appear. Try not to get the leaves wet. Gloxinias will do well in a room whose temperature is normal or cool, but the air should be fairly humid, and the plant should have bright light but not blazing sun. Like other members of the gesneriad family, which includes African violets and streptocarpus, gloxinias do superbly under broad-spectrum fluorescent lights (give them 14 to 16 hours per day). You might want to bring them into bloom under lights, then place them in a more sociable environment when they're at their best. Feed with a balanced or high-phosphorus fertilizer once a month while plants are growing.

After bloom, stop feeding and gradually stop watering. When the leaves turn yellow and the plant goes dormant, you can either leave the tuber in the pot or repot it in a slightly larger one, then store it in a dark, cool place (about 50 degrees), keeping the soil almost dry until a few months later when new growth begins. New plants can be propagated by dividing the tubers just when they show eyes, making sure there is an eye for each division, or by taking leaf cuttings.

JADE PLANT
Crassula argentea

Description: This almost indestructible South African plant has fat, oval, usually dark green leaves. It is a succulent, so the leaves hold water, helping it to survive droughts in its native land and forgetful waterers elsewhere. It also tolerates low humidity and low light. It is very long-lived, and will grow into a thick-trunked, treelike shape. My friend Chip has a magnificent old one that has always sat at one end of her dining table, like a member of the family. It has even doubled as a Christmas tree. But you can also keep your jade plant smaller and bushier by pinching the stem tips. Though plants rarely bloom while young, an old one will suddenly cover itself with fragrant, star-like white flowers if it is potbound.

How to Grow: Give a jade plant the average-to-cool temperatures it prefers—though it will tolerate a very wide temperature range. Sun or bright light is best but not necessary. Let plants dry out slightly between waterings in spring and summer, then water less and less as winter comes, giving the plants only enough in winter to keep the leaves from shriveling. Feed every two weeks or so during spring and summer. Jade plants will do fine if potbound, though it's best to repot them every few years using an average soil mix. If the plant looks graceless and overburdened, remove pendulous growth as needed. Use the cut stems or single leaves for propagation (both are easily rooted).

PALMS
Many genera

parlor palm

lady palm

sentry palm

Description: Palms make great indoor plants because of their graceful shapes and because they tolerate a multitude of ills: dry air, overheating, cold drafts, low light.

Palm fronds are divided into leaflets, and while some plants grow on a single stem, others have many stems coming up from the base. There seems to be a palm for every situation—here are some to try. The parlor palm, or Neanthe Bella palm (*Chamaedorea elegans*), is a fine-textured, fairly slow growing plant that makes clumps up to 4 feet, sometimes taller. It prefers a warm, humid room and an evenly moist soil, and does best when potbound. The lady palm (*Rhapis excelsa*) is also slow growing but can eventually reach the ceiling, with fan-shaped dark green fronds on hairy, bamboolike canes. There are variegated forms with yellow stripes. This is a very tolerant palm that will even take fairly cool temperatures. The kentia palm (*Howea*) is another graceful, feathery palm that grows slowly and adapts to either low or bright light, though it needs a warm room. Species include *H. forsteriana*, also called paradise palm, whose long fronds arch out in a vase shape, and the sentry palm (*H. belmoreana*), which is more compact. Both are single stemmed and can be potted in clumps of several plants.

How to Grow: Picture the filtered light of a tropical jungle, then see if you can find a site like that for your palm. Try to give it a warm spot with fairly high humidity, even though it may tolerate dry air to some extent. (Humidity also helps it to avoid red spider mites.) Use a standard potting mix, not soilless but with some loam. Keep the soil consistently moist (again, like a jungle), but let the top inch dry out just a bit between waterings in wintertime; overwatering a palm in winter can cause the roots to rot. There's no dormant period, but growth does slow in winter and palms should not be fed then, though a monthly feeding in spring and summer with a balanced fertilizer will benefit them.

PEPEROMIA
Peperomia

baby rubber plant

watermelon peperomia

emerald ripple

Description: Peperomias are dainty little plants, rarely more than a foot tall, well suited terrariums, dish gardens, or wherever a small plant seems appropriate. Though they produce little spiky flowers, they are grown for their thick leaves—sometimes heart-shaped, sometimes more elongated. These can be smooth or wrinkled and range in color from very dark green to reddish to almost silver—sometimes in combinations when the leaves are variegated. There are many peperomias you can try. One popular one is *Peperomia caperata*, emerald ripple, which has crinkled dark green leaves and is very easy to grow. Another is *P. argyreia* (*P. sandersii*), often called watermelon peperomia because its leaves, held on red stems, are striped like a watermelon. *P. obtusifolia* is sometimes called baby rubber plant because the shape and texture of its leaves are a bit like those of a rubber plant. Its leaves often have white markings. But this is only a small selection of these delightful plants, some of which are trailing and grow well in hanging baskets.

How to Grow: Peperomias are not fussy about temperature, though they do appreciate a humid atmosphere. They like a bright, sunny spot. Many are epiphytes (air plants) and so prefer a light, very well drained soil or soilless mix. It's most important not to overwater peperomias, especially in winter. Let the soil dry out slightly on the surface between waterings. They can be fed monthly with a balanced liquid fertilizer during spring and summer, but not in fall or winter, and overfeeding should always be avoided. Peperomias do not need frequent repotting, since they are so small and compact, but you can repot them in early spring. This is also the time to propagate them by division if they make offsets, or by tip, stem, or leaf cuttings.

PHILODENDRON

Philodendron

Description: The name "philodendron" means "tree-loving," and was inspired by the tree-climbing habit of many of these South and Central American jungle plants. Some species are not so vining in their habit, however, forming new growth at the base, branching, and creeping along the ground; these are known as the self-heading types. Philodendrons may seem like mundane plants simply because they are so common—common because they're so easy to grow. *Anyone* can grow

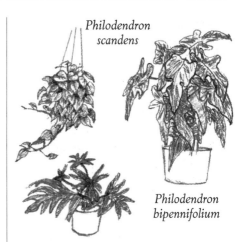

Philodendron scandens

Philodendron bipennifolium

Philodendron selloum

a philodendron. But they can be used in interesting ways—cascading from indoor balconies, for instance. And there are many species and cultivars you've probably never heard of but might like to grow once you start to explore them.

Heart-leaf philodendrons are the most common type. Two species, *Philodendron scandens* and *P. cordatum*, are both known by this name. They are vining plants with smooth, heart-shaped leaves. You also might try the vining *P. bipennifolium*, or fiddle-leaved philodendron, which has large, violin-shaped leaves when full grown. Like many vining plants it is often grown on a bark-covered support (usually a piece of wood). *P. selloum*, saddle-leaved philodendron, has deeply lobed leaves and is a self-heading type, as is *P. wendlandii*, which looks something like a bird's-nest fern. There are also philodendron varieties with brightly colored or variegated leaves.

How to Grow: Give philodendrons bright light if possible but not strong, direct sun. Average warmth and humidity are fine, though they prefer quite humid air, and the variegated ones like it pretty warm. Keep the soil evenly moist but not too wet, and feed about twice a month with a liquid houseplant fertilizer in spring and summer. Stop feeding in winter, when the plants like to take a rest, and water less. Philodendrons like an average potting soil with organic matter and should be repotted only when very rootbound. Pinch straggly, vining specimens if you want them bushier. They are propagated very easily from stem cuttings (tip cuttings for vining types).

SCHEFFLERA

Schefflera actinophylla
(Brassaia actinophylla)

Description: This plant is sometimes called umbrella tree, because of the umbrella-like shade it casts in the wild. Its leaves grow in hand-shaped leaf clusters. Schefflera is the classic, easy-to-grow indoor tree, branching nicely. It grows fairly slowly and can be easily kept to a manageable size, though in its native Australia it grows to 20 feet.

How to Grow: Grow schefflera in a room of average temperature but with a humid atmosphere if possible, misting as needed. It likes a bright, sunny window, although it will tolerate somewhat dimmer conditions. Pot it in a standard potting mixture, and repot anytime it seems potbound, unless you're trying to keep the plant small. You can let the top inch or so of soil dry out between waterings, especially in fall and winter when growth is slower. When you water, give the plant a good soaking but don't let water stand in the saucer. Feed twice a month in spring and summer, but don't overfeed, especially if the plant is not in bright light. I find that dusting and washing the leaves regularly is one of the most important things you can do to keep a schefflera healthy.

SPIDER PLANT

Chlorophytum comosum, C. elatum

Description: Ah, the spider plant. During the 1970s it crept into the health-food restaurants, then into all the other restaurants, then into the car dealerships, the travel agencies, the government agencies, and probably heaven, hell, and purgatory. But cliché or not, the spider plant will always be with us because it's attractive and outrageously easy to grow. Narrow, grassy green leaves with a central white (sometimes yellow) stripe erupt in rosettes at the tips of hanging stems that can get 5 feet long, looking much like a spider's legs. It is most often grown as a hanging plant.

How to Grow: Spider plant likes an average room temperature and humid air but will survive in fairly dry air, too. It likes bright light but not blazing sun, and will tolerate somewhat dimmer conditions. Rotate the pot from time to time, or you'll have a lopsided spider. Give it an all-purpose potting soil, and repot it anytime you think it looks crowded. Water the plant thoroughly, then let it dry out on the surface or even a bit deeper; it will tolerate dry soil much better than wet. Feed your spider plant every two weeks in spring and summer if you want to encourage growth. Plants can be divided, but the simplest way to propagate is to remove a leaf cluster from the end of a stem and root it in a small pot. You can put many clusters in one pot if you're impatient to get a big, lush plant.

STREPTOCARPUS

Streptocarpus × hybridus

Description: The common name for this plant is Cape primrose (because it comes from the Cape of Good Hope in South Africa), but most people these days call it by its Latin name. Streptocarpus may sound like a disease, but it's an excellent indoor plant—compact, easy to grow, and in bloom for most of the year. The 2- to 5-inch flowers are most typically blue-violet

but can also be red, pink, purple, lavender, and white. Some have frilly edges or throats of contrasting colors. The flowers' shape is much like that of an azalea bloom, but they are borne on wiry stems above a large rosette of stemless, crinkled, primroselike leaves. The varieties available are far too numerous to name. *Streptocarpus saxorum* (sometimes called *Streptocarpella saxorum*) is a trailing type, with a violet color, often used in hanging baskets.

How to Grow: Streptocarpuses are in some ways similar to African violets, but they will take cooler temperatures (usually down to 50 degrees—below that they may go dormant). They need good, bright light, although they don't like direct sun, and they do very well under fluorescent lighting. Plant them in shallow clay pots in a light soil mix like that used for African violets, and keep the soil moist. If the plant stops blooming, however, let it rest for at least a month or two, giving it just enough water so that the leaves do not wilt. Feed once or twice a month in spring and summer, with a balanced or high-phosphorus liquid fertilizer, but don't overfeed, and never feed while the plant is resting. Wait till new growth appears, repot if necessary, and then resume the standard feeding and watering routine. To propagate streptocarpus, divide mature plants while they are dormant.

Appendix

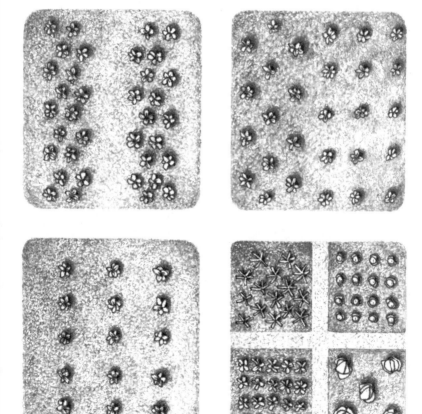

Plant Hardiness Zone Map
Agricultural Research Service, USDA

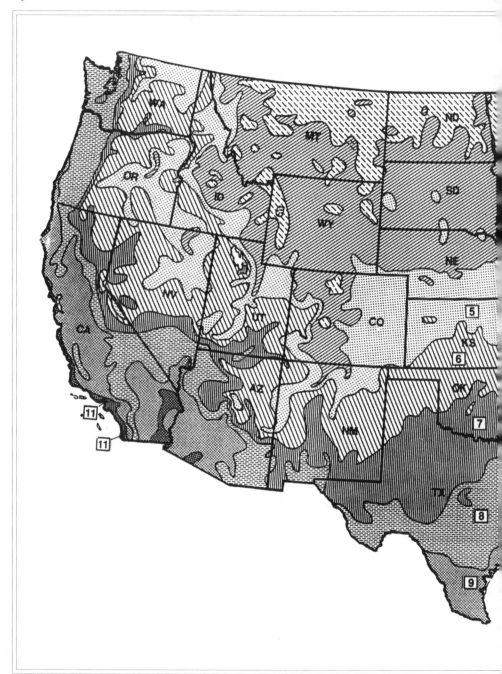

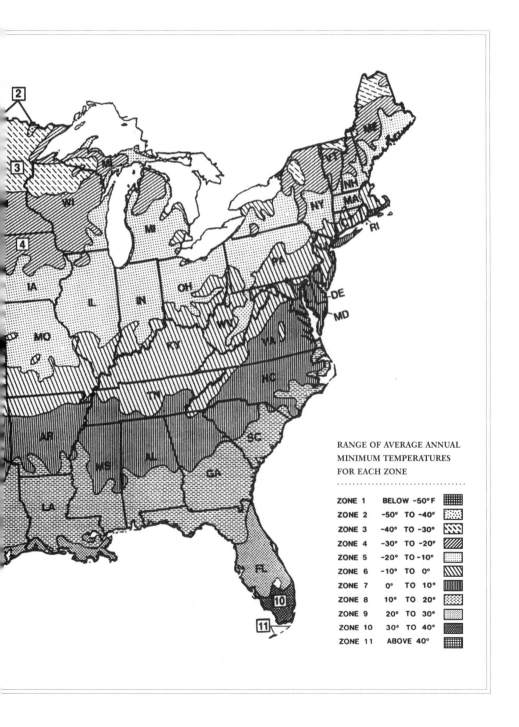

RANGE OF AVERAGE ANNUAL
MINIMUM TEMPERATURES
FOR EACH ZONE

ZONE 1	BELOW -50°F
ZONE 2	-50° TO -40°
ZONE 3	-40° TO -30°
ZONE 4	-30° TO -20°
ZONE 5	-20° TO -10°
ZONE 6	-10° TO 0°
ZONE 7	0° TO 10°
ZONE 8	10° TO 20°
ZONE 9	20° TO 30°
ZONE 10	30° TO 40°
ZONE 11	ABOVE 40°

Organizations and Societies

GROUPS DEVOTED TO SPECIFIC PLANTS

African Violet Society of America
PO Box 3609
Beaumont, TX 77702
www.avsa.org

American Bamboo Society
315 S. Coastal Highway 101 Ste. U
PMB 212
Encinitas, CA 92024-3555
www.american bamboo.org

American Begonia Society
PO Box 471651
San Francisco, CA 94147-1651
www.begonias.org

American Bonsai Society
PO Box 351604
Toledo, OH 43635-1604
www.absbonsai.org

American Boxwood Society
PO Box 85
Boyce, VA 22620-4942
www.boxwoodsociety.org

American Camellia Society
100 Massee Ln.
Fort Valley, GA 31030
www.camellias-acs.org

American Clematis Society
Edith Malek
PO Box 17085
Irvine, CA 92623-7085
www.clematis.org

American Conifer Society
John Martin
175 Charisma Ln.
Lewisville, NC 27023-9611
www.conifersociety.org

American Daffodil Society
Jaydee Atkins Ager
PO Box 522
Hawkinsville, GA 31036
www.daffodilusa.org

American Dahlia Society
Alan A. Fisher
1 Rock Falls Ct.
Rockville, MD 20854
www.dahlia.org

American Fern Society
Dr. George Yatskievych
Missouri Botanical Garden
P.O. Box 299
St. Louis, MO 63166-0299
www.amerfernsoc.org

American Gourd Society
PO Box 2186
Kokomo, IN 46904-2186
www.americangourdsociety.org

American Hemerocallis Society
Pat Mercer
Dept. WWW
PO Box 10
Dexter, GA 31019
www.daylilies.org

American Hosta Society
Sandie Markland
8702 Pinnacle Rock Ct.
Lorton, VA 22079-3029
www.hosta.org

American Hydrangea Society
PO Box 986
Grayson, CA 30017
www.americanhydrangeasociety.org

American Iris Society
Tom Gormley
10606 Timber Ridge St.
Dubuque, IA 52001-8266
www.irises.org

American Ivy Society
PO Box 2123
Naples, FL 34106-2123
www.ivy.org

American Orchid Society
16700 AOS Ln.
Delray Beach, FL 33446-4351
www.aos.org

American Penstemon Society
Dale Lindgren
West Central Research Center
Rte. 4, Box 46A
North Platte, NE 69101
www.penstemon.org

American Peony Society
c/o Claudia Schroer
713 White Oak Ln.
Gladstone, MO 64116-4607
www.americanpeonysociety.org

American Primrose Society
Jon Kawaguchi
3524 Bowman Ct.
Alameda, CA 94502
www.americanprimrosesociety.org

American Rhododendron Society
PO Box 525
Niagara Falls, NY 14304
www.rhododendron.org

American Rose Society
PO Box 30,000
Shreveport, LA 71130-0030
www.ars.org

American Violet Society
Gary W. Sherwin
PO Box 342
Yukon, PA 15698-0342
www.americanvioletsociety.org

Azalea Society of America
Carol Flowers, Apt. 1011
700 New Hampshire Ave. NW
Washington, DC 20037
www.azaleas.org

Bromeliad Society International
Dan Kinnard
6901 Kellyn Ln.
Vista, CA 92084-1243
www.bsi.org

Cactus & Succulent Society of America
PO Box 2615
Pahrump, NV 89041-2615
www.cssainc.org

Canadian Rose Society
c/o Marie Farnady
504-334 Queen Mary Rd.
Kingston, ON KJM 7E7
Canada
www.canadianrosesociety.org

The Cycad Society
Craig Nazor
11701 Barchetta Dr.
Austin, TX 78758
www.cycad.org

Gesneriad Society
1122 East Pike St., PMB 637
Seattle, WA 98122-3916
www.gesneriadsociety.org

Heritage Roses Group
Bev Dobson
916 Union St., #302
Alameda, CA 94501
www.heritagerosegroup.org

Holly Society of America
PO Box 803
Millville, NJ 68332-0803
www.hollysocam.org

International Carnivorous Plant Society
PMB 322
1564-A Fitzgerald Dr.
Pirole, CA 94564-2229
www.carnivorousplants.org

International Lilac Society
William Tschumi
3 Paradise Ct.
Cohoes, NY 12047-1422
www.internationallilacsociety.org

International Palm Society
PO Box 7075
Lawrence, KS 66044-7075
www.palms.org

International Waterlily & Water Gardening
Society
PO Box 602
Greenville, VA 24440
www.iwgs.org

Magnolia Society
Beth Edward
3000 Henneberry Rd.
Jamesville, NY 13078-9640
www.magnoliasociety.org

National Chrysanthemum Society
Galen L. Goss
10107 Homar Pond Dr.
Fairfax Station, VA 22039-1650
www.mums.org

North American Lily Society
Stephanie Sims
PO Box W
Bonners Ferry, ID 83805
www.lilies.org

North American Rock Garden Society
PO Box 67
Millwood, NY 10546
www.nargs.org

Sedum Society
Sue Haffner
3015 Timmy
Clovis, CA 93612-4849
www.cactus-mall/sedum

EDIBLES

At the time of this writing, there are few organizations dedicated to home vegetable and fruit growers. Associations devoted to individual crops are, for the most part, industry groups. Your local Cooperative Extension Service or Land Grant University will often be your nearest resource. Locate these through the US Cooperative State Research, Education, and Extension Service or the American Horticultural Society, both listed below under Broad-Based Groups. The AHS has a website for the popular Master Gardener program, which offers locally based gardening instruction in exchange for volunteer service.

In addition, state and regional organic farming organizations are an excellent resource. Most include home gardeners in their membership and hold conferences, fairs, and other events that are instructive and fun for all. I have included a few; others can be found through the Extension Service or through ATTRA, listed below.

American Pomological Society (Fruit)
R. M. Crassweller
103 Tyson Building
University Park, PA 16802-4200
www.americanpomological.org

ATTRA—National Sustainable Agriculture
Information Service
PO Box 3657
Fayetteville, AR 72702
www.attra.ncat.org

California Rare Fruit Growers
Fullerton Arboretum—CSUF
PO Box 6850
Fullerton, CA 92834-6850
www.crfg.org

Canadian Organic Growers
323 Chapel St.
Ottawa, ON K1N 7Z2
Canada
www.cog.ca

Chez Panisse Foundation
1517 Shattuck Ave.
Berkeley, CA 94709
www.chezpanissefoundation.org
*Information and links about gardening
education, including the Edible Schoolyard.*

Herb Society of America
9019 Kirtland Chardon Rd.
Kirtland, OH 44094
www.herbsociety.org

Home Orchard Society
PO Box 230192
Tigard, OR 97281-0192
www.homeorchardsociety.org

Kitchen Gardeners International
www.kitchengardeners.org
Online resource for home gardeners.

Maine Organic Farmers and Gardeners Assn.
PO Box 170
Unity, ME 04988
www.mofga.org

Native Seeds/SEARCH
526 N. Fourth Ave.
Tucson, AZ 85705
www.nativeseeds.org

North American Fruit Explorers
1716 Apples Rd.
Chapin, IL 62628
www.nafex.org

Northeast Organic Farming Assn.
    Includes 7 state chapters: CT, MA,
    NH, NJ, NY, RI, and VT, linked by the
    Interstate Council.
Bill Duesing
PO Box 135
Stevenson, CT 06491
www.nofa.org

Ohio Ecological Food and Farm Assn.
41 Croswell Rd.
Columbus, OH 43214
www.oeffa.org

Oregon Tilth
470 Lancaster Dr. NE
Salem, OR 97301
www.tilth.org

The Scatterseed Project
Will Bonsall
PO Box 1167
Farmington, ME 04938
www.gardeningplaces.com/scatterseed.htm
Preservation of seed diversity and heritage crops.

Slow Food USA
20 Jay St., No. 313
Brooklyn, NY 11201
www.slowfoodusa.org
*Preserves and promotes traditional crops and
practices, gardening education.*

Texas Organic Farmers and Gardeners Assn.
288 SW County Rd. 20
Corsicana, TX 75110
www.tofga.org

NATIVE PLANTS

There are a great many regional native plant societies throughout the United States and Canada. The New England Wild Flower Society, below, offers a good list.

Lady Bird Johnson Wildflower Center
4801 La Crosse Ave.
Austin, TX 78739
www.wildflower.org

New England Wild Flower Society
180 Hemenway Rd.
Framingham, MA 01701-2699
www.newfs.org

North American Native Plant Society
PO Box 84, Station D
Etobicoke, ON 4X1 M9A
Canada
www.nanps.org

PLANTS AND WILDLIFE

eNature: America's Wildlife Resource
1811 36th St. NW
Washington, DC 20007
www.enature.com
*Offers online field guides to thousands of plant
and animal species.*

Flora and Fauna International
PO Box 42575
Washington, DC 20015-0575
www.fauna-flora.org

National Audubon Society
225 Varick St.
New York, NY 10014
www.audubon.org

North American Butterfly Assn.
4 Delaware Rd.
Morristown, NJ 07960
www.naba.org

The Xerces Society for Invertebrate
   Conservation
4828 SE Hawthorne Blvd.
Portland, OR 97215
www.xerces.org

BROAD-BASED GROUPS

American Community Gardening Assn.
1777 East Broad St.
Columbus, OH 43203-2040
www.communitygarden.org

American Forests
PO Box 2000
Washington, DC 20013
www.americanforests.org

American Horticultural Society
7931 E. Boulevard Dr.
Alexandria, VA 22308
www.ahs.org

American Society for Horticultural Science
113 S. West St., Ste. 200
Alexandria, VA 22314-2851
www.ashs.org

Botanical Society of America
PO Box 299
St. Louis, MO 63166-0299
www.botany.org

Dave's Garden
www.davesgarden.com
Online databases and forums for gardeners.

The Garden Club of America
14 E. 60th St.
New York, NY 10022-1006
www.gcamerica.org

The Garden Conservancy
PO Box 219
Cold Spring, NY 10516
www.gardenconservancy.org

Garden Web
www.gardenweb.com
Online information resource.

Horticultural Society of New York
148 W. 37th St.
New York, NY 10018-6909
www.hsny.org

International Bulb Society
PO Box 336
Sanger, CA 93657-0336
www.bulbsociety.org

Massachusetts Horticultural Society
Elm Bank Horticultural Center
900 Washington St.
Wellesley, MA 02482-5725
www.masshort.org

National Garden Clubs
4401 Magnolia Ave.
St. Louis, MO 63110
www.gardenclub.org

National Gardening Association
1100 Dorset St.
South Burlington, VT 05403
www.nationalgardening.com

National Junior Horticulture Association
Carole Carney
15 Railroad Ave.
Homer City, PA 15748-1378
www.njha.org

National Plant Database
www.plants.usda.gov

National Woodland Owners Association
374 Maple Ave. East, Ste. 310
Vienna, VA 22180
www.woodlandowners.org

Northwest Horticultural Society
Karin Kravitz
PO Box 4597
Rolling Bay, WA 98061
www.northwesthort.org

Pennsylvania Horticultural Society
100 N. 20th St.
Philadelphia, PA 19103-1495
www.pennsylvaniahorticulturalsociety.org

Perennial Plant Association
3383 Schirtzinger Rd.
Hilliard, OH 43026
www.perennialplant.org

Rain Garden Network
773-774-5333
www.raingardennetwork.com

SafeLawns
60 Pineland Dr., Bldg. 3, Ste. 207
New Gloucester, ME 04260
www.safelawns.org

Seed Savers Exchange
3094 North Winn Rd.
Decorah, IA 52101
www.seedsavers.org

Soil and Water Conservation Society
945 SW Ankeny Rd.
Ankeny, IA 50023
www.swcs.org

U.S. Dept. of Agriculture
Cooperative State Research, Education, and
    Extension Service
1400 Independence Ave. SW, Stop 2201
Washington, DC 20250-2201
www.csrees.usda.gov
*Locates Cooperative Extension Service offices in
your area and other regional links.*

USDA Natural Resources Conservation
    Service
www.plants.usda.gov
*The PLANTS Database provides useful plant
guides and fact sheets.*

Mail-Order Sources of Plants, Seeds, and Supplies

Whenever possible it is best to buy plants, seeds, and supplies sold locally, as these are often best adapted to your area. You'll also waste less fuel and help sustain your regional economy. For those times when you must go farther afield to find something special, this list will put you in touch with some good companies. But even among these, try to choose the ones closest to home.

BULBS

Antonelli Brothers
407 Hecker Pass
Watsonville, CA 95076
888-423-4664
www.antonellibegonias.com
Specializing in tuberous begonias; other plants available.

B & D Lilies/Snow Creek Daylily Gardens
PO Box 2007
Port Townsend, WA 98368
360-765-4341
www.bdlilies.com

Brent and Becky's Bulbs
7900 Daffodil La.
Gloucester, VA 23061
877-661-2852
www.brentandbeckysbulbs.com

McClure & Zimmerman
PO Box 368
Friesland, WI 53935-0368
800-883-6998
www.mzbulb.com
Large selection of bulbs, some uncommon.

Old House Gardens
536 Third St.
Ann Arbor, MI 48103
734-995-1468
www.oldhousegardens.com
Unusual heirloom varieties.

John Scheepers
PO Box 638
Bantam, CT 06750-0638
860-567-0838
www.johnscheepers.com
Spring, summer, and indoor bulbs; lilies.

The Southern Bulb Company
PO Box 350
Golden, TX 75444-0350
903-768-2530
www.southernbulbs.com
Rare and heirloom bulbs for warm climates.

Swan's Island Dahlias
PO Box 700
Canby, OR 97013
800-410-6540
www.dahlias.com

TyTy Nursery
PO Box 130
TyTy, GA 31795
800-972-2101
www.tytyga.com
Unusual summer bulbs such as calla and crinum lily.

Van Engelen
PO Box 638
Bantam, CT 06750
860-567-5323
www.vanengelen.com
Large quantities at economical prices.

FRUITS

Adams County Nursery
PO Box 108
Aspers, PA 17304
717-677-8105
www.acnursery.com
Fruit trees.

Applesource
1716 Apples Rd.
Chaplin, IL 62628
800-588-3854
www.applesource.com
Ships antique and specialty apples for tasting.

The Banana Tree
715 Northampton St.
Easton, PA 18042
610-253-9589
www.banana-tree.com
*Plants and seeds of bananas and
other tropical fruits.*

Double A Vineyards
10277 Christy Rd.
Fredonia, NY 14063
716-672-8493
www.doubleavineyards.com

Edible Landscaping
361 Spirit Ridge Ln.
Afton, VA 22920
434-361-9134
www.ediblelandscaping.com
Wide range of interesting fruit-bearing plants.

Johnson Nursery
1352 Big Creek Rd.
Ellijay, GA 30536
888-276-3187
www.johnsonnursery.com
*Includes antique and unusual varieties,
southern apples, muscadines.*

Lawson's Nursery
2730 Yellow Creek Rd.
Ball Ground, GA 30107
770-893-2141
www.lawsonsnursery.com
Old-fashioned and unusual fruit trees.

Miller Nurseries
5060 West Lake Rd.
Canandaigua, NY 14424-8904
www.millernurseries.com
Includes tree fruits, small fruits, nut trees.

Nourse Farms
41 River Rd.
South Deerfield, MA 01373
413-665-2658
www.noursefarms.com
*Specializing in strawberry plants and
other small fruits.*

Oikos Tree Crops
PO Box 19425
Kalamazoo, MI 40019-0425
269-624-6233
www.oikostreecrops.com
Native fruits, nuts, and more.

One Green World
(Northwoods Nursery)
28696 S. Cramer Rd.
Molalla, OR 97038-8576
877-353-4028
www.onegreenworld.com
Wide and unusual selection.

Peterson Pawpaws
PO Box 1011
Harpers Ferry, WV 25425
www.petersonpawpaws.com

Raintree Nursery
391 Butts Rd.
Morton, WA 98356
360-496-6400
www.raintreenursery.com

St. Lawrence Nurseries
325 State Hwy. 345
Potsdam, NY 13676
315-265-6739
www.sln.potsdam.ny.us
Fruit and nut trees for cold climates.

Trees of Antiquity
20 Wellsona Rd.
Paso Robles, CA 93446
805-467-9909
www.treesofantiquity.com
Heirloom fruit trees, rootstocks.

Van Well Nursery
PO Box 1339
Wenatchee, WA 98807
800-572-1553
www.vanwell.net
Large selection of standard and dwarf fruit trees, some small fruits.

GARDEN GEAR

Charley's Greenhouse & Garden
17979 State Rte. 536
Mount Vernon, WA 98273-3269
800-322-4709
www.charleysgreenhouse.com

Dripworks
190 Sanhedrin Cir.
Willits, CA 95490-8753
800-522-3747
www.dripworks.com
Drip irrigation supplies.

Gardener's Supply
128 Intervale Rd.
Burlington, VT 05401
800-429-3363
www.gardeners.com
Employee-owned purveyor of tools, equipment, and supplies, with an emphasis on organic methods.

Indoor Gardening Supplies
PO Box 527
Dexter, MI 48130
800-823-5740
www.indoorgardeningsupplies.com

Lee Valley Tools
US: PO Box 1780
Ogdensburg, NY 13669-6780
800-871-8158
Canada: PO Box 6295 Station J
Ottawa, ON K2A 1T4
Canada
800-267-8767
www.leevalley.com

A. M. Leonard
PO Box 816
Piqua, OH 45356-0816
800-543-8955
www.amleo.com
Encyclopedic array of tools and supplies for home gardeners and professionals.

Gardens Alive!
5100 Schenley Pl.
Lawrenceburg, IN 47025
513-354-1482
www.gardensalive.com
Environmentally responsible gardening products.

Growers Supply
1440 Field of Dreams Way
Dyersville, IA 52040
800-476-9715
www.growerssupply.com
Serious gardening equipment, greenhouses.

Walter F. Nicke
PO Box 433
Topsfield, MA 01983
978-887-3388
www.gardentalk.com
Garden tools and equipment; many unusual items.

Peaceful Valley Farm & Garden Supply
PO Box 2209
125 Clydesdale Ct.
Grass Valley, CA 95945
888-784-1722
www.groworganic.com
Main catalog has a wide selection of equipment and supplies. Also organic plants and seeds.

Premier
2031 300th St.
Washington, IA 52353
800-282-6631
www.premier1supplies.com
Fence systems for gardens and livestock.

Womanswork
PO Box 728
Pawling, NY 12564
800-639-2709
www.womanswork.com
Gardening gloves sized for women.

HERBS

Goodwin Creek Gardens
PO Box 83
Williams, OR 97544
800-846-7359
www.goodwincreekgardens.com
*Herb seeds and plants, native plants,
and more.*

Horizon Herbs
PO Box 69
Williams, OR 97544
541-846-6704
www.horizonherbs.com
Organic medicinal herb seeds and plants.

Nichols Garden Nursery
1190 Old Salem Rd. NE
Albany, OR 97321-4580
800-422-3985
www.nicholsgardennursery.com
Herb seeds, vegetables, flowers.

Papa Geno's Herb Farm &
    Prairie Home Perennials
6005 West Roca Rd.
Martell, NE 68404
402-794-0400
www.papagenos.com
Herb plants and others.

Richter's
Box 26
Goodwood, ON L0C 1A0
Canada
905-640-6677
www.richters.com
*Very large selection of herb seeds, many rare,
some medicinal. Some wildflower and gourmet
vegetable seeds, herb plants.*

Sandy Mush Herb Nursery
316 Surrett Cove Rd.
Leicester, NC 28748
828-683-2014
www.sandymush.com
*Very large selection of herbs and other plants,
specializing in scented-leaved geraniums.*

Well-Sweep Herb Farm
205 Mount Bethel Rd.
Port Murray, NJ 07865
908-852-5390
www.wellsweep.com
Herb plants and perennials.

HOUSEPLANTS

Cape Cod Violetry
587 Shawmut Ave.
New Bedford, MA 02740
508-993-2386
Very extensive list of African violet varieties.

Glasshouse Works
PO Box 97
Stewart, OH 45978-0097
740-662-2142
www.glasshouseworks.com
*Very extensive selection of plants, both hardy
and tropical.*

Grigsby Cactus Gardens
2326 Bella Vista Dr.
Vista, CA 92084-7836
760-727-1323
www.cactus-mall.com/grigsby
Large selection of cacti and other succulents.

K & L Cactus Nursery
9500 Brook Ranch Rd. East
Ione, CA 95640-9417
209-274-0360
www.klcactus.com
Extensive offering of cacti and other succulents.

Kartuz Greenhouses
1408 Sunset Dr.
Vista, CA 92081
760-941-3613
www.kartuz.com
Rare and unusual plants.

Lauray of Salisbury
432 Undermountain Rd.
Salisbury, CT 06068
860-435-2263
www.lauray.com
Large selection includes cacti and other succulents, begonias, orchids, gesneriads, and others.

Logee's Greenhouses
141 North St.
Danielson, CT 06239
888-330-8038
www.logees.com
Huge selection of houseplants with a specialty in begonias.

Lyndon Lyon Greenhouses
14 Mutchler St.
Dolgeville, NY 13329-0249
315-429-8291
www.lyndonlyon.com
African violets and more.

Orchids by Hausermann
2N 134 Addison Rd.
Villa Park, IL 60181-1191
630-543-6855
www.orchidsbyhausermann.com

Shady Hill Gardens
42W075 Rte. 38
Ellburn, IL 60119
630-365-5665
www.shadyhill.com
Specializing in geraniums.

PERENNIALS

Asiatica
PO Box 270
Lewisberry, PA 17339
717-938-8677
www.asiaticanursery.com
Large selection of rare choice plants, mostly from Asia.

Kurt Bluemel
2740 Greene Ln.
Baldwin, MD 21013
800-498-1560
www.kurtbluemel.com
Specializes in ornamental grasses.

Bluestone Perennials
7211 Middle Ridge Rd.
Madison, OH 44057
800-852-5243
www.bluestoneperennials.com
Large selection of perennials; small container-grown plants at affordable prices; also shrubs, herbs, and bulbs.

Bridgewood Gardens
PO Box 391
Strasburg, VA 22657
540-631-9311
www.bridgewoodgardens.com
Hostas.

Bloomingfields Farm
PO Box 5, Rte. 55
Gaylordsville, CT 06755
203-354-6951
www.bloomingfieldsfarm.com
Choice selection of organically grown daylilies, reasonably priced.

Canyon Creek Nursery
3527 Dry Creek Rd.
Oroville, CA 95965
530-533-2166
www.canyoncreeknursery.com
Very large selection, emphasizing dry-climate plants.

Cooley's Gardens
PO Box 126 NT
Silverton, OR 97381
503-873-5463
www.cooleysgardens.com
Extensive selection of bearded irises.

The Crownsville Nursery
PO Box 309
Strasburg, VA 22657
540-631-9411
www.crownsvillenursery.com
Varied selection of ferns, perennials, shrubs.

Digging Dog Nursery
See "Miscellaneous"

Forest Farm
See "Shrubs and Trees"

Garden Vision
63 Williamsville Rd.
Hubbardston, MA 01452-1315
978-928-4808
www.home.earthlink.net/~darrellpro
Fascinating array of epimediums and other shade plants.

Russell Graham, Purveyor of Plants
4030 Eagle Crest Rd. NW
Salem, OR 97304-9787
503-362-1135
Interesting selection of unusual perennials, bulbs, and wildflowers.

High Country Gardens
2902 Rufina St.
Santa Fe, NM 87507
800-925-9387
www.highcountrygardens.com
Wide selection of perennials and grasses, with an emphasis on dry western areas.

King's Mums
PO Box 368
Clements, CA 95227
209-759-3571
www.kingsmums.com

Extensive list of chrysanthemums for the exhibitor or gardener.

Klehm's Song Sparrow
13101 E Rye Rd.
Avalon, WI 53505
800-553-3715
www.songsparrow.com
Specializing in herbaceous and tree peonies; also daylilies, hostas, bearded iris, others.

Niche Gardens
See "Wildflowers"

Plant Delights Nursery
9241 Saul's Rd.
Raleigh, NC 27603
919-772-4794
www.plantdelights.com
Very large selection of unusual perennials; specialty in hostas.

Reath's Nursery
N 195 County Rd. 577
Vulcan, MI 49892
906-563-9777
www.reathsnursery.com
Specializing in herbaceous and tree peonies, Siberian iris.

Schreiner's Gardens
3625 Quinaby Rd. NE.
Salem, OR 97303
800-525-2367
www.schreinersgardens.com
Large selection of bearded iris, including new introductions, dwarf and intermediate varieties.

Siskiyou Rare Plant Nursery
See "Wildflowers"

Wayside Gardens
See "Miscellaneous"

White Flower Farm
PO Box 50, Rte. 63
Litchfield, CT 06759-0050
800-503-9624

www.whiteflowerfarm.com
Renowned for perennials; also carries bulbs, shrubs, vines.

ROSES

The Antique Rose Emporium
9300 Lueckemeyer Rd.
Brenham, TX 77833
800-441-0002
www.antiqueroseemporium.com
Very extensive selection of antique roses; also companion perennials.

David Austin Roses
15059 State Hwy. 64 West
Tyler, TX 75704
800-328-8893
www.davidaustinroses.com
Modern roses with an old rose look.

High Country Roses
PO Box 448
Jensen, UT 84035
800-552-2082
www.highcountryroses.com
Antique and modern roses grown on their own roots; cold hardy, high altitude, drought tolerant.

Jackson and Perkins
84 Rose Ln.
Medford, OR 97501
877-322-2300
www.jacksonandperkins.com
Primarily modern roses; new introductions.

Lowe's Roses
6 Sheffield Rd.
Nashua, NH 03062
603-888-2214
www.loweroses.com
Old garden and shrub roses; their own introductions.

Nor'East Miniature Roses
PO Box 520
Arroyo Grande, CA 93421
800-426-6485
www.noreast-miniroses.com

North Creek Farm
PO Box 35
Sebasco Estates, ME 04565
To visit: 24 Sebasco Rd.
Phippsburg, ME 04562
207-389-1341
www.northcreekfarm.com
Old and antique roses, clematis; specializing in rugosas.

Pickering Nurseries
3043 County Rd. 2, RR 1
Port Hope, ON L1A 3V5
Canada
866-269-9282
www.pickeringnurseries.com
Ships to US and Canada.

Roses of Yesterday and Today
803 Brown's Valley Rd.
Watsonville, CA 95076-0398
831-728-1901
www.rosesofyesterday.com
Very large selection of old, rare, and unusual roses, some modern.

SEEDS

Abundant Life Seeds
PO Box 157
Saginaw, OR 97472-0157
541-767-9606
www.abundantlifeseeds.com
Organic heirloom vegetable, flower, and herb seeds.

Allen, Sterling & Lothrop
191 U.S. Rte. 1
Falmouth, ME 04105
207-781-4142
www.allensterlinglothrop.com
Unusual heirloom vegetable seeds, some flowers.

Baker Creek Heirloom Seeds
2278 Baker Creek Rd.
Mansfield, MO 65704
417-924-8917
www.rareseeds.com
Old and unusual vegetable varieties, some flowers.

Bountiful Gardens
18001 Shafer Ranch Rd.
Willits, CA 95490
707-459-6410
www.bountifulgardens.org
Organically grown, open-pollinated seeds of vegetables herbs, flowers, grains, green manures; rare and unusual varieties.

W. Atlee Burpee
300 Park Ave.
Warminster, PA 18974
800-888-1447
www.burpee.com
Extensive collection of vegetable and flower seeds.

D. V. Burrell Seed Growers
PO Box 150
Rocky Ford, CO 81067
866-254-7333
www.burrellseeds.com
Basic selection of vegetable seeds available in both small quantities and bulk.

Comstock, Ferre
263 Main St.
Wethersfield, CT 06109
860-571-6590
www.comstockferre.com
Very old company with wide selection of vegetable, flower, and herb seeds.

The Cook's Garden
PO Box 65
Londonderry, VT 05148
802-824-3400
www.cooksgarden.com
Vegetable, herb, and flower seeds, including many unusual varieties, especially lettuces and other salad greens; some organic.

William Dam Seeds
279 Hwy. 8 RR 1
Dundas, ON L9H 5E1
Canada
905-628-6641
www.damseeds.com
Wide selection of untreated vegetable seeds; many varieties for northern gardens. Cover crops, trees, grasses, herbs, wildflowers, flowers, bulbs.

E & R Seed
1356 E 200 S
Monroe, IN 46772
866-510-3337
Fax: 715-265-7004
Amish company with good selection.

Evergreen Y. H. Enterprises
PO Box 17538
Anaheim, CA 92817
714-637-5769
www.evergreenseeds.com
Very wide selection of Asian vegetable seeds.

Fedco Seeds
See "Miscellaneous"

Filaree Farm
182 Conconully Hwy.
Okanogan, WA 98840
509-422-6940
www.filareefarm.com
Organic seed, garlic.

The Fragrant Path
PO Box 328
Fort Calhoun, NE 68023
www.fragrantpathseeds.com
Seeds for fragrant, rare and old-fashioned plants. Annuals, perennials, herbs, vines, trees, and shrubs.

Good Seed
195 Bolster Rd.
Oroville, WA 98844
www.goodseedco.net
Modern and heirloom seeds adapted for northern and mountain gardeners; vegetables, herbs, flowers.

Gourmet Seed International
HC 12, Box 510
Tatum, NM 88267-9700
575-398-6111
www.gourmetseed.com
Wide selection of unusual vegetable seed varieties.

Harris Seeds
PO Box 24966
Rochester, NY 14624-0966
800-514-4441
www.harrisseeds.com
Complete selection of vegetable and flower seeds; plants, supplies.

High Mowing Seeds
76 Quarry Rd.
PO Box 180
Wolcott, VT 05860
802-472-6174
www.highmowingseeds.com
Organic vegetables, herbs, flowers, cover crops.

J. L. Hudson
Box 337
La Honda, CA 94020-0337
www.jlhudsonseeds.com
Encyclopedic collection of rare and unusual seeds—vegetables, herbs, flowers, fruits, shrubs, trees, ferns, grasses—from around the world.

Johnny's Selected Seeds
955 Benton Ave.
Winslow, ME 04901-2601
To visit: Foss Hill Rd.
Albion, ME
877-564-6697
www.johnnyseeds.com
Large selection of new and traditional varieties, many unusual. Vegetables, herbs, flowers, books, supplies.

Kitazawa Seed Company
PO Box 13220
Oakland, CA 94661-3220
510-595-1188
www.kitazawaseeds.com
Wide selection of Asian vegetables.

Le Jardin du Gourmet & Artistic Gardens
PO Box 75
St. Johnsbury, VT 05863-0075
802-748-1446
www.artisticgardens.com
Gourmet vegetable seeds, many from France. Small sample packets available.

Nichols Garden Nursery
See "Herbs"

Park Seed
1 Parkton Ave.
Greenwood, SC 29647
800-213-0076
www.parkseed.com
Large selection of annual and perennial flower and vegetable seeds, herb and wildflower seeds, bulbs, perennial plants, small fruits, supplies.

Pinetree Garden Seeds
PO Box 300
New Gloucester, ME 04260
888-527-3337
www.superseeds.com
Large selection of vegetable seeds, including gourmet and heirloom varieties.

Plants of the Southwest
3095 Agua Fria Rd.
Santa Fe, NM 87507
800-788-7333
www.plantsofthesouthwest.com
Unusual seed catalog features grasses, wildflowers, trees, shrubs, modern and ancient American vegetables, herbs, books.

Redwood City Seed
PO Box 361
Redwood City, CA 94064
650-325-7333
www.ecoseeds.com
Heirloom vegetables, specializing in hot peppers.

Ronniger Potato Farm
12101 2135 Rd.
Austin, CO 81410
877-204-8704
www.ronnigers.com
Seed potatoes from Colorado.

John Scheepers Kitchen Garden Seeds
PO Box 638
23 Tulip Dr.
Bantam, CT 06750-0638
860-567-6086

www.kitchengardenseeds.com
*Gourmet vegetable and herb seeds with an
international flavor; old-fashioned flowers.*

Seed Savers Exchange
3094 North Winn Rd.
Decorah, IA 52101
563-382-5990
www.seedsavers.org
*Wide array of heirloom vegetable and flower
seeds; also has a huge seed-swapping network.*

Seeds from Italy
PO Box 149
Winchester, MA 01890
781-721-5904
www.growitalian.com
*US distributor of Franchi seeds; Italian vegetable
varieties.*

Seeds of Change
PO Box 15700
Santa Fe, NM 87592-1500
888-762-7333
www.seedsofchange.com
*Organic vegetable, herb, and flower seeds, many
heirloom and unusual.*

Southern Exposure Seed Exchange
PO Box 460
Mineral, VA 23117
540-894-9480
www.southernexposure.com
*Seeds of heirloom and other open-pollinated
varieties; emphasis on mid-Atlantic states.*

Stokes Seeds
US: PO Box 548
Buffalo, NY 14240
Canada: PO Box 10
Thorold, ON L2V 5E9
Canada
800-396-9238
www.stokeseeds.com
*Very large, basic selection of vegetable and
flower seeds.*

Territorial Seed
PO Box 158
Cottage Grove, OR 97424-0061
800-626-0866
www.territorialseed.com
*Vegetables, herbs, flowers, specialty fruits.
Company does extensive trials.*

Thompson and Morgan Seedsmen
220 Faraday Ave.
Jackson, NJ 08527-5073
888-466-4769
www.tmseeds.com
*English company with very large selection of
seeds; both ornamentals and edibles.*

Tomato Growers Supply
PO Box 60015
Fort Myers, FL 33906
888-478-7333
www.tomatogrowers.com
*Huge selection of tomato varieties; sweet and hot
peppers; books and supplies.*

Vesey's Seed
US: PO Box 9000
Calais, ME 04619-6102
Canada: PO Box 9000
Charlottetown, PE C1A 8K6
Canada
800-363-7333
www.veseys.com
*Vegetable and flower seeds from Canada, with
an emphasis on short growing seasons.*

Willhite Seed
PO Box 23
Poolville, TX 76407-0023
817-599-8656
www.willhiteseed.com
*Seeds from Texas, with a specialty in
watermelons.*

Wood Prairie Farm
49 Kinney Rd.
Bridgewater, ME 04736
207-425-7741
www.woodprairie.com
Organic seed potatoes from Maine.

SHRUBS AND TREES

Carlson's Gardens
PO Box 305
South Salem, NY 10590
914-763-5958
www.carlsonsgardens.com
*Large selection of azaleas and rhododendrons.
Boxwood and mountain laurel.*

Cascade Forestry Service
1621 McCabe Ln.
Cascade, IA 52033
800-586-9437
www.cascadeforestry.com
Northern hardwood trees.

Fairweather Gardens
PO Box 330
Greenwich, NJ 08323
856-451-6261
www.fairweathergardens.com
Uncommon shrubs and trees.

Forest Farm
990 Thetherow Rd.
Williams, OR 97544-9599
541-846-7269
www.forestfarm.com
*Extraordinary selection of shrubs and trees.
Also perennials, ornamental grasses, ferns,
fruits, hardy palms.*

Girard Nurseries
PO Box 428
Geneva, OH 44041
440-466-2881
www.girardnurseries.com
Wide range of trees and shrubs.

Gossler Farms Nursery
1200 Weaver Rd.
Springfield, OR 97478
541-746-3922
www.gosslerfarms.com
*Specializing in magnolias and unusual shrubs
and trees.*

Greer Gardens
1280 Goodpasture Island Rd.
Eugene, OR 97401
800-548-0111
www.greergardens.com
*Huge selection of unusual shrubs, trees,
and perennials. Specializing in azaleas and
rhododendrons.*

Musser Forests
1880 Rte. 119 Hwy N
Indiana, PA 15701
800-643-8319
www.musserforests.com
*Evergreens, ornamental and shade trees, shrubs,
hedge plants, ground covers, perennials.*

Niche Gardens
See "Wildflowers"

Oikos Tree Crops
See "Fruits"

Plants of the Southwest
See "Seeds"

Rare Find Nursery
957 Patterson Rd.
Jackson, NJ 08527
732-833-0613
www.rarefindnursery.com
*Extensive collection of shrubs, trees, herbaceous
plants. Specialty in rhododendrons.*

Rock Spray Nursery
PO Box 3025
Truro, MA 02666
508-349-6769
www.rockspray.com
Heaths and heathers.

WILDFLOWERS

Forest Farm
See "Shrubs and Trees"

Grow Wild!
35 Cedar Tree Ln.
Bobcaygeon, ON K0M 1A0
Canada
705-738-5496
www.grow-wild.com
Canadian native plants.

Las Pilitas Nursery
3232 Las Pilitas Rd.
Santa Margarita, CA 93453
805-438-5992
www.laspilitas.com
California native plants, primarily shrubs and trees. Also herbaceous plants.

Meadowbrook Nursery/We-Du Natives
2055 Polly Spout Rd.
Marion, NC 28752
828-287-9348
www.we-du.com
Extensive selection of native woody and herbaceous plants, with an emphasis on the southwest.

Niche Gardens
1111 Dawson Rd.
Chapel Hill, NC 27516
919-967-0078
www.nichegardens.com
Fine selection of unusual perennials, shrubs, and trees, emphasizing natives.

Plants of the Southwest
See "Seeds"

Prairie Nursery
PO Box 306
Westfield, WI 53964
608-296-2741
www.prairienursery.com
Native midwestern prairie plants and seeds; wildflowers, grasses, wetland species.

Siskiyou Rare Plant Nursery
2115 Talent Ave.
Talent, OR 97540
541-535-7103
www.srpn.net
Rare alpines, rock-garden plants, ferns, shrubs, perennials, with an emphasis on western natives.

Southwestern Native Seeds
PO Box 50503
Tucson, AZ 85703
www.southwesternnativeseeds.com
Southwestern native wildflowers, trees, shrubs, succulents.

Woodlanders
1128 Colleton Ave.
Aiken, SC 29801
803-648-7522
www.woodlanders.net
Extensive selection of woody and herbaceous plants, focusing on American natives.

Yerba Buena Nursery
19500 Skyline Blvd.
Woodside, CA 94062
650-851-1668
www.yerbabuenanursery.com
California native plants; primarily trees and shrubs, also many perennials and ferns.

MISCELLANEOUS

Vernon Barnes & Son Nursery
PO Box 250S2
McMinnville, TN 37111
931-668-8576
Economical source of shrubs, trees, fruits, vines, bulbs, perennials, wildflowers.

Cross Country Nurseries
PO Box 170
Rosemont, NJ 08556-0170
Fax: 908-996-4638
www.chileplant.com
Big selection of hot and sweet pepper plants, also tomatoes.

Digging Dog Nursery
PO Box 471
Albion, CA 95410
707-937-1130
www.diggingdog.com
Hard-to-find perennials, shrubs, trees, vines, ornamental grasses, many suitable for dry climates. Good clematis selection.

Fedco
PO Box 520
Waterville, ME 04903
207-873-7333
www.fedcoseeds.com
Cooperatively owned company has 5 divisions: Fedco Seeds, Fedco Trees, Fedco Bulbs, Organic Growers Supply, and Moose Tubers (organic seed potatoes, onion sets, shallots, and sunchokes). The delightful seed catalog focuses on cold climates.

Heronswood
30 Park Ave.
Warminster, PA 18974
866-578-7948
www.heronswood.com
Encyclopedic plant offerings, many unusual.

Lilypons Water Gardens
6800 Lilypons Rd.
PO Box 10
Adamston, MD 21710-0010
800-999-5459
www.lilypons.com
Large selection of hardy and tropical water lilies, bog plants, water-gardening supplies.

Natural Gardening Co.
PO Box 750776
Petaluma, CA 94975-0776
707-766-9303
www.naturalgardening.com.
Organic plants and seeds, drip irrigation equipment.

Steele Plant Co.
202 Collins St.
Gleason, TN 38229
731-648-5476
www.sweetpotatoplant.com
Sweet potato and onion plants.

William Tricker
PO Box 31267
7125 Tanglewood Dr.
Independence, OH 44131
800-524-3492
www.tricker.com
Large selection of hardy and tropical water lilies, bog plants, water-gardening supplies.

Wayside Gardens
1 Garden Lane
Hodges, SC 29695-0001
800-845-1124
www.waysidegardens.com
Wide variety of perennials, shrubs, roses, trees, vines, ground covers, bulbs, fruits, herbs.

For Further Reading

BOOKS

The following offer more detail about specific plants, practices, and regional perspectives. Out of print books can be found in libraries and at www.bookfinder.com.

REFERENCE

Batson, Wade T. *Landscape Plants for the Southeast*. Columbia, SC: University of South Carolina Press, 1984.

Bender, Steve, ed. *The Southern Living Gardening Book*. Birmingham, AL: Oxmoor House, 2004.

Bradley, Fern Marshall, and Barbara W. Ellis. *Rodale's All-New Encyclopedia of Organic Gardening*. Emmaus, PA: Rodale Press, 1993.

Breuzel, Kathleen Norris, ed. *Sunset Western Garden Book*, 8th ed. Menlo Park, CA: Sunset Books, 2007.

Capon, Brian. *Botany for Gardeners*. Portland, OR: Timber Press, 2004.

Cathey, H. Marc. *Heat-Zone Gardening: How to Choose Plants That Grow in Your Region's Warmest Weather*. Alexandria, VA: Time-Life Books, 1998.

Ellis, Barbara, et al. *The Organic Gardener's Handbook of Natural Insect and Disease Control*. New York: St. Martin's Press, 1996.

Favretti, Rudy and Joy. *For Every House a Garden: A Guide for Reproducing Period Gardens*. Danvers, MA: University Press of New England, 1990.

Flint, Mary Louise. *Pests of the Garden and Small Farm*. Berkeley, CA: University of California Press, 1999.

Griffiths, Mark. *Index of Garden Plants* (derived from *The New Royal Horticultural Society Dictionary of Gardening*). Portland, OR: Timber Press, 1994.

Hyams, Edward. *A History of Gardens and Gardening*. New York: Praeger Publishers, 1971.

Neal, Bill. *Gardener's Latin*. Chapel Hill, NC: Algonquin Books, 2003.

Pleasant, Barbara. *The Gardener's Bug Book: Harmless Insect Controls*. North Adams, MA: Storey Publishing, 1994.

Randall, J. M., and Janet Marinelli, eds. *Invasive Plants*. New York: Brooklyn Botanic Garden, 1996.

Raven, Peter H., et al. *The Biology of Plants*, 6th ed. New York: W. H. Freeman Publishers, 1999 (I prefer this to the 7th ed., 2005).

Staff of L. H. Bailey Hortorium, Cornell University. *Hortus Third: A Concise Dictionary of Plants Cultivated in the United States and Canada*. New York: Macmillan Publishing, 1976.

Stearn, William T. *Stearn's Dictionary of Plant Names for Gardeners*. Portland, OR: Timber Press, 2002.

Taylor, Norman, ed. *Taylor's Encyclopedia of Gardening, Horticulture and Landscape Design*. 4th ed. Boston: Houghton Mifflin, 1961.

Waters, George, and Nora Harlow. *The Pacific Horticulture Book of Western Gardening*. Boston: David R. Godine, Publisher, 1990.

Wyman, Donald. *Wyman's Gardening Encyclopedia*. New York: Simon & Schuster, 1987.

VEGETABLES, FRUITS, AND HERBS

Ashworth, Suzanne. *Seed to Seed: Seed Saving Techniques for the Vegetable Gardener*. White River Junction, VT: Chelsea Green Publishing, 2002.

Chan, Peter. *Better Vegetable Gardens the Chinese Way.* North Adams, MA: Storey Publishing, 1985.

Coleman, Eliot. *Four-Season Harvest.* White River Junction, VT: Chelsea Green Publishing, 1999.

———. *The New Organic Grower.* White River Junction, VT: Chelsea Green Publishing, 1995.

Creasy, Rosalind. *The Complete Book of Edible Landscaping.* San Francisco: Sierra Club Books, 1982

Engeland, Ron L. *Growing Great Garlic.* Okanogan, WA: Filaree Farm, 1991.

Foster, Catherine O. *The Organic Gardener.* New York: Alfred A. Knopf, 1972.

Foster, Gertrude B., and Rosemary F. Louden. *Park's Success With Herbs.* Greenwood, SC: George W. Park Seed Co., 1980.

Goldman, Amy. *Melons for the Passionate Grower.* New York: Artisan, 2002.

Hill, Lewis. *Fruits and Berries for the Home Garden.* North Adams, MA: Storey Publishing, 1992.

Hunter, Beatrice T. *Gardening Without Poisons.* New York: Berkley Books, 1977.

Jabs, Carolyn. *The Heirloom Gardener.* San Francisco: Sierra Club Books, 1984.

Kourik, Robert. *Designing and Maintaining Your Edible Landscape Naturally.* White River Junction, VT: Chelsea Green Publishing, 2005.

Larkcom, Joy. *Oriental Vegetables.* New York: Kodansha International, 2008.

———. *The Organic Salad Garden.* London: Frances Lincoln, 2006.

Male, Carolyn. *100 Heirloom Tomatoes for the American Garden.* New York: Workman Publishing, 1999.

McGee, Rose Marie Nichols, and Maggie Stuckey. *The Bountiful Container.* New York: Workman Publishing, 2002.

McNaughton, Virginia. *Lavender: The Grower's Guide.* Portland, OR: Timber Press, 2000.

McVicar, Jekka. *Jekka's Complete Herb Book.* Vancouver, BC: Raincoast Books, 2007.

Ogden, Shepherd. *Straight-Ahead Organic.* White River Junction, VT: Chelsea Green Publishing, 1999.

Owen, Millie. *A Cook's Guide to Growing Herbs, Greens, and Aromatics.* New York: Alfred A. Knopf, 1978.

Phillips, Michael. *The Apple Grower.* White River Junction, VT: Chelsea Green Publishing, 2005.

Proulx, E. Annie. *The Gourmet Gardener.* New York: Ballantine Books, 1987.

Reich, Lee. *Uncommon Fruits for Every Garden.* Portland, OR: Timber Press, 1994.

Rodale, J. I. *How to Grow Vegetables and Fruits by the Organic Method.* Emmaus, PA: Rodale Press. 1976.

Rombaugh, Lon. *The Grape Grower.* White River Junction, VT: Chelsea Green Publishing, 2002.

Seymour, John. *The New Self-Sufficient Gardener.* New York: Dorling Kindersley, 2008.

Simmons, Adelma G. *Herb Gardening in Five Seasons.* New York: E. P. Dutton, 1977.

Stout, Ruth. *Gardening Without Work.* New York: Simon & Schuster, 1974.

Taylor, Norman. *Taylor's Guide to Vegetables and Herbs,* ed. and rev. by Gordon P. DeWolf Jr. Boston: Houghton Mifflin, 1987.

Toensmeier, Eric. *Perennial Vegetables.* White River Junction, VT: Chelsea Green Publishing, 2007.

Weaver, William Woys. *Heirloom Vegetable Gardening.* New York: Henry Holt, 1997.

ANNUALS, PERENNIALS, AND BULBS

Armitage, Alan M. *Armitage's Manual of Annuals, Biennials and Half-Hardy Perennials.* Portland, OR: Timber Press, 2001.

———. *Herbaceous Perennial Plants.* Champaign, IL: Stipes Publishing, 1997.

Clausen, Ruth Rogers, and Nicholas H. Eckstrom. *Perennials for American Gardens.* New York: Random House, 1989.

Darke, Rick. *The Encyclopedia of Grasses for Livable Landscapes.* Portland, OR: Timber Press, 2007.

DiSabato-Aust, Tracy. *The Well-Tended Perennial Garden.* Portland, OR: Timber Press, 2006.

Free, Montague. *All About the Perennial Garden.* New York: Doubleday, 1955.

Hays, Robert M., and Janet Marinelli. *Bulbs for Indoors.* New York: Brooklyn Botanic Garden, 1996.

Lawrence, Elizabeth. *The Little Bulbs.* Durham, NC: Duke University Press, 1986.

Lord, Tony. *Best Borders.* New York: Viking Penguin, 1995.

McGourty, Frederick. *The Perennial Gardener.* Boston: Houghton Mifflin, 1989.

Olsen, Sue. *Encyclopedia of Garden Ferns.* Portland OR: Timber Press, 2007.

Phillips, Roger, and Martyn Rix. *The Random House Book of Perennials,* 2 vols. New York: Random House, 1991.

Raven, Sarah. *The Cutting Garden.* Pleasantville, NY: Reader's Digest, 1996.

Rix, Martyn, and Roger Phillips. *The Random House Book of Bulbs.* New York: Random House, 1989.

Scheider, Alfred E. *Park's Success With Bulbs.* Greenwood, SC: George W. Park Seed Co., 1981.

Welch, William C. *Perennial Garden Color for Texas and the South.* Dallas: Taylor Publishing, 1989.

Winterrowd, Wayne. *Annuals for Connoisseurs.* Indianapolis: Macmillan General Reference, 1996.

SHRUBS, TREES, AND VINES

Cullina, William. *Native Trees, Shrubs, and Vines.* New York: Houghton Mifflin, 2002.

Dirr, Michael A. *Manual of Woody Landscape Plants,* 3rd ed. Champaign, IL: Stipes Publishing Co., 1990.

———. *Dirr's Hardy Trees and Shrubs.* Portland, OR: Timber Press, 1997.

———. *Dirr's Trees and Shrubs for Warm Climates.* Portland, OR: Timber Press, 2002.

Grant, John A. and Carol L. *Trees and Shrubs for Pacific Northwest Gardens.* Portland, OR: Timber Press, 1990.

Lamb, Samuel H. *Woody Plants of the Southwest.* Santa Fe, NM: Sunstone Press, 1989.

Minckler, Leon S. *Woodland Ecology.* Syracuse, NY: Syracuse University Press, 1980.

Poor, Janet M., and Nancy P. Brewster. *Plants That Merit Attention, Vol. 1: Trees.* Portland, OR: Timber Press, 1994.

———. *Plants That Merit Attention, Vol. 2: Shrubs.* Portland, OR: Timber Press, 1996.

Rogers, David J. and Constance R. *Woody Ornamentals for Deep South Gardens.* Pensacola, FL: University of West Florida Press, 1991.

Shigo, Alex L. *A New Tree Biology.* Durham, NH: Shigo and Trees Associates, 1986.

Symonds. George W. *The Shrub Identification Book.* New York: William Morrow, 1973.

———. *The Tree Identification Book.* New York: William Morrow, 1973.

Wyman, Donald. *Shrubs and Vines for American Gardens.* New York: Macmillan Publishing, 1969.

———. *Trees for American Gardens.* New York: Macmillan Publishing, 1990.

ROSES

Beales, Peter. *Roses.* New York: Henry Holt, 1992.

Jekyll, Gertrude, and Edward Mawley. *Roses,* rev. by Graham Stuart Thomas. Salem, NH: Ayer Company, 1985.

Osborne Robert A. *Hardy Roses.* North Adams, MA: Storey Publishing, 1995.

Scaniello, Stephen, ed. *Easy-Care Roses.* New York: Brooklyn Botanic Garden, 1995.

Shepherd, Roy E. *The History of the Rose.* New York: Earl M. Coleman, Publisher, 1978.

Verrier, Suzanne. *Rosa Rugosa.* Richmond Hill, ON: Firefly Books, 1999.

———. *Rosa Gallica.* Richmond Hill, ON: Firefly Books, 1999.

Young, Marily, and Phillip Schorr, eds. *Modern Roses 12.* Vancouver, WA: Pediment Publishing, 2007. Available from the American Rose Society.

NATIVE PLANTS

Cullina, William. *The New England Wild Flower Society Guide to Growing and Propagating Wildflowers of the United States and Canada.* Boston: Houghton Mifflin, 2000.

Diekelmann, John, and Robert Schuster. *Natural Landscaping.* Madison, WI: University of Wisconsin Press, 2002.

Druse, Ken. *The Natural Habitat Garden.* Portland, OR: Timber Press, 2004.

Foote, Leonard E., and Samuel B. Jones, Jr. *Native Shrubs and Woody Vines of the Southwest: Landscape Uses and Identification.* Portland, OR: Timber Press, 2005.

Houk, Rose, and George H. H. Huey. *Wild Cactus.* New York: Artisan, 1996.

Johnson, Lorraine. *Grow Wild: Native Plant Gardening in Canada and the Northern United States.* Toronto: Random House, 1998.

Lowry, Judith L. *Gardening with a Wild Heart: Restoring California's Native Landscapes at Home.* Berkeley: University of California Press, 1999.

National Audubon Society. *The Audubon Society Field Guide to North American Wildflowers: Eastern Region.* New York: Alfred A. Knopf, 2001.

———. *The Audubon Society Field Guide to North American Wildflowers: Western Region.* New York: Alfred A. Knopf, 2001.

Otteson, Carole. *The Native Plant Primer.* New York: Harmony Books, 1995.

Phillips, Harry R. *Growing and Propagating Wild Flowers.* Chapel Hill: University of North Carolina Press, 1985.

Robson, Kathleen A., et al. *Encyclopedia of Northwest Native Plants for Gardens and Landscapes.* Portland, OR: Timber Press, 2005.

Smith, J. Robert and Beatrice S. *The Prairie Garden.* Madison, WI: University of Wisconsin Press, 1980.

Taylor, Patricia. *Easy Care Native Plants.* New York: Henry Holt, 1996.

Wasowski, Sally, with Andy Wasowski. *Native Gardens for Dry Climates.* New York: Clarkson Potter, 1995.

———. *Gardening with Native Plants of the South.* Dallas: Taylor Publishing, 1994.

WILDLIFE AND GARDENS

Arbib, Robert, and Tony Soper. *The Hungry Bird Book: How to Make Your Garden Their Heaven on Earth.* New York: Taplinger Publishing, 1970.

Buchmann, Stephen L., and Gary P. Nabhan. *The Forgotten Pollinators.* Washington, DC: Island Press, 1997.

Carroll, Steven B., and Steven D. Salt. *Ecology for Gardeners.* Portland, OR: Timber Press, 2004.

DeGraaf, Richard M. *Trees, Shrubs and Vines for Attracting Birds: A Manual for the Northeast.* Lebanon, NH: University Press of New England, 2002.

Dennis, John V. *The Wildlife Gardener.* New York: Alfred A. Knopf, 1985.

Martin, Alexander C., et al. *American Wildlife and Plants: A Guide to Wildlife Food Habits.* New York: Dover Publications, 1961.

Starcher, Allison Mia. *Good Bugs for Your Garden.* Chapel Hill, NC: Algonquin Books, 1998.

Stein, Sara. *Noah's Garden.* New York: Houghton Mifflin, 1995.

Terres, John K. *Songbirds in Your Garden.* Chapel Hill, NC: Algonquin Books, 1994.

The Xerces Society and the Smithsonian Institution. *Butterfly Gardening.* San Francisco: Sierra Club Books, 1998.

HOUSEPLANTS

Banks, David P. *Orchid Grower's Companion.* Portland, OR: Timber Press, 2004.

Crockett, James U., and the Editors of Time-Life Books. *The Time-Life Book of Flowering Houseplants.* New York: Henry Holt, 1986.

———. *The Time-Life Book of Foliage Houseplants.* New York: Henry Holt, 1986.

Cruso, Thalassa. *Making Things Grow.* New York: Van Nostrand Reinhold, 1983.

McDonald, Elvin. *The New Houseplant.* New York: Macmillan Publishing, 1993.

GARDENING TECHNIQUES

Bormann, F. Herbert, et al. *Redesigning the American Lawn.* New Haven: Yale University Press, 2001.

Foster, H. Lincoln. *Rock Gardening: A Guide to Growing Alpines and Other Wildflowers in the American Garden.* Portland, OR: Timber Press, 1982.

Gallup, Barbara, and Deborah Reich. *The Complete Book of Topiary.* New York: Workman Publishing, 1994.

Giles, Floyd. *Landscape Construction Procedures, Techniques and Design.* Champaign, IL: Stipes Publishing, 2000.

Hill, Lewis. *Pruning Made Easy.* North Adams, MA: Storey Publishing, 1998.

———. *Secrets of Plant Propagation.* North Adams, MA: Storey Publishing, 1985.

Hylton, William, ed. *Projects for Outdoor Living.* Emmaus, PA: Rodale Press, 1990.

Jennings, Karen Park. *Park's Success with Seed.* Greenwood, SC: George W. Park Seed, 2006.

Kramer, Jack. *Drip System Watering for Bigger and Better Plants.* New York: W. W. Norton, 1980.

North American Rock Garden Society. *Rock Garden Design and Construction.* Portland, OR: Timber Press, 2003.

Schultz, Warren. *The Chemical-Free Lawn.* Emmaus, PA: Rodale Press, 1996.

Swindells, Phillip, and David Mason. *The Complete Book of the Water Garden.* New York: Sterling Publishing, 2002.

Yang, Linda. *The City Gardener's Handbook.* North Adams, MA: Storey Publishing, 2002.

Young, James A. and Cheryl G. *Collecting, Processing and Germinating Seeds of Wildland Plants.* Portland, OR: Timber Press, 1986.

FOR INSPIRATION

Brookes, John. *The Small Garden.* New York: Dorling Kindersley, 2006.

Damrosch, Barbara. *Theme Gardens*, rev. ed. New York: Workman Publishing, 2001.

Druse, Ken. *The Natural Shade Garden.* New York: Clarkson Potter, 1992.

Fairbrother, Nan. *Men and Gardens.* Guilford, CT: Lyons Press, 1997.

Hobhouse, Penelope. *Color in Your Garden.* Boston: Little, Brown, 1985.

Jekyll, Gertrude. *Gertrude Jekyll's Colour Schemes for the Flower Garden.* London: Frances Lincoln, 2008.

Lloyd, Christopher. *The Well Chosen Garden.* New York: Harper & Row, 1984.

Lowenfels, Jeff. *Teaming with Microbes: A Gardener's Guide to the Soil Food Web.* Portland, OR: Timber Press, 2006.

Page, Russell. *The Education of a Gardener.* New York: New York Review of Books, 2007.

Phillips, Judith. *Natural by Design: Beauty and Balance in Southwest Gardens.* Santa Fe, NM: Museum of New Mexico Press, 1995.

Pollan, Michael. *Second Nature.* New York: Grove Press, 2003.

Schenk, George. *The Complete Shade Garden.* Portland, OR: Timber Press, 2003.

Tasker, Georgia B. *Enchanted Ground: Gardening with Nature in the Subtropics.* Kansas City, MO: Andrews McMeel Publishing, 1994.

Verey, Rosemary, and Ellen Samuels, eds. *The American Woman's Garden.* Boston: New York Graphic Society/Little, Brown, 1985.

Wilder, Louise Beebe. *The Fragrant Garden: A Book About Sweet Scented Flowers and Leaves.* New York: Dover Publications, 1974.

PERIODICALS

In addition to the following periodicals, many plant societies beginning on page 758 publish informative journals.

All Region Guides. 3 issues/yr. on specific topics. Brooklyn Botanic Garden, 1000 Washington Ave., Brooklyn, NY 11225. www.bbg.org.

The Avant Gardener. Monthly. Horticultural Data Processors, PO Box 489, New York, NY 10028.

Canadian Gardening. Monthly. 225 Sheppard Ave. W., Toronto, ON M2N 6S7, Canada. www.canadiangardening.com.

Garden Design Magazine. 7 issues/yr. 460 N. Orlando Ave., Ste. 200, Winter Park, FL 32789. www.gardendesign.com.

Horticulture. Monthly. 98 N. Washington St., Boston, MA 02114. www.hortmag.com.

HortIdeas. Bimonthly. 750 Black Lick Rd., Gravel Switch, KY 40328.

Organic Gardening. Bimonthly. Rodale, 33 E. Minor St., Emmaus, PA 18098. www.organicgardening.com.

Index